Instructor's Annotated Edition

SECOND EDITION

PANORAMA

Introducción a la lengua española

José A. Blanco

Philip Redwine Donley, Late
Austin Community College

VISTA
HIGHER LEARNING

Boston, Massachusetts

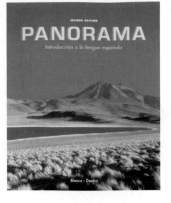

The **PANORAMA, Second Edition,** cover celebrates the natural beauty of the Spanish-speaking world you will discover throughout this program. The cover photo is an image of **Laguna Miscanti** and **Cerro Miñiques** in Chile.

Publisher: José A. Blanco

President: Stephen Pekich

Editorial Director: Denise St. Jean

Art Director: Linda Jurras

Design Manager: Polo Barrera

Project Manager: Kristen Chapron

Staff Editors: Gabriela Ferland, Sarah Kenney

Contributing Writers and Editors: Mary Ann Dellinger, Adriana Lavergne

Design, Production, and Manufacturing Team: Linde Gee; Niki Birbilis, Oscar Díez, Jonathan Gorey, Mauricio Henao, Ray Levesque; Gustavo Cinci

Technology Team: Andrew Paradise, Thomas Ziegelbauer

Student Text ISBN 1-59334-520-8

Instructor's Annotated Edition ISBN 1-59334-521-6

1 2 3 4 5 6 7 8 9 VH 09 08 07 06 05 04

Instructor's Annotated Edition

Table of Contents

The PANORAMA Story

Vista Higher Learning, the publisher of **PANORAMA**, was founded with one mission: to raise the teaching of Spanish to a higher level. Years of experience working with textbook publishers convinced us that more could be done to offer you superior tools and to give your students a more profound learning experience. Along the way, we questioned everything about the way textbooks support the teaching of Spanish.

In the fall of 2000, the result was **VISTAS**, a textbook and coordinated package of print and technology ancillaries that looked different and *were* different. **PANORAMA**, a briefer text based on **VISTAS**, followed in fall 2001. We took a fresh look at introductory college Spanish and found that hundreds of Spanish instructors nationwide liked what they saw. In just three years, **VISTAS** and **PANORAMA** became the most successful new introductory Spanish textbooks to be published in the last decade, having been adopted at more than 400 schools across the country and used by well over 150,000 students to learn Spanish.

Over the last three years, we have been listening to the instructors and students using the first edition, gathering their invaluable feedback in order to incorporate it into the second edition. The result is **PANORAMA 2/e**, an even better and more comprehensive program that will work more effectively and seamlessly in your classes.

To those instructors who used **PANORAMA 1/e** and are continuing with the second edition, we thank you for partnering with us these past few years and for your ongoing belief both in the program and in us as a new enterprise dedicated to innovative, focused, and captivating products. To those who are new to the second edition, we welcome you and thank you for choosing **PANORAMA.**

We hope that you and your students enjoy using **PANORAMA 2/e**. Please contact us with your questions, comments, and reactions.

Vista Higher Learning
31 St. James Avenue
Boston, MA 02116-4104
TOLLFREE: 800-618-7375
TELEPHONE: 617-426-4910
FAX: 617-426-5215
www.vistahigherlearning.com

Getting to Know PANORAMA

PANORAMA 2/e retains the highly successful underpinnings of the first edition. It takes a fresh, student-friendly approach to introductory Spanish aimed at making students' learning and instructors' teaching easier, more enjoyable, and more successful. At the same time, **PANORAMA** takes a communicative approach to language learning. It develops students' speaking, listening, reading, and writing skills so that they will be able to express their own ideas and interact with others in meaningful, real-life contexts. It emphasizes frequently used vocabulary and presents grammar as a tool for effective communication. Finally, because cultural knowledge is an integral part of both language learning and successful communication, **PANORAMA** introduces students to the everyday lives of Spanish speakers, as well as the countries of the Spanish-speaking world.

Whereas other introductory college Spanish programs are based on many of these same pedagogical principals, **PANORAMA** continues to offer features that make it truly different.

- **PANORAMA,** and its parent program **VISTAS**, were the first introductory college Spanish textbooks to incorporate graphic design—page layout, use of colors, typefaces, and other graphic elements—as an integral part of the learning process. To enhance learning and make navigation easy, lesson sections were created from their inception—not retrofitted—to be color-coded and to appear either completely on one page or on spreads of two facing pages. The textbook pages themselves are also visually dramatic, with an array of photos, drawings, realia, charts, graphs, diagrams, and word lists, all designed for both instructional impact and visual appeal.

- **PANORAMA** offers student sidebars with on-the-spot linguistic and cultural information, as well as **recursos** boxes with on-page correlations of student supplements, to increase students' comfort level and to save them time.

- **PANORAMA** integrates video with the student textbook up-front in each lesson's **Fotonovela** section and throughout every lesson's **Estructura** section.

- **PANORAMA** provides a unique four-part practice sequence for virtually every grammar point. It moves from form-focused **¡Inténtalo!** exercises to directed, yet meaningful, **Práctica** exercises to communicative, interactive **Comunicación** activities, and lastly to cumulative, open-ended **Síntesis** activities.

- **PANORAMA** incorporates groundbreaking, text-specific technology, specially designed to expand students' learning and instructors' teaching options. In its first edition, with **VISTAS,** it was the first program to include a Video CD-ROM. Now, in its second edition, it offers a unique, interactive online version of the textbook: **PANORAMA** eText.

Before you read the rest of the front matter in your Instructor's Annotated Edition (pages IAE-6 – IAE-16), it is recommended that you familiarize yourself with these pages of the Student Text front matter: p. iii (To the Student), pp. xii–xxiii (**PANORAMA**-At-A-Glance), pp. xxiv–xxv (Video Programs), and pp. xxvi–xxvii (Ancillaries).

Getting to Know Your Instructor's Annotated Edition

Like **VISTAS 2/e**, its parent textbook, **PANORAMA 2/e** offers you the most thoroughly developed Instructor's Annotated Edition ever written for introductory college Spanish. In response to instructor input, the second edition IAE features a new trim size larger than that of the student text, as well as enhanced surrounding side and bottom panels for increased readability. It features slightly reduced student text pages, overprinted with answers to all activities with discrete responses, and it places a wealth of teaching resources at your fingertips. The annotations were written to complement and support varied teaching styles, to extend the already rich contents of the student textbook, and to save you time in class preparation and course management.

Because the **PANORAMA 2/e** IAE is a relatively new kind of teaching resource, this section is designed as a quick orientation to the principal types of instructor annotations you will find in it. As you familiarize yourself with them, it is important to know that the annotations are suggestions only. Any Spanish questions, sentences, models, or simulated instructor-student exchanges are not meant to be prescriptive or limiting. You are encouraged to view these suggested "scripts" as flexible points of departure that will help you achieve your instructional goals.

On the Lesson Opening Page

- **Lesson Goals** A list of the lexical, grammatical, and socio-cultural goals of the lesson, including language-learning strategies and skill-building techniques

- **A primera vista** Personalized questions based on the full-page photograph for jump-starting the lesson

- **Instructional Resources** A correlation, including page references, to all student and instructor supplements available to reinforce the lesson

In the Side Panels

- **Section Goals** A list of the lexical, grammatical, and/or socio-cultural goals of the corresponding section

- **Instructional Resources** A correlation, including page references, to all ancillaries

- **Suggestion** Teaching suggestions for leading into the corresponding section, working with on-page materials, and carrying out specific activities, as well as quick ways to start classes or activities by recycling language or ideas

- **Expansion** Expansion and variations on activities

- **Script** Printed transcripts of the audio recordings on the Textbook Activities CD for the first **Práctica** activity in each **Contextos** section and the **Estrategia** and **Ahora escucha** features in the **Escuchar** sections in **Lecciones 3, 6, 9, 12,** and **15**

- **Possible Response** Answers based on known vocabulary, grammar, and language functions that students might produce

- **Video Recap** Questions to help students recall the events of the previous lesson's **Fotonovela** episode

- **Video Synopsis** Summaries in the **Fotonovela** sections that recap that lesson's video module

- **Expresiones útiles** Suggestions for introducing upcoming **Estructura** grammar points incorporated into the **Fotonovela** episode

- **Estrategia** Suggestions for working with the reading, writing, and listening strategies presented in the **Lectura, Escritura,** and **Escuchar** sections, respectively

- **Tema** Ideas for presenting and expanding the writing assignment topic in **Escritura**

- **El país en cifras** Additional information expanding on the data presented for each Spanish-speaking country featured in the **Panorama** sections

- **¡Increíble pero cierto!** Curious facts about a lesser-known aspect of the country featured in the **Panorama** sections

- **Section-specific Annotations** Suggestions for presenting, expanding, varying, and reinforcing individual instructional elements

- **Student Text Sidebar Annotations** Suggestions for incorporating the information provided in sidebars (**¡Atención!, Ayuda, Nota cultural,** etc.)

- **Successful Language Learning** Tips and strategies to enhance students' language-learning experience

- **The Affective Dimension** Suggestions for managing and/or reducing students' language-learning anxieties

In the *Teaching Options* Boxes

- **Extra Practice, Pairs, Small Groups, and Large Groups** Additional activities over and above those already in the student textbook

- **Game** Games that practice the language of the section and/or recycle previously learned language

- **TPR** Total Physical Response activities that engage students physically in learning Spanish

- **Enfoque cultural** Additional cultural information related to the **Enfoque cultural** in **Fotonovela**

- **Variación léxica** Extra information related to the **Variación léxica** in **Contextos** and/or the Spanish-speaking countries in **Panorama**

- **Worth Noting** More detailed information about an interesting aspect of the history, geography, culture, or people of the Spanish-speaking countries in **Panorama**

- **Heritage Speakers** Suggestions and activities tailored to heritage speakers, who in many colleges and universities are enrolled in the same introductory courses as non-heritage speakers

- **Video** Techniques and activities for using the **Fotonovela** video program with the **Fotonovela** sections as well as other lesson sections

- **Proofreading Activity** Activities exclusive to the **Escritura** sections that guide students in the development of good proofreading skills. Each item contains errors related to a structure taught in the lesson's **Estructura** section or, in **Lecciones 10–15,** a spelling rule taught in **Ortografía**

Please check our website (**www.vistahigherlearning.com**) for additional teaching support and program updates.

General Teaching Considerations

Orienting Students to the Student Textbook

Because **PANORAMA 2/e** treats interior and graphic design as an integral part of students' language-learning experience, you may want to take a few minutes to orient students to the student textbook. Have them flip through one lesson, and point out that all fifteen lessons are organized in six major sections, each color-coded for easy navigation: red for **Contextos**, purple for **Fotonovela**, blue for **Estructura**, green for **Adelante**, orange for **Panorama**, and gold for **Vocabulario**. Mention that, in each lesson, **Adelante** consists of a two-page **Lectura** section, but that in **Lecciones 3, 6, 9, 12,** and **15**, it also includes one-page **Escritura** and **Escuchar** sections. Tell them that, because of these design elements, they can be confident that they will always know "where they are" in **PANORAMA**.

Emphasize that sections are self-contained, occupying either a full page or a spread of two facing pages, thereby eliminating "bad breaks" and the need to flip back and forth to do activities. Finally, call students' attention to the use of color to highlight key information in elements such as charts, diagrams, word lists, sidebars, and activity **modelos** and titles.

Flexible Lesson Organization

PANORAMA 2/e uses a flexible lesson organization designed to meet the needs of diverse teaching styles, institutions, and instructional goals. For example, you can begin with the lesson opening page and progress sequentially through a lesson. If you do not want to devote class time to grammar, you can assign the **Estructura** explanations for outside study, freeing up class time for other purposes like developing oral communication skills; building listening, reading, or writing skills; learning more about the Spanish-speaking world; or working with the video program. You might decide to work extensively with the **Adelante** and **Panorama** sections in order to focus on students' reading, writing, and listening skills as well as their knowledge of the Spanish-speaking world. On the other hand, you might prefer to skip these sections entirely, exploiting them periodically in response to your students' interests as the opportunity arises. If you plan on using the **PANORAMA** Testing Program, however, be aware that its tests and exams check language presented in **Contextos**, **Estructura**, and the **Expresiones útiles** boxes of **Fotonovela**.

Identifying Active Vocabulary

All words and expressions taught in the illustrations and **Más vocabulario** lists in **Contextos** are considered active, testable vocabulary. Any items in the **Variación léxica** boxes, however, are intended for receptive learning and are presented for enrichment only. The words and expressions in the **Expresiones útiles** boxes in **Fotonovela**, as well as words in charts, word lists, **¡Atención!** sidebars, and sample sentences in **Estructura** are also part of the active vocabulary load. At the end of each lesson, **Vocabulario** provides a convenient one-page summary of the items students should know and that may appear on tests and exams. You will want to point this out to students. You might also tell them that an easy way to study from **Vocabulario** is to cover up the Spanish half of each section, leaving only the English equivalents exposed. They can then quiz themselves on the Spanish items. To focus on the English equivalents of the Spanish entries, they simply reverse this process.

Taking into Account the Affective Dimension

While many factors contribute to the quality and success rate of learning experiences, two factors are particularly germane to language learning. One is students' beliefs about how language is learned; the other is language-learning anxiety.

As studies show and experienced instructors know, students often come to modern languages courses either with a lack of knowledge about how to approach language learning or with mistaken notions about how to do so. For example, many students believe that making mistakes when speaking the target language must be avoided because doing so will lead to permanent errors. Others are convinced that learning another language is like learning any other academic subject. In other words, they believe that success is guaranteed, provided they attend class regularly, learn the assigned vocabulary words and grammar rules, and study for exams. In fact, in a study of college-level beginning language learners in the United States, over one-third of the participants thought that they could become fluent if they studied the language for only one hour a day for two years or less. Mistaken and unrealistic beliefs such as these can cause frustration and ultimately demotivation, thereby significantly undermining students' ability to achieve a successful language-learning experience.

Another factor that can negatively impact students' language-learning experiences is language-learning anxiety. As Professor Elaine K. Horwitz of The University of Texas at Austin and Senior Consulting Editor of **VISTAS 1/e** and **PANORAMA 1/e** wrote, "Surveys indicate that up to one-third of American foreign language students feel moderately to highly anxious about studying another language. Physical symptoms of foreign language anxiety can include heart-pounding or palpitations, sweating, trembling, fast breathing, and general feelings of unease." The late Dr. Philip Redwine Donley, **VISTAS** and **PANORAMA** co-author and author of articles on language-learning anxiety, spoke with many students who reported feeling nervous or apprehensive in their classes. They mentioned freezing when called on by their instructors or going inexplicably blank when taking tests. Some so dreaded their classes that they skipped them or dropped the course.

PANORAMA contains several features aimed at reducing students' language anxiety and supporting their successful language-learning. First of all, its highly structured, visually dramatic interior design was conceived as a learning tool to make students feel comfortable with the content and confident about navigating the lessons. The Instructor's Annotated Edition includes recurring *Affective Dimension* annotations with suggestions for managing and/or reducing language-learning anxieties, as well as *Successful Language Learning* annotations with learning strategies for enhancing students' learning experiences. In addition, the student text provides a wealth of helpful sidebars that assist students by making immediately relevant connections with new information or reminding them of previously learned concepts.

Student Sidebars

¡Atención!	Provides active, testable information about the vocabulary or grammar point
Ayuda	Offers specific grammar and vocabulary reminders related to a particular activity
Consejos	Suggests pertinent language-learning strategies
Consúltalo	References related material introduced in previous or upcoming lessons
¡Lengua viva!	Presents immediately relevant information on everyday language use
Nota cultural	Provides a wide range of cultural information relevant to the topic of an activity or section

General Suggestions for Using the *Panorama cultural* Video

The **Panorama cultural** video contains documentary and travelogue footage of each country featured in the lessons' **Panorama** sections. The images were chosen for visual appeal, diversity of topics, and information of interest that goes beyond the materials about each country that are presented in the textbook. Like the conversations in the **Fotonovela** video, the voice-overs for the video segments represent comprehensible input. Each was written to make the most of the vocabulary and grammar students learned in the corresponding and previous lessons while still providing a small amount of unknown language. The effect on students as they watch will be that of viewing a documentary in their second language, because all footage is authentic and all narration is exclusively in Spanish. A special effort was also made to concentrate on one unique social or historical aspect of each country in such a way as to avoid promoting stereotypes of Spanish-speaking cultures.

Panorama cultural Video Table of Contents

Lesson	Country	Topic	Lesson	Country	Topic
1	Los Estados Unidos	Los hispanos en Nueva York	10	Nicaragua	Masaya
1	Canadá	Los hispanos en Montreal	11	Argentina	El tango
2	España	El Festival de San Fermín	11	Uruguay	Las estancias
3	Ecuador	Las islas Galápagos	12	Panamá	Los deportes en el mar
4	México	Teotihuacán	12	El Salvador	El maíz
5	Puerto Rico	El Viejo San Juan	13	Colombia	Las fiestas y los parques
6	Cuba	La santería	13	Honduras	Copán
7	Perú	Los deportes de aventura	14	Venezuela	Las costas y las montañas
8	Guatemala	Antigua y Chichicastenango	14	La República Dominicana	El merengue y la bachata
9	Chile	La isla de Pascua	15	Bolivia	El salar de Uyuni
10	Costa Rica	Monteverde y Tortuguero	15	Paraguay	El mate

Activities for the **Panorama cultural** video are located in the Video Manual section of the **PANORAMA 2/e** Workbook/Video Manual. They follow a process approach of pre-viewing, while-viewing, and post-viewing and use a variety of formats to prepare students for watching the video segments, to focus them while viewing, and to check comprehension after they have seen the footage.

When showing the **Panorama cultural** video in your classes, you might also want to implement a process approach. You could start with an activity that prepares students for the video segment by taking advantage of what they learned in previous lessons. This could be followed by an activity that students do while you play parts or all of the video segment. The final activity, done in the same class period or in the next one as warm-up, could recap what students saw and heard and move beyond the video segment's topic. The following suggestions for working with the **Panorama cultural** video in class can be carried out as described or expanded upon in any number of ways.

Before viewing

- After students have practiced the lesson's vocabulary and grammar and worked through the **Panorama** section of the student textbook, mention the video segment's title and ask them to guess what the segment might be about.

- Have pairs make a list of vocabulary they expect to hear in the video segment.

- Read the class a list of true-false or multiple-choice questions about the video. Students must use what they learned in the **Panorama** section to guess the answers. Confirm their guesses after watching the segment.

While viewing

- Show the video segment with the audio turned off and ask students to use lesson vocabulary and structures to describe what is happening. Have them confirm their guesses by showing the segment again with the audio on.

- Have students refer to the list of words they brainstormed before viewing the video and put a check in front of any words they actually see in the segment.

- First, have students simply watch the video. Then, show it again and ask students to take notes on what they see and hear. Finally, have them compare their notes in pairs or groups for confirmation.

- Photocopy the segment's videoscript from the Instructor's Resource Manual and white out words and expressions. Distribute the scripts for pairs or groups to complete as cloze paragraphs.

- After having introduced the lesson's theme using the lesson-opening page, show the video segment *before* moving on to **Contextos** to jump-start the lesson's language and cultural focus. Have students tell you what vocabulary and grammar they recognize from previous lessons. Briefly present the new lesson's theme and grammar structures for recognition.

After viewing

- Have students say what aspects of the information presented in the **Panorama** section of their textbook are observable in the video segment.

- Ask groups to write a brief summary of the content of the video segment. Have them exchange papers with another group for peer editing.

- Ask students to discuss any aspects of the featured country of which they were unaware before watching. Encourage them to say why they did not expect those aspects to be true of the country in question.

- Have students pick one characteristic about the country that they learned from watching the video segment. Have them research more about that topic and write a brief composition to expand on it.

General Suggestions for Using the PANORAMA *Fotonovela* Video

The **Fotonovela** section in each of the student textbook's lessons and the **PANORAMA** **Fotonovela** video were created as interlocking pieces. All photos in **Fotonovela** are actual video stills from the corresponding video module, while the printed conversations are abbreviated versions of the video module's dramatic segment. Both the **Fotonovela** conversations and their expanded video versions represent comprehensible input at the discourse level; they were purposely written to use language from the corresponding lesson's **Contextos** and **Estructura** sections. Thus, as of **Lección 2**, they recycle known language, preview grammar points students will study later in the lesson, and, in keeping with the concept of "i + 1," contain a small amount of unknown language.

Because the **Fotonovela** sections and the **PANORAMA** **Fotonovela** video are so closely connected, you may use them in many different ways. For instance, you can use **Fotonovela** as an advance organizer, presenting it before showing the video module. You can also show the video module first and follow up with **Fotonovela**. You can even use **Fotonovela** as a stand-alone, video-independent section.

Depending on your teaching preferences and campus facilities, you might decide to show all video modules in class or to assign them solely for viewing outside of the classroom. You could begin by showing the first one or two modules in class to familiarize yourself and students with the characters, storyline, style, "flashbacks," and **Resumen** sections. After that, you could work in class only with **Fotonovela** and have students view the remaining video modules outside of class. No matter which approach you choose, students have ample materials to support viewing the video independently and processing it in a meaningful way. For each video module, there are **Reacciona a la fotonovela** activities in the **Fotonovela** section of the corresponding textbook lesson and video activities in the Student Activities Manual.

You might also want to use the **PANORAMA** **Fotonovela** video in class when working with the **Estructura** sections. You could play the parts of the dramatic episode that correspond to the video stills in the grammar explanations or show selected scenes and ask students to identify certain grammar points.

You could also focus on the video's **Resumen** sections. In these, one of the main video characters recaps the dramatic episode by reminiscing about its key events. These reminiscences, which emphasize the lesson's active vocabulary and grammar points, take the form of footage pulled out of the dramatic episode and repeated in black and white images. The main character who "hosts" each **Resumen** begins and ends the section with a few lines that do not appear in the live segment. These sentences provide a new, often humorous setting for the host character's reminiscences, as well as additional opportunities for students to process language they have been studying within the context of the video storyline.

In class, you could play the parts of the **Resumen** section that exemplify individual grammar points as you progress through each **Estructura** section. You could also wait until you complete an **Estructura** section and review it by showing the corresponding **Resumen** section in its entirety.

PANORAMA and *the Standards for Foreign Language Learning*

Since 1982, when the *ACTFL Proficiency Guidelines* were first published, that seminal document and its subsequent revisions have influenced the teaching of modern languages in the United States. **VISTAS**, the parent book from which **PANORAMA** is derived, was written with the concerns and philosophy of the *ACTFL Proficiency Guidelines* in mind, incorporating a proficiency-oriented approach from its planning stages.

VISTAS', and consequently **PANORAMA**'s, pedagogy was also informed from its inception by the *Standards for Foreign Language Learning in the 21st Century*. First published in 1996 under the auspices of the National Standards in Foreign Language Education Project, the Standards are organized into five goal areas, often called the Five Cs: Communication, Cultures, Connections, Comparisons, and Communities.

The Communication goal is central to the **VISTAS** and **PANORAMA** student texts. For example, the diverse formats used in **Comunicación** and **Síntesis** activities—pair work, small group work, class circulation, information gap, task-based, and so forth—engage students in communicative exchanges, providing and obtaining information, and expressing feelings and emotions.

The Cultures goal is most evident in the lessons' **Enfoque cultural** boxes **Nota cultural** student sidebars, and **Panorama** sections, but **PANORAMA** also weaves culture into virtually every page, exposing students to the multiple facets of practices, products, and perspectives of the Spanish-speaking world. In keeping with the Connections goal, students can connect with other disciplines such as geography, history, fine arts, and science in the **Panorama** sections; they can acquire information and recognize distinctive cultural viewpoints in the non-literary and literary texts of the **Lectura** sections. The **Estructura** sections, with their clear explanations and special *Compare & Contrast* sections, reflect the Comparisons goal, and students can work toward the Connections and Communities goals when they do the **Panorama** sections' **Conexión Internet** activities, as well as the activities and information on the **PANORAMA** website. In addition, special Standards icons appear on the student text pages of your IAE to call out sections that have a particularly strong relationship with the Standards.

All in all, these features are a few examples of how **PANORAMA** was written with the Standards firmly in mind, but you will find many more as you work with the student textbook and its ancillaries.

COURSE PLANNING

The entire **PANORAMA** program was developed with an eye to flexibility and ease of use in a wide variety of course configurations. Here are some sample course plans that illustrate how the program can be used in a variety of academic situations. Visit the **PANORAMA** website (**www.vistahigherlearning.com**) for more course planning tips and detailed suggestions, as well as an essay on course planning by the late Dr. Philip Redwine Donley, **PANORAMA** co-author. You should, of course, feel free to organize your courses in the way that best suits your students' needs and your instructional objectives.

Two-Semester System

This chart illustrates how **PANORAMA** can be completed in a two-semester course. This division of material allows the present and the present progressive, including reflexive verbs, and the preterite tenses to be presented in the first semester; the second semester focuses on the imperfect tense, the subjunctive, and the perfect tenses, as well as the future and the conditional.

Semester 1	Semester 2
Lecciones 1–8	Lecciones 10–15

Three-Semester System

This chart shows how **PANORAMA** can be used in a three-semester course. The lessons are equally divided among the three semesters, allowing students to absorb the material at a steady pace.

Semester 1	Semester 2	Semester 3
Lecciones 1–5	Lecciones 6–10	Lecciones 11–15

Quarter System

In this chart, the **PANORAMA** materials are organized in three balanced segments for use in the quarter system, allowing ample time for learning and review in each quarter.

First Quarter	Second Quarter	Third Quarter
Lecciones 1–5	Lecciones 6–10	Lecciones 11–15

LESSON PLANNING

Like **VISTAS**, its parent textbook, **PANORAMA** has been carefully planned to meet your instructional needs, whether you teach on a semester or quarter system and whether you plan to use the textbook for two, three, or four semesters or over three quarters. Vocabulary presentations and grammar topics have been methodically designed for maximum instructional flexibility.

This lesson plan for **Lección 1** illustrates how **PANORAMA 2/e** can be used in a two-semester program with four contact hours per week. It deals with order of presentation rather than specific instructional techniques and suggestions because those are provided in the annotations of the **PANORAMA 2/e** IAE and because complete, detailed lesson plans are posted on the **PANORAMA 2/e** website (www.vistahigherlearning.com). There you will find lesson plans for two-semester courses, quarter courses, and essays by the late Dr. Philip Redwine Donley, **PANORAMA** co-author, about how to use **PANORAMA** with the following types of course configurations: two-semester courses with four contact hours per week; quarter courses with five contact hours per week; and courses that meet over three and four semesters.

Sample Lesson Plan for *Lección 1*

Day 1

1. Introduce yourself and present the course syllabus.
2. Present the **Lección 1** objectives.
3. Preview the **Contextos** section; present the **Contextos** vocabulary.
4. Work through the **Práctica** activities with the class; have students read over the **Comunicación** activities for the next class.
5. Preview the **Fotonovela** and the **Expresiones útiles**.
6. Have students read through the **Fotonovela** and prepare the first **Reacciona a la fotonovela** activity for the next class.

Day 2

1. Review **Contextos** vocabulary; have the class do the **Comunicación** activities.
2. Present the **Fotonovela** and **Expresiones útiles**.
3. Do the first **Reacciona a la fotonovela** activity with the class.
4. Have your students do the next three **Reacciona a la fotonovela** activities.
5. Preview the **Pronunciación** section and **Estructura 1.1**.
6. Have students read **Estructura 1.1** and prepare the **Inténtalo** and **Práctica** activities for the next class.

Day 3

1. Review the **Expresiones útiles**.
2. Go over the **Pronunciación** section with the class and work through the corresponding activities.
3. Present **Estructura 1.1**.
4. Work through the **Inténtalo** and **Práctica** activities with the class.
5. Have your students do the **Comunicación** activity in class.
6. Preview **Estructura 1.2**.
7. Have students read **Estructura 1.2** and prepare the **Inténtalo** and **Práctica** activities for the next class.

Day 4

1. Review **Estructura 1.1.**
2. Present **Estructura 1.2** and work through the **Inténtalo** and **Práctica** activities with the class.
3. Have your students do the **Comunicación** activities during class.
4. Preview **Estructura 1.3.**
5. Have your students read **Estructura 1.3** and prepare the **Inténtalo** and **Práctica** activities for the next class.

Day 5

1. Review **Estructura 1.2.**
2. Present **Estructura 1.3** and work through the **Inténtalo** and **Práctica** activities with the class.
3. Have your students do the **Comunicación** activities during class.
4. Preview **Estructura 1.4.**
5. Have your students read **Estructura 1.4** and prepare the **Inténtalo** and **Práctica** activities for the next class.

Day 6

1. Quickly review **Estructura 1.3.**
2. Present **Estructura 1.4** and work through the **Inténtalo** and **Práctica** activities with the class.
3. Have your students do the **Comunicación** activities and the **Síntesis** activity.
4. Assign material from the **Lectura** section as desired for integrated practice and review.

Day 7

1. Go over assigned material from the **Lectura** section.
2. Present the **Panorama** section.
3. Review **Lección 1** with the class.
4. Have your students prepare to take **Prueba A** or **Prueba B** for **Lección 1** during the next class session.

Day 8

1. Administer **Prueba A** or **Prueba B** for **Lección 1.**
2. Preview the **Lección 2** objectives.
3. Have your students read the **Contextos** section and prepare the **Práctica** activities for the next class.

The lesson plan presented here is not prescriptive. You should feel free to present lesson materials as you see fit, tailoring them to your own teaching preferences and to your students' learning styles. You may, for example, want to allow extra time for concepts students find challenging. You may want to allot less time to topics they comprehend without difficulty or to group topics together when making assignments. Based on your students' needs, you may want to omit certain topics or activities altogether. If you have fewer than five contact hours per semester or are on a quarter system, you will find the **PANORAMA** program very flexible: simply pick and choose from its array of instructional resources and sequence them in the way that makes the most sense for your program.

SECOND EDITION

PANORAMA

Introducción a la lengua española

SECOND EDITION

PANORAMA

Introducción a la lengua española

José A. Blanco

Philip Redwine Donley, Late

Austin Community College

VISTA
HIGHER LEARNING

Boston, Massachusetts

The **PANORAMA, Second Edition,** cover celebrates the natural beauty of the Spanish-speaking world you will discover throughout this program. The cover photo is an image of **Laguna Miscanti** and **Cerro Miñiques** in Chile.

Publisher: José A. Blanco

President: Stephen Pekich

Editorial Director: Denise St. Jean

Art Director: Linda Jurras

Design Manager: Polo Barrera

Project Manager: Kristen Odlum Chapron

Staff Editors: María Cinta Aparisi, Armando Brito, Gabriela Ferland, María Isabel García, Sarah Kenney, Paola Ríos Schaaf, Alicia Spinner

Contributing Writers and Editors: Mary Ann Dellinger, Carmela Fazzino-Farah, Adriana Lavergne, Magdalena Malinowska, Lourdes Murray-Eljach, Angélica Solares, Ana Yáñez

Design, Production, and Manufacturing Team: Linde Gee; Oscar Díez, Mauricio Henao, Jonathan Gorey; Gustavo Cinci

Student Text ISBN 1-59334-520-8

Instructor's Annotated Edition ISBN 1-59334-521-6

Library of Congress Card Number: 2004114832

1 2 3 4 5 6 7 8 9 VH 09 08 07 06 05 04

TO THE STUDENT

To Vista Higher Learning's great pride and gratification, **PANORAMA** and **VISTAS,** the parent text from which **PANORAMA** is derived, became the best-selling new introductory college Spanish programs in more than a decade in their first editions. It is now our distinct pleasure to welcome you to **PANORAMA, Second Edition,** your point of entry to the Spanish language and to the vibrant, diverse cultures of the Spanish-speaking world.

The direct result of extensive reviews and ongoing input from students and instructors using the first edition, **PANORAMA 2/e** includes both the highly successful, ground-breaking features of the original program, plus many exciting new features. Here are just a few of the elements you will encounter:

Original, hallmark features

- An innovative, easy-to-navigate design built around color-coded sections that appear either completely on one page or on spreads of two facing pages
- Integration of an appealing video up-front in each lesson of the student text
- Practical, high-frequency vocabulary presented in meaningful contexts
- Clear, comprehensive grammar explanations with high-impact graphics and other special features that make structures easier to learn and use
- Ample guided, focused practice to make you comfortable with the vocabulary and grammar you are learning and to give you a solid foundation for communication
- An emphasis on communicative interactions with a classmate, small groups, the full class, and your instructor
- Careful development of reading, writing, and listening skills that integrates learning strategies and a process approach
- Integration of the culture of the everyday lives of Spanish speakers and coverage of the entire Spanish-speaking world
- Unprecedented learning support through on-the-spot student sidebars and on-page correlations to the print and technology ancillaries for each lesson section
- A complete set of coordinated print and technology ancillaries to help you learn Spanish more easily

New to the Second Edition

- Revised grammar scope and sequence for improved coverage within and across lessons
- Jump-start **A primera vista** activities on each lesson's opening page
- Engaging information gap activities in diverse formats
- Increased opportunities for reading and coverage of culture
- New ancillaries like the Vocabulary CDs, the **Panorama cultural** Video, DVDs, and the online **PANORAMA** eText, all closely integrated with your student text

To familiarize yourself with the organization of the text, as well as its *original* and *new* features, turn to page xii and take the **at-a-glance** tour.

table of contents

	contextos	fotonovela

estructura	adelante	panorama

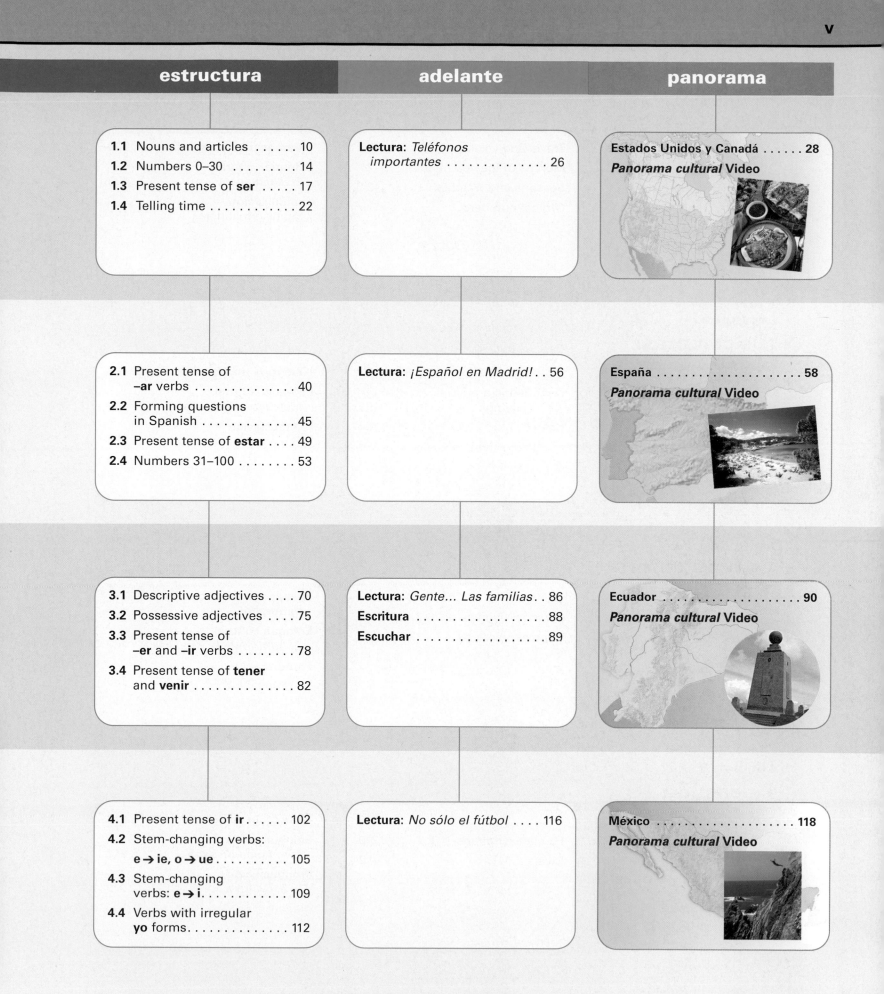

table of contents

	contextos	fotonovela

estructura	adelante	panorama

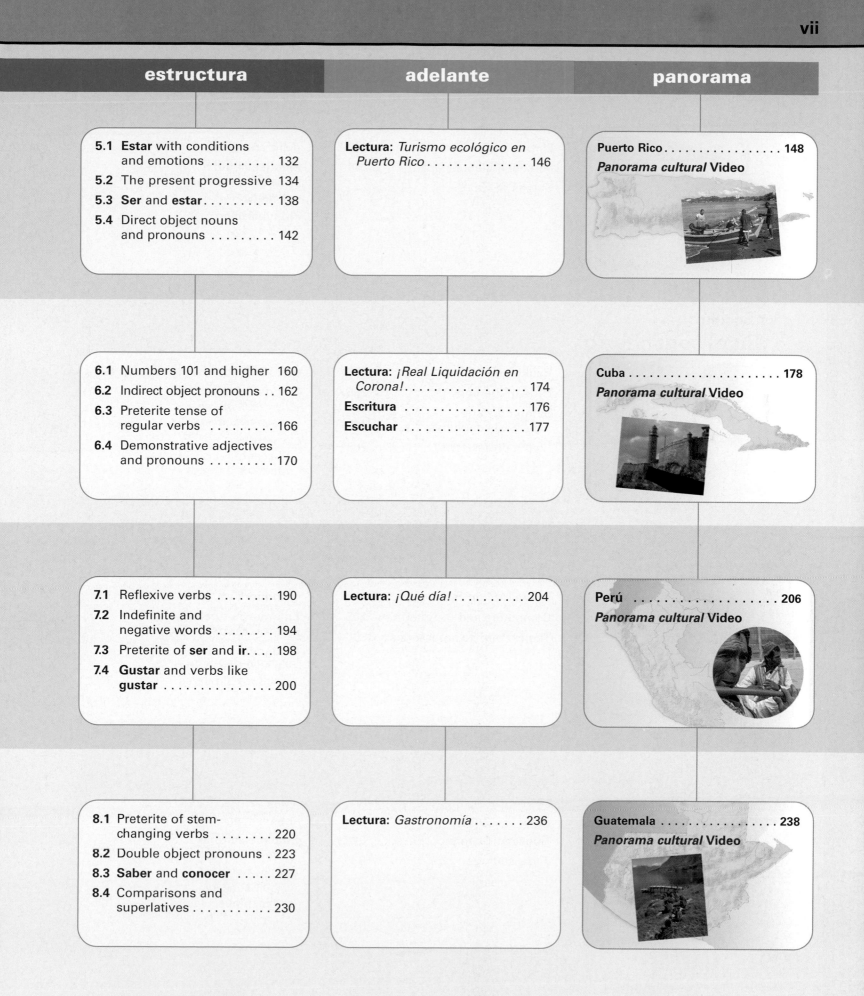

table of contents

	contexts	fotonovela

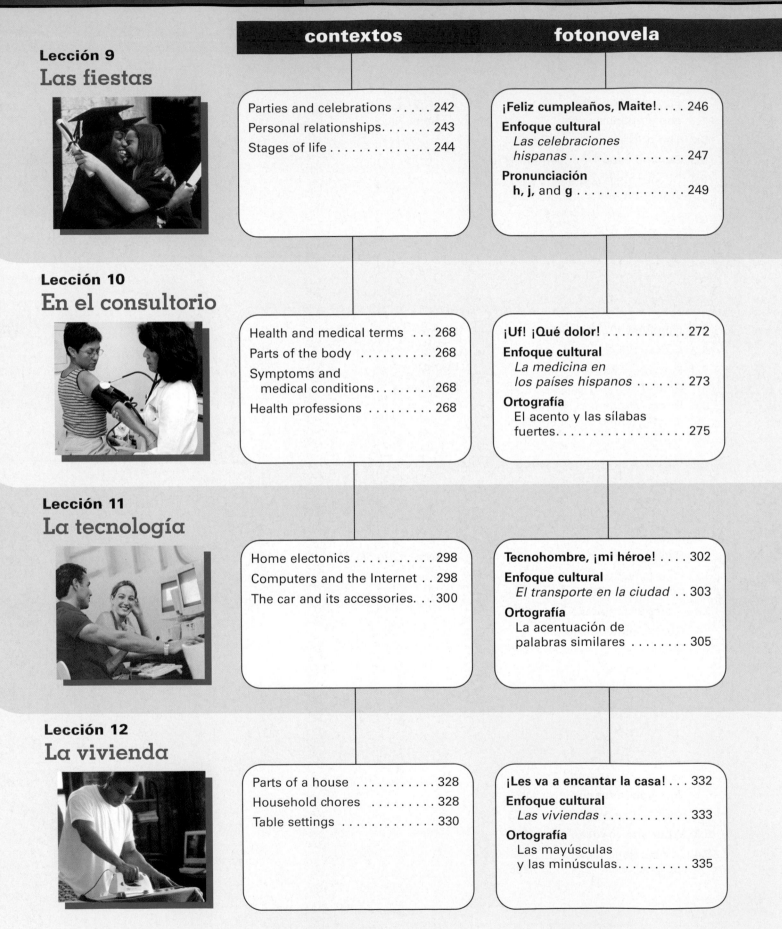

estructura	adelante	panorama

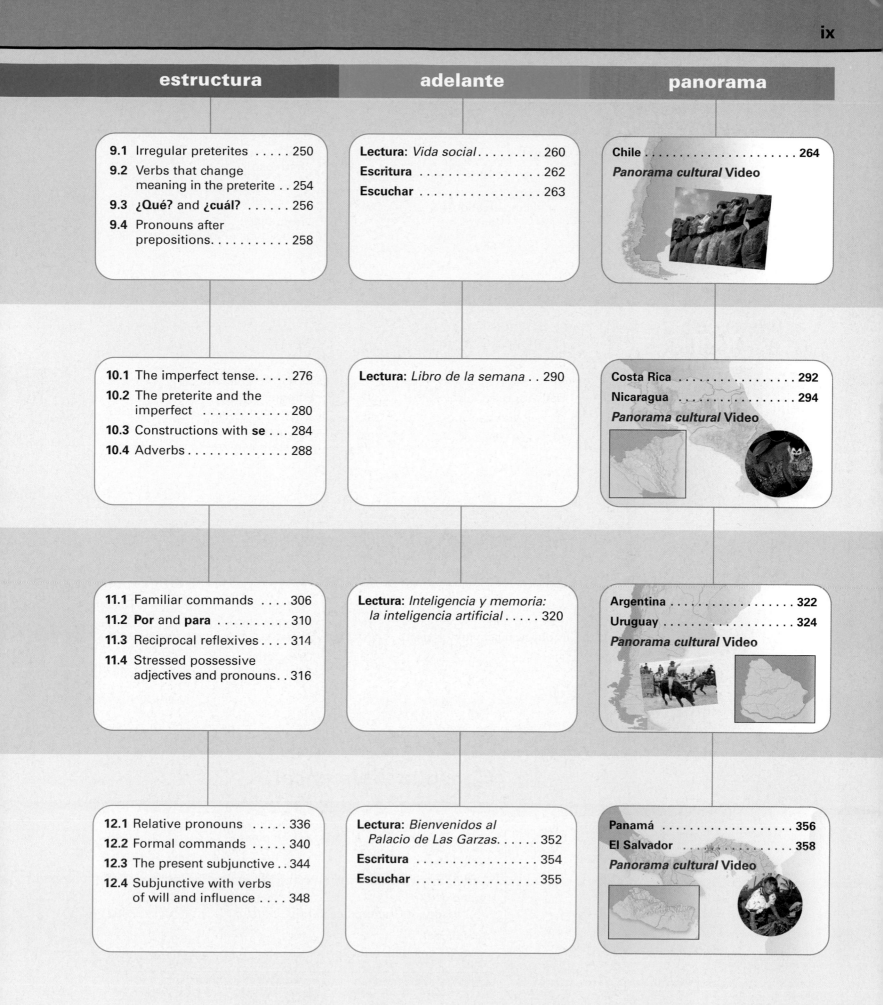

table of contents

	contextos	fotonovela

Consulta (*Reference*)

estructura	adelante	panorama

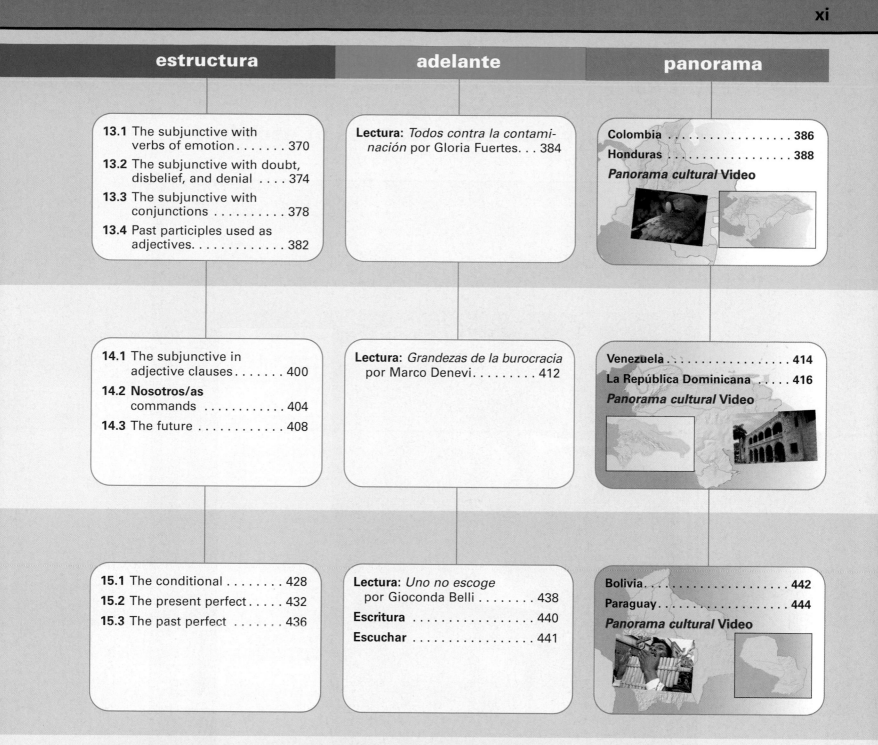

PANORAMA-at-a-glance

Lesson Openers
outline the content and features of each lesson.

La comida

8

Communicative Goals

You will learn how to:
- Order food in a restaurant
- Talk about and describe food

contextos

pages 210–215
- Food
- Food descriptions
- Meals

fotonovela

pages 216–219
The students and Don Francisco stop for a lunch break in the town of Cotacachi. They decide to eat at El Cráter, a restaurant owned by Don Francisco's friend, Doña Rita.

estructura

pages 220–235
- Preterite of stem-changing verbs
- Double object pronouns
- **Saber** and **conocer**
- Comparisons and superlatives

adelante

pages 236–237
Lectura: Read a menu and restaurant review.

panorama

pages 238–239
Featured country: Guatemala
- Antigua Guatemala
- The quetzal: a national symbol
- The Mayan civilization
- Mayan clothing

A PRIMERA VISTA
- ¿Está ella en un restaurante?
- ¿Trabaja ella?
- ¿Es parte de su rutina diaria?
- ¿Qué colores hay en la foto?

New! A primera vista activities jump-start the lessons, allowing you to use the Spanish you know to talk about the photos.

Communicative goals highlights the real-life tasks you will be able to carry out in Spanish by the end of each lesson.

Contextos
presents vocabulary in meaningful contexts.

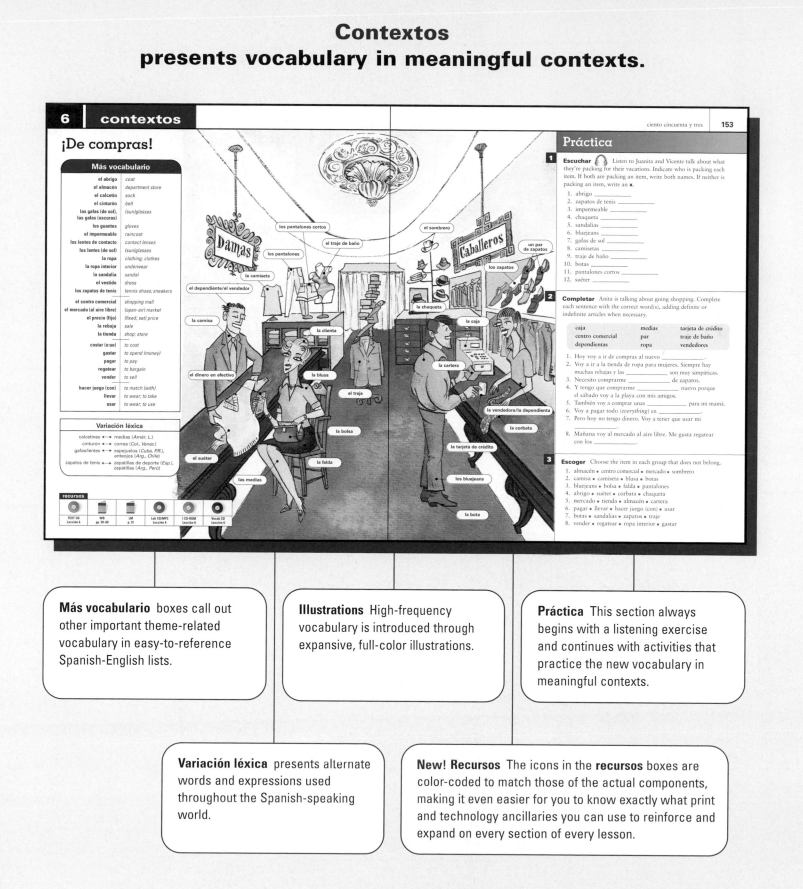

6 **contextos**

¡De compras!

Más vocabulario

el abrigo	coat
el almacén	department store
el calcetín	sock
el cinturón	belt
las gafas (de sol)	(sun)glasses
las gafas (oscuras)	
los guantes	gloves
el impermeable	raincoat
los lentes de contacto	contact lenses
los lentes (de sol)	(sun)glasses
la ropa	clothing; clothes
la ropa interior	underwear
la sandalia	sandal
el vestido	dress
los zapatos de tenis	tennis shoes; sneakers
el centro comercial	shopping mall
el mercado (al aire libre)	(open-air) market
el precio (fijo)	(fixed; set) price
la rebaja	sale
la tienda	shop; store
costar (o:ue)	to cost
gastar	to spend (money)
pagar	to pay
regatear	to bargain
vender	to sell
hacer juego (con)	to match (with)
llevar	to wear; to take
usar	to wear; to use

Variación léxica

calcetines ←→ medias (Amér. L.)
cinturón ←→ correa (Col., Venez.)
gafas/lentes ←→ espejuelos (Cuba, P.R.),
anteojos (Arg., Chile)
zapatos de tenis ←→ zapatillas de deporte (Esp.),
zapatillas (Arg., Perú)

recursos

TEXT CD Lección 6	WB pp. 59–60	LM p. 31	Lab CD/MP3 Lección 6	I CD-ROM Lección 6	Vocab CD Lección 6

Práctica

1 **Escuchar** Listen to Juanita and Vicente talk about what they're packing for their vacations. Indicate who is packing each item. If both are packing an item, write both names. If neither is packing an item, write an **x**.

1. abrigo _____
2. zapatos de tenis _____
3. impermeable _____
4. chaqueta _____
5. sandalias _____
6. bluejeans _____
7. gafas de sol _____
8. camisetas _____
9. traje de baño _____
10. botas _____
11. pantalones cortos _____
12. suéter _____

2 **Completar** Anita is talking about going shopping. Complete each sentence with the correct word(s), adding definite or indefinite articles when necessary.

caja	medias	tarjeta de crédito
centro comercial	par	traje de baño
dependientas	ropa	vendedores

1. Hoy voy a ir de compras al nuevo _____.
2. Voy a ir a la tienda de ropa para mujeres. Siempre hay muchas rebajas y las _____ son muy simpáticas.
3. Necesito comprarme _____ de zapatos.
4. Y tengo que comprarme _____ nuevo porque el sábado voy a la playa con mis amigos.
5. También voy a comprar unas _____ para mi mamá.
6. Voy a pagar todo (*everything*) en _____.
7. Pero hoy no tengo dinero. Voy a tener que usar mi _____.
8. Mañana voy al mercado al aire libre. Me gusta regatear con los _____.

3 **Escoger** Choose the item in each group that does not belong.

1. almacén • centro comercial • mercado • sombrero
2. camisa • camiseta • blusa • botas
3. bluejeans • bolsa • falda • pantalones
4. abrigo • suéter • corbata • chaqueta
5. mercado • tienda • almacén • cartera
6. pagar • llevar • hacer juego (con) • usar
7. botas • sandalias • zapatos • traje
8. vender • regatear • ropa interior • gastar

Más vocabulario boxes call out other important theme-related vocabulary in easy-to-reference Spanish-English lists.

Illustrations High-frequency vocabulary is introduced through expansive, full-color illustrations.

Práctica This section always begins with a listening exercise and continues with activities that practice the new vocabulary in meaningful contexts.

Variación léxica presents alternate words and expressions used throughout the Spanish-speaking world.

New! Recursos The icons in the **recursos** boxes are color-coded to match those of the actual components, making it even easier for you to know exactly what print and technology ancillaries you can use to reinforce and expand on every section of every lesson.

PANORAMA-at-a-glance

Contextos
practices vocabulary in a variety of formats.

Los días de la semana

¿Qué día es hoy (today)?

Hoy es martes.

¿Cuándo (when) es el examen?

Es el viernes.

septiembre

lunes	martes	miércoles	jueves	viernes	sábado	domingo
		1	2	3	4	5	6
7	8	9	10			

¡LENGUA VIVA!
The days of the week are never capitalized in Spanish.
• • •
Monday is considered the first day of the week in Spanish–speaking countries.

CONSÚLTALO
Note that September in Spanish is **septiembre**. To see all of the months of the year, go to **Contextos, Lección 5**, p. 124.

AYUDA
Ayer fue...
Yesterday was...

5 **¿Qué día es hoy?** Complete each statement with the correct day of the week.
1. Hoy es martes. Mañana es _____. Ayer fue _____.
2. Ayer fue sábado. Mañana es _____. Hoy es _____.
3. Mañana es viernes. Hoy es _____. Ayer fue _____.
4. Ayer fue domingo. Hoy es _____. Mañana es _____.
5. Hoy es jueves. Ayer fue _____. Mañana es _____.
6. Mañana es lunes. Hoy es _____. Ayer fue _____.

6 **Analogías** Use these words to complete the analogies. Some words will not be used.

arte	día	martes	pizarra
biblioteca	domingo	matemáticas	profesor
catorce	estudiante	mujer	reloj

1. maleta ←→ pasajero ⊙ mochila ←→ _____
2. chico ←→ chica ⊙ hombre ←→ _____
3. pluma ←→ papel ⊙ tiza ←→ _____
4. inglés ←→ lengua ⊙ miércoles ←→ _____
5. papel ←→ cuaderno ⊙ libro ←→ _____
6. quince ←→ dieciséis ⊙ lunes ←→ _____
7. Cervantes ←→ literatura ⊙ Dalí ←→ _____
8. autobús ←→ conductor ⊙ clase ←→ _____
9. EE.UU. ←→ mapa ⊙ hora ←→ _____
10. veinte ←→ veintitrés ⊙ jueves ←→ _____

Comunicación

7 **Horario** Choose three classes to create your own class schedule, then discuss it with a classmate.

¡ATENCIÓN!
Use **el** + [day of the week] when an activity occurs on a specific day and **los** + [day of the week] when an activity occurs regularly:
El lunes tengo un examen.
On Monday I have an exam.
Los lunes y miércoles tomo biología.
On Mondays and Wednesdays I take biology.
• • •
Except for **sábados** and **domingos**, the singular and plural forms for days of the week are the same.

materia	hora	días	profesor(a)
historia	9-10	lunes, miércoles	Ordóñez
biología	12-1	lunes, jueves	Dávila
periodismo	2-3	martes, jueves	Quiñones
matemáticas	2-3	miércoles, jueves	Jiménez
arte	12-1:30	lunes, miércoles	Molina

modelo
Estudiante 1: Tomo (*I take*) biología los lunes y jueves con la profesora Dávila.
Estudiante 2: ¿Sí? Yo no tomo biología. Yo tomo arte los lunes y miércoles con el profesor Molina.

8 **La clase** First, look around your classroom to get a mental image, then close your eyes. Your partner will then use these words or other vocabulary to ask you questions about the classroom. After you have answered six questions, switch roles.

modelo
Estudiante 1: ¿Cuántas ventanas hay?
Estudiante 2: Hay cuatro ventanas.

escritorio	mochila	puerta
estudiante	pizarra	reloj
libro	profesor(a)	silla

9 **Nuevos amigos** During the first week of class, you meet a new student in the cafeteria. With a partner, prepare a conversation using these cues.

Estudiante 1	**Estudiante 2**
Greet your new acquaintance.	Introduce yourself.
Find out about him or her.	Tell him or her about yourself.
Ask about your partner's class schedule.	Compare your schedule to your partner's.
Say nice to meet you and goodbye.	Say nice to meet you and goodbye.

Práctica exercises reinforce the vocabulary through varied and engaging formats.

Student sidebars provide handy, on-the-spot information that helps you complete the activities.

Comunicación activities allow you to use the vocabulary creatively in interactions with a partner, a small group, or the entire class.

Icons provide on-the-spot visual cues for various types of activities: pair, small group, listening-based, video-related, handout-based, and information gap. For a legend explaining all icons used in the student text, see page xxiii.

Fotonovela
tells the story of four students traveling in Ecuador.

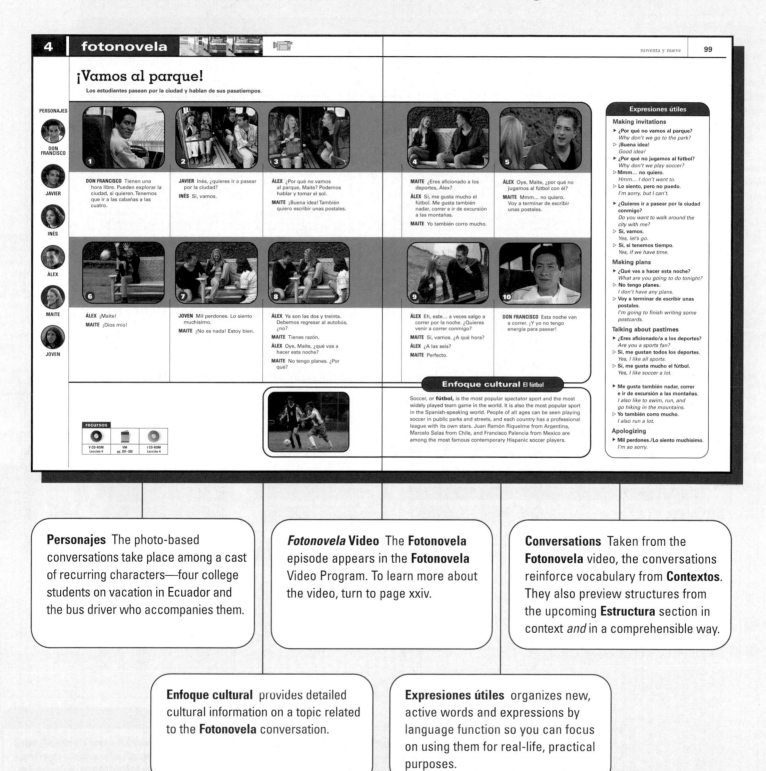

Personajes The photo-based conversations take place among a cast of recurring characters—four college students on vacation in Ecuador and the bus driver who accompanies them.

***Fotonovela* Video** The **Fotonovela** episode appears in the **Fotonovela** Video Program. To learn more about the video, turn to page xxiv.

Conversations Taken from the **Fotonovela** video, the conversations reinforce vocabulary from **Contextos**. They also preview structures from the upcoming **Estructura** section in context *and* in a comprehensible way.

Enfoque cultural provides detailed cultural information on a topic related to the **Fotonovela** conversation.

Expresiones útiles organizes new, active words and expressions by language function so you can focus on using them for real-life, practical purposes.

PANORAMA-at-a-glance

Pronunciación & Ortografía
present the rules of Spanish pronunciation and spelling.

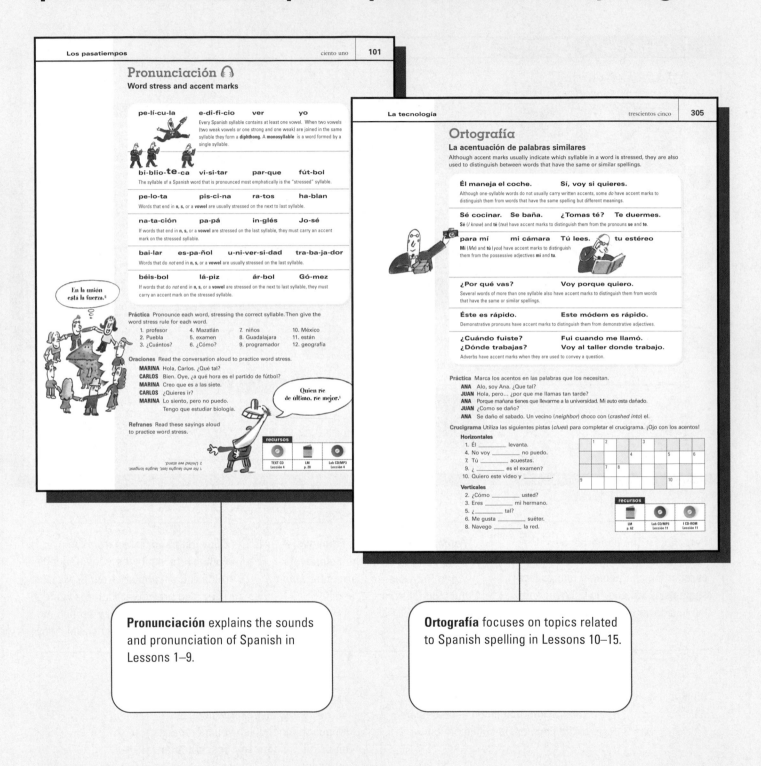

Pronunciación
Word stress and accent marks

pe-lí-cu-la   e-di-fi-cio   ver   yo

Every Spanish syllable contains at least one vowel. When two vowels (two weak vowels or one strong and one weak) are joined in the same syllable they form a **diphthong**. A **monosyllable** is a word formed by a single syllable.

bi-blio-**te**-ca   vi-si-tar   par-que   fút-bol

The syllable of a Spanish word that is pronounced most emphatically is the "stressed" syllable.

pe-lo-ta   pis-ci-na   ra-tos   ha-blan

Words that end in **n**, **s**, or a **vowel** are usually stressed on the next to last syllable.

na-ta-ción   pa-pá   in-glés   Jo-sé

If words that end in **n**, **s**, or a **vowel** are stressed on the last syllable, they must carry an accent mark on the stressed syllable.

bai-lar   es-pa-ñol   u-ni-ver-si-dad   tra-ba-ja-dor

Words that do *not* end in **n**, **s**, or a **vowel** are usually stressed on the last syllable.

béis-bol   lá-piz   ár-bol   Gó-mez

If words that do *not* end in **n**, **s**, or a **vowel** are stressed on the next to last syllable, they must carry an accent mark on the stressed syllable.

En la unión está la fuerza.²

Práctica Pronounce each word, stressing the correct syllable. Then give the word stress rule for each word.

1. profesor
2. Puebla
3. ¿Cuántos?
4. Mazatlán
5. examen
6. ¿Cómo?
7. niños
8. Guadalajara
9. programador
10. México
11. están
12. geografía

Oraciones Read the conversation aloud to practice word stress.

MARINA Hola, Carlos. ¿Qué tal?
CARLOS Bien. Oye, ¿a qué hora es el partido de fútbol?
MARINA Creo que es a las siete.
CARLOS ¿Quieres ir?
MARINA Lo siento, pero no puedo. Tengo que estudiar biología.

Quien ríe de último, ríe mejor.¹

Refranes Read these sayings aloud to practice word stress.

recursos

| TEXT CD Lección 4 | LM p. 29 | Lab CD/MP3 Lección 4 |

¹ *He who laughs last, laughs longest.* ² *United we stand.*

Ortografía
La acentuación de palabras similares

Although accent marks usually indicate which syllable in a word is stressed, they are also used to distinguish between words that have the same or similar spellings.

Él maneja el coche.   Sí, voy si quieres.

Although one-syllable words do not usually carry written accents, some *do* have accent marks to distinguish them from words that have the same spelling but different meanings.

Sé cocinar.   Se baña.   ¿Tomas té?   Te duermes.

Sé (*I know*) and **té** (*tea*) have accent marks to distinguish them from the pronouns **se** and **te**.

para mí   mi cámara   Tú lees.   tu estéreo

Mí (*Me*) and **tú** (*you*) have accent marks to distinguish them from the possessive adjectives **mi** and **tu**.

¿Por qué vas?   Voy porque quiero.

Several words of more than one syllable also have accent marks to distinguish them from words that have the same or similar spellings.

Éste es rápido.   Este módem es rápido.

Demonstrative pronouns have accent marks to distinguish them from demonstrative adjectives.

¿Cuándo fuiste?   Fui cuando me llamó.
¿Dónde trabajas?   Voy al taller donde trabajo.

Adverbs have accent marks when they are used to convey a question.

Práctica Marca los acentos en las palabras que los necesitan.

ANA Alo, soy Ana. ¿Que tal?
JUAN Hola, pero... ¿por que me llamas tan tarde?
ANA Porque mañana tienes que llevarme a la universidad. Mi auto esta dañado.
JUAN ¿Como se daño?
ANA Se daño el sabado. Un vecino (*neighbor*) choco con (*crashed into*) el.

Crucigrama Utiliza las siguientes pistas (*clues*) para completar el crucigrama. ¡Ojo con los acentos!

Horizontales
1. Él _____ levanta.
4. No voy _____ no puedo.
7. Tú _____ acuestas.
9. ¿_____ es el examen?
10. Quiero este video y _____.

Verticales
2. ¿Cómo _____ usted?
3. Eres _____ mi hermano.
5. ¿_____ tal?
6. Me gusta _____ suéter.
8. Navego _____ la red.

recursos

| LM p. 62 | Lab CD/MP3 Lección 11 | I CD-ROM Lección 11 |

Pronunciación explains the sounds and pronunciation of Spanish in Lessons 1–9.

Ortografía focuses on topics related to Spanish spelling in Lessons 10–15.

Estructura
presents Spanish grammar in a graphic-intensive format.

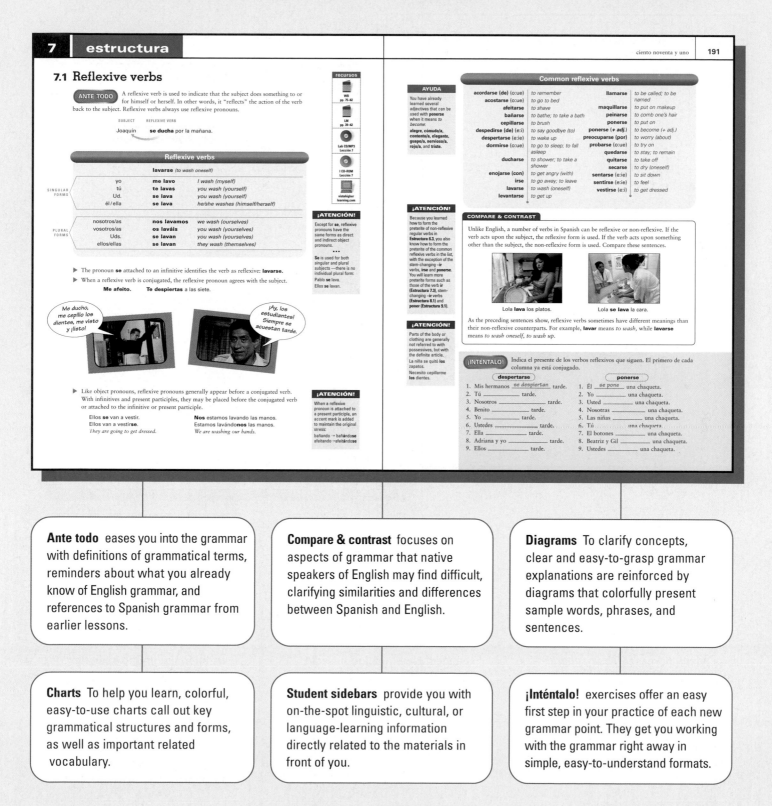

Ante todo eases you into the grammar with definitions of grammatical terms, reminders about what you already know of English grammar, and references to Spanish grammar from earlier lessons.

Compare & contrast focuses on aspects of grammar that native speakers of English may find difficult, clarifying similarities and differences between Spanish and English.

Diagrams To clarify concepts, clear and easy-to-grasp grammar explanations are reinforced by diagrams that colorfully present sample words, phrases, and sentences.

Charts To help you learn, colorful, easy-to-use charts call out key grammatical structures and forms, as well as important related vocabulary.

Student sidebars provide you with on-the-spot linguistic, cultural, or language-learning information directly related to the materials in front of you.

¡Inténtalo! exercises offer an easy first step in your practice of each new grammar point. They get you working with the grammar right away in simple, easy-to-understand formats.

Estructura
provides directed and communicative practice.

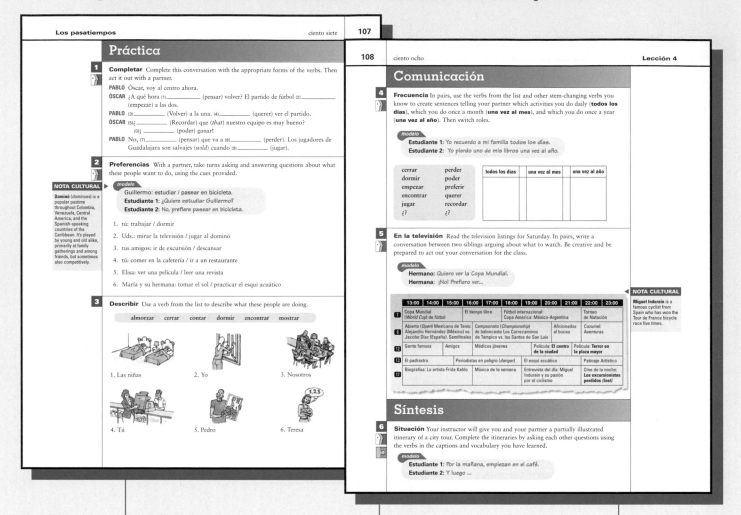

Práctica activities provide a wide range of guided, yet meaningful exercises that weave current and previously learned vocabulary together with the current grammar point.

Comunicación offers opportunities for creative expression using the lesson's grammar and vocabulary. These take place with a partner, in small groups, or with the whole class.

Síntesis integrates the current grammar point with previously learned points, providing built-in, consistent review and recycling as you progress through the text.

Expanded! Increased *Nota cultural* **sidebars** expand coverage of the cultures of the Spanish-speaking peoples and countries with a special emphasis on everyday-life practices. In Spanish as of Lesson 7, the cultural notes also provide additional reading practice.

Expanded! New reading-based activities involving authentic documents, dialogues, and other brief texts provide increased reading opportunities throughout the textbook.

New! Information Gap activities engage you and a partner in problem-solving and other situations based on handouts your instructor gives you. However, you and your partner each have only half of the information you need, so you must work together to accomplish the task at hand.

Adelante

In every lesson, *Lectura* develops reading skills in the context of the lesson theme.

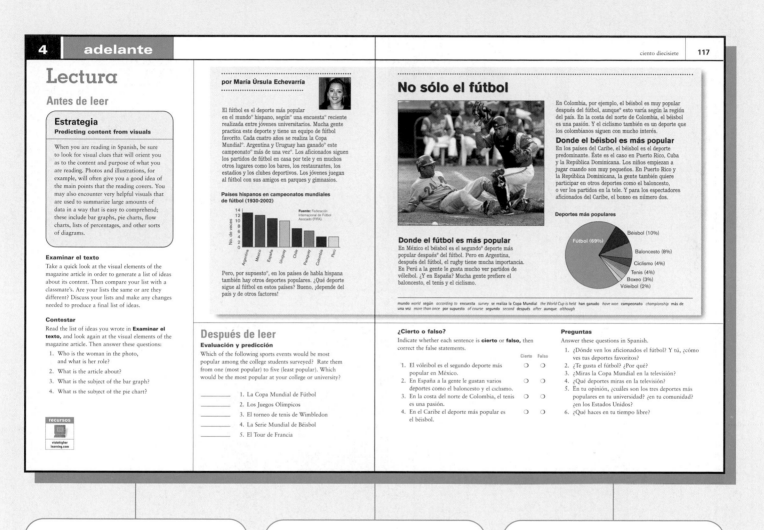

Antes de leer presents valuable reading strategies and pre-reading activities that strengthen your reading abilities in Spanish.

Readings are specifically related to the lesson theme and recycle vocabulary and grammar you have learned. The selections in Lessons 1–12 are cultural texts, while those in Lessons 13–15 are literary pieces.

Después de leer includes post-reading exercises that review and check your comprehension of the reading.

New! Three cultural and two literary readings are new to **PANORAMA 2/e.** Lessons 4, 7, and 11 feature high-interest, culturally-oriented texts; Lessons 13 and 15 offer new highly accessible, theme-related poems.

PANORAMA-at-a-glance

Adelante

In Lessons 3, 6, 9, 12, and 15, *Escritura* and *Escuchar* develop writing and listening skills.

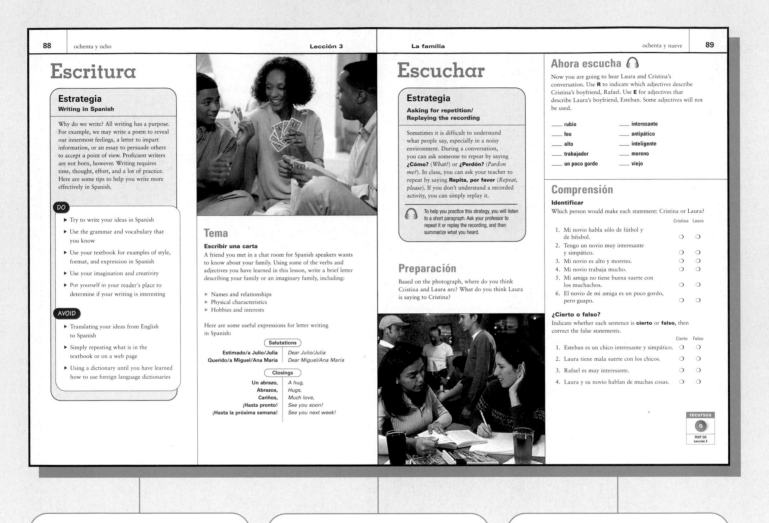

Escritura

Estrategia
Writing in Spanish

Why do we write? All writing has a purpose. For example, we may write a poem to reveal our innermost feelings, a letter to impart information, or an essay to persuade others to accept a point of view. Proficient writers are not born, however. Writing requires time, thought, effort, and a lot of practice. Here are some tips to help you write more effectively in Spanish.

DO

▶ Try to write your ideas in Spanish
▶ Use the grammar and vocabulary that you know
▶ Use your textbook for examples of style, format, and expression in Spanish
▶ Use your imagination and creativity
▶ Put yourself in your reader's place to determine if your writing is interesting

AVOID

▶ Translating your ideas from English to Spanish
▶ Simply repeating what is in the textbook or on a web page
▶ Using a dictionary until you have learned how to use foreign language dictionaries

Tema

Escribir una carta

A friend you met in a chat room for Spanish speakers wants to know about your family. Using some of the verbs and adjectives you have learned in this lesson, write a brief letter describing your family or an imaginary family, including:

▶ Names and relationships
▶ Physical characteristics
▶ Hobbies and interests

Here are some useful expressions for letter writing in Spanish:

Salutations

Estimado/a Julio/Julia	Dear Julio/Julia
Querido/a Miguel/Ana María	Dear Miguel/Ana María

Closings

Un abrazo,	A hug,
Abrazos,	Hugs,
Cariños,	Much love,
¡Hasta pronto!	See you soon!
¡Hasta la próxima semana!	See you next week!

Escuchar

Estrategia
Asking for repetition/
Replaying the recording

Sometimes it is difficult to understand what people say, especially in a noisy environment. During a conversation, you can ask someone to repeat by saying **¿Cómo?** (*What?*) or **¿Perdón?** (*Pardon me?*). In class, you can ask your teacher to repeat by saying **Repita, por favor** (*Repeat, please*). If you don't understand a recorded activity, you can simply replay it.

To help you practice this strategy, you will listen to a short paragraph. Ask your professor to repeat it or replay the recording, and then summarize what you heard.

Preparación

Based on the photograph, where do you think Cristina and Laura are? What do you think Laura is saying to Cristina?

Ahora escucha

Now you are going to hear Laura and Cristina's conversation. Use **R** to indicate which adjectives describe Cristina's boyfriend, Rafael. Use **E** for adjectives that describe Laura's boyfriend, Esteban. Some adjectives will not be used.

___ rubio		___ interesante
___ feo		___ antipático
___ alto		___ inteligente
___ trabajador		___ moreno
___ un poco gordo		___ viejo

Comprensión

Identificar
Which person would make each statement: Cristina or Laura?

	Cristina	Laura
1. Mi novio habla sólo de fútbol y de béisbol.	○	○
2. Tengo un novio muy interesante y simpático.	○	○
3. Mi novio es alto y moreno.	○	○
4. Mi novio trabaja mucho.	○	○
5. Mi amiga no tiene buena suerte con los muchachos.	○	○
6. El novio de mi amiga es un poco gordo, pero guapo.	○	○

¿Cierto o falso?
Indicate whether each sentence is **cierto** or **falso,** then correct the false statements.

	Cierto	Falso
1. Esteban es un chico interesante y simpático.	○	○
2. Laura tiene mala suerte con los chicos.	○	○
3. Rafael es muy interesante.	○	○
4. Laura y su novio hablan de muchas cosas.	○	○

recursos
TEXT CD
Lección 3

88 ochenta y ocho Lección 3   La familia ochenta y nueve 89

Estrategia provides strategies that help you prepare for the writing task presented in this section.

Tema describes the writing topic and includes suggestions for approaching it.

Escuchar presents a recorded conversation or narration to develop your listening skills in Spanish. **Estrategia** and **Preparación** prepare you for listening to the recorded passage.

Ahora escucha tracks you through the passage, and **Comprensión** checks your understanding of what you heard.

Panorama
presents the nations of the Spanish-speaking world.

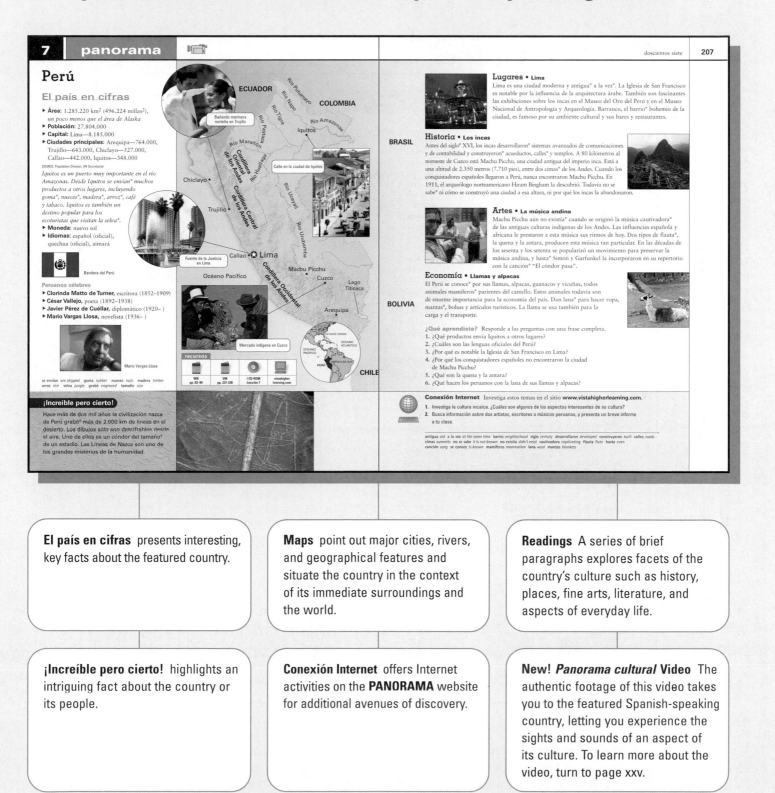

El país en cifras presents interesting, key facts about the featured country.

Maps point out major cities, rivers, and geographical features and situate the country in the context of its immediate surroundings and the world.

Readings A series of brief paragraphs explores facets of the country's culture such as history, places, fine arts, literature, and aspects of everyday life.

¡Increíble pero cierto! highlights an intriguing fact about the country or its people.

Conexión Internet offers Internet activities on the **PANORAMA** website for additional avenues of discovery.

New! *Panorama cultural* Video The authentic footage of this video takes you to the featured Spanish-speaking country, letting you experience the sights and sounds of an aspect of its culture. To learn more about the video, turn to page xxv.

PANORAMA-at-a-glance

Vocabulario
summarizes all the active vocabulary of the lesson.

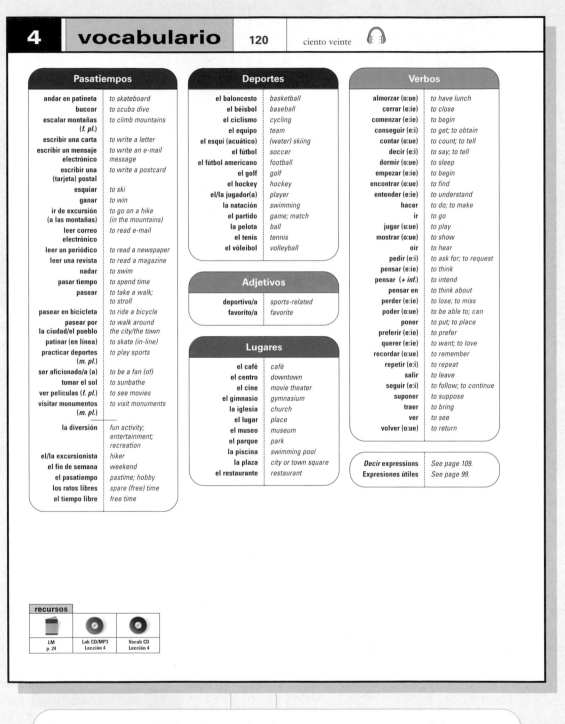

4 vocabulario 120 ciento veinte

Pasatiempos

andar en patineta	to skateboard
bucear	to scuba dive
escalar montañas (f. pl.)	to climb mountains
escribir una carta	to write a letter
escribir un mensaje electrónico	to write an e-mail message
escribir una (tarjeta) postal	to write a postcard
esquiar	to ski
ganar	to win
ir de excursión (a las montañas)	to go on a hike (in the mountains)
leer correo electrónico	to read e-mail
leer un periódico	to read a newspaper
leer una revista	to read a magazine
nadar	to swim
pasar tiempo	to spend time
pasear	to take a walk; to stroll
pasear en bicicleta	to ride a bicycle
pasear por la ciudad/el pueblo	to walk around the city/the town
patinar (en línea)	to skate (in-line)
practicar deportes (m. pl.)	to play sports
ser aficionado/a (a)	to be a fan (of)
tomar el sol	to sunbathe
ver películas (f. pl.)	to see movies
visitar monumentos (m. pl.)	to visit monuments
la diversión	fun activity; entertainment; recreation
el/la excursionista	hiker
el fin de semana	weekend
el pasatiempo	pastime; hobby
los ratos libres	spare (free) time
el tiempo libre	free time

Deportes

el baloncesto	basketball
el béisbol	baseball
el ciclismo	cycling
el equipo	team
el esquí (acuático)	(water) skiing
el fútbol	soccer
el fútbol americano	football
el golf	golf
el hockey	hockey
el/la jugador(a)	player
la natación	swimming
el partido	game; match
la pelota	ball
el tenis	tennis
el vóleibol	volleyball

Adjetivos

deportivo/a	sports-related
favorito/a	favorite

Lugares

el café	café
el centro	downtown
el cine	movie theater
el gimnasio	gymnasium
la iglesia	church
el lugar	place
el museo	museum
el parque	park
la piscina	swimming pool
la plaza	city or town square
el restaurante	restaurant

Verbos

almorzar (o:ue)	to have lunch
cerrar (e:ie)	to close
comenzar (e:ie)	to begin
conseguir (e:i)	to get; to obtain
contar (o:ue)	to count; to tell
decir (e:i)	to say; to tell
dormir (o:ue)	to sleep
empezar (e:ie)	to begin
encontrar (o:ue)	to find
entender (e:ie)	to understand
hacer	to do; to make
ir	to go
jugar (u:ue)	to play
mostrar (o:ue)	to show
oír	to hear
pedir (e:i)	to ask for; to request
pensar (e:ie)	to think
pensar (+ inf.)	to intend
pensar en	to think about
perder (e:ie)	to lose; to miss
poder (o:ue)	to be able to; can
poner	to put; to place
preferir (e:ie)	to prefer
querer (e:ie)	to want; to love
recordar (o:ue)	to remember
repetir (e:i)	to repeat
salir	to leave
seguir (e:i)	to follow; to continue
suponer	to suppose
traer	to bring
ver	to see
volver (o:ue)	to return

Decir expressions	See page 109.
Expresiones útiles	See page 99.

recursos

LM p. 24 · Lab CD/MP3 Lección 4 · Vocab CD Lección 4

New! Recorded vocabulary The headset icon at the top of the page and the **recursos** box at the bottom of the page highlight that the active lesson vocabulary is recorded for convenient study on both the Lab Audio Program and the new Vocabulary CDs.

ICONS AND RECURSOS BOXES

Icons

Icons provide on-the-spot support throughout the student text. They appear at the beginning of sections or next to activities in **PANORAMA, Second Edition**.

Icons legend			
🎧	Listening activity/section	📹	Video-based activity/section
	Pair activity		Information Gap activity
	Group activity		Hoja de actividades

- The Information Gap activities and those involving **Hojas de actividades** (*activity sheets*) require handouts that your instructor will give you.
- You will see the listening icon in each lesson's **Contextos**, **Pronunciación**, **Escuchar** and **Vocabulario** sections.
- The video icon appears in the **Fotonovela** and the **Panorama** sections of each lesson.

Recursos

Recursos boxes let you know exactly what print and technology ancillaries you can use to reinforce and expand on every section of the lessons in your textbook. They even include page numbers when applicable. In **PANORAMA 2/e**, the colors of the icons for the CDs and CD-ROMs match those of the actual ancillaries, making it even easier for you to use the complete program. See page xxvi for a description of the ancillaries.

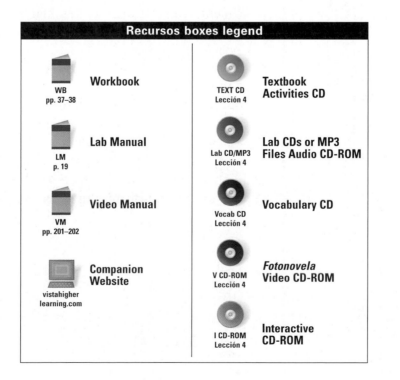

Recursos boxes legend			
WB pp. 37–38	Workbook	TEXT CD Lección 4	Textbook Activities CD
LM p. 19	Lab Manual	Lab CD/MP3 Lección 4	Lab CDs or MP3 Files Audio CD-ROM
VM pp. 201–202	Video Manual	Vocab CD Lección 4	Vocabulary CD
vistahigher learning.com	Companion Website	V CD-ROM Lección 4	*Fotonovela* Video CD-ROM
		I CD-ROM Lección 4	Interactive CD-ROM

FOTONOVELA VIDEO PROGRAM

Fully integrated with your textbook, the **PANORAMA** video contains fifteen episodes, one for each lesson of the text. The episodes present the adventures of four college students who are studying at the **Universidad de San Francisco** in Quito, Ecuador. They decide to spend their vacation break on a bus tour of the Ecuadorian countryside with the ultimate goal of hiking up a volcano. The video, shot in various locations in Ecuador, tells their story and the story of Don Francisco, the tour bus driver who accompanies them.

The **Fotonovela** section in each textbook lesson is actually an abbreviated version of the dramatic episode featured in the video. Therefore, each **Fotonovela** section can be done before you see the corresponding video episode, after it, or as a section that stands alone in its own right.

As you watch each video episode, you will first see a live segment in which the characters interact using vocabulary and grammar you are studying. As the video progresses, the live segments carefully combine new vocabulary and grammar with previously taught language. You will then see a **Resumen** section in which one of the main video characters recaps the live segment, emphasizing the grammar and vocabulary you are studying within the context of the episode's key events.

In addition, in most of the video episodes, there are brief pauses to allow the characters to reminisce about their home country. These flashbacks—montages of real-life images shot in Spain, Mexico, Puerto Rico, and various parts of Ecuador—connect the theme of the video to everyday life in various parts of the Spanish-speaking world.

THE CAST

Here are the main characters you will meet when you watch the **PANORAMA** video:

From Ecuador,
Inés Ayala Loor

From Spain,
María Teresa (Maite) Fuentes de Alba

From Mexico,
Alejandro (Álex) Morales Paredes

From Puerto Rico,
Javier Gómez Lozano

And, also from Ecuador,
don Francisco Castillo Moreno

PANORAMA CULTURAL VIDEO PROGRAM

The new **Panorama cultural** video is integrated with the **Panorama** section in each lesson of **PANORAMA, Second Edition**. Each segment is 2–3 minutes long and consists of documentary footage from each of the countries featured. The images were specially chosen for interest level and visual appeal, while the all-Spanish narrations were carefully written to reflect the vocabulary and grammar covered in the textbook.

As you watch the video segments, you will experience a diversity of images and topics: cities, monuments, traditions, festivals, archaeological sites, geographical wonders, and more. You will be transported to each Spanish-speaking country including the United States and Canada, thereby having the opportunity to expand your cultural perspectives with information directly related to the content of **PANORAMA, Second Edition**.

STUDENT ANCILLARIES

▶ **Workbook/Video Manual**
The Workbook/Video Manual contains the workbook activities for each textbook lesson, activities for the **Fotonovela** Video, and new pre-, while-, and post-viewing activities for the **Panorama cultural** Video.

▶ **Lab Manual**
The Lab Manual contains lab activities for each textbook lesson for use with the Lab Audio Program.

▶ **Lab Audio Program**
15 CDs or 1 MP3 Files Audio CD-ROM

▶ **Textbook Activities CD***
The Textbook Activities CD contains the audio recordings for the listening-based activities in the student text.

▶ **New! Vocabulary CDs***
The Vocabulary CDs contain recordings of the active vocabulary in each lesson of the student text.

▶ ***Fotonovela* Video CD-ROM***
The **Fotonovela** Video CD-ROM provides the complete **Fotonovela** Video Program with videoscripts, note-taking capabilities, and navigation tools.

▶ **Significant Revision! Interactive CD-ROMs***
These Interactive CD-ROMs, overwhelmingly popular among students, contain multimedia practice of the language taught in each lesson, as well as practice quizzes with autoscoring and feedback. Improved **Panorama** sections feature interactive geographical maps, comprehension checks, and the entire **Panorama Cultural** Video Program.

▶ **VHL Intro Spanish Pocket Dictionary and Language Guide***
The VHL Intro Spanish Pocket Dictionary and Language Guide is a portable reference for Spanish words, expressions, idioms, and more, created expressly to complement and extend the student text.

▶ **Web-SAM** (online Workbook/Video Manual/Lab Manual)

▶ **New! PANORAMA eText**
(www.vistahigherlearning.com)
Accessed through the **PANORAMA 2/e** website, the eText is a ground-breaking online version of **PANORAMA 2/e.** It delivers the contents of the printed textbook, plus the Textbook Activities CDs and the **Fotonovela** and **Panorama cultural** Videos, in interactive formats ideal for online courses and distance learning applications, or as a supplement to **PANORAMA 2/e.** Students can interact with the textbook, access specially designed step-by-step vocabulary and grammar tutorials, do practice activities, complete tests, and communicate orally and in writing with their instructor and e-partners. Instructors have access to powerful electronic gradebook and classroom management tools for tracking students' performance and administering tests.

▶ **Expanded! Companion Website***
(www.vistahigherlearning.com)
The **PANORAMA 2/e** website provides an abundance of activities and resources specially created to reinforce and expand on the language and culture presented in each lesson of the student text. Auto-scored exercises review the vocabulary and grammar; cultural activities explore the theme and country of focus; **Conexión Internet** activities support directly their corresponding activities in the textbook's **Panorama** sections; and a new reading with pre- and post-reading exercises provides increased reading practice. Among the resources included are an electronic verb wheel, an online dictionary, links to the entire Spanish-speaking world, and entryways to the **PANORAMA 2/e** Web-SAM and eText.

*Free with purchase of a new Student Text

INSTRUCTOR ANCILLARIES

▶ **New! Instructor's Annotated Edition (IAE)**
The expanded trim size and enhanced design of the **PANORAMA 2/e IAE** make the annotations and facsimile student pages easier to read and reference in the classroom.

▶ **Expanded! Instructor's Resource Manual (IRM)**
The IRM contains Tapescripts, Videoscripts, English translations of both the **Fotonovela** conversations and the **Panorama cultural** Video, **Hojas de actividades** for selected textbook activities, **Vocabulario adicional** handouts for each lesson, and answers to the ¡**Inténtalo!** and **Práctica** activities in the student text.

▶ **New! Information Gap Activities Booklet**
This booklet contains the handouts for the information gap activities in the student text, plus additional info gap activities.

▶ **New! Workbook/Video Manual/Lab Manual Answer Key**

▶ **Major Revision! Testing Program**
Four different tests are now provided for each lesson, as well as two midterm and final exams for the semester and quarter systems. All tests and exams have been thoroughly revised to make them more contextualized and communicative and to include reading sections. Two new communicative tests have been added for each lesson, as well as optional sections with alternate listening sections and test items for the **Fotonovela** Video, the **Panorama** textbook sections, and the **Panorama cultural** Video.

▶ **Major Revision! Testing Program Audio CD**
The CD contains the listening passages to be used in conjunction with the listening sections on the tests and exams. Scripts for the passages are located in the printed Testing Program and on the Test Files CD-ROM.

▶ **Major Revision! Test Files CD-ROM**
The Test Files CD-ROM (for Windows® and Macintosh®) contains the tests, exams, listening scripts, optional sections, and answer keys of the printed Testing Program as Microsoft Word® files. Instructors can customize the materials to suit their curricula and/or teaching styles.

▶ **New! Test Generator** BROWNSTONE
The Test Generator provides a test bank of the entire **PANORAMA 2/e** Testing Program on CD-ROM and includes a robust online testing component. Instructors can modify existing tests, create their own tests, and randomly generate new tests. Test items with discrete answers are automatically scored, and all grades are easily exported to WebCT and Blackboard.

▶ **New! *Panorama cultural* Video Program (VHS)**
The **Panorama cultural** Video Program consists of authentic footage from each of the Spanish-speaking countries featured in each lesson's **Panorama** section. The images were specifically chosen for interest level and visual appeal, while the all-Spanish narrations were specially written to reflect the vocabulary and grammar taught in the text.

▶ ***Fotonovela* Video Program (VHS)**
This specially-shot video, a favorite among students using **PANORAMA 1/e**, is closely and distinctively integrated with each lesson of the textbook.

▶ **New! DVD**
The complete **Fotonovela** Video and the new **Panorama cultural** Video are available on DVD.

▶ **New! *Contextos* and *Estructura* Presentations CD-ROM**
This CD-ROM contains PDFs of the Overhead Transparencies (the **Contextos** illustrations, maps, and more); a Microsoft PowerPoint® presentation for each **Estructura** grammar point; and selected photographs from each textbook lesson.

▶ **Overhead Transparencies**
The Transparencies consist of the maps of the countries of the Spanish-speaking world, the **Contextos** vocabulary drawings, and other selected illustrations from the student text.

▶ **Expanded! Companion Website***
(www.vistahigherlearning.com)
The **PANORAMA 2/e** website supports instructors with a wide range of online resources—cultural information and links, lyrics to the music on the **Fotonovela** Video, a professional center, teaching suggestions, course syllabi, lesson plans, and more—that directly correlate to the textbook and go beyond it.

ACKNOWLEDGMENTS

On behalf of its authors and editors, Vista Higher Learning expresses its sincere appreciation to the many college professors nationwide who contributed their ideas and suggestions to **VISTAS**, our flagship program from which **PANORAMA** is derived. We are grateful to the more than fifty members of the Spanish-teaching community who participated in focus groups and class-tested materials at the initial stages of the program, as well as the more than sixty instructors who reviewed it. Their insights and detailed comments were invaluable to **VISTAS** and **PANORAMA** in their final published forms.

VISTAS, Second Edition, and **PANORAMA, Second Edition**, are the direct result of extensive reviews and ongoing input from both students and instructors using the first editions. Accordingly, we gratefully acknowledge these educators and students who shared their suggestions, recommendations, and ideas:

- Mary Ellen Brines of Alma College and her students for their valuable feedback
- Julio Rivera and his students at Foothill College for their generous input
- Dr. Antonio Velásquez of McMaster University in Ontario, Canada for his contributions regarding the presence and influence of the Spanish language and Hispanic cultures in Canada
- Dr. Mary Ann Dellinger of Virginia Military Institute for her work on the first editions and her contributions to the Instructor's Annotated Editions of the second editions
- Dr. Mercedes Valle of the University of Massachusetts, Amherst and Smith College for her contributions to the Testing Program
- José Cruz of Fayetteville Technical Community College for his thorough suggestions for the Web-SAM that have resulted in enhanced Web-SAMs for the second editions
- Yolanda González of Valencia Community College for her thoughtful remarks about and cogent advice for improving **PANORAMA**

We also extend a special thank you to the following teaching professionals:
- The almost one hundred instructors who completed reviews of **VISTAS**. Their comments and suggestions were instrumental in shaping the second editions of both **VISTAS** and **PANORAMA**.
- The six instructors who provided in-depth reviews of **VISTAS** based on the everyday use of the materials in their classrooms. Their practical, detailed comments and constructive ideas were critical in helping us to fine-tune virtually every page of every lesson in **VISTAS** and **PANORAMA**.

VISTAS In-depth Reviewers

María I. Fleck
  Cerritos College, CA

Jerome Miner
  Knox College, IL

Michael Panbehchi
  Virginia Commonwealth
  University, VA

Joyce Pinkard
  Fresno City College, CA

Claire Reetz
  Florida Community College,
  Jacksonville, FL

Julio C. Rivera
  Foothill College, CA

VISTAS Reviewers

Amanda Amend
  St. Michael's College, VT

Renée Andrade
  Mount San Antonio College, CA

David Arbesú Fernández
  University of Massachusetts,
  Amherst, MA

Rafael Arias
  Los Angeles Valley College, LA

Emily Ballou
  University of Calgary,
  Canada

Amy R. Barber
  Grove City College, PA

Allen Bertsche
  Augustana College, IL

Jane Harrington Bethune
  Salve Regina University, RI

Patrick Brady
  Tidewater Community College, VA

Mary Ellen Brines
  Alma College, MI

Veronica Burke
  Lyon College, AR

Karen Burrell
  Mary Washington College, VA

Billy Bussell-Thompson
  Hofstra University, NY

Danielle Cahill
  Christopher Newport University, VA

Fernando Canto-Lugo
  Yuba Community College, CA

Patricia H. Carlin
  University of Central Arkansas, AR

Irene Chico-Wyatt
  University of Kentucky, KY

Kimberly Contag
  Minnesota State University,
  Mankato MN

Lisa Contreras
  Transylvania University, KY

Marzia Corni-Benson
  Indian Hills Community College, IA

Linda Crawford
  Salve Regina University, RI

José Cruz
  Fayetteville Technical
  Community College, NC

Maria D. Delgado-Hellin
  Willamette University, OR

Rocío Domínguez
  Carnegie Mellon University, PA

Deborah M. Edson
  Tidewater Community College, VA

John L. Finan
  William Rainey Harper College, IL

María I. Fleck
  Cerritos College, CA

Roberto Fuertes-Manjón
  Midwestern State University, TX

Adalberto García
  Midwestern State University, TX

Lourdes Girardi
  Glendale Community College, CA

James Grabowska
  Minnesota State University,
  Mankato MN

Linda Hollabaugh
  Midwestern State University, TX

Patricia G. Horner
  Stanly Community College, NC

Nan Hussey
  Houghton College, NY

Chuck Hutchings
  Central Oregon Community
  College, OR

Alfonso Illingworth-Rico
  Eastern Michigan University, MI

Franklin Inojosa
  Richard J. Daley College, IL

Joseph C. Jeter
  Alabama A & M University, AL

Eric Jewell
  Truman State University, MO

Steven D. Kirby
  Eastern Michigan University, MI

M. Phillip Kristiansen
  University of the Ozarks, AR

Lora Looney
  University of Portland, OR

acknowledgments

VISTAS Reviewers

Esteban E. Loustaunau
Augustana College, IL

Bernard Manker
Grand Rapids Community
College, MI

Carol Marshall
Truman State University, MO

Gianna M. Martella
Western Oregon University, OR

Vidal Martín
Everett Community College, WA

Laurie Mattas
College of DuPage, IL

Haven McBee
Middle Tennessee State
University, TN

Suzanne McLaughlin
Chemeketa Community
College, OR

Jerome Miner
Knox College, IL

Carrie Mittleman
University of Massachusetts,
Amherst, MA

Charles H. Molano
Dodge City Community
College, KS

Karen-Jean Muñoz
Florida Community College,
Jacksonville, FL

Nancy C. Mustafa
Virginia Commonwealth
University, VA

M. Margarita Nodarse
Barry University, FL

Kathleen D. O'Connor
Tidewater Community College, VA

Milagros Ojermark
Diablo Valley College, CA

Daniel Onorato
Modesto Junior College, CA

Michael Panbehchi
Virginia Commonwealth
University, VA

John Parrack
University of Central
Arkansas, AR

Peregrina Pereiro
Washburn University, KS

Gladys A. Perez
University of Portland, OR

Martha Perez
Kirkwood Community College,
Iowa City, IA

Inmaculada Pertusa
University of Kentucky, KY

Joyce Pinkard
Fresno City College, CA

Ruth Ellen Porter
Brewton-Parker College, GA

Karry Putzy
Kirkwood Community College,
Iowa City, IA

Richard Reid
Grand Rapids Community
College, MI

Claire Reetz
Florida Community College,
Jacksonville, FL

Rita Ricaurte
Nebraska Wesleyan
University, NE

Julio C. Rivera
Foothill College, CA

Anthony J. Robb
Rowan University, NJ

Cathy A. Robison
Clemson University, SC

Theresa E. Ruiz-Velasco
College of Lake County, IL

José Carlos Saa-Ramos
Washburn University, KS

Jan Satterlee
Richland Community College, IL

Kathy Schmidt
Minneapolis Community Technical
College, MN

Mary Shea
Napa Valley College, CA

Juanita Shettlesworth
Tennessee Technological
University, TN

Roger Simpson
Clemson University, SC

Laurel Sparks
North Dakota State University, ND

Daniela Stewart
Everett Community College, WA

Cristobal Trillo
Joliet Junior College, IL

Alejandro Varderi
Borough of Manhattan Community
College of CUNY, NY

David J. Viera
Tennessee Technological
University, TN

Keith Watts
Grand Valley State
University, MI

James Reese Weckler
Minnesota State University,
Moorhead, MN

Georgina Whittingham
Oswego, State University of New
York, NY

Terri Wilbanks
University of South Alabama, AL

Diane Wright
Grand Valley State University, MI

Laura Yocom
Centralia College, WA

Mary F. Yudin
Mary Washington College, VA

Hola, ¿qué tal?

1

Communicative Goals

You will learn how to:

- **Greet people in Spanish**
- **Say goodbye**
- **Identify yourself and others**
- **Talk about the time of day**

A PRIMERA VISTA
- **Guess what the people in the photo are saying:**
  a. Café b. Hola c. Salsa
- **Most likely they would also say:**
  a. Gracias b. Fiesta c. Buenos días
- **The women are:**
  a. amigas b. chicos c. señores

contextos

fotonovela

estructura

adelante

panorama

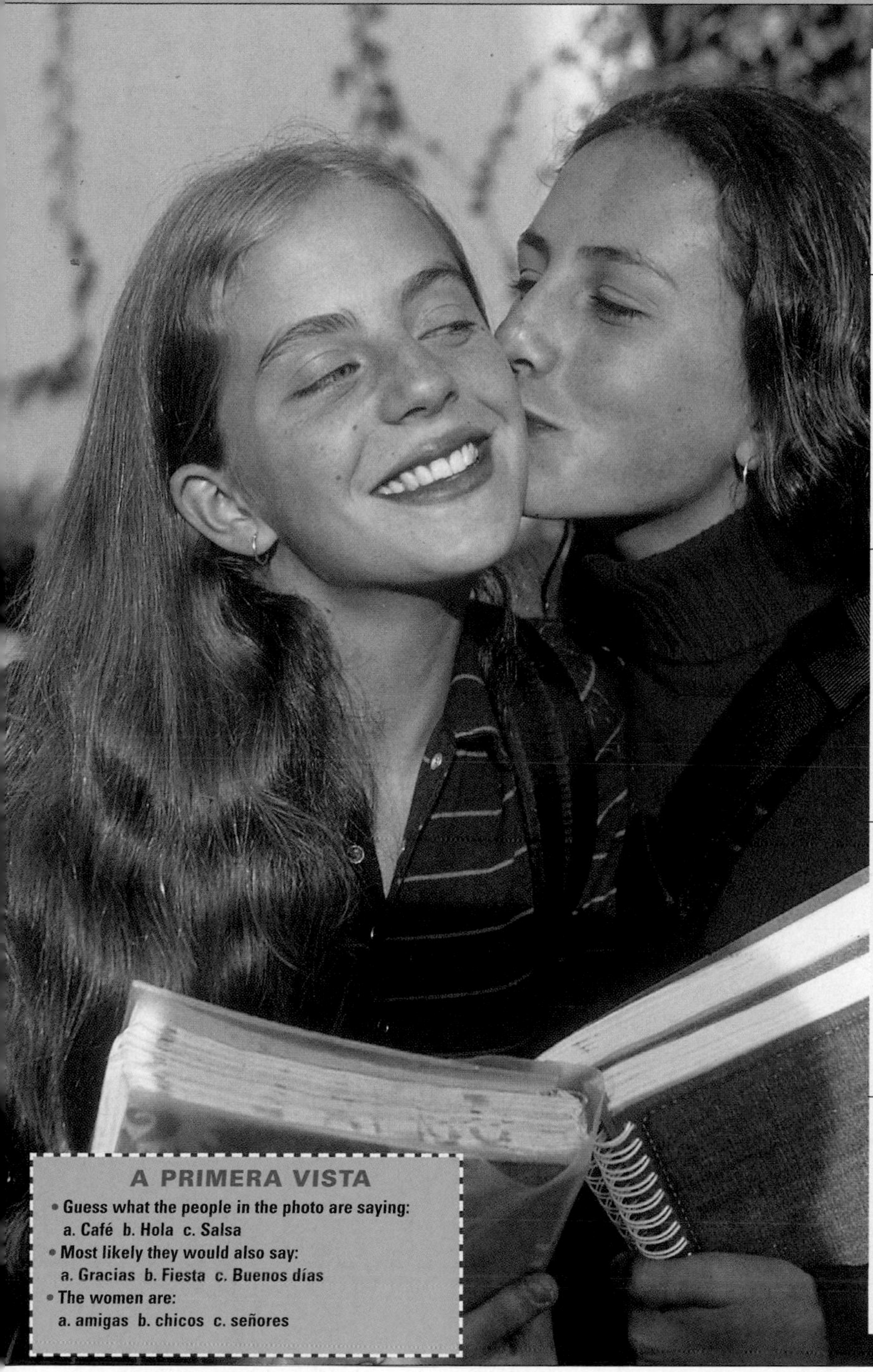

Lesson Goals

In **Lección 1** students will be introduced to the following:
- terms for greetings and leave-takings
- identifying where one is from
- expressions of courtesy
- nouns and articles (definite and indefinite)
- numbers 0–30
- present tense of **ser**
- telling time
- recognizing cognates
- reading a telephone list rich in cognates
- cultural and demographic information about Hispanics in the United States and Canada

A primera vista Have students look at the photo. Ask: *What do you think the young women are doing?* Say: *It is common in Hispanic cultures for friends to greet each other with a kiss (or two) on the cheek.* Ask: *How do you greet your friends?*

INSTRUCTIONAL RESOURCES

Workbook/Video Manual: WB Activities, pp. 1–10
Laboratory Manual: Lab Activities, pp. 1–6
Workbook/Video Manual: Video Activities, pp. 195–196; pp. 225–226
Instructor's Resource Manual: **Vocabulario adicional**, pp. 153–154; **¡Inténtalo!** & **Práctica** Answers, pp. 171–172; **Fotonovela** Translations, p. 119; Textbook CD Tapescript, p. 71; Lab CDs Tapescript, pp. 1–5; **Fotonovela** Videoscript, p. 87; **Panorama cultural** Videoscript, p. 107; **Pan. cult.** Translations, p. 129
Info Gap Activities Booklet, pp. 1–4
Overhead Transparencies: #9, #10, #11, #12
Lab Audio CD/MP3 **Lección 1**
Panorama cultural DVD/Video
Fotonovela DVD/Video
Testing Program, pp. 1–12
Testing Program Audio CD
Test Files CD-ROM
Test Generator
Companion website
Presentations CD-ROM
Textbook CD
Vocabulary CD
Interactive CD-ROM
Video CD-ROM
Web-SAM

Hola, ¿qué tal?

Section Goals

In **Contextos**, students will learn and practice:
• basic greetings
• introductions
• courtesy expressions

Instructional Resources
Transparencies, #9, #10
Textbook Activities CD
Vocabulary CD
WB/VM: Workbook, pp. 1–2
Lab Manual, p. 1
*Lab CD/MP3 **Lección 1***
*IRM: **Vocab. adicional**, p. 153;*
***Práctica** Answers, p. 171;*
Tapescript, pp. 1–5; p. 71
Interactive CD-ROM
Companion website:
www.vistahigherlearning.com
Presentations CD-ROM

Suggestions

• To familiarize students right away with the meanings of headings used in the lessons and important vocabulary for classroom interactions, you can pass out **Vocabulario adicional: Más vocabulario para la clase de español**, from the IRM.

• For complete lesson plans, go to **www.vistahigherlearning.com** to access the instructor's part of the **PANORAMA** companion website.

• With books closed, write a few greetings, farewells, and courtesy expressions on the board, explain their meaning, and model their pronunciation. Go around the class greeting students, making introductions, and encouraging responses. Then have students open to pages 2–3 or project **Transparency #9** and ask them to identify which conversations seem to be exchanges between friends and which seem more formal. Overlay **Transparency #10** or use the printed text to draw attention to the use of **Ud.** vs. **tú** in these conversations. Explain situations in which each form is appropriate.

Successful Language
Learning Encourage your students to make flash cards to help them memorize new vocabulary words.

Más vocabulario

Buenos días.	*Good morning.*
Buenas tardes.	*Good afternoon.*
Buenas noches.	*Good evening./night.*
Hasta la vista.	*See you later.*
Hasta pronto.	*See you soon.*
¿Cómo se llama usted?	*What's your name? (form.)*
Le presento a…	*I would like to introduce (name) to you. (form.)*
Te presento a…	*I would like to introduce (name) to you. (fam.)*
nombre	*name*
¿Cómo estás?	*How are you? (fam.)*
No muy bien.	*Not very well.*
¿Qué pasa?	*What's happening?; What's going on?*
por favor	*please*
De nada.	*You're welcome.*
No hay de qué.	*You're welcome.*
Lo siento.	*I'm sorry.*
(Muchas) gracias.	*Thank you (very much).; Thanks (a lot).*

Variación léxica

Items are presented for recognition purposes only.

Buenos días. ⟷ Buenas.
De nada. ⟷ A la orden.
Lo siento. ⟷ Perdón.
¿Qué tal? ⟷ ¿Qué hubo? (*Col.*)
chau ⟷ ciao

recursos

TEXT CD Lección 1	WB pp. 1–2	LM p. 1	Lab CD/MP3 Lección 1	I CD-ROM Lección 1	Vocab CD Lección 1

ELENA Patricia, éste es el señor Perales.
PATRICIA Encantada.
SEÑOR PERALES Igualmente. ¿De dónde es usted, señorita?
PATRICIA Soy de México. ¿Y usted?
SEÑOR PERALES De Puerto Rico.

TOMÁS ¿Qué tal, Alberto?
ALBERTO Regular. ¿Y tú?
TOMÁS Bien. ¿Qué hay de nuevo?
ALBERTO Nada.

SEÑOR VARGAS Buenas tardes, señora Wong. ¿Cómo está usted?
SEÑORA WONG Muy bien, gracias. ¿Y usted, señor Vargas?
SEÑOR VARGAS Bien, gracias.
SEÑORA WONG Hasta mañana, señor Vargas. Saludos a la señora Vargas.
SEÑOR VARGAS Adiós.

TEACHING OPTIONS

Variación léxica Point out that **Buenas, Chévere,** and **¿Qué hubo?** (often pronounced **¿Quihubo?**) are all colloquial. You may add that another common equivalent of **¿Qué tal?** is **¿Cómo te va?**
Extra Practice Bring family photos or magazine photos in which people are shown greeting each other. Ask groups to write dialogue captions for each photo. Remind the class to use formal and informal expressions as appropriate.

Small Groups Have small groups role-play an original conversation in which older adults, children, and college-age people interact. Verify that the groups are using formal and informal expressions as appropriate. Have a few groups present their conversations to the class.
Extra Practice After calling a name, greet that student and ask a question related to the day's lesson.

BERTA Hasta luego, Tere.

TERESA Chau, Berta. Nos vemos mañana.

CARMEN Hola. Me llamo Carmen. ¿Cómo te llamas tú?

ANTONIO Buenas tardes. Me llamo Antonio. Mucho gusto.

CARMEN El gusto es mío. ¿De dónde eres?

ANTONIO Soy de los Estados Unidos, de California.

Práctica

1

Escuchar Listen to each question or statement, then choose the correct response.

1. a. Muy bien, gracias.   b. Me llamo Graciela. b
2. a. Lo siento.   b. Mucho gusto. b
3. a. Soy de Puerto Rico.   b. No muy bien. a
4. a. No hay de qué.   b. Regular. a
5. a. Mucho gusto.   b. Hasta pronto. b
6. a. Nada.   b. Igualmente. a
7. a. Me llamo Guillermo Montero.   b. Muy bien, gracias. b
8. a. Buenas tardes. ¿Cómo estás?   b. El gusto es mío. a
9. a. Saludos a la señora Ramírez.   b. Encantada. b
10. a. Adiós.   b. Regular. b

2

Escoger For each expression, write another word or phrase that expresses a similar idea.

> *modelo*
> ¿Cómo estás?
> ¿Qué tal?

1. De nada. ___No hay de qué.___
2. Encantado. ___Mucho gusto.___
3. Adiós. ___Chau./Hasta luego/mañana/pronto.___
4. Te presento a Antonio. ___Éste es Antonio.___
5. Hasta la vista. ___Hasta luego.___
6. Mucho gusto. ___El gusto es mío.___

3

Ordenar Work with a classmate to put this scrambled conversation in order. Then act it out.

—Muy bien, gracias. Soy Rosabel.

—Soy del Ecuador. ¿Y tú?

—Mucho gusto, Rosabel.

—Hola. Me llamo Carlos. ¿Cómo estás?

—Soy de Argentina.

—Igualmente. ¿De dónde eres, Carlos?

CARLOS	Hola. Me llamo Carlos. ¿Cómo estás?
ROSABEL	Muy bien, gracias. Soy Rosabel.
CARLOS	Mucho gusto, Rosabel.
ROSABEL	Igualmente. ¿De dónde eres, Carlos?
CARLOS	Soy del Ecuador. ¿Y tú?
ROSABEL	Soy de Argentina.

4 Suggestion Review the pairs' responses with the class.

4 Expansion Have pairs or small groups create conversations that include the expressions used in **Actividad 4**. Ask volunteers to present their conversations to the class.

5 Suggestions
• Be sure to discuss the **modelo** with the whole class before assigning the activity to pairs. After students have completed the activity, have eight pairs of students role-play one of the corrected mini-conversations. Ask them to substitute their own names and personal information where possible.
• Have volunteers write each conversation on the board. Work together as a class to identify and explain any errors.

¡Lengua viva! Have students locate examples of the titles in **Actividad 5**. Then have them create short sentences in which they use the titles with people they know.

4 **Completar** Work with a partner to complete these exchanges. Some answers will vary.

> **modelo**
> **Estudiante 1:** ¿Cómo estás?
> **Estudiante 2:** _Muy bien, gracias._

1. **Estudiante 1:** _Buenos días._
   Estudiante 2: Buenos días. ¿Qué tal?
2. **Estudiante 1:** _¿Cómo te llamas?_
   Estudiante 2: Me llamo Carmen Sánchez.
3. **Estudiante 1:** _¿De dónde eres?_
   Estudiante 2: De México.
4. **Estudiante 1:** Te presento a Marisol.
   Estudiante 2: _Encantado/a._

5. **Estudiante 1:** Gracias.
   Estudiante 2: _De nada._
6. **Estudiante 1:** _¿Qué tal?_
   Estudiante 2: Regular.
7. **Estudiante 1:** _¿Qué pasa?_
   Estudiante 2: Nada.
8. **Estudiante 1:** ¡Hasta la vista!
   Estudiante 2: _Adiós._

5 **Cambiar** Work with a partner and correct the second part of each conversation to make it logical. Answers will vary.

> **modelo**
> **Estudiante 1:** ¿Qué tal?
> **Estudiante 2:** ~~No hay de qué.~~ Bien. ¿Y tú?

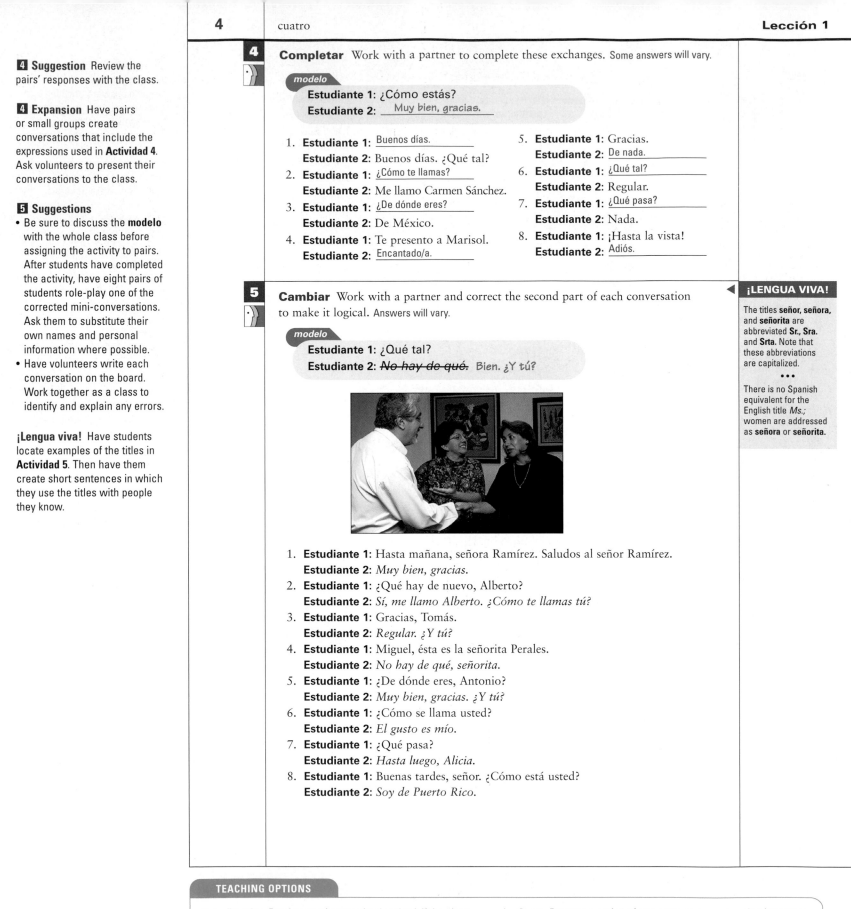

1. **Estudiante 1:** Hasta mañana, señora Ramírez. Saludos al señor Ramírez.
   Estudiante 2: *Muy bien, gracias.*
2. **Estudiante 1:** ¿Qué hay de nuevo, Alberto?
   Estudiante 2: *Sí, me llamo Alberto. ¿Cómo te llamas tú?*
3. **Estudiante 1:** Gracias, Tomás.
   Estudiante 2: *Regular. ¿Y tú?*
4. **Estudiante 1:** Miguel, ésta es la señorita Perales.
   Estudiante 2: *No hay de qué, señorita.*
5. **Estudiante 1:** ¿De dónde eres, Antonio?
   Estudiante 2: *Muy bien, gracias. ¿Y tú?*
6. **Estudiante 1:** ¿Cómo se llama usted?
   Estudiante 2: *El gusto es mío.*
7. **Estudiante 1:** ¿Qué pasa?
   Estudiante 2: *Hasta luego, Alicia.*
8. **Estudiante 1:** Buenas tardes, señor. ¿Cómo está usted?
   Estudiante 2: *Soy de Puerto Rico.*

► ¡LENGUA VIVA!

The titles **señor, señora,** and **señorita** are abbreviated **Sr., Sra.** and **Srta.** Note that these abbreviations are capitalized.

• • •

There is no Spanish equivalent for the English title *Ms.;* women are addressed as **señora** or **señorita**.

TEACHING OPTIONS

Extra Practice Read some phrases aloud and ask if the class would use them with another student of the same age or with an older person. Ex: **1. Te presento a Luis.** (student) **2. Muchas gracias, señor.** (older person) **3. ¿Cómo estás?** (student) **4. Buenos días, doctor Soto.** (older person) **5. ¿De dónde es usted, señora?** (older person) **6. Chau, Teresa.** (student) **7. ¿Cómo se llama usted?** (older person) **8. No hay de qué, señor Perales.** (older person)

Game Prepare a series of response statements using language in **Contextos**. Divide the class into two teams and invite students to guess the question or statement that would have elicited each of your response statements. Read a statement at a time. The team to correctly guess the question or statement first wins the point. Ex: **Me llamo Lupe Torres Garza. (¿Cómo se llama usted? / ¿Cómo te llamas?)** The team with the most correct guesses wins.

Comunicación

6 **Diálogos** With a partner, complete and act out these conversations. Answers will vary.

Conversación 1

—Hola. Me llamo Teresa. ¿Cómo te llamas tú?

—_____

—Soy de Puerto Rico. ¿Y tú?

—_____

Conversación 2

—_____

—Muy bien, gracias. ¿Y usted, señora López?

—_____

—Hasta luego, señora. Saludos al señor López.

—_____

Conversación 3

—_____

—Regular. ¿Y tú?

—_____

—Nada.

7 **Conversaciones** This is the first day of class. Write four short conversations based on what the people in this scene would say. Answers will vary.

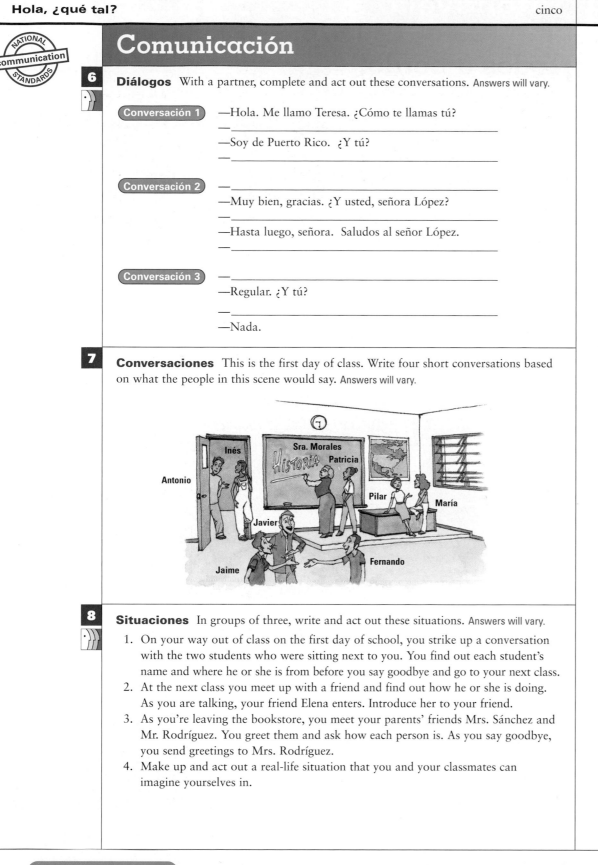

8 **Situaciones** In groups of three, write and act out these situations. Answers will vary.

1. On your way out of class on the first day of school, you strike up a conversation with the two students who were sitting next to you. You find out each student's name and where he or she is from before you say goodbye and go to your next class.
2. At the next class you meet up with a friend and find out how he or she is doing. As you are talking, your friend Elena enters. Introduce her to your friend.
3. As you're leaving the bookstore, you meet your parents' friends Mrs. Sánchez and Mr. Rodríguez. You greet them and ask how each person is. As you say goodbye, you send greetings to Mrs. Rodríguez.
4. Make up and act out a real-life situation that you and your classmates can imagine yourselves in.

6 Expansion

• Have the class work in small groups to write a few mini-conversations modeled on this activity. Then ask them to copy the dialogues, omitting a few exchanges. Each group should exchange its mini-conversations with another group, which will fill in the blanks.

• Have students rephrase **Conversaciones 1** and **3** in the formal register and **Conversación 2** in the informal register.

7 Suggestion Have students brainstorm who the people in the illustration are and what they are talking about. Ask students which groups would be speaking to each other in the **Ud.** form, and which would be using the **tú** form.

8 Suggestion Have each group pick a situation to prepare and perform. Tell groups not to memorize the conversations, but to recreate them.

The Affective Dimension Point out that if students rehearse the situations a few times, they will feel more comfortable with the material and less anxious when they are asked to present it before the class.

TEACHING OPTIONS

Extra Practice Have students circulate around the classroom and conduct unrehearsed mini-conversations in Spanish with other students, using the words and expressions that they have learned on pages 2–3. As students are carrying out the activity, circulate around the room, monitoring your students' work and offering assistance if requested.

Heritage Speakers Ask heritage speakers to role-play some of the conversations and situations in these **Comunicación** activities, modeling correct pronunciation and intonation for the class. Remind students that there are regional differences in the way English is pronounced, and that the same is true of Spanish. Help clarify unfamiliar vocabulary as necessary.

¡Todos a bordo!

communication cultures **NATIONAL STANDARDS**

Los cuatro estudiantes, don Francisco y la Sra. Ramos se reúnen (*meet*) en la universidad.

Section Goals

In **Fotonovela** students will:
• receive comprehensible input from free-flowing discourse
• learn functional phrases that preview lesson grammatical structures

Instructional Resources
WB/VM: Video Activities, pp. 195–196
Fotonovela *DVD/Video (Start 00:02:18)*
Fotonovela *Video CD-ROM*
IRM: **Fotonovela** *Translations, p. 119, Videoscript, p. 87*
Interactive CD-ROM

Video Synopsis Don Francisco, the bus driver, and Sra. Ramos, a representative of Ecuatur, meet the four travelers at the university. Sra. Ramos passes out travel documents. Inés and Maite introduce themselves, as do Javier and Álex. The travelers board the bus.

Suggestions

• Have students cover the Spanish captions and guess the plot based only on the video stills. Record their predictions, and, after students have watched the video, compare their predictions to what actually happened in the episode.
• Tell students that all items in **Expresiones útiles** on page 7 are active vocabulary for which they are responsible. Pronounce each item and have the class repeat. Also, practice the **Expresiones útiles** by using them in short conversations with individual students.

PERSONAJES

DON FRANCISCO

SRA. RAMOS

ÁLEX

JAVIER

INÉS

MAITE

1
SRA. RAMOS Buenos días, chicos. Yo soy Isabel Ramos de la agencia Ecuatur.
DON FRANCISCO Y yo soy don Francisco, el conductor.

2
SRA. RAMOS Bueno, ¿quién es María Teresa Fuentes de Alba?
MAITE ¡Soy yo!
SRA. RAMOS Ah, bien. Aquí tienes los documentos de viaje.
MAITE Gracias.

3
SRA. RAMOS ¿Javier Gómez Lozano?
JAVIER Aquí... soy yo.

6
JAVIER ¿Qué tal? Me llamo Javier.
ÁLEX Mucho gusto, Javier. Yo soy Álex. ¿De dónde eres?
JAVIER De Puerto Rico. ¿Y tú?
ÁLEX Yo soy de México.

7
DON FRANCISCO Bueno, chicos, ¡todos a bordo!

8
INÉS Con permiso.

recursos

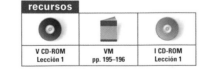

| V CD-ROM Lección 1 | VM pp. 195–196 | I CD-ROM Lección 1 |

TEACHING OPTIONS

Video Tips General suggestions for using video clips in the classroom can be found on page IAE-12 of this Instructor's Annotated Edition.
¡Todos a bordo! Play the **¡Todos a bordo!** segment of this video module once and ask the class to write down the basic greetings they hear. Play this segment a second time and ask the class to make a list of all the expressions the characters use to identify

themselves. Then play the **¡Todos a bordo!** segment for a third time, asking the class to write down all the courtesy expressions they hear, including ways to say "pleased to meet you" and "excuse me."

SRA. RAMOS Y tú eres Inés Ayala Loor, ¿verdad?

INÉS Sí, yo soy Inés.

SRA. RAMOS Y tú eres Alejandro Morales Paredes, ¿no?

ÁLEX Sí, señora.

INÉS Hola. Soy Inés.

MAITE Encantada. Yo me llamo Maite. ¿De dónde eres?

INÉS Soy del Ecuador, de Portoviejo. ¿Y tú?

MAITE De España. Soy de Madrid, la capital. Oye, ¿qué hora es?

INÉS Son las diez y tres minutos.

ÁLEX Perdón.

DON FRANCISCO ¿Y los otros?

SRA. RAMOS Son todos.

DON FRANCISCO Está bien.

Enfoque cultural Saludos y presentaciones

In the Hispanic world, it is customary for men and women to shake hands when meeting someone for the first time and when saying hello and goodbye to people they already know. Men greet female friends and family members with a brief kiss on the cheek, and they greet males they know well with an **abrazo**—a quick hug and pat on the back. Women of all ages frequently greet good friends, family members, and other loved ones with a brief kiss on one or both cheeks.

Expresiones útiles

Identifying yourself and others
▶ **¿Cómo se llama usted?**
What's your name?
▷ **Yo soy don Francisco, el conductor.**
I'm Don Francisco, the driver.

▶ **¿Cómo te llamas?**
What's your name?
▷ **Me llamo Javier.**
My name is Javier.

▶ **¿Quién es... ?**
Who is... ?
▷ **Aquí... soy yo.**
Here... that's me.

▶ **Tú eres... , ¿verdad?/¿no?**
You are ..., right?/no?
▷ **Sí, señora.**
Yes, ma'am.

Saying what time it is
▶ **¿Qué hora es?**
What time is it?
▷ **Es la una.**
It's one o'clock.
▷ **Son las dos.**
It's two o'clock.
▷ **Son las diez y tres minutos.**
It's 10:03.

Saying "excuse me"
▶ **Con permiso.**
Pardon me.; Excuse me.
(to request permission)
▶ **Perdón.**
Pardon me.; Excuse me.
(to get someone's attention or to ask forgiveness)

When starting a trip
▶ **¡Todos a bordo!**
All aboard!
▶ **¡Buen viaje!**
Have a good trip!

Getting a friend's attention
▶ **Oye...**
Listen...

1 **Expansion** Give these true-false statements to the class as items 8–10: **8. Maite es de la capital de España.** (Cierto) **9. Son las tres y diez minutos.** (Falso. Son las diez y tres minutos.) **10. Inés es de Quito, la capital del Ecuador.** (Falso. Inés es de Portoviejo.)

2 **Expansion** Ask students to call out additional statements that were made in the **Fotonovela**; the class should guess who made each statement.

¡Lengua viva! Ask students how they might address **Sra. Ramos** (doña Isabel).

3 **Suggestion** Go over the activity by asking volunteers to take the roles of Maite and Inés.

4 **Possible Response**
E1: **Buenas tardes. ¿Cómo te llamas?**
E2: **Hola. Me llamo Felipe. Y tú, ¿cómo te llamas?**
E1: **Me llamo Denisa. Mucho gusto.**
E2: **El gusto es mío.**
E1: **¿Cómo estás?**
E2: **Bien, gracias.**
E1: **¿De dónde eres?**
E2: **Soy de Venezuela.**
E1: **¡Buen viaje!**
E2: **Gracias. ¡Adiós!**

The Affective Dimension Point out that many people feel a bit nervous about speaking in front of a group. Encourage your students to think of anxious feelings as extra energy that will help them accomplish their goals.

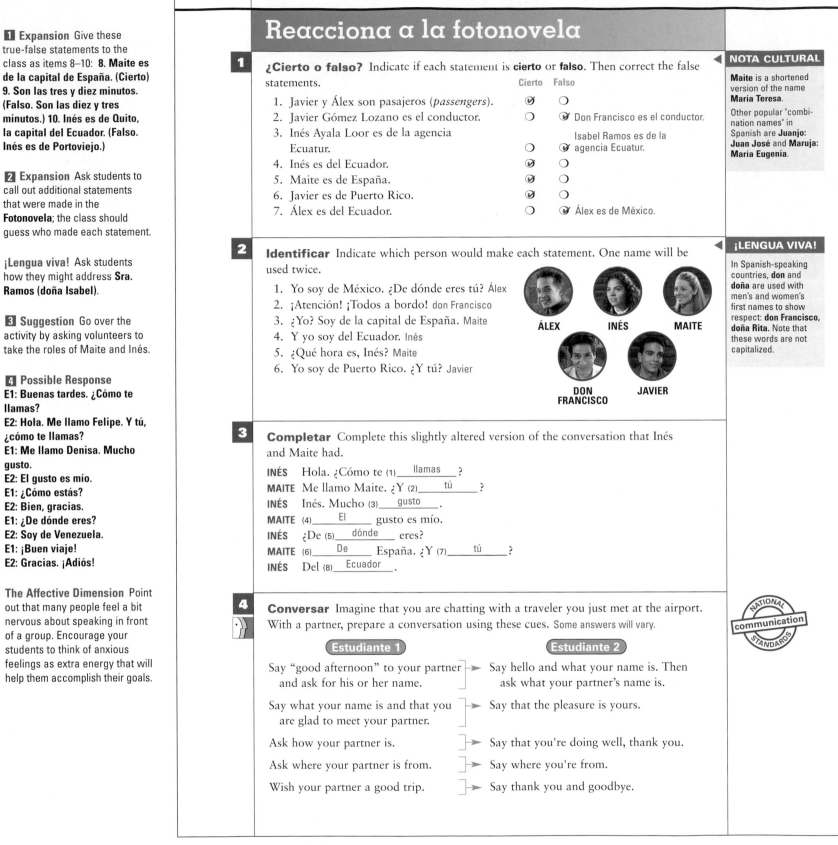

Reacciona a la fotonovela

1 **¿Cierto o falso?** Indicate if each statement is **cierto** or **falso**. Then correct the false statements.

	Cierto	Falso	
1. Javier y Álex son pasajeros (*passengers*).	☑	○	
2. Javier Gómez Lozano es el conductor.	○	☑	Don Francisco es el conductor.
3. Inés Ayala Loor es de la agencia Ecuatur.	○	☑	Isabel Ramos es de la agencia Ecuatur.
4. Inés es del Ecuador.	☑	○	
5. Maite es de España.	☑	○	
6. Javier es de Puerto Rico.	☑	○	
7. Álex es del Ecuador.	○	☑	Álex es de México.

> **NOTA CULTURAL**
>
> **Maite** is a shortened version of the name **María Teresa**.
>
> Other popular "combination names" in Spanish are **Juanjo: Juan José** and **Maruja: María Eugenia**.

2 **Identificar** Indicate which person would make each statement. One name will be used twice.

1. Yo soy de México. ¿De dónde eres tú? Álex
2. ¡Atención! ¡Todos a bordo! don Francisco
3. ¿Yo? Soy de la capital de España. Maite
4. Y yo soy del Ecuador. Inés
5. ¿Qué hora es, Inés? Maite
6. Yo soy de Puerto Rico. ¿Y tú? Javier

ÁLEX   INÉS   MAITE
DON FRANCISCO   JAVIER

> **¡LENGUA VIVA!**
>
> In Spanish-speaking countries, **don** and **doña** are used with men's and women's first names to show respect: **don Francisco, doña Rita.** Note that these words are not capitalized.

3 **Completar** Complete this slightly altered version of the conversation that Inés and Maite had.

INÉS Hola. ¿Cómo te (1)__llamas__ ?
MAITE Me llamo Maite. ¿Y (2)__tú__ ?
INÉS Inés. Mucho (3)__gusto__ .
MAITE (4)__El__ gusto es mío.
INÉS ¿De (5)__dónde__ eres?
MAITE (6)__De__ España. ¿Y (7)__tú__ ?
INÉS Del (8)__Ecuador__ .

4 **Conversar** Imagine that you are chatting with a traveler you just met at the airport. With a partner, prepare a conversation using these cues. Some answers will vary.

Estudiante 1	Estudiante 2
Say "good afternoon" to your partner and ask for his or her name.	Say hello and what your name is. Then ask what your partner's name is.
Say what your name is and that you are glad to meet your partner.	Say that the pleasure is yours.
Ask how your partner is.	Say that you're doing well, thank you.
Ask where your partner is from.	Say where you're from.
Wish your partner a good trip.	Say thank you and goodbye.

(NATIONAL communication STANDARDS)

TEACHING OPTIONS

Pairs Ask students to work in pairs to ad-lib the exchanges between don Francisco and Sra. Ramos, Inés and Maite, and Álex and Javier. Tell them to convey the general meaning using vocabulary and expressions they know, and assure them that they do not have to stick to the original exchanges word for word. Then, ask volunteers to present their exchanges to the class.

Extra Practice Choose four or five lines of the **Fotonovela** to use as a dictation. Read the lines twice slowly to give students an opportunity to write. Then read them again at normal speed to allow students to correct any errors or fill in any gaps. You may have students correct their own work by checking it against the **Fotonovela** text.

NOTA CULTURAL

The **Real Academia Española** (Royal Spanish Academy) is based in Madrid, Spain. Founded in 1713, the goal of the RAE is to preserve and update the Spanish language throughout the Spanish-speaking world.

Pronunciación

The Spanish alphabet

The Spanish alphabet consisted of 29 letters until 1994, when the **Real Academia Española** removed **ch (che)** and **ll (elle)**. You may still see **ch** and **ll** listed as separate letters in reference works printed before 1994. The Spanish letter, **ñ (eñe)**, doesn't appear in the English alphabet. The letters **k (ka)** and **w (doble ve)** are used only in words of foreign origin.

Letra	Nombre(s)	Ejemplos	Letra	Nombre(s)	Ejemplos
a	a	adiós	ñ	eñe	mañana
b	be	bien, problema	o	o	once
c	ce	cosa, cero	p	pe	profesor
d	de	diario, nada	q	cu	qué
e	e	estudiante	r	ere	regular, señora
f	efe	foto	s	ese	señor
g	ge	gracias, Gerardo, regular	t	te	tú
			u	u	usted
h	hache	hola	v	ve	vista, nuevo
i	i	igualmente	w	doble ve	*walkman*
j	jota	Javier	x	equis	existir, México
k	ka, ca	kilómetro	y	i griega, ye	yo
l	ele	lápiz			
m	eme	mapa	z	zeta, ceta	zona
n	ene	nacionalidad			

El alfabeto Repeat the Spanish alphabet and example words after your instructor.

Práctica Spell these words aloud in Spanish.

1. nada
2. maleta
3. quince
4. muy
5. hombre
6. por favor
7. San Fernando
8. Estados Unidos
9. Puerto Rico
10. España
11. Javier
12. Ecuador
13. Maite
14. gracias
15. Nueva York

Refranes Read these sayings aloud.

Ver es creer.[1]

En boca cerrada no entran moscas.[2]

1 Seeing is believing. 2 Silence is golden.

recursos

TEXT CD Lección 1	LM p. 2	Lab CD/MP3 Lección 1	I CD-ROM Lección 1

---

estructura

1.1 Nouns and articles

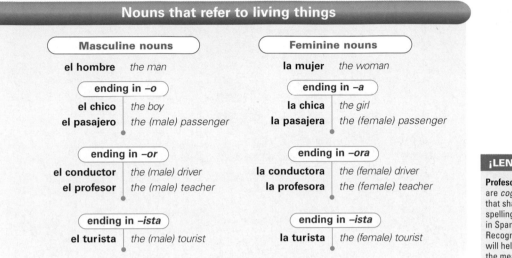

Spanish nouns

ANTE TODO A noun is a word used to identify people, animals, places, things, or ideas. Unlike English, all Spanish nouns, even those that refer to non-living things, have gender; that is, they are considered either masculine or feminine. As in English, nouns in Spanish also have number, meaning that they are either singular or plural.

Nouns that refer to living things

Masculine nouns		Feminine nouns	
el hombre	*the man*	**la mujer**	*the woman*
ending in –o		*ending in –a*	
el chico	*the boy*	**la chica**	*the girl*
el pasajero	*the (male) passenger*	**la pasajera**	*the (female) passenger*
ending in –or		*ending in –ora*	
el conductor	*the (male) driver*	**la conductora**	*the (female) driver*
el profesor	*the (male) teacher*	**la profesora**	*the (female) teacher*
ending in –ista		*ending in –ista*	
el turista	*the (male) tourist*	**la turista**	*the (female) tourist*

▶ As shown above, nouns that refer to males, like **el hombre**, are generally masculine, while nouns that refer to females, like **la mujer**, are generally feminine.

▶ Many nouns that refer to male beings end in **–o** or **–or**. Their corresponding feminine forms end in **–a** and **–ora**, respectively.

el conductor   la profesora

▶ The masculine and feminine forms of nouns that end in **–ista,** like **turista**, are the same, so gender is indicated by the article **el** (masculine) or **la** (feminine). Some other nouns have identical masculine and feminine forms.

el joven	**la** joven
the youth; the young man	*the youth; the young woman*
el estudiante	**la** estudiante
the (male) student	*the (female) student*

¡LENGUA VIVA!

Profesor(a) and **turista** are *cognates*— words that share similar spellings and meanings in Spanish and English. Recognizing cognates will help you determine the meaning of many Spanish words. Here are some other cognates:
la administración,
el animal,
el apartamento,
el cálculo, el color,
la decisión, la historia,
la música,
el restaurante,
el/la secretario/a

CONSEJOS

Cognates can certainly be very helpful in your study of Spanish. Beware, however, of "false" cognates, those that have similar spellings in Spanish and English, but different meanings:
la carpeta *file folder*
el conductor *driver*
el éxito *success*
la fábrica *factory*

Nouns that refer to non-living things

Masculine nouns

ending in –o

el cuaderno	the notebook
el diario	the diary
el diccionario	the dictionary
el número	the number
el video	the video

ending in –ma

el problema	the problem
el programa	the program

ending in –s

el autobús	the bus
el país	the country

Feminine nouns

ending in –a

la cosa	the thing
la escuela	the school
la grabadora	the tape recorder
la maleta	the suitcase
la palabra	the word

ending in –ción

la lección	the lesson
la conversación	the conversation

ending in –dad

la nacionalidad	the nationality
la comunidad	the community

¡LENGUA VIVA!

The Spanish word for *video* can be pronounced with the stress on the **i** or the **e**. For that reason, you might see the word written with or without an accent: **video** or **vídeo**.

▶ As shown above, certain noun endings are strongly associated with a specific gender, so you can use them to determine if a noun is masculine or feminine.

▶ Because the gender of nouns that refer to non-living things cannot be determined by foolproof rules, you should memorize the gender of each noun you learn. It is helpful to memorize each noun with its corresponding article, **el** for masculine and **la** for feminine.

▶ Another reason to memorize the gender of every noun is that there are common exceptions to the rules of gender. For example, **el mapa** (*map*) and **el día** (*day*) end in **–a,** but are masculine. **La mano** (*hand*) ends in **-o,** but is feminine.

Plural of nouns

¡ATENCIÓN!

In general, when a singular noun has an accent mark on the last syllable, the accent is dropped from the plural form:

la lección →
  las lecciones
el autobús →
  los autobuses

You will learn more about accent marks in **Lección 4, Pronunciación**, p. 101.

▶ In Spanish, nouns that end in a vowel form the plural by adding **–s.** Nouns that end in a consonant add **–es.** Nouns that end in **–z** change the **–z** to **–c,** then add **–es.**

el chico → los chicos	la nacionalidad → las nacionalidades
el diario → los diarios	el país → los países
la palabra → las palabras	el profesor → los profesores
el problema → los problemas	el lápiz (*pencil*) → los lápices

▶ You use the masculine plural form of the noun to refer to a group that includes both males and females.

1 pasajero + 2 pasajeras = 3 pasajeros

2 chicos + 2 chicas = 4 chicos

Suggestions
- Work through the list of nouns, modeling their pronunciation. Point out patterns of gender, including word endings **–ma**, **–ción**, and **–dad**. Give cognate nouns with these endings and ask students to indicate the gender. Ex: **diagrama, acción, personalidad**. Point out common exceptions to gender agreement rules for **el mapa**, **el día**, and **la mano**.
- Stress the addition of **–s** to nouns that end in vowels and **–es** to nouns that end in consonants. Write ten nouns on the board and ask volunteers to give the plural forms, along with the appropriate articles.
- Stress that even if a group contains 100 women and one man, the masculine plural form and article are used. Point to three male students and ask if the group is **los** or **las estudiantes** (**los**). Next, point to three female students and ask the same question (**las**). Then indicate a group of males and females and ask for the correct term to refer to them (**los estudiantes**).

¡Atención! Point out that these words lose the written accent in the plural form in order to keep the stress on the same syllable as in the singular noun.

The Affective Dimension
Tell your students that many people feel anxious when learning grammar. Tell them that grammar will seem less intimidating if they think of it as a description of how the language works instead of a list of strict rules.

TEACHING OPTIONS

TPR Assign a different definite article to each of four students. Then line up ten students, each of whom is assigned a noun. Include a mix of masculine, feminine, singular, and plural nouns. Say one of the nouns (without the article), and that student must step forward. The student assigned the corresponding article has five seconds to join the noun student.

Game Divide the class into two teams, A and B. Indicate one team member at a time, alternating between teams. Give a singular noun to the member of team A. He or she must repeat it, preceded by the correct definite article. The corresponding member of team B must correctly supply the plural and definite article. Give a point per correct answer. Deduct a point for each wrong answer. The team with the most points at the end wins.

Spanish articles

ANTE TODO   As you know, English often uses definite articles (**the**) and indefinite articles (**a, an**) before nouns. Spanish also has definite and indefinite articles. Unlike English, Spanish articles vary in form because they agree in gender and number with the nouns they modify.

Definite articles

	Masculine		Feminine	
	SINGULAR	PLURAL	SINGULAR	PLURAL

el diccionario
the dictionary

los diccionarios
the dictionaries

la computadora
the computer

las computadoras
the computers

▶ Spanish has four forms that are equivalent to the English definite article *the*. You use definite articles to refer to specific nouns.

Indefinite articles

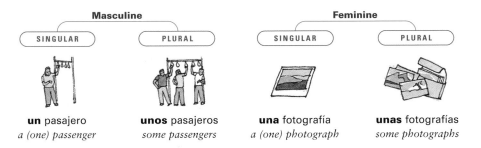

	Masculine		Feminine	
	SINGULAR	PLURAL	SINGULAR	PLURAL

un pasajero
a (one) passenger

unos pasajeros
some passengers

una fotografía
a (one) photograph

unas fotografías
some photographs

▶ Spanish has four forms that are equivalent to the English indefinite article, which according to context may mean *a*, *an*, or *some*. You use indefinite articles to refer to unspecified persons or things.

¡LENGUA VIVA!

Feminine singular nouns that begin with **a-** or **ha-** require the masculine articles **el** and **un**. This is done in order to avoid repetition of the **a** sound:

el agua *water*
las aguas *waters*
un hacha *ax*
unas hachas *axes*

¡LENGUA VIVA!

Since **la fotografía** is feminine, so is its shortened form, **la foto**, even though it ends in **–o**.

¡INTÉNTALO!   Provide a definite article for each noun in the first column and an indefinite article for each noun in the second column. The first item has been done for you.

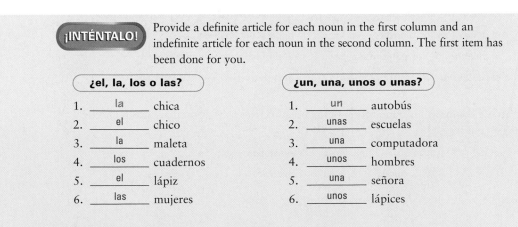

¿el, la, los o las?

1. ___la___ chica
2. ___el___ chico
3. ___la___ maleta
4. ___los___ cuadernos
5. ___el___ lápiz
6. ___las___ mujeres

¿un, una, unos o unas?

1. ___un___ autobús
2. ___unas___ escuelas
3. ___una___ computadora
4. ___unos___ hombres
5. ___una___ señora
6. ___unos___ lápices

Práctica

1 **¿Singular o plural?** If the word is singular, make it plural. If it is plural, make it singular.

1. el número los números
2. un diario unos diarios
3. la estudiante las estudiantes
4. el conductor los conductores
5. el país los países
6. las cosas la cosa
7. unos turistas un turista
8. las nacionalidades la nacionalidad
9. unas computadoras una computadora
10. los problemas el problema
11. una fotografía unas fotografías
12. los profesores el profesor
13. unas señoritas una señorita
14. el hombre los hombres
15. la grabadora las grabadoras
16. la señora las señoras

2 **Identificar** For each drawing, provide the noun with its corresponding definite and indefinite articles.

modelo
las maletas, unas maletas

1. la computadora, una computadora
2. los cuadernos, unos cuadernos
3. las mujeres, unas mujeres
4. el chico, un chico
5. la escuela, una escuela
6. las fotos, unas fotos
7. los autobuses, unos autobuses
8. el diario, un diario

Comunicación

NATIONAL communication STANDARDS

3 **Charadas** In groups, play a game of charades. Individually, think of two nouns for each charade, for example, a boy using a computer (**un chico; una computadora**). The first person to guess correctly acts out the next charade. Answers will vary.

---

1 **Expansion** Reverse the activity by reading the on-page answers and having students convert the singular to plural and vice versa. Make sure they close their books. Give the nouns in random order.

2 **Expansion** Bring in photos or magazine pictures that illustrate items whose names students know. Ask students to indicate the definite article and the noun. Include a mix of singular and plural nouns. Repeat the exercise with indefinite articles.

3 **Suggestion** Explain the basic rules of charades relevant to what students know at this point: (1) the student acting out the charade may not speak and (2) he or she may show the number of syllables by using fingers.

3 **Expansion** Split the class into two teams with volunteers from each team acting out the charades. Give a point to each team for correctly guessing the charade. Deduct a point for incorrect guesses. The team with the most points wins.

TEACHING OPTIONS

Video Show the **Fotonovela** video again to offer more input on singular and plural nouns and their articles. With their books closed, have students write down every noun and article that they hear. After viewing the video, ask volunteers to list the nouns and articles they heard. Explain that the **las** used when telling time refers to **las horas** (Ex: **Son las cinco** = **Son las cinco horas**).

Extra Practice Slowly read a short passage from a novel, story, or poem written in Spanish, preferably one with a great number of nouns and articles. As a listening exercise, have students write down every noun and article they hear, even unfamiliar ones (the articles may cue when nouns appear).

Section Goals

In **Estructura 1.2** students will be introduced to:
- numbers 0–30
- the verb form **hay**

Instructional Resources
WB/VM: Workbook, p. 4
Lab Manual, p. 4
Lab CD/MP3 Lección 1
IRM: ¡Inténtalo! & Práctica
Answers, pp. 171–172;
Tapescript, pp. 1–5
Info Gap Activities Booklet,
pp. 1–2
Interactive CD-ROM
Companion website:
www.vistahigherlearning.com
Presentations CD-ROM

Suggestions

- Introduce numbers by asking students how many of them can count to ten in Spanish. Hold up varying numbers of fingers and ask students to shout out the corresponding number in Spanish.
- Assign each student a number which they must remember. When finished, have the student assigned **uno** recite his or her number aloud, then **dos, tres,** etc. Help anyone who struggles with his or her number.
- Go through the numbers, modeling the pronunciation of each. Write individual numbers on the board and call on students at random to say the number.
- Emphasize the variable forms of **uno** and **veintiuno**, giving examples of each. Ex: **veintiún profesores, veintiuna profesoras**.
- Ask questions like the following: **¿Cuántos estudiantes hay en la clase? (Hay quince estudiantes en la clase.)**

1.2 Numbers 0–30

Los números 0–30

0	cero	11	once	21	veintiuno
1	uno	12	doce	22	veintidós
2	dos	13	trece	23	veintitrés
3	tres	14	catorce	24	veinticuatro
4	cuatro	15	quince	25	veinticinco
5	cinco	16	dieciséis	26	veintiséis
6	seis	17	diecisiete	27	veintisiete
7	siete	18	dieciocho	28	veintiocho
8	ocho	19	diecinueve	29	veintinueve
9	nueve	20	veinte	30	treinta
10	diez				

▶ The number **uno** (*one*) and numbers ending in **–uno**, such as **veintiuno**, have more than one form. Before masculine nouns, **uno** shortens to **un**. Before feminine nouns, **uno** changes to **una**.

un hombre → veinti**ún** hombres   **una** mujer → veinti**una** mujeres

▶ To ask *how many* people or things there are, use **cuántos** before masculine nouns and **cuántas** before feminine nouns.

▶ The Spanish equivalent of both *there is* and *there are* is **hay**. Use **¿Hay...?** to ask *Is there...?* or *Are there...?* Use **no hay** to express *there is not* or *there are not*.

—¿**Cuántos** estudiantes **hay**?
How many students are there?

—**Hay** tres estudiantes en la foto.
There are three students in the photo.

—¿**Hay** chicas en la fotografía?
Are there girls in the picture?

—**Hay** cuatro chicos, y **no hay** chicas.
There are four guys, and there are no girls.

> **¡ATENCIÓN!**
>
> The numbers sixteen through nineteen can also be written as three words: **diez y seis, diez y siete**…
>
> • • •
>
> The forms **uno** and **veintiuno** are used when counting (**uno, dos, tres…veinte, veintiuno, veintidós…**). They are also used when the number *follows* a noun, even if the noun is feminine: **la lección uno**.

¡INTÉNTALO!   Provide the Spanish words for these numbers.

1. **7** siete
2. **16** dieciséis
3. **29** veintinueve
4. **1** uno
5. **0** cero

6. **15** quince
7. **21** veintiuno
8. **9** nueve
9. **23** veintitrés
10. **11** once

11. **30** treinta
12. **4** cuatro
13. **12** doce
14. **28** veintiocho
15. **14** catorce

16. **10** diez
17. **2** dos
18. **5** cinco
19. **22** veintidós
20. **13** trece

TEACHING OPTIONS

TPR Assign ten students a number from 0–30 and line them up in front of the class. Call out one of the numbers at random, and have the student assigned that number take a step forward. When two students have stepped forward, ask them to repeat their numbers. Then ask individuals to add (Say: **Suma**) or subtract (Say: **Resta**) the two numbers.

Game Have students write B-I-N-G-O at the top of a blank piece of paper. They should draw five squares underneath each column and randomly fill in the squares with numbers from 0-30 without repeating numbers. From a hat, draw numbers and call them out in Spanish. The first student to get five in a row (horizontally, vertically or diagonally) yells '**¡Bingo!**' and wins.

Práctica

1

Contar Following the pattern, provide the missing numbers in Spanish.

1. 1, 3, 5, .., 29   7, 9, 11, 13, 15, 17, 19, 21, 23, 25, 27
2. 2, 4, 6, .., 30   8, 10, 12, 14, 16, 18, 20, 22, 24, 26, 28
3. 3, 6, 9, .., 30   12, 15, 18, 21, 24, 27
4. 30, 28, 26, .., 0   24, 22, 20, 18, 16, 14, 12, 10, 8, 6, 4, 2
5. 30, 25, 20, .., 0   15, 10, 5
6. 28, 24, 20, .., 0   16, 12, 8, 4

2

Resolver Solve these math problems with a partner.

modelo

$5 + 3 =$

Estudiante 1: cinco más tres son…
Estudiante 2: ocho

AYUDA
$+$ → más
$-$ → menos
$=$ → es/son

1. **2 + 15 =** Dos más quince son diecisiete.
2. **20 – 1 =** Veinte menos uno son diecinueve.
3. **5 + 7 =** Cinco más siete son doce.
4. **18 + 12 =** Dieciocho más doce son treinta.
5. **3 + 22 =** Tres más veintidós son veinticinco.
6. **6 – 3 =** Seis menos tres son tres.
7. **11 + 12 =** Once más doce son veintitrés.
8. **7 – 7 =** Siete menos siete es cero.
9. **8 + 5 =** Ocho más cinco son trece.
10. **23 – 14 =** Veintitrés menos catorce son nueve.

3

¿Cuántos hay? How many persons or things are there in these drawings?

modelo

Hay cuatro maletas.

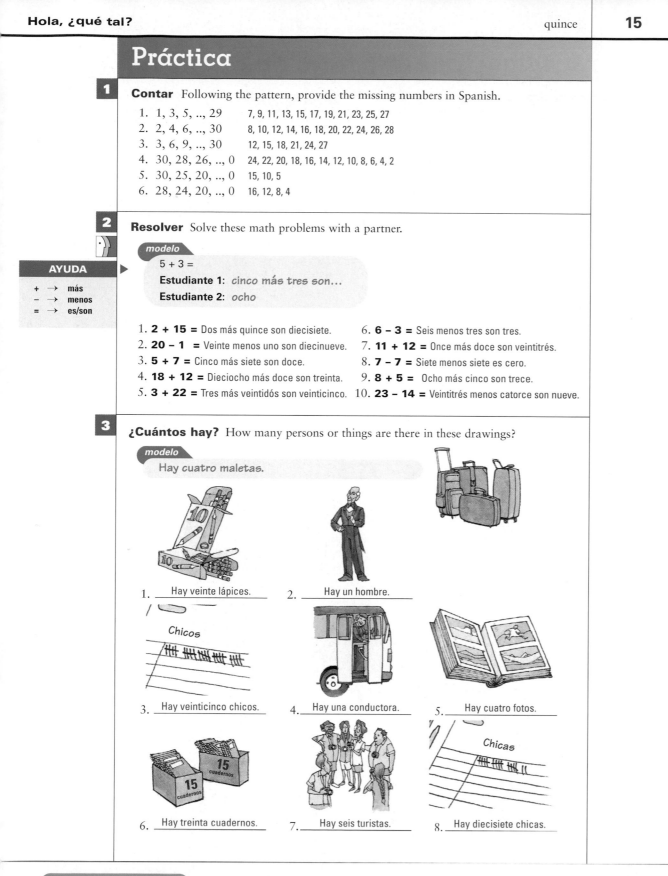

1. _Hay veinte lápices._
2. _Hay un hombre._
3. _Hay veinticinco chicos._
4. _Hay una conductora._
5. _Hay cuatro fotos._
6. _Hay treinta cuadernos._
7. _Hay seis turistas._
8. _Hay diecisiete chicas._

1 Suggestion Before beginning the activity, make sure students know these patterns: odds (**los números impares**), evens (**los números pares**), count by threes (**contar de tres en tres**).

1 Expansion Ask the class to list the prime numbers (**los números primos**) up to 30. Explain that a prime number is any number that can only be divided by itself and 1. Prime numbers to 30 are: 1, 2, 3, 5, 7, 11, 13, 17, 19, 23, 29.

2 Expansion Do simple multiplication problems. Introduce the phrase (**multiplicado**) **por**. Ex: **Cinco multiplicado por cinco son…** (**veinticinco**) or **Cinco por cinco son…** (**veinticinco**).

3 Suggestion Have students read the directions and model sentence. Cue student responses by asking questions related to the drawings. Ex: **¿Cuántos lápices hay?** (**Hay veinte lápices.**)

3 Expansion Hold up or point to classroom objects and ask how many there are. Since students will not know the names of many of the items, a simple number or **hay** + the number will suffice to signal comprehension. Ex: —**¿Cuántos bolígrafos hay aquí?** —(**Hay**) **Dos.**

TEACHING OPTIONS

TPR Give ten students each a card that contains a different number from 0–30 (you may want to assign numbers in fives to simplify the activity). The cards must be visible to the other students. Then call out simple math problems (addition, subtraction) involving the assigned numbers. When the first two numbers are called, each student steps forward. The student whose assigned number completes the math problem then has five seconds to join them.

Extra Practice Ask questions about the university and the town or city in which it is located. Ex: **¿Cuántos profesores hay en el departamento de español? ¿Cuántas universidades hay en _____?** **¿Cuántas pizzerías hay en ___?** Encourage students to guess the number. If a number exceeds 30, write that number on the board and model its pronunciation.

4 Suggestion For items 3, 4, 7, and 9, ask students **¿Cuántos/as hay?** If there are no examples of the item listed, students should say **No hay ____**.

4 Expansion After completing the activity, call on individual students to give rapid responses to the same items. Mix up the order of items to make the activity more challenging. See if the students can remember the number of items from the first time through the activity.

5 Suggestion Remind students that they will be forming sentences with **hay** and a number. Give them four minutes to do the activity. You might also have them write out their answers.

5 Expansion After pairs have finished analyzing the drawing, call on individual students to respond. Convert the statements into questions in Spanish. Ask: **¿Cuántos chicos hay? ¿Cuántas mujeres hay?**

Suggestion See the Information Gap Activities Booklet for an additional activity to practice the material presented in this section.

Comunicación

4 En la clase With a classmate, take turns asking and answering these questions about your classroom. Answers will vary.

1. ¿Cuántos estudiantes hay?
2. ¿Cuántos profesores hay?
3. ¿Hay una computadora?
4. ¿Hay una maleta?
5. ¿Cuántos mapas hay?

6. ¿Cuántos lápices hay?
7. ¿Hay cuadernos?
8. ¿Cuántas grabadoras hay?
9. ¿Hay hombres?
10. ¿Cuántas mujeres hay?

5 Preguntas With a classmate, take turns asking and answering questions about the drawing. Talk about:
Answers will vary.

1. How many children there are
2. How many women there are
3. If there are some photographs
4. If there is a boy
5. How many notebooks there are

6. If there is a bus
7. If there are tourists
8. How many pencils there are
9. If there is a man
10. How many computers there are

TEACHING OPTIONS

Pairs Have each student draw a scene similar to the one on this page. Of course, stick figures are perfectly acceptable! Give them three minutes to draw the scene. Then pairs take turns describing what is in their partner's picture. Encourage students to include multiple numbers of particular items (**cuadernos, maletas, lápices**).

Pairs Divide students into pairs. Give half of the pairs magazine pictures that contain images of words that are familiar to them or that are close cognates. Give the other half descriptions of those pictures, including **hay** in the description. Ex: **En esta foto hay dos mujeres, un chico y una chica.** Pairs walk around the room to match the descriptions with the corresponding pictures.

1.3 Present tense of ser

Subject pronouns

ANTE TODO   In order to use verbs, you will need to learn about subject pronouns. A subject pronoun replaces the name or title of a person, place, or thing, and acts as the subject of a verb. In both Spanish and English, subject pronouns are divided into three groups: first person, second person, and third person.

Subject pronouns

	SINGULAR		PLURAL	
FIRST PERSON	yo	*I*	nosotros	*we* (masculine)
			nosotras	*we* (feminine)
SECOND PERSON	tú	*you* (familiar)	vosotros	*you* (masc., fam.)
	usted (Ud.)	*you* (formal)	vosotras	*you* (fem., fam.)
			ustedes (Uds.)	*you* (form.)
THIRD PERSON	él	*he*	ellos	*they* (masc.)
	ella	*she*	ellas	*they* (fem.)

¡LENGUA VIVA!

In Latin America, **ustedes** is used as the plural for both **tú** and **usted**. In Spain, however, **vosotros** and **vosotras** are used as the plural of **tú**, and **ustedes** is used only as the plural of **usted**.

• • •

Usted and **ustedes** are abbreviated as **Ud.** and **Uds.**, or occasionally as **Vd.** and **Vds.**

▶ Spanish has two subject pronouns that mean *you* (singular). Use **tú** when addressing a friend, a family member, or a child you know well. Use **usted** to address a person with whom you have a formal or more distant relationship, such as a superior at work, a professor, or an older person.

▶ The masculine plural forms **nosotros**, **vosotros**, and **ellos** refer to a group of males or to a group of males and females. The feminine plural forms **nosotras**, **vosotras**, and **ellas** can refer only to groups made up exclusively of females.

nosotros, vosotros, ellos

nosotros, vosotros, ellos

nosotras, vosotras, ellas

▶ There is no Spanish equivalent of the English subject pronoun *it*. Generally it is not expressed in Spanish.

Es un problema.
It's a problem.

Es una computadora.
It's a computer.

Section Goals

In **Estructura 1.3** students will be introduced to:
• subject pronouns
• present tense of the verb **ser**
• using **ser** to identify, to indicate possession, to describe origin, and to talk about professions or occupations

Instructional Resources
WB/VM: Workbook, pp. 5–6
Lab Manual, p. 5
*Lab CD/MP3 **Lección 1***
*IRM: **Vocab. adicional**, p. 154;*
***¡Inténtalo!** & **Práctica** Answers,*
pp. 171–172; Tapescript, pp. 1–5
Interactive CD-ROM
Companion website:
www.vistahigherlearning.com
Presentations CD-ROM

Suggestions
• Point to yourself and say: **Yo soy profesor(a).** Then walk up to a student and say: **Tú eres…** Correct student response should be **estudiante.** Once the pattern has been established, include other subject pronouns and forms of **ser** while indicating other students. Ex: **Él es…, Ella es…, Ellos son…**
• Remind students of familiar and formal forms of address they learned in **Contextos.**
• You may want to point out that while **Ud.** and **Uds.** are part of the second person *you*, they use third person forms.
• While the **vosotros/as** forms are listed in verb paradigms in **PANORAMA,** they will not be actively practiced.

TEACHING OPTIONS

Extra Practice Explain that students are to give subject pronouns based on your (the instructor's) point of view. Ex: Point to yourself (**yo**), a female student (**ella**), everyone in the class (**nosotros**). **Extra Practice** Ask students to indicate whether certain people would be addressed as **tú** or **Ud.** Ex: a roommate, a friend's grandfather, a doctor, a neighbor's child

Heritage Speakers Ask heritage speakers how they address elder members of their family such as parents, grandparents, aunts and uncles—whether they use **tú** or **Ud.** Also ask them if they use **vosotros/as** or not (they typically do not unless they or their family are from Spain).

Suggestions

- Work through the explanation and the forms of **ser** in the chart. Emphasize that **es** is used for **Ud.**, **él**, and **ella**, and that **son** is used for **Uds.**, **ellos**, and **ellas**. Context or the use of subject pronouns or names will determine who is being addressed or talked about.
- Explain that **ser** is used to identify people and things. At this point there is no need to explain that **estar** also means *to be*; it will be introduced in **Lección 2**.
- Explain the meaning of **¿quién?** and ask questions about who students in the class are. Ex: ____, **¿quién es ella? (Es ____.) ¿Quién soy yo? (Soy el profesor/la profesora ____.)** Introduce **¿qué?** and ask questions about items in the class. Ex: **¿Qué es esto? (Es un mapa.)**
- Point out the construction of **ser** + **de** to indicate possession. Stress that there is no *'s* in Spanish. (Direct students to the **¡Atención!** sidebar.) Pick up objects belonging to students and ask questions. Ex: **¿De quién es este cuaderno? (Es de ____.) ¿De quién son estos libros? (Son de ____.)**

¡Atención! Introduce the contraction **de + el = del.** Emphasize that **de** and other definite articles do not make contractions and support with examples. Ex: **Soy del estado de ____. El diccionario no es de la profesora de ____.** Also use examples of possession to illustrate the contraction. Ex: **¿Es este mapa del presidente de la universidad?**

The present tense of *ser*

ANTE TODO In **Contextos** and **Fotonovela**, you have already used several forms of the present tense of **ser** (*to be*) to identify yourself and others and to talk about where you and others are from. **Ser** is an irregular verb, which means its forms don't follow the regular patterns that most verbs follow. You need to memorize the forms, which appear in the following chart.

ser			
	ser *(to be)*		
SINGULAR FORMS	yo	**soy**	*I am*
	tú	**eres**	*you are* (fam.)
	Ud./él/ella	**es**	*you are* (form.); *he/she is*
PLURAL FORMS	nosotros/as	**somos**	*we are*
	vosotros/as	**sois**	*you are* (fam.)
	Uds./ellos/ellas	**son**	*you are* (form.); *they are*

Uses of *ser*

▶ To identify people and things

—¿Quién **es** él?
Who is he?

—**Es** Javier Gómez Lozano.
He's Javier Gómez Lozano.

—¿Qué **es**?
What is it?

—**Es** un mapa de España.
It's a map of Spain.

Es Maite.

Es un autobús.

▶ To express possession, with the preposition **de**

—¿**De** quién **es**?
Whose is it?

—**Es** el diario **de** Maite.
It's Maite's diary.

—**Es** la computadora **de** Álex.
It's Alex's computer.

—¿**De** quiénes **son**?
Whose are they?

—**Son** los lápices **de** la chica.
They are the girl's pencils.

—**Son** las maletas **del** chico.
They are the boy's suitcases.

¡ATENCIÓN!

When **de** is followed by the article **el**, the two combine to form the contraction **del**. **De** does *not* contract with **la, las,** or **los**.

• • •

There is no Spanish equivalent of the English construction [*noun*] +'s (*Maite's*). In its place, Spanish uses [*noun*] + **de** + [*owner*]: **el diario de Maite**.

▶ To express origin, using the preposition **de**

— ¿**De** dónde **es** Javier?
Where is Javier from?

— **Es de** Puerto Rico.
He's from Puerto Rico.

— ¿**De** dónde **es** Inés?
Where is Inés from?

— **Es del** Ecuador.
She's from Ecuador.

▶ To express profession or occupation

Don Francisco **es conductor.**
Don Francisco is a driver.

Yo **soy estudiante.**
I am a student.

Somos Perú
✈ AeroPerú

¡INTÉNTALO! Provide the correct present forms of **ser** in the column. The first item has been done for you.

1. Gabriel — *es*
2. Juan y yo — *somos*
3. Óscar y Flora — *son*
4. Adriana — *es*
5. las turistas — *son*
6. el chico — *es*
7. los conductores — *son*
8. el señor y la señora Ruiz — *son*

Práctica

1

Pronombres What subject pronouns would you use to a) talk to these people directly and b) talk about them?

1. una chica tú, ella
2. el presidente de México usted, él
3. tres chicas y un chico ustedes, ellos
4. un estudiante tú, él
5. la señora Ochoa usted, ella
6. dos profesoras ustedes, ellas

2

Identidad y origen With a partner, take turns asking and answering questions about these people: **¿Quién es?/¿Quiénes son?** and **¿De dónde es?/¿De dónde son?**

> **modelo**
> Ricky Martin (Puerto Rico)
> **Estudiante 1:** ¿Quién es?   **Estudiante 1:** ¿De dónde es?
> **Estudiante 2:** Es Ricky Martin.   **Estudiante 2:** Es de Puerto Rico.

1. Enrique Iglesias (España)
   E1: ¿Quién es? E2: Es Enrique Iglesias. E1: ¿De dónde es? E2: Es de España.
2. Sammy Sosa (República Dominicana)
   E2: ¿Quién es? E1: Es Sammy Sosa. E2: ¿De dónde es? E1: Es de la República Dominicana.
3. Rebecca Lobo y Martin Sheen (Estados Unidos) E1: ¿Quiénes son? E2: Son Rebecca Lobo y Martin Sheen. E1: ¿De dónde son? E2: Son de los Estados Unidos.
4. Carlos Santana y Salma Hayek (México) E2: ¿Quiénes son? E1: Son Carlos Santana y Salma Hayek. E2: ¿De dónde son? E1: Son de México.
5. Shakira (Colombia)
   E1: ¿Quién es? E2: Es Shakira. E1: ¿De dónde es? E2: Es de Colombia.
6. Antonio Banderas y Penélope Cruz (España) E2: ¿Quiénes son? E1: Son Antonio Banderas y Penélope Cruz. E2: ¿De dónde son? E1: Son de España.
7. Edward James Olmos y Jimmy Smits (Estados Unidos) E1: ¿Quiénes son? E2: Son Edward James Olmos y Jimmy Smits. E1: ¿De dónde son? E2: Son de los Estados Unidos.
8. Gloria Estefan (Cuba) E2: ¿Quién es? E1: Es Gloria Estefan. E1: ¿De dónde es? E1: Es de Cuba.

3

¿Qué es? Ask your partner what each object is and to whom it belongs.

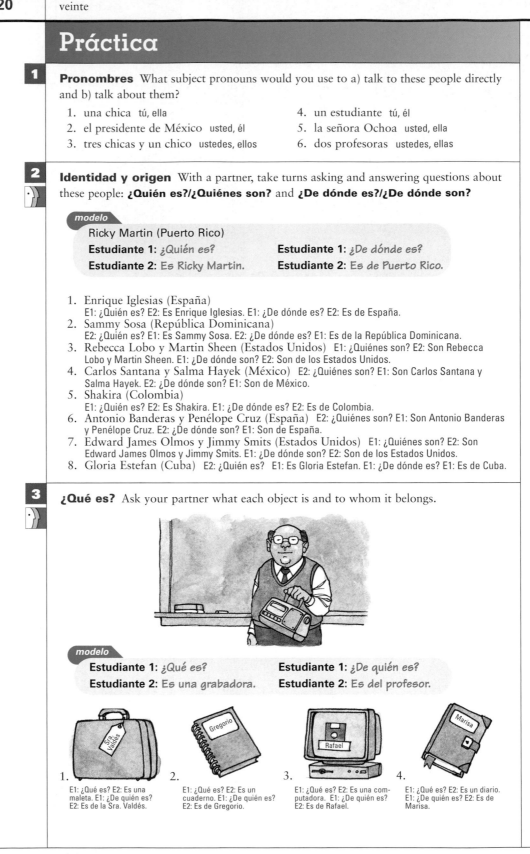

> **modelo**
> **Estudiante 1:** ¿Qué es?   **Estudiante 1:** ¿De quién es?
> **Estudiante 2:** Es una grabadora.   **Estudiante 2:** Es del profesor.

1. E1: ¿Qué es? E2: Es una maleta. E1: ¿De quién es? E2: Es de la Sra. Valdés.
2. E1: ¿Qué es? E2: Es un cuaderno. E1: ¿De quién es? E2: Es de Gregorio.
3. E1: ¿Qué es? E2: Es una computadora. E1: ¿De quién es? E2: Es de Rafael.
4. E1: ¿Qué es? E2: Es un diario. E1: ¿De quién es? E2: Es de Marisa.

Comunicación

4 Preguntas Using the items in the word bank, ask your partner questions about the ad.
Be imaginative in your responses. Answers will vary.

¿Quién?	¿De dónde?	¿Cuántos?
¿Qué?	¿De quién?	¿Cuántas?

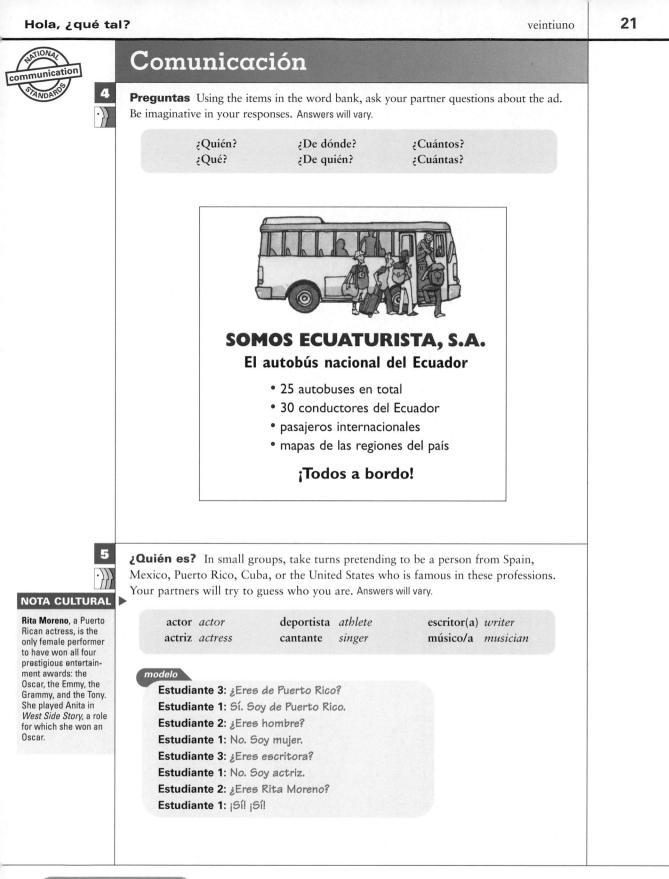

SOMOS ECUATURISTA, S.A.
El autobús nacional del Ecuador

- 25 autobuses en total
- 30 conductores del Ecuador
- pasajeros internacionales
- mapas de las regiones del país

¡Todos a bordo!

5 ¿Quién es? In small groups, take turns pretending to be a person from Spain,
Mexico, Puerto Rico, Cuba, or the United States who is famous in these professions.
Your partners will try to guess who you are. Answers will vary.

actor	*actor*	**deportista**	*athlete*	**escritor(a)**	*writer*
actriz	*actress*	**cantante**	*singer*	**músico/a**	*musician*

modelo

> **Estudiante 3:** ¿Eres de Puerto Rico?
> **Estudiante 1:** Sí. Soy de Puerto Rico.
> **Estudiante 2:** ¿Eres hombre?
> **Estudiante 1:** No. Soy mujer.
> **Estudiante 3:** ¿Eres escritora?
> **Estudiante 1:** No. Soy actriz.
> **Estudiante 2:** ¿Eres Rita Moreno?
> **Estudiante 1:** ¡Sí! ¡Sí!

NOTA CULTURAL

Rita Moreno, a Puerto Rican actress, is the only female performer to have won all four prestigious entertainment awards: the Oscar, the Emmy, the Grammy, and the Tony. She played Anita in *West Side Story*, a role for which she won an Oscar.

---

4 Suggestion If students ask, explain that the abbreviation **S.A.** in the ad stands for **sociedad anónima** and is equivalent to English *Inc.* (*Incorporated*).

4 Expansion Ask volunteers to make true-false statements about the ad. Classmates have to indicate whether the statements are true or false and correct false statements.

5 Suggestion You may want to have students brainstorm a list of names in the categories suggested and have three students read the **modelo** aloud.

TEACHING OPTIONS

Small Groups Bring in personal photos or magazine pictures that show people. In small groups, have students invent stories about the people: who they are, where they are from, what they do. Circulate around the room and assist with unfamiliar vocabulary as necessary, but encourage students to use terms they already know.

Game Hand out individual strips of paper with names of famous people on them. There should be several duplicates of each name. Then give descriptions of one of the famous people (**Es de ____,** **Es** [*profession*]), including cognate adjectives if you wish (**inteligente, pesimista**). The first person to stand and indicate that the name they have is the one you are describing (**¡Yo lo tengo!**) wins that round.

1.4 Telling time

ANTE TODO In both English and Spanish, the verb *to be* (**ser**) and numbers are used to tell time.

▶ To ask what time it is, use **¿Qué hora es?** When telling time, use **es + la** with **una** and **son + las** with all other hours.

Es la una.   Son las dos.   Son las seis.

▶ As in English, you express time from the hour to the half-hour in Spanish by adding minutes.

Son las cuatro **y cinco.**   Son las once **y veinte.**

▶ You may use either **y cuarto** or **y quince** to express fifteen minutes or quarter past the hour. For thirty minutes or half past the hour, you may use either **y media** or **y treinta.**

Es la una **y cuarto.**

Son las doce **y media.**

Son las nueve **y quince.**

Son las siete **y treinta.**

▶ You express time from the half-hour to the hour in Spanish by subtracting minutes or a portion of an hour from the next hour.

Es la una **menos cuarto.**   Son las tres **menos quince.**   Son las ocho **menos veinte.**   Son las tres **menos diez.**

► To ask at what time a particular event takes place, use the phrase **¿A qué hora (...)?**
To state at what time something takes place, use the construction **a la(s)** + *time*.

¿A qué hora es la clase de biología?
(At) what time is biology class?

La clase es **a las dos**.
The class is at two o'clock.

¿A qué hora es la fiesta?
(At) what time is the party?

A las ocho
At eight

► Here are some useful words and phrases associated with telling time:

Son las ocho **en punto**.
It's 8 o'clock on the dot/sharp.

Es **el mediodía**.
It's noon.

Es **la medianoche**.
It's midnight.

Son las nueve **de la mañana**.
It's 9 a.m. (in the morning).

Son las cuatro y cuarto **de la tarde**.
It's 4:15 p.m. (in the afternoon).

Son las diez y media **de la noche**.
It's 10:30 p.m. (at night).

Oye, ¿qué hora es?

Son las diez y tres minutos.

Oiga, ¿qué hora es?

Son las diez.

¡INTÉNTALO! Practice telling time by completing these sentences. The first item has been done for you.

1. (1:00 a.m.) Es la ____una____ de la mañana.
2. (2:50 a.m.) Son las tres ____menos____ diez de la mañana.
3. (4:15 p.m.) Son las cuatro y ___cuarto/quince___ de la tarde.
4. (8:30 p.m.) Son las ocho y ___media/treinta___ de la noche.
5. (9:15 a.m.) Son las nueve y quince de la ___mañana___.
6. (12:00 p.m.) Es el __mediodía/Son las doce__.
7. (6:00 a.m.) Son las seis de la ___mañana___.
8. (4:05 p.m.) Son las cuatro y cinco de la ___tarde___.
9. (12:00 a.m.) Es la __medianoche/Son las doce__.
10. (3:45 a.m.) Son las cuatro menos ___cuarto/quince___ de la mañana.

1 Expansion Have students draw clock faces showing the times presented in the activity. Then they exchange their drawings with a partner to verify accuracy.

2 Suggestion Model the pronunciation of the two ways of saying 4:15 in the model sentence. Point out that some of the clocks and watches also indicate the part of day (morning, afternoon, or evening) as well as the hour. Have students include this information in their responses.

2 Expansion At random, give times shown in the activity. Students must give the number of the clock or watch described. Ex: **Es la una de la mañana. (Es el número 2.)**

3 Expansion

• Have partners switch roles and ask and answer the questions again. Alternatively, have each student who asked questions the first time pair up with a student from another pair who answered questions. The new pair then switches roles.

• Have students come up with three original items to ask their partner, similar to the items in the activity. The partner should respond with actual times. Ex: —**¿A qué hora es el programa *ER*? —Es a las diez.**

Práctica

1 Ordenar Put these times in order, from the earliest to the latest.

a. Son las dos de la tarde. 4
b. Son las once de la mañana. 2
c. Son las siete y media de la noche. 6
d. Son las seis menos cuarto de la tarde. 5
e. Son las dos menos diez de la tarde. 3
f. Son las ocho y veintidós de la mañana. 1

2 ¿Qué hora es? Give the times shown on each clock or watch.

modelo
Son las cuatro y cuarto/quince de la tarde.

1. Son las doce y media.
2. Es la una de la mañana.
3. Son las cinco y cuarto.
4. Son las ocho y diez.
5. Son las cinco y media/treinta.
6. Son las once menos cuarto/quince.
7. Son las dos y doce de la tarde.
8. Son las siete y cinco.
9. Son las cuatro menos cinco.
10. Son las doce menos veinticinco de la noche.

NOTA CULTURAL

Many Spanish-speaking countries use both the 12-hour clock and the 24-hour clock (that is, military time). The 24-hour clock is commonly used in written form on signs and schedules. For example, 1p.m. is 13h, 2 p.m. is 14h and so on.

3 ¿A qué hora? Ask your partner at what time these events take place. Your partner will answer according to the cues provided.

modelo
la clase de matemáticas (2:30 p.m.)
Estudiante 1: *¿A qué hora es la clase de matemáticas?*
Estudiante 2: *Es a las dos y media de la tarde.*

1. el programa *Las cuatro amigas* (*11:30 a.m.*)
2. el drama *La casa de Bernarda Alba* (*7:00 p.m.*)
3. el programa *Los turistas* (*8:30 a.m.*)
4. la clase de español (*10:30 a.m.*)
5. la clase de biología (*9:40 a.m. sharp*)
6. la clase de historia (*10:50 a.m.*)
7. el partido (*game*) de béisbol (*5:15 p.m.*)
8. el partido de tenis (*12:45 p.m. sharp*)
9. el partido de baloncesto (*basketball*) (*7:45 p.m.*)
10. la fiesta (*8:30 p.m.*)

1. E1: ¿A qué hora es el programa *Las cuatro amigas*?
   E2: Es a las once y media/treinta de la mañana.
2. E1: ¿A qué hora es el drama *La casa de Bernada Alba*?
   E2: Es a las siete de la noche.
3. E1: ¿A qué hora es el programa *Los turistas*?
   E2: Es a las ocho y media/treinta de la mañana.
4. E1: ¿A qué hora es la clase de español?
   E2: Es a las diez y media/treinta de la mañana.
5. E1: ¿A qué hora es la clase de biología?
   E2: Es a las diez menos veinte de la mañana en punto.
6. E1: ¿A qué hora es la clase de historia?
   E2: Es a las once menos diez de la mañana.
7. E1: ¿A qué hora es el partido de béisbol?
   E2: Es a las cinco y cuarto de la tarde.
8. E1: ¿A qué hora es el partido de tenis?
   E2: Es a la una menos cuarto de la tarde en punto.
9. E1: ¿A qué hora es el partido de baloncesto?
   E2: Es a las ocho menos cuarto de la noche.
10. E1: ¿A qué hora es la fiesta?
    E2: Es a las ocho y media/treinta de la noche.

NOTA CULTURAL

La casa de Bernarda Alba is a famous play by Spanish poet and playwright **Federico García Lorca** (1898-1936). Lorca was one of the most famous writers of the 20th century and a close friend of Spain's most talented artists, including the painter Salvador Dalí and the filmmaker Luis Buñuel.

TEACHING OPTIONS

Pairs Have students work with a partner to create an original conversation similar to the one in **Actividad 3**. They should do at least the following in their conversation: (1) greet each other appropriately, (2) ask for the time, (3) ask what time a particular class is, (4) say goodbye. Have pairs present their conversations in front of the rest of the class.

Extra Practice Give certain times of the day and ask students whether those times are typical times to be awake for **un(a) médico/a, un(a) estudiante,** or **los/las dos** (*both*). Ex: **Son las cinco menos cuarto de la mañana. (un(a) médico/a) Es la medianoche. (un(a) estudiante)**

Comunicación

4 **En la televisión** With a partner, take turns asking and answering questions about these television listings. *Answers will vary.*

modelo

> **Estudiante 1:** ¿A qué hora es el documental *Las computadoras?*
> **Estudiante 2:** Es a las nueve en punto de la noche.

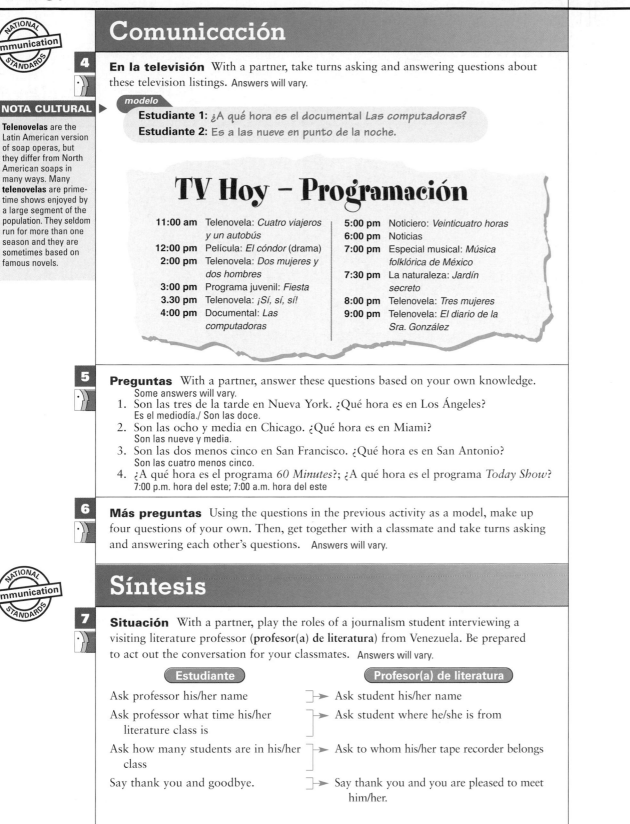

TV Hoy – Programación

11:00 am Telenovela: *Cuatro viajeros y un autobús*	**5:00 pm** Noticiero: *Veinticuatro horas*
12:00 pm Película: *El cóndor* (drama)	**6:00 pm** Noticias
2:00 pm Telenovela: *Dos mujeres y dos hombres*	**7:00 pm** Especial musical: *Música folklórica de México*
3:00 pm Programa juvenil: *Fiesta*	**7:30 pm** La naturaleza: *Jardín secreto*
3.30 pm Telenovela: *¡Sí, sí, sí!*	**8:00 pm** Telenovela: *Tres mujeres*
4:00 pm Documental: *Las computadoras*	**9:00 pm** Telenovela: *El diario de la Sra. González*

5 **Preguntas** With a partner, answer these questions based on your own knowledge. *Some answers will vary.*

1. Son las tres de la tarde en Nueva York. ¿Qué hora es en Los Ángeles?
   Es el mediodía./ Son las doce.
2. Son las ocho y media en Chicago. ¿Qué hora es en Miami?
   Son las nueve y media.
3. Son las dos menos cinco en San Francisco. ¿Qué hora es en San Antonio?
   Son las cuatro menos cinco.
4. ¿A qué hora es el programa *60 Minutes*?; ¿A qué hora es el programa *Today Show*?
   7:00 p.m. hora del este; 7:00 a.m. hora del este

6 **Más preguntas** Using the questions in the previous activity as a model, make up four questions of your own. Then, get together with a classmate and take turns asking and answering each other's questions. *Answers will vary.*

Síntesis

7 **Situación** With a partner, play the roles of a journalism student interviewing a visiting literature professor (**profesor(a) de literatura**) from Venezuela. Be prepared to act out the conversation for your classmates. *Answers will vary.*

Estudiante	Profesor(a) de literatura
Ask professor his/her name	→ Ask student his/her name
Ask professor what time his/her literature class is	→ Ask student where he/she is from
Ask how many students are in his/her class	→ Ask to whom his/her tape recorder belongs
Say thank you and goodbye.	→ Say thank you and you are pleased to meet him/her.

TEACHING OPTIONS

Small Groups Have small groups of students prepare skits. Groups can choose any situation they wish, provided that they use material presented in the **Contextos** and **Estructura** sections. Possible situations include: meeting to go on an excursion (as in the **Fotonovela**), meeting in between classes, introducing friends to professors, and so forth.

Heritage Speakers Have heritage speakers interview class-mates. They should use vocabulary and structures presented in **Lección 1**. Have them report their findings to the class.
Heritage Speakers Ask heritage speakers what **novelas** are currently featured on Spanish-language television and the channel (**canal**) and time when they are shown.

---

4 Suggestion Before beginning the activity, have students look over the schedule and point out cognates and predict their meanings. Help them with the meanings of other programming categories: **película, programa juvenil, noticias/noticiero.**

4 Expansion Ask students questions about what time some popular TV programs are shown. Ex: —¿A qué hora es el programa "Will y Grace"? —Es a las nueve.

5 Suggestion Remind students that there are four time zones in the continental United States, and that when it is noon in the Eastern Time zone, it is three hours earlier in the Pacific Time zone.

6 Expansion Have pairs choose the two most challenging questions to share with the class.

7 Suggestion Point out that this activity synthesizes everything students have learned in this chapter: greetings and leave-takings, nouns and articles, numbers 0–30 and **hay**, the verb **ser**, and telling time. Spend a few moments reviewing these topics.

Suggestion See the Information Gap Activities Booklet for an additional activity to practice the material presented in this section.

Section Goals

In **Lectura** students will:
- learn to recognize cognates
- use suffixes to recognize cognates
- read a telephone list rich in cognates

Instructional Resource
Companion website:
www.vistahigherlearning.com

Estrategia Tell students that cognates are words in one language that have identical or similar counterparts in another language. True cognates are close in meaning, so recognizing Spanish words that are cognates of English words can help them read Spanish. Have students look at the cognates in this **Estrategia** box. Write some of the common suffix correspondences between Spanish and English on the board: **–ción/–sión** = *–tion/–sion* (**nación, decisión**); **–ante/–ente** = *–ant/–ent* (**importante, inteligente, elegante**); **–ia/–ía** = *–y* (**farmacia, sociología, historia**); **–dad** = *–ty* (**oportunidad, universidad**).

The Affective Dimension Tell students that reading in Spanish will be less anxiety-provoking if they follow the advice in the **Estrategia** sections, which are designed to reinforce and improve reading comprehension skills.

Examinar el texto Ask students to tell you what type of text **Teléfonos importantes** is and how they can tell. (It is a list and it contains names and telephone numbers.)

Cognados Ask students to mention any cognates they see in the phone list. Discuss the cognates and explain any discrepancies with the list of corresponding suffixes given above. Ex: **policía** = police, *not* policy

Lectura

Antes de leer

Estrategia
Recognizing cognates

As you learned earlier in this lesson, cognates are words that share similar meanings and spellings in two or more languages. When reading in Spanish, it's helpful to look for cognates and use them to guess the meaning of what you're reading. But watch out for false cognates. For example, **librería** means *bookstore*, not *library*, and **embarazada** means *pregnant*, not *embarrassed*. Look at this list of Spanish words, paying special attention to prefixes and suffixes. Can you guess the meaning of each word?

importante	oportunidad
farmacia	cultura
inteligente	activo
dentista	sociología
decisión	espectacular
televisión	restaurante
médico	policía

Examinar el texto

Glance quickly at the reading selection and guess what type of document it is. Explain your answer.

Cognados

Read the document and make a list of the cognates you find. Guess their English equivalents, then compare your answers with those of a classmate.

recursos

vistahigher learning.com

Teléfonos importantes

- Policía
- Médico
- Dentista
- Pediatra
- Farmacia
- Banco Central
- Aerolíneas Nacionales
- Cine Metro
- Hora/Temperatura
- Profesora Salgado (universidad)
- Felipe (oficina)
- Gimnasio Gente Activa
- Restaurante Roma
- Supermercado Famoso
- Librería El Inteligente

TEACHING OPTIONS

Heritage Speakers Ask heritage speakers to model reading and writing the numbers in **Teléfonos importantes**, and to discuss how digits are grouped and punctuated (periods instead of hyphens). For example, 732.5722 may be pronounced by a combination of tens, **siete, treinta y dos, cincuenta y siete, veintidós**, or hundreds and tens, **setecientos treinta y dos, cincuenta y siete, veintidós**.

Extra Practice Write some of these Spanish words on the board and have students name the English cognate: **democracia, actor, eficiente, nacionalidad, diferencia, guitarrista, artista, doctora, dificultad, exploración**. Then write on the board some of these words with less obvious cognates: **ciencia, población, número, signo, remedio**.

54.11.11

54.36.92

54.87.11

53.14.57

54.03.06

54.90.83

54.87.40

53.45.96

53.24.81

54.15.33

54.84.99

54.36.04

53.75.44

54.77.23

54.66.04

Después de leer

¿Cierto o falso?

Indicate whether each statement is **cierto** or **falso**.
Then correct the false statements.

1. There is a child in this household.
   Cierto

2. To renew a prescription you would dial 54.90.83.
   Falso. To renew a prescription you would dial 54.03.06.

3. If you wanted the exact time and information about the weather you'd dial 53.24.81.
   Cierto

4. Felipe probably works outdoors.
   Falso. Felipe works in an office.

5. This household probably orders a lot of Chinese food.
   Falso. They probably order a lot of Italian food.

6. If you had a toothache, you would dial 54.87.11.
   Cierto

7. You would dial 54.87.40 to make a flight reservation.
   Cierto

8. To find out if a best-selling book was in stock, you would dial 54.66.04.
   Cierto

9. If you needed information about aerobics classes, you would dial 54.15.33.
   Falso. If you needed information about aerobics class you would call Gimnasio Gente Activa at 54.36.04.

10. You would call **Cine Metro** to find out what time a movie starts.
    Cierto

Hacer una lista

Make your own list of phone numbers like the one shown in this reading. Include emergency phone numbers as well as frequently called numbers. Use as many cognates from the reading as you can. Answers will vary.

¿Cierto o falso?
- Go over Items 1–10 orally with the whole class. If students have trouble inferring the answer to any question, help them identify the cognate or provide additional corresponding context clues.
- Ask students to work with a partner to use cognates and context clues to determine whether each statement is **cierto** or **falso**. Go over the answers with the whole class.

Hacer una lista
- With the whole class, brainstorm possible categories of phone numbers students may wish to include in their lists. Begin an idea map on the board or overhead projector, jotting down the students' responses in Spanish, explaining unfamiliar vocabulary as necessary.
- You may wish to have students include e-mail addesses (**direcciones electrónicas**) in their lists.

TEACHING OPTIONS

Variación léxica How a Spanish speaker answers the telephone may reveal where that person is from. A telephone call in Mexico is likely answered **¿Bueno?** In other parts of the Spanish-speaking world you may hear the greetings **Diga, Dígame, Óigame,** and even **Aló.**
Small Groups In groups of three, have students read aloud entries from their lists. The listeners should copy down the items

they hear. Have group members switch roles so each has a chance to read. Have groups compare and contrast their lists.
Heritage Speakers Ask heritage speakers to share phone etiquette they may know, such as answering the phone or the equivalents of "Is ____ there?" (**¿Está ____?**), "Speaking" (**Soy yo.** or **Al habla.**), and identifying oneself, "This is ____." (**Habla ____.** or **Soy ____.**)

Section Goal

In **Panorama** students will read statistics and cultural information about Hispanics in the United States and Canada.

Instructional Resources
Transparency #12
WB/VM: Workbook, pp. 9–10;
Video Activities, pp. 225–226
***Panorama cultural** DVD/Video*
Interactive CD-ROM
IRM: Videoscript, p. 107;
***Panorama cultural** Translations,*
p. 129
Companion website:
www.vistahigherlearning.com
Presentations CD-ROM

Suggestion Have students look at the map of the United States and Canada or project **Transparency #12**. Have volunteers read aloud the labeled cities and geographic features. Model Spanish pronunciation of names as necessary. Have students jot down as many names of places and geographic features with Hispanic origins as they can. Ask volunteers to share their lists with the class. Write the names they mention on the board and model their pronunciation. Ex: **Alamosa está en Colorado.**

El país en cifras Have volunteers read the bulleted headings in **El país en cifras**. Point out cognates and clarify unfamiliar words. Explain that numerals in Spanish have a comma where English would use a decimal point (**3,5%**) and have a period where English would use a comma (**12.268.000**). Explain that **EE.UU.** is the abbreviation of **Estados Unidos**, the doubling of the initial letters indicating plural. Model the pronunciation of **Florida** (accent on the second syllable) and point out that it is often used with an article (**la Florida**) by Spanish speakers.

¡Increíble pero cierto! Do not expect students to produce numbers greater than 30 at this point. Explain phrases such as **se estima** and **grupo minoritario**.

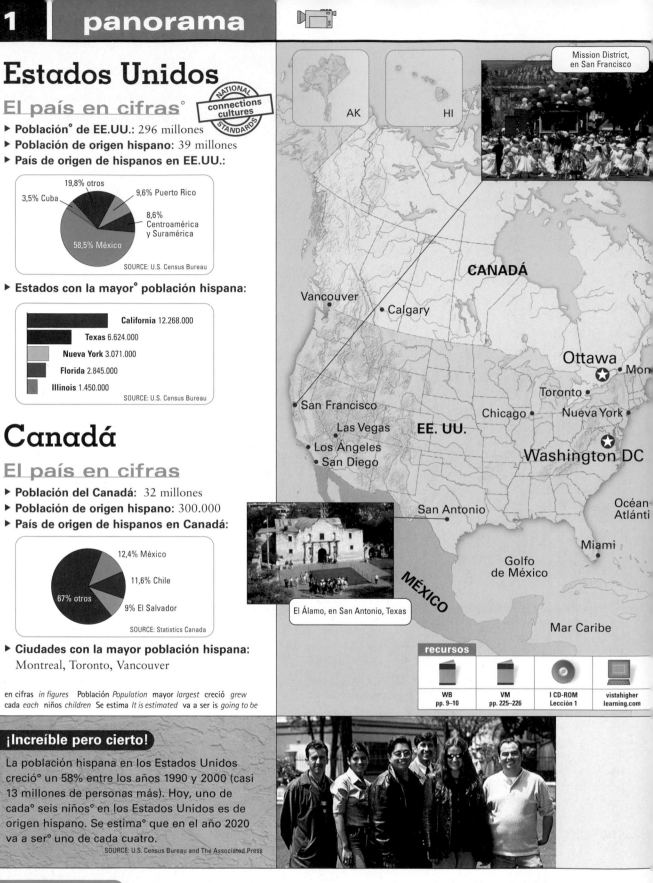

Estados Unidos

El país en cifras°

► **Población° de EE.UU.:** 296 millones
► **Población de origen hispano:** 39 millones
► **País de origen de hispanos en EE.UU.:**

Pie chart:
- 19,8% otros
- 3,5% Cuba
- 9,6% Puerto Rico
- 8,6% Centroamérica y Suramérica
- 58,5% México

SOURCE: U.S. Census Bureau

► **Estados con la mayor° población hispana:**

- California 12.268.000
- Texas 6.624.000
- Nueva York 3.071.000
- Florida 2.845.000
- Illinois 1.450.000

SOURCE: U.S. Census Bureau

Canadá

El país en cifras

► **Población del Canadá:** 32 millones
► **Población de origen hispano:** 300.000
► **País de origen de hispanos en Canadá:**

Pie chart:
- 12,4% México
- 11,6% Chile
- 9% El Salvador
- 67% otros

SOURCE: Statistics Canada

► **Ciudades con la mayor población hispana:**
Montreal, Toronto, Vancouver

en cifras in figures Población Population mayor largest creció grew cada each niños children Se estima It is estimated va a ser is going to be

¡Increíble pero cierto!

La población hispana en los Estados Unidos creció° un 58% entre los años 1990 y 2000 (casi 13 millones de personas más). Hoy, uno de cada° seis niños° en los Estados Unidos es de origen hispano. Se estima° que en el año 2020 va a ser° uno de cada cuatro.

SOURCE: U.S. Census Bureau and The Associated Press

Map labels: Mission District, en San Francisco; AK; HI; CANADÁ; Vancouver; Calgary; Ottawa; Mon; Toronto; San Francisco; Chicago; Nueva York; Las Vegas; EE. UU.; Los Ángeles; San Diego; Washington DC; San Antonio; Océano Atlánti; Miami; MÉXICO; El Álamo, en San Antonio, Texas; Golfo de México; Mar Caribe

recursos

| WB pp. 9–10 | VM pp. 225–226 | I CD-ROM Lección 1 | vistahigher learning.com |

TEACHING OPTIONS

Heritage Speakers Ask heritage speakers to describe for the class the Hispanic celebrations that are held in the region where they come from. Ask them to tell the date when the celebration takes place, the event it commemorates, and some of the particulars of the celebration. Possible celebrations: **Cinco de Mayo, Día de la Raza, Día de los Muertos, Fiesta de San Juan, Carnaval**

Game Divide the class into teams of five students. Give teams five minutes to brainstorm place names (cities, states, lakes, rivers, montain ranges) in the United States that have Spanish origins. One member of the team should take down the names in a numbered list. After five minutes, go over the names with the whole class, confirming the accuracy of each name. The team with the greatest number wins.

Comida • La comida mexicana

La comida° mexicana es muy popular en los Estados Unidos. Los tacos, las enchiladas, las quesadillas y los frijoles son platos° mexicanos que frecuentemente forman parte de las comidas de muchos norteamericanos. También° son populares las variaciones de la comida mexicana en los Estados Unidos... el tex-mex y el cali-mex.

Lugares • La Pequeña Habana

La Pequeña Habana° es un barrio° de Miami, Florida, donde viven° muchos cubanoamericanos. Es un lugar° donde se encuentran° las costumbres° de la cultura cubana, los aromas y sabores° de su comida y la música salsa. La Pequeña Habana es una parte de Cuba en los Estados Unidos.

Costumbres • Desfile puertorriqueño

Cada junio desde° 1951 (mil novecientos cincuenta y uno), los puertorriqueños celebran su cultura con un desfile° en Nueva York. Es un gran espectáculo con carrozas° y música salsa, flamenco y hip-hop. Muchos espectadores llevan° la bandera° de Puerto Rico en su ropa° o pintada en la cara°.

Sociedad° • La influencia hispánica en Canadá

La presencia hispana en Canadá es importante en la cultura del país. En 1998 (mil novecientos noventa y ocho) se establecieron° los *Latin American Achievement Awards Canada*, para reconocer° los logros° de la comunidad en varios campos°. Dos figuras importantes de origen argentino son Alberto Manguel (novelista) y Sergio Marchi (Embajador° de Canadá en las Naciones Unidas°). Hay grupos musicales que son parte de la cultura hispana en Canadá: Dominicanada, Bomba, Norteño y Rasca.

¿Qué aprendiste? Completa las frases con la información adecuada (*appropriate*).

1. Hay __39 millones__ de personas de origen hispano en los Estados Unidos.
2. Los cuatro estados con las poblaciones hispanas más grandes son (en orden) __California__, Texas, __Nueva York__ y Florida.
3. Toronto, Montreal y __Vancouver__ son las tres ciudades con mayor población hispana del Canadá.
4. Las quesadillas y las enchiladas son platos __mexicanos__.
5. La Pequeña __Habana__ es un barrio de Miami.
6. En Miami hay muchas personas de origen __cubano__.
7. Cada junio se celebra en Nueva York un gran desfile para personas de origen __puertorriqueño__.
8. Dominicanada es un __grupo musical__ del Canadá.

Conexión Internet Investiga estos temas en el sitio **www.vistahigherlearning.com**.

1. Haz (*Make*) una lista de seis hispanos célebres de EE.UU. o Canadá. Explica (*Explain*) por qué (*why*) son célebres.
2. Escoge (*Choose*) seis lugares en los Estados Unidos con nombres hispanos y busca información sobre el origen y el significado (*meaning*) de cada nombre.

Comida *Food* platos *dishes* También *Also* La Pequeña Habana *Little Havana* barrio *neighborhood* viven *live* lugar *place* se encuentran *are found* costumbres *customs* sabores *flavors* Cada junio desde *Each June since* desfile *parade* con carrozas *with floats* llevan *wear* bandera *flag* ropa *clothing* cara *face* Sociedad *Society* se establecieron *were established* reconocer *to recognize* logros *achievements* campos *fields* Embajador *Ambassador* Naciones Unidas *United Nations*

Instructional Resources
Vocabulary CD
Lab Manual, p. 6
Lab CD/MP3 Lección 1
IRM: Tapescript, pp. 1–5
Testing Program: Pruebas,
pp. 1–12
Testing Program Audio CD
Test Files CD-ROM
Test Generator

Suggestion Tell students that
this is active vocabulary for
which they are responsible and
that it will appear on tests and
exams.

Saludos

Hola.	Hello; Hi.
Buenos días.	Good morning.
Buenas tardes.	Good afternoon.
Buenas noches.	Good evening.; Good night.

Despedidas

Adiós.	Goodbye.
Nos vemos.	See you.
Hasta luego.	See you later.
Hasta la vista.	See you later.
Hasta pronto.	See you soon.
Hasta mañana.	See you tomorrow.
Saludos a...	Greetings to …
Chau.	Bye.

¿Cómo está?

¿Cómo está usted?	How are you? (form.)
¿Cómo estás?	How are you? (fam.)
¿Qué hay de nuevo?	What's new?
¿Qué pasa?	What's happening?; What's going on?
¿Qué tal?	How are you?; How is it going?
(Muy) bien, gracias.	(Very) well, thanks.
Nada.	Nothing.
No muy bien.	Not very well.
Regular.	So so; OK.

Expresiones de cortesía

Con permiso.	Pardon me; Excuse me.
De nada.	You're welcome.
Lo siento.	I'm sorry.
(Muchas) gracias.	Thank you (very much).; Thanks (a lot).
No hay de qué.	You're welcome.
Perdón.	Pardon me.; Excuse me.
por favor	please

Títulos

señor (Sr.); don	Mr.; sir
señora (Sra.)	Mrs.; ma'am
señorita (Srta.)	Miss

Presentaciones

¿Cómo se llama usted?	What's your name? (form.)
¿Cómo te llamas (tú)?	What's your name? (fam.)
Me llamo...	My name is …
¿Y tú?	And you? (fam.)
¿Y usted?	And you? (form.)
Mucho gusto.	Pleased to meet you.
El gusto es mío.	The pleasure is mine.
Encantado/a.	Delighted.; Pleased to meet you.
Igualmente.	Likewise.
Éste/Ésta es...	This is …
Le presento a...	I would like to introduce (name) to you… (form.)
Te presento a...	I would like to introduce (name) to you… (fam.)
nombre	name

¿De dónde es?

¿De dónde es usted?	Where are you from? (form.)
¿De dónde eres?	Where are you from? (fam.)
Soy de...	I'm from …

Palabras adicionales

¿cuánto(s)/a(s)?	how much/many?
¿de quién...?	whose …? (sing.)
¿de quiénes...?	whose …? (plural)
(no) hay	there is (not); there are (not)

Países

Ecuador	Ecuador
España	Spain
Estados Unidos (EE.UU.; E.U.)	United States
México	Mexico
Puerto Rico	Puerto Rico

Verbos

ser	to be

Sustantivos

el autobús	bus
la capital	capital (city)
el chico	boy
la chica	girl
la computadora	computer
la comunidad	community
el/la conductor(a)	driver
la conversación	conversation
la cosa	thing
el cuaderno	notebook
el día	day
el diario	diary
el diccionario	dictionary
la escuela	school
el/la estudiante	student
la foto(grafía)	photograph
la grabadora	tape recorder
el hombre	man
el/la joven	youth; young person
el lápiz	pencil
la lección	lesson
la maleta	suitcase
la mano	hand
la mujer	woman
la nacionalidad	nationality
el número	number
el país	country
la palabra	word
el/la pasajero/a	passenger
el problema	problem
el/la profesor(a)	teacher
el programa	program
el/la turista	tourist
el video	video

Numbers 0–30	See page 14.
Telling time	See pages 22–23.
Expresiones útiles	See page 7.

recursos

LM p. 6	Lab CD/MP3 Lección 1	Vocab CD Lección 1

En la universidad

2

Communicative Goals

You will learn how to:

- Talk about your classes and school life
- Discuss everyday activities
- Ask questions in Spanish
- Describe the location of people and things

Lesson Goals

In **Lección 2** students will be introduced to the following:

- classroom- and university-related words
- names of academic courses and fields of study
- class schedules
- days of the week
- present tense of regular –**ar** verbs
- forming negative sentences
- forming questions
- the present tense of **estar**
- prepositions of location
- numbers 31–100
- using text formats to predict content
- cultural and historical information about Spain

A primera vista Have students look at the photo. Say: **Es una foto de dos jóvenes en la universidad.** Then ask: **¿Qué son los jóvenes? (Son estudiantes.) ¿Qué hay en la mano del chico? (Hay un diccionario/libro.)**

INSTRUCTIONAL RESOURCES

Workbook/Video Manual: WB Activities, pp. 11–22
Laboratory Manual: Lab Activities, pp. 7–12
Workbook/Video Manual: Video Activities, pp. 197–198; pp. 227–228
Instructor's Resource Manual: **Hojas de actividades**, p. 141; **Vocabulario adicional**, p. 155; **¡Inténtalo!** & **Práctica** Answers, pp. 173–174; **Fotonovela**

Translations, pp. 119–120; Textbook CD Tapescript, p. 72; Lab CDs Tapescript, pp. 6–10; **Fotonovela** Videoscript, p. 88; **Panorama cultural** Videoscript, p. 108; **Pan. cult.** Translations p. 130.
Info Gap Activities Booklet, pp. 5–8
Overhead Transparencies: #7, #8, #13, #14, #15
Lab Audio CD/MP3 **Lección 2**

Panorama cultural DVD/Video
Fotonovela DVD/Video
Testing Program, pp. 13–24
Testing Program Audio CD
Test Files CD-ROM
Test Generator
Companion website

Presentations CD-ROM
Textbook CD
Vocabulary CD
Interactive CD-ROM
Video CD-ROM
Web-SAM

Section Goals

In **Contextos**, students will learn and practice:
• names for people, places, and things at the university
• names of academic courses

Instructional Resources
Transparency #13
Textbook Activities CD
Vocabulary CD
WB/VM: Workbook, pp. 11–12
Lab Manual, p. 7
Lab CD/MP3 **Lección 2**
IRM: **Vocab. adicional**, *p. 155;*
Práctica *Answers, p. 173;*
Tapescript, pp. 6–10; p. 72
Interactive CD-ROM
Companion website:
www.vistahigherlearning.com
Presentations CD-ROM

Suggestions

• Introduce vocabulary for classroom objects such as **mesa, libro, pluma, lápiz, papel.** Hold up or point to an object and say: **Es un lápiz.** Ask questions that include **¿Hay/No hay… ?** and **¿Cuántos/as… ?**
• Using either objects in the classroom or **Transparency #13**, point to items and ask questions such as: **¿Qué es? ¿Es una mesa? ¿Es un reloj?** Vary by asking: **¿Qué hay en el escritorio? ¿Qué hay en la mesa? ¿Cuántas tizas hay en la pizarra? ¿Hay una pluma en el escritorio de _____?**

Note: At this point you may want to present **Vocabulario adicional: Más vocabulario para las clases**, from the IRM.

En la universidad

Más vocabulario

la biblioteca	*library*
la cafetería	*cafeteria*
la casa	*house; home*
el estadio	*stadium*
el laboratorio	*laboratory*
la librería	*bookstore*
la residencia estudiantil	*dormitory*
la universidad	*university; college*
el/la compañero/a de clase	*classmate*
el/la compañero/a de cuarto	*roommate*
la clase	*class*
el examen	*test; exam*
el horario	*schedule*
la prueba	*test; quiz*
el semestre	*semester*
la tarea	*homework*
el trimestre	*trimester; quarter*
la administración de empresas	*business administration*
el arte	*art*
la especialización	*major*
la biología	*biology*
las ciencias	*sciences*
la computación	*computer science*
la contabilidad	*accounting*
el curso	*course*
la economía	*economics*
el español	*Spanish*
la física	*physics*
la geografía	*geography*
la música	*music*

Variación léxica

pluma ←→ bolígrafo
pizarra ←→ tablero (*Col.*)

recursos

TEXT CD Lección 2	WB pp. 11–12	LM p. 7	Lab CD/MP3 Lección 2	I CD-ROM Lección 2	Vocab CD Lección 2

TEACHING OPTIONS

Variación léxica Ask heritage speakers to tell the class any other terms they use to talk about people, places, or things at the university. Ask them to tell where these terms are used. Possible responses: **el boli, la ciudad universitaria, el profe, el catedrático, la facultad, el profesorado, la asignatura, el gimnasio, el pizarrón, el salón de clases, el aula, el pupitre, el gis, el alumno**

Game Divide the class into teams. Then, in English, read aloud the name of an academic course and ask one of the teams to provide the Spanish equivalent. If the team provides the correct term, it gets a point. If not, the second team gets a chance at the same item. Alternate asking questions of the two teams until you have read all the course names. The team that has the most points at the end wins.

el mapa
la pizarra

LAS MATERIAS	COURSES
la historia	history
las humanidades	humanities
el inglés	English
las lenguas extranjeras	foreign languages
la literatura	literature
las matemáticas	mathematics
el periodismo	journalism
la psicología	psychology
la química	chemistry
la sociología	sociology

el papel

el borrador
la tiza

la papelera

el escritorio

la estudiante

la silla

Práctica

1

Escuchar Listen to Professor Morales talk about her Spanish classroom, then check the items she mentions.

puerta	✔	sillas	○
ventanas	✔	libros	✔
pizarra	✔	plumas	✔
borrador	○	mochilas	○
tiza	✔	papel	✔
escritorios	✔	reloj	✔

2

Emparejar Match each question with its most logical response. **¡Ojo!** (*Careful!*) Two of the responses will not be used.

1. ¿Qué clase es? d
2. ¿Quiénes son? h
3. ¿Quién es? e
4. ¿De dónde es? c
5. ¿A qué hora es la clase de inglés? g
6. ¿Cuántos estudiantes hay? a

a. Hay veinticinco.
b. Es un reloj.
c. Es del Perú.
d. Es la clase de química.
e. Es el señor Bastos.
f. Mucho gusto.
g. Es a las nueve en punto.
h. Son los profesores.

3

Identificar Identify the word that does not fit in each group.

1. examen • grabadora • tarea • prueba grabadora
2. economía • matemáticas • biblioteca • contabilidad biblioteca
3. pizarra • tiza • borrador • librería librería
4. lápiz • cafetería • papel • cuaderno cafetería
5. veinte • diez • pluma • treinta pluma
6. conductor • laboratorio • autobús • pasajero laboratorio
7. humanidades • mesa • ciencias • lenguas extranjeras mesa
8. papelera • casa • residencia estudiantil • biblioteca papelera

4

¿Qué clase es? Use the clues to name the subject matter of each class.

> **modelo**
> los elementos, los átomos
> Es la clase de química.

1. Abraham Lincoln, Winston Churchill Es la clase de historia.
2. Picasso, Leonardo da Vinci Es la clase de arte.
3. Freud, Jung Es la clase de psicología.
4. África, el océano Pacífico Es la clase de geografía.
5. la cultura de España, verbos Es la clase de español.
6. Hemingway, Shakespeare Es la clase de literatura.
7. geometría, trigonometría Es la clase de matemáticas.
8. las plantas, los animales Es la clase de biología.

1 Suggestion Have students check their answers by going over **Actividad 1** with the whole class.

1 Tapescript ¿Qué hay en mi clase de español? ¡Muchas cosas! Hay una puerta y cinco ventanas. Hay una pizarra con tiza. Hay muchos escritorios para los estudiantes. En los escritorios de los estudiantes hay libros y plumas. En la mesa de la profesora hay papel. Hay un mapa y un reloj en la clase también.
Textbook Activities CD

2 Expansion Items b and f were not used. Ask the class to come up with questions or statements that would elicit these two items as responses.

3 Expansion Read the following as items 9 and 10: **9. pluma, lápiz, silla, tiza (silla); 10. ventana, estudiante, profesor, compañera de cuarto (ventana).**

4 Expansion Have the class brainstorm a list of famous people that they would associate with these fields: **periodismo** (Ex: Dan Rather, Barbara Walters), **computación** (Ex: Bill Gates, Michael Dell), **humanidades** (Ex: Maya Angelou, Sandra Cisneros). Then have the class guess the field associated with each of these people: Albert Einstein (**física**), Charles Darwin (**biología**), Alan Greenspan (**economía**).

TEACHING OPTIONS

Extra Practice Ask students what phrases or vocabulary words they associate with items such as the following: **1. la pizarra** (Ex: **la tiza, el borrador**), **2. la residencia estudiantil** (Ex: **el compañero de cuarto, la compañera de cuarto, el/la estudiante**), **3. el reloj** (Ex: **¿Qué hora es?, Son las…, Es la…**), **4. la biblioteca** (Ex: **los libros, los exámenes, las materias**).

Extra Practice On the board, write **¿Qué clases tomas?** and **Tomo…** . Explain the meaning of these phrases and ask your students to circulate around the classroom and imagine that they are meeting their classmates for the first time. Tell them to introduce themselves, find out where each person is from, and what classes he or she is taking. Follow up by asking individual students about what their classmates are taking.

Suggestions
- Write the following questions and answers on the board, explaining their meaning as you do so:
  —**¿Qué día es hoy?**
  —**Hoy es ____.**
  —**¿Qué día es mañana?**
  (Students learned **mañana** in **Lección 1**.)
  —**Mañana es ____.**
  —**¿Cuándo es la prueba?**
  —**Es el ____.**
  Then ask students the questions on the board.
- Tell students that Monday is traditionally the first day of the week in the Spanish-speaking world and usually appears as such on calendars.

5 **Expansion** Ask the class questions such as: **Mañana es viernes… ¿qué día fue ayer?** (miércoles); Ayer fue domingo… ¿qué día es mañana? (martes)

6 **Suggestion** Have the class review the list of **sustantivos** on page 30 and the numbers 0–30 on page 14 before doing this activity.

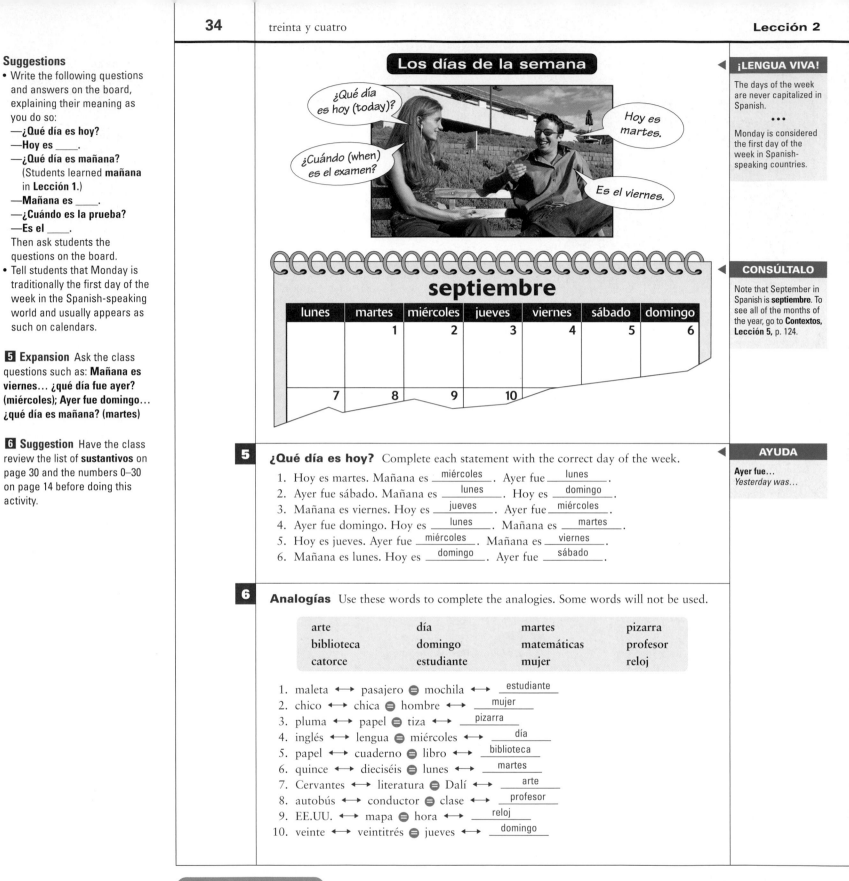

Los días de la semana

¿Qué día es hoy (today)?

Hoy es martes.

¿Cuándo (when) es el examen?

Es el viernes.

septiembre

lunes	martes	miércoles	jueves	viernes	sábado	domingo
	1	2	3	4	5	6
7	8	9	10			

¡LENGUA VIVA!
The days of the week are never capitalized in Spanish.
• • •
Monday is considered the first day of the week in Spanish-speaking countries.

CONSÚLTALO
Note that September in Spanish is **septiembre**. To see all of the months of the year, go to **Contextos, Lección 5**, p. 124.

AYUDA
Ayer fue…
Yesterday was…

5 **¿Qué día es hoy?** Complete each statement with the correct day of the week.
1. Hoy es martes. Mañana es __miércoles__. Ayer fue __lunes__.
2. Ayer fue sábado. Mañana es __lunes__. Hoy es __domingo__.
3. Mañana es viernes. Hoy es __jueves__. Ayer fue __miércoles__.
4. Ayer fue domingo. Hoy es __lunes__. Mañana es __martes__.
5. Hoy es jueves. Ayer fue __miércoles__. Mañana es __viernes__.
6. Mañana es lunes. Hoy es __domingo__. Ayer fue __sábado__.

6 **Analogías** Use these words to complete the analogies. Some words will not be used.

arte	día	martes	pizarra
biblioteca	domingo	matemáticas	profesor
catorce	estudiante	mujer	reloj

1. maleta ⟷ pasajero ⊜ mochila ⟷ __estudiante__
2. chico ⟷ chica ⊜ hombre ⟷ __mujer__
3. pluma ⟷ papel ⊜ tiza ⟷ __pizarra__
4. inglés ⟷ lengua ⊜ miércoles ⟷ __día__
5. papel ⟷ cuaderno ⊜ libro ⟷ __biblioteca__
6. quince ⟷ dieciséis ⊜ lunes ⟷ __martes__
7. Cervantes ⟷ literatura ⊜ Dalí ⟷ __arte__
8. autobús ⟷ conductor ⊜ clase ⟷ __profesor__
9. EE.UU. ⟷ mapa ⊜ hora ⟷ __reloj__
10. veinte ⟷ veintitrés ⊜ jueves ⟷ __domingo__

TEACHING OPTIONS

Heritage Speakers Have heritage speakers prepare a day-planner for the upcoming week. Tell them to list each day of the week and the things they expect to do each day, including classes, homework, tests, appointments, and social events. Tell them to include the time each activity takes place. Have them exchange their day-planners with a partner and check each other's work for errors.

Game Have the class play a chain-forming game in which the first student says a word in Spanish (e.g., **estudiante**). The next student has to think of a word that begins with the last letter of the first person's word (e.g., **español**). If a student cannot think of a word, he or she is out of the game and it is the next student's turn. The last student left in the game is the winner.

Comunicación

7

Horario Choose three classes to create your own class schedule, then discuss it with a classmate. *Answers will vary.*

materia	hora	días	profesor(a)
historia	9–10	lunes, miércoles	Ordóñez
biología	12–1	lunes, jueves	Dávila
periodismo	2–3	martes, jueves	Quiñones
matemáticas	2–3	miércoles, jueves	Jiménez
arte	12–1:30	lunes, miércoles	Molina

modelo

Estudiante 1: Tomo (*I take*) biología los lunes y jueves con la profesora Dávila.

Estudiante 2: ¿Sí? Yo no tomo biología. Yo tomo arte los lunes y miércoles con el profesor Molina.

8

La clase First, look around your classroom to get a mental image, then close your eyes. Your partner will then use these words or other vocabulary to ask you questions about the classroom. After you have answered six questions, switch roles. *Answers will vary.*

modelo

Estudiante 1: ¿Cuántas ventanas hay?

Estudiante 2: Hay cuatro ventanas.

escritorio	mochila	puerta
estudiante	pizarra	reloj
libro	profesor(a)	silla

9

Nuevos amigos During the first week of class, you meet a new student in the cafeteria. With a partner, prepare a conversation using these cues. *Answers will vary.*

Estudiante 1

Greet your new acquaintance.

Find out about him or her.

Ask about your partner's class schedule.

Say nice to meet you and goodbye.

Estudiante 2

Introduce yourself.

Tell him or her about yourself.

Compare your schedule to your partner's.

Say nice to meet you and goodbye.

¡ATENCIÓN!

Use **el** + [*day of the week*] when an activity occurs on a specific day and **los** + [*day of the week*] when an activity occurs regularly:

El lunes tengo un examen.
On Monday I have an exam.

Los lunes y miércoles tomo biología.
On Mondays and Wednesdays I take biology.

•••

Except for **sábados** and **domingos,** the singular and plural forms for days of the week are the same.

---

7 Expansion Tell pairs to exchange schedules with another pair. Then have them repeat the activity with the new schedules, asking and answering questions in the third person. Ex: —**¿Qué clases toma _____?** —**Los lunes y jueves _____ toma biología.**

8 Expansion Repeat the exercise with campus-related vocabulary.

Successful Language Learning Remind the class that errors are a natural part of language learning. Point out that it is impossible to speak "perfectly" in any language. Emphasize that their spoken and written Spanish will improve if they make the effort to practice.

9 Suggestion Quickly review the basic greetings, courtesy expressions, and introductions taught in **Lección 1, Contextos,** pages 2–3.

TEACHING OPTIONS

Groups Have students do **Actividad 9** in groups, imagining that they are going to meet several new students in the cafeteria and find out about them. Have the groups prepare and present this activity as a skit in front of the class. Give the groups time to prepare and rehearse their skit, and tell them that they will be presenting it without a script or any other kind of notes.

Game Teach the class the word **con** (*with*). Then have your students write down a few simple sentences that describe their course schedules. Ex: **Los lunes, miércoles y viernes tomo español con la profesora Dávalos. Los martes y jueves tomo arte con el profesor Casas.** Then collect the descriptions and read them to the class. The class should try to guess who wrote each description.

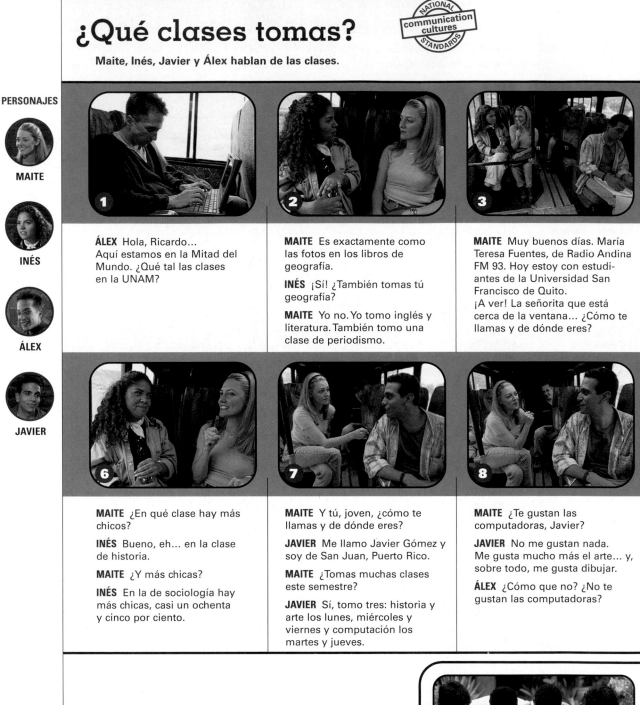

¿Qué clases tomas?

Maite, Inés, Javier y Álex hablan de las clases.

Section Goals

In **Fotonovela** students will:
- receive comprehensible input from free-flowing discourse
- learn functional phrases that preview lesson grammatical structures

Instructional Resources
WB/VM: Video Activities,
pp. 197–198
***Fotonovela** DVD/Video*
(Start 00:06:10)
***Fotonovela** Video CD-ROM*
*IRM: **Fotonovela** Translations,*
pp. 119–120, Videoscript, p. 88
Interactive CD-ROM

Video Recap: Lección 1

Before doing this **Fotonovela** section, review the previous one with this activity.
1. **¿Quiénes son Maite, Inés, Javier y Álex? (estudiantes)**
2. **¿Cómo se llama el conductor? (don Francisco)**
3. **¿Quiénes son del Ecuador? (don Francisco e Inés)**
4. **¿De dónde es Maite? (España) ¿Y Álex? (México) ¿Y Javier? (Puerto Rico)**

Video Synopsis

While Álex writes an e-mail, Maite pretends to be a radio reporter and asks Inés and Javier a few questions about school. Álex is shocked that Javier does not like computers.

Suggestions

- Have students cover the **Expresiones útiles**. Then have them scan the captions under the video stills and find two phrases about classes and two phrases that express likes and dislikes.
- Ask a few basic questions that use the **Expresiones útiles**. Ex: **¿Qué clases tomas? ¿Te gusta la clase de _____?**

PERSONAJES

MAITE

INÉS

ÁLEX

JAVIER

1
ÁLEX Hola, Ricardo… Aquí estamos en la Mitad del Mundo. ¿Qué tal las clases en la UNAM?

2
MAITE Es exactamente como las fotos en los libros de geografía.

INÉS ¡Sí! ¿También tomas tú geografía?

MAITE Yo no. Yo tomo inglés y literatura. También tomo una clase de periodismo.

3
MAITE Muy buenos días. María Teresa Fuentes, de Radio Andina FM 93. Hoy estoy con estudiantes de la Universidad San Francisco de Quito.
¡A ver! La señorita que está cerca de la ventana… ¿Cómo te llamas y de dónde eres?

6
MAITE ¿En qué clase hay más chicos?

INÉS Bueno, eh… en la clase de historia.

MAITE ¿Y más chicas?

INÉS En la de sociología hay más chicas, casi un ochenta y cinco por ciento.

7
MAITE Y tú, joven, ¿cómo te llamas y de dónde eres?

JAVIER Me llamo Javier Gómez y soy de San Juan, Puerto Rico.

MAITE ¿Tomas muchas clases este semestre?

JAVIER Sí, tomo tres: historia y arte los lunes, miércoles y viernes y computación los martes y jueves.

8
MAITE ¿Te gustan las computadoras, Javier?

JAVIER No me gustan nada. Me gusta mucho más el arte… y, sobre todo, me gusta dibujar.

ÁLEX ¿Cómo que no? ¿No te gustan las computadoras?

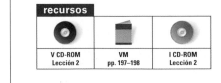

recursos

| V CD-ROM Lección 2 | VM pp. 197–198 | I CD-ROM Lección 2 |

TEACHING OPTIONS

Video Tips General suggestions for using video clips in the classroom can be found on page IAE-12 of this Instructor's Annotated Edition.
¿Qué clases tomas? Play the **¿Qué clases tomas?** segment of this video module and have students give you a "play-by-play" description of the action. Write their descriptions on the board. After playing this segment of the video module, give the class a moment to read the descriptions you have written on the board. Then play the **¿Qué clases tomas?** segment a second time so students can add more details to the descriptions on the board, if necessary, or simply consolidate information. Finally, discuss the material on the board with the class and call attention to any incorrect information. Help your students prepare a brief plot summary.

INÉS Hola. Me llamo Inés Ayala Loor y soy del Ecuador... de Portoviejo.

MAITE Encantada. ¿Qué clases tomas en la universidad?

INÉS Tomo geografía, inglés, historia, sociología y arte.

MAITE Tomas muchas clases, ¿no?

INÉS Pues sí, me gusta estudiar mucho.

ÁLEX Pero si son muy interesantes, hombre.

JAVIER Sí, ¡muy interesantes!

Expresiones útiles

Talking about classes
▶ **¿Qué tal las clases en la UNAM?**
How are classes going at UNAM?
▶ **¿También tomas tú geografía?**
Are you also taking geography?
▷ **No, tomo inglés y literatura.**
No, I'm taking English and literature.

▶ **Tomas muchas clases, ¿no?**
You're taking lots of classes, aren't you?
▷ **Pues sí.** *Well, yes.*

▶ **¿En qué clase hay más chicos?**
In which class are there more guys?
▷ **En la clase de historia.**
In history class.

Talking about likes/dislikes
▶ **¿Te gusta estudiar?**
Do you like to study?
▷ **Sí, me gusta mucho. Pero también me gusta mirar la televisión.**
Yes, I like it a lot. But I also like to watch television.

▶ **¿Te gusta la clase de sociología?**
Do you like sociology class?
▷ **Sí, me gusta muchísimo.**
Yes, I like it very much.

▶ **¿Te gustan las computadoras?**
Do you like computers?
▷ **No, no me gustan nada.**
No, I don't like them at all.

Talking about location
▶ **Aquí estamos en...**
Here we are at/in...
▶ **¿Dónde está la señorita?**
Where is the young woman?
▷ **Está cerca de la ventana.**
She's near the window.

Expressing hesitation
▶ **A ver...** *Let's see...*
▶ **Bueno...** *Well...*

Enfoque cultural La vida universitaria

Universities in Spanish-speaking countries differ from those in the United States. In most cases students enroll in programs that prepare them for a specific career, rather than choosing a major. The courses for these programs are standardized within each country, so students take few elective courses. The classes themselves are also taught differently. Most are conducted as lectures that meet one or two times weekly. Grades are often based on a scale of one to ten, where five is passing.

Reacciona a la fotonovela

1 **Escoger** Choose the answer that best completes each sentence.

1. Maite toma (*is taking*) _____c_____ en la universidad.
   a. geografía, inglés y periodismo   b. economía, periodismo y literatura
   c. periodismo, inglés y literatura

2. Inés toma sociología, geografía, _____a_____.
   a. inglés, historia y arte   b. periodismo, computación y arte
   c. historia, literatura y biología

3. Javier toma _____b_____ clases este semestre.
   a. cuatro   b. tres   c. dos

4. Javier toma historia y _____c_____ los _____c_____.
   a. computación; martes y jueves   b. arte; lunes, martes y miércoles
   c. arte; lunes, miércoles y viernes

2 **Identificar** Indicate which person would make each statement.
The names may be used more than once.

1. Sí, me gusta estudiar. Inés
2. ¡Hola! ¿Te gustan las clases en la UNAM? Álex
3. ¿La clase de periodismo? Sí, me gusta mucho. Maite
4. Hay más chicas en la clase de sociología. Inés
5. Buenos días. Yo soy de Radio Andina FM 93. Maite
6. ¡Uf! ¡No me gustan las computadoras! Javier
7. Las computadoras son muy interesantes.
   Me gustan muchísimo. Álex
8. Me gusta dibujar en la clase de arte. Javier

INÉS

JAVIER   MAITE

ÁLEX

◀ **NOTA CULTURAL**

Álex is a student at **la UNAM,** or **Universidad Nacional Autónoma de México** (*National Autonomous University of Mexico*). Founded in 1551, it is now one of the largest universities in the world, with an annual enrollment of over 250,000 students.

3 **Completar** These sentences are similar to things said in the **Fotonovela**.
Complete each sentence with the correct word(s).

| el arte | geografía | la Mitad del Mundo |
| la clase de historia | la sociología | la Universidad San Francisco de Quito |

1. Maite, Javier, Inés y yo estamos en… la Mitad del Mundo
2. Hay fotos impresionantes de la Mitad del Mundo en los libros de… geografía
3. Me llamo Maite. Estoy aquí con estudiantes de… la Universidad San Francisco de Quito
4. Hay muchos chicos en… la clase de historia
5. No me gustan las computadoras. Me gusta más… el arte

◀ **NOTA CULTURAL**

In the **Fotonovela**, Álex, Maite, Javier, and Inés visit **la Mitad del Mundo** (*Center of the World*), a monument north of Quito, Ecuador. It marks the line at which the equator divides the Earth's northern and southern hemispheres.

4 **Preguntas personales** Interview a classmate about his/her likes and dislikes of the university and university life. Answers will vary.

modelo
Estudiante 1: ¿Te gusta la cafetería?
Estudiante 2: No, no me gusta la cafetería. Pero me gusta la residencia estudiantil.
Estudiante 1: ¿Te gustan las computadoras?
Estudiante 2: Sí, me gustan mucho. Tomo una clase de computación.

NATIONAL
communication
STANDARDS

Pronunciación 🎧

Spanish vowels

a   **e**   **i**   **o**   **u**

Spanish vowels are never silent; they are always pronounced in a short, crisp way without the glide sounds used in English.

Álex	**clase**	**nada**	**encantada**

The letter **a** is pronounced like the *a* in *father*, but shorter.

el	**ene**	**mesa**	**elefante**

The letter **e** is pronounced like the *e* in *they*, but shorter.

Inés	**chica**	**tiza**	**señorita**

The letter **i** sounds like the *ee* in *beet*, but shorter.

hola	**con**	**libro**	**don Francisco**

The letter **o** is pronounced like the *o* in *tone*, but shorter.

uno	**regular**	**saludos**	**gusto**

The letter **u** sounds like the *oo* in *room*, but shorter.

Práctica   Practice the vowels by saying the names of these places in Spain.

1. Madrid
2. Alicante
3. Tenerife
4. Toledo
5. Barcelona
6. Granada
7. Burgos
8. La Coruña

Oraciones   Read the sentences aloud, focusing on the vowels.

1. Hola. Me llamo Ramiro Morgado.
2. Estudio arte en la Universidad de Salamanca.
3. Tomo también literatura y contabilidad.
4. Ay, tengo clase en cinco minutos. ¡Nos vemos!

Refranes   Practice the vowels by reading these sayings aloud.

> Cada loco con su tema.[2]

> Del dicho al hecho hay un gran trecho.[1]

1 Easier said than done.
2 To each his own.

AYUDA

Although **ay** and **hay** are pronounced identically, they do not have the same meaning. **¡Ay!** is an exclamation expressing pain, shock, or affliction: *Oh, dear; Woe is me!* As you learned in **Lección 1**, **hay** is a verb form that means *there is, there are.* **Hay veinte libros.** (*There are twenty books.*)

recursos

TEXT CD Lección 2	LM p. 8	Lab CD/MP3 Lección 2	I CD-ROM Lección 2

Section Goal

In **Pronunciación** students will be introduced to the Spanish vowels and how they are pronounced.

Instructional Resources
Textbook Activities CD
Lab Manual, p. 8
Lab CD/MP3 Lección 2
IRM: Tapescript, pp. 6–10; p. 72
Interactive CD-ROM

Suggestions
- Point out that the drawings above the vowels on this page indicate the approximate position of the mouth as the vowels are pronounced.
- Model the pronunciation of each vowel and have students watch the shape of your mouth. Have them repeat the vowel after you. Then go through the example words.
- Pronounce a few of the example words and have the students write them on the board with their books closed.

Práctica/Oraciones/Refranes
These exercises are recorded on the Textbook Activities CD. You may want to play the CD so students practice the pronunciation point by listening to Spanish spoken by speakers other than yourself.

TEACHING OPTIONS

Extra Practice   Supply the class with the names of more places in Spain. Have your students spell each name aloud in Spanish, then ask them to pronounce each one. Avoid names that contain diphthongs. Ex: **Sevilla, Salamanca, Santander, Albacete, Gerona, Lugo, Badajoz, Tarragona, Logroño, Valladolid, Orense, Pamplona.**

Small Groups   Have the class turn to the **Fotonovela**, pages 36–37, and work in groups of four to read all or part of the **Fotonovela** aloud, focusing on the correct pronunciation of the vowels. Circulate among the groups and model the correct pronunciation and intonation of words and phrases as needed.

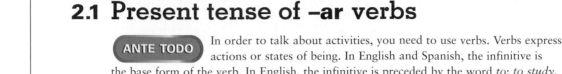

Section Goals

In **Estructura 2.1** students will learn:

• the present tense of regular **–ar** verbs

• the formation of negative sentences

Instructional Resources

WB/VM: Workbook, pp. 13–14
Lab Manual, p. 9
Lab CD/MP3 Lección 2
IRM: ¡Inténtalo! & Práctica
Answers, pp. 173–174;
Tapescript, pp. 6–10
Interactive CD-ROM
Companion website:
www.vistahigherlearning.com
Presentations CD-ROM

Suggestions

• Point out that students have been using verbs and verb constructions from the start. Ex: **¿Cómo te llamas?, hay, ser**. Ask a student: **¿Qué clases tomas?** Model the answer as **Yo tomo...** Then ask another student: **¿Qué clases toma ____? (Toma ____.)**

• Explain that because the verb endings mark the person speaking or spoken about, subject pronouns are usually optional in Spanish.

• Remind students that **vosotros/as** forms will not be actively practiced in **PANORAMA**.

2.1 Present tense of –ar verbs

In order to talk about activities, you need to use verbs. Verbs express actions or states of being. In English and Spanish, the infinitive is the base form of the verb. In English, the infinitive is preceded by the word *to*: *to study, to be*. The infinitive in Spanish is a one-word form and can be recognized by its endings: **–ar, –er,** or **–ir**. In this lesson, you will learn the forms of regular **–ar** verbs.

–ar verb	**–er verb**	**–ir verb**
estudiar *to study*	**comer** *to eat*	**escribir** *to write*

estudiar

estudiar *(to study)*		
SINGULAR FORMS		
yo	estudi**o**	*I study*
tú	estudi**as**	*you* (fam.) *study*
Ud./él/ella	estudi**a**	*you* (form.) *study; he/she studies*
PLURAL FORMS		
nosotros/as	estudi**amos**	*we study*
vosotros/as	estudi**áis**	*you* (fam.) *study*
Uds./ellos/ellas	estudi**an**	*you* (form.) *study; they study*

¿Tomas muchas clases este semestre?

Sí, tomo tres.

▶ To create the forms of most regular verbs in Spanish, you drop the infinitive endings (**–ar, –er, –ir**). You then add to the stem the endings that correspond to the different subject pronouns. The following diagram will help you visualize the process by which verb forms are created.

Conjugation of –ar verbs

INFINITIVE	VERB STEM	CONJUGATED FORM
estudi**ar**	estudi-	yo estudi**o**
bail**ar**	bail-	tú bail**as**
trabaj**ar**	trabaj-	nosotros trabaj**amos**

TEACHING OPTIONS

Extra Practice Do a pattern practice drill. Write an infinitive from the list of common **–ar** verbs on page 41 on the board and ask individual students to provide conjugations for the different subject pronouns and/or names you suggest. Reverse the activity by saying a conjugated form and asking students to give the appropriate subject pronoun.

Extra Practice Ask questions, using **estudiar, bailar,** and **trabajar**. Students should answer in complete sentences. Ask additional questions to get more information. Ex: —____, ¿trabajas? —Sí, trabajo. —¿Dónde trabajas? —Trabajo en ____. • —¿Quién baila los sábados? —Yo bailo los sábados. —¿Bailas merengue? • —¿Estudian ustedes mucho? —¿Quién estudia más? —¿Cuántas horas estudias los lunes? ¿Y los sábados?

Common –ar verbs

bailar	to dance	**estudiar**	to study
buscar	to look for	**explicar**	to explain
caminar	to walk	**hablar**	to talk; to speak
cantar	to sing	**llegar**	to arrive
cenar	to have dinner	**llevar**	to carry
comprar	to buy	**mirar**	to look (at); to watch
contestar	to answer	**necesitar (+ inf.)**	to need
conversar	to converse; to chat	**practicar**	to practice
desayunar	to have breakfast	**preguntar**	to ask (a question)
descansar	to rest	**preparar**	to prepare
desear (+ inf.)	to desire; to wish	**regresar**	to return
dibujar	to draw	**terminar**	to end; to finish
enseñar	to teach	**tomar**	to take; to drink
escuchar	to listen (to)	**trabajar**	to work
esperar (+ inf.)	to wait (for); to hope	**viajar**	to travel

COMPARE & CONTRAST

Compare the verbs in the English sentences to the verb in the Spanish equivalent.

Paco **trabaja** en la cafetería.

1. *Paco works in the cafeteria.*
2. *Paco is working in the cafeteria.*
3. *Paco does work in the cafeteria.*

English uses three sets of forms to talk about the present: 1) the simple present (*Paco works*), 2) the present progressive (*Paco is working*), and 3) the emphatic present (*Paco does work*). In Spanish, the simple present can be used in all three cases.

In both Spanish and English, the present tense is also sometimes used to express future action.

Marina **viaja** a Madrid mañana.

1. *Marina travels to Madrid tomorrow.*
2. *Marina will travel to Madrid tomorrow.*
3. *Marina is traveling to Madrid tomorrow.*

▶ In Spanish, as in English, when two verbs are used together with no change of subject, the second verb is generally in the infinitive.

Deseo hablar con don Francisco.
I want to speak with Don Francisco.

Necesitamos comprar cuadernos
We need to buy notebooks.

▶ To make a sentence negative in Spanish, the word **no** is placed before the conjugated verb. In this case, **no** means *not*.

Ellos **no** miran la televisión.
They don't watch television.

Alicia **no** desea bailar ahora.
Alicia doesn't want to dance now.

¿Hablas japonés?

No, no hablo japonés.

▶ Note that no subject pronouns were used in the Spanish conversation depicted above. Spanish speakers often omit them because the verb endings indicate who the subject is. In Spanish, subject pronouns are used for emphasis, clarification, or contrast, as in the examples below.

Clarification/Contrast

—¿Qué enseñan **ellos**?
What do they teach?

—**Ella** enseña arte y **él** enseña física.
She teaches art, and he teaches physics.

Emphasis

—¿Quién desea trabajar hoy?
Who wants to work today?

—**Yo** no deseo trabajar hoy.
I don't want to work today.

¡INTÉNTALO! Provide the present tense forms of these verbs. The first items have been done for you.

hablar

1. Yo ___hablo___ español.
2. Ellos ___hablan___ español.
3. Inés ___habla___ español.
4. Nosotras ___hablamos___ español.
5. Tú ___hablas___ español.
6. Los estudiantes ___hablan___ español.
7. Usted ___habla___ español.
8. Javier y yo ___hablamos___ español.

trabajar

1. Ustedes ___trabajan___ mucho.
2. Juanita y yo ___trabajamos___ mucho.
3. Nuestra profesora ___trabaja___ mucho.
4. Tú ___trabajas___ mucho.
5. Yo ___trabajo___ mucho.
6. Las chicas ___trabajan___ mucho.
7. Él ___trabaja___ mucho.
8. Tú y Álex ___trabajan___ mucho.

desear

1. Usted ___desea___ viajar.
2. Yo ___deseo___ viajar.
3. Nosotros ___deseamos___ viajar.
4. Lourdes y Luz ___desean___ viajar.
5. Tú ___deseas___ viajar.
6. Ella ___desea___ viajar.
7. Marco y yo ___deseamos___ viajar.
8. Ustedes ___desean___ viajar.

Práctica

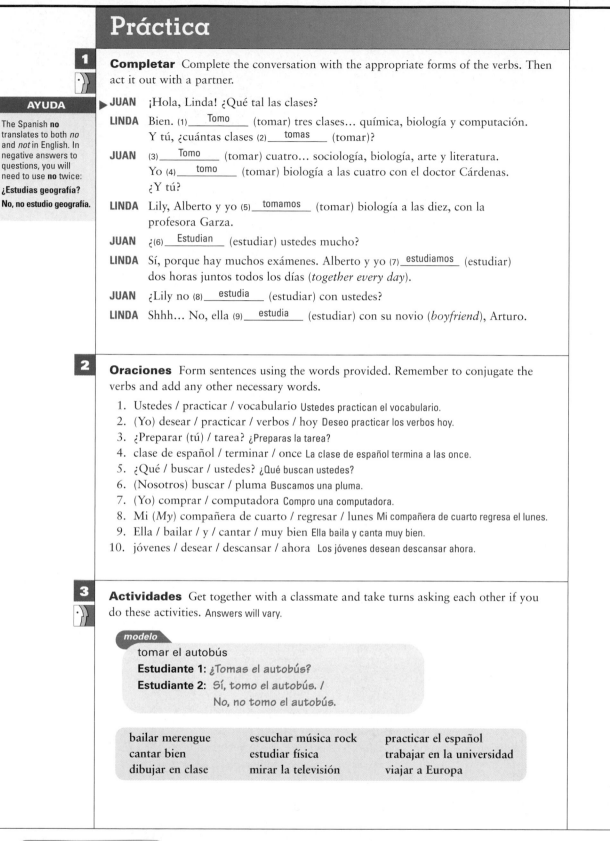

1 Completar Complete the conversation with the appropriate forms of the verbs. Then act it out with a partner.

JUAN ¡Hola, Linda! ¿Qué tal las clases?

LINDA Bien. (1)____Tomo____ (tomar) tres clases… química, biología y computación. Y tú, ¿cuántas clases (2)____tomas____ (tomar)?

JUAN (3)____Tomo____ (tomar) cuatro… sociología, biología, arte y literatura. Yo (4)____tomo____ (tomar) biología a las cuatro con el doctor Cárdenas. ¿Y tú?

LINDA Lily, Alberto y yo (5)____tomamos____ (tomar) biología a las diez, con la profesora Garza.

JUAN ¿(6)____Estudian____ (estudiar) ustedes mucho?

LINDA Sí, porque hay muchos exámenes. Alberto y yo (7)____estudiamos____ (estudiar) dos horas juntos todos los días (*together every day*).

JUAN ¿Lily no (8)____estudia____ (estudiar) con ustedes?

LINDA Shhh… No, ella (9)____estudia____ (estudiar) con su novio (*boyfriend*), Arturo.

2 Oraciones Form sentences using the words provided. Remember to conjugate the verbs and add any other necessary words.

1. Ustedes / practicar / vocabulario Ustedes practican el vocabulario.
2. (Yo) desear / practicar / verbos / hoy Deseo practicar los verbos hoy.
3. ¿Preparar (tú) / tarea? ¿Preparas la tarea?
4. clase de español / terminar / once La clase de español termina a las once.
5. ¿Qué / buscar / ustedes? ¿Qué buscan ustedes?
6. (Nosotros) buscar / pluma Buscamos una pluma.
7. (Yo) comprar / computadora Compro una computadora.
8. Mi (*My*) compañera de cuarto / regresar / lunes Mi compañera de cuarto regresa el lunes.
9. Ella / bailar / y / cantar / muy bien Ella baila y canta muy bien.
10. jóvenes / desear / descansar / ahora Los jóvenes desean descansar ahora.

3 Actividades Get together with a classmate and take turns asking each other if you do these activities. Answers will vary.

modelo

tomar el autobús
Estudiante 1: ¿Tomas el autobús?
Estudiante 2: Sí, tomo el autobús. /
          No, no tomo el autobús.

bailar merengue	escuchar música rock	practicar el español
cantar bien	estudiar física	trabajar en la universidad
dibujar en clase	mirar la televisión	viajar a Europa

4 Suggestion Encourage students to offer additional descriptions of the drawings. Ex: **La profesora habla en clase. Hay números y letras en la pizarra y un libro en la mesa.** Ask volunteers to share their descriptions with the class.

5 Expansion You may want to split the class into two teams with volunteers from each team acting out the charades. Give points for correct guesses. Deduct points for incorrect guesses. The team with the most points at the end wins.

6 Suggestion Point out that, in addition to practicing **–ar** verbs, this activity recycles and reviews material from **Lección 1**: greetings, leave-takings, and telling time. Give students several minutes to plan their conversation before they begin speaking.

6 Expansion Have pairs of students present their conversations in front of the class.

Comunicación

4 Describir With a partner, describe what you see in the pictures using the given verbs. Answers will vary.

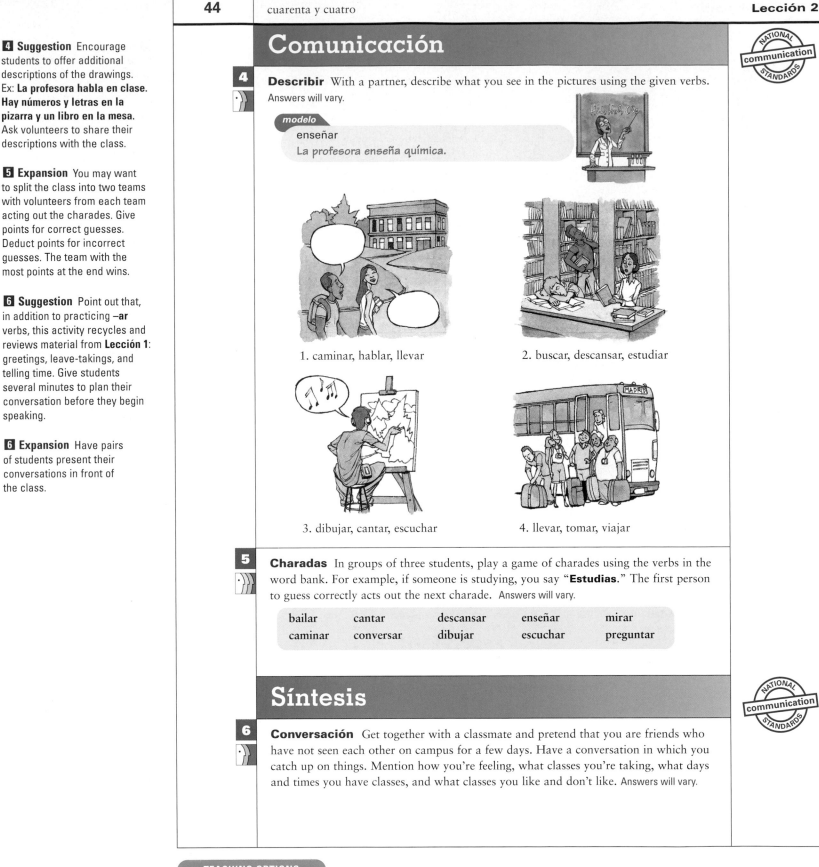

> modelo
> enseñar
> La profesora enseña química.

1. caminar, hablar, llevar

2. buscar, descansar, estudiar

3. dibujar, cantar, escuchar

4. llevar, tomar, viajar

5 Charadas In groups of three students, play a game of charades using the verbs in the word bank. For example, if someone is studying, you say "**Estudias.**" The first person to guess correctly acts out the next charade. Answers will vary.

bailar	cantar	descansar	enseñar	mirar
caminar	conversar	dibujar	escuchar	preguntar

Síntesis

6 Conversación Get together with a classmate and pretend that you are friends who have not seen each other on campus for a few days. Have a conversation in which you catch up on things. Mention how you're feeling, what classes you're taking, what days and times you have classes, and what classes you like and don't like. Answers will vary.

TEACHING OPTIONS

Extra Practice Have students write a description of themselves made up of activities they like or do not like to do, using sentences containing **me gusta…** and **no me gusta…** . Collect the descriptions and read a few of them to the class. Have the class guess who wrote each description.

Game Play **Concentración**. Choose eight infinitives taught in this section, and write each one on a separate card. On another eight cards, draw or paste a picture that illustrates the action of each infinitive. Place the cards face-down in four rows of four. Play with even-numbered groups of students. In pairs, students select two cards. If the two cards match, the pair keeps them. If the cards do not match, students replace them in their original position. The pair with the most cards at the end wins.

2.2 Forming questions in Spanish

ANTE TODO There are three basic ways to ask questions in Spanish. Can you guess what they are by looking at the photos and photo captions on this page?

¿Dibujas mucho?

Las computadoras son muy interesantes, ¿no?

¿También tomas tú geografía?

▶ One way to form a question is to raise the pitch of your voice at the end of a declarative sentence. When writing any question in Spanish, be sure to use an upside down question mark (¿) at the beginning and a regular question mark (?) at the end of the sentence.

Statement	Question
Ustedes trabajan los sábados.	¿Ustedes trabajan los sábados?
You work on Saturdays.	*Do you work on Saturdays?*
Miguel busca un mapa.	¿Miguel busca un mapa?
Miguel is looking for a map.	*Is Miguel looking for a map?*

▶ As in English, you can form a question by inverting the order of the subject and the verb of a declarative statement. The subject may even be placed at the end of the sentence.

Statement	Question
SUBJECT VERB	VERB SUBJECT
Ustedes trabajan los sábados.	¿**Trabajan ustedes** los sábados?
You work on Saturdays.	*Do you work on Saturdays?*
SUBJECT VERB	VERB SUBJECT
Carlota regresa a las seis.	¿**Regresa** a las seis **Carlota**?
Carlota returns at six.	*Does Carlota return at six?*

▶ Questions can also be formed by adding the tags **¿no?** or **¿verdad?** at the end of a statement.

Statement	Question
Ustedes trabajan los sábados.	Ustedes trabajan los sábados, **¿verdad?**
You work on Saturdays.	*You work on Saturdays, right?*
Carlota regresa a las seis.	Carlota regresa a las seis, **¿no?**
Carlota returns at six.	*Carlota returns at six, doesn't she?*

Suggestions

- Model pronunciation by asking questions. Ex: **¿Cómo estás?** **¿Cuál es tu clase favorita?**
- Point out written accent marks on interrogative words.
- Point out that **¿qué?** and **¿cuál?** are not used interchangeably. The word **¿qué?** generally precedes a noun while **¿cuál?** is typically used with a verb. Compare and contrast the following: **¿Qué clase te gusta? ¿Cuál es tu clase favorita?** Write similar questions on the board but leave out the interrogative word. Ask students to tell whether **¿qué?** or **¿cuál?** is used for each.
- Point out **¿cuáles?** and **¿quiénes?** and give examples for each.
- Explain that the answer to the question **¿por qué?** is **porque**.
- Point out singular/plural and masculine/feminine variants for **¿cuánto/a?** and **¿cuántos/as?** Ex: **¿Cuánta tarea hay?** **¿Cuántos libros hay?**
- Model pronunciation of example sentences, asking similar questions of students. Ex: ___, **¿dónde trabajas?** Ask other students to verify their classmates' answers. Ex: ____ **trabaja en ____.**

Question words

Interrogative words

¿Adónde?	Where (to)?	**¿De dónde?**	From where?
¿Cómo?	How?	**¿Dónde?**	Where?
¿Cuál?, ¿Cuáles?	Which?; Which one(s)?	**¿Por qué?**	Why?
¿Cuándo?	When?	**¿Qué?**	What?; Which?
¿Cuánto/a?	How much?	**¿Quién?**	Who?
¿Cuántos/as?	How many?	**¿Quiénes?**	Who (plural)?

▶ To ask a question that requires more than a simple *yes* or *no* answer, an interrogative word is used.

¿Cuál de ellos estudia en la biblioteca?
Which of them studies in the library?

¿Cuándo descansan ustedes?
When do you rest?

¿Cuántos estudiantes hablan español?
How many students speak Spanish?

¿Dónde trabaja Ricardo?
Where does Ricardo work?

¿Qué clases tomas?
What classes are you taking?

¿Adónde caminamos?
Where are we walking?

¿De dónde son Álex y Javier?
Where are Álex and Javier from?

¿Por qué necesitas hablar con ella?
Why do you need to talk to her?

¿Quién enseña la clase de arte?
Who teaches the art class?

¿Cuánta tarea hay?
How much homework is there?

▶ When pronouncing this type of question, the pitch of your voice falls at the end of the sentence.

¿Cómo llegas a clase?
How do you get to class?

¿Por qué necesitas estudiar?
Why do you need to study?

▶ In Spanish **no** can mean both *no* and *not*. Therefore, when answering a yes/no question in the negative, you need to use **no** twice.

¿Caminan a la universidad?
Do you walk to the university?

No, no caminamos a la universidad.
No, we do not walk to the university.

> **CONSÚLTALO**
>
> **¿Qué?** and **¿cuál(es)?** You will learn more about the difference between **qué** and **cuál** in **Estructura 9.3**, pp. 256–257.

¡INTÉNTALO! Make questions out of these statements. Use intonation in column 1 and the tag **¿no?** in column 2. The first item has been done for you.

Statement	Intonation	Tag questions
1. Hablas inglés.	¿Hablas inglés?	Hablas inglés, ¿no?
2. Trabajamos mañana.	¿Trabajamos mañana?	Trabajamos mañana, ¿no?
3. Ustedes desean bailar.	¿Ustedes desean bailar?	Ustedes desean bailar, ¿no?
4. Raúl estudia mucho.	¿Raúl estudia mucho?	Raúl estudia mucho, ¿no?
5. Enseño a las nueve.	¿Enseño a las nueve?	Enseño a las nueve, ¿no?
6. Luz mira la televisión.	¿Luz mira la televisión?	Luz mira la televisión, ¿no?
7. Los chicos descansan.	¿Los chicos descansan?	Los chicos descansan, ¿no?
8. Él prepara la prueba.	¿Él prepara la prueba?	Él prepara la prueba, ¿no?

TEACHING OPTIONS

Video Show the **Fotonovela** video again to give students more input on forming questions. Stop the video where appropriate to discuss how certain questions, including tag questions, are formed. Have students focus on characters' rising and falling intonation in questions and statements.

Heritage Speakers Ask heritage speakers to give original statements and questions at random. Have the rest of the class determine whether each sentence is a statement or a question.
Pairs Give pairs of students five minutes to write original questions using as many interrogative words as they can. Can any pair come up with questions using all interrogative words?

Práctica

1 **Preguntas** Change these sentences into questions by inverting the word order.

> **modelo**
>
> Ernesto habla con su compañero de clase.
>
> ¿Habla Ernesto con su compañero de clase? /
>
> ¿Habla con su compañero de clase Ernesto?

1. La profesora Cruz prepara la prueba.
   ¿Prepara la profesora Cruz la prueba? / ¿Prepara la prueba la profesora Cruz?
2. Sandra y yo necesitamos estudiar.
   ¿Necesitamos Sandra y yo estudiar? / ¿Necesitamos estudiar Sandra y yo?
3. Los chicos practican el vocabulario.
   ¿Practican los chicos el vocabulario? / ¿Practican el vocabulario los chicos?
4. Jaime termina la tarea.
   ¿Termina Jaime la tarea? / ¿Termina la tarea Jaime?
5. Tú trabajas en la biblioteca. ¿Trabajas tú en la biblioteca? / ¿Trabajas en la biblioteca tú?

2 **Completar** Irene and Manolo are chatting in the library. Complete their conversation with the appropriate questions. Answers will vary.

IRENE   Hola, Manolo. (1)¿Cómo estás?/¿Qué tal?

MANOLO   Bien, gracias. (2)¿Y tú?

IRENE   Muy bien. (3)¿Qué hora es?

MANOLO   Son las nueve.

IRENE   (4)¿Qué estudias?

MANOLO   Estudio historia.

IRENE   (5)¿Por qué?

MANOLO   Porque hay un examen mañana.

IRENE   (6)¿Te gusta la clase?

MANOLO   Sí, me gusta mucho la clase.

IRENE   (7)¿Quién enseña la clase?

MANOLO   El profesor Padilla enseña la clase.

IRENE   (8)¿Tomas psicología este semestre?

MANOLO   No, no tomo psicología este semestre.

IRENE   (9)¿A qué hora regresas a la residencia?

MANOLO   Regreso a la residencia a las once.

IRENE   (10)¿Deseas tomar una soda?

MANOLO   No, no deseo tomar soda. ¡Deseo estudiar!

3 **Dos profesores** In pairs, create a dialogue, similar to the one in **Actividad 2**, between profesor Padilla and his colleague profesora Martínez. Use question words. Answers will vary.

> **modelo**
>
> **Prof. Padilla:** ¿Qué enseñas este semestre?
>
> **Prof. Martínez:** Enseño dos cursos de sociología.

4 Suggestions
• Because this is the first activity in which the **Hojas de actividades** (found in the IRM) are used, explain to students that they use the **Hojas** to complete the corresponding activity.
• Distribute the **Hojas de actividades** and explain that students must actively approach their classmates with their **Hoja** in hand. When they find someone who answers affirmatively, that student signs his or her name.

4 Expansion Ask students to say the name of someone who signed their **Hoja**. Then ask that student for more information. Ex: **¿Quién estudia computación? Ah, ¿sí? _____ estudia computación. ¿Dónde estudias computación, _____? ¿Quién es el profesor/la profesora?**

5 Expansion Play this with the entire class, selecting a few students to play the contestants and to "buzz in" their answers.

6 Suggestion Brainstorm ideas for interview questions and write them on the board, or have students prepare their questions as homework for an in-class interview session.

Comunicación

4 **Encuesta** Your instructor will give you a worksheet. Change the categories in the first column into questions, then use them to survey your classmates. Find at least one person for each category. Be prepared to report the results of your survey to the class. Answers will vary.

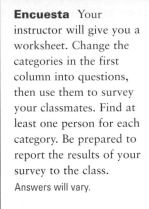

Categorías	Nombres
1. Estudiar computación	
2. Tomar una clase de psicología	
3. Dibujar bien	
4. Cantar bien	
5. Escuchar música clásica	
6. Escuchar jazz	
7. Hablar mucho en clase	
8. Desear viajar a España	

5 **Un juego** (*A game*) In groups of four or five, play a game of *Jeopardy.*® Each person has to write two clues. Then take turns reading the clues and guessing the questions. The person who guesses correctly reads the next clue. Answers will vary.

Es algo que...	**Es un lugar donde...**	**Es una persona que...**
It's something that...	*It's a place where...*	*It's a person that...*

modelo

Estudiante 1: Es un lugar donde estudiamos.
Estudiante 2: ¿Qué es la biblioteca?

Estudiante 1: Es algo que escuchamos.
Estudiante 2: ¿Qué es la música?

Estudiante 1: Es un director de España.
Estudiante 2: ¿Quién es Pedro Almodóvar?

NOTA CULTURAL

Pedro Almodóvar is an award-winning film director from Spain. His films are full of both humor and melodrama, and their controversial subject matter has often sparked great debate. His 1999 film **Todo sobre mi madre** (*All About My Mother*) received an Oscar for Best Foreign Film and Best Director at the Cannes Film Festival.

Síntesis

6 **Entrevista** Imagine that you are a reporter for the school newspaper. Write five questions about student life at your school and use them to interview two classmates. Be prepared to report your findings to the class. Answers will vary.

TEACHING OPTIONS

Extra Practice Have students go back to the **Fotonovela** on pages 36–37 and write as many questions as they can about what they see in the photos. Ask volunteers to share their questions as you write them on the board. Then call on individual students to answer them.

Extra Practice Prepare eight questions and answers. Write the answers, but not the questions, on the board in random order. Then read your questions, having students match the question to the appropriate answer. Ex: **¿Cuándo es la clase de español? (Es los lunes, miércoles y viernes.)**

2.3 Present tense of estar

NATIONAL comparisons STANDARDS

CONSÚLTALO

To review the forms of **ser**, see **Estructura 1.3**, pp. 17–18.

ANTE TODO In **Lección 1**, you learned how to conjugate and use the ver **ser** *(to be)*. You will now learn a second verb which means *to be*, the verb **estar**. Although **estar** ends in **–ar**, it does not follow the pattern of regular **–ar** verbs. The **yo** form (**estoy**) is irregular. Also, all forms have an accented **á** except the **yo** and **nosotros/as** forms.

estar

		estar *(to be)*	
SINGULAR FORMS	yo	est**oy**	*I am*
	tú	est**ás**	*you* (fam.) *are*
	Ud./él/ella	est**á**	*you* (form.) *are; he/she is*
PLURAL FORMS	nosotros/as	est**amos**	*we are*
	vosotros/as	est**áis**	*you* (fam.) *are*
	Uds./ellos/ellas	est**án**	*you* (form.) *are; they are*

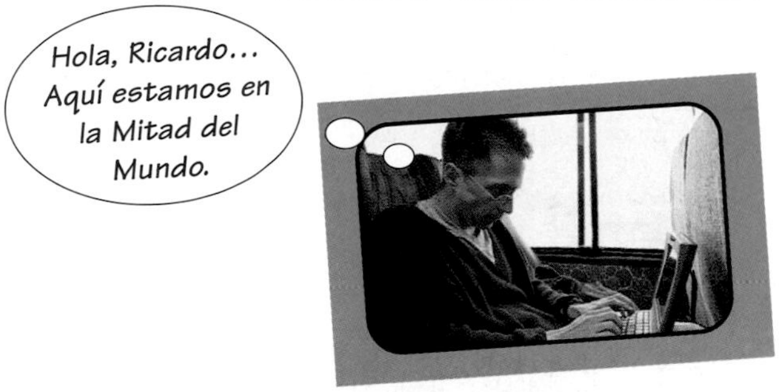

Hola, Ricardo... Aquí estamos en la Mitad del Mundo.

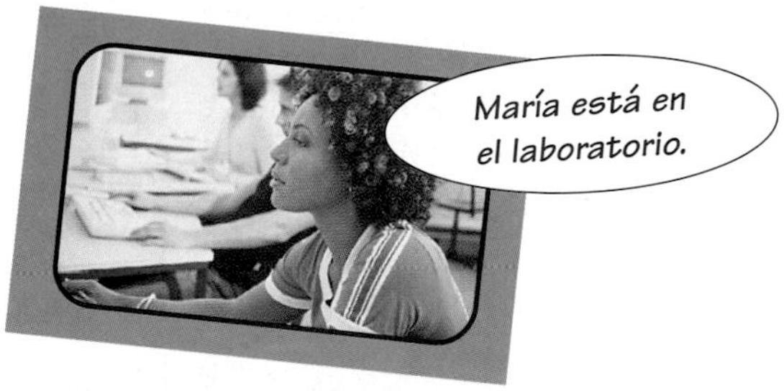

María está en el laboratorio.

COMPARE & CONTRAST

In the following chart, compare the uses of the verb **estar** to those of the verb **ser**.

Uses of *estar*

Location
Estoy en casa
I am at home.
Inés **está** al lado de Javier.
Inés is next to Javier.

Health
Álex **está** enfermo hoy.
Álex is sick today.

Well-being
—¿Cómo **estás**, Maite?
How are you, Maite?
—**Estoy** muy bien, gracias.
I'm very well, thank you.

Uses of *ser*

Identity
Hola, **soy** Maite.
Hello, I'm Maite.

Occupation
Soy estudiante.
I'm a student.

Origins
—¿**Eres** de España?
Are you from Spain?
—Sí, **soy** de España.
Yes, I'm from Spain.

Time-telling
Son las cuatro.
It's four o'clock.

¡ATENCIÓN!

You use **la casa** to express *the house*, but **en casa** to express *at home*.

Section Goals

In **Estructura 2.3** students will be introduced to:
- the present tense of **estar**
- contrasts between **ser** and **estar**
- prepositions of location used with **estar**

Instructional Resources
Transparency #14
WB/VM: Workbook, pp. 17–18
Lab Manual, p. 11
Lab CD/MP3 ***Lección 2***
IRM: ***¡Inténtalo! & Práctica***
Answers, pp. 173–174;
Tapescript, pp. 6–10
Interactive CD-ROM
Companion website:
www.vistahigherlearning.com
Presentations CD-ROM

Suggestions
- Point out that only the **yo** and **nosotros/as** forms do not have a written accent.
- Emphasize that the principal distinction between **estar** and **ser** is that **estar** is generally used to express temporary conditions (**Álex está enfermo hoy.**) and **ser** is generally used to express inherent qualities (**Álex es inteligente.**).
- Students will learn to compare **ser** and **estar** formally in **Estructura 5.3**.

TEACHING OPTIONS

Extra Practice Give statements in English and have students say if they would use **ser** or **estar** in each. Ex: *I'm at home.* (**estar**) *I'm a student.* (**ser**) *I'm tired.* (**estar**) *I'm glad.* (**estar**) *I'm generous.* (**ser**)
Extra Practice Ask students where certain people are or probably are at this moment. Ex: **¿Dónde estás? (Estoy en la clase.) ¿Dónde está el presidente? (Está en Washington, D.C.)**

Heritage Speakers Ask heritage speakers whether they know of any instances where either **ser** or **estar** may be used. (They may point out more advanced uses, such as with certain adjectives: **Es aburrido.** vs. **Está aburrido.**) This may help to compare and contrast inherent vs. temporary conditions and qualities.

Prepositions often used with *estar*

al lado de	next to; beside		**delante de**	in front of
a la derecha de	to the right of		**detrás de**	behind
a la izquierda de	to the left of		**encima de**	on top of
en	in; on		**entre**	between; among
cerca de	near		**lejos de**	far from
con	with		**sin**	without
debajo de	below		**sobre**	on; over

▶ **Estar** is often used with certain prepositions to describe the location of a person or an object.

La clase **está al lado de** la biblioteca.
The class is next to the library.

Los libros **están encima del** escritorio.
The books are on top of the desk.

El laboratorio **está cerca de** la clase.
The lab is near the classroom.

Maribel **está delante de** José.
Maribel is in front of José.

El estadio no **está lejos de** la librería.
The stadium isn't far from the bookstore.

El mapa está **entre** la pizarra y la puerta.
The map is between the blackboard and the door.

Los estudiantes **están en** la clase.
The students are in class.

El libro **está sobre** la mesa.
The book is on the table.

¡A ver! La señorita que está cerca de la ventana...

Aquí estoy con cuatro estudiantes de la universidad... ¡Qué aventura!

¡INTÉNTALO! Provide the present tense forms of **estar**. The first item has been done for you.

1. Ustedes ___están___ en la clase.
2. José ___está___ en la biblioteca.
3. Yo ___estoy___ en el estadio.
4. Nosotras ___estamos___ en la cafetería.
5. Tú ___estás___ en el laboratorio.
6. Elena ___está___ en la librería.
7. Ellas ___están___ en la clase.

8. Ana y yo ___estamos___ en la clase.
9. Usted ___está___ en la biblioteca.
10. Javier y Maribel ___están___ en el estadio.
11. Nosotros ___estamos___ en la cafetería.
12. Yo ___estoy___ en el laboratorio.
13. Carmen y María ___están___ en la librería.
14. Tú ___estás___ en la clase.

Práctica

1

Completar Daniela has just returned home from her classes at the local university.
▶ Complete this conversation with the appropriate forms of **ser** or **estar**.

MAMÁ   Hola, Daniela. ¿Cómo (1)____estás____?

DANIELA   Hola, mamá. (2)____Estoy____ bien. ¿Dónde (3)____está____ papá?
               ¡Ya (*already*) (4)____son____ las ocho de la noche!

MAMÁ   No (5)____está____ aquí. (6)____Está____ en la oficina.

DANIELA   Y Andrés y Margarita, ¿dónde (7)____están____ ellos?

MAMÁ   (8)____Están____ en el restaurante La Palma con Martín.

DANIELA   ¿Quién (9)____es____ Martín?

MAMÁ   (10)____Es____ un compañero de clase. (11)____Es____ de México.

DANIELA   Ah. Y el restaurante La Palma, ¿dónde (12)____está____?

MAMÁ   (13)____Está____ cerca de la Plaza Mayor, en San Modesto.

DANIELA   Gracias, mamá. Voy (*I'm going*) al restaurante. ¡Hasta pronto!

2

Escoger Choose the preposition that best completes each sentence.
1. La pluma está (encima de / detrás de) la mesa. encima de
2. La ventana está (a la izquierda de / debajo de) la puerta. a la izquierda de
3. La pizarra está (debajo de / delante de) los estudiantes. delante de
4. Las sillas están (encima de / detrás de) los escritorios. detrás de
5. Los estudiantes llevan los libros (en / sobre) la mochila. en
6. La biblioteca está (sobre / al lado de) la residencia estudiantil. al lado de
7. España está (cerca de / lejos de) Puerto Rico. lejos de
8. Cuba está (cerca de / lejos de) los Estados Unidos. cerca de
9. Felipe trabaja (con / en) Ricardo en la cafetería. con

3

¿Dónde está...? Imagine that you are in the school bookstore and can't find various items. Ask the clerk (your partner) where the items in the drawing are located. Then switch roles.   Answers will vary.

modelo
> **Estudiante 1:** ¿Dónde están los diccionarios?
> **Estudiante 2:** Los diccionarios están debajo de los libros de literatura.

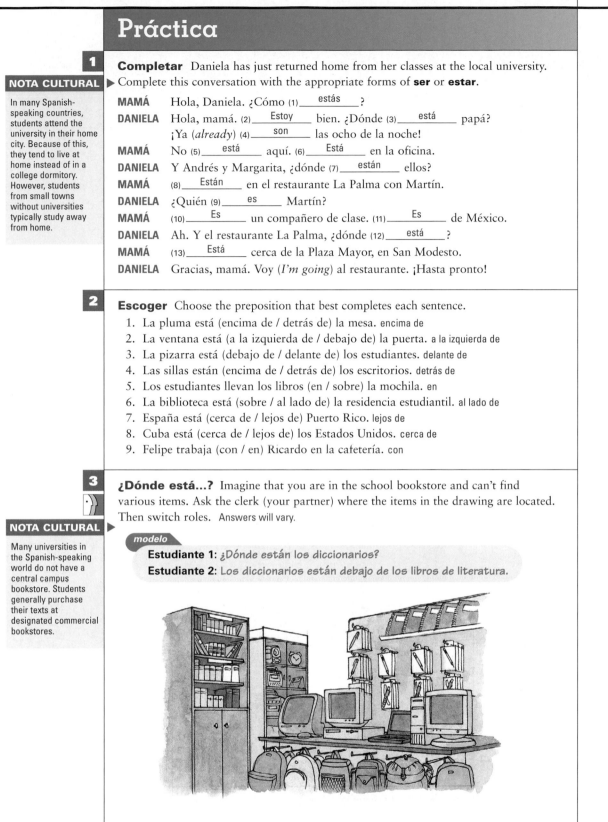

TEACHING OPTIONS

Extra Practice Use a large world map (one with Spanish labels is best), **Transparencies #1–#8**, and/or the maps on the inside covers of the textbook to ask students where countries and cities are in relation to each other on the map. Ex: **¿Bolivia está a la derecha del Brasil? ¿Uruguay está más cerca de Chile o del Ecuador? ¿Qué país está entre Colombia y Costa Rica? ¿Está Puerto Rico a la izquierda de la República Dominicana?**

Small Groups Have each group member think of a country or well-known location on campus and describe it with progressively more specific statements. After each statement, the other group members guess what country or location it is. Ex: **Es un país. Está en Europa. Está cerca de España. Está a la izquierda de Italia y Suiza. Es Francia.**

Comunicación

4 **¿Dónde estás...?** Get together with a partner and take turns asking each other where you are at these times.   Answers will vary.

> **modelo**
>
> lunes / 10:00 a.m.
> **Estudiante 1:** ¿Dónde estás los lunes a las *diez de la mañana*?
> **Estudiante 2:** Estoy en *la clase de español.*

1. sábados / 6:00 a.m.
2. miércoles / 9:15 a.m.
3. lunes / 11:10 a.m.
4. jueves / 12:30 a.m.

5. viernes / 2:25 p.m.
6. martes / 3:50 p.m.
7. jueves / 5:45 p.m.
8. miércoles / 8:20 p.m.

5 **La ciudad universitaria** You are an exchange student at a Spanish university. Tell a classmate which buildings you are looking for and ask for their location relative to where you are.   Answers will vary.

> **modelo**
>
> **Estudiante 1:** ¿La Facultad de Medicina está lejos?
> **Estudiante 2:** No, está cerca. Está a la izquierda de la Facultad
> de Administración de Empresas.

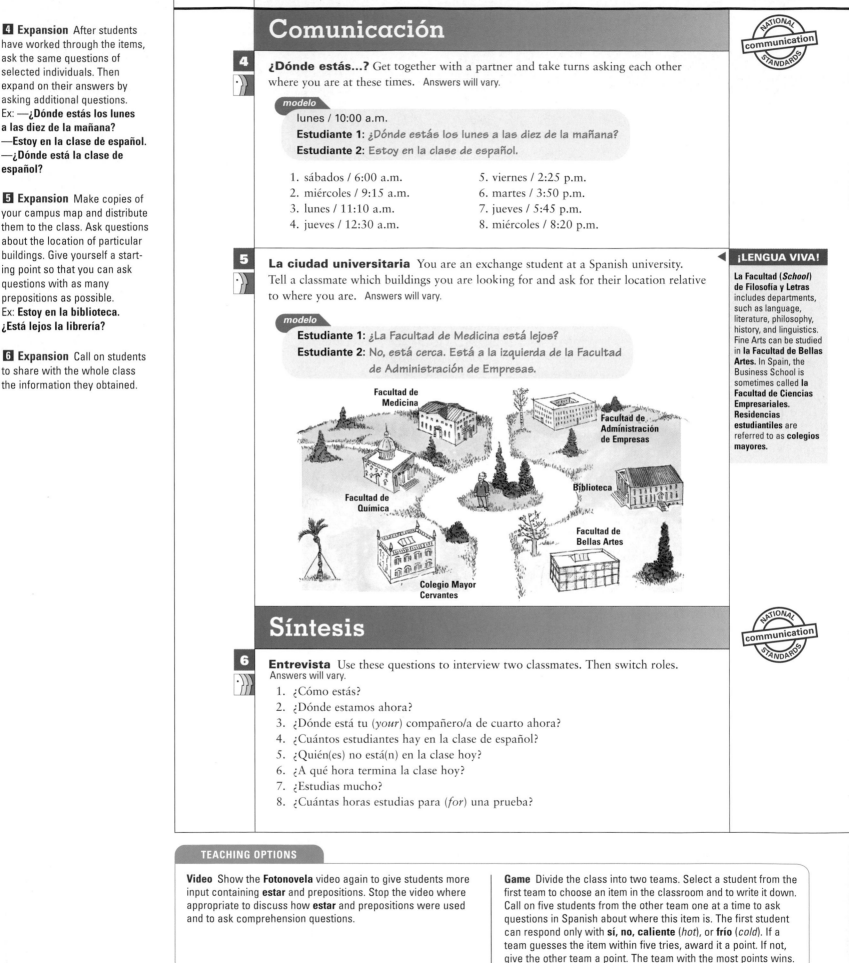

Facultad de Medicina
Facultad de Administración de Empresas
Facultad de Química
Biblioteca
Facultad de Bellas Artes
Colegio Mayor Cervantes

¡LENGUA VIVA!

La Facultad (*School*) **de Filosofía y Letras** includes departments, such as language, literature, philosophy, history, and linguistics. Fine Arts can be studied in **la Facultad de Bellas Artes.** In Spain, the Business School is sometimes called **la Facultad de Ciencias Empresariales. Residencias estudiantiles** are referred to as **colegios mayores.**

Síntesis

6 **Entrevista** Use these questions to interview two classmates. Then switch roles.
Answers will vary.

1. ¿Cómo estás?
2. ¿Dónde estamos ahora?
3. ¿Dónde está tu (*your*) compañero/a de cuarto ahora?
4. ¿Cuántos estudiantes hay en la clase de español?
5. ¿Quién(es) no está(n) en la clase hoy?
6. ¿A qué hora termina la clase hoy?
7. ¿Estudias mucho?
8. ¿Cuántas horas estudias para (*for*) una prueba?

TEACHING OPTIONS

Video Show the **Fotonovela** video again to give students more input containing **estar** and prepositions. Stop the video where appropriate to discuss how **estar** and prepositions were used and to ask comprehension questions.

Game Divide the class into two teams. Select a student from the first team to choose an item in the classroom and to write it down. Call on five students from the other team one at a time to ask questions in Spanish about where this item is. The first student can respond only with **sí, no, caliente** (*hot*), or **frío** (*cold*). If a team guesses the item within five tries, award it a point. If not, give the other team a point. The team with the most points wins.

2.4 Numbers 31–100

NATIONAL comparisons STANDARDS

Section Goal

In **Estructura 2.4**, students will be introduced to numbers 31–100.

Instructional Resources
WB/VM: Workbook, pp. 19–20
Lab Manual, p. 12
Lab CD/MP3 Lección 2
IRM: ¡Inténtalo! & Práctica
Answers, pp. 173–174;
Tapescript, pp. 6–10
Info Gap Activities Booklet,
pp. 5–8
Interactive CD-ROM
Companion website:
www.vistahigherlearning.com
Presentations CD-ROM

Los números 31–100					
31	treinta y uno	37	treinta y siete	50	cincuenta
32	treinta y dos	38	treinta y ocho	60	sesenta
33	treinta y tres	39	treinta y nueve	70	setenta
34	treinta y cuatro	40	cuarenta	80	ochenta
35	treinta y cinco	41	cuarenta y uno	90	noventa
36	treinta y seis	42	cuarenta y dos *(and so on)*	100	cien, ciento

▶ **Y** is used in most numbers from **31** through **99**.

Hay **ochenta y cinco** exámenes.
There are eighty-five exams.

Hay **cuarenta y dos** estudiantes.
There are forty-two students.

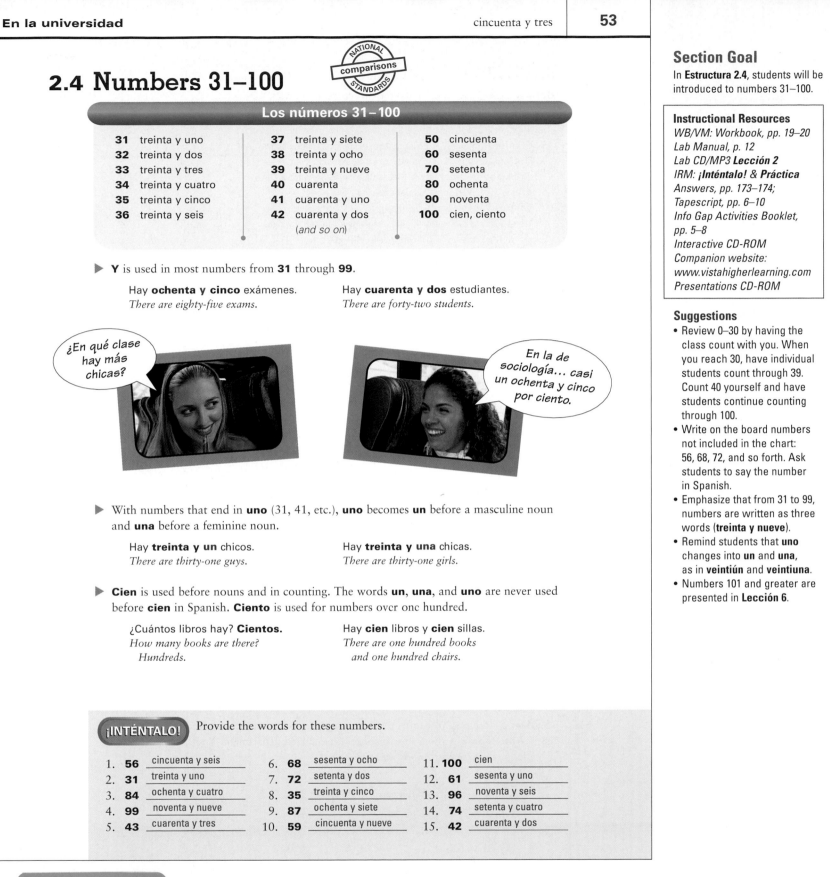

¿En qué clase hay más chicas?

En la de sociología… casi un ochenta y cinco por ciento.

▶ With numbers that end in **uno** (31, 41, etc.), **uno** becomes **un** before a masculine noun and **una** before a feminine noun.

Hay **treinta y un** chicos.
There are thirty-one guys.

Hay **treinta y una** chicas.
There are thirty-one girls.

▶ **Cien** is used before nouns and in counting. The words **un**, **una**, and **uno** are never used before **cien** in Spanish. **Ciento** is used for numbers over one hundred.

¿Cuántos libros hay? **Cientos.**
How many books are there?
Hundreds.

Hay **cien** libros y **cien** sillas.
There are one hundred books
and one hundred chairs.

Suggestions
• Review 0–30 by having the class count with you. When you reach 30, have individual students count through 39. Count 40 yourself and have students continue counting through 100.
• Write on the board numbers not included in the chart: 56, 68, 72, and so forth. Ask students to say the number in Spanish.
• Emphasize that from 31 to 99, numbers are written as three words (**treinta y nueve**).
• Remind students that **uno** changes into **un** and **una**, as in **veintiún** and **veintiuna**.
• Numbers 101 and greater are presented in **Lección 6**.

¡INTÉNTALO!   Provide the words for these numbers.

1. **56** cincuenta y seis
2. **31** treinta y uno
3. **84** ochenta y cuatro
4. **99** noventa y nueve
5. **43** cuarenta y tres
6. **68** sesenta y ocho
7. **72** setenta y dos
8. **35** treinta y cinco
9. **87** ochenta y siete
10. **59** cincuenta y nueve
11. **100** cien
12. **61** sesenta y uno
13. **96** noventa y seis
14. **74** setenta y cuatro
15. **42** cuarenta y dos

TEACHING OPTIONS

Extra Practice Do simple math problems (addition and subtraction) with numbers to 100. Include numbers 0–30 as well, for a well-balanced review. Remind students that **más** = *plus*, **menos** = *minus*, and **es/son** = *equals*.
Extra Practice Write the beginning of a series of numbers on the board and have students continue the sequence.
Ex: **5, 10, 15,…** or **3, 6, 9, 12,…**

Heritage Speakers Ask heritage speakers to give the house or apartment number where they live (they do not have to give the street name). Ask them to give the addresses in tens (**1471 = catorce setenta y uno**). Have volunteers write the numbers they say on the board.

Práctica

1 Baloncesto Provide these basketball scores in Spanish.

1. Ohio State 76, Michigan 65 setenta y seis, sesenta y cinco
2. Florida 92, Florida State 84 noventa y dos, ochenta y cuatro
3. Stanford 58, UCLA 49 cincuenta y ocho, cuarenta y nueve
4. Purdue 81, Indiana 78 ochenta y uno, setenta y ocho
5. Princeton 67, Harvard 55 sesenta y siete, cincuenta y cinco
6. Duke 100, Virginia 91 cien, noventa y uno
7. Kansas 95, Colorado 53 noventa y cinco, cincuenta y tres
8. Texas 79, Oklahoma 47 setenta y nueve, cuarenta y siete
9. Army 86, Navy 71 ochenta y seis, setenta y uno
10. Kentucky 98, Tennessee 74 noventa y ocho, setenta y cuatro

2 Números de teléfono What courses would you take if you were studying at a university in Spain? Take turns deciding and having your partner give you the phone number for enrollment information. Answers will vary.

> **modelo**
> **Estudiante 1:** Necesito tomar una clase de química.
> **Estudiante 2:** El número del departamento es el noventa y uno, cuarenta y siete, uno, veintinueve, ochenta y siete.

DIRECTORIO

Departamento	Número de teléfono
Administración de empresas	(91) 758-6562
Arte	(91) 944-1216
Biología	(91) 634-3211
Computación	(91) 472-2350
Contabilidad	(91) 419-7660
Economía	(91) 773-1382
Español	(91) 944-3915
Física	(91) 634-7148
Geografía	(91) 834-5238
Historia	(91) 834-3371
Literatura	(91) 552-6359
Psicología	(91) 564-8799
Química	(91) 471-2987
Sociología	(91) 837-2225

3 Números In pairs, take turns reading aloud telephone numbers at random from the list in **Actividad 2** without mentioning the associated department. Your partner must provide the department. Answers will vary.

> **modelo**
> **Estudiante 1:** (91) 564-8799.
> **Estudiante 2:** Es el departamento de psicología.

NOTA CULTURAL

Basketball (**baloncesto** or **básquetbol**) is a popular sport in many Spanish-speaking countries. Spain, Puerto Rico, Argentina, and Mexico, for example, have national leagues and champion teams often go on to international competitions.

NOTA CULTURAL

In Spanish-speaking countries, the number of digits in phone numbers may vary from four to seven; they are often said in pairs.

TEACHING OPTIONS

Heritage Speakers Ask heritage speakers if they or members of their families say phone numbers in any particular manner other than the one presented.

Game Ask for two volunteers and station them at opposite ends of the board so neither one can see what the other is writing. Give a number from 0–100 for them to write on the board. If both students are correct, continue to give numbers until one writes an incorrect number. The winner continues on to play against another student.

Comunicación

4

Precios (*Prices*) With a partner, take turns asking how much the items in the ad cost.

Answers will vary.

modelo

Estudiante 1: Deseo comprar papel.
¿Cuánto cuesta (*How much does it cost*)?

Estudiante 2: Un paquete cuesta (*it costs*) cuatro dólares
y cuarenta y un centavos.

$5,31 caja

$4,98

$36

$19,50

$5,59 caja

$87

$4,41 paquete

AYUDA

una caja de *a box of*

un paquete de *a package of*

• • •

Note that in Spanish, a comma is used in place of a decimal point, which is the standard in the U.S.

U.S.	Spanish
$4.95	$4,95
$12.50	$12,50

Conversely, Spanish uses a period instead of a comma to indicate thousands.

U.S.	Spanish
1,500	1.500
50,000	50.000

5

Entrevista Find out the telephone numbers and e-mail addresses of four classmates.

Answers will vary.

modelo

Estudiante 1: ¿Cuál es tu (*your*) número de teléfono?

Estudiante 2: Es el 6-35-19-51.

Estudiante 1: ¿Y tu dirección de correo electrónico?

Estudiante 2: Es jota-Smith-arroba-pe-ele-punto-
e-de-u. (jsmith@pl.edu)

AYUDA

arroba *at* (@)

punto *dot* (.)

Síntesis

6

¿A qué distancia...? Your instructor will give you and a partner incomplete charts that indicate the distances between Madrid and various locations. Fill in the missing information on your chart by asking your partner questions. Answers will vary.

modelo

Estudiante 1: ¿A qué distancia está Arganda del Rey?

Estudiante 2: Está a veintisiete kilómetros de Madrid.

---

4 Suggestion Explain **¿cuánto cuesta...?** and present **dólares** and **centavos**.

4 Expansion Ask students how much they think common items cost. Ex: **un disco compacto, un video**

5 Suggestions
• Write your own e-mail address on the board as you pronounce it.
• Point out that **el correo electrónico** means e-mail.
• If students are reluctant to reveal their personal information, ask them to invent a phone number and e-mail address.
• Ask volunteers to share their phone numbers and e-mail addresses. Have other students write them on the board.

6 Suggestions
• Divide the class into pairs and distribute the handouts from the Information Gap Activities Booklet that correspond to this activity. Explain that this type of activity is called an information gap activity. In it, each partner has information that the other needs, and the way to get this information is by asking each other questions.
• Point out and model **está a** [*distance*] **de...** to express distance.

Suggestion See the Information Gap Activities Booklet for an additional activity to practice the material presented in this section.

TEACHING OPTIONS

Small Groups In groups of three or four, have students think of a city or town within a 100-mile radius of your university city or town. They need to figure out how many miles away it is and what other cities or towns are nearby (**está cerca de...**). Then they get together with another group and read their descriptions. The other group has to guess which city or town is being described.

TPR Assign ten students a number from 0–100 and line them up in front of the class. Call out a number at random, and that student is to take a step forward. When two students have stepped forward, ask them to repeat their numbers. Then ask volunteers to add or subtract the two numbers given. Make sure the resulting sum is not greater than 100.

Section Goals

In **Lectura** students will:
- learn to use text formats to predict content
- read documents in Spanish

Instructional Resource
Companion website:
www.vistahigherlearning.com

Estrategia Introduce the strategy. Point out that many documents have easily identifiable formats that can help readers predict content. Have students look at the document in the **Estrategia** box and ask them to name the recognizable elements:
- days of the week
- time
- classes

Ask what kind of document it is (a student's weekly schedule).

Cognados Have pairs of students scan **¡Español en Madrid!** and identify cognates and guess their meanings.

Examinar el texto Ask students what type of information is contained in **¡Español en Madrid!** (It's a brochure for a summer intensive Spanish language program.) Discuss elements of the recognizable format that helped them predict the content, such as headings, list of courses, course schedule with dates, etc.

Lectura

Antes de leer

Estrategia

Predicting Content Through Formats

Recognizing the format of a document can help you to predict its content. For instance, invitations, greeting cards, and classified ads follow an easily identifiable format, which usually gives you a general idea of the information they contain. Look at the text and identify it based on its format.

	lunes	martes	miércoles	jueves	viernes
8:30	biología		biología		biología
9:00		historia		historia	
9:30	inglés		inglés		inglés
10:00					
10:30					
11:00					
12:00					
12:30					
1:00					
2:00	arte		arte		arte

If you guessed that this is a page from a student's schedule, you are correct. You can now infer that the document contains information about a student's weekly schedule, including days, times, and activities.

Cognados

With a classmate, make a list of the cognates in the text and guess their English meanings. What do cognates reveal about the content of the document?

Examinar el texto

Look at the format of the document entitled *¡Español en Madrid!* What type of text is it? What information do you expect to find in a document of this kind?

recursos

vistahigher
learning.com

¡ESPAÑOL EN MADRID!

UAM

Programa de Cursos Intensivos de Español
Universidad Autónoma de Madrid

Madrid, la capital cultural de Europa, y la UAM te ofrecen cursos intensivos de verano° para aprender° español como nunca antes°.

Después de leer

Correspondencias

Provide the letter of each item in Column B that matches the words in Column A. Two items will not be used.

A	B
1. profesores f	a. (34) 91 523 4500
2. vivienda h	b. (34) 91 524 0210
3. Madrid d	c. 23 junio – 30 julio
4. número de teléfono a	d. capital cultural de Europa
5. Español 2B c	e. 16 junio – 22 julio
6. número de fax g	f. especializados en enseñar español como lengua extranjera
	g. (34) 91 523 4623
	h. familias españolas

TEACHING OPTIONS

Extra Practice Have students write as homework a weekly schedule (**horario semanal**) of a friend or family member. Ask them to label the days of the week in Spanish and add notes for that person's appointments and activities as well. In class, ask students questions about the schedules they wrote.
Ex: **¿Qué clase toma _____ hoy? ¿Trabaja _____ mañana?**
¿Cuántos días trabaja _____ esta semana?

Heritage Speakers Ask heritage speakers who have attended a university or institution of higher education in the Spanish-speaking world to describe what their schedule there was like, comparing and contrasting it with their schedule now. Invite them to make other comparisons between American or Canadian institutions of higher education and those in the Spanish-speaking world.

Correspondencias Go over the answers with the whole class or assign pairs of students to work together to check each other's answers.

¿Dónde?
En el campus de la UAM, edificio° de la Facultad de Filosofía y Letras.

¿Quiénes son los profesores?
Son todos hablantes nativos del español y catedráticos° de la UAM especializados en enseñar el español como lengua extranjera.

¿Qué niveles se ofrecen?
Se ofrecen tres niveles° básicos:
1. Español Elemental, A, B y C
2. Español Intermedio, A y B
3. Español Avanzado, A y B

Viviendas
Para estudiantes extranjeros se ofrece vivienda° con familias españolas.

¿Cuándo?
Este verano desde° el 16 de junio hasta el 10 de agosto. Los cursos tienen una duración de 6 semanas.

Cursos	Empieza°	Termina
Español 1A	16 junio	22 julio
Español 1B	23 junio	30 julio
Español 1C	30 junio	10 agosto
Español 2A	16 junio	22 julio
Español 2B	23 junio	30 julio
Español 3A	16 junio	22 julio
Español 3B	23 junio	30 julio

Información
Para mayor información, sirvan comunicarse con la siguiente° oficina:

Universidad Autónoma de Madrid
Programa de Español como Lengua Extranjera
Ctra. Colmenar Viejo, Km. 15
28049 Madrid, ESPAÑA
Tel. (34) 91 523 4500
Fax (34) 91 523 4623
www.uam.es

verano *summer* aprender *to learn* nunca antes *never before* edificio *building* catedráticos *professors* niveles *levels*
vivienda *housing* desde *from* Empieza *Begins* siguiente *following*

¿Cierto o falso? Continue the activity with true-false statements such as these: **1. El campus de la UAM está en la Ciudad de México. (Falso; está en Madrid.) 2. Los cursos terminan en junio. (Falso; terminan en julio y agosto.) 3. Hay tres cursos de español intermedio. (Falso; hay dos cursos.) 4. Los cursos se ofrecen en el verano. (Cierto) 5. Hay una residencia estudiantil para los estudiantes extranjeros en el campus. (Falso; los estudiantes extranjeros viven con familias españolas.) 6. Hay un número en la universidad para más información. (Cierto) 7. Todos los profesores son hablantes nativos. (Cierto) 8. Los cursos tienen una duración de doce semanas. (Falso; tienen una duración de seis semanas.)**

¿Cierto o falso?

Indicate whether each statement is **cierto** (*true*) or **falso** (*false*). Then correct the false statements.

	Cierto	Falso
1. La Universidad Autónoma de Madrid ofrece (*offers*) cursos intensivos de italiano. Ofrece cursos intensivos de español.	○	⊘
2. La lengua nativa de los profesores del programa es el inglés. La lengua nativa de los profesores es el español.	○	⊘
3. Los cursos de español son en la Facultad de Ciencias. Son en el edificio de la Facultad de Filosofía y Letras.	○	⊘
4. Los estudiantes pueden vivir (*can live*) con familias españolas.	⊘	○

	Cierto	Falso
5. La universidad que ofrece los cursos intensivos está en Salamanca. Está en Madrid.	○	⊘
6. Español 3B termina en agosto. Termina en julio.	○	⊘
7. Si deseas información sobre (*about*) los cursos intensivos de español, es posible llamar al (34) 91 523 4500.	⊘	○
8. Español 1A empieza en julio. Empieza en junio.	○	⊘

TEACHING OPTIONS

Variación léxica Explain that in Spanish dates are usually written in the order of day/month/year rather than month/day/year, as they are in the United States and Canada. Someone from Mexico with a birthdate of July 5, 1986, therefore, would write his or her birthdate as 5/7/86. To avoid confusion, the month is often written with a roman numeral, 5/VII/86.

Pairs Provide students with magazines and newspapers in Spanish. Have pairs of students work together to look for documents in Spanish with easily recognizable formats, such as classified ads or advertisements in periodicals or on the Internet. Ask them to use cognates and other context clues to predict the content. Then have partners present their examples and findings to the class.

Section Goal

In **Panorama**, students will receive comprehensible input by reading about the culture and economy of Spain.

Instructional Resources
Transparencies, #7, #8, #15
WB/VM: Workbook, pp. 21–22;
Video Activities, pp. 227–228
Panorama cultural *DVD/Video*
Interactive CD-ROM
IRM: Videoscript, p. 108;
Panorama cultural *Translations,*
p. 130
Companion website:
www.vistahigherlearning.com
Presentations CD-ROM

Suggestion Project **Transparency #15** or have students use the map in their books to find the places mentioned. Explain that the Canary Islands are located in the Atlantic Ocean off the northwestern coast of Africa. Point out the photos that accompany the map on this page.

El país en cifras After **Idiomas** has been read, associate the regional languages with the larger map by asking questions such as: **¿Hablan catalán en Barcelona? ¿Qué idioma hablan en Madrid?** Point out that the names of languages may be capitalized as labels on maps, but are not capitalized when they appear in running text.

¡Increíble pero cierto! In addition to festivals related to economic and agricultural resources, Spain has many festivals rooted in its deep Catholic tradition. Among the most famous is **Semana Santa** (*Holy Week*) which is celebrated annually in Seville, and many other towns and cities, with great reverence and pageantry.

Note: Population figures represent metropolitan areas.

España

connections cultures NATIONAL STANDARDS

El país en cifras

▶ **Área:** 504.750 km² (kilómetros cuadrados) ó 194.884 millas cuadradas°, incluyendo las islas Baleares y las islas Canarias

▶ **Población:** 39.874.000

▶ **Capital:** Madrid—3.976.000

▶ **Ciudades principales:** Barcelona—2.729.000, Valencia—2.149.171, Sevilla—1.727.304, Zaragoza—827.730

SOURCE: Population Division, UN Secretariat

▶ **Moneda°:** euro

▶ **Idiomas°:** español o castellano, catalán, gallego, valenciano, eusquera

Gallego
Eusquera
Catalán
Español
Valenciano

Regiones lingüísticas

Bandera de España

Españoles célebres

▶ **Miguel de Cervantes,** escritor° (1547–1616)
▶ **Pedro Almodóvar,** director de cine° (1949–)
▶ **Rosa Montero,** escritora y periodista° (1951–)
▶ **Pedro Duque,** astronauta (1963–)
▶ **Arantxa Sánchez Vicario,** tenista (1971–)

millas cuadradas *square miles* Moneda *Currency* Idiomas *Languages*
escritor *writer* cine *film* periodista *reporter* pueblo *town*
Cada año *Every year* Durante todo un día *All day long* miles *thousands*
se tiran *throw at each other* varias toneladas *many tons*

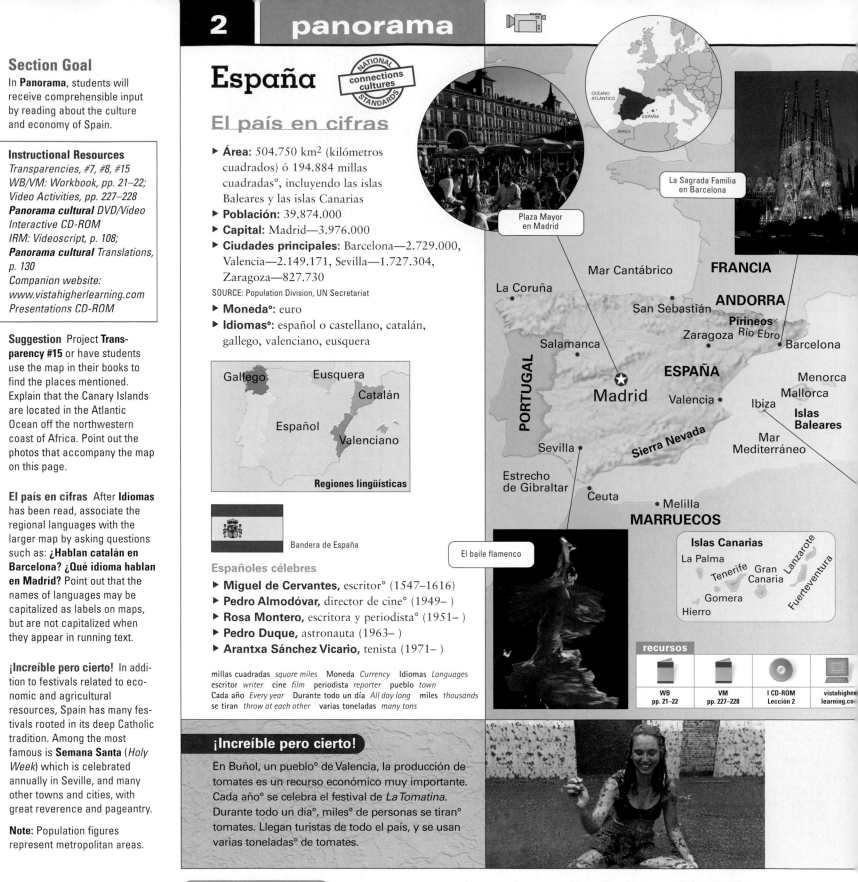

La Sagrada Familia en Barcelona

Plaza Mayor en Madrid

OCÉANO ATLÁNTICO
EUROPA
ESPAÑA
ÁFRICA

Mar Cantábrico
FRANCIA
La Coruña
San Sebastián
ANDORRA
Pirineos
Zaragoza Río Ebro
Salamanca
Barcelona
ESPAÑA
Menorca
Mallorca
Ibiza
Islas Baleares
Madrid
Valencia
Sevilla
Sierra Nevada
Mar Mediterráneo
Estrecho de Gibraltar
Ceuta
Melilla
MARRUECOS

El baile flamenco

Islas Canarias
La Palma
Tenerife
Gran Canaria
Lanzarote
Fuerteventura
Gomera
Hierro

recursos

| WB pp. 21–22 | VM pp. 227–228 | I CD-ROM Lección 2 | vistahigher learning.co |

¡Increíble pero cierto!

En Buñol, un pueblo° de Valencia, la producción de tomates es un recurso económico muy importante. Cada año° se celebra el festival de *La Tomatina*. Durante todo un día°, miles° de personas se tiran° tomates. Llegan turistas de todo el país, y se usan varias toneladas° de tomates.

TEACHING OPTIONS

Heritage Speakers **Paella,** the national dish of Spain, is the ancestor of the popular Latin American dish, **arroz con pollo.** Ask heritage speakers if they know of any dishes traditional in their families that have their roots in Spanish cuisine. Invite them to describe the dishes to the class.

Variación léxica Tell students that they may also see the word **eusquera** spelled **euskera** and **euskara.** The letter **k** is used in Spanish only in words of foreign origin. **Euskera,** or **euskara,** is the name of the Basque language in Basque, a language that linguists believe is unrelated to any other known language. **Euskera** is sometimes spelled **eusquera,** following the principles of Spanish orthography. The Spanish name for Basque is **vascuence** or **vasco.**

Lugares • La Universidad de Salamanca

La Universidad de Salamanca, fundada en 1218 (mil doscientos dieciocho), es la más antigua° de España. Más de 35.000 (treinta y cinco mil) estudiantes toman clases en la universidad. La universidad está en la ciudad de Salamanca, famosa por sus edificios° históricos.

Economía • La Unión Europea

Desde° 1992 (mil novecientos noventa y dos) España es miembro de la Unión Europea, un grupo de países europeos que trabaja para desarrollar° una política° económica y social común en Europa. La moneda de los países de la Unión Europea es el euro.

Artes • Velázquez y el Prado

Las meninas, Diego Velázquez, 1656.

El Prado, en Madrid, es uno de los museos más famosos del mundo°. En el Prado hay pinturas° importantes de Botticelli, del Greco, y de los españoles Goya y Velázquez. *Las Meninas* es la obra más conocida° de Diego Velázquez, pintor° oficial de la corte real° durante el siglo° XVII.

Comida • La paella

La paella es uno de los platos típicos de España. Siempre se prepara° con arroz° y azafrán°, pero hay diferentes recetas°. La paella valenciana, por ejemplo, es de pollo° y conejo°, y la paella marinera es de mariscos°.

Una playa de Ibiza

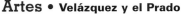

¿Qué aprendiste? Completa las frases con la información adecuada.

1. La <u>Unión Europea</u> trabaja para desarrollar una política económica común en Europa.
2. El arroz y el azafrán son ingredientes básicos de la <u>paella</u>.
3. El Prado está en <u>Madrid</u>.
4. La universidad más antigua de España es la <u>Universidad de Salamanca</u>.
5. La ciudad de <u>Salamanca</u> es famosa por sus edificios históricos.
6. El gallego es una de las lenguas oficiales de <u>España</u>.

Conexión Internet Investiga estos temas en el sitio **www.vistahigherlearning.com.**

1. Busca (*Look for*) información sobre la Universidad de Salamanca u otra universidad española. ¿Qué cursos ofrece (*does it offer*)? ¿Ofrece tu universidad cursos similares?
2. Busca información sobre un español o una española célebre (por ejemplo, un(a) político/a, un actor, una actriz, un(a) artista). ¿De qué parte de España es, y por qué es célebre?

---

más antigua *oldest*	**edificios** *buildings*	**Desde** *Since*	**desarrollar** *develop*	**política** *policy*	**mundo** *world*	**pinturas** *paintings*

más antigua *oldest* **edificios** *buildings* **Desde** *Since* **desarrollar** *develop* **política** *policy* **mundo** *world* **pinturas** *paintings*
más conocida *best-known* **pintor** *painter* **corte real** *royal court* **siglo** *century* **Siempre se prepara** *It is always prepared*
arroz *rice* **azafrán** *saffron* **recetas** *recipes* **pollo** *chicken* **conejo** *rabbit* **mariscos** *seafood*

Instructional Resources
Vocabulary CD
Lab Manual, p. 12
Lab CD/MP3 Lección 2
IRM: Tapescript, pp. 6–10
Testing Program: Pruebas, pp. 13–24
Testing Program Audio CD
Test Files CD-ROM
Test Generator

La clase y la universidad

el borrador	eraser
la clase	class
el/la compañero/a de clase	classmate
el/la compañero/a de cuarto	roommate
el escritorio	desk
el/la estudiante	student
el libro	book
el mapa	map
la mesa	table
la mochila	backpack
el papel	paper
la papelera	wastebasket
la pizarra	blackboard
la pluma	pen
el/la profesor(a)	teacher
la puerta	door
el reloj	clock; watch
la silla	seat
la tiza	chalk
la ventana	window
la biblioteca	library
la cafetería	cafeteria
la casa	house; home
el estadio	stadium
el laboratorio	laboratory
la librería	bookstore
la residencia estudiantil	dormitory
la universidad	university; college
el curso, la materia	course
la especialización	major
el examen	test; exam
el horario	schedule
la prueba	test; quiz
el semestre	semester
la tarea	homework
el trimestre	trimester; quarter

Las materias

la administración de empresas	business administration
el arte	art
la biología	biology
las ciencias	sciences
la computación	computer science
la contabilidad	accounting
la economía	economics
el español	Spanish
la física	physics
la geografía	geography
la historia	history
las humanidades	humanities
el inglés	English
las lenguas extranjeras	foreign languages
la literatura	literature
las matemáticas	mathematics
la música	music
el periodismo	journalism
la psicología	psychology
la química	chemistry
la sociología	sociology

Preposiciones

al lado de	next to; beside
a la derecha de	to the right of
a la izquierda de	to the left of
en	in; on
cerca de	near
con	with
debajo de	below; under
delante de	in front of
detrás de	behind
encima de	on top of
entre	between; among
lejos de	far from
sin	without
sobre	on; over

Palabras adicionales

¿Adónde?	(to) Where?
ahora	now
¿Cuál?, ¿Cuáles?	Which?; Which one(s)?
¿Por qué?	Why?
porque	because

Verbos

bailar	to dance
buscar	to look for
caminar	to walk
cantar	to sing
cenar	to have dinner
comprar	to buy
contestar	to answer
conversar	to converse; to chat
desayunar	to have breakfast
descansar	to rest
desear	to wish; to desire
dibujar	to draw
enseñar	to teach
escuchar la radio/música	to listen (to) the radio/music
esperar (+ inf.)	to wait (for); to hope
estar	to be
estudiar	to study
explicar	to explain
hablar	to talk; to speak
llegar	to arrive
llevar	to carry
mirar	to look (at); to watch
necesitar (+ inf.)	to need
practicar	to practice
preguntar	to ask (a question)
preparar	to prepare
regresar	to return
terminar	to end; to finish
tomar	to take; to drink
trabajar	to work
viajar	to travel

Los días de la semana

¿Cuándo?	When?
¿Qué día es hoy?	What day is it?
Hoy es…	Today is …
la semana	week
lunes	Monday
martes	Tuesday
miércoles	Wednesday
jueves	Thursday
viernes	Friday
sábado	Saturday
domingo	Sunday

Numbers 31–100	See page 53.
Expresiones útiles	See page 37.

recursos

LM p. 12 | Lab CD/MP3 Lección 2 | Vocab CD Lección 2

La familia

3

Communicative Goals

You will learn how to:

- **Talk about your family and friends**
- **Describe people and things**
- **Express ownership**

Lesson Goals

In **Lección 3** students will be introduced to the following:

- terms for family relationships
- names of various professions
- descriptive adjectives
- possessive adjectives
- the present tense of common regular **–er** and **–ir** verbs
- the present tense of **tener** and **venir**
- context clues to unlock meaning of unfamiliar words
- basic dos and don'ts of writing
- how to write a friendly letter
- strategies for asking clarification in oral communication
- cultural and historical information about Ecuador

A primera vista Here are some additional questions you can ask based on the photo: **¿Cuántas personas hay en tu familia? ¿De qué conversas con ellos? ¿Estudias lejos o cerca de la casa de tu familia? ¿Viajas mucho con ellos?**

A PRIMERA VISTA

- ¿Hay cuatro personas en la foto?
- ¿Hay una mujer a la izquierda? ¿Y a la derecha?
- ¿Está el hombre al lado de ella?
- ¿Conversan ellos? ¿Caminan?

INSTRUCTIONAL RESOURCES

Workbook/Video Manual: WB Activities, pp. 23–36
Laboratory Manual: Lab Activities, pp. 13–18
Workbook/Video Manual: Video Activities, pp. 199–200; pp. 229–230
Instructor's Resource Manual: **Hojas de actividades**, p. 142; **Vocabulario adicional**, pp. 156–157; **¡Inténtalo!** & **Práctica** Answers, p. 175; **Fotonovela**

Translations, p. 120; Textbook CD Tapescript, p. 73; Lab CDs Tapescript, pp. 11–15; **Fotonovela** Videoscript, p. 89; **Panorama cultural** Videoscript, p. 108; **Pan. cult**. Translations, p. 130
Info Gap Activities Booklet, pp. 9–12
Overhead Transparencies: #5, #6, #16, #17, #18
Lab Audio CD/MP3 **Lección 3**

Panorama cultural DVD/Video
Fotonovela DVD/Video
Testing Program, pp. 25–36
Testing Program Audio CD
Test Files CD-ROM
Test Generator
Companion website

Presentations CD-ROM
Textbook CD
Vocabulary CD
Interactive CD-ROM
Video CD-ROM
Web-SAM

Section Goals

In **Contextos**, students will learn and practice
• terms for family relationships
• names of professions

Instructional Resources
Transparencies, #16, #17
Textbook Activities CD
Vocabulary CD
WB/VM: Workbook, pp. 23–24
Lab Manual, p. 13
Lab CD/MP3 **Lección 3**
IRM: **Vocab. adicional**, pp.
156–157; **Práctica** *Answers*, p.
175; *Tapescript*, pp. 11–15; p. 73
Interactive CD-ROM
Companion website:
www.vistahigherlearning.com
Presentations CD-ROM

Suggestions

• Point out the meanings of plural family terms to students so they are aware that the masculine plural forms can refer to mixed groups of males and females:
los hermanos *brothers; siblings; brothers and sisters*
los primos *male cousins; male and female cousins*
los sobrinos *nephews; nieces and nephews*
los tíos *uncles; aunts and uncles*

• Introduce active lesson vocabulary. Ask: **¿Cómo se llama tu hermano?** Ask another student **¿Cómo se llama el hermano de ____?** Work your way through various family relationships.

• Project **Transparency #16.** Point out that the family tree is drawn from the point of view of José Miguel Pérez Santoro. Have students refer to the family tree to answer your questions about it. Ex: **¿Cómo se llama la madre de Víctor?**

• Discuss the pattern of Hispanic last names (**apellidos**). If your name follows this pattern, you may wish to use it as an example. Then ask volunteers to say what their names would be.

• You can find vocabulary on more professions and on pets, should students inquire about it, in **Vocabulario adicional** from the IRM. pp. 156–157.

La familia

Más vocabulario

los abuelos	*grandparents*
el/la bisabuelo/a	*great-grandfather/great-grandmother*
la familia	*family*
el/la gemelo/a	*twin*
el/la hermanastro/a	*stepbrother/stepsister*
el/la hijastro/a	*stepson/stepdaughter*
la madrastra	*stepmother*
el medio hermano/ la media hermana	*half-brother/ half-sister*
el padrastro	*stepfather*
los padres	*parents*
los parientes	*relatives*
el/la cuñado/a	*brother-in-law/ sister-in-law*
la nuera	*daughter-in-law*
el/la suegro/a	*father-in-law/ mother-in-law*
el yerno	*son-in-law*
el/la amigo/a	*friend*
el apellido	*last name*
la gente	*people*
el/la muchacho/a	*boy/girl*
el/la niño/a	*child*
el/la novio/a	*boyfriend/girlfriend*
la persona	*person*
el/la artista	*artist*
el/la doctor(a), el/la médico/a	*doctor; physician*
el/la ingeniero/a	*engineer*
el/la periodista	*journalist*
el/la programador(a)	*computer programmer*

Variación léxica

madre ⟷ mamá, mami (*colloquial*)
padre ⟷ papá, papi (*colloquial*)
muchacho/a ⟷ chico/a

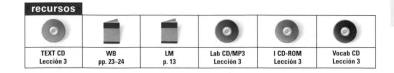

recursos					
TEXT CD Lección 3	WB pp. 23–24	LM p. 13	Lab CD/MP3 Lección 3	I CD-ROM Lección 3	Vocab CD Lección 3

La familia de José Miguel Pérez Santoro

Juan Santoro Sánchez
mi abuelo (*my grandfather*)

Ernesto Santoro González
mi tío (*uncle*)
hijo (*son*) **de Juan y Socorro**

Marina Gutiérrez de Santoro
mi tía (*aunt*)
esposa (*wife*) **de Ernesto**

Silvia Socorro Santoro Gutiérrez
mi prima (*cousin*)
hija (*daughter*) **de Ernesto y Marina**

Héctor Manuel Santoro Gutiérrez
mi primo (*cousin*)
nieto (*grandson*) **de Juan y Socorro**

Carmen Santoro Gutiérrez
mi prima
hija de Ernesto y Marina

¡LENGUA VIVA!

In Spanish-speaking countries, it is common:
• for people to go by both first name and middle name, such as **José Miguel.**
• for people to have two last names: first the father's, then the mother's (the first last name of each parent) such as **Pérez Soto.**
• for wives sometimes to replace their second last name with their husband's first last name, preceded by **de: Mirta Santoro de Pérez.**

TEACHING OPTIONS

Extra Practice Draw your own family tree on a transparency or the board and label it with names. Ask students questions about it. Ex: **¿Es ____ mi tío o mi abuelo? ¿Cómo se llama mi madre? ____ es el primo de ____, ¿verdad? ¿____ es el sobrino o el hermano de ____? ¿Quién es el cuñado de ____?** Help them identify the relationships between members. Then invite them to ask you questions.

Variación léxica Ask heritage speakers to tell the class any other terms they use to refer to members of their families. These may include terms of endearment. Ask them to tell where these terms are used. Possible responses: **nene/nena, guagua, m'hijo/m'hija, chamaco/chamaca, chaval/chavala, cielo, cariño, corazón**

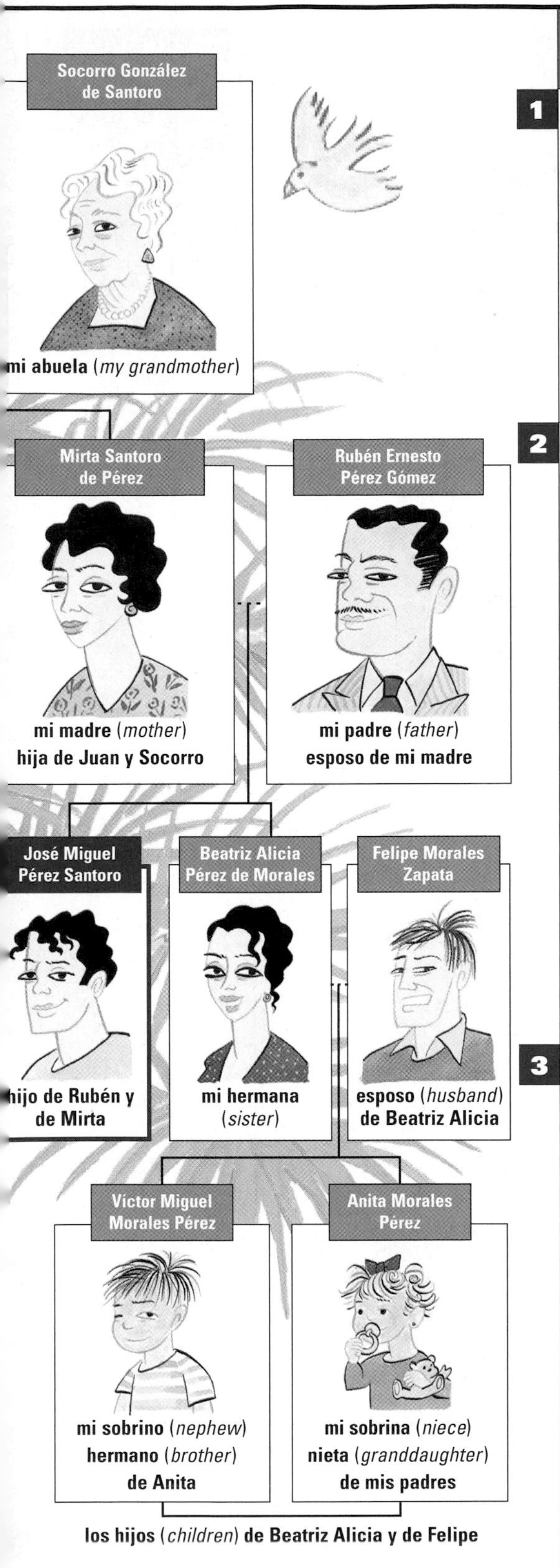

Family tree (left column)

Socorro González de Santoro
mi abuela (*my grandmother*)

Mirta Santoro de Pérez
mi madre (*mother*) **hija de Juan y Socorro**

Rubén Ernesto Pérez Gómez
mi padre (*father*) **esposo de mi madre**

José Miguel Pérez Santoro
hijo de Rubén y de Mirta

Beatriz Alicia Pérez de Morales
mi hermana (*sister*)

Felipe Morales Zapata
esposo (*husband*) **de Beatriz Alicia**

Víctor Miguel Morales Pérez
mi sobrino (*nephew*) **hermano** (*brother*) **de Anita**

Anita Morales Pérez
mi sobrina (*niece*) **nieta** (*granddaughter*) **de mis padres**

los hijos (*children*) **de Beatriz Alicia y de Felipe**

Práctica

1 Escuchar 🎧 Listen to each statement made by José Miguel Pérez Santoro, then indicate whether it is **cierto** or **falso,** based on his family tree.

	Cierto	Falso		Cierto	Falso
1.	✓	○	6.	✓	○
2.	✓	○	7.	✓	○
3.	○	✓	8.	○	✓
4.	✓	○	9.	○	✓
5.	○	✓	10.	✓	○

2 Emparejar Provide the letter of the phrase that matches each description. Two items will not be used.

1. Mi hermano programa las computadoras. c
2. Son los padres de mi esposo. e
3. Son los hijos de mis (*my*) tíos. h
4. Mi tía trabaja en un hospital. a
5. Es el hijo de mi madrastra y el hijastro de mi padre. b
6. Es el esposo de mi hija. l
7. Es el hijo de mi hermana. k
8. Mi primo dibuja y pinta mucho. i
9. Mi hermanastra da (*gives*) clases en la universidad. j
10. Mi padre trabaja con planos (*blueprints*). d

a. Es médica.
b. Es mi hermanastro.
c. Es programador.
d. Es ingeniero.
e. Son mis suegros.
f. Es mi novio.
g. Es mi padrastro.
h. Son mis primos.
i. Es artista.
j. Es profesora.
k. Es mi sobrino.
l. Es mi yerno.

3 Definiciones Define these family terms in Spanish.

modelo
hijastro
Es el hijo de mi esposo/a, pero no es mi hijo.

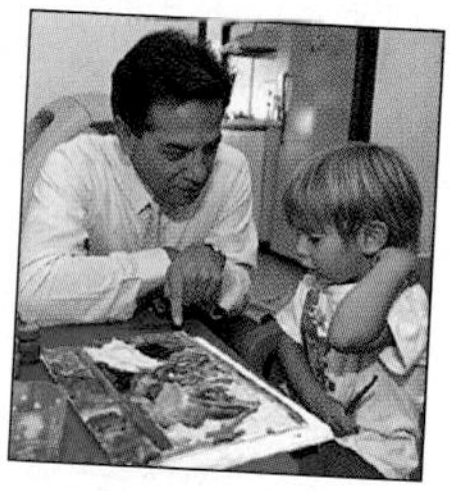

1. abuela la madre de mi madre/padre
2. bisabuelo el abuelo de mi madre/padre
3. tío el hermano de mi madre/padre
4. parientes la familia extendida
5. suegra la madre de mi esposo/a
6. cuñado el esposo de mi hermana
7. nietos los hijos de mis hijos
8. yerno el esposo de mi hija
9. medio hermano el hijo de mi padre pero no de mi madre
10. hermanastro el hijo de mi madrastra/padrastro

4

Escoger Complete the description of each photo using words you learned in **Contextos**. Some answers will vary.

1. La ____familia____ de Sara es muy grande.

2. Héctor y Lupita son ____novios____.

3. Alberto Díaz es ____médico____.

4. Rubén camina con su ____hijo/padre____.

5. Los dos ____hermanos____ están en el parque.

6. Don Manuel es el ____abuelo____ de Martín.

7. Elena Vargas Soto es ____artista____.

8. Irene es ____programadora____.

Comunicación

5 **Una familia** With a classmate, identify the members in the family tree by asking questions about how each family member is related to Graciela Vargas García.

CONSÚLTALO

Cities and towns where family members are from can be seen in **Panorama** on p.90.

modelo
> **Estudiante 1:** ¿Quién es Beatriz Pardo de Vargas?
> **Estudiante 2:** Es la abuela de Graciela.

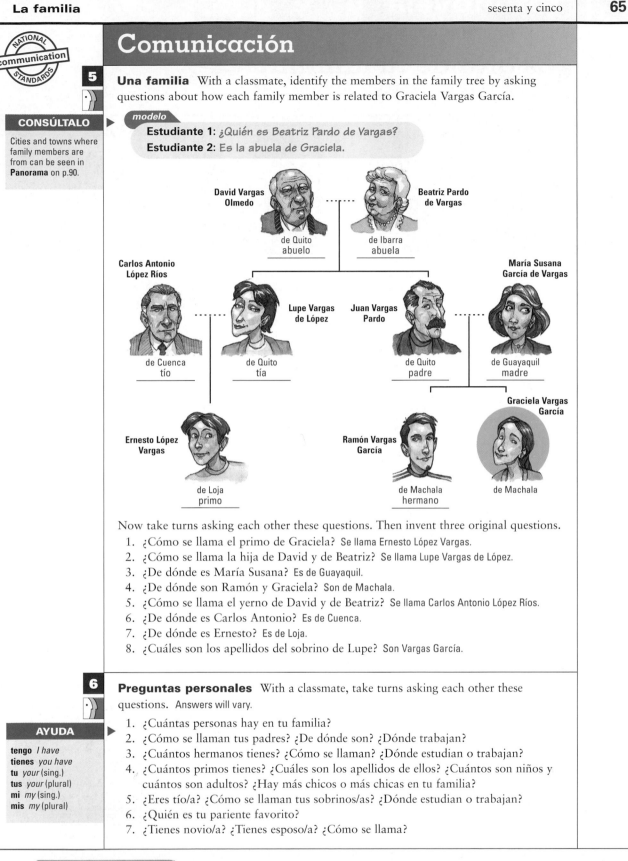

David Vargas Olmedo
de Quito
abuelo

Beatriz Pardo de Vargas
de Ibarra
abuela

Carlos Antonio López Ríos
de Cuenca
tío

Lupe Vargas de López
de Quito
tía

Juan Vargas Pardo
de Quito
padre

María Susana García de Vargas
de Guayaquil
madre

Ernesto López Vargas
de Loja
primo

Ramón Vargas García
de Machala
hermano

Graciela Vargas García
de Machala

Now take turns asking each other these questions. Then invent three original questions.

1. ¿Cómo se llama el primo de Graciela? Se llama Ernesto López Vargas.
2. ¿Cómo se llama la hija de David y de Beatriz? Se llama Lupe Vargas de López.
3. ¿De dónde es María Susana? Es de Guayaquil.
4. ¿De dónde son Ramón y Graciela? Son de Machala.
5. ¿Cómo se llama el yerno de David y de Beatriz? Se llama Carlos Antonio López Ríos.
6. ¿De dónde es Carlos Antonio? Es de Cuenca.
7. ¿De dónde es Ernesto? Es de Loja.
8. ¿Cuáles son los apellidos del sobrino de Lupe? Son Vargas García.

6 **Preguntas personales** With a classmate, take turns asking each other these questions. Answers will vary.

1. ¿Cuántas personas hay en tu familia?
2. ¿Cómo se llaman tus padres? ¿De dónde son? ¿Dónde trabajan?
3. ¿Cuántos hermanos tienes? ¿Cómo se llaman? ¿Dónde estudian o trabajan?
4. ¿Cuántos primos tienes? ¿Cuáles son los apellidos de ellos? ¿Cuántos son niños y cuántos son adultos? ¿Hay más chicos o más chicas en tu familia?
5. ¿Eres tío/a? ¿Cómo se llaman tus sobrinos/as? ¿Dónde estudian o trabajan?
6. ¿Quién es tu pariente favorito?
7. ¿Tienes novio/a? ¿Tienes esposo/a? ¿Cómo se llama?

AYUDA

tengo *I have*
tienes *you have*
tu *your* (sing.)
tus *your* (plural)
mi *my* (sing.)
mis *my* (plural)

5 **Suggestion** Project **Transparency #17** to do this activity.

5 **Expansion** Model the pronunciation of the Ecuadorian cities mentioned. Ask students to locate each on the map of Ecuador, page 90. Ask students to talk about each city based on the map.
Ex: **Guayaquil y Machala son ciudades de la costa del Pacífico. Quito, Loja y Cuenca son ciudades de la cordillera de los Andes. Quito es la capital del Ecuador.**

6 **Expansion**
• After modeling the activity with the whole class, have students circulate around the classroom asking their classmates these questions.
• Have pairs of students ask each other these questions, writing down the answers. After they have finished, ask students questions about their partners' answers.
Ex: **¿Cuántas personas hay en la familia de ____? ¿Cómo se llaman los padres de ____? ¿De dónde son ellos? ¿Cuántos hermanos tiene ____?**

TEACHING OPTIONS

Extra Practice Ask students to draw their own family tree as homework. Have them label each position on the tree with the appropriate Spanish family term and the name of their family member. In class, ask students questions about their families. Ex: **¿Cómo se llama tu prima? ¿Cómo es ella? ¿Ella es estudiante? ¿Cómo se llama tu madre? ¿Quién es tu cuñado?**

TPR Make a family tree using the whole class. Have each student write down the family designation you assign him or her on a note card or sheet of paper, then arrange students as in a family tree, with each one displaying the note card. Then, ask questions about relationships. Ex: **¿Quién es la madre de ____? ¿Cómo se llama el tío de ____?**

¿Es grande tu familia?

Los chicos hablan de sus familias en el autobús.

NATIONAL
communication
cultures
STANDARDS

PERSONAJES

MAITE

INÉS

DON FRANCISCO

ÁLEX

JAVIER

1

MAITE Inés, ¿tienes una familia grande?

INÉS Pues, sí... mis papás, mis abuelos, cuatro hermanas y muchos tíos y primos.

2

INÉS Sólo tengo un hermano mayor, Pablo. Su esposa, Francesca, es médica. No es ecuatoriana, es italiana. Sus papás viven en Roma, creo. Vienen de visita cada año. Ah... y Pablo es periodista.

MAITE ¡Qué interesante!

3

INÉS ¿Y tú, Javier? ¿Tienes hermanos?

JAVIER No, pero aquí tengo unas fotos de mi familia.

INÉS ¡Ah! ¡Qué bien! ¡A ver!

6

INÉS ¿Y cómo es él?

JAVIER Es muy simpático. Él es viejo pero es un hombre muy trabajador.

7

MAITE Oye, Javier, ¿qué dibujas?

JAVIER ¿Eh? ¿Quién? ¿Yo? ¡Nada!

MAITE ¡Venga! ¡No seas tonto!

8

MAITE Jaaavieeer... Oye, pero ¡qué bien dibujas!

JAVIER Este... pues... ¡Sí! ¡Gracias!

recursos

V CD-ROM Lección 3	VM pp. 199–200	I CD-ROM Lección 3

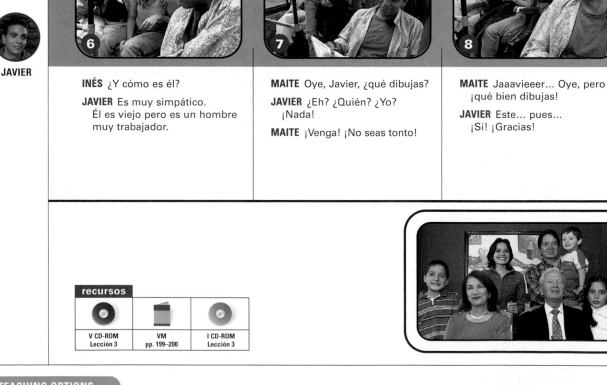

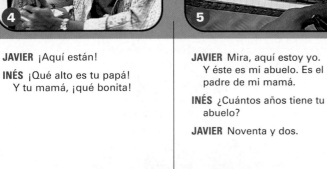

JAVIER ¡Aquí están!

INÉS ¡Qué alto es tu papá! Y tu mamá, ¡qué bonita!

JAVIER Mira, aquí estoy yo. Y éste es mi abuelo. Es el padre de mi mamá.

INÉS ¿Cuántos años tiene tu abuelo?

JAVIER Noventa y dos.

MAITE Álex, mira, ¿te gusta?

ÁLEX Sí, mucho. ¡Es muy bonito!

DON FRANCISCO Epa, ¿qué pasa con Inés y Javier?

Expresiones útiles

Talking about your family

▶ **¿Tienes una familia grande?**
  Do you have a large family?

▷ **Sí... mis papás, mis abuelos, cuatro hermanas y muchos tíos.**
  Yes... my parents, my grandparents, four sisters, and many (aunts and) uncles.

▷ **Sólo tengo un hermano mayor/ menor.**
  I only have one older/younger brother.

▶ **¿Tienes hermanos?**
  Do you have siblings (brothers or sisters)?

▷ **No, soy hijo único.**
  No, I'm an only (male) child.

▶ **Su esposa, Francesca, es médica.**
  His wife, Francesca, is a doctor.

▶ **No es ecuatoriana, es italiana.**
  She's not Ecuadorian; she's Italian.

▶ **Pablo es periodista.**
  Pablo is a journalist.

▶ **Es el padre de mi mamá.**
  He is my mother's father.

Describing people

▶ **¡Qué alto es tu papá!**
  How tall your father is!

▶ **Y tu mamá, ¡qué bonita!**
  And your mother, how pretty!

▶ **¿Cómo es tu abuelo?**
  What is your grandfather like?

▷ **Es simpático.**
  He's nice.

▷ **Es viejo.**
  He's old.

▷ **Es un hombre muy trabajador.**
  He's a very hard-working man.

Saying how old people are

▶ **¿Cuántos años tienes?**
  How old are you?

▶ **¿Cuántos años tiene tu abuelo?**
  How old is your grandfather?

▷ **Noventa y dos.**
  Ninety-two.

Enfoque cultural La familia hispana

It is difficult to generalize about families in any culture, not just among Spanish speakers. There are many kinds of Hispanic families—large and small, close-knit and distant, loving and contentious. Traditionally, however, the family is one of the most important social institutions for Spanish speakers. Extended families, consisting of nuclear families and grandparents, aunts, and uncles, may reside in the same dwelling. Unmarried children often may live with their parents while attending college or working full-time.

Suggestion Ask students to read the **Fotonovela** conversation in groups of five. Ask one or two groups to present the script to the rest of the class.

Expresiones útiles Draw attention to the masculine, feminine, singular, and plural forms of descriptive adjectives and the present tense of **tener** in the video-still captions, **Expresiones útiles**, and as they occur in your conversation with the students. Point out that this material will be formally presented in **Estructura**. Correct students when they ask for correction, but do not expect them to be able to produce the forms correctly at this time.

TEACHING OPTIONS

Enfoque cultural The influence of Hispanic families frequently extends beyond the household. In the entertainment business, for instance, it is not unusual to find children following in the footsteps of their famous parents. Though theatrical families are not unheard of in the United States, Canada, or Great Britain, the phenomenon of children reaping the benefits of a parent's fame and connections is probably more frequent in the Spanish-speaking world. Students may recognize some of these stars of popular music whose parents were/are stars: Enrique Iglesias (Julio Iglesias), Christian Castro (Verónica Castro), Alejandro Fernández (Vicente Fernández).

1 Expansion Give these true-false statements to the class as items 8–10: **7. El padre de Javier es alto. (Cierto.) 8. Javier tiene tres hermanos. (Falso; Javier no tiene hermanos.) 9. Javier tiene unas fotos de su familia. (Cierto.) 10. Inés es italiana. (Falso; Inés es del Ecuador.)**

2 Expansion Álex is the only student not associated with a statement. Ask the class to look at **Fotonovela** and **Expresiones útiles** on pages 66–67 and invent a statement for him. Remind students not to use his exact words. Ex: **¡Qué bonito! ¡Me gusta mucho!**

3 Expansion Have pairs who wrote about the same family exchange papers and compare their descriptions. Ask them to share the differences with the class.

4 Expansion Ask volunteers to share their partner's answers with the class.

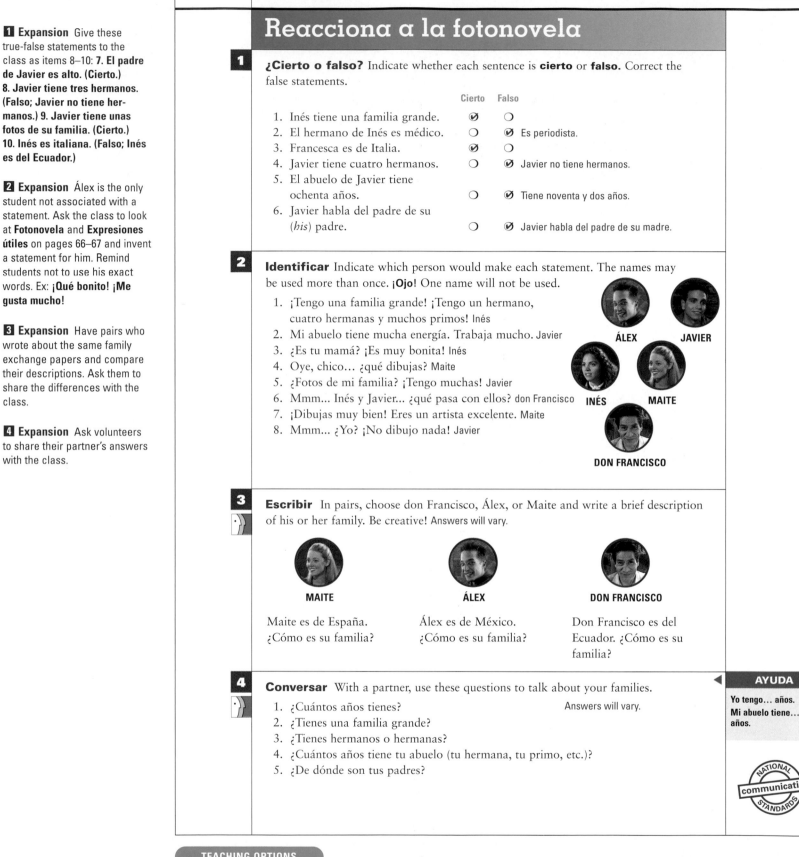

Reacciona a la fotonovela

1 **¿Cierto o falso?** Indicate whether each sentence is **cierto** or **falso**. Correct the false statements.

	Cierto	Falso	
1. Inés tiene una familia grande.	☑	○	
2. El hermano de Inés es médico.	○	☑	Es periodista.
3. Francesca es de Italia.	☑	○	
4. Javier tiene cuatro hermanos.	○	☑	Javier no tiene hermanos.
5. El abuelo de Javier tiene ochenta años.	○	☑	Tiene noventa y dos años.
6. Javier habla del padre de su (*his*) padre.	○	☑	Javier habla del padre de su madre.

2 **Identificar** Indicate which person would make each statement. The names may be used more than once. **¡Ojo!** One name will not be used.

1. ¡Tengo una familia grande! ¡Tengo un hermano, cuatro hermanas y muchos primos! Inés
2. Mi abuelo tiene mucha energía. Trabaja mucho. Javier
3. ¿Es tu mamá? ¡Es muy bonita! Inés
4. Oye, chico… ¿qué dibujas? Maite
5. ¿Fotos de mi familia? ¡Tengo muchas! Javier
6. Mmm… Inés y Javier… ¿qué pasa con ellos? don Francisco
7. ¡Dibujas muy bien! Eres un artista excelente. Maite
8. Mmm… ¿Yo? ¡No dibujo nada! Javier

ÁLEX   **JAVIER**

INÉS   **MAITE**

DON FRANCISCO

3 **Escribir** In pairs, choose don Francisco, Álex, or Maite and write a brief description of his or her family. Be creative! Answers will vary.

MAITE   **ÁLEX**   **DON FRANCISCO**

Maite es de España. ¿Cómo es su familia?

Álex es de México. ¿Cómo es su familia?

Don Francisco es del Ecuador. ¿Cómo es su familia?

4 **Conversar** With a partner, use these questions to talk about your families.

1. ¿Cuántos años tienes?
2. ¿Tienes una familia grande?
3. ¿Tienes hermanos o hermanas?
4. ¿Cuántos años tiene tu abuelo (tu hermana, tu primo, etc.)?
5. ¿De dónde son tus padres?

Answers will vary.

TEACHING OPTIONS

Extra Practice Ask volunteers to ad-lib the **Fotonovela** episode for the class. Assure them that it is not necessary to memorize the **Fotonovela** or stick strictly to its content. They should try to get the general meaning across with the vocabulary and expressions they know, and they should also feel free to be creative. Give them time to prepare.

Variación léxica Clarify that in Spanish the adjective **americano/a** applies to all inhabitants of North and South America, not just citizens of the United States. In Spanish, residents of the United States are usually referred to with the adjective **norteamericano/a** or, more formally, with the adjective **estadounidense**.

Pronunciación 🎧

Diphthongs and linking

hermano	niña	cuñado

In Spanish, **a**, **e**, and **o** are considered strong vowels. The weak vowels are **i** and **u**.

ruido	parientes	periodista

A diphthong is a combination of two weak vowels or of a strong vowel and a weak vowel. Diphthongs are pronounced as a single syllable.

mi hijo	una clase excelente

Two identical vowel sounds that appear together are pronounced like one long vowel.

la abuela

con Natalia	sus sobrinos	las sillas

Two identical consonants together sound like a single consonant.

es ingeniera	mis abuelos	sus hijos

A consonant at the end of a word is linked with the vowel at the beginning of the next word.

mi hermano	su esposa	nuestro amigo

A vowel at the end of a word is linked with the vowel at the beginning of the next word.

Práctica Say these words aloud, focusing on the diphthongs.

1. historia
2. nieto
3. parientes
4. novia
5. residencia
6. prueba
7. puerta
8. ciencias
9. lenguas
10. estudiar
11. izquierda
12. ecuatoriano

Oraciones Read these sentences aloud to practice diphthongs and linking words.

1. Hola. Me llamo Anita Amaral. Soy del Ecuador.
2. Somos seis en mi familia.
3. Tengo dos hermanos y una hermana.
4. Mi papá es del Ecuador y mi mamá es de España.

Refranes Read these sayings aloud to practice diphthongs and linking sounds.

Cuando una puerta se cierra, otra se abre.[1]

Hablando del rey de Roma, por la puerta se asoma.[2]

1 When one door closes, another opens. 2 Speak of the devil and he will appear.

recursos			
TEXT CD Lección 3	LM p. 14	Lab CD/MP3 Lección 3	I CD-ROM Lección 3

Section Goals

In **Pronunciación** students will be introduced to
• the strong and weak vowels
• common diphthongs
• linking in pronunciation

Instructional Resources
Textbook Activities CD
Lab Manual, p. 14
Lab CD/MP3 Lección 3
IRM: Tapescript, pp. 11–15; p. 73
Interactive CD-ROM

Suggestions
• Write **hermano, niña**, and **cuñado** on the board. Ask students to identify the strong and weak vowels.
• Pronounce **ruido, parientes**, and **periodista**, and have students identify the diphthong in each word. Point out that the strong vowels (**a, e, o**) do not combine with each other to form diphthongs. When two strong vowels come together, they are in different syllables.
• Point out that the letter **h** is silent.
• Pronounce **mi hermano** and **su esposa** and ask volunteers to write them on the board. Point out that the resulting linked vowels form a diphthong and are pronounced as one syllable.
• Follow the same procedure with **es ingeniera** and **mis abuelos**. You may want to introduce linking involving the other final consonants (l, n, r, z). Ex: **Son hermanos. El hermano mayor está aquí. ¿Cuál es tu hermana?**
• Ask students to provide words they learned in **Lecciones 1** and **2** and **Contextos** and **Fotonovela** of this lesson that exemplify each point.

Práctica/Oraciones/Refranes
These exercises are recorded on the Textbook Activities CD. You may want to play the CD so students practice the pronunciation point by listening to Spanish spoken by speakers other than yourself.

TEACHING OPTIONS

Heritage Speakers Ask heritage speakers if they know of other **refranes**. Write each new **refrán** on the board and have the student who volunteered it explain what it means. Ex: **A quien Dios no le dio hijos, el diablo le da sobrinos. Más sabe el diablo por viejo que por diablo.**

Extra Practice Here are additional sentences to use for extra practice with diphthongs and linking: **Los estudiantes extranjeros hablan inglés. Mi abuela Ana tiene ochenta años. Juan y Enrique son hermanos. ¿Tu esposa aprende una lengua extranjera? Tengo un examen en la clase de español hoy.**

3.1 Descriptive adjectives

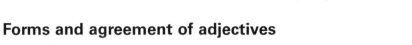

ANTE TODO Adjectives are words that describe people, places, and things. In Spanish, descriptive adjectives are often used with the verb **ser** to point out the characteristics or qualities of nouns or pronouns, such as nationality, size, color, shape, personality, and appearance.

NOUN	ADJECTIVE	PRONOUN	ADJECTIVE
El abuelo de Maite es **alto.**		**Él** es muy **simpático** también.	

Forms and agreement of adjectives

COMPARE & CONTRAST

In English, the forms of descriptive adjectives do not change to reflect the gender (masculine/feminine) and number (singular/plural) of the noun or pronoun they describe.

*Juan is **nice.*** *Elena is **nice.*** *They are **nice.***

In Spanish, the forms of descriptive adjectives agree in gender and/or number with the nouns or pronouns they describe.

Juan es simpátic**o**. Elena es simpátic**a**. Ellos son simpátic**os**.

▶ Adjectives that end in **–o** have four different forms. The feminine singular is formed by changing the **–o** to **–a**. The plural is formed by adding **–s** to the singular forms.

Masculine		Feminine	
SINGULAR	PLURAL	SINGULAR	PLURAL
el muchach**o** alt**o**	los muchach**os** alt**os**	la muchach**a** alt**a**	las muchach**as** alt**as**

> Mi abuelo es muy simpático.

> ¡Qué alto es tu papá! Y tu mamá, ¡qué bonita!

▶ Adjectives that end in **–e** or a consonant have the same masculine and feminine forms.

Masculine		Feminine	
SINGULAR	PLURAL	SINGULAR	PLURAL
el muchacho inteligent**e**	los muchachos inteligent**es**	la muchacha inteligent**e**	las muchachas inteligent**es**
el examen difícil	los exámenes difíc**iles**	la clase difícil	las clases difíc**iles**

Section Goals

In **Estructura 3.1**, students will learn:
• forms, agreement, and position of adjectives ending in –o/–a, –e, or a consonant
• high-frequency descriptive adjectives and some adjectives of nationality

Instructional Resources
WB/VM: Workbook, pp. 25–26
Lab Manual, p. 15
*Lab CD/MP3 **Lección 3***
*IRM: **Vocab. adicional**, pp. 156–157; **¡Inténtalo!** & **Práctica** Answers, p. 175; Tapescript, pp. 11–15*
Info Gap Activities Booklet, pp. 9–10
Interactive CD-ROM
Companion website:
www.vistahigherlearning.com
Presentations CD-ROM

Suggestions

• Write these adjectives on the board: **ecuatoriana, alto, bonito, viejo, trabajador.** Ask volunteers to tell what each means and say whether it is masculine or feminine. Model one of the adjectives in a sentence and ask volunteers to use the others in sentences. Correct any agreement errors.
• Work through the discussion of adjective forms point by point, writing examples on the board. Test comprehension as you proceed by asking volunteers to supply the correct form of adjectives for nouns you suggest. Remind students that grammatical gender does not necessarily reflect the actual gender.

recursos

WB
pp. 25–32

LM
pp. 15–18

Lab CD/MP3
Lección 3

I CD-ROM
Lección 3

vistahigher
learning.com

TEACHING OPTIONS

Extra Practice Have pairs of students write sentences using adjectives such as **inteligente, alto, joven**. When they have finished, ask volunteers to dictate their sentences to you to write on the board. After you have written a sentence and corrected any errors, ask volunteers to suggest a sentence that uses the antonym of the adjective.

Heritage Speakers Have heritage speakers create short conversations in which they use as many of the descriptive adjectives as they can. Ask them to read their conversations to the class. Conversations may also be assigned to pairs of heritage speakers.

▶ Adjectives that end in **–or** are variable in both gender and number.

Masculine		Feminine	
SINGULAR	PLURAL	SINGULAR	PLURAL
el hombre trabajad**or**	los hombres trabajad**ores**	la mujer trabajad**ora**	las mujeres trabajad**oras**

▶ Adjectives that refer to nouns of different genders use the masculine plural form.

Manuel es alt**o**.   Lola es alt**a**.   Manuel y Lola son alt**os**.

Common adjectives

alto/a	tall	**gordo/a**	fat	**moreno/a**	brunet(te)
antipático/a	unpleasant	**grande**	big; large	**mucho/a**	much; many; a lot of
bajo/a	short (in height)	**guapo/a**	handsome; good-looking	**pelirrojo/a**	red-haired
bonito/a	pretty	**importante**	important	**pequeño/a**	small
bueno/a	good	**inteligente**	intelligent	**rubio/a**	blond(e)
delgado/a	thin; slender	**interesante**	interesting	**simpático/a**	nice; likeable
difícil	hard; difficult	**joven**	young	**tonto/a**	silly; foolish
fácil	easy	**malo/a**	bad	**trabajador(a)**	hard-working
feo/a	ugly	**mismo/a**	same	**viejo/a**	old

Adjectives of nationality

▶ Adjectives of nationality are formed like other descriptive adjectives. Adjectives of nationality that end in **–o** form the feminine by changing the **–o** to **–a**.

chin**o** ⟶ chin**a**   mexican**o** ⟶ mexican**a**

The plural is formed by adding an **–s** to the masculine or feminine form.

chin**o** ⟶ chin**os**   mexican**a** ⟶ mexican**as**

▶ Adjectives of nationality that end in **–e** have only two forms, singular and plural.

canadiens**e** ⟶ canadiens**es**   estadounidens**e** ⟶ estadounidens**es**

▶ Adjectives of nationality that end in a consonant form the feminine by adding **–a**.

alemá**n** ⟶ alema**na**   españo**l** ⟶ españo**la**
japoné**s** ⟶ japone**sa**   inglé**s** ⟶ ingle**sa**

Some adjectives of nationality

alemán, alemana	German	**inglés, inglesa**	English
canadiense	Canadian	**italiano/a**	Italian
chino/a	Chinese	**japonés, japonesa**	Japanese
ecuatoriano/a	Ecuadorian	**mexicano/a**	Mexican
español(a)	Spanish	**norteamericano/a**	(North) American
estadounidense	from the U. S.	**puertorriqueño/a**	Puerto Rican
francés, francesa	French	**ruso/a**	Russian

AYUDA

Remember to be aware of cognates, that is words that share similar spellings and meanings in Spanish and English.
A cognate can be a noun like **profesor** or a descriptive adjective like **interesante**.

¡ATENCIÓN!

Unlike in English, Spanish adjectives of nationality are **not** capitalized. Proper names of countries, however, are capitalized.

**México   Canadá
China   Perú**

• • •

Note that adjectives of nationality which carry an accent mark on the last syllable, drop it in the feminine and plural forms.

inglés → inglesa
alemán → alemanes

Suggestions
• Use pictures and the names of celebrities to teach descriptive adjectives in semantic pairs. Use either/or questions, yes/no questions, or a combination. Ex: **¿Michael Jordan es alto o bajo? (Es alto.) ¿Cindy Crawford es fea? (No, es bonita.) ¿Los candidatos son inteligentes o tontos? (Son inteligentes.)**
• Use pictures and the names of celebrities to practice adjectives of nationality. Ex: **Tony Blair, ¿es canadiense? (No, es inglés.) Madeleine Albright, ¿es francesa? (No, es norteamericana.)**
• Point out that adjectives with an accent mark on the last syllable are spelled without it when they add another syllable to form the feminine or the plural. Ex: **irlandés, irlandesa, irlandeses, irlandesas.**
• Point out that adjectives of nationality can be used as nouns as well as adjectives. Ex: **La chica ecuatoriana es guapa. La ecuatoriana es guapa.** Like adjectives, nouns of nationality are not capitalized in Spanish.
• At this point you may want to present **Vocabulario adicional: Más adjetivos de nacionalidad** and **Más adjetivos,** from the IRM.
• Add the nationalities of students and celebrities not on the list. When you introduce another nationality, write one of its forms on the board and ask what the other forms would be. Ex: **¿Los chicos del grupo *The Cardigans* son suecos? (Sí, son suecos.) ¿Cuáles son las formas singulares de *suecos*? (sueco/sueca)**

TEACHING OPTIONS

Extra Practice Write on the board the Spanish country name corresponding to each adjective of nationality that students have learned. Practice the adjectives by indicating a student, saying the country, and having the student come up with the corresponding adjective.
Heritage Speakers Ask heritage speakers to tell what countries their families have come from.

Game Divide the class into two teams. Indicate one team member at a time, alternating between teams. Give a certain form of an adjective and name another form which the team member should give. Ex: **ecuatorianos;** feminine singular (**ecuatoriana**). Give a point per correct answer. Deduct a point for each wrong answer. The team with the most points at the end wins.

Position of adjectives

▶ Descriptive adjectives and adjectives of nationality generally follow the nouns they modify.

El niño **rubio** es de España.
The blond boy is from Spain.

La mujer **española** habla inglés.
The Spanish woman speaks English.

▶ Unlike descriptive adjectives, adjectives of quantity are placed before the modified noun.

Hay **muchos** libros en la biblioteca.
There are many books in the library.

Hablo con **dos** turistas puertorriqueños.
I am talking with two Puerto Rican tourists.

▶ **Bueno/a** and **malo/a** can be placed before or after a noun. When placed before a masculine singular noun, the forms are shortened: **bueno ➞ buen; malo ➞ mal**.

Joaquín es un **buen** amigo.
Joaquín es un amigo **bueno.**   ⟶   *Joaquín is a good friend.*

Hoy es un **mal** día.
Hoy es un día **malo.**   ⟶   *Today is a bad day.*

▶ When **grande** appears before a singular noun, it is shortened to **gran,** and the meaning of the word changes: **gran** = *great* and **grande** = *big, large*.

Don Francisco es un **gran** hombre.
Don Francisco is a great man.

La familia de Inés es **grande**.
Inés' family is large.

¡INTÉNTALO! Provide the appropriate forms of the adjectives. The first item in each group has been done for you.

simpático
1. Mi hermano es *simpático* .
2. La profesora Martínez es *simpática* .
3. Rosa y Teresa son *simpáticas* .
4. Nosotros somos *simpáticos* .

español
1. Luis es *español* .
2. Mis primas son *españolas* .
3. Rafael y yo somos *españoles* .
4. Mi tía es *española* .

difícil
1. Clara es *difícil* .
2. El periodista es *difícil* .
3. Ellas son *difíciles* .
4. Los turistas son *difíciles* .

guapo
1. Su esposo es *guapo* .
2. Mis sobrinas son *guapas* .
3. Los padres de ella son *guapos* .
4. Marta es *guapa* .

Práctica

1 **Emparejar** Find the words in column B that are the opposite of the words in column A. One word in B will not be used, and another will be used twice.

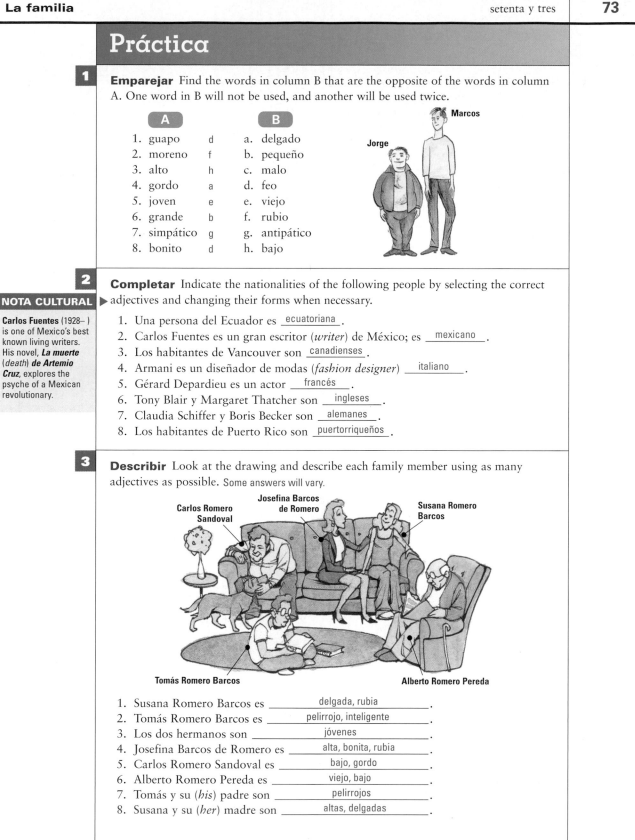

Marcos

Jorge

A		B
1. guapo	d	a. delgado
2. moreno	f	b. pequeño
3. alto	h	c. malo
4. gordo	a	d. feo
5. joven	e	e. viejo
6. grande	b	f. rubio
7. simpático	g	g. antipático
8. bonito	d	h. bajo

2 **Completar** Indicate the nationalities of the following people by selecting the correct adjectives and changing their forms when necessary.

1. Una persona del Ecuador es ___ecuatoriana___ .
2. Carlos Fuentes es un gran escritor (*writer*) de México; es ___mexicano___ .
3. Los habitantes de Vancouver son ___canadienses___ .
4. Armani es un diseñador de modas (*fashion designer*) ___italiano___ .
5. Gérard Depardieu es un actor ___francés___ .
6. Tony Blair y Margaret Thatcher son ___ingleses___ .
7. Claudia Schiffer y Boris Becker son ___alemanes___ .
8. Los habitantes de Puerto Rico son ___puertorriqueños___ .

3 **Describir** Look at the drawing and describe each family member using as many adjectives as possible. Some answers will vary.

Josefina Barcos de Romero

Carlos Romero Sandoval

Susana Romero Barcos

Tomás Romero Barcos

Alberto Romero Pereda

1. Susana Romero Barcos es ___delgada, rubia___ .
2. Tomás Romero Barcos es ___pelirrojo, inteligente___ .
3. Los dos hermanos son ___jóvenes___ .
4. Josefina Barcos de Romero es ___alta, bonita, rubia___ .
5. Carlos Romero Sandoval es ___bajo, gordo___ .
6. Alberto Romero Pereda es ___viejo, bajo___ .
7. Tomás y su (*his*) padre son ___pelirrojos___ .
8. Susana y su (*her*) madre son ___altas, delgadas___ .

1 **Expansion**
- Ask volunteers to create sentences describing famous people, using an adjective from column A and its opposite from B. Ex: **Tom Cruise no es gordo, es delgado. Cristina Saralegui no es morena, es rubia.**
- Have students describe Jorge and Marcos using as many of the antonyms as they can. Ex: **Jorge es muy simpático, pero Marcos es antipático.**

2 **Expansion** Ask pairs of students to write four more statements modeled on the activity. Have them leave a space where the adjectives of nationality should go. Ask each pair to exchange its sentences with another pair, who will fill in the adjectives of nationality.

3 **Expansion**
- Have students say what each person in the drawing is not. Ex: **Susana Romero Barcos no es vieja. Tomás Romero Barcos no es moreno.**
- Have students ask each other questions about the family relationships shown in the illustration. Ex: —**¿Tomás Romero Barcos es el hijo de Alberto Romero Pereda? —No, Tomás es el hijo de Carlos Romero Sandoval.**

TEACHING OPTIONS

Extra Practice Have students write short descriptions of themselves. Tell them to mention where they are from and what they are studying, as well as describing their personalities and what they look like. Collect the descriptions and read a few of them to the class. Have the class guess who wrote each description.

Extra Practice Prepare short descriptions of five easily recognizable people. Write their names on the board in random order. Then read your descriptions as a dictation, having students copy your description and match the description to the appropriate name. Ex: **Ella es joven, morena, atlética e inteligente. (Serena Williams)**

Comunicación

4 Expansion Have small groups brainstorm a list of famous people, places, and things not in the activity. Ask them to include some plural items. Then ask the groups to exchange lists and describe the people, places, and things on the lists they receive.

5 Suggestion Have students divide a sheet of paper into two columns, labeling one **Yo** and the other **Mi novio/a ideal** or **Mi esposo/a ideal**. Have them brainstorm Spanish adjectives for each column. Ask them to rank each adjective in the second column in terms of its importance to them.

5 Expansion Ask small groups to write a personal ad describing a fictional person and his or her ideal mate. Have groups exchange and respond to each other's ads.

6 Suggestion Divide the class into pairs and distribute the handouts from the Information Gap Activities Booklet that correspond to this activity. Give the students ten minutes to complete this activity.

6 Expansion
• Ask questions based on the artwork. Ex: **¿Es alto el abuelo? ¿Es delgado el hijo menor?**
• Have volunteers take turns stating the differences. Then have them invent their own stories based on these families.

4 **¿Cómo es?** With a partner, take turns describing each item on the list. Tell your partner whether you agree (**Estoy de acuerdo.**) or disagree (**No estoy de acuerdo.**) with the descriptions. Answers will vary.

modelo
San Francisco
Estudiante 1: San Francisco es una ciudad muy bonita.
Estudiante 2: No estoy de acuerdo. Es muy fea.

1. Nueva York
2. Jim Carrey
3. Celine Dion
4. El presidente de los Estados Unidos
5. Steven Spielberg
6. La primera dama (*first lady*) de los Estados Unidos
7. El/La profesor(a) de español
8. Los Ángeles
9. Mi universidad
10. Mi clase de español

AYUDA
Here are some tips to help you complete the descriptions:
• Jim Carrey es actor de cine.
• Celine Dion es cantante.
• Steven Spielberg es director de cine.

5 **Anuncio personal** Write a personal ad that describes yourself and your ideal boyfriend, girlfriend, or mate. Then compare your ad with a classmate's. How are you similar and how are you different? Are you looking for the same things in a boyfriend, girlfriend, or mate? Answers will vary.

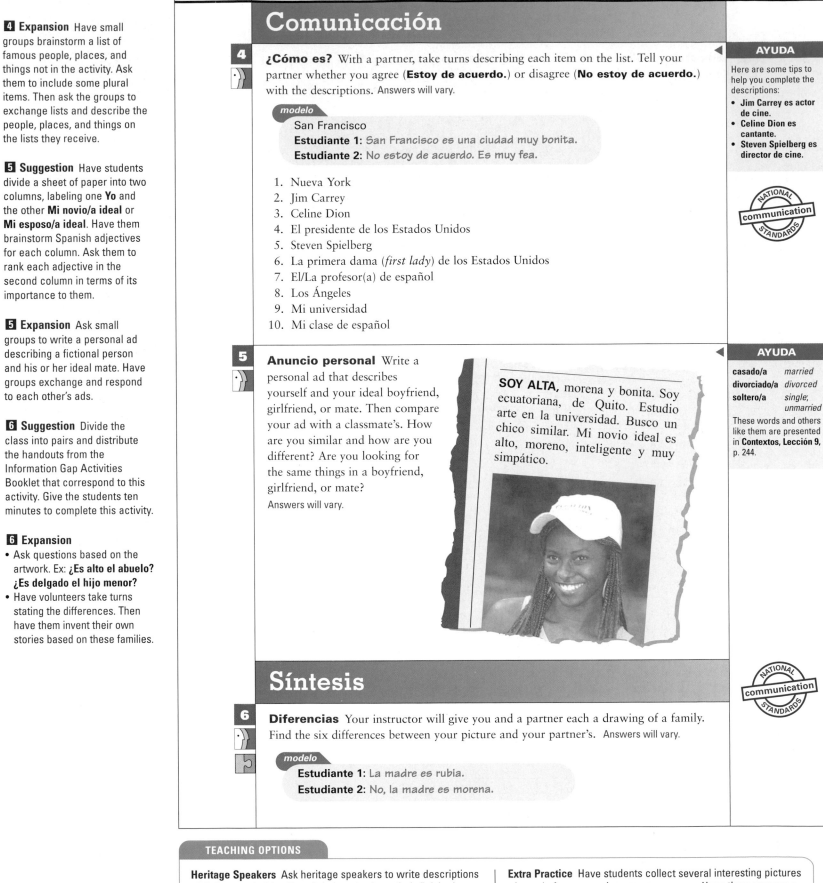

SOY ALTA, morena y bonita. Soy ecuatoriana, de Quito. Estudio arte en la universidad. Busco un chico similar. Mi novio ideal es alto, moreno, inteligente y muy simpático.

AYUDA
casado/a *married*
divorciado/a *divorced*
soltero/a *single; unmarried*
These words and others like them are presented in **Contextos, Lección 9,** p. 244.

Síntesis

6 **Diferencias** Your instructor will give you and a partner each a drawing of a family. Find the six differences between your picture and your partner's. Answers will vary.

modelo
Estudiante 1: La madre es rubia.
Estudiante 2: No, la madre es morena.

3.2 Possessive adjectives

ANTE TODO Possessive adjectives, like descriptive adjectives, are words that are used to qualify people, places, or things. Possessive adjectives express the quality of ownership or possession.

Forms of possessive adjectives

SINGULAR FORMS	PLURAL FORMS	
mi	**mis**	*my*
tu	**tus**	*your* (fam.)
su	**sus**	*his, her, its, your* (form.)
nuestro/a	**nuestros/as**	*our*
vuestro/a	**vuestros/as**	*your* (fam.)
su	**sus**	*their, your* (form.)

COMPARE & CONTRAST

In English, possessive adjectives are invariable; that is, they do not agree in gender and number with the nouns they modify. Spanish possessive adjectives, however, do agree in number with the nouns they modify.

my cousin	*my cousins*	*my aunt*	*my aunts*
mi primo	**mis** primos	**mi** tía	**mis** tías

The forms **nuestro** and **vuestro** agree in both gender and number with the nouns they modify.

nuestr**o** prim**o**	nuestr**os** prim**os**	nuestr**a** tía	nuestr**as** tías

▶ Possessive adjectives are always placed before the nouns they modify.

—¿Está **tu novio** aquí?   —No, **mi novio** está en la biblioteca.
Is your boyfriend here?   *No, my boyfriend is in the library.*

CONSEJOS

Look at the context, focusing on nouns and pronouns, to help you determine the meaning of **su(s)**.

▶ Because **su** and **sus** have multiple meanings (*your, his, her, their, its*), you can avoid confusion by using this construction instead: [*article*] + [*noun*] + **de** + [*subject pronoun*].

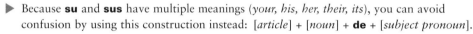

sus parientes

los parientes **de él/ella**	*his/her relatives*
los parientes **de Ud./Uds.**	*your relatives*
los parientes **de ellos/ellas**	*their relatives*

¡INTÉNTALO! Provide the appropriate form of each possessive adjective. The first item in each column has been done for you.

1. Es _____ mi _____ (*my*) libro.
2. _____ Mi _____ (*My*) familia es ecuatoriana.
3. _____ Tu _____ (*Your*, fam.) esposo es italiano.
4. _____ Nuestro _____ (*Our*) profesor es español.
5. Es _____ su _____ (*her*) reloj.
6. Es _____ tu _____ (*your*, fam.) mochila.
7. Es _____ su _____ (*your*, form.) maleta.
8. _____ Su _____ (*Their*) sobrina es alemana.
9. _____ Sus _____ (*Her*) primos son franceses.
10. _____ Nuestros _____ (*Our*) primos son canadienses.
11. Son _____ sus _____ (*their*) lápices.
12. _____ Sus _____ (*Their*) nietos son japoneses.
13. Son _____ nuestras _____ (*our*) plumas.
14. Son _____ mis _____ (*my*) papeles.
15. _____ Mis _____ (*My*) amigas son inglesas.
16. Son _____ sus _____ (*his*) cuadernos.

TEACHING OPTIONS

Video Replay the **Fotonovela** video segment, having students focus on possessive adjectives. Ask them to write down each one they hear, with the noun it modifies. Afterward, ask the class to describe the families of Inés and Javier. Remind them to use definite articles and **de** if necessary to avoid confusion with the possessive **su**.

Small Groups Give small groups three minutes to brainstorm how many words they can associate with the phrases **nuestro país, nuestro estado, nuestra universidad,** and **nuestra clase de español**. Have them model their responses on **En nuestra clase hay _____** and **Nuestro país es _____**. Have the groups share their associations with the rest of the class.

Section Goals

In **Estructura 3.2** students will be introduced to:
- possessive adjectives
- ways of clarifying **su(s)** when referent is ambiguous

Instructional Resources
WB/VM: Workbook, pp. 27–28
Lab Manual, p. 16
*Lab CD/MP3 **Lección 3***
*IRM: ¡**Inténtalo!** & **Práctica***
Answers, p. 175;
Tapescript, pp. 11–15
Interactive CD-ROM
Companion website:
www.vistahigherlearning.com
Presentations CD-ROM

Suggestions
- Introduce the concept of possessive adjectives. Ask volunteers questions. Ex: **¿Es simpática tu madre? ¿Cómo es tu profesor(a) favorito/a?**
- List the possessive adjectives on the board. Use each with a noun to illustrate agreement. Point out that all possessive adjectives agree in number with the noun they modify but that only **nuestro/a** and **vuestro/a** show gender. Point out that **tú** (subject) has an accent mark; **tu** (possessive) does not.
- Ask students to give the plural or singular of possessive adjectives with nouns. Say: **Da el plural: mi profesor, nuestra clase.** Say: **Da el singular: mis manos, nuestras abuelas.**
- Write **su familia** and **sus amigos** on the board and ask the class to tell you the possible meanings. Then ask for volunteers to supply the equivalent clarifying phrases.

Práctica

1

La familia de Manolo Complete each sentence with the correct possessive adjective. Use the subject of each sentence as a guide.

1. Me llamo Manolo, y ____mi____ (nuestro, mi, sus) hermano es Federico.
2. ____Nuestra____ (Nuestra, Sus, Mis) madre Silvia es profesora y enseña química.
3. Ella admira mucho a ____sus____ (tu, nuestro, sus) estudiantes porque trabajan mucho.
4. Yo estudio en la misma universidad, pero no tomo clases con ____mi____ (mi, nuestras, tus) madre.
5. Federico trabaja en una oficina con ____nuestro____ (mis, tu, nuestro) padre.
6. ____Su____ (Mi, Su, Tu) oficina está en el centro de Quito.
7. Javier y Óscar son ____mis____ (mis, mi, sus) tíos de Guayaquil.
8. ¿Y tú? ¿Cómo es ____tu____ (mi, su, tu) familia?

2

Clarificar Clarify each sentence with a prepositional phrase. Follow the model.

> **modelo**
> Su hermana es muy bonita. (ella)
> *La hermana de ella es muy bonita.*

1. Su casa es muy grande. (ellos) ____La casa de ellos es muy grande.____
2. ¿Cómo se llama su hermano? (ellas) ____¿Cómo se llama el hermano de ellas?____
3. Sus padres trabajan en el centro. (ella) ____Los padres de ella trabajan en el centro.____
4. Sus abuelos son muy simpáticos. (él) ____Los abuelos de él son muy simpáticos.____
5. Maribel es su prima. (ella) ____Maribel es la prima de ella.____
6. Su primo lee los libros. (ellos) ____El primo de ellos lee los libros.____

3

¿Dónde está? With a partner, imagine that you can't remember where you put some of the belongings you see in the pictures. Your partner will help you by reminding you where your things are. Take turns playing each role. Answers will vary.

> **modelo**
> **Estudiante 1:** ¿Dónde está mi mochila?
> **Estudiante 2:** Tu mochila está encima del escritorio.

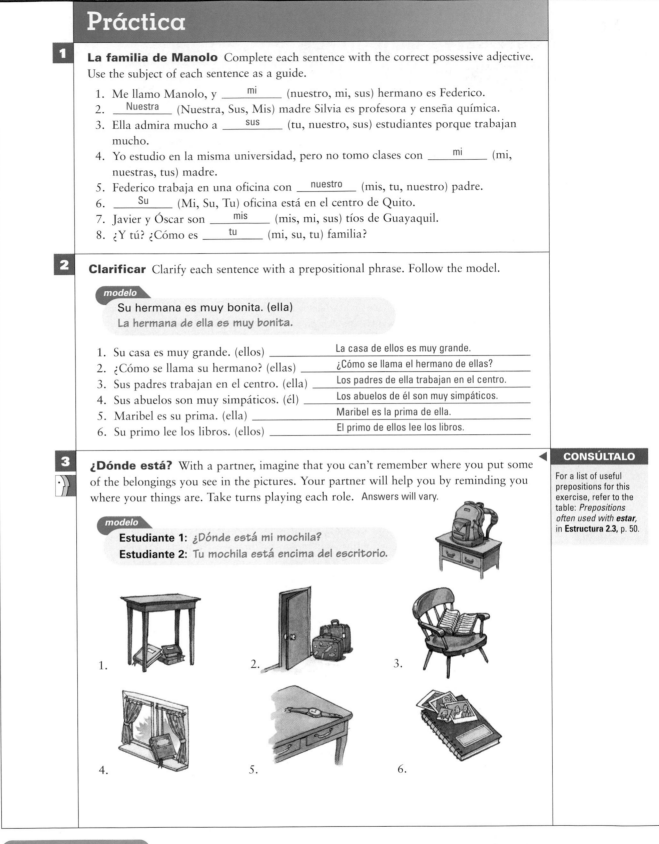

1.
2.
3.
4.
5.
6.

---

1 Expansion
- Have students replace the nouns with nouns of a different number and gender. Then have them say each new sentence, changing the possessives as necessary.
- Have students respond to the question in item 8.

2 Expansion
- Replace the subject pronouns in parentheses with others and have the class provide new answers. Then have groups of students provide new nouns and the corresponding answers.
- Give the class sentences such as **Es su libro** and have volunteers rephrase them with a clarifying prepositional phrase.

3 Suggestions
- Before doing the activity, quickly review **estar** by writing the present-tense forms on the board.
- Remind students that **estar** is used to indicate location.

3 Expansion Ask questions about objects that are in the classroom. Ex: **¿Dónde está mi escritorio? ¿Dónde está el libro de _____? ¿Dónde están las plumas de _____? ¿Dónde están tus lápices?**

TEACHING OPTIONS

Extra Practice Ask students a few questions about the members of their immediate and extended families. Ex: **¿Cómo son tus padres? ¿Cómo se llama tu tío favorito? ¿Es el hermano de tu madre o de tu padre? ¿Tienes muchos primos? ¿Cómo se llaman tus primos? ¿De dónde son tus abuelos? ¿Hablas mucho con tus abuelos?**

Heritage Speakers Ask heritage speakers to write a paragraph about a favorite relative. Ask them to include the characteristics that make that relative their favorite. Have them explain what they have learned from their relative.

Comunicación

4

Describir Get together with a partner and take turns describing the people and places on the list. Answers will vary.

> *modelo*
> La biblioteca de su universidad
> La *biblioteca de nuestra universidad es muy grande. Hay muchos libros en la biblioteca. Mis amigos y yo estudiamos en la biblioteca.*

1. Tu profesor favorito
2. Tu profesora favorita
3. Su clase de español
4. La librería de su universidad
5. Tus padres
6. Tus abuelos
7. Tu mejor (*best*) amigo
8. Tu mejor amiga
9. Su universidad
10. Tu país de origen

5

Una familia In small groups, each student pretends to be a different member of the family pictured and shares that person's private thoughts about the others in the family. Make two positive comments and two negative ones. Answers will vary.

> *modelo*
> **Estudiante 1:** Mi hijo Roberto es muy trabajador. Estudia mucho y termina su tarea.
> **Estudiante 2:** Nuestra familia es difícil. Mis padres no escuchan mis opiniones.

Síntesis

6

Describe a tu familia Get together with two classmates and describe your family to them in several sentences (**Mi padre es alto y moreno. Mi madre es delgada y muy bonita. Mis hermanos son...**). They will work together to try to repeat your description (**Su padre es alto y moreno. Su madre...**). If they forget any details, they will ask you questions (**¿Es alto tu hermano?**). Alternate roles until all of you have described your families. Answers will vary.

TEACHING OPTIONS

Extra Practice Have students work in small groups to prepare a description of a famous person, such as a politician, a movie star, or a sports figure, and his or her extended family. Tell them to feel free to invent family members as necessary. Have groups present their descriptions to the rest of the class.

Heritage Speakers Ask heritage speakers to describe their home country (**país de origen**) for the whole class. As they are giving their descriptions, ask them questions that elicit more information. Also, clarify for the class any unfamiliar words and expressions they may use.

Estructura **77**

---

4 Suggestion Ask students to suggest a few other details to add to the **modelo**. Then tell them to work in pairs, taking turns describing three or four of the items.

5 Suggestions
• Quickly review the descriptive adjectives on page 71. You can do this by saying an adjective and having volunteers give its opposite (**palabra opuesta**).
• Explain the activity to the class. Have students give names to the people in the photo following Hispanic naming conventions.

5 Expansion Ask a couple of groups to perform the activity for the class.

6 Suggestions
• Review the family vocabulary on pages 62–63.
• Explain that the class will divide into groups of three. One student will describe his or her own family (using **mi**), and then the other two will describe the first student's family to one another (using **su**) and ask for clarification as necessary (using **tu**). Before beginning, ask students to list the family members they plan to describe.

3.3 Present tense of –er and –ir verbs

ANTE TODO

In **Lección 2,** you learned how to form the present tense of regular **–ar** verbs. You also learned about the importance of verb forms, which change to show who is performing the action. The chart below shows the forms of verbs from two other important verb groups, **–er** verbs, and **–ir** verbs.

CONSÚLTALO

To review the conjugation of –ar verbs, see **Estructura 2.1**, p. 40.

Present tense of –er, and –ir verbs

		comer (to eat)	**escribir** (to write)
SINGULAR FORMS	yo	com**o**	escrib**o**
	tú	com**es**	escrib**es**
	Ud./él/ella	com**e**	escrib**e**
PLURAL FORMS	nosotros/as	com**emos**	escrib**imos**
	vosotros/as	com**éis**	escrib**ís**
	Uds./ellos/ellas	com**en**	escrib**en**

▶ **–Er** and **–ir** verbs have very similar endings. Study the preceding chart to detect the patterns that make it easier for you to use them to communicate in Spanish.

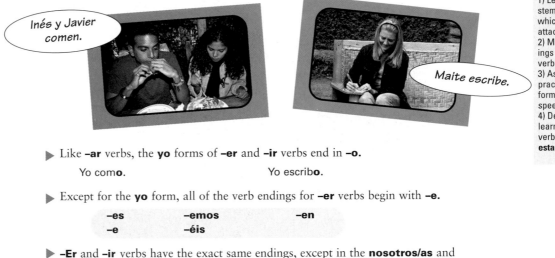

Inés y Javier comen.

Maite escribe.

CONSEJOS

Here are some tips on learning Spanish verbs:
1) Learn to identify the stem of each verb, to which all endings attach.
2) Memorize the endings that go with each verb and verb tense.
3) As often as possible, practice using different forms of each verb in speech and writing.
4) Devote extra time to learning irregular verbs, such as **ser** and **estar**.

▶ Like **–ar** verbs, the **yo** forms of **–er** and **–ir** verbs end in **–o.**

Yo com**o**.   Yo escrib**o**.

▶ Except for the **yo** form, all of the verb endings for **–er** verbs begin with **–e.**

–es   –emos   –en
–e   –éis

▶ **–Er** and **–ir** verbs have the exact same endings, except in the **nosotros/as** and **vosotros/as** forms.

nosotros ◀ com**emos** / escrib**imos**   vosotros ◀ com**éis** / escrib**ís**

Section Goals

In **Estructura 3.3** students will learn:
• the present-tense forms of regular **–er/–ir** verbs
• some high-frequency regular **–er/–ir** verbs

Instructional Resources
WB/VM: Workbook, pp. 29–30
Lab Manual, p. 17
Lab CD/MP3 **Lección 3**
IRM: ¡**Inténtalo!** & **Práctica**
Answers, p. 175;
Tapescript, pp. 11–15;
Hojas de actividades, p. 142
Info Gap Activities Booklet, pp. 11–12
Interactive CD-ROM
Companion website:
www.vistahigherlearning.com
Presentations CD-ROM

Suggestions
• Write **trabajo** on the board and ask for the corresponding subject pronoun. (**yo**) Continue until you have the entire paradigm. Underline the endings, pointing out the characteristic vowel (**–a–**) where it appears and the personal endings.
• Ask questions and make statements that use the verb **comer** to elicit all the present-tense forms.
Ex: ¿**Comes en la cafetería o en un restaurante? Yo no como en la cafetería. ¿Come _____ en casa o en un bar?** As you elicit responses, write just the verbs on the board until you have the complete conjugation. Do the same with **escribir.**
Ex: ¿**Quién escribe muchas cartas? ¿A quién escribes?** When you have a complete paradigm of both verbs, contrast it with the paradigm of **trabajar.** Help students identify the ending that is the same in all three conjugations. **yo** = (**–o**)

TEACHING OPTIONS

Heritage Speakers Have heritage speakers write ten statements about themselves, their family, and people that they know using ten different **–er/–ir** verbs introduced on pages 78–79.
Game Divide the class into two teams. Announce an infinitive and a subject pronoun (Ex: **creer/yo**) and have the first member of Team A give the appropriate conjugated form of the verb. If the team member answers correctly, his or her team gets one point. If he or she does not know the answer, give the first member of Team B the same infinitive and pronoun. If he or she does not know the answer, say the correct verb form and move on to the next team member of Team A. The team with the most points at the end wins.

Common –er and –ir verbs

–er verbs		–ir verbs	
aprender (a + *inf.*)	to learn	abrir	to open
beber	to drink	asistir (a)	to attend
comer	to eat	compartir	to share
comprender	to understand	decidir (+ *inf.*)	to decide
correr	to run	describir	to describe
creer (en)	to believe (in)	escribir	to write
deber (+ *inf.*)	should; must; ought to	recibir	to receive
leer	to read	vivir	to live

Ellos **corren** en el parque.

Él **escribe** una carta.

¡INTÉNTALO! Provide the appropriate present tense forms of these verbs. The first item in each column has been done for you.

correr
1. Graciela __corre__ .
2. Tú __corres__ .
3. Yo __corro__ .
4. Sara y Ana __corren__ .
5. Usted __corre__ .
6. Ustedes __corren__ .
7. La gente __corre__ .
8. Marcos y yo __corremos__ .

abrir
1. Ellos __abren__ la puerta.
2. Carolina __abre__ la maleta.
3. Yo __abro__ las ventanas.
4. Nosotras __abrimos__ los libros.
5. Usted __abre__ el cuaderno.
6. Tú __abres__ la ventana.
7. Ustedes __abren__ las maletas.
8. Los muchachos __abren__ los cuadernos.

aprender
1. Él __aprende__ español.
2. Maribel y yo __aprendemos__ inglés.
3. Tú __aprendes__ japonés.
4. Tú y tu hermanastra __aprenden__ francés.
5. Mi hijo __aprende__ chino.
6. Yo __aprendo__ alemán.
7. Usted __aprende__ inglés.
8. Nosotros __aprendemos__ italiano.

1 Expansion
• Working with the whole class, come up with the questions that would elicit the statements in this activity. Ex: **¿Dónde viven tú y tu familia? ¿Cuántos libros tienes? ¿Por qué tienes muchos libros? ¿Cómo es tu hermano Alfredo? ¿Cuándo asiste Alfredo a sus clases? ¿Cuándo corren ustedes? ¿Cuánto comen tus padres? ¿Cuánto deben comer tus padres?**
• Have small groups describe the family pictured here. Ask the groups to invent each person's name, using Hispanic naming conventions, and include his or her physical description, place of origin, and family relationship to the other people in the photo.

2 Expansion Have pairs create two original dehydrated sentences for another pair to write out.

3 Expansion Write these words on the board for students to add to the activity: **aprender historia japonesa, escribir más cartas, comer más sushi, describir su viaje**.

Práctica

1

Completar Complete Susana's sentences about her family with the correct forms of the verbs in parentheses. One of the verbs will remain in the infinitive.

1. Mi familia y yo ___vivimos___ (vivir) en Guayaquil.
2. Tengo muchos libros. Me gusta ___leer___ (leer).
3. Mi hermano Alfredo es muy inteligente. Alfredo ___asiste___ (asistir) a clases los lunes, miércoles y viernes.
4. Los martes y jueves Alfredo y yo ___corremos___ (correr).
5. Mis padres ___comen___ (comer) mucho.
6. Yo ___creo___ (creer) que (*that*) mis padres deben comer menos (*less*).

2

Oraciones Juan is talking about what he and his friends do after school. Form complete sentences.

> **modelo**
>
> Yo / correr / amigos / lunes y miércoles
> *Yo corro con mis amigos los lunes y miércoles.*

1. Manuela / asistir / clase / yoga Manuela asiste a la clase de yoga.
2. Eugenio / abrir / correo electrónico (*e-mail*) Eugenio abre su correo electrónico.
3. Isabel y yo / leer / biblioteca Isabel y yo leemos en la biblioteca.
4. Sofía y Roberto / aprender / hablar / inglés Sofía y Roberto aprenden a hablar inglés.
5. Tú / comer / cafetería / universidad Tú comes en la cafetería de la universidad.
6. Mi novia y yo / compartir / libro de historia Mi novia y yo compartimos el libro de historia.

3

Consejos Mario teaches Japanese at a university in Quito and is spending a year in Tokyo with his family. In pairs, use the words below to say what he and/or his family members are doing or should do to adjust to life in Japan. Then, create one more sentence using a verb not in the list.   Answers will vary.

> **modelo**
>
> recibir libros / deber practicar japonés
> **Estudiante 1:** *Mario y su esposa reciben muchos libros en japonés.*
> **Estudiante 2:** *Los hijos deben practicar japonés.*

aprender japonés	decidir explorar el país
asistir a clases	escribir listas de palabras en japonés
beber sake	leer novelas japonesas
deber comer cosas nuevas	vivir con una familia japonesa
¿?	¿?

TEACHING OPTIONS

Pairs Have pairs of students play the roles of interviewer and movie star. Students can review previous lesson vocabulary lists in preparation. Give pairs sufficient time to plan and practice. When all pairs have completed the activity, ask a few of them to introduce their characters and perform the interview for the whole class.

Heritage Speakers Have heritage speakers brainstorm a list of things that a study-abroad student in a Spanish-speaking country might want to do. Have them base their list on **Actividad 3** using as many **–er/–ir** verbs as they can. Then have the rest of the class write full sentences based on the list.

Comunicación

4

Entrevista Get together with a classmate and use these questions to interview each other. Be prepared to report the results of your interviews to the class. Answers will vary.

1. ¿Dónde comes al mediodía? ¿Comes mucho?
2. ¿Debes comer más (*more*) o menos (*less*)?
3. ¿Cuándo asistes a tus clases?
4. ¿Cuál es tu clase favorita? ¿Por qué?
5. ¿Dónde vives?
6. ¿Con quién vives?
7. ¿Qué cursos debes tomar el próximo (*next*) semestre?
8. ¿Lees el periódico (*newspaper*)? ¿Qué periódico lees y cuándo?
9. ¿Recibes muchas cartas (*letters*)? ¿De quién(es)?
10. ¿Escribes poemas?

5

Encuesta Your instructor will give you a worksheet. Walk around the class and ask a different classmate each question about his/her family members. Be prepared to report the results of your survey to the class. Answers will vary.

Actividades

1. Vivir en una casa
2. Beber café
3. Correr todos los días (every day)
4. Comer mucho en restaurantes
5. Recibir mucho correo electrónico (e-mail)
6. Comprender tres lenguas
7. Deber estudiar más (more)
8. Leer muchos libros

Miembros de la familia

Los padres de Juan.

Síntesis

6

Horario Your instructor will give you and a partner incomplete versions of Alicia's schedule. Fill in the missing information on the schedule by talking to your partner. Be prepared to reconstruct Alicia's complete schedule with the class. Answers will vary.

modelo

Estudiante 1: A las ocho, Alicia corre.
Estudiante 2: ¡Ah, sí! (*Writes down information*)
Estudiante 2: A las nueve, ella ...

---

4 Suggestions
- Tell students that after one of them has interviewed his or her partner, they should switch roles.
- This activity is also suited to a group of three students, one of whom acts as note taker. They should switch roles at the end of each interview until each has played all three roles.

5 Suggestions
- Model one or two of the questions. Then distribute the **Hojas de actividades**.
- The activity can also be done in pairs. Have students change the heading of the second column to **¿Sí o no?**

5 Expansion Go through the survey (**encuesta**) to find out how the items apply to the class. Record the results on the board. Ask: **¿Quiénes viven en una casa?**

6 Suggestion Divide the class into pairs and distribute the handouts from the Information Gap Activities Booklet that correspond to this activity. Give students ten minutes to complete this activity.

6 Expansion
- Ask questions based on Alicia's schedule. Ex: **¿Qué hace Alicia a las nueve? (Ella desayuna.)**
- Have volunteers take turns reading aloud Alicia's schedule. Then have them write their own schedules using as many –er/–ir verbs as they can.

Small Groups Have small groups talk about their favorite classes and teachers. They should describe the classes and the teachers and indicate why they like them. They should also mention what days and times they attend each class. A few volunteers may present a summary of their conversations.

Extra Practice Here are four sentences containing –er/–ir verbs to use as a dictation. Read each twice, pausing after the second time for students to write. **1. Mi hermana Juana y yo asistimos a la Universidad de Quito. 2. Ella vive en la casa de mis padres y yo vivo en una residencia. 3. Juana es estudiante de letras y lee mucho. 4. Yo estudio computación y aprendo a programar computadoras.**

3.4 Present tense of **tener** and **venir**

ANTE TODO The verbs **tener** (*to have*) and **venir** (*to come*) are among the most frequently used in Spanish. Because most of their forms are irregular, you will have to learn each one individually.

		tener and *venir*	
		tener	**venir**
SINGULAR FORMS	yo	ten**go**	ven**go**
	tú	tien**es**	vien**es**
	Ud./él/ella	tien**e**	vien**e**
PLURAL FORMS	nosotros/as	ten**emos**	ven**imos**
	vosotros/as	ten**éis**	ven**ís**
	Uds./ellos/ellas	tien**en**	vien**en**

▶ The endings are the same as those of regular **–er** and **–ir** verbs, except for the **yo** forms, which are irregular: **tengo, vengo.**

▶ In the **tú, Ud.,** and **Uds.** forms, the **e** of the stem changes to **ie** as shown below.

INFINITIVE	VERB STEM	VERB FORM
tener →	ten- →	tú t**ie**nes
		él/ella/Ud. t**ie**ne
		ellos/ellas/Uds. t**ie**nen
venir →	ven- →	tú v**ie**nes
		él/ella/Ud. v**ie**ne
		ellos/ellas/Uds. v**ie**nen

¿Tienes hermanos?

Sí, tengo cuatro hermanas y un hermano mayor.

▶ The **nosotros** and **vosotros** forms are the only ones which are regular. Compare them to the forms of **comer** and **escribir** that you learned on page 78.

	tener	comer	venir	escribir
nosotros/as	ten**emos**	com**emos**	ven**imos**	escrib**imos**
vosotros/as	ten**éis**	com**éis**	ven**ís**	escrib**ís**

TEACHING OPTIONS

Heritage Speakers Have heritage speakers work in pairs to invent a short conversation in which they use forms of **tener, venir,** and other –ir/–er verbs they know. Tell them their conversations should involve the family and should include some descriptions of family members. Have pairs present their conversations to the whole class.

Extra Practice Use sentences such as the following for further practice with the conjugation of **tener** and **venir.** First write a sentence on the board and have students say it. Then say a new subject and have students repeat the sentence, substituting the new subject and making all necessary changes. **Yo tengo una familia grande. (Ernesto y yo, Ud., Tú, Ellos) Claudia y Pilar vienen a la clase de historia. (Nosotras, Ernesto, Uds., Tú)**

Expressions with *tener*

tener... años	to be... years old	**tener (mucha) prisa**	to be in a (big) hurry
tener (mucho) calor	to be (very) hot	**tener razón**	to be right
tener (mucho) cuidado	to be (very) careful	**no tener razón**	to be wrong
tener (mucho) frío	to be (very) cold	**tener (mucha) sed**	to be (very) thirsty
tener (mucha) hambre	to be (very) hungry	**tener (mucho) sueño**	to be (very) sleepy
tener (mucho) miedo (de)	to be (very) afraid/ scared (of)	**tener (mucha) suerte**	to be (very) lucky

▶ In certain idiomatic or set expressions in Spanish, you use the construction **tener** + [*noun*] to express *to be* + [*adjective*]. The chart above contains a list of the most common expressions with **tener.**

—¿**Tienen** hambre ustedes?
Are you hungry?

—Sí, y **tenemos** sed también.
Yes, and we're thirsty, too.

▶ To express an obligation, use **tener que** (*to have to*) + [*infinitive*].

—¿Qué **tienes que** estudiar hoy?
What do you have to study today?

—**Tengo que** estudiar biología.
I have to study biology.

▶ To ask people if they feel like doing something, use **tener ganas de** (*to feel like*) + [*infinitive*].

—¿**Tienes ganas de** comer?
Do you feel like eating?

—No, **tengo ganas de** dormir.
No, I feel like sleeping.

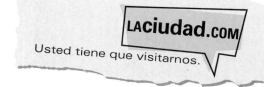

LAciudad.COM
Usted tiene que visitarnos.

¡INTÉNTALO! Provide the appropriate forms of **tener** and **venir**. The first item in each column has been done for you.

tener
1. Ellos __tienen__ dos hermanos.
2. Yo __tengo__ una hermana.
3. El artista __tiene__ tres primos.
4. Nosotros __tenemos__ diez tíos.
5. Eva y Diana __tienen__ un sobrino.
6. Usted __tiene__ cinco nietos.
7. Tú __tienes__ dos hermanastras.
8. Ustedes __tienen__ cuatro hijos.
9. Ella __tiene__ una hija.

venir
1. Mis padres __vienen__ de México.
2. Tú __vienes__ de España.
3. Nosotras __venimos__ de Cuba.
4. Pepe __viene__ de Italia.
5. Yo __vengo__ de Francia.
6. Ustedes __vienen__ del Canadá.
7. Alfonso y yo __venimos__ de Portugal.
8. Ellos __vienen__ de Alemania.
9. Usted __viene__ de Venezuela.

Suggestions
• Remind the class that Spanish uses **tener** + [*noun*] in many cases where English uses *to be* + [*adjective*].
• Model the use of the expressions by talking about yourself and asking students questions about themselves. Ex: **Tengo ____ años. Y tú, ¿cuántos años tienes? Esta mañana tengo frío. ¿Tienen frío ustedes? Y tú, ____, ¿tienes frío también o tienes calor? Yo no tengo sueño esta mañana. Me gusta enseñar por la mañana.**
• Present **tener que** + [*infinitive*] and **tener ganas de** + [*infinitive*] together. Go around the class asking questions that use the expressions, having students answer in complete sentences. Ex: **____, ¿tienes que estudiar más para la clase de español?**

TEACHING OPTIONS

Small Groups Have groups of three write nine sentences, each of which uses a different expression with **tener**, including **tener que** + [*infinitive*] and **tener ganas de** + [*infinitive*]. Ask volunteers to write some of their group's best sentences on the board. Work with the whole class to read the sentences and correct any errors.

Variación léxica Point out that **tener que** + [*infinitive*] not only expresses obligation, but also need. **Tengo que estudiar más** can mean either *I have to (am obligated to) study more* or *I need to study more*. Another way of expressing need is with the regular –ar verb **necesitar** + [*infinitive*]. Ex: **Necesito estudiar más.** This can also be said with **deber** + [*infinitive*]. Ex: **Debo estudiar más.**

1 **Suggestion** Go over the activity with the class, reading a statement in Column A and having volunteers give the corresponding phrase in Column B. **Tener ganas de** does not match any items in Column A. Help students think of a word or phrase that would match it. Ex: **comer una pizza, asistir a un concierto**

1 **Expansion** Have pairs of students write sentences by combining elements from the two columns. Ex: **Sonia está en el Polo Norte y tiene mucho frío. José es una persona muy inteligente pero no tiene razón.**

2 **Expansion** Have students answer questions based on the completed activity. Ex: **¿Qué tienen ellos hoy? ¿Cómo viene el narrador a la reunión? ¿Quién no viene?**

3 **Suggestion** Before doing this activity with the whole class, have students identify which picture is referred to in each of these statements. (Have them answer: **La(s) persona(s) del dibujo número _____.**) Ask: **¿Quién bebe Coca-Cola?** (6), **¿Quién asiste a una fiesta?** (3), **¿Quiénes comen pizza?** (4), **¿Quiénes esperan el autobús?** (5), **¿Quién corre a la oficina?** (1), **¿Quién hace ejercicio en una bicicleta?** (2)

3 **Expansion** Orally give students situations to elicit a response with a **tener** expression. Ex: **Pedro come mucho. ¿Por qué? (Porque tiene hambre.)**

Práctica

1

Emparejar Find the phrase in column B that matches best with the phrase in column A. One phrase in column B will not be used.

A		B
1. el Polo Norte	c	a. tener calor
2. una sauna	a	b. tener sed
3. la comida salada (*salty food*)	b	c. tener frío
4. una persona muy inteligente	d	d. tener razón
5. un abuelo	g	e. tener ganas de
6. una dieta	f	f. tener hambre
		g. tener 75 años

2

Completar Complete the sentences with the forms of **tener** or **venir**.

1. Hoy nosotros ___tenemos___ una reunión familiar (*family reunion*).
2. Yo ___vengo___ en autobús de la Universidad de Quito.
3. Todos mis parientes ___vienen___, excepto mi tío Manolo y su esposa.
4. Ellos no ___tienen___ ganas de venir porque viven en Portoviejo.
5. Mi prima Susana y su novio no ___vienen___ hasta las ocho porque ella ___tiene___ que trabajar.
6. En las fiestas, mi hermana siempre ___viene___ muy tarde.
7. Nosotros ___tenemos___ mucha suerte porque las reuniones son divertidas (*fun*).
8. Mi madre cree que mis sobrinos son muy simpáticos. Creo que ella ___tiene___ razón.

3

Describir Look at the drawings and describe what people are doing using an expression with **tener.**

1. ___Tiene (mucha) prisa.___
2. ___Tiene (mucho) calor.___
3. ___Tiene veintiún años.___
4. ___Tienen (mucha) hambre.___
5. ___Tienen (mucho) frío.___
6. ___Tiene (mucha) sed.___

TEACHING OPTIONS

Extra Practice Create sentences with **tener** and **venir** such as these: **1. Paula y Luis no tienen hambre, pero yo sí ____ mucha hambre. 2. Mis padres vienen del Ecuador, pero mis hermanos y yo ____ de los Estados Unidos. 3. ¿Tienes frío, Marta? Pues, Carlos y yo ____ calor. 4. Enrique viene de la residencia. ¿De dónde ____ tú, Angélica? 5. ¿Ustedes tienen que trabajar hoy? Yo no ____ que trabajar.**

TPR Assign gestures to each expression with **tener**. Ex: **tener calor**: *wipe brow*, **tener cuidado**: *look around suspiciously*, **tener frío**: *wrap arms around oneself and shiver*, **tener miedo**: *hold hand over mouth in fear*. Have students stand. Say an expression at random (**Tienes sueño**) and point at a student who should perform the appropriate gesture. Vary by pointing to more than one student (**Ustedes tienen hambre**).

Comunicación

4 **¿Sí o no?** Using complete sentences, indicate whether these statements apply to you. Answers will vary.

1. Mi padre tiene 50 años.
2. Mis amigos vienen a mi casa todos los días (*every day*).
3. Vengo a la universidad los martes.
4. Tengo hambre.
5. Tengo dos computadoras.
6. Tengo sed.
7. Tengo que estudiar los domingos.
8. Tengo una familia grande.

Now interview a classmate by transforming each statement into a question. Be prepared to report the results of your interview to the class. Answers will vary.

> **modelo**
>
> **Estudiante 1:** ¿Tiene tu padre 50 años?
> **Estudiante 2:** No, no tiene 50 años. Tiene 65.

5 **Preguntas** Get together with a classmate and ask each other these questions. Answers will vary.

1. ¿Tienes que estudiar hoy?
2. ¿Cuántos años tienes? ¿Y tus hermanos/as?
3. ¿Cuándo vienes a la clase de español?
4. ¿Cuándo vienen tus amigos a tu casa, apartamento o residencia estudiantil?
5. ¿De qué tienes miedo? ¿Por qué?
6. ¿Qué tienes ganas de hacer esta noche (*tonight*)?

6 **Conversación** Use an expression with **tener** to hint at what's on your mind. Your partner will ask questions to find out why you feel that way. If your partner cannot guess what's on your mind after three attempts, tell him/her. Then switch roles. Answers will vary.

> **modelo**
>
> **Estudiante 1:** Tengo miedo.
> **Estudiante 2:** ¿Tienes que hablar en público?
> **Estudiante 1:** No.
> **Estudiante 2:** ¿Tienes un examen hoy?
> **Estudiante 1:** Sí, y no tengo tiempo para estudiar.

Síntesis

7 **Minidrama** Act out this situation with a partner: you are introducing your boyfriend/girlfriend to your extended family. To avoid any surprises before you go, talk about who is coming and what each family member is like. Switch roles. Answers will vary.

4 Suggestion Give students three minutes to read the statements. Have them rephrase any statement that does not apply to them so that it does. Ex: **Mi padre tiene 80 años.** Then read the **modelo** and make clear the transformations involved.

5 Suggestion Remind students that each partner should both ask and answer all the questions. Ask volunteers to summarize the responses. Record these responses on the board as a survey (**encuesta**) about the class's characteristics.

6 Suggestion Give an expression with **tener**. (Ex: **Tengo mucha prisa.**) Encourage students to guess the reason using **tener** and **venir**. If they guess incorrectly, give them more specific clues. Ex: **Tengo mucho que hacer hoy. Es un día especial. (Viene un amigo.)**

6 Expansion In pairs, have students use **tener** and **venir** to invent a conversation between the characters in the drawing.

7 Suggestion Before doing **Síntesis**, have students quickly refamiliarize themselves with the following material: family vocabulary on pages 62–63; descriptive adjectives on pages 70–71; possessive adjectives on page 75; and the forms of **tener** and **venir** on page 82.

TEACHING OPTIONS

Small Groups Have small groups prepare skits in which one person takes a few friends to a family reunion. The introducer should make polite introductions and tell the people he or she is introducing a few facts about each other. All the people involved should attempt to make small talk.

Game Give pairs of students five minutes to write a conversation in which they use as many of the expressions with **tener** as they can in a logical manner. After the time is up ask pairs the number of **tener** expressions they used in their conversations. Have the top three or four perform their conversations before the whole class.

Section Goals

In **Lectura** students will:
- learn to use context clues in reading
- read context-rich selections about Hispanic families

Instructional Resource
Companion website:
www.vistahigherlearning.com

Estrategia Tell students that they can often infer the meaning of an unfamiliar Spanish word by looking at the word's context and by using their common sense. Five types of context clues are:
- synonyms
- antonyms
- clarifications
- definitions
- additional details

Have students read the sentence **Ayer fui a ver a mi tía abuela, la hermana de mi abuela** from the letter. Point out that the meaning of **tía abuela** can be inferred from its similarity to the known word **abuela** and from the clarification that follows in the letter.

Examinar el texto Have students read Paragraph 1 silently. Point out the phrase **salgo a pasear** and ask a volunteer to explain how the context might give clues to the meaning. Afterward, point out that **salgo** is the first-person singular form of **salir** (*to go out*). Tell students they will learn all the forms of **salir** in **Lección 4**.

Examinar el formato Guide students to see that the photos and captions reveal that the paragraphs are about several different families.

Lectura

Antes de leer

Estrategia
Guessing meaning from context

As you read in Spanish, you'll often come across words you haven't learned. You can guess what they mean by looking at the surrounding words and sentences. Look at the following text and guess what **tía abuela** means, based on the context.

¡Hola, Claudia!
  ¿Qué hay de nuevo?
¿Sabes qué? Ayer fui a ver a mi tía abuela, la hermana de mi abuela. Tiene 85 años pero es muy independiente. Vive en un apartamento en Quito con su prima Lorena, quien también tiene 85 años.

If you guessed *great-aunt*, you are correct, and you can conclude from this word and the format clues that this is a letter about someone's visit with his or her great-aunt.

Examinar el texto

Quickly read through the paragraphs and find two or three words you don't know. Using the context as your guide, guess what these words mean. Then glance at the paragraphs where these words appear and try to predict what the paragraphs are about.

Examinar el formato

Look at the format of the reading. What clues do the captions, photos, and layout give you about its content?

recursos

vistahigher
learning.com

Gente · · · Las familias

1. Me llamo Armando y tengo setenta años pero no me considero viejo. Tengo seis nietas y un nieto. Vivo con mi hija y tengo la oportunidad de pasar mucho tiempo con ella y con mi nieto. Por las tardes salgo a pasear° por el parque con mi nieto y por la noche le leo cuentos°.

Armando. Tiene seis nietas y un nieto.

2. Mi prima Victoria y yo nos llevamos muy bien. Estudiamos juntas° en la universidad y compartimos un apartamento. Ella es muy inteligente y me ayuda con los estudios. Además, es muy simpática y generosa. Si no tengo dinero°, ¡ella me lo presta!

Diana. Vive con su prima.

3. Me llamo Ramona y soy paraguaya, aunque ahora vivo en los Estados Unidos. Tengo tres hijos, uno de nueve años, uno de doce y el mayor de quince. Es difícil a veces, pero mi esposo y yo tratamos° de ayudarlos y comprenderlos siempre.

Ramona. Sus hijos son muy importantes para ella.

4. Tengo mucha suerte. Aunque° mis padres están divorciados, tengo una familia muy unida. Tengo dos hermanos y dos hermanas. Me gusta hablar y salir a fiestas con ellos. Ahora tengo novio en la universidad y él no conoce a mis hermanos. ¡Espero que se lleven bien!

Ana María.
Su familia es
muy unida.

5. Antes quería° tener hermanos pero ya no es tan importante. Ser hijo único tiene muchas ventajas°:

no tengo que compartir mis cosas con hermanos, no hay discusiones° y, como soy nieto único también, ¡mis abuelos piensan que soy perfecto!

Fernando.
Es hijo único.

6. Como soy joven todavía°, no tengo ni esposa ni hijos. Pero tengo un sobrino, el hijo de mi hermano, que es muy especial para mí. Se llama Benjamín y tiene diez años. Es un muchacho muy simpático. Siempre tiene hambre y por lo tanto vamos frecuentemente a comer hamburguesas. Nos gusta también ir al cine° a ver películas de acción. Hablamos de todo. Creo que ser tío es mejor que ser padre!

Santiago. Ser tío es divertido.

voy a pasear *I go take a walk* cuentos *stories* juntas *together* dinero *money* tratamos *we try* Aunque *Although* quería *I wanted* ventajas *advantages* discusiones *arguments* todavía *still* ir al cine *go to the movies*

Después de leer

Emparejar

Glance at the paragraphs and see how the words and phrases in column A are used in context. Then find their definitions in column B.

A

1. me lo presta   d
2. nos llevamos bien   h
3. no conoce   g
4. películas   b
5. mejor que   j
6. el mayor   a

B

a. the oldest
b. movies
c. the youngest
d. loans it to me
e. borrows it from me
f. we see each other
g. doesn't know
h. we get along
i. portraits
j. better than

Seleccionar

Choose the sentence that best summarizes each paragraph.

1. Párrafo 1 a
   a. Me gusta mucho ser abuelo.
   b. No hablo mucho con mi nieto.
   c. No tengo nietos.
2. Párrafo 2 c
   a. Mi prima es antipática.
   b. Mi prima no es muy trabajadora.
   c. Mi prima y yo somos muy buenas amigas.
3. Párrafo 3 a
   a. Tener hijos es un gran sacrificio pero es muy bonito también.
   b. No comprendo a mis hijos.
   c. Mi esposo y yo no tenemos hijos.
4. Párrafo 4 c
   a. No hablo mucho con mis hermanos.
   b. Comparto mis cosas con mis hermanos.
   c. Mis hermanos y yo somos como (*like*) amigos.
5. Párrafo 5 a
   a. Me gusta ser hijo único.
   b. Tengo hermanos y hermanas.
   c. Vivo con mis abuelos.
6. Párrafo 6 b
   a. Mi sobrino tiene diez años.
   b. Me gusta mucho ser tío.
   c. Mi esposa y yo no tenemos hijos.

Escritura

Estrategia
Writing in Spanish

Why do we write? All writing has a purpose. For example, we may write a poem to reveal our innermost feelings, a letter to impart information, or an essay to persuade others to accept a point of view. Proficient writers are not born, however. Writing requires time, thought, effort, and a lot of practice. Here are some tips to help you write more effectively in Spanish.

DO

▸ Try to write your ideas in Spanish

▸ Use the grammar and vocabulary that you know

▸ Use your textbook for examples of style, format, and expression in Spanish

▸ Use your imagination and creativity

▸ Put yourself in your reader's place to determine if your writing is interesting

AVOID

▸ Translating your ideas from English to Spanish

▸ Simply repeating what is in the textbook or on a web page

▸ Using a dictionary until you have learned how to use foreign language dictionaries

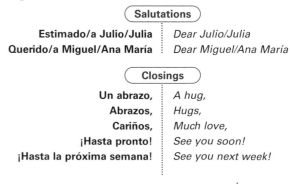

Tema

Escribir una carta

A friend you met in a chat room for Spanish speakers wants to know about your family. Using some of the verbs and adjectives you have learned in this lesson, write a brief letter describing your family or an imaginary family, including:

▸ Names and relationships
▸ Physical characteristics
▸ Hobbies and interests

Here are some useful expressions for letter writing in Spanish:

Salutations	
Estimado/a Julio/Julia	*Dear Julio/Julia*
Querido/a Miguel/Ana María	*Dear Miguel/Ana María*

Closings	
Un abrazo,	*A hug,*
Abrazos,	*Hugs,*
Cariños,	*Much love,*
¡Hasta pronto!	*See you soon!*
¡Hasta la próxima semana!	*See you next week!*

Section Goals

In **Escritura** students will:
• learn to write a friendly letter in Spanish
• integrate vocabulary and structures taught in **Lección 3** and before

Estrategia Go over the dos and don'ts of writing with the class. Explain to students that they can avoid many errors by writing in Spanish rather than translating word for word from English. Emphasize that they should be creative when they write, but that they should also take reasonable risks, using vocabulary and structures they know.

Tema Introduce students to the common salutations (**saludos**) and closings (**despedidas**) used in friendly letters in Spanish. Point out that the salutation **Estimado/a** is more formal than **Querido/a**, which is rather familiar. Also point out that **Un abrazo** is less familiar in Spanish than its translation *a hug* would be in English.

The Affective Dimension Tell the class that they will feel less anxious about writing in a foreign language if they use the strategies and suggestions that appear in each **Escritura** section.

Suggestion Tell students to consult the **Plan de Escritura** in **Apéndice A**, page 448, for step-by-step writing instructions.

Proofreading Activity Copy as many of the following sentences containing mistakes onto the board or a transparency as you think appropriate for a proofreading activity to do with the whole class.
1. **Mis hermana Paula es una persona muy simpático y inteligente.**
2. **Ella es estudiante y asista a clases en una grande universidad.**
3. **Viva en una residencia estudiantil y lea muchos libros.**
4. **Tiene cinco clase y tiene de estudiar mucho.**
5. **A ella le gusta más tu clase de literatura inglésa.**

Escuchar

NATIONAL communication STANDARDS

Estrategia

Asking for repetition/ Replaying the recording

Sometimes it is difficult to understand what people say, especially in a noisy environment. During a conversation, you can ask someone to repeat by saying **¿Cómo?** (*What?*) or **¿Perdón?** (*Pardon me?*). In class, you can ask your teacher to repeat by saying **Repita, por favor** (*Repeat, please*). If you don't understand a recorded activity, you can simply replay it.

🎧 To help you practice this strategy, you will listen to a short paragraph. Ask your professor to repeat it or replay the recording, and then summarize what you heard.

Preparación

Based on the photograph, where do you think Cristina and Laura are? What do you think Laura is saying to Cristina?

Ahora escucha 🎧

Now you are going to hear Laura and Cristina's conversation. Use **R** to indicate which adjectives describe Cristina's boyfriend, Rafael. Use **E** for adjectives that describe Laura's boyfriend, Esteban. Some adjectives will not be used.

____ rubio	_E_ interesante
____ feo	____ antipático
_R_ alto	_R_ inteligente
_E_ trabajador	_R_ moreno
_E_ un poco gordo	____ viejo

Comprensión

Identificar

Which person would make each statement: Cristina or Laura?

	Cristina	Laura
1. Mi novio habla sólo de fútbol y de béisbol.	⊘	○
2. Tengo un novio muy interesante y simpático.	○	⊘
3. Mi novio es alto y moreno.	⊘	○
4. Mi novio trabaja mucho.	○	⊘
5. Mi amiga no tiene buena suerte con los muchachos.	○	⊘
6. El novio de mi amiga es un poco gordo, pero guapo.	⊘	○

¿Cierto o falso?

Indicate whether each sentence is **cierto** or **falso,** then correct the false statements.

	Cierto	Falso
1. Esteban es un chico interesante y simpático.	⊘	○
2. Laura tiene mala suerte con los chicos. Cristina tiene mala suerte con los chicos.	○	⊘
3. Rafael es muy interesante. Esteban es muy interesante.	○	⊘
4. Laura y su novio hablan de muchas cosas.	⊘	○

recursos

TEXT CD Lección 3

Section Goal

In **Panorama**, students will receive comprehensible input by reading about the geography and culture of Ecuador.

Instructional Resources
Transparencies, #5, #6, #18
WB/VM: Workbook, pp. 33–34;
Video Activities, pp. 229–230
***Panorama cultural** DVD/Video*
Interactive CD-ROM
IRM: Videoscript, p. 108;
***Panorama cultural** Translations,*
p. 130
Companion website:
www.vistahigherlearning.com
Presentations CD-ROM

Suggestion Have students look at the map of Ecuador or project **Transparency #18**. Then have them look at the call-out photos and read the captions. Encourage students to mention anything they may know about Ecuador.

El país en cifras

- Ask students to glance at the headings. Establish the kind of information contained in each and clarify unfamiliar words. Point out that every word in the headings has an English cognate.
- Ask volunteers to read the sections. After each section, ask other students questions about the content. Point out that where hundreds, thousands, and millions are separated by commas in English, most Spanish-speaking countries use periods. Model the pronunciation of the numbers.
- Point out that in September 2000 the U.S. dollar became the official currency of Ecuador.

¡Increíble pero cierto!

Mt. St. Helens in Washington and Cotopaxi in Ecuador are just two of a chain of volcanoes that stretches along the entire Pacific coast of North and South America, from Mt. McKinley in Alaska to Monte Sarmiento in Tierra del Fuego of southern Chile.

---

3 panorama

Ecuador

NATIONAL STANDARDS connections cultures

El país en cifras

▶ **Área:** 283.560 km² (109.483 millas²), *incluyendo las islas Galápagos, aproximadamente el área de Colorado*
▶ **Población:** 13.798.000
▶ **Capital:** Quito— 1.832.000
▶ **Ciudades principales:**
  Guayaquil—2.359.000, Cuenca—247.000, Machala—191.000, Portoviejo—164.000

SOURCE: Population Division, UN Secretariat

▶ **Moneda:** dólar estadounidense
▶ **Idiomas:** español (oficial), quichua

La lengua° oficial del Ecuador es el español, pero también se hablan° otras° lenguas en el país. Aproximadamente unos 4.000.000 de ecuatorianos hablan lenguas indígenas; la mayoría° de ellos habla quichua. El quichua es el dialecto ecuatoriano del quechua, la lengua de los incas.

Bandera del Ecuador

Ecuatorianos célebres

▶ **Francisco Eugenio De Santa Cruz y Espejo,** médico, periodista y patriota (1747–1795)
▶ **Juan León Mera,** novelista (1832–1894)
▶ **Eduardo Kingman,** pintor° (1913–1998)
▶ **Rosalía Arteaga,** abogada°, política y ex-vicepresidenta (1956–)

lengua *language* se hablan *are spoken* otras *other* mayoría *majority*
pintor *painter* abogada *lawyer* sur *south* mundo *world* pies *feet*
dos veces más alto *twice as tall*

¡Increíble pero cierto!

El volcán Cotopaxi, situado a unos 60 kilómetros al sur° de Quito, es considerado el volcán activo más alto del mundo°. Tiene una altura de 5.897 metros (19.340 pies°). Es dos veces más alto° que el monte St. Helens (2.550 metros o 9.215 pies) en el estado de Washington.

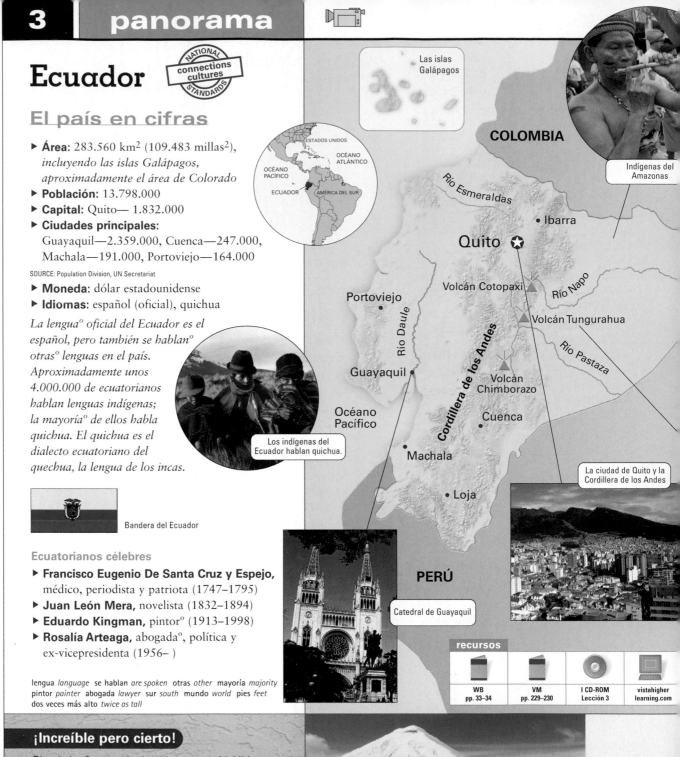

Las islas Galápagos

COLOMBIA

Indígenas del Amazonas

ESTADOS UNIDOS
OCÉANO ATLÁNTICO
OCÉANO PACÍFICO
ECUADOR
AMÉRICA DEL SUR

Río Esmeraldas

• Ibarra

Quito ✪

Portoviejo •

Volcán Cotopaxi
Río Napo

Volcán Tungurahua

Río Daule
Río Pastaza

Cordillera de los Andes

Guayaquil •

Volcán Chimborazo

Cuenca

Océano Pacífico

Los indígenas del Ecuador hablan quichua.

• Machala

La ciudad de Quito y la Cordillera de los Andes

• Loja

PERÚ

Catedral de Guayaquil

recursos

WB pp. 33–34	VM pp. 229–230	I CD-ROM Lección 3	vistahigher learning.com

---

TEACHING OPTIONS

Heritage Speakers If a Spanish speaker has visited Ecuador, ask him or her to prepare a short presentation about his or her experiences there. If possible, the presentation should be illustrated with photos and articles of the country.

Extra Practice Remind students that **km²** is the abbreviation for **kilómetros cuadrados** and that **millas²** is the abbreviation for **millas cuadradas**. Ask a volunteer to explain why **kilómetros** takes **cuadrados** and **millas** takes **cuadradas**.

Lugares • Las islas Galápagos

Muchas personas vienen de lejos a visitar las islas Galápagos porque son un verdadero tesoro° ecológico. Aquí Charles Darwin estudió° las especies que inspiraron° sus ideas sobre la evolución. Como las islas están lejos del continente, sus plantas y animales son únicos. Las islas son famosas por sus tortugas° gigantes.

Artes • Oswaldo Guayasamín

Oswaldo Guayasamín fue° uno de los artistas latinoamericanos más famosos del mundo. Fue escultor° y muralista. Su expresivo estilo viene del cubismo y sus temas preferidos son la injusticia y la pobreza° sufridas° por los indígenas de su país.

Madre y niño en azul,
Oswaldo Guayasamín,1986.

Deportes • El *trekking*

El sistema montañoso de los Andes cruza° y divide el Ecuador en varias regiones. La Sierra, que tiene volcanes, grandes valles y una variedad increíble de plantas y animales, es perfecta para el *trekking*. Muchos turistas visitan el Ecuador cada° año para hacer° *trekking* y escalar montañas°.

Lugares • Latitud 0

Hay un monumento en el Ecuador, a unos 22 kilómetros (14 millas) de Quito, donde los visitantes están en el hemisferio norte y el hemisferio sur a la misma vez°. Este monumento se llama la Mitad del Mundo°, y es un destino turístico muy popular.

Explosión del volcán
Tungurahua en 1999

¿Qué aprendiste? Completa las frases con la información correcta.

1. La ciudad más grande (*biggest*) del Ecuador es ___Guayaquil___.
2. La capital del Ecuador es ___Quito___.
3. Unos 4.000.000 de ecuatorianos hablan ___quichua___.
4. Darwin estudió el proceso de la evolución en ___las islas Galápagos___.
5. Dos temas del arte de ___Guayasamín___ son la pobreza y la ___injusticia___.
6. Un destino turístico muy popular es ___la Mitad del Mundo___.
7. La Sierra es un lugar perfecto para el ___trekking___.
8. El volcán ___Cotopaxi___ es el volcán activo más alto del mundo.

Conexión Internet Investiga estos temas en el sitio **www.vistahigherlearning.com**.

1. Busca información sobre una ciudad del Ecuador.
   ¿Te gustaría (*would you like*) visitar la ciudad? ¿Por qué?
2. Haz una lista de tres animales o plantas que viven sólo en las islas Galápagos.
   ¿Dónde hay animales o plantas similares?

....

verdadero tesoro *true treasure* **estudió** *studied* **inspiraron** *inspired* **tortugas** *tortoises* **fue** *was* **escultor** *sculptor* **pobreza** *poverty* **sufridas** *suffered* **cruza** *crosses* **cada** *every* **hacer** *to do* **escalar montañas** *to climb mountains* **a la misma vez** *at the same time* **Mitad del Mundo** *Equatorial Line Monument (lit. Midpoint of the World)*

Las islas Galápagos Show magazine and book articles that give an idea of the Galapagos Islands.
For more information about **Las Islas Galápagos**, you may want to play the **Panorama cultural** video for this lesson.

Oswaldo Guayasamín (1919–1999) The name **Guayasamín** means *white bird* in Quichua. The artist took this name out of solidarity with his Incan ancestors. Bring reproductions of some of Guayasamín's work to class. Show a variety of his often disturbing paintings and encourage students to talk about what the artist's social and political stance might be.

El *trekking* *Trekking* is one of several English words that have been accepted into Spanish. These words name phenomena whose popularity originated in the English-speaking world. Some words like these enter Spanish without much change: **camping**, **marketing**. Others are changed to match Spanish spelling patterns, as **líder** (*leader*) or **mítin** (*meeting*).

Latitud 0 Bring in a globe and have students find Ecuador and point out its location on the equator.

Conexión Internet Students will find supporting Internet activities and links at **www.vistahigherlearning.com**.

TEACHING OPTIONS

Variación léxica A word that the Quichua language has contributed to English is *jerky* (salted, dried meat), which comes from the Quichua word **charqui**. The Quichua-speaking peoples of the Andean highlands had perfected techniques for "freeze-drying" both vegetable tubers and meat before the first Spaniards arrived in the region. Freeze-dried potatoes, called **chuño**, are a staple in the diet of the inhabitants of the Andes.

In Ecuador and throughout the rest of South America, **charqui** is the word used to name meat preserved by drying. **Charqui** is an important component in the national cuisines of South America, and in Argentina, Uruguay, and Brazil its production is a major industry. In other parts of the Spanish-speaking world you may hear the terms **tasajo** or **carne seca** used instead of **charqui**.

Instructional Resources
Vocabulary CD
Lab Manual, p. 18
Lab CD/MP3 **Lección 3**
IRM: Tapescript, pp. 11–15
Testing Program: ***Pruebas,***
pp. 25–36
Testing Program Audio CD
Test Files CD-ROM
Test Generator

La familia

el/la abuelo/a	grandfather/grandmother
los abuelos	grandparents
el apellido	last name
el/la bisabuelo/a	great-grandfather/great-grandmother
el/la cuñado/a	brother-in-law/sister-in-law
el/la esposo/a	husband; wife; spouse
la familia	family
el/la gemelo/a	twin
el/la hermanastro/a	stepbrother/stepsister
el/la hermano/a	brother/sister
el/la hijastro/a	stepson/stepdaughter
el/la hijo/a	son/daughter
los hijos	children
la madrastra	stepmother
la madre	mother
el/la medio/a hermano/a	half-brother/half-sister
el/la nieto/a	grandson/granddaughter
la nuera	daughter-in-law
el padrastro	stepfather
el padre	father
los padres	parents
los parientes	relatives
el/la primo/a	cousin
el/la sobrino/a	nephew/niece
el/la suegro/a	father-in-law/mother-in-law
el/la tío/a	uncle/aunt
el yerno	son-in-law

Otras personas

el/la amigo/a	friend
la gente	people
el/la muchacho/a	boy/girl
el/la niño/a	child
el/la novio/a	boyfriend/girlfriend
la persona	person

Profesiones

el/la artista	artist
el/la doctor(a), el/la médico/a	doctor; physician
el/la ingeniero/a	engineer
el/la periodista	journalist
el/la programador(a)	computer programmer

Adjetivos

alto/a	tall
antipático/a	unpleasant
bajo/a	short (in height)
bonito/a	pretty
buen, bueno/a	good
delgado/a	thin; slender
difícil	difficult; hard
fácil	easy
feo/a	ugly
gordo/a	fat
gran, grande	big
guapo/a	handsome; good-looking
importante	important
inteligente	intelligent
interesante	interesting
joven	young
mal, malo/a	bad
mismo/a	same
moreno/a	brunet(te)
mucho/a	much; many; a lot of
pelirrojo/a	red-haired
pequeño/a	small
rubio/a	blond(e)
simpático/a	nice; likeable
tonto/a	silly; foolish
trabajador(a)	hard-working
viejo/a	old

Nacionalidades

alemán, alemana	German
canadiense	Canadian
chino/a	Chinese
ecuatoriano/a	Ecuadorian
español(a)	Spanish
estadounidense	from the U. S.
francés, francesa	French
inglés, inglesa	English
italiano/a	Italian
japonés, japonesa	Japanese
mexicano/a	Mexican
norteamericano/a	(North) American
puertorriqueño/a	Puerto Rican
ruso/a	Russian

Verbos

abrir	to open
aprender (a + *inf.*)	to learn
asistir (a)	to attend
beber	to drink
comer	to eat
compartir	to share
comprender	to understand
correr	to run
creer (en)	to believe (in)
deber (+ *inf.*)	should; must
decidir (+ *inf.*)	to decide
describir	to describe
escribir	to write
leer	to read
recibir	to receive
tener	to have
venir	to come
vivir	to live

Possessive adjectives	See page 75.
Expressions with *tener*	See page 83.
Expresiones útiles	See page 67.

recursos

LM p. 18 | Lab CD/MP3 Lección 3 | Vocab CD Lección 3

Los pasatiempos

4

Lesson Goals

In **Lección 4** students will be introduced to the following:
• names of sports and other pastimes
• names of places in a city
• present tense of **ir**
• the contraction **al**
• **ir a** + [*infinitive*]
• present tense of common stem-changing verbs
• verbs with irregular **yo** forms
• predicting content by surveying graphic elements
• cultural, historical, and geographic information about Mexico

A primera vista Here are some additional questions you can ask based on the photo: **¿Te gusta el fútbol? ¿Crees que son importantes los pasatiempos? ¿Trabajas mucho los sábados y domingos? ¿Bailas? ¿Lees? ¿Escuchas música?**

A PRIMERA VISTA
• ¿Qué son estas personas, atletas o artistas?
• ¿En qué tienen interés, en el fútbol o el tenis?
• ¿Son viejos? ¿Son delgados?
• ¿Tienen frío o calor?

INSTRUCTIONAL RESOURCES

Workbook/Video Manual: WB Activities, pp. 37–48
Laboratory Manual: Lab Activities, pp. 19–24
Workbook/Video Manual: Video Activities, pp. 201–202; pp. 231–232
Instructor's Resource Manual: **Hojas de actividades**, p. 143; **Vocabulario adicional**, p. 158; **¡Inténtalo!** & **Práctica** Answers, pp. 176–177; **Fotonovela**

Translations, pp. 120–121; Textbook CD Tapescript, p. 74; Lab CDs Tapescript, pp. 16–19; **Fotonovela** Videoscript, p. 90; **Panorama cultural** Videoscript, p. 109; **Pan. cult.** Translations, p. 131
Info Gap Activities Booklet, pp. 13–16
Overhead Transparencies: #1, #2, #19, #20, #21
Lab Audio CD/MP3 **Lección 4**

Panorama cultural DVD/Video
Fotonovela DVD/Video
Testing Program, pp. 37–48
Testing Program Audio CD
Test Files CD-ROM
Test Generator
Companion website

Presentations CD-ROM
Textbook CD
Vocabulary CD
Interactive CD-ROM
Video CD-ROM
Web-SAM

Section Goals

In **Contextos**, students will learn and practice:
- names of sports, pastimes, and other activities
- names of places in a city

Instructional Resources

Transparencies, #19, #20
Textbook Activities CD
Vocabulary CD
WB/VM: Workbook, pp. 37–38
Lab Manual, p. 19
Lab CD/MP3 **Lección 4**
IRM: **Vocab. adicional**,
p. 158; **Práctica** *Answers,*
p. 176; Tapescript, pp. 16–19;
p. 74
Interactive CD-ROM
Companion website:
www.vistahigherlearning.com
Presentations CD-ROM

Suggestions

- Beginning in English, ask volunteers about sports they may enjoy. Ask: *Who likes to play a sport?* Write **practicar un deporte** on the board and explain what it means. Ask a student who answers: **¿Qué deportes practicas?** Offer some cognates as suggestions: **¿Practicas el béisbol?, ¿el vóleibol?, ¿el tenis?, ¿el golf?** After the student has answered, ask another student: **¿Qué deporte practica ____?**
- Project **Transparency #19**. Have students refer to the scene to answer your true-false questions about it. Ex: **¿Cierto o falso? Dos hombres juegan al baloncesto. (Cierto.) Una chica nada en la piscina. (Falso. Es un chico.)** Next, give names of famous athletes and ask students the sport with which each one is associated.
  Ex: **¿Qué deporte practica Pedro Martínez?**
- Point out that except for the **nosotros/as** and **vosotros/as** forms, all present tense forms of **esquiar** carry an accent over the **i**: **esquío, esquías, esquía, esquían**.

Note: At this point you may want to present **Vocabulario adicional: Más vocabulario para el fin de semana**, from the IRM.

Los pasatiempos

Más vocabulario

el béisbol	*baseball*
el ciclismo	*cycling*
el esquí (acuático)	*(water) skiing*
el fútbol americano	*football*
el golf	*golf*
el hockey	*hockey*
la natación	*swimming*
el tenis	*tennis*
el vóleibol	*volleyball*
el equipo	*team*
el/la excursionista	*hiker*
el parque	*park*
el partido	*game; match*
la plaza	*city or town square*
andar en patineta	*to skateboard*
bucear	*to scuba dive*
escalar montañas	*to climb mountains*
esquiar	*to ski*
ganar	*to win*
ir de excursión (a las montañas)	*to go on a hike (in the mountains)*
practicar deportes (*m. pl.*)	*to play sports*
ser aficionado/a (a)	*to be a fan (of)*
escribir una carta/ un mensaje electrónico/ una (tarjeta) postal	*to write a letter/ an e-mail message/ a postcard*
leer correo electrónico	*to read e-mail*
leer una revista	*to read a magazine*
deportivo/a	*sports-related*

Lee el periódico. (leer)

Pasea en bicicleta. (pasear)

la pelota

el fútbol

la jugadora

Visitan el monumento. (visitar)

Pasean. (pasear)

Toma el sol. (tomar)

Nada. (nadar)

la piscina

PARQUE MUNICIPAL

Variación léxica

piscina ⟷ pileta (*Arg.*); alberca (*Méx.*)
baloncesto ⟷ básquetbol (*Amér. L.*)
béisbol ⟷ pelota (*P. Rico, Rep. Dom.*)

recursos

| TEXT CD Lección 4 | WB pp. 37–38 | LM p. 19 | Lab CD/MP3 Lección 4 | I CD-ROM Lección 4 | Vocab CD Lección 4 |

TEACHING OPTIONS

Game Have students work in pairs. Ask each to write down in Spanish his or her three favorite sports or leisure activities. Each student shares his or her information with the other, who must remember what his or her partner has said without writing it down. With the whole class, ask students to report their partners' activities. The partner confirms whether all three reported activities were correct or not.

Variación léxica Point out that many sports in Spanish are referred to by names derived from English (**básquetbol, béisbol, fútbol**), including many in **Más vocabulario**: **el golf, el hockey, el vóleibol**. Ask students to guess the meaning of these activities (be sure to use Spanish pronunciation): **el footing** (*jogging*), **el camping, el surf(ing), el windsurf**.

Práctica

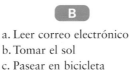

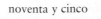

1 Escuchar Indicate the letter of the activity in Column B that best corresponds to each statement you hear. Two items in Column B will not be used.

A	B
1. __b__	a. Leer correo electrónico
2. __d__	b. Tomar el sol
3. __f__	c. Pasear en bicicleta
4. __c__	d. Ir a un partido de fútbol americano
5. __g__	e. Escribir una tarjeta postal
6. __h__	f. Practicar muchos deportes
	g. Nadar
	h. Ir de excursión a las montañas

2 ¿Cierto o falso? Indicate whether each statement is **cierto** or **falso** based on the illustration.

	Cierto	Falso
1. Un hombre nada en la piscina.	☑	○
2. Un hombre lee una revista.	○	☑
3. Un chico pasea en bicicleta.	☑	○
4. Hay un partido de baloncesto en el parque.	☑	○
5. Dos muchachos esquían.	○	☑
6. Dos mujeres practican el golf.	○	☑
7. Una mujer y dos niños visitan un monumento.	☑	○
8. Un hombre bucea.	○	☑
9. Hay un excursionista.	○	☑
10. Una mujer toma el sol.	☑	○

tina en línea.
(patinar)

el jugador

el baloncesto

3 Clasificar Fill in the chart below with as many terms from **Contextos** as you can.
Answers will vary.

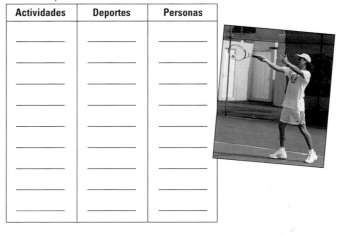

Actividades	Deportes	Personas
_____	_____	_____
_____	_____	_____
_____	_____	_____
_____	_____	_____
_____	_____	_____
_____	_____	_____
_____	_____	_____
_____	_____	_____

---

1 Suggestion Have students check their answers by going over **Actividad 1** with the whole class.

1 Tapescript 1. No me gusta nadar pero paso mucho tiempo al lado de la piscina. 2. Alicia y yo vamos al estadio a las cuatro. Creemos que nuestro equipo va a ganar. 3. Me gusta patinar en línea, esquiar y practicar el tenis. 4. El ciclismo es mi deporte favorito. 5. Me gusta mucho la natación. Paso mucho tiempo en la piscina. 6. Mi hermana es una gran excursionista.
Textbook Activities CD

2 Expansion Ask students to write three additional true-false statements based on the drawing. Ask volunteers to read their sentences aloud. The rest of the class indicates whether the statements are true or false.

3 Expansion Ask students to provide complete sentences based on the categories. You may wish to cue them to create different responses. Ex: **¿Qué es la natación? (La natación es un deporte.) ¿Dónde nadan las personas? (Nadan en una piscina.)**

Extra Practice Narrate a brief series of activities you want or need to do. Students have to guess the place to which you will have to go. Ex: **Necesito estudiar en un lugar tranquilo. También deseo leer una revista y unos periódicos. ¿Adónde voy?** (Write on board and explain meaning of **voy**.) **(la biblioteca)**

Game Play a modified version of Twenty Questions. Ask a volunteer to think of a sport, activity, person, or place (the item must come from the vocabulary drawing or list). Other students get one chance each to ask a yes-no question until someone guesses the item correctly. Limit attempts to ten questions per item. You may want to write some phrases on the board to cue students' questions.

el cine

el museo

el gimnasio

el restaurante

el café

En el centro

4 Identificar Identify the place where these activities would take place.

modelo
Esquiamos.
Es una montaña.

1. Tomamos una limonada. Es un café./Es un restaurante.
2. Vemos una película. Es un cine.
3. Nadamos y tomamos el sol. Es una piscina./Es un parque.
4. Hay muchos monumentos. Es un parque./Es una ciudad.
5. Comemos tacos y fajitas. Es un restaurante.
6. Miramos pinturas (*paintings*) de Diego Rivera y Frida Kahlo. Es un museo.
7. Hay mucho tráfico. Es una ciudad./Es el centro.
8. Practicamos deportes. Es un gimnasio./Es un parque.

Más vocabulario

la diversión	fun activity; entertainment; recreation
el fin de semana	weekend
el pasatiempo	pastime; hobby
los ratos libres	spare (free) time
el tiempo libre	free time
la iglesia	church
el lugar	place
pasar tiempo	to spend time
pasear por la ciudad/el pueblo	to walk around the city/the town
ver películas (*f. pl.*)	to see movies
favorito/a	favorite

5 Entrevista In pairs, take turns asking each other and answering the questions.

1. ¿Hay un café cerca de la universidad? ¿Dónde está? Answers will vary.
2. ¿Cuál es tu restaurante favorito?
3. ¿Te gusta viajar y visitar monumentos? ¿Por qué?
4. ¿Te gusta ir al cine los fines de semana?
5. ¿Cuáles son tus películas favoritas?
6. ¿Te gusta practicar deportes?
7. ¿Cuáles son tus deportes favoritos? ¿Por qué?
8. ¿Cuáles son tus pasatiempos favoritos?

CONSÚLTALO

To review expressions with **gustar**, see **Lección 2, Expresiones útiles**, p. 37.

UN DÍA CON ÁNGELA

Un día inolvidable.

Comunicación

6 **Preguntar** Ask a classmate what he or she does in the places mentioned below. Your classmate will respond using verbs from the word bank. Answers will vary.

> **modelo**
> un pueblo interesante
> **Estudiante 1:** ¿Qué haces *(do you do)* cuando estás en un pueblo interesante?
> **Estudiante 2:** Paseo por el pueblo y busco lugares bonitos.

beber	leer	patinar
correr	mirar	practicar
escalar	nadar	tomar
escribir	pasear	visitar

1. una biblioteca
2. un estadio
3. una plaza
4. una piscina
5. las montañas
6. un parque
7. un café
8. un museo

7 **Conversación** Using the words and expressions provided, work with a partner to prepare a short conversation about your pastimes. Answers will vary.

> **modelo**
> **Estudiante 1:** ¿Cuándo patinas en línea?
> **Estudiante 2:** Patino en línea los domingos. Y tú, ¿patinas en línea?
> **Estudiante 1:** No, no me gusta patinar en línea. Me gusta practicar el béisbol.

¿a qué hora?	¿cuándo?	¿qué?
¿cómo?	¿dónde?	¿con quién(es)?

8 **Pasatiempos** In pairs, tell each other what pastimes three of your friends and family members enjoy. Be prepared to share with the class any pastimes you noticed they have in common. Answers will vary.

> **modelo**
> **Estudiante 1:** Mi hermana pasea mucho en bicicleta. Pero mis padres practican la natación. Mi hermano no nada, pero visita muchos museos.
> **Estudiante 2:** Mi primo lee muchas revistas, pero no practica muchos deportes. Mis tíos esquían y practican el golf...

---

6 Suggestion Quickly review some of the verbs listed. Make sure students understand the meaning of **¿Qué haces... ?** and that they will use it throughout the activity.

6 Expansion
- Ask additional questions and have volunteers answer. Ex: **¿Qué haces en la residencia estudiantil (el apartamento, la casa)?** Suggested places: **la casa de un amigo/una amiga, el centro de la ciudad, el gimnasio**
- Have students share their responses with the class. Then have them create a table based on the responses. Ex: **En la biblioteca: yo (leo, trabajo en la computadora)**

7 Suggestion Remind students of the forms of **gustar** that they learned in **Lección 2 Expresiones útiles**, page 37.

7 Expansion After students have asked and answered questions, ask volunteers to report their partners' activities back to the class. The partner should verify whether the information is correct.

8 Expansion
- Ask volunteers to share any pastimes they and their partners, friends, and families have in common. Ask for a show of hands to find out which activities are most popular and where they do them. What are the general tendencies of the class?
- In pairs, have students write sentences about the pastimes of a famous person. Then have them work with another pair who will guess who is the famous person being described.

TEACHING OPTIONS

Extra Practice On a sheet of paper, students write down six activities they like to do. Then they circulate around the room trying to find other students who also like to do those activities (**¿Te gusta... ?**). Once a student finds someone that shares a particular activity in common, he or she asks that student to sign his or her name (**Firma aquí, por favor.**). How many signatures can each student collect?

Game On a slip of paper, each student writes down the one activity that best corresponds to him or her without writing down his or her name. Collect the slips of paper and mix them up in a hat. Pull out each slip of paper and read the activity. The rest of the class has to guess who the student is. If a particular activity corresponds to more than one student, ask them to elaborate: With whom do they do the activity? Where? When?

Section Goals

In **Fotonovela** students will:
- receive comprehensible input from free-flowing discourse
- learn functional phrases for making invitations and plans, talking about pastimes, and apologizing

Instructional Resources
WB/VM: Video Activities, pp. 201–202
***Fotonovela** DVD/Video (Start 00:17:00)*
***Fotonovela** Video CD-ROM*
*IRM: **Fotonovela** Translations, pp. 120–121, Videoscript, p. 90*
Interactive CD-ROM

Video Recap: Lección 3
Before doing this **Fotonovela** section, review the previous one with this activity.
1. _____ tiene una familia grande. (Inés)
2. El _____ de Javier es viejo y trabajador. (abuelo)
3. _____ no tiene hermanos. (Javier)
4. Inés tiene _____ hermanas. (cuatro)

Video Synopsis The travelers have an hour to explore the city before heading to the cabins. Javier and Inés decide to stroll around the city. Álex and Maite go to the park. While Maite writes postcards, Álex and a young man play soccer. A stray ball hits Maite. Álex and Maite return to the bus, and Álex invites her to go running with him that evening.

Suggestions

- Have students quickly glance over the **Fotonovela** and make a list of the cognates they find. Then, have them guess what this episode is about.
- Have students tell you a few expressions used to talk about pastimes. Then ask a few questions. Ex: **¿Eres aficionado/a a un deporte? ¿Te gusta el fútbol?**

¡Vamos al parque!

Los estudiantes pasean por la ciudad y hablan de sus pasatiempos.

PERSONAJES

DON FRANCISCO

JAVIER

INÉS

ÁLEX

MAITE

JOVEN

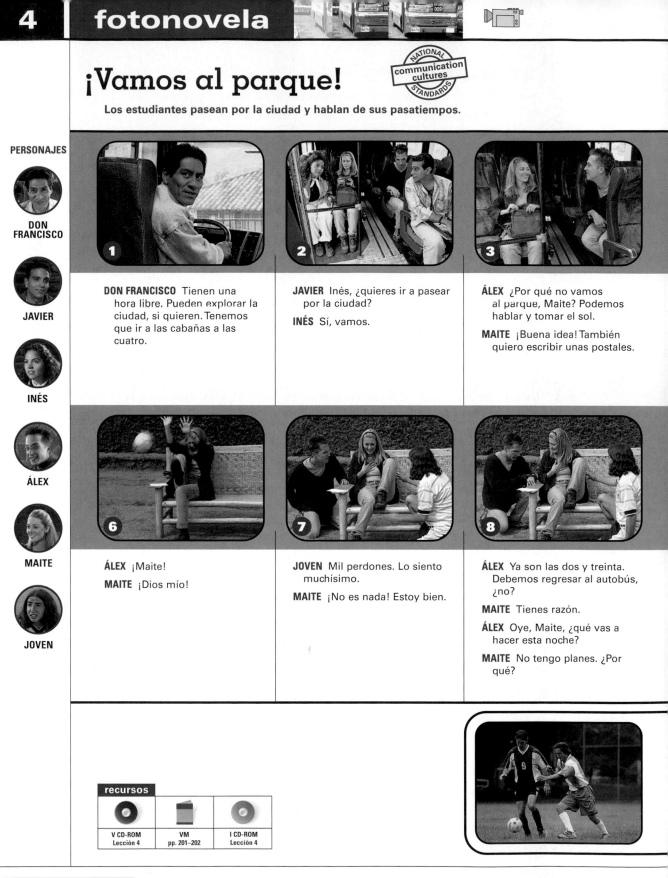

DON FRANCISCO Tienen una hora libre. Pueden explorar la ciudad, si quieren. Tenemos que ir a las cabañas a las cuatro.

JAVIER Inés, ¿quieres ir a pasear por la ciudad?
INÉS Sí, vamos.

ÁLEX ¿Por qué no vamos al parque, Maite? Podemos hablar y tomar el sol.
MAITE ¡Buena idea! También quiero escribir unas postales.

ÁLEX ¡Maite!
MAITE ¡Dios mío!

JOVEN Mil perdones. Lo siento muchísimo.
MAITE ¡No es nada! Estoy bien.

ÁLEX Ya son las dos y treinta. Debemos regresar al autobús, ¿no?
MAITE Tienes razón.
ÁLEX Oye, Maite, ¿qué vas a hacer esta noche?
MAITE No tengo planes. ¿Por qué?

recursos

| V CD-ROM Lección 4 | VM pp. 201–202 | I CD-ROM Lección 4 |

Suggestion Have the class read through the entire **Fotonovela**, with volunteers playing the parts of Don Francisco, Javier, Inés, Álex, Maite, and the **Joven**. Have students take turns playing the roles so that more participate.

Expresiones útiles Point out the written accents in the words **¿qué?, ¿por qué?,** and **también**. Explain that accents indicate a stressed syllable in a word (**también**) and that all question words have accent marks. Then mention that **voy, vas, va,** and **vamos** are present-tense forms of the verb **ir**. Point out that **ir a** is used with an infinitive to tell what is going to happen. Ask: **¿Qué vas a hacer esta noche? ¿Por qué no vamos al parque?** Explain that **quiero, quieres,** and **siento** are forms of **querer** and **sentir**, which undergo a stem change from **e** to **ie** in certain forms. Tell your students that they will learn more about these concepts in **Estructura**.

MAITE ¿Eres aficionado a los deportes, Álex?

ÁLEX Sí, me gusta mucho el fútbol. Me gusta también nadar, correr e ir de excursión a las montañas.

MAITE Yo también corro mucho.

ÁLEX Oye, Maite, ¿por qué no jugamos al fútbol con él?

MAITE Mmm... no quiero. Voy a terminar de escribir unas postales.

ÁLEX Eh, este... a veces salgo a correr por la noche. ¿Quieres venir a correr conmigo?

MAITE Sí, vamos. ¿A qué hora?

ÁLEX ¿A las seis?

MAITE Perfecto.

DON FRANCISCO Esta noche van a correr. ¡Y yo no tengo energía para pasear!

Enfoque cultural El fútbol

Soccer, or **fútbol,** is the most popular spectator sport and the most widely played team game in the world. It is also the most popular sport in the Spanish-speaking world. People of all ages can be seen playing soccer in public parks and streets, and each country has a professional league with its own stars. Juan Ramón Riquelme from Argentina, Marcelo Salas from Chile, and Francisco Palencia from Mexico are among the most famous contemporary Hispanic soccer players.

Expresiones útiles

Making invitations

▶ **¿Por qué no vamos al parque?**
Why don't we go to the park?
▷ **¡Buena idea!**
Good idea!
▶ **¿Por qué no jugamos al fútbol?**
Why don't we play soccer?
▷ **Mmm... no quiero.**
Hmm... I don't want to.
▷ **Lo siento, pero no puedo.**
I'm sorry, but I can't.

▶ **¿Quieres ir a pasear por la ciudad conmigo?**
Do you want to walk around the city with me?
▷ **Sí, vamos.**
Yes, let's go.
▷ **Sí, si tenemos tiempo.**
Yes, if we have time.

Making plans

▶ **¿Qué vas a hacer esta noche?**
What are you going to do tonight?
▷ **No tengo planes.**
I don't have any plans.
▷ **Voy a terminar de escribir unas postales.**
I'm going to finish writing some postcards.

Talking about pastimes

▶ **¿Eres aficionado/a a los deportes?**
Are you a sports fan?
▷ **Sí, me gustan todos los deportes.**
Yes, I like all sports.
▷ **Sí, me gusta mucho el fútbol.**
Yes, I like soccer a lot.

▶ **Me gusta también nadar, correr e ir de excursión a las montañas.**
I also like to swim, run, and go hiking in the mountains.
▷ **Yo también corro mucho.**
I also run a lot.

Apologizing

▶ **Mil perdones./Lo siento muchísimo.**
I'm so sorry.

TEACHING OPTIONS

Enfoque cultural Tell the class that children—generally boys—in Spanish-speaking countries often take up soccer at a very early age, playing on pick-up soccer teams in their neighborhoods. Many people continue to participate as players or spectators in local soccer clubs through adulthood. Explain that nearly every town or city has its own club and that larger cities have professional clubs that may be well-known throughout the nation. Team rivalries can be fierce. Mention that excitement about soccer often rises to a fever pitch every four years during the **Copa Mundial** (*World Cup*), which is the sport's international championship. At that time, top-notch professional players, who may be members of teams in other countries, form national teams to compete with other national teams. Spanish-speaking countries have competed regularly in the World Cup, which was first played in Uruguay in 1930.

Reacciona a la fotonovela

1

Escoger Choose the answer that best completes each sentence.

1. Inés y Javier ___b___.
   a. toman el sol b. pasean por la ciudad c. corren por el parque

2. Álex desea ___a___ en el parque.
   a. hablar y tomar el sol b. hablar y leer el periódico c. nadar y tomar el sol

3. A Álex le gusta nadar, ___c___.
   a. jugar al fútbol y escribir postales b. escalar montañas y esquiar
   c. ir de excursión y correr

4. A Maite le gusta ___b___.
   a. nadar y correr b. correr y escribir postales c. correr y jugar al fútbol

5. Maite desea ___c___.
   a. ir de excursión b. jugar al fútbol c. ir al parque

2

Identificar Identify the person who would make each statement.

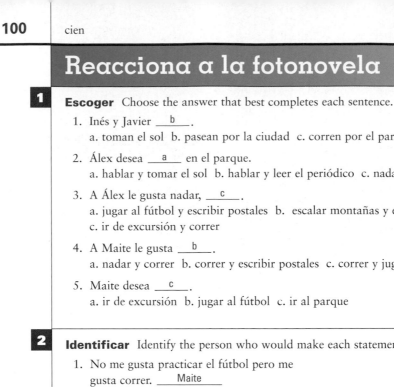

1. No me gusta practicar el fútbol pero me gusta correr. ___Maite___

2. ¿Por qué no vamos a pasear por la ciudad? ___Javier___

3. ¿Por qué no exploran ustedes la ciudad? Tienen tiempo. ___don Francisco___

4. ¿Por qué no corres conmigo esta noche? ___Álex___

5. No voy al parque. Prefiero estar con mi amigo. ___Inés___

JAVIER

INÉS

MAITE

ÁLEX

DON FRANCISCO

3

Preguntas Answer the questions using the information from the **Fotonovela**.

1. ¿Qué desean hacer Inés y Javier?
   Desean pasear por la ciudad.
2. ¿Qué desea hacer Álex en el parque?
   Desea jugar al fútbol.
3. ¿Qué desea hacer Maite en el parque?
   Maite desea escribir postales./Maite desea terminar de escribir unas postales.
4. ¿Qué deciden hacer Maite y Álex esta noche?
   Deciden ir a correr.

4

Conversación With a partner, prepare a conversation in which you talk about pastimes and invite each other to do some activity together. Use these expressions:

Answers will vary.

▶ ¿Eres aficionado/a a...?
▶ ¿Te gusta...?
▶ ¿Qué vas a hacer esta noche?
▶ ¿Por qué no...?
▶ ¿Quieres... conmigo?

AYUDA

contigo *with you*
¿A qué hora? *(At) What time?*
¿Dónde? *Where?*
No puedo porque... *I can't because...*
Nos vemos a las siete. *See you at seven.*

Pronunciación 🎧

Word stress and accent marks

pe-lí-cu-la	e-di-fi-cio	ver	yo

Every Spanish syllable contains at least one vowel. When two vowels (two weak vowels or one strong and one weak) are joined in the same syllable they form a **diphthong**. A **monosyllable** is a word formed by a single syllable.

bi-blio-te-ca	vi-si-tar	par-que	fút-bol

The syllable of a Spanish word that is pronounced most emphatically is the "stressed" syllable.

pe-lo-ta	pis-ci-na	ra-tos	ha-blan

Words that end in **n**, **s**, or a **vowel** are usually stressed on the next to last syllable.

na-ta-ción	pa-pá	in-glés	Jo-sé

If words that end in **n**, **s**, or a **vowel** are stressed on the last syllable, they must carry an accent mark on the stressed syllable.

bai-lar	es-pa-ñol	u-ni-ver-si-dad	tra-ba-ja-dor

Words that do *not* end in **n**, **s**, or a **vowel** are usually stressed on the last syllable.

béis-bol	lá-piz	ár-bol	Gó-mez

If words that do *not* end in **n**, **s**, or a **vowel** are stressed on the next to last syllable, they must carry an accent mark on the stressed syllable.

En la unión está la fuerza.²

Práctica Pronounce each word, stressing the correct syllable. Then give the word stress rule for each word.

1. profesor
2. Puebla
3. ¿Cuántos?
4. Mazatlán
5. examen
6. ¿Cómo?
7. niños
8. Guadalajara
9. programador
10. México
11. están
12. geografía

Oraciones Read the conversation aloud to practice word stress.

MARINA Hola, Carlos. ¿Qué tal?
CARLOS Bien. Oye, ¿a qué hora es el partido de fútbol?
MARINA Creo que es a las siete.
CARLOS ¿Quieres ir?
MARINA Lo siento, pero no puedo.
Tengo que estudiar biología.

Quien ríe de último, ríe mejor.¹

Refranes Read these sayings aloud to practice word stress.

¹ He who laughs last, laughs longest.
² United we stand.

recursos

TEXT CD Lección 4	LM p. 20	Lab CD/MP3 Lección 4	I CD-ROM Lección 4

In **Estructura 4.1**, students will learn:
• the present tense of **ir**
• the contraction **al**
• **ir a** + [*infinitive*] to express future events
• **vamos a** to express *Let's ...*

Instructional Resources
WB/VM: Workbook, pp. 39–40
Lab Manual, p. 21
Lab CD/MP3 Lección 4
IRM: ¡Inténtalo! & Práctica
Answers, pp. 176–177;
Tapescript, pp. 16–19;
***Hojas de actividades**, p. 143*
Info Gap Activities Booklet,
pp. 13–14
Interactive CD-ROM
Companion website:
www.vistahigherlearning.com
Presentations CD-ROM

Suggestions
• Write your next day's schedule on the board, mixing infinitives with nouns. Ex: **8:00—la biblioteca; 12:00—comer.** Explain what you are going to do using the verb **ir.** Ask volunteers questions about their schedules using forms of **ir.**
• Ask individuals questions about their future plans using **ir.** Ex: **¿Adónde vas el sábado? ¿Cuándo vas a viajar a México?** Point out the difference in usage between **dónde** and **adónde.** Ex: **¿Dónde está la casa de los Franco? ¿Adónde va José Franco?**
• After you have presented the use of **ir** to express the idea of *let's,* ask volunteers to respond to your prompts with suggestions of things to do. Ex: **Tengo hambre. (Vamos a la cafetería.) Quiero ver una buena película. (Vamos al cine.)**

4.1 Present tense of **ir**

ANTE TODO The verb **ir** (*to go*) is irregular in the present tense. Note that, except for the **yo** form (**voy**) and the lack of a written accent on the **vosotros** form (**vais**), the endings are the same as those for **–ar** verbs.

ir

Singular forms		Plural forms	
yo	**voy**	nosotros/as	**vamos**
tú	**vas**	vosotros/as	**vais**
Ud./él/ella	**va**	Uds./ellos/ellas	**van**

▶ **Ir** is often used with the preposition **a** (*to*). If **a** is followed by the definite article **el**, they combine to form the contraction **al**. If **a** is followed by the other definite articles (**la, las, los**), there is no contraction.

$$a + el = al$$

Voy **al** parque con Juan.
I'm going to the park with Juan.

Los excursionistas van **a las** montañas.
The hikers are going to the mountains.

▶ The construction **ir a** + [*infinitive*] is used to talk about actions that are going to happen in the future. It is equivalent to the English *to be going to* + [*infinitive*].

Va a leer el periódico.
He is going to read the newspaper.

Van a pasear por el pueblo.
They are going to walk around town.

Voy a escribir unas postales.

Álex y Maite van a volver al autobús.

▶ **Vamos a** + [*infinitive*] can also express the idea of *let's (do something)*.

Vamos a pasear.
Let's take a stroll.

¡Vamos a ver!
Let's see!

¡INTÉNTALO! Provide the present tense forms of **ir.** The first item has been done for you.

1. Ellos ___van___.
2. Yo ___voy___.
3. Tu novio ___va___.
4. Adela ___va___.
5. Mi prima y yo ___vamos___.
6. Tú ___vas___.
7. Ustedes ___van___.
8. Nosotros ___vamos___.
9. Usted ___va___.
10. Nosotras ___vamos___.
11. Miguel ___va___.
12. Ellos ___van___.

recursos

WB
pp. 39–46

LM
pp. 21–24

Lab CD/MP3
Lección 4

I CD-ROM
Lección 4

vistahigher learning.com

CONSÚLTALO
To review the contraction **de + el**, see **Estructura 1.3**, pp. 18–19.

¡ATENCIÓN!
Remember to use **adónde** instead of **dónde** when asking a question that contains a form of the verb **ir:**
¿Adónde vas?
(To) Where are you going?

TEACHING OPTIONS

TPR Invent gestures to pantomime activities mentioned in **Lección 4**. Ex: **poner la televisión** (press the button on a remote control), **patinar** (skate), **nadar** (move arms as if swimming). Signal individuals to gesture appropriately as you cue activities with **Vamos a...** . Keep the pace brisk.
Heritage Speakers Have heritage speakers make a list of public or commercial places where people go in their home country.

Have them write these names on the board and explain their meaning to the class.
Extra Practice To provide oral practice with the verb **ir**, provide prompts similar to those in **¡Inténtalo!** Say the subject and the verb, have students repeat it, then say a different subject, varying the gender and number. Have students then say the phrase with the new subject, changing the verb as necessary.

Práctica

1

¿Adónde van? Everyone in your neighborhood is dashing off to various places. Say where they are going.

1. la señora Castillo / el centro La señora Castillo va al centro.
2. las hermanas Gómez / la piscina Las hermanas Gómez van a la piscina.
3. tu tío y tu papá / el partido de fútbol Tu tío y tu papá van al partido de fútbol.
4. yo / el Museo de Arte Moderno (Yo) Voy al Museo de Arte Moderno.
5. nosotros / el restaurante Miramar (Nosotros) Vamos al restaurante Miramar.

2

¿Qué van a hacer? These sentences describe what several students in a college hiking club are doing today. Use **ir a** + [*infinitive*] to say that they are also going to do the same activities tomorrow.

> **modelo**
> Martín y Rodolfo nadan en la piscina.
> *Van a nadar en la piscina mañana también.*

1. Sara lee una revista. Va a leer una revista mañana también.
2. Yo practico deportes. Voy a practicar deportes mañana también.
3. Ustedes van de excursión. Van a ir de excursión mañana también.
4. El presidente del club patina. Va a patinar mañana también.
5. Tú tomas el sol. Vas a tomar el sol mañana también.
6. Paseamos con nuestros amigos. Vamos a pasear con nuestros amigos mañana también.

3

Preguntas With a partner, take turns asking and answering questions about where the people are going and what they are going to do there. Some answers will vary.

> **modelo**
> **Estudiante 1:** ¿Adónde va Estela?
> **Estudiante 2:** Va a la Librería Sol.
> **Estudiante 1:** Va a comprar un libro.

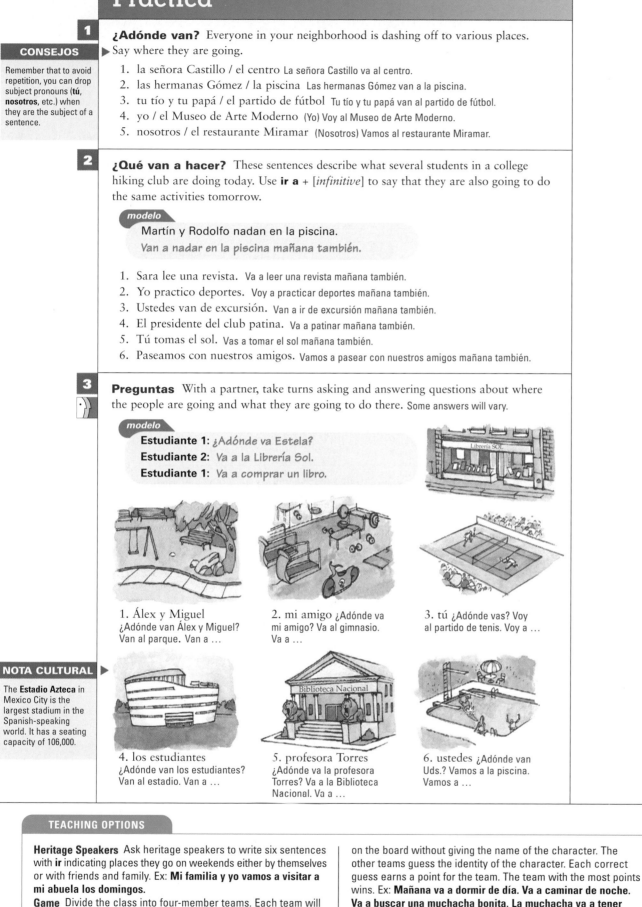

1. Álex y Miguel ¿Adónde van Álex y Miguel? Van al parque. Van a …
2. mi amigo ¿Adónde va mi amigo? Va al gimnasio. Va a …
3. tú ¿Adónde vas? Voy al partido de tenis. Voy a …
4. los estudiantes ¿Adónde van los estudiantes? Van al estadio. Van a …
5. profesora Torres ¿Adónde va la profesora Torres? Va a la Biblioteca Nacional. Va a …
6. ustedes ¿Adónde van Uds.? Vamos a la piscina. Vamos a …

4 Expansion Have students convert the dependent clause to its negative form and create a new independent clause. Ex: **Cuando no deseo descansar, voy al gimnasio.**

5 Suggestion Model turning the first phrase into a question. Ex: **¿Vas a comer en un restaurante chino hoy?** Then distribute the **Hojas de actividades** from the IRM that correspond to this activity. Give students five minutes to fill out the surveys.

5 Expansion After collecting the surveys, ask individuals about their plans. Ex: If someone's name appears by **ver una película**, ask him or her: **¿Qué película vas a ver hoy?**

6 Suggestion Have each student use an idea map to brainstorm a trip he or she would like to take. Write **lugar** in the central circle and in surrounding circles write: **visitar**, **deportes**, **otras actividades**, **comida**, **compañeros/as**.

7 Suggestions
• Brainstorm useful expressions with your students before beginning the activity. Ex: —**¿Quieres jugar al tenis conmigo?** —**Lo siento, pero no puedo./Sí, vamos.**
• Have students make two columns on a sheet of paper. The first one should be headed **El fin de semana tengo que...** and the other **El fin de semana deseo...** Give students a few minutes to brainstorm about their activities for the weekend.

Suggestion See the Information Gap Activities Booklet for an additional activity to practice the material presented in this section.

Comunicación

4 Situaciones Work with a partner and say where you and your friends go in the following situations. Answers will vary.

1. Cuando deseo descansar…
2. Cuando mi novio/a tiene que estudiar…
3. Si mis compañeros de clase necesitan practicar el español…
4. Si deseo hablar con unos amigos…
5. Cuando tengo dinero (*money*)…
6. Cuando mis amigos y yo tenemos hambre…
7. Si tengo tiempo libre…
8. Cuando mis amigos desean esquiar…
9. Si estoy de vacaciones…
10. Si quiero leer…

5 Encuesta Your instructor will give you a worksheet. Walk around the class and ask your classmates if they are going to do these activities today. Find one person to answer **Sí** and one to answer **No** for each item and note their names on the worksheet in the appropriate column. Be prepared to report your findings to the class.
Answers will vary.

modelo
Tú: ¿Vas a leer el periódico hoy?
Ana: Sí, voy a leer el periódico hoy.
Luis: No, no voy a leer el periódico hoy.

Actividades	Sí	No
1. Comer en un restaurante chino		
2. Leer el periódico		
3. Escribir un mensaje electrónico	Ana	Luis
4. Correr 20 kilómetros		
5. Ver una película de horror		
6. Pasear en bicicleta		

6 Entrevista Interview two classmates to find out where they are going and what they are going to do on their next vacation. Answers will vary.

modelo
Estudiante 1: ¿Adónde vas de vacaciones (*for vacation*)?
Estudiante 2: Voy a Guadalajara con mis amigos.
Estudiante 1: ¿Y qué van a hacer (*to do*) ustedes en Guadalajara?
Estudiante 2: Vamos a visitar unos monumentos y museos.

Síntesis

7 El fin de semana Create a schedule with your activities for this weekend. Answers will vary.
▶ For each day, list at least three things you have to do.
▶ For each day, list at least two things you will do for fun.
▶ Tell a classmate what your weekend schedule is like. He or she will write down what you say.
▶ Switch roles to see if you have any plans in common.
▶ Take turns asking each other to participate in some of the activities you listed.

TEACHING OPTIONS

Pairs Divide the class into pairs. Have the members of each pair take turns reading a time which you write on the board and making a suggestion of something to do. Ex: Write: **12:00.** **E1: Son las doce en punto. E2: Vamos a la cafetería.** Write: **12:45. E2: Es la una menos quince. E1: Vamos a la biblioteca.**
Game Divide the class into teams of three. Each team has a piece of paper on which to write the answers. Name a category.

Ex: **lugares públicos.** The first team member will write one answer and pass the paper to the next person. The paper will continue to circulate for two minutes. The team with the most words wins.
Video Show the **Fotonovela** video again to give students more input containing the verb **ir.** Stop the video where appropriate to discuss how **ir** is used to express different ideas.

4.2 Stem-changing verbs: e→ie, o→ue

comparisons NATIONAL STANDARDS

CONSÚLTALO

To review the present tense of regular –ar verbs, see **Estructura 2.1**, p. 40.

• • •

To review the present tense of regular –er and –ir verbs, see **Estructura 3.3**, p. 78.

ANTE TODO Stem-changing verbs deviate from the normal pattern of regular verbs. In stem-changing verbs, the stressed vowel of the stem changes when the verb is conjugated.

INFINITIVE	VERB STEM	STEM CHANGE	CONJUGATED FORM
empezar	emp**ez**-	emp**iez**-	emp**ie**zo
volver	v**o**lv-	v**ue**lv-	v**ue**lvo

▶ In many verbs, such as **empezar** *(to begin)*, the stem vowel changes from **e** to **ie**. Note that the **nosotros/as** and **vosotros/as** forms don't have a stem change.

empezar (e:ie)

Singular forms		Plural forms	
yo	emp**ie**zo	nosotros/as	empezamos
tú	emp**ie**zas	vosotros/as	empezáis
Ud./él/ella	emp**ie**za	Uds./ellos/ellas	emp**ie**zan

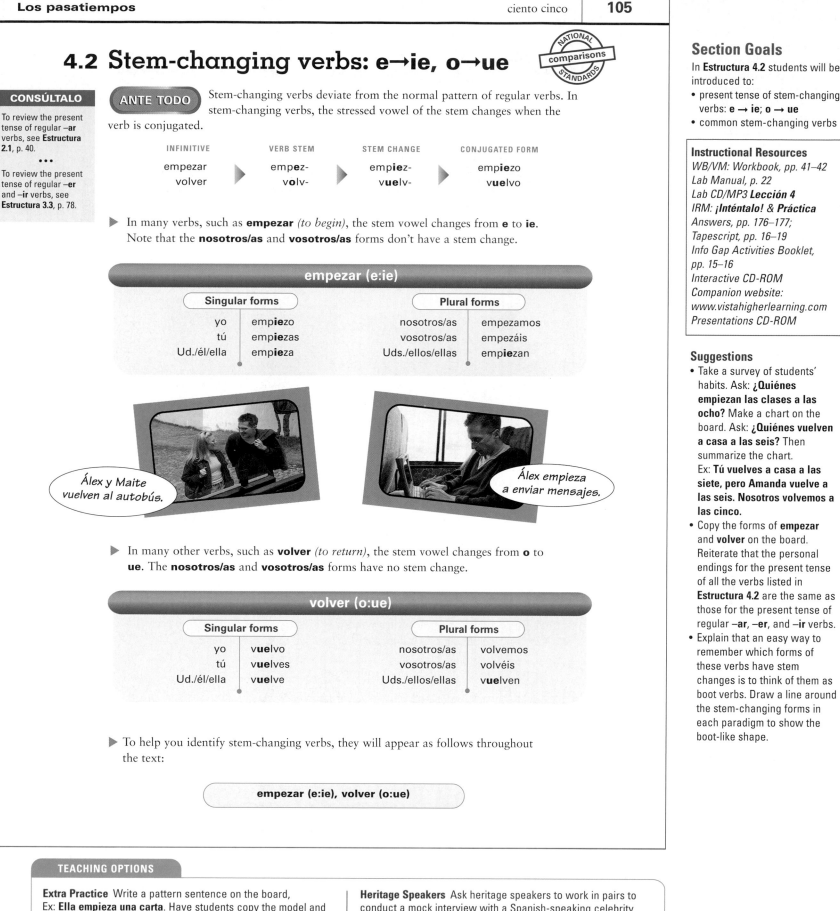

Álex y Maite vuelven al autobús.

Álex empieza a enviar mensajes.

▶ In many other verbs, such as **volver** *(to return)*, the stem vowel changes from **o** to **ue**. The **nosotros/as** and **vosotros/as** forms have no stem change.

volver (o:ue)

Singular forms		Plural forms	
yo	v**ue**lvo	nosotros/as	volvemos
tú	v**ue**lves	vosotros/as	volvéis
Ud./él/ella	v**ue**lve	Uds./ellos/ellas	v**ue**lven

▶ To help you identify stem-changing verbs, they will appear as follows throughout the text:

> **empezar (e:ie), volver (o:ue)**

Section Goals

In **Estructura 4.2** students will be introduced to:
• present tense of stem-changing verbs: **e → ie**; **o → ue**
• common stem-changing verbs

Instructional Resources
WB/VM: Workbook, pp. 41–42
Lab Manual, p. 22
Lab CD/MP3 Lección 4
IRM: ¡Inténtalo! & Práctica Answers, pp. 176–177;
Tapescript, pp. 16–19
Info Gap Activities Booklet, pp. 15–16
Interactive CD-ROM
Companion website:
www.vistahigherlearning.com
Presentations CD-ROM

Suggestions
• Take a survey of students' habits. Ask: **¿Quiénes empiezan las clases a las ocho?** Make a chart on the board. Ask: **¿Quiénes vuelven a casa a las seis?** Then summarize the chart.
Ex: **Tú vuelves a casa a las siete, pero Amanda vuelve a las seis. Nosotros volvemos a las cinco.**
• Copy the forms of **empezar** and **volver** on the board. Reiterate that the personal endings for the present tense of all the verbs listed in **Estructura 4.2** are the same as those for the present tense of regular **–ar**, **–er**, and **–ir** verbs.
• Explain that an easy way to remember which forms of these verbs have stem changes is to think of them as boot verbs. Draw a line around the stem-changing forms in each paradigm to show the boot-like shape.

TEACHING OPTIONS

Extra Practice Write a pattern sentence on the board, Ex: **Ella empieza una carta**. Have students copy the model and then dictate a list of different subjects. Ex: **Maite, nosotras, don Francisco**. Have students write down the subjects and supply the correct verb form. Ask volunteers to read their answers aloud.

Heritage Speakers Ask heritage speakers to work in pairs to conduct a mock interview with a Spanish-speaking celebrity such as Ricky Martin, Arantxa Sánchez-Vicario, Luis Miguel, and so forth, in which they use the verbs **empezar**, **volver**, **querer**, and **recordar**. Ask them to present their interview for the class and have students write down the forms of **empezar**, **volver**, **querer**, and **recordar** that they hear.

Suggestions

- Write **e:ie** and **o:ue** on the board and explain that some very common verbs have these types of stem changes. Point out that all the verbs listed are conjugated like **empezar** or **volver**. Model the pronunciation of the verbs and ask students a few questions using verbs of each type, having them answer in complete sentences. Ex: **¿A qué hora cierra la biblioteca? ¿Duermen los estudiantes tarde, por lo general? ¿Qué piensan hacer este fin de semana? ¿Quién quiere comer en un restaurante esta noche?**

- Point out the structure **jugar al** used with sports. Practice it by asking students about the sports they play. Have them answer in complete sentences. Ex: ____, **¿te gusta jugar al fútbol? Y tú, ____, ¿juegas al fútbol? ¿Prefieres jugar al fútbol o ver un partido en el estadio? ¿Cuántos juegan al tenis? ¿Qué prefieres, ____, jugar al tenis o jugar al fútbol?**

- Prepare "dehydrated" sentences such as these: **Maite / empezar / la lección; Uds. / mostrar / los trabajos; Nosotros / jugar / al fútbol.** Write them on the board one at a time, and have students "hydrate" them.

Common stem-changing verbs

e:ie		o:ue	
cerrar	*to close*	**almorzar**	*to have lunch*
comenzar (a + inf.)	*to begin*	**contar**	*to count; to tell*
empezar (a + inf.)	*to begin*	**dormir**	*to sleep*
entender	*to understand*	**encontrar**	*to find*
pensar (+ inf.)	*to think*	**mostrar**	*to show*
perder	*to lose; to miss*	**poder (+ inf.)**	*to be able; can*
preferir (+ inf.)	*to prefer*	**recordar**	*to remember*
querer (+ inf.)	*to want; to love*	**volver**	*to return*

¡LENGUA VIVA!

The verb **perder** can mean *to lose* or *to miss*, in the sense of "to miss a train":

Siempre pierdo mis llaves.
I always lose my keys.

Es importante no perder el autobús.
It's important not to miss the bus.

▶ **Jugar** (*to play* a sport or game), is the only Spanish verb that has a **u:ue** stem change.
    Jugar is followed by **a** + [*definite article*] when the name of a sport or game is mentioned.

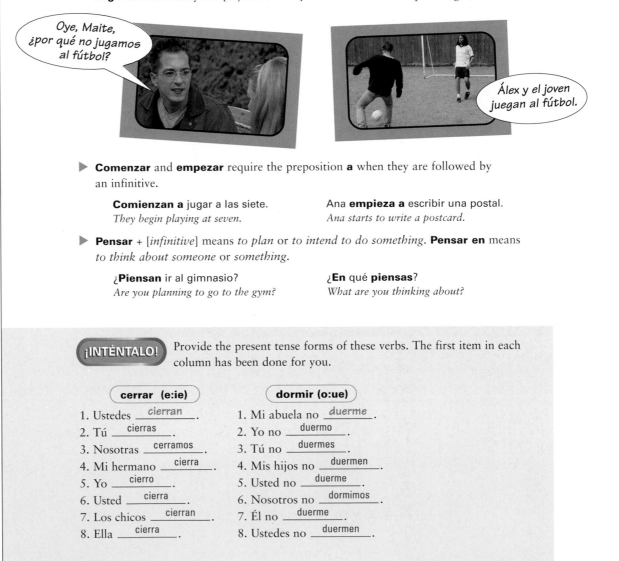

Oye, Maite, ¿por qué no jugamos al fútbol?

Álex y el joven juegan al fútbol.

▶ **Comenzar** and **empezar** require the preposition **a** when they are followed by an infinitive.

    Comienzan a jugar a las siete.   Ana **empieza a** escribir una postal.
    They begin playing at seven.   *Ana starts to write a postcard.*

▶ **Pensar** + [*infinitive*] means *to plan* or *to intend to do something*. **Pensar en** means *to think about someone* or *something*.

    ¿Piensan ir al gimnasio?   **¿En** qué **piensas**?
    Are you planning to go to the gym?   *What are you thinking about?*

¡INTÉNTALO!   Provide the present tense forms of these verbs. The first item in each column has been done for you.

cerrar (e:ie)

1. Ustedes _____cierran_____.
2. Tú _____cierras_____.
3. Nosotras _____cerramos_____.
4. Mi hermano _____cierra_____.
5. Yo _____cierro_____.
6. Usted _____cierra_____.
7. Los chicos _____cierran_____.
8. Ella _____cierra_____.

dormir (o:ue)

1. Mi abuela no _____duerme_____.
2. Yo no _____duermo_____.
3. Tú no _____duermes_____.
4. Mis hijos no _____duermen_____.
5. Usted no _____duerme_____.
6. Nosotros no _____dormimos_____.
7. Él no _____duerme_____.
8. Ustedes no _____duermen_____.

TEACHING OPTIONS

Extra Practice For additional drills of stem-changing verbs with the whole class or with students who need extra practice, do **¡Inténtalo!** orally using infinitives other than **cerrar** and **dormir**. Keep the pace rapid.

Large Group Arrange all the classroom chairs in a circle and use a ball (or balled-up piece of paper) for this activity. Begin by naming the infinitive of a common stem-changing verb.

Then name a pronoun. Ex: **querer / tú**. Then throw the ball to a student. The student catches the ball and says the appropriate form of the verb (**quieres**). Then he or she names a different pronoun and throws the ball to another student who must catch it and give the appropriate form of the verb. Continue until all subject pronouns have been covered, and then begin again with another infinitive.

Práctica

1 Completar Complete this conversation with the appropriate forms of the verbs. Then act it out with a partner.

PABLO Óscar, voy al centro ahora.

ÓSCAR ¿A qué hora (1)___piensas___ (pensar) volver? El partido de fútbol (2)___empieza___ (empezar) a las dos.

PABLO (3)___Vuelvo___ (Volver) a la una. (4)___Quiero___ (querer) ver el partido.

ÓSCAR (5)¿___Recuerdas___ (Recordar) que (*that*) nuestro equipo es muy bueno? (6)¡___Puede___ (poder) ganar!

PABLO No, (7)___pienso___ (pensar) que va a (8)___perder___ (perder). Los jugadores de Guadalajara son salvajes (*wild*) cuando (9)___juegan___ (jugar).

2 Preferencias With a partner, take turns asking and answering questions about what these people want to do, using the cues provided.

NOTA CULTURAL

Dominó (*dominoes*) is a popular pastime throughout Colombia, Venezuela, Central America, and the Spanish-speaking countries of the Caribbean. It's played by young and old alike, primarily at family gatherings and among friends, but sometimes also competitively.

> **modelo**
> Guillermo: estudiar / pasear en bicicleta.
> **Estudiante 1:** ¿Quiere estudiar Guillermo?
> **Estudiante 2:** No, prefiere pasear en bicicleta.

1. tú: trabajar / dormir
¿Quieres trabajar? No, prefiero dormir.
2. Uds.: mirar la televisión / jugar al dominó
¿Quieren ustedes mirar la televisión? No, preferimos jugar al dominó.
3. tus amigos: ir de excursión / descansar
¿Quieren ir de excursión tus amigos? No, mis amigos prefieren descansar.
4. tú: comer en la cafetería / ir a un restaurante
¿Quieres comer en la cafetería? No, prefiero ir a un restaurante.
5. Elisa: ver una película / leer una revista
¿Quiere ver una película Elisa? No, (Elisa) prefiere leer una revista.
6. María y su hermana: tomar el sol / practicar el esquí acuático
¿Quieren tomar el sol María y su hermana? No, (María y su hermana) prefieren practicar el esquí acuático.

3 Describir Use a verb from the list to describe what these people are doing.

almorzar   cerrar   contar   dormir   encontrar   mostrar

1. Las niñas Las niñas duermen.   2. Yo (Yo) Cierro la ventana.   3. Nosotros (Nosotros) Almorzamos.

4. Tú (Tú) Encuentras una maleta.   5. Pedro Pedro muestra una foto.   6. Teresa Teresa cuenta.

1 Suggestion Divide the class into pairs and give them three minutes to act out the conversation. Then have partners switch roles.

1 Expansion
• Supply students with short-answer prompts based on the conversation. Ask students to give the questions that would have elicited the answers. Ex: **A las dos. (¿A qué hora empieza el partido de fútbol?) Porque no quiere perderse el partido. (¿Por qué vuelve Pablo a la una?)**
• Ask questions using **pensar** + [*infinitive*]; **pensar en**, and **perder** (in both senses). Ex: **¿Qué piensas hacer mañana? ¿En qué piensas ahora? ¿Cuándo pierdes las cosas?**

2 Suggestion Model the activity by reading the **modelo** and giving other examples in the **yo** form before assigning the activity to pairs. Ex: **¿Quiero descansar en casa? No, prefiero enseñar la clase.**

2 Expansion Have students ask one another questions of their own using the same pattern. Ex: —**¿Quieres jugar al baloncesto? —No, prefiero jugar al tenis.**

3 Expansion Bring in photos or magazine pictures to extend this activity. Choose pictures that lend themselves to being described by the common stem-changing verbs.

TEACHING OPTIONS

TPR Brainstorm gestures to go with each of the stem-changing verbs. Have students mime the activity you mention. Tell them that only male students should respond to **él/ellos** and only females to **ella/ellas**. Everyone should respond to **nosotros**. **Game** Arrange students in rows of five or six (depending on whether you use **vosotros**), one behind the other. The first person in the row has a piece of paper. Call out the infinitive of a stem-changing verb. The first person writes the **yo** form and passes the paper to the student behind. That student writes the **tú** form and passes the paper on. There is to be no talking. The last person in the row holds up the paper to show the team has finished. The first team to finish the conjugation correctly gets a point. Have students rotate positions in their row before calling out another verb. The team with the most points wins.

Comunicación

4 **Frecuencia** In pairs, use the verbs from the list and other stem-changing verbs you know to create sentences telling your partner which activities you do daily (**todos los días**), which you do once a month (**una vez al mes**), and which you do once a year (**una vez al año**). Then switch roles.   Answers will vary.

> **modelo**
> **Estudiante 1:** Yo recuerdo a mi familia todos los días.
> **Estudiante 2:** Yo pierdo uno de mis libros una vez al año.

cerrar	perder
dormir	poder
empezar	preferir
encontrar	querer
jugar	recordar
¿?	¿?

todos los días	una vez al mes		una vez al año

5 **En la televisión** Read the television listings for Saturday. In pairs, write a conversation between two siblings arguing about what to watch. Be creative and be prepared to act out your conversation for the class.   Answers will vary.

> **modelo**
> **Hermano:** Quiero ver la Copa Mundial.
> **Hermana:** ¡No! Prefiero ver...

	13:00	14:00	15:00	16:00	17:00	18:00	19:00	20:00	21:00	22:00	23:00
7	Copa Mundial (*World Cup*) de fútbol		El tiempo libre		Fútbol internacional: Copa América: México-Argentina					Torneo de Natación	
8	Abierto (*Open*) Mexicano de Tenis: Alejandro Hernández (México) vs. Jacobo Díaz (España). Semifinales			Campeonato (*Championship*) de baloncesto Los Correcaminos de Tampico vs. los Santos de San Luis				Aficionados al buceo		Cozumel: Aventuras	
12	Gente famosa		Amigos	Médicos jóvenes				Película: **El centro de la ciudad**		Película: **Terror en la plaza mayor**	
13	El padrastro			Periodistas en peligro (*danger*)		El esquí acuático				Patinaje Artístico	
17	Biografías: La artista Frida Kahlo			Música de la semana		Entrevista del día: Miguel Indurain y su pasión por el ciclismo				Cine de la noche: **Los excursionistas perdidos** (*lost*)	

Síntesis

6 **Situación** Your instructor will give you and your partner a partially illustrated itinerary of a city tour. Complete the itineraries by asking each other questions using the verbs in the captions and vocabulary you have learned.   Answers will vary.

> **modelo**
> **Estudiante 1:** Por la mañana, empiezan en el café.
> **Estudiante 2:** Y luego ...

NOTA CULTURAL

Miguel Indurain is a famous cyclist from Spain who has won the Tour de France bicycle race five times.

4.3 Stem-changing verbs: e→i

ANTE TODO You've already seen that many verbs in Spanish change their stem vowel when conjugated. There is a third kind of stem-vowel change in some verbs, such as **pedir** (*to ask for; to request*). In these verbs, the stressed vowel in the stem changes from **e** to **i**, as shown in the diagram.

INFINITIVE	VERB STEM	STEM CHANGE	CONJUGATED FORM
pedir	p**e**d-	p**i**d-	p**i**do

▶ As with other stem-changing verbs you have learned, there is no stem change in the **nosotros/as** or **vosotros/as** forms in the present tense.

pedir (e:i)

Singular forms		Plural forms	
yo	p**i**do	nosotros/as	pedimos
tú	p**i**des	vosotros/as	pedís
Ud./él/ella	p**i**de	Uds./ellos/ellas	p**i**den

▶ To help you identify verbs with the **e:i** stem change, they will appear as follows throughout the text:

pedir (e:i)

▶ The following are the most common **e:i** stem-changing verbs:

conseguir	**decir**	**repetir**	**seguir**
to get; to obtain	*to say; to tell*	*to repeat*	*to follow; to continue; to keep (doing something)*

Pido favores cuando es necesario.
I ask for favors when it's necessary.

Javier **dice** la verdad.
Javier is telling the truth.

Sigue esperando.
He keeps waiting.

Consiguen ver buenas películas.
They get to see good movies.

▶ The **yo** forms of **seguir** and **conseguir** have a spelling change as well as the stem change **e→i**.

Sigo su plan.
I'm following their plan.

Consigo novelas en la librería.
I get novels at the bookstore.

¡INTÉNTALO! Provide the correct forms of the verbs.

repetir (e:i)
1. Arturo y Eva _repiten_.
2. Yo _repito_.
3. Nosotros _repetimos_.
4. Julia _repite_.
5. Sofía y yo _repetimos_.
6. Tú _repites_.

decir (e:i)
1. Yo _digo_.
2. Él _dice_.
3. Tú _dices_.
4. Usted _dice_.
5. Ellas _dicen_.
6. Nosotros _decimos_.

seguir (e:i)
1. Yo _sigo_.
2. Nosotros _seguimos_.
3. Tú _sigues_.
4. Los chicos _siguen_.
5. Usted _sigue_.
6. Anita _sigue_.

¡LENGUA VIVA!

As you learned in **Lección 2, preguntar** *means to ask a question.* **Pedir**, however, means *to ask for something:*

Ella me pregunta cuántos años tengo.
She asks me how old I am.

Él me pide ayuda.
He asks me for help.

¡ATENCIÓN!

While **decir** follows the stem-change pattern of **e** to **i**, its **yo** form is irregular: **yo digo**. You will learn other verbs whose **yo** forms end in **–go** in **Estructura 4.4**, pp. 112–113.

• • •

Here are some common expressions with **decir**:

decir la verdad *to tell the truth*

decir mentiras *to tell lies*

decir que *to say that*

Section Goal

In **Estructura 4.3** students will learn the present tense of **e → i** stem-changing verbs.

Instructional Resources
WB/VM: Workbook, pp. 43–44
Lab Manual, p. 23
*Lab CD/MP3 **Lección 4***
IRM: ¡Inténtalo! & Práctica
Answers, pp. 176–177;
Tapescript, pp. 16–19
Interactive CD-ROM
Companion website:
www.vistahigherlearning.com
Presentations CD-ROM

Suggestions
• Take a survey of students' habits. Make a chart on the board. Ask questions like: **¿Quiénes piden Coca-Cola?** Then summarize the chart.
• Ask for volunteers to answer questions using **conseguir, decir, pedir, repetir,** and **seguir**.
• Reiterate that the personal endings for the present tense of all the verbs listed are the same as those for the present tense of regular **–ir** verbs.
• Point out the spelling changes in the **yo** forms of **seguir → sigo** and **conseguir → consigo**.
• Prepare "dehydrated" sentences, write them on the board one at a time, and have students "hydrate" them. Ex: **Tú / pedir / café; Ustedes / repetir / la pregunta; Nosotros / decir / la verdad**
• For additional drills with stem-changing verbs, complete the **¡Inténtalo!** activity orally using other infinitives such as **conseguir, impedir, pedir,** and **servir**. Keep the pace rapid.

¡Atención! Since they are active vocabulary, go over the common expressions used with **decir**. In pairs, have students practice the different expressions by asking each other questions. Ex: **¿En qué circunstancias dices mentiras?**

Note: Students will learn more about **decir** with indirect object pronouns in **Estructura 6.2**.

Práctica

1 **Completar** Complete these sentences with the correct form of the verb provided.

1. Cuando mi familia pasea por la ciudad, mi madre siempre va al café y __pide__ (pedir) una soda.
2. Pero mi padre __dice__ (decir) que perdemos mucho tiempo. Tiene prisa por llegar al bosque de Chapultepec.
3. Mi padre tiene suerte, porque él siempre __consigue__ (conseguir) lo que (*that which*) desea.
4. Cuando llegamos al parque, mis hermanos y yo __seguimos__ (seguir) conversando (*talking*) con nuestros padres.
5. Mis padres siempre __repiten__ (repetir) la misma cosa: "Nosotros tomamos el sol aquí sin ustedes."
6. Yo siempre __pido__ (pedir) permiso para volver a casa un poco más tarde porque me gusta mucho el parque.

2 **Combinar** Combine words from the columns to create sentences about yourself and people you know. Answers will vary.

A	B
Yo	(no) pedir muchos favores
Mi compañero/a de cuarto	nunca (*never*) pedir perdón
Mi mejor (*best*) amigo/a	nunca seguir las instrucciones
Mi familia	siempre seguir las instrucciones
Mis amigos/as	conseguir libros en Internet
Mis amigos y yo	repetir el vocabulario
Mis padres	(no) decir mentiras
Mi hermano/a	
Mi profesor(a) de español	

3 **Opiniones** Work in pairs to guess how your partner completed the sentences from **Actividad 2**. If you guess incorrectly, your partner must supply the correct answer. Switch roles. Answers will vary.

modelo

Estudiante 1: En mi opinión, tus padres consiguen libros en Internet.
Estudiante 2: ¡No! Mi hermana consigue libros en Internet.

Comunicación

4

Las películas Use these questions to interview a classmate. Answers will vary.

1. ¿Prefieres las películas románticas, las películas de acción o las películas de horror? ¿Por qué?

2. ¿Dónde consigues información sobre (*about*) una película?

3. ¿Dónde consigues las entradas (*tickets*) para una película?

4. Para decidir qué películas vas a ver, ¿sigues las recomendaciones de los críticos? ¿Qué dicen los críticos en general?

5. ¿Qué cines en tu comunidad muestran las mejores (*best*) películas?

6. ¿Vas a ver una película esta semana? ¿A qué hora empieza la película?

Síntesis

5

El cine In pairs, first scan the ad and jot down all the stem-changing verbs. Then answer the questions. Be prepared to share your answers with the class. Answers will vary.

1. ¿Qué palabras indican que *Un mundo azul oscuro* (*Dark Blue World*) es una película dramática?

2. ¿Cuántas personas hay en el póster?

3. ¿Cómo son las personas del póster? ¿Qué relación tienen?

4. ¿Te gustan las películas como ésta (*this one*)?

5. Describe tu película favorita con los verbos de la **Lección 4.**

4 Suggestions
• Have students report to the class what their partners said. After the presentation, encourage them to ask each other questions.
• Take a class poll to find out students' film genre and local movie theater preferences.

5 Suggestions
• Write the stem-changing verbs from the ad on the board. Have students conjugate the verbs using different subjects.
• In pairs, have students use the verbs from the ad to write a dramatic dialogue.
• Go over student responses to item 5.

TEACHING OPTIONS

Small Groups First, have students talk about how they would advertise fun activities in town. Then, have them create a poster similar to the movie poster using stem-changing verbs from **Estructura 4.2** and **4.3.**

Heritage Speakers Ask heritage speakers to talk about popular Spanish-language films. Brainstorm with the class a list of questions about the films using stem-changing verbs from **Estructura 4.2** and **4.3.** Have students ask the heritage speakers the questions. Ex: **¿Dónde podemos conseguir la película aquí? ¿Dices que es tu película favorita? ¿Prefieres películas en español o en inglés?**

Section Goal

In **Estructura 4.4** students will learn verbs with irregular **yo** forms.

Instructional Resources
*WB/VM: Workbook, pp. 45–46
Lab Manual, p. 24
Lab CD/MP3 **Lección 4**
IRM: **¡Inténtalo!** & **Práctica**
Answers, pp. 176–177;
Tapescript, pp. 16–19
Interactive CD-ROM
Companion website:
www.vistahigherlearning.com
Presentations CD-ROM*

Suggestions
• Quickly review the present tense of **tener**, pointing out the **–go** ending of the **yo** form.
• Ask questions and make statements that elicit the **yo** forms of the verbs.
Ex: **¿Haces la tarea en casa o en la biblioteca? (Hago la tarea en la biblioteca.) ¿Traes un diccionario a la clase? (Sí, traigo un diccionario a la clase.)** As you elicit responses, write just the verbs on the board until you have listed all the irregular **yo** forms.
• Go over the different uses of **salir** as outlined. Then model an additional example of each usage.
• You might want to tell students that the verb **prender**, not **poner**, is used to express *to turn on an electrical device or appliance* in many Latin American countries (for example, Mexico, Venezuela, Colombia, and Peru).

Successful Language Learning Point out that students should learn the verbs with irregular **yo** forms thoroughly because these will often be used in conversation.

4.4 Verbs with irregular yo forms

ANTE TODO   In Spanish, several verbs have irregular **yo** forms in the present tense. You have already seen three verbs with the **–go** ending in the **yo** form: **decir → digo**, **tener → tengo**, and **venir → vengo**. Now you will learn several more.

Verbs with irregular *yo* forms

	hacer *(to do; to make)*	poner *(to put; to place)*	salir *(to leave)*	suponer *(to suppose)*	traer *(to bring)*
SINGULAR FORMS	**hago** haces hace	**pongo** pones pone	**salgo** sales sale	**supongo** supones supone	**traigo** traes trae
PLURAL FORMS	hacemos hacéis hacen	ponemos ponéis ponen	salimos salís salen	suponemos suponéis suponen	traemos traéis traen

▶ The verbs **hacer**, **poner**, **salir**, **suponer**, and **traer** have **yo** forms that end in **–go**. The other forms are regular.

A veces salgo a correr por la noche.

Nunca salgo a correr, no hago ejercicio, pero sí tengo energía... ¡para leer el periódico y tomar un café!

▶ **Poner** can also mean *to turn on* a household appliance.

    Carlos **pone** la radio.   María **pone** la televisión.
    Carlos turns on the radio.   *María turns on the television.*

▶ **Salir de** is used to indicate that someone is leaving a particular place.

    Hoy **salgo del** hospital.   **Sale de** la clase a las cuatro.
    Today I leave the hospital.   *He leaves class at four.*

▶ **Salir para** is used to indicate someone's destination.

    Mañana **salgo para** México.   Hoy **salen para** España.
    Tomorrow I leave for Mexico.   *Today they leave for Spain.*

▶ **Salir con** means *to leave with someone or something*, or *to date someone*.

    Alberto **sale con** su mochila.   Margarita **sale con** Guillermo.
    Alberto is leaving with his backpack.   *Margarita is going out with Guillermo.*

    Hoy voy a **salir con** mi hermana.   Mi primo **sale con** una chica muy bonita.
    Today I'm going out with my sister.   *My cousin is going out with a very pretty girl.*

TEACHING OPTIONS

TPR Use the verbs with irregular **yo** forms in different sentences. Students will mime what you are saying. Ex: **Hago la tarea.** (Students mime writing their homework.) **Pongo la radio.** (They mime turning on a radio.)
Game Divide the class into teams of three. Each team has a piece of paper. Call out an infinitive and a person. Ex: **traer / primera persona plural.** Each team has to compose a sentence with

each person writing one part. The first team member writes a subject (Ex: **nosotras**). The second writes the correct form of the verb (Ex: **traemos**). The third gives a direct or indirect object (Ex: **el libro**). The first team to write a logical and correct sentence wins. Team members should rotate positions each time a new verb is given.

Suggestions
• Point out that **oír** is irregular in all forms except **nosotros** and **vosotros**. Write a model sentence on the board. Ex: **Ustedes oyen el programa de radio todos los viernes**. Then change the subject, and have students give the new sentence. Ex: **tú (Tú oyes el programa de radio todos los viernes.)**
• Call out different forms of the verbs in **Estructura 4.4** and have volunteers say the infinitive. Ex: **oyen (oír)**. Keep the pace rapid.
• Explain the difference between **escuchar** (*to listen*) and **oír** (*to hear*). Ex: **Escucho la radio. No oigo el perro.**

The verbs **ver** and **oír**

▶ The verb **ver** (*to see*) has an irregular **yo** form. The other forms of **ver** are regular, but note that the **vosotros/as** form does not carry an accent mark.

ver			
Singular forms		**Plural forms**	
yo	**veo**	nosotros/as	vemos
tú	ves	vosotros/as	veis
Ud./él/ella	ve	Uds./ellos/ellas	ven

Oye, ¿por qué no jugamos al fútbol?

Maite ve la pelota.

▶ The verb **oír** (*to hear*) has an irregular **yo** form and the spelling change **i→y** in the **tú, usted, él, ella, ustedes, ellos,** and **ellas** forms. The **nosotros/as** and **vosotros/as** forms have an accent mark.

oír			
Singular forms		**Plural forms**	
yo	**oigo**	nosotros/as	oímos
tú	oyes	vosotros/as	oís
Ud./él/ella	oye	Uds./ellos/ellas	oyen

Oigo a unas personas en la otra sala.
I hear some people in the other room.

¿Oyes música latina?
Do you hear Latin music?

¡INTÉNTALO! Provide the appropriate forms of these verbs. The first item has been done for you.

1. salir   Isabel ___sale___   Nosotros ___salimos___   Yo ___salgo___
2. ver   Yo ___veo___   Ustedes ___ven___   Tú ___ves___
3. poner   Rita y yo ___ponemos___   Yo ___pongo___   Los niños ___ponen___
4. hacer   Yo ___hago___   Tú ___haces___   Usted ___hace___
5. oír   Él ___oye___   Nosotros ___oímos___   Yo ___oigo___
6. traer   Ellas ___traen___   Yo ___traigo___   Tú ___traes___
7. suponer   Yo ___supongo___   Mi amigo ___supone___   Nosotras ___suponemos___

TEACHING OPTIONS

Extra Practice For oral practice, call out subject pronouns and have students respond with the correct form of **ver** or **oír**. Reverse the drill by starting with forms of **ver** and **oír** and asking students to give the corresponding subject pronouns.

Pairs In pairs, have students create and then ask each other questions about their habits. Ex: **¿Sales a comer a restaurantes con tus amigos? ¿Ves la televisión en español? ¿Supones que una clase de matemáticas es muy difícil? ¿Haces ejercicio por la mañana?** Have students record their partners' answers and be prepared to share the information with the class.

1 Suggestion Quickly review the new verbs with irregular **yo** forms. Ask pairs to complete and act out the conversation, then switch roles.

1 Expansion Ask questions about the conversation. **¿Qué hace David hoy? ¿Qué hace Diana? ¿Por qué tienen que hacer las maletas Andrés y Javier? ¿Por qué pone Ernesto la televisión?**

2 Suggestion Model the activity by completing the **modelo** orally. Ask volunteers to say aloud each complete sentence.

2 Expansion Change the subjects of the dehydrated sentences in the activity and have students write or say aloud the new sentences.

3 Expansion Use magazine pictures which elicit the target verbs to extend the activity. Encourage students to add further descriptions if they can.

Práctica

1 Completar
Complete this conversation with the appropriate forms of the verbs. Then act it out with a partner.

ERNESTO David, ¿qué (1)_____haces_____ (hacer) hoy?

DAVID Ahora estudio biología, pero esta noche (2)_____salgo_____ (salir) con Luisa. Vamos al cine. Los críticos (3)_____dicen_____ (decir) que la nueva (*new*) película de Almodóvar es buena.

ERNESTO ¿Y Diana? ¿Qué (4)_____hace_____ (hacer) ella?

DAVID (5)_____Sale_____ (Salir) a comer con sus padres.

ERNESTO ¿Qué (6)_____hacen_____ (hacer) Andrés y Javier?

DAVID Tienen que (7)_____hacer_____ (hacer) las maletas. (8)_____Salen_____ (Salir) para Monterrey mañana.

ERNESTO Pues, ¿qué (9)_____hago_____ (hacer) yo?

DAVID (10)_____Supongo_____ (Suponer) que puedes estudiar o (11)_____ver_____ (ver) la televisión.

ERNESTO No quiero estudiar. Mejor (12)_____pongo_____ (poner) el televisor. Mi programa favorito empieza en unos minutos.

2 Oraciones
Form sentences using the cues provided and verbs from **Estructura 4.4**.

> **modelo**
> Tú / _____ / cosas / en / su lugar / antes de (*before*) / salir
> *Tú pones las cosas en su lugar antes de salir.*

1. Mis amigos / _____ / conmigo / centro Mis amigos salen conmigo al centro.
2. Tú / _____ / cámara Tú traes una cámara.
3. Alberto / _____ / música del café Pasatiempos Alberto oye la música del café Pasatiempos.
4. Yo / no / _____ / muchas películas Yo no veo muchas películas.
5. domingo / nosotros / _____ / mucha / tarea El domingo, nosotros hacemos mucha tarea.
6. Si / yo / _____ / que / yo / querer / ir / cine / mis amigos / ir / también Si yo digo que quiero ir al cine, mis amigos van también.

3 Describir
Use a verb from **Estructura 4.4** to describe what these people are doing.
Some answers will vary.

1. Fernán Fernán pone la mochila en el escritorio.

2. Los aficionados Los aficionados salen del estadio.

3. Yo Yo traigo una cámara.

4. Nosotros Nosotros vemos el monumento.

5. La señora Vargas La señora Vargas no oye bien.

6. El estudiante El estudiante hace su tarea.

Pairs Have students write three sentences in each of which they use one of the target verbs from **Estructura 4.4**. Then ask them to copy their sentences onto a sheet of paper in "dehydrated" form, following the model of the sentences in **Actividad 2**. Students exchange their sentences with a partner, who writes the complete sentences on the paper. Finally, have partners check each other's work.

Extra Practice Have students use five of the target verbs from **Estructura 4.4** to write sentences about habits or likes they have that they think are somewhat unusual. Ex: **Traigo doce bolígrafos en la mochila. Hago la tarea en un café del centro. No pongo la televisión hasta las diez de la noche.**

Comunicación

4 **Preguntas** Get together with a classmate and ask each other these questions. Answers will vary.

1. ¿Qué traes a clase?
2. ¿Quiénes traen un diccionario a clase? ¿Por qué traen un diccionario?
3. ¿A qué hora sales de tu residencia o de tu casa por la mañana? ¿A qué hora sale tu compañero/a de cuarto o tu esposo/a?
4. ¿Dónde pones tus libros cuando regresas de clase? ¿Siempre (*Always*) pones tus cosas en su lugar?
5. ¿Pones fotos de tu familia en tu casa? ¿Quiénes son las personas que están en las fotos?
6. ¿Oyes la radio cuando estudias?
7. ¿En qué circunstancias dices mentiras?
8. ¿Haces mucha tarea los fines de semana?
9. ¿Sales con tus amigos los fines de semana? ¿A qué hora? ¿Qué hacen?
10. ¿Te gusta ver deportes en la televisión o prefieres ver otros programas? ¿Cuáles?

5 **Charadas** In groups, play a game of charades. Each person should think of two phrases using the verbs **hacer, poner, salir, oír, traer,** or **ver**. The first person to guess correctly acts out the next charade. Answers will vary.

6 **Entrevista** You are doing a market research report on lifestyles. Interview a classmate to find out when he or she goes out with the following people and what they do for entertainment. Answers will vary.

- ▶ los amigos
- ▶ el/la novio/a
- ▶ el/la esposo/a
- ▶ la familia

Síntesis

7 **Situación** Imagine that you are speaking with your roommate. With a partner, prepare a conversation using these cues. Answers will vary.

Estudiante 1	Estudiante 2
Ask your partner what he or she is doing.	→ Tell your partner that you are watching TV.
Say what you suppose he or she is watching.	→ Say that you like the show _____. Ask if he or she wants to watch.
Say no, because you are going out with friends and tell where you are going.	→ Say you think it's a good idea, and ask what your partner and his or her friends are doing there.
Say what you are going to do, and ask your partner whether her or she wants to come along.	→ Say no and tell your partner what you prefer to do.

4 Suggestion Model the activity for the class by asking volunteers the first two items.

4 Expansion Ask students questions about their own and their classmates' responses to the activity questions. Ex: **¿Tu compañera trae un diccionario a clase? ¿Por qué?**

5 Suggestions
- Model the activity by doing a charade and having the class guess. Ex: **Pongo un lápiz en la mesa.** Then divide the class into groups of five to seven students.
- Ask each group to pick out the best **charada**. Then ask the students to present them to the whole class, having the other groups guess what activities they are miming.

6 Suggestion Model the activity for the class, giving a report on your own lifestyle. Ex: **Salgo al cine con mis amigas. Me gusta comer en restaurantes con mi esposo. En familia vemos deportes en la televisión.** Remind students that a market researcher and his or her interviewee would address each other with the **Ud.** verb forms.

7 Possible Response
E1: **¿Qué haces?**
E2: **Veo la tele.**
E1: **Supongo que ves el programa *Amigos*.**
E2: **Sí. Me gusta el programa. ¿Quieres ver la tele conmigo?**
E1: **No puedo. Salgo con mis amigos a la plaza mayor.**
E2: **Buena idea. ¿Qué hacen en la plaza?**
E1: **Vamos a escuchar música y a pasear. ¿Quieres venir?**
E2: **No. Prefiero descansar.**

TEACHING OPTIONS

Pairs Have pairs of students role-play the perfect date. Students should write their script first, then present it to the class. Encourage students to use descriptive adjectives as well as the new verbs learned in **Estructura 4.4**.

Heritage Speakers Ask heritage speakers to make an oral presentation to the class about social customs in their home communities. Remind them to use familiar vocabulary and simple sentences.

Lectura

Antes de leer

Estrategia
Predicting content from visuals

When you are reading in Spanish, be sure to look for visual clues that will orient you as to the content and purpose of what you are reading. Photos and illustrations, for example, will often give you a good idea of the main points that the reading covers. You may also encounter very helpful visuals that are used to summarize large amounts of data in a way that is easy to comprehend; these include bar graphs, pie charts, flow charts, lists of percentages, and other sorts of diagrams.

Examinar el texto

Take a quick look at the visual elements of the magazine article in order to generate a list of ideas about its content. Then compare your list with a classmate's. Are your lists the same or are they different? Discuss your lists and make any changes needed to produce a final list of ideas.

Contestar

Read the list of ideas you wrote in **Examinar el texto,** and look again at the visual elements of the magazine article. Then answer these questions:

1. Who is the woman in the photo, and what is her role?

2. What is the article about?

3. What is the subject of the bar graph?

4. What is the subject of the pie chart?

recursos

vistahigher
learning.com

---

por María Úrsula Echevarría

El fútbol es el deporte más popular en el mundo° hispano, según° una encuesta° reciente realizada entre jóvenes universitarios. Mucha gente practica este deporte y tiene un equipo de fútbol favorito. Cada cuatro años se realiza la Copa Mundial°. Argentina y Uruguay han ganado° este campeonato° más de una vez°. Los aficionados siguen los partidos de fútbol en casa por tele y en muchos otros lugares como los bares, los restaurantes, los estadios y los clubes deportivos. Los jóvenes juegan al fútbol con sus amigos en parques y gimnasios.

Países hispanos en campeonatos mundiales de fútbol (1930-2002)

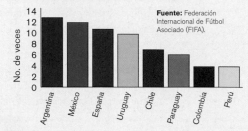

Fuente: Federación Internacional de Fútbol Asociado (FIFA).

Pero, por supuesto°, en los países de habla hispana también hay otros deportes populares. ¿Qué deporte sigue al fútbol en estos países? Bueno, ¡depende del país y de otros factores!

Después de leer

Evaluación y predicción

Which of the following sports events would be most popular among the college students surveyed? Rate them from one (most popular) to five (least popular). Which would be the most popular at your college or university? Answers will vary.

_____ 1. La Copa Mundial de Fútbol

_____ 2. Los Juegos Olímpicos

_____ 3. El torneo de tenis de Wimbledon

_____ 4. La Serie Mundial de Béisbol

_____ 5. El Tour de Francia

No sólo el fútbol

En Colombia, por ejemplo, el béisbol es muy popular después del fútbol, aunque° esto varía según la región del país. En la costa del norte de Colombia, el béisbol es una pasión. Y el ciclismo también es un deporte que los colombianos siguen con mucho interés.

Donde el béisbol es más popular

En los países del Caribe, el béisbol es el deporte predominante. Éste es el caso en Puerto Rico, Cuba y la República Dominicana. Los niños empiezan a jugar cuando son muy pequeños. En Puerto Rico y la República Dominicana, la gente también quiere participar en otros deportes como el baloncesto, o ver los partidos en la tele. Y para los espectadores aficionados del Caribe, el boxeo es número dos.

Donde el fútbol es más popular

En México el béisbol es el segundo° deporte más popular después° del fútbol. Pero en Argentina, después del fútbol, el rugby tiene mucha importancia. En Perú a la gente le gusta mucho ver partidos de vóleibol. ¿Y en España? Mucha gente prefiere el baloncesto, el tenis y el ciclismo.

Deportes más populares

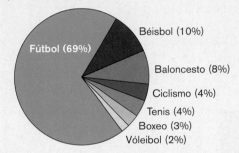

- Fútbol (69%)
- Béisbol (10%)
- Baloncesto (8%)
- Ciclismo (4%)
- Tenis (4%)
- Boxeo (3%)
- Vóleibol (2%)

mundo *world* según *according to* encuesta *survey* se realiza la Copa Mundial *the World Cup is held* han ganado *have won* campeonato *championship* más de una vez *more than once* por supuesto *of course* segundo *second* después *after* aunque *although*

¿Cierto o falso?

Indicate whether each sentence is **cierto** or **falso,** then correct the false statements.

	Cierto	Falso
1. El vóleibol es el segundo deporte más popular en México. Es el béisbol.	○	☑
2. En España a la gente le gustan varios deportes como el baloncesto y el ciclismo.	☑	○
3. En la costa del norte de Colombia, el tenis es una pasión. El béisbol es una pasión.	○	☑
4. En el Caribe el deporte más popular es el béisbol.	☑	○

Preguntas

Answer these questions in Spanish. Answers will vary.

1. ¿Dónde ven los aficionados el fútbol? Y tú, ¿cómo ves tus deportes favoritos?
2. ¿Te gusta el fútbol? ¿Por qué?
3. ¿Miras la Copa Mundial en la televisión?
4. ¿Qué deportes miras en la televisión?
5. En tu opinión, ¿cuáles son los tres deportes más populares en tu universidad? ¿en tu comunidad? ¿en los Estados Unidos?
6. ¿Qué haces en tu tiempo libre?

4 | **panorama**

Section Goals

In **Panorama**, students will read about:
• the geography, history, and culture of Mexico
• Mexico's relationship with the United States

Instructional Resources
Transparencies, #1, #2, #21
WB/VM: Workbook, pp. 47–48;
Video Activities, pp. 231–232
Panorama cultural *DVD/Video*
Interactive CD-ROM
IRM: Videoscript, p. 109;
Panorama cultural *Translations,*
p. 131
Companion website:
www.vistahigherlearning.com
Presentations CD-ROM

Suggestion Have students look at the map of Mexico or project **Transparency #21**. Ask questions about the locations of cities and natural features of Mexico. Ex: **¿Dónde está la capital? (en el centro del país)**

El país en cifras Because students will learn numbers over 100 in **Lección 6**, be sure to read aloud the numbers and dates in this section. Expand with questions related to section content. Ex: After **Área**, ask: **¿Qué ciudad mexicana está en la frontera con El Paso, Texas? (Ciudad Juárez)** Ask students if they can name other sister cities (**ciudades hermanas**) on the Mexico-U.S. border. (Tijuana/San Diego, Calexico/Mexicali, Laredo/Nuevo Laredo, Piedras Negras/Eagle Pass, Matamoros/Brownsville). Follow the same procedure with other sections.

¡Increíble pero cierto! Streets in the ever-expanding Mexico City are also named for bodies of water, scientists, philosophers, professions, zodiac signs, and colors.

México

connections cultures
NATIONAL STANDARDS

El país en cifras

▶ **Área:** 1.972.550 km² (761.603 millas²), casi° tres veces° el área de Texas.

La situación geográfica de México, al sur° de los Estados Unidos, ha influido en° la economía y la sociedad de los dos países. Una de las consecuencias es la emigración de la población mexicana al país vecino°. Hoy día, más de 20 millones de personas de descendencia mexicana viven en los Estados Unidos.

▶ **Población:** 110.139.000
▶ **Capital:** México, D.F.—18.934.000
▶ **Ciudades principales:** Guadalajara—3.889.000, Monterrey—3.502.000, Puebla—1.888.000, Ciudad Juárez—1.462.000

SOURCE: Population Division, UN Secretariat

▶ **Moneda:** peso mexicano
▶ **Idiomas:** español (oficial), náhuatl, idiomas mayas

La bandera de México

Mexicanos célebres

▶ **Benito Juárez,** héroe nacional (1806–1872)
▶ **Octavio Paz,** poeta (1914–1998)
▶ **Elena Poniatowska,** periodista y escritora (1932–)
▶ **Julio César Chávez,** boxeador (1962–)

casi *almost* veces *times* sur *south* ha influido en *has influenced* vecino *neighboring* vecindario *neighborhood* calles *streets* ha elegido *has chosen* Atún *tuna* cortas *short* nunca *never*

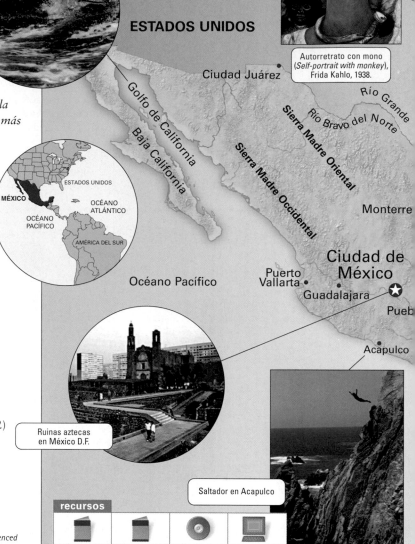

Un delfín en Baja California

Autorretrato con mono (Self-portrait with monkey), Frida Kahlo, 1938.

ESTADOS UNIDOS

Ciudad Juárez

Río Grande

Río Bravo del Norte

Golfo de California

Baja California

Sierra Madre Oriental

Sierra Madre Occidental

ESTADOS UNIDOS

MÉXICO

OCÉANO PACÍFICO

OCÉANO ATLÁNTICO

AMÉRICA DEL SUR

Monterre

Ciudad de México

Puerto Vallarta

Guadalajara

Pueb

Océano Pacífico

Acapulco

Ruinas aztecas en México D.F.

Saltador en Acapulco

recursos

| WB pp. 47–48 | VM pp. 231–232 | I CD-ROM Lección 4 | vistahigher learning.com |

¡Increíble pero cierto!

En la Ciudad de México cada vecindario° nombra sus calles° en honor a un tema especial. Un vecindario ha elegido° la literatura, y tiene calles llamadas *Dickens, Dante* y *Shakespeare*. En otro están las calles del *Atún°* y del *Cilantro*. Irónicamente, las calles del *Amor* y la *Felicidad* son cortas°, mientras que la calle del *Trabajo* nunca° termina.

TEACHING OPTIONS

Heritage Speakers Mexico is a large and diverse nation, with many regions and regional cultures. Have heritage speakers who have visited Mexico describe the region which they visited in a short oral report to the class. Encourage them to include information about the cities, art, history, geography, customs, and cuisine of the region.

Small Groups Many of the dishes that distinguish Mexican cuisine have pre-Hispanic origins. To these native dishes have been added elements of Spanish and French cuisines, making Mexican food, like Mexican civilization, a dynamic mix of ingredients. Have groups of students look through Mexican cookbooks to find some striking examples of Mexican cuisine and describe them to the class.

Ciudades • México D.F.

La Ciudad de México, fundada° en 1525 (mil quinientos veinticinco), también se llama el D.F. o Distrito Federal. Muchos turistas e inmigrantes vienen a la ciudad porque es el centro cultural y económico del país. El crecimiento° de la población es de los más altos° del mundo. El D.F. tiene una población mayor que las de Nueva York, Madrid o París.

Artes • Diego Rivera y Frida Kahlo

Frida Kahlo y Diego Rivera eran° artistas mexicanos muy famosos. Casados° en 1929 (mil novecientos veintinueve), los dos se interesaron° en las condiciones sociales de la gente indígena de su país. Puedes ver algunas de sus obras° en el Museo de Arte Moderno de la Ciudad de México.

Historia • Los aztecas

Los aztecas dominaron° en México del siglo° XIV hasta el siglo XVI. Sus canales, puentes° y pirámides con templos religiosos eran° muy importantes. El imperio azteca terminó° cuando llegaron° los conquistadores en 1519 (mil quinientos diecinueve), pero la presencia azteca sigue hoy. La Ciudad de México está situada en la capital azteca de Tenochtitlán, y muchos turistas van a visitar sus ruinas°.

Comida • Las tortillas

La base de la comida mexicana es la tortilla, que se hace° con maíz° y con harina°. Los tacos, las enchiladas y las quesadillas se hacen con tortillas y son tan populares en México como en los Estados Unidos. Puedes conseguir tortillas muy buenas en muchos restaurantes mexicanos.

Golfo de México

Península de Yucatán

Mérida

Cancún

Bahía de Campeche

ruz

Istmo de ehuantepec

BELICE

GUATEMALA

¿Qué aprendiste? Responde a las preguntas (*questions*) con una frase completa.

1. ¿Qué lenguas hablan los mexicanos? Los mexicanos hablan español, náhuatl e idiomas mayas.
2. ¿Cómo es la población del D.F. en comparación a otras ciudades? La población del D.F. es mayor.
3. ¿En qué se interesaron Kahlo y Rivera? Se interesaron en las condiciones sociales de la gente indígena de su país.
4. Nombra algunas (*some*) de las estructuras de la arquitectura azteca. Muchos canales, puentes y pirámides con templos religiosos.
5. ¿Dónde está situada la capital de México? Está situada en la capital azteca, Tenochtitlán.
6. ¿Por qué es importante la tortilla? Es la base de la comida mexicana.

Conexión Internet Investiga estos temas en el sitio **www.vistahigherlearning.com**.

1. Busca información sobre dos lugares de México. ¿Te gustaría (*Would you like*) vivir allí? ¿Por qué?
2. Busca información sobre dos artistas mexicanos. ¿Cómo se llaman sus obras (*works*) más famosas?

fundada *founded* crecimiento *growth* más altos *highest* eran *were* casados *married* se interesaron *were interested in* obras *works* dominaron *dominated* siglo *century* puentes *bridges* eran *were* terminó *ended* llegaron *arrived* ruinas *ruins* se hace *is made* maíz *corn* harina *flour*

TEACHING OPTIONS

Variación léxica Over 52 languages are spoken by indigenous communities in Mexico today. Not all of these languages have a written form. The speakers of Mayan languages are the most numerous non-Spanish speakers in Mexico. Náhuatl, the language of the Aztecs, is still spoken by many, and a number of Náhuatl words have entered Mexican Spanish. A few have also entered other languages. Mexican Spanish words derived from Náhuatl include **aguacate** (*avocado*), **guajolote** (*turkey*), **cacahuate** (*peanut*), **ejote** (*green bean*), **chile** (*chili pepper*), and **elote** (*corn*). Two words Náhuatl has given to other world languages are *tomato* and *chocolate*, products native to Mexico and brought to Europe only in the sixteenth century.

Instructional Resources
Vocabulary CD
Lab Manual, p. 24
*Lab CD/MP3 **Lección 4***
IRM: Tapescript, pp. 16–19
*Testing Program: **Pruebas**, pp. 37–48*
Testing Program Audio CD
Test Files CD-ROM
Test Generator

Pasatiempos

andar en patineta	*to skateboard*
bucear	*to scuba dive*
escalar montañas (*f. pl.*)	*to climb mountains*
escribir una carta	*to write a letter*
escribir un mensaje electrónico	*to write an e-mail message*
escribir una (tarjeta) postal	*to write a postcard*
esquiar	*to ski*
ganar	*to win*
ir de excursión (a las montañas)	*to go on a hike (in the mountains)*
leer correo electrónico	*to read e-mail*
leer un periódico	*to read a newspaper*
leer una revista	*to read a magazine*
nadar	*to swim*
pasar tiempo	*to spend time*
pasear	*to take a walk; to stroll*
pasear en bicicleta	*to ride a bicycle*
pasear por la ciudad/el pueblo	*to walk around the city/the town*
patinar (en línea)	*to skate (in-line)*
practicar deportes (*m. pl.*)	*to play sports*
ser aficionado/a (a)	*to be a fan (of)*
tomar el sol	*to sunbathe*
ver películas (*f. pl.*)	*to see movies*
visitar monumentos (*m. pl.*)	*to visit monuments*
la diversión	*fun activity; entertainment; recreation*
el/la excursionista	*hiker*
el fin de semana	*weekend*
el pasatiempo	*pastime; hobby*
los ratos libres	*spare (free) time*
el tiempo libre	*free time*

Deportes

el baloncesto	*basketball*
el béisbol	*baseball*
el ciclismo	*cycling*
el equipo	*team*
el esquí (acuático)	*(water) skiing*
el fútbol	*soccer*
el fútbol americano	*football*
el golf	*golf*
el hockey	*hockey*
el/la jugador(a)	*player*
la natación	*swimming*
el partido	*game; match*
la pelota	*ball*
el tenis	*tennis*
el vóleibol	*volleyball*

Adjetivos

deportivo/a	*sports-related*
favorito/a	*favorite*

Lugares

el café	*café*
el centro	*downtown*
el cine	*movie theater*
el gimnasio	*gymnasium*
la iglesia	*church*
el lugar	*place*
el museo	*museum*
el parque	*park*
la piscina	*swimming pool*
la plaza	*city or town square*
el restaurante	*restaurant*

Verbos

almorzar (o:ue)	*to have lunch*
cerrar (e:ie)	*to close*
comenzar (e:ie)	*to begin*
conseguir (e:i)	*to get; to obtain*
contar (o:ue)	*to count; to tell*
decir (e:i)	*to say; to tell*
dormir (o:ue)	*to sleep*
empezar (e:ie)	*to begin*
encontrar (o:ue)	*to find*
entender (e:ie)	*to understand*
hacer	*to do; to make*
ir	*to go*
jugar (u:ue)	*to play*
mostrar (o:ue)	*to show*
oír	*to hear*
pedir (e:i)	*to ask for; to request*
pensar (e:ie)	*to think*
pensar (+ *inf.*)	*to intend*
pensar en	*to think about*
perder (e:ie)	*to lose; to miss*
poder (o:ue)	*to be able to; can*
poner	*to put; to place*
preferir (e:ie)	*to prefer*
querer (e:ie)	*to want; to love*
recordar (o:ue)	*to remember*
repetir (e:i)	*to repeat*
salir	*to leave*
seguir (e:i)	*to follow; to continue*
suponer	*to suppose*
traer	*to bring*
ver	*to see*
volver (o:ue)	*to return*

***Decir* expressions**	*See page 109.*
Expresiones útiles	*See page 99.*

recursos

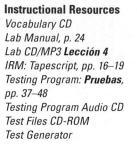

LM p. 24	Lab CD/MP3 Lección 4	Vocab CD Lección 4

Las vacaciones

Communicative Goals

You will learn how to:

• Discuss and plan a vacation

• Describe a hotel

• Talk about how you feel

• Talk about the seasons and the weather

Lesson Goals

In **Lección 5** students will be introduced to the following:

• terms for traveling and vacations
• seasons and months of the year
• weather expressions
• ordinal numbers (1st–10th)
• **estar** with conditions and emotions
• adjectives for conditions and emotions
• present progressive of regular and irregular verbs
• comparison of the uses of **ser** and **estar**
• direct object nouns and pronouns
• personal **a**
• scanning to find specific information
• cultural, geographic, and historical information about Puerto Rico

A primera vista Here are some additional questions you can ask based on the photo: **¿Dónde te gusta pasar tus ratos libres? ¿Qué haces en tus ratos libres? ¿Te gusta nadar? ¿Puedes nadar en una piscina todo el año?**

A PRIMERA VISTA

• ¿Dónde está la pareja: en una piscina o en el mar?
• ¿Son viejos o jóvenes?
• ¿Nadan o toman el sol?

INSTRUCTIONAL RESOURCES

Workbook/Video Manual: WB Activities, pp. 49–58
Laboratory Manual: Lab Activities, pp. 25–30
Workbook/Video Manual: Video Activities, pp. 203–204; pp. 233–234
Instructor's Resource Manual: **Hojas de actividades**, p. 144; **Vocabulario adicional**, p. 159; **¡Inténtalo!** & **Práctica** Answers, pp. 178–179;

Fotonovela Translations, p. 121; Textbook CD Tapescript, p. 75; Lab CDs Tapescript, pp. 20–24; **Fotonovela** Videoscript, p. 91; **Panorama cultural** Videoscript, p. 109; **Pan. cult.** Translations, p. 131
Info Gap Activities Booklet, pp. 17–20
Overhead Transparencies: #3, #4, #22–#27
Lab Audio CD/MP3 **Lección 5**

Panorama cultural DVD/Video
Fotonovela DVD/Video
Testing Program, pp. 49–60; pp. 205-216
Testing Program Audio CD
Test Generator
Test Files CD-ROM

Companion website
Presentations CD-ROM
Textbook CD
Vocabulary CD
Interactive CD-ROM
Video CD-ROM
Web-SAM

Las vacaciones

Más vocabulario

la cabaña	*cabin*
la cama	*bed*
la habitación individual, doble	*single, double room*
el piso	*floor (of a building)*
la planta baja	*ground floor*
el campo	*countryside*
el paisaje	*landscape*
el equipaje	*luggage*
la estación de autobuses, del metro, de tren	*bus, subway, train station*
la llegada	*arrival*
el pasaje (de ida y vuelta)	*(round-trip) ticket*
la salida	*departure; exit*
acampar	*to camp*
estar de vacaciones	*to be on vacation*
hacer las maletas	*to pack (one's suitcases)*
hacer una excursión	*to go on a hike; to go on a tour*
hacer turismo (m.)	*to go sightseeing*
hacer un viaje	*to take a trip*
ir de compras	*to go shopping*
ir de pesca	*to go fishing*
ir de vacaciones	*to go on vacation*
ir en autobús (m.), auto(móvil) (m.), avión (m.), barco (m.), motocicleta (f.), taxi (m.)	*to go by bus, car, plane, boat, motorcycle, taxi*

Variación léxica

automóvil ⟷ coche (*Esp.*), carro (*Amér. L.*)
autobús ⟷ camión (*Méx.*), guagua (*P. Rico*)
motocicleta ⟷ moto (*coloquial*)

la agente de viajes

el pasaporte

Confirma una reservación. (confirmar)

En la agencia de viajes

la habitación

el ascensor

el empleado

la llave

la huésped

el botones

el huésped

En el hotel

recursos

TEXT CD Lección 5	WB pp. 49–50	LM p. 25	Lab CD/MP3 Lección 5	I CD-ROM Lección 5	Vocab CD Lección 5

TEACHING OPTIONS

Extra Practice Ask questions about the people, places, and activities in **Contextos**. Ex: **¿Qué actividades pueden hacer los turistas en una playa? ¿Pueden nadar? ¿tomar el sol? ¿sacar fotos?** Then expand questions to ask students what they specifically do at these places. Ex: **¿Qué haces tú cuando vas a la playa?** Students should respond in complete sentences.

Variación léxica Point out that these are just some of the different Spanish names for vehicles. Ask heritage speakers in class if they are familiar with other terms. While some of these terms are mutually understood in different regions (**el coche, el carro, el auto, el automóvil**), others are specific to a region and may not be understood by others (**la guagua, el camión**). Stress that the feminine article **la** is used with the abbreviation **moto**.

Práctica

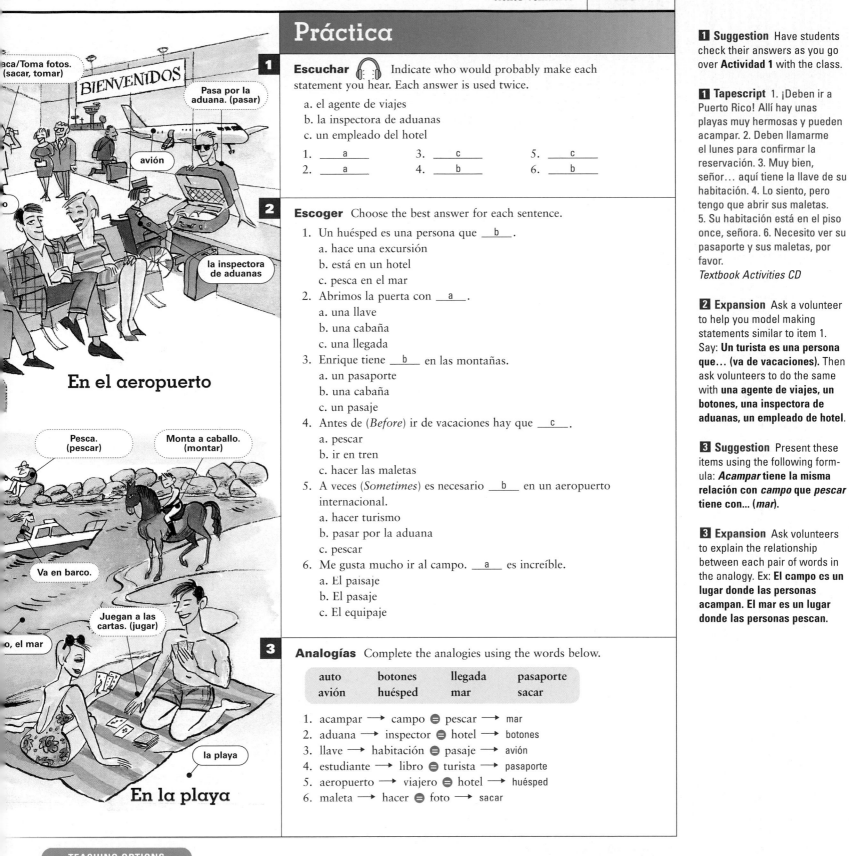

Pasa por la aduana. (pasar)

...aca/Toma fotos. (sacar, tomar)

BIENVENIDOS

avión

la inspectora de aduanas

En el aeropuerto

Pesca. (pescar)

Monta a caballo. (montar)

Va en barco.

Juegan a las cartas. (jugar)

...o, el mar

la playa

En la playa

1 **Escuchar** Indicate who would probably make each statement you hear. Each answer is used twice.

a. el agente de viajes
b. la inspectora de aduanas
c. un empleado del hotel

1. __a__   3. __c__   5. __c__
2. __a__   4. __b__   6. __b__

2 **Escoger** Choose the best answer for each sentence.

1. Un huésped es una persona que __b__.
   a. hace una excursión
   b. está en un hotel
   c. pesca en el mar
2. Abrimos la puerta con __a__.
   a. una llave
   b. una cabaña
   c. una llegada
3. Enrique tiene __b__ en las montañas.
   a. un pasaporte
   b. una cabaña
   c. un pasaje
4. Antes de (*Before*) ir de vacaciones hay que __c__.
   a. pescar
   b. ir en tren
   c. hacer las maletas
5. A veces (*Sometimes*) es necesario __b__ en un aeropuerto internacional.
   a. hacer turismo
   b. pasar por la aduana
   c. pescar
6. Me gusta mucho ir al campo. __a__ es increíble.
   a. El paisaje
   b. El pasaje
   c. El equipaje

3 **Analogías** Complete the analogies using the words below.

| auto | botones | llegada | pasaporte |
| avión | huésped | mar | sacar |

1. acampar → campo ⊖ pescar → mar
2. aduana → inspector ⊖ hotel → botones
3. llave → habitación ⊖ pasaje → avión
4. estudiante → libro ⊖ turista → pasaporte
5. aeropuerto → viajero ⊖ hotel → huésped
6. maleta → hacer ⊖ foto → sacar

1 Suggestion Have students check their answers as you go over **Actividad 1** with the class.

1 Tapescript 1. ¡Deben ir a Puerto Rico! Allí hay unas playas muy hermosas y pueden acampar. 2. Deben llamarme el lunes para confirmar la reservación. 3. Muy bien, señor… aquí tiene la llave de su habitación. 4. Lo siento, pero tengo que abrir sus maletas. 5. Su habitación está en el piso once, señora. 6. Necesito ver su pasaporte y sus maletas, por favor.
Textbook Activities CD

2 Expansion Ask a volunteer to help you model making statements similar to item 1. Say: **Un turista es una persona que… (va de vacaciones).** Then ask volunteers to do the same with **una agente de viajes, un botones, una inspectora de aduanas, un empleado de hotel.**

3 Suggestion Present these items using the following formula: *Acampar* **tiene la misma relación con** *campo* **que** *pescar* **tiene con… (***mar***).**

3 Expansion Ask volunteers to explain the relationship between each pair of words in the analogy. Ex: **El campo es un lugar donde las personas acampan. El mar es un lugar donde las personas pescan.**

Suggestions

- Project **Transparency #23** and have students look over the seasons and months of the year. Call out the names of holidays or campus events and ask students to say the month or season in which they occur.
- Introduce weather-related vocabulary by discussing the weather in your area today. Write the expressions on the board. Ex: **Hoy hace sol.**
- Project **Transparency #24** and use magazine pictures to cover as many weather conditions as possible from this page. Begin describing one of the pictures using one of the weather expressions. Then, ask volunteers further questions that elicit other expressions. Point out the use of **mucho/a** before nouns and **muy** before adjectives in these expressions.
- Review the shortened forms **buen** and **mal** and their use before **tiempo**.
- Use pictures that include human beings to illustrate the distinction between **tener calor/frío** and **hacer calor/frío**.

Successful Language Learning
Remind students that the weather expressions are used very frequently in conversation and that they should make a special effort to learn them.

Las estaciones y los meses del año

el invierno: diciembre, enero, febrero

la primavera: marzo, abril, mayo

el verano: junio, julio, agosto

el otoño: septiembre, octubre, noviembre

—**¿Cuál es la fecha de hoy?**   *What is today's date?*
—**Es el primero de octubre.**   *It's the first of October.*
—**Es el diez de noviembre.**   *It's November 10th.*

El tiempo

—**¿Qué tiempo hace?**   *How's the weather?*
—**Hace buen/mal tiempo.**   *The weather is good/bad.*

Hace (mucho) calor.
It's (very) hot.

Hace (mucho) frío.
It's (very) cold.

Llueve.
It's raining.

Nieva.
It's snowing.

Más vocabulario

Está (muy) nublado.	*It's (very) cloudy.*
Hace fresco.	*It's cool.*
Hace (mucho) sol.	*It's (very) sunny.*
Hace (mucho) viento.	*It's (very) windy.*
Hay (mucha) niebla.	*It's (very) foggy.*

TEACHING OPTIONS

Pairs Have pairs of students work together to create sentences for each of the drawings on this page. Ask one student to write sentences for the first four drawings and the other to write sentences for the next four. When each pair has finished, ask them to exchange their sentences and correct their partners' work.

Extra Practice Create a number of cloze sentences about the weather that require the verb forms **hace, hay**, and **está** to be completed. Ex: **1. San Juan _____ en Puerto Rico. (está) 2. _____ mucho calor. (Hace) 3. No _____ muy nublado cuando _____ sol. (está, hace) 4. Cuando llueve, _____ nublado, pero no _____ niebla. (está, hay)**

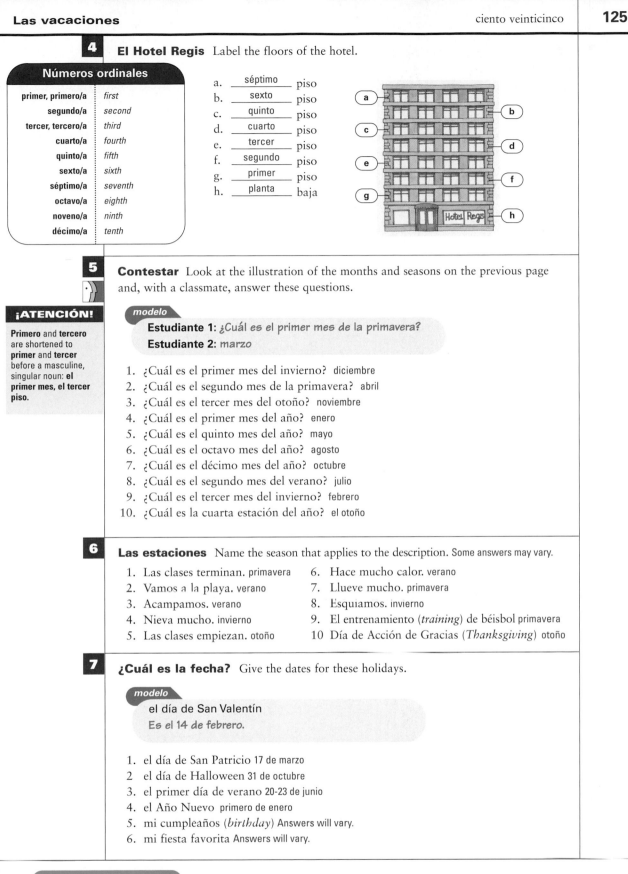

4 **El Hotel Regis** Label the floors of the hotel.

Números ordinales

primer, primero/a	first
segundo/a	second
tercer, tercero/a	third
cuarto/a	fourth
quinto/a	fifth
sexto/a	sixth
séptimo/a	seventh
octavo/a	eighth
noveno/a	ninth
décimo/a	tenth

a. <u>séptimo</u> piso
b. <u>sexto</u> piso
c. <u>quinto</u> piso
d. <u>cuarto</u> piso
e. <u>tercer</u> piso
f. <u>segundo</u> piso
g. <u>primer</u> piso
h. <u>planta</u> baja

5 **Contestar** Look at the illustration of the months and seasons on the previous page and, with a classmate, answer these questions.

¡ATENCIÓN!

Primero and **tercero** are shortened to **primer** and **tercer** before a masculine, singular noun: **el primer mes, el tercer piso.**

> **modelo**
> **Estudiante 1:** ¿Cuál es el primer mes de la primavera?
> **Estudiante 2:** marzo

1. ¿Cuál es el primer mes del invierno? diciembre
2. ¿Cuál es el segundo mes de la primavera? abril
3. ¿Cuál es el tercer mes del otoño? noviembre
4. ¿Cuál es el primer mes del año? enero
5. ¿Cuál es el quinto mes del año? mayo
6. ¿Cuál es el octavo mes del año? agosto
7. ¿Cuál es el décimo mes del año? octubre
8. ¿Cuál es el segundo mes del verano? julio
9. ¿Cuál es el tercer mes del invierno? febrero
10. ¿Cuál es la cuarta estación del año? el otoño

6 **Las estaciones** Name the season that applies to the description. Some answers may vary.

1. Las clases terminan. primavera
2. Vamos a la playa. verano
3. Acampamos. verano
4. Nieva mucho. invierno
5. Las clases empiezan. otoño
6. Hace mucho calor. verano
7. Llueve mucho. primavera
8. Esquiamos. invierno
9. El entrenamiento (*training*) de béisbol primavera
10 Día de Acción de Gracias (*Thanksgiving*) otoño

7 **¿Cuál es la fecha?** Give the dates for these holidays.

> **modelo**
> el día de San Valentín
> *Es el 14 de febrero.*

1. el día de San Patricio 17 de marzo
2. el día de Halloween 31 de octubre
3. el primer día de verano 20-23 de junio
4. el Año Nuevo primero de enero
5. mi cumpleaños (*birthday*) Answers will vary.
6. mi fiesta favorita Answers will vary.

8 Seleccionar Paco is talking about his family and friends. Choose the word or phrase that best completes each sentence.

1. A mis padres les gusta ir a Cancún porque (hace sol, nieva). hace sol
2. Mi primo de Kansas dice que durante (*during*) un tornado, hace mucho (sol, viento). viento
3. Mis amigos van a esquiar si (nieva, está nublado). nieva
4. Tomo el sol cuando (hace calor, hay niebla). hace calor
5. Nosotros vamos a ver una película si hace (buen, mal) tiempo. mal
6. Mi hermana prefiere correr cuando (hace mucho calor, hace fresco). hace fresco
7. Mis tíos van de excursión si hace (buen, mal) tiempo. buen
8. Mi padre no quiere jugar al golf si (hace fresco, llueve). llueve
9. Cuando hace mucho (sol, frío) no salgo de casa y tomo chocolate caliente (*hot*). frío
10. Hoy mi sobrino va al parque porque (llueve, hace buen tiempo). hace buen tiempo

9 El clima With a partner, take turns asking and answering questions about the weather and temperatures in these cities. Answers will vary.

> **modelo**
> **Estudiante 1:** ¿Qué tiempo hace hoy en Nueva York?
> **Estudiante 2:** Hace frío y hace viento.
> **Estudiante 1:** ¿Cuál es la temperatura máxima?
> **Estudiante 2:** Treinta y un grados (*degrees*).
> **Estudiante 1:** ¿Y la temperatura mínima?
> **Estudiante 2:** Diez grados.

soleado   lluvia   nieve   nublado   viento

Nueva York	Miami	Chicago	París	Madrid	Tokio
Máx. 31° Mín. 10°	Máx. 84° Mín. 62°	Máx. 23° Mín. 5°	Máx. 38° Mín. 26°	Máx. 42° Mín. 27°	Máx. 49° Mín. 34°

Montreal	México D.F.	Cozumel	Caracas	Quito	Buenos Aires
Máx. 18° Mín. 2°	Máx. 76° Mín. 41°	Máx. 91° Mín. 73°	Máx. 80° Mín. 72°	Máx. 60° Mín. 51°	Máx. 85° Mín. 59°

10 Completar Complete these sentences with your own ideas. Answers will vary.

1. Cuando hace sol, yo…
2. Cuando llueve, mis amigos y yo…
3. Cuando hace calor, mi familia…
4. Cuando hay niebla, la gente…
5. Cuando hace frío, yo…
6. Cuando hace mal tiempo, mis amigos…
7. Cuando nieva, muchas personas…
8. Cuando está nublado, mis amigos y yo…
9. Cuando hace fresco, mis padres…
10. Cuando hace buen tiempo, mis amigos…

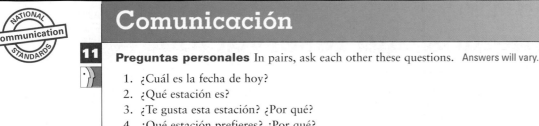

Comunicación

11 Preguntas personales In pairs, ask each other these questions. Answers will vary.

1. ¿Cuál es la fecha de hoy?
2. ¿Qué estación es?
3. ¿Te gusta esta estación? ¿Por qué?
4. ¿Qué estación prefieres? ¿Por qué?
5. ¿Prefieres el mar o las montañas? ¿La playa o el campo? ¿Por qué?
6. Cuando estás de vacaciones, ¿qué haces?
7. Cuando haces turismo, ¿qué te gusta hacer y ver?
8. ¿Piensas ir de vacaciones este verano? ¿Adónde quieres ir? ¿Por qué?
9. ¿Qué deseas ver?
10. ¿Cómo te gusta viajar ... en avión, en motocicleta ...?

12 Encuesta Your instructor will give you a worksheet. How does the weather affect what you do? Walk around the class and ask your classmates what they prefer or like to do in the following weather conditions. Note their responses on your worksheet. Make sure to personalize your survey by adding a few original questions to the list. Be prepared to report your findings to the class.
Answers will vary.

CONSÚLTALO

Calor and **frío** can apply to both weather and people. **Hacer** is used to describe weather conditions or climate (**Hace frío en Santiago.** *It's cold in Santiago.*). **Tener** is used to refer to people (**El viajero tiene frío.** *The traveler is cold.*). See **Estructura 3.4** p. 82.

Tiempo	Actividades
1. Hace mucho calor.	
2. Nieva.	
3. Hace buen tiempo.	
4. Hace fresco.	
5. Llueve.	
6. Está nublado.	
7. Hace mucho frío.	

13 Minidrama With two or three classmates, prepare and act out a skit about people who are on vacation or are planning a vacation. The skit should take place in one of the areas mentioned below. Answers will vary.

1. Una agencia de viajes
2. Una casa
3. Un aeropuerto, una estación de tren o una estación de autobuses
4. Un hotel
5. El campo o la playa

Síntesis

14 Un viaje You are planning a trip to Mexico and have many questions about your itinerary on which your partner, a travel agent, will advise you. Your instructor will give you and your partner each a sheet with different instructions for acting out the roles. Answers will vary.

11 Expansion Have students write the answers to questions 3–10 on a sheet of paper anonymously. Collect the sheets, shuffle them, and redistribute them for pairs to guess who wrote what.

12 Suggestion Model the activity by asking volunteers what they enjoy doing in hot weather. Ex: **Cuando hace calor, ¿qué haces? (Nado.)** Then distribute the **Hojas de actividades** from the IRM.

13 Suggestion With the whole class, brainstorm a list of people and topics that may be encountered in each situation and write it on the board.

13 Expansion Have students judge the skits in categories such as most original, funniest, most realistic, etc.

14 Suggestion Divide the class into pairs and distribute the handouts from the Information Gap Activities Booklet that correspond to this activity. Give students ten minutes to complete this activity.

14 Expansion Have pairs put together the ideal itinerary for someone else traveling to Mexico, like a classmate, a relative, someone famous, or even **el/la profesor(a)**.

TEACHING OPTIONS

Pairs Tell students they are part of a scientific expedition to Antarctica (**la Antártida**). Have them write a letter back home about the weather conditions and their activities there. Begin the letter for them by writing **Queridos amigos** on the board.
Game Have each student draw a Bingo card with 25 squares (five rows of five). Tell them to write **GRATIS** (*free*) in the center square and the name of a different city in each of the other

squares. Have them exchange cards. Call out different weather expressions. Ex: **Hace viento.** Students who think this description fits a city or cities on their board should mark the square with the weather condition. In order to win, a student must have marked five squares in a row and be able to give the weather condition for each one. Ex: **Hace mucho viento en Chicago.**

Tenemos una reservación.

Don Francisco y los estudiantes llegan al hotel.

communication
cultures
NATIONAL STANDARDS

PERSONAJES

MAITE

INÉS

DON FRANCISCO

ÁLEX

JAVIER

EMPLEADA

BOTONES

1

EMPLEADA ¿En qué puedo servirles?

DON FRANCISCO Mire, yo soy Francisco Castillo Moreno y tenemos una reservación a mi nombre.

EMPLEADA Mmm... no veo su nombre aquí. No está.

2

DON FRANCISCO ¿Está segura, señorita? Quizás la reservación está a nombre de la agencia de viajes, Ecuatur.

EMPLEADA Pues sí, aquí está... dos habitaciones dobles y una individual, de la ciento uno a la ciento tres,... todas en las primeras cabañas.

DON FRANCISCO Gracias, señorita. Muy amable.

3

BOTONES Bueno, la habitación ciento dos... Por favor.

6

INÉS Oigan, yo estoy aburrida. ¿Quieren hacer algo?

JAVIER ¿Por qué no vamos a explorar la ciudad un poco más?

INÉS ¡Excelente idea! ¡Vamos!

7

MAITE No, yo no voy. Estoy cansada y quiero descansar un poco porque a las seis voy a correr con Álex.

ÁLEX Y yo quiero escribir un mensaje electrónico antes de ir a correr.

8

JAVIER Pues nosotros estamos listos, ¿verdad, Inés?

INÉS Sí, vamos.

MAITE Adiós.

INÉS & JAVIER ¡Chau!

recursos

V CD-ROM	VM	I CD-ROM
Lección 5	pp. 203–204	Lección 5

Suggestion Work through the scenes that correspond to video stills 1–3 with the whole class, asking volunteers to play each part. Have students work together in groups of four to read scenes 4–10 aloud.

Expresiones útiles Remind the class that **estoy**, **está**, and **están** are present tense forms of the verb **estar**, which is often used with adjectives that describe conditions and emotions. Remind students that **es** and **son** are present tense forms of the verb **ser**, which is often used to describe the characteristics of people and things and to make generalizations. Draw students' attention to video still 4 of the **Fotonovela**. Point out that **están haciendo** and **estamos descansando** are examples of the present progressive, which is used to emphasize that an action is in progress. Tell your students that they will learn more about these concepts in **Estructura**.

ÁLEX Hola, chicas. ¿Qué están haciendo?

MAITE Estamos descansando.

JAVIER Oigan, no están nada mal las cabañas, ¿verdad?

INÉS Y todo está muy limpio y ordenado.

ÁLEX Sí, es excelente.

MAITE Y las camas son tan cómodas.

ÁLEX Bueno, nos vemos a las seis.

MAITE Sí, hasta luego.

ÁLEX Adiós.

MAITE ¿Inés y Javier? Juntos otra vez.

Expresiones útiles

Talking to hotel personnel

▶ **¿En qué puedo servirles?**
How can I help you?

▷ **Tenemos una reservación a mi nombre.**
We have a reservation in my name.

▶ **Mmm... no veo su nombre. No está.**
I don't see your name. It's not here.

▷ **¿Está seguro/a? Quizás/Tal vez está a nombre de Ecuatur.**
Are you sure? Maybe it's under the name of Ecuatur.

▶ **Aquí está... dos habitaciones dobles y una individual.**
Here it is, two double rooms and one single.

▶ **Aquí tienen las llaves.**
Here are your keys.

▷ **Gracias, señorita. Muy amable.**
Thank you, miss. You're very kind.

▶ **¿Dónde pongo las maletas?**
Where do I put the suitcases?

▷ **Allí, encima de la cama.**
There, on the bed.

Describing a hotel

▶ **No están nada mal las cabañas.**
The cabins aren't bad at all.

▶ **Todo está muy limpio y ordenado.**
Everything is very clean and orderly.

▶ **Es excelente/estupendo/ fabuloso/fenomenal.**
It's excellent/stupendous/ fabulous/great.

▶ **Es increíble/magnífico/ maravilloso/perfecto.**
It's incredible/magnificent/ marvelous/perfect.

▶ **Las camas son tan cómodas.**
The beds are so comfortable.

Talking about how you feel

▶ **Estoy un poco aburrido/a/ cansado/a.**
I'm a little bored/tired.

Enfoque cultural El alojamiento

There are many different types of lodging (**alojamiento**) for travelers in Hispanic countries. In major cities there are traditional hotels, but a more economical choice is a youth hostel, or **albergue juvenil,** where people can stay in a large, barracks-type room for a very low fee. Another option is an inn, or **hostal,** usually a privately owned residence. A unique type of lodging in Spain is a **parador,** which is usually a converted castle, palace, or villa that has been preserved and emphasizes the culture and cuisine of the region.

TEACHING OPTIONS

Enfoque cultural Point out to the class that a private residence that serves as an inn is sometimes called **una pensión.** Mention also that through exchange programs (**programas de intercambio**), many students travel to Spanish-speaking countries and live with host families. Tell the class that for long-term visits, travelers often save money by renting an apartment (**apartamento** or **departamento**) and cooking for themselves. In addition, encourage students to think critically about this information by discussing which type of lodging they would prefer if they were traveling to a Spanish-speaking country, and why.

Reacciona a la fotonovela

1 **Completar** Complete these sentences with the correct term from the word bank.

aburrida	cansada	habitaciones individuales
la agencia de viajes	descansar	hacer las maletas
las camas	habitaciones dobles	las maletas

1. La reservación para el hotel está a nombre de _la agencia de viajes_ .
2. Los estudiantes tienen dos _habitaciones dobles_ .
3. Maite va a _descansar_ porque está _cansada_ .
4. El botones lleva _las maletas_ a las habitaciones.
5. Las habitaciones son buenas y _las camas_ son cómodas.

2 **Identificar** Identify the person who would make each statement.

1. Antes de correr voy a trabajar en la computadora un poco. Álex
2. Estoy aburrido. Tengo ganas de explorar la ciudad. ¿Vienes tú también? Javier
3. Lo siento mucho, señor, pero su nombre no está en la lista. Empleada
4. Creo que la reservación está a mi nombre, señorita. Don Francisco
5. Oye, el hotel es maravilloso, ¿no? Las habitaciones están muy limpias. Inés

EMPLEADA   **ÁLEX**   **DON FRANCISCO**   **JAVIER**   **INÉS**

3 **Ordenar** Place these events in correct order.

a. Las chicas descansan en su habitación. __3__
b. Javier e Inés deciden ir a explorar la ciudad. __5__
c. Don Francisco habla con la empleada del hotel. __1__
d. Javier, Maite, Inés y Álex hablan en la habitación de las chicas. __4__
e. El botones pone las maletas en la cama. __2__

4 **Conversar** With a partner use these cues to create a conversation between a bellhop and a hotel guest in Spain.

Huésped	Botones
Ask the bellhop to carry your suitcases to your room.	→ Say "yes, sir/ma'am/miss."
Comment that the hotel is excellent and that everything is very clean.	→ Agree, then point out the guest's room, a single room on the sixth floor.
Ask if the bellhop is sure. You think you have room 96.	→ Confirm that the guest has room 69. Ask where you should put the suitcases.
Tell the bellhop to put them on the bed and thank him or her.	→ Say "you're welcome" and "goodbye."

---

1 **Expansion** To expand on the information contained in the items, have students create a follow-up sentence for each one, based on the **Fotonovela**.

2 **Expansion** Tell the class to add the **Botones** to the list of possible answers. Then, give these statements to the class as items 6–8: **6. Yo no voy. Necesito descansar. (Maite) 7. Ah, sí. Aquí tienen ustedes las llaves. (Empleada) 8. Bueno, aquí estamos… ésta es su habitación. (Botones)**

3 **Expansion** After students have determined the correct order, have pairs write sentences to describe what happens chronologically between items.

4 **Possible Response**
E1: **¿Puede llevar mis maletas a mi habitación?**
E2: **Sí, señorita.**
E1: **El hotel es excelente. Me gusta muchísimo. Todo está muy limpio.**
E2: **Sí, es un hotel maravilloso. Bueno, aquí estamos… la habitación sesenta y nueve, una habitación individual en el sexto piso.**
E1: **¿Está usted seguro? Creo que tengo la habitación número noventa y seis.**
E2: **No, señorita. Usted tiene la habitación sesenta y nueve. ¿Dónde pongo las maletas?**
E1: **Puede ponerlas encima de la cama. Gracias.**
E2: **De nada. Adiós, señorita.**

¡ATENCIÓN!

The meanings of some adjectives, such as **aburrido**, change depending on whether they are used with **ser** or **estar**. See **Estructura 5.3**, pp. 138–139.

NOTA CULTURAL

You might have difficulty finding a hotel room in parts of Spain during the month of August.

As in many other European countries, a large portion of the population goes on vacation for the entire month. Many shops and offices close. Life resumes its usual pace in September.

NATIONAL **communication** STANDARDS

TEACHING OPTIONS

Extra Practice Give your students some true-false items about the **Fotonovela**. Have them correct the false items. Ex: **1. Maite quiere ir a explorar la ciudad. (Falso. Maite quiere descansar.) 2. Álex y Maite van a correr a las seis. (Cierto.) 3. Las reservaciones están a nombre de Ecuatur. (Cierto.) 4. Inés no quiere explorar la ciudad porque está cansada. (Falso. Está aburrida y quiere explorar.)**

Small Groups Have students work in groups of four to prepare a skit to present to the class. In the skit, two friends check into a hotel, have a bellhop carry their suitcases to their rooms, and decide what to do for the rest of the day. Have students decide what city they are visiting, describe the hotel and their rooms, and explain what activities they want to do while they are visiting the city.

NATIONAL comparisons STANDARDS

Pronunciación
Spanish b and v

bueno   **vóleibol**   **biblioteca**   **vivir**

There is no difference in pronunciation between the Spanish letters **b** and **v**. However, each letter can be pronounced two different ways, depending on which letters appear next to them.

bonito   **viajar**   **también**   **investigar**

B and **v** are pronounced like the English hard *b* when they appear either as the first letter of a word, at the beginning of a phrase, or after **m** or **n**.

deber   **novio**   **abril**   **cerveza**

In all other positions, **b** and **v** have a softer pronunciation, which has no equivalent in English. Unlike the hard **b**, which is produced by tightly closing the lips and stopping the flow of air, the soft **b** is produced by keeping the lips slightly open.

bola   **vela**   **Caribe**   **declive**

In both pronunciations, there is no difference in sound between **b** and **v**. The English *v* sound, produced by friction between the upper teeth and lower lip, does not exist in Spanish. Instead, the soft **b** comes from friction between the two lips.

Verónica y su esposo cantan boleros.

When **b** or **v** begins a word, its pronunciation depends on the previous word. At the beginning of a phrase or after a word that ends in **m** or **n**, it is pronounced as a hard **b**.

Benito   **es de Boquerón**   **pero vive**   **en Victoria.**

Words that begin with **b** or **v** are pronounced with a soft **b** if they appear immediately after a word that ends in a vowel or any consonant other than **m** or **n**.

Práctica Read these words aloud to practice the **b** and the **v**.

1. hablamos
2. trabajar
3. botones
4. van
5. contabilidad
6. bien
7. doble
8. novia
9. béisbol
10. cabaña
11. llave
12. invierno

No hay mal que por bien no venga.[1]

Hombre prevenido vale por dos.[2]

Oraciones Read these sentences aloud to practice the **b** and the **v**.

1. Vamos a Guaynabo en autobús.
2. Voy de vacaciones a la Isla Culebra.
3. Tengo una habitación individual en el octavo piso.
4. Víctor y Eva van en avión al Caribe.
5. La planta baja es bonita también.
6. ¿Qué vamos a ver en Bayamón?
7. Beatriz, la novia de Víctor, es de Arecibo, Puerto Rico.

Refranes Read these sayings aloud to practice the **b** and the **v**.

[1] *Every cloud has a silver lining.*
[2] *An ounce of prevention equals a pound of cure.*

recursos

TEXT CD Lección 5	LM p. 26	Lab CD/MP3 Lección 5	I CD-ROM Lección 5

Section Goal
In **Pronunciación** students will be introduced to the pronunciation of **b** and **v**.

Instructional Resources
Textbook Activities CD
Lab Manual, p. 26
Lab CD/MP3 **Lección 5**
IRM: Tapescript, pp. 20–24; p. 75
Interactive CD-ROM

Suggestions
• Emphasize that **b (alta)** and **v (baja)** are pronounced identically in Spanish but that, depending on the letter's position in a word, each is pronounced two ways. Pronounce **vóleibol** and **vivir** several times, asking students to listen for the difference between the initial and medial sounds represented by **b** and **v**.
• Explain the cases in which **b** and **v** are pronounced like English **b** in *boy* and model the pronunciation of **bonito**, **viajar**, **también**, and **investigar**.
• Point out that before **b** or **v**, **n** is usually pronounced **m**.
• Explain that in all other positions, **b** and **v** are fricatives. Pronounce **deber**, **novio**, **abril**, and **cerveza** as students watch your lips.
• Remind the class that Spanish has no sound like the English **v**. Pronounce **vida**, **vacaciones**, **avión**, **automóvil**.
• Explain that the same rules apply in connected speech. Practice with phrases like **de vacaciones**, **de ida y vuelta**.

Práctica/Oraciones/Refranes
These exercises are recorded on the Textbook Activities CD. You may want to play the CD so students practice the pronunciation point by listening to Spanish spoken by speakers other than yourself.

TEACHING OPTIONS

Extra Practice Write some additional proverbs on the board and have the class practice saying each one. Ex: **Más vale que sobre y no que falte.** (*Better too much than too little.*) **No sólo de pan vive el hombre.** (*Man doesn't live by bread alone.*) **A caballo regalado no se le ve el colmillo.** (*Don't look a gift horse in the mouth.*)

Small Groups Have students work in small groups and take turns reading aloud sentences from the **Fotonovela** on pages 128–129, focusing on the correct pronunciation of **b** and **v**. If a group member gets stuck on a word that contains **b** or **v**, the rest of the group should supply the rule that explains how it should be pronounced.

Section Goals

In **Estructura 5.1**, students will learn:
- to use **estar** to describe conditions and emotions
- adjectives that describe conditions and emotions

Instructional Resources

WB/VM: Workbook, pp. 51–52
Lab Manual, p. 27
Lab CD/MP3 Lección 5
IRM: ¡Inténtalo! & Práctica
Answers, pp. 178–179;
Tapescript, pp. 20–24
Interactive CD-ROM
Companion website:
www.vistahigherlearning.com
Presentations CD-ROM

Suggestions

- Ask students to find examples of **estar** used with adjectives in the **Fotonovela**.
- Draw attention to the caption for video still 5 and compare the use of **estar** in the first two sentences with the use of **ser** in the third.
- Use TPR to practice the adjectives. Have the class stand and signal a student. Say: _____, **estás enojado/a**. (Student will make an angry face.) Continue signaling individuals until you have introduced most of the adjectives. Then vary the procedure by indicating more than one student. Keep the pace rapid so the drill seems like a game.

5.1 Estar with conditions and emotions

ANTE TODO As you learned in **Lecciones 1** and **2**, the verb **estar** is used to talk about how you feel and to say where people, places, and things are located. **Estar** is also used with adjectives to talk about certain emotional and physical conditions.

▶ **Estar** is used with adjectives to describe the physical condition of places and things.

La habitación **está** sucia.
The room is dirty.

La puerta **está** cerrada.
The door is closed.

▶ **Estar** is also used with adjectives to describe how people feel, both mentally and physically.

Estoy aburrida. ¿Quieren hacer algo?

No, estoy cansada.

recursos

WB
pp. 51–56

LM
pp. 27–30

Lab CD/MP3
Lección 5

I CD-ROM
Lección 5

vistahigher
learning.com

CONSÚLTALO

To review the present tense of **ser**, see **Estructura 1.3**, p. 18.

• • •

To review the present tense of **estar**, see **Estructura 2.3**, p. 49.

¡ATENCIÓN!

Two important expressions with **estar** that you can use to talk about conditions and emotions are **estar de buen humor** (*to be in a good mood*) and **estar de mal humor** (*to be in a bad mood*).

Adjectives that describe emotions and conditions

abierto/a	open	**contento/a**	happy; content	**listo/a**	ready
aburrido/a	bored	**desordenado/a**	disorderly	**nervioso/a**	nervous
alegre	happy; joyful	**enamorado/a (de)**	in love (with)	**ocupado/a**	busy
avergonzado/a	embarrassed			**ordenado/a**	orderly
cansado/a	tired	**enojado/a**	mad; angry	**preocupado/a (por)**	worried (about)
cerrado/a	closed	**equivocado/a**	wrong	**seguro/a**	sure
cómodo/a	comfortable	**feliz**	happy	**sucio/a**	dirty
confundido/a	confused	**limpio/a**	clean	**triste**	sad

¡INTÉNTALO! Provide the present tense forms of **estar**, and choose which adjective best completes the sentence. The first item has been done for you.

1. La biblioteca ___está___ (cerrada / nerviosa) los domingos por la noche. *cerrada*
2. Nosotros ___estamos___ muy (ocupados / equivocados) todos los lunes. *ocupados*
3. Ellas ___están___ (alegres / confundidas) porque tienen tiempo libre. *alegres*
4. Javier ___está___ (enamorado / ordenado) de Maribel. *enamorado*
5. Diana ___está___ (enojada / limpia) con su novio. *enojada*
6. Yo ___estoy___ (nerviosa / abierta) por el viaje. *nerviosa*
7. La habitación siempre ___está___ (ordenada / segura) cuando vienen sus padres. *ordenada*
8. Ustedes no comprenden; ___están___ (equivocados / tristes). *equivocados*
9. Marina y yo ___estamos___ (preocupados / aburridos) por el examen. *preocupados*
10. Usted ___está___ muy (cansado / sucio) los lunes por la mañana. *cansado*

TEACHING OPTIONS

TPR Call out a sentence using an adjective and have students mime the emotion or show the condition. Ex: **Sus libros están abiertos.** (Students show their open books.) **Ustedes están alegres.** (Students act happy.) Next, call on volunteers to act out an emotion or condition and have the class tell what is going on. Ex: A student pretends to cry. (**Carlos está triste.**)

Video Show the **Fotonovela** video again and ask comprehension questions using **estar** and adjectives expressing emotions or conditions. Ex: **¿Cómo está la cabaña? (Todo está muy limpio y ordenado.) ¿Está cansado Javier? (No, no está cansado.) ¿Quién está cansado? (Maite está cansada.)**

Práctica

1

¿Cómo están? Complete Martín's statements about how he and other people are feeling. In the first blank, fill in the correct form of **estar**. In the second blank, fill in the adjective that best fits the context. Some answers may vary.

1. Yo ___estoy___ un poco ___nervioso___ porque tengo un examen mañana.
2. Mi hermana Patricia ___está___ muy ___contenta___ porque mañana va a hacer una excursión al campo.
3. Mis hermanos Juan y José salen de la casa a las cinco de la mañana. Por la noche, siempre ___están___ muy ___cansados___.
4. Mi amigo Ramiro ___está___ ___enamorado___; su novia se llama Adela.
5. Mi papá y sus colegas ___están___ muy ___ocupados___ hoy. ¡Hay mucho trabajo!
6. Patricia y yo ___estamos___ un poco ___preocupados___ por ellos porque trabajan mucho.
7. Mi amiga Mónica ___está___ un poco ___triste/enojada___ porque su novio no puede salir esta noche.
8. Esta clase no es muy interesante. ¿Tú ___estás___ ___aburrido___ también?

2

Describir Describe these people and places. Answers will vary.

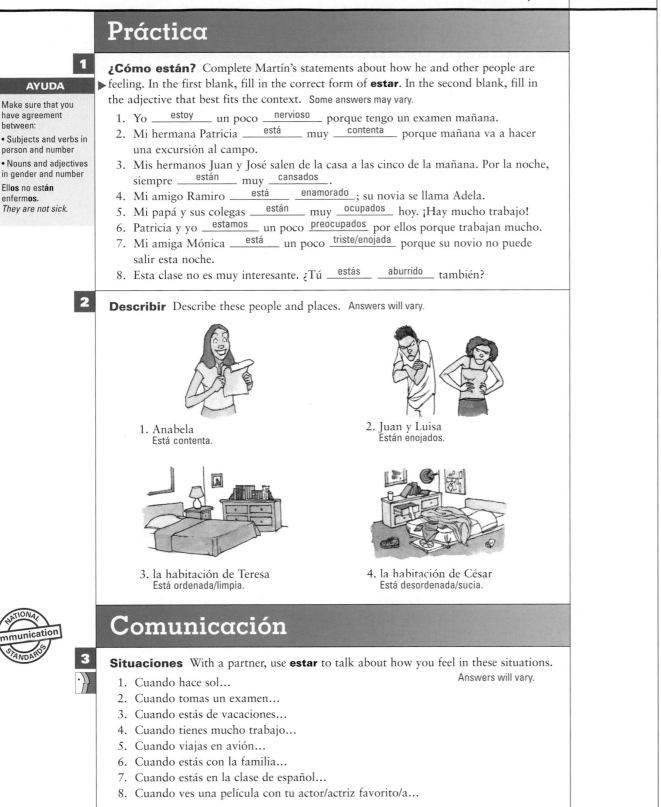

1. Anabela
   Está contenta.

2. Juan y Luisa
   Están enojados.

3. la habitación de Teresa
   Está ordenada/limpia.

4. la habitación de César
   Está desordenada/sucia.

Comunicación

3

Situaciones With a partner, use **estar** to talk about how you feel in these situations.

Answers will vary.

1. Cuando hace sol...
2. Cuando tomas un examen...
3. Cuando estás de vacaciones...
4. Cuando tienes mucho trabajo...
5. Cuando viajas en avión...
6. Cuando estás con la familia...
7. Cuando estás en la clase de español...
8. Cuando ves una película con tu actor/actriz favorito/a...

---

1 Suggestion Have a volunteer model the first sentence by supplying the correct form of **estar** and an appropriate adjective. Ask the student to explain his or her choices.

1 Expansion Have students write five more sentences missing **estar** and an adjective like those in the activity. Then have them exchange papers and complete one another's sentence.

2 Expansion
• Have students write a sentence explaining why the people feel the way they do and why the rooms are the way they are.
• Have students pretend they are Anabela, Juan, or Luisa and give a short oral presentation describing who they are and how they feel today.

3 Suggestion Have partners alternate asking and answering questions until each has answered all items.

3 Expansion Ask students to keep a record of their partners' responses. Take a classroom poll to see what percentage of students felt a particular way for each situation.

TEACHING OPTIONS

Pairs Have students write a list of four questions using different conjugations of **estar** and four adjectives that have an opposite from the list on page 132. Students ask partners their questions. They respond negatively, then use the opposite adjective in an affirmative statement. Ex: **¿Está abierta la biblioteca? (No, no está abierta. Está cerrada.)**

Heritage Speakers Ask heritage speakers to work with a partner to play with word associations. Student A calls out an adjective. Student B calls out all the words that come to mind. After partners have each taken several turns, have them choose one set of associations to include in a poem or haiku.

5.2 The present progressive

ANTE TODO Both Spanish and English use the present progressive. In both languages, it consists of the present tense of the verb *to be* and the present participle (the *-ing* form of the verb in English).

Estoy escuchando.	Carlos **está corriendo**.	Ella **está escribiendo** una carta.
I am listening.	*Carlos is running.*	*She is writing a letter.*

Hola, chicas. ¿Qué están haciendo?

Estamos descansando.

▶ The present progressive is formed with the present tense of **estar** and the present participle of the main verb.

FORM OF **ESTAR** + PRESENT PARTICIPLE	FORM OF **ESTAR** + PRESENT PARTICIPLE
Estoy **pescando.**	**Estamos** **comiendo.**
I am *fishing.*	*We are* *eating.*

▶ The present participle of regular **–ar**, **–er**, and **–ir** verbs is formed as follows:

INFINITIVE	STEM	ENDING	PRESENT PARTICIPLE
hablar	habl-	-ando	habl**ando**
comer	com-	-iendo	com**iendo**
escribir	escrib-	-iendo	escrib**iendo**

▶ **Ir**, **poder**, and **venir** have irregular present participles (**yendo, pudiendo, viniendo**), but these verbs are rarely used in the present progressive. Several other verbs have irregular present participles that you will need to learn.

▶ **–Ir** stem-changing verbs have a stem change in the present participle.

–*ir* stem-changing verbs

e:ie in the present tense	**e → i** in the present participle
preferir	pref**i**riendo
sentir	s**i**ntiendo

e:i in the present tense	**e → i** in the present participle
conseguir	cons**i**guiendo
pedir	p**i**diendo
seguir	s**i**guiendo

o:ue in the present tense	**o → u** in the present participle
dormir	d**u**rmiendo

Section Goals

In **Estructura 5.2**, students will learn:
- the present progressive of regular and irregular verbs
- the present progressive versus the simple present tense in Spanish

Instructional Resources
Transparency #25
WB/VM: Workbook, p. 53
Lab Manual, p. 28
Lab CD/MP3 **Lección 5**
IRM: ¡Inténtalo! & Práctica
Answers, pp. 178–179;
Tapescript, pp. 20–24
Info Gap Activities Booklet, pp. 19–20
Interactive CD-ROM
Companion website:
www.vistahigherlearning.com
Presentations CD-ROM

Suggestions
- Have students read the caption under video still 4 on page 129. Focus attention on **estar** + [*present participle*] to express what is going on at the moment. Then have students use the present progressive to describe what is happening in the rest of the **Fotonovela** episode.
- To elicit the present progressive, use regular verbs to ask questions about things students are not doing. Ex: **¿Estás comiendo pizza? (No, no estoy comiendo pizza.)**
- Explain the formation of the present progressive of regular verbs, writing examples on the board.
- Use pictures to elicit sentences with the present progressive. Ex: **¿Qué está haciendo el hombre alto? (Está sacando fotos.)** Continue until most students have had an opportunity to respond, and include present participles ending in **–yendo** as well as those with stem changes.

TEACHING OPTIONS

Large Groups Divide the class into three groups. Appoint leaders and give them a list of verbs. Leaders call out a verb and a subject (**seguir / yo**), then toss a ball (or a balled-up piece of paper) to someone in the group. That student says the appropriate present progressive form of the verb (**estoy siguiendo**) and tosses the ball back. Leaders should call out all verbs on the list and toss the ball to every member of the group.

Extra Practice Mime an action. Ask students what you are doing. Students respond using the present progressive. Ex: Pick up a newspaper and pretend to read it. Ask: _____, **¿qué estoy haciendo? (Está leyendo el periódico.)** Also ask leading questions that may require either affirmative or negative answers depending on what you mime. **Y ahora, ¿estoy haciendo las maletas? (No, está bebiendo café.)**

COMPARE & CONTRAST

The use of the present progressive is much more restricted in Spanish than in English. In Spanish, the present progressive is mainly used to emphasize that an action is in progress at the time of speaking.

Inés **está escuchando** música latina **ahora mismo**.
Inés is listening to Latin music right now.

Álex y su amigo **todavía están jugando** al fútbol.
Álex and his friend are still playing soccer.

In English, the present progressive is often used to talk about situations and actions that occur over an extended period of time or in the future. In Spanish, the simple present tense is often used instead.

Javier **estudia** computación este semestre.
Javier is studying computer science this semester.

Inés y Maite **salen** mañana para los Estados Unidos.
Inés and Maite are leaving tomorrow for the United States.

Estamos pensando en lo mismo:

su **F**uturo

Su asesor para ganar
FIDUCOLOMBIA
Sociedad Fiduciaria S.A.

¡INTÉNTALO! Create complete sentences by putting the verbs in the present progressive. The first item has been done for you.

1. Mis amigos / descansar en la playa Mis amigos están descansando en la playa.
2. Nosotros / practicar deportes Estamos practicando deportes.
3. Carmen / comer en casa Carmen está comiendo en casa.
4. Nuestro equipo / ganar el partido Nuestro equipo está ganando el partido.
5. Yo / leer el periódico Estoy leyendo el periódico.
6. Él / pensar en comprar una bicicleta Está pensando en comprar una bicicleta.
7. Ustedes / jugar a las cartas Ustedes están jugando a las cartas.
8. José y Francisco / dormir José y Francisco están durmiendo.
9. Marisa / leer correo electrónico Marisa está leyendo correo electrónico.
10. Yo / preparar sándwiches Estoy preparando sándwiches.
11. Carlos / tomar fotos Carlos está tomando fotos.
12. ¿dormir / tú? ¿Estás durmiendo?

Suggestions
- Discuss each point in the **Compare & Contrast** box.
- Point out that the present progressive is rarely used with the verbs **ir, poder,** and **venir** since they already imply an action in progress.
- Write the following statements on the board. Ask students if they would use the present or the present progressive in Spanish for each item. 1. I'm going on vacation tomorrow. 2. She is packing her suitcase right now. 3. They are sightseeing in Madrid this week. 4. Roberto is still working. Then ask students to translate the items. (**1. Voy de vacaciones mañana. 2. Está haciendo la maleta ahora mismo. 3. Hacen turismo en Madrid esta semana. 4. Roberto todavía está trabajando.**)
- In this lesson, students learn **todavía** to mean *still* in the present progressive tense. You may want to point out that **todavía** also means *yet*. They will be able to use that meaning in later lessons, as they learn the past tenses.
- Have students rewrite the sentences in the ¡**Inténtalo!** activity using the simple present. Ask volunteers to explain how the sentences change depending on whether the verb is in the present progressive or the simple present.

TEACHING OPTIONS

Pairs Have students write eight sentences in Spanish modeled after the examples in the **Compare & Contrast** box. There should be two sentences modeled after each example. Ask students to replace the verbs with blanks. Then, have students exchange their sentences with a partner for completion.

Extra Practice Ask students to find five photos from a magazine or create five drawings of people performing different activities. Have them write one sentence telling what the people in the photo/drawing are doing and one describing how they feel. Ex: **Juan está trabajando. Está cansado.**

Práctica

1

Completar Alfredo's Spanish class is preparing to travel to Puerto Rico. Use the present progressive of the verb in parentheses to complete Alfredo's description of what everyone is doing.

1. Yo <u>estoy investigando</u> (investigar) la situación política de la isla (*island*).
2. La esposa del profesor <u>está haciendo</u> (hacer) las maletas.
3. Marta y José Luis <u>están buscando</u> (buscar) información sobre San Juan en Internet.
4. Enrique y yo <u>estamos leyendo</u> (leer) un correo electrónico de nuestro amigo puertorriqueño.
5. Javier <u>está aprendiendo</u> (aprender) mucho sobre la cultura puertorriqueña.
6. Y tú <u>estás practicando</u> (practicar) tu español, ¿verdad?

2

¿Qué están haciendo? María and her friends are vacationing at a resort in San Juan, Puerto Rico. Complete her description of what everyone is doing right now.

CONSÚLTALO

For more information about Puerto Rico, see **Panorama**, pp. 148–149.

1. Yo estoy escribiendo una carta.
2. Javier está buceando en el mar.
3. Alejandro y Rebeca están jugando a las cartas.
4. Celia y yo estamos tomando el sol.
5. Samuel está escuchando música.
6. Lorenzo está durmiendo.

3

Personajes famosos Say what these celebrities are doing right now, using the cues provided. Answers will vary.

modelo
Serena Williams está jugando al tenis ahora mismo.

A

John Grisham — Mikhail Baryshnikov
Sarah McLachlan — Picabo Street
James Cameron — Regis Philbin
Venus Williams — ¿?
Tiger Woods — ¿?

B

bailar — hablar
cantar — hacer
correr — jugar
escribir — ¿?
esquiar — ¿?

AYUDA

John Grisham - **novelas**
Sarah McLachlan - **canciones**
James Cameron - **cine**
Venus Williams - **tenis**
Tiger Woods - **golf**
Mikhail Baryshnikov - **ballet**
Picabo Street - **esquí**
Regis Philbin - **televisión**

TEACHING OPTIONS

Heritage Speakers Have students bring in photos (photocopies or magazine illustrations will also do) from a vacation. Ask them to describe the photos to a partner. Students should explain who is in the photo, what they are doing, and where they are. After students have practiced with a partner, have them present their descriptions to the class.

Game Student A mimes an action and states what he or she is doing. Student B states what the first student is doing, mimes the action, and then mimes a different action and states what he or she is doing. Students continue to add actions to the chain until it breaks. A new chain begins with the student following the breakdown. After five minutes of play, the group of students comprising the longest chain wins.

Comunicación

4 **Un amigo preguntón** You have a friend who calls you at all hours to see what you're doing. What do you tell him or her if he or she calls you at these times?

Answers will vary.

> **modelo**
> 8:00 a.m.
> Estoy desayunando.

1. 5:00 a.m.	3. 9:30 a.m.	5. 11:00 a.m.	7. 12:00 p.m.
2. 2:00 p.m.	4. 5:00 p.m.	6. 9:00 p.m.	8. 11:30 p.m.

5 **Describir** Work with a partner and use the present progressive to describe what's going on in this Spanish beach scene. Answers will vary.

NOTA CULTURAL ▶

Drawn by its warm climate and attractive coasts, more tourists flock to Spain annually than to practically any other country in the world. In the summer months, the arrival of tourists makes the country's population swell to over twice its year-round population.

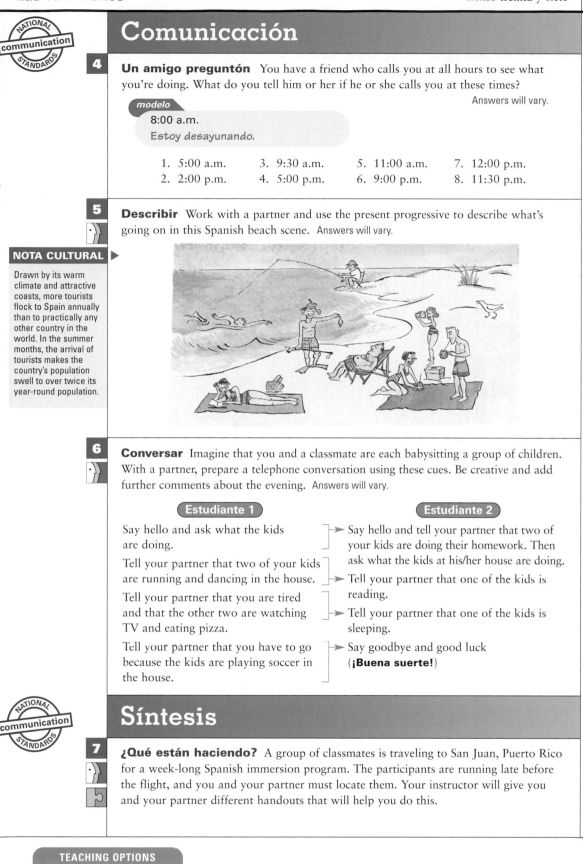

6 **Conversar** Imagine that you and a classmate are each babysitting a group of children. With a partner, prepare a telephone conversation using these cues. Be creative and add further comments about the evening. Answers will vary.

Estudiante 1

Say hello and ask what the kids are doing.

Tell your partner that two of your kids are running and dancing in the house.

Tell your partner that you are tired and that the other two are watching TV and eating pizza.

Tell your partner that you have to go because the kids are playing soccer in the house.

Estudiante 2

→ Say hello and tell your partner that two of your kids are doing their homework. Then ask what the kids at his/her house are doing.

→ Tell your partner that one of the kids is reading.

→ Tell your partner that one of the kids is sleeping.

→ Say goodbye and good luck (**¡Buena suerte!**)

Síntesis

7 **¿Qué están haciendo?** A group of classmates is traveling to San Juan, Puerto Rico for a week-long Spanish immersion program. The participants are running late before the flight, and you and your partner must locate them. Your instructor will give you and your partner different handouts that will help you do this.

---

4 **Suggestions**
- Have students outline their daily activities and what time they do them before beginning the activity.
- Remind students to use **a la(s)** when expressing time.
- Convert **Actividad 1** into a pair activity. Ex: E1: **¡Hola Andrés! Son las ocho de la mañana. ¿Qué estás haciendo?** E2: **Estoy desayunando.**

5 **Suggestion** Project **Transparency #25** and have students do the activity with their books closed.

5 **Expansion** In pairs, have students write a conversation between two or more of the people in the drawing. Conversations should consist of at least three exchanges.

6 **Suggestion** Before beginning their conversation, have students brainstorm two lists: one with verbs that describe what children do at home and the other with adjectives that describe how each of the babysitters feels.

6 **Expansion** Ask pairs to tell each other what the parents of the two sets of children are doing. Ex: **Los padres de los niños buenos están visitando el museo. Los padres de los niños malos están en una fiesta.**

7 **Suggestion** Divide the class into pairs and distribute the handouts from the Information Gap Activities Booklet that correspond to this activity. Give students ten minutes to complete this activity.

7 **Expansion** Have students work in pairs to say what each program participant is doing in flight. Ex: **Pedro está leyendo una novela.**

TEACHING OPTIONS

Video Show the **Fotonovela** video again, pausing after each exchange. Ask students to describe what each person in the shot is doing right at that moment.
TPR Write sentences with the present progressive on strips of paper. Call on a volunteer to pick a strip out of a hat to act out. The class tries to guess what the sentence is. Ex: **Yo estoy durmiendo en la cama.**

Pairs Ask students to write five sentences using the present progressive. Students should try to make their sentences as complex as possible. Have students dictate their sentences to their partners. After both partners have finished dictating their sentences, have them exchange papers for correction.

Section Goal

In **Estructura 5.3** students will review and compare the uses of **ser** and **estar**.

Instructional Resources

Transparency #26
WB/VM: Workbook, pp. 54–55
Lab Manual, p. 29
Lab CD/MP3 Lección 5
IRM: ¡Inténtalo! & Práctica
Answers, pp. 178–179;
Tapescript, pp. 20–24
Interactive CD-ROM
Companion website:
www.vistahigherlearning.com
Presentations CD-ROM

Suggestions

- Have pairs brainstorm as many uses of **ser** with examples as they can. Compile a list on the board, and repeat for **estar**. Ask students where there might be some confusion about which verb to use.
- On the board or an overhead transparency, write two columns. Column one will have sentences using **ser** and **estar** in random order. Ex: **Álex es de México.** Column two will have the uses of **ser** and **estar** taught so far, also in random order. Ex: **g. place of origin.** Call on individual students to match the sentence with its corresponding use.
- Write sentences with **ser** and **estar** on the board, but omitting the verb. Ask students to supply the correct form of **ser** or **estar**. Ex: **Mi casa ____ lejos de aquí. (estar, location; está)** If either **ser** or **estar** could be used, ask students to explain how the meaning of the sentence would change.

The Affective Dimension

If students feel anxious that Spanish has two verbs that mean *to be*, reassure them that they will soon feel more comfortable with this concept. Point out that Spanish speakers express rich shades of meaning by the way they use **ser** and **estar**.

5.3 Ser and estar

ANTE TODO You have already learned that **ser** and **estar** both mean *to be* but are used for different purposes. The following charts summarize the key differences in usage between **ser** and **estar**.

Uses of *ser*

1. Nationality and place of origin	Martín **es** argentino. **Es** de Buenos Aires.
2. Profession or occupation	Adela **es** agente de viajes. Francisco **es** médico.
3. Characteristics of people and things . . .	José y Clara **son** simpáticos. El clima de Puerto Rico **es** agradable.
4. Generalizations	¡**Es** fabuloso viajar! **Es** difícil estudiar a la una de la mañana.
5. Possession	**Es** la pluma de Maite. **Son** las llaves de don Francisco.
6. What something is made of	La bicicleta **es** de metal. Los pasajes **son** de papel.
7. Time and date	Hoy **es** martes. **Son** las dos. Hoy **es** el primero de julio.
8. Where or when an event takes place . .	El partido **es** en el estadio Santa Fe. La conferencia **es** a las siete.

¡ATENCIÓN!

Note that **de** is generally used after **ser** to express not only origin (**Es de Buenos Aires.**) and possession (**Es la pluma de Maite.**), but also what material something is made of (**La bicicleta es de metal.**).

Soy Francisco Castillo Moreno. Yo soy de la agencia Ecuatur.

Su nombre no está en mi lista.

Uses of *estar*

1. Location or spatial relationships	El aeropuerto **está** lejos de la ciudad. Tu habitación **está** en el tercer piso.
2. Health	¿Cómo **estás**? **Estoy** bien, gracias.
3. Physical states and conditions	El profesor **está** ocupado. Las ventanas **están** abiertas.
4. Emotional states	Marisa **está** feliz hoy. **Estoy** muy enojado con Javier.
5. Certain weather expressions	**Está** lloviendo. **Está** nublado.
6. Ongoing actions (progressive tenses) . .	**Estamos** estudiando para un examen. Ana **está** leyendo una novela.

TEACHING OPTIONS

Extra Practice Call out sentences containing forms of **ser** or **estar**. Ask students to identify the use of the verb.
Heritage Speakers Ask heritage speakers to write a postcard home about a vacation in Puerto Rico, incorporating as many of the uses of **ser** and **estar** as they can.

Game Divide the class into teams. Call out a purpose for either **ser** or **estar**. The first member of each team runs to the board and writes a sample sentence. If the sentence of the team finishing first is correct, the team gets a point. If not, check the next team, and so on. Practice all purposes for each verb, making sure each team member has had at least two turns, then tally the points to see which team wins.

Ser and *estar* with adjectives

▶ With many descriptive adjectives, **ser** and **estar** can both be used, but the meaning will change.

Juan **es** delgado.
Juan is thin.

Juan **está** más delgado hoy.
Juan looks thinner today.

Ana **es** nerviosa.
Ana is a nervous person.

Ana **está** nerviosa por el examen.
Ana is nervous because of the exam.

▶ In the examples above, the statements with **ser** are general observations about the inherent qualities of Juan and Ana. The statements with **estar** describe conditions that are variable.

▶ Here are some adjectives that change in meaning when used with **ser** and **estar**.

With *ser*	With *estar*
El chico **es listo**.	El chico **está listo**.
The boy is smart.	*The boy is ready.*
La profesora **es mala**.	La profesora **está mala**.
The professor is bad.	*The professor is sick.*
Jaime **es aburrido**.	Jaime **está aburrido**.
Jaime is boring.	*Jaime is bored.*
Las peras **son verdes**.	Las peras **están verdes**.
The pears are green.	*The pears are not ripe.*
El gato **es muy vivo**.	El gato **está vivo**.
The cat is very lively.	*The cat is alive.*
El puente **es seguro**.	Él no **está seguro**.
The bridge is safe.	*He's not sure.*

¡INTÉNTALO! Form complete sentences by using the correct form of **ser** or **estar**, the correct form of each adjective, and any other necessary words. The first item has been done for you.

1. Alejandra / cansado
   Alejandra está cansada.

2. Ellos / pelirrojo
   Ellos son pelirrojos.

3. Carmen / alto
   Carmen es alta.

4. Yo / la clase de español
   Estoy en la clase de español.

5. Película / a las once
   La película es a las once.

6. Hoy / viernes
   Hoy es viernes.

7. Nosotras / enojado
   Nosotras estamos enojadas.

8. Antonio / médico
   Antonio es médico.

9. Romeo y Julieta / enamorado
   Romeo y Julieta están enamorados.

10. Libros / de Ana
    Los libros son de Ana.

11. Marisa y Juan / estudiando
    Marisa y Juan están estudiando.

12. Partido de baloncesto / gimnasio
    El partido de baloncesto es en el gimnasio.

Suggestions
- Ask students if they notice any context clues in the examples that would help them choose between **ser** and **estar**.
- Write sentences like these on the board: 1. Pilar is worried because she has a test tomorrow. (**Pilar está preocupada porque tiene una prueba mañana.**) 2. The bellman is very busy right now. (**El botones está muy ocupado ahora.**) 3. The beach is pretty. (**La playa es bonita.**) 4. Juan is very handsome today. (**Juan está muy guapo hoy.**) Have students translate the sentences into Spanish and ask them why they chose either **ser** or **estar** for their translation.
- Ask students questions like these to practice the different meanings of adjectives depending on whether they are used with **ser** or **estar**. **1. Manuel es un muchacho muy inteligente. ¿Está listo o es listo? 2. No me gusta la clase de física. ¿Está aburrida o es aburrida? 3. No sé si Carlos tiene 50 ó 51 años. ¿No estoy seguro/a o no soy seguro/a? 4. ¿El color del taxi es verde o está verde? 5. El profesor no enseña muy bien. ¿Está malo o es malo?**

TEACHING OPTIONS

Extra Practice Have students write sentences illustrating the contrasting meanings of adjectives that change meaning when used with **ser** or **estar**. Have students trade sentences for peer-editing before going over them with the class.
Video Show the **Fotonovela** video again. Have students jot down every time they hear a form of **ser** or **estar**. Discuss each use of **ser** and **estar** in the **Fotonovela**.

Pairs Tell students to imagine that they are to interview a celebrity visiting their hometown. Ask them to write questions employing at least ten different uses of **ser** and **estar**. Next, have them interview a partner, recording his or her answers. Students should then write a summary of their interviews.

Práctica

1 Completar Complete this conversation with the appropriate forms of **ser** and **estar**.

EDUARDO ¡Hola, Ceci! ¿Cómo (1)___estás___?

CECILIA Hola, Eduardo. Bien, gracias. ¡Qué guapo (2)___estás___ hoy!

EDUARDO Gracias. (3)___Eres___ muy amable. Oye, ¿qué (4)___estás___ haciendo? (5)¿___Estás___ ocupada?

CECILIA No, sólo le (6)___estoy___ escribiendo una carta a mi prima Pilar.

EDUARDO ¿De dónde (7)___es___ ella?

CECILIA Pilar (8)___es___ del Ecuador. Su papá (9)___es___ médico en Quito. Pero ahora Pilar y su familia (10)___están___ de vacaciones en Ponce, Puerto Rico.

EDUARDO Y… ¿cómo (11)___es___ Pilar?

CECILIA (12)___Es___ muy lista. Y también (13)___es___ alta, rubia y muy bonita.

2 Describir With a partner, describe the people in the drawing. Your descriptions should answer the questions. Answers will vary.

1. ¿Quiénes son las personas en el dibujo?
2. ¿Dónde están?
3. ¿Cómo son?
4. ¿Cómo están?
5. ¿Qué están haciendo?
6. ¿Qué estación es?
7. ¿Qué tiempo hace?
8. ¿Quiénes están de vacaciones?

Comunicación

communication

3 **Describir** With a classmate, take turns describing people. First mention where each person is from. Then describe what each person is like, how each person is feeling, and what he or she is doing right now.   Answers will vary.

> **modelo**
>
> tu compañero/a de cuarto
>
> *Mi compañera de cuarto es de San Juan, Puerto Rico. Es muy inteligente.*
> *Está cansada pero está estudiando porque tiene un examen.*

1. tu mejor (*best*) amigo/a
2. tus padres
3. tu profesor(a) favorito/a
4. tu novio/a o esposo/a
5. tu primo/a favorito/a
6. tus abuelos

4 **Adivinar** Get together with a partner and describe a celebrity to him or her using these questions as a guide. Don't mention the celebrity's name. Can your partner guess who you are describing?   Answers will vary.

1. ¿Cómo es?
2. ¿Cómo está?
3. ¿De dónde es?
4. ¿Dónde está?
5. ¿Qué está haciendo?
6. ¿Cuál es su profesión?

5 **En el aeropuerto** In small groups, take turns using **ser** and **estar** to describe this scene at Luis Muñoz Marín International Airport. What do the people in the picture look like? How are they feeling? What are they doing?   Answers will vary.

NOTA CULTURAL ▶

Luis Muñoz Marín International Airport in San Juan, Puerto Rico is a major transportation hub of the Caribbean. The airport connects the region with the rest of the world.

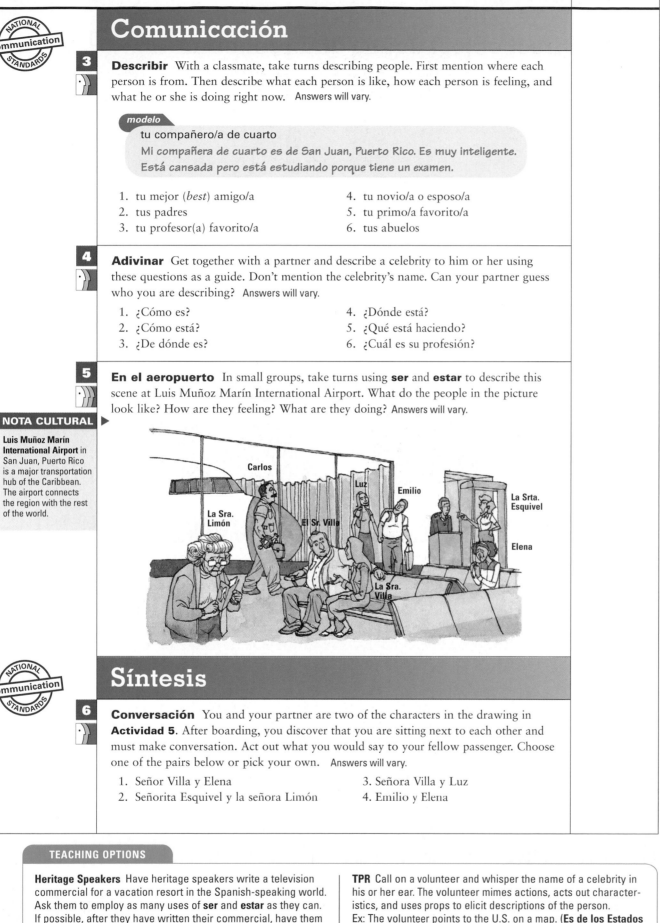

Síntesis

communication

6 **Conversación** You and your partner are two of the characters in the drawing in **Actividad 5**. After boarding, you discover that you are sitting next to each other and must make conversation. Act out what you would say to your fellow passenger. Choose one of the pairs below or pick your own.   Answers will vary.

1. Señor Villa y Elena
2. Señorita Esquivel y la señora Limón
3. Señora Villa y Luz
4. Emilio y Elena

TEACHING OPTIONS

Heritage Speakers Have heritage speakers write a television commercial for a vacation resort in the Spanish-speaking world. Ask them to employ as many uses of **ser** and **estar** as they can. If possible, after they have written their commercial, have them videotape it to show to the class.

TPR Call on a volunteer and whisper the name of a celebrity in his or her ear. The volunteer mimes actions, acts out characteristics, and uses props to elicit descriptions of the person. Ex: The volunteer points to the U.S. on a map. (**Es de los Estados Unidos.**) She then indicates a short man. (**Es un hombre bajo.**) She mimes riding a bicycle. (**Está paseando en bicicleta. ¿Es Lance Armstrong?**)

---

3 Suggestion Have students suggest names of celebrities to add to the list.

3 Expansion After pairs have practiced their descriptions, have them select two to present to the class.

4 Suggestion Assign the name of each student in the class to another student. Students circulate around the room asking the activity questions to determine the identity of the student assigned to each person. Students record the names of the students interviewed and their assigned students. After five minutes, see how many identities students were able to discover.

5 Suggestion Ask groups to choose a leader to moderate the activity, a secretary to record the group's description, and a proofreader to check that the written description is accurate. Then project **Transparency #26**. All students should take turns adding one sentence at a time to the group's description.

5 Expansion Have students pick one of the individuals pictured and write a one-paragraph description of that person, employing as many different uses of **ser** and **estar** as possible.

6 Suggestions
- Before starting, have students work in pairs to describe the character they will be playing to their partner.
- Make sure that students use **ser** and **estar**, the present progressive, and stem-changing verbs in their conversation, as well as vacation-, pastime-, and family-related vocabulary.

The Affective Dimension
Ask your students if they are more comfortable speaking Spanish with students they already know or students they do not know very well. Encourage them to consider pair and group activities as a cooperative venture in which group members support and encourage each other.

142 Instructor's Annotated Edition • Lesson Five

Section Goals

In **Estructura 5.4** students will study:
- direct object nouns
- the personal **a**
- direct object pronouns

Instructional Resources
WB/VM: Workbook, p. 56
Lab Manual, p. 30
*Lab CD/MP3 **Lección 5***
IRM: ¡Inténtalo! & Práctica
Answers, pp. 178–179;
Tapescript, pp. 20–24
Interactive CD-ROM
Companion website:
www.vistahigherlearning.com
Presentations CD-ROM

Suggestions

- Write these sentences on the board: **—¿Quién tiene el pasaporte? —Juan lo tiene.** Underline **pasaporte** and explain that it is a direct object. Then underline **lo** and explain that it is the masculine singular direct object pronoun. Translate both sentences. Follow the same procedure with these sentences: **—¿Quién hace turismo? —Simón lo hace. —¿Quién tiene la llave? —Pilar la tiene. —¿Quién escribe postales? —Jorge las escribe.**
- Ask individuals questions to elicit the personal **a**: **¿Tienes que esperar a tu novio con frecuencia? ¿Visitas a tu abuela los fines de semana? ¿Llamas a tu padre los sábados?**
- Continue by asking a series of questions to elicit the **lo, la, los**, and **las** pronouns. Ask: **¿Quién ve el lápiz de Marcos? ¿Ves el libro de Daniela? ¿Quién quiere este diccionario? ¿Escuchas al profesor de matemáticas?**

5.4 Direct object nouns and pronouns

SUBJECT	VERB	DIRECT OBJECT NOUN
Álex y Javier	están tomando	fotos.
Álex and Javier	*are taking*	*photos.*

▶ A direct object noun receives the action of the verb directly and generally follows the verb. In the example above, the direct object noun answers the question *What are Javier and Álex taking?*

▶ When a direct object noun in Spanish is a person or a pet, it is preceded by the word **a**. This is called the personal **a**; there is no English equivalent for this construction.

Don Francisco visita **a** la señora Ramos.   Don Francisco visita el Hotel Prado.
Don Francisco is visiting Mrs. Ramos.   *Don Francisco is visiting the Hotel Prado.*

▶ In the first sentence above, the personal **a** is required because the direct object is a person. In the second sentence, the personal **a** is not required because the direct object is a place, not a person.

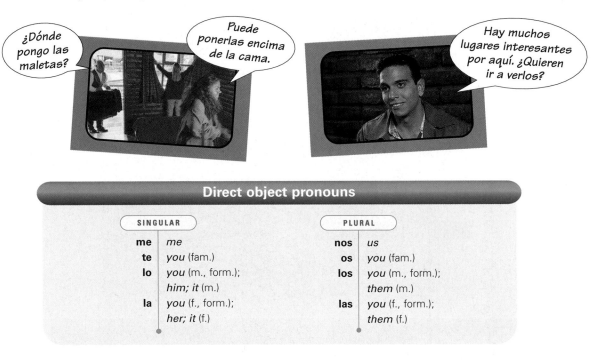

Direct object pronouns

SINGULAR		PLURAL	
me	*me*	**nos**	*us*
te	*you* (fam.)	**os**	*you* (fam.)
lo	*you* (m., form.); *him; it* (m.)	**los**	*you* (m., form.); *them* (m.)
la	*you* (f., form.); *her; it* (f.)	**las**	*you* (f., form.); *them* (f.)

▶ Direct object pronouns are words that replace direct object nouns. Like English, Spanish sometimes uses a direct object pronoun to avoid repeating a noun already mentioned.

	DIRECT OBJECT			DIRECT OBJECT PRONOUN
Maribel hace	las maletas.		Maribel las	hace.
Felipe compra	el sombrero.		Felipe lo	compra.
Vicky tiene	la llave.		Vicky la	tiene.

▶ In affirmative sentences, direct object pronouns generally appear before the conjugated verb. In negative sentences, the pronoun is placed between the word **no** and the verb.

Adela practica **el tenis**.	Adela no tiene **las llaves**.
Adela **lo** practica.	Adela **no las** tiene.
Carmen compra **los pasajes**.	Diego no hace **las maletas**.
Carmen **los** compra.	Diego **no las** hace.

▶ When the verb is an infinitive construction, such as **ir a** + [*infinitive*], the direct object pronoun can be placed before the conjugated form or attached to the infinitive.

Ellos van a escribir **unas postales**.
— Ellos **las** van a escribir.
— Ellos van a escribir**las**.

Lidia quiere ver **una película**.
— Lidia **la** quiere ver.
— Lidia quiere ver**la**.

▶ When the verb is in the present progressive, the direct object pronoun can be placed before the conjugated form or attached to the present participle.

Gerardo está leyendo **la lección**.
— Gerardo **la** está leyendo.
— Gerardo está leyéndo**la**.

Toni está mirando **el partido**.
— Toni **lo** está mirando.
— Toni está mirándo**lo**.

¡INTÉNTALO!   Choose the correct response to each question. The first one has been done for you.

1. ¿Tienes el libro de español? *c*
   a. Sí, la tengo. b. No, no los tengo. c. Sí, lo tengo.
2. ¿Me puedes llevar al partido de baloncesto? *b*
   a. Sí, los puedo llevar. b. Sí, te puedo llevar. c. No, no las puedo llevar.
3. El artista quiere dibujarte con tu mamá, ¿no? *b*
   a. Sí, quiere dibujarlos mañana. b. Sí, nos quiere dibujar mañana.
   c. Sí, quiere dibujarte mañana.
4. ¿Quién tiene las llaves de nuestra habitación? *a*
   a. Yo no las tengo. b. Amalia los tiene, ¿no? c. Yo la tengo.
5. ¿Quién te lleva al aeropuerto? *c*
   a. Yo te llevo al aeropuerto. b. Rita los lleva al aeropuerto.
   c. Mónica me lleva al aeropuerto a las seis.
6. ¿Puedes oírme? *a*
   a. Sí, te puedo oír bien. b. No, no los oigo. c. Sí, las oigo bien.
7. ¿Estudia ella los verbos irregulares? *c*
   a. No, no la estudia. b. Sí, lo estudia. c. Sí, los estudia.
8. ¿Practican ellos la pronunciación todos los días? *b*
   a. Sí, lo practican. b. Sí, la practican. c. No, no los practican.

1 Suggestion Ask individual students to identify the direct object in each sentence before assigning the activity.

2 Expansion Ask questions using direct objects included and not included in the activity to elicit **Sí/No** answers. Ex: **¿Tiene Ramón reservaciones en el hotel?** (Sí, las tiene.) **¿Tiene su mochila?** (No, no la tiene.)

3 Expansion
- Ask additional questions about the family's preparations, allowing students to decide who does what. Ex: **¿Quién compra una revista para leer en el avión? ¿Quién llama al taxi? ¿Quién practica el español?**
- Ask students true-false questions about who does what in the activity. Have them respond orally, correcting the false statements. Ex: **¿La señora Garza busca la cámara?** (No, María la busca.)

Práctica

1 **Sustitución** Professor Vega's class is planning a trip to Costa Rica. Describe their preparations by changing the direct object nouns into direct object pronouns.

> **modelo**
> La profesora Vega tiene su pasaporte.
> *La profesora Vega lo tiene.*

1. Gustavo y Héctor confirman las reservaciones. Gustavo y Héctor las confirman.
2. Nosotros leemos los folletos (*brochures*). Nosotros los leemos.
3. Ana María estudia el mapa. Ana María lo estudia.
4. Yo aprendo los nombres de los monumentos de San José. Yo los aprendo.
5. Alicia escucha a la profesora. Alicia la escucha.
6. Miguel escribe las direcciones para ir al hotel. Miguel las escribe.
7. Esteban busca el pasaje. Esteban lo busca.
8. Nosotros planeamos una excursión. Nosotros la planeamos.

◀ **¡LENGUA VIVA!**

There are many Spanish words that correspond to *ticket*. **Billete** and **pasaje** usually refer to a ticket for travel, such as an airplane ticket. **Entrada** refers to a ticket to an event, such as a concert or a movie. **Boleto** can be used in either case.

2 **Vacaciones** Ramón is going to San Juan, Puerto Rico with his friends, Javier and Marcos. Express his thoughts more succinctly using direct object pronouns.

> **modelo**
> Quiero hacer una excursión.
> *Quiero hacerla./La quiero hacer.*

1. Voy a hacer mi maleta. Voy a hacerla./La voy a hacer.
2. Necesitamos llevar los pasaportes. Necesitamos llevarlos./Los necesitamos llevar.
3. Marcos está pidiendo el folleto turístico. Marcos está pidiéndolo./Marcos lo está pidiendo.
4. Javier debe llamar a sus padres. Javier debe llamarlos./Javier los debe llamar.
5. Ellos esperan visitar el Viejo San Juan. Ellos esperan visitarlo./Ellos lo esperan visitar.
6. Puedo llamar a Javier por la mañana. Puedo llamarlo./Lo puedo llamar.
7. Prefiero traer mi cámara. Prefiero traerla./La prefiero traer.
8. No queremos perder nuestras reservaciones de hotel. No queremos perderlas./No las queremos perder.

◀ **NOTA CULTURAL**

Because Puerto Rico is a U.S. territory, passengers traveling there from the U.S. mainland do not need passports or visas. Passengers traveling to Puerto Rico from a foreign country, however, must meet travel requirements identical to those required for travel to the U.S. mainland. Puerto Ricans are U.S. citizens and can therefore travel to the U.S. mainland without any travel documents.

3 **¿Quién?** The Garza family is preparing to go on a vacation to Puerto Rico. Based on the clues, answer the questions. Use direct object pronouns in your answers.

> **modelo**
> ¿Quién hace las reservaciones para el hotel? (El Sr. Garza)
> *El Sr. Garza las hace.*

1. ¿Quién compra los pasajes para el vuelo (*flight*)? (La Sra. Garza)
   La Sra. Garza los compra.
2. ¿Quién tiene que hacer las maletas de los niños? (María)
   María tiene que hacerlas./María las tiene que hacer.
3. ¿Quiénes buscan los pasaportes? (Antonio y María)
   Antonio y María los buscan.
4. ¿Quién va a confirmar las reservaciones para el hotel? (La Sra. Garza)
   La Sra. Garza va a confirmarlas./La Sra. Garza las va a confirmar.
5. ¿Quién busca la cámara? (María)
   María la busca.
6. ¿Quién compra un mapa de Puerto Rico? (Antonio)
   Antonio lo compra.

TEACHING OPTIONS

Pairs Have students take turns asking each other who they know who does these activities: **leer revistas, practicar el ciclismo, ganar siempre los partidos, visitar a sus padres durante las vacaciones, leer el periódico, escribir cartas, escuchar a sus profesores, practicar la natación.** Ex: **—¿Quién lee revistas? —Yo las leo.**

Heritage Speakers Have heritage speakers create a dialogue between a travel agent and client. The client would like to go to Puerto Rico and wants to know what he or she needs for the trip, how to prepare for it, and what to do once there. Have partners take turns playing both roles, choosing one of their role-plays to present to the class.

Comunicación

4 Entrevista Interview a classmate using these questions. Be sure to use direct object pronouns in your responses.   Answers will vary.

1. ¿Ves mucho la televisión?
2. ¿Cuándo vas a ver tu programa favorito?
3. ¿Quién prepara la comida (*food*) en tu casa?
4. ¿Te visita mucho tu familia?
5. ¿Visitas mucho a tus abuelos?
6. ¿Nos entienden nuestros padres a nosotros?
7. ¿Cuándo ves a tus amigos/as?
8. ¿Cuándo te llaman tus amigos/as?

5 En el aeropuerto Get together with a partner and take turns asking each other questions about the drawing. Use the word bank and direct object pronouns.
Answers will vary.

> **modelo**
>
> **Estudiante 1:** ¿Quién está leyendo el libro?
> **Estudiante 2:** Susana está leyéndolo.

buscar	confirmar	escribir	leer	tener	vender
comprar	encontrar	escuchar	llevar	traer	¿?

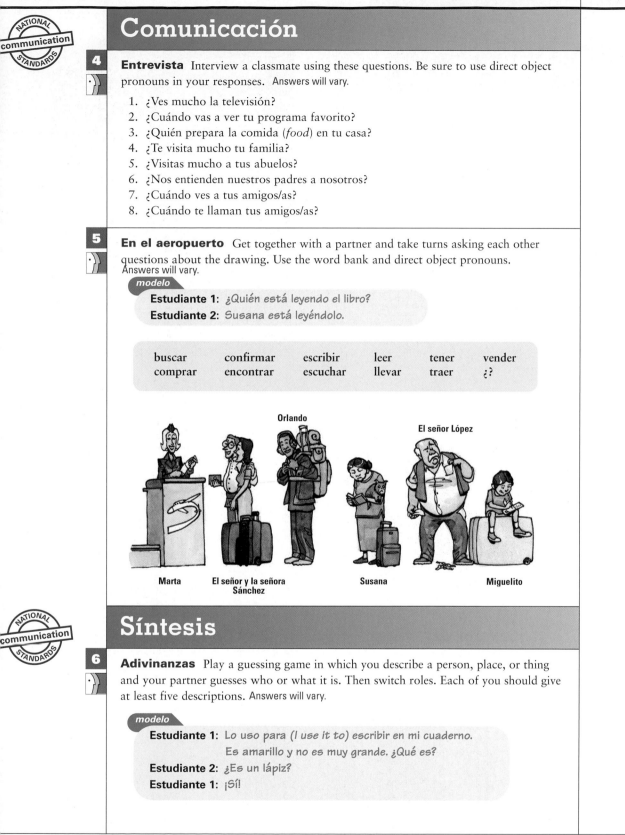

Orlando

El señor López

Marta   El señor y la señora   Susana   Miguelito
        Sánchez

Síntesis

6 Adivinanzas Play a guessing game in which you describe a person, place, or thing and your partner guesses who or what it is. Then switch roles. Each of you should give at least five descriptions. Answers will vary.

> **modelo**
>
> **Estudiante 1:** Lo uso para (*I use it to*) escribir en mi cuaderno.
>   Es amarillo y no es muy grande. ¿Qué es?
> **Estudiante 2:** ¿Es un lápiz?
> **Estudiante 1:** ¡Sí!

---

4 Suggestion Ask students to take notes on their partners' answers. After the interviews, have them review answers in groups and report the most common answers to the class.

4 Expansion Have students write five more questions like the ones in the activity, then continue their interviews.

5 Suggestion Before assigning the activity, ask individual students to identify different objects in the picture that might be used as direct objects in questions and answers.

6 Expansion Have pairs write out five additional riddles like that in **Actividad 6**. Have them present their riddles for the rest of the class to answer.

TEACHING OPTIONS

Game Play a game of **20 Preguntas** with the class. Divide the class into two teams. Think of an object in the room. Alternate calling on teams to ask questions. Once a team knows the answer, the team captain should raise his or her hand. If right, the team gets a point. If wrong, the team loses a point. Play until one team has earned five points.

Pairs Have students create five questions that include the direct object pronouns **me**, **te**, and **nos**. Then have them ask their partners the questions on their list. Ex: —¿Quién te llama **mucho?** —Mi novia me llama mucho. —¿Quién nos escucha **cuando hacemos preguntas en español?** —El/La profesor(a) y **los estudiantes nos escuchan.**

Lectura

NATIONAL STANDARDS communication cultures

Antes de leer

Estrategia
Scanning

Scanning involves glancing over a document in search of specific information. For example, you can scan a document to identify its format, to find cognates, to locate visual clues about the document's content, or to find specific facts. Scanning allows you to learn a great deal about a text without having to read it word for word.

Examinar el texto

Scan the reading selection for cognates and write a few of them down.

1. _____   4. _____
2. _____   5. _____
3. _____   6. _____

Based on the cognates you found, what do you think this document is about?

_____

Preguntas

Read the following questions. Then scan the document again to look for answers to the questions.

1. What is the format of the reading selection?

   _____

2. Which place is the document about?

   _____

3. What are some of the visual cues this document provides? What do they tell you about the content of the document?

   _____

4. Who produced the document, and what do you think it is for?

   _____

recursos

vistahigher
learning.com

Section Goals

In **Lectura** students will:
• learn the strategy of scanning to find specific information in reading matter
• read a brochure about eco-tourism in Puerto Rico

Instructional Resource
Companion website:
www.vistahigherlearning.com

Estrategia Explain to students that a good way to get an idea of what an article or other text is about is to scan it before reading. Scanning means running one's eyes over a text in search of specific information that can be used to infer the content of the text. Explain that scanning a text before reading it is a good way to improve Spanish reading comprehension.

The Affective Dimension
Point out to students that becoming familiar with cognates will help them feel less overwhelmed when they encounter new Spanish texts.

Examinar el texto Do the activity orally with the whole class. Some cognates that give a clue to the content of the text are: **turismo ecológico, hotel, aire acondicionado, perfecto, Parque Nacional Foresta, Museo de Arte Nativo, Reserva, Biosfera, Santuario.** These clues should tell a reader scanning the text that it is about a hotel promoting eco-tourism.

Preguntas Ask the questions orally of the whole class. Possible responses: 1. travel brochure 2. Puerto Rico 3. photos of beautiful tropical beaches, bays, and forests; the document is trying to attract the reader 4. Hotel La Cabaña in Lajas, Puerto Rico; attract guests

---

Turismo ecológico en Puerto Rico

Hotel La Cabaña
~ Lajas, Puerto Rico ~

Habitaciones

• 40 individuales   • Restaurante (Bar)
• 15 dobles   • Piscina
• Teléfono / TV / Cable   • Área de juegos
• Aire acondicionado   • Cajero automático°

*E*l hotel está situado en Playa Grande, un pequeño pueblo de pescadores del mar Caribe. Es el lugar perfecto para el viajero que viene de vacaciones. Las playas son seguras y limpias, ideales para tomar el sol, descansar, tomar fotografías y nadar. Está abierto los 365 días del año. Hay una rebaja° especial para estudiantes universitarios.

DIRECCIÓN: Playa Grande 406, Lajas, PR 00667, cerca del Parque Nacional Foresta.

Cajero automático *ATM*   rebaja *discount*

Heritage Speakers Ask heritage speakers of Puerto Rican descent who have lived on or visited the island to prepare a short presentation about the climate, geography, or people of Puerto Rico. Ask them to illustrate their presentations with photos they have taken or illustrations from magazines, if possible.
Small Groups Have five students work together to brainstorm a list of what would constitute an ideal tropical vacation for them.

Each student should contribute at least one idea. Opinions will vary. Ask the group to designate one student to take notes and another to present the information to the class. When each group has its list, ask the designated presenter to share the information with the rest of the class. How do the groups differ? How are they similar?

Atracciones cercanas

Playa Grande ¿Busca la playa perfecta? Playa Grande es la playa que está buscando. Usted puede ir de pesca, sacar fotos, nadar y pasear en bicicleta. Playa Grande es un paraíso para el turista que quiere practicar deportes acuáticos. El lugar es bonito e interesante y usted tiene muchas oportunidades para descansar y disfrutar en familia.

Valle Niebla Ir de excursión, tomar café, montar a caballo, caminar, acampar, hacer picnic. Más de 100 lugares para acampar.

Bahía Fosforescente Sacar fotos, pescar, salidas de noche, excursión en barco. Una maravillosa experiencia con peces° fosforescentes.

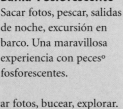

Arrecifes de Coral Sacar fotos, bucear, explorar. Es un lugar único en el Caribe.

Playa Vieja Tomar el sol, pasear en bicicleta, jugar a las cartas, escuchar música. Ideal para la familia.

Parque Nacional Foresta Sacar fotos, visitar el Museo de Arte Nativo. Reserva Mundial de la Biosfera.

Santuario de las Aves Sacar fotos, observar aves°, seguir rutas de excursión.

peces *fish* aves *birds*

Después de leer

Listas

Which of the amenities of the Hotel La Cabaña would most interest these potential guests? Explain your choices. Answers will vary.

1. Dos padres con un hijo de seis años y una hija de ocho años

   _____

2. Un hombre y una mujer en su luna de miel (*honeymoon*)

   _____

3. Una persona en un viaje de negocios (*business trip*)

   _____

Conversaciones

With a partner, take turns asking each other the following questions. Answers will vary.

1. ¿Quieres visitar el Hotel La Cabaña? ¿Por qué?
2. Tienes tiempo de visitar sólo tres de las atracciones turísticas que están cerca del hotel. ¿Cuáles vas a visitar? ¿Por qué?
3. ¿Qué prefieres hacer en Valle Niebla? ¿En Playa Vieja? ¿En el Parque Nacional Foresta?

Situaciones

You have just arrived at the Hotel La Cabaña. Your classmate is the concierge. Use the phrases below to express your interests and ask him or her for suggestions about where to go. Answers will vary.

1. montar a caballo
2. bucear
3. pasear en bicicleta
4. pescar
5. observar aves

Contestar

Answer the following questions. Answers will vary.

1. ¿Quieres visitar Puerto Rico? Explica tu respuesta.

   _____

2. ¿Adónde quieres ir de vacaciones el verano que viene? Explica tu respuesta.

   _____

Puerto Rico

connections cultures NATIONAL STANDARDS

El país en cifras

- ▶ **Área:** 8.959 km² (3.459 millas²) *menor° que el área de Connecticut*
- ▶ **Población:** 4.091.000

Puerto Rico es una de las islas más densamente pobladas° del mundo. Cerca de la mitad° de la población vive en San Juan, la capital.

- ▶ **Capital:** San Juan—1.466.000

SOURCE: Population Division, UN Secretariat

- ▶ **Ciudades principales:** Arecibo—100.000, Bayamón—222.815, Fajardo—40.000, Mayagüez—100.371, Ponce—187.749
- ▶ **Moneda:** dólar estadounidense
- ▶ **Idiomas:** español (oficial); inglés (oficial)

Aproximadamente la cuarta parte de la población puertorriqueña habla inglés. Pero, en las zonas turísticas este porcentaje es mucho más alto. El uso del inglés es obligatorio para documentos federales.

Bandera de Puerto Rico

Puertorriqueños célebres

- ▶ **Raúl Juliá,** actor (1940–1994)
- ▶ **Roberto Clemente,** beisbolista (1934–1972)
- ▶ **Luis Rafael Sánchez,** escritor (1936–)
- ▶ **Ricky Martin,** cantante y actor (1971–)
- ▶ **Rita Moreno,** actriz, cantante, bailarina (1931–)

menor *less* pobladas *populated* mitad *half* río subterráneo *underground river* más largo *longest* sistema de cuevas *cave system* bóveda *vault* fortaleza *fort* caber *fit*

¡Increíble pero cierto!

El río *Camuy* es el tercer río subterráneo° más largo° del mundo y tiene el sistema de cuevas° más grande en el hemisferio occidental. La *Cueva de los Tres Pueblos* es una gigantesca bóveda°, tan grande que toda la fortaleza° del Morro puede caber° en su interior.

Hoteles en El Condado, San Juan

Plaza de Arecibo

Océano Atlántico

Arecibo

San Juan ✪

Bayamón

Río Grande de Añasco

Mayagüez

Cordillera Central

Ponce

Sierra de Cay

Mar Caribe

Parque de Bombas, Ponce

Pescadores en Mayagüez

OCÉANO ATLÁNT

PUERTO R

OCÉANO PACÍFICO

recursos

| WB pp. 57–58 | VM pp. 233–234 | I CD-ROM Lección 5 | vistahigher learning.com |

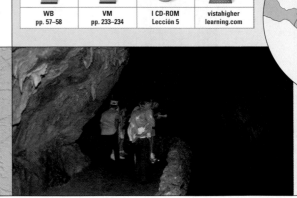

Lugares • El Morro

El Morro es una fortaleza que protegía° la bahía° de San Juan entre los años 1500 (mil quinientos) y 1900 (mil novecientos). Hoy día muchos turistas visitan este lugar, que ahora es un museo. Es el sitio más fotografiado de Puerto Rico. La arquitectura de la fortaleza es impresionante. Tiene misteriosos túneles, oscuras mazmorras° y vistas fabulosas de la bahía.

Artes • Salsa

Este estilo musical, de orígenes puertorriqueños y cubanos, nació° en la ciudad de Nueva York. Dos de los músicos de salsa más famosos son Tito Puente (1923–2000) y Willie Colón (1950–), los dos de Nueva York. Las estrellas° de la salsa en Puerto Rico son Felipe Rodríguez y Héctor Lavoe. Hoy, Puerto Rico es el centro universal de la salsa; el Gran Combo de Puerto Rico es una de las orquestas de salsa más famosas.

Ciencias • El Observatorio de Arecibo

El Observatorio de Arecibo tiene el radiotelescopio más grande del mundo. Gracias al telescopio los científicos° pueden estudiar la atmósfera de la Tierra° y la Luna°, fenómenos celestiales como los quasares y pulsares y escuchar emisiones de radio de otras galaxias, buscando inteligencia extraterrestre.

Isla de Culebra

Fajardo

Isla de Vieques

Historia • Relación con los Estados Unidos

Puerto Rico pasó a ser° parte de los Estados Unidos después de° la Guerra° de 1898 (mil ochocientos noventa y ocho) y se hizo° un estado libre asociado en 1952 (mil novecientos cincuenta y dos). Los puertorriqueños, ciudadanos° estadounidenses desde° 1917 (mil novecientos diecisiete), tienen representación en el Congreso pero no votan en las elecciones presidenciales y no pagan impuestos° federales. Hay un debate entre los puertorriqueños: ¿debe la isla seguir como estado libre asociado, hacerse un estado como los otros o hacerse independiente?

¿Qué aprendiste? Responde a las preguntas con una frase completa.

1. ¿Cuál es la moneda de Puerto Rico? La moneda de Puerto Rico es el dólar estadounidense.
2. ¿Qué idiomas se hablan (*are spoken*) en Puerto Rico? Se hablan español e inglés en Puerto Rico.
3. ¿Cuál es el sitio más fotografiado de Puerto Rico? El Morro es el sitio más fotografiado de Puerto Rico.
4. ¿Qué es el Gran Combo? Es una orquesta de Puerto Rico.
5. ¿Qué hacen los científicos en el Observatorio de Arecibo? Los científicos estudian la atmósfera de la Tierra y la Luna y escuchan emisiones de otras galaxias.

Conexión Internet Investiga estos temas en el sitio **www.vistahigherlearning.com.**

1. Describe a dos puertorriqueños famosos. ¿Cómo son? ¿Qué hacen? ¿Dónde viven? ¿Por qué son célebres?
2. Busca información sobre lugares buenos para el ecoturismo en Puerto Rico. Luego presenta un informe a la clase.

protegía *protected* bahía *bay* mazmorras *dungeons* nació *was born* estrellas *stars* científicos *scientists* Tierra *Earth* Luna *Moon* pasó a ser *became* después de *after* Guerra *War* se hizo *became* ciudadanos *citizens* desde *since* pagan impuestos *pay taxes*

El Morro Remind students that at the time **El Morro** was built, piracy was a major concern for Spain and its Caribbean colonies. If possible, show other photos of **El Morro**, San Juan Bay, and **El Viejo San Juan**. For more information about **El Morro** and **Viejo San Juan**, you may want to play the **Panorama cultural** video for this lesson.

Salsa With students, listen to **salsa** or **merengue** from the Dominican Republic, and **rumba** or **mambo** from Cuba. Encourage them to identify common elements in the music (strong percussion patterns rooted in African traditions, alternating structure of soloist and ensemble, incorporation of Western instruments and musical vocabulary). Then, have them point out contrasts.

El Observatorio de Arecibo The Arecibo Ionospheric Observatory has the world's most sensitive radio telescope. It can detect objects up to 13 billion light years away. The telescope dish is 1,000 feet in diameter and covers 20 acres. The dish is made of about 40,000 aluminum mesh panels.

Relación con los Estados Unidos Point out that only Puerto Ricans living on the island vote in plebiscites on the question of the island's political relationship to the United States.

Conexión Internet Students will find supporting Internet activities and links at **www.vistahigherlearning.com.**

Variación léxica When the first Spanish colonists arrived on the island they were to name Puerto Rico, they found it inhabited by the Taínos, who called the island **Borinquen**. Puerto Ricans still use that name to refer to the island, and they frequently call themselves **borinqueños** or **boricuas**. The Puerto Rican national anthem is ***La borinqueña***. Some other Taíno words that have entered Spanish (and English) are **huracán**, **hamaca**, **canoa**, and

iguana. **Juracán** was the name of the Taíno god of the winds whose anger stirred up the great storms that periodically devastated the island. The hammock, of course, was the device the Taínos slept in, and canoes were the boats made of great hollowed-out logs with which they paddled between islands. The Taíno language also survives in many Puerto Rican place names: **Arecibo, Bayamón, Guayama, Sierra de Cayey, Yauco,** and **Coamo**.

Los viajes y las vacaciones

acampar	to camp
confirmar una reservación	to confirm a reservation
estar de vacaciones (f. pl.)	to be on vacation
hacer las maletas	to pack (one's suitcases)
hacer turismo (m.)	to go sightseeing
hacer un viaje	to take a trip
hacer una excursión	to go on a hike; to go on a tour
ir de compras (f. pl.)	to go shopping
ir de pesca (f.)	to go fishing
ir de vacaciones	to go on vacation
ir en autobús (m.), auto(móvil)(m.), avión (m.), barco (m.), motocicleta (f.), taxi (m.)	to go by bus, car, plane, boat, motorcycle, taxi
jugar a las cartas	to play cards
montar a caballo (m.)	to ride a horse
pasar por la aduana	to go through customs
pescar	to fish
sacar/tomar fotos (f. pl.)	to take photos
el/la agente de viajes	travel agent
el/la inspector(a) de aduanas	customs inspector
el/la viajero/a	traveler
el aeropuerto	airport
la agencia de viajes	travel agency
la cabaña	cabin
el campo	countryside
el equipaje	luggage
la estación de autobuses, del metro, de tren	bus, subway, train station
la llegada	arrival
el mar	sea
el océano	ocean
el paisaje	landscape
el pasaje (de ida y vuelta)	(round-trip) ticket
el pasaporte	passport
la playa	beach
la salida	departure; exit

El hotel

el ascensor	elevator
el/la botones	bellhop
la cama	bed
el/la empleado/a	employee
la habitación individual, doble	single, double room
el hotel	hotel
el/la huésped	guest
la llave	key
el piso	floor (of a building)
la planta baja	ground floor

Adjetivos

abierto/a	open
aburrido/a	bored; boring
alegre	happy; joyful
amable	nice; friendly
avergonzado/a	embarrassed
cansado/a	tired
cerrado/a	closed
cómodo/a	comfortable
confundido/a	confused
contento/a	happy; content
desordenado/a	disorderly
enamorado/a (de)	in love (with)
enojado/a	mad; angry
equivocado/a	wrong
feliz	happy
limpio/a	clean
listo/a	ready; smart
nervioso/a	nervous
ocupado/a	busy
ordenado/a	orderly
preocupado/a (por)	worried (about)
seguro/a	sure; safe
sucio/a	dirty
triste	sad

Los números ordinales

primer, primero/a	first
segundo/a	second
tercer, tercero/a	third
cuarto/a	fourth
quinto/a	fifth
sexto/a	sixth
séptimo/a	seventh
octavo/a	eighth
noveno/a	ninth
décimo/a	tenth

Palabras adicionales

ahora mismo	right now
el año	year
¿Cuál es la fecha (de hoy)?	What is the date (today)?
de buen/mal humor	in a good/bad mood
la estación	season
el mes	month
todavía	yet; still

Seasons, months, and dates	See page 124.
Weather Expressions	See page 124.
Direct object pronouns	See page 142.
Expresiones útiles	See page 129.

recursos

LM p. 30	Lab CD/MP3 Lección 5	Vocab CD Lección 5

¡De compras!

6

Communicative Goals

You will learn how to:

- Talk about and describe clothing
- Express preferences in a store
- Negotiate and pay for items you buy

Lesson Goals

In **Lección 6** students will be introduced to the following:

- terms for clothing and shopping
- colors
- numbers 101 and higher
- indirect object pronouns
- preterite tense of regular verbs
- demonstrative adjectives and pronouns
- skimming a text
- brainstorming ideas for writing
- preparing interview questions
- writing a report
- listening for linguistic cues
- cultural, geographic, economic, and historical information about Cuba

A primera vista Here are some additional questions you can ask based on the photo: ¿**Te gusta ir de compras? ¿Por qué? ¿Estás de buen humor cuando vas de compras? ¿Qué compras cuando estás de vacaciones? ¿Estás pensando salir de vacaciones en el verano?**

---

contextos

pages 152–155
- Clothing and shopping
- Negotiating a price and buying
- Colors
- More adjectives

fotonovela

pages 156–159
Inés and Javier explore the market in Otavalo, looking for something to buy. Inés purchases a gift for her sister. Javier must bargain for a better price in order to get what he wants.

estructura

pages 160–173
- Numbers 101 and higher
- Indirect object pronouns
- Preterite tense of regular verbs
- Demonstrative adjectives and pronouns

adelante

pages 174–177
Lectura: Read an advertisement for a sale in a store.
Escritura: Write a report for the school newspaper.
Escuchar: Listen to a conversation between two shoppers.

panorama

pages 178–179
Featured Country: Cuba
- The Cuban National Ballet
- Sugar cane and tobacco
- The Taíno culture
- Celia Cruz: Queen of Salsa

A PRIMERA VISTA
- ¿Está comprando algo la mujer?
- ¿Está buscando una maleta o una mochila?
- ¿Es delgada?
- ¿Es morena o rubia?

INSTRUCTIONAL RESOURCES

Workbook/Video Manual: WB Activities, pp. 59–72
Laboratory Manual: Lab Activities, pp. 31–36
Workbook/Video Manual: Video Activities, pp. 205–206; pp. 235–236
Instructor's Resource Manual: **Vocabulario adicional,** p. 160; **¡Inténtalo!** & **Práctica** Answers, pp. 180–181; **Fotonovela** Translations, pp. 121–122; Textbook CD

Tapescript, p. 76; Lab CDs Tapescript, pp. 25–29; **Fotonovela** Videoscript, p. 92; **Panorama cultural** Videoscript, p. 110; **Pan. cult.** translations, p. 132
Info Gap Activities Booklet, pp. 21–24
Overhead Transparencies: #3, #4, #28, #29, #30
Lab Audio CD/MP3 **Lección 6**
Panorama cultural DVD/Video

Fotonovela DVD/Video
Testing Program, pp. 61–72
Testing Program Audio CD
Test Files CD-ROM
Test Generator
Companion website
Presentations CD-ROM

Textbook CD
Vocabulary CD
Interactive CD-ROM
Video CD-ROM
Web-SAM

Section Goals

In **Contextos**, students will learn and practice:
- clothing vocabulary
- vocabulary to use while shopping
- colors

Instructional Resources
Transparencies, #28, #29
Textbook Activities CD
Vocabulary CD
WB/VM: Workbook, pp. 59–60
Lab Manual, p. 31
Lab CD/MP3 **Lección 6**
IRM: **Vocab. adicional,** *p. 160;*
Práctica *Answers, p. 180;*
Tapescript, pp. 25–29; p. 76
Interactive CD-ROM
Companion website:
www.vistahigherlearning.com
Presentations CD-ROM

Suggestions

- Ask volunteers about shopping preferences and habits. Say: **¿Qué te gusta comprar? ¿Discos compactos? ¿Programas para la computadora? ¿Ropa?** (point to your own clothing) **¿Adónde vas para comprar esas cosas? ¿Cuánto dinero gastas** (mime reaching in your pocket and paying for something) **normalmente?** Ask another student: **¿Adónde va de compras ____? (Va a ____.) ¿Y qué compra allí? (Compra ____.)**
- Project **Transparency #28**. Have students guess the meanings of **damas** and **caballeros**. Have them refer to the scene to answer your true-false questions about it. Ex: **El hombre paga con tarjeta de crédito. (Cierto) No venden zapatos en la tienda. (Falso) Se puede regatear en el almacén. (Falso)** Use as many clothing items and verbs from **Más vocabulario** as you can.

Note: At this point you may want to present **Vocabulario adicional: Más vocabulario para ir de compras**, from the IRM.

¡De compras!

Más vocabulario

el abrigo	*coat*
el almacén	*department store*
el calcetín	*sock*
el cinturón	*belt*
las gafas (de sol), las gafas (oscuras)	*(sun)glasses*
los guantes	*gloves*
el impermeable	*raincoat*
los lentes de contacto	*contact lenses*
los lentes (de sol)	*(sun)glasses*
la ropa	*clothing; clothes*
la ropa interior	*underwear*
la sandalia	*sandal*
el vestido	*dress*
los zapatos de tenis	*tennis shoes; sneakers*
el centro comercial	*shopping mall*
el mercado (al aire libre)	*(open-air) market*
el precio (fijo)	*(fixed; set) price*
la rebaja	*sale*
la tienda	*shop; store*
costar (o:ue)	*to cost*
gastar	*to spend (money)*
pagar	*to pay*
regatear	*to bargain*
vender	*to sell*
hacer juego (con)	*to match (with)*
llevar	*to wear; to take*
usar	*to wear; to use*

Variación léxica

calcetines ⟷ medias (*Amér. L.*)
cinturón ⟷ correa (*Col., Venez.*)
gafas/lentes ⟷ espejuelos (*Cuba, P.R.*), anteojos (*Arg., Chile*)
zapatos de tenis ⟷ zapatillas de deporte (*Esp.*), zapatillas (*Arg., Perú*)

recursos

| TEXT CD Lección 6 | WB pp. 59–60 | LM p. 31 | Lab CD/MP3 Lección 6 | I CD-ROM Lección 6 | Vocab CD Lección 6 |

TEACHING OPTIONS

Small Groups In groups of three or four, students close their books and make a list of as many of the articles of clothing that appear in the store scene as they can. Then have all groups call out their lists as you write down the items on the board. Did the groups remember all of the items pictured in the drawing?

Variación léxica Point out that terms for clothing vary widely throughout the Spanish-speaking world. For the most part, Spanish speakers of different regions can mutually understand each other when talking about clothing. Other variations include **los bluejeans = los vaqueros, los jeans; zapatos de tenis = los tenis; los pantalones = el pantalón; el suéter = el pulóver, el jersey; la chaqueta = la chamarra.**

el sombrero

Caballeros

un par de zapatos

los zapatos

a chaqueta

la caja

la cartera

la vendedora/la dependienta

la corbata

la tarjeta de crédito

los bluejeans

la bota

Práctica

1 Escuchar 🎧 Listen to Juanita and Vicente talk about what they're packing for their vacations. Indicate who is packing each item. If both are packing an item, write both names. If neither is packing an item, write an **x**.

1. abrigo _____Vicente_____
2. zapatos de tenis __Juanita, Vicente__
3. impermeable _____x_____
4. chaqueta _____Vicente_____
5. sandalias _____Juanita_____
6. bluejeans __Juanita, Vicente__
7. gafas de sol _____Vicente_____
8. camisetas __Juanita, Vicente__
9. traje de baño _____Juanita_____
10. botas _____Vicente_____
11. pantalones cortos _____Juanita_____
12. suéter _____Vicente_____

2 Completar Anita is talking about going shopping. Complete each sentence with the correct word(s), adding definite or indefinite articles when necessary.

caja	medias	tarjeta de crédito
centro comercial	par	traje de baño
dependientas	ropa	vendedores

1. Hoy voy a ir de compras al nuevo ____centro comercial____.
2. Voy a ir a la tienda de ropa para mujeres. Siempre hay muchas rebajas y las ____dependientas____ son muy simpáticas.
3. Necesito comprarme ____un par____ de zapatos.
4. Y tengo que comprarme ____un traje de baño____ nuevo porque el sábado voy a la playa con mis amigos.
5. También voy a comprar unas ____medias____ para mi mamá.
6. Voy a pagar todo (*everything*) en ____la caja____.
7. Pero hoy no tengo dinero. Voy a tener que usar mi ____tarjeta de crédito____.
8. Mañana voy al mercado al aire libre. Me gusta regatear con los ____vendedores____.

3 Escoger Choose the item in each group that does not belong.

1. almacén • centro comercial • mercado • sombrero sombrero
2. camisa • camiseta • blusa • botas botas
3. bluejeans • bolsa • falda • pantalones bolsa
4. abrigo • suéter • corbata • chaqueta corbata
5. mercado • tienda • almacén • cartera cartera
6. pagar • llevar • hacer juego (con) • usar pagar
7. botas • sandalias • zapatos • traje traje
8. vender • regatear • ropa interior • gastar ropa interior

1 Suggestion Have students check their answers by going over **Actividad 1** with the class.

1 Tapescript JUANITA: Hola. Me llamo Juanita. Mi familia y yo salimos de vacaciones mañana y estoy haciendo mis maletas. Para nuestra excursión al campo ya tengo bluejeans, camisetas y zapatos de tenis. También vamos a la playa… ¡no puedo esperar! Para ir a la playa necesito un traje de baño, pantalones cortos y sandalias. ¿Qué más necesito? Creo que es todo.
VICENTE: Buenos días. Soy Vicente. Estoy haciendo mis maletas porque mi familia y yo vamos a las montañas a esquiar. Los primeros dos días vamos a hacer una excursión por las montañas. Necesito zapatos de tenis, camisetas, una chaqueta y bluejeans. El tercer día vamos a esquiar. Necesito un abrigo, un suéter y botas… y gafas de sol.
Textbook Activities CD

1 Expansion Have students indicate where these two are going: ¿**Por qué necesita llevar sandalias Juanita?**

2 Expansion Ask pairs to write three additional fill-in-the-blank sentences based on Anita's shopping. Ask volunteers to read their sentences aloud. The rest of the class provides the correct answers.

3 Expansion Go over answers quickly in class. After each answer, indicate why a particular item does not belong. Ex: **1. El sombrero. No puedes ir de compras a un sombrero.**

TEACHING OPTIONS

Extra Practice Suggest a vacation spot and then ask students at random what clothing they need to take. Make it a continuing narration whereby the next student must say all of the items of clothing that came before and add one. Ex: **Vas a la playa. ¿Qué vas a llevar? E1: Voy a llevar un traje de baño. E2: Voy a llevar un traje de baño y lentes de sol.**

TPR Play a game of Simon Says (**Simón dice…**). Write on the board **levántense** and **siéntense** and explain that they mean stand up and sit down, respectively. Then start by saying: **Simón dice… los que llevan bluejeans, levántense.** Students wearing blue jeans stand up and remain standing until further instruction. Work through various articles of clothing. Be sure to give instructions without saying **Simón dice…** once in a while.

Suggestion Project
Suggestion Project **Transparency #29** and review the color words. Point to a drawing and say: **¿De qué color es esta camiseta?** After you go through several colors, ask: **Si mezclo el rojo y el azul, ¿qué color resulta? (el morado) Y si yo mezclo el amarillo y el rojo, ¿qué color resulta? (el anaranjado)** Then point to objects in the classroom and clothes you and students are wearing to elicit color words. Point out that color words are adjectives and agree with the nouns they modify.

4 Suggestion Before beginning the activity, ask several brief comprehension questions. Ex: **¿Quién lleva una camiseta roja? (_____ lleva una camiseta roja.) ¿Son baratos o caros los trajes de Armani? (Son caros.)**

4 Expansion Show magazine pictures of various products (cars, computers, etc.) and ask students: **¿Es cara esta computadora o es barata? (Es barata.)**

5 Expansion Point to various students in the class and ask others what color of clothing each is wearing. Ex: _____, **¿de qué color es la falda de _____? (Es _____.)**

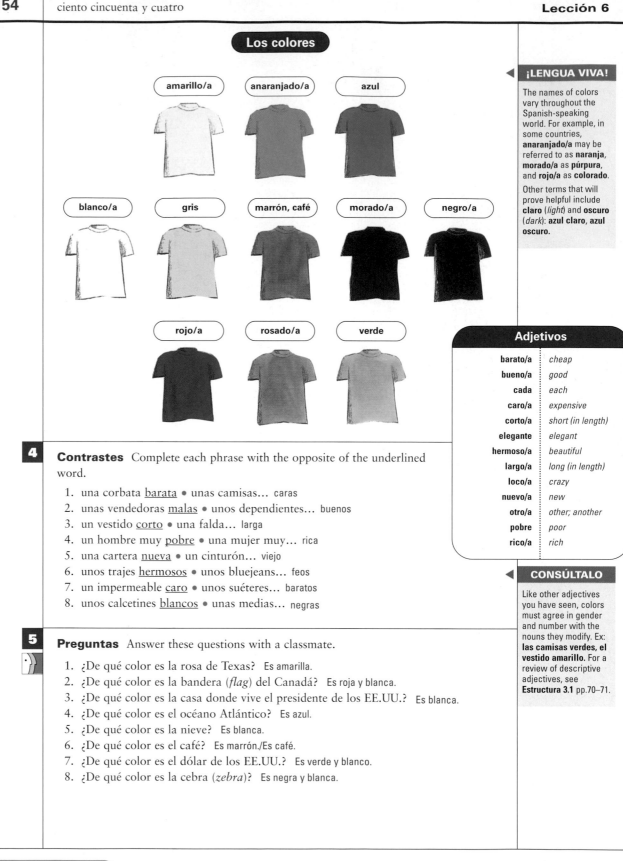

Los colores

amarillo/a · anaranjado/a · azul

blanco/a · gris · marrón, café · morado/a · negro/a

rojo/a · rosado/a · verde

¡LENGUA VIVA!

The names of colors vary throughout the Spanish-speaking world. For example, in some countries, **anaranjado/a** may be referred to as **naranja**, **morado/a** as **púrpura**, and **rojo/a** as **colorado**.

Other terms that will prove helpful include **claro** (*light*) and **oscuro** (*dark*): **azul claro, azul oscuro**.

Adjetivos

barato/a	cheap
bueno/a	good
cada	each
caro/a	expensive
corto/a	short (in length)
elegante	elegant
hermoso/a	beautiful
largo/a	long (in length)
loco/a	crazy
nuevo/a	new
otro/a	other; another
pobre	poor
rico/a	rich

4 **Contrastes** Complete each phrase with the opposite of the underlined word.

1. una corbata <u>barata</u> • unas camisas... caras
2. unas vendedoras <u>malas</u> • unos dependientes... buenos
3. un vestido <u>corto</u> • una falda... larga
4. un hombre muy <u>pobre</u> • una mujer muy... rica
5. una cartera <u>nueva</u> • un cinturón... viejo
6. unos trajes <u>hermosos</u> • unos bluejeans... feos
7. un impermeable <u>caro</u> • unos suéteres... baratos
8. unos calcetines <u>blancos</u> • unas medias... negras

CONSÚLTALO

Like other adjectives you have seen, colors must agree in gender and number with the nouns they modify. Ex: **las camisas verdes, el vestido amarillo.** For a review of descriptive adjectives, see **Estructura 3.1** pp.70–71.

5 **Preguntas** Answer these questions with a classmate.

1. ¿De qué color es la rosa de Texas? Es amarilla.
2. ¿De qué color es la bandera (*flag*) del Canadá? Es roja y blanca.
3. ¿De qué color es la casa donde vive el presidente de los EE.UU.? Es blanca.
4. ¿De qué color es el océano Atlántico? Es azul.
5. ¿De qué color es la nieve? Es blanca.
6. ¿De qué color es el café? Es marrón./Es café.
7. ¿De qué color es el dólar de los EE.UU.? Es verde y blanco.
8. ¿De qué color es la cebra (*zebra*)? Es negra y blanca.

TEACHING OPTIONS

Pairs In pairs, students spend a few minutes creating a physical description of a well-known TV or cartoon character. Then they read their descriptions while the rest of the class guesses who the character is. Ex: **Soy bajo y un poco gordo. Llevo pantalones cortos azules y una camiseta anaranjada. Tengo el pelo amarillo. También soy amarillo. ¿Quién soy? (Bart Simpson)**

Game Play **Concentración**. On eight cards, write descriptions of clothing, including colors (Ex: **unos pantalones negros**). On another eight cards, draw pictures that match the descriptions. Place the cards face-down in four rows of four. In pairs, students select two cards. If the two cards match, the pair keeps them. If the two cards do not match, students replace them in their original position. The pair with the most cards at the end wins.

Comunicación

NATIONAL communication STANDARDS

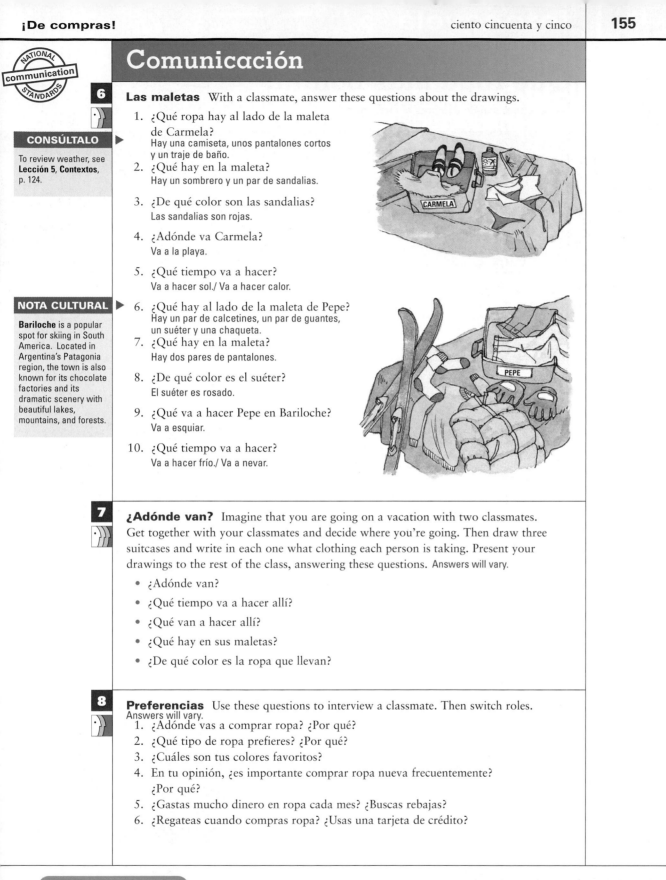

6

Las maletas With a classmate, answer these questions about the drawings.

CONSÚLTALO
To review weather, see **Lección 5, Contextos,** p. 124.

1. ¿Qué ropa hay al lado de la maleta de Carmela?
   Hay una camiseta, unos pantalones cortos y un traje de baño.
2. ¿Qué hay en la maleta?
   Hay un sombrero y un par de sandalias.
3. ¿De qué color son las sandalias?
   Las sandalias son rojas.
4. ¿Adónde va Carmela?
   Va a la playa.
5. ¿Qué tiempo va a hacer?
   Va a hacer sol./ Va a hacer calor.

NOTA CULTURAL
Bariloche is a popular spot for skiing in South America. Located in Argentina's Patagonia region, the town is also known for its chocolate factories and its dramatic scenery with beautiful lakes, mountains, and forests.

6. ¿Qué hay al lado de la maleta de Pepe?
   Hay un par de calcetines, un par de guantes, un suéter y una chaqueta.
7. ¿Qué hay en la maleta?
   Hay dos pares de pantalones.
8. ¿De qué color es el suéter?
   El suéter es rosado.
9. ¿Qué va a hacer Pepe en Bariloche?
   Va a esquiar.
10. ¿Qué tiempo va a hacer?
    Va a hacer frío./ Va a nevar.

7

¿Adónde van? Imagine that you are going on a vacation with two classmates. Get together with your classmates and decide where you're going. Then draw three suitcases and write in each one what clothing each person is taking. Present your drawings to the rest of the class, answering these questions. Answers will vary.

- ¿Adónde van?
- ¿Qué tiempo va a hacer allí?
- ¿Qué van a hacer allí?
- ¿Qué hay en sus maletas?
- ¿De qué color es la ropa que llevan?

8

Preferencias Use these questions to interview a classmate. Then switch roles.
Answers will vary.

1. ¿Adónde vas a comprar ropa? ¿Por qué?
2. ¿Qué tipo de ropa prefieres? ¿Por qué?
3. ¿Cuáles son tus colores favoritos?
4. En tu opinión, ¿es importante comprar ropa nueva frecuentemente? ¿Por qué?
5. ¿Gastas mucho dinero en ropa cada mes? ¿Buscas rebajas?
6. ¿Regateas cuando compras ropa? ¿Usas una tarjeta de crédito?

---

6 Expansion Ask volunteers what kind of clothing they take with them when they visit these places at these times: **Seattle en la primavera, la Florida en el verano, Minnesota en el invierno, San Francisco en el otoño.**

7 Suggestion Assign groups and have them discuss where they are going the day before you do this activity in class.

7 Expansion Have students guess where the groups are going, based on the content of the suitcases. Facilitate guessing by asking the questions listed on the page.

8 Expansion Students report the findings of their interviews to the class. Ex: ____ va a **The Gap para comprar ropa porque allí la ropa no es cara. Prefiere la ropa informal…**

TEACHING OPTIONS

Extra Practice Students write a paragraph about the next vacation they plan to take and what clothing they plan to take with them. If students do not have a vacation planned, ask them to invent one. They should also include what kind of weather they expect at their destination and any weather-specific clothing they will need. Ask volunteers to share their paragraphs with the class.

Extra Practice Students write descriptions of the one article of clothing or complete outfit that best describes them without indicating who they are. Collect the papers and read the descriptions aloud. The rest of the class has to guess who each student is based on his or her defining article or outfit.

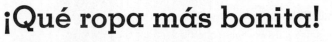

¡Qué ropa más bonita!

Javier e Inés van de compras al mercado.

Section Goals

In **Fotonovela** students will:
• receive comprehensible input from free-flowing discourse
• learn functional phrases involving clothing and how much things cost

---

Instructional Resources
WB/VM: Video Activities, pp. 205–206
Fotonovela *DVD/Video (Start 00:28:02)*
Fotonovela *Video CD-ROM*
*IRM: **Fotonovela** Translations, pp. 121–122, Videoscript, p. 92*
Interactive CD-ROM

Video Recap: Lección 5

Before doing this **Fotonovela** section, review the previous one with this activity.
1. ¿Qué pasa cuando llegan al hotel? (la empleada no encuentra la reservación)
2. ¿Qué piensan Javier, Inés, Maite y Álex de las cabañas? (no están nada mal; son muy limpias y ordenadas)
3. ¿Por qué quiere Maite descansar? (a las seis va a correr con Álex)
4. ¿Qué está pensando Maite cuando los demás salen de la habitación? (Inés y Javier están juntos otra vez)

Video Synopsis
Inés and Javier go to an open-air market. Inés browses the market and eventually buys a purse for her sister, as well as a shirt and a hat for herself. Javier buys a sweater for the hike in the mountains.

Suggestions
• Have students scan the **Fotonovela** captions for vocabulary related to clothing or colors.
• Bring color photographs from magazines and ask the class questions about what the people in the photographs are wearing. Ex: **¿Qué lleva la señorita? ¿De qué color es?**
• Point out the clothing that a few individual students are wearing and ask them some questions about it. Ex: **Me gusta esa camisa azul. ¿Es de algodón? ¿Dónde la compraste?**
• Point out that in September 2000 the U.S. dollar became the official currency of Ecuador.

PERSONAJES

INÉS

JAVIER

EL VENDEDOR

INÉS Javier, ¡qué ropa más bonita! A mí me gusta esa camisa blanca y azul. Debe ser de algodón. ¿Te gusta?

JAVIER Yo prefiero la camisa de la izquierda... la gris con rayas rojas. Hace juego con mis botas marrones.

INÉS Está bien, Javier. Mira, necesito comprarle un regalo a mi hermana Graciela. Acaba de empezar un nuevo trabajo...

JAVIER ¿Tal vez una bolsa?

VENDEDOR Esas bolsas son típicas de las montañas. ¿Le gustan?

INÉS Sí. Quiero comprarle una a mi hermana.

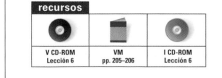

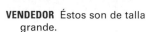

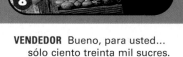

VENDEDOR Buenas tardes, joven. ¿Le puedo servir en algo?

JAVIER Sí. Voy a ir de excursión a las montañas y necesito un buen suéter.

VENDEDOR ¿Qué talla usa usted?

JAVIER Uso talla grande.

VENDEDOR Éstos son de talla grande.

JAVIER ¿Qué precio tiene ése?

VENDEDOR ¿Le gusta este suéter? Le cuesta ciento cincuenta mil sucres.

JAVIER Quiero comprarlo, pero, señor, no soy rico. ¿Ciento veinte mil sucres?

VENDEDOR Bueno, para usted... sólo ciento treinta mil sucres.

JAVIER Está bien, señor.

recursos

V CD-ROM Lección 6	VM pp. 205–206	I CD-ROM Lección 6

TEACHING OPTIONS

Video Tips General suggestions for using video clips in the classroom can be found on page IAE-12 of this Instructor's Annotated Edition.
¡Qué ropa más bonita! Photocopy the videoscript and opaque out 7–10 words with white correction fluid in order to create a master for a cloze activity. Hand out photocopies of the master to your students and have them fill in the missing words as they watch the **¡Qué ropa más bonita!** segment of this video module. You may want to show the segment twice or more if your students experience difficulties with this activity. You may also want your students to share their pages in small groups and help each other fill in any gaps.

INÉS Me gusta aquélla. ¿Cuánto cuesta?

VENDEDOR Ésa cuesta ciento sesenta mil sucres. ¡Es de muy buena calidad!

INÉS Uy, demasiado cara. Quizás otro día.

JAVIER Acabo de comprarme un suéter. Y tú, ¿qué compraste?

INÉS Compré esta bolsa para mi hermana.

INÉS También compré una camisa y un sombrero. ¿Qué tal me veo?

JAVIER ¡Guapa, muy guapa!

Enfoque cultural Mercados al aire libre

Open-air markets, or **mercados al aire libre,** are an important part of the commerce and culture of many Hispanic countries. Fresh fruits and vegetables, tapestries, clothing, pottery and crafts are commonly seen among the vendors' wares. One of the most famous is the market in Otavalo, Ecuador, which has taken place every Saturday since pre-Incan times. Another popular market is **El Rastro** in Madrid, held every Sunday, where tourists can buy antiques and many other goods.

Expresiones útiles

Talking about clothing

▶ **¡Qué ropa más bonita!**
What nice clothing!
▶ **Me gusta esta/esa camisa blanca de rayas negras.**
I like this/that white shirt with black stripes.
▶ **Está de moda.**
It's in fashion.
▶ **Debe ser de algodón/lana/seda.**
It must be cotton/wool/silk.
▶ **Es de cuadros/lunares/rayas.**
It's plaid/polka-dotted/striped.
▶ **Me gusta este/ese suéter.**
I like this/that sweater.
▶ **Es de muy buena calidad.**
It's very good quality.
▶ **¿Qué talla lleva/usa usted?**
What size do you wear?
▷ **Llevo/Uso talla grande.**
I wear a large.
▶ **¿Qué número calza usted?**
What (shoe) size do you wear?
▷ **Calzo el treinta y seis.**
I wear a size thirty-six.

Talking about how much things cost

▶ **¿Cuánto cuesta?**
How much does it cost?
▷ **Sólo cuesta noventa mil sucres.**
It only costs ninety thousand sucres.
▷ **Demasiado caro/a.**
Too expensive.
▷ **Es una ganga.**
It's a bargain.

Saying what you bought

▶ **¿Qué compró Ud./él/ella?**
What did you (form.)/he/she buy?
▷ **Compré esta bolsa para mi hermana.**
I bought this purse for my sister.
▶ **¿Qué compraste?**
What did you buy?
▷ **Acabo de comprarme un sombrero.**
I have just bought myself a hat.

158

Reacciona a la fotonovela

1 **¿Cierto o falso?** Indicate whether each sentence is **cierto** or **falso**. Correct the false statements.

	Cierto	Falso
1. A Inés le gusta la camisa verde y amarilla.	○	⊘
A Inés le gusta la camisa blanca y azul.		
2. Javier necesita comprarle un regalo a su hermana.	○	⊘
Inés necesita comprarle un regalo a su hermana.		
3. Las bolsas en el mercado son típicas de las montañas.	⊘	○
4. Javier busca un traje de baño.	○	⊘
Javier busca un suéter.		
5. Inés compró un sombrero, un suéter y una bolsa.	○	⊘
Inés compró una bolsa, una camisa y un sombrero.		
6. Javier regatea con el vendedor.	⊘	○

2 **Identificar** Provide the name of the person who would make each statement. The names may be used more than once.

1. ¿Te gusta el sombrero que compré? _____Inés_____
2. Estos suéteres son de talla grande. ¿Qué talla usa usted? _____el vendedor_____
3. ¿Por qué no compras una bolsa para Graciela? _____Javier_____
4. Creo que mis botas hacen juego con la camisa. _____Javier_____
5. Estas bolsas son excelentes, de muy buena calidad. _____el vendedor_____
6. Creo que las blusas aquí son de algodón. _____Inés_____

INÉS

JAVIER

EL VENDEDOR

3 **Contestar** Answer the questions using the information in the **Fotonovela**.

1. Inés quiere comprarle un regalo a su hermana. ¿Por qué? Inés quiere comprarle un regalo a su hermana porque ella acaba de empezar un nuevo trabajo.
2. ¿Cuánto cuesta la bolsa de las montañas? La bolsa de las montañas cuesta ciento cincuenta mil sucres.
3. ¿Por qué necesita Javier un buen suéter? Javier necesita un buen suéter porque va de excursión a las montañas.
4. ¿Cuál es el precio final del suéter? El precio final del suéter es ciento treinta mil sucres.
5. ¿Qué compra Inés en el mercado? Inés compra una bolsa, una camisa y un sombrero.
6. ¿Qué talla usa Javier? Javier usa talla grande.

4 **Conversar** With a partner, role-play a conversation between a customer and a sales person in an open-air market. Answers will vary.

Cliente/a	Vendedor(a)
Say good afternoon.	Greet the customer and ask what he or she would like.
Explain that you are looking for a particular item of clothing.	Show him or her some items and ask what he or she prefers.
Discuss colors and sizes.	Discuss colors and sizes.
Ask for the price and begin bargaining.	Tell him or her a price. Negotiate a price.
Settle on a price and purchase the item.	Accept a price and say thank you.

NATIONAL communication STANDARDS

CONSEJOS

When discussing prices, it's important to keep in mind singular and plural forms of verbs.

La **camisa cuesta** diez dólares.

Las **botas cuestan** sesenta dólares.

El **precio** de las botas **es** sesenta dólares.

Los **precios** de la ropa **son** altos.

AYUDA

¿Qué desea?
What would you like?

Estoy buscando...
I'm looking for...

Prefiero el/la rojo/a.
I prefer the red one.

¿Cuánto cuesta?
How much does it cost?

Es demasiado.
It's too much.

---

1 **Expansion** Once all statements have been corrected, ask pairs to find the places in the **Fotonovela** episode that support their answers. Have pairs play out the scenes for the class.

2 **Expansion** Present these as items 7-9: **7. Pero, señor... no traigo mucho dinero. (Javier) 8. Señor, para usted... ochenta mil sucres. (el vendedor) 9. Me gusta mucho esta camisa blanca de algodón. (Inés)**

3 **Expansion** Have pairs write two additional questions. Then in groups of four, pairs take turns asking, answering, and correcting each other's questions. Call on volunteers to share their questions with the rest of the class.

4 **Possible Response**
E1: Buenas tardes.
E2: Buenas tardes. ¿Le puedo servir en algo?
E1: Necesito una camisa.
E2: Pues, tengo estas camisas de algodón y estas camisas de seda. Son de muy buena calidad. ¿Cuál prefiere usted?
E1: Busco una camisa blanca o azul de algodón. Uso talla mediana.
E2: Las camisas de algodón son de talla mediana. Tengo esta camisa azul de algodón.
E1: Quiero comprarla, pero no soy rico/a. ¿Cuánto cuesta?
E2: Veinte dólares. Pero para usted... sólo quince dólares.
E1: Muy bien. La compro, pero sólo tengo diez dólares.
E2: Está bien. Muchas gracias, y adiós.

Successful Language Learning Tell students to devote extra effort and attention to **Actividad 4**. This activity sums up the vocabulary and functional phrases that the students have learned earlier in the lesson. In addition, this activity explores a real-life situation that travelers might encounter when visiting a Spanish-speaking country.

TEACHING OPTIONS

Extra Practice Have the class answer questions about **Fotonovela**. Ex: **1. ¿Quién necesita una bolsa nueva para su trabajo? (Graciela, la hermana de Inés) 2. ¿Quién cree que las bolsas son demasiado caras? (Inés) 3. ¿De qué color son las botas de Javier? (marrón) 4. ¿Quién acaba de comprarse un suéter? (Javier)**

Small Groups Have the class work in small groups to write statements about the **Fotonovela**. Ask each group to exchange its statements with another group. Each group will then write out the question that would have elicited each statement. Ex: G1: **Graciela acaba de empezar un nuevo trabajo.** G2: **¿Quién acaba de empezar un nuevo trabajo?**

Pronunciación 🎧

The consonants **d** and **t**

¿Dónde?	vender	nadar	verdad

Like **b** and **v**, the Spanish **d** can also have a hard sound or a soft sound, depending on which letters appear next to it.

Don	dinero	tienda	falda

At the beginning of a phrase and after **n** or **l**, the letter **d** is pronounced with a hard sound. This sound is similar to the English *d* in *dog*, but a little softer and duller. The tongue should touch the back of the upper teeth, not the roof of the mouth.

medias	verde	vestido	huésped

In all other positions, **d** has a soft sound. It is similar to the English *th* in *there*, but a little softer.

Don Diego no tiene el diccionario.

When **d** begins a word, its pronunciation depends on the previous word. At the beginning of a phrase or after a word that ends in **n** or **l**, it is pronounced as a hard **d**.

Doña Dolores es de la capital.

Words that begin with **d** are pronounced with a soft **d** if they appear immediately after a word that ends in a vowel or any consonant other than **n** or **l**.

traje	pantalones	tarjeta	tienda

When pronouncing the Spanish **t**, the tongue should touch the back of the upper teeth, not the roof of the mouth. Unlike the English *t*, no air is expelled from the mouth.

Práctica Read these phrases aloud to practice the **d** and the **t**.

1. Hasta pronto.
2. De nada.
3. Mucho gusto.
4. Lo siento.
5. No hay de qué.
6. ¿De dónde es usted?
7. ¡Todos a bordo!
8. No puedo.
9. Es estupendo.
10. No tengo computadora.
11. ¿Cuándo vienen?
12. Son las tres y media.

Oraciones Read these sentences aloud to practice the **d** and the **t**.

1. Don Teodoro tiene una tienda en un almacén en La Habana.
2. Don Teodoro vende muchos trajes, vestidos y zapatos todos los días.
3. Un día un turista, Federico Machado, entra en la tienda para comprar un par de botas.
4. Federico regatea con don Teodoro y compra las botas y también un par de sandalias.

Refranes Read these sayings aloud to practice the **d** and the **t**.

En la variedad está el gusto.[1]

Aunque la mona se vista de seda, mona se queda.[2]

[1] *Variety is the spice of life.*
[2] *You can't make a silk purse out of a sow's ear.*

recursos			
💿	📘	💿	💿
TEXT CD Lección 6	LM p. 32	Lab CD/MP3 Lección 6	I CD-ROM Lección 6

Section Goal

In **Pronunciación** students will be introduced to the pronunciation of the letters **d** and **t**.

Instructional Resources
Textbook Activities CD
Lab Manual, p. 32
Lab CD/MP3 Lección 6
IRM: Tapescript, pp. 25–29; p. 76
Interactive CD-ROM

Suggestions

• Say that **d** has a hard sound at the beginning of a phrase or after **n** or **l**. Write **don, dinero, tienda,** and **falda** on the board and have the class pronounce them.

• Explain that **d** has a soft sound in all other situations. Pronounce the words **medias, verde, vestido,** and **huésped** and have the class repeat.

• Point out that within phrases, **d** at the beginning of a word has a hard or soft sound depending on the last sound of the word that precedes it, according to the same rules described above for **d** at the beginning of a phrase. Read the example sentences aloud and have the class repeat.

• Explain that **t** is pronounced with the tongue at the back of the upper teeth and that, unlike English, no air is expelled from the mouth. Pronounce **traje, pantalones, tarjeta,** and **tienda** and have the class repeat. Then pronounce pairs of similar-sounding Spanish and English words, having students focus on the difference between the sounds of **t**: ti/*tea*; tal/*tall*; todo/*toad*; tema/*tame*, tela/*tell*.

Práctica/Oraciones/Refranes
These exercises are recorded on the Textbook Activities CD. You may want to play the CD so students practice the pronunciation point by listening to Spanish spoken by speakers other than yourself.

TEACHING OPTIONS

Extra Practice Write some additional proverbs on the board and have the class practice saying each one. Ex: **De tal padre, tal hijo.** (*Like father, like son.*) **El que tiene tejado de cristal no tira piedras al vecino.** (*People who live in glass houses shouldn't throw stones.*) **Cuatro ojos ven más que dos.** (*Two heads are better than one.*)

Extra Practice Write on the board the names of these famous Cuban literary figures: **José Martí, Julián del Casal, Gertrudis Gómez de Avellaneda,** and **Dulce María Loynaz.** Say the names aloud and have the class repeat after you. Then ask the class to explain the pronunciation of each **d** and **t** in these names.

6.1 Numbers 101 and higher

101	ciento uno	**1.000**	mil
200	doscientos/as	**1.100**	mil cien
300	trescientos/as	**2.000**	dos mil
400	cuatrocientos/as	**5.000**	cinco mil
500	quinientos/as	**100.000**	cien mil
600	seiscientos/as	**200.000**	doscientos mil
700	setecientos/as	**550.000**	quinientos cincuenta mil
800	ochocientos/as	**1.000.000**	un millón (de)
900	novecientos/as	**8.000.000**	ocho millones (de)

▶ As shown in the preceding chart, Spanish uses a period to indicate thousands and millions, rather than a comma as used in English.

▶ The numbers 200 through 999 agree in gender with the nouns they modify.

324 bolsas
trescientas veinticuatro bolsas

605 sombreros
seiscientos cinco sombreros

La bolsa cuesta ciento sesenta mil sucres.

▶ The word **mil**, which can mean *a thousand* and *one thousand*, is not usually used in the plural form when referring to numbers. **Un millón** (*a million* or *one million*), has the plural form **millones** in which the accent is dropped.

1.000 zapatos
mil zapatos

25.000 faldas
veinticinco mil faldas

2.000.000 de clientes
dos millones de clientes

▶ To express a more complex number, string together its component parts.

55.422
cincuenta y cinco mil cuatrocientos veintidós

¡INTÉNTALO! Give the Spanish equivalent of each number. The first item has been done for you.

1. **102** _ciento dos_
2. **5.000.000** cinco millones
3. **2001** dos mil uno
4. **1776** mil setecientos setenta y seis
5. **345** trescientos cuarenta y cinco
6. **550.300** quinientos cincuenta mil trescientos
7. **235** doscientos treinta y cinco
8. **1999** mil novecientos noventa y nueve
9. **113** ciento trece
10. **205** doscientos cinco
11. **17.123** diecisiete mil ciento veintitrés
12. **497** cuatrocientos noventa y siete

¡LENGUA VIVA!

In Spanish, the years of dates (**fechas**) are not expressed as pairs of 2-digit numbers as they are in English (1979, *nineteen seventy-nine*): 1876, **mil ochocientos setenta y seis**; 1945, **mil novecientos cuarenta y cinco**; 2004, **dos mil cuatro.**

¡ATENCIÓN!

When **millón** or **millones** is used before a noun, the word **de** is placed between the two:

1.000.000 de hombres = un millón de hombres

12.000.000 de aviones = doce millones de aviones

• • •

See **Estructura 2.4**, p. 53 to review the difference between **cien** and **ciento**:

100.000 = cien mil

2.101 = dos mil ciento uno

Práctica

1 **Completar** Complete the following sequences of numbers.
  1. 50, 150, 250 ... 1.050 trescientos cincuenta, cuatrocientos cincuenta, quinientos cincuenta,
     seiscientos cincuenta, setecientos cincuenta, ochocientos cincuenta, novecientos cincuenta
  2. 5.000, 20.000, 35.000 ... 95.000
     cincuenta mil, sesenta y cinco mil, ochenta mil
  3. 100.000, 200.000, 300.000 ... 1.000.000
     cuatrocientos mil, quinientos mil, seiscientos mil, setecientos mil, ochocientos mil, novecientos mil
  4. 100.000.000, 90.000.000, 80.000.000 ... 0 setenta millones, sesenta millones,
     cincuenta millones, cuarenta millones, treinta millones, veinte millones, diez millones

2 **Resolver** Read the math problems aloud and solve them.

  modelo
  $200 + 300 =$
  Doscientos más trescientos son quinientos.

+	más
–	menos
=	son

  1. $1000 + 753 =$ Mil más setecientos cincuenta y tres son mil setecientos cincuenta y tres.
  2. $1.000.000 - 30.000 =$ Un millón menos treinta mil son novecientos setenta mil.
  3. $10.000 + 555 =$ Diez mil más quinientos cincuenta y cinco son diez mil quinientos cincuenta y cinco.
  4. $150 + 150 =$ Ciento cincuenta más ciento cincuenta son trescientos.
  5. $100.000 + 205.000 =$ Cien mil más doscientos cinco mil son trescientos cinco mil.
  6. $29.000 - 10.000 =$ Veintinueve mil menos diez mil son diecinueve mil.

Comunicación

NATIONAL
communication
STANDARDS

3 **En la librería** In pairs look at the ad and answer the questions.

> **¡Librería TU ACENTO tiene rebajas en toda la tienda!**
> Puedes comprar libros populares como:
>
> **El planeta rojo,** 154 pesos, 210 páginas
> **Un billón de pesos y dónde lo gastan,** 130 pesos, 455 páginas
> **Misterio en el almacén,** 268 pesos, 379 páginas
> **Historia de la Segunda Guerra Mundial, 1939–1945,**
>   324 pesos, 802 páginas
> **El béisbol: Pasión en La Habana,** 249 pesos, 101 páginas
> **El loco del impermeable,** 247 pesos, 290 páginas

  1. ¿Qué libro tiene más páginas? ¿Cuántas tiene?
     Historia de la Segunda Guerra Mundial, 1939–1945; 802 páginas
  2. ¿Qué libro tiene menos (*least*) páginas? ¿Cuántas tiene?
     El béisbol: Pasión en La Habana; 101 páginas
  3. ¿Qué libro tiene una fecha en su título? ¿Cuál es la fecha?
     Historia de la Segunda Guerra Mundial, 1939–1945
  4. ¿Qué libro es más caro? ¿Cuánto cuesta?
     Historia de la Segunda Guerra Mundial, 1939–1945; 324 pesos
  5. ¿Qué libro es menos caro? ¿Cuánto cuesta?
     Un billón de pesos y dónde lo gastan; 130 pesos
  6. ¿Qué libro quieren ustedes comprar en la librería *Tu acento*? ¿Por qué?
     Answers will vary.
  7. ¿Cuál es su libro favorito? ¿Cuántas páginas tiene?
     Answers will vary.

¡ATENCIÓN!

Note this difference between Spanish and English:
mil millones
a billion (*1,000,000,000*)
un billón
a trillion
(*1,000,000,000,000*)

1 **Suggestion** Practice listening comprehension by having students read numbers from the activity to a partner, who writes them down.

1 **Expansion** Have pairs write three new number sequences like those in the activity. Then have them exchange their papers with another pair.

2 **Expansion** Have pairs convert one of the problems into a word problem. Ex: **Tengo doscientos dólares. Mi hermana tiene trescientos. ¿Cuántos dólares tenemos?**

3 **Suggestion** Ask questions about the ad before assigning the activity. Ex: **¿Dónde hay rebajas? (Hay rebajas en la librería *Tu acento*.) ¿Qué tipos de libros venden? (Venden libros de historia, de ciencia y de deportes.) ¿Cuánto cuestan los libros? (Cuestan entre 130 y 324 pesos.)**

3 **Expansion** Have small groups write a newspaper ad for a local business, incorporating numbers 101 and higher.

6.2 Indirect object pronouns

ANTE TODO In **Lección 5**, you learned that a direct object is a noun or pronoun that receives the action of the verb directly. In contrast, indirect objects are nouns or pronouns that receive the action of the verb indirectly. Note the following example:

SUBJECT	I.O. PRONOUN	VERB	DIRECT OBJECT	INDIRECT OBJECT
Roberto	**le**	presta	cien pesos	**a Luisa**.
Roberto		*lends*	*100 pesos*	*to Luisa.*

An indirect object is a noun or pronoun that answers the question *to whom* or *for whom* an action is done. In the preceding example, the indirect object answers this question: **¿A quién le presta Roberto cien pesos?** *To whom does Roberto lend 100 pesos?*

Indirect object pronouns

SINGULAR		PLURAL	
me	(to, for) *me*	**nos**	(to, for) *us*
te	(to, for) *you* (fam.)	**os**	(to, for) *you* (fam.)
le	(to, for) *you* (form.) (to, for) *him; her*	**les**	(to, for) *you* (form.) (to, for) *them*

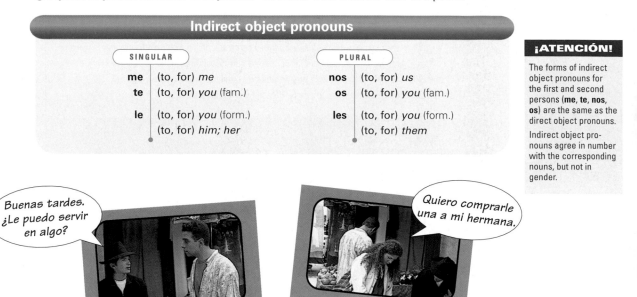

Buenas tardes. ¿Le puedo servir en algo?

Quiero comprarle una a mi hermana.

Using indirect object pronouns

▶ Spanish speakers commonly use both an indirect object pronoun and the noun to which it refers in the same sentence. This is done to emphasize and clarify to whom the pronoun refers.

I.O. PRONOUN		INDIRECT OBJECT		I.O. PRONOUN		INDIRECT OBJECT
Ella **le** vende la ropa a **Elena**.				**Les** prestamos el dinero a **Inés y Álex**.		

▶ Indirect object pronouns are also used without the indirect object noun when the person for whom the action is being done is known.

Ana **le** presta la falda **a Elena**.
Ana lends her skirt to Elena.

También **le** presta unos bluejeans.
She also lends her a pair of blue jeans.

▶ Indirect object pronouns are usually placed before the conjugated form of the verb. In negative sentences the pronoun is placed between **no** and the conjugated verb.

Martín **me** compra un regalo.	Eva **no me** escribe cartas.
Martín buys me a gift.	*Eva doesn't write me letters.*

¡ATENCIÓN!

When an indirect object pronoun is attached to a present participle, an accent mark is added to maintain the proper stress. For more information on accents, see **Pronunciación**, p. 101, **Ortografía**, p. 275, and p. 305.

▶ When a conjugated verb is followed by an infinitive or the present progressive, the indirect object pronoun may be placed before the conjugated verb or attached to the infinitive or present participle.

Él no quiere **pagarte**.	Él está **escribiéndole** una postal a ella.
He does not want to pay you.	*He is writing a postcard to her.*
Él no **te** quiere pagar.	Él **le** está escribiendo una postal a ella.
He does not want to pay you.	*He is writing a postcard to her.*

▶ Because the indirect object pronouns **le** and **les** have multiple meanings, Spanish speakers often clarify to whom the pronouns refer with the preposition **a** + [*pronoun*] or **a** + [*noun*].

UNCLARIFIED STATEMENTS	CLARIFIED STATEMENTS
Yo **le** compro un abrigo.	Yo **le** compro un abrigo **a él/ella/usted.**
Ella **le** describe un libro.	Ella **le** describe un libro **a Juan.**

UNCLARIFIED STATEMENTS	CLARIFIED STATEMENTS
Él **les** vende unos sombreros.	Él **les** vende unos sombreros a **ellos/ellas/ustedes.**
Ellos **les** hablan muy claro.	Ellos **les** hablan muy claro **a los clientes.**

▶ The irregular verb **dar** (*to give*), as well as **decir**, are often used with indirect object pronouns.

dar			
Singular forms		**Plural forms**	
yo	**doy**	nosotros/as	**damos**
tú	**das**	vosotros/as	**dais**
Ud./él/ella	**da**	Uds./ellos/ellas	**dan**

¡ATENCIÓN!

Here are some common expressions with **dar**:

dar consejos
to give advice

dar un regalo
to give a present

dar una fiesta
to throw a party

Mi abuela **me da** muchos regalos.	**Te digo** la verdad.
My grandmother gives me lots of gifts.	*I'm telling you the truth.*
Voy a **darle** consejos.	No **les digo** mentiras a mis padres.
I'm going to give her advice.	*I don't tell lies to my parents.*

CONSÚLTALO

Remember that **decir** is a stem-changing verb (**e:i**) with an irregular **yo** form: **digo**. To review the present tense of **decir**, see **Estructura 4.3**, p. 109.

¡INTÉNTALO! Use the cues in parentheses to provide the indirect object pronoun for the sentence. The first item has been done for you.

1. Juan ___le___ quiere dar un regalo. (*to Elena*)
2. María ___nos___ prepara un café. (*for us*)
3. Beatriz y Felipe ___me___ escriben desde Cuba. (*to me*)
4. Marta y yo ___les___ compramos unos guantes. (*for them*)
5. Los vendedores ___te___ venden ropa. (*to you, fam. sing.*)
6. La dependienta ___nos___ enseña los guantes. (*to us*)

TEACHING OPTIONS

Video Have students read along as you replay the **Fotonovela**. Ask them to note each time an indirect object pronoun is used. Point out that the pronouns used with the verb **gustar** are indirect objects because they answer the question (*is pleasing*) *to whom?* Next, have students find each use of **le** and **les** and state to whom or what the pronouns refer.

Game Have students write a sentence with an indirect object pronoun. Each word is written on a separate slip of paper, then placed in an envelope. Students trade envelopes. After putting the sentences together, students write them down. Students continue trading envelopes and writing sentences. At the end of three minutes, the student with the most correctly deciphered sentences wins.

Suggestions

• Point out that the position of indirect object pronouns in a sentence is the same as that of direct object pronouns.

• After going over the **¡Inténtalo!** orally with the class, ask students which items might require clarification (items 1 and 4). Ask them what they would add to each sentence in order to clarify **le** or **les**.

• As a comprehension check, have students write answers to these questions: **1. Necesitas comprar un regalo para tu mejor amigo. ¿Qué vas a comprarle? 2. ¿A quiénes les hablas todos los días? 3. ¿Quién te presta dinero cuando lo necesitas? 4. ¿Quién les está enseñando español a ustedes?**

Práctica

1 Completar Fill in the correct pronouns to complete Mónica's description of her family's holiday shopping.

1. Juan y yo __le__ damos una blusa a nuestra hermana Gisela.
2. Mi tía __nos__ da a nosotros una mesa para la casa.
3. Gisela __le__ da dos corbatas a su novio.
4. A mi mamá yo __le__ doy un par de guantes negros.
5. A mi profesora __le__ doy dos libros de José Martí.
6. Juan __les__ da un regalo a mis padres.
7. Mis padres __me__ dan a mí un traje nuevo.
8. Y a ti, yo __te__ doy un regalo también. ¿Quieres verlo?

2 Combinar Use an item from each column and an indirect object pronoun to create logical sentences. Answers will vary.

modelo
Mis padres les dan regalos a mis primos.

A	B	C	D
Yo	comprar	correo electrónico	mí
El dependiente	dar	corbata	ustedes
El profesor Arce	decir	dinero en efectivo	clienta
La vendedora	escribir	ejercicio	la novia
Mis padres	explicar	problemas	mis primos
Tú	pagar	regalos	ti
Nosotros/as	prestar	ropa	nosotros
¿?	vender	¿?	¿?

3 Describir Describe what's happening in these photos based on the cues provided.

1. escribir / mensaje electrónico Álex le escribe un mensaje electrónico (a Ricardo).

2. mostrar / fotos Javier les muestra fotos (a Inés y Maite).

3. dar / documentos La Sra. Ramos le da los documentos (a Maite).

4. pedir / llaves Don Francisco le pide las llaves (a la empleada).

5. vender / suéter El vendedor le vende un suéter (a Javier).

6. comprar / bolsa Inés le compra una bolsa (a su hermana).

Comunicación

4 **Entrevista** Take turns with a classmate asking and answering questions using the word bank. Answers will vary.

modelo

escribir mensajes electrónicos
Estudiante 1: ¿A quién le escribes mensajes electrónicos?
Estudiante 2: Le escribo mensajes electrónicos a mi hermano.

cantar canciones de amor (*love songs*)	escribir mensajes electrónicos
comprar ropa	pedir dinero
dar consejos	preparar comida (*food*) mexicana
decir mentiras	prestar dinero

5 **¡Somos ricos!** You and your classmates chipped in on a lottery ticket and you won! Now you want to spend money on your loved ones. In groups of three, discuss what each person is buying for family and friends. Answers will vary.

modelo

Estudiante 1: Quiero comprarle un vestido de Carolina Herrera a mi madre.
Estudiante 2: Y yo voy a darles un carro nuevo a mis padres.
Estudiante 3: Voy a comprarles una casa a mis padres, pero a mis amigos no les voy a dar nada.

NOTA CULTURAL

Carolina Herrera (1941–) is a Venezuelan fashion designer known worldwide for her elegant, understated designs. In the past two decades, she has become very successful and even has a fragrance line.

6 **Entrevista** Use these questions to interview a classmate. Answers will vary.

1. ¿Qué tiendas, almacenes o centros comerciales prefieres?
2. ¿A quién le compras regalos cuando hay rebajas?
3. ¿A quién le prestas dinero cuando esa persona lo necesita?
4. Quiero ir de compras. ¿Cuánto dinero me puedes prestar?
5. ¿Te dan tus padres su tarjeta de crédito cuando vas de compras?

Síntesis

7 **Minidrama** With two classmates, take turns playing the roles of two shoppers and a clerk in a clothing store. The shoppers should take turns talking about the articles of clothing they are looking for, for whom they are buying the clothes, and what they bought for the same people last year. The clerk should recommend several items based on the shoppers' descriptions. Answers will vary.

AYUDA

Here are some useful sentences in addition to the **Expresiones útiles** on p.157.

Me queda grande/pequeño.
It's big/small on me.

¿Tiene otro color?
Do you have another color?

¿Está en rebaja?
Is it on sale?

---

4 **Expansion** Give students five minutes to work in groups of three to brainstorm as many questions as they can using different forms of the verbs listed in the word bank. Invite two groups to come to the front of the class. Each group takes a turn asking the other its questions.

5 **Expansion** Have students research information about national lotteries in Spanish-speaking countries.

6 **Expansion** Take a class survey of the answers and write the results on the board.

7 **Suggestions**
• Have students rehearse their mini-dramas.
• Videotape the scenes in or outside of class.

TEACHING OPTIONS

Small Groups Have students write a conversation between two friends. One friend tries to convince the other to go shopping with him or her this weekend. The other friend explains that he or she cannot and lists all the things he or she is going to do this weekend. Students should try to incorporate as many different indirect object pronouns in their conversations as possible.

Pairs Ask students to imagine they are going on an extended trip. Have them make a list of five things they are going to do (people they are going to write to, things they are going to buy for themselves or others, money they are going to borrow, etc.) before leaving. Ex: **Voy a comprarme unos zapatos nuevos.**

6.3 Preterite tense of regular verbs

ANTE TODO In order to talk about events in the past, Spanish uses two simple tenses: the preterite and the imperfect. In this lesson, you will learn how to form the preterite tense, which is used to express actions or states completed in the past.

Preterite of regular –*ar*, –*er*, and –*ir* verbs

		–*ar* verbs **comprar**	–*er* verbs **vender**	–*ir* verbs **escribir**
SINGULAR FORMS	yo	compr**é** *I bought*	vend**í** *I sold*	escrib**í** *I wrote*
	tú	compr**aste**	vend**iste**	escrib**iste**
	Ud./él/ella	compr**ó**	vend**ió**	escrib**ió**
PLURAL FORMS	nosotros/as	compr**amos**	vend**imos**	escrib**imos**
	vosotros/as	compr**asteis**	vend**isteis**	escrib**isteis**
	Uds./ellos/ellas	compr**aron**	vend**ieron**	escrib**ieron**

▶ As the preceding chart shows, the endings for regular –**er** and –**ir** verbs are identical in the preterite.

¿Qué compraste?

Compré esta bolsa.

▶ Note that the **nosotros/as** forms of regular –**ar** and –**ir** verbs in the preterite are identical to the present tense forms. Context will help you determine which tense is being used.

En invierno **compramos** la ropa
   en la tienda de la universidad.
In the winter, we buy clothing
   at the university store.

Anoche **compramos** unos zapatos
   de tenis y unas sandalias.
Last night we bought a pair of tennis shoes
   and a pair of sandals.

▶ –**Ar** and –**er** verbs that have a stem change in the present tense are regular in the preterite. They do *not* have a stem change.

	PRESENT	PRETERITE
cerrar (e:ie)	La tienda **cierra** a las seis.	La tienda **cerró** a las seis.
volver (o:ue)	Carlitos **vuelve** tarde.	Carlitos **volvió** tarde.
jugar (u:ue)	Él **juega** al fútbol.	Él **jugó** al fútbol.

▶ Verbs that end in **–car**, **–gar**, and **–zar** have a spelling change in the first person singular (**yo** form) in the preterite.

bus**car**	bus**c-**	**qu-**	yo bus**qu**é
lle**gar**	lle**g-**	**gu-**	yo lle**gu**é
empe**zar**	empe**z-**	**c-**	yo empe**c**é

▶ Except for the **yo** form, all other forms of **–car**, **–gar**, and **–zar** verbs are regular in the preterite.

▶ Three other verbs —**creer**, **leer**, and **oír** — have spelling changes in the preterite. The **i** of the verb endings of **creer**, **leer**, and **oír** carries an accent in the **yo, tú, nosotros/as,** and **vosotros/as** forms, and changes to **y** in the **Ud./él/ella** and **Uds./ellos/ellas** forms.

creer	cre-	cre**í**, cre**í**ste, cre**y**ó, cre**í**mos, cre**í**steis, cre**y**eron
leer	le-	le**í**, le**í**ste, le**y**ó, le**í**mos, le**í**steis, le**y**eron
oír	o-	o**í**, o**í**ste, o**y**ó, o**í**mos, o**í**steis, o**y**eron

▶ **Ver** is regular in the preterite, but none of its forms has an accent. **ver** ⟶ **vi, viste, vio, vimos, visteis, vieron.**

Words commonly used with the preterite

anoche	last night	pasado/a (*adj.*)	last; past
anteayer	the day before yesterday	el año pasado	last year
		la semana pasada	last week
ayer	yesterday	una vez	once; one time
de repente	suddenly	dos veces	twice; two times
desde... hasta...	from... until...	ya	already

Ayer llegué a Santiago de Cuba.
Yesterday I arrived in Santiago de Cuba.

Anoche oí un ruido extraño.
Last night I heard a strange noise.

▶ **Acabar de** + [*infinitive*] is used to say that something has just occurred. Note that **acabar** is in the present tense in this construction.

Acabo de comprar una falda.
I just bought a skirt.

Acabas de ir de compras.
You just went shopping.

¡INTÉNTALO! Provide the appropriate preterite forms of the verbs. The first item in each column has been done for you.

celebrar
1. Elena celebró .
2. Yo celebré .
3. Los chicos celebraron .
4. Emilio y yo celebramos .
5. Tú celebraste .

comer
1. Los niños comieron .
2. Tú comiste .
3. Usted comió .
4. Nosotros comimos .
5. Yo comí .

salir
1. Tú y yo salimos .
2. Ella salió .
3. Pablo y Elena salieron .
4. Nosotros salimos .
5. Yo salí .

comenzar
1. Ustedes comenzaron .
2. Nosotras comenzamos .
3. Yo comencé .
4. Marcos comenzó .
5. Tú comenzaste .

Suggestions
• Practice verbs with spelling changes in the preterite by asking students about things they read, heard, and saw yesterday. Ex: **¿Leíste el periódico ayer? ¿Quiénes vieron el pronóstico del tiempo? Yo oí que va a llover hoy. ¿Qué oyeron ustedes?**
• Use magazine pictures to demonstrate **acabar de.** Ex: **¿Quién acaba de ganar? (Tiger Woods acaba de ganar.) ¿Qué acaban de ver ellos? (Acaban de ver un fantasma.)**

TEACHING OPTIONS

Game Divide the class into teams of six, arranged in rows. Call out the infinitive of a verb. The first person writes the **yo** form on a sheet of paper and passes it to the second person, who writes the **tú** form. The third writes the **él/ella/Ud.** form, and so on. The sixth checks spelling. If all forms are correct, the team gets a point. Continue play, starting with a different person each time. The team with the most points after six rounds wins.

Extra Practice Have students write five things they did yesterday. Ask students questions about what they did to elicit as many different conjugations as possible. Ex: **Carlos, ¿leíste el periódico ayer? ¿Quién más leyó el periódico ayer?... Carlos y Ana, ustedes dos leyeron el periódico ayer, ¿verdad? ¿Quiénes leyeron el periódico ayer?**

1 Expansion Ask questions about Andrea's weekend. Have students answer with complete sentences. Ex: **¿Quién asistió a una reunión? ¿Qué compraron los amigos?**

2 Suggestion After item 8 have pairs switch roles and repeat the activity.

2 Expansion Have students redo the activity, using **Uds.** as the subject of the questions and **nosotros** in the answers.

3 Suggestions
• Have students work with a partner to quickly review the preterite forms of the verbs in the activity.
• Divide the class into groups of four. Give students five minutes to see how many different sentences they can write. Have groups exchange their work with another group for peer editing. The group with the most sentences free of errors wins.

Práctica

1

Completar Andrea is talking about what happened last weekend. Complete each sentence by choosing the correct verb and putting it in the preterite.

1. El sábado a las diez de la mañana, la profesora Mora ___asistió___ (asistir, costar, usar) a una reunión (*meeting*) de profesores.
2. A la una, yo ___llegué___ (llegar, bucear, llevar) a la tienda con mis amigos.
3. Mis amigos y yo ___compramos___ (comprar, regatear, gastar) dos o tres cosas.
4. Yo ___compré___ (costar, comprar, escribir) unos pantalones negros y mi amigo Mateo ___compró___ (gastar, pasear, comprar) una camisa azul.
5. Después, nosotros ___comimos___ (llevar, vivir, comer) cerca de un mercado.
6. A las nueve, Pepe ___habló___ (hablar, pasear, nadar) con su novia por teléfono.
7. El sábado por la tarde, mi mamá les ___escribió___ (escribir, beber, vivir) una carta a nuestros parientes en Cuba.
8. El domingo por la mañana mi tía Manuela ___decidió___ (decidir, salir, escribir) comprarme un traje elegante.
9. A las cuatro de la tarde, mi tía ___encontró___ (beber, salir, encontrar) un traje para mí y después ___vimos___ (acabar, ver, salir) una película.

2

Preguntas Imagine that you have a pesky friend who keeps asking you questions. Respond that you already did or have just done what he or she asks.

> **modelo**
> leer la lección
> **Estudiante 1:** ¿Leíste la lección?
> **Estudiante 2:** Sí, ya la leí./Sí, acabo de leerla.

1. escribir el correo electrónico
   —¿Escribiste el correo electrónico?
   —Sí, ya lo escribí./Acabo de escribirlo.
2. lavar (*to wash*) la ropa
   —¿Lavaste la ropa?
   —Sí, ya la lavé./Acabo de lavarla.
3. oír las noticias (*news*)
   —¿Oíste las noticias?
   —Sí, ya las oí./Acabo de oírlas.
4. comprar pantalones cortos
   —¿Compraste pantalones cortos?
   —Sí, ya los compré./Acabo de comprarlos.
5. practicar los verbos
   —¿Practicaste los verbos?
   —Sí, ya los practiqué./Acabo de practicarlos.
6. pagar la cuenta (*bill*)
   —¿Pagaste la cuenta?
   —Sí, ya la pagué./Acabo de pagarla.
7. empezar la composición
   —¿Empezaste la composición?
   —Sí, ya la empecé./Acabo de empezarla.
8. ver la película *Buena Vista Social Club*
   —¿Viste la película *Buena Vista Social Club*?
   —Sí, ya la vi./Acabo de verla.

NOTA CULTURAL

The **Buena Vista Social Club** is a musical phenomenon that has been taking the world by storm since the group's rise to stardom in the 1990s. A number of Cuban musicians, popular decades earlier but almost forgotten, recorded a Grammy-winning album of traditional Cuban music. Later, a documentary about their comeback story was released, along with subsequent albums featuring the group's music.

3

Combinar Combine words and phrases from each column to talk about what you and others did. Be sure to use the correct form of each verb. Answers will vary.

> **modelo**
> Mis amigos y yo llegamos tarde a clase una vez.

yo	ver televisión	anoche
mi compañero/a de cuarto	hablar con un(a)	anteayer
mis amigos y yo	chico/a guapo/a	ayer
mi mejor (*best*) amigo/a	llevar un traje/vestido	la semana pasada
mis padres	comprar ropa nueva	el año pasado
el/la profesor(a) de español	leer un buen libro	una vez
el presidente de los	llegar tarde a clase	dos veces
Estados Unidos	gastar mucho dinero	
	compartir ropa	

TEACHING OPTIONS

Heritage Speakers Ask heritage speakers to imagine they have just visited an open-air market for the first time. Have them write a letter to a friend describing what they saw and did in the market. Then, ask students to exchange their letters with another person who will respond to them.

TPR Have groups of three students write out three sentences that use verbs in the preterite, with a verb from a different conjugation in each sentence. After they have finished writing, have each group mime its sentences for the class. When someone guesses the mimed action, the group writes its sentence on the board.

Comunicación

4 **Las vacaciones** Imagine that you took these photos on a vacation with friends. Get together with a partner and use the pictures to tell him or her about your trip.
Answers will vary.

5 **El fin de semana** Your instructor will give you and your partner different incomplete charts about what four employees at **Almacén Gigante** did last weekend. After you fill out the chart based on each other's information, you will fill out the final column about your partner. Answers will vary.

Síntesis

6 **Conversación** Get together with a partner and have a conversation about what you did last week using verbs from the word bank. Don't forget to include school activities, shopping, and pastimes. Answers will vary.

acampar	buscar	escribir	jugar	trabajar
asistir	comer	estudiar	leer	vender
bailar	comprar	gastar	oír	ver
beber	correr	hablar	tomar	viajar

4 **Suggestion** Have students first state where they traveled and when. Then have them identify the people in the photos, stating their names and their relationship to them and describing their personalities. Finally, students should tell what everyone did on the trip.

4 **Expansion** After completing the activity orally, have partners write a paragraph about their vacation, basing their account on the photos.

5 **Suggestion** Divide the class into pairs and distribute the handouts from the Information Gap Activities Booklet that correspond to this activity. Give students ten minutes to complete this activity.

5 **Expansion** Have students tell the class about any activities that both their partner and one of the **Almacén Gigante** employees did. Ex: **La señora Zapata leyó un libro y mi compañero/a, _____, también. Los dos leyeron un libro.**

6 **Suggestion** Have volunteers rehearse their conversation, then present it to the class.

6 **Expansion** Have volunteers report orally to the class what their partners did last week.

TEACHING OPTIONS

Large Group Have students create a story chain about a student who had a very bad day. Begin the story by saying: **Ayer, Rigoberto pasó un día desastroso.** Call on a student at one corner of the class to continue the story by telling how Rigoberto began his day. The second person tells what happened next. Different students continue adding sentences until only one student remains. That person must conclude the story.

Extra Practice Have students make a "to do" list at the beginning of their day. Then, ask students to return to their list at the end of the day and write sentences stating which activities they completed. Ex: **limpiar mi habitación; No, no limpié mi habitación.**

Section Goal

In **Estructura 6.4** students will learn to use demonstrative adjectives and pronouns.

Instructional Resources
WB/VM: Workbook, pp. 67–68
Lab Manual, p. 36
Lab CD/MP3 **Lección 6**
IRM: ¡Inténtalo! & Práctica
Answers, pp. 180–181;
Tapescript, pp. 25–29
Info Gap Activities Booklet,
pp. 23–24
Interactive CD-ROM
Companion website:
www.vistahigherlearning.com
Presentations CD-ROM

Suggestions
- Point to the book on your desk. Say: **Este libro está en la mesa.** Point to a book on a student's desk. Say: **Ese libro está encima del escritorio de ___** . Then point to a book on the window ledge. Say: **Aquel libro está cerca de la ventana**. Follow the same procedure with **tiza, papeles,** and **plumas**.
- Point out that although the masculine singular forms **este** and **ese** do not end in **–o**, their plural forms end in **–os**: **estos, esos**.
- Hold up or point to objects and have students give the plural: **este libro, esta mochila, este traje, este zapato**. Repeat with forms of **ese** and **aquel** with other nouns.

6.4 Demonstrative adjectives and pronouns

Demonstrative adjectives

 In Spanish, as in English, demonstrative adjectives are words that "demonstrate" or "point out" nouns. Demonstrative adjectives precede the nouns they modify and, like other Spanish adjectives you have studied, agree with them in gender and number. Observe these examples, then study the chart.

esta camisa	**ese** vendedor	**aquellos** zapatos
this shirt	*that salesman*	*those shoes (over there)*

Demonstrative adjectives

Singular		Plural		
MASCULINE	FEMININE	MASCULINE	FEMININE	
este	**esta**	**estos**	**estas**	*this; these*
ese	**esa**	**esos**	**esas**	*that; those*
aquel	**aquella**	**aquellos**	**aquellas**	*that; those (over there)*

▶ There are three sets of demonstrative adjectives. To determine which one to use, you must establish the relationship between the speaker and the noun(s) being pointed out.

▶ The demonstrative adjectives **este, esta, estos,** and **estas** are used to point out nouns that are close to the speaker and the listener.

Me gustan estos zapatos.

▶ The demonstrative adjectives **ese, esa, esos,** and **esas** are used to point out nouns that are not close in space and/or time to the speaker. They may, however, be close to the listener.

Prefiero esos zapatos.

Extra Practice Hold up one or two items of clothing or classroom objects. Have students write all three forms of the demonstrative pronouns that would apply. Ex: **estos zapatos, esos zapatos, aquellos zapatos.**

Pairs Refer students to **Contextos** on pages 152–153. Have them work with a partner to comment on the articles of clothing pictured. Ex: **Este suéter es bonito, ¿no? (No, ese suéter no es bonito. Es feo.)** or **Aquella camiseta es muy cara. (Sí, aquella camiseta es cara.)**

▶ The demonstrative adjectives **aquel, aquella, aquellos,** and **aquellas** are used to point out nouns that are far away from the speaker and the listener.

Aquel auto es de mi hermana.

Demonstrative pronouns

▶ Demonstrative pronouns are identical to their corresponding demonstrative adjectives, with the exception that they carry an accent mark on the stressed vowel.

—¿Quieres comprar **este suéter**?
Do you want to buy this sweater?

—No, no quiero **éste**. Quiero **ése**.
No, I don't want this one. I want that one.

—¿Vas a leer **estas revistas**?
Are you going to read these magazines?

—Sí, voy a leer **éstas**. También voy a leer **aquéllas**.
Yes, I'm going to read these. I'll also read those (over there).

Demonstrative pronouns

Singular		Plural	
MASCULINE	FEMININE	MASCULINE	FEMININE
éste	ésta	éstos	éstas
ése	ésa	ésos	ésas
aquél	aquélla	aquéllos	aquéllas

▶ There are three neuter demonstrative pronouns: **esto, eso,** and **aquello**. These forms refer to unidentified or unspecified nouns, situations, ideas, and concepts. They do not change in gender or number and never carry an accent mark.

—¿Qué es **esto**?
What's this?

—**Eso** es interesante.
That's interesting.

—**Aquello** es bonito.
That's pretty.

¡ATENCIÓN!

Like demonstrative adjectives, demonstrative pronouns agree in gender and number with the corresponding noun.

Este libro es de Pablito.

Éstos son de Juana.

¡INTÉNTALO! Provide the correct form of the demonstrative adjective for these nouns. The first item has been done for you.

1. la falda / este ___esta falda___
2. los estudiantes / este ___estos estudiantes___
3. los países / aquel ___aquellos países___
4. la ventana / ese ___esa ventana___
5. los periodistas / ese ___esos periodistas___
6. las empleadas / ese ___esas empleadas___
7. el chico / aquel ___aquel chico___
8. las sandalias / este ___estas sandalias___
9. el autobús / ese ___ese autobús___
10. las chicas / aquel ___aquellas chicas___

Práctica

1 **Cambiar** Make the singular sentences plural and the plural sentences singular.

> *modelo*
> Estas camisas son blancas.
> *Esta camisa es blanca.*

1. Aquellos sombreros son muy elegantes. Aquel sombrero es muy elegante.
2. Ese abrigo es muy caro. Esos abrigos son muy caros.
3. Estos cinturones son hermosos. Este cinturón es hermoso.
4. Esos precios son muy buenos. Ese precio es muy bueno.
5. Estas faldas son muy cortas. Esta falda es muy corta.
6. ¿Quieres ir a aquel almacén? ¿Quieres ir a aquellos almacenes?
7. Esas blusas son baratas. Esa blusa es barata.
8. Esta corbata hace juego con mi traje. Estas corbatas hacen juego con mi traje.

2 **Completar** Here are some things people might say while shopping. Complete the sentences with the correct demonstrative pronouns.

1. No me gustan esos zapatos. Voy a comprar _____éstos_____. (*these*)
2. ¿Vas a comprar ese traje o _____éste_____? (*this one*)
3. Esta guayabera es bonita pero prefiero _____ésa_____. (*that one*)
4. Estas corbatas rojas son muy bonitas pero _____ésas_____ son fabulosas. (*those*)
5. Estos cinturones cuestan demasiado. Prefiero _____aquéllos_____. (*those over there*)
6. ¿Te gustan esas botas o _____éstas_____? (*these*)
7. Esa bolsa roja es bonita pero prefiero _____aquélla_____. (*that one over there*)
8. No voy a comprar estas botas, voy a comprar _____aquéllas_____. (*those over there*)
9. ¿Prefieres estos pantalones o _____ésos_____? (*those*)
10. Me gusta este vestido pero voy a comprar _____ése_____. (*that one*)
11. Me gusta ese almacén pero _____aquél_____ es mejor (*better*). (*that one over there*)
12. Esa blusa es bonita pero cuesta demasiado. Voy a comprar _____ésta_____. (*this one*)

3 **Describir** With your partner, look for two items in the classroom that are one of these colors: **amarillo, azul, blanco, marrón, negro, verde, rojo.** Take turns pointing them out to each other, first using demonstrative adjectives, and then demonstrative pronouns. Answers will vary.

> *modelo*
> azul
> **Estudiante 1:** *Esta silla es azul. Aquella mochila es azul.*
> **Estudiante 2:** *Ésta es azul. Aquélla es azul.*

Now use demonstrative adjectives and pronouns to discuss the colors of your classmates' clothing. One of you can ask a question about an article of clothing, using the wrong color. Your partner will correct you and point out that color somewhere else in the room.

> *modelo*
> **Estudiante 1:** *¿Esa camisa es negra?*
> **Estudiante 2:** *No, ésa es azul. Aquélla es negra.*

NOTA CULTURAL

The **guayabera** is a men's shirt typically worn in some parts of the Caribbean. Never tucked in, it is casual wear, but variations exist for more formal occasions, such as weddings, parties, or the office.

Comunicación

4 **Conversación** With a classmate, use demonstrative adjectives and pronouns to ask each other questions about the people around you. Use words and expressions from the word bank and/or your own ideas. Answers will vary.

> **modelo**
>
> **Estudiante 1:** ¿Cómo se llama esa chica?
> **Estudiante 2:** Se llama Rebeca.
> **Estudiante 1:** ¿A qué hora llegó aquel chico a la clase?
> **Estudiante 2:** A las nueve.

¿A qué hora...?	¿Cómo se llama...?
¿Cuándo...?	¿De dónde es/son...?
¿Cuántos años tiene(n)...?	¿De quién es/son...?
¿Cómo es/son...?	¿Qué clases toma(n)...?

5 **En una tienda** Imagine that you and a classmate are in Madrid shopping at **Zara**. Study the floor plan, then have a conversation about what you see around you. Use demonstrative adjectives and pronouns as much as possible. Answers will vary.

> **modelo**
>
> **Estudiante 1:** Me gusta este suéter azul.
> **Estudiante 2:** Yo prefiero aquella chaqueta.

NOTA CULTURAL ▶

Zara is an international company based in Spain. It manufactures clothing and accessories for men, women, and children and also markets a popular fragrance line. While Zara makes both casual and sophisticated clothing, it is best-known for its trendy and classy lines that appeal to young professional women.

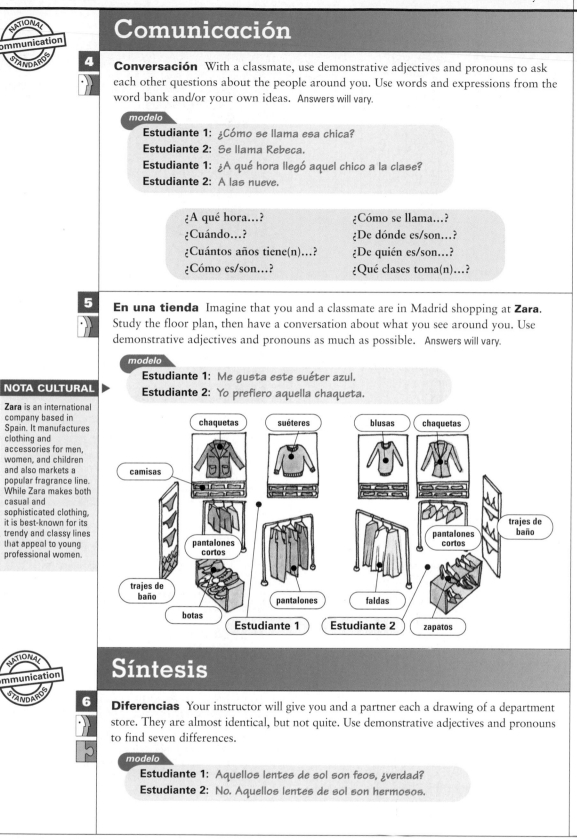

chaquetas   suéteres   blusas   chaquetas

camisas

pantalones cortos

trajes de baño

pantalones cortos   trajes de baño

trajes de baño

botas   **Estudiante 1**   pantalones   **Estudiante 2**   faldas   zapatos

Síntesis

6 **Diferencias** Your instructor will give you and a partner each a drawing of a department store. They are almost identical, but not quite. Use demonstrative adjectives and pronouns to find seven differences.

> **modelo**
>
> **Estudiante 1:** Aquellos lentes de sol son feos, ¿verdad?
> **Estudiante 2:** No. Aquellos lentes de sol son hermosos.

---

4 Suggestion Challenge both partners to ask a question for each item in the word bank and to ask at least one other question using an interrogative expression that is not included.

5 Expansion Divide students into groups of three to role-play a scene between a salesperson and two customers. The customers should ask about the different items of clothing pictured and the salesperson will answer. They talk about how the items fit and their cost. The customers then express their preferences and decide which items to buy.

6 Suggestion Divide the class into pairs and distribute the handouts from the Information Gap Activities Booklet that correspond to this activity. Give students ten minutes to complete this activity.

6 Expansion Have pairs work together with another pair to compare the seven responses that confirmed the seven differences. Ex: **No. Aquellos lentes de sol no son feos. Aquéllos son hermosos.** Ask a few groups to share some of the sentences with the class.

TEACHING OPTIONS

Pairs Ask students to write a conversation between two people sitting at a busy sidewalk café in the city. They are watching the people who walk by, asking each other questions about what the passersby are doing, and making comments on their clothing. Students should use as many demonstrative adjectives and pronouns as possible in their conversations. Invite several pairs to present their conversation to the whole class.

Small Groups Ask students to bring in pictures of their families, a sports team, a group of friends, etc. Have them take turns asking about and identifying the people in the pictures.
Ex: —¿Quién es aquella mujer? (¿Cuál?)
—Aquélla con la camiseta roja. (Es mi...)

Section Goals

In **Lectura** students will:
- learn to skim a text
- use what they know about text format to predict a document's content
- read a text rich in cognates and recognizable format elements

Instructional Resource
Companion website:
www.vistahigherlearning.com

Estrategia Tell students that they can often predict the content of an unfamiliar document in Spanish by skimming it and looking for recognizable format elements.

Examinar el texto Have students skim the text at the top of the ad. Point out the cognate **Liquidación** and the series of percentages. Ask them to predict what type of document it is. (advertisement for a liquidation sale) Then ask students to scan the rest of the ad.

Buscar cognados Ask volunteers to point out cognates they notice.

Impresiones generales Ask students to sum up their general impression of the document by answering the three questions at the bottom.

Lectura

Antes de leer

Estrategia

Skimming

Skimming involves quickly reading through a document to absorb its general meaning. This practice allows you to understand the main ideas without having to read word for word. When you skim a text, you might want to look at its title and subtitles. You might also want to read the first sentence of each paragraph.

Examinar el texto

Look at the format of the reading selection. How is it organized? What does the organization of the document tell you about its content?

Buscar cognados

Scan the reading selection to locate at least five cognates. Based on the cognates, what do you think the reading selection is about?

1. _____   4. _____
2. _____   5. _____
3. _____

The reading selection is about _____.

Impresiones generales

Now skim the reading selection to understand its general meaning. Jot down your impressions. What new information did you learn about the document by skimming it? Based on all the information you now have, answer these questions.

1. Who produced this document?
2. What is its purpose?
3. Who is its intended audience?

recursos

vistahigher
learning.com

¡Real° Liquidación° en Corona!

¡Grandes rebajas!
¡La rebaja está de moda en Corona!

SEÑORAS	CABALLEROS
Falda larga **ROPA BONITA** Algodón. De cuadros y rayas Talla mediana **Precio especial: $8.000**	**Pantalones** **OCÉANO** Colores blanco, azul y café Ahora: $11.550 **30% de rebaja**
Blusas de seda **BAMBÚ** Seda. De cuadros y de lunares Ahora: $21.000 **40% de rebaja**	**Zapatos** **COLOR** Italianos y franceses Números del 40 al 45 **Sólo $20.000 el par**
Sandalias de playa **GINO** Números del 35 al 38 Ahora: $12.000 el par **50% de rebaja**	**Chaqueta** **CASINO** Microfibra. Colores negro, blanco y gris Tallas P-M-G-XG **Ahora: $22.500**
Carteras **ELEGANCIA** Colores anaranjado, blanco, rosado y amarillo Ahora: $15.000 **50% de rebaja**	**Traje inglés** **GALES** Modelos originales Ahora: $105.000 **30% de rebaja**
Vestido de algodón **PANAMÁ** Colores blanco, azul y verde Ahora: $18.000 **30% de rebaja**	**Ropa interior** **ATLÁNTICO** Talla mediana Colores blanco, negro, gris **40% de rebaja**

Lunes a sábado de 9 a 21 horas.
Domingo de 10 a 14 horas.

TEACHING OPTIONS

Heritage Speakers Ask heritage speakers to create an ad for one or two items of clothing. Have them use the **¡Real Liquidación en Corona!** advertisement as a model. Have them share their ads with the class. Discuss the ads with the class.
Small Groups Have small groups of students work together to write a cloze paragraph about shopping for clothing, modeled on the **Completar** paragraph. Ask each group member to contribute

two sentences to the paragraph. Then have the group make a clean copy, omitting several words or phrases, and writing the omitted words and phrases above the paragraph. Each group then exchanges its paragraph with another group, which, in turn, completes it. Finally, the groups that exchanged paragraphs get together to check and discuss the completed paragraphs.

Almacén Corona (advertisement)

¡Corona tiene las ofertas más locas del verano!

30% 40% 50%

La tienda más elegante de la ciudad con precios increíbles y con la tarjeta de crédito más conveniente del mercado.

JÓVENES

Bluejeans chicos y chicas
PACOS
Americanos. Tradicional
Ahora: $9.000 el par
30% de rebaja

Suéteres
CARAMELO
Algodón y lana.
Colores blanco, gris y negro
Antes: $10.500
Ahora: $6.825

Lentes de contacto
VISIÓN
Americanos. Colores azul, verde y morado
Antes: $15.000 el par
Ahora $10.000

Trajes de baño chicos y chicas
SUBMARINO
Microfibra. Todas las tallas
Ahora: $12.500
50% de rebaja

Gafas de sol
VISIÓN
Origen canadiense
Antes: $23.000
Ahora: $14.950

NIÑOS

Vestido de niña
GIRASOL
Tallas de la 2 a la 12.
De cuadros y rayas
Ahora: $8.625
30% de rebaja

Pantalón deportivo de niño
MILÁN
Tallas de la 4 a la 16
Ahora: $13.500
30% de rebaja

Zapatos de tenis
ACUARIO
Números del 20 al 25
Ahora: $15.000 el par
30% de rebaja

Pantalones cortos
MACARENA
Talla mediana
Ahora: $15.000
30% de rebaja

Camisetas de algodón
POLO
Antes: $15.000
Ahora: $7.500
50% de rebaja

Por la compra de $40.000, puede llevar un regalo gratis.
• Un hermoso cinturón de señora
• Un par de calcetines
• Una corbata de seda
• Una bolsa para la playa
• Una mochila
• Unas medias

real *royal* liquidación *clearance sale* antes *before*

Después de leer

Completar

Complete this paragraph about the reading selection with the correct forms of the words from the word bank.

almacén	hacer juego	tarjeta de crédito
caro	increíble	tienda
dinero	pantalones	verano
falda	rebaja	zapato

En este anuncio (*advertisement*) de periódico el _____almacén_____ Corona anuncia la liquidación de _____verano_____ con grandes _____rebajas_____ en todos los departamentos. Con muy poco _____dinero_____ usted puede equipar a toda su familia. Si no tiene dinero en efectivo, puede utilizar su _____tarjeta de crédito_____ y pagar luego. Para el caballero con gustos refinados, hay _____zapatos_____ importados de París y Roma. La señora elegante puede encontrar blusas de seda que _____hacen juego_____ con todo tipo de _____pantalones/faldas_____ o _____faldas/pantalones_____. Los precios de esta liquidación son realmente _____increíbles_____.

¿Cierto o falso?

Indicate whether each statement is **cierto** or **falso**. Correct the false statements.

1. Hay ropa de algodón para jóvenes.
   Cierto.
2. La ropa interior tiene una rebaja del 30%.
   Falso. Tiene una rebaja del 40%.
3. El almacén Corona tiene un departamento de zapatos.
   Cierto.
4. Normalmente las sandalias cuestan $22.000 el par.
   Falso. Normalmente cuestan $24.000.

Preguntas

Answer these questions in Spanish. Answers will vary.

1. Imagina que vas a ir a la tienda Corona. ¿Qué departamentos vas a visitar? ¿el departamento de ropa para señoras, el departamento de ropa para caballeros…?
2. ¿Qué vas a buscar en Corona?
3. ¿Hay tiendas similares a la tienda Corona en tu pueblo o ciudad? ¿Cómo se llaman? ¿Tienen muchas gangas?

Completar Have students quickly review the lesson vocabulary on pages 152–153 before they do this activity. Make sure that they understand the meaning of **dinero en efectivo** and **el caballero de gustos refinados**.

¿Cierto o falso? Present these as items 5–8: **5. Las camisetas Polo no tienen una rebaja grande. (Falso. Tienen una rebaja del 50%.) 6. Hay regalos con compras de $40.000. (Cierto.) 7. El almacén Corona está cerrado los domingos. (Falso. El almacén Corona está abierto de 10:00 a 14:00 los domingos.) 8. Se puede conseguir lentes de contacto verdes y morados en rebaja. (Cierto.)**

Preguntas Have small groups put together an ad for a store where they shop. Have them use the **Almacén Corona** ad as a model. If two or more groups chose the same store, compare their ads in a follow-up discussion with the class.

TEACHING OPTIONS

TPR Write items of clothing on slips of paper. Divide the class into two teams. Have a member of Team A draw a slip. That team member mimes putting on the item of clothing. Team Bz guesses what it is. Give points for correct answers. The team with the most points wins.
Variación léxica Ask heritage speakers to tell the class phrases they use to ask the price of items. Ex: **¿Cuánto vale?**

Game Ask students to work in pairs to play a game of **Diez preguntas**. Student A thinks of an item of clothing. Student B asks questions and guesses the name of the item. Student A keeps track of the number of questions and guesses. Allow partners to ask a total of ten questions and attempt to guess three times before moving on to the next item. The pair with the fewest questions overall wins.

Escritura

Section Goals

In **Escritura** students will:
- conduct an interview
- integrate vocabulary and structures taught in **Lección 6** into a written report
- report on an interview

Estrategia Go over this writing strategy with the class, then help your students brainstorm a few questions that they could use to interview someone about shopping habits and clothing preferences, using the information in **Preparing interview questions** and **Tema** as a guide.

Tema Tell students that they may interview another member of their class or they may interview a Spanish-speaking student they know. Encourage them to take notes as they conduct the interview or tape record it. They might want to work with a classmate they are not going to interview to brainstorm the questions. Introduce terms such as **entrevista, entrevistar, diálogo,** and **citas** as you present the activity.

The Affective Dimension

Emphasize to students that they should not feel inhibited while they brainstorm. Remind them that the purpose of brainstorming is to accumulate a large number of ideas that they will be able to organize and edit later.

Suggestion Tell students to consult the **Plan de Escritura** in **Apéndice A**, page 448, for step-by-step writing instructions.

Estrategia

Brainstorming

How do you find ideas to write about? In the early stages of writing, brainstorming can help you generate ideas on a specific topic. Before writing your first draft, you should spend ten to fifteen minutes brainstorming and jotting down any ideas about the topic that occur to you. Whenever possible, try to write down your ideas in Spanish. Express your ideas in single words or phrases, and jot them down in any order. While brainstorming, do not worry about whether your ideas are good or bad. Selecting and organizing ideas should be the second stage of your writing. Remember that the more ideas you write down while you are brainstorming, the more options you will have to choose from later when you start to organize your ideas.

Preparing interview questions

Before conducting an interview, you may find it helpful to brainstorm a list of interview questions, remembering to include the five W's (*who, when, where, what, why*) and the H (*how*). For example:

- ► ¿Cuándo vas de compras?
- ► ¿Con quién(es) vas de compras?
- ► ¿Adónde vas de compras?
- ► ¿Por qué te gusta ir de compras a ese almacén?
- ► ¿Qué compras normalmente?
- ► ¿Cómo pagas? ¿Con un cheque, con una tarjeta de crédito…?

Tema

Escribe un informe

Write a report for the school newspaper about an interview you conducted with a student about his or her shopping habits and clothing preferences. First, brainstorm a list of interview questions. Then conduct the interview using the questions below as a guide, but feel free to ask other questions as they occur to you.

Examples of questions:

- ► ¿Qué tiendas, almacenes o centros comerciales prefieres?
- ► ¿Compras ropa de catálogos o por Internet?
- ► ¿Prefieres comprar ropa cara o barata? ¿Por qué?
- ► ¿Te gusta buscar gangas?
- ► ¿Qué ropa llevas cuando vas a clase?
- ► ¿Qué ropa llevas cuando sales a bailar?
- ► ¿Qué ropa llevas cuando practicas un deporte?
- ► ¿Cuáles son tus colores favoritos? ¿Compras mucha ropa de esos colores?
- ► ¿Les das ropa a tu familia o a tus amigos/as?

TEACHING OPTIONS

Proofreading Activity Copy the following interview questions and answers containing mistakes onto the board or a transparency as a proofreading activity to do with the whole class.
1. Este blusa me costó veinte dólores y esta veinticinco.
2. Luis no creó que los pantalones cuestaron sólo treinta dólares.
3. Ayer buscé gangas en el almacén Corona pero no encuentré nada interestante.

4. ¿Cuál prefieres, éste sombrero elegante pero caro o aquello sombrero barato?
5. No compré me nada ayer pero pensé comprar un par de bluejeans hoy.
6. El dependiente quiere le vender los zapatos caros pero mi tío busca aquéllas en rebaja.

Escuchar

NATIONAL communication STANDARDS

Estrategia

Listening for linguistic cues

You can enhance your listening comprehension by listening for specific linguistic cues. For example, if you listen for the endings of conjugated verbs, or for familiar constructions, such as **acabar de** + [*infinitive*] or **ir a** + [*infinitive*], you can find out whether an event already took place, is taking place now, or will take place in the future. Verb endings also give clues about who is participating in the action.

To practice listening for linguistic cues, you will now listen to four sentences. As you listen, note whether each sentence refers to a past, present, or future action. Also jot down the subject of each sentence.

reparación

sed on the photograph below, what do you nk Marisol has recently done? What do you nk Marisol and Alicia are talking about? What e can you guess about their conversation from visual clues in the photograph?

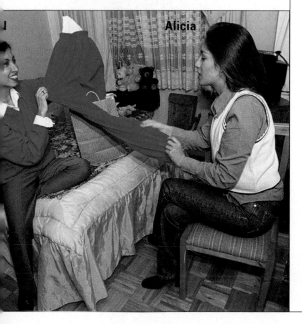

Alicia

Ahora escucha

Now you are going to hear Marisol and Alicia's conversation. Make a list of the clothing items that each person mentions. Then put a check mark after the item if the person actually purchased it.

Marisol	Alicia
1. pantalones ✓	1. falda
2. blusa ✓	2. blusa
3. _____	3. zapatos
4. _____	4. cinturón

Comprensión

¿Cierto o falso?

Indicate whether each statement is **cierto** or **falso**. Then correct the false statements.

1. Marisol y Alicia acaban de ir de compras juntas (*together*). Falso. Marisol acaba de ir de compras.
2. Marisol va a comprar unos pantalones y una blusa mañana. Falso. Marisol ya los compró.
3. Marisol compró una blusa de cuadros. Cierto.
4. Alicia compró unos zapatos nuevos hoy. Falso. Alicia va a comprar unos zapatos nuevos.
5. Alicia y Marisol van a ir al café. Cierto.
6. Marisol gastó todo el dinero de la semana en ropa nueva. Cierto.

Preguntas

Discuss these questions with a classmate. Be sure to explain your answers. Answers will vary.

1. ¿Crees que Alicia y Marisol son buenas amigas? ¿Por qué?
2. ¿Cuál de las dos estudiantes es más ahorradora (*frugal*)? ¿Por qué?
3. ¿Crees que a Alicia le gusta la ropa que Marisol compró?
4. ¿Crees que la moda es importante para Alicia? ¿Para Marisol? ¿Por qué?
5. ¿Es importante para ti estar a la moda? ¿Por qué?

recursos

TEXT CD
Lección 6

Section Goals

In **Escuchar** students will:
- listen for specific linguistic cues in oral sentences
- answer questions based on a recorded conversation

Instructional Resources
Textbook Activities CD
IRM: Tapescript, p. 76

Estrategia
Script 1. Acabamos de pasear por la ciudad y encontramos unos monumentos fenomenales. 2. Estoy haciendo las maletas. 3. Carmen y Alejandro decidieron ir a un restaurante. 4. Mi familia y yo vamos a ir a la playa.

Suggestion Ask students to look at the photo of Marisol and Alicia and predict what they are talking about.

Ahora escucha
Script MARISOL: Oye, Alicia, ¿qué estás haciendo?
ALICIA: Estudiando no más. ¿Qué hay de nuevo?
M: Acabo de comprarme esos pantalones que andaba buscando.
A: ¿Los encontraste en el centro comercial? ¿Y cuánto te costaron?
M: Míralos. ¿Te gustan? En el almacén Melo tienen tremenda rebaja. Como estaban baratos me compré una blusa también. Es de cuadros pero creo que hace juego con los pantalones por el color rojo. ¿Qué piensas?
A: Es de los mismos colores que la falda y la blusa que llevaste cuando fuimos al cine anoche. La verdad es que te quedan muy bien esos colores. ¿No encontraste unos zapatos y un cinturón para completar el juego?
M: No lo digas ni de chiste. Mi tarjeta de crédito está que no aguanta más. Y trabajé poco la semana pasada. ¡Acabo de gastar todo el dinero para la semana!

A: ¡Ay, chica! Fui al centro comercial el mes pasado y encontré unos zapatos muy, pero muy de moda. Muy caros... pero buenos. No me los compré porque no los tenían en mi número. Voy a comprarlos cuando lleguen más.... el vendedor me va a llamar.
M: Ajá... ¿Y va a invitarte a salir con él?

A: ¡Ay! ¡No seas así! Ven, vamos al café. Te ves muy bien y no hay que gastar eso aquí.
M: De acuerdo. Vamos.

(Script continues at far left in the bottom panels.)

Section Goal

In **Panorama**, students will read about the geography, culture, and economy of Cuba.

Instructional Resources
Transparencies, #3, #4, #30
WB/VM: Workbook, pp. 69–70;
Video Activities, pp. 235–236
Panorama cultural *DVD/Video*
Interactive CD-ROM
IRM: Videoscript, p. 110;
Panorama cultural *translations*
p. 132
Companion website:
www.vistahigherlearning.com
Presentations CD-ROM

Suggestion Ask students to look at the map or project **Transparency #30.** Ask volunteers to read the captions on each call-out. Then discuss the call-out photos with the class.

The Affective Dimension
Some students may have strong feelings about Cuba. Ask your students to discuss their feelings.

El país en cifras
• After reading about **La Habana Vieja**, if possible, show students illustrations or photos of this part of the city.
• Draw attention to the design and colors of the Cuban flag. Compare the Cuban flag to the Puerto Rican flag (page 148). Explain that Puerto Rico and Cuba, the last Spanish colonies in the western hemisphere, both gained their independence from Spain in 1898 in part through the intervention of the United States.

¡Increíble pero cierto! Due to the patterns of evolution and adaptation common to islands, Cuba has many examples of unique flora and fauna. Students may wish to research other examples.

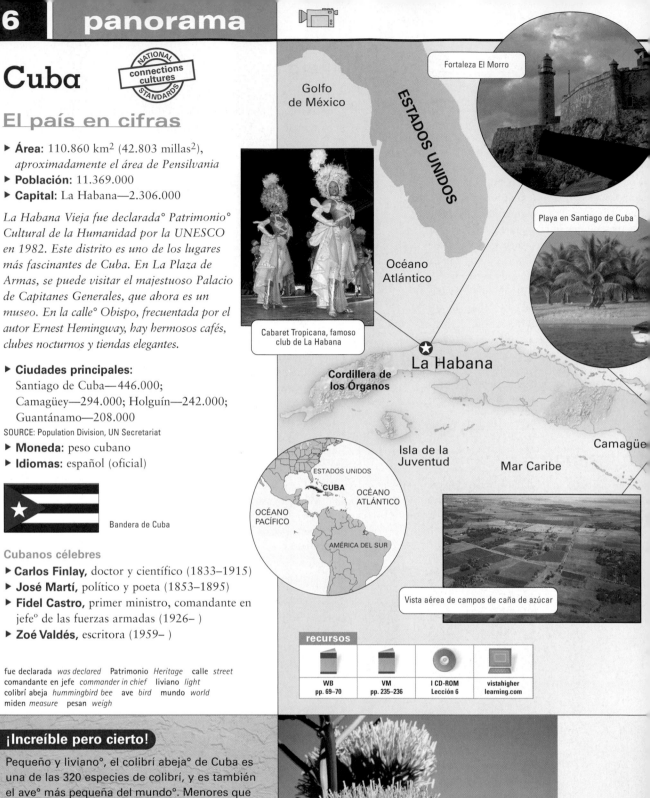

6 panorama

Cuba

connections cultures NATIONAL STANDARDS

El país en cifras

▶ **Área:** 110.860 km² (42.803 millas²), *aproximadamente el área de Pensilvania*
▶ **Población:** 11.369.000
▶ **Capital:** La Habana—2.306.000

La Habana Vieja fue declarada° Patrimonio° Cultural de la Humanidad por la UNESCO en 1982. Este distrito es uno de los lugares más fascinantes de Cuba. En La Plaza de Armas, se puede visitar el majestuoso Palacio de Capitanes Generales, que ahora es un museo. En la calle° Obispo, frecuentada por el autor Ernest Hemingway, hay hermosos cafés, clubes nocturnos y tiendas elegantes.

▶ **Ciudades principales:**
    Santiago de Cuba—446.000;
    Camagüey—294.000; Holguín—242.000;
    Guantánamo—208.000
    SOURCE: Population Division, UN Secretariat
▶ **Moneda:** peso cubano
▶ **Idiomas:** español (oficial)

Bandera de Cuba

Cubanos célebres
▶ **Carlos Finlay,** doctor y científico (1833–1915)
▶ **José Martí,** político y poeta (1853–1895)
▶ **Fidel Castro,** primer ministro, comandante en jefe° de las fuerzas armadas (1926–)
▶ **Zoé Valdés,** escritora (1959–)

fue declarada *was declared* Patrimonio *Heritage* calle *street*
comandante en jefe *commander in chief* liviano *light*
colibrí abeja *hummingbird bee* ave *bird* mundo *world*
miden *measure* pesan *weigh*

recursos

| WB pp. 69–70 | VM pp. 235–236 | I CD-ROM Lección 6 | vistahigher learning.com |

Fortaleza El Morro

Golfo de México

ESTADOS UNIDOS

Playa en Santiago de Cuba

Cabaret Tropicana, famoso club de La Habana

Océano Atlántico

La Habana

Cordillera de los Órganos

ESTADOS UNIDOS
CUBA OCÉANO ATLÁNTICO
OCÉANO PACÍFICO
AMÉRICA DEL SUR

Isla de la Juventud

Mar Caribe

Camagüe

Vista aérea de campos de caña de azúcar

¡Increíble pero cierto!

Pequeño y liviano°, el colibrí abeja° de Cuba es una de las 320 especies de colibrí, y es también el ave° más pequeña del mundo°. Menores que muchos insectos, estas aves minúsculas miden° 5 centímetros y pesan° sólo 1,95 gramos.

TEACHING OPTIONS

Variación léxica An item of clothing that you will see everywhere if you visit Cuba (or any of the other countries bordering the Caribbean) is the **guayabera.** A loose-fitting, short-sleeved shirt made of natural fibers, the **guayabera** is perfect for hot, humid climates. **Guayaberas** generally have large pockets and may be decorated with embroidery. They are worn open at the neck and never tucked in.

Extra Practice Introduce students to two stanzas of José Martí's poem **"Versos sencillos."** Some students may recognize these as verses from the song **"Guantanamera."**

*Yo soy un hombre sincero
de donde crece la palma;
y, antes de morirme, quiero
echar mis versos del alma.*

*Yo vengo de todas partes,
y hacia todas partes voy;
arte soy entre las artes;
en los montes monte soy.*

Baile • **Ballet Nacional de Cuba**

La bailarina Alicia Alonso fundó el Ballet Nacional de Cuba en 1948, después de° convertirse en una estrella° internacional en el Ballet de Nueva York y en Broadway. El Ballet Nacional de Cuba es famoso en todo el mundo por su creatividad y perfección técnica.

Economía • **La caña de azúcar y el tabaco**

La caña de azúcar° es el producto agrícola más cultivado° de la isla y su exportación es muy importante para la economía del país. El tabaco, que se usa para fabricar los famosos puros° cubanos, es otro cultivo de mucha importancia.

Historia • **Los taínos**

Los taínos eran° una de las tres tribus indígenas que vivían° en la isla cuando llegaron los españoles en el siglo XV. Los taínos también vivían en Puerto Rico, la República Dominicana, Haití, Trinidad, Jamaica y en partes de las Bahamas y la Florida.

Música • **Celia Cruz**

La cantante Celia Cruz (1924-2003) es considerada la reina° de la música salsa. Su carrera empezó en Cuba en los años cincuenta. Aunque° Celia Cruz salió de Cuba en 1960, siempre cantó en español. Su forma de cantar atrae a oyentes° de todo el mundo. Ganó un *Grammy* en 1990.

Holguín

Santiago de Cuba
Guantánamo

rra Maestra

¿Qué aprendiste? Responde a las preguntas con una frase completa.
1. ¿Quién es el líder del gobierno de Cuba? El líder de Cuba es Fidel Castro.
2. ¿Qué autor está asociado con la Habana Vieja? Ernest Hemingway está asociado con la Habana Vieja.
3. ¿Por qué es famoso el Ballet Nacional de Cuba? Es famoso por su creatividad y perfección técnica.
4. ¿Cuáles son los dos cultivos más importantes para la economía cubana? Los cultivos más importantes son la caña de azúcar y el tabaco.
5. ¿Qué fabrican los cubanos con la planta del tabaco? Los cubanos fabrican puros.
6. ¿Quiénes eran (*were*) los taínos? Eran una tribu indígena.
7. ¿Cuándo empezó Celia Cruz su carrera musical? Empezó su carrera en los años cincuenta.

Conexión Internet Investiga estos temas en el sitio **www.vistahigherlearning.com.**

1. Busca información sobre un(a) cubano/a célebre. ¿Por qué es célebre? ¿Qué hace? ¿Todavía vive en Cuba?
2. Busca información sobre una de las ciudades principales de Cuba. ¿Qué atracciones hay en esta ciudad?

....

después de *after* estrella *star* caña de azúcar *sugar cane* cultivado *grown* puros *cigars* eran *were* vivían *lived*
reina *queen* Aunque *Although* atrae a oyentes *attracts listeners*

Ballet Nacional de Cuba
Although the **Ballet Nacional de Cuba** specializes in classical dance, Cuban popular dances (**habanera, mambo, rumba**) have gained worldwide popularity. Students can interview parents or others to see what they remember about Cuban dances.

La caña de azúcar y el tabaco
The collapse of the Soviet bloc and the end of subsidies that sustained its economy dealt Cuba a blow. Since 1990, Cuba has been in **el período especial en tiempo de paz**. Government planners have decided to develop tourism, formerly seen as bourgeois and corrupting, as a means of gaining badly-needed foreign currency.

Los taínos The Taínos had a deep understanding of the use of native plants for medicinal purposes. Traditional Taíno healing arts have been preserved and handed down across generations in Cuba. Today, ethnobotanists are exploring this traditional knowledge as they search for modern medical resources.

Celia Cruz Bring in some of Celia Cruz's music for students to hear. Read song titles and make predictions about songs before listening to them, then confirm and revise predictions.

Conexión Internet Students will find supporting Internet activities and links at **www.vistahigherlearning.com**.

Suggestion You may want to wrap up this section by playing the **Panorama cultural** video footage for this lesson.

TEACHING OPTIONS

Variación léxica Some Cuban songs mention beings with names that do not sound Spanish, such as **Obatalá, Elegguá,** and **Babaluayé**. These are divinities (**orichas**) of the Afro-Cuban religion, which has its origins in Yoruba-speaking West Africa. Forcibly converted to Catholicism upon their arrival in Cuba, Africans developed a syncretized religion in which they worshiped the gods they had brought from Africa in the form of Catholic saints. **Babaluayé**, for instance, is worshiped as **San Lázaro**. **Obatalá** is **Nuestra Señora de las Mercedes**. Cuban popular music is deeply rooted in the songs and dances with which Afro-Cubans expressed their devotion to the **orichas**. It is not surprising then that these gods should be so frequently invoked in this music.

La ropa

el abrigo	coat
los bluejeans	jeans
la blusa	blouse
la bolsa	purse; bag
la bota	boot
el calcetín	sock
la camisa	shirt
la camiseta	t-shirt
la cartera	wallet
la chaqueta	jacket
el cinturón	belt
la corbata	tie
la falda	skirt
las gafas (de sol), las gafas (oscuras)	(sun)glasses
los guantes	gloves
el impermeable	raincoat
los lentes de contacto	contact lenses
los lentes (de sol)	(sun)glasses
las medias	pantyhose; stockings
los pantalones	pants
los pantalones cortos	shorts
la ropa	clothing; clothes
la ropa interior	underwear
la sandalia	sandal
el sombrero	hat
el suéter	sweater
el traje	suit
el traje (de baño)	(bathing) suit
el vestido	dress
los zapatos de tenis	tennis shoes, sneakers

Ir de compras

el almacén	department store
la caja	cash register
el centro comercial	shopping mall
el/la cliente/a	customer
el/la dependiente/a	clerk
el dinero	money
(en) efectivo	cash
el mercado (al aire libre)	(open-air) market
un par de zapatos	a pair of (shoes)
el precio (fijo)	(fixed; set) price
la rebaja	sale
el regalo	gift
la tarjeta de crédito	credit card
la tienda	shop; store
el/la vendedor(a)	salesperson
costar (o:ue)	to cost
gastar	to spend (money)
hacer juego (con)	to match (with)
llevar	to wear; to take
pagar	to pay
regatear	to bargain
usar	to wear; to use
vender	to sell

Adjetivos

barato/a	cheap
bueno/a	good
cada	each
caro/a	expensive
corto/a	short (in length)
elegante	elegant
hermoso/a	beautiful
largo/a	long (in length)
loco/a	crazy
nuevo/a	new
otro/a	other; another
pobre	poor
rico/a	rich

Los colores

el color	color
amarillo/a	yellow
anaranjado/a	orange
azul	blue
blanco/a	white
gris	gray
marrón, café	brown
morado/a	purple
negro/a	black
rojo/a	red
rosado/a	pink
verde	green

Palabras adicionales

acabar de (+ inf.)	to have just done something
anoche	last night
anteayer	the day before yesterday
ayer	yesterday
de repente	suddenly
desde	from
dos veces	twice; two times
hasta	until
pasado/a (*adj.*)	last; past
el año pasado	last year
la semana pasada	last week
prestar	to lend; to loan
una vez	once; one time
ya	already

Numbers 101 and higher	See page 160.
Indirect object pronouns	See page 162.
Dar expressions	See page 163.
Demonstrative adjectives and pronouns	See page 170.
Expresiones útiles	See page 157.

recursos
LM p. 36 | Lab CD/MP3 Lección 6 | Vocab CD Lección 6

La rutina diaria

7

Communicative Goals

You will learn how to:
- **Describe your daily routine**
- **Talk about personal hygiene**
- **Reassure someone**

Lesson Goals

In **Lección 7** students will be introduced to the following:
- terms for daily routines
- reflexive verbs
- adverbs of time
- indefinite and negative words
- preterite of **ser** and **ir**
- forms of **gustar** and verbs like **gustar**
- predicting content from the title
- sequencing events
- cultural, geographic, and historical information about Peru

A primera vista Here are some additional questions you can ask based on the photo: **¿Con quién vives? ¿Qué le dices antes de salir de casa? ¿Qué tipo de ropa llevas para ir a tus clases? ¿Les prestas esta ropa a tus amigos/as? ¿Qué ropa usaste en el verano? ¿Y en el invierno?**

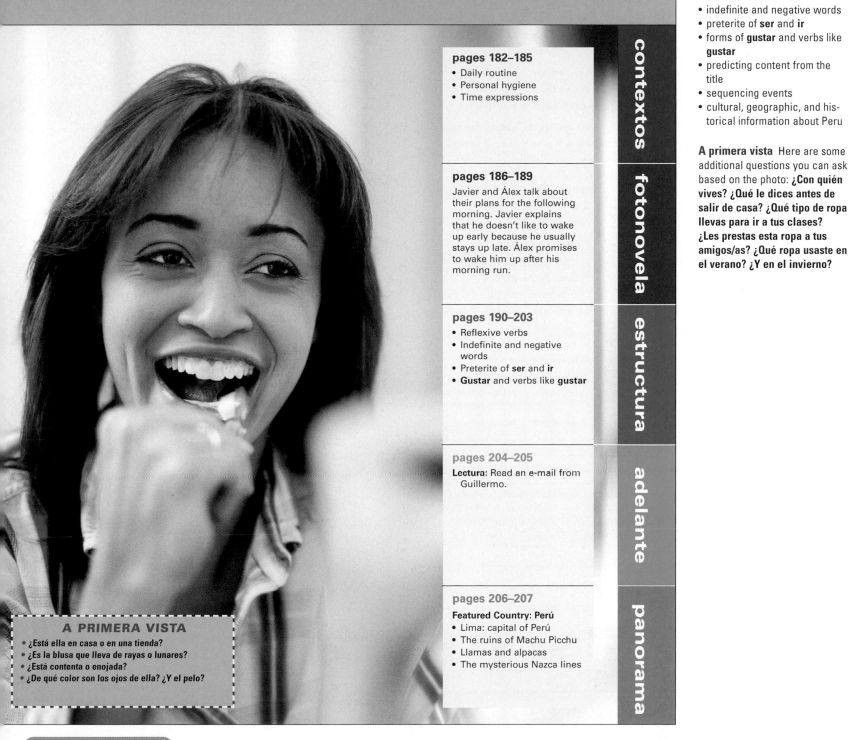

contextos

pages 182–185
- Daily routine
- Personal hygiene
- Time expressions

fotonovela

pages 186–189

Javier and Álex talk about their plans for the following morning. Javier explains that he doesn't like to wake up early because he usually stays up late. Álex promises to wake him up after his morning run.

estructura

pages 190–203
- Reflexive verbs
- Indefinite and negative words
- Preterite of **ser** and **ir**
- **Gustar** and verbs like **gustar**

adelante

pages 204–205

Lectura: Read an e-mail from Guillermo.

panorama

pages 206–207

Featured Country: Perú
- Lima: capital of Perú
- The ruins of Machu Picchu
- Llamas and alpacas
- The mysterious Nazca lines

A PRIMERA VISTA
- ¿Está ella en casa o en una tienda?
- ¿Es la blusa que lleva de rayas o lunares?
- ¿Está contenta o enojada?
- ¿De qué color son los ojos de ella? ¿Y el pelo?

INSTRUCTIONAL RESOURCES

Workbook/Video Manual: WB Activities, pp. 73–84
Laboratory Manual: Lab Activities, pp. 37–42
Workbook/Video Manual: Video Activities, pp. 207–208; pp. 237–238
Instructor's Resource Manual: **Hojas de actividades**, p. 145; **Vocabulario adicional**, p. 161; **¡Inténtalo!** & **Práctica** Answers, pp. 182–183; **Fotonovela**

Translations, p. 122; Textbook CD Tapescript, p. 77; Lab CDs Tapescript, pp. 30–34; **Fotonovela** Videoscript, p. 93; **Panorama cultural** Videoscript, p. 110; **Pan. cult.** translations, p. 132
Info Gap Activities Booklet, pp. 25–28
Overhead Transparencies: #5, #6, #31, #32
Lab Audio CD/MP3 **Lección 7**

Panorama cultural DVD/Video
Fotonovela DVD/Video
Testing Program, pp. 73–84; pp. 181–192
Testing Program Audio CD
Test Files CD-ROM
Test Generator

Companion website
Presentations CD-ROM
Textbook CD
Vocabulary CD
Interactive CD-ROM
Video CD-ROM
Web-SAM

La rutina diaria

Más vocabulario

el baño, el cuarto de baño	bathroom
el inodoro	toilet
el jabón	soap
el despertador	alarm clock
el maquillaje	makeup
la rutina diaria	daily routine
bañarse	to bathe; to take a bath
cepillarse el pelo	to brush one's hair
dormirse (o:ue)	to go to sleep; to fall asleep
lavarse la cara	to wash one's face
levantarse	to get up
maquillarse	to put on makeup
antes (de)	before
después	afterwards; then
después (de)	after
durante	during
entonces	then
luego	then
más tarde	later
por la mañana	in the morning
por la noche	at night
por la tarde	in the afternoon; in the evening
por último	finally

Variación léxica

afeitarse ⟷ rasurarse *(Méx., Amér. C.)*
ducha ⟷ regadera *(Col., Méx., Venez.)*
ducharse ⟷ bañarse *(Amér. L.)*
pantuflas ⟷ chancletas *(Méx., Col.);* zapatillas *(Esp.)*

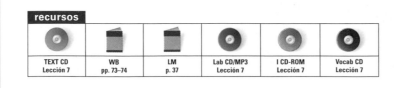

recursos

TEXT CD Lección 7 | WB pp. 73–74 | LM p. 37 | Lab CD/MP3 Lección 7 | I CD-ROM Lección 7 | Vocab CD Lección 7

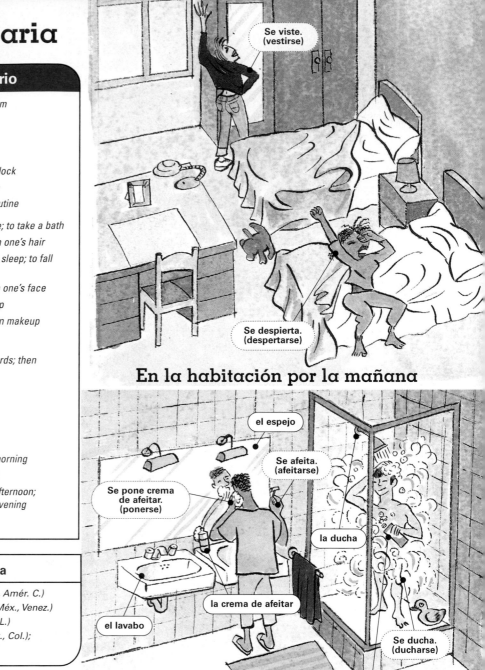

En la habitación por la mañana

Por la mañana

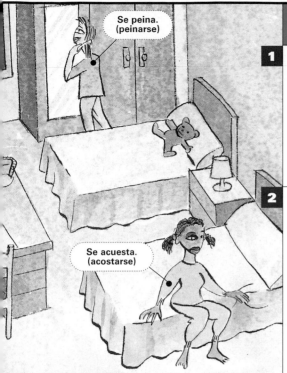

Se peina. (peinarse)

Se acuesta. (acostarse)

n la habitación por la noche

Se lava las manos. (lavarse las manos)

Se cepilla los dientes. (cepillarse los dientes)

la toalla

la pasta de dientes

ntuflas

Por la noche

Práctica

1 Escuchar 🎧 Escucha las frases e indica si cada frase es **cierta** o **falsa,** según el dibujo.

1. _falsa_
2. _cierta_
3. _falsa_
4. _cierta_
5. _falsa_
6. _falsa_
7. _falsa_
8. _cierta_
9. _falsa_
10. _cierta_

2 Seleccionar Selecciona las palabras que no están relacionadas con su grupo.

1. lavabo • toalla • despertador • jabón   despertador
2. manos • antes de • después de • por último   manos
3. acostarse • jabón • despertarse • dormirse   jabón
4. espejo • lavabo • despertador • entonces   entonces
5. dormirse • toalla • vestirse • levantarse   toalla
6. pelo • cara • manos • inodoro   inodoro
7. espejo • champú • jabón • pasta de dientes   espejo
8. maquillarse • vestirse • peinarse • dientes   dientes
9. baño • dormirse • despertador • acostarse   baño
10. ducharse • crema de afeitar • bañarse   crema de afeitar

3 Identificar Con un(a) compañero/a, identifica las cosas que cada persona necesita. Sigue el modelo. Some answers will vary.

> **modelo**
> Jorge / lavarse la cara
> **Estudiante 1:** ¿Qué necesita Jorge para lavarse la cara?
> **Estudiante 2:** Necesita jabón y una toalla.

1. Mariana / maquillarse ¿Qué necesita Mariana para maquillarse? Necesita maquillaje.
2. Gerardo / despertarse ¿Qué necesita Gerardo para despertarse? Necesita un despertador.
3. Celia / bañarse ¿Qué necesita Celia para bañarse? Necesita jabón y una toalla.
4. Gabriel / ducharse ¿Qué necesita Gabriel para ducharse? Necesita una ducha, una toalla y jabón.
5. Roberto / afeitarse ¿Qué necesita Roberto para afeitarse? Necesita crema de afeitar.
6. Sonia / lavarse el pelo ¿Qué necesita Sonia para lavarse el pelo? Necesita champú y una toalla.
7. Vanesa / lavarse las manos ¿Qué necesita Vanesa para lavarse las manos? Necesita jabón y una toalla.
8. Manuel / vestirse ¿Qué necesita Manuel para vestirse? Necesita su ropa/una camiseta/unos pantalones/etc.
9. Simón / acostarse ¿Qué necesita Simón para acostarse? Necesita una cama.
10. Daniela / lavarse la cara ¿Qué necesita Daniela para lavarse la cara? Necesita jabón y una toalla.

1 Suggestion Have students check their answers by going over **Actividad 1** with the whole class. Then, have volunteers correct the false statements.

1 Tapescript 1. Hay dos despertadores en la habitación de las chicas. 2. Un chico se pone crema de afeitar en la cara. 3. Una de las chicas se ducha. 4. Uno de los chicos se afeita. 5. Hay una toalla en la habitación de las chicas. 6. Una de las chicas se maquilla. 7. Las chicas están en el baño. 8. Uno de los chicos se cepilla los dientes en el baño. 9. Uno de los chicos se viste. 10. Una de las chicas se despierta. *Textbook Activities CD*

2 Expansion Go over answers and indicate why a particular item does not belong. Ex: **El lavabo, la toalla y el jabón son para lavarse. El despertador es para despertarse.**

3 Suggestion Do this as a whole-class activity, giving different students the opportunity to ask and answer questions.

3 Expansion Have students make statements about the people's actions, then ask a question. Ex: **Jorge se lava la cara. ¿Qué necesita?**

TEACHING OPTIONS

Pairs Have students write out three daily routine activities without showing them to their partner. The partner asks questions that contain adverbs of time in order to figure out what the action is. Ex: —¿Es antes o después de ducharse? —Antes de ducharse. —¿Es *levantarse*? —Sí.

Small Groups Hand out strips of paper with verbs used to describe daily routines written on them. Small groups of students place them in the most logical order in which the actions occur.

4 Expansion Ask students if Andrés's schedule represents that of a "typical" student. Ask: **Un estudiante típico, ¿se despierta normalmente a las seis y media de la mañana? ¿A qué hora se despiertan ustedes?**

5 Expansion
- Ask brief comprehension questions about the actions in the drawings. Ex: **¿Quién se maquilla? (Lupe) ¿Quién se cepilla el pelo? (Ángel)**
- If students ask, point out that in drawing number 7, **Ángel se mira en el espejo**. Reflexive pronouns and verbs will be formally presented in **Estructura 7.1**. For now it is enough just to explain that *he is looking at himself*, hence the use of the pronoun **se**.

4 **Ordenar** Pon (*Put*) esta historia (*story*) en orden.

a. Se afeita después de cepillarse los dientes. __4__
b. Se acuesta a las once y media de la noche. __9__
c. Por último, se duerme. __10__
d. Después de afeitarse, sale para las clases. __5__
e. Asiste a todas sus clases y vuelve a su casa. __6__
f. Andrés se despierta a las seis y media de la mañana. __1__
g. Después de volver a casa, come un poco. Luego estudia en su habitación. __7__
h. Se viste y entonces se cepilla los dientes. __3__
i. Se cepilla los dientes antes de acostarse. __8__
j. Se ducha antes de vestirse. __2__

5 **La rutina diaria** Con un(a) compañero/a, mira los dibujos y describe lo que hacen Ángel y Lupe.

1.
Ángel se afeita y mira la televisión.

2.
Lupe se maquilla y escucha la radio.

3.
Ángel se ducha y canta.

4.
Lupe se baña y lee.

5.
Ángel se lava la cara con jabón.

6.
Lupe se lava el pelo con champú en la ducha.

7.

Ángel se cepilla el pelo.

8.
Lupe se cepilla los dientes.

TEACHING OPTIONS

Extra Practice Name daily routine activities and have students give a list of all the words that they associate with each activity. They can be things, places, and parts of the body.
Ex: **lavarse las manos: el jabón, el cuarto de baño, el agua, la toalla.** How many associations can the class make for each activity?

Small Groups In groups of three or four, students think of a famous person or character and describe his or her daily routine. In their descriptions, students may use names of friends or family of the famous person or character. The rest of the class has to guess who is being described.

Comunicación

6 **La farmacia** Lee el anuncio (*ad*) y responde a las preguntas con un(a) compañero/a.

LA FARMACIA NUEVO SOL tiene todo
lo que necesitas para la vida diaria.

Esta semana tenemos grandes rebajas.

Por poco dinero puedes comprar lo que necesitas para el cuarto de baño ideal.

Para los hombres ofrecemos...
Buenas cremas de afeitar de Guapo y Máximo

Para las mujeres ofrecemos...
Nuevos maquillajes de Marisol y jabones de baño Ilusiones y Belleza

Y para todos tenemos los mejores jabones, pastas de dientes y cepillos de dientes.

¡Visita **LA FARMACIA NUEVO SOL**!
Te ofrecemos los mejores precios. Tenemos una tienda cerca de tu casa.

1. ¿Qué tipo de tienda es?
   Es una farmacia.
2. ¿Qué productos ofrecen para las mujeres?
   maquillajes, jabones de baño
3. ¿Qué productos ofrecen para los hombres?
   cremas de afeitar
4. Haz (*make*) una lista de los verbos que asocias con los productos del anuncio.
   Suggested answers: afeitarse, maquillarse, cepillarse los dientes
5. ¿Dónde compras tus productos de higiene?
   Answers will vary.
6. ¿Tienes una tienda favorita? ¿Cuál es?
   Answers will vary.

7 **Rutinas diarias** Trabajen en parejas (*pairs*) para describir la rutina diaria de dos o tres de estas personas. Pueden usar palabras de la lista. Answers will vary.

antes (de)	entonces	primero
después (de)	luego	tarde
durante el día	por último	temprano

1. un(a) profesor(a) de la universidad
2. un(a) turista
3. un hombre o una mujer de negocios (*businessman/woman*)
4. un vigilante (*night watchman*)
5. un(a) jubilado/a (*retired person*)
6. el presidente de los Estados Unidos
7. un niño de cuatro años
8. la reina (*queen*) Sofía de España

NOTA CULTURAL ▶

La Reina Doña Sofía de España, esposa del rey (*king*) Don Juan Carlos, nació en Grecia en 1938. Su familia, una de las más antiguas de Europa, está emparentada con (*related to*) los zares (*czars*) de Rusia, los emperadores germanos y la reina Victoria de Inglaterra.

6 Expansion Have small groups write a competing ad for another pharmacy. Then, every group should present its ad to the class, who will pick the most persuasive one of all.

7 Expansion Ask volunteers to read their descriptions of the people they chose. Ask other pairs who chose the same people if their descriptions are similar and how they differ.

TEACHING OPTIONS

Small Groups In groups of three or four, students act out a brief skit. The situation: they are all roommates who are trying to get ready for their morning classes at the same time. The problem: there is only one bathroom in the house or apartment. You may wish for the class to vote for the most original or funniest skit.

Heritage Speakers Have heritage speakers write paragraphs in which they describe their daily routine when living with their family. If they are not talking about their current situation, be sure that they keep their narration in the historical present. Students then present their paragraphs orally to the class. Verify comprehension by asking other students to relate aspects of the speaker's description.

¡Jamás me levanto temprano!

communication
cultures
NATIONAL STANDARDS

Álex y Javier hablan de sus rutinas diarias.

PERSONAJES

DON FRANCISCO

ÁLEX

JAVIER

1

JAVIER Hola, Álex. ¿Qué estás haciendo?

ÁLEX Nada... sólo estoy leyendo mi correo electrónico. ¿Adónde fueron?

2

JAVIER Inés y yo fuimos a un mercado. Fue muy divertido. Mira, compré este suéter. Me encanta. No fue barato pero es chévere, ¿no?

ÁLEX Sí, es ideal para las montañas.

3

JAVIER ¡Qué interesantes son los mercados al aire libre! Me gustaría volver pero ya es tarde. Oye, Álex, sabes que mañana tenemos que levantarnos temprano.

ÁLEX Ningún problema.

6

JAVIER ¡Increíble! ¡Álex, el superhombre!

ÁLEX Oye, Javier, ¿por qué no puedes levantarte temprano?

JAVIER Es que por la noche no quiero dormir, sino dibujar y escuchar música. Por eso es difícil despertarme por la mañana.

7

JAVIER El autobús no sale hasta las ocho y media. ¿Vas a levantarte mañana a las seis también?

ÁLEX No, pero tengo que levantarme a las siete menos cuarto porque voy a correr.

8

JAVIER Ah, ya... ¿Puedes despertarme después de correr?

ÁLEX Éste es el plan para mañana. Me levanto a las siete menos cuarto y corro por treinta minutos. Vuelvo, me ducho, me visto y a las siete y media te despierto. ¿De acuerdo?

JAVIER ¡Absolutamente ninguna objeción!

recursos

V CD-ROM	VM	I CD-ROM
Lección 7	pp. 207–208	Lección 7

Suggestion Have students get together in groups of three to act out the episode. Have one or two groups present it to the class.

Expresiones útiles Draw the class' attention to the verb forms **fui, fuiste, fue,** and **fuimos.** Explain that these are forms of the verbs **ir** and **ser** in the preterite tense. The context always makes clear which is meant. Then point out the phrases **me levanto, me despierto, me ducho, me cepillo, me afeito,** and **No te preocupes.** Tell the class that these are forms of the reflexive verbs **levantarse, despertarse, ducharse, cepillarse, afeitarse,** and **preocuparse.** Also, point out the words **siempre, nunca, jamás,** and **ningún.** Explain that **siempre** is called an indefinite word and that the other three are called negative words. Tell students that they will learn more about these concepts in **Estructura.**

JAVIER ¿Seguro? Pues yo jamás me levanto temprano. Nunca oigo el despertador cuando estoy en casa y mi mamá se enoja mucho.

ÁLEX Tranquilo, Javier. Yo tengo una solución.

ÁLEX Cuando estoy en casa en la Ciudad de México, siempre me despierto a las seis en punto. Me ducho en cinco minutos y luego me cepillo los dientes. Después me afeito, me visto y ¡listo! ¡Me voy!

DON FRANCISCO Hola, chicos. Mañana salimos temprano, a las ocho y media... ni un minuto antes ni un minuto después.

ÁLEX No se preocupe, don Francisco. Todo está bajo control.

DON FRANCISCO Bueno, pues, hasta mañana.

DON FRANCISCO ¡Ay, los estudiantes! Siempre se acuestan tarde. ¡Qué vida!

Enfoque cultural El horario de la vida diaria

En algunos países hispanos, el horario de la vida diaria es muy diferente al de EE.UU. En estos países, muchas personas trabajan de las ocho de la mañana a las dos de la tarde. A las dos salen del trabajo para ir a almorzar. Vuelven a las cuatro y salen a las seis de la tarde. Muchos utilizan esas dos horas para almorzar en casa con sus familias y, a veces (*sometimes*), dormir una siesta. También, frecuentemente la gente cena más tarde que en los EE.UU.

Expresiones útiles

Telling where you went

▶ **¿Adónde fuiste/fue usted?**
   Where did you go?
▷ **Fui a un mercado.**
   I went to a market.
▶ **¿Adónde fueron ustedes?**
   Where did you go?
▷ **Fuimos a un mercado.**
   Fue muy divertido.
   We went to a market.
   It was a lot of fun.

Talking about morning routines

▶ **(Jamás) me levanto temprano/tarde.**
   I (never) get up early/late.
▶ **Nunca oigo el despertador.**
   I never hear the alarm clock.
▶ **Es difícil/fácil despertarme.**
   It's hard/easy to wake up.
▶ **Cuando estoy en casa, siempre me despierto a las seis en punto.**
   When I'm home, I always wake up at six on the dot.
▶ **Me ducho y luego me cepillo los dientes.**
   I take a shower and then I brush my teeth.
▶ **Después me afeito y me visto.**
   Afterwards, I shave and get dressed.

Reassuring someone

▶ **Ningún problema.**
   No problem.
▶ **No te preocupes.** *(fam.)/*
   No se preocupe. *(form.)*
   Don't worry.
▶ **Todo está bajo control.**
   Everything is under control.
▶ **Tranquilo.**
   Don't worry.; Be cool.

Additional vocabulary

▶ **sino**
   but (rather)

Enfoque cultural The two-hour "lunch" break (2:00 p.m. to 4:00 p.m.), which includes the day's largest meal and a period of rest afterward, is observed in many Spanish-speaking countries as the **siesta.** Explain to the class that although the **siesta** is part of the daily routine of many people in Spanish-speaking countries, the observance of this tradition is not universal. For example, when Spain entered the European Union, many Spanish businesspeople began to adjust their work schedules to mirror those of their counterparts in other European countries. Ask your students to discuss the custom of the **siesta** and its impact on businesses and on individual workers. Ask them if they think the **siesta** should be incorporated into the schedules of businesses in the United States, and why.

■ Expansion Present these true-false statements as items 6–7:
6. Javier siempre se despierta temprano. (Falso. Álex siempre se despierta temprano.) 7. Don Francisco cree que los estudiantes siempre se acuestan temprano. (Falso. Don Francisco cree que los estudiantes siempre se acuestan tarde.)

② Expansion Give these additional items to the class:
7. Quiero volver al mercado pero no hay tiempo. (Javier) 8. Cuando estoy en casa, siempre me despierto muy temprano. (Álex)

③ Suggestion Have your students quickly glance over the caption to video still 8, page 186, before doing this activity.

③ Expansion Ask pairs to imagine another character's plans for the following day and list them using the **yo** form of the verbs as in the activity. Then have pairs share their lists with the class.

④ Suggestion Encourage students to use as many reflexive infinitives from **Contextos** as they can. They will learn to conjugate them formally in **Estructura 7.1**.

④ Possible Response
E1: ¿Prefieres levantarte tarde o temprano?
E2: Prefiero levantarme tarde... muy tarde.
E1: ¿A qué hora te levantas durante la semana?
E2: A las siete. ¿Y tú?
E1: Siempre me levanto muy temprano... a las cinco y media.
E2: Y ¿a qué hora te acuestas?
E1: Siempre me acuesto temprano, a las diez o a las once. ¿Y tú?
E2: Yo prefiero acostarme a las doce.

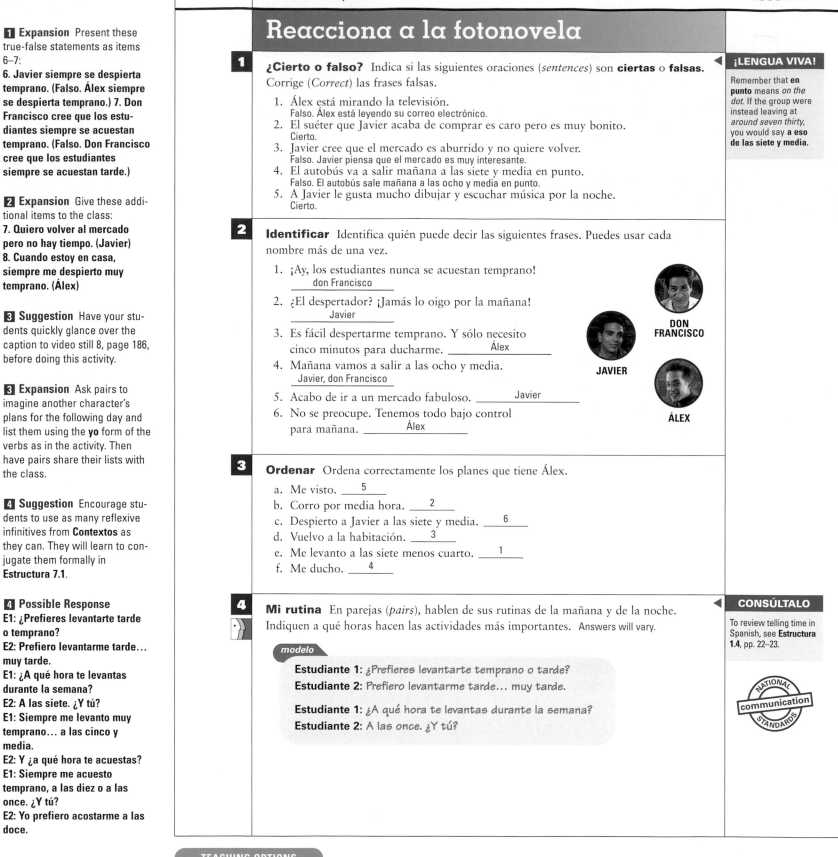

Reacciona a la fotonovela

1 **¿Cierto o falso?** Indica si las siguientes oraciones (*sentences*) son **ciertas** o **falsas**. Corrige (*Correct*) las frases falsas.

1. Álex está mirando la televisión.
Falso. Álex está leyendo su correo electrónico.
2. El suéter que Javier acaba de comprar es caro pero es muy bonito.
Cierto.
3. Javier cree que el mercado es aburrido y no quiere volver.
Falso. Javier piensa que el mercado es muy interesante.
4. El autobús va a salir mañana a las siete y media en punto.
Falso. El autobús sale mañana a las ocho y media en punto.
5. A Javier le gusta mucho dibujar y escuchar música por la noche.
Cierto.

2 **Identificar** Identifica quién puede decir las siguientes frases. Puedes usar cada nombre más de una vez.

1. ¡Ay, los estudiantes nunca se acuestan temprano!
____don Francisco____
2. ¿El despertador? ¡Jamás lo oigo por la mañana!
____Javier____
3. Es fácil despertarme temprano. Y sólo necesito cinco minutos para ducharme. ____Álex____
4. Mañana vamos a salir a las ocho y media.
____Javier, don Francisco____
5. Acabo de ir a un mercado fabuloso. ____Javier____
6. No se preocupe. Tenemos todo bajo control para mañana. ____Álex____

DON FRANCISCO

JAVIER

ÁLEX

3 **Ordenar** Ordena correctamente los planes que tiene Álex.

a. Me visto. ____5____
b. Corro por media hora. ____2____
c. Despierto a Javier a las siete y media. ____6____
d. Vuelvo a la habitación. ____3____
e. Me levanto a las siete menos cuarto. ____1____
f. Me ducho. ____4____

4 **Mi rutina** En parejas (*pairs*), hablen de sus rutinas de la mañana y de la noche. Indiquen a qué horas hacen las actividades más importantes. Answers will vary.

modelo

Estudiante 1: ¿Prefieres levantarte temprano o tarde?
Estudiante 2: Prefiero levantarme tarde... muy tarde.

Estudiante 1: ¿A qué hora te levantas durante la semana?
Estudiante 2: A las once. ¿Y tú?

¡LENGUA VIVA!

Remember that **en punto** means *on the dot*. If the group were instead leaving at *around seven thirty*, you would say **a eso de las siete y media.**

CONSÚLTALO

To review telling time in Spanish, see **Estructura 1.4**, pp. 22–23.

NATIONAL
communication
STANDARDS

TEACHING OPTIONS

Extra Practice Have your students close their books. Then use the sentences from **Actividad 3**, in the correct order, as a dictation activity. Read each sentence twice slowly to give students an opportunity to write. Then read them again at normal speed, without pausing, to allow students to correct any errors or fill in any gaps.

Small Groups Have your students get together in groups of three to discuss and compare their daily routines. Tell your students to use as many of the words and expressions they have learned in this lesson as they can. Then ask for a few volunteers to describe the daily routine of one of their group members.

Pronunciación 🎧

The consonant **r**

ropa	**rutina**	**rico**	**Ramón**

In Spanish, **r** has a strong trilled sound at the beginning of a word. No English words have a trill, but English speakers often produce a trill when they imitate the sound of a motor.

gustar	**durante**	**primero**	**crema**

In any other position, **r** has a weak sound similar to the English *tt* in *better* or the English *dd* in *ladder*. In contrast to English, the tongue touches the roof of the mouth behind the teeth.

pizarra	**corro**	**marrón**	**aburrido**

The letter combination **rr,** which only appears between vowels, always has a strong trilled sound.

caro	**carro**	**pero**	**perro**

Between vowels, the difference between the strong trilled **rr** and the weak **r** is very important, as a mispronunciation could lead to confusion between two different words.

Práctica Lee las palabras en voz alta, prestando (*paying*) atención a la pronunciación de la **r** y la **rr**.

1. Perú	4. madre	7. rubio	10. tarde
2. Rosa	5. comprar	8. reloj	11. cerrar
3. borrador	6. favor	9. Arequipa	12. despertador

Oraciones Lee las oraciones en voz alta, prestando atención a la pronunciación de la **r** y la **rr**.

1. Ramón Robles Ruiz es programador. Su esposa Rosaura es artista.
2. A Rosaura Robles le encanta regatear en el mercado.
3. Ramón nunca regatea… le aburre regatear.
4. Rosaura siempre compra cosas baratas.
5. Ramón no es rico pero prefiere comprar cosas muy caras.
6. ¡El martes Ramón compró un carro nuevo!

Refranes Lee en voz alta los refranes, prestando atención a la **r** y a la **rr**.

> Perro que ladra no muerde.[1]

> No se ganó Zamora en una hora.[2]

[1] A dog's bark is worse than its bite.
[2] Rome wasn't built in a day.

recursos

TEXT CD Lección 7	LM p. 38	Lab CD/MP3 Lección 7	I CD-ROM Lección 7

Section Goals

In **Estructura 7.1** students will learn:
- the conjugation of reflexive verbs
- common reflexive verbs

Instructional Resources
WB/VM: Workbook, pp. 75–76
Lab Manual, p. 39
Lab CD/MP3 Lección 7
IRM: ¡Inténtalo! & Práctica
Answers, pp. 182–183;
Tapescript, pp. 30–34
Info Gap Activities Booklet,
pp. 25–26
Interactive CD-ROM
Companion website:
www.vistahigherlearning.com
Presentations CD-ROM

Suggestions

- Model the first-person reflexive by talking about yourself. Ex: **Me levanto muy temprano. Me levanto a las cinco de la mañana.**
- Model the second person by asking questions with a verb you have already used in the first person. Ex: **Y tú, _____ , ¿a qué hora te levantas? (Me levanto a las ocho.)**
- Introduce the third person by making statements and asking questions about what a student has told you. Ex: _____ **se levanta muy tarde, ¿no? (Sí, se levanta muy tarde.)**
- Write the paradigm of **lavarse** on the board and model its pronunciation.
- Use magazine pictures to clarify meanings between third-person singular and third-person plural forms. Ex: **Se lava las manos.** and **Se lavan las manos.**

7.1 Reflexive verbs

ANTE TODO A reflexive verb is used to indicate that the subject does something to or for himself or herself. In other words, it "reflects" the action of the verb back to the subject. Reflexive verbs always use reflexive pronouns.

SUBJECT   REFLEXIVE VERB

Joaquín   **se ducha** por la mañana.

Reflexive verbs

lavarse *(to wash oneself)*

SINGULAR FORMS	yo	**me lavo**	*I wash (myself)*
	tú	**te lavas**	*you wash (yourself)*
	Ud.	**se lava**	*you wash (yourself)*
	él / ella	**se lava**	*he/she washes (himself/herself)*
PLURAL FORMS	nosotros/as	**nos lavamos**	*we wash (ourselves)*
	vosotros/as	**os laváis**	*you wash (yourselves)*
	Uds.	**se lavan**	*you wash (yourselves)*
	ellos/ellas	**se lavan**	*they wash (themselves)*

▶ The pronoun **se** attached to an infinitive identifies the verb as reflexive: **lavarse.**

▶ When a reflexive verb is conjugated, the reflexive pronoun agrees with the subject.

Me afeito.   **Te despiertas** a las siete.

Me ducho, me cepillo los dientes, me visto y ¡listo!

¡Ay, los estudiantes! Siempre se acuestan tarde.

▶ Like object pronouns, reflexive pronouns generally appear before a conjugated verb. With infinitives and present participles, they may be placed before the conjugated verb or attached to the infinitive or present participle.

Ellos **se** van a vestir.   **Nos** estamos lavando las manos.
Ellos van a vestir**se**.   Estamos lavándo**nos** las manos.
They are going to get dressed.   *We are washing our hands.*

¡ATENCIÓN!

Except for **se**, reflexive pronouns have the same forms as direct and indirect object pronouns.

• • •

Se is used for both singular and plural subjects —there is no individual plural form:
Pablo **se** lava.
Ellos **se** lavan.

¡ATENCIÓN!

When a reflexive pronoun is attached to a present participle, an accent mark is added to maintain the original stress:
bañando → bañándo**se**
afeitando →afeitándo**se**

TEACHING OPTIONS

Extra Practice To provide oral practice with reflexive verbs, create sentences that follow the pattern of the sentences in the examples. Say the sentence, have students repeat it, then say a different subject, varying the gender and number. Have students then say the sentence with the new subject, changing pronouns and verbs as necessary.

Heritage Speakers Have heritage speakers describe daily routines in their home communities. Encourage them to use their own linguistic variation of words presented in this lesson. Ex: **regarse (e:ie)**, **pintarse**. Have heritage speakers work together to compare and contrast activities as well as lexical variations.

Suggestions

- Go through the list of common reflexive verbs asking students closed-answer questions.
  Ex: ¿**Te acuerdas de tu primer día en la universidad? (Sí, me acuerdo.) ¿Los niños pequeños se acuestan tarde o temprano? (Los niños pequeños se acuestan temprano.)**
- To practice reflexive verbs in the preterite and periphrastic future (**ir a** + [*infinitive*]), talk and ask questions about what you and your students did yesterday and plan to do tomorrow. Ex: **Ayer me levanté a las seis. Pero el sábado me voy a levantar a las nueve.**
- Compare and contrast reflexive and non-reflexive verbs by giving examples. Ex: **Me ducho por la mañana. Nunca ducho al gato. Me pongo un suéter. Pongo la radio.**
- Ask volunteers to translate sentences such as: *He wakes the children at seven. He wakes up at seven.*

AYUDA

You have already learned several adjectives that can be used with **ponerse** when it means *to become*:
alegre, cómodo/a, contento/a, elegante, guapo/a, nervioso/a, rojo/a, and **triste.**

Common reflexive verbs

acordarse (de) (o:ue)	to remember	**llamarse**	to be called; to be named
acostarse (o:ue)	to go to bed	**maquillarse**	to put on makeup
afeitarse	to shave	**peinarse**	to comb one's hair
bañarse	to bathe; to take a bath	**ponerse**	to put on
cepillarse	to brush	**ponerse** (*+ adj.*)	to become (*+ adj.*)
despedirse (de) (e:i)	to say goodbye (to)	**preocuparse (por)**	to worry (about)
despertarse (e:ie)	to wake up	**probarse** (o:ue)	to try on
dormirse (o:ue)	to go to sleep; to fall asleep	**quedarse**	to stay; to remain
ducharse	to shower; to take a shower	**quitarse**	to take off
		secarse	to dry (oneself)
enojarse (con)	to get angry (with)	**sentarse** (e:ie)	to sit down
irse	to go away; to leave	**sentirse** (e:ie)	to feel
lavarse	to wash (oneself)	**vestirse** (e:i)	to get dressed
levantarse	to get up		

¡ATENCIÓN!

Because you learned how to form the preterite of non-reflexive regular verbs in **Estructura 6.3**, you also know how to form the preterite of the common reflexive verbs in the list, with the exception of the stem-changing **–ir** verbs, **irse** and **ponerse.** You will learn more preterite forms such as those of the verb **ir** (**Estructura 7.3**), stem-changing **–ir** verbs (**Estructura 8.1**) and **poner** (**Estructura 9.1**).

COMPARE & CONTRAST

Unlike English, a number of verbs in Spanish can be reflexive or non-reflexive. If the verb acts upon the subject, the reflexive form is used. If the verb acts upon something other than the subject, the non-reflexive form is used. Compare these sentences.

Lola **lava** los platos.   Lola **se lava** la cara.

As the preceding sentences show, reflexive verbs sometimes have different meanings than their non-reflexive counterparts. For example, **lavar** means *to wash*, while **lavarse** means *to wash oneself, to wash up.*

¡ATENCIÓN!

Parts of the body or clothing are generally not referred to with possessives, but with the definite article.
La niña se quitó **los** zapatos.
Necesito cepillarme **los** dientes.

¡INTÉNTALO! Indica el presente de los verbos reflexivos que siguen. El primero de cada columna ya está conjugado.

despertarse

1. Mis hermanos <u>se despiertan</u> tarde.
2. Tú <u>te despiertas</u> tarde.
3. Nosotros <u>nos despertamos</u> tarde.
4. Benito <u>se despierta</u> tarde.
5. Yo <u>me despierto</u> tarde.
6. Ustedes <u>se despiertan</u> tarde.
7. Ella <u>se despierta</u> tarde.
8. Adriana y yo <u>nos despertamos</u> tarde.
9. Ellos <u>se despiertan</u> tarde.

ponerse

1. Él <u>se pone</u> una chaqueta.
2. Yo <u>me pongo</u> una chaqueta.
3. Usted <u>se pone</u> una chaqueta.
4. Nosotras <u>nos ponemos</u> una chaqueta.
5. Las niñas <u>se ponen</u> una chaqueta.
6. Tú <u>te pones</u> una chaqueta.
7. El botones <u>se pone</u> una chaqueta.
8. Beatriz y Gil <u>se ponen</u> una chaqueta.
9. Ustedes <u>se ponen</u> una chaqueta.

TEACHING OPTIONS

TPR Model gestures for a few of the reflexive verbs. Ex: **acordarse** (tap side of head), **acostarse** (lay head on folded hands). Have students stand. Begin by practicing as a class using only the **nosotros** form, saying an expression at random (**Nos lavamos la cara.**). Then vary the verb forms and point to a student who should perform an appropriate gesture. Keep the pace rapid. Vary by pointing to more than one student (**Ustedes se peinan.**).

Pairs Have students write a short account of their own daily routine. Then have pairs compare and contrast their routines using a Venn Diagram. Have the pair write one of their names in the left circle and one in the right circle, writing **Los/Las dos** where the circles overlap. Then have them list their activities in the appropriate location. Remember verbs under **Los/Las dos** should be in the first-person plural.

Práctica

1

Nuestra rutina La familia de Blanca sigue la misma rutina todos los días. Según (*According to*) Blanca, ¿qué hacen ellos?

> **modelo**
> mamá / despertarse a las 5:00
> Mamá *se despierta a las cinco.*

1. Roberto y yo / levantarse a las 7:00 Roberto y yo nos levantamos a las siete.
2. papá / ducharse primero y / luego afeitarse Papá se ducha primero y luego se afeita.
3. yo / lavarse la cara y / vestirse antes de tomar café Yo me lavo la cara y me visto antes de tomar café.
4. mamá / peinarse y / luego maquillarse Mamá se peina y luego se maquilla.
5. todos / sentarse a la mesa para comer Todos nos sentamos a la mesa para comer.
6. Roberto / cepillarse los dientes después de comer Roberto se cepilla los dientes después de comer.
7. yo / ponerse el abrigo antes de salir Yo me pongo el abrigo antes de salir.
8. nosotros / despedirse de mamá Nosotros nos despedimos de mamá.

2

La fiesta elegante Selecciona el verbo apropiado y completa las frases con la forma correcta.

1. Tú ____lavas____ (lavar / lavarse) el auto antes de ir a la fiesta.
2. Nosotros no __nos acordamos__ (acordar / acordarse) de comprar regalos.
3. Para llegar a tiempo, Raúl y Marta ___acuestan___ (acostar / acostarse) a los niños antes de irse.
4. Yo __me siento__ (sentir / sentirse) bien hoy.
5. Mis amigos siempre ___se visten___ (vestir / vestirse) con ropa muy cara.
6. ¿__Se prueban__ (probar / probarse) ustedes la ropa antes de comprarla?
7. Usted __se preocupa__ (preocupar / preocuparse) mucho por sus amigos, ¿no?
8. En general, __me afeito__ (afeitar / afeitarse) yo mismo, pero hoy el barbero (*barber*) me ___afeita___ (afeitar / afeitarse).

3

Describir Mira los dibujos y describe lo que estas personas hacen. Some answers may vary.

1. El joven se quita los zapatos.
2. Carmen se duerme.
3. Juan se pone la camiseta.
4. Ellos se despiden.
5. Estrella se maquilla.
6. Toni se enoja con el perro.

Comunicación

4 Preguntas personales En parejas, túrnense (*take turns*) para hacerse estas preguntas.

Answers will vary.

1. ¿A qué hora te levantas durante la semana?
2. ¿A qué hora te levantas los fines de semana?
3. ¿Prefieres levantarte tarde o temprano? ¿Por qué?
4. ¿Te enojas frecuentemente con tus amigos?
5. ¿Te preocupas fácilmente? ¿Qué te preocupa?
6. ¿Qué cosas te ponen contento/a?
7. ¿Qué haces cuando te sientes triste?
8. ¿Y cuando te sientes alegre?
9. ¿Te acuestas tarde o temprano durante la semana?
10. ¿A qué hora te acuestas los fines de semana?

5 Charadas En grupos, jueguen a las charadas. Cada (*Each*) persona debe pensar en dos frases con verbos reflexivos. La primera persona que adivina (*guesses*) la charada dramatiza la próxima (*next*). Answers will vary.

6 Debate En grupos, discutan (*discuss*) este tema (*topic*): ¿Quiénes necesitan más tiempo para arreglarse (*to get ready*) antes de salir, los hombres o las mujeres? Hagan una lista de las razones (*reasons*) que tienen para defender sus ideas e informen a la clase.
Answers will vary.

Síntesis

7 La familia ocupada Tú y tu compañero/a asisten a un programa de verano en Lima, Perú. Viven con la familia Ramos. Tu profesor(a) te va a dar la rutina incompleta que la familia sigue en las mañanas. Trabaja con tu compañero/a para completarla.
Answers will vary.

> **modelo**
>
> **Estudiante 1:** ¿Qué hace el señor Ramos a las seis y cuarto?
> **Estudiante 2:** El señor Ramos se levanta.

Sidebar:

4 Expansion Ask volunteers to call out some of their answers. The class must add information by speculating on the reason behind each answer. Have the volunteer confirm or refute the speculation. Ex: **Hablas por teléfono con tus amigos cuando te sientes triste porque ellos te comprenden muy bien.**

5 Expansion Ask each group to present their best **charada** to the class.

6 Suggestion Before assigning groups, go over some of the things men and women do to get ready to go out. Ex: **Las mujeres se maquillan. Los hombres se afeitan.** Then ask students to indicate their opinion on the question and divide the class into groups accordingly.

7 Suggestion Divide the class into pairs and distribute the handouts from the Information Gap Activities Booklet that correspond to this activity. Give students ten minutes to complete this activity.

7 Expansion Ask groups of four to imagine they all live in the same house and have them put together a message board to reflect their different schedules.

TEACHING OPTIONS

Game Divide the class into teams of three. Each member should tell his or her team about the strangest, funniest, or most exciting thing that he or she has done. The team chooses one account and writes it on a slip of paper. For each team's turn, you read the description aloud. The class has two minutes to ask team members questions to find out who did the activity. The teams that guess win one point. The team with the most points wins.

Extra Practice Prepare descriptions of five celebrities, using reflexives. Write their names randomly on the board. Then read the descriptions as a dictation, having students match each to a name. Ex: **Su deporte es el tenis, pero no juega en competiciones ahora. Se pone nervioso en los torneos y se enoja con frecuencia. (John McEnroe)**

Section Goals

In **Estructura 7.2** students will learn:
- high-frequency indefinite and negative words
- the placement and use of indefinite and negative words

Instructional Resources
WB/VM: Workbook, pp. 77–78
Lab Manual, p. 40
Lab CD/MP3 **Lección 7**
IRM: ¡Inténtalo! & Práctica
Answers, pp. 182–183;
Tapescript, pp. 30–34; **Hojas de actividades**, *p. 145*
Interactive CD-ROM
Companion website:
www.vistahigherlearning.com
Presentations CD-ROM

Suggestions
- Write **alguien** and **nadie** on the board and ask questions about what students are wearing today. Ex: **Hoy alguien lleva una camiseta de Puerto Rico. ¿Quién es? ¿Alguien lleva pantalones anaranjados? No, nadie los lleva.**
- Use magazine pictures to compare and contrast indefinite and negative words. Ex: **La señora de la foto tiene algo en las manos. ¿El señor tiene algo en las manos también? No, el señor no tiene nada en las manos.**
- Ask volunteers questions about their activities since the last class, reiterating the answers by using the targeted structures. Ex: **¿Quién compró algo nuevo? Sólo dos personas. Nadie más compró algo nuevo. Los otros no compraron nada nuevo. Yo no compré nada nuevo tampoco.**
- Give further examples to consolidate the information presented in **¡Atención!** Ex: **¿Buscas a algún compañero? No, no busco a ningún compañero.**
- Point out that **uno/a(s)** can be used as an indefinite pronoun. Ex: **¿Tienes un lápiz? Sí, tengo uno.**

7.2 Indefinite and negative words

ANTE TODO Indefinite words refer to people and things that are not specific, for example, *someone* or *something*. Negative words deny the existence of people and things or contradict statements, for instance, *no one* or *nothing*. As the following chart shows, Spanish indefinite words have corresponding negative words, which are opposite in meaning.

Indefinite and negative words

Indefinite words		Negative words	
algo	*something; anything*	**nada**	*nothing; not anything*
alguien	*someone; somebody; anyone*	**nadie**	*no one; nobody; not anyone*
alguno/a(s), algún	*some; any*	**ninguno/a, ningún**	*no; none; not any*
o... o	*either... or*	**ni... ni**	*neither... nor*
siempre	*always*	**nunca, jamás**	*never, not ever*
también	*also; too*	**tampoco**	*neither; not either*

▶ There are two ways to form negative sentences in Spanish: 1) You can place the negative word before the verb, or 2) you can place **no** before the verb and the negative word after the verb.

Nadie se levanta temprano.
No one gets up early.

No se levanta nadie temprano.
No one gets up early.

Ellos **nunca se enojan**.
They never get angry.

Ellos **no se enojan nunca**.
They never get angry.

▶ Because they refer to people, **alguien** and **nadie** are often used with the personal **a**. The personal **a** is also used before the pronouns **alguno/a, algunos/as**, and **ninguno/a** when these words refer to people and they are the direct object of the verb.

—Perdón, señor, ¿busca usted **a alguien**?
—No, gracias, señorita, no busco **a nadie**.

—Tomás, ¿buscas **a alguno** de tus hermanos?
—No, mamá, no busco **a ninguno**.

¡ATENCIÓN!

Before a masculine, singular noun, **alguno** and **ninguno** are shortened to **algún** and **ningún**.

—¿Tienen ustedes **algún** amigo peruano?
—**No**, no tenemos **ningún** amigo peruano.

• • •

Alguno/a, algunos/as are not always used in the same way English uses *some* or *any*. Often, **algún** is used where *a* would be used in English.

¿Tienes algún libro que hable de los incas?
Do you have a book that talks about the Incas?

TEACHING OPTIONS

Extra Practice Write sentences like the following on the board and have the students complete them with an indefinite or negative word. Ex: **1. Los vegetarianos no comen carne ____.** (nunca) **2. Las madres ____ se preocupan por sus hijos.** (siempre) **3. En las fiestas ella no es sociable, ____ baila ____ habla con ____.** (ni, ni, nadie)

Pairs Have students practice by taking turns giving one-word indefinite and negative word prompts and having the other respond in complete sentences. Ex: **E1: siempre. E2: Siempre le mando un mensaje electrónico a mi madre por la mañana. E2: tampoco E1: Yo no me levanto temprano tampoco.**

COMPARE & CONTRAST

In English, it is incorrect to use more than one negative word in a sentence. In Spanish, however, sentences frequently contain two or more negative words. Compare the following Spanish and English sentences.

Nunca le escribo a **nadie**.
I never write to anyone.

No me preocupo por **nada nunca**.
I do not ever worry about anything.

As the preceding sentences show, once an English sentence contains one negative word (for example, *not* or *never*), no other negative word may be used. Instead, indefinite (or affirmative) words are used. In Spanish, however, once a sentence is negative, no other affirmative (that is, indefinite) word may be used. Instead, all indefinite ideas must be expressed in the negative.

▶ Although in Spanish **pero** and **sino** both mean *but*, they are not interchangeable. **Sino** is used when the first part of a sentence is negative and the second part contradicts it. In this context, **sino** means *but rather* or *on the contrary*. In all other cases, **pero** is used to mean *but*.

Los estudiantes no se acuestan
  temprano **sino** tarde.
*The students don't go to bed
  early, but rather late.*

Las toallas son caras,
  pero bonitas.
*The towels are expensive,
  but beautiful.*

María no habla francés
  sino español.
*María doesn't speak French,
  but rather Spanish.*

José es inteligente, **pero**
  no saca buenas notas.
*José is intelligent but
  doesn't get good grades.*

¡INTÉNTALO! Cambia las siguientes frases para que sean negativas. La primera frase se da *(is given)* como ejemplo.

1. Siempre se viste bien.
   __Nunca__ se viste bien.
   __No__ se viste bien __nunca__.
2. Alguien se ducha.
   __Nadie__ se ducha.
   __No__ se ducha __nadie__.
3. Ellas van también.
   Ellas __tampoco__ van.
   Ellas __no__ van __tampoco__.
4. Alguien se pone nervioso.
   __Nadie__ se pone nervioso.
   __No__ se pone nervioso __nadie__.
5. Tú siempre te lavas las manos.
   Tú __nunca / jamás__ te lavas las manos.
   Tú __no__ te lavas las manos __nunca / jamás__.
6. Voy a traer algo.
   __No__ voy a traer __nada__.

7. Juan se afeita también.
   Juan __tampoco__ se afeita.
   Juan __no__ se afeita __tampoco__.
8. Mis amigos viven en una residencia
   o en casa.
   Mis amigos __no__ viven __ni__ en
   una residencia __ni__ en casa.
9. La profesora hace algo en su escritorio.
   La profesora __no__ hace __nada__ en su
   escritorio.
10. Tú y yo vamos al mercado.
    __Ni__ tú __ni__ yo vamos al mercado.
11. Tienen un espejo en su casa.
    __No__ tienen __ningún__ espejo en su casa.
12. Algunos niños se ponen el abrigo.
    __Ningún__ niño se pone el abrigo.

Suggestions
• Reiterate that there is no limit to the number of negative words that can be strung together in a sentence in Spanish. Ex: **No hablo con nadie nunca de ningún problema, ni con mi familia ni con mis amigos.**
• Elicit negative responses by asking questions whose answers will clearly be negative. Ex: **¿Alguien lleva zapatos de lunares? (No, nadie lleva zapatos de lunares.) ¿Alguien tiene una moto en la mochila? (No, nadie tiene una moto en la mochila.)**
• Give examples of **pero** and **sino** using the seating of the students. Ex: ___ **se sienta al lado de** ___ **, pero no al lado de** ___ **. No se sienta a la izquierda de** ___ **, sino a la derecha.** ___ **no se sienta al lado de la ventana, pero está cerca de la puerta.**

TEACHING OPTIONS

Video Show the **Fotonovela** video again to give students more input containing indefinite and negative words. Stop the video where appropriate to discuss how these words are used.

Small Groups Give small groups five minutes to write a description of **un(a) señor(a) muy, pero muy antipático/a**. Tell students to use as many indefinite and negative words as possible to describe what makes this person so unpleasant.

Práctica

1

¿Pero o sino? Forma frases sobre los estudiantes usando **pero** o **sino**.

> **modelo**
>
> Muchos estudiantes viven en residencias estudiantiles / muchos de ellos quieren vivir fuera del campus.
>
> *Muchos estudiantes viven en residencias estudiantiles, pero muchos de ellos quieren vivir fuera del campus.*

1. Marcos nunca se despierta temprano / siempre llega puntual a clase.
   Marcos nunca se despierta temprano, pero siempre llega puntual a clase.
2. Lisa y Katarina no se acuestan temprano / muy tarde.
   Lisa y Katarina no se acuestan temprano sino muy tarde.
3. Alfonso es inteligente / algunas veces es antipático.
   Alfonso es inteligente, pero algunas veces es antipático.
4. Los directores de la residencia no son ecuatorianos / peruanos.
   Los directores de la residencia no son ecuatorianos sino peruanos.
5. No nos acordamos de comprar champú / compramos jabón.
   No nos acordamos de comprar champú, pero compramos jabón.
6. Emilia no es estudiante / profesora.
   Emilia no es estudiante sino profesora.
7. No quiero levantarme / tengo que ir a clase.
   No quiero levantarme, pero tengo que ir a clase.
8. Miguel no se afeita por la mañana / por la noche.
   Miguel no se afeita por la mañana sino por la noche.

2

Completar Completa esta conversación. Usa expresiones negativas en tus respuestas. Luego, dramatiza la conversación con un(a) compañero/a. Answers will vary.

AURELIO Ana María, ¿encontraste algún regalo para Eliana?
ANA MARÍA (1) No, no encontré ningún regalo/nada para Eliana.

AURELIO ¿Viste a algunas amigas en el centro comercial?
ANA MARÍA (2) No, no vi a ninguna amiga/ninguna/nadie en el centro comercial.

AURELIO ¿Me llamó alguien?
ANA MARÍA (3) No, nadie te llamó./No, no te llamó nadie.

AURELIO ¿Quieres ir al teatro o al cine esta noche?
ANA MARÍA (4) No, no quiero ir ni al teatro ni al cine.

AURELIO ¿No quieres salir a comer?
ANA MARÍA (5) No, no quiero salir a comer (tampoco).

AURELIO ¿Hay algo interesante en la televisión esta noche?
ANA MARÍA (6) No, no hay nada interesante en la televisión.

AURELIO ¿Tienes algún problema?
ANA MARÍA (7) No, no tengo ningún problema/ninguno.

Comunicación

3

Opiniones Completa estas frases de una manera lógica. Luego, compara tus respuestas con las de un(a) compañero/a.   Answers will vary.

1. Mi habitación es _____ pero _____.
2. Mis padres no son _____ sino _____.
3. Mi compañero/a es _____ pero _____.
4. Por la noche me gusta _____ pero _____.
5. Un(a) profesor(a) ideal no es _____ sino _____.
6. Mis amigos son _____ pero _____.

4

Quejas (*Complaints*) En parejas hagan (*make*) una lista de cinco quejas comunes (*common*) que tienen los estudiantes. Usen expresiones negativas. Answers will vary.

> **modelo**
> Nadie me entiende.

Ahora hagan (*make*) una lista de cinco quejas que los padres tienen de sus hijos.

> **modelo**
> Nunca limpian sus habitaciones.

5

Anuncio (*Ad*) En parejas, lean el anuncio y respondan a las preguntas.

1. ¿Es el anuncio positivo o negativo? ¿Por qué?
   Answers will vary.

2. ¿Cuáles son las palabras indefinidas en el anuncio?
   algún, siempre, algo

3. Escriban el texto del anuncio cambiando todo por expresiones negativas. ¿No buscas ningún producto especial? ¡Nunca hay nada para nadie en las tiendas García!

4. Ahora preparen su propio (*own*) anuncio usando expresiones afirmativas y negativas para compartir con la clase. Answers will vary.

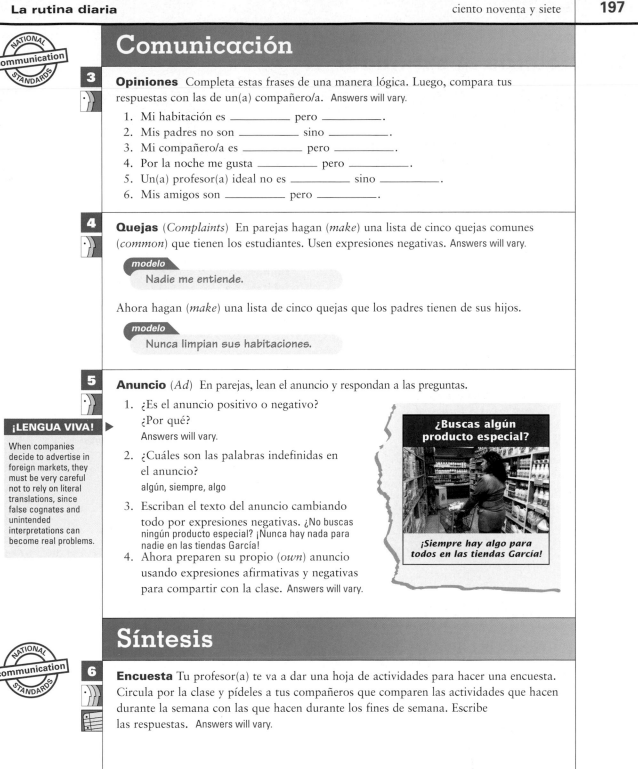

¿Buscas algún producto especial?

¡Siempre hay algo para todos en las tiendas García!

¡LENGUA VIVA!

When companies decide to advertise in foreign markets, they must be very careful not to rely on literal translations, since false cognates and unintended interpretations can become real problems.

Síntesis

6

Encuesta Tu profesor(a) te va a dar una hoja de actividades para hacer una encuesta. Circula por la clase y pídeles a tus compañeros que comparen las actividades que hacen durante la semana con las que hacen durante los fines de semana. Escribe las respuestas. Answers will vary.

3 Suggestion Before assigning the activity, give some personal examples using different subjects. Ex: **1. Mi hijo es inteligente, pero no le gusta estudiar. 2. Mi amiga no es norteamericana, sino española.**

4 Expansion Divide the class into all-male and all-female groups. Then have each group make two different lists: **Quejas que tienen los hombres de las mujeres** and **Quejas que tienen las mujeres de los hombres**. After five minutes, compare and contrast the answers and perceptions.

5 Expansion Have pairs work with another pair to combine the best aspects of each of their individual ads. Then have them present the "fused" ads to the class.

6 Suggestion Distribute the **Hojas de actividades** from the IRM that correspond to this activity.

6 Expansion Have students write five sentences using the information obtained through the **encuesta**. Ex: **1. Nadie va a la biblioteca durante el fin de semana, pero muchos vamos durante la semana. 2. No estudiamos los sábados sino los domingos.**

TEACHING OPTIONS

Large Groups Write the names of four vacation spots on four slips of paper and post them in different corners of the room. Ask students to pick their vacation preference by going to one of the corners. Then, have each group produce five reasons for their choice as well as one complaint about each of the other places.

Extra Practice Have students complete the following cloze activity using **pero, sino,** and **tampoco:** Yo me levanto temprano y hago mi tarea, ___ mi compañera de apartamento prefiere hacerla por la noche y acostarse muy tarde. (pero) Ella no tiene exámenes este semestre ___ proyectos. (sino) Yo no tengo exámenes ___. (tampoco) Sólo tengo mucha, mucha tarea.

7.3 Preterite of ser and ir

ANTE TODO   In **Lección 6**, you learned how to form the preterite tense of regular –ar, –er, and –ir verbs. The following chart contains the preterite forms of **ser** (*to be*) and **ir** (*to go*). Since these forms are irregular, you will need to memorize them.

Preterite of *ser* and *ir*

		ser	ir
SINGULAR FORMS	yo	fui	fui
	tú	fuiste	fuiste
	Ud./él/ella	fue	fue
PLURAL FORMS	nosotros/as	fuimos	fuimos
	vosotros/as	fuisteis	fuisteis
	Uds./ellos/ellas	fueron	fueron

¡ATENCIÓN!

Note that, whereas regular –er and –ir verbs have accent marks in the **yo** and **Ud.** forms of the preterite, **ser** and **ir** do not.

▶ Since the preterite forms of **ser** and **ir** are identical, context clarifies which of the two verbs is being used.

Él **fue** a comprar champú y jabón.
He went to buy shampoo and soap.

—¿Cómo **fue** la película anoche?
How was the movie last night?

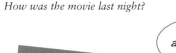
¿Adónde fueron ustedes?

Inés y yo fuimos a un mercado. Fue muy divertido.

¡INTÉNTALO!   Completa las siguientes frases usando el pretérito de **ser** e **ir**. La primera frase de cada columna se da (*is given*) como ejemplo.

ir
1. Los viajeros _fueron_ a Perú.
2. Patricia _fue_ a Cuzco.
3. Tú _fuiste_ a Iquitos.
4. Gregorio y yo _fuimos_ a Lima.
5. Yo _fui_ a Trujillo.
6. Ustedes _fueron_ a Arequipa.
7. Mi padre _fue_ a Lima.
8. Nosotras _fuimos_ a Cuzco.
9. Él _fue_ a Machu Picchu.
10. Usted _fue_ a Nazca.

ser
1. Usted _fue_ muy amable.
2. Yo _fui_ muy cordial.
3. Ellos _fueron_ muy simpáticos.
4. Nosotros _fuimos_ muy desagradables.
5. Ella _fue_ muy antipática.
6. Tú _fuiste_ muy chistoso.
7. Ustedes _fueron_ muy cordiales.
8. La gente _fue_ muy agradable.
9. Tomás y yo _fuimos_ muy corteses.
10. Los profesores _fueron_ muy buenos.

Práctica

1

Completar Completa estas conversaciones con la forma correcta del pretérito de **ser** o **ir**. Indica el infinitivo de cada forma verbal.

Conversación 1

RAÚL ¿Adónde (1)_____fueron/ir_____ ustedes de vacaciones?

▶ **PILAR** (2)_____Fuimos/ir_____ al Perú.

RAÚL ¿Cómo (3)_____fue/ser_____ el viaje?

PILAR ¡(4)_____Fue/ser_____ estupendo! Machu Picchu y la Plaza de Armas son increíbles.

RAÚL ¿(5)_____Fue/ser_____ caro el viaje?

PILAR No, el precio (6)_____fue/ser_____ muy bajo, sólo costó tres mil dólares.

Conversación 2

ISABEL Tina y Vicente (7)_____fueron/ser_____ novios, ¿no?

LUCÍA Sí, pero ahora no. Anoche Tina (8)_____fue/ir_____ a comer con Gregorio y la semana pasada ellos (9)_____fueron/ir_____ al partido de fútbol.

ISABEL ¿Ah sí? Javier y yo (10)_____fuimos/ir_____ al partido y no los vimos.

2

Descripciones Forma frases con los siguientes elementos. Usa el pretérito.   Answers will vary.

A	B	C	D
yo	(no) ir	a un restaurante	ayer
tú	(no) ser	en autobús	anoche
mi compañero/a		estudiante	anteayer
nosotros		muy simpático	la semana pasada
mis amigos/as		a la playa	el año pasado
ustedes		dependiente/a en una tienda	
		en avión	

Comunicación

3

Preguntas En parejas, túrnense (*take turns*) para hacerse estas preguntas.   Answers will vary.

1. ¿Adónde fuiste de vacaciones este año? ¿Con quién fuiste?
2. ¿Cómo fueron tus vacaciones?
3. ¿Fuiste de compras esta semana? ¿Adónde? ¿Qué compraste?
4. ¿Fuiste al cine la semana pasada? ¿Fueron tus amigos también?
5. ¿Qué película viste? ¿Cómo fue?
6. ¿Fuiste a la cafetería hoy? ¿A qué hora?
7. ¿Adónde fuiste durante el fin de semana? ¿Por qué?
8. ¿Quién fue tu profesor(a) favorito/a el semestre pasado? ¿Por qué?

4

El viaje En parejas, escriban un diálogo de un(a) viajero/a hablando con el/la agente de viajes sobre un viaje que tomó recientemente. Tienen cinco minutos para escribirlo. La pareja con más usos del pretérito de **ser** e **ir** y con menos errores gana. Answers will vary.

> **modelo**
>
> **Agente:** ¿Cómo fue el viaje?
> **Viajero:** El viaje fue maravilloso/horrible...

Section Goals

In **Estructura 7.4** students will learn:
• all forms of **gustar**
• other verbs that follow the pattern of **gustar**

Instructional Resources
WB/VM: Workbook, pp. 80–82
Lab Manual, p. 42
*Lab CD/MP3 **Lección 7***
IRM: ¡Inténtalo! & Práctica
Answers, pp. 182–183;
Tapescript, pp. 30–34
Info Gap Activities Booklet,
pp. 27–28
Interactive CD-ROM
Companion website:
www.vistahigherlearning.com
Presentations CD-ROM

Suggestions
• Use realia to compare different products using the verb **gustar**. Ex: (with clothing) **Me gustan estos pantalones, pero no me gustan estos zapatos.** Then ask volunteers questions using different indirect object pronouns. Ex: ____ , ¿te gusta este suéter? ____ , ¿le gusta a ____ este suéter?
• Write the headings **Gustos** and **Disgustos** on the board. Have the class brainstorm a list of likes and dislikes among the college population including music artists, movies, clothes, or hobbies. Use the lists to form statements and questions illustrating the use of the verb **gustar**. Use different indirect object pronouns. Ex: **A los estudiantes universitarios no les gustan los Beatles. A mis amigos y a mí, sí nos gustan los Beatles. A los estudiantes no les gustan las películas infantiles.**

7.4 Gustar and verbs like gustar

ANTE TODO   In **Lección 2**, you learned that the expressions **me gusta(n)** and **te gusta(n)** express the English concepts of *I like* and *you like*. You will now learn more about the verb **gustar** and other similar verbs. Observe the following examples.

Me gusta ese champú.
> ENGLISH EQUIVALENT
> *I like that shampoo.*
> LITERAL MEANING
> *That shampoo is pleasing to me.*

¿**Te gustaron** las clases?
> ENGLISH EQUIVALENT
> *Did you like the classes?*
> LITERAL MEANING
> *Were the classes pleasing to you?*

▶ As the examples show, the construction **me gusta(n)** does not have a direct equivalent in English. The literal meaning of this construction is *to be pleasing to (someone)*, and it requires the use of an indirect object pronoun.

INDIRECT OBJECT PRONOUN		SUBJECT	SUBJECT		DIRECT OBJECT
Me	**gusta**	ese champú.	*I*	*like*	*that shampoo.*

▶ In the diagram above, observe how in the Spanish sentence the object being liked **(ese champú)** is really the subject of the sentence. The person who likes the object, in turn, is an indirect object because it answers the question: *To whom is the shampoo pleasing?*

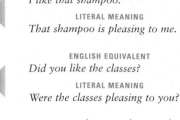
¿No te gustan las computadoras?

Me gustan mucho los parques.

▶ The forms most commonly used with **gustar** and similar verbs are the third person (singular and plural). When the object or person being liked is singular, the singular form **(gusta)** is used. When two or more objects or persons are being liked, the plural form **(gustan)** is used. Observe this diagram:

me, te, le, nos, os, les

SINGULAR
gusta → la película
gustó → el concierto

PLURAL
gustan → las vacaciones
gustaron → los museos de Lima

▶ To express what someone likes or does not like to do, **gustar** is followed by an infinitive. The singular form of **gustar** is used even if there is more than one infinitive.

No **nos gusta comer** a las nueve.
We don't like to eat at nine o'clock.

Les gusta cantar y **bailar** en las fiestas.
They like to sing and dance at parties.

TEACHING OPTIONS

Heritage Speakers Have heritage speakers compare and contrast activities they like to do with activities their parents/grandparents like to do. Encourage them to use the verb **gustar** and others that follow the same pattern, referring them to the list of verbs on page 201.

Game Divide the class into small teams. Give a prompt including subject and object. Ex: **ella/películas de horror**. Teams will have one minute to construct a sentence using **gustar** or one of the verbs that follow the pattern of **gustar**. Then one member from each team will write the sentence on the board. Award one point to each team for every correct response. The team with the most points at the end wins.

▶ The construction **a** + [*pronoun*] (**a mí, a ti, a Ud., a él,** etc.) is used to clarify or to emphasize who is pleased.

> **A ella** le gustan las toallas verdes, pero **a él** no le gustan.
> *She likes green towels, but he doesn't like them.*

> **A ti** te gusta cenar en casa, pero **a mí** no me gusta.
> *You like to eat dinner at home, but I don't like to.*

▶ The construction **a** + [*noun*] can also be used before the indirect object pronoun to clarify or to emphasize who is pleased.

> **A los turistas** les gustó mucho Machu Picchu.
> *The tourists liked Machu Picchu a lot.*

> **A Juanita** le gustaron mucho los mercados al aire libre.
> *Juanita liked the open-air markets a lot.*

▶ Other verbs in Spanish are used in the same way as **gustar**. Here is a list of the most common ones.

Verbs like *gustar*

aburrir	to bore	**importar**	to be important to; to matter
encantar	to like very much; to love (inanimate objects)	**interesar**	to be interesting to; to interest
faltar	to lack; to need	**molestar**	to bother; to annoy
fascinar	to fascinate	**quedar**	to be left over; to fit (clothing)

¡INTÉNTALO! Indica el pronombre del objeto indirecto y la forma del tiempo presente adecuados en cada frase. La primera frase de cada columna se da (*is given*) como ejemplo.

gustar

1. A él <u>le gusta</u> viajar.
2. A mí <u>me gusta</u> bailar.
3. A nosotras <u>nos gusta</u> cantar.
4. A ustedes <u>les gusta</u> leer.
5. A ti <u>te gusta</u> correr.
6. A Pedro <u>le gusta</u> gritar.
7. A mis padres <u>les gusta</u> caminar.
8. A usted <u>le gusta</u> jugar tenis.
9. A mi esposo y a mí <u>nos gusta</u> dormir.
10. A Alberto <u>le gusta</u> dibujar.
11. A todos <u>nos/les gusta</u> opinar.
12. A Pili no <u>le gusta</u> ir de compras.

encantar

1. A ellos <u>les encantan</u> los deportes.
2. A ti <u>te encantan</u> las películas.
3. A usted <u>le encantan</u> los viajes.
4. A mí <u>me encantan</u> las revistas.
5. A Jorge y a Luis <u>les encantan</u> los perros.
6. A nosotros <u>nos encantan</u> las vacaciones.
7. A ustedes <u>les encantan</u> las fiestas.
8. A Marcela <u>le encantan</u> los libros.
9. A mis amigos <u>les encantan</u> los museos.
10. A ella <u>le encanta</u> el ciclismo.
11. A Pedro <u>le encanta</u> el limón.
12. A ti y a mí <u>nos encanta</u> el baile.

Práctica

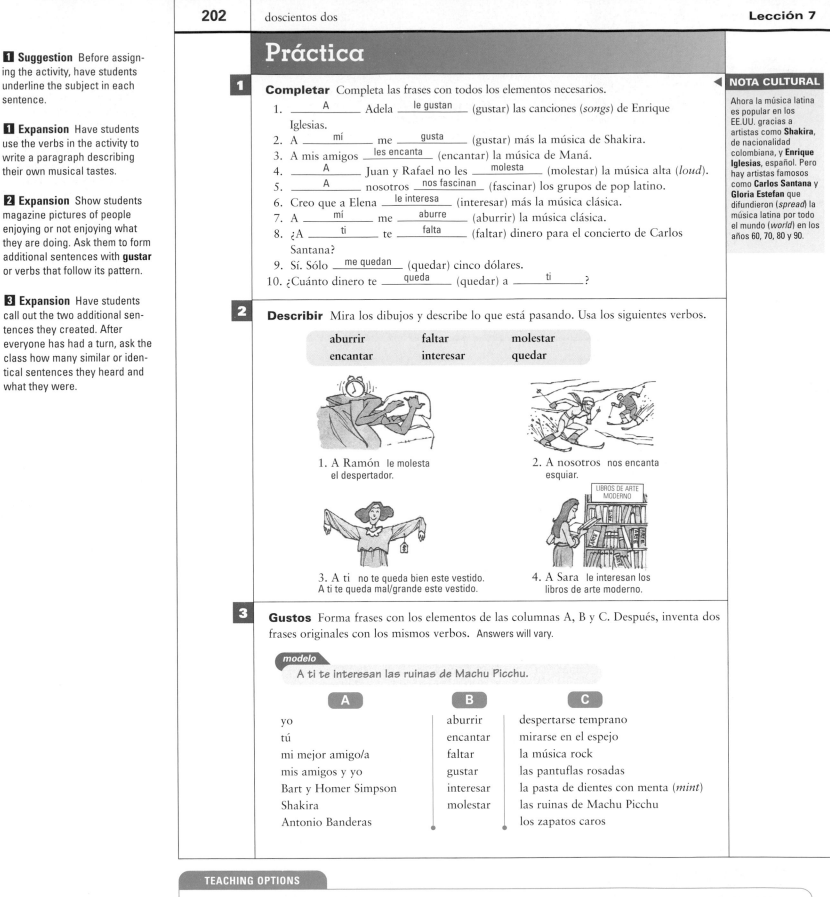

1 Completar Completa las frases con todos los elementos necesarios.

1. ____A____ Adela __le gustan__ (gustar) las canciones (*songs*) de Enrique Iglesias.
2. A ____mí____ me __gusta__ (gustar) más la música de Shakira.
3. A mis amigos __les encanta__ (encantar) la música de Maná.
4. ____A____ Juan y Rafael no les __molesta__ (molestar) la música alta (*loud*).
5. ____A____ nosotros __nos fascinan__ (fascinar) los grupos de pop latino.
6. Creo que a Elena __le interesa__ (interesar) más la música clásica.
7. A ____mí____ me __aburre__ (aburrir) la música clásica.
8. ¿A ____ti____ te __falta__ (faltar) dinero para el concierto de Carlos Santana?
9. Sí. Sólo __me quedan__ (quedar) cinco dólares.
10. ¿Cuánto dinero te __queda__ (quedar) a ____ti____?

2 Describir Mira los dibujos y describe lo que está pasando. Usa los siguientes verbos.

aburrir	faltar	molestar
encantar	interesar	quedar

1. A Ramón le molesta el despertador.

2. A nosotros nos encanta esquiar.

3. A ti no te queda bien este vestido.
A ti te queda mal/grande este vestido.

4. A Sara le interesan los libros de arte moderno.

LIBROS DE ARTE MODERNO

3 Gustos Forma frases con los elementos de las columnas A, B y C. Después, inventa dos frases originales con los mismos verbos. Answers will vary.

modelo
A ti te interesan las ruinas de Machu Picchu.

A	B	C
yo	aburrir	despertarse temprano
tú	encantar	mirarse en el espejo
mi mejor amigo/a	faltar	la música rock
mis amigos y yo	gustar	las pantuflas rosadas
Bart y Homer Simpson	interesar	la pasta de dientes con menta (*mint*)
Shakira	molestar	las ruinas de Machu Picchu
Antonio Banderas		los zapatos caros

Comunicación

NATIONAL communication STANDARDS

4 **Preguntas** En parejas, túrnense para hacer y contestar estas preguntas. Answers will vary.

1. ¿Te gusta levantarte temprano o tarde? ¿Por qué? ¿Y tu compañero/a de cuarto?
2. ¿Te gusta acostarte temprano o tarde? ¿Y tu compañero/a de cuarto?
3. ¿Te gusta dormir la siesta?
4. ¿Te gusta acampar o prefieres quedarte en un hotel cuando estás de vacaciones?
5. ¿Qué te gusta hacer en el verano?
6. ¿Qué te gusta más de esta universidad? ¿Qué te molesta?
7. ¿Te interesan más las ciencias o las humanidades? ¿Por qué?
8. ¿Qué cosas te molestan?

NOTA CULTURAL ▶

La siesta (un descanso de dos o tres horas) no es hoy tan común como antes.

Cuando España entró en la Unión Europea, muchas empresas (*businesses*) redujeron (*reduced*) la siesta.

5 **Completar** Completa estas frases de una manera lógica. Answers will vary.

1. A mi novio/a le fascina(n)…
2. A mi mejor (*best*) amigo/a no le interesa(n)…
3. A mis padres les importa(n)…
4. A nosotros nos molesta(n)…
5. A mis hermanos les aburre(n)…
6. A mi compañero/a de cuarto le aburre(n)…
7. A los turistas les interesa(n)…
8. A los jugadores profesionales les encanta(n)…
9. A nuestro/a profesor(a) le molesta(n)…

6 **La residencia** Tú y tu compañero/a de clase son los directores de una residencia estudiantil en Perú. Su profesor(a) les va a dar a cada uno de ustedes las descripciones de cinco estudiantes. Con la información tienen que escoger (*choose*) quiénes van a ser compañeros de cuarto. Después, completen la lista. Answers will vary.

NATIONAL communication STANDARDS

Síntesis

7 **Situación** Trabajen en parejas para representar los papeles (*roles*) de un(a) cliente/a y un(a) dependiente/a. Usen las instrucciones como guía. Answers will vary.

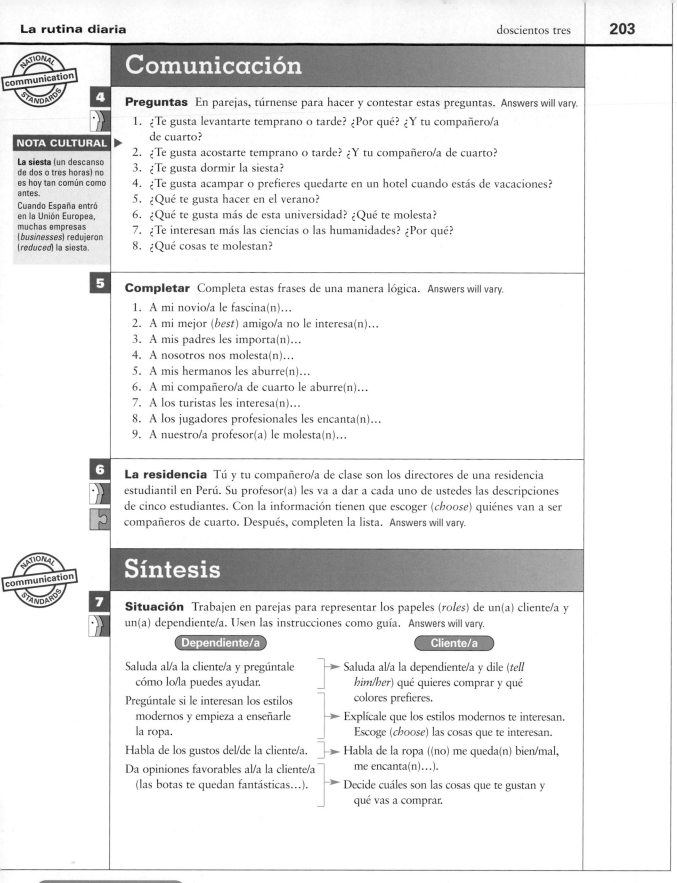

Dependiente/a	Cliente/a
Saluda al/a la cliente/a y pregúntale cómo lo/la puedes ayudar.	Saluda al/a la dependiente/a y dile (*tell him/her*) qué quieres comprar y qué colores prefieres.
Pregúntale si le interesan los estilos modernos y empieza a enseñarle la ropa.	Explícale que los estilos modernos te interesan. Escoge (*choose*) las cosas que te interesan.
Habla de los gustos del/de la cliente/a.	Habla de la ropa ((no) me queda(n) bien/mal, me encanta(n)…).
Da opiniones favorables al/a la cliente/a (las botas te quedan fantásticas…).	Decide cuáles son las cosas que te gustan y qué vas a comprar.

4 **Expansion** Take a class survey of the answers and write the results on the board. Ask volunteers to use verbs like **gustar** to summarize them.

5 **Suggestion** For items that start with **A mi(s)…** , have pairs compare their answers and then report to the class: first answers in common, then answers that differed. Ex: **A mis padres les importan los estudios, pero a los padres de _____ les importa más el dinero.**

6 **Suggestion** Divide the class into pairs and distribute the handouts from the Information Gap Activities Booklet that correspond to this activity. Give students ten minutes to complete this activity.

6 **Expansion**
• Have pairs compare their matches by walking around the classroom until they have all compared their answers with one another.
• Have pairs choose one of the students and write his or her want ad looking for a suitable roommate.

7 **Expansion** Ask pairs to perform their conversation for the class or have them videotape it outside of class.

TEACHING OPTIONS

Pairs Have pairs prepare short TV commercials in which they use the target verbs presented in **Estructura 7.4** to sell a particular product. Group three pairs together so that each pair presents its skit to four other students.

Game Give groups of students five minutes to write a description of social life during a specific historical period such as the French Revolution or prehistoric times using as many of the target verbs presented in **Estructura 7.4** as possible. After the time is up ask groups the number of these verbs they used in their descriptions. Have the top three read their descriptions for the class. Students vote for the best description.

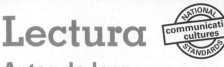

Lectura

Antes de leer

Estrategia
Predicting content from the title

Prediction is an invaluable strategy in reading for comprehension. We can usually predict the content of a newspaper article from its headline, for example. More often than not, we decide whether or not to read the article based on its headline. Predicting content from the title will help you increase your reading comprehension in Spanish.

Examinar el texto

Lee el título de la lectura y haz tres predicciones sobre el contenido. Escribe tus predicciones en una hoja de papel.

Compartir

Comparte tus ideas con un(a) compañero/a de clase.

Cognados

Haz una lista de seis cognados que encuentres en la lectura.

1. _____.
2. _____.
3. _____.
4. _____.
5. _____.
6. _____.

¿Qué te dicen los cognados sobre el tema de la lectura?

recursos

vistahigher learning.com

¡Qué día!

Anterior ▼ ⬇Siguiente ▼ 📧 Responder | Responder a todos

Fecha: Lunes, 10 de mayo
De: Guillermo Zamora
Asunto: ¡Qué día!
Para: Lupe; Marcos; Sandra; Jorge

Hola chicos:

La semana pasada me di cuenta° de que necesito organizar mejor mi rutina... pero especialmente necesito prepararme mejor para los exámenes. Me falta mucha disciplina, me molesta no tener control de mi tiempo y nunca deseo repetir los eventos de esta semana.

El miércoles pasé todo el día y toda la noche estudiando para el examen de biología del jueves por la mañana. Me aburre la biología y no empecé a estudiar hasta el día antes del examen. El jueves a las 8, después de no dormir en toda la noche, fui exhausto al examen. Fue difícil, pero afortunadamente° me acordé de todo el material. Esa noche me acosté temprano y dormí mucho.

Me desperté a las 9, y fue extraño° ver a mi compañero de

cuarto, Andrés, preparándose para ir a dormir. Nunca hablamos mucho y no comenté nada. Fui al baño a cepillarme los dientes para ir a clase. ¿Y Andrés? Él se acostó. "¡Qué extraño es este chico!," pensé.

Mi clase es a las 10, y fue necesario hacer las cosas rápido. Todo empezó a ir mal... eso pasa siempre cuando uno tiene prisa. Cuando busqué mis cosas para el baño, no las encontré. Entonces me duché sin jabón, me cepillé los dientes sin cepillo de dientes y me peiné con las manos. Tampoco encontré ropa limpia, y usé la sucia. Rápido, tomé mis libros. ¿Y Andrés? Roncando°... ¡a las 9:50!

Cuando salí corriendo para la clase, la prisa no me permitió ver el campus desierto. Cuando llegué a la clase, no vi a nadie. No vi al profesor ni a los estudiantes. Por último miré mi reloj, y vi la hora. Las 10 en punto... ¡de la noche!

¡Dormí 24 horas!

Guillermo

me di cuenta *I realized* afortunadamente *fortunately* extraño *strange* Roncando *snoring*

Después de leer

Seleccionar
Selecciona la respuesta (*answer*) correcta.

1. ¿Quién es el/la narrador(a)? __c__.
   a. Andrés
   b. una profesora
   c. Guillermo
2. ¿Qué le molesta al narrador? __b__.
   a. Le molestan los exámenes de biología.
   b. Le molesta no tener control de su tiempo.
   c. Le molesta mucho organizar su rutina.
3. ¿Por qué está exhausto? __c__.
   a. Porque fue a una fiesta la noche anterior.
   b. Porque no le gusta la biología.
   c. Porque pasó la noche anterior estudiando.
4. ¿Por qué no hay nadie en clase? __a__.
   a. Porque es de noche.
   b. Porque todos están de vacaciones.
   c. Porque el profesor canceló la clase.
5. ¿Cómo es la relación de Guillermo y Andrés? __b__
   a. Son buenos amigos.
   b. No hablan mucho.
   c. Tienen una buena relación.

Ordenar
Ordena los sucesos de la narración. Utiliza los números del 1 al 9.

a. Toma el examen de biología. __2__
b. No encuentra la bolsa para el baño. __5__
c. Andrés se duerme. __7__
d. Pasa todo el día y toda la noche estudiando para un examen. __1__
e. Se ducha sin jabón. __6__
f. Se acuesta temprano. __3__
g. Vuelve a su cuarto a las 10 de la noche. __9__
h. Se despierta a las 9 y su compañero de cuarto se prepara para dormir. __4__
i. Va a clase y no hay nadie. __8__

Contestar
Contesta estas preguntas. Answers will vary.

1. ¿Cómo es tu rutina diaria? ¿Muy organizada?
2. ¿Cuándo empiezas a estudiar para los exámenes?
3. ¿Tienes compañero/a de cuarto? ¿Son amigos/as?
4. Para comunicarte con tus amigos/as, ¿prefieres el teléfono o el correo electrónico? ¿Por qué?

Section Goal
In **Panorama**, students will read about the geography, culture, and history of Peru.

Instructional Resources
Transparencies, #5, #6, #32
WB/VM: Workbook, pp. 83–84;
Video Activities, pp. 237–238
Panorama cultural *DVD/Video*
Interactive CD-ROM
IRM: Videoscript, p. 110;
Panorama cultural *translations,*
p. 132
Companion website:
www.vistahigherlearning.com
Presentations CD-ROM

Suggestion Have students look at the map of Peru or project **Transparency #32**. Ask them to find the **Río Amazonas** and the **Cordillera de los Andes**, and to speculate about the types of climate found in Peru. As a mountainous country near the equator, climate varies according to elevation and ranges from tropical to arctic. Point out that well over half of the territory of Peru lies within the Amazon Basin. Encourage students to tell what they know about Peru.

El país en cifras After each section, ask students questions about the content of what has been read. Point out that Iquitos, Peru's port city on the Amazon River, is a destination for ships that travel 2,300 miles up the Amazon from the Atlantic Ocean.

¡Increíble pero cierto! In recent years, the **El Niño** weather phenomenon has caused flooding in the deserts of southern Peru. The Peruvian government is currently taking steps to preserve the **Líneas de Nazca** from further deterioration due to floods in the hope that scientists will someday discover more about their origins and meaning.

Perú

connections cultures — NATIONAL STANDARDS

El país en cifras

▶ **Área:** 1.285.220 km² (496.224 millas²), *un poco menos que el área de Alaska*
▶ **Población:** 27.804.000
▶ **Capital:** Lima—8.185.000
▶ **Ciudades principales:** Arequipa—764.000, Trujillo—643.000, Chiclayo—527.000, Callao—442.000, Iquitos—348.000

SOURCE: Population Division, UN Secretariat

Iquitos es un puerto muy importante en el río Amazonas. Desde Iquitos se envían° muchos productos a otros lugares, incluyendo goma°, nueces°, madera°, arroz°, café y tabaco. Iquitos es también un destino popular para los ecoturistas que visitan la selva°.

▶ **Moneda:** nuevo sol
▶ **Idiomas:** español (oficial), quechua (oficial), aimará

Bandera del Perú

Peruanos célebres
▶ **Clorinda Matto de Turner,** escritora (1852–1909)
▶ **César Vallejo,** poeta (1892–1938)
▶ **Javier Pérez de Cuéllar,** diplomático (1920–)
▶ **Mario Vargas Llosa,** novelista (1936–)

Mario Vargas Llosa

se envían *are shipped* goma *rubber* nueces *nuts* madera *timber*
arroz *rice* selva *jungle* grabó *engraved* tamaño *size*

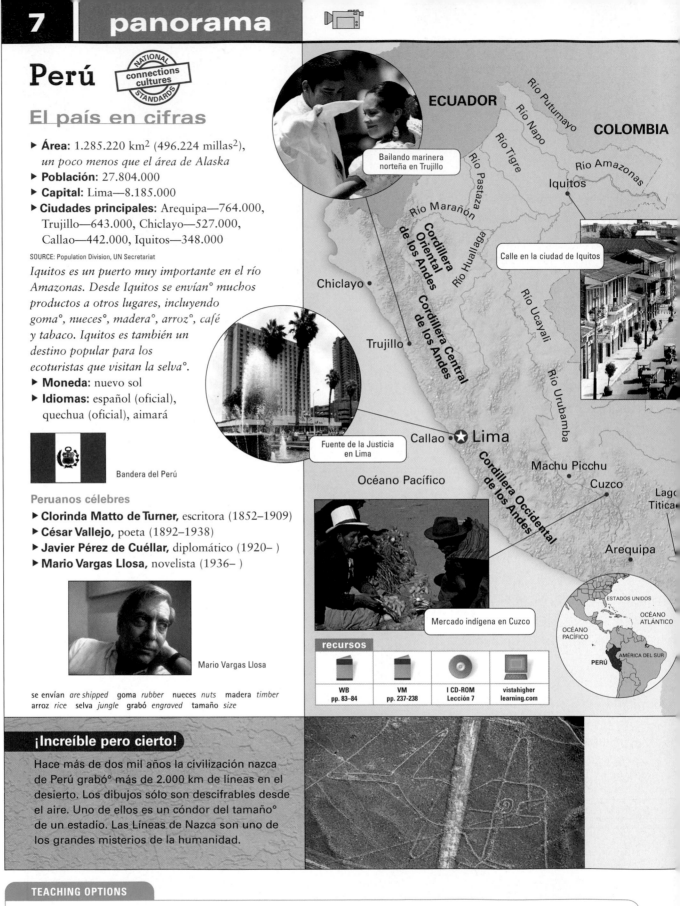

ECUADOR — COLOMBIA
Río Putumayo — Río Napo — Río Amazonas
Río Tigre — Río Pastaza — Río Marañón
Río Huallaga

Bailando marinera norteña en Trujillo

Iquitos

Calle en la ciudad de Iquitos

Cordillera Oriental de los Andes
Cordillera Central de los Andes
Cordillera Occidental de los Andes

Chiclayo

Río Ucayali

Río Urubamba

Trujillo

Fuente de la Justicia en Lima

Callao — Lima

Océano Pacífico

Machu Picchu
Cuzco
Lago Titicaca
Arequipa

Mercado indígena en Cuzco

ESTADOS UNIDOS
OCÉANO ATLÁNTICO
OCÉANO PACÍFICO
AMÉRICA DEL SUR
PERÚ

recursos

WB pp. 83–84	VM pp. 237–238	I CD-ROM Lección 7	vistahigher learning.com

¡Increíble pero cierto!

Hace más de dos mil años la civilización nazca de Perú grabó° más de 2.000 km de líneas en el desierto. Los dibujos sólo son descifrables desde el aire. Uno de ellos es un cóndor del tamaño° de un estadio. Las Líneas de Nazca son uno de los grandes misterios de la humanidad.

TEACHING OPTIONS

Heritage Speakers Ask heritage speakers from Peru or who have visited Peru to make a short presentation to the class about their impressions. Encourage them to speak of the region they are from or have visited and how it differs from other regions in this vast country. If they have photographs, ask them to bring them to class to illustrate their talk.

TPR Invite students to take turns guiding the class on tours of Peru's waterways: one student gives directions, and the others follow by tracing the route on their map of Peru. For example: **Comenzamos en el río Amazonas, pasando por Iquitos hasta llegar al río Ucayali.**

Lugares • Lima

Lima es una ciudad moderna y antigua° a la vez°. La Iglesia de San Francisco es notable por la influencia de la arquitectura árabe. También son fascinantes las exhibiciones sobre los incas en el Museo del Oro del Perú y en el Museo Nacional de Antropología y Arqueología. Barranco, el barrio° bohemio de la ciudad, es famoso por su ambiente cultural y sus bares y restaurantes.

Historia • Los incas

Antes del siglo° XVI, los incas desarrollaron° sistemas avanzados de comunicaciones y de contabilidad y construyeron° acueductos, calles° y templos. A 80 kilómetros al noroeste de Cuzco está Machu Picchu, una ciudad antigua del imperio inca. Está a una altitud de 2.350 metros (7.710 pies), entre dos cimas° de los Andes. Cuando los conquistadores españoles llegaron a Perú, nunca encontraron Machu Picchu. En 1911, el arqueólogo norteamericano Hiram Bingham la descubrió. Todavía no se sabe° ni cómo se construyó una ciudad a esa altura, ni por qué los incas la abandonaron.

Artes • La música andina

Machu Picchu aún no existía° cuando se originó la música cautivadora° de las antiguas culturas indígenas de los Andes. Las influencias española y africana le prestaron a esta música sus ritmos de hoy. Dos tipos de flauta°, la quena y la antara, producen esta música tan particular. En las décadas de los sesenta y los setenta se popularizó un movimiento para preservar la música andina, y hasta° Simon y Garfunkel la incorporaron en su repertorio con la canción° "El cóndor pasa".

Economía • Llamas y alpacas

El Perú se conoce° por sus llamas, alpacas, guanacos y vicuñas, todos animales mamíferos° parientes del camello. Estos animales todavía son de enorme importancia para la economía del país. Dan lana° para hacer ropa, mantas°, bolsas y artículos turísticos. La llama se usa también para la carga y el transporte.

¿Qué aprendiste? Responde a las preguntas con una frase completa.

1. ¿Qué productos envía Iquitos a otros lugares? Iquitos envía goma, nueces, madera, arroz, café y tabaco.
2. ¿Cuáles son las lenguas oficiales del Perú? Las lenguas oficiales del Perú son el español y el quechua.
3. ¿Por qué es notable la Iglesia de San Francisco en Lima? Es notable por la influencia de la arquitectura árabe.
4. ¿Por qué los conquistadores españoles no encontraron la ciudad de Machu Picchu? No la encontraron porque está entre dos cimas.
5. ¿Qué son la quena y la antara? Son dos tipos de flauta.
6. ¿Qué hacen los peruanos con la lana de sus llamas y alpacas? Hacen ropa, mantas, bolsas y artículos turísticos.

Conexión Internet Investiga estos temas en el sitio **www.vistahigherlearning.com**.

1. Investiga la cultura incaica. ¿Cuáles son algunos de los aspectos interesantes de su cultura?
2. Busca información sobre dos artistas, escritores o músicos peruanos, y presenta un breve informe a tu clase.

----

antigua *old* a la vez *at the same time* barrio *neighborhood* siglo *century* desarrollaron *developed* construyeron *built* calles *roads* cimas *summits* no se sabe *it is not known* no existía *didn't exist* cautivadora *captivating* flauta *flute* hasta *even* canción *song* se conoce *is known* mamíferos *mammalian* lana *wool* mantas *blankets*

Lima Lima is rich in colonial architecture. It is also the home of the University of San Marcos, established in 1551, the oldest university in South America.

Los incas Another invention of the Incas were the **quipus**, clusters of knotted strings that were a means of keeping records and sending messages. A **quipu** consisted of a series of small cords with knots in them attached to a larger cord. A cord's color, place, size, and the knots in it all had significance.

La música andina Ancient tombs, belonging to pre-Columbian cultures like the Nasca and Moche and pre-dating even the Incan civilization, have yielded instruments and other artifacts indicating that the precursors of Andean music go back at least as far as two millenia.

Llamas y alpacas Of the camel-like animals of the Andes, only the sturdy llama has been domesticated as a pack animal. Its long, thick coat also provides fiber that is woven into a coarser grade of cloth. The more delicate alpaca and vicuña are raised only for their beautiful coats, used to create extremely high-quality cloth. The guanaco has never been domesticated.

Conexión Internet Students will find supporting Internet activities and links at **www.vistahigherlearning.com**.

Suggestion You may want to wrap up this section by playing the **Panorama cultural** video footage for this lesson.

Variación léxica Some of the most familiar words to have entered Spanish from the Quechua language are the names of animals native to the Andean region, such as **el cóndor, la llama, el puma,** and **la vicuña**. These words later passed from Spanish to a number of European languages, including English. **La alpaca** comes not from Quechua, the language of the Incas and their descendants, who inhabit most of the Andean region, but from Aymara, the language of native American people who live near Lake Titicaca on the Peruvian-Bolivian border. Most students are probably familiar with the traditional Quechua tune, *El cóndor pasa*, popularized in a version by Simon and Garfunkel.

Instructional Resources
Vocabulary CD
Lab Manual, p. 42
*Lab CD/MP3 **Lección 7***
IRM: Tapescript, pp. 30–34
*Testing Program: **Pruebas**,*
*pp. 73–84; **Exámenes**, pp.*
181–192
Testing Program Audio CD
Test Files CD-ROM
Test Generator

Los verbos reflexivos

acordarse (de) (o:ue)	*to remember*
acostarse (o:ue)	*to go to bed*
afeitarse	*to shave*
bañarse	*to bathe; take a bath*
cepillarse el pelo	*to brush one's hair*
cepillarse los dientes	*to brush one's teeth*
despedirse (de) (e:i)	*to say goodbye (to)*
despertarse (e:ie)	*to wake up*
dormirse (o:ue)	*to go to sleep; to fall asleep*
ducharse	*to shower; to take a shower*
enojarse (con)	*to get angry (with)*
irse	*to go away; to leave*
lavarse la cara	*to wash one's face*
lavarse las manos	*to wash one's hands*
levantarse	*to get up*
llamarse	*to be called; to be named*
maquillarse	*to put on makeup*
peinarse	*to comb one's hair*
ponerse	*to put on*
ponerse (+ *adj.*)	*to become (+ adj.)*
preocuparse (por)	*to worry (about)*
probarse (o:ue)	*to try on*
quedarse	*to stay; to remain*
quitarse	*to take off*
secarse	*to dry (oneself)*
sentarse (e:ie)	*to sit down*
sentirse (e:ie)	*to feel*
vestirse (e:i)	*to get dressed*

Palabras de secuencia

antes (de)	*before*
después (de)	*afterwards; then*
después de	*after*
durante	*during*
entonces	*then*
luego	*then*
más tarde	*later*
por último	*finally*

Palabras afirmativas y negativas

algo	*something; anything*
alguien	*someone; somebody; anyone*
alguno/a(s), algún	*some; any*
jamás	*never; not ever*
nada	*nothing; not anything*
nadie	*no one; nobody; not anyone*
ni... ni	*neither... nor*
ninguno/a, ningún	*no; none; not any*
nunca	*never; not ever*
o... o	*either... or*
siempre	*always*
también	*also; too*
tampoco	*neither; not either*

En el baño

el baño, el cuarto de baño	*bathroom*
el champú	*shampoo*
la crema de afeitar	*shaving cream*
la ducha	*shower*
el espejo	*mirror*
el inodoro	*toilet*
el jabón	*soap*
el lavabo	*sink*
el maquillaje	*makeup*
la pasta de dientes	*toothpaste*
la toalla	*towel*

Gustar y verbos similares

aburrir	*to bore*
encantar	*to like very much; to love (inanimate objects)*
faltar	*to lack; to need*
fascinar	*to fascinate*
gustar	*to be pleasing to; to like*
importar	*to be important to; to matter*
interesar	*to be interesting to; to interest*
molestar	*to bother; to annoy*
quedar	*to be left over; to fit (clothing)*

Palabras adicionales

el despertador	*alarm clock*
las pantuflas	*slippers*
la rutina diaria	*daily routine*
por la mañana	*in the morning*
por la noche	*at night*
por la tarde	*in the afternoon; in the evening*

Expresiones útiles	*See page 187.*

recursos

LM p. 42	Lab CD/MP3 Lección 7	Vocab CD Lección 7

La comida

8

Communicative Goals

You will learn how to:
- Order food in a restaurant
- Talk about and describe food

Lesson Goals

In **Lección 8** students will be introduced to the following:
- food terms
- meal-related words
- preterite of stem-changing verbs
- double object pronouns
- converting **le** and **les** to **se** with double object pronouns
- uses of **saber** and **conocer**
- more uses of the personal **a**
- comparatives and superlatives
- reading for the main idea
- cultural, geographic, and historical information about Guatemala

A primera vista Here are some additional questions you can ask based on the photo: **¿Dónde prefieres comer, en tu casa o en un restaurante? ¿Por qué? ¿Fuiste a algún lugar especial para comer el año pasado? ¿Adónde fuiste y quién fue? ¿Dónde te encanta comer? ¿Por qué? ¿Qué ropa te pones para salir a comer en una ocasión especial? ¿Qué más haces antes de salir?**

A PRIMERA VISTA

- ¿Está ella en un restaurante?
- ¿Trabaja ella?
- ¿Es parte de su rutina diaria?
- ¿Qué colores hay en la foto?

INSTRUCTIONAL RESOURCES

Workbook/Video Manual: WB Activities, pp. 85–96
Laboratory Manual: Lab Activities, pp. 43–48
Workbook/Video Manual: Video Activities, pp. 209–210;
pp. 239–240
Instructor's Resource Manual: **Hojas de actividades**,
p. 146; **Vocabulario adicional**, p. 162; **¡Inténtalo!** &
Práctica Answers, pp. 184–185; **Fotonovela**

Translations, pp. 122–123; Textbook CD Tapescript,
p. 78; Lab CDs Tapescript, pp. 35–39; **Fotonovela**
Videoscript, pp. 94–95; **Panorama cultural** Videoscript,
p. 111; **Pan. cult.** Translations, p. 133
Info Gap Activities Booklet, pp. 29–32
Overhead Transparencies: #3, #4, #33, #34, #35
Lab Audio CD/MP3 **Lección 8**

Panorama cultural DVD/
Video
Fotonovela DVD/Video
Testing Program, pp. 85–96
Testing Program Audio CD
Test Files CD-ROM
Test Generator

Companion website
Presentations CD-ROM
Textbook CD
Vocabulary CD
Interactive CD-ROM
Video CD-ROM
Web-SAM

Section Goals

In **Contextos** students will learn and practice:
• food names
• meal-related vocabulary

Instructional Resources

Transparencies, #33, #34
Textbook Activities CD
Vocabulary CD
WB/VM: Workbook, pp. 85–86
Lab Manual, p. 43
Lab CD/MP3 Lección 8
IRM: Vocab. adicional, p. 162;
Práctica Answers, p. 184;
Tapescript, pp. 35–39; p. 78
Info Gap Activities Booklet,
pp. 29–30
Interactive CD-ROM
Companion website:
www.vistahigherlearning.com
Presentations CD-ROM

Suggestions

• Tell what you are going to have for lunch, writing food vocabulary on the board. Ex: **Tengo hambre y voy a preparar una hamburguesa. ¿Qué ingredientes necesito? Pues, carne de res molida, queso, tomates, lechuga y mayonesa. También voy a preparar una ensalada. ¿Con qué ingredientes preparo la ensalada? A ver, lechuga, tomates, zanahorias,…**
• Project **Transparency #33.** Ask: **¿Sí o no? ¿Hay bananas en el dibujo del mercado? (Sí.) ¿Qué otras frutas hay? Y, ¿hay cerveza? (No.)** Next mention typical dishes and ask students to tell what ingredients are used to make them. Suggestions: **una ensalada verde, una ensalada de fruta, un sándwich.**
• Ask students what some of their favorite foods are. Ex: **Y a ti, _____, ¿qué te gusta comer?**

La comida

Más vocabulario

el/la camarero/a	*waiter*
la comida	*food; meal*
el/la dueño/a	*owner; landlord*
los entremeses	*hors d'oeuvres*
el menú	*menu*
el plato (principal)	*(main) dish*
la sección de (no) fumar	*(non) smoking section*
el agua (mineral)	*(mineral) water*
la bebida	*drink*
la cerveza	*beer*
la leche	*milk*
el ajo	*garlic*
las arvejas	*peas*
los cereales	*cereal; grain*
los frijoles	*beans*
el melocotón	*peach*
las papas/patatas (fritas)	*(fried) potatoes; French fries*
el pollo (asado)	*(roast) chicken*
el queso	*cheese*
la sandía	*watermelon*
el sándwich	*sandwich*
el yogur	*yogurt*
el aceite	*oil*
la margarina	*margarine*
la mayonesa	*mayonnaise*
el refresco	*soft drink*
el vinagre	*vinegar*
delicioso/a	*delicious*
rico/a	*tasty; delicious*
sabroso/a	*tasty; delicious*

Variación léxica

camarones ⟷ gambas (*Esp.*)

camarero ⟷ mesero (*Amér. L.*), mesonero (*Ven.*), mozo (*Arg., Chile, Urug., Perú*)

refresco ⟷ gaseosa (*Amér. C., Amér. S.*)

recursos					
TEXT CD Lección 8	WB pp. 85–86	LM p. 43	Lab CD/MP3 Lección 8	I CD-ROM Lección 8	Vocab CD Lección 8

TEACHING OPTIONS

Extra Practice To review vocabulary for colors, ask students what colors the following food items are: **las bananas (amarillas), las uvas (verdes o moradas), las zanahorias (anaranjadas), los tomates (rojos), los frijoles (blancos, marrones, rojos o negros).**

Variación léxica Point out that food vocabulary varies from region to region in the Spanish-speaking world. When the Spanish visited the New World, they introduced many foods unknown to the indigenous peoples, and likewise they took back many food items previously unknown in Europe. Also point out the different names for fruits and vegetables in **¡Lengua viva!** on page 211.

Práctica

¡LENGUA VIVA!

Many fruits and vegetables have a variety of names:

arveja ↔ guisante, chícharo

banana ↔ banano, plátano, guineo

champiñón ↔ seta, hongo

frijol ↔ habichuela

maíz ↔ choclo, elote

papa ↔ patata

tomate ↔ jitomate

1 Escuchar 🎧 Indica si las frases que vas a escuchar son **ciertas** o **falsas**, según el dibujo. Después, corrige (*correct*) las frases falsas.

1. ___Cierta___
2. ___Falsa___ El hombre compra una naranja.
3. ___Cierta___
4. ___Falsa___ El pollo es una carne y la zanahoria es una verdura.
5. ___Cierta___
6. ___Falsa___ El hombre y la mujer no compran vinagre.
7. ___Falsa___ La naranja es una fruta.
8. ___Falsa___ La chuleta de cerdo es una carne.
9. ___Falsa___ El limón es una fruta y el jamón es una carne.
10. ___Cierta___

2 Identificar Identifica la palabra que no está relacionada con su grupo.

1. champiñón • cebolla • banana • zanahoria ___banana___
2. camarones • ajo • atún • salmón ___ajo___
3. aceite • leche • refresco • agua mineral ___aceite___
4. jamón • chuleta de cerdo • vinagre • carne de res ___vinagre___
5. cerveza • lechuga • arvejas • frijoles ___cerveza___
6. carne • pescado • mariscos • camarero ___camarero___
7. pollo • naranja • limón • melocotón ___pollo___
8. maíz • queso • tomate • champiñón ___queso___
9. rico • sabroso • menú • delicioso ___menú___
10. pescado • mariscos • salmón • bebida ___bebida___

3 Completar Completa las frases con las palabras más lógicas.

1. ¡Me gusta mucho este plato! Es ___b___.
   a. feo b. sabroso c. antipático
2. Camarero, ¿puedo ver el ___c___, por favor?
   a. aceite b. maíz c. menú
3. A Elena no le gusta la ___a___ pero le gusta mucho la fruta.
   a. carne b. uva c. naranja
4. Carlos y yo bebemos siempre agua ___b___.
   a. cómodo b. mineral c. principal
5. Antes de su plato principal, Maribel comió ___b___.
   a. cereales b. entremeses c. cerveza
6. El plato del día es ___a___.
   a. el pollo asado b. la mayonesa c. el ajo
7. Margarita es vegetariana. Ella come ___a___.
   a. frijoles b. chuletas c. jamón
8. Mi hermana le sirve ___c___ a su niña.
   a. ajo b. vinagre c. yogur

TEACHING OPTIONS

Game Play **Concentración**. On eight cards, write names of food items. On another eight cards, draw or paste a picture that matches each food item. Place the cards face-down in four rows of four. In pairs, students select two cards. If the two cards match, the pair keeps them. If the two cards do not match, students replace them in their original positions. The group with the most cards at the end wins.

Game Play a modified version of **20 Preguntas**. Ask a volunteer to think of a food item from the vocabulary drawing or list. Other students get one chance each to ask a yes-no question until someone guesses the item correctly. Limit attempts to ten questions per item. You may want to write some phrases on the board to cue students' questions. Ex: **¿Es una fruta? ¿Es roja?**

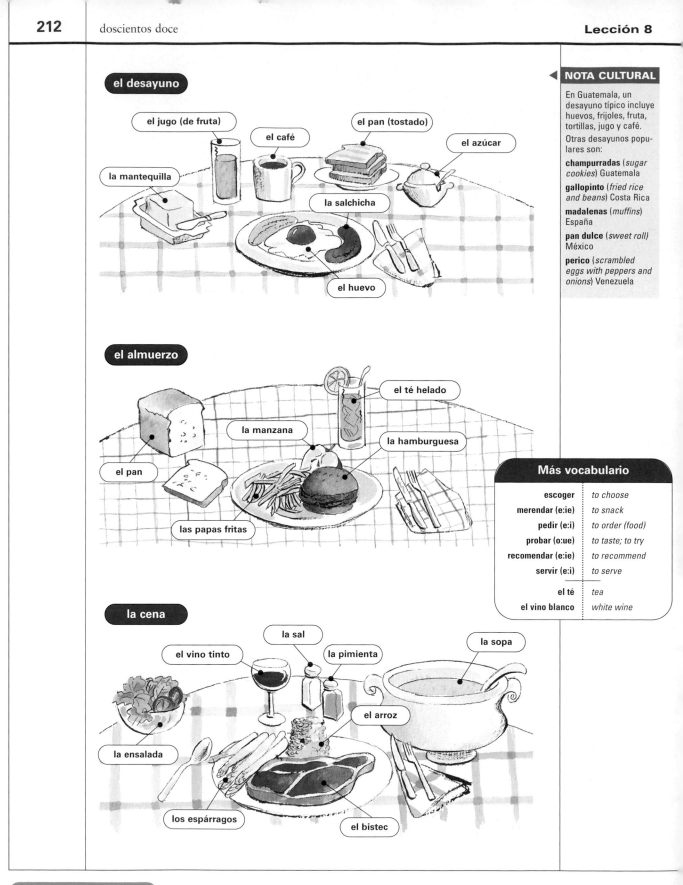

Más vocabulario

escoger	to choose
merendar (e:ie)	to snack
pedir (e:i)	to order (food)
probar (o:ue)	to taste; to try
recomendar (e:ie)	to recommend
servir (e:i)	to serve
el té	tea
el vino blanco	white wine

4

Completar Trabaja con un(a) compañero/a de clase para relacionar cada producto con el grupo alimenticio (*food group*) correcto.

modelo

<u>La carne</u> es del grupo uno.

el aceite	las bananas	los cereales	la leche
el arroz	el café	los espárragos	el pescado
el azúcar	la carne	los frijoles	el vino

1. <u>La leche</u> y el queso son del grupo cuatro.
2. <u>Los frijoles</u> son del grupo ocho.
3. <u>El pescado</u> y el pollo son del grupo tres.
4. <u>El aceite</u> es del grupo cinco.
5. <u>El azúcar</u> es del grupo dos.
6. Las manzanas y <u>las bananas</u> son del grupo siete.
7. <u>El café</u> es del grupo seis.
8. <u>Los cereales</u> son del grupo diez.
9. <u>Los espárragos</u> y los tomates son del grupo nueve.
10. El pan y <u>el arroz</u> son del grupo diez.

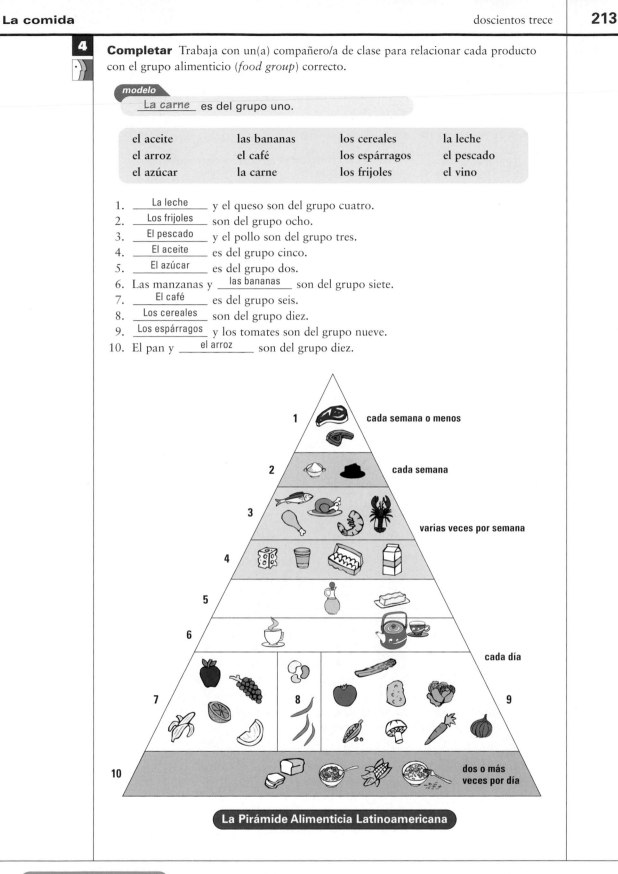

La Pirámide Alimenticia Latinoamericana

1 — cada semana o menos
2 — cada semana
3 — varias veces por semana
4
5
6 — cada día
7
8
9
10 — dos o más veces por día

4 Suggestion Ask students to compare foods at the base of the pyramid with those at the top. (The foods at the bottom of the pyramid are essential dietary requirements. As one moves closer to the top, the food items become less essential to daily requirements but help to balance out a diet.)

4 Expansion
- Ask additional questions about the **pirámide alimenticia.** Ask: **¿Qué se debe comer varias veces por semana? ¿Qué se debe comer todos los días? ¿Cuáles son los productos que aparecen en el grupo cuatro? ¿y en el grupo siete?** Get students to talk about what they eat. **¿Comen ustedes carne sólo una vez a la semana o menos? ¿Qué comidas comen ustedes dos o más veces al día? ¿Toman café todos los días?**
- Ask students if they know which food groups and food products comprise the food pyramid used in this country. If you can get a copy of one, bring it to class and compare similarities and differences between the dietary requirements among cultures.

TEACHING OPTIONS

Heritage Speakers Ask heritage speakers to talk about food items or dishes unique to their country of origin that are not typically found in this country. Have them describe what the item looks and tastes like. If the item is a dish, they should briefly describe how to prepare it if they know how to do so.

Extra Practice Have students draw food pyramids based not on what they should eat but on what they actually do eat as part of their diet. Encourage them to include drawings or magazine cutouts to enhance the visual presentation. Then have students present their pyramids to the class.

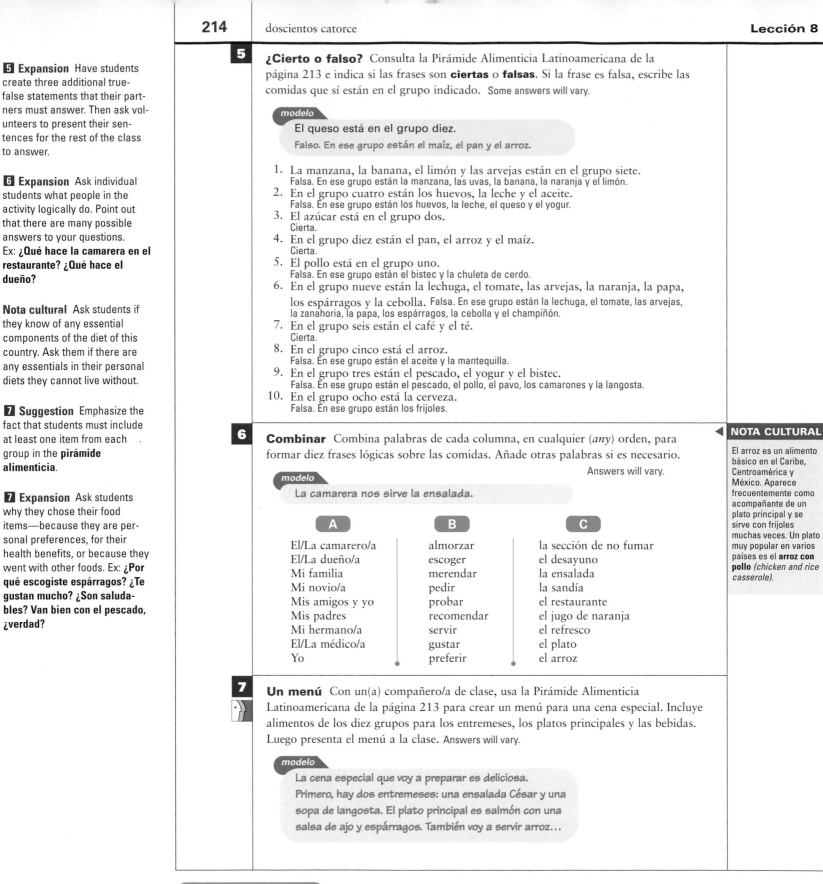

5 Expansion Have students create three additional true-false statements that their partners must answer. Then ask volunteers to present their sentences for the rest of the class to answer.

6 Expansion Ask individual students what people in the activity logically do. Point out that there are many possible answers to your questions. Ex: **¿Qué hace la camarera en el restaurante? ¿Qué hace el dueño?**

Nota cultural Ask students if they know of any essential components of the diet of this country. Ask them if there are any essentials in their personal diets they cannot live without.

7 Suggestion Emphasize the fact that students must include at least one item from each group in the **pirámide alimenticia**.

7 Expansion Ask students why they chose their food items—because they are personal preferences, for their health benefits, or because they went with other foods. Ex: **¿Por qué escogiste espárragos? ¿Te gustan mucho? ¿Son saludables? Van bien con el pescado, ¿verdad?**

5 **¿Cierto o falso?** Consulta la Pirámide Alimenticia Latinoamericana de la página 213 e indica si las frases son **ciertas** o **falsas**. Si la frase es falsa, escribe las comidas que sí están en el grupo indicado. Some answers will vary.

modelo
El queso está en el grupo diez.
Falso. En ese grupo están el maíz, el pan y el arroz.

1. La manzana, la banana, el limón y las arvejas están en el grupo siete.
   Falsa. En ese grupo están la manzana, las uvas, la banana, la naranja y el limón.
2. En el grupo cuatro están los huevos, la leche y el aceite.
   Falsa. En ese grupo están los huevos, la leche, el queso y el yogur.
3. El azúcar está en el grupo dos.
   Cierta.
4. En el grupo diez están el pan, el arroz y el maíz.
   Cierta.
5. El pollo está en el grupo uno.
   Falsa. En ese grupo están el bistec y la chuleta de cerdo.
6. En el grupo nueve están la lechuga, el tomate, las arvejas, la naranja, la papa,
   los espárragos y la cebolla. Falsa. En ese grupo están la lechuga, el tomate, las arvejas,
   la zanahoria, la papa, los espárragos, la cebolla y el champiñón.
7. En el grupo seis están el café y el té.
   Cierta.
8. En el grupo cinco está el arroz.
   Falsa. En ese grupo están el aceite y la mantequilla.
9. En el grupo tres están el pescado, el yogur y el bistec.
   Falsa. En ese grupo están el pescado, el pollo, el pavo, los camarones y la langosta.
10. En el grupo ocho está la cerveza.
    Falsa. En ese grupo están los frijoles.

6 **Combinar** Combina palabras de cada columna, en cualquier (*any*) orden, para formar diez frases lógicas sobre las comidas. Añade otras palabras si es necesario.

Answers will vary.

modelo
La camarera nos sirve la ensalada.

A	B	C
El/La camarero/a	almorzar	la sección de no fumar
El/La dueño/a	escoger	el desayuno
Mi familia	merendar	la ensalada
Mi novio/a	pedir	la sandía
Mis amigos y yo	probar	el restaurante
Mis padres	recomendar	el jugo de naranja
Mi hermano/a	servir	el refresco
El/La médico/a	gustar	el plato
Yo	preferir	el arroz

7 **Un menú** Con un(a) compañero/a de clase, usa la Pirámide Alimenticia Latinoamericana de la página 213 para crear un menú para una cena especial. Incluye alimentos de los diez grupos para los entremeses, los platos principales y las bebidas. Luego presenta el menú a la clase. Answers will vary.

modelo
La cena especial que voy a preparar es deliciosa.
Primero, hay dos entremeses: una ensalada César y una
sopa de langosta. El plato principal es salmón con una
salsa de ajo y espárragos. También voy a servir arroz...

NOTA CULTURAL

El arroz es un alimento básico en el Caribe, Centroamérica y México. Aparece frecuentemente como acompañante de un plato principal y se sirve con frijoles muchas veces. Un plato muy popular en varios países es el **arroz con pollo** *(chicken and rice casserole)*.

TEACHING OPTIONS

Extra Practice To review and practice the preterite along with food vocabulary, have students write a paragraph in which they describe what they ate up to this point today. Students should also indicate whether this meal or collection of meals represents a typical day for them. If not, they should explain why.

Small Groups In groups of two or three, students role-play a situation in a restaurant. One or two students play the customers and the other plays the **camarero/a**. Offer the following sentences on the board as suggested phrases: **¿Están listos para pedir?, ¿Qué nos recomienda usted?, ¿Me trae _____, por favor?, ¿Y para empezar?, A sus órdenes, La especialidad de la casa es _____.**

Comunicación

NATIONAL communication STANDARDS

8 **Conversación** En grupos, contesten las siguientes preguntas. Answers will vary.

1. ¿Meriendas mucho durante el día? ¿Qué comes? ¿A qué hora?
2. ¿Qué comidas te gustan más para la cena?
3. ¿A qué hora, dónde y con quién almuerzas?
4. ¿Cuáles son las comidas más (*most*) típicas de tu almuerzo?
5. ¿Desayunas? ¿Qué comes y bebes por la mañana?
6. ¿Qué comida deseas probar?
7. ¿Comes cada día comidas de los diferentes grupos de la pirámide alimenticia? ¿Cuáles son las comidas y bebidas más frecuentes en tu dieta?
8. ¿Qué comida recomiendas a tus amigos? ¿Por qué?
9. ¿Eres vegetariano/a? ¿Crees que ser vegetariano/a es una buena idea? ¿Por qué?
10. ¿Te gusta cocinar (*cook*)? ¿Qué comidas preparas para tus amigos? ¿Para tu familia?

¡LENGUA VIVA!

In addition to **beber**, the verb **tomar** is often used to express *to drink*.

9 **Describir** Con dos compañeros/as de clase, describe las dos fotos, contestando las siguientes preguntas. Answers will vary.

▶ ¿Quiénes están en las fotos?

▶ ¿Dónde están?

▶ ¿Qué hora es?

▶ ¿Qué comen y qué beben?

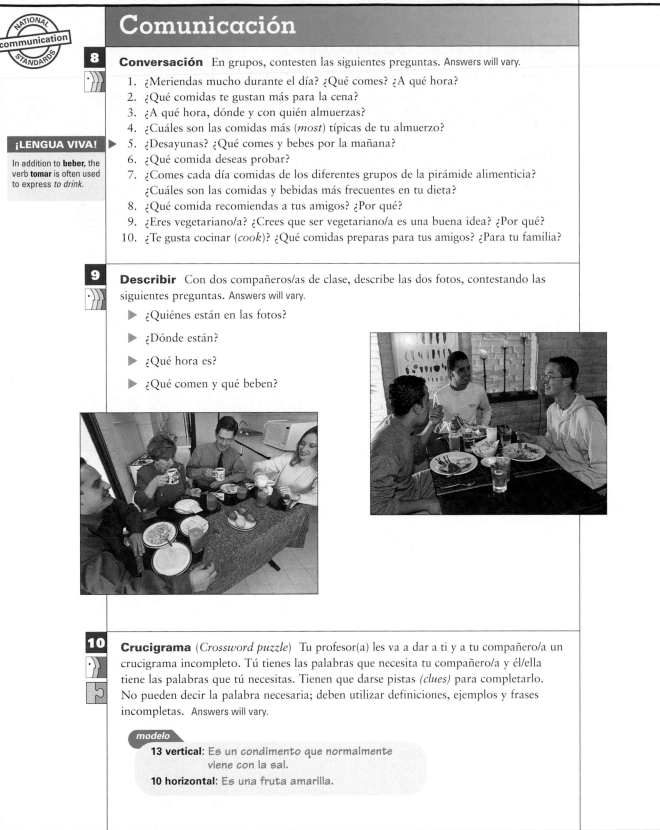

10 **Crucigrama** (*Crossword puzzle*) Tu profesor(a) les va a dar a ti y a tu compañero/a un crucigrama incompleto. Tú tienes las palabras que necesita tu compañero/a y él/ella tiene las palabras que tú necesitas. Tienen que darse pistas (*clues*) para completarlo. No pueden decir la palabra necesaria; deben utilizar definiciones, ejemplos y frases incompletas. Answers will vary.

> **modelo**
> **13 vertical:** Es un condimento que normalmente
> viene con la sal.
> **10 horizontal:** Es una fruta amarilla.

8 **Expansion** Ask the same questions of individual students. Ask other students to restate what their classmates answered.

¡Lengua viva! Explain that students already know several uses of **tomar (tomar clases, tomar fotos, tomar el sol)**. Explain that **tomar** with beverages is common in all Spanish-speaking countries. Ex: **¿Quieres tomar un café?**

9 **Expansion** Using magazine pictures that show people in eating situations, have students describe what is going on: who the people are, what they are eating and drinking, and so forth.

10 **Suggestion** Divide the class into pairs and distribute the handouts from the Information Gap Activities Booklet that correspond to this activity. Give students ten minutes to complete this activity.

10 **Expansion** Have groups create another type of word puzzle, such as a word-find, to share with the class. It should contain additional food- and meal-related vocabulary.

TEACHING OPTIONS

Small Groups In groups of two to four, students prepare brief skits that have something to do with food. The skits may involve being in a market, in a restaurant, in a café, inviting people over for dinner, and so forth. Videotape the skits and play them back for the class to select the most creative one.

Game Play a game of continuous narration. Student A begins with: **Voy a preparar** (*name of dish*) **y voy al mercado. Necesito comprar...** and names one food item. Student B then repeats the entire narration, adding another food item. Continue on through various students. When the possibilities for that particular dish are used up, have another student begin with another dish, repeating the process.

¿Qué tal la comida?

communication cultures — NATIONAL STANDARDS

Don Francisco y los estudiantes van al restaurante El Cráter.

PERSONAJES

MAITE

INÉS

DON FRANCISCO

ÁLEX

JAVIER

DOÑA RITA

CAMARERO

1

JAVIER ¿Sabes dónde estamos?

INÉS Mmm, no sé. Oiga, don Francisco, ¿sabe usted dónde estamos?

DON FRANCISCO Estamos cerca de Cotacachi.

2

ÁLEX ¿Dónde vamos a almorzar, don Francisco? ¿Conoce un buen restaurante en Cotacachi?

DON FRANCISCO Pues, conozco a doña Rita Perales, la dueña del mejor restaurante de la ciudad, el restaurante El Cráter.

3

DOÑA RITA Hombre, don Paco, ¿Usted por aquí?

DON FRANCISCO Sí, doña Rita... y hoy le traigo clientes. Le presento a Maite, Inés, Álex y Javier. Los llevo a las montañas para ir de excursión.

6

MAITE Voy a tomar un caldo de patas y un lomo a la plancha.

JAVIER Para mí las tortillas de maíz y el ceviche de camarón.

ÁLEX Yo también quisiera las tortillas de maíz y el ceviche.

INÉS Voy a pedir caldo de patas y lomo a la plancha.

7

DON FRANCISCO Yo quiero tortillas de maíz y una fuente de fritada, por favor.

DOÑA RITA Y de tomar, les recomiendo el jugo de piña, frutilla y mora. ¿Se lo traigo a todos?

TODOS Sí, perfecto.

8

CAMARERO ¿Qué plato pidió usted?

MAITE Un caldo de patas y lomo a la plancha.

recursos

V CD-ROM Lección 8	VM pp. 209–210	I CD-ROM Lección 8

DOÑA RITA ¡Bienvenidos al restaurante El Cráter! Están en muy buenas manos... don Francisco es el mejor conductor del país. Y no hay nada más bonito que nuestras montañas. Pero si van a ir de excursión deben comer bien. Vengan chicos, por aquí.

JAVIER ¿Qué nos recomienda Ud.?

DOÑA RITA Bueno, las tortillas de maíz son riquísimas. La especialidad de la casa es el caldo de patas... ¡tienen que probarlo! El lomo a la plancha es un poquito más caro que el caldo pero es sabrosísimo. También les recomiendo el ceviche y la fuente de fritada.

DOÑA RITA ¿Qué tal la comida? ¿Rica?

JAVIER Rica, no. ¡Riquísima!

ÁLEX Sí. ¡Y nos la sirvieron tan rápidamente!

MAITE Una comida deliciosa, gracias.

DON FRANCISCO Hoy es el cumpleaños de Maite...

DOÑA RITA ¡Ah! Tenemos unos pasteles que están como para chuparse los dedos...

Enfoque cultural La comida hispana

La cocina (*cuisine*) hispana es una combinación de comidas e ingredientes de varias regiones. La carne de res, la papa, el maíz y el chile, por ejemplo, son característicos de los países andinos. Los frijoles, el arroz, la caña de azúcar y la banana son productos típicos de los países del Caribe. La cocina española incorpora pescados y carnes cocinados (*cooked*) con condimentos como el ajo y la cebolla. La comida típica de Centroamérica es similar a la mexicana y consta de (*consists of*) carne, pescados, chile, tortillas y salsas.

Expresiones útiles

Finding out where you are
▶ **¿Sabe Ud./Sabes dónde estamos?**
Do you know where we are?
▷ **Estamos cerca de Cotacachi.**
We're near Cotacachi.

Talking about people and places you're familiar with
▶ **¿Conoce usted/Conoces un buen restaurante en Cotacachi?**
Do you know a good restaurant in Cotacachi?
▷ **Sí, conozco varios.**
Yes, I know several.
▶ **¿Conoce/Conoces a doña Rita?**
Do you know doña Rita?

Ordering food
▶ **¿Qué le puedo traer?**
What can I bring you?
▷ **Voy a tomar/pedir un caldo de patas y un lomo a la plancha.**
I am going to have/to order the beef soup and grilled flank steak.
▷ **Para mí las tortillas de maíz y el ceviche de camarón, por favor.**
Corn tortillas and lemon-marinated shrimp for me, please.
▷ **Yo también quisiera...**
I also would like...
▷ **Y de tomar, el jugo de piña, frutilla y mora.**
And pineapple/strawberry/blackberry juice to drink.
▶ **¿Qué plato pidió usted?**
What did you order?
▷ **Yo pedí un caldo de patas.**
I ordered the beef soup.

Talking about the food at a restaurant
▶ **¿Qué tal la comida?**
How is the food?
▷ **Muy rica, gracias.**
Very tasty, thanks.
▷ **¡Riquísima!**
Extremely delicious!

Suggestion Have the class read through the entire **Fotonovela**, with volunteers playing the parts of Don Francisco, Javier, Inés, Álex, Maite, Doña Rita, and the **Camarero**. Have students take turns playing the roles so that more students participate.

Expresiones útiles Point out some of the unfamiliar structures, which will be taught in detail in **Estructura**. Draw attention to the verb **pidió**. Explain that this is a form of the verb **pedir**, which has a stem change in the **Ud./él/ella** and **Uds./ellos/ellas** forms of the preterite. Have the class read the caption for video still 5, and explain that **más caro que** is an example of a comparison. Point out that in caption 9, **nos la** is an example of an indirect object pronoun and a direct object pronoun used together. Tell your students that they will learn more about these concepts in **Estructura**.

TEACHING OPTIONS

Enfoque cultural Point out that meal times in Spanish-speaking countries differ from country to country. Breakfast (**el desayuno**) is often eaten between the hours of 7 and 9 in the morning, while lunch (**el almuerzo**) is usually eaten around 2 or 3 p.m. Late in the afternoon, some families have a snack (**merienda**) to tide them over until the last meal of the day (**la cena**), which is typically not very large and is served between 8 and 11 in the evening. Your students might also be interested to know that it is customary for family members to remain at the dinner table after the meal is over for an after-meal chat, **la sobremesa**. Tell students that in Spanish-speaking countries it is not common for people to eat their meals on the run and separately from other members of the family.

1 Suggestion Ask your students these questions before having them complete this activity: **¿Qué es El Cráter? ¿Quién es doña Rita? ¿Cuáles son algunas de las comidas del menú?**

2 Suggestion Have your students close their books. Then read each item aloud and have the class guess who would have made each statement.

2 Expansion Present these items as 7-9: **7. Les van a gustar muchísimo nuestras montañas. (doña Rita) 8. ¿Les gustó la comida? (doña Rita) 9. Para mí, las tortillas de maíz y la fuente de fritada. (don Francisco)**

3 Suggestion Change the questions' focus by rephrasing them. Ex: **¿Qué es El Cráter? (Es el restaurante donde comieron don Francisco y los estudiantes.)**

4 Possible Responses
Conversation 1:
E1: Oye, María, ¿conoces un buen restaurante en esta ciudad?
E2: Sí... el restaurante El Pescador sirve comida sabrosísima.
E1: ¿Por qué no vamos a El Pescador esta noche?
E2: ¿A qué hora?
E1: ¿A las ocho?
E2: Perfecto.
E1: Está bien. Nos vemos a las ocho.
E2: Adiós.
Conversation 2:
E1: ¿Qué le puedo traer?
E2: Bueno, ¿cuáles son las especialidades de la casa?
E1: La especialidad de la casa es el lomo a la plancha. También, le recomiendo el caldo de patas.
E2: Mmm... voy a pedir los camarones y el lomo a la plancha. De tomar, voy a pedir el jugo de piña.
E1: Gracias, señor.

Reacciona a la fotonovela

1

Escoger Escoge la respuesta (*answer*) que completa mejor (*best*) cada oración.

1. Don Francisco lleva a los estudiantes a ___c___ al restaurante de una amiga.
   a. cenar   b. desayunar   c. almorzar
2. Doña Rita es ___b___.
   a. la hermana de don Francisco   b. la dueña del restaurante
   c. una camarera que trabaja en El Cráter
3. Doña Rita les recomienda a los viajeros ___a___.
   a. el caldo de patas y el lomo a la plancha
   b. el bistec, las verduras frescas y el vino tinto   c. unos pasteles (*cakes*)
4. Inés va a pedir ___c___.
   a. las tortillas de maíz y una fuente de fritada (*mixed grill*)
   b. el ceviche de camarón y el caldo de patas
   c. el caldo de patas y el lomo a la plancha

▶ **NOTA CULTURAL**

El **ceviche** es un plato típico de Suramérica. Se prepara con jugo de limón, cebolla, chiles y pescado crudo (*raw*) o mariscos.

2

Identificar Indica quién puede decir las siguientes frases.

1. No me gusta esperar en los restaurantes. ¡Qué bueno que nos sirvieron rápidamente! Álex
2. Les recomiendo la especialidad de la casa. doña Rita
3. ¡Maite y yo pedimos los mismos platos! Inés
4. Disculpe, señora... ¿qué platos recomienda usted? Javier
5. Yo conozco a una señora que tiene un restaurante excelente. Les va a gustar mucho. don Francisco
6. Hoy es mi cumpleaños (*birthday*). Maite

ÁLEX   INÉS   DOÑA RITA   MAITE   DON FRANCISCO   JAVIER

3

Preguntas Contesta las siguientes preguntas sobre la **Fotonovela**.

1. ¿Dónde comieron don Francisco y los estudiantes?
   Comieron en el restaurante de doña Rita/El Cráter.
2. ¿Cuál es la especialidad de El Cráter?
   La especialidad de la casa es el caldo de patas.
3. ¿Qué pidió Javier? ¿Y Álex? ¿Qué tomaron todos? Javier pidió tortillas de maíz y el ceviche. Álex también pidió las tortillas de maíz y el ceviche. Todos tomaron jugo.
4. ¿Qué tal los pasteles en El Cráter?
   Los pasteles en El Cráter son sabrosísimos.

4

En el restaurante Answers will vary.

1. Prepara con un(a) compañero/a una conversación en la que le preguntas si conoce algún buen restaurante en tu comunidad. Tu compañero/a responde que él/ella sí conoce un restaurante que sirve una comida deliciosa. Lo/La invitas a cenar y tu compañero/a acepta. Determinan la hora para verse en el restaurante y se despiden.
2. Trabaja con un(a) compañero/a para representar los papeles (*roles*) de un(a) cliente/a y un(a) camarero/a en un restaurante. El/La camarero/a te pregunta qué te puede servir y tú preguntas cuál es la especialidad de la casa. El/La camarero/a te dice cuál es la especialidad y te recomienda algunos platos del menú. Tú pides entremeses, un plato principal y escoges una bebida. El/La camarero/a te da las gracias y luego te sirve la comida.

◀ **CONSÚLTALO**

To review indefinite words like **algún**, see **Estructura 7.2**, p. 194.

NATIONAL communication STANDARDS

TEACHING OPTIONS

Extra Practice Ask your students these questions about the **Fotonovela**. Ex: **1. ¿En qué ciudad está el restaurante El Cráter? (Cotacachi) 2. ¿Qué pidió Javier en el restaurante? (tortillas de maíz, ceviche de camarón) 3. ¿Qué pidió don Francisco? (tortillas de maíz, fuente de fritada) 4. ¿Cuándo es el cumpleaños de Maite? (hoy)**

Small Groups Have your students work in groups to prepare a skit in which a family goes to a restaurant, is seated by a waitperson, examines the menu, and orders dinner. Each family member should ask a few questions about the menu and then order an entrée and a drink. Have one or two groups perform the skit in front of the class.

Pronunciación

ll, ñ, c, and z

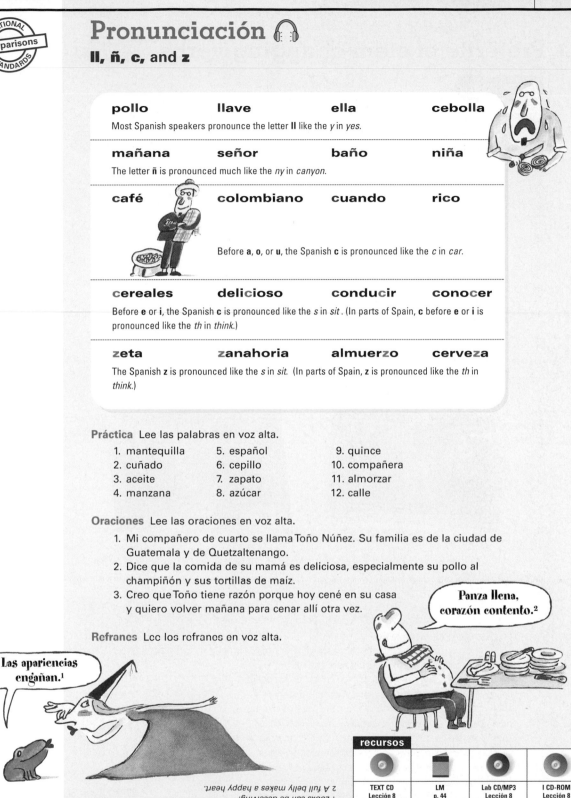

pollo	llave	ella	cebolla

Most Spanish speakers pronounce the letter **ll** like the *y* in *yes*.

mañana	señor	baño	niña

The letter **ñ** is pronounced much like the *ny* in *canyon*.

café	colombiano	cuando	rico

Before **a**, **o**, or **u**, the Spanish **c** is pronounced like the *c* in *car*.

cereales	delicioso	conducir	conocer

Before **e** or **i**, the Spanish **c** is pronounced like the *s* in *sit*. (In parts of Spain, **c** before **e** or **i** is pronounced like the *th* in *think*.)

zeta	zanahoria	almuerzo	cerveza

The Spanish **z** is pronounced like the *s* in *sit*. (In parts of Spain, **z** is pronounced like the *th* in *think*.)

Práctica Lee las palabras en voz alta.

1. mantequilla
2. cuñado
3. aceite
4. manzana
5. español
6. cepillo
7. zapato
8. azúcar
9. quince
10. compañera
11. almorzar
12. calle

Oraciones Lee las oraciones en voz alta.

1. Mi compañero de cuarto se llama Toño Núñez. Su familia es de la ciudad de Guatemala y de Quetzaltenango.
2. Dice que la comida de su mamá es deliciosa, especialmente su pollo al champiñón y sus tortillas de maíz.
3. Creo que Toño tiene razón porque hoy cené en su casa y quiero volver mañana para cenar allí otra vez.

Refranes Lee los refranes en voz alta.

Las apariencias engañan.[1]

Panza llena, corazón contento.[2]

1 Looks can be deceiving.
2 A full belly makes a happy heart.

recursos

TEXT CD Lección 8	LM p. 44	Lab CD/MP3 Lección 8	I CD-ROM Lección 8

Section Goal

In **Pronunciación** students will be introduced to the pronunciation of the letters **ll**, **ñ**, **c**, and **z**.

Instructional Resources

Textbook Activities CD
Lab Manual, p. 44
Lab CD/MP3 **Lección 8**
IRM: Tapescript, pp. 35–39; p. 78
Interactive CD-ROM

Suggestions

- Point out that the Spanish letter **ll** is usually pronounced like the English *y* in *you*.
- Ask the class how the letter **ñ** is pronounced (like the *ny* in *canyon*).
- Tell the class that **c** is pronounced like the English *c* in *car* before **a**, **o**, or **u**.
- Ask the class how most Spanish speakers pronounce the letter **c** when it appears before **e** or **i** (like the English *s* in *some*). Then point out that **c** before **e** or **i** is pronounced like the English *th* in *think* in some parts of Spain.
- Explain that the Spanish **z** is usually pronounced like the English *s* in *some*. Mention that in parts of Spain, **z** is pronounced like the English *th* in *think*.
- As you explain the pronunciation of these sounds, write a few of the example words on the board and have students pronounce them.

Práctica/Oraciones/Refranes

These exercises are recorded on the Textbook Activities CD. You may want to play the CD so students practice the pronunciation point by listening to Spanish spoken by speakers other than yourself.

TEACHING OPTIONS

Extra Practice Write the names of a few distinguished Guatemalans on the board and ask for a volunteer to pronounce each one. Ex: **Luis Cardoza y Aragón** (writer), **Carlos Mérida** (painter), **Enrique Gómez Carrillo** (writer), **José Milla** (writer), **Alonso de la Paz** (sculptor). Repeat the process with a few city names: **Villanueva**, **Zacapa**, **Escuintla**, **Cobán**.

Pairs Have the class work in pairs to practice the pronunciation of the sentences given in **Actividad 2** (**Identificar**) on page 218. Encourage your students to help their partner if they have trouble pronouncing a particular word. Circulate around the class and model correct pronunciation as needed, focusing on the letters **ll**, **ñ**, **c**, and **z**.

8.1 Preterite of stem-changing verbs

ANTE TODO As you learned in **Lección 6**, **–ar** and **–er** stem-changing verbs have no stem change in the preterite. **–Ir** stem-changing verbs, however, do have a stem change. Study the following charts and observe where the stem changes occur.

Preterite of *–ir* stem-changing verbs

		servir (to serve)	**dormir** (to sleep)
SINGULAR FORMS	yo	serví	dormí
	tú	serviste	dormiste
	Ud./él/ella	si**rv**ió	d**u**rmió
PLURAL FORMS	nosotros/as	servimos	dormimos
	vosotros/as	servisteis	dormisteis
	Uds./ellos/ellas	si**rv**ieron	d**u**rmieron

▶ Stem-changing **–ir** verbs, in the preterite only, have a stem change in the **Ud./él/ella** and **Uds./ellos/ellas** forms. The stem change consists of either **e** to **i** or **o** to **u**.

(e → i) pedir: p**i**dió, p**i**dieron   (o → u) morir (*to die*): m**u**rió, m**u**rieron

Perdón, ¿quiénes pidieron las tortillas de maíz?

¿Y qué plato pidió usted?

recursos

WB
pp. 87–94

LM
pp. 45–48

Lab CD/MP3
Lección 8

I CD-ROM
Lección 8

vistahigher learning.com

¡INTÉNTALO! Cambia los infinitivos al pretérito.

1. Yo _____serví_____. (servir, dormir, pedir, preferir, repetir, seguir)
   dormí, pedí, preferí, repetí, seguí
2. Usted _____. (morir, conseguir, pedir, sentirse, despedirse, vestirse)
   murió, consiguió, pidió, se sintió, se despidió, se vistió
3. Tú _____. (conseguir, servir, morir, pedir, dormir, repetir)
   conseguiste, serviste, moriste, pediste, dormiste, repetiste
4. Ellas _____. (repetir, dormir, seguir, preferir, morir, servir)
   repitieron, durmieron, siguieron, prefirieron, murieron, sirvieron
5. Nosotros _____. (seguir, preferir, servir, vestirse, despedirse, dormirse)
   seguimos, preferimos, servimos, nos vestimos, nos despedimos, nos dormimos
6. Ustedes _____. (sentirse, vestirse, conseguir, pedir, despedirse, dormirse)
   se sintieron, se vistieron, consiguieron, pidieron, se despidieron, se durmieron
7. Él _____. (dormir, morir, preferir, repetir, seguir, pedir)
   durmió, murió, prefirió, repitió, siguió, pidió

Práctica

NOTA CULTURAL

El horario de las comidas en España es muy distinto al de los EE.UU. El desayuno es muy ligero (*light*). La hora de la comida, o el almuerzo, es entre las 2 y las 3 de la tarde. Es la comida más importante del día. Mucha gente come una merienda o tapas por la tarde. La cena, normalmente ligera, suele ser entre las 9 y 11 de la noche.

1 Completar Completa las siguientes frases para describir lo que pasó anoche en el restaurante El Famoso.

1. Paula y Humberto Suárez llegaron al restaurante El Famoso a las ocho y ___siguieron___ (seguir) al camarero a una mesa en la sección de no fumar.
2. El señor Suárez ___pidió___ (pedir) una chuleta de cerdo. La señora Suárez decidió probar los camarones.
3. Para tomar, los dos ___pidieron___ (pedir) vino tinto.
4. El camarero ___repitió___ (repetir) el pedido (*the order*) para confirmarlo.
5. La comida tardó mucho (*took a long time*) en llegar y los señores Suárez ___se durmieron___ (dormirse) esperando la comida.
6. A las nueve el camarero les ___sirvió___ (servir) la comida.
7. Después de comer la chuleta de cerdo, el señor Suárez ___se sintió___ (sentirse) muy mal.
8. De repente, el señor Suárez se ___murió___ (morir).
9. Pobre señor Suárez... ¿por qué no ___pidió___ (pedir) los camarones?

2 El camarero loco En el restaurante La Hermosa trabaja un camarero muy loco que siempre comete muchos errores. Indica lo que los clientes pidieron y lo que el camarero les sirvió.

> **modelo**
> Armando / papas fritas
> Armando pidió papas fritas, pero el camarero le sirvió maíz.

1. Nosotros / jugo de naranja Nosotros pedimos jugo de naranja, pero el camarero nos sirvió papas.
2. Beatriz / queso Beatriz pidió queso, pero el camarero le sirvió uvas.
3. Tú / arroz Tú pediste arroz, pero el camarero te sirvió arvejas/sopa.
4. Elena y Alejandro /atún Elena y Alejandro pidieron atún, pero el camarero les sirvió camarones (mariscos).
5. Usted / agua mineral Usted pidió agua mineral, pero el camarero le sirvió vino tinto.
6. Yo / hamburguesa Yo pedí una hamburguesa, pero el camarero me sirvió zanahorias.

1 Expansion Ask students to work in pairs to come up with an alternate ending to the narration, using stem-changing –ir verbs in the preterite. Pairs then share their endings with the class. The class can vote on the most original ending.

2 Expansion In pairs, students redo the activity, this time role-playing the customer and the waiter. Model the possible interaction between the students. Ex: **E1: Perdón, pero pedí papas fritas y usted me sirvió maíz. E2: ¡Ay perdón! Le traigo papas fritas enseguida.** Students take turns playing the role of the customer and waiter.

TEACHING OPTIONS

Video Show the **Fotonovela** video again to give students more input with stem-changing –ir verbs in the preterite. Have them write down all the stem-changing forms they hear. Stop the video where appropriate to discuss how certain verbs were used and to ask comprehension questions. Ex: **¿Qué pidió Maite? ¿Cómo sirvieron la comida?**

Extra Practice Prepare descriptions of five easily recognizable people in which you use the stem-changing forms of –ir verbs in the preterite. Write their names on the board in random order. Then read your descriptions, having students match the description to the appropriate name. Ex: **Murió en un accidente de avión en 1999.** (John F. Kennedy, Jr.)

Comunicación

3

El almuerzo Completa las oraciones de César de una manera lógica. Answers will vary.

> **modelo**
>
> Mi compañero de cuarto se despertó temprano, pero yo...
> *Mi compañero de cuarto se despertó temprano, pero yo me desperté tarde.*

1. Yo llegué al restaurante a tiempo, pero mis amigos...
2. Beatriz pidió la ensalada de frutas, pero yo...
3. Yolanda les recomendó el bistec, pero Eva y Paco...
4. Nosotros preferimos las papas fritas, pero Yolanda...
5. El camarero sirvió la carne, pero yo...
6. Beatriz y yo pedimos café, pero Yolanda y Paco...
7. Eva se sintió enferma, pero Paco y yo...
8. Nosotros repetimos el postre, pero Eva...
9. Ellos salieron tarde, pero yo...
10. Yo me dormí temprano, pero mi compañero de cuarto...

4

Entrevista Trabajen en parejas y túrnense para entrevistar a su compañero/a. Answers will vary.

1. ¿Te acostaste tarde o temprano anoche? ¿A qué hora te dormiste? ¿Dormiste bien?
2. ¿A qué hora te despertaste esta mañana? Y ¿a qué hora te levantaste?
3. ¿A qué hora vas a acostarte esta noche?
4. ¿Qué almorzaste ayer? ¿Quién te sirvió el almuerzo?
5. ¿Qué cenaste ayer?
6. ¿Cenaste en un restaurante recientemente? ¿Con quién?
7. ¿Qué pediste en el restaurante? ¿Qué pidieron los demás?
8. ¿Se durmió alguien en alguna de tus clases la semana pasada? ¿En qué clase?

Síntesis

5

Describir En grupos, estudien la foto y las preguntas que siguen. Luego, describan la cena romántica de Eduardo y Rosa. Answers will vary.

▶ ¿Adónde salieron a cenar?

▶ ¿Qué pidieron?

▶ ¿Les sirvieron la comida rápidamente?

▶ ¿Les gustó la comida?

▶ ¿Cuánto costó?

▶ ¿Van a volver a este restaurante en el futuro?

▶ ¿Recomiendas el restaurante?

NATIONAL communication STANDARDS

NATIONAL communication STANDARDS

8.2 Double object pronouns

ANTE TODO In **Lecciones 5** and **6**, you learned that direct and indirect object pronouns replace nouns and that they often refer to nouns that have already been referenced. You will now learn how to use direct and indirect object pronouns together. Observe the following diagram.

Indirect Object Pronouns			Direct Object Pronouns	
me	nos		lo	los
te	os	**+**	la	las
le (se)	les (se)			

▶ When direct and indirect object pronouns are used together, the indirect object pronoun always precedes the direct object pronoun.

    I.O.   D.O.

El camarero **me** muestra **el menú**.
The waiter shows me the menu.

⟶   **DOUBLE OBJECT PRONOUNS**
El camarero **me lo** muestra.
The waiter shows it to me.

    I.O.   D.O.

Nos sirven **los platos**.
They serve us the dishes.

⟶   **DOUBLE OBJECT PRONOUNS**
Nos los sirven.
They serve them to us.

    I.O.   D.O.

Maribel **te** pidió **una hamburguesa**.
Maribel ordered a hamburger for you.

⟶   **DOUBLE OBJECT PRONOUNS**
Maribel **te la** pidió.
Maribel ordered it for you.

Y de tomar, les recomiendo el jugo de piña... ¿Se lo traigo a todos?

Sí, perfecto.

▶ In Spanish, two pronouns that begin with the letter **l** cannot be used together. Therefore, the indirect object pronouns **le** and **les** always change to **se** when they are used with **lo, los, la,** and **las.**

    I.O.   D.O.

Le escribí **la carta**.
I wrote him the letter.

⟶   **DOUBLE OBJECT PRONOUNS**
Se la escribí.
I wrote it to him.

    I.O.   D.O.

Les sirvió **los entremeses**.
He served them the hors d'oeuvres.

⟶   **DOUBLE OBJECT PRONOUNS**
Se los sirvió.
He served them to them.

Extra Practice Write six sentences on the board for students to express using double object pronouns. Ex: **Rita les sirvió la cena a los viajeros. (Rita se la sirvió.)**
Pairs In pairs, students write five sentences that contain both direct and indirect objects (not pronouns). Their partners must express the sentences using double object pronouns.

Video Show the **Fotonovela** video again to give students more input containing double object pronouns. Stop the video where appropriate to discuss how double object pronouns were used and to ask comprehension questions.

Section Goals

In **Estructura 8.2** students will be introduced to:
• the use of double object pronouns
• converting **le** and **les** into **se** when used with direct object pronouns **lo, la, los** and **las**

Instructional Resources
WB/VM: Workbook, pp. 89–90
Lab Manual, p. 46
*Lab CD/MP3 **Lección 8***
IRM: ¡Inténtalo! & Práctica
Answers, pp. 184–185;
Tapescript, pp. 35–39
Info Gap Activities Booklet,
pp. 31–32
Interactive CD-ROM
Companion website:
www.vistahigherlearning.com
Presentations CD-ROM

Suggestions
• Briefly review direct object pronouns (**Estructura 5.4**) and indirect object pronouns (**Estructura 6.2**). Give sentences and have students convert objects into object pronouns. Ex: **Sara escribió la carta. (Sara la escribió.) Mis padres escribieron una carta. (yo) (Mis padres me escribieron una carta.)**
• Model additional examples for the students, asking them to make the conversion with **se**. Ex: **Le pedí papas fritas. (Se las pedí.) Les servimos café. (Se lo servimos.)**

▶ Because **se** has multiple meanings, Spanish speakers often clarify to whom the pronoun refers by adding **a usted, a él, a ella, a ustedes, a ellos,** or **a ellas.**

¿El sombrero? Carlos **se** lo vendió **a ella.**
The hat? Carlos sold it to her.

¿Las verduras? Ellos **se** las compran a **usted.**
The vegetables? They buy them for you.

▶ Double object pronouns are placed before a conjugated verb. With infinitives and present participles, they may be placed before the conjugated verb or attached to the end of the infinitive or present participle.

DOUBLE OBJECT PRONOUNS
Te   lo   voy a mostrar.

DOUBLE OBJECT PRONOUNS
Voy a mostrár**telo**.

DOUBLE OBJECT PRONOUNS
Nos las están sirviendo.

DOUBLE OBJECT PRONOUNS
Están sirviéndo**noslas**.

▶ As you can see above, when double object pronouns are attached to an infinitive or a present participle, an accent mark is added to maintain the original stress.

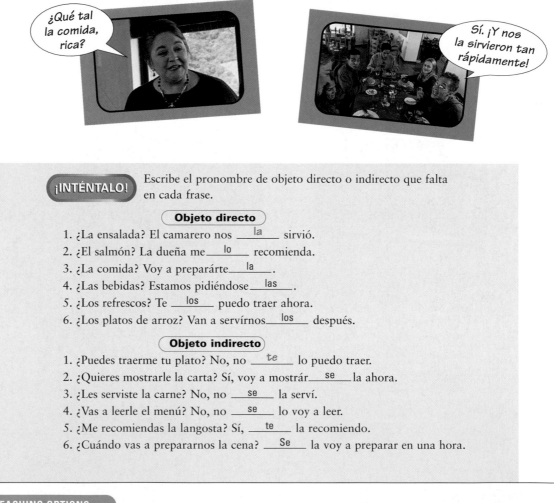

¿Qué tal la comida, rica?

Sí. ¡Y nos la sirvieron tan rápidamente!

¡INTÉNTALO! Escribe el pronombre de objeto directo o indirecto que falta en cada frase.

Objeto directo

1. ¿La ensalada? El camarero nos ___la___ sirvió.
2. ¿El salmón? La dueña me___lo___ recomienda.
3. ¿La comida? Voy a preparárte___la___.
4. ¿Las bebidas? Estamos pidiéndose___las___.
5. ¿Los refrescos? Te ___los___ puedo traer ahora.
6. ¿Los platos de arroz? Van a servírnos___los___ después.

Objeto indirecto

1. ¿Puedes traerme tu plato? No, no ___te___ lo puedo traer.
2. ¿Quieres mostrarle la carta? Sí, voy a mostrár___se___la ahora.
3. ¿Les serviste la carne? No, no ___se___ la serví.
4. ¿Vas a leerle el menú? No, no ___se___ lo voy a leer.
5. ¿Me recomiendas la langosta? Sí, ___te___ la recomiendo.
6. ¿Cuándo vas a prepararnos la cena? ___Se___ la voy a preparar en una hora.

Práctica

1 **Responder** Imagínate que trabajas de camarero/a en un restaurante. Responde a las
▶ órdenes de estos clientes usando pronombres.

modelo

Sra. Gómez: Una ensalada, por favor.
Sí, señora. Enseguida (Right away) se la traigo.

1. Sr. López: La mantequilla, por favor. Sí, señor. Enseguida se la traigo.
2. Srta. Rivas: Los camarones, por favor. Sí, señorita. Enseguida se los traigo.
3. Sra. Lugones: El pollo asado, por favor. Sí, señora. Enseguida se lo traigo.
4. Tus compañeros/as de cuarto: Café, por favor. Sí, chicos. Enseguida se lo traigo.
5. Tu profesor(a) de español: Papas fritas, por favor. Sí, profesor(a). Enseguida se las traigo.
6. Dra. González: La chuleta de cerdo, por favor. Sí, doctora. Enseguida se la traigo.
7. Tus padres: Los champiñones, por favor. Sí, señores. Enseguida se los traigo.
8. Dr. Torres: La cuenta (*check*), por favor. Sí, doctor. Enseguida se la traigo.

2 **¿Quién?** La señora Cevallos está planeando una cena. Se pregunta cómo va a resolver
ciertas situaciones. En parejas, túrnense (*take turns*) para decir lo que ella está pensando.
Cambien los sustantivos (*nouns*) subrayados por pronombres de objeto directo y hagan
(*make*) los otros cambios necesarios.

modelo

¡No tengo carne! ¿Quién va a traerme la <u>carne</u> del
supermercado? (Mi esposo)
Mi esposo va a traérmela./Mi esposo me la va a traer.

1. ¡Las invitaciones! ¿Quién les manda <u>las invitaciones</u> a los invitados (*guests*)?
(Mi hija) Mi hija se las manda.
2. No tengo tiempo de ir a la bodega. ¿Quién me puede comprar <u>el vino</u>?
(Mi hijo) Mi hijo puede comprármelo./Mi hijo me lo puede comprar.
3. ¡Ay! No tengo suficientes platos. ¿Quién puede prestarme <u>los platos</u> que necesito?
(Mi mamá) Mi mamá puede prestármelos./Mi mamá me los puede prestar.
4. Nos falta mantequilla. ¿Quién nos trae <u>la mantequilla</u>?
(Mi cuñada) Mi cuñada nos la trae.
5. ¡Los postres (*desserts*)! ¿Quién está preparándonos <u>los postres</u>?
(Silvia y Renata) Silvia y Renata están preparándonoslos./Silvia y Renata nos los están preparando.
6. No hay suficientes sillas. ¿Quiénes nos traen <u>las sillas</u> que faltan?
(Héctor y Lorena) Héctor y Lorena nos las traen.
7. No tengo tiempo de pedirle el azúcar a Mónica. ¿Quién puede pedirle <u>el azúcar</u>?
(Mi hijo) Mi hijo puede pedírselo./Mi hijo se lo puede pedir.
8. ¿Quién va a servirles <u>la cena</u> a los invitados? (Mis hijos)
Mis hijos van a servírsela./Mis hijos se la van a servir.

AYUDA

Here are some other useful expressions:
ahora mismo *right now*
inmediatamente *immediately*
¡A la orden! *At your service!*
¡Ya voy! *I'm on my way!*

NOTA CULTURAL

Los vinos de Chile son conocidos internacionalmente. **Concha y Toro** es el productor y exportador más grande de vinos de Chile. Las zonas más productivas de vino están al norte de Santiago, en el Valle Central.

1 Expansion Do the activity with the whole class, selecting a student to play the role of customer and another to play the role of waiter for each item.

Ayuda Model the helpful phrases in sentences. Point out that **ahora mismo, inmediatamente,** and **ya** can replace **enseguida** in the **modelo** for **Actividad 1**.

2 Expansion
• Change the subjects in parentheses for students to use different forms of the verbs.
• Use magazine pictures and ask students who is doing what to or for whom in the pictures. Ex: **La señora les muestra la casa a los jóvenes. Se la muestra a los jóvenes.**

TEACHING OPTIONS

Heritage Speakers Ask heritage speakers to talk about a favorite gift they received. Write **regalar** on the board and explain that it means *to give (a gift)*. Students should talk about what they received, who gave it to them (**regalar**), and why. Ask the rest of the class comprehension questions.

Game Play **Concentración**. Write sentences that use double object pronouns on each of eight cards. On another eight cards, draw or paste a picture that matches each sentence. Place the cards face-down in four rows of four. In pairs, students select two cards. If the two cards match, the pair keeps them. If they do not match, students replace them in their original position. The pair with the most cards at the end wins.

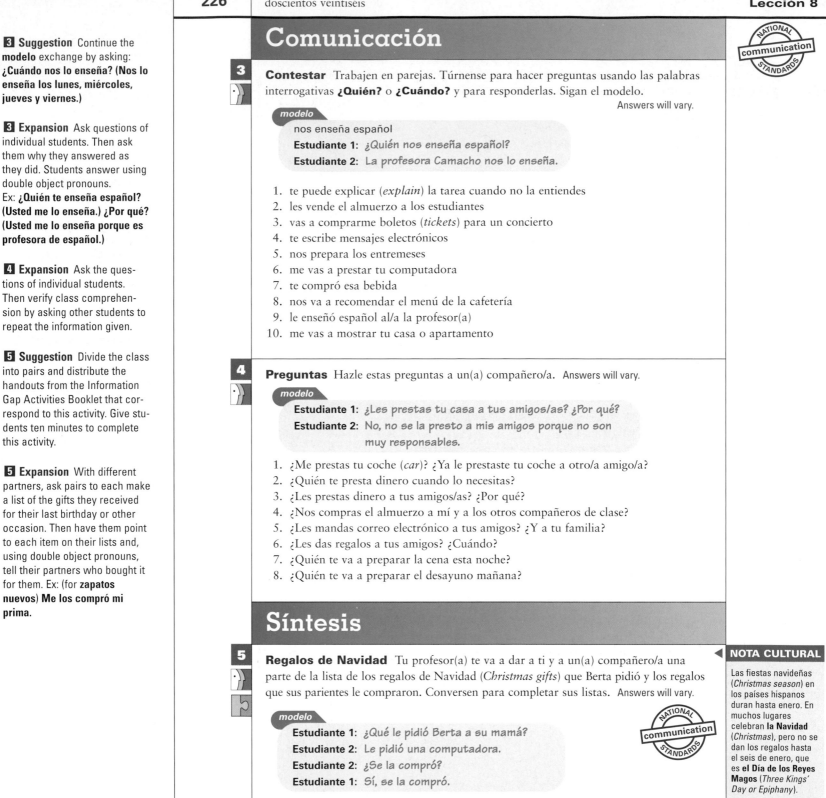

Comunicación

3

Contestar Trabajen en parejas. Túrnense para hacer preguntas usando las palabras interrogativas **¿Quién?** o **¿Cuándo?** y para responderlas. Sigan el modelo.

Answers will vary.

modelo

nos enseña español

Estudiante 1: ¿Quién nos enseña español?

Estudiante 2: La profesora Camacho nos lo enseña.

1. te puede explicar (*explain*) la tarea cuando no la entiendes
2. les vende el almuerzo a los estudiantes
3. vas a comprarme boletos (*tickets*) para un concierto
4. te escribe mensajes electrónicos
5. nos prepara los entremeses
6. me vas a prestar tu computadora
7. te compró esa bebida
8. nos va a recomendar el menú de la cafetería
9. le enseñó español al/a la profesor(a)
10. me vas a mostrar tu casa o apartamento

4

Preguntas Hazle estas preguntas a un(a) compañero/a. Answers will vary.

modelo

Estudiante 1: ¿Les prestas tu casa a tus amigos/as? ¿Por qué?

Estudiante 2: No, no se la presto a mis amigos porque no son muy responsables.

1. ¿Me prestas tu coche (*car*)? ¿Ya le prestaste tu coche a otro/a amigo/a?
2. ¿Quién te presta dinero cuando lo necesitas?
3. ¿Les prestas dinero a tus amigos/as? ¿Por qué?
4. ¿Nos compras el almuerzo a mí y a los otros compañeros de clase?
5. ¿Les mandas correo electrónico a tus amigos? ¿Y a tu familia?
6. ¿Les das regalos a tus amigos? ¿Cuándo?
7. ¿Quién te va a preparar la cena esta noche?
8. ¿Quién te va a preparar el desayuno mañana?

Síntesis

5

Regalos de Navidad Tu profesor(a) te va a dar a ti y a un(a) compañero/a una parte de la lista de los regalos de Navidad (*Christmas gifts*) que Berta pidió y los regalos que sus parientes le compraron. Conversen para completar sus listas. Answers will vary.

modelo

Estudiante 1: ¿Qué le pidió Berta a su mamá?

Estudiante 2: Le pidió una computadora.

Estudiante 2: ¿Se la compró?

Estudiante 1: Sí, se la compró.

NOTA CULTURAL

Las fiestas navideñas (*Christmas season*) en los países hispanos duran hasta enero. En muchos lugares celebran **la Navidad** (*Christmas*), pero no se dan los regalos hasta el seis de enero, que es **el Día de los Reyes Magos** (*Three Kings' Day or Epiphany*).

---

3 Suggestion Continue the **modelo** exchange by asking: **¿Cuándo nos lo enseña? (Nos lo enseña los lunes, miércoles, jueves y viernes.)**

3 Expansion Ask questions of individual students. Then ask them why they answered as they did. Students answer using double object pronouns. Ex: **¿Quién te enseña español? (Usted me lo enseña.) ¿Por qué? (Usted me lo enseña porque es profesora de español.)**

4 Expansion Ask the questions of individual students. Then verify class comprehension by asking other students to repeat the information given.

5 Suggestion Divide the class into pairs and distribute the handouts from the Information Gap Activities Booklet that correspond to this activity. Give students ten minutes to complete this activity.

5 Expansion With different partners, ask pairs to each make a list of the gifts they received for their last birthday or other occasion. Then have them point to each item on their lists and, using double object pronouns, tell their partners who bought it for them. Ex: (for **zapatos nuevos**) **Me los compró mi prima.**

TEACHING OPTIONS

Heritage Speakers Ask heritage speakers if they or their families celebrate **el Día de los Reyes Magos** (Epiphany, January 6). Ask them to expand on the information given in the **Nota cultural** sidebar and to tell whether **el Día de los Reyes** is more important for them than **la Navidad**.

Large Groups Divide the class in half. To each member of one half of the class give a strip of paper with a question on it. Ex: **¿Te compró ese suéter tu novia?** To each member of the other half of the class give the answer to one of the questions. Ex: **Sí, ella me lo compró.** Students must find their partners. Take care not to create sentences that can have more than one match.

8.3 Saber and conocer

ANTE TODO Spanish has two verbs that mean *to know*: **saber** and **conocer**. They cannot be used interchangeably. Note that all forms of **saber** and **conocer** are regular in the present tense except their **yo** forms.

Saber and conocer

		saber *(to know)*	**conocer** *(to know)*
SINGULAR FORMS	yo	**sé**	**conozco**
	tú	**sabes**	**conoces**
	Ud./él/ella	**sabe**	**conoce**
PLURAL FORMS	nosotros/as	**sabemos**	**conocemos**
	vosotros/as	**sabéis**	**conocéis**
	Uds./ellos/ellas	**saben**	**conocen**

¡ATENCIÓN!

Saber + [*adjective*] is used to explain how something *tastes*.

Sabe muy dulce/bien/amargo.
It tastes very sweet/nice/bitter.

Saber + a means *to taste like.*

Sabe a ajo.
It tastes like garlic.

No sabe a nada.
It doesn't taste like anything.

▶ **Saber** means *to know a fact or piece(s) of information* or *to know how to do something.*

No **sé** tu número de teléfono.
I don't know your telephone number.

Mi hermana **sabe** hablar francés.
My sister knows how to speak French.

▶ **Conocer** means *to know* or *be familiar/acquainted* with a person, place, or thing.

¿**Conoces** la ciudad de Nueva York?
Do you know New York City?

No **conozco** a tu amigo Esteban.
I don't know your friend Esteban.

▶ When the direct object of **conocer** is a person or pet, the personal **a** is used.

¿Conoces los restaurantes de Tegucigalpa?   *but*   ¿Conoces **a** Rigoberta Menchú?

¡ATENCIÓN!

The following verbs are also conjugated like **conocer**:

conducir *to drive*
ofrecer *to offer*
parecer *to seem*
traducir *to translate*

¡INTÉNTALO! Escribe las formas apropiadas de los siguientes verbos.

saber

1. José no ___sabe___ la hora.
2. Sara y yo ___sabemos___ jugar al tenis.
3. ¿Por qué no ___sabes___ tú estos verbos?
4. Mis padres ___saben___ hablar japonés.
5. Yo ___sé___ a qué hora es la clase.
6. Usted no ___sabe___ dónde vivo.
7. Mi hermano no ___sabe___ nadar.
8. Nosotros ___sabemos___ muchas cosas.
9. Carlos nunca ___sabe___ qué hora es.
10. Yo ___sé___ dónde comer bien.

verbos como conocer

1. Usted y yo ___conocemos___ (conocer) bien Miami.
2. Mi compañero ___conduce___ (conducir) muy mal.
3. Esta clase ___parece___ (parecer) muy buena.
4. Ellos siempre me ___ofrecen___ (ofrecer) ayuda.
5. Yo ___traduzco___ (traducir) del chino al inglés.
6. Ana, ¿___conoces___ (conocer) los poemas de Mistral?
7. Luis, ___pareces___ (parecer) triste.
8. Ustedes ___conducen___ (conducir) con cuidado.
9. Yo siempre les ___ofrezco___ (ofrecer) café a mis amigos.
10. Nadie me ___conoce___ (conocer) bien.

Section Goals

In **Estructura 8.3** students will learn:
• the uses of **saber** and **conocer**
• more uses of the personal **a**

Instructional Resources
WB/VM: Workbook, p. 91
Lab Manual, p. 47
Lab CD/MP3 Lección 8
IRM: ¡Inténtalo! & Práctica
Answers, pp. 184–185;
Tapescript, pp. 35–39
Interactive CD-ROM
Companion website:
www.vistahigherlearning.com
Presentations CD-ROM

Suggestion Model **saber** by asking several questions with it. Ex: _____, ¿sabes mi número de teléfono? ¿Sabes dónde está la biblioteca? Next write **conocer** on the board and ask questions such as: _____, ¿conoces a esta persona? ¿Me conoces a mí? Ask students further questions using both verbs and help them infer the difference in use between the two.

¡Atención! Point out the **yo** forms of the verbs listed in the second **¡Atención!** sidebar.

TEACHING OPTIONS

Video Show the **Fotonovela** video again to give students more input with **saber** and **conocer**. Stop the video where appropriate to discuss how **saber** and **conocer** were used and to ask comprehension questions.

Extra Practice Call out several sentences in English which use *to know*. Have students say whether they would use **saber** or **conocer** to translate it. Ex: I know the answer to that question. (**saber**) He does not know the president. (**conocer**)

Práctica

1 Completar
Completa las frases con la forma apropiada de **saber** o **conocer**.

CONSÚLTALO
Locate the Guatemalan cities mentioned here, in **Panorama**, p. 238.

1. Mi hermana mayor ___sabe___ conducir, pero yo no ___sé___.
2. —¿___Conoces___ a Carla, mi sobrina? —No, no la ___conozco___.
3. —¿___Saben___ ustedes el número de Marta? —Nosotras no lo ___sabemos___.
4. —Nosotros no ___conocemos___ Guatemala. —Ah, ¿no? Yo ___conozco___ bien las ciudades de Escuintla, Mazatenango, Quetzaltenango y Antigua.
5. —Todavía no ___conozco___ a tu novio. —Sí, ya lo ___sé___. Mañana te lo presento.
6. Yo ___sé___ esquiar, pero Tino y Luis son pequeños y no ___saben___.
7. Roberto ___conoce___ bien el Popol Vuh, el libro sagrado de los mayas, y también ___sabe___ leer los jeroglíficos de los templos mayas.

2 Emparejar
Escoge la oracion de la lista A que corresponde con la de la lista B y escribe la forma correcta de los verbos en la lista B.

A
1. María del Carmen tiene mucha sed. b
2. ¿Puedes traducir el menú? No entiendo francés. d
3. ¿Sabes cuándo sirven los entremeses? a
4. Gloria, tú no tienes automóvil para ir a la fiesta, ¿verdad? f
5. Aquel camarero es el hijastro de mi cuñada María José. c
6. ¿De dónde es el dueño del restaurante? ¿Es francés? e

B
a. No lo sé, pero ___parece___ (parecer) que van a servirlos pronto.
b. Con gusto le ___ofrezco___ (ofrecer) una bebida.
c. ¿Ah, sí? Pues, no lo ___conozco___ (conocer). ¡Qué guapo!
d. Sí, te lo ___traduzco___ (traducir). Me gusta mucho practicar el francés.
e. No ___sé___ (saber). No me acuerdo, pero conozco a su esposa. Es de Guatemala.
f. No, pero ___conduzco___ (conducir) el de mis padres.

3 Combinar
Combina las columnas A, B y C para hacer oraciones completas. *Answers will vary.*

modelo
No conozco a Stephen King. / Stephen King conoce a Meg Ryan.

A	B	C
Katie Couric	(no) conocer	Cameron Diaz
Bill Gates	(no) saber	Andy García
Shakira y Enrique Iglesias		cantar
Mike Myers		el lago de Atitlán en Guatemala
Stephen King		hablar dos lenguas extranjeras
Salma Hayek		hacer reír (laugh) a la gente
yo		preparar buenas comidas
tú		escribir novelas de horror
tu compañero/a		programar computadoras
nosotras		muchas personas importantes

Comunicación

4

Preguntas Con un(a) compañero/a, háganse y respondan a las siguientes preguntas. Answers will vary.

1. ¿Qué restaurantes buenos conoces? ¿Vas mucho a comer a restaurantes?
2. En tu familia, ¿quién sabe cantar? ¿Tu opinión es objetiva?
3. ¿Conoces a algún artista hispano?
4. ¿Sabes usar bien Internet? ¿Te parece fácil o difícil?
5. ¿Sabes escuchar cuando alguien te habla de sus problemas?
6. ¿Conoces a algún/alguna chef famoso/a? ¿Qué tipo de comida prepara?
7. ¿Conoces a algún/alguna escritor(a) famoso/a?
8. ¿Sabes si ofrecen cursos de administración de empresas en la universidad?

AYUDA

Whereas in English we make contrasts by using *do/does*, in Spanish it is common to use **sí/no**.
Yo no lo conozco, pero mi novio **sí lo conoce**.
I don't know him, but my boyfriend does.

5

Entrevista Hazle preguntas a un(a) compañero/a sobre los siguientes temas. Utiliza los verbos **saber** y **conocer**. Answers will vary.

modelo

Estudiante 1: *¿Conoces un buen restaurante argentino?*
Estudiante 2: *Sí, conozco La parrilla ardiente.*
Estudiante 1: *¿Sabes cocinar comida argentina?*
Estudiante 2: *Sí, sé preparar un buen asado.*

actividades	deportes	recetas (*recipes*)
ciudades	lenguas	restaurantes
compras	países	viajes

NOTA CULTURAL

El **asado** es la barbacoa (*barbecue*) argentina. Un asado típico consiste en chorizos y otras carnes a la parrilla (*grill*). Según los argentinos, el secreto de un buen asado es el corte (*cut*) de la carne y el control del fuego (*fire*).

Síntesis

6

Anuncio En grupos, lean el anuncio (*advertisement*). Después, contesten las preguntas. Answers will vary.

1. Busquen ejemplos de los verbos **saber** y **conocer**.
2. ¿Qué saben del Centro Comercial Oviedo?
3. ¿Qué pueden hacer en el Centro Comercial Oviedo?
4. ¿Conocen otros centros comerciales como éste? ¿Cómo se llaman? ¿Dónde están?
5. ¿Conocen algún centro comercial en otro país? ¿Cómo es?

NOTA CULTURAL

Los centros comerciales son muy populares en los países hispanos y en casi todas las principales ciudades hay varios. El Centro Sambil en Caracas, Venezuela, es el centro comercial más grande de Suramérica. Además de muchísimas tiendas, tiene una terraza con restaurantes, cafés y una vista espectacular de la ciudad.

Él sabe dónde comer
lo que más le gusta

Él sabe cómo jugar
cuatro horas seguidas

Él sabe dónde
está su regalo
de cumpleaños

Él sabe dónde divertirse

... y usted sabe dónde puede
encontrar un poco de todo.
¿Conoce algún otro lugar como éste?

Oviedo
Centro Comercial

Sabe lo que te gusta

Right margin:

4 Expansion Ask these questions of the whole class. Ask students who answer in the affirmative for additional information. Ex: **¿Quién conoce un buen restaurante? ¿Cuál es? ¿Por qué es tan bueno?**

5 Expansion Write on the board the topics listed. Then have students call out the names of the cities, recipes, etc. that their partner mentioned and write them under their respective topic. Have students divide up into groups accordingly and share additional information about what they know using **saber** and **conocer**.

6 Suggestion Before assigning groups, ask general questions about the ad. Ex: **¿De quién es el anuncio? ¿Qué venden?**

6 Expansion Have students generate their own poster using two examples each of **conocer** and **saber**.

TEACHING OPTIONS

Pairs Ask students to individually write brief paragraphs in which they use the verbs presented in this section. Then they exchange their papers with a partner. Students should help each other to make the paragraphs as error-free as possible. Collect the papers for grading.

Extra Practice Ask individual students questions that are most likely not true for them. When students give a negative answer, they should indicate someone else who *would* answer in the affirmative. Ex: _____, **¿conoces a Martin Sheen? No, no lo conozco, pero Rob Lowe sí lo conoce.**

8.4 Comparisons and superlatives

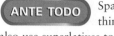

ANTE TODO Spanish and English use comparisons to indicate which of two people or things has a lesser, equal, or greater degree of a quality. Both languages also use superlatives to express the highest or lowest degree of a quality.

Comparisons

menos interesante	más grande	tan sabroso como
less interesting	*bigger*	*as delicious as*

Superlatives

la/el mejor	la/el peor	la más alta
the best	*the worst*	*the tallest*

Comparisons of inequality

▶ Comparisons of inequality are formed by placing **más** (*more*) or **menos** (*less*) before adjectives, adverbs, and nouns and **que** (*than*) after them.

$$\text{más/menos} + \begin{bmatrix} adjective \\ adverb \\ noun \end{bmatrix} + que$$

adjectives

Los bistecs son **más caros que** el pollo. | Estas uvas son **menos sabrosas que** esa pera.
Steaks are more expensive than chicken. | *These grapes are less tasty than that pear.*

adverbs

Me acuesto **más tarde que** tú. | Mi hermano se despierta **menos temprano que** yo.
I go to bed later than you (do). | *My brother wakes up less early than I (do).*

nouns

Juan prepara **más platos que** José. | Susana come **menos carne que** Enrique.
Juan prepares more dishes than José (does). | *Susana eats less meat than Enrique (does).*

> **¡ATENCIÓN!**
>
> Note that while English has a comparative form for short adjectives and adverbs (*taller*, *later*), such forms do not exist in Spanish (**más** alto, **más** tarde).
>
> • • •
>
> When the comparison involves a numerical expression, **de** is used before the number instead of **que**.
>
> Hay más **de** cincuenta naranjas.
>
> Llego en menos **de** diez minutos.

Tengo más hambre que un elefante.

El lomo a la plancha es un poquito más caro pero es sabrosísimo.

▶ With verbs, the following construction is used to make comparisons of inequality:

$$[\text{verb}] + \text{más/menos que}$$

Mis hermanos **comen más que** yo. | Arturo **duerme menos que** su padre.
My brothers eat more than I (do). | *Arturo sleeps less than his father (does).*

Section Goals

In **Estructura 8.4** students will be introduced to:
• comparisons of inequality
• comparisons of equality
• superlatives
• irregular comparative and superlative words

Instructional Resources
WB/VM: Workbook, pp. 92–94
Lab Manual, p. 48
Lab CD/MP3 Lección 8
IRM: ¡Inténtalo! & Práctica
Answers, pp. 184–185;
Tapescript, pp. 35–39; Hojas de actividades, p. 146
Interactive CD-ROM
Companion website:
www.vistahigherlearning.com
Presentations CD-ROM

Suggestions

• Write **más** + [*adjective*] + **que** and **menos** + [*adjective*] + **que** on the board, explaining their meaning. Illustrate with examples. Ex: **Esta clase es más grande que la clase de la tarde. La clase de la tarde es menos trabajadora que ésta.**
• Practice the structures by asking volunteers questions about classroom objects. **El lápiz de ____, ¿es más largo que el lápiz de ____? (No, es menos largo que el lápiz de ____.)**
• Point out that **que** and what follows it are optional if the items being compared are evident. Ex: **Los bistecs son más caros (que el pollo).**

TEACHING OPTIONS

Extra Practice Ask students questions that make comparisons of inequality using adjectives, adverbs, and nouns. Ex: **¿Qué es más sabroso que una ensalada de frutas? ¿Quién se despierta más tarde que tú? ¿Quién tiene más libros que yo?** Then ask questions that use verbs in their construction. Ex: **¿Quién habla más que yo en la clase?**

Heritage Speakers Ask heritage speakers to give four to five sentences in which they compare themselves to members of their families. Make sure that the comparisons are ones of inequality. Ask other students in the class to report what the heritage speakers said to verify comprehension.

Comparisons of equality

The following constructions are used to make comparisons of equality.

$$\textbf{tan} + \begin{bmatrix} adjective \\ adverb \end{bmatrix} + \textbf{como} \qquad \textbf{tanto/a(s)} + \begin{bmatrix} singular\ noun \\ plural\ noun \end{bmatrix} + \textbf{como}$$

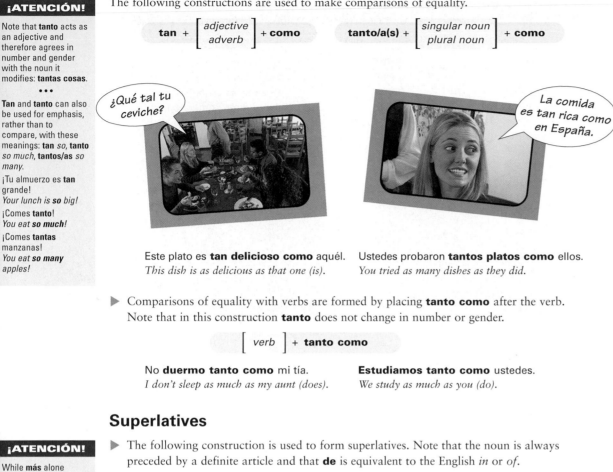

Este plato es **tan delicioso como** aquél.
This dish is as delicious as that one (is).

Ustedes probaron **tantos platos como** ellos.
You tried as many dishes as they did.

▶ Comparisons of equality with verbs are formed by placing **tanto como** after the verb. Note that in this construction **tanto** does not change in number or gender.

$$\begin{bmatrix} verb \end{bmatrix} + \textbf{tanto como}$$

No **duermo tanto como** mi tía.
I don't sleep as much as my aunt (does).

Estudiamos tanto como ustedes.
We study as much as you (do).

Superlatives

▶ The following construction is used to form superlatives. Note that the noun is always preceded by a definite article and that **de** is equivalent to the English *in* or *of*.

$$\textbf{el/la/los/las} + \begin{bmatrix} noun \end{bmatrix} + \textbf{más/menos} + \begin{bmatrix} adjective \end{bmatrix} + \textbf{de}$$

Es **el café más rico del** país.
It's the most delicious coffee in the country.

Es el menú **menos caro de** todos éstos.
It is the least expensive menu of all of these.

▶ The noun in a superlative construction can be omitted if the person, place, or thing referred to is clear.

¿El restaurante El Cráter?
   Es **el más elegante** de la ciudad.
The El Cráter restaurant?
   It's the most elegant (one) in the city.

Recomiendo el pollo asado.
   Es **el más sabroso** del menú.
I recommend the roast chicken.
   It's the most delicious (thing) on the menu.

Irregular comparisons and superlatives

Irregular comparative and superlative forms

Adjective		Comparative form		Superlative form	
bueno/a	good	mejor	better	el/la mejor	(the) best
malo/a	bad	peor	worse	el/la peor	(the) worst
grande	big	mayor	bigger	el/la mayor	(the) biggest
pequeño/a	small	menor	smaller	el/la menor	(the) smallest
joven	young	menor	younger	el/la menor	(the) youngest
viejo/a	old	mayor	older	el/la mayor	(the) eldest

Inés, ¿tienes hermanos?

Sí, tengo un hermano mayor.

¿Adónde vamos a almorzar, don F?

Pues, conozco el mejor restaurante de la ciudad, el restaurante El Cráter.

▶ When **grande** and **pequeño/a** refer to age, the irregular comparative and superlative forms, **mayor** and **menor**, are used. However, when these adjectives refer to size, the regular forms, **más grande** and **más pequeño/a**, are used.

> Isabel es **la mayor** de su familia.
> *Isabel is the eldest in her family.*

> Tu ensalada es **más grande** que ésa.
> *Your salad is bigger than that one.*

> Yo soy **menor** que tú.
> *I'm younger than you.*

> Pedí **el plato más pequeño** del menú.
> *I ordered the smallest dish on the menu.*

▶ The adverbs **bien** and **mal** have the same irregular comparative forms as the adjectives **bueno/a** and **malo/a**.

> Julio nada **mejor** que los otros chicos.
> *Julio swims better than the other boys.*

> Ellas cantan **peor** que las otras chicas.
> *They sing worse than the other girls.*

CONSÚLTALO

To review how descriptive adjectives like **bueno, malo,** and **grande** shorten before nouns, see **Estructura 3.1**, p. 70.

TEACHING OPTIONS

Absolute superlatives

▶ In Spanish the absolute superlative is equivalent to *extremely, exceptionally, super,* or *very* before an adjective or adverb. You encountered an absolute superlative when you learned how to say **Me gusta(n) muchísimo...**

▶ To form the absolute superlative of most adjectives and adverbs, drop the final vowel, if there is one, and add **-ísimo/a(s).**

malo → **mal-** → **malísimo**   **mucho** → **much-** → **muchísimo**

¡El bistec está **malísimo**!   Comes **muchísimo**.
The steak is very bad!   *You eat a lot (very, very much).*

difícil + -ísimo → **dificilísimo**   **fácil + ísimo** → **facilísimo**

Esta prueba es **dificilísima**.   Los exámenes son **facilísimos**.
This quiz is exceptionally difficult.   *The tests are extremely easy.*

▶ Adjectives and adverbs whose stem ends in **c, g,** or **z** change spelling to **qu, gu,** and **c** in the absolute superlative.

rico → **riquísimo**   **largo** → **larguísimo**   **feliz** → **felicísimo**

▶ Adjectives that end in **–n** or **–r** normally form the absolute superlative by adding **-císimo.**

joven + -císimo → **jovencísimo**   **trabajador + -císimo** → **trabajadorcísimo**

¡INTÉNTALO! Escribe el equivalente de las palabras en inglés.

Comparativos
1. (*than*) Ernesto mira más televisión __que__ Alberto.
2. (*less*) Tú eres __menos__ simpático que Federico.
3. (*as much*) La camarera sirve __tanta__ carne como pescado.
4. (*more*) Conozco __más__ restaurantes que tú.
5. (*as much as*) No estudio __tanto como__ tú.
6. (*as*) ¿Sabes jugar al tenis tan bien __como__ tu hermana?
7. (*as many*) ¿Puedes beber __tantos__ refrescos como yo?
8. (*as*) Mis amigos parecen __tan__ simpáticos como ustedes.

Superlativos
1. (*the most intelligent*) Marisa es __la más inteligente__ de todas.
2. (*the least boring*) Ricardo y Tomás son __los menos aburridos__ de la fiesta.
3. (*the worst*) Miguel y Antonio son __los peores__ estudiantes de la clase.
4. (*the eldest*) Mi profesor de biología es __el mayor__ de la universidad.
5. (*extremely delicious*) El pollo de este supermercado es __riquísimo__.
6. (*the youngest*) Carlos es __el menor__ de mis hermanos.
7. (*the best*) Este plato es __el mejor__ del restaurante.
8. (*extremely tall*) Sara es __altísima__.

Suggestions
• Use magazine pictures to compare and contrast absolute superlatives. Ex: **Este edificio parece modernísimo, pero éste no. Parece viejísimo.**
• Ask volunteers to identify people you describe using absolute superlatives. Ex: **Es riquísima. (Oprah Winfrey) Es graciosísimo. (Robin Williams)**

TEACHING OPTIONS

Extra Practice Give ten comparative and superlative sentences orally to practice listening comprehension. Dictate the sentences, then give students about 30 seconds per sentence to write the direct opposite. Ask volunteers to present their opposite sentences. Ex: **Ernesto mira más televisión que Alberto. (Alberto mira menos televisión que Ernesto.)**

Heritage Speakers Ask heritage speakers to discuss whether absolute superlatives are common in their culture or not (some regions and countries use them less frequently than others). Also have them discuss under what circumstances absolute superlatives are most frequently used, such as when talking about food, people, events, and so forth.

1 Suggestion Quickly review the use of **de** before numerals in comparisons.

1 Expansion
- Ask two students a question, then have another student compare them. Ex: **¿Cuántas horas de televisión miras cada día? ¿Y tú, ____? ____ , haz una comparación.**
- Ask several pairs of students different types of questions for comparison later. Ex: **¿Cuáles prefieres, las películas de aventura o los dramas? ¿Estudias más para la clase de español o para la clase de matemáticas?**

2 Expansion Turn the activity statements into questions and ask them of students. Have them make up answers that involve comparisons. Ex: **¿Cómo es Mario?**

3 Suggestion Distribute the **Hojas de actividades** from the IRM that correspond to this activity.

3 Expansion In pairs, have students select a family member or a close friend and describe him or her using comparatives and superlatives. Ask volunteers to share their descriptions with the class.

Práctica

1 Escoger De las palabras que están entre paréntesis, escoge la correcta para comparar a dos hermanas muy diferentes. Haz (*Make*) las adaptaciones necesarias.

1. Lucila es más alta y más bonita ___que___ Tita. (de, más, menos, que)
2. Tita es más delgada porque come ___más___ verduras que su hermana. (de, más, menos, que)
3. Lucila es más ___simpática___ que Tita porque es alegre. (listo, simpático, bajo)
4. A Tita le gusta comer en casa. Va a ___menos___ restaurantes que su hermana. (más, menos, que) Es tímida, pero activa. Hace ___más___ ejercicio que su hermana. (más, tanto, menos) Todos los días toma más ___de___ cinco vasos de agua mineral. (que, tan, de)
5. Lucila come muchas papas fritas y se preocupa ___menos___ que Tita por comer frutas. (de, más, menos) Son ___tan___ diferentes, pero se llevan bien. (como, tan, tanto)

2 Emparejar Completa las oraciones (*sentences*) de la columna A con información de la columna B para comparar a Mario y a Luis, los novios de Lucila y Tita.

A	B
1. Mario es ___tan interesante___ como Luis.	amigos extranjeros
2. Mario viaja tanto ___como___ Luis.	como
3. Luis escoge ___tantas___ clases de cocina (*cooking*) como Mario.	diferencia
4. Luis habla ___francés___ tan bien como Mario.	francés
5. Mario tiene tantos ___amigos extranjeros___ como Luis.	tan interesante
6. ¡Qué casualidad (*coincidence*)! Mario y Luis también son hermanos, pero no hay tanta ___diferencia___ entre ellos como entre Lucila y Tita.	tantas

3 Completar Tu profesor(a) va a darte (*to give you*) una hoja de actividades con descripciones de José Valenzuela Carranza y Ana Orozco Hoffman. Completa las oraciones acerca de (*about*) Ana, José y sus familias con las palabras de la lista.

atlética	del	mejor	peor
altísima	la	menor	periodista
bajo	más	guapísimo	trabajadorcísimo
de	mayor	Orozco	Valenzuela

1. José es el ___menor___ y el más ___bajo___ de su familia. Es ___guapísimo___ y ___trabajadorcísimo___. Es el mejor ___periodista___ de la ciudad y el ___peor___ jugador de baloncesto.
2. Ana es la más ___atlética___ y ___la___ mejor jugadora de baloncesto del estado. Es la ___mayor___ de sus hermanos y es ___altísima___. Estudió la profesión ___más___ difícil ___de___ todas.
3. Jorge es el ___mejor___ jugador de juegos electrónicos de su familia.
4. Mauricio es el menor de la familia ___Orozco___.
5. El abuelo es el ___mayor___ de todos los miembros de la familia Valenzuela.
6. Fifí es la perra más antipática ___del___ mundo.

Extra Practice Using magazine pictures or your own drawings, show a family whose members vary widely in different aspects: age (write a number on each person that indicates how old he or she is), height, weight, and so forth. Ask students to make comparisons about that family. Give names to each family member so that they are easier to identify.

Large Groups Divide the class into two groups. Survey each group to get information about various topics. Ex: **¿Cuántos hacen ejercicio todos los días? ¿Cuántos van al cine cada fin de semana? ¿Cuántos comen comida rápida tres veces a la semana?** Ask for a show of hands and tally the number of hands. Then have students make comparisons between the two groups based on the information given.

Comunicación

4   **Intercambiar**   En parejas, hagan comparaciones sobre diferentes cosas. Pueden usar las sugerencias de la lista u otras ideas.   Answers will vary.

AYUDA

You can use the following adjectives in your comparisons:
bonito/a
caro/a
elegante
interesante
inteligente

> **modelo**
>
> **Estudiante 1:** Los pollos de *Pollitos del Corral* son los mejores del mundo.
> **Estudiante 2:** Pues yo creo que los pollos de *Rostipollos* son tan buenos como los pollos de *Pollitos del Corral*.
> **Estudiante 1:** Mmm... no tienen tanta mantequilla como los pollos de *Pollitos del Corral*. Tienes razón. Son sabrosísimos.

cafés en tu ciudad/pueblo
restaurantes en tu ciudad/pueblo
tiendas en tu ciudad/pueblo

libros favoritos
periódicos en tu ciudad/pueblo
revistas favoritas

comidas favoritas
cursos que toman
profesores

5   **Conversar**   En grupos, túrnense (*take turns*) para hacer comparaciones entre ustedes mismos (*yourselves*) y una persona de cada categoría de la lista.   Answers will vary.

▶ una persona de tu familia

▶ un(a) amigo/a especial

▶ una persona famosa

Síntesis

6   **La familia López**   En grupos, túrnense para hablar de Sara, Sabrina, Cristina, Ricardo y David y hacer comparaciones entre ellos.   Answers will vary.

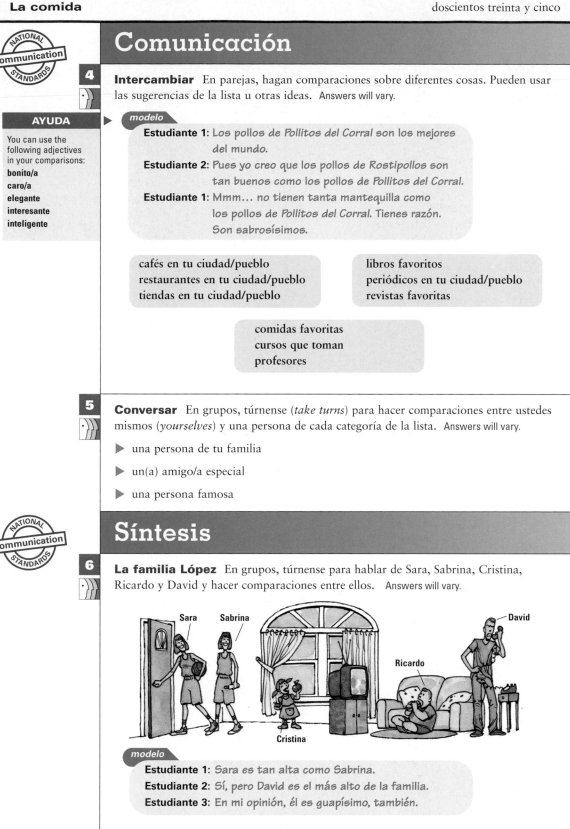

> **modelo**
>
> **Estudiante 1:** Sara es tan alta como Sabrina.
> **Estudiante 2:** Sí, pero David es el más alto de la familia.
> **Estudiante 3:** En mi opinión, él es guapísimo, también.

4 Expansion Ask pairs of volunteers to present one of their conversations to the class. Then survey the class to see with which of the students the class agrees more.

5 Suggestion Model the activity by making a few comparisons between yourself and a celebrity.

5 Expansion Ask a volunteer to share his or her comparisons. Then make comparisons between yourself and the student or yourself and the person the student mentioned. Continue to do this with different students, asking them to make similar comparisons as well.

6 Expansion Have students create a drawing of a family similar to the one on this page. Tell them not to let anyone see their drawings. Then pair students up and have them describe their drawings to one another. Each student must draw the family described by his or her partner.

TEACHING OPTIONS

Extra Practice As a listening comprehension activity, prepare short descriptions of five easily recognizable people in which you compare them to other recognizable people. Write their names on the board in random order. Then read your descriptions, having students match the description to the appropriate name. Ex: **Esta persona es más famosa que Enrique Iglesias pero es tan guapa como él. (Ricky Martin)**

TPR Give the same types of objects to different students but in different numbers. For example, hand out three books to one student, one book to another, and four to another. Then call on individuals to make comparisons between the students based on the number of objects they have.

Lectura

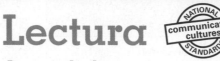

Antes de leer

Estrategia
Reading for the main idea

As you know, you can learn a great deal about a reading selection by looking at the format and looking for cognates, titles, and subtitles. You can skim to get the gist of the reading selection and scan it for specific information. Reading for the main idea is another useful strategy; it involves locating the topic sentences of each paragraph to determine the author's purpose for writing a particular piece. Topic sentences can provide clues about the content of each paragraph, as well as the general organization of the reading. Your choice of which reading strategies to use will depend on the style and format of each reading selection.

Examinar el texto

En esta sección tenemos dos textos diferentes. ¿Qué estrategias puedes usar para leer la crítica culinaria? ¿Cuáles son las apropiadas para familiarizarte con el menú? Utiliza las estrategias más eficaces° para cada texto. ¿Qué tienen en común? ¿Qué tipo de comida sirven en el restaurante?

Identificar la idea principal

Lee la primera frase de cada párrafo de la crítica culinaria del restaurante **La feria del maíz**. Apunta° el tema principal de cada párrafo. Luego lee todo el primer párrafo. ¿Crees que el restaurante le gustó al/a la autor(a) de la crítica culinaria? ¿Por qué? Ahora lee la crítica entera. En tu opinión, ¿cuál es la idea principal de la crítica? ¿Por qué la escribió el/la autor(a)? Compara tus opiniones con las de un(a) compañero/a.

recursos

vistahigher
learning.com

eficaces *efficient*   Apunta *Jot down*

MENÚ

Entremeses
Tortilla servida con
• Ajiaceite (chile, aceite) • Ajicomino (chile, comino)

Pan tostado servido con
• Queso frito a la pimienta • Salsa de ajo y mayonesa

Sopas
• Tomate • Cebolla • Verduras • Pollo y huevo
• Carne de res • Mariscos

Entradas
Tomaticán
(tomate, papas, maíz, chile, arvejas, zanahorias y verduras)

Tamales
(maíz, azúcar, ajo, cebolla)

Frijoles enchilados
(frijoles negros, carne de cerdo o de res, arroz, chile)

Chilaquil
(tortilla de maíz, queso, hierbas y chile)

Tacos
(tortillas, pollo, verduras y mole)

Cóctel de mariscos
(camarones, langostas, vinagre, sal, pimienta, aceite)

Postres
• Plátanos caribeños • Cóctel de frutas al ron
• Uvate (uvas, azúcar de caña y ron) • Flan napolitano
• Helado de piña y naranja • Pastel de yogur

Después de leer

Preguntas

En parejas, contesten las siguientes preguntas sobre la crítica culinaria de **La feria del maíz.**

1. ¿Quién es el dueño y chef de **La feria del maíz**?
   Ernesto Sandoval

2. ¿Qué tipo de comida se sirve en el restaurante?
   tradicional

3. ¿Cuál es el problema con el servicio?
   Se necesitan más camareros.

4. ¿Cómo es el ambiente del restaurante?
   agradable

5. ¿Qué comidas probó el autor de la crítica culinaria? las tortillas, el ajiaceite, la sopa de mariscos, los tamales, los tacos de pollo y el fla

6. ¿Quieren probar ustedes el restaurante **La feria del maíz**? ¿Por qué? Answers will vary.

Section Goals

In **Lectura** students will:
• learn to identify the main idea in a text
• read a content-rich menu and restaurant review

Instructional Resource
Companion website:
www.vistahigherlearning.com

Estrategia Tell students that recognizing the main idea of a text will help them unlock the meaning of unfamiliar words and phrases they come across while reading. Tell them to check the title first. The main idea is often expressed in the title. Tell them to read the topic sentence of each paragraph before they read the full text, so they will get a sense of the main idea.

Examinar el texto First, have students scan the menu. Ask how the title and subheadings help predict the content. Ask volunteers to state the meaning of each category of food served. Then have students scan the newspaper article. Ask them how the title and the format (the box with ratings) of the text give clues to the content.

Identificar la idea principal Ask students to read the column heading and the title of the article and predict the subject of the article and the author's purpose. Then have students read the topic sentence of the first paragraph and state the main idea. Finally, have them read the entire paragraph.

TEACHING OPTIONS

Heritage Speakers Ask heritage speakers to create a dinner menu featuring their favorite dishes, including lists of ingredients similar to those in the menu above. Have heritage speakers make copies of their menus, distribute them, and answer questions from classmates about unfamiliar vocabulary or how dishes are prepared.

Heritage Speakers Ask a heritage speaker who has visited Guatemala and dined in restaurants or cafés to prepare a short presentation about his or her experiences there. Of particular interest would be a comparison and contrast of city vs. small-town restaurants. If possible, the presentation should be illustrated with menus from the restaurants, advertisements, or photos of and articles about the country.

23F

Gastronomía

La feria del maíz

Sobresaliente°. En el nuevo restaurante **La feria del maíz** va a encontrar la perfecta combinación entre la comida tradicional y el encanto de la vieja ciudad de Antigua. Ernesto Sandoval, antiguo jefe de cocina° del famoso restaurante **El fogón**, está teniendo mucho éxito° en su nueva aventura culinaria.

El gerente°, el experimentado José Sierra, controla a la perfección la calidad del servicio. El camarero que me atendió esa noche fue muy amable en todo momento. Sólo hay

La feria del maíz
13 calle 4-41 Zona 1
La Antigua, Guatemala
2329912

lunes a sábado
10:30am-11:30pm
domingo 10:00am-10:00pm

Comida ♉♉♉♉♉

Servicio ♉♉♉

Ambiente ♉♉♉♉

Precio ♉♉♉

que comentar que, debido al éxito inmediato de **La feria del maíz**, se necesitan más camareros para atender a los clientes de una forma más eficaz. En esta ocasión, el

mesero tardó unos veinte minutos en traerme la bebida.

Afortunadamente, no me importó mucho la espera entre plato y plato, pues el ambiente es tan agradable que me sentí como en casa. El restaurante mantiene el estilo colonial de Antigua. Por dentro°, el estilo es elegante y rústico a la vez. Cuando el tiempo lo permite, se puede comer también en el patio, donde hay muchas flores.

El servicio de camareros y el ambiente agradable del local pasan a un segundo plano cuando llega la comida, de una calidad extraordinaria. Las tortillas de casa se sirven

con un ajiaceite delicioso. La sopa de mariscos es excelente, y los tamales, pues, tengo que confesar que son mejores que los de mi abuelita. También recomiendo los tacos de pollo, servidos con un mole buenísimo. De postre, don Ernesto me preparó su especialidad, un flan napolitano sabrosísimo.

Los precios pueden parecer altos° para una comida tradicional, pero, la calidad de los productos con que se cocinan los platos y el exquisito ambiente de **La feria del maíz** le garantizan° una experiencia inolvidable.

Bebidas
• Cerveza negra • Chilate (bebida de maíz, chile y cacao)
• Jugos de fruta • Agua mineral • Té helado
• Vino tinto/blanco • Ron

Sobresaliente *Outstanding* **jefe de cocina** *head chef* **éxito** *success*
gerente *manager* **Por dentro** *Inside* **altos** *high* **garantizan** *guarantee*

Un(a) guía turístico/a

Tú eres un(a) guía turístico/a en Guatemala. Estás en el restaurante **La feria del maíz** con un grupo de turistas norteamericanos. Ellos no hablan español y quieren pedir de comer, pero necesitan tu ayuda. Lee nuevamente el menú e indica qué error comete cada turista.

1. La señora Johnson es diabética y no puede comer azúcar. Pide sopa de verdura y tamales. No pide nada de postre.
   No debe pedir los tamales porque tienen azúcar.

2. Los señores Petit son vegeterianos y piden sopa de tomate, frijoles enchilados y plátanos caribeños.
   No deben pedir los frijoles enchilados porque tienen carne.

3. El señor Smith, que es alérgico al chocolate, pide tortilla servida con ajiaceite, chilaquil y chilate para beber.
   No debe pedir chilate porque tiene cacao.

4. La adorable hija del señor Smith tiene sólo cuatro años y le gustan mucho las verduras y las frutas naturales. Su papá le pide tomaticán y un cóctel de frutas.
   No debe pedir el cóctel de frutas porque tiene ron.

5. La señorita Jackson está a dieta y pide uvate, flan napolitano y helado.
   No debe pedir postres porque está a dieta.

Preguntas
• Have students quickly review the article before answering the questions. Suggest that pairs take turns answering them. The student who does not answer a question should find the line of text that contains the answer.
• Expand the activity with these questions. **7. ¿Cómo fue el mesero que atendió al crítico? (Fue muy amable, pero estaba muy ocupado con otros clientes del restaurante.) 8. ¿Cuál fue la opinión del crítico con respecto a la comida? (La encontró toda de muy alta calidad.) 9. ¿Cómo son los precios de La feria del maíz? (Son altos, pero la calidad de la comida los justifica.)**

Un(a) guía turístico/a Ask pairs to work together to check the menu and state why each customer should not order the item(s) he or she has selected.

The Affective Dimension
A source of discomfort in travel can be unfamiliar foods. Tell students that by learning about the foods of a country they are going to visit, they can make that part of their visit even more enjoyable.

TEACHING OPTIONS

Extra Practice Ask students to review the items in **Un(a) guía turístico/a**, write a conversation, and act out the scene involving a tour guide eating lunch in a Guatemalan restaurant with several tourists. Have them work in groups of eight to assign the following roles: **mesero, guía turístico/a, la señora Johnson, los señores Petit, el señor Smith, la hija del señor Smith,** and **la señorita Jackson.** Each group can perform for the class.

Variación léxica Tell students that the adjective of place or nationality for Guatemala is **guatemalteco/a**. Guatemalans often use a more colloquial term, **chapín**, as a synonym for **guatemalteco/a**.
Heritage Speakers Ask heritage speakers to describe restaurant etiquette in Spanish-speaking countries. Have them discuss how to order, call a food server, ask for the check, tip, and so forth.

Section Goal

In **Panorama**, students will read about the geography and culture of Guatemala.

Instructional Resources
Transparencies, #3, #4, #35
WB/VM: Workbook, pp. 95–96;
Video Activities, pp. 239–240
Panorama cultural *DVD/Video*
Interactive CD-ROM
IRM: Videoscript, p. 111;
Panorama cultural *translations,*
p. 133
Companion website:
www.vistahigherlearning.com
Presentations CD-ROM

Suggestion Have students use the map in their books or project **Transparency #35**. Point out that Guatemala has three main climatic regions: the tropical Pacific and Caribbean coasts, the highlands (southwest), and jungle lowlands (north). Ask volunteers to read aloud the names of the cities, mountains, and rivers of Guatemala. Point out that indigenous languages are the source of many place names.

El país en cifras As you read about the languages of Guatemala, you might point out that there are many Guatemalans who are monolingual in either Spanish or a Mayan language. Many are bilingual, speaking an indigenous language and Spanish. When students look at the Guatemalan flag, point out that the quetzal is featured prominently in the shield in the center.

¡Increíble pero cierto!
Guatemala is internationally renowned for the incredible wealth and diversity of its textile arts. Each village has a traditional "signature" weaving style that allows those in the know to quickly identify where each beautiful piece comes from.

Guatemala

NATIONAL STANDARDS — connections cultures

El país en cifras

▶ **Área:** 108.890 km² (42.042 millas²), *un poco más pequeño que Tennessee*

▶ **Población:** 12.952.000

▶ **Capital:** la Ciudad de Guatemala—3.869.000

▶ **Ciudades principales:**
Quetzaltenango—101.000, Escuintla—68.000,
Mazatenango—42.000, Puerto Barrios—39.000
SOURCE: Population Division, UN Secretariat

▶ **Moneda:** quetzal

▶ **Idiomas:** español (oficial), lenguas mayas
El español es la lengua de un 60 por ciento° de la población; el otro 40 por ciento tiene una de las lenguas mayas (cakchiquel, quiché y kekchícomo entre otras) como lengua materna. Una palabra que las lenguas mayas tienen en común es ixim, que significa maíz, un cultivo° de mucha importancia en estas culturas.

Bandera de Guatemala

Guatemaltecos célebres

▶ **Carlos Mérida,** pintor (1891–1984)
▶ **Miguel Ángel Asturias,** escritor (1899–1974)
▶ **Margarita Carrera,** poeta y ensayista (1929–)
▶ **Rigoberta Menchú Tum,** activista (1959–)

por ciento *percent* cultivo *crop* telas *fabrics*
tinte *dye* aplastados *crushed*
hace... destiñan *keeps the colors from running*

Vista de una calle céntrica en la Ciudad de Guatemala

Mujeres indígenas limpiando cebollas

MÉXICO

Sierra de Lacandón

Lago Petén Itzá

Río Usumacinta

Río de la Pasión

Sierra de las Minas

Lago de Izabal

Río Mota

Sierra Madre

Quetzaltenango

Lago de Atitlán

★ Guatemala
Antigua Guatemala

Mazatenango

Escuintla

Iglesia de la Merced en Antigua Guatemala

EL SALVADOR

Océano Pacífico

recursos

WB pp. 95–96	VM pp. 239–240	I CD-ROM Lección 8	vi... lea...

¡Increíble pero cierto!

¿Qué ingrediente secreto se encuentra en las telas° tradicionales de Guatemala? ¡El mosquito! El excepcional tínte° de estas telas es producto de una combinación de flores y de mosquitos aplastados°. El insecto hace que los colores no se destiñan°. Quizás es por ésto que los artesanos representan la figura del mosquito en muchas de sus telas.

TEACHING OPTIONS

Worth Noting Although the indigenous population of Guatemala is Mayan, many place names in southwestern Guatemala are in Nahuatl, the language of the Aztecs of central Mexico. How did this happen? In the sixteenth century, Guatemala was conquered by Spaniards who came from the Valley of Mexico after having overthrown the Aztec rulers there. These conquistadors were accompanied by large numbers of Nahuatl-speaking allies, and it was these allies who renamed the captured Mayan strongholds with Nahuatl names. The suffix **–tenango**, which appears in many of these names, means "place with a wall," that is, a fortified place. **Quetzaltenango**, then, means fortified place of the quetzal bird; **Mazatenango** means fortified place of the deer.

Ciudades • La Antigua Guatemala

La Antigua Guatemala fue fundada en 1543. Fue una capital de gran importancia hasta 1773, cuando un terremoto° la destruyó. La Antigua Guatemala conserva el carácter original de su arquitectura y hoy es uno de los centros turísticos del país. Su celebración de la Semana Santa° es, para muchas personas, la más importante del hemisferio.

Naturaleza • El quetzal

El quetzal simbolizó la libertad para los antiguos° mayas porque creían° que este pájaro° no podía vivir en cautividad°. Hoy el quetzal es el símbolo nacional. El pájaro da su nombre a la moneda nacional y aparece en los billetes° del país. Desafortunadamente, está en peligro° de extinción. Para su protección, el gobierno mantiene una reserva biológica especial.

Historia • Los mayas

Desde 1500 a.C. hasta 900 d.C. los mayas habitaron gran parte de lo que ahora es Guatemala. Su civilización fue muy avanzada. Fueron arquitectos y constructores de pirámides, templos y observatorios. Descubrieron° y usaron el cero antes que los europeos, e inventaron un calendario complejo° y preciso.

Artesanía • La ropa tradicional

La ropa tradicional de los guatemaltecos se llama *huipil* y muestra el amor de la cultura maya por la naturaleza. Ellos se inspiran en las flores, plantas y animales para hacer sus diseños°. Es de colores vivos° y tiene formas geométricas. El diseño y los colores de cada *huipil* indican el pueblo de origen y a veces el sexo y la edad° de la persona que lo lleva.

¿Qué aprendiste? Responde a las preguntas con una frase completa.

1. ¿Qué significa la palabra *ixim*?
   La palabra *ixim* significa maíz.
2. ¿Quién es Rigoberta Menchú?
   Rigoberta Menchú es una activista de Guatemala.
3. ¿Qué pájaro representa a Guatemala?
   El quetzal representa a Guatemala.
4. ¿Qué simbolizó el quetzal para los mayas?
   El quetzal simbolizó la libertad para los mayas.
5. ¿Cuál es la moneda nacional de Guatemala?
   La moneda nacional de Guatemala es el quetzal.
6. ¿De qué fueron arquitectos los mayas?
   Los mayas fueron arquitectos de pirámides, templos y observatorios.
7. ¿Qué celebración de la Antigua Guatemala es la más importante del hemisferio para muchas personas? La celebración de la Semana Santa de la Antigua Guatemala es la más importante del hemisferio.
8. ¿Qué descubrieron los mayas antes que los europeos? Los mayas descubrieron el cero antes que los europeos.
9. ¿Qué muestra la ropa tradicional de los guatemaltecos? La ropa muestra el amor a la naturaleza.
10. ¿Qué indica un *huipil* con su diseño y sus colores? Con su diseño y colores, un *huipil* indica el pueblo de origen, el sexo y la edad de la persona.

Conexión Internet Investiga estos temas en el sitio **www.vistahigherlearning.com**.

1. Busca información sobre Rigoberta Menchú. ¿De dónde es? ¿Qué libros publicó? ¿Por qué es famosa?
2. Estudia un sitio arqueológico en Guatemala para aprender más sobre los mayas, y prepara un breve informe para tu clase.

---

terremoto *earthquake*   **Semana Santa** *Holy Week*   **antiguos** *ancient*   **creían** *they believed*   **pájaro** *bird*   **cautividad** *captivity*
los billetes *bills*   **peligro** *danger*   **descubrieron** *discovered*   **complejo** *complex*   **diseños** *designs*   **vivos** *bright*   **edad** *age*

(side margin, left)
Mar Caribe

fo de
duras

(side margin, left)
URAS

(right margin)

La Antigua Guatemala Students can use tour books and the Internet to learn more about **Semana Santa** celebrations in this Guatemalan city, usually referred to simply as Antigua. Encourage short presentations to the class. Also, you may want to play the **Panorama cultural** video for this lesson that focuses on **Antigua** and **Chichicastenango**.

El quetzal Recent conservation efforts in Guatemala, Costa Rica, and other Central American nations have focused on preserving the cloud forests (**bosque nuboso**) that are home to the quetzal.

Los mayas Today ethnobotanists are working with Mayan traditional healers to learn about medicinal uses of plants of the region.

La ropa tradicional Many indigenous Guatemalans still wear traditional garb richly decorated with embroidery. The **huipil** is a long, sleeveless tunic worn by women. A distinctively woven **faja**, or waist sash, identifies the town or village each woman comes from.

Conexión Internet Students will find supporting Internet activities and links at **www.vistahigherlearning.com**.

Worth Noting Spanish is a second language for more than 40% of Guatemalans. Students may be interested to learn that Guatemala has many bilingual education programs, where native languages are used in addition to Spanish for instructional purposes. There are also many government-sponsored Spanish as a Second Language (SSL) programs, offered through schools and radio or television. Speakers of Guatemala's indigenous languages often encounter problems similar to those found by other learners of Spanish: difficulty with agreement of number and gender.

Instructional Resources
Vocabulary CD
Lab Manual, p. 48
*Lab CD/MP3 **Lección 8***
IRM: Tapescript, pp. 35–39
*Testing Program: **Pruebas**,*
pp. 85–96
Testing Program Audio CD
Test Files CD-ROM
Test Generator

Las comidas

el/la camarero/a	*waiter*
la comida	*food; meal*
el/la dueño/a	*owner; landlord*
el menú	*menu*
la sección de (no) fumar	*(non) smoking section*
el almuerzo	*lunch*
la cena	*dinner*
el desayuno	*breakfast*
los entremeses	*hors d'oeuvres*
el plato (principal)	*(main) dish*
delicioso/a	*delicious*
rico/a	*tasty; delicious*
sabroso/a	*tasty; delicious*
escoger	*to choose*
merendar (e:ie)	*to snack*
pedir (e:i)	*to order (food)*
probar (o:ue)	*to taste; to try*
recomendar (e:ie)	*to recommend*
servir (e:i)	*to serve*

Las frutas

la banana	*banana*
las frutas	*fruits*
el limón	*lemon*
la manzana	*apple*
el melocotón	*peach*
la naranja	*orange*
la pera	*pear*
la sandía	*watermelon*
la uva	*grape*

Las verduras

las arvejas	*peas*
la cebolla	*onion*
el champiñón	*mushroom*
la ensalada	*salad*
los espárragos	*asparagus*
los frijoles	*beans*
la lechuga	*lettuce*
el maíz	*corn*
las papas/patatas (fritas)	*(fried) potatoes; French fries*
el tomate	*tomato*
las verduras	*vegetables*
la zanahoria	*carrot*

La carne y el pescado

el atún	*tuna*
el bistec	*steak*
los camarones	*shrimp*
la carne	*meat*
la carne de res	*beef*
la chuleta (de cerdo)	*(pork) chop*
la hamburguesa	*hamburger*
el jamón	*ham*
la langosta	*lobster*
los mariscos	*shellfish*
el pavo	*turkey*
el pescado	*fish*
el pollo (asado)	*(roast) chicken*
la salchicha	*sausage*
el salmón	*salmon*

Otras comidas

el aceite	*oil*
el ajo	*garlic*
el arroz	*rice*
el azúcar	*sugar*
los cereales	*cereal; grains*
el huevo	*egg*
la mantequilla	*butter*
la margarina	*margarine*
la mayonesa	*mayonnaise*
el pan (tostado)	*(toasted) bread*
la pimienta	*black pepper*
el queso	*cheese*
la sal	*salt*
el sándwich	*sandwich*
la sopa	*soup*
el vinagre	*vinegar*
el yogur	*yogurt*

Las bebidas

el agua (mineral)	*(mineral) water*
la bebida	*drink*
el café	*coffee*
la cerveza	*beer*
el jugo (de fruta)	*(fruit) juice*
la leche	*milk*
el refresco	*soft drink*
el té (helado)	*(iced) tea*
el vino (blanco/tinto)	*(white/red) wine*

Verbos

conducir	*to drive*
conocer	*to know; to be acquainted with*
morir (o:ue)	*to die*
ofrecer	*to offer*
parecer	*to seem*
saber	*to know; to know how*
traducir	*to translate*

Las comparaciones

como	*like; as*
más de *(+ number)*	*more than*
más... que	*more ... than*
menos de *(+ number)*	*fewer than*
menos... que	*less ... than*
tan... como	*as ... as*
tantos/as... como	*as many... as*
tanto... como	*as much... as*
el/la mayor	*the eldest*
el/la mejor	*the best*
el/la menor	*the youngest*
el/la peor	*the worst*
mejor	*better*
peor	*worse*

Expresiones útiles	*See page 217.*

recursos

LM p. 48	Lab CD/MP3 Lección 8	Vocab CD Lección 8

Las fiestas

Communicative Goals

You will learn how to:
- Express congratulations
- Express gratitude
- Ask for and pay the bill at a restaurant

Lesson Goals

In **Lección 9** students will be introduced to the following:
- terms for parties and celebrations
- words for stages of life and interpersonal relations
- irregular preterites
- verbs that change meaning in the preterite
- uses of **¿qué?** and **¿cuál?**
- pronouns after prepositions
- recognizing word families
- using a Spanish-English dictionary
- writing a comparative analysis
- using context to infer the meaning of unfamiliar words
- cultural, geographic, and economic information about Chile

A primera vista Here are some additional questions you can ask based on the photo: **¿Fuiste a una fiesta importante el año pasado? ¿Cuál fue la ocasión? ¿Sirvieron comida en la fiesta? ¿Qué sirvieron? En tu opinión, ¿qué fiestas son las más divertidas? ¿Por qué? ¿Conoces algún buen lugar para hacer una fiesta? ¿Por qué es bueno?**

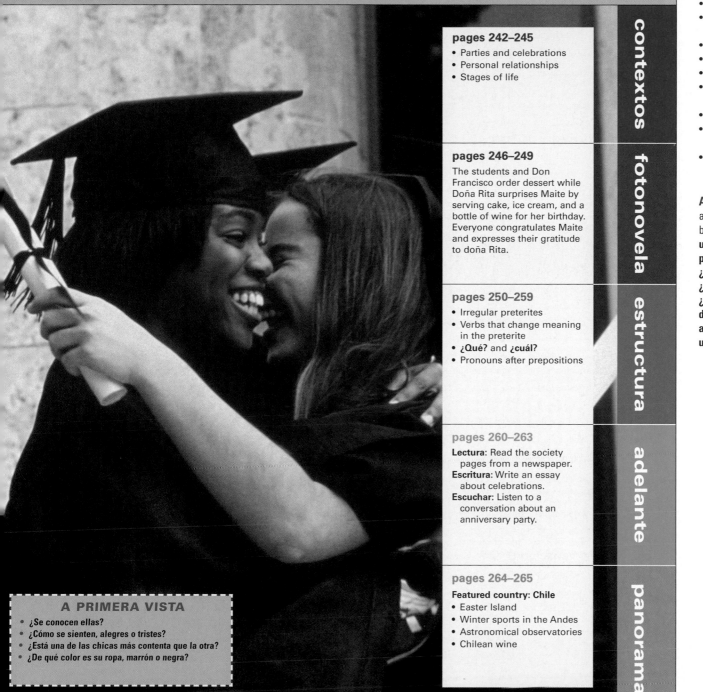

A PRIMERA VISTA
- ¿Se conocen ellas?
- ¿Cómo se sienten, alegres o tristes?
- ¿Está una de las chicas más contenta que la otra?
- ¿De qué color es su ropa, marrón o negra?

INSTRUCTIONAL RESOURCES

Workbook/Video Manual: WB Activities, pp. 97–108
Laboratory Manual: Lab Activities, pp. 49–54
Workbook/Video Manual: Video Activities, pp. 211–212; pp. 241–242
Instructor's Resource Manual: **Hojas de actividades**, pp. 147–148; **Vocabulario adicional**, p. 163; **¡Inténtalo!** & **Práctica** Answers, p. 186; **Fotonovela**

Translations, pp. 123–124; Textbook CD Tapescript, p. 79; Lab CDs Tapescript, pp. 40–44; **Fotonovela** Videoscript, p. 96; **Panorama cultural** Videoscript, p. 111; **Pan. cult.** translations, p.133
Info Gap Activities Booklet, pp. 33–36
Overhead Transparencies: #5, #6, #36, #37
Lab Audio CD/MP3 **Lección 9**

Panorama cultural DVD/Video
Fotonovela DVD/Video
Testing Program, pp. 97–108
Testing Program Audio CD
Test Files CD-ROM
Test Generator
Companion website

Presentations CD-ROM
Textbook CD
Vocabulary CD
Interactive CD-ROM
Video CD-ROM
Web-SAM

Las fiestas

Más vocabulario

la alegría	*happiness*
la amistad	*friendship*
el amor	*love*
el beso	*kiss*
la sorpresa	*surprise*
el aniversario (de bodas)	*(wedding) anniversary*
la boda	*wedding*
el cumpleaños	*birthday*
el día de fiesta	*holiday*
el divorcio	*divorce*
el matrimonio	*marriage*
la Navidad	*Christmas*
el/la recién casado/a	*newlywed*
la quinceañera	*young woman's fifteenth birthday celebration*
celebrar	*to celebrate*
cumplir años	*to have a birthday*
divertirse (e:ie)	*to have fun*
graduarse (de/en)	*to graduate (from/in)*
invitar	*to invite*
jubilarse	*to retire (from work)*
nacer	*to be born*
odiar	*to hate*
pasarlo bien/mal	*to have a good/bad time*
reírse (e:i)	*to laugh*
relajarse	*to relax*
sorprender	*to surprise*
sonreír (e:i)	*to smile*
cambiar (de)	*to change*
dejar una propina	*to leave a tip*
pagar la cuenta	*to pay the bill*
juntos/as	*together*

Variación léxica

pastel ←→ torta (*Arg., Venez.*)
comprometerse ←→ prometerse (*Esp.*)

la pareja

el pastel de chocolate

la botella de vino

el flan de caramelo

las galletas

los postres

el champán

los dulces

Práctica

FELIZ CUMPLEAÑOS

brindar

el invitado

Relaciones personales

casarse (con)	*to get married (to)*
comprometerse (con)	*to get engaged (to)*
divorciarse (de)	*to get divorced (from)*
enamorarse (de)	*to fall in love (with)*
llevarse bien/mal (con)	*to get along well/badly (with)*
romper (con)	*to break up (with)*
salir (con)	*to go out (with); to date*
separarse (de)	*to separate (from)*
tener una cita	*to have a date; to have an appointment*

el helado

1 Escuchar 🎧 Escucha la conversación e indica si las oraciones son **ciertas** o **falsas**.

1. A Silvia no le gusta mucho el chocolate. Falsa.
2. Silvia sabe que sus amigos le van a hacer una fiesta. Falsa.
3. Los amigos de Silvia le compraron un pastel de chocolate. Cierta.
4. Los amigos brindan por Silvia con refrescos. Falsa.
5. Silvia y sus amigos van a comer helado. Cierta.
6. Los amigos de Silvia le van a servir flan y galletas. Falsa.

2 Emparejar Indica la letra de la frase que mejor completa cada oración.

a. se jubiló	d. nos divertimos	g. se llevan bien
b. dejó una propina	e. nació	h. lo pasaron mal
c. sonrió	f. se casaron	i. tenemos una cita

1. María y sus compañeras de cuarto __g__ . Son buenas amigas.
2. Pablo y yo __d__ en la fiesta. Bailamos y comimos mucho.
3. Manuel y Felipe __h__ en el cine. La película fue muy mala.
4. ¡Tengo una nueva sobrina! Ella __e__ ayer por la mañana.
5. Mi madre le __b__ muy grande al camarero.
6. Mi padre __a__ hace un año. Ahora no trabaja.
7. A Elena le gustan las galletas. Ella __c__ después de comérselas todas.
8. Jorge y yo __i__ esta noche. Vamos a ir a un restaurante muy elegante.
9. Jaime y Laura __f__ el septiembre pasado. La boda fue maravillosa.

3 Definiciones En parejas, definan las palabras y escriban una frase para cada ejemplo. Answers will vary. Suggested answers below.

> **modelo**
> romper (con) una pareja termina la relación
> Marta rompió con su novio.

1. regalar dar un regalo
2. helado una comida fría y dulce
3. pareja dos personas enamoradas
4. invitado una persona que va a una fiesta
5. casarse ellos deciden estar juntos para siempre
6. quinceañera la fiesta de cumpleaños de una chica de 15 años
7. sorpresa la persona no sabe lo que va a pasar
8. pasarlo bien divertirse

1 Suggestion Have students check their answers by going over **Actividad 1** with the whole class.

1 Tapescript E1: ¿Estamos listos, amigos? E2: Creo que sí. Aquí tenemos el pastel y el helado… E3: De chocolate, espero. Ustedes saben cómo le encanta a Silvia el chocolate… E2: Por supuesto, el chocolate para Silvia. Bueno, un pastel de chocolate, el helado… E3: ¿El helado es de la cafetería o lo compraste cerca de la residencia estudiantil? E2: Lo compré en la tienda que está al lado de nuestra residencia. Es mejor que el helado de la cafetería. E1: Psstt… aquí viene Silvia… E1, E2, E3: ¡Sorpresa! ¡Sorpresa, Silvia! ¡Felicidades! E4: ¡Qué sorpresa! E3: ¿Y cuántos años cumples? E4: Dieciocho. ¡Gracias, amigos, muchas gracias! E1: Y ahora, ¡brindamos por nuestra amiga! E3: ¿Con qué brindamos? ¿Con el champán? E1: ¡Cómo no! ¡Por nuestra amiga Silvia, la más joven de todos nosotros! *Textbook Activities CD*

2 Expansion Have students write three sentences based on the drawing on pages 242–243, leaving out a word or phrase from the vocabulary. In pairs, students complete their partners' sentences. Ex: **Dos personas ____ con champán. (brindan)**

3 Expansion Ask students personalized questions using verbs from the **Relaciones personales** box on this page. Ex: **¿Con quién te llevas muy bien? ¿Con quién te llevas mal?**

TEACHING OPTIONS

Heritage Speakers Ask heritage speakers about some Hispanic holidays or other celebrations that they or their families typically celebrate, such as **el Día de los Reyes Magos, el día del santo, la quinceañera, el Cinco de Mayo,** and **el Día de los Muertos**. Ask speakers to elaborate on what the celebrations are like: who attends, what they eat and drink, why those days are celebrated, and so forth.

Game Play **Concentración**. Write vocabulary items that pertain to parties and celebrations on each of eight cards. On another eight cards, draw or paste a picture that matches each description. Place the cards face-down in four rows of four. In pairs, students select two cards. If the two cards match, the pair keeps them. If the two cards do not match, students replace them in their original position. The pair with the most cards at the end wins.

Suggestion Engage students in a conversation about the stages in Sergio's life. Say: **Mira al bebé en el primer dibujo. ¡Qué contento está! ¿Qué hace en el segundo dibujo? Está paseando en un triciclo, ¿no? ¿Quiénes se acuerdan de su niñez?** Cover all the vocabulary in **Más vocabulario**.

4 Suggestion Before beginning, ask several true-false questions. Have students correct false statements. Ex: **1. Un soltero es un hombre que no está casado. (Cierto.) 2. La vejez ocurre antes de la niñez. (Falso. La vejez ocurre después de la madurez.)**

4 Expansion Have students create three original sentences that describe events mentioned in **Más vocabulario** on page 242. Then have partners name the events described. Ex: **E1: Lourdes y Mario llevan diez años de casados. E2: el aniversario de bodas**

5 Suggestion Explain that students are to give the opposite of the underlined words in their answers.

5 Expansion Have students use words and expressions with opposite meanings to share sentences about their families with partners, who will then report the information to the class. Ex: **Mi abuelo se jubiló el año pasado, pero mi hermana mayor empezó a trabajar la semana pasada.**

Las etapas de la vida de Sergio

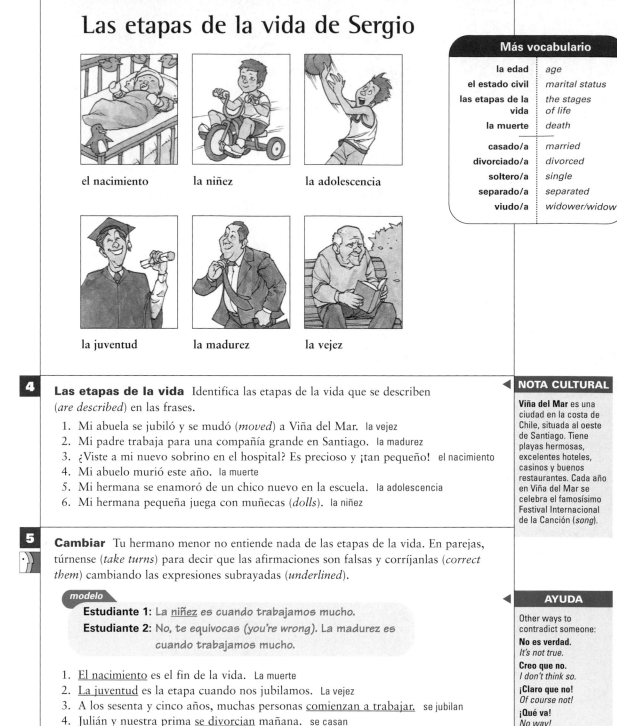

el nacimiento   la niñez   la adolescencia

la juventud   la madurez   la vejez

Más vocabulario	
la edad	age
el estado civil	marital status
las etapas de la vida	the stages of life
la muerte	death
casado/a	married
divorciado/a	divorced
soltero/a	single
separado/a	separated
viudo/a	widower/widow

4 **Las etapas de la vida** Identifica las etapas de la vida que se describen (*are described*) en las frases.

1. Mi abuela se jubiló y se mudó (*moved*) a Viña del Mar. la vejez
2. Mi padre trabaja para una compañía grande en Santiago. la madurez
3. ¿Viste a mi nuevo sobrino en el hospital? Es precioso y ¡tan pequeño! el nacimiento
4. Mi abuelo murió este año. la muerte
5. Mi hermana se enamoró de un chico nuevo en la escuela. la adolescencia
6. Mi hermana pequeña juega con muñecas (*dolls*). la niñez

5 **Cambiar** Tu hermano menor no entiende nada de las etapas de la vida. En parejas, túrnense (*take turns*) para decir que las afirmaciones son falsas y corríjanlas (*correct them*) cambiando las expresiones subrayadas (*underlined*).

> **modelo**
> **Estudiante 1:** La niñez es cuando trabajamos mucho.
> **Estudiante 2:** No, te equivocas (*you're wrong*). La madurez es cuando trabajamos mucho.

1. El nacimiento es el fin de la vida. La muerte
2. La juventud es la etapa cuando nos jubilamos. La vejez
3. A los sesenta y cinco años, muchas personas comienzan a trabajar. se jubilan
4. Julián y nuestra prima se divorcian mañana. se casan
5. Mamá odia a su hermana. quiere / se lleva bien con
6. El abuelo murió, por eso la abuela es separada. viuda
7. Cuando te gradúas de la universidad, estás en la etapa de la adolescencia. la juventud
8. Mi tío nunca se casó, es viudo. soltero

NOTA CULTURAL

Viña del Mar es una ciudad en la costa de Chile, situada al oeste de Santiago. Tiene playas hermosas, excelentes hoteles, casinos y buenos restaurantes. Cada año en Viña del Mar se celebra el famosísimo Festival Internacional de la Canción (*song*).

AYUDA

Other ways to contradict someone:
No es verdad.
It's not true.
Creo que no.
I don't think so.
¡Claro que no!
Of course not!
¡Qué va!
No way!

TEACHING OPTIONS

Small Groups In groups of two to four, have students perform a skit whose content describes and/or displays a particular stage of life (youth, old age, etc.) or marital status (married, single, divorced). The rest of the class has to try to figure out what the group is displaying.

Game Play a modified version of **20 Preguntas**. Ask a volunteer to think of a famous person. Other students get one chance each to ask a yes-no question until someone guesses the item correctly. Limit attempts to ten questions per famous person. Point out that students can narrow down their selection by using vocabulary about the stages of life and marital status.

Comunicación

6 **Una fiesta** Trabaja con dos compañeros/as para planear una fiesta. Recuerda incluir la siguiente (*following*) información.   Answers will vary.

1. ¿Qué tipo de fiesta es? ¿Dónde va a ser? ¿Cuándo va a ser?
2. ¿A quiénes van a invitar?
3. ¿Qué van a comer? ¿Quiénes van a llevar o a preparar la comida?
4. ¿Qué van a beber? ¿Quiénes van a llevar las bebidas?
5. ¿Qué van a hacer todos durante la fiesta?

7 **Encuesta** Tu profesor(a) va a darte una hoja de actividades. Haz las preguntas de la hoja a dos o tres compañeros/as de clase para saber qué actitudes tienen en sus relaciones personales. Luego comparte los resultados de la encuesta (*survey*) con la clase y comenta tus conclusiones. Answers will vary.

Preguntas	Nombres	Actitudes
1. ¿Te importa la amistad? ¿Por qué?		
2. ¿Es mejor tener un(a) buen(a) amigo/a o muchos/as amigos/as?		
3. ¿Cuáles son las características que buscas en tus amigos/as?		
4. ¿Tienes novio/a? ¿A qué edad es posible enamorarse?		
5. ¿Deben las parejas hacer todo juntos? ¿Deben tener las mismas opiniones? ¿Por qué?		

¡LENGUA VIVA!

While a **buen(a) amigo/a** is a *good friend*, the term **amigo/a íntimo/a** refers to a *close friend*, or a very good friend, without any romantic overtones.

8 **Minidrama** En parejas, consulten la ilustración en la página 244, y luego, usando las palabras de la lista, preparen un minidrama para representar (*to act out*) las etapas de la vida de Sergio. Pueden ser creativos e inventar más información sobre su vida. Answers will vary.

amor	celebrar	enamorarse	romper
boda	comprometerse	graduarse	salir
cambiar	cumpleaños	jubilarse	separarse
casarse	divorciarse	nacer	tener una cita

6 Expansion
- Ask volunteer groups to talk to the class about the party they have just planned.
- Have students make invitations for their party. Ask the class to judge which invitation is the cleverest, funniest, most elegant, and so forth.

7 Suggestion Distribute the **Hojas de actividades**. Give students eight minutes to ask other group members the questions.

7 Expansion Take a survey of the attitudes found in the entire class. Ex: **¿Quiénes creen que es más importante tener un buen amigo que muchos amigos? ¿Quiénes creen que es más importante tener muchos amigos que un buen amigo?**

8 Expansion After all skits have been presented, have the class vote on the most original, funniest, truest to life, and so forth.

TEACHING OPTIONS

Extra Practice Using magazine pictures, display images that pertain to parties or celebrations, stages of life, or interpersonal relations. Have students describe the pictures and make guesses about who the people are, how they are feeling, and so forth.

Extra Practice As a listening comprehension activity, prepare short descriptions of five easily recognizable people. Use as much active lesson vocabulary as possible. Write their names on the board in random order. Then read your descriptions, having students match the description to the appropriate name.

Section Goals

In **Fotonovela** students will:
• receive comprehensible input from free-flowing discourse
• learn functional phrases that preview lesson grammatical structures

Instructional Resources
WB/VM: Video Activities, pp. 211–212
Fotonovela *DVD/Video (Start 00:47:00)*
Fotonovela *Video CD-ROM*
IRM: **Fotonovela** *Translations, pp. 123–124, Videoscript, p. 96 Interactive CD-ROM*

Video Recap: Lección 8
Before doing this **Fotonovela** section, review the previous one with this activity.
1. ¿Quién es doña Rita Perales? (la dueña del restaurante El Cráter)
2. ¿Qué platos sirven en El Cráter? (tortillas de maíz, caldo de patas, lomo a la plancha, ceviche, fuente de fritada, pasteles)
3. ¿Qué opinión tienen los estudiantes de la comida? (es riquísima)
4. ¿Cuál es la ocasión especial ese día? (el cumpleaños de Maite)

Video Synopsis While the travelers are looking at the dessert menu, Doña Rita and the waiter bring in some flan, a cake, and some wine to celebrate Maite's birthday. The group leaves Doña Rita a nice tip, thanks her, and says goodbye.

Suggestions

• Have students read the first line of dialogue in each **Fotonovela** segment and then make an educated guess about what happens in this episode.
• Quickly review the guesses your students made about the **Fotonovela**, and guide the class to a correct summary of the plot.

¡Feliz cumpleaños, Maite!

Don Francisco y los estudiantes celebran el cumpleaños de Maite en el restaurante El Cráter.

PERSONAJES

MAITE

INÉS

DON FRANCISCO

ÁLEX

JAVIER

DOÑA RITA

CAMARERO

1
INÉS A mí me encantan los dulces. Maite, ¿tú qué vas a pedir?
MAITE Ay, no sé. Todo parece tan delicioso. Quizás el pastel de chocolate.

2
JAVIER Para mí el pastel de chocolate con helado. Me encanta el chocolate. Y tú, Álex, ¿qué vas a pedir?
ÁLEX Generalmente prefiero la fruta, pero hoy creo que voy a probar el pastel de chocolate.
DON FRANCISCO Yo siempre tomo un flan y un café.

3
DOÑA RITA & CAMARERO ¡Feliz cumpleaños, Maite!
INÉS ¿Hoy es tu cumpleaños, Maite?
MAITE Sí, el 22 de junio. Y parece que vamos a celebrarlo.
TODOS MENOS MAITE ¡Felicidades!

6
ÁLEX Yo también acabo de cumplir los veintitrés años.
MAITE ¿Cuándo?
ÁLEX El cuatro de mayo.

7
DOÑA RITA Aquí tienen un flan, pastel de chocolate con helado... y una botella de vino para dar alegría.
MAITE ¡Qué sorpresa! ¡No sé qué decir! Muchísimas gracias.

8
DON FRANCISCO El conductor no puede tomar vino. Doña Rita, gracias por todo. ¿Puede traernos la cuenta?
DOÑA RITA Enseguida, Paco.

recursos

V CD-ROM	VM	I CD-ROM
Lección 9	pp. 211–212	Lección 9

TEACHING OPTIONS

Video Tips General suggestions for using video clips in the classroom can be found on page IAE-12 of this Instructor's Annotated Edition.
¡Feliz cumpleaños, Maite! Ask your students to brainstorm a list of things that might happen during a surprise birthday party. Then play the **¡Feliz cumpleaños, Maite!** segment of this video module once, asking your students to take notes about what they see and hear. After viewing this video segment, have students use their notes to tell you what happened in this episode. Then play the segment again to allow your students to refine their notes. Repeat the discussion process and lead the class to an accurate summary of the plot.

Suggestion Go through the **Fotonovela**, asking for volunteers to read the various parts.

Expresiones útiles Draw attention to the forms **dijo** and **supe**. Explain that these are irregular preterite forms of the verbs **decir** and **saber**. Point out the phrase **no quisiste decírmelo** under video still 5 of the **Fotonovela**. Explain that **quisiste** is an irregular preterite form of the verb **querer**. Tell the class that **no querer** in the preterite means *to refuse*. Tell your students that they will learn more about these concepts in **Estructura**.

MAITE ¡Gracias! Pero, ¿quién le dijo que es mi cumpleaños?

DOÑA RITA Lo supe por don Francisco.

ÁLEX Ayer te lo pregunté, ¡y no quisiste decírmelo! ¿Eh? ¡Qué mala eres!

JAVIER ¿Cuántos años cumples?

MAITE Veintitrés.

INÉS Creo que debemos dejar una buena propina. ¿Qué les parece?

MAITE Sí, vamos a darle una buena propina a la señora Perales. Es simpatiquísima.

DON FRANCISCO Gracias una vez más. Siempre lo paso muy bien aquí.

MAITE Muchísimas gracias, señora Perales. Por la comida, por la sorpresa y por ser tan amable con nosotros.

Enfoque cultural Las celebraciones hispanas

Las celebraciones de la independencia, los carnavales y la Semana Santa son fiestas importantísimas en los países hispanos. Las fechas de Navidad y Noche Vieja (*New Year's Eve*) son, quizás, las más festejadas (*celebrated*). Otra celebración importante es el santo. Cada día del año tiene un santo asignado, y algunas personas que se llaman igual que el santo del día (*who have the same name as the day's saint*) lo celebran. El 19 de marzo, por ejemplo, los que se llaman José o Josefa celebran el día de San José.

Expresiones útiles

Celebrating a birthday party

▶ **¡Feliz cumpleaños!**
  Happy birthday!
▶ **¡Felicidades!/¡Felicitaciones!**
  Congratulations!

▶ **¿Quién le dijo que es mi cumpleaños?**
  Who told you (form.) *that it's my birthday?*
▷ **Lo supe por don Francisco.**
  I found out through don Francisco.

▶ **¿Cuántos años cumples/cumple Ud.?**
  How old are you now?
▷ **Veintitrés.**
  Twenty-three.

Asking for and getting the bill

▶ **¿Puede traernos la cuenta?**
  Can you bring us the bill?
▶ **La cuenta, por favor.**
  The bill, please.
▷ **Enseguida, señor/señora/señorita.**
  Right away, sir/ma'am/miss.

Expressing gratitude

▶ **¡(Muchas) gracias!**
  Thank you (very much)!
▶ **Muchísimas gracias.**
  Thank you very, very much.
▶ **Gracias por todo.**
  Thanks for everything.
▶ **Gracias una vez más.**
  Thanks again. (lit. Thanks one more time.)

Leaving a tip

▶ **Creo que debemos dejar una buena propina. ¿Qué les parece?**
  I think we should leave a good tip. What do you guys think?
▷ **Sí, vamos a darle una buena propina.**
  Yes, let's give her a good tip.

TEACHING OPTIONS

Enfoque cultural Tell the class that many young girls eagerly anticipate their **quinceañera**, or fifteenth birthday party, which celebrates their transition into adulthood. The **quinceañera** is frequently a lavish event with live music, catered food, and a long list of guests, who include people of all ages, especially the girl's parents, grandparents, aunts, uncles, and not just friends of the girl's own age. You might want to mention that for young men, the coming-of-age party traditionally coincides with the eighteenth or twenty-first birthday. Tell the class that many other events are celebrated by families in the Spanish-speaking world, including weddings, anniversaries, and graduations. Ask heritage speakers if they are aware of any other specific celebrations or festivals in the Hispanic world.

Reacciona a la fotonovela

1 **Completar** Completa las frases con la información correcta, según la fotonovela.

1. De postre, don Francisco siempre pide ____un café y un flan____.
2. A Javier le encanta ____el chocolate____.
3. Álex cumplió los ____veintitrés____ años ____el cuatro de mayo____.
4. Hoy Álex quiere tomar algo diferente. De postre, quiere pedir ____un pastel de chocolate____.
5. Los estudiantes le van a dejar ____una buena propina____ a doña Rita.

2 **Identificar** Identifica quién puede decir las siguientes frases.

1. Gracias, doña Rita, pero no puedo tomar vino. don Francisco
2. ¡Qué simpática es doña Rita! Fue tan amable conmigo. Maite
3. A mí me encantan los dulces y los pasteles, ¡especialmente si son de chocolate! Javier
4. Mi amigo acaba de informarme que hoy es el cumpleaños de Maite. doña Rita
5. ¿Tienen algún postre de fruta? Los postres de fruta son los mejores. Álex
6. Me parece una buena idea dejarle una buena propina a la dueña. ¿Qué piensan ustedes? Inés

JAVIER ÁLEX

INÉS MAITE

DON FRANCISCO DOÑA RITA

NOTA CULTURAL

En los países hispanos los camareros no dependen tanto de **las propinas** como en los EE.UU. Por eso, en estos países no es común dejar propina. Pero siempre es buena idea dejar una buena propina cuando el grupo es grande o el servicio es excepcional.

3 **Completar** Selecciona algunas de las opciones de la lista para completar las frases.

el amor	la cuenta	la galleta	la quinceañera
una botella de vino	día de fiesta	pedir	¡Qué sorpresa!
celebrar	el divorcio	un postre	una sorpresa

1. Maite no sabe que van a celebrar su cumpleaños porque es ____una sorpresa____.
2. Cuando una pareja celebra su aniversario y quiere tomar algo especial, compra ____una botella de vino____.
3. Después de una cena o un almuerzo, es normal pedir ____postre/la cuenta____.
4. Inés y Maite no saben exactamente lo que van a ____pedir____ de postre.
5. Después de comer en un restaurante, tienes que pagar ____la cuenta____.
6. Una pareja de enamorados nunca piensa en ____el divorcio____.
7. Hoy no trabajamos porque es un ____día de fiesta____.

CONSÚLTALO

Some Latin American countries mark a girl's fifteenth birthday by celebrating a **quinceañera**, a party in her honor in which she is "presented" to society. To read more, see **Lectura** p. 261.

4 **Fiesta sorpresa** Trabajen en grupos para representar una conversación en la que uno/a de ustedes está celebrando su cumpleaños en un restaurante. Answers will vary.

- Una persona le desea feliz cumpleaños a su compañero/a y le pregunta cuántos años cumple.
- Cada persona del grupo le pide al/a la camarero/a un postre y algo de beber.
- Después de terminar los postres, una persona pide la cuenta.
- Otra persona habla de dejar una propina.
- Los amigos que no cumplen años dicen que quieren pagar la cuenta.
- El/la que cumple años les da las gracias por todo.

---

1 **Expansion** Have students work in pairs or small groups to write questions that would have elicited these statements.

2 **Suggestion** Ask students these questions before doing this activity: **¿A quién le gusta mucho la fruta?** (a Álex) **¿A quién le gusta muchísimo el chocolate?** (a Javier) **¿Quién no puede tomar vino?** (don Francisco)

2 **Expansion** Give these additional items to your students: **7. ¡No me lo puedo creer! ¿Pastel de chocolate y flan para mí?** (Maite) **8. ¿Mi cumpleaños? Es el cuatro de mayo.** (Álex)

3 **Suggestion** Have the class review the vocabulary items on pages 242–243 before doing this activity.

3 **Expansion** Have pairs create additional sentences with the leftover items from the word bank.

4 **Possible Response**
E1: ¡Feliz cumpleaños! ¿Cuántos años cumples hoy?
E2: ¡Muchas gracias! Cumplo diecinueve.
E3: Buenas tardes. ¿En qué les puedo servir?
E1: Quisiera el pastel de chocolate y un café, por favor.
E2: Voy a pedir un pastel de chocolate con helado, y de tomar, un café.
[LATER...]
E1: ¿Puede usted traernos la cuenta?
E3: Enseguida, señor.
E2: La camarera fue muy amable. Debemos dejarle una buena propina, ¿no crees?
E1: Sí. Y yo voy a pagar la cuenta, porque es tu cumpleaños.
E2: Yo te ayudo. Gracias por todo…

TEACHING OPTIONS

Extra Practice Ask volunteers to ad-lib the **Fotonovela** episode for the class. Assure them that it is not necessary to memorize the **Fotonovela** or stick strictly to its content. They should try to get the general meaning across with the vocabulary and expressions they know, and they should also feel free to be creative.

Pairs Have your students work in pairs to tell each other about celebrations in their families. Remind them to use as many expressions as possible from the **Expresiones útiles** on page 247, as well as the vocabulary on pages 242–243. Follow up by asking a few students to describe celebrations in their partners' families.

Pronunciación 🎧

The letters **h**, **j**, and **g**

helado	**hombre**	**hola**	**hermosa**

The Spanish **h** is always silent.

José	**jubilarse**	**dejar**	**pareja**

The letter **j** is pronounced much like the English *h* in *his*.

agencia	**general**	**Gil**	**Gisela**

The letter **g** can be pronounced three different ways. Before **e** or **i**, the letter **g** is pronounced much like the English *h*.

Gustavo, gracias por llamar el domingo.

At the beginning of a phrase or after the letter **n**, the Spanish **g** is pronounced like the English *g* in *girl*.

Me gradué en agosto.

In any other position, the Spanish **g** has a somewhat softer sound.

Guerra	**conseguir**	**guantes**	**agua**

In the combinations **gue** and **gui**, the **g** has a hard sound and the **u** is silent. In the combination **gua**, the **g** has a hard sound and the **u** is pronounced like the English *w*.

Práctica Lee las palabras en voz alta, prestando atención a la **h**, la **j** y la **g**.

1. hamburguesa	5. geografía	9. seguir	13. Jorge
2. jugar	6. magnífico	10. gracias	14. tengo
3. oreja	7. espejo	11. hijo	15. ahora
4. guapa	8. hago	12. galleta	16. guantes

Oraciones Lee las oraciones en voz alta, prestando atención a la **h**, la **j** y la **g**.

1. Hola. Me llamo Gustavo Hinojosa Lugones y vivo en Santiago de Chile.
2. Tengo una familia grande; somos tres hermanos y tres hermanas.
3. Voy a graduarme en mayo.
4. Para celebrar mi graduación mis padres van a regalarme un viaje a Egipto.
5. ¡Qué generosos son!

Refranes Lee los refranes en voz alta, prestando atención a la **h**, la **j** y la **g**.

A la larga, lo más dulce amarga.[1]

El hábito no hace al monje.[2]

1 *Too much of a good thing.*
2 *The clothes don't make the man.*

recursos			
TEXT CD Lección 9	LM p. 50	Lab CD/MP3 Lección 9	I CD-ROM Lección 9

Section Goal

In **Pronunciación** students will be introduced to the pronunciation of **h**, **j**, and **g**.

Instructional Resources
Textbook Activities CD
Lab Manual, p. 50
Lab CD/MP3 **Lección 9**
IRM: Tapescript, pp. 40–44; p. 79
Interactive CD-ROM

Suggestions
- Ask the class how the Spanish **h** is pronounced. Ask volunteers to pronounce the example words.
- Explain that **j** is pronounced much like the English *h*.
- Draw attention to the fact that the letter **g** is pronounced like the English *h* before **e** or **i**. Write the example words on the board and ask volunteers to pronounce them.
- Point out that the letter **g** is pronounced like the English *g* in *good* at the beginning of a phrase or after the letter **n**.
- Explain that in any other position, particularly between vowels, **g** has a softer sound.
- Tell the class that in the combinations **gue** and **gui**, **g** has a hard sound and **u** is not pronounced. Explain that in the combinations **gua** and **guo**, the **u** sounds like the English *w*.

Práctica/Oraciones/Refranes
These exercises are recorded on the Textbook Activities CD. You may want to play the CD so students practice the pronunciation point by listening to Spanish spoken by speakers other than yourself.

TEACHING OPTIONS

Extra Practice Write the names of these Chilean cities on the board and ask for a volunteer to pronounce each one: **Santiago, Antofagasta, Rancagua, Coihaique**. Repeat the process with the names of these Chilean writers: **Alberto Blest Gana, Vicente Huidobro, Gabriela Mistral, Juan Modesto Castro**.

Pairs Have your students work in pairs to read aloud the sentences in **Actividad 2**, **Identificar**, page 248. Encourage your students to help their partners if they have trouble pronouncing a particular word.

9.1 Irregular preterites

ANTE TODO You already know that the verbs **ir** and **ser** are irregular in the preterite. You will now learn other verbs whose preterite forms are also irregular.

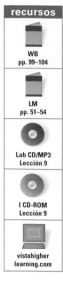

Preterite of *tener, venir,* and *decir*

		tener (u-stem)	venir (i-stem)	decir (j-stem)
SINGULAR FORMS	yo	tuve	vine	dije
	tú	tuviste	viniste	dijiste
	Ud./él/ella	tuvo	vino	dijo
PLURAL FORMS	nosotros/as	tuvimos	vinimos	dijimos
	vosotros/as	tuvisteis	vinisteis	dijisteis
	Uds./ellos/ellas	tuvieron	vinieron	dijeron

▶ The following verbs observe similar stem-changes to **tener, venir,** and **decir**.

INFINITIVE	U-STEM	PRETERITE FORMS
poder	pud-	pude, pudiste, pudo, pudimos, pudisteis, pudieron
poner	pus-	puse, pusiste, puso, pusimos, pusisteis, pusieron
saber	sup-	supe, supiste, supo, supimos, supisteis, supieron
estar	estuv-	estuve, estuviste, estuvo, estuvimos, estuvisteis, estuvieron

INFINITIVE	I-STEM	PRETERITE FORMS
querer	quis-	quise, quisiste, quiso, quisimos, quisisteis, quisieron
hacer	hic-	hice, hiciste, hizo, hicimos, hicisteis, hicieron

INFINITIVE	J-STEM	PRETERITE FORMS
traer	traj-	traje, trajiste, trajo, trajimos, trajisteis, trajeron
conducir	conduj-	conduje, condujiste, condujo, condujimos, condujisteis, condujeron
traducir	traduj-	traduje, tradujiste, tradujo, tradujimos, tradujisteis, tradujeron

¡ATENCIÓN!

The endings of these verbs are the regular preterite endings of **–er/–ir** verbs, except for the **yo** and **Ud./él/ella** forms. Note that these endings are unaccented.

¡ATENCIÓN!

Most verbs that end in **–cir** are **j**-stem verbs in the preterite. For example, **producir → produje, produjiste,** etc.

▶ Notice that the preterites with **j**-stems omit the letter **i** in the **ellos, ellas,** and **ustedes** form.

Mis amigos **trajeron** comida a la fiesta.   Ellos **comieron** muchos dulces.

ORBITEL
Larga distancia prepagada
$5.000
$10.000
$20.000

¿Dijiste larga distancia?

En tarjetas prepagadas ninguna te da más minutos para hablar

The preterite of *dar*

Singular forms		Plural forms	
yo	**di**	nosotros/as	**dimos**
tú	**diste**	vosotros/as	**disteis**
Ud./él/ella	**dio**	Uds./ellos/ellas	**dieron**

▶ The endings for **dar** are the same as the regular preterite endings for **–er** and **–ir** verbs, except that there are no accent marks.

La camarera me **dio** el menú.
The waitress gave me the menu.

Le **di** a Juan algunos consejos.
I gave Juan some advice.

Los invitados le **dieron** un regalo.
The guests gave him/her a gift.

Nosotros **dimos** una gran fiesta.
We gave a great party.

CONSÚLTALO

Note that there are other ways to say *there was* or *there were* in Spanish. See **Estructura 10.1**, p. 276.

▶ The preterite of **hay** (*inf.* **haber**) is **hubo** (*there was; there were*).

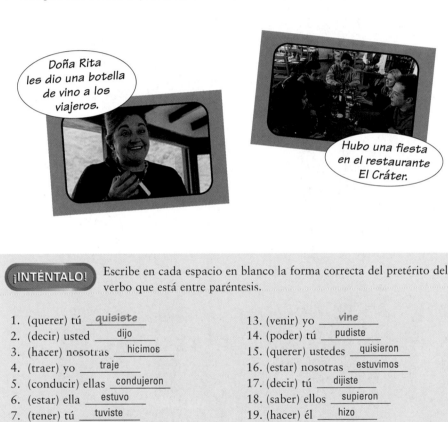

Doña Rita les dio una botella de vino a los viajeros.

Hubo una fiesta en el restaurante El Cráter.

¡INTÉNTALO! Escribe en cada espacio en blanco la forma correcta del pretérito del verbo que está entre paréntesis.

1. (querer) tú __quisiste__
2. (decir) usted __dijo__
3. (hacer) nosotras __hicimos__
4. (traer) yo __traje__
5. (conducir) ellas __condujeron__
6. (estar) ella __estuvo__
7. (tener) tú __tuviste__
8. (dar) ella y yo __dimos__
9. (traducir) yo __traduje__
10. (haber) ayer __hubo__
11. (saber) usted __supo__
12. (poner) ellos __pusieron__
13. (venir) yo __vine__
14. (poder) tú __pudiste__
15. (querer) ustedes __quisieron__
16. (estar) nosotras __estuvimos__
17. (decir) tú __dijiste__
18. (saber) ellos __supieron__
19. (hacer) él __hizo__
20. (poner) yo __puse__
21. (traer) nosotras __trajimos__
22. (tener) yo __tuve__
23. (dar) tú __diste__
24. (poder) ustedes __pudieron__

Suggestions
• Test comprehension by randomly calling out the infinitive of one of these verbs and a subject pronoun. Signal a student to give you the corresponding preterite form. Continue until you have covered a majority of the forms and given most of the class an opportunity to respond.
• Use the preterite forms of all these verbs by talking about what you did in the recent past and then asking students questions that involve them in a conversation about what they did in the recent past. You may want to avoid the preterite of **poder, saber**, and **querer** for the moment. Ex: **El sábado pasado tuve que ir a la fiesta de cumpleaños de mi sobrina. Cumplió siete años. Le di un bonito regalo. ____, ¿tuviste que ir a una fiesta el sábado? ¿No? Pues, ¿qué hiciste el sábado?**

TEACHING OPTIONS

Video Show the **Fotonovela** video again to give students more input containing irregular preterite forms. Stop the video where appropriate to discuss how certain verbs were used and to ask comprehension questions.

Extra Practice Have students write down six things they brought to class today. Then have them walk around the room asking other students if they also brought those items (**¿Trajiste tus llaves a clase hoy?**). When they find a student that answers **sí**, have them ask that student to sign his or her name next to that item (**Firma aquí, por favor.**). Can students get signatures for all the items they brought to class?

1 Expansion
• Ask individual students about the last time they threw a party. Ex: **La última vez que diste una fiesta, ¿quiénes estuvieron allí? ¿Fue alguien que no invitaste? ¿Qué llevaron los invitados?**

• Assign students to groups of three. Tell them they are going to write a narrative about a wedding. You will begin the story, then each student will add a sentence using a stem-changing verb in the preterite. Each group member should have at least two turns. Ex: **El domingo se casaron Carlos y Susana. (E1: Tuvieron una boda muy grande. E2: Vinieron muchos invitados. E3: Hubo un pastel enorme y elegante.)**

2 Suggestion There are several possible answers other than those given in the annotations. Encourage the class to see how many sentences they can come up with to describe each drawing using the target verbs.

2 Expansion Using magazine pictures, show images similar to those in the activity. Students narrate what is happening in the images using irregular preterite verb forms.

Práctica

1 **Completar** Completa estas frases con el pretérito de los verbos entre paréntesis.

1. El sábado ___hubo___ (haber) una fiesta sorpresa para Elsa en mi casa.
2. Sofía ___hizo___ (hacer) un pastel para la fiesta y Miguel ___trajo___ (traer) un flan.
3. Los amigos y parientes de Elsa ___vinieron___ (venir) y ___trajeron___ (traer) regalos.
4. El hermano de Elsa no ___vino___ (venir) porque ___tuvo___ (tener) que trabajar.
5. Su tía María Dolores tampoco ___pudo___ (poder) venir.
6. Cuando Elsa abrió la puerta, todos gritaron (*shouted*): "¡Feliz cumpleaños!" y su esposo le ___dio___ (dar) un beso.
7. Al final de la fiesta, todos ___dijeron___ (decir) que se divirtieron mucho.
8. La historia (*story*) le ___dio___ (dar) a Elsa tanta risa (*laughter*) que no ___pudo___ (poder) dejar de reírse durante toda la noche.

NOTA CULTURAL

El **flan** es un postre muy popular en los países de habla hispana. Se prepara con huevos y se sirve con salsa de caramelo. Existen variedades deliciosas como el flan de queso o el flan de coco.

2 **Describir** En parejas, usen verbos de la lista para describir lo que estas personas hicieron. Deben dar por lo menos dos frases por cada dibujo. *Some answers will vary.*

dar	hacer	tener	traer
estar	poner	traducir	venir

1. El señor López
El señor López le dio dinero a su hijo.

2. Norma
Norma puso el pavo en la mesa.

3. Anoche nosotros
Anoche nosotros tuvimos (hicimos/dimos) una fiesta de Navidad./Anoche nosotros estuvimos en una fiesta de Navidad.

4. Roberto y Elena
Roberto y Elena le trajeron/dieron un regalo a su amigo.

TEACHING OPTIONS

Heritage Speakers Ask heritage speakers to talk about a party they once attended. They should include information on what kind of party it was, who was there, what people brought, what the guests did, and so forth. Verify comprehension by asking other students in the class to relate what was said.

Small Groups In groups of three or four, each student writes three sentences using irregular preterites. Two of the sentences must be true for them and the third must be false. The other members of the group have to guess which of the sentences is the false one. This can also be done with the whole class.

Comunicación

3 **Preguntas** En parejas, túrnense para hacerse y responder a estas preguntas.
Answers will vary.
1. ¿Fuiste a una fiesta de cumpleaños el año pasado? ¿De quién?
2. ¿Quiénes fueron a la fiesta?
3. ¿Quién condujo el carro?
4. ¿Cómo estuvo la fiesta?
5. ¿Quién llevó regalos, bebidas o comida? ¿Llevaste algo especial?
6. ¿Hubo comida? ¿Quién la hizo? ¿Hubo champán?
7. ¿Qué regalo diste tú? ¿Qué otros regalos dieron los invitados?
8. ¿Cuántos invitados hubo en la fiesta?
9. ¿Qué tipo de música hubo?
10. ¿Qué dijeron los invitados de la fiesta?

4 **Encuesta** Tu profesor(a) va a darte una hoja de actividades. Para cada una de las actividades de la lista, encuentra a alguien que hizo esa actividad en el tiempo indicado.
Answers will vary.

> **modelo**
> Traer dulces a clase
> **Estudiante 1:** ¿Trajiste dulces a clase?
> **Estudiante 2:** Sí, traje galletas y helado a la fiesta del fin del semestre.

Actividades   **Nombres**
1. Ponerse un disfraz (costume) de Halloween
2. Traer dulces a clase
3. Conducir su carro a clase
4. Estar en la biblioteca ayer
5. Dar un beso a alguien ayer
6. Poder levantarse temprano esta mañana
7. Hacer un viaje a un país hispano en el verano
8. Tener una cita anoche
9. Ir a una fiesta el fin de semana pasado
10. Tener que trabajar el sábado pasado

NOTA CULTURAL

Halloween es una fiesta que también se celebra en algunos países hispanos, como México, por su proximidad con los Estados Unidos, pero no es parte de la cultura hispana. Sin embargo, sí lo es el Día de todos los Santos (1 de noviembre) y el Día de los Muertos (2 de noviembre). Según la tradición mexicana, el Día de los Muertos los espíritus de los muertos regresan para visitar a los vivos. Muchas personas van al cementerio ese día y algunas pasan la noche allí. También es costumbre comer pan y dulces en forma de calaveras (*skulls*) y esqueletos (*skeletons*).

Síntesis

5 **Conversación** En parejas, preparen una conversación en la que un(a) hermano/a va a visitar a su hermano/a para explicarle por qué no fue a su fiesta de graduación y para saber cómo estuvo la fiesta. Incluyan la siguiente información en la conversación:
Answers will vary.
- Cuál fue el menú
- Quiénes vinieron a la fiesta y quiénes no pudieron venir
- Quiénes prepararon la comida o trajeron algo
- Si él/ella tuvo que preparar algo
- Lo que la gente hizo antes y después de comer
- Cómo lo pasaron, bien o mal

---

3 **Suggestion** Instead of having students take turns, ask them to go through all the questions with their partners, writing down the information the partners give them. Later, have them write a third-person description about their partners' experiences.

3 **Expansion** To practice the formal register, call on different students to ask you the questions in the activity. Ex: **¿Fue usted a una fiesta de cumpleaños el año pasado? (Sí, fui a fiesta de la cumpleaños de Lisa.)**

4 **Suggestion** Distribute the **Hojas de actividades**. Point out that to get information, students must form questions using the **tú** forms of the infinitives. Ex: **¿Trajiste dulces a clase?**

4 **Expansion** Write items 1–10 on the board and ask for a show of hands for each item. Ex: **¿Quién trajo dulces a clase?** Write tally marks next to each item to find out which activity was the most popular.

5 **Expansion** Have pairs work in groups of four to write a paragraph combining the most interesting or unusual aspects of each pair's conversation. Ask a group representative to read the paragraph to the class, who will later vote for the most creative or funniest paragraph.

TEACHING OPTIONS

Extra Practice Ask students to write a brief composition on the **Fotonovela** from this lesson. Students should write about where the characters were, what they were doing, who ordered what, what they said to each other, and so forth. (Note: Students should stick to completed actions in the past [preterite]. The use of the imperfect for narrating a story will not be presented until **Lección 10.**)

Large Groups Divide the class in half. To each member of the first half give a strip of paper that has a question on it. Ex: **¿Quién me trajo el pastel de cumpleaños?** To each member of the second half give the answer to that question. Ex: **Marta te lo trajo.** Students must find their partners.

Section Goal

In **Estructura 9.2** students will be introduced to verbs that change meaning in the preterite tense.

Instructional Resources

WB/VM: Workbook, p. 101
Lab Manual, p. 52
*Lab CD/MP3 **Lección 9***
IRM: ¡Inténtalo! & Práctica
Answers, p. 186; Tapescript,
pp. 40–44
Interactive CD-ROM
Companion website:
www.vistahigherlearning.com
Presentations CD-ROM

Suggestions

• Introduce the preterite of **conocer**. Say: **Los conozco a ustedes muy bien ahora. Pero me acuerdo del día en que los conocí. ¿Ustedes se acuerdan del día en que nos conocimos?** Ask volunteers to compare and contrast the meanings of **conocer** in your example.

• Stress the meaning of **poder** in the preterite by giving both affirmative (*to manage; to succeed*) and negative (*to try and fail*) examples. Ex: **Pude leer todas sus composiciones anoche, pero no pude leer las composiciones de la otra clase.**

• Stress the meaning of **querer** in the preterite by giving both affirmative (*to try*) and negative (*to refuse*) examples. Ex: **Quisimos ver una película el sábado, pero no quise ver ninguna película violenta.**

9.2 Verbs that change meaning in the preterite

ANTE TODO The verbs **conocer**, **saber**, **poder**, and **querer** change meanings when used in the preterite. Because of this, each of them corresponds to more than one verb in English, depending on its tense.

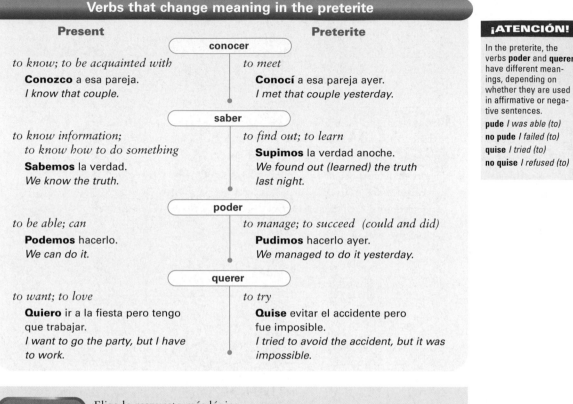

Verbs that change meaning in the preterite

Present	Preterite
conocer	
to know; to be acquainted with	*to meet*
Conozco a esa pareja.	**Conocí** a esa pareja ayer.
I know that couple.	*I met that couple yesterday.*
saber	
to know information; to know how to do something	*to find out; to learn*
Sabemos la verdad.	**Supimos** la verdad anoche.
We know the truth.	*We found out (learned) the truth last night.*
poder	
to be able; can	*to manage; to succeed (could and did)*
Podemos hacerlo.	**Pudimos** hacerlo ayer.
We can do it.	*We managed to do it yesterday.*
querer	
to want; to love	*to try*
Quiero ir a la fiesta pero tengo que trabajar.	**Quise** evitar el accidente pero fue imposible.
I want to go the party, but I have to work.	*I tried to avoid the accident, but it was impossible.*

¡ATENCIÓN!

In the preterite, the verbs **poder** and **querer** have different meanings, depending on whether they are used in affirmative or negative sentences.

pude *I was able (to)*
no pude *I failed (to)*
quise *I tried (to)*
no quise *I refused (to)*

¡INTÉNTALO! Elige la respuesta más lógica.

1. Yo no hice lo que me pidieron mis padres. ¡Tengo mis principios! a
   a. No quise hacerlo.   b. No supe hacerlo.

2. Hablamos por primera vez con Nuria y Ana en la boda. a
   a. Las conocimos en la boda.   b. Las supimos en la boda.

3. Por fin hablé con mi hermano después de llamarlo siete veces. b
   a. No quise hablar con él.   b. Pude hablar con él.

4. Josefina se acostó para relajarse. Se durmió inmediatamente. a
   a. Pudo relajarse.   b. No pudo relajarse.

5. Después de mucho buscar, encontraste la definición en el diccionario. b
   a. No supiste la respuesta.   b. Supiste la repuesta.

6. Las chicas fueron a la fiesta. Cantaron, bailaron mucho y hablaron con todos los invitados. a
   a. Ellas pudieron divertirse.   b. Ellas no supieron divertirse.

TEACHING OPTIONS

Extra Practice Give sentences using **conocer**, **saber**, **poder**, and **querer** in the present tense that will be logical when converted into the preterite. Have students convert them and explain how the meanings of the sentences change. Ex: **Sé la fecha de la fiesta. Gustavo puede comprar un regalo bonito. Queremos conocer a los invitados. Felipe y Paula no quieren ir a la fiesta. No puedo hacer un flan.**

Heritage Speakers Ask heritage speakers to talk about one of the following situations in the past: (1) when they found out there was no Santa Claus (**saber**), (2) when they met their best friend (**conocer**), or (3) something they tried to do but could not (**querer/no poder**). Verify student comprehension by asking other students to relate what was said.

Práctica

1

Carlos y Eva Forma frases con los siguientes elementos. Usa el pretérito. Al final, inventa la razón del divorcio de Carlos y Eva.

1. Anoche / mi esposa y yo / saber / que / Carlos y Eva / divorciarse
   Anoche mi esposa y yo supimos que Carlos y Eva se divorciaron.

NOTA CULTURAL

La Isla de Pascua es un remoto territorio chileno situado en el océano Pacífico Sur. Sus inmensas estatuas son uno de los mayores misterios del mundo: nadie sabe cómo o por qué se construyeron. Para más información, véase **Panorama**, p. 265.

▶ 2. Los / conocer / viaje / Isla de Pascua
   Los conocimos en un viaje a la Isla de Pascua.
3. No / poder / hablar / mucho / con / ellos / ese / día
   No pudimos hablar mucho con ellos ese día.
4. Pero / ellos / ser / simpático / y / nosotros / hacer planes / vernos / con más / frecuencia
   Pero ellos fueron simpáticos y nosotros hicimos planes para vernos con más frecuencia.
5. Yo / poder / su / número / teléfono / encontrar / páginas / amarillo
   Yo pude encontrar su número de teléfono en las páginas amarillas.
. 6. (Yo) querer / llamar / les / ese día / pero / no / tener / tiempo.
   Quise llamarles ese día pero no tuve tiempo.
7. Cuando / los / llamar / nosotros / poder / hablar / Eva.
   Cuando los llamé, nosotros pudimos hablar con Eva.
8. Nosotros / saber / razón / divorcio / después / hablar / ella
   Nosotros supimos la razón del divorcio después de hablar con ella.

Comunicación

2

Completar Completa estas frases de una manera lógica. Answers will vary.

1. Ayer mi compañero/a de cuarto supo...
2. Esta mañana no pude...
3. Conocí a mi mejor amigo/a en...
4. Mis padres no quisieron...
5. Mi mejor amigo/a no pudo...
6. Mi novio/a y yo nos conocimos en...
7. La semana pasada supe...
8. Ayer mis amigos quisieron...

3

Telenovela (*Soap opera*) En parejas, escriban el diálogo para una escena de una telenovela. La escena trata de (*is about*) una situación amorosa entre tres personas: Mirta, Daniel y Raúl. Usen el pretérito de **conocer, poder, querer** y **saber** en su diálogo. Answers will vary.

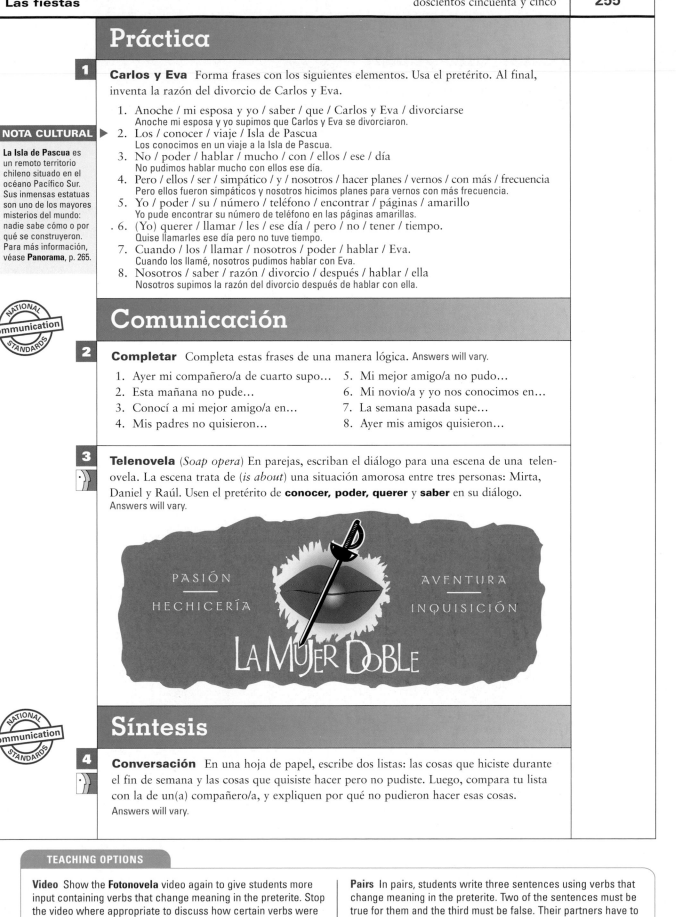

PASIÓN — HECHICERÍA — AVENTURA — INQUISICIÓN

LA MUJER DOBLE

Síntesis

4

Conversación En una hoja de papel, escribe dos listas: las cosas que hiciste durante el fin de semana y las cosas que quisiste hacer pero no pudiste. Luego, compara tu lista con la de un(a) compañero/a, y expliquen por qué no pudieron hacer esas cosas. Answers will vary.

TEACHING OPTIONS

Video Show the **Fotonovela** video again to give students more input containing verbs that change meaning in the preterite. Stop the video where appropriate to discuss how certain verbs were used and to ask comprehension questions.

Pairs In pairs, students write three sentences using verbs that change meaning in the preterite. Two of the sentences must be true for them and the third must be false. Their partners have to guess which of the sentences are false.

---

1 Suggestion This activity can also be done in pairs.

1 Expansion
• In pairs, students create five similar dehydrated sentences for their partners to complete, using the verbs **conocer, saber, poder,** and **querer**. After pairs have completed this, ask volunteers to share some of their dehydrated sentences. Write them on the board and have the rest of the class "hydrate" them.
• Have pairs use preterite forms of **conocer, saber, poder,** and **querer** to role-play Carlos and Eva explaining their separate versions of the divorce to their friends.

2 Suggestion Before assigning the activity, share with the class some recent things you found out, tried to do but could not, or the names of people you met, inviting students to respond.

3 Suggestion Point out that unlike their U.S. counterparts, Hispanic soap operas run for a limited period of time, like a miniseries, and then end.

4 Expansion Have pairs repeat the activity, this time describing another person. Ask students to share their descriptions with the class, who will guess who is being described.

Section Goals

In **Estructura 9.3** students will review:
• the uses of ¿qué? and ¿cuál?
• interrogative words and phrases

Instructional Resources

WB/VM: Workbook, pp. 102–103
Lab Manual, p. 53
Lab CD/MP3 **Lección 9**
IRM: ¡Inténtalo! & Práctica
Answers, p. 186; Tapescript, pp. 40–44
Info Gap Activities Booklet, pp. 33–34
Interactive CD-ROM
Companion website: www.vistahigherlearning.com
Presentations CD-ROM

Suggestions

• Review the question words ¿qué? and ¿cuál? Write incomplete questions on the board and ask students which interrogative word best completes each sentence. Ex: **1. ¿____ es tu número de teléfono? (Cuál) 2. ¿____ es esto? (Qué)**
• Point out that while both question words mean *what?* or *which?*, ¿qué? is used with a noun, whereas ¿cuál? is used with a verb. Ex: **¿Qué clase te gusta más? ¿Cuál es tu clase favorita?**
• Review the chart of interrogative words and phrases. Ask students personalized questions using each of them and invite them to ask you questions. Ex: **¿Cuál es tu película favorita? (*Como agua para chocolate*) ¿Qué director es tu favorito? (Pedro Almodóvar)**

9.3 ¿Qué? and ¿cuál?

ANTE TODO   You've already learned how to use interrogative words and phrases. As you know, **¿qué?** and **¿cuál?** or **¿cuáles?** mean *what?* or *which?* However, they are not interchangeable.

▶ **¿Qué?** is used to ask for a definition or an explanation.

¿Qué es el flan?	**¿Qué** estudias?
What is flan?	*What do you study?*

▶ **¿Cuál(es)?** is used when there is a choice among several possibilities.

¿Cuál de los dos prefieres, el vino o el champán?	**¿Cuáles** son tus medias, las negras o las blancas?
Which of these (two) do you prefer, wine or champagne?	*Which ones are your socks, the black ones or the white ones?*

▶ **¿Cuál?** cannot be used before a noun; in this case, **¿qué?** is used.

¿Qué sorpresa te dieron tus amigos?	**¿Qué** colores te gustan?
What surprise did your friends give you?	*What colors do you like?*

▶ **¿Qué?** used before a noun has the same meaning as **¿cuál?**

¿Qué regalo te gusta?	**¿Qué dulces** quieren ustedes?
What (Which) gift do you like?	*What (Which) sweets do you want?*

Review of interrogative words and phrases

¿a qué hora?	*at what time?*	**¿cuánto/a?**	*how much?*
¿adónde?	*(to) where?*	**¿cuántos/as?**	*how many?*
¿cómo?	*how?*	**¿de dónde?**	*from where?*
¿cuál(es)?	*what?; which?*	**¿dónde?**	*where?*
¿cuándo?	*when?*	**¿qué?**	*what?; which?*
		¿quién(es)?	*who?*

¡INTÉNTALO!   Completa las preguntas con **¿qué?** o **¿cuál(es)?**, según el contexto.

1. ¿ __Cuál__ de los dos te gusta más?
2. ¿ __Cuál__ es tu teléfono?
3. ¿ __Qué__ tipo de pastel pediste?
4. ¿ __Qué__ es una quinceañera?
5. ¿ __Qué__ haces ahora?
6. ¿ __Cuáles__ son tus platos favoritos?
7. ¿ __Qué__ bebidas te gustan más?
8. ¿ __Qué__ es esto?
9. ¿ __Cuál__ es el mejor?
10. ¿ __Cuál__ es tu opinión?
11. ¿ __Qué__ fiestas celebras tú?
12. ¿ __Qué__ botella de vino prefieres?
13. ¿ __Cuál__ es tu helado favorito?
14. ¿ __Qué__ pones en la mesa?
15. ¿ __Qué__ restaurante prefieres?
16. ¿ __Qué__ estudiantes estudian más?
17. ¿ __Qué__ quieres comer esta noche?
18. ¿ __Cuál__ es la sorpresa mañana?
19. ¿ __Qué__ postre prefieres?
20. ¿ __Qué__ opinas?

TEACHING OPTIONS

Extra Practice Ask questions of individual students, using ¿qué? and ¿cuál? Make sure a portion of the questions are general and information-seeking in nature (¿qué?). Ex: **¿Qué es una guitarra? ¿Qué es un elefante?** This is also a good way for students to practice circumlocution (**Es algo que…**).

Extra Practice Students write one question using each of the interrogative words or phrases in the chart on this page. Then they ask those questions of a partner, who must answer in complete sentences.

Práctica

1

Completar Tu clase de español va a crear un sitio web. Completa estas frases con alguna(s) palabra(s) interrogativa(s). Luego, con un(a) compañero/a hagan y contesten las preguntas para obtener la información para el sitio web.

1. ¿____Cuál____ es la fecha de tu cumpleaños?
2. ¿___Dónde___ naciste?
3. ¿____Cuál____ es tu estado civil?
4. ¿_____ te relajas? Cómo/Cuándo/Dónde
5. ¿___Quién___ es tu mejor amigo/a?
6. ¿____Qué____ cosas te hacen reír?
7. ¿____Qué____ postres te gustan? ¿____Cuál____ te gusta más?
8. ¿____Qué____ problemas tuviste en la primera cita con alguien?

Comunicación

2

Una invitación En parejas, lean esta invitación. Luego, túrnense para hacer y contestar preguntas con **qué** y **cuál** basadas en la información de la invitación. Answers will vary.

modelo

> **Estudiante 1:** ¿Cuál es el nombre del padre de la novia?
> **Estudiante 2:** Su nombre es Fernando Sandoval Valera.

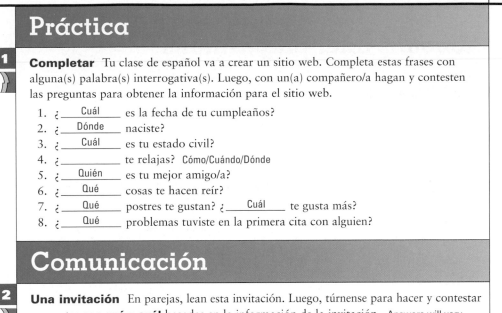

Fernando Sandoval Valera   Lorenzo Vásquez Amaral
Isabel Arzipe de Sandoval   Elena Soto de Vásquez

tienen el agrado de invitarlos
a la boda de sus hijos

María Luisa y José Antonio

La ceremonia religiosa tendrá lugar
el sábado 10 de junio a las dos de la tarde
en el Templo de Santo Domingo
(Calle Santo Domingo, 961).

Después de la ceremonia sírvanse pasar a la recepción en el salón
de baile del Hotel Metrópoli (Sotero del Río, 465).

3

Quinceañera Trabaja con un(a) compañero/a. Uno/a de ustedes es el/la director(a) del salón de fiestas "Renacimiento". El/la otro/a es el padre/la madre de Ana María, quien quiere hacer la fiesta de quinceañera de su hija sin gastar más de $25 por invitado/a. Su profesor(a) va a darles la información necesaria para confirmar la reservación.

Answers will vary.

modelo

> **Estudiante 1:** ¿Cuánto cuestan los entremeses?
> **Estudiante 2:** Depende. Puede escoger champiñones por 50 centavos o camarones por dos dólares.
> **Estudiante 1:** ¡Uf! A mi hija le gustan los camarones, pero son muy caros.
> **Estudiante 2:** Bueno, también puede escoger quesos por un dólar por invitado.

TEACHING OPTIONS

Pairs In pairs, students prepare a skit between two friends talking. One of the friends is planning a surprise party (**fiesta sorpresa**) for a mutual friend. However, the other person reveals that he or she does not care all that much for the party honoree and tells why. The class can vote for the funniest or most original skit.

Game Play a game of *Jeopardy*®. Prepare five answers for each of six categories (30 questions in all), each in varying degrees of difficulty. Ask for three volunteers to play. Students must give their answers in the form of a question. You may also decrease the number of questions and have additional volunteers participate in the game.

---

1 Expansion Conduct a conversation with the whole class to find consensus on some of the questions.

2 Expansion
- Ask students to share some of the questions they asked their partner, which other students answer in complete sentences.
- Have pairs design an invitation to a party, wedding, **quinceañera**, or other social event. Then have them answer questions from the class about their invitation without showing it. The class guesses what kind of social event is announced. Ex: ¿**Dónde es el evento? (En el salón de baile "Cosmopolita") ¿A qué hora es? (A las ocho de la noche) ¿De quiénes es la invitación? (de los señores López Pujol) Es una quinceañera. (Sí)** Finally, have pairs reveal their design to the class.

3 Suggestion Divide the class into pairs and distribute the handouts from the Information Gap Activities Booklet that correspond to this activity. Give students ten minutes to complete this activity.

3 Expansion With the same partner or in small groups, have students prepare a **telenovela** skit with characters from the **quinceañera** activity. Encourage students to use interrogative words as well as verbs that change meaning in the preterite.

Section Goals

In **Estructura 9.4** students will be
introduced to:
• pronouns as objects of
  prepositions
• the pronoun-preposition combinations **conmigo** and **contigo**

Instructional Resources
WB/VM: Workbook, p. 104
Lab Manual, p. 54
Lab CD/MP3 **Lección 9**
IRM: **¡Inténtalo!** & **Práctica**
Answers, p. 186; Tapescript,
pp. 40–44
Info Gap Activities Booklet,
pp. 35–36
Interactive CD-ROM
Companion website:
www.vistahigherlearning.com
Presentations CD-ROM

Suggestions
• Review the chart "Prepositions often used with **estar**" in
  Estructura 2.3. Use prepositional pronouns as you
  describe yourself and others
  in relation to people and
  things. Say: **¿Quién está
  delante de mí? Sí, _____ está
  delante de mí. ¿Y quién está
  detrás de ella? Sí, _____ está
  detrás de ella.**
• Ask students which pronouns
  they recognize and which are
  new. Ask the class to deduce
  the rules for pronouns after
  prepositions.

9.4 Pronouns after prepositions

ANTE TODO   In Spanish, as in English, the object of a preposition is the noun or
pronoun that follows a preposition. Observe the following diagram.

PREPOSITION	NOUN	PREPOSITION	PRONOUN
La sopa es para	Alicia	y para	él.

Prepositional pronouns

	Singular			Plural	
	mí	me		**nosotros/as**	us
	ti	you (fam.)		**vosotros/as**	you (fam.)
preposition +	**Ud.**	you (form.)		**Uds.**	you (form.)
	él	him		**ellos**	them (m.)
	ella	her		**ellas**	them (f.)

▶ Note that, except for **mí** and **ti,** these pronouns are the same as the subject pronouns.

▶ The preposition **con** combines with **mí** and **ti** to form **conmigo** and **contigo,** respectively.

—¿Quieres venir **conmigo** a Concepción?   —Sí, gracias, me gustaría ir **contigo.**
Do you want to come with me to Concepción?   *Yes, thanks, I would like to go with you.*

▶ The preposition **entre** is followed by **tú** and **yo** instead of **ti** and **mí.**

Papá va a sentarse **entre tú y yo.**
Dad is going to sit between you and me.

¡ATENCIÓN!

Remember that **mí** (*me*)
has an accent mark to
distinguish it from the
possessive adjective
mi (*my*).

CONSÚLTALO

For more prepositions,
refer to **Estructura 2.3,**
p. 50.

¡INTÉNTALO!   Completa las frases con las preposiciones y los
pronombres apropiados.

1. *(with him)* No quiero ir ___con él___ .
2. *(for her)* Las galletas son ___para ella___ .
3. *(for me)* Los mariscos son ___para mí___ .
4. *(with you, pl. form.)* Preferimos estar ___con ustedes___ .
5. *(with you, fam.)* Me gusta salir ___contigo___ .
6. *(with me)* ¿Por qué no quieres tener una cita ___conmigo___ ?
7. *(for her)* La cuenta es ___para ella___ .
8. *(for them, m.)* La habitación es muy pequeña ___para ellos___ .
9. *(with them, f.)* Anoche celebré la Navidad ___con ellas___ .
10. *(for you, fam.)* Este beso es ___para ti___ .
11. *(with you, fam.)* Nunca me aburro ___contigo___ .
12. *(with you, pl. form.)* ¡Qué bien que vamos ___con ustedes___ !
13. *(for you, fam.)* ___Para ti___ la vida es muy fácil.
14. *(for them, f.)* ___Para ellas___ no hay sorpresas.

TEACHING OPTIONS

Extra Practice Describe someone in the classroom using
prepositions of location, but do not indicate who that person is.
Ex: **Esta persona está entre la ventana y _____. Y está enfrente
de mí.** The rest of the class has to guess the person being
described. Once students have this model, ask individuals to
create similar descriptions so that their classmates may guess
who is being described.

Game Divide the class into two teams. One student from team A
chooses an item that is in the classroom and writes it down. Call
on five students from team B one at a time to ask questions
about where this item is. Ex: **¿Está cerca de mí?** The first student can respond with **sí, no, caliente,** or **frío.** If a team guesses
the item within five tries, give them a point. If not, give the other
team a point. The team with the most points wins.

Práctica

1 **Completar** David sale con sus amigos a comer. Para saber quién come qué, lee el mensaje electrónico que David le envió (*sent*) a Cecilia dos días después y completa el diálogo en el restaurante con los pronombres apropiados.

> **modelo**
> **Camarero:** Los camarones en salsa verde, ¿para quién son?
> **David:** Son para ___ella___.

NOTA CULTURAL

Las **machas a la parmesana** es un plato muy típico de Chile. Se prepara con machas, un tipo de almeja (*clam*) que se encuentra en Suramérica. Las machas a la parmesana se hacen con queso parmesano, limón, sal, pimienta y mantequilla, y luego se ponen en el horno (*oven*).

Para	Asunto

Hola, Cecilia:
¿Recuerdas la comida del viernes? Quiero repetir el menú en mi casa el miércoles. Ahora voy a escribir lo que comimos, luego me dices si falta algún plato. Yo pedí el filete de pescado y Maribel camarones en salsa verde. Tatiana pidió un plato grandísimo de machas a la parmesana. Diana y Silvia pidieron langostas, ¿te acuerdas? Y tú, ¿qué pediste? Ah, sí, un bistec grande con papas. Héctor también pidió un bistec, pero más pequeño. Miguel pidió pollo y vino tinto para todos. Y la profesora comió ensalada verde porque está a dieta. ¿Falta algo? Espero tu mensaje. Hasta pronto. David.

CAMARERO	El filete de pescado, ¿para quién es?
DAVID	Es para (1)___mí___.
CAMARERO	Aquí está. ¿Y las machas a la parmesana y las langostas?
DAVID	Las machas son para (2)___ella___.
SILVIA Y DIANA	Las langostas son para (3)___nosotras___.
CAMARERO	Tengo un bistec grande...
DAVID	Cecilia, es para (4)___ti___, ¿no es cierto? (*Cecilia nods.*) Y el bistec más pequeño es para (5)___él___.
CAMARERO	¿Y la botella de vino?
MIGUEL	Es para todos (6)___nosotros___, y el pollo es para (7)___mí___.
CAMARERO	(*a la profesora*) Entonces la ensalada verde es para (8)___usted___.

Comunicación

2 **Compartir** Tu profesor(a) va a darte una hoja de actividades en la que hay un dibujo. En parejas, hagan preguntas para saber dónde está cada una de las personas en el dibujo. Ustedes tienen dos versiones diferentes de la ilustración. Al final (*end*) deben saber dónde está cada persona.

AYUDA

Here are some other useful prepositions: **al lado de, debajo de, a la derecha de, a la izquierda de, cerca de, lejos de, delante de, detrás de, entre.**

> **modelo**
> **Estudiante 1:** ¿Quién está al lado de Óscar?
> **Estudiante 2:** Alfredo está al lado de él.

Alfredo	Dolores	Graciela	Raúl
Sra. Blanco	Enrique	Leonor	Rubén
Carlos	Sra. Gómez	Óscar	Yolanda

1 Suggestion Remind students that they are to fill in the blanks with prepositional pronouns, not names of the characters in the conversation.

1 Expansion In small groups, have students play the roles of the people mentioned in the e-mail message. Ex: **E1: ¿Para quién son los camarones? E2: Son para mí. E1: ¿Y el bistec? E2: Es para él.**

2 Suggestion Divide the class into pairs and distribute the handouts from the Information Gap Activities Booklet that correspond to this activity. Give students ten minutes to complete this activity.

2 Expansion
• Using both versions of the drawing as a guide, ask questions of the whole class to find out where the people are. Ex: **¿Quién sabe dónde está la señora Blanco?**
• Verify that all students labeled the characters correctly by suggesting changes to the drawing and using prepositions to ask about their new locations. Ex: **Yolanda y Carlos cambian de lugar. ¿Quién está al lado de Yolanda ahora? (Rubén)**

TEACHING OPTIONS

Video Show the **Fotonovela** video module again to give students more input containing prepositional pronouns. Stop the video where appropriate to discuss how certain pronouns were used and to ask comprehension questions.

Large Groups Give half of the class cards that contain an activity (Ex: **jugar al baloncesto**) and give the other half cards that contain a place (Ex: **el gimnasio**). Activity card students circulate around the room to find places that match their activities. Ex: **E1: Voy a jugar al baloncesto. ¿Puedo ir contigo? E2: Pues, yo voy al museo. No puedes ir conmigo.** or **Voy al gimnasio. Sí, puedes ir conmigo.**

Lectura

Antes de leer

communication cultures — NATIONAL STANDARDS

Estrategia
Recognizing word families

Recognizing root words can help you guess the meaning of words in context, ensuring better comprehension of a reading selection. Using this strategy will enrich your Spanish vocabulary as you will see below.

Examinar el texto

Familiarízate con el texto usando las estrategias de lectura más efectivas para ti. ¿Qué tipo de documento es? ¿De qué tratan° las cuatro secciones del documento? Explica tus respuestas.

Raíces°

Completa el siguiente cuadro° para ampliar tu vocabulario. Usa palabras de la lectura de esta lección y el vocabulario de las lecciones anteriores. ¿Qué significan las palabras que escribiste en el cuadro? Answers will vary.

modelo

Verbo	Sustantivos	Otras formas
agradecer	agradecimiento/gracias	agradecido

	Verbo	Sustantivos	Otras formas
1.	estudiar	estudiante *student*	estudiado *studied*
2.	celebrar *to celebrate*	celebración *celebration*	celebrado
3.	bailar *to dance*	baile	bailable *danceable*
4.	bautizar	bautismo *baptism*	bautizado *baptized*

recursos

vistahigher
learning.com

¿De qué tratan...? *What are they about?*
Raíces *Roots* cuadro *chart*

Vida social

Matrimonio
Espinoza Álvarez-Reyes Salazar

El día sábado 12 de junio de 2004 a las 19 horas, se celebró el matrimonio de Silvia Reyes y Carlos Espinoza en la Catedral de Santiago. La ceremonia fue oficiada por el pastor Federico Salas y participaron los padres de los novios, el señor Jorge Espinoza y señora y el señor José Alfredo Reyes y señora. Después de la ceremonia, los padres de los recién casados ofrecieron una fiesta bailable en el restaurante Doña Mercedes.

Bautismo

José María recibió el bautismo el 26 de junio de 2004.

Sus padres, don Roberto Lagos Moreno y doña María Angélica Sánchez, compartieron la alegría de la fiesta con todos sus parientes y amigos. La ceremonia religiosa tuvo lugar° en la Catedral de Aguas Blancas. Después de la ceremonia, padres, parientes y amigos celebraron una fiesta en la residencia de la familia Lagos.

32B

Fiesta quinceañera

El doctor don Amador Larenas Fernández y la señora Felisa Vera de Larenas celebraron los quince años de su hija Ana Ester junto a sus parientes y amigos. La quinceañera° reside en la ciudad de Valparaíso y es estudiante del Colegio Francés. La fiesta de presentación en sociedad de la señorita Ana Ester fue el día viernes 4 de mayo a las 19 horas, en el Club Español. Entre los invitados especiales asistieron el alcalde° de la ciudad, don Pedro Castedo, y su esposa. La música estuvo a cargo de la Orquesta Americana. ¡Feliz cumpleaños le deseamos a la señorita Ana Ester en su fiesta bailable!

Expresión de gracias
Carmen Godoy Tapia

Agradecemos° sinceramente a todas las personas que nos acompañaron en el último adiós a nuestra apreciada esposa, madre, abuela y tía, la señora Carmen Godoy Tapia. El funeral tuvo lugar el día 28 de junio de 2004 en la ciudad de Viña del Mar. La vida de Carmen Godoy fue un ejemplo de trabajo, amistad, alegría y amor para todos nosotros. La familia agradece de todo corazón° su asistencia° al funeral a todos los parientes y amigos. Su esposo, hijos y familia.

tuvo lugar *took place* quinceañera *fifteen year-old girl* alcalde *mayor* Agradecemos *We thank* de todo corazón *sincerely* asistencia *attendance*

Después de leer

Corregir
Escribe estos comentarios otra vez para corregir la información errónea.

1. El alcalde y su esposa asistieron a la boda de Silvia y Carlos. El alcalde y su esposa asistieron a la fiesta de quinceañera de Ana Ester.
2. Todos los anuncios° describen eventos felices. Tres de los anuncios tratan de eventos felices. Uno trata de una muerte.
3. Ana Ester Larenas cumple dieciséis años. Ana Ester Larenas cumple quince años.
4. Roberto Lagos y María Angélica Sánchez son hermanos. Roberto Lagos y María Angélica Sánchez están casados/son esposos.
5. Carmen Godoy Tapia les dio las gracias a las personas que asistieron al funeral. La familia de Carmen Godoy Tapia les dio las gracias a las personas que asistieron al funeral.

Identificar
Escribe el nombre de la(s) persona(s) descrita(s)°.

1. Dejó viudo a su esposo en junio de 2004. Carmen Godoy Tapia
2. Sus padres y todos los invitados brindaron por él, pero él no entendió por qué. José María
3. El Club Español les presentó una cuenta considerable para pagar. don Amador Larenas Fernández y doña Felisa Vera de Larenas
4. Unió a los novios en santo matrimonio. el pastor Federico Salas
5. La celebración de su cumpleaños marcó el comienzo de su vida adulta. Ana Ester

Un anuncio
Trabaja con dos o tres compañeros/as de clase e inventen un anuncio breve sobre una celebración importante. Esta celebración puede ser una graduación, un matrimonio o una gran fiesta en la que ustedes participan. Incluyan la siguiente información. Answers will vary.

1. Nombres de los participantes
2. La fecha, la hora y el lugar
3. Qué se celebra
4. Otros detalles de interés

anuncios *announcements* descritas *described*

Section Goals

In **Escritura** students will:
- learn how to use a Spanish-English dictionary.
- learn words and phrases that signal similarity and difference
- write a comparative analysis

Estrategia Work through this writing strategy with your students, emphasizing that bilingual dictionaries are valuable tools when used properly. Also, point out that not all Spanish-English dictionaries are alike. Encourage students to compare several Spanish-English dictionaries and use the one whose format makes the most sense to them.

Tema Explain to students that to write a comparative analysis, they will need to use words or phrases that signal similarities (**similitudes**) and differences (**diferencias**). Model the pronunciation of the words and expressions under **Escribir una composición** with the whole class.

Suggestion Tell students to consult the **Plan de Escritura** in **Apéndice A**, page 448, for step-by-step writing instructions. Remind them to use the dictionary properly as they write. You might also tell them to refer to the **Doing a comparative analysis** strategy in **Apéndice A**, page 449.

Escritura

Estrategia
Using a dictionary

A common mistake made by beginning language learners is to embrace the dictionary as the ultimate resource for reading, writing, and speaking. While it is true that the dictionary is a useful tool that can provide valuable information about vocabulary, using the dictionary correctly requires that you understand the elements of each entry.

If you glance at a Spanish-English dictionary, you will notice that its format is similar to that of an English dictionary. The word is listed first, usually followed by its pronunciation. Then come the definitions, organized by parts of speech. Sometimes the most frequently used definitions are listed first.

To find the best word for your needs, you should refer to the abbreviations and the explanatory notes that appear next to the entries. For example, imagine that you are writing about your pastimes. You want to write, "I want to buy a new racket for my match tomorrow," but you don't know the Spanish word for "racket." In the dictionary, you may find an entry like this:

> **racket** s 1. alboroto; 2. raqueta *(dep.)*

The abbreviation key at the front of the dictionary says that *s* corresponds to **sustantivo** *(noun)*. Then, the first word you see is **alboroto**. The definition of **alboroto** is *noise* or *racket*, so **alboroto** is probably not the word you're looking for. The second word is **raqueta**, followed by the abbreviation *dep.*, which stands for **deportes**. This indicates that the word **raqueta** is the best choice for your needs.

Tema

Escribir una composición

Compara una celebración familiar (como una boda, una fiesta de cumpleaños o una graduación) a la que tú asististe recientemente, con otro tipo de celebración. Utiliza palabras y expresiones de la siguiente lista.

Para expresar similitudes	
además; también	*in addition; also*
al igual que	*the same as*
como	*as; like*
de la misma manera	*in the same manner (way)*
del mismo modo	*in the same manner (way)*
tan + [*adjetivo*] + como	*as + [adjective] + as*
tanto/a(s) + [*sustantivo*] + como	*as many/much + [noun] + as*

Para expresar diferencias	
a diferencia de	*unlike*
a pesar de	*in spite of*
aunque	*although*
en cambio	*on the other hand*
más/menos... que	*more/less . . . than*
no obstante	*nevertheless; however*
por otro lado	*on the other hand*
por el contrario	*on the other hand*
sin embargo	*nevertheless; however*

TEACHING OPTIONS

Proofreading Activity Copy on the board or onto a transparency the following items containing mistakes as a proofreading activity to do with the whole class.
1. Concepción me deció que habió muchos invitados en su fiesta de cumpleaños.
2. ¿Cuáles consejos siempre los dan a los recien casados?
3. Los invitados trajieron muchos regalos cuando venieron a la fiesta.
4. ¿Cuál pensaste cuando sabiste las noticias de la boda?
5. Viné a la fiesta pero no pasé lo bien.
6. ¿Qué me deces si te do un regalo bonito?
7. Me dijieron que Isabel rompió con Mario. ¿Cuál piensas tú?

Escuchar

Estrategia

Guessing the meaning of words through context

When you hear an unfamiliar word, you can often guess its meaning by listening to the words and phrases around it.

To practice this strategy, you will now listen to a paragraph. Jot down the unfamiliar words that you hear. Then listen to the paragraph again and jot down the word or words that are the most useful clues to the meaning of each unfamiliar word.

Preparación

Lee la invitación. ¿De qué crees que van a hablar Rosa y Josefina?

Margarita Robles de García
y Roberto García Olmos

Piden su presencia en la celebración
del décimo aniversario de bodas
el día 13 de marzo de 2004
con una misa en la Iglesia Virgen del Coromoto
a las 6:30

❧

seguida por cena y baile
en el restaurante El Campanero,
Calle Principal, Las Mercedes
a las 8:30

Ahora escucha

Ahora escucha la conversación entre Josefina y Rosa. Cuando oigas una de las palabras de la columna A, usa el contexto para identificar el sinónimo o la definición en la columna B.

A	
_d_	festejar
_c_	dicha
_h_	bien parecido
_g_	finge (fingir)
_b_	soporta (soportar)
_e_	yo lo disfruté (disfrutar)

B	
a.	conmemoración religiosa de una muerte
b.	tolera
c.	suerte
d.	celebrar
e.	me divertí
f.	horror
g.	crea una ficción
h.	guapo

Comprensión

¿Cierto o falso?

Lee cada frase e indica si lo que dice es **cierto** o **falso**. Corrige las frases falsas.

1. No invitaron a mucha gente a la fiesta de Margarita y Roberto porque ellos no conocen a muchas personas.
   Falso. Fueron muchos invitados.
2. Algunos fueron a la fiesta con pareja y otros fueron sin compañero/a.
   Cierto.
3. Margarita y Roberto decidieron celebrar el décimo aniversario porque no tuvieron ninguna celebración en su matrimonio.   Falso. Celebraron el décimo aniversario. porque les gustan las fiestas.
4. A Rosa y a Josefina les parece interesante Rafael.
   Cierto
5. Josefina se divirtió mucho en la fiesta porque bailó toda la noche con Rafael.   Falso. Josefina se divirtió mucho. pero bailó con otros, no con Rafael.

Preguntas Answers will vary.

1. ¿Son solteras Rosa y Josefina? ¿Cómo lo sabes?
2. ¿Tienen las chicas una amistad de mucho tiempo con la pareja que celebra su aniversario? ¿Cómo lo sabes?

recursos

TEXT CD
Lección 9

Section Goals

In **Escuchar** students will:
• use context to infer meaning of unfamiliar words
• answer questions based on a recorded conversation

Instructional Resources
Textbook Activities CD
IRM: Tapescript, p. 79

Estrategia
Script Hoy mi sobrino Gabriel cumplió seis años. Antes de la fiesta, ayudé a mi hermana a decorar la sala con globos de todos los colores, pero ¡qué bulla después!, cuando los niños se pusieron a estallarlos todos. El pastel de cumpleaños estaba riquísimo y cuando Gabriel sopló las velas, apagó las seis. Los otros niños le regalaron un montón de juguetes, y nos divertimos mucho.

Suggestion Have students read the invitation and guess what Rosa and Josefina will be talking about in the recorded conversation.

Ahora escucha
Script JOSEFINA: Rosa, ¿te divertiste anoche en la fiesta? ROSA: Sí, me divertí más en el aniversario que en la boda. ¡La fiesta estuvo fenomenal! Fue buena idea festejar el aniversario en un restaurante. Así todos pudieron relajarse. J: En parte, yo lo disfruté porque son una pareja tan linda; qué dicha que estén tan enamorados después de diez años de matrimonio. Me gustaría tener una relación como la de ellos. Y también saberlo celebrar con tanta alegría. ¡Pero qué cantidad de comida y bebida! R: Es verdad que Margarita y Roberto exageran un poco con sus fiestas, pero son de la clase de gente que le gusta celebrar los eventos de la vida. Y como tienen tantas amistades y dos familias tan grandes....

(Script continues at far left in the bottom panels.)

J: Oye, Rosa, hablando de familia, ¿llegaste a conocer al cuñado de Magali? Es soltero, ¿no? Quise bailar con él pero no me sacó a bailar.
R: Hablas de Rafael. Es muy bien parecido; ¡ese pelo...! Estuve hablando con él después del brindis. Me dijo que

no le gusta ni el champán ni el vino; él finge tomar cuando brindan porque no lo soporta. No te sacó a bailar porque él y Susana estaban juntos en la fiesta.
J: De todos modos, aun sin Rafael, bailé toda la noche. Lo pasé muy, pero muy bien.

Section Goal

In **Panorama**, students will read about the geography, culture, and economy of Chile.

Instructional Resources

Transparencies, #5, #6, #37
WB/VM: Workbook, pp. 105–106;
Video Activities, pp. 241–242
***Panorama cultural** DVD/Video*
Interactive CD-ROM
IRM: Videoscript, p. 111;
***Panorama cultural** Translations;*
p. 133
Companion website:
www.vistahigherlearning.com
Presentations CD-ROM

Suggestion Ask students to look at the map of Chile, or project **Transparency #37**, and to talk about the physical features of the country. Point out that Chile is 2,880 miles from north to south, but no more than 264 miles from east to west. Point out that Chile has a variety of climates.

El país en cifras After reading **Chilenos célebres,** give students more information about O'Higgins. They can probably guess correctly that his father was an Irish immigrant, but should also know that he is considered one of the founders of modern Latin America, along with Simón Bolívar and José de San Martín. These "founding fathers" are called **los próceres**.

¡Increíble pero cierto! Chile lies in a seismically active zone and has developed state-of-the-art seismic engineering in order to address architectural vulnerability and other issues that impact this earthquake-prone region.

Chile

connections cultures NATIONAL STANDARDS

El país en cifras

▶ **Área:** 756.950 km² (292.259 millas²), *dos veces el área de Montana*

▶ **Población:** 16.136.000
Aproximadamente el 80 por ciento de la población es urbana, y la tercera parte° de los chilenos vive en la capital.

▶ **Capital:** Santiago de Chile—5.867.000

▶ **Ciudades principales:**
Concepción—356.000,
Viña del Mar—326.000,
Valparaíso—283.000, Temuco—246.000

SOURCE: Population Division, UN Secretariat

▶ **Moneda:** peso chileno

▶ **Idiomas:** español (oficial), mapuche

Bandera de Chile

Chilenos célebres

▶ **Bernardo O'Higgins,** militar° y héroe nacional (1778–1842)

▶ **Gabriela Mistral,** Premio Nobel de Literatura, 1945; poeta y diplomática (1889–1957)

▶ **Pablo Neruda,** Premio Nobel de Literatura, 1971; poeta (1904–1973)

▶ **Isabel Allende,** novelista (1942–)

Pablo Neruda

la tercera parte *a third*   militar *soldier*   el terremoto *earthquake*
heridas *wounded*   hogar *home*

¡Increíble pero cierto!

El terremoto° más grande de la historia tuvo lugar en Chile el 22 de mayo de 1960. Registró una intensidad récord de 9.5 en la escala de Richter. Murieron 2.000 personas, 3.000 resultaron heridas° y 2.000.000 perdieron su hogar°. La geografía del país se modificó notablemente.

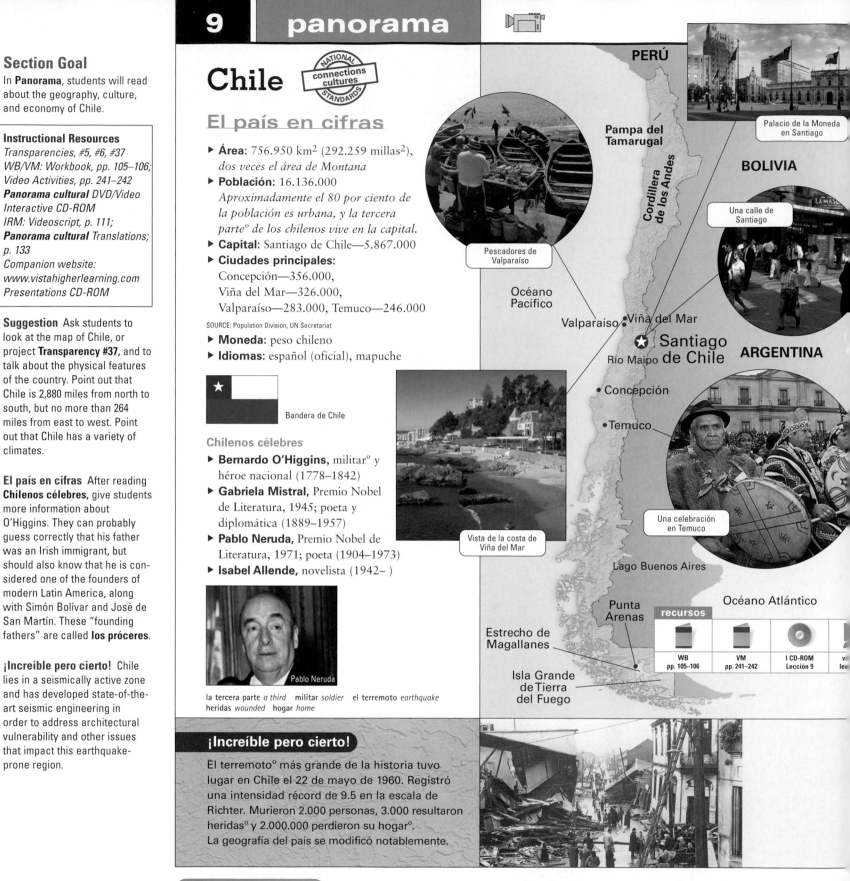

Palacio de la Moneda en Santiago

Una calle de Santiago

Pescadores de Valparaíso

PERÚ

BOLIVIA

Cordillera de los Andes

Pampa del Tamarugal

Océano Pacífico

Valparaíso • Viña del Mar
✪ Santiago de Chile
Río Maipo

ARGENTINA

• Concepción

• Temuco

Una celebración en Temuco

Vista de la costa de Viña del Mar

Lago Buenos Aires

Océano Atlántico

Punta Arenas

Estrecho de Magallanes

Isla Grande de Tierra del Fuego

recursos			
WB pp. 105–106	VM pp. 241–242	I CD-ROM Lección 9	

TEACHING OPTIONS

Heritage Speakers Invite heritage speakers to prepare a poem by **Pablo Neruda** to read aloud for the class. Many of the **Odas elementales,** such as **"Oda a la alcachofa"**, **"Oda al tomate"**, and **"Oda a la cebolla"**, are written in simple language. Prepare copies of the poem beforehand and go over unfamiliar vocabulary with the class.

Worth Noting Though Chile is the second smallest Spanish-speaking country in South America (only Ecuador is smaller), it has 2,800 miles of coastline. In the north is the Desert of Atacama, the driest region on earth. Some of the highest peaks in the Andes lie on Chile's border with Argentina. Chile's agricultural region is a valley the size of central California's. The southern archipelago is cool, foggy, and rainy, like the Alaska panhandle.

Lugares • La Isla de Pascua

La Isla de Pascua° recibió ese nombre porque los exploradores holandeses° llegaron a la isla por primera vez el día de Pascua de 1722. Ahora es parte del territorio de Chile. La Isla de Pascua es famosa por los *moai*, estatuas enormes que representan personas con rasgos° muy exagerados. Estas estatuas las construyeron los *rapa nui*, los antiguos habitantes de la zona. Todavía no se sabe mucho sobre los *rapa nui*, ni tampoco se sabe por qué decidieron abandonar la isla.

Deportes • Los deportes de invierno

Hay muchos lugares para practicar los deportes de invierno en Chile porque las montañas nevadas de los Andes ocupan gran parte del país. El Parque Nacional de Villarrica, por ejemplo, situado al pie de un volcán y junto a° un lago, es un sitio popular para el esquí y el *snowboard*. Para los que prefieren deportes más extremos, el centro de esquí Valle Nevado organiza excursiones del heli-esquí.

Ciencias • Astronomía

Los observatorios chilenos, situados en los Andes, son lugares excelentes para las observaciones astronómicas. Científicos° de todo el mundo van a Chile para estudiar las estrellas° y otros fenómenos de la galaxia. Hoy día Chile está construyendo nuevos observatorios y telescopios para mejorar las imágenes del universo.

Economía • El vino

La producción de vino comenzó en Chile en el siglo° XVI. Ahora la industria del vino constituye una parte importante de la actividad agrícola del país y la exportación de sus productos está subiendo° cada vez más. Los vinos chilenos reciben el aprecio internacional por su gran variedad, sus ricos y complejos sabores° y su precio moderado. Los más conocidos internacionalmente son los vinos de Aconcagua, de Santiago y de Huasco.

¿Qué aprendiste? Responde a las preguntas con una frase completa.

1. ¿Qué porcentaje (*percentage*) de la población chilena es urbana?
   El 80 por ciento de la población chilena es urbana.

2. ¿Qué son los *moai*? ¿Dónde están? Los *moai* son estatuas enormes. Están en la Isla de Pascua.

3. ¿Qué deporte extremo ofrece el centro de esquí Valle Nevado?
   Se practica el *heli-esquí*.

4. ¿Por qué van a Chile científicos de todo el mundo? Porque los observatorios chilenos son excelentes para las observaciones astronómicas.

5. ¿Cuándo comenzó la producción de vino en Chile?
   Comenzó en el siglo XVI.

6. ¿Por qué reciben los vinos chilenos el aprecio internacional? Lo reciben por su variedad, sus ricos y complejos sabores y su precio moderado.

Conexión Internet Investiga estos temas en el sitio **www.vistahigherlearning.com**.

1. Busca información sobre Pablo Neruda e Isabel Allende. ¿Dónde y cuándo nacieron? ¿Cuáles son algunas de sus obras (*works*)? ¿Cuáles son algunos de los temas de sus obras?

2. Busca información sobre sitios donde los chilenos y los turistas practican deportes de invierno en Chile. Selecciona un sitio y descríbeselo a tu clase.

La Isla de Pascua *Easter Island*   holandeses *Dutch*   rasgos *features*   junto a *beside*   Científicos *Scientists*   estrellas *stars*
siglo *century*   subiendo *increasing*   complejos sabores *complex flavors*

La Isla de Pascua With its vibrant Polynesian culture, Easter Island is unlike anywhere else in Chile. Located 2,000 miles from the nearest island and 3,800 kilometers from the Chilean coast, it is one of the most isolated places on earth. Until the 1960s, it was visited once a year by a Chilean warship bringing supplies. Now there are regular air connections to Santiago.
For more information about **La Isla de Pascua**, you may want to play the **Panorama cultural** video for this lesson.

Los deportes de invierno Remind students that some of the highest mountains in South America lie along the border Chile shares with Argentina. In the south is the **Parque Nacional Torres del Paine**, a national park featuring ice caverns, deep glacial trenches, and other spectacular features.

Astronomía In 1962, the Cerro Tololo Inter-American Observatory was founded as a joint project between Chilean and American astronomers. Since that time, so many other major telescopes have been installed for research purposes that Chile can now claim to have the highest concentration of telescopes in the world.

El vino Invite students to research the wine-growing regions of Chile and to compare them to wine-growing regions in California, France, or other wine-producing areas.

Conexión Internet Students will find supporting Internet activities and links at **www.vistahigherlearning.com**.

TEACHING OPTIONS

Worth Noting The native Mapuche people of southern Chile are a small minority of the Chilean population today, but have maintained a strong cultural identity since the time of their first contact with Europeans. In fact, they resisted conquest so well that it was only in the late 19th century that the government of Chile could assert actual sovereignty over the region south of the river Bío-bío. However, the majority of Chileans are of European descent. Chilean Spanish is much less infused with indigenous lexical items than is the Spanish of countries such as Guatemala and Mexico, where the larger indigenous population has made a greater impact on the language.

Instructional Resources
Vocabulary CD
Lab Manual, p. 54
Lab CD/MP3 **Lección 9**
IRM: Tapescript, pp. 40–44
Testing Program: **Pruebas**, *pp. 97–108*
Testing Program Audio CD
Test Files CD-ROM
Test Generator

Las celebraciones

el aniversario (de bodas)	(wedding) anniversary
la boda	wedding
el cumpleaños	birthday
el día de fiesta	holiday
la fiesta	party
el/la invitado/a	guest
la Navidad	Christmas
la quinceañera	young woman's fifteenth birthday celebration
la sorpresa	surprise
brindar	to toast (drink)
celebrar	to celebrate
cumplir años	to have a birthday
dejar una propina	to leave a tip
divertirse (e:ie)	to have fun
invitar	to invite
pagar la cuenta	to pay the bill
pasarlo bien/mal	to have a good/bad time
regalar	to give (a gift)
reírse (e:i)	to laugh
relajarse	to relax
sonreír (e:i)	to smile
sorprender	to surprise

Los postres y otras comidas

la botella (de vino)	bottle (of wine)
el champán	champagne
los dulces	sweets; candy
el flan (de caramelo)	baked (caramel) custard
la galleta	cookie
el helado	ice cream
el pastel (de chocolate)	(chocolate) cake; pie
el postre	dessert

Las relaciones personales

la amistad	friendship
el amor	love
el divorcio	divorce
el estado civil	marital status
el matrimonio	marriage
la pareja	(married) couple; partner
el/la recién casado/a	newlywed
casarse (con)	to get married (to)
comprometerse (con)	to get engaged (to)
divorciarse (de)	to get divorced (from)
enamorarse (de)	to fall in love (with)
llevarse bien/mal (con)	to get along well/badly (with)
odiar	to hate
romper (con)	to break up (with)
salir (con)	to go out (with); to date
separarse (de)	to separate (from)
tener una cita	to have a date; to have an appointment
casado/a	married
divorciado/a	divorced
juntos/as	together
separado/a	separated
soltero/a	single
viudo/a	widower/widow

Las etapas de la vida

la adolescencia	adolescence
la edad	age
el estado civil	marital status
las etapas de la vida	the stages of life
la juventud	youth
la madurez	maturity; middle age
la muerte	death
el nacimiento	birth
la niñez	childhood
la vejez	old age
cambiar (de)	to change
graduarse (de/en)	to graduate (from/in)
jubilarse	to retire (from work)
nacer	to be born

Palabras adicionales

la alegría	happiness
el beso	kiss
conmigo	with me
contigo	with you

Expresiones útiles	See page 247.

recursos

LM p. 54	Lab CD/MP3 Lección 9	Vocab CD Lección 9

En el consultorio

Communicative Goals

You will learn how to:

- Describe how you feel physically
- Talk about health and medical conditions

Lesson Goals

In **Lección 10** students will be introduced to the following:
- names of parts of the body
- health-related terms
- imperfect tense
- uses of the preterite and imperfect tenses
- impersonal constructions with **se**
- using **se** for unplanned events
- forming adverbs using [*adjective*] + **–mente**
- common adverbs and adverbial expressions
- activating background knowledge
- cultural, geographic, and economic information about Costa Rica
- cultural, geographic, and historical information about Nicaragua

A primera vista Here are some additional questions you can ask based on the photo: **¿Cuándo conociste a tu médico/a? ¿Vas mucho a verlo/a? ¿Estuviste en su oficina la semana pasada? ¿El año pasado? ¿Cuándo? ¿Cuáles son las mejores comidas para sentirte bien? ¿Cuáles son las peores?**

A PRIMERA VISTA

- ¿Cuál de ellas es la doctora? ¿La mujer de pelo largo o de pelo corto?
- ¿En qué etapa de la vida está la doctora, la vejez o la madurez?
- ¿Es una de ellas mayor que la otra o son aproximadamente de la misma edad?

INSTRUCTIONAL RESOURCES

Workbook/Video Manual: WB Activities, pp. 109–124
Laboratory Manual: Lab Activities, pp. 55–60
Workbook/Video Manual: Video Activities, pp. 213–214; pp. 243–246
Instructor's Resource Manual: **Vocabulario adicional**, p. 164; **¡Inténtalo!** & **Práctica** Answers, pp. 187–188;
Fotonovela Translations, p. 124; Textbook CD

Tapescript, p. 80; Lab CDs Tapescript, pp. 45–48;
Fotonovela Videoscript, p. 97; **Panorama cultural** Videoscript, p. 112; **Pan. cult.** translations, p.134
Info Gap Activities Booklet, pp. 37–40
Overhead Transparencies: #3, #4, #38, #39, #40
Lab Audio CD/MP3 **Lección 10**
Panorama cultural DVD/Video

Fotonovela DVD/Video
Testing Program, pp. 109–120; pp. 217–228
Testing Program Audio CD
Test Files CD-ROM
Test Generator
Companion website

Presentations CD-ROM
Textbook CD
Vocabulary CD
Interactive CD-ROM
Video CD-ROM
Web-SAM

Section Goals

In **Contextos**, students will learn and practice:
- names of parts of the body
- vocabulary for talking about illnesses and accidents
- vocabulary associated with medical visits

Instructional Resources

Transparency #38
Textbook Activities CD
Vocabulary CD
WB/VM: Workbook, pp. 109–110
Lab Manual, p. 55
Lab CD/MP3 **Lección 10**
IRM: **Vocab. adicional**, *p. 164;*
Práctica *Answers, pp. 187–188;*
Tapescript, pp. 45–48; p. 80
Info Gap Activities Booklet,
pp. 37–38
Interactive CD-ROM
Companion website:
www.vistahigherlearning.com
Presentations CD-ROM

Suggestions

- Using cognate vocabulary, pointing to parts of your body, and miming procedures, talk about a hospital visit, real or imaginary. Use the imperfect as input before it is presented in **Estructura 10.1**. Ex: **Recientemente fui al hospital. Me dolían la cabeza, la garganta, los ojos, la nariz… El médico me puso una inyección con antibióticos.** Ask comprehension questions and point to body parts. Ex: **¿Me dolía la nariz? ¿el brazo? ¿la cabeza?**

- Project **Transparency #38.** Have students refer to the scene and the vocabulary boxes as you give yes-no statements about the new vocabulary. Ex: **¿Sí o no? La enfermera le toma la temperatura a la paciente. (Sí.) La doctora le pone una inyección al hombre. (No.)** Then ask volunteers to describe what is going on in the scene, using as much of the new vocabulary as possible.

En el consultorio

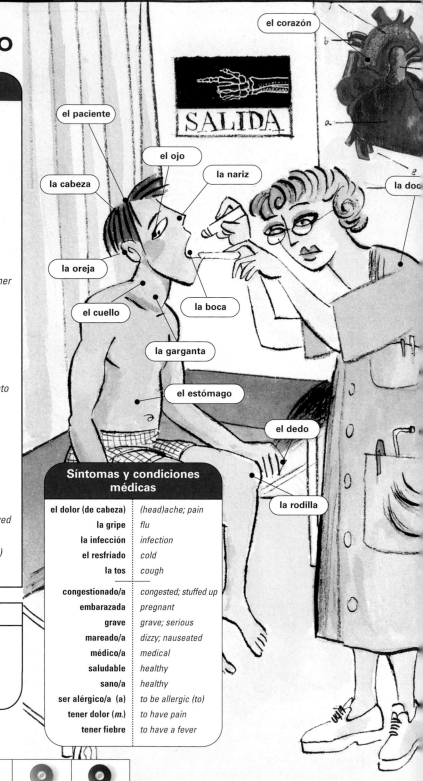

Más vocabulario

la clínica	*clinic*
el consultorio	*doctor's office*
el/la dentista	*dentist*
el examen médico	*physical exam*
la farmacia	*pharmacy*
el hospital	*hospital*
la operación	*operation*
la sala de emergencia(s)	*emergency room*
el cuerpo	*body*
la muela	*molar*
el oído	*(sense of) hearing; inner ear*
el accidente	*accident*
la salud	*health*
el síntoma	*symptom*
caerse	*to fall (down)*
darse con	*to bump into; to run into*
doler (o:ue)	*to hurt*
enfermarse	*to get sick*
estar enfermo/a	*to be sick*
lastimarse (el pie)	*to injure (one's foot)*
poner una inyección	*to give an injection*
recetar	*to prescribe*
romperse (la pierna)	*to break (one's leg)*
sacar(se) una muela	*to have a tooth removed*
sufrir una enfermedad	*to suffer an illness*
torcerse (o:ue) (el tobillo)	*to sprain (one's ankle)*
toser	*to cough*

Variación léxica

gripe ⟷ gripa (*Col., Gua., Méx.*)
resfriado ⟷ catarro (*Cuba, Esp., Gua.*)
sala de ⟷ sala de urgencias
emergencia(s) (*Arg., Esp., Méx.*)
romperse ⟷ quebrarse (*Arg., Gua.*)

Síntomas y condiciones médicas

el dolor (de cabeza)	*(head)ache; pain*
la gripe	*flu*
la infección	*infection*
el resfriado	*cold*
la tos	*cough*
congestionado/a	*congested; stuffed up*
embarazada	*pregnant*
grave	*grave; serious*
mareado/a	*dizzy; nauseated*
médico/a	*medical*
saludable	*healthy*
sano/a	*healthy*
ser alérgico/a (a)	*to be allergic (to)*
tener dolor (m.)	*to have pain*
tener fiebre	*to have a fever*

recursos

TEXT CD Lección 10	WB pp. 109–110	LM p. 55	Lab CD/MP3 Lección 10	I CD-ROM Lección 10	Vocab CD Lección 10

Labels on illustration: el corazón, el paciente, el ojo, la nariz, la doc..., la cabeza, la oreja, el cuello, la boca, la garganta, el estómago, el dedo, la rodilla

---

TEACHING OPTIONS

TPR Play a game of Simon Says (**Simón dice…**). Write **señalen** on the board and explain that it means *point*. Start by saying: **Simón dice… señalen la nariz.** Students are to touch their noses and keep their hands there until instructed to do otherwise. Work through various parts of the body. Be sure to give instructions without saying **Simón dice…** once in a while.

Variación léxica Point out differences in vocabulary related to health, as well as some false cognates students should be aware of. **Embarazada** means *pregnant*, not *embarrassed.* You may also want to present **constipado/a** and explain that it does not mean *constipated*, but rather *congested,* or *stuffed up.*

la radiografía

el hueso

la enfermera

Estornuda.

la paciente

Toma la temperatura.

el brazo

la pierna

el tobillo

Práctica

1 Escuchar 🎧 Escucha las frases y selecciona la respuesta más adecuada.

a. Tengo dolor de cabeza y fiebre.
b. No fui a la clase porque estaba enfermo.
c. Me caí la semana pasada jugando al tenis.
d. Debes ir a la farmacia.
e. Porque tengo gripe.
f. Sí, tengo mucha tos por las noches.
g. Lo llevaron directamente a la sala de emergencia.
h. No sé. Todavía tienen que tomarme la temperatura.

1. ___c___   5. ___f___
2. ___e___   6. ___h___
3. ___g___   7. ___a___
4. ___d___   8. ___b___

2 Completar Completa las siguientes frases con una palabra de la misma familia de la palabra subrayada. Usa la forma correcta de cada palabra.

1. Cuando <u>oyes</u> algo, usas el ___oído___, que es uno de los cinco sentidos.
2. Cuando te <u>enfermas</u>, te sientes ___enfermo/a___ y necesitas ir al consultorio para ver a la ___enfermera___.
3. El médico <u>examina</u> tu salud durante tu ___examen médico___ anual.
4. ¿Alguien ___estornudó___? Creo que oí un <u>estornudo</u> (*sneeze*).
5. No puedo <u>arrodillarme</u> (*kneel down*) porque me lastimé la ___rodilla___ en un accidente de coche.
6. ¿Vas al ___consultorio___ para <u>consultar</u> al médico?
7. Si te rompes un <u>diente</u>, vas al ___dentista___.
8. Si tienes una ___infección___ de garganta, tu garganta está <u>infectada</u>.

3 Contestar Mira el dibujo de las páginas 268 y 269 y contesta las preguntas. Answers will vary.

1. ¿Qué hace la doctora?
2. ¿Qué hay en la pared?
3. ¿Qué hace la enfermera?
4. ¿Qué hace el paciente?
5. ¿A quién le duele la garganta?
6. ¿Qué hace la paciente?
7. ¿Qué tiene la paciente?
8. ¿Quién toma la temperatura?

La medicina

el antibiótico	*antibiotic*
la aspirina	*aspirin*
el medicamento	*medication*
la pastilla	*pill; tablet*
la receta	*prescription*

1 Suggestion Have students check their answers as you go over **Actividad 1** with the whole class.

1 Tapescript 1. ¿Cuándo te caíste? 2. ¿Por qué vas al médico? 3. ¿Adónde llevaron a Juan después del accidente? 4. ¿Adónde debo ir para conseguir estas pastillas? 5. ¿Tienes mucha tos? 6. ¿Tienes fiebre? 7. ¿Cuáles son sus síntomas, señor? 8. Ayer no te vi en la clase de biología. ¿Por qué? *Textbook Activities CD*

2 Suggestion Have students say which part of speech the underlined word is and which part of speech the word they write on the blank is.

2 Expansion Have students write two additional sentences following the pattern of those in the activity. Their partners have to come up with the correct missing words.

3 Expansion Ask additional questions about the doctor's office scene for volunteers to answer. Ex: **9. ¿Quiénes trabajan en el consultorio? (la médica/doctora, la enfermera) 10. ¿Qué hace la chica? (Estornuda.)**

TEACHING OPTIONS

Game Play **Concentración**. On eight cards, write names for parts of the body or items found in a doctor's office. On another eight cards, draw or paste a picture that matches each description. Place the cards face-down in four rows of four. In pairs, students select two cards. If the two cards match, the pair keeps them. If the two cards do not match, students replace them in their original position. The pair with the most cards at the end wins.

Heritage Speakers Ask heritage speakers to describe a visit they made to a doctor's office. Verify comprehension by having students relate what was said. On the board write any nonactive vocabulary that the native speakers may use, such as **auscultar los pulmones, sacar la lengua, tomar la presión arterial, la sangre,** and so forth.

4 Suggestion Point out that there are often several parts of the body that may be associated with each activity. Encourage students to list as many as they can.

4 Expansion Say parts of the body and ask pairs of students to associate them with as many activities as they can.

5 Expansion
• Write the three categories with their point totals on the board. Ask for a show of hands for those who fall into the different groups based on their point totals. Analyze the trends of the class—are your students healthy or unhealthy?
• Ask for volunteers from each of the three groups to explain whether they think the results of the survey are accurate or not. Ask them to give examples based on their own eating, exercise, and other health habits.

Note: At this point you may want to present **Vocabulario adicional: Más vocabulario para el consultorio**, from the IRM.

---

4 **Asociaciones** Trabajen en parejas para identificar las partes del cuerpo que ustedes asocian con las siguientes actividades. Sigan el modelo. *Answers will vary.*

> **modelo**
> nadar
> **Estudiante 1:** *Usamos los brazos para nadar.*
> **Estudiante 2:** *Usamos las piernas también.*

1. hablar por teléfono
2. tocar el piano
3. correr en el parque
4. escuchar música
5. ver una película
6. toser
7. llevar zapatos
8. comprar perfume
9. estudiar biología
10. comer lomo a la plancha

5 **Cuestionario** Contesta el cuestionario seleccionando las respuestas que reflejen mejor tus experiencias. Suma (*Add*) los puntos de cada respuesta y anota el resultado. Después, con el resto de la clase, compara y analiza los resultados del cuestionario y comenta lo que dicen de la salud y de los hábitos de todo el grupo. *Answers will vary.*

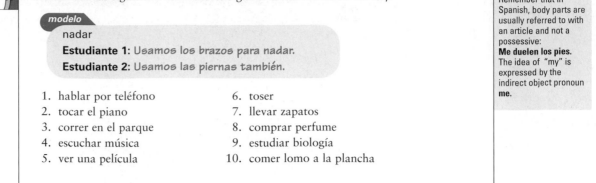

¿Tienes buena salud?

27-30 puntos	Salud y hábitos excelentes
23-26 puntos	Salud y hábitos buenos
22 puntos o menos	Salud y hábitos problemáticos

1. **¿Con qué frecuencia te enfermas? (resfriados, gripe, etc.)**
   Cuatro veces por año o más. (1 punto)
   Dos o tres veces por año. (2 puntos)
   Casi nunca. (3 puntos)

2. **¿Con qué frecuencia tienes dolores de estómago o problemas digestivos?**
   Con mucha frecuencia. (1 punto)
   A veces. (2 puntos)
   Casi nunca. (3 puntos)

3. **¿Con qué frecuencia sufres de dolores de cabeza?**
   Frecuentemente. (1 punto)
   A veces. (2 puntos)
   Casi nunca. (3 puntos)

4. **¿Comes verduras y frutas?**
   No, casi nunca como verduras ni frutas. (1 punto)
   Sí, a veces. (2 puntos)
   Sí, todos los días. (3 puntos)

5. **¿Eres alérgico/a a algo?**
   Sí, a muchas cosas. (1 punto)
   Sí, a algunas cosas. (2 puntos)
   No. (3 puntos)

6. **¿Haces ejercicios aeróbicos?**
   No, casi nunca hago ejercicios aeróbicos. (1 punto)
   Sí, a veces. (2 puntos)
   Sí, con frecuencia. (3 puntos)

7. **¿Con qué frecuencia te haces un examen médico?**
   Nunca o casi nunca. (1 punto)
   Cada dos años. (2 puntos)
   Cada año y/o antes de practicar un deporte. (3 puntos)

8. **¿Con qué frecuencia vas al dentista?**
   Nunca voy al dentista. (1 punto)
   Sólo cuando me duele una muela. (2 puntos)
   Por lo menos una vez por año. (3 puntos)

9. **¿Qué comes normalmente por la mañana?**
   No como nada por la mañana. (1 punto)
   Tomo una bebida dietética. (2 puntos)
   Como cereal y fruta. (3 puntos)

10. **¿Con qué frecuencia te sientes mareado/a?**
    Frecuentemente. (1 punto)
    A veces. (2 puntos)
    Casi nunca. (3 puntos)

TEACHING OPTIONS

Pairs In pairs, students interview each other using the questions from the realia piece in **Actividad 5**. However, students are not limited to the choices given for answers if they can make other statements that are true for them. Then have students present the results of their interview in class. Does the interviewer think that his or her partner is in great health, relatively good health, or poor health?

Game Play a modified version of **20 Preguntas**. Ask a volunteer to think of a part of the body. Other students get one chance each to ask a yes-no question until someone guesses the item correctly. Limit attempts to ten questions per item. You may want to write some phrases on the board to cue students' questions. Encourage students to guess by associating activities with various parts of the body.

Comunicación

6

¿Qué le pasó? Trabajen en un grupo de dos o tres personas. Hablen de lo que les pasó y de cómo se sienten las personas que aparecen en los dibujos. Answers will vary.

1. Adela
2. Francisco
3. Pilar
4. Pedro
5. Cristina
6. Félix

7

Un accidente Cuéntale (*Tell*) a la clase de un accidente o una enfermedad que tuviste. Incluye información que conteste las siguientes preguntas. Answers will vary.

✓ ¿Qué ocurrió?
✓ ¿Dónde ocurrió?
✓ ¿Cuándo ocurrió?
✓ ¿Cómo ocurrió?
✓ ¿Quién te ayudó y cómo?
✓ ¿Tuviste algún problema después del accidente o después de la enfermedad?
✓ ¿Cuánto tiempo tuviste el problema?

8

Crucigrama (*Crossword*) Tu profesor(a) les va a dar a ti y a tu compañero/a un crucigrama incompleto. Tú tienes las palabras que necesita tu compañero/a y él/ella tiene las palabras que tú necesitas. Tienen que darse pistas (*clues*) para completarlo. No pueden decir la palabra necesaria; deben utilizar definiciones, ejemplos y frases incompletas.

> **modelo**   Answers will vary.
> **10 horizontal:** La usamos para hablar.
> **14 vertical:** Es el médico que examina los dientes.

Successful Language Learning
Tell your students to imagine situations in which they commonly see a doctor and to think about what they would say in Spanish in each of these situations.

6 Expansion
• Ask students to list the various possibilities of what happened to these people and how they feel. Have them name possible treatments for each.
• Bring in magazine pictures related to illness, medicine, and medical appointments. Have students describe what is going on in the images.

7 Suggestion Talk about an illness or accident you have had.

7 Expansion To practice more verb forms, have students talk about an illness or accident that someone they know has had.

8 Suggestion Divide the class into pairs and distribute the handouts from the Information Gap Activities Booklet that correspond to this activity. Give students ten minutes to complete this activity.

8 Expansion Have pairs use words from the crossword to role-play a visit to a doctor's office. One partner can play the role of doctor and the other that of patient.

TEACHING OPTIONS

Small Groups Prepare four different descriptions of a fantastical beast or alien. Ex: **Tiene dos narices y tres ojos. Los ojos están encima de la cabeza,** and so forth. Read each description line by line to groups of three or four. Members of the group take turns drawing the description on the board. Did they get the description right?

Extra Practice Have students write physical descriptions of themselves. Students should use as much vocabulary from this lesson as they can. Collect the papers and read the descriptions aloud. The rest of the class has to guess who is being described. Write **Mido ____ pies y ____ pulgadas** on the board and explain what it means.

Section Goals

In **Fotonovela** students will:
- receive comprehensible input from free-flowing discourse
- learn functional phrases that preview lesson grammatical structures

Instructional Resources
WB/VM: Video Activities, pp. 213–214
Fotonovela *DVD/Video (Start 00:52:19)*
Fotonovela *Video CD-ROM*
IRM: **Fotonovela** *Translations, p. 124, Videoscript, p. 97*
Interactive CD-ROM

Video Recap: Lección 9
Before doing this **Fotonovela** section, review the previous one with this activity.
1. ¿De quién fue el cumpleaños? (de Maite)
2. ¿Cómo supo doña Rita del cumpleaños? (se lo dijo don Francisco)
3. ¿Qué trajo doña Rita de comer para celebrar el cumpleaños? (flan, pastel de chocolate con helado y vino)
4. ¿Quién no tomó vino? ¿Por qué no? (don Francisco, porque es el conductor)

Video Synopsis While on the bus, Javier injures his foot. Don Francisco tells the group they are close to the clinic of his friend, Doctora Márquez. Doctora Márquez determines that Javier simply twisted his ankle. She prescribes some pain medication and sends Javier and Don Francisco on their way.

Suggestions
- Have students scan the **Fotonovela** for words and expressions related to health care. Then have them predict what will happen in this episode.
- Review the predictions, asking a few questions that guide students in summarizing this episode.

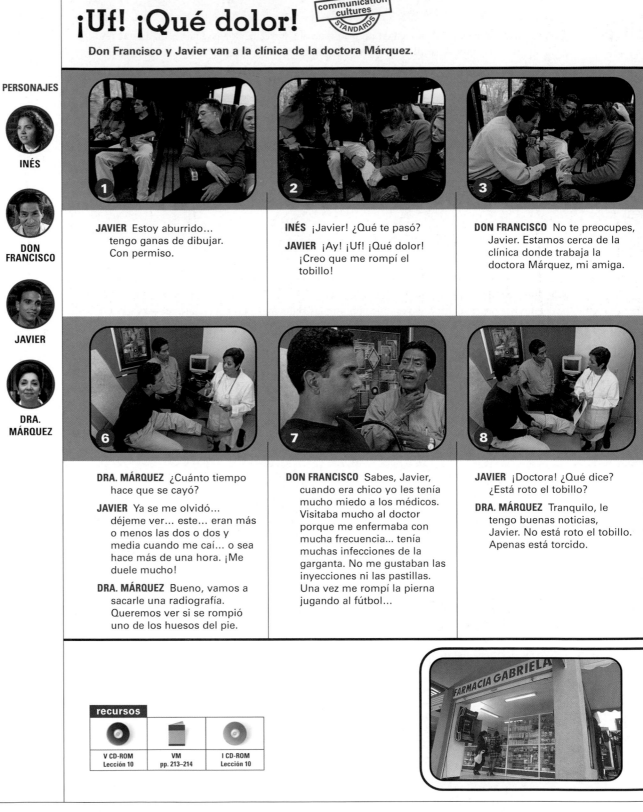

¡Uf! ¡Qué dolor!

Don Francisco y Javier van a la clínica de la doctora Márquez.

PERSONAJES

INÉS

DON FRANCISCO

JAVIER

DRA. MÁRQUEZ

1 JAVIER Estoy aburrido... tengo ganas de dibujar. Con permiso.

2 INÉS ¡Javier! ¿Qué te pasó?
JAVIER ¡Ay! ¡Uf! ¡Qué dolor! ¡Creo que me rompí el tobillo!

3 DON FRANCISCO No te preocupes, Javier. Estamos cerca de la clínica donde trabaja la doctora Márquez, mi amiga.

6 DRA. MÁRQUEZ ¿Cuánto tiempo hace que se cayó?
JAVIER Ya se me olvidó... déjeme ver... este... eran más o menos las dos o dos y media cuando me caí... o sea hace más de una hora. ¡Me duele mucho!
DRA. MÁRQUEZ Bueno, vamos a sacarle una radiografía. Queremos ver si se rompió uno de los huesos del pie.

7 DON FRANCISCO Sabes, Javier, cuando era chico yo les tenía mucho miedo a los médicos. Visitaba mucho al doctor porque me enfermaba con mucha frecuencia... tenía muchas infecciones de la garganta. No me gustaban las inyecciones ni las pastillas. Una vez me rompí la pierna jugando al fútbol...

8 JAVIER ¡Doctora! ¿Qué dice? ¿Está roto el tobillo?
DRA. MÁRQUEZ Tranquilo, le tengo buenas noticias, Javier. No está roto el tobillo. Apenas está torcido.

recursos

V CD-ROM	VM	I CD-ROM
Lección 10	pp. 213–214	Lección 10

FARMACIA GABRIELA

TEACHING OPTIONS

Video Tips General suggestions for using video clips in the classroom can be found on page IAE-12 of this Instructor's Annotated Edition.
¡Uf! ¡Qué dolor! Play the **¡Uf! ¡Qué dolor!** segment of this video module and have your students jot down key words that they hear. Then have them work in small groups to prepare a brief plot summary based on their lists of key words. Play the seg-

ment again and have students return to their groups to refine their summaries. Finally, discuss the plot of this episode with the entire class and correct any errors of fact or sequencing that students may have.

JAVIER ¿Tengo dolor? Sí, mucho. ¿Dónde? En el tobillo. ¿Tengo fiebre? No lo creo. ¿Estoy mareado? Un poco. ¿Soy alérgico a algún medicamento? No. ¿Embarazada? Definitivamente NO.

DRA. MÁRQUEZ ¿Cómo se lastimó el pie?

JAVIER Me caí cuando estaba en el autobús.

JAVIER Pero, ¿voy a poder ir de excursión con mis amigos?

DRA. MÁRQUEZ Creo que sí. Pero debe descansar y no caminar mucho durante un par de días. Le receto unas pastillas para el dolor.

DRA. MÁRQUEZ Adiós, Francisco. Adiós, Javier. ¡Cuidado! ¡Buena suerte en las montañas!

Enfoque cultural La medicina en los países hispanos

Varios factores económicos y culturales hacen el sistema de sanidad de los países hispanos diferente del sistema estadounidense. En las farmacias, muchas veces las personas le consultan sus síntomas al farmacéutico y él mismo (*he himself*) les da el medicamento, sin necesidad de recetas médicas. La influencia de las culturas indígenas se refleja en la importancia que tienen los curanderos (*folk medicine practitioners*) en muchas regiones. Éstos combinan hierbas medicinales y elementos religiosos para curar las enfermedades.

Expresiones útiles

Discussing medical conditions

▶ **¿Cómo se lastimó el pie?**
How did you hurt your foot?
▷ **Me caí en el autobús.**
I fell when I was on the bus.

▶ **¿Te duele el tobillo?**
Does your ankle hurt? (fam.)
▶ **¿Le duele el tobillo?**
Does your ankle hurt? (form.)
▷ **Sí, (me duele) mucho.**
Yes, (it hurts) a lot.

▶ **¿Es usted alérgico/a a algún medicamento?**
Are you allergic to any medication?
▷ **Sí, soy alérgico/a a la penicilina.**
Yes, I'm allergic to penicillin.

▶ **¿Está roto el tobillo?**
Is my ankle broken?
▷ **No está roto. Apenas está torcido.**
It's not broken. It's just twisted.

▶ **¿Te enfermabas frecuentemente?**
Did you get sick frequently? (fam.)
▷ **Sí, me enfermaba frecuentemente.**
Yes, I used to get sick frequently.
▷ **Tenía muchas infecciones.**
I used to get a lot of infections.

Other expressions

▶ **hace + [*period of time*] + que + [*present tense*]:**
▶ **¿Cuánto tiempo hace que te duele?**
How long has it been hurting?
▷ **Hace una hora que me duele.**
It's been hurting for an hour.

▶ **hace + [*period of time*] + que + [*preterite*]:**
▶ **¿Cuánto tiempo hace que se cayó?**
How long ago did you fall?
▷ **Me caí hace más de una hora./Hace más de una hora que me caí.**
I fell more than an hour ago.

Suggestion Ask students to read the **Fotonovela** conversation in groups of four. Ask one or two groups to present the episode to the class.

Expresiones útiles Point out the verb forms **enfermaba, enfermabas,** and **tenía.** Explain that these are imperfect tense forms, used here to talk about habitual events in the past. Point out the adverb **frecuentemente** and tell the class that many adverbs end in –**mente.** In frame 6 of the **Fotonovela,** point out the phrase **se me olvidó** and inform the class that **se** constructions are often used to talk about unplanned events. Tell students that they will learn more about these concepts in **Estructura.**

Successful Language Learning Tell students that before traveling to a Spanish-speaking country, they should make a list of their allergies and medical needs and learn how to say them in Spanish.

TEACHING OPTIONS

Enfoque cultural Explain to the class that most Spanish-speaking countries, including Spain, Mexico, and Costa Rica, offer free health care to all citizens through systems of state-run hospitals and clinics. Point out that residents of large, cosmopolitan areas generally have access to a wide variety of medical specialists and to the latest advances in health care. The same cannot usually be said about people who live in rural areas.

Although many residents of rural areas have access to doctors, hospitals, and public health clinics, some, either by necessity or by choice, seek medical assistance from **curanderos** (*folk medicine practitioners*) and **parteras** (*midwives*).

Reacciona a la fotonovela

1 Expansion Give these additional items to the class:
6. Javier tiene el tobillo roto. (Falso. El tobillo no está roto. Está torcido.) 7. La doctora Márquez le receta un poco de penicilina. (Falso. Le receta unas pastillas para el dolor.)

2 Expansion Give these additional items to the class: 7. Le voy a recetar unas pastillas para el dolor. (Dra. Márquez) 8. Cuando era niño no me gustaba mucho ir al doctor. (don Francisco)

3 Suggestion Divide the class into small groups and distribute six strips of paper to each. Each strip should contain one of the sentences in the activity. Distribute the strips to each group in random order so that every member receives at least two sentences. Have groups put the sentences in correct order and then return them to a group representative, who will read them aloud.

4 Possible Response
E1: Buenos días. ¿Cómo se lastimó?
E2: Bueno, doctor, me caí en casa.
E1: ¿Y cuánto tiempo hace que se cayó?
E2: Hace más de dos horas. Creo que me rompí el dedo.
E1: ¿Ah, sí? ¿Le duele mucho?
E2: Me duele muchísimo, doctor. Y estoy mareada.
E1: Bueno, le voy a sacar una radiografía primero.
E2: ¿Está roto el dedo?
E1: No se preocupe. No está roto el dedo. Como le duele mucho, le receto unas pastillas para el dolor.
E2: Sí, doctor. Gracias.

The Affective Dimension Point out to your students that they are more likely to feel anxious about speaking Spanish during a medical emergency. Tell them to rehearse phrases that they might use in such a situation and to visualize themselves remaining calm.

1 **¿Cierto o falso?** Decide si lo que dicen las siguientes frases sobre Javier es **cierto** o **falso**. Corrige las frases falsas.

	Cierto	Falso
1. Está aburrido y tiene ganas de hacer algo creativo.	☑	○
2. Cree que se rompió la rodilla.	○	☑ Cree que se rompió el tobillo.
3. Se lastimó cuando se cayó en el autobús.	☑	○
4. Es alérgico a dos medicamentos.	○	☑ No es alérgico a ningún medicamento.
5. No está mareado pero sí tiene un poco de fiebre.	○	☑ Está un poco mareado pero no tiene fiebre.

2 **Identificar** Identifica quién puede decir las siguientes frases.

1. Hace años me rompí la pierna cuando estaba jugando al fútbol. don Francisco
2. Hace más de una hora que me rompí la pierna. Me duele muchísimo. Javier
3. Tengo que sacarle una radiografía. No sé si se rompió uno de los huesos del pie. Dra. Márquez
4. No hay problema, vamos a ver a mi amiga, la doctora Márquez. don Francisco
5. Bueno, parece que el tobillo no está roto. Qué bueno, ¿no? Dra. Márquez
6. No sé si voy a poder ir de excursión con el grupo. Javier

DRA. MÁRQUEZ

DON FRANCISCO

JAVIER

3 **Ordenar** Pon los siguientes eventos en el orden correcto.

a. La doctora le saca una radiografía. __4__
b. La doctora le receta unas pastillas para el dolor. __6__
c. Javier se lastima el tobillo en el autobús. __2__
d. Don Francisco le habla a Javier de cuando era chico. __5__
e. Javier quiere dibujar un rato (*a while*). __1__
f. Don Francisco lo lleva a una clínica. __3__

NATIONAL communication STANDARDS

4 **En el consultorio** Trabajen en parejas para representar los papeles (*roles*) de un(a) médico/a y su paciente. Usen las instrucciones como guía. Answers will vary.

Médico/a	Paciente
Pregúntale al / a la paciente si le duele. →	Te caíste en casa. Describe tu dolor.
Pregúntale cuánto tiempo hace que se cayó. →	Describe la situación. Piensas que te rompiste el dedo.
Mira el dedo. Debes recomendar un tratamiento (*treatment*) al / a la paciente. →	Debes hacer preguntas al / a la médico/a sobre el tratamiento (*treatment*).

AYUDA

Here are some useful expressions:

¿Cómo se lastimó...?
¿Le duele...?
¿Cuánto tiempo hace que...?
Tengo...
Estoy...
¿Es usted alérgico/a a algún medicamento?
Usted debe...

TEACHING OPTIONS

Heritage Speakers Ask heritage speakers in your class to prepare a poster that gives information about the health care system of their country of origin or other Spanish-speaking countries they have visited. You may want to display the posters in your classroom.

Extra Practice Ask your students a few questions about the **Fotonovela**. Ex: **1. ¿Quién se lastimó en el autobús? (Javier) 2. ¿Cómo se llama la amiga de don Francisco? (Dra. Márquez) 3. ¿Adónde lleva don Francisco a Javier? (a la clínica de la doctora Márquez) 4. ¿Quién tenía muchas infecciones de la garganta? (don Francisco)**

Ortografía

El acento y las sílabas fuertes

In Spanish, written accent marks are used on many words. Here is a review of some of the principles governing word stress and the use of written accents.

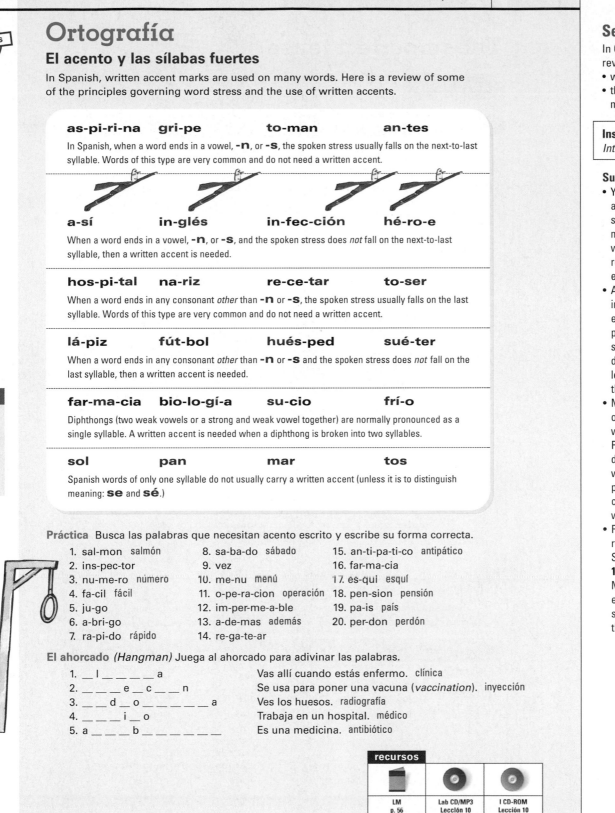

as-pi-ri-na   gri-pe   to-man   an-tes

In Spanish, when a word ends in a vowel, **-n**, or **-s**, the spoken stress usually falls on the next-to-last syllable. Words of this type are very common and do not need a written accent.

a-sí   in-glés   in-fec-ción   hé-ro-e

When a word ends in a vowel, **-n**, or **-s**, and the spoken stress does *not* fall on the next-to-last syllable, then a written accent is needed.

hos-pi-tal   na-riz   re-ce-tar   to-ser

When a word ends in any consonant *other* than **-n** or **-s**, the spoken stress usually falls on the last syllable. Words of this type are very common and do not need a written accent.

lá-piz   fút-bol   hués-ped   sué-ter

When a word ends in any consonant *other* than **-n** or **-s** and the spoken stress does *not* fall on the last syllable, then a written accent is needed.

far-ma-cia   bio-lo-gí-a   su-cio   frí-o

Diphthongs (two weak vowels or a strong and weak vowel together) are normally pronounced as a single syllable. A written accent is needed when a diphthong is broken into two syllables.

sol   pan   mar   tos

Spanish words of only one syllable do not usually carry a written accent (unless it is to distinguish meaning: **se** and **sé**.)

CONSÚLTALO

In Spanish, **a**, **e** and **o** are considered strong vowels while **i** and **u** are weak vowels. To review this concept, see **Lección 3**, **Pronunciación** p. 69.

Práctica Busca las palabras que necesitan acento escrito y escribe su forma correcta.

1. sal-mon   salmón
2. ins-pec-tor
3. nu-me-ro   número
4. fa-cil   fácil
5. ju-go
6. a-bri-go
7. ra-pi-do   rápido
8. sa-ba-do   sábado
9. vez
10. me-nu   menú
11. o-pe-ra-cion   operación
12. im-per-me-a-ble
13. a-de-mas   además
14. re-ga-te-ar
15. an-ti-pa-ti-co   antipático
16. far-ma-cia
17. es-qui   esquí
18. pen-sion   pensión
19. pa-is   país
20. per-don   perdón

El ahorcado *(Hangman)* Juega al ahorcado para adivinar las palabras.

1. _ l _ _ _ _ _ _ a   Vas allí cuando estás enfermo.   clínica
2. _ _ _ _ e _ c _ _ _ n   Se usa para poner una vacuna (*vaccination*).   inyección
3. _ _ _ d _ o _ _ _ _ _ _ a   Ves los huesos.   radiografía
4. _ _ _ _ i _ o   Trabaja en un hospital.   médico
5. a _ _ _ _ b _ _ _ _ _ _ _ o   Es una medicina.   antibiótico

recursos		
LM p. 56	**Lab CD/MP3** Lección 10	**I CD-ROM** Lección 10

Section Goals

In **Ortografía** students will review:
- word stress
- the use of written accent marks

Instructional Resource
Interactive CD-ROM

Suggestions
- You may want to explain that all words in which the spoken stress falls on the antepenultimate syllable or one before will carry a written accent, regardless of the letter they end in.
- As you go through each point in the explanation, write the example words on the board, pronounce them, and have students repeat. Then, ask students to provide words they learned in previous lessons that exemplify each point.
- Make a list of unfamiliar words on the board, leaving out any written accent marks. Pronounce them, and ask students whether and where a written accent mark should be placed. Include words that carry a written accent mark as well as some that do not.
- Point out that **Ortografía** replaces **Pronunciación** in the Student Edition for **Lecciones 10–15**, but not in the Lab Manual. The **Recursos** box references the **Pronunciación** sections found in all lessons of the Lab Manual.

TEACHING OPTIONS

Extra Practice Have your students close their books. Then give them the sentences in **Actividad 1, ¿Cierto o falso?**, page 274 as a dictation. Say each sentence twice slowly and once at normal speed to give your students enough time to write. Then have them open their books and check their work.

Pairs Ask your students to work in pairs to explain why each word in the **Práctica** activity does or does not have a written accent mark. The same process can be followed with the words in the **El ahorcado** activity.

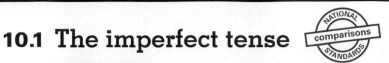

10.1 The imperfect tense

ANTE TODO In **Lección 6** you learned the preterite tense. You will now learn the imperfect, used to describe past activities in a different way.

recursos

WB
pp. 111–120

LM
pp. 57–60

Lab CD/MP3
Lección 10

I CD-ROM
Lección 10

vistahigher
learning.com

The imperfect of regular verbs

		cantar	**beber**	**escribir**
SINGULAR FORMS	yo	cant**aba**	beb**ía**	escrib**ía**
	tú	cant**abas**	beb**ías**	escrib**ías**
	Ud./él/ella	cant**aba**	beb**ía**	escrib**ía**
PLURAL FORMS	nosotros/as	cant**ábamos**	beb**íamos**	escrib**íamos**
	vosotros/as	cant**abais**	beb**íais**	escrib**íais**
	Uds./ellos/ellas	cant**aban**	beb**ían**	escrib**ían**

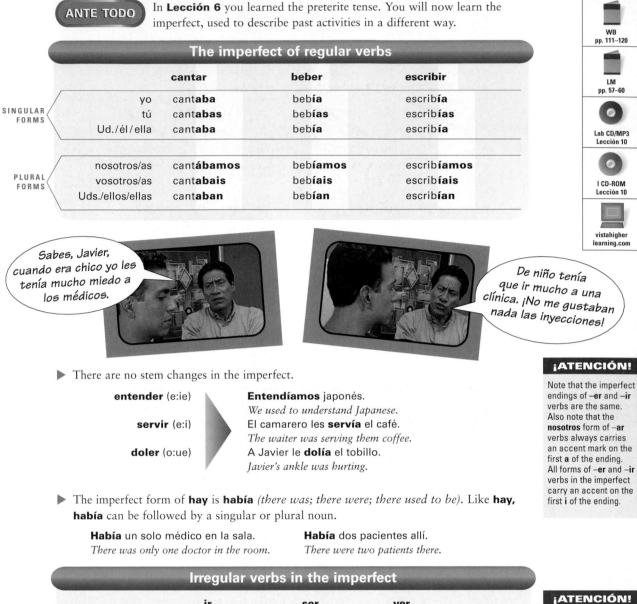

Sabes, Javier, cuando era chico yo les tenía mucho miedo a los médicos.

De niño tenía que ir mucho a una clínica. ¡No me gustaban nada las inyecciones!

▶ There are no stem changes in the imperfect.

entender (e:ie)

servir (e:i)

doler (o:ue)

Entendíamos japonés.
We used to understand Japanese.
El camarero les **servía** el café.
The waiter was serving them coffee.
A Javier le **dolía** el tobillo.
Javier's ankle was hurting.

¡ATENCIÓN!

Note that the imperfect endings of –**er** and –**ir** verbs are the same. Also note that the **nosotros** form of –**ar** verbs always carries an accent mark on the first **a** of the ending. All forms of –**er** and –**ir** verbs in the imperfect carry an accent on the first **i** of the ending.

▶ The imperfect form of **hay** is **había** (*there was; there were; there used to be*). Like **hay, había** can be followed by a singular or plural noun.

Había un solo médico en la sala.
There was only one doctor in the room.

Había dos pacientes allí.
There were two patients there.

Irregular verbs in the imperfect

		ir	**ser**	**ver**
SINGULAR FORMS	yo	ib**a**	er**a**	ve**ía**
	tú	ib**as**	er**as**	ve**ías**
	Ud./él/ella	ib**a**	er**a**	ve**ía**
PLURAL FORMS	nosotros/as	**íb**amos	**ér**amos	ve**íamos**
	vosotros/as	ib**ais**	er**ais**	ve**íais**
	Uds./ellos/ellas	ib**an**	er**an**	ve**ían**

¡ATENCIÓN!

Ir, ser, and **ver** are the only verbs in Spanish that are irregular in the imperfect.

CONSÚLTALO

You will learn more about the contrast between the preterite and the imperfect in **Estructura 10.2**, pp. 280–281.

Uses of the imperfect

▶ The imperfect is used to describe past events in a different way than the preterite. As a general rule, the imperfect is used to describe actions which are seen by the speaker as incomplete or "continuing," while the preterite is used to describe actions which have been completed. The imperfect expresses what was happening at a certain time or how things used to be. The preterite, in contrast, expresses a completed action.

—¿Qué te **pasó**?
What happened to you?

—Me **torcí** el tobillo.
I sprained my ankle.

—¿Dónde **vivías** de niño?
Where did you live as a child?

—**Vivía** en San José.
I lived in San José.

▶ The following words and expressions are often used with the imperfect because they express habitual or repeated actions: **de niño/a** (*as a child*), **todos los días** (*every day*), **mientras** (*while*).

Uses of the imperfect

1. **Habitual or repeated actions** . . . . **Íbamos** al parque los domingos.
   We used to go to the park on Sundays.

2. **Events or actions that were in progress** Yo **leía** mientras él **estudiaba**.
   I was reading while he was studying.

3. **Physical characteristics** . . . . **Era** alto y guapo.
   He was tall and handsome.

4. **Mental or emotional states** . . . . **Quería** mucho a su familia.
   He loved his family very much.

5. **Time-telling** . . . . **Eran** las tres y media.
   It was 3:30.

6. **Age** . . . . Los niños **tenían** seis años.
   The children were six years old.

¡INTÉNTALO! Indica la forma correcta de cada verbo en el imperfecto.

1. Yo ___hablaba___ (hablar, bailar, recetar, correr, comer, decidir, vivir)
   bailaba, recetaba, corría, comía, decidía, vivía

2. Tú _____ (nadar, encontrar, comprender, venir, ir, ser, ver)
   nadabas, encontrabas, comprendías, venías, ibas, eras, veías

3. Usted _____ (hacer, doler, asistir, ser, pasear, poder, ir)
   hacía, dolía, asistía, era, paseaba, podía, iba

4. Nosotras _____ (ser, tomar, ir, poner, seguir, ver, pensar)
   éramos, tomábamos, íbamos, poníamos, seguíamos, veíamos, pensábamos

5. Ellos _____ (salir, viajar, ir, querer, ser, pedir, empezar)
   salían, viajaban, iban, querían, eran, pedían, empezaban

6. Yo _____ (ver, estornudar, sufrir, ir, dar, ser, toser)
   veía, estornudaba, sufría, iba, daba, era, tosía

Suggestions

• Ask students to compare and contrast a home video with a snapshot in the family picture album. Then call their attention to the brief description of uses of the imperfect. Which actions would be best captured by a home video? (Continuing actions; incomplete actions; what was happening; how things used to be.) Which actions are best captured in a snapshot? (A completed action.)

• Ask students to answer questions about themselves in the past. Ex: **Y tú, _____ , ¿ibas al parque los domingos cuando eras niño/a? ¿Qué hacías mientras tu madre preparaba la comida? ¿Cómo eras de niño/a?**

• Ask questions about the **Fotonovela** characters using the imperfect.

Successful Language Learning
Ask students to think about what they used to do when they were younger and imagine how to say it in Spanish. This is good practice for real-life conversations because people often talk about their childhood when making new friends.

TEACHING OPTIONS

Video Show the **Fotonovela** video again to give students more input about the use of the imperfect. Stop the video at appropriate moments to contrast the use of preterite and imperfect tenses.

Game Divide the class into two teams. Indicate one team member at a time, alternating between teams. Give a certain infinitive and name a subject for which the team member should supply the correct form of the verb in the imperfect. Give a point per correct answer. Deduct a point for each wrong answer. The team with the most points at the end wins.

Práctica

1 Completar Primero, completa las frases con el imperfecto de los verbos. Luego, pon las oraciones en orden lógico y compáralas con las de un(a) compañero/a.

a. El doctor dijo que no ___era___ (ser) nada grave. 7
b. El doctor ___quería___ (querer) ver la nariz del niño. 6
c. Su mamá ___estaba___ (estar) dibujando cuando Miguelito entró llorando. 3
d. Miguelito ___tenía___ (tener) la nariz hinchada (*swollen*). Fueron al hospital. 4
e. Miguelito no ___iba___ (ir) a jugar más. Ahora quería ir a casa a descansar. 8
f. Miguelito y sus amigos ___jugaban___ (jugar) al béisbol en el patio. 2
g. ___Eran___ (ser) las dos de la tarde. 1
h. Miguelito le dijo a la enfermera que ___le dolía___ (dolerle) la nariz. 5

2 Transformar Forma oraciones completas. Usa las formas correctas del imperfecto y añade (*add*) todas las palabras necesarias.

1. Julieta y César / ser / paramédicos
   Julieta y César eran paramédicos.
2. trabajar / juntos y / llevarse / bien
   Trabajaban juntos y se llevaban muy bien.
3. cuando / haber / accidente, / siempre / analizar / situación / con cuidado
   Cuando había un accidente, siempre analizaban la situación con cuidado.
4. preocuparse / mucho / por / pacientes
   Se preocupaban mucho por los pacientes.
5. si / paciente / tener / mucho / dolor, / ponerle / inyección
   Si el paciente tenía mucho dolor, le ponían una inyección.

3 En la escuela de medicina Usa los verbos de la lista para completar las frases con las formas correctas del imperfecto. Algunos verbos se usan más de una vez. Some answers will vary.

caerse	enfermarse	ir	querer	tener
comprender	estornudar	pensar	sentirse	tomar
doler	hacer	poder	ser	toser

1. Cuando Javier y Victoria ___eran___ estudiantes de medicina, siempre ___tenían___ que ir al médico.
2. Cada vez que él ___tomaba___ un examen, a Javier le ___dolía___ mucho la cabeza.
3. Cuando Victoria ___hacía___ ejercicio aeróbico, siempre ___se sentía___ mareada.
4. Todas las primaveras, Javier ___estornudaba/tosía___ mucho porque es alérgico al polen.
5. Victoria también ___se caía___ de su bicicleta en camino a clase.
6. Después de comer en la cafetería, a Victoria siempre le ___dolía___ el estómago.
7. Javier ___quería/pensaba___ ser médico para ayudar a los demás.
8. Pero no ___comprendía___ por qué él ___se enfermaba___ con tanta frecuencia.
9. Cuando Victoria ___tenía___ fiebre, no ___podía___ ni leer el termómetro.
10. Javier ___tenía___ dolor de muelas, pero nunca ___quería___ ir al dentista.
11. Victoria ___tosía/estornudaba___ mucho cuando ___se sentía___ congestionada.
12. Javier y Victoria ___pensaban___ que nunca ___iban___ a graduarse.

Comunicación

4 Entrevista Trabajen en parejas. Un(a) estudiante usa estas preguntas para entrevistar a su compañero/a. Luego compartan los resultados de la entrevista con la clase. *Answers will vary.*

1. Cuando eras estudiante de primaria, ¿te gustaban tus profesores/as?
2. ¿Veías mucha televisión cuando eras niño/a?
3. Cuando tenías diez años, ¿cuál era tu programa de televisión favorito?
4. Cuando eras niño/a, ¿qué hacía tu familia durante las vacaciones?
5. ¿Cuántos años tenías en 1996?
6. Cuando eras estudiante de secundaria, ¿qué hacías con tus amigos/as?
7. Cuando tenías quince años, ¿cuál era tu grupo musical favorito?
8. Antes de tomar esta clase, ¿sabías hablar español?

5 Describir En parejas, túrnense para describir cómo eran sus vidas cuando eran niños. Pueden usar las sugerencias de la lista u otras ideas. Luego informen a la clase sobre la vida del/de la compañero/a. *Answers will vary.*

NOTA CULTURAL

El Parque Nacional Tortuguero está en la costa del Caribe, al norte de la ciudad de Limón, en Costa Rica. Varias especies de tortuga (*turtle*) utilizan las playas del parque para poner (*lay*) sus huevos. Esto ocurre de noche, y hay guías que llevan pequeños grupos de turistas a observar este fenómeno biológico.

> **modelo**
>
> De niña, mi familia y yo siempre íbamos a Tortuguero. Tomábamos un barco desde Limón, y por las noches mirábamos las tortugas (*turtles*) en la playa. Algunas veces teníamos suerte, porque las tortugas venían a poner (*lay*) huevos. Otras veces, volvíamos al hotel sin ver ninguna tortuga.

- Las vacaciones
- Ocasiones especiales
- Qué hacías durante el verano
- Celebraciones con tus amigos/as
- Celebraciones con tu familia
- Cómo era tu escuela
- Cómo eran tus amigos/as
- Los viajes que hacías
- A qué jugabas
- Qué hacías cuando te sentías enfermo/a

Síntesis

6 En el consultorio Tu profesor(a) te va a dar una lista incompleta con los pacientes que fueron al consultorio del doctor Donoso ayer. En parejas, conversen para completar sus listas y saber a qué hora llegaron las personas al consultorio y cuáles eran sus problemas. *Answers will vary.*

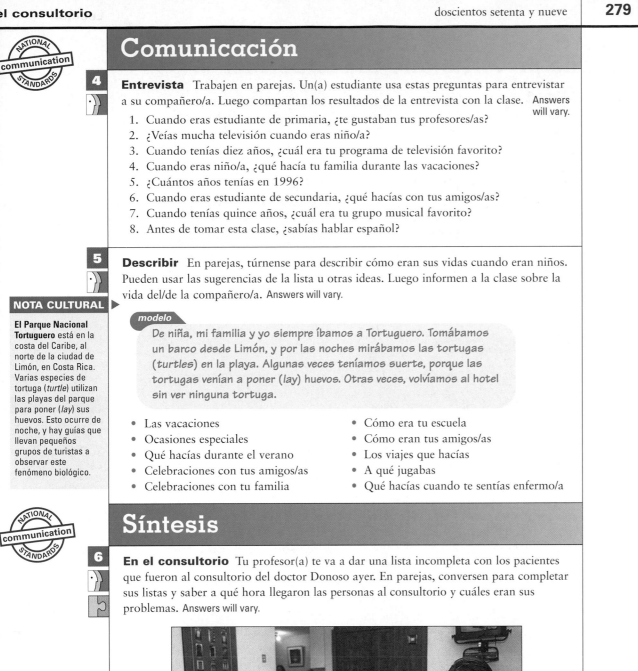

---

4 Suggestion Students should record the results of their interviews in a Venn diagram, which they can use to present the information to the class.

5 Suggestions
- Before students report to the class, divide the class into groups of four. After each report, the groups decide on a question for the presenter. Then have the groups take turns asking the student about his or her experience.
- Assign this activity as a short written composition.

6 Suggestion Divide the class into pairs and distribute the handouts from the Information Gap Activities Booklet that correspond to this activity. Give students ten minutes to complete this activity.

6 Expansion Have pairs write Dr. Donoso's advice for three of the patients. Later, have them read the advice to the class and compare it with what other pairs wrote for the same patients.

TEACHING OPTIONS

Large Groups Label the four corners of the room **La Revolución Americana, Tiempos prehistóricos, El Imperio Romano,** and **El Japón de los samurai.** Have students go to the corner that best describes what historical period they would visit if they could. Each group should then discuss their reasons for choosing that period using the imperfect tense. A spokesperson will summarize the group response to the rest of the class.

Game Divide the class into teams of three. Each team should decide on a historical or fictional villain. When it is their turn, they will give the class one hint. The other teams are allowed three questions, which must be answered truthfully. At the end of the question/answer session, teams must guess the identity. Award one point for each correct guess. The team with the most points wins.

Section Goal

In **Estructura 10.2** students will compare and contrast the uses and meanings of the preterite and imperfect tenses.

Instructional Resources

WB/VM: Workbook, pp. 113–116
Lab Manual, p. 58
*Lab CD/MP3 **Lección 10***
*IRM: ¡Inténtalo! & **Práctica***
Answers, pp. 187–188;
Tapescript, pp. 45–48
Interactive CD-ROM
Companion website:
www.vistahigherlearning.com
Presentations CD-ROM

Suggestions

• Have a volunteer read Javier's words in the caption of the left-hand video still on this page. Ask which verb is imperfect (**estaba**) and which is preterite (**Me caí**). Repeat for the right-hand video still showing Don Francisco (**jugaba/me rompí**).

• Give personalized examples as you contrast the preterite and the imperfect. Ex: **La semana pasada tuve que ir al dentista. Me dolía mucho la muela.**

10.2 The preterite and the imperfect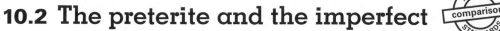

ANTE TODO   Now that you have learned the forms of the preterite and the imperfect, you will learn more about how they are used. The preterite and the imperfect are not interchangeable. In Spanish, the choice between these two tenses depends on the context and on the point of view of the speaker.

Me caí cuando estaba en el autobús.

De niño jugaba mucho al fútbol. Una vez me rompí la pierna.

COMPARE & CONTRAST

Uses of the preterite	Uses of the imperfect
1. To express actions that are viewed by the speaker as completed Don Francisco **se rompió** la pierna. *Don Francisco broke his leg.* **Fueron** a Buenos Aires ayer. *They went to Buenos Aires yesterday.*	**1.** To describe an ongoing past action with no reference to its beginning or end Don Francisco **esperaba** a Javier. *Don Francisco was waiting for Javier.* El médico **se preocupaba** por sus pacientes. *The doctor worried about his patients.*
2. To express the beginning or end of a past action La película **empezó** a las nueve. *The movie began at nine o'clock.* Ayer **terminé** el proyecto para la clase de química. *Yesterday I finished the project for chemistry class.*	**2.** To express habitual past actions and events Cuando **era** joven, **jugaba** al tenis. *When I was young, I used to play tennis.* De niño, don Francisco **se enfermaba** con mucha frecuencia. *As a child, Don Francisco used to get sick very frequently.*
3. To narrate a series of past actions or events La doctora me **miró** los oídos, me **hizo** unas preguntas y **escribió** la receta. *The doctor looked in my ears, asked me some questions, and wrote the prescription.* **Me di** con la mesa, **me caí** y **me lastimé** el pie. *I bumped into the table, I fell, and I injured my foot.*	**3.** To describe physical and emotional states or characteristics La chica **quería** descansar. **Se sentía** mal y **tenía** dolor de cabeza. *The girl wanted to rest. She felt ill and had a headache.* Ellos **eran** altos y **tenían** ojos verdes. *They were tall and had green eyes.* **Estábamos** felices de ver a la familia. *We were happy to see the family.*

AYUDA

These words and expressions, as well as similar ones, commonly occur with the preterite: **ayer, anteayer, una vez, dos veces, tres veces, el año pasado, de repente**.

They usually imply that an action has happened at a specific point in time. For a review, see **Estructura 6.3**, p. 166.

AYUDA

These words and expressions, as well as similar ones, commonly occur with the imperfect: **de niño/a, todos los días, mientras, siempre, con frecuencia, todas las semanas**. They usually express habitual or repeated actions in the past.

TEACHING OPTIONS

Extra Practice Write in English a simple, humorous retelling of a well-known fairy tale. Read it to the class, pausing after each verb in the past to ask the class whether the imperfect or preterite would be used in Spanish. Ex: Once upon a time there was a girl named Little Red Riding Hood. She wanted to take lunch to her ailing grandmother. She put a loaf of bread, a wedge of cheese, and a bottle of Beaujolais in a basket and set off through the

woods. Meanwhile, farther down the path, a big, ugly, snaggle-toothed wolf was leaning against a tree, filing his nails . . .
Pairs On separate slips of paper, have students write six true statements, one for each of the uses of the preterite and imperfect in **Compare & Contrast**. Have them mix up the slips and exchange them with a partner, who will identify the preterite or imperfect use the sentence illustrates.

▶ The preterite and the imperfect often appear in the same sentence. In such cases the imperfect describes what *was happening*, while the preterite describes the action that "interrupted" the ongoing activity.

Miraba la tele cuando **sonó** el teléfono.
I was watching TV when the phone rang.

Maite **leía** el periódico cuando **llegó** Álex.
Maite was reading the newspaper when Álex arrived.

▶ You will also see the preterite and the imperfect together in narratives such as fiction, news, and retelling of events. In these cases the imperfect provides all of the background information, such as time, weather, and location, while the preterite indicates the specific events that occurred to advance the plot.

Eran las dos de la mañana y el detective ya no **podía** mantenerse despierto. **Se bajó** lentamente del coche, **estiró** las piernas y **levantó** los brazos hacia el cielo oscuro.
It was two in the morning, and the detective could no longer stay awake. He slowly stepped out of the car, stretched his legs, and raised his arms toward the dark sky.

La luna **estaba** llena y no **había** en el cielo ni una sola nube. De repente, el detective **escuchó** un grito espeluznante proveniente del parque.
The moon was full and there wasn't a single cloud in the sky. Suddenly, the detective heard a piercing scream coming from the park.

Un médico colombiano descubrió la vacuna contra la malaria

El doctor colombiano Manuel Elkin Patarroyo descubrió una vacuna contra la malaria. Esta enfermedad se erradicó hace décadas en muchas partes del mundo. Sin embargo, los casos de malaria empezaban a aumentar otra vez, justo cuando salió la vacuna de Patarroyo. En mayo de 1993, el doctor Patarroyo donó la vacuna, a nombre de Colombia, a la Organización Mundial de la Salud. Los grandes laboratorios farmacéuticos presionaron a la OMS porque querían la vacuna. Pero en 1995 las dos partes, el doctor Patarroyo y la OMS, ratificaron el pacto original.

¡INTÉNTALO! Elige el pretérito o el imperfecto para completar la historia. Explica por qué se usa ese tiempo verbal en cada ocasión. Answers will vary. Suggested answers.

1. ___Eran___ (Fueron/Eran) las doce.
2. ___Había___ (Hubo/Había) mucha gente en la calle.
3. A las doce y media, Tomás y yo ___entramos___ (entramos/entrábamos) en el Restaurante Tárcoles.
4. Todos los días yo ___almorzaba___ (almorcé/almorzaba) con Tomás al mediodía.
5. El camarero ___llegó___ (llegó/llegaba) inmediatamente, para darnos el menú.
6. Nosotros ___empezamos___ (empezamos/empezábamos) a leerlo.
7. Yo ___pedí___ (pedí/pedía) el pescado.
8. De repente, el camarero ___volvió___ (volvió/volvía) a nuestra mesa.
9. Y nos ___dio___ (dio/daba) una mala noticia.
10. Desafortunadamente, no ___tenían___ (tuvieron/tenían) más pescado.
11. Por eso Tomás y yo ___decidimos___ (decidimos/decidíamos) comer en otro lugar.
12. ___Llovía___ (Llovió/Llovía) muy fuerte cuando ___salimos___ (salimos/salíamos) del café.
13. Así que ___regresamos___ (regresamos/regresábamos) al Restaurante Tárcoles.
14. Esta vez, ___pedí___ (pedí/pedía) el arroz con pollo.

Suggestions

• Give further examples from your own experience that contrast the imperfect and the preterite. Ex: **Quería ver la nueva película ____, pero anoche sólo pude ir a las diez de la noche. La película estaba buena, pero terminó muy tarde. Era la una cuando llegué a casa. Me acosté muy tarde y esta mañana, cuando me levanté, estaba cansadísimo/a.**

• Have students find the example of an interrupted action in the realia.

• Involve the class in a conversation about what they did in the past. Ask: ____, **¿paseabas en bicicleta cuando eras niño/a? ¿Te caíste alguna vez? ____, ¿cuando eras niño/a iba tu familia de vacaciones todos los años? ¿Adónde iban?**

• After completing **¡Inténtalo!**, have students explain why the preterite or imperfect was used in each case. Then call on different students to create other sentences illustrating the same uses.

TEACHING OPTIONS

Pairs Ask students to narrate the most interesting, embarrassing, exciting, or annoying thing that has happened to them recently. Tell them to describe what happened and how they felt, using preterite and imperfect verbs.

Heritage Speakers Ask heritage speakers to write a summary of what happened in the **Fotonovela**. Tell them that their summaries should first set the scene and establish background information about the characters, where they are, and what they were doing, then explain what happened.

Práctica

1 Seleccionar Utiliza el tiempo verbal adecuado, según (*according to*) el contexto.

1. La semana pasada, Manolo y Aurora __querían__ (querer) dar una fiesta. __Decidieron__ (Decidir) invitar a seis amigos y servirles mucha comida.
2. Manolo y Aurora __estaban__ (estar) preparando la comida cuando Elena __llamó__ (llamar). Como siempre, __tenía__ (tener) que estudiar para un examen.
3. A las seis, __volvió__ (volver) a sonar el teléfono. Su amigo Francisco tampoco __podía__ (poder) ir a la fiesta, porque __tenía__ (tener) fiebre. Manolo y Aurora __se sentían__ (sentirse) muy tristes, pero __tenían__ (tener) que preparar la comida.
4. Después de otros 15 minutos, __sonó__ (sonar) el teléfono. Sus amigos, los señores Vega, __estaban__ (estar) en camino (*en route*) al hospital: a su hijo le __dolía__ (doler) mucho el estómago. Sólo dos de los amigos __podían__ (poder) ir a la cena.
5. Por supuesto, __iban__ (ir) a tener demasiada comida. Finalmente, cinco minutos antes de las ocho, __llamaron__ (llamar) Ramón y Javier. Ellos __pensaban__ (pensar) que la fiesta __era__ (ser) la próxima semana.
6. Tristes, Manolo y Aurora __se sentaron__ (sentarse) a comer solos. Mientras __comían__ (comer) pronto __llegaron__ (llegar) a la conclusión de que __era__ (ser) mejor estar solos: ¡La comida __estaba__ (estar) malísima!

2 Completar Completa esta noticia con la forma correcta del pretérito o el imperfecto.

Un accidente trágico

Ayer temprano por la mañana (1)__hubo__ (haber) un trágico accidente en el centro de Buenos Aires cuando un autobús no (2)__vio__ (ver) venir un auto. La mujer que (3)__conducía__ (conducir) el auto (4)__murió__ (morir) al instante y los paramédicos (5)__tuvieron__ (tener) que llevar al pasajero al hospital porque (6)__sufrió__ (sufrir) varias fracturas. El conductor del autobús (7)__dijo__ (decir) que no (8)__vio__ (ver) el auto hasta el último (*last*) momento porque (9)__había__ (haber) mucha niebla y (10)__estaba__ (estar) lloviendo. Él (11)__intentó__ (intentar) (*to attempt*) dar un viraje brusco (*to swerve*), pero (12)__perdió__ (perder) el control del autobús y no (13)__pudo__ (poder) evitar (*to avoid*) el accidente. Según nos informaron, no (14)__se lastimó__ (lastimarse) ningún pasajero del autobús.

3 Completar Completa las frases de una manera lógica. Usa el pretérito o el imperfecto. En parejas, comparen sus respuestas. Answers will vary.

1. De niño/a, yo...
2. Yo conducía el auto mientras...
3. Anoche mi novio/a...
4. Ayer el/la profesor(a)...
5. La semana pasada un(a) amigo/a...
6. Con frecuencia mis padres...
7. Esta mañana en la cafetería...
8. Hablábamos con el doctor cuando...

Comunicación

4 Entrevista Usa estas preguntas para entrevistar a un(a) compañero/a acerca de su primer(a) novio/a. Si quieres, puedes añadir (*to add*) otras preguntas. Answers will vary.

1. ¿Quién fue tu primer(a) novio/a?
2. ¿Cuántos años tenían ustedes cuando se conocieron?
3. ¿Cómo era él/ella?
4. ¿Qué le gustaba hacer? ¿Le interesaban los deportes?
5. ¿Por cuánto tiempo salieron ustedes?
6. ¿Qué hacían ustedes cuando salían?
7. ¿Pensaban casarse?
8. ¿Cuándo y por qué rompieron ustedes?

5 La sala de emergencia En parejas, miren la lista e inventen qué les pasó a estas personas que están en la sala de emergencias. Answers will vary.

> **modelo**
>
> *Eran las tres de la tarde. Como todos los días, Pablo jugaba al fútbol con sus amigos. Estaba muy contento. De repente, se cayó y se rompió el brazo. Después fue a la sala de emergencias.*

Paciente	Edad	Hora	Condición
1. Pablo Romero	9 años	15:20	hueso roto (el brazo)
2. Estela Rodríguez	45 años	15:25	tobillo torcido
3. Lupe Quintana	29 años	15:37	embarazada, dolores
4. Manuel López	52 años	15:45	infección de garganta
5. Marta Díaz	3 años	16:00	temperatura muy alta, fiebre
6. Roberto Salazar	32 años	16:06	dolor de muelas
7. Marco Brito	18 años	16:18	daño en el cuello, posible fractura
8. Ana María Ortiz	66 años	16:29	reacción alérgica a un medicamento

6 Situación Anoche alguien robó (*stole*) el examen de la **Lección 10** de la oficina de tu profesor(a) y tú tienes que averiguar (*to find out*) quién lo hizo. Pregúntales a tres compañeros dónde estaban, con quién estaban y qué hicieron entre las ocho y las doce de la noche. Answers will vary.

Síntesis

7 La primera vez En grupos, cuéntense cómo fue la primera vez que les pusieron una inyección, se rompieron un hueso, pasaron la noche en un hospital, estuvieron mareados/as, etc. Incluyan los siguientes puntos en su conversación: una descripción del día que hacía, sus edades, qué pasó y cómo se sentían. Answers will vary.

---

4 Suggestion Before the interviews, have students prepare a few notes to help them in their responses.

4 Expansion Have students write a summary of their partners' responses, omitting all names. Collect the summaries, then read them to the class. Have students guess who had the relationship described in the summary.

5 Expansion Have pairs share their answers with the class, but without mentioning the name of the character. The class must guess which one is being described.

6 Expansion Have students decide who in their group would be the most likely thief based on his or her responses. Ask the group to prepare a police report explaining why they believe their suspect is the culprit.

7 Suggestion Before assigning groups, have students list information they can include in their descriptions such as their age, the time, the date, what the weather was like, and so forth. Next have them list the events of the day in the order they happened.

7 Expansion Have students decide who in their group is most accident prone on the basis of his or her responses. Ask the group to prepare a doctor's account of his or her treatments in the emergency room.

TEACHING OPTIONS

Small Groups Have students write and perform a conversation for the class. Three students walk into the campus clinic. They are all trying to explain to the doctor what happened to them and why they should be seen first. Students should use the preterite and imperfect.

Game Create a short narrative in the past based on a well-known story. Allow space between each sentence so they may be easily cut apart into strips. Print two copies and cut apart the sentences. Then make a copy of the file and edit it, changing all preterites to imperfects and vice versa. Print two copies of this version and cut the sentences apart. Into each of two bags put a full set of each version of the story, mix the strips up, and challenge two teams to reconstruct the correct version. The team that does so first wins.

10.3 Constructions with *se*

ANTE TODO In **Lección 7** you learned how to use **se** as the third person reflexive pronoun (**El se despierta. Ellos se visten. Ella se baña.**). **Se** can also be used to form constructions in which the person performing the action is not expressed or is de-emphasized.

Impersonal constructions with *se*

▶ In Spanish, verbs that are not reflexive can be used with **se** to form impersonal constructions. These are statements in which the person performing the action is not expressed or defined. In English, the passive voice or indefinite subjects *(you, they, one)* are used.

Se habla español en Costa Rica.
Spanish is spoken in Costa Rica.

Se hacen operaciones aquí.
They perform operations here.

Se puede leer en la sala de espera.
You can read in the waiting room.

Se necesitan medicinas enseguida.
They need medicine right away.

> **¡ATENCIÓN!**
>
> Note that the third person singular verb form is used with singular nouns and the third person plural form is used with plural nouns:
>
> **Se vende ropa.**
>
> **Se venden camisas.**

▶ You often see the impersonal **se** in signs, advertisements, and directions.

SE PROHÍBE NADAR

Se necesitan programadores
GRUPO TECNO
Tel. 778-34-34

ENTRADA

Se entra por la izquierda

Se for unplanned events

¿Cuánto tiempo hace que se cayó?

Ya se me olvidó.

Bueno, vamos a sacarle una radiografía para ver si se le rompió el hueso.

▶ **Se** is also used to form statements that describe accidental or unplanned events. In this construction, the person who performs the action is de-emphasized, so as to imply that the accident or unplanned event is not his or her direct responsibility. These statements are constructed using the following pattern.

se + [INDIRECT OBJECT PRONOUN] + [VERB] + [SUBJECT]

Se   me   cayó   la pluma.

TEACHING OPTIONS

TPR Use impersonal constructions with **se** to have students draw what you say. Ex: You say: **Se prohíbe entrar**, and students draw a door with a diagonal line through it. Other possible expressions could be: **Se sale por la derecha. Se permiten perros. Se prohíben botellas.**

Extra Practice Have students bring in common icons or international signs. They can find these on the Internet. Then pair students to write directions using **se** for each of the icons and signs. Ex: **Se prohíbe entrar. Se prohíbe pasar. Se habla español.**

▶ In this type of construction, what would normally be the direct object of the sentence becomes the subject, and it agrees with the verb, not with the indirect object pronoun.

I.O. PRONOUN	VERB		SUBJECT
me, te, le	quedó / cayó / dañó	SINGULAR	la receta. / la taza. / el radio.
Se			
nos, os, les	rompieron / olvidaron / perdieron	PLURAL	las botellas. / las pastillas. / las llaves.

▶ The following verbs are the ones most frequently used with **se** to describe unplanned events.

Verbs commonly used with *se*

caer	to fall; to drop	**perder** (e:ie)	to lose
dañar	to damage; to break down	**quedar**	to be left behind
olvidar	to forget	**romper**	to break

Se me perdió el teléfono de la farmacia.
I lost the pharmacy's phone number.

Se nos olvidaron los pasajes.
We forgot the tickets.

▶ To clarify or emphasize who the person involved in the action is, this construction commonly begins with the preposition **a** + [*noun*] or **a** + [*prepositional pronoun*].

Al paciente se le perdió la receta.
The patient lost his prescription.

A Diana se le olvidó ir al consultorio ayer.
Diana forgot to go to the doctor's office yesterday.

A mí se me cayeron los cuadernos.
I dropped the notebooks.

A ustedes se les quedaron los libros en casa.
You left the books at home.

 ¡INTÉNTALO! Completa las frases de la columna A con **se** impersonal y los verbos correspondientes en presente.

A

1. *Se enseñan* (enseñar) cinco lenguas en esta universidad.
2. *Se come* (comer) muy bien en El Cráter.
3. *Se venden* (vender) muchas camisetas allí.
4. *Se sirven* (servir) platos exquisitos cada noche.
5. *Se necesita* (necesitar) mucho dinero.
6. *Se busca* (buscar) secretaria.

Completa las frases de la columna B con **se** y los verbos en pretérito para expresar sucesos imprevistos.

B

1. *Se me rompieron* (*I broke*) las gafas.
2. *Se te cayeron* (*You* (fam.) *dropped*) las pastillas.
3. *Se les perdió* (*They lost*) la receta.
4. *Se le quedó* (*You* (form.) *left*) aquí la radiografía.
5. *Se nos olvidó* (*We forgot*) pagar la medicina.
6. *Se les quedaron* (*They left*) los antibióticos en la clínica.

¡ATENCIÓN!

While Spanish has a verb for *to fall* (**caer**), there is no direct translation for *to drop*. **Dejar caer** (*let fall*) is often used to mean *to drop*.
El médico dejó caer la aspirina. *The doctor dropped the aspirin.*

CONSÚLTALO

For an explanation of prepositional pronouns, refer to **Estructura 9.4**, p. 258.

Successful Language Learning
Tell your students that this construction has no exact equivalent in English. Tell them to examine the examples in the textbook and make up some of their own in order to get a feel for how this construction works.

Suggestions
• Test comprehension by asking volunteers to change sentences from plural to singular and vice versa. Ex: **Se me perdieron las llaves. (Se me perdió la llave.)**
• Have students finish sentences using a construction with **se** to express an unplanned event. Ex: **1. Al doctor ____. (se le cayó el termómetro) 2. A la profesora ____. (se le quedaron los papeles en casa)**
• Involve students in a conversation about unplanned events that happened to them recently. Say: **Se me olvidaron los lentes oscuros esta mañana. Y a ti, ____, ¿se te olvidó algo esta mañana? ¿Qué se te olvidó?** Continue with other verbs. Ex: **¿A quién se le perdió algo importante esta semana? ¿Qué se te perdió, ____?**

TEACHING OPTIONS

Video Show the **Fotonovela** video again to give students more input containing constructions with **se**. Have students write down as many of the examples of the construction as they can. After viewing the video, have students edit their lists and cross out any reflexive verbs that they mistakenly understood to be constructions with **se**.

Heritage Speakers Ask heritage speakers to write a fictional or true account of a day in which everything went wrong. Ask them to include as many constructions with **se** as possible. Have them read their accounts aloud to the class to give extra practice to their classmates.

1 Expansion
• Change the date from 1901 to 2004 and go through the exercise again orally.
• Have students work in pairs and, using constructions with **se**, write a description of a period in history such as the French or American Revolution, the Sixties, Prohibition, and so forth. Then have pairs form groups of six to read their descriptions aloud to their group.
• Have students use **se** constructions to compare cultural differences between Spanish-speaking countries and their own. Ex: **Aquí se habla inglés, pero en _____ se habla español.**

2 Suggestions
• Model the activity by asking volunteers to translate similar sentences. Ex: Nurse sought. **(Se busca enfermera.)** Used books bought. **(Se compran libros usados.)**
• Ask students to describe where these signs could be found locally.

3 Suggestion Have students work in pairs to brainstorm verbs that could be used to complete this activity.

3 Expansion Use magazine pictures to have students continue describing past events using constructions with **se**.

Práctica

1

¿Cierto o falso? Lee estas oraciones sobre la vida en 1901. Indica si lo que dice cada oración es **cierto** o **falso**. Luego corrige las oraciones falsas.

1. Se veía mucha televisión. Falso. No se veía televisión. Se leía mucho.
2. Se escribían muchos libros. Cierto.
3. Se viajaba mucho en tren. Cierto.
4. Se montaba a caballo. Cierto.
5. Se mandaba mucho correo electrónico. Falso. No se mandaba correo electrónico. Se mandaban muchas cartas y postales.
6. Se preparaban muchas comidas en casa. Cierto.
7. Se llevaban minifaldas. Falso. No se llevaban minifaldas. Se llevaban faldas largas.
8. Se pasaba mucho tiempo con la familia. Cierto.

2

Traducir Traduce estos letreros (*signs*) y anuncios (*ads*) al español.

1. Nurses needed Se necesitan enfermeros/as
2. Eating and drinking prohibited Se prohíbe comer y beber
3. Programmers sought Se buscan programadores
4. English is spoken Se habla inglés
5. Computers sold Se venden computadoras
6. No talking Se prohíbe hablar
7. Teacher needed Se necesita profesor / profesora
8. Books sold Se venden libros
9. Do not enter Se prohíbe entrar
10. Spanish is spoken Se habla español

3

¿Qué pasó? Mira los dibujos e indica lo que pasó en cada uno. Some answers will vary.

1. camarero / pastel

Al camarero se le cayó el pastel.

2. Sr. Álvarez / espejo

Al señor Álvarez se le rompió el espejo.

3. Arturo / tarea

A Arturo se le olvidó la tarea.

4. Sra. Domínguez / llaves

A la Sra. Domínguez se le perdieron las llaves.

5. Carla y Lupe / botellas de vino

A Carla y Lupe se les rompieron dos botellas de vino.

6. Juana / platos

A Juana se le rompieron los platos.

TEACHING OPTIONS

Extra Practice Have students imagine that they have just seen a movie about the future. Have them work in groups to prepare a description of the way of life portrayed in the movie using the imperfect tense and constructions with **se**. Ex: **No se necesitaba trabajar. Se usaban robots para hacer todo. Se viajaba por telepatía. No se comía nada sino en los fines de semana**.

Game Divide the class into teams of four. Have each team think of a famous place or public building and compose four signs that could be found on the premises. Teams will take turns reading their signs aloud. Each team that correctly identifies the place or building receives a point. The team with the most points wins.

Comunicación

4 **Preguntas** Trabajen en parejas y usen estas preguntas para entrevistarse. Answers will vary.

1. ¿Qué comidas se sirven en tu restaurante favorito?
2. ¿Se te olvidó invitar a alguien a tu última fiesta o comida? ¿A quién?
3. ¿A qué hora se abre la cafetería de tu universidad?
4. ¿Alguna vez se te quedó algo importante en la casa? ¿Qué?
5. ¿Alguna vez se te perdió algo importante durante un viaje?
6. ¿Qué se vende en una farmacia?
7. ¿Sabes si en la farmacia se aceptan cheques?
8. ¿Alguna vez se te rompió algo muy caro? ¿Qué?

5 **Opiniones** En parejas, terminen cada oración con ideas originales. Después, comparen los resultados con la clase para ver qué pareja tuvo las mejores ideas. Answers will vary.

1. No se tiene que dejar propina cuando…
2. Antes de viajar, se debe…
3. Si se come bien, …
4. Para tener una vida sana, se debe...
5. Se sirve la mejor comida en…
6. Se hablan muchas lenguas en…

Síntesis

6 **Anuncios** En grupos, preparen dos anuncios de televisión para presentar a la clase. Usen el imperfecto y por lo menos dos construcciones con **se** en cada uno. Answers will vary.

modelo

Se me cayeron unos libros en el pie y me dolía mucho. Pero ahora no, gracias a SuperAspirina 500. ¡Dos pastillas y se me fue el dolor! Se puede comprar SuperAspirina 500 en todas las farmacias Recetamax.

NOTA CULTURAL

En muchos países de Latinoamérica es posible conseguir medicinas en **las farmacias**, sin la receta de un médico.

Comúnmente, los farmacéuticos (*pharmacists*) diagnostican el problema del/de la cliente/a y le venden el medicamento adecuado.

TEACHING OPTIONS

Extra Practice Write the following sentence fragments on the board and ask students to supply several logical endings using a construction with **se**: **1.** Cuando subía al avión, ____. (se le cayó la maleta; se le torció el pie) **2.** Una vez, cuando comía en un restaurante elegante, ____. (se me rompió un vaso; me dio un dolor de estómago) **3.** Ayer cuando venía a clase, ____. (se me quedó la tarea en el autobús; me caí y se me rompió el brazo)

4. Cuando era niño/a, ____. (siempre se me olvidaban las cosas; se me perdían siempre las cosas) **5.** El otro día cuando lavaba los platos, ____. (se me rompieron tres vasos; se me terminó el detergente)

Section Goals

In **Estructura 10.4** students will learn:
- the formation of adverbs using [*adjective*] + **–mente**
- common adverbs and adverbial expressions

Instructional Resources
*WB/VM: Workbook, pp. 119–120
Lab Manual, p. 60
Lab CD/MP3 Lección 10
IRM: ¡Inténtalo! & Práctica
Answers, pp. 187–188;
Tapescript, pp. 45–48
Interactive CD-ROM
Companion website:
www.vistahigherlearning.com
Presentations CD-ROM*

Suggestions

- Use magazine pictures to review known adverbs. Ex: **Mira la foto que tengo *aquí*. *Hoy* esta chica se siente *bien*, pero *ayer* se sentía *mal*.** Write the adverbs on the board as you proceed.
- After presenting the formation of adverbs that end in **–mente**, ask volunteers to convert known adjectives into adverbs and then use them in a sentence. Ex: **cómodo/cómoda-mente: Alberto se sentó cómodamente en la silla.**

10.4 Adverbs

ANTE TODO Adverbs are words that describe how, when, and where actions take place. They can modify verbs, adjectives, and even other adverbs. In previous lessons, you have already learned many Spanish adverbs, such as the ones below.

aquí	hoy	nunca
ayer	mal	siempre
bien	muy	temprano

▶ The most common adverbs are those which end in **–mente**. These are equivalent to the English adverbs which end in *-ly*.

fácilmente *easily*	**generalmente** *generally*
verdaderamente *truly; really*	**simplemente** *simply*

▶ To form adverbs which end in **–mente**, add **–mente** to the feminine form of the adjective. If the adjective does not have a special feminine form, just add **–mente** to the standard form.

ADJECTIVE	FEMININE FORM	SUFFIX	ADVERB
seguro	segura	-mente	seguramente
fabuloso	fabulosa	-mente	fabulosamente
enorme		-mente	enormemente
feliz		-mente	felizmente

▶ Adverbs that end in **–mente** generally follow the verb, while adverbs that modify an adjective or another adverb precede the word they modify.

Javier dibuja **maravillosamente**.
Javier draws wonderfully.

Inés está **casi siempre** ocupada.
Inés is almost always busy.

¡ATENCIÓN!

When a sentence contains two or more adverbs in sequence, the suffix **–mente** is dropped from all but the last adverb.

El médico nos habló simple y abiertamente.
The doctor spoke to us simply and openly.

• • •

Adjectives do not lose their accents when adding **–mente**.

fácil ⟶ fácilmente
débil ⟶ débilmente

Common adverbs and adverbial expressions

a menudo	*often*	**así**	*like this; so*	**menos**	*less*
a tiempo	*on time*	**bastante**	*enough; rather*	**muchas veces**	*a lot; many times*
a veces	*sometimes*	**casi**	*almost*		
además (de)	*furthermore; besides*	**con frecuencia**	*frequently*	**poco**	*little*
		de vez en cuando	*from time to time*	**por lo menos**	*at least*
apenas	*hardly; scarcely*			**pronto**	*soon*
		despacio	*slowly*	**rápido**	*quickly*

¡ATENCIÓN!

Rápido functions as an adjective (**Ella tiene una computadora rápida.**) as well as an adverb (**Ella corre rápido.**). Note that as an adverb, **rápido** does not need to agree with any other word in the sentence. You can also use the adverb **rápidamente** (**Ella corre rápidamente**).

¡INTÉNTALO! Transforma los adjetivos en adverbios.

1. alegre ___alegremente___
2. constante ___constantemente___
3. gradual ___gradualmente___
4. perfecto ___perfectamente___
5. real ___realmente___
6. frecuente ___frecuentemente___
7. tranquilo ___tranquilamente___
8. regular ___regularmente___
9. maravilloso ___maravillosamente___
10. normal ___normalmente___
11. básico ___básicamente___
12. afortunado ___afortunadamente___

TEACHING OPTIONS

Heritage Speakers Have heritage speakers interview an older member of their home community about daily life when he or she was a young adult. Students should write a summary of the information, using at least eight of the common adverbs and adverbial expressions listed.

Extra Practice Have pairs of students write sentences using adverbs such as **nunca, hoy, lentamente,** and so forth. When they have finished, ask volunteers to dictate their sentences to you to write on the board. After you have written a sentence and corrected any errors, ask volunteers to suggest a sentence that uses the antonym of the adverb.

Práctica

1 **Suggestion** Review common adverbs and adverbial expressions by drawing a three-column chart on the board. Title the columns **¿Cómo?**, **¿Cuándo?**, and **¿Dónde?** Ask volunteers to call out adverbs for each column. Write the correct answers on the board. Ex: **¿Cómo? (a tiempo, lentamente, temprano) ¿Cuándo? (nunca, siempre, a menudo) ¿Dónde? (aquí, allí)**

1 **Escoger** Completa las oraciones con los adverbios adecuados.

1. La cita era para las dos pero llegamos ___tarde___. (mientras, nunca, tarde)
2. El problema fue que ___ayer___ se nos descompuso el despertador. (aquí, ayer, despacio)
3. La recepcionista no se enojó porque sabe que normalmente llego ___a tiempo___. (a veces, a tiempo, poco)
4. ___Por lo menos___ el doctor estaba listo. (por lo menos, muchas veces, casi)
5. ___Apenas___ tuvimos que esperar cinco minutos. (así, además, apenas)
6. El doctor dijo que nuestra hija Irene necesitaba cambiar su rutina diaria ___inmediatamente___. (temprano, menos, inmediatamente)
7. El doctor nos explicó ___bien___ las recomendaciones del Cirujano General (*Surgeon General*) sobre la salud de los jóvenes. (de vez en cuando, bien, apenas)
8. ___Afortunadamente___ nos dijo que Irene estaba bien, pero tenía que hacer más ejercicio y comer mejor. (bastante, afortunadamete, a menudo)

NOTA CULTURAL ▶

La doctora Antonia Novello, de Puerto Rico, fue la primera mujer y la primera hispana en tomar el cargo de **Cirujana General** de los Estados Unidos (1990–1993).

NATIONAL
communication
STANDARDS

Comunicación

2 **Suggestion** Before assigning the activity, ask some general questions about the ad. Ex: **¿Qué producto se vende? (aspirina) ¿Dónde se encuentra un anuncio de este tipo? (en una revista)**

2 **Expansion** Have pairs do a similar ad for a different pharmaceutical product. Collect the ads and read the descriptions aloud. The rest of the class will guess what product is being advertised.

2 **Aspirina** Lee el anuncio y responde a las preguntas con un(a) compañero/a.

Answers will vary.

No Hay Tiempo Para el Dolor de Cabeza

Si tienes prisa, o simplemente quieres que tu dolor de cabeza se vaya muy pronto, piensa en Bayer. Se asimila mejor y actúa rápidamente. Ya no se puede perder tiempo por un dolor de cabeza.

ASPIRINA

Bayer
Siempre a tu lado.

1. ¿Cuáles son los adverbios que aparecen en el anuncio?
2. Según el anuncio, ¿cuáles son las ventajas (*advantages*) de este tipo de aspirina? ¿Cuáles son sus cualidades?
3. ¿Tienen ustedes muchos dolores de cabeza? ¿Qué toman para curarlos?
4. ¿Qué medicamentos ven con frecuencia en los anuncios de televisión? Escriban descripciones de varios de estos anuncios. Usen adverbios en sus descripciones.

TEACHING OPTIONS

Extra Practice Here are five sentences containing adverbs to use as a dictation. **1. A mi profesor de español siempre se le olvidan las cosas. 2. Con frecuencia se pone dos zapatos diferentes por la mañana. 3. De vez en cuando trae un calcetín negro y otro blanco. 4. De vez en cuando se le pierden los papeles. 5. Felizmente es un profesor excelente y siempre aprendemos mucho en su clase.**

Game Divide the class into teams of three. Each team should have a piece of paper or a transparency. Say the name of a historical figure and give teams three minutes to write down as many facts as they can about that person, using adverbs and adverbial expressions. At the end of each round, have teams project their answers or read them aloud. Award one point to the team with the most correct answers for each historical figure.

Section Goals

In **Lectura** students will:
- learn to activate background knowledge to understand a reading selection
- read a content-rich text on health care while traveling

Instructional Resource
Companion website:
www.vistahigherlearning.com

Estrategia Tell students that they will find it easier to understand the content of a reading selection on a particular topic by reviewing what they know about the subject before reading. Then ask students to brainstorm ways to stay healthy while traveling. Possible responses: don't drink the water, don't eat raw fruit or vegetables, pack personal medical supplies that may not be available at the destination.

Examinar el texto Students should mention that the text is an interview (**entrevista**) by a journalist (**periodista**) of an author (**autora**) whose book is about health care while traveling.

Conocimiento previo Have small groups write a paragraph summarizing ways to safeguard health while traveling. Their recommendations should be based on their collective experiences. Encourage them to draw on the experiences of people they know if no one in the group can relate personally to one of the situations mentioned in the items. Have groups share their paragraphs with the class.

The Affective Dimension Remind your students that they will probably feel less anxious about reading in Spanish if they follow the suggestions in the **Estrategia** sections, which are designed to reinforce and increase reading comprehension skills.

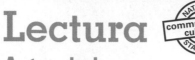

Lectura

Antes de leer

Estrategia
Activating background knowledge

Using what you already know about a particular subject will often help you better understand a reading selection. For example, if you read an article about a recent medical discovery, you might think about what you already know about health in order to understand unfamiliar words or concepts.

Examinar el texto

Utiliza las estrategias de lectura que tú consideras las más efectivas para hacer unas observaciones preliminares acerca del texto. Después trabajen en parejas para comparar sus observaciones acerca del texto. Luego contesten las siguientes preguntas:

- Analiza el formato del texto. ¿Qué tipo de texto es? ¿Dónde crees que se publicó este artículo?
- ¿Quiénes son Carla Baron y Tomás Monterrey?
- Mira la foto del libro. ¿Qué sugiere el título del libro sobre su contenido?

Conocimiento previo

Ahora piensen en su conocimiento previo° sobre el cuidado de la salud en los viajes. Consideren las siguientes preguntas:

- ¿Viajaste alguna vez a otro estado o a otro país?
- ¿Tuviste algunos problemas durante tus viajes con el agua, la comida o el clima del país?
- ¿Olvidaste poner en tu maleta algún medicamento que después necesitaste?
- Imagina que tu amigo/a se va de viaje. Dile por lo menos cinco cosas que debe hacer para prevenir cualquier problema de salud.

recursos

vistahigher
learning.com

conocimiento previo *background knowledge*

Libro de la semana

Cómo hacer un viaje saludable y feliz

Carla Baron

Después de leer

Correspondencias Busca las correspondencias entre los problemas y las recomendaciones.

Problemas
1. el agua ___b___
2. el sol ___d___
3. la comida ___a___
4. la identificación ___e___
5. el clima ___c___

Recomendaciones
a. Hay que adaptarse a los ingredientes no familiares.
b. Toma sólo productos purificados (*purified*).
c. Es importante llevar ropa adecuada cuando viajas.
d. Lleva loción o crema con alta protección solar.
e. Lleva tu pasaporte.

TEACHING OPTIONS

Heritage Speakers Have pairs of heritage speakers interview each other about health problems they have encountered while traveling. First, have them brainstorm a list of pertinent questions, then have them take turns asking and answering them. After the interview have each student write a short paragraph about his or her own experience.

Small Groups Have groups of three select a country they would like to visit. Ask students to research what food and beverage precautions should be taken (**precauciones que se deben tomar**) by visitors to that country. Students should mention precautions such as not eating undercooked meat, uncooked seafood or vegetables, raw fruits, or unpasteurized dairy products, and not drinking tap water or drinks with ice or mixed with water.

Correspondencias Ask students to work together in pairs to use cognates and context clues to match **Problemas** with **Recomendaciones**.

Seleccionar
- Have students check their work by locating the sections in the text where the answers can be found.
- Ask the questions of the whole class. Ask volunteers to answer orally or to write their answers on the board.

Entrevista a Carla Baron
por Tomás Monterrey

Tomás: ¿Por qué escribió su libro *Cómo hacer un viaje saludable y feliz?*

Carla: Me encanta viajar, conocer otras culturas y escribir. Mi primer viaje lo hice cuando era estudiante universitaria. Todavía recuerdo el día en que llegamos a San Juan, Puerto Rico. Era el panorama ideal para unas vacaciones maravillosas, pero al llegar a la habitación del hotel, bebí mucha agua de la llave° y luego pedí un jugo de frutas con mucho hielo°. El clima en San Juan es tropical y yo tenía mucha sed y calor. Los síntomas llegaron en menos de media hora: pasé dos días con dolor de estómago y corriendo al cuarto de baño cada 10 minutos. Desde entonces, siempre que viajo sólo bebo agua mineral y llevo un pequeño bolso con medicinas necesarias como pastillas para el dolor y también bloqueador solar, una crema repelente de mosquitos y un desinfectante.

Tomás: ¿Son reales° las situaciones que se narran en su libro?

Carla: Sí, son reales y son mis propias° historias°. A menudo los autores crean caricaturas divertidas de un turista en dificultades. ¡En mi libro la turista en dificultades soy yo!

Tomás: ¿Qué recomendaciones puede encontrar el lector en su libro?

Carla: Bueno, mi libro es anecdótico y humorístico, pero el tema de la salud se trata° de manera seria. En general, se dan recomendaciones sobre ropa adecuada para cada sitio, consejos para protegerse del sol, y comidas y bebidas adecuadas para el turista que viaja al Caribe o a la América del Sur.

Tomás: ¿Tiene algún consejo para las personas que se enferman cuando viajan?

Carla: Muchas veces los turistas toman el avión sin saber nada acerca del país que van a visitar. Ponen toda su ropa en la maleta, toman el pasaporte, la cámara fotográfica y ¡a volar°! Es necesario tomar precauciones porque nuestro cuerpo necesita adaptarse al clima, al sol, a la humedad, al agua y a la comida. Se trata de° viajar, admirar las maravillas del mundo y regresar a casa con hermosos recuerdos. En resumen, el secreto es "prevenir en vez de° curar".

llave *faucet* **hielo** *ice* **reales** *true* **propias** *own* **historias** *stories* **se trata** *is treated* **¡a volar!** *off they go!* **Se trata de** *It's a question of* **en vez de** *instead of*

Seleccionar Selecciona la respuesta correcta.

1. El tema principal de este libro es ___d___.
   a. Puerto Rico b. la salud y el agua c. otras culturas
   d. el cuidado de la salud en los viajes
2. Las situaciones narradas en el libro son ___a___.
   a. autobiográficas b. inventadas c. ficticias
3. ¿Qué recomendaciones no vas a encontrar en este libro? ___d___
   a. cómo vestirse adecuadamente
   b. cómo prevenir las quemaduras solares
   c. consejos sobre la comida y la bebida
   d. cómo dar propina en los países del Caribe o de América del Sur

4. En opinión de la señorita Baron, ___b___.
   a. es bueno tomar agua de la llave y beber jugo de frutas con mucho hielo
   b. es mejor tomar solamente agua embotellada (*bottled*)
   c. los minerales son buenos para el dolor abdominal
   d. es importante visitar el cuarto de baño cada 10 minutos
5. ¿Cuál de los siguientes productos no lleva la autora cuando viaja a otros países? ___c___
   a. desinfectante
   b. crema repelente
   c. detergente
   d. pastillas medicinales

TEACHING OPTIONS

Pairs Ask pairs to use the items in **Correspondencias** on page 290 as a model. Have them work together to write additional possibilities for **Problemas** and **Recomendaciones**. Ex: **Problema: el dinero; Recomendación: lleva cheques de viajero o una tarjeta de crédito internacional**. When pairs have completed five more items, have them exchange their items with another pair who can match them.

Heritage Speakers Ask heritage speakers to prepare a short presentation of health tips for traveling in their countries. Students should include information on any immunizations that may be required; appropriate clothing, particularly for countries in which the seasons are opposite ours; spicy regional foods or dishes that may cause digestive problems; and so forth.

Costa Rica

NATIONAL connections cultures STANDARDS

El país en cifras

▶ **Área:** 51.100 km² (19.730 millas²),
aproximadamente el área de Virginia Occidental°

▶ **Población:** 4.454.000

*Costa Rica es el país de Centroamérica con la
población más homogénea. El 98% de sus
habitantes es blanco y mestizo°. Más del 50% de
la población es de descendencia° española y un alto
porcentaje tiene sus orígenes en otros países europeos.*

▶ **Capital:** San José —1.080.000

▶ **Ciudades principales:**
Alajuela —173.000, Cartago —119.000,
Puntarenas —102.000, Heredia —73.000

SOURCE: Population Division, UN Secretariat

▶ **Moneda:** colón costarricense°

▶ **Idioma:** español (oficial)

Bandera de Costa Rica

Costarricenses célebres

▶ **Carmen Lyra,** escritora (1888–1949)
▶ **Chavela Vargas,** cantante (1919–)
▶ **Óscar Arias Sánchez,** político (1941–)
▶ **Claudia Poll,** nadadora° olímpica (1972–)

Óscar Arias recibió
el Premio Nobel
de la Paz en 1987.

Virginia Occidental *West Virginia* mestizo *of indigenous and white
parentage* descendencia *descent* costarricense *Costa Rican* nadadora
swimmer ejército *army* gastos *expenditures* cuartel *barracks*

¡Increíble pero cierto!

Costa Rica es el único país latinoamericano
que no tiene ejército°. Sin gastos° militares, el
gobierno puede poner más dinero en la
educación y las artes. En la foto aparece el
Museo Nacional de Costa Rica, antiguo cuartel
del ejército.

Celebración del
Viernes Santo

Cráter del
Volcán Poás

NICARAGUA

Río Tempisque
Cordillera de Guanacaste
Río San Juan
Cordillera Central
Volcán Poás
Cordillera
de Tilarán
Alajuela
Puntarenas
Heredia
Río Grande
de Tárcoles
Volcán Irazú
San José · Cartago

Edificio Metálico
en San José

Océano
Pacífico

Cordill

Basílica de Nuestra Señora
de los Ángeles en Cartago

ESTADOS UNIDOS

OCÉANO
ATLÁNTICO

COSTA RICA

OCÉANO
PACÍFICO
AMÉRICA DEL SUR

recursos

| WB pp. 121–122 | VM pp. 243–244 | I CD-ROM Lección 10 | vistahigher learning.com |

MUSEO NACIONAL

Section Goal

In **Panorama**, students will read
about the geography and culture
of Costa Rica.

Instructional Resources
Transparencies, #3, #4, #39
WB/VM: Workbook, pp. 121–122;
Video Activities, pp. 243–244
***Panorama cultural** DVD/Video*
Interactive CD-ROM
IRM: Videoscript, p. 112;
***Panorama cultural** Translations,*
p. 134
Companion website:
www.vistahigherlearning.com
Presentations CD-ROM

Suggestion Have students look
at the map of Costa Rica or
project **Transparency #39.**
Encourage them to mention the
physical features that they
notice. Discuss the images in
the call-out photos.

El país en cifras After each
section, ask students questions
about the content. Ex: **¿Entre
qué masas de agua está Costa
Rica? ¿Las ciudades principales, en qué lado de la
Cordillera Central están?** When
reading about Costa Rica's population, point out that the country has over a 90% literacy rate,
the best in Latin America. Point
out that Óscar Arias received
the Nobel Peace Prize for his
work in resolving civil wars in
the other Central American
countries during the 1970s.

¡Increíble pero cierto! Costa
Rica has one of the most long-
standing democratic traditions
in America. Although it has no
army, it does have a national
police force and a rural guard.

TEACHING OPTIONS

Heritage Speakers Invite students of Costa Rican background
or from other countries of Central America to share information
about the national nicknames that Central Americans use for
each other. Costa Ricans are called **ticos**, Nicaraguans are
called **nicas**, and Guatemalans are called **chapines**.

Variación léxica If you visit Costa Rica, you may hear a few
interesting colloquialisms such as these. **Pulpería** is the word
for the *corner grocery store*. A gas station is called a **bomba**, literally a *pump*. A city block is called **cien metros**, literally *a hundred meters.*

Lugares • Los parques nacionales

Establecido° para la protección de los delicados ecosistemas de la región y su biodiversidad, el sistema de parques nacionales ocupa el 12% del territorio de Costa Rica. En los parques, los ecoturistas pueden ver hermosas cataratas°, montañas y una multitud de plantas exóticas. Algunos parques ofrecen también la oportunidad de ver quetzales, monos°, jaguares, armadillos y elegantes mariposas° en su hábitat natural.

Economía • Las plantaciones de café

Costa Rica fue el primer país centroamericano en desarrollar° la industria del café. En el siglo° XIX los costarricenses empezaron a exportar su delicioso café, de rico aroma, a Inglaterra°, lo cual contribuyó mucho a la prosperidad de la nación. Hoy día, más de 50.000 costarricenses trabajan en el cultivo de café. El café representa cerca del 15% de las exportaciones anuales del país.

Sociedad • Una nación progresista

Un modelo de democracia y de estabilidad, Costa Rica es también uno de los países más progresistas del mundo°. Ofrece servicios médicos gratuitos° a todos sus ciudadanos° y también a los turistas. En 1870 Costa Rica eliminó la pena de muerte° y en 1948 eliminó el ejército° e hizo obligatoria y gratuita la educación para todos los costarricenses.

PANAMÁ

Bañistas en Limón

¿Qué aprendiste? Responde a las preguntas con una frase completa.

1. ¿Cómo se llama la capital de Costa Rica? La capital de Costa Rica se llama San José.
2. ¿Quién es Claudia Poll? Claudia Poll es una nadadora olímpica.
3. ¿Qué porcentaje del territorio de Costa Rica ocupan los parques nacionales? Los parques nacionales ocupan el 12% del territorio de Costa Rica.
4. ¿Qué hacen los parques nacionales? Los parques nacionales protegen los ecosistemas de la región y su biodiversidad.
5. ¿Qué pueden ver los turistas en los parques nacionales? En los parques nacionales, los turistas pueden ver cataratas, montañas y muchas plantas exóticas.
6. ¿Cuántos costarricenses trabajan en las plantaciones de café hoy día? Más de 50.000 costarricenses trabajan en las plantaciones de café hoy día.
7. ¿Cuándo eliminó Costa Rica la pena de muerte? Costa Rica eliminó la pena de muerte en 1870.

Conexión Internet Investiga estos temas en el sitio **www.vistahigherlearning.com.**

1. Busca información sobre Óscar Arias Sánchez. ¿Quién es? ¿Por qué se le considera (*is he considered*) un costarricense célebre?
2. Busca información sobre los artistas de Costa Rica. ¿Qué artista, escritor o cantante te interesa más? ¿Por qué?

Establecido *Established* cataratas *waterfalls* monos *monkeys* mariposas *butterflies* desarrollar *develop* siglo *century* Inglaterra *England* mundo *world* gratuitos *free* ciudadanos *citizens* pena de muerte *death penalty* ejército *army*

Los parques nacionales Costa Rica's system of national parks was begun in the 1960s. With the addition of buffer zones in which some logging and farming are allowed, the percentage of Costa Rica's territory protected by environmental legislation rose to 27%.

Las plantaciones de café Invite students to prepare a coffee-tasting session, where they sample the coffees of Central America. You may wish to compare them to South American or African coffees as well. Teach vocabulary to describe the flavors: **rico, amargo, fuerte,** and so forth.

Una nación progresista Because of its mild climate (in terms of weather *and* politics), Costa Rica has become a major destination for retired and expatriate Americans. Survey students to see how many have visited Costa Rica already, and how many know of friends or family who have visited or live there.

Conexión Internet Students will find supporting Internet activities and links at **www.vistahigherlearning.com.**

Suggestion You may want to wrap up this section by playing the **Panorama cultural** video footage for this lesson.

TEACHING OPTIONS

Worth Noting Costa Rica has three types of lands protected by ecological legislation: **parques nacionales, refugios silvestres,** and **reservas biológicas.** Costa Rica's most famous protected area is the **Reserva Biológica Bosque Nuboso Monteverde** (Monteverde Cloud Forest Biological Reserve), where over 400 different species of birds have been recorded. The town of Monteverde was founded by Quakers from the United States in 1951 who began dairy farming and cheese-making there. In order to protect the watershed, the settlers decided to preserve about a third of their property as a biological reserve. In 1972 this area was more than doubled, and this became the **Reserva Biológica.** Today Monteverde still has a cheese factory (**La Fábrica**) and its cheeses are sold throughout the country.

Section Goal

In **Panorama**, students will read about the history and culture of Nicaragua.

Instructional Resources
Transparencies, #3, #4, #40
WB/VM: Workbook, pp. 123–124;
Video Activities, pp. 245–246
Panorama cultural *DVD/Video*
Interactive CD-ROM
IRM: Videoscript, p. 112;
Panorama cutural *Translations,*
p.134
Companion website:
www.vistahigherlearning.com
Presentations CD-ROM

Suggestion Have students look at the map of Nicaragua or project **Transparency #40** and talk about the physical features of the country. Point out the concentration of cities along the country's Pacific Coast, and note the sparse settlement in the eastern part of the country and along the Caribbean coast. Remind students that before the construction of the Panama Canal, Nicaragua was the proposed site for an interoceanic canal.

El país en cifras

• After reading about the country's varied terrain and many volcanoes, tell students that Nicaragua's national slogan is **"El país de lagos y volcanes."** After students read about the capital, ask: **¿Qué porcentaje de nicaragüenses vive en Managua? (el 20%)** Tell students that one reason so many Nicaraguans live in the capital is due to the devastation experienced in much of the rest of the country over the past two decades due to war and natural disasters, such as Hurricane Mitch in 1998, and earthquakes and volcanic eruptions in 1999.

• You may want to tell students that they will read one of Gioconda Belli's poems in **Lección 15**.

¡Increíble pero cierto! Lake Nicaragua is the largest lake in Central America. Over 40 rivers drain into the lake.

Nicaragua

connections cultures NATIONAL STANDARDS

El país en cifras

▶ **Área:** 129.494 km² (49.998 millas²), *aproximadamente el área de Nueva York Nicaragua es el país más grande de Centroamérica. Su terreno es muy variado e incluye bosques tropicales, montañas, sabanas° y marismas°, además de unos 40 volcanes.*

▶ **Población:** 5.774.000

▶ **Capital:** Managua—1.166.000
Managua está en una región de una notable inestabilidad geográfica, con muchos volcanes y terremotos°. En décadas recientes, los nicaragüenses han decidido que no vale la pena° construir rascacielos° porque no resisten los terremotos.

▶ **Ciudades principales:** León—249.000, Masaya—149.000, Granada—113.000

SOURCE: Population Division, UN Secretariat

▶ **Moneda:** córdoba

▶ **Idiomas:** español (oficial), misquito, inglés

Bandera de Nicaragua

Nicaragüenses célebres

▶ **Rubén Darío,** poeta (1867–1916)
▶ **Violeta Barrios de Chamorro,** política y ex-presidenta (1929–)
▶ **Daniel Ortega,** político y ex-presidente (1945–)
▶ **Gioconda Belli,** poeta (1948–)

sabanas *grasslands* marismas *marshes* terremoto *earthquake*
no vale la pena *it's not worthwhile* rascacielos *skyscrapers* tiburón *shark*
agua dulce *freshwater* bahía *bay* fue cercada *was closed off* atunes *tuna*

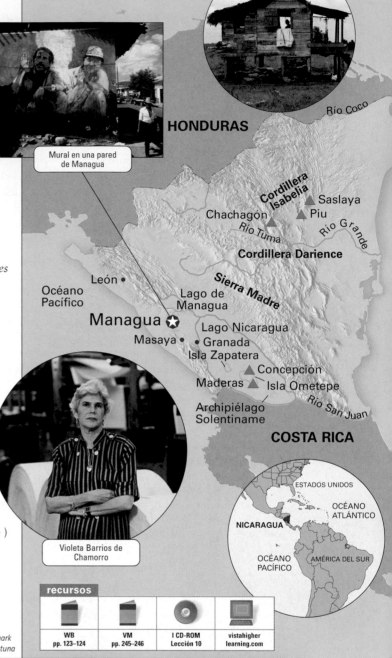
Típico hogar misquito en la costa atlántica
Mural en una pared de Managua
Violeta Barrios de Chamorro

recursos	

WB pp. 123–124 · VM pp. 245–246 · I CD-ROM Lección 10 · vistahigher learning.com

¡Increíble pero cierto!

En el lago Nicaragua está la única especie de tiburón° de agua dulce° del mundo. Los científicos creen que el lago fue antes una enorme bahía° que luego fue cercada° por erupciones volcánicas. Esta teoría explicaría la presencia de tiburones, atunes° y otras especies de peces que normalmente sólo viven en mares y océanos.

TEACHING OPTIONS

Worth Noting Managua is a city that has been destroyed and rebuilt multiple times due to wars and natural disasters. This has contributed to the unusual method used for listing street addresses in this capital city. Many places do not have an address that includes an actual building number and street name. Instead, the address includes a reference to a local landmark, and its relationship to other permanent features of the landscape, such as Lake

Managua. Here's a typical Managua address: **De la Clínica Don Bosco, 2 cuadras al norte, 3 y media al sur.** Invite students who have lived in Managua to share other "typical" addresses.
Extra Practice Invite students to compare the romantic poetry of Rubén Darío to the contemporary work of Ernesto Cardenal and Gioconda Belli. Students can choose several poems to read aloud to the class, and then comment on differences in style and content.

Historia • Las huellas de Acahualinca

La región de Managua se caracteriza por tener un gran número de sitios prehistóricos. Las huellas° de Acahualinca son uno de los restos° más famosos y antiguos°. Se formaron hace más de 6.000 años, a orillas° del lago Managua. Las huellas, tanto de humanos como de animales, se dirigen° hacia una misma dirección. Esto hace pensar a los expertos que corrían hacia el lago para escapar de una erupción volcánica.

Artes • Ernesto Cardenal (1925–)

Ernesto Cardenal, poeta, escultor y sacerdote° católico, es uno de los escritores más famosos de Nicaragua, país conocido por sus grandes poetas. Ha escrito° más de 35 libros y se le considera uno de los principales autores de Latinoamérica. Desde joven creyó en el poder° de la poesía°. En los años 60, Cardenal organizó la comunidad artística del archipiélago Solentiname en el lago Nicaragua. Fue ministro de cultura del país desde 1979 hasta 1988, y también fue vicepresidente de Casa de los Tres Mundos, una organización creada para el intercambio cultural internacional.

Naturaleza • El lago Nicaragua

El lago Nicaragua, con un área de más de 8.000 km² (3.100 millas²), es el lago más grande de Centroamérica. Dentro del lago hay más de 370 islas°, formadas por las erupciones del volcán Mombacho. La isla Zapatera, casi deshabitada ahora, fue un cementerio° indígena donde todavía se encuentran estatuas prehistóricas que parecen representar dioses. En el lago también se encuentran muchos peces exóticos.

¿Qué aprendiste? Responde a las preguntas con una frase completa.

1. ¿Por qué no hay muchos rascacielos en Managua?
   No hay muchos rascacielos en Managua porque no resisten los terremotos.
2. Nombra dos ex-presidentes de Nicaragua.
   Violeta Barrios de Chamorro y Daniel Ortega son dos ex-presidentes de Nicaragua.
3. ¿Qué especie única vive en el lago Nicaragua?
   La única especie de tiburón de agua dulce vive en el lago Nicaragua.
4. ¿Cuál es una de las teorías sobre la formación de las huellas de Acahualinca?
   Una teoría dice que las personas y los animales corrían para escapar de la erupción del volcán.
5. ¿Por qué es famoso el archipiélago Solentiname?
   El archipiélago Solentiname es famoso por su comunidad artística.
6. ¿Quién es Ernesto Cardenal?
   Es un poeta, escultor y sacerdote de Nicaragua.
7. ¿Cómo se formaron las islas del lago Nicaragua?
   Las islas se formaron por erupciones volcánicas.
8. ¿Qué hay de interés arqueológico en la isla Zapatera?
   En la isla Zapatera existió un cementerio indígena en que todavía se encuentran estatuas prehistóricas.

Conexión Internet Investiga estos temas en el sitio **www.vistahigherlearning.com**.

1. ¿Dónde se habla inglés en Nicaragua y por qué?
2. ¿Qué información hay ahora sobre la economía y/o los derechos humanos en Nicaragua?

----

huellas *footprints*   restos *remains*   antiguos *ancient*   orillas *shores*   se dirigen *are headed*   sacerdote *priest*   Ha escrito *He has written*   poder *power*   poesía *poetry*   islas *island*   cementerio *cemetery*

Las huellas de Acahualinca The **huellas de Acahualinca** were preserved in soft mud that was then covered with volcanic ash which became petrified, preserving the prints of bison, otter, deer, lizards, and birds— as well as humans.

Ernesto Cardenal After completing undergraduate studies in Nicaragua, **Ernesto Cardenal** studied in Mexico and in the United States, where he studied with religious poet Thomas Merton at the Trappist seminary in Kentucky. He later studied theology in Colombia, and was ordained in Nicaragua in 1965. It was shortly after that he founded the faith-based community of artists on **Solentiname** in **Lago Nicaragua**.

El lago Nicaragua Environmental groups in Nicaragua have been concerned about the recent introduction of a variety of **tilapia** into Lake Nicaragua. Although **tilapia** are native to the lake, this variety is a more prolific species. Environmentalists are concerned that the Nicaraguan-Norwegian joint venture responsible for this initiative has not done an adequate environmental impact study, and that the delicate and unique ecology of the lake may be negatively impacted.

Conexión Internet Students will find supporting Internet activities and links at **www.vistahigherlearning.com**.

Suggestion You may want to wrap up this section by playing the **Panorama cultural** video footage for this lesson.

TEACHING OPTIONS

Worth Noting On July 19, 1979, the FSLN (Frente Sandinista de Liberación Nacional), known as the Sandinistas, came to power in Nicaragua after winning a revolutionary struggle against the dictatorship of Anastasio Somoza. The Sandinistas began a program of economic and social reform that threatened the power of Nicaragua's traditional elite, leading to a civil war known as the **Contra** war. The United States became enmeshed in this conflict, illegally providing funding and arms to the **Contras**, who fought to oust the Sandinistas. The Sandinistas were ultimately voted out of power in 1990.

Instructional Resources
Vocabulary CD
Lab Manual, p. 60
*Lab CD/MP3 **Lección 10***
IRM: Tapescript, pp. 45–48
*Testing Program: **Pruebas**,*
*pp. 109–120; **Exámenes**,*
pp. 217–228
Testing Program Audio CD
Test Files CD-ROM
Test Generator

El cuerpo

la boca	mouth
el brazo	arm
la cabeza	head
el corazón	heart
el cuello	neck
el cuerpo	body
el dedo	finger
el estómago	stomach
la garganta	throat
el hueso	bone
la muela	molar
la nariz	nose
el oído	(sense of) hearing; inner ear
el ojo	eye
la oreja	(outer) ear
el pie	foot
la pierna	leg
la rodilla	knee
el tobillo	ankle

La salud

el accidente	accident
el antibiótico	antibiotic
la aspirina	aspirin
la clínica	clinic
el consultorio	doctor's office
el/la dentista	dentist
el/la doctor(a)	doctor
el dolor (de cabeza)	(head)ache; pain
el/la enfermero/a	nurse
el examen médico	physical exam
la farmacia	pharmacy
la gripe	flu
el hospital	hospital
la infección	infection
el medicamento	medication
la medicina	medicine
la operación	operation
el/la paciente	patient
la pastilla	pill; tablet
la radiografía	X-ray
la receta	prescription
el resfriado	cold (illness)
la sala de emergencia(s)	emergency room
la salud	health
el síntoma	symptom
la tos	cough

Verbos

caerse	to fall (down)
dañar	to damage; to break down
darse con	to bump into; to run into
doler (o:ue)	to hurt
enfermarse	to get sick
estar enfermo/a	to be sick
estornudar	to sneeze
lastimarse (el pie)	to injure (one's foot)
olvidar	to forget
poner una inyección	to give an injection
prohibir	to prohibit
recetar	to prescribe
romper	to break
romperse (la pierna)	to break (one's leg)
sacar(se) una muela	to have a tooth removed
ser alérgico/a (a)	to be allergic (to)
sufrir una enfermedad	to suffer an illness
tener dolor (m.)	to have a pain
tener fiebre	to have a fever
tomar la temperatura	to take someone's temperature
torcerse (o:ue) (el tobillo)	to sprain (one's ankle)
toser	to cough

Adjetivos

congestionado/a	congested; stuffed-up
embarazada	pregnant
grave	grave; serious
mareado/a	dizzy; nauseated
médico/a	medical
saludable	healthy
sano/a	healthy

Adverbios

a menudo	often
a tiempo	on time
a veces	sometimes
además (de)	furthermore; besides
apenas	hardly; scarcely
así	like this; so
bastante	enough; rather
casi	almost
con frecuencia	frequently
de niño/a	as a child
de vez en cuando	from time to time
despacio	slowly
menos	less
mientras	while
muchas veces	a lot; many times
poco	little
por lo menos	at least
pronto	soon
rápido	quickly
todos los días	every day

Expresiones útiles	See page 273.

recursos		
LM p. 60	Lab CD/MP3 Lección 10	Vocab CD Lección 10

La tecnología

11

Communicative Goals

You will learn how to:

- Talk about using technology and electronic products
- Use common expressions on the telephone
- Talk about car trouble

Lesson Goals

In **Lección 11** students will be introduced to the following:
- terms related to home electronics and the Internet
- terms related to cars and their accessories
- familiar (**tú**) commands
- uses of **por** and **para**
- reciprocal reflexive verbs
- stressed possessive adjectives and pronouns
- recognizing borrowed words
- cultural, geographic, and historical information about Argentina
- cultural, geographic, and historical information about Uruguay

A primera vista Here are some additional questions you can ask based on the photo: **¿Te gustan las computadoras? ¿Para qué usas el correo electrónico? ¿Cómo se escribían tus padres cuando no existía el correo electrónico? ¿Se hablaban tus abuelos por teléfono con frecuencia? ¿Cuánto tiempo hace que sabes conducir? ¿Tienes auto?**

---

contextos

fotonovela

estructura

adelante

panorama

A PRIMERA VISTA

- ¿Se llevan ellos bien o mal?
- ¿Crees que hace mucho tiempo que se conocen?
- ¿Están saludables?
- ¿Qué partes del cuerpo se ven en la foto?

INSTRUCTIONAL RESOURCES

Workbook/Video Manual: WB Activities, pp. 125–138
Laboratory Manual: Lab Activities, pp. 61–66
Workbook/Video Manual: Video Activities, pp. 215–216; pp. 247–250
Instructor's Resource Manual: **Vocabulario adicional,** p. 165; **¡Inténtalo! & Práctica** Answers, pp. 189–190; **Fotonovela** Translations, pp. 124–125; Textbook CD

Tapescript, p. 81; Lab CDs Tapescript, pp. 49–53; **Fotonovela** Videoscript, pp. 98–99; **Panorama cultural** Videoscript, p. 113; **Pan. cult.** Translations, p.135
Info Gap Activities Booklet, pp. 41–44
Overhead Transparencies: #5, #6, #41, #42, #43, #44
Lab Audio CD/MP3 **Lección 11**

Panorama cultural DVD/Video
Fotonovela DVD/Video
Testing Program, pp. 121–132
Testing Program Audio CD
Test Files CD-ROM
Test Generator
Companion website

Presentations CD-ROM
Textbook CD
Vocabulary CD
Interactive CD-ROM
Video CD-ROM
Web-SAM

Section Goals

In **Contextos**, students will learn and practice:
- vocabulary related to home electronics and the Internet
- terms related to cars and their accessories

Instructional Resources
Transparencies, #41, #42
Textbook Activities CD
Vocabulary CD
WB/VM: Workbook, pp. 125–126
Lab Manual, p. 61
*Lab CD/MP3 **Lección 11***
*IRM: **Vocab. adicional**,*
*p. 165; **Práctica** Answers,*
p. 189; Tapescript,
pp. 49–53; p. 81
Interactive CD-ROM
Companion website:
www.vistahigherlearning.com
Presentations CD-ROM

Suggestions

- Ask students about electronic items they may have.
  Ex: **¿Cuántos de ustedes tienen cámara digital? ¿Cuántos tienen un sitio web? ¿Cuántos tienen teléfono celular? ¿Cuántas veces al día lo usas?**
- Have students open their books to the drawing on pages 298–299 or project **Transparency #41**. Ask students questions to elicit computer vocabulary and involve them in a conversation about their computer use. Ex: **¿Es portátil la computadora? ¿Qué se usa para mover el cursor? ¿Quiénes navegan en la red? ¿Cuál es tu sitio web favorito?**
- Ask students about electronic items by giving true-false statements about associations. Ex: **El control remoto se usa con el televisor. (Cierto.)**

La tecnología

Más vocabulario

la calculadora	calculator
la cámara de video, digital	video, digital camera
el canal	(TV) channel
el cederrón	CD-ROM
la contestadora	answering machine
el estéreo	stereo
el *fax*	fax (machine)
la televisión por cable	cable television
el tocadiscos compacto	compact disc player
el video(casete)	video(cassette)
el archivo	file
arroba	@ symbol
la dirección electrónica	e-mail address
Internet	Internet
la página principal	home page
el programa de computación	software
la red	network; Web
el sitio web	Website
apagar	to turn off
borrar	to erase
descargar	to download
funcionar	to work
grabar	to record
guardar	to save
imprimir	to print
llamar	to call
navegar (en Internet)	to surf (the Internet)
poner, prender	to turn on
quemar	to burn (a CD)
sonar (o:ue)	to ring
descompuesto/a	not working; out of order
lento/a	slow
lleno/a	full

Variación léxica

computadora ⟷ ordenador (*Esp.*), computador (*Col.*)

descargar ⟷ bajar (*Esp., Col., Arg., Ven.*)

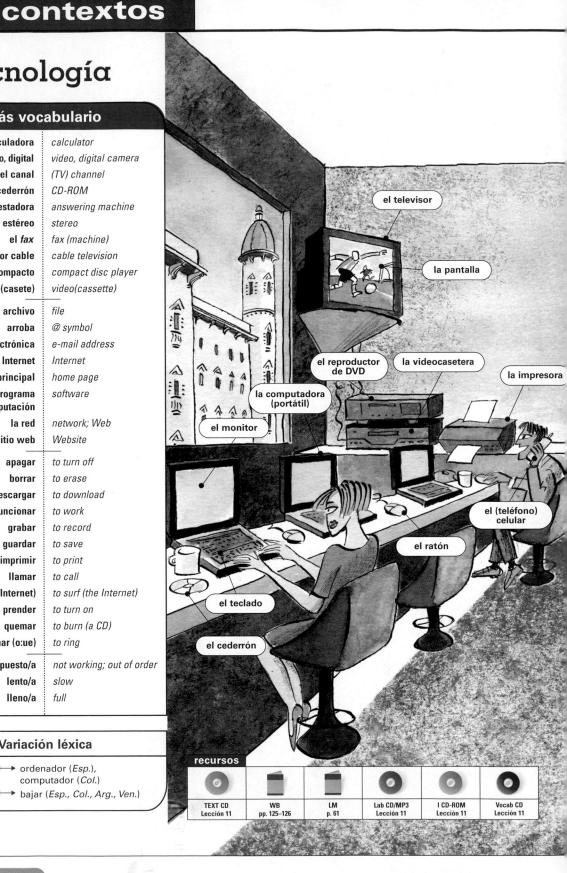

el televisor

la pantalla

el reproductor de DVD

la videocasetera

la impresora

la computadora (portátil)

el monitor

el (teléfono) celular

el ratón

el teclado

el cederrón

recursos

TEXT CD Lección 11	WB pp. 125–126	LM p. 61	Lab CD/MP3 Lección 11	I CD-ROM Lección 11	Vocab CD Lección 11

TEACHING OPTIONS

Extra Practice Students write down a list of six electronic or other technology items they have or use frequently. Then they circulate around the room asking others if they have those items too. When someone answers affirmatively, the student asks for his or her signature (**Firma aquí, por favor**). Students should try to get a different signature for each item.

Game Play **Concentración**. On eight cards, write names of electronic items. On another eight cards, draw or paste a picture that matches each of the first eight cards. Place the cards face-down in four rows of four. In pairs, students select two cards. If the two cards match, the pair keeps them. If the two cards do not match, students replace them in their original position. The pair with the most cards at the end wins.

Práctica

1 **Escuchar** Escucha esta conversación entre dos amigas. Después completa las oraciones.

1. María y Ana están en ___b___.
   a. una tienda   b. un cibercafé   c. un restaurante
2. El hijo de Ana le mandó ___a___.
   a. unas fotos digitales   b. un cederrón   c. un disco compacto
3. A María le encantan ___b___.
   a. los celulares   b. las cámaras digitales   c. los cibercafés
4. Ana prefiere guardar las fotos en ___c___.
   a. la pantalla   b. un archivo   c. un cederrón
5. María quiere tomar un café y ___c___.
   a. poner la computadora   b. sacar fotos digitales
   c. navegar en Internet
6. Ana paga por el café y ___a___.
   a. el uso de Internet   b. la impresora   c. el cederrón

2 **Oraciones** Escribe oraciones usando los elementos siguientes. Usa el pretérito y agrega (*add*) las palabras necesarias.

1. Yo / descargar / fotos digitales / Internet
   Yo descargué las fotos digitales por Internet.
2. Yo / apagar / televisor / diez / noche
   Yo apagué el televisor a las diez de la noche.
3. ¿Quién / poner / videocasetera?
   ¿Quién puso la videocasetera?
4. Daniel y su esposa / comprar / computadora portátil / ayer
   Daniel y su esposa compraron una computadora portátil ayer.
5. Sara y yo / ir / cibercafé / para / navegar en Internet
   Sara y yo fuimos al cibercafé para navegar en Internet.
6. Jaime / decidir / comprar / calculadora / nuevo
   Jaime decidió comprar una calculadora nueva.
7. Sandra / perder / control remoto
   Sandra perdió el control remoto.
8. David / poner / contestadora / y / acostarse
   David puso la contestadora y se acostó.
9. teléfono celular / sonar / pero / yo / no contestar
   El teléfono celular sonó pero yo no contesté.
10. Yo / sacar / fotos / cámara digital
    Yo saqué fotos con una cámara digital.

3 **Preguntas** Mira el dibujo de **Contextos** y contesta las preguntas.

Answers will vary.

1. ¿Qué tipo de café es?
2. ¿Cuántas impresoras hay? ¿Cuántos ratones?
3. ¿Por qué vinieron estas personas al café?
4. ¿Qué hace el camarero?
5. ¿Qué hace la mujer en la computadora? ¿Y el hombre?
6. ¿Qué máquinas están cerca del televisor?
7. ¿Dónde hay un cibercafé en tu ciudad?
8. ¿Por qué puedes tú necesitar un cibercafé?

Cibercafé CORRIENTES

el control remoto

el *walkman*

el disco compacto

1 **Suggestion** Have students check their answers by going over **Actividad 1** with the whole class.

1 **Tapescript** ANA: ¿María? ¿Qué haces aquí en el cibercafé? ¿No tienes Internet en casa?
MARÍA: Pues, sí, pero la computadora está descompuesta. Tengo que esperar unos días más.
A: Te entiendo. Me pasó lo mismo con la computadora portátil hace poco. Todavía no funciona bien . . . por eso vine aquí.
M: ¿Recibiste algún mensaje interesante?
A: Sí. Mi hijo está de vacaciones con unos amigos en Argentina. Tiene una cámara digital y me mandó unas fotos digitales.
M: ¡Qué bien! Me encantan las cámaras digitales. Normalmente imprimimos las fotos con nuestra impresora y no tenemos que ir a ninguna tienda. Es muy conveniente.
A: Claro que sí. También imprimo fotos, pero no voy a imprimirlas ahora. Prefiero guardarlas en un cederrón.
M: Buena idea. Ahí está mi café. Voy a navegar en Internet mientras tomo mi cafecito.
A: Bueno. Tengo que irme. Voy a pagar por el café y el uso de Internet. ¿No es muy caro, verdad?
M: Para nada, es muy barato. Hasta luego.
A: Chau. Nos vemos.
Textbook Activities CD

2 **Expansion** In pairs, students create three similar dehydrated sentences for their partners to complete. Write some on the board and have the class "hydrate" them.

3 **Expansion** Have small groups discuss how they would design and run their own cybercafés. Encourage them to be creative with as many details as possible. What would they name it? Where would it be located? What would customers find there? How much would the services cost?

TEACHING OPTIONS

Pairs Have pairs of students role-play one of these situations taking place in a cybercafé. 1. One student plays an irate customer who claims to have been overcharged for brief Internet use. The second plays the employee who insists on being paid the full amount, claiming that the customer spent quite a bit of time online. 2. One student plays a customer who has been waiting over an hour to use a computer and must ask another customer to log off and give him or her a chance. The second customer becomes annoyed at the request and the two must sort it all out.

Heritage Speakers Ask heritage speakers to describe their experiences with cybercafés in Spanish-speaking countries: where they were, how much the visits cost, what the cybercafés were like, etc. Ask other students to relate what was said.

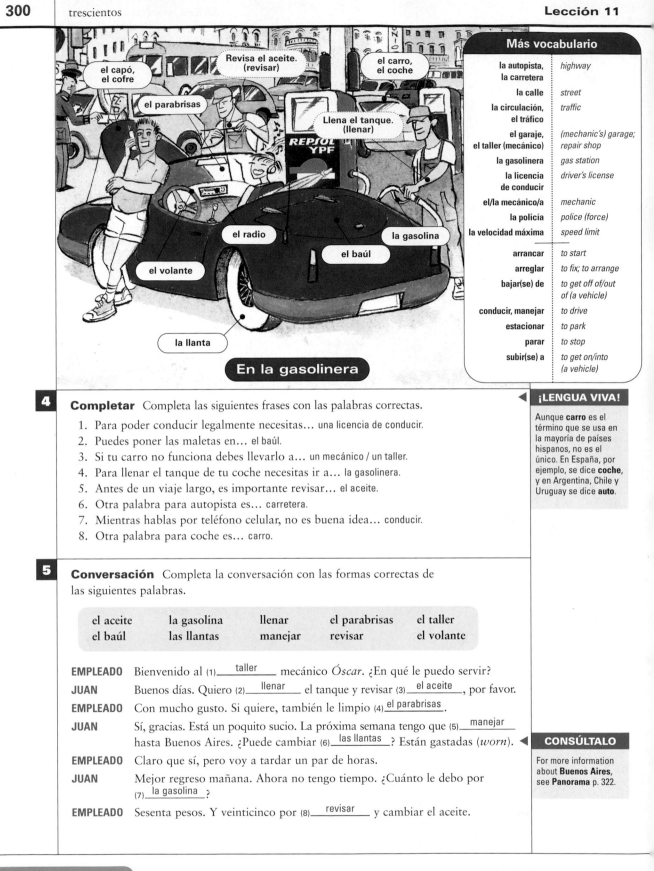

Más vocabulario

la autopista, la carretera	highway
la calle	street
la circulación, el tráfico	traffic
el garaje, el taller (mecánico)	(mechanic's) garage; repair shop
la gasolinera	gas station
la licencia de conducir	driver's license
el/la mecánico/a	mechanic
la policía	police (force)
la velocidad máxima	speed limit
arrancar	to start
arreglar	to fix; to arrange
bajar(se) de	to get off of/out of (a vehicle)
conducir, manejar	to drive
estacionar	to park
parar	to stop
subir(se) a	to get on/into (a vehicle)

En la gasolinera

4 Completar Completa las siguientes frases con las palabras correctas.

1. Para poder conducir legalmente necesitas… una licencia de conducir.
2. Puedes poner las maletas en… el baúl.
3. Si tu carro no funciona debes llevarlo a… un mecánico / un taller.
4. Para llenar el tanque de tu coche necesitas ir a… la gasolinera.
5. Antes de un viaje largo, es importante revisar… el aceite.
6. Otra palabra para autopista es… carretera.
7. Mientras hablas por teléfono celular, no es buena idea… conducir.
8. Otra palabra para coche es… carro.

5 Conversación Completa la conversación con las formas correctas de las siguientes palabras.

el aceite	la gasolina	llenar	el parabrisas	el taller
el baúl	las llantas	manejar	revisar	el volante

EMPLEADO Bienvenido al (1)___taller___ mecánico Óscar. ¿En qué le puedo servir?

JUAN Buenos días. Quiero (2)___llenar___ el tanque y revisar (3)___el aceite___, por favor.

EMPLEADO Con mucho gusto. Si quiere, también le limpio (4)___el parabrisas___.

JUAN Sí, gracias. Está un poquito sucio. La próxima semana tengo que (5)___manejar___ hasta Buenos Aires. ¿Puede cambiar (6)___las llantas___? Están gastadas (worn).

EMPLEADO Claro que sí, pero voy a tardar un par de horas.

JUAN Mejor regreso mañana. Ahora no tengo tiempo. ¿Cuánto le debo por (7)___la gasolina___?

EMPLEADO Sesenta pesos. Y veinticinco por (8)___revisar___ y cambiar el aceite.

Comunicación

6

Preguntas Trabajen en grupos para contestar las siguientes preguntas. Después compartan sus respuestas con la clase. Answers will vary.

1. a. ¿Tienes un teléfono celular? ¿Para qué lo usas?
   b. ¿Qué utilizas más: el teléfono o el correo electrónico? ¿Por qué?
   c. En tu opinión, ¿cuáles son las ventajas (*advantages*) y desventajas de los diferentes modos de comunicación?
2. a. ¿Con qué frecuencia usas la computadora?
   b. ¿Para qué usas Internet?
   c. ¿Tienes tu propio sitio web? ¿Cómo es?
3. a. ¿Miras la televisión con frecuencia? ¿Qué programas ves?
   b. ¿Tienes televisión por cable? ¿Por qué?
   c. ¿Tienes una videocasetera? ¿Un reproductor de DVD? ¿Un reproductor de DVD en la computadora?
   d. ¿A través de (*By*) qué medio escuchas música? ¿Radio, estéreo, tocadiscos compacto o computadora?
4. a. ¿Tienes licencia de conducir?
   b. ¿Cuánto tiempo hace que la conseguiste?
   c. ¿Tienes carro? Descríbelo.
   d. ¿Llevas tu carro al taller? ¿Para qué?

NOTA CULTURAL

Algunos sitios web utilizan códigos para identificar su país de origen. Éstos son los códigos para algunos países hispanohablantes.

Argentina   .ar
Colombia   .co
México   .mx
España   .es
Venezuela   .ve

CONSÚLTALO

To review expressions like **hace…que**, see **Lección 10, Expresiones útiles**, p. 273.

7

Postal En parejas, lean la tarjeta postal. Después contesten las preguntas.

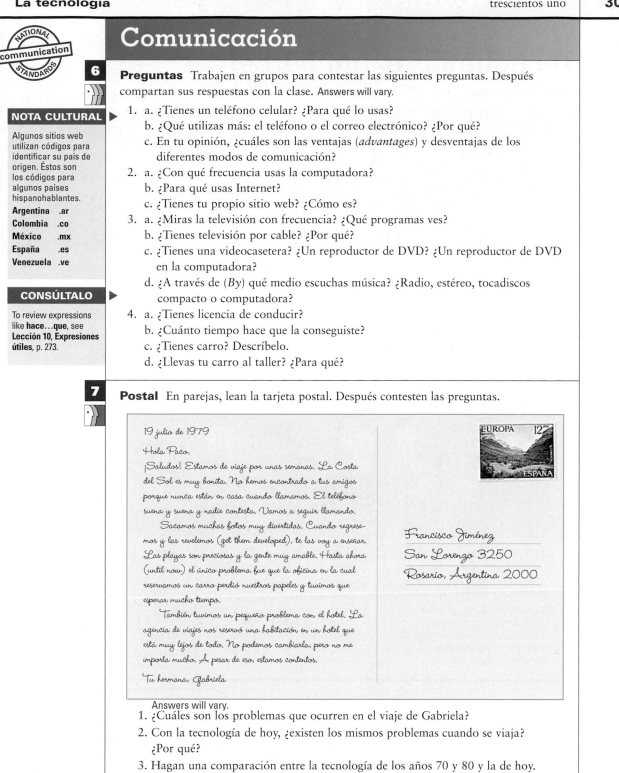

19 julio de 1979

Hola Paco,

¡Saludos! Estamos de viaje por unas semanas. La Costa del Sol es muy bonita. No hemos encontrado a tus amigos porque nunca están en casa cuando llamamos. El teléfono suena y suena y nadie contesta. Vamos a seguir llamando.

Sacamos muchas fotos muy divertidas. Cuando regresemos y las revelemos (*get them developed*), te las voy a enseñar. Las playas son preciosas y la gente muy amable. Hasta ahora (*until now*) el único problema fue que la oficina en la cual reservamos un carro perdió nuestros papeles y tuvimos que esperar mucho tiempo.

También tuvimos un pequeño problema con el hotel. La agencia de viajes nos reservó una habitación en un hotel que está muy lejos de todo. No podemos cambiarla, pero no me importa mucho. A pesar de eso, estamos contentos.

Tu hermana, Gabriela

Francisco Jiménez
San Lorenzo 3250
Rosario, Argentina 2000

EUROPA   12ᵖᵗᵃˢ
ESPAÑA

Answers will vary.
1. ¿Cuáles son los problemas que ocurren en el viaje de Gabriela?
2. Con la tecnología de hoy, ¿existen los mismos problemas cuando se viaja? ¿Por qué?
3. Hagan una comparación entre la tecnología de los años 70 y 80 y la de hoy.
4. Imaginen que la hija de Gabriela escribe un correo electrónico sobre el mismo tema con fecha de hoy. Escriban ese correo, incorporando la tecnología de hoy (teléfonos celulares, Internet, cámaras digitales, etc.). Inventen nuevos problemas.

---

6 Expansion Write names of electronic communication devices on the board (**teléfono celular, fax, computadora**, and so forth). Then survey the class to find out how many people own or use these items. Analyze the trends of the class.

7 Suggestion Possible answers: **1. Gabriela no encuentra a los amigos de Paco porque nunca están en casa, tuvo que esperar mucho por el carro y su hotel estaba muy lejos de todo. 2. No existen los mismos problemas porque existen las contestadoras y los teléfonos celulares, se puede reservar un carro en Internet y se puede buscar información sobre un hotel en la red antes del viaje.**

7 Expansion Ask groups to write a postcard similar to the one in the activity, except that in theirs the problems encountered during the trip are a direct result of the existence of technology, not its absence.

Note: At this point you may want to present **Vocabulario adicional: Más vocabulario para el carro y la tecnología**, from the IRM.

TEACHING OPTIONS

Extra Practice Have students do an Internet research project on technology and technology terminology in the Spanish-speaking world. Suggest possible topics and sites where students may look for information. Have students write out their reports and present them to the class.

Small/Large Groups Stage a debate about the role of technology in today's world. Propose this debate topic: **La tecnología: ¿beneficio o no?** Divide each group in half, assigning each side a position. Allow groups time to plan their arguments before staging the debate. You may also divide the class into two large groups to have the debate with the entire class.

Section Goals

In **Fotonovela** students will:
- receive comprehensible input from free-flowing discourse
- learn functional phrases that preview lesson grammatical structures

Instructional Resources
WB/VM: Video Activities, pp. 215–216
Fotonovela *DVD/Video (Start 00:58:05)*
Fotonovela *Video CD-ROM*
IRM: **Fotonovela** *Translations, pp. 124–125, Videoscript, pp. 98–99*
Interactive CD-ROM

Video Recap: Lección 10
Before doing this **Fotonovela** section, review the previous one with this activity.
1. ¿Qué le pasó a Javier en el autobús? (se lastimó el tobillo)
2. ¿Adónde llevó don Francisco a Javier? (a ver a su amiga, la doctora Márquez)
3. ¿Qué mostró la radiografía? (el tobillo de Javier estaba torcido)
4. ¿Qué le recetó la doctora a Javier? (unas pastillas para el dolor)

Video Synopsis On the way to Ibarra, the bus breaks down. Don Francisco cannot locate the problem, but Inés, an experienced mechanic, diagnoses it as a burned-out alternator. Álex uses his cell phone to call Don Francisco's friend, Sr. Fonseca, who is a mechanic. Maite and Don Francisco praise Inés and Álex for saving the day.

Suggestions
- Have your students predict the **Fotonovela** content based on the video stills only.
- Quickly review the predictions your students made. Ask them a few questions to guide them in summarizing this episode.

Tecnohombre, ¡mi héroe!

El autobús se daña.

PERSONAJES

MAITE

INÉS

DON FRANCISCO

ÁLEX

JAVIER

SR. FONSECA

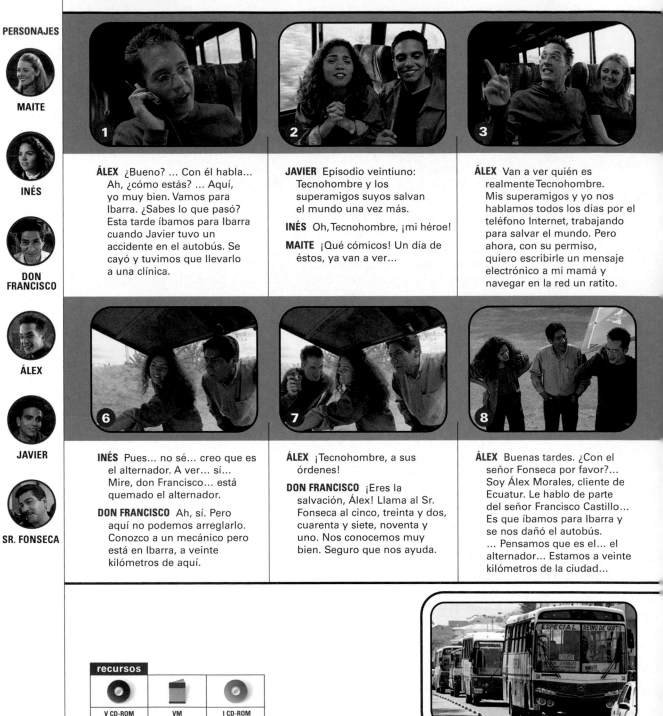

ÁLEX ¿Bueno? ... Con él habla... Ah, ¿cómo estás? ... Aquí, yo muy bien. Vamos para Ibarra. ¿Sabes lo que pasó? Esta tarde íbamos para Ibarra cuando Javier tuvo un accidente en el autobús. Se cayó y tuvimos que llevarlo a una clínica.

JAVIER Episodio veintiuno: Tecnohombre y los superamigos suyos salvan el mundo una vez más.

INÉS Oh, Tecnohombre, ¡mi héroe!

MAITE ¡Qué cómicos! Un día de éstos, ya van a ver...

ÁLEX Van a ver quién es realmente Tecnohombre. Mis superamigos y yo nos hablamos todos los días por el teléfono Internet, trabajando para salvar el mundo. Pero ahora, con su permiso, quiero escribirle un mensaje electrónico a mi mamá y navegar en la red un ratito.

INÉS Pues... no sé... creo que es el alternador. A ver... sí... Mire, don Francisco... está quemado el alternador.

DON FRANCISCO Ah, sí. Pero aquí no podemos arreglarlo. Conozco a un mecánico pero está en Ibarra, a veinte kilómetros de aquí.

ÁLEX ¡Tecnohombre, a sus órdenes!

DON FRANCISCO ¡Eres la salvación, Álex! Llama al Sr. Fonseca al cinco, treinta y dos, cuarenta y siete, noventa y uno. Nos conocemos muy bien. Seguro que nos ayuda.

ÁLEX Buenas tardes. ¿Con el señor Fonseca por favor?... Soy Álex Morales, cliente de Ecuatur. Le hablo de parte del señor Francisco Castillo... Es que íbamos para Ibarra y se nos dañó el autobús. ... Pensamos que es el... el alternador... Estamos a veinte kilómetros de la ciudad...

recursos

| V CD-ROM Lección 11 | VM pp. 215–216 | I CD-ROM Lección 11 |

TEACHING OPTIONS

Video Tips General suggestions for using video clips in the classroom can be found on page IAE-12 of this Instructor's Annotated Edition.
Tecnohombre, ¡mi héroe! Make a photocopy of the videoscript and white out ten words to create a master for a cloze activity. Hand out photocopies of the master to your students and have them fill in the missing words as they watch the **Tecnohombre, ¡mi héroe!** video module. You may want to show the segment twice or more if your students experience difficulties with this activity. You may also want your students to share their pages in small groups and help each other fill in any gaps.

Suggestion Have the class read through the entire **Fotonovela**, with volunteers playing the various roles. Have students take turns playing the roles so that more of them participate.

Expresiones útiles Draw the attention of the class to the phrase **nos hablamos** in the caption of video still 3. Explain that this is a reciprocal reflexive construction that expresses a shared action between Álex and his friends. Point out the words **llama al Sr. Fonseca** in video still 7 and explain that **llama** is a **tú** command. Point out the words **los míos** in the caption of video still 10 and tell the class that this is an example of a possessive pronoun. Tell your students that they will learn more about these concepts in **Estructura**.

DON FRANCISCO Chicos, creo que tenemos un problema con el autobús. ¿Por qué no se bajan?

DON FRANCISCO Mmm, no veo el problema.

INÉS Cuando estaba en la escuela secundaria, trabajé en el taller de mi tío. Me enseñó mucho sobre mecánica. Por suerte, arreglé unos autobuses como éste.

DON FRANCISCO ¡No me digas! Bueno, ¿qué piensas?

SR. FONSECA Creo que va a ser mejor arreglar el autobús allí mismo. Tranquilo, enseguida salgo.

ÁLEX Buenas noticias. El señor Fonseca viene enseguida. Piensa que puede arreglar el autobús aquí mismo.

MAITE ¡La Mujer Mecánica y Tecnohombre, mis héroes!

DON FRANCISCO ¡Y los míos también!

Enfoque cultural El transporte en la ciudad

En las ciudades hispanas suele haber (*there is usually*) más transporte público que en las estadounidenses y sus habitantes dependen menos de los carros. En los países hispanos también es más frecuente el uso de carros pequeños y de motocicletas que gastan poca gasolina. En las ciudades españolas, por ejemplo, la gasolina es muy cara y también hay poco espacio para el estacionamiento (*parking*); por eso es tan frecuente el uso de vehículos pequeños y económicos.

Expresiones útiles

Talking on the telephone
▶ **Aló./¿Bueno?/Diga.**
Hello.
▶ **¿Quién habla?**
Who is speaking?
▶ **¿De parte de quién?**
Who is calling?
▷ **Con él/ella habla.**
This is he/she.
▷ **Le hablo de parte de Francisco Castillo.**
I'm speaking to you on behalf of Francisco Castillo.
▶ **¿Puedo dejar un recado?**
May I leave a message?
▷ **Está bien. Llamo más tarde.**
That's fine. I'll call later.

Talking about bus or car problems
▶ **¿Qué pasó?**
What happened?
▷ **Se nos dañó el autobús.**
The bus broke down.
▷ **Se nos pinchó una llanta.**
We had a flat tire.
▷ **Está quemado el alternador.**
The alternator is burned out.

Saying how far away things are
▶ **Está a veinte kilómetros de aquí.**
It's twenty kilometers from here.
▶ **Estamos a veinte millas de la ciudad.**
We're twenty miles from the city.

Expressing surprise
▶ **¡No me digas!**
You don't say! (fam.)
▶ **¡No me diga!**
You don't say! (form.)

Offering assistance
▶ **A sus órdenes.**
At your service.

Additional vocabulary
▶ **aquí mismo**
right here

Enfoque cultural Like anywhere else, large cities in the Spanish-speaking world often experience traffic gridlock. To address this problem, these cities have emphasized public transportation. Mexico City, with a population estimated at over 20 million, has been singled out for particular praise because of its **metro** (*subway*) system. The Mexico City metro, which is efficient and well-maintained, costs very little to ride and provides transportation to approximately four million riders on its eleven lines each day. Though its 175 stations are notably attractive, two downtown stations are of more than transportation interest. The **Insurgentes** station is packed with market stalls of every type, and the **Pino Suárez** station, near the national palace, houses an Aztec pyramid, unearthed during the excavations when the metro was built.

Reacciona a la fotonovela

1 **Seleccionar** Selecciona las respuestas que completan correctamente las siguientes frases.

1. Álex quiere __b__.
   a. llamar a su mamá por teléfono celular b. escribirle a su mamá y navegar en la red
   c. hablar por teléfono Internet y navegar en la red
2. Se les dañó el autobús. Inés dice que __a__.
   a. el alternador está quemado b. se pinchó una llanta c. el taller está lejos
3. Álex llama al mecánico, el señor __c__.
   a. Castillo b. Ibarra c. Fonseca
4. Maite llama a Inés la "Mujer Mecánica" porque antes __a__.
   a. trabajaba en el taller de su tío b. arreglaba computadoras
   c. conocía a muchos mecánicos
5. El grupo está a __c__ de la ciudad.
   a. veinte millas b. veinte grados centígrados c. veinte kilómetros

2 **Identificar** Identifica quién puede decir las siguientes frases.

1. Gracias a mi tío tengo un poco de experiencia arreglando autobuses. Inés
2. Sé manejar un autobús pero no sé arreglarlo. ¿Por qué no llamamos a mi amigo? don Francisco
3. Sabes, admiro mucho a la Mujer Mecánica y a Tecnohombre. Maite
4. Aló... Sí, ¿de parte de quién? Álex
5. El nombre de Tecnohombre fue idea mía. ¡Qué cómico!, ¿no? Javier

JAVIER   ÁLEX   MAITE   INÉS   DON FRANCISCO

3 **Problema mecánico** Trabajen en parejas para representar los papeles (*roles*) de un(a) mecánico/a y un(a) cliente/a que está llamando al taller porque su carro está descompuesto. Usen las instrucciones como guía. Answers will vary.

Mecánico/a	Cliente/a
Contesta el teléfono con un saludo y el nombre del taller.	Saluda y explica que tu carro está descompuesto.
Pregunta qué tipo de problema tiene exactamente.	Explica que tu carro no arranca cuando hace frío.
Di que debe traer el carro al taller.	Pregunta cuándo puedes llevarlo.
Ofrece una hora para revisar el carro.	Acepta la hora que ofrece el/la mecánico/a.
Da las gracias y despídete.	Despídete y cuelga (*hang up*) el teléfono.

Ahora cambien los papeles y representen otra conversación. Ustedes son un(a) técnico/a y un(a) cliente/a. Usen estas ideas:

> el celular no guarda mensajes   la impresora imprime muy lentamente
> la computadora no descarga fotos   el reproductor de DVD está descompuesto

NATIONAL communication STANDARDS

Ortografía

La acentuación de palabras similares

Although accent marks usually indicate which syllable in a word is stressed, they are also used to distinguish between words that have the same or similar spellings.

Él maneja el coche.   **Sí, voy si quieres.**

Although one-syllable words do not usually carry written accents, some *do* have accent marks to distinguish them from words that have the same spelling but different meanings.

Sé cocinar.   **Se baña.**   **¿Tomas té?**   **Te duermes.**

Sé (*I know*) and **té** (*tea*) have accent marks to distinguish them from the pronouns **se** and **te**.

---

para mí   **mi cámara**   **Tú lees.**    **tu estéreo**

Mí (*Me*) and **tú** (*you*) have accent marks to distinguish them from the possessive adjectives **mi** and **tu**.

¿Por qué vas?   **Voy porque quiero.**

Several words of more than one syllable also have accent marks to distinguish them from words that have the same or similar spellings.

Éste es rápido.   **Este módem es rápido.**

Demonstrative pronouns have accent marks to distinguish them from demonstrative adjectives.

¿Cuándo fuiste?   **Fui cuando me llamó.**

¿Dónde trabajas?   **Voy al taller donde trabajo.**

Adverbs have accent marks when they are used to convey a question.

Práctica Marca los acentos en las palabras que los necesitan.

ANA Alo, soy Ana. ¿Que tal? *Aló/¿Qué?*

JUAN Hola, pero... ¿por que me llamas tan tarde? *¿por qué?*

ANA Porque mañana tienes que llevarme a la universidad. Mi auto esta dañado. *está*

JUAN ¿Como se daño? *¿Cómo?/dañó*

ANA Se daño el sabado. Un vecino (*neighbor*) choco con (*crashed into*) el. *dañó/sábado/chocó/él*

Crucigrama Utiliza las siguientes pistas (*clues*) para completar el crucigrama. ¡Ojo con los acentos!

Horizontales

1. Él _____ levanta.
4. No voy _____ no puedo.
7. Tú _____ acuestas.
9. ¿ _____ es el examen?
10. Quiero este video y _____.

Verticales

2. ¿Cómo _____ usted?
3. Eres _____ mi hermano.
5. ¿_____ tal?
6. Me gusta _____ suéter.
8. Navego _____ la red.

		¹S	²E			³C			
			S		⁴P	O	R	⁵Q	U	⁶E
				⁷T	⁸E		M	U		S
	⁹C	U	Á	N	D	O		¹⁰É	S	E

recursos

| LM p. 62 | Lab CD/MP3 Lección 11 | I CD-ROM Lección 11 |

Section Goal

In **Ortografía** students will learn about the use of accent marks to distinguish between words that have the same or similar spellings.

Instructional Resource
Interactive CD-ROM

Suggestions

- As you go through each point in the explanation, pronounce the example sentences, as well as some of your own, and have students write them on the board.
- Write the example sentences, as well as some of your own, on the board without accent marks. Ask students where the written accents should go.
- Emphasize the difference in stress between **por qué** and **porque**.
- Ask students to provide words they learned in previous lessons that exemplify each point.
- Point out that **Ortografía** replaces **Pronunciación** in the Student Edition for **Lecciones 10–15**, but not in the Lab Manual. The **Recursos** box references the **Pronunciación** sections found in all lessons of the Lab Manual.

TEACHING OPTIONS

Small Groups Have your students work in groups to explain which words in the **Práctica** activity need written accents and why. If necessary, have your students quickly review the information about accents in the **Ortografía** section of **Lección 10**, page 275.

Extra Practice Write these examples on the board or on a transparency without accent marks. **1. Esta es mi camara. Papa la trajo del Japon para mi. 2. ¿Donde encontraste mi mochila? ¡Pues, donde la dejaste, claro! 3. ¿Cuando visito Buenos Aires Mario? Se que Lourdes fue alli el año pasado, pero ¿cuando fue el? 4. ¿Me explicas por que llegas tarde? Porque mi coche esta descompuesto.**

11.1 Familiar commands

ANTE TODO In Spanish, the command forms are used to give orders or advice. You use **tú** commands when you want to give an order or advice to someone you normally address with the familiar **tú**.

Affirmative *tú* commands

Infinitive	Present tense *él/ella* form	Affirmative *tú* command
hablar	habla	**habla** (tú)
guardar	guarda	**guarda** (tú)
prender	prende	**prende** (tú)
volver	vuelve	**vuelve** (tú)
pedir	pide	**pide** (tú)
imprimir	imprime	**imprime** (tú)

▶ Affirmative **tú** commands usually have the same form as the **él/ella** form of the present indicative.

Guarda el documento antes de cerrarlo.
Save the document before closing it.

Imprime tu tarea para la clase de inglés.
Print your homework for English class.

▶ There are eight irregular affirmative **tú** commands.

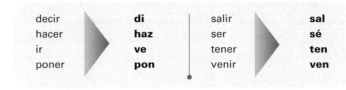

decir	**di**	salir	**sal**
hacer	**haz**	ser	**sé**
ir	**ve**	tener	**ten**
poner	**pon**	venir	**ven**

¡Sal de aquí ahora mismo!
Leave here at once!

Haz los ejercicios.
Do the exercises.

▶ Since **ir** and **ver** have the same **tú** command (**ve**), context will determine the meaning.

Ve al cibercafé con Yolanda.
Go to the cybercafé with Yolanda.

Ve ese programa... es muy interesante.
See that program... it's very interesting.

Apaga ese walkman y contesta el teléfono.

¡No me digas!

¡LENGUA VIVA!

To form affirmative **vosotros** commands, drop the –r from the infinitive and add –d:

parar → **parad**
poner → **poned**
salir → **salid**

Negative **vosotros** commands have the same form as the **vosotros** forms of the present subjunctive, which is introduced in **Estructura 12.3**:

no paréis
no pongáis
no salgáis

Section Goals

In **Estructura 11.1** students will learn:
• negative **tú** commands
• affirmative **tú** commands

Instructional Resources
WB/VM: Workbook, pp. 127–128
Lab Manual, p. 63
*Lab CD/MP3 **Lección 11***
IRM: ¡Inténtalo! & Práctica
Answers, pp. 189–190;
Tapescript, pp. 49–53
Info Gap Activities Booklet, pp. 41–42
Interactive CD-ROM
Companion website: www.vistahigherlearning.com
Presentations CD-ROM

Suggestions
• Model the use of informal commands with simple examples using TPR and gestures. Ex: Point to a student and say: _____ , **levántate. Gracias, ahora siéntate.** Give other commands using **camina, vuelve, toca,** and **corre.**
• Help students recognize that the affirmative **tú** command forms of regular verbs are the same as the third-person singular forms.
• Make clear to students that **tú** commands are spoken to people one addresses as **tú**.

TEACHING OPTIONS

TPR Ask individual students to comply with a series of commands requiring them to perform actions or move around the room. While the student follows the command, the class writes it down as a volunteer writes it on the board. Be sure to use both affirmative and negative commands. Ex: **Recoge ese papel. Ponlo en la basura. Regresa a tu escritorio. No te sientes. Siéntate ahora.**

Pairs Ask students to imagine they are starting a computer club. Have them make a list of five things to do in order to get ready for the first meeting and five things not to do to make sure everything runs smoothly, using infinitives. Then have students take turns telling their partners what to do or not do.

Suggestions
- Contrast the negative forms of **tú** commands by giving an affirmative command followed by a negative command. Ex: **Camina a la puerta. No camines rápidamente.** Write the examples on the board as you go along.
- Test comprehension and practice negative **tú** commands by calling out the infinitives of a variety of regular verbs the students already know and asking individual students to convert them into negative commands. Ex: **toser: no tosas; pedir: no pidas; pensar: no pienses.**
- Ask volunteers to convert affirmative **tú** commands with reflexive and object pronouns into negative forms. Ex: **Imprímelo. (No lo imprimas.) Vete. (No te vayas.)**

Negative *tú* commands

Infinitive	Present tense *yo* form	Negative *tú* command
hablar	hablo	**no hables** (tú)
guardar	guardo	**no guardes** (tú)
prender	prendo	**no prendas** (tú)
volver	vuelvo	**no vuelvas** (tú)
pedir	pido	**no pidas** (tú)

▶ The negative **tú** commands are formed by dropping the final –**o** of the **yo** form of the present tense. For –**ar** verbs, add –**es**. For –**er** and –**ir** verbs, add –**as**.

Héctor, **no pares** el carro en el medio de la calle.
Héctor, don't stop the car in the middle of the street.

No prendas la computadora todavía.
Don't turn on the computer yet.

No pierdas tu licencia de conducir.
Don't lose your driver's license.

No repitas las instrucciones.
Don't repeat the instructions.

▶ Verbs with irregular **yo** forms maintain the same irregularity in their negative **tú** commands. These verbs include **conducir, conocer, decir, hacer, ofrecer, oír, poner, salir, tener, traducir, traer, venir,** and **ver**.

No pongas aquel cederrón en la computadora portátil.
Don't put that CD-ROM in the laptop.

No conduzcas tan rápido.
Don't drive so fast.

▶ Verbs ending in –**car**, –**gar**, and –**zar** have a spelling change in the negative **tú** commands.

sa**car**	c → **qu**	no sa**qu**es
apa**gar**	g → **gu**	no apa**gu**es
almor**zar**	z → **c**	no almuer**c**es

▶ The following verbs have irregular negative **tú** commands.

Infinitive	Negative *tú* command
dar	**no des**
estar	**no estés**
ir	**no vayas**
saber	**no sepas**
ser	**no seas**

¡ATENCIÓN!

In affirmative commands, reflexive, indirect, and direct object pronouns are always attached to the end of the verb. In negative commands, these pronouns always precede the verb.

Bórralos. /No los borres.

Escríbeles un correo electrónico./**No les escribas** un correo electrónico.

• • •

When a pronoun is attached to an affirmative command that has two or more syllables, an accent mark is added to maintain the original stress:

borra → **bórralos**
prende → **préndela**
imprime → **imprímelo**

¡LENGUA VIVA!

Reflexive **vosotros** commands drop the –**d** and attach **os**:

sentaos
levantaos

The negative forms follow the normal pattern:

no os sentéis
no os levantéis

¡INTÉNTALO! Indica los mandatos (*commands*) familiares afirmativos y negativos de estos verbos.

1. correr — _Corre_ más rápido. — No _corras_ más rápido.
2. llenar — _Llena_ el tanque. — No _llenes_ el tanque.
3. salir — _Sal_ ahora. — No _salgas_ ahora.
4. descargar — _Descarga_ ese documento. — No _descargues_ ese documento.
5. venir — _Ven_ aquí. — No _vengas_ aquí.
6. levantarse — _Levántate_ temprano. — No _te levantes_ temprano.
7. volver — _Vuelve_ pronto. — No _vuelvas_ pronto.
8. hacerlo — _Hazlo_ ya. — No _lo hagas_ ahora.

TEACHING OPTIONS

Heritage Speakers Ask heritage speakers to look for an advertisement in Spanish-language magazines or newspapers in which they find informal commands used. Have students bring copies of the ads to class. Ask them to share them with the class and explain why they think informal commands were used instead of formal ones.

Extra Practice Have pairs imagine that they are in charge of a computer lab at a university in a Spanish-speaking country. Have them make a handout of four things students must do and four things they must not do while in the lab. Instruct them to use **tú** commands throughout. Then, write **Mandatos afirmativos** and **Mandatos negativos** on the board and ask individuals to write one of their commands in the appropriate column.

Práctica

1 Completar Tu mejor amigo no entiende nada de tecnología y te pide ayuda. Completa los comentarios de tu amigo con el mandato de cada verbo.

1. No ___vengas___ en una hora. ___Ven___ ahora mismo. (venir)
2. ___Haz___ tu tarea después. No la ___hagas___ ahora. (hacer)
3. No ___vayas___ a la tienda a comprar papel para la impresora. ___Ve___ a la cafetería a comprarme algo de comer. (ir)
4. No ___me digas___ que no sabes abrir un archivo. ___Dime___ que el programa de computación funciona sin problemas. (decirme)
5. ___Sé___ generoso con tu tiempo, y no ___seas___ antipático si no entiendo fácilmente. (ser)
6. ___Ten___ mucha paciencia y no ___tengas___ prisa. (tener)
7. ___Apaga___ tu teléfono celular, pero no ___apagues___ la computadora. (apagar)

2 Cambiar Pedro y Marina no pueden ponerse de acuerdo (*agree*) cuando viajan en su carro. Cuando Pedro dice que algo es necesario, Marina expresa una opinión diferente. Usa la información entre paréntesis para formar las órdenes que Marina le da a Pedro.

> **modelo**
> **Pedro:** Necesito revisar el aceite del carro. (seguir hasta el próximo pueblo)
> **Marina:** No revises el aceite del carro. Sigue hasta el próximo pueblo.

1. Necesito conducir más rápido. (parar el carro) No conduzcas más rápido. Para el carro.
2. Necesito poner el radio. (hablarme) No pongas el radio. Háblame.
3. Necesito almorzar ahora. (comer más tarde) No almuerces ahora. Come más tarde.
4. Necesito sacar los discos compactos. (manejar con cuidado) No saques... Maneja...
5. Necesito estacionar el carro en esta calle. (pensar en otra opción) No estaciones... Piensa...
6. Necesito volver a esa gasolinera. (arreglar el carro en un taller) No vuelvas... Arregla...
7. Necesito leer el mapa. (pedirle ayuda a aquella señora) No leas... Pídele...
8. Necesito dormir en el carro. (acostarse en una cama) No duermas... Acuéstate...

3 Problemas Tú y tu compañero/a trabajan en el centro de computadoras de la universidad. Muchos estudiantes están llamando con problemas. Denles órdenes para ayudarlos a resolverlos. Answers will vary; suggested answers below.

> **modelo**
> **Problema:** No veo nada en la pantalla.
> **Tu respuesta:** Prende la pantalla de tu computadora.

apagar...	descargar...	grabar...	imprimir...	prender...
borrar...	funcionar...	guardar...	navegar...	quemar...

1. No me gusta este programa de computación. Descarga otro.
2. Tengo miedo de perder mi documento. Guárdalo.
3. Prefiero leer este sitio web en papel. Imprímelo.
4. Mi correo electrónico funciona muy lentamente. Borra los mensajes más viejos.
5. Busco información sobre los gauchos de Argentina. Navega en Internet.
6. Tengo demasiados archivos en mi computadora. Borra algunos archivos.
7. Mi computadora se congeló (*froze*). Apaga la computadora y luego préndela.
8. Quiero ver las fotos del cumpleaños de mi hermana. Descárgalas.

Comunicación

4 **Órdenes** Circula por la clase e intercambia órdenes negativas y afirmativas con tus compañeros/as. Debes seguir las órdenes que ellos te dan o reaccionar apropiadamente. Answers will vary.

> **modelo**
>
> **Estudiante 1:** Dame todo tu dinero.
> **Estudiante 2:** No, no quiero dártelo. Muéstrame tu cuaderno.
> **Estudiante 1:** Aquí está.
> **Estudiante 3:** Ve a la pizarra y escribe tu nombre.
> **Estudiante 4:** No quiero. Hazlo tú.

5 **Anuncios** Miren este anuncio (*ad*). Luego, en grupos pequeños, preparen tres anuncios adicionales para tres escuelas que compiten (*compete*) con ésta. Answers will vary.

INFORMÁTICA ARGENTINA

Toma nuestros cursos y aprende
a usar la computadora

abre y lee tus archivos

imprime tus documentos

entra al campo de la tecnología

¡Ponte en contacto con nosotros llamando al **11-4-129-1508** HOY!

Síntesis

6 **¡Tanto que hacer!** Tu profesor(a) te va a dar una lista de diligencias (*errands*). Algunas las hiciste tú y algunas las hizo tu compañero/a. Las diligencias que ya hicieron tienen esta marca ✔. Pero quedan cuatro diligencias por hacer. Dale mandatos a tu compañero/a, y él/ella responde para confirmar si hay que hacerla o ya la hizo. Answers will vary.

> **modelo**
>
> **Estudiante 1:** Llena el tanque.
> **Estudiante 2:** Ya llené el tanque. / ¡Oh, no! Tenemos que
> llenar el tanque.

TEACHING OPTIONS

Pairs Have pairs prepare a conversation between two roommates, both of whom are hurrying to get ready for a party. Students should use affirmative and negative **tú** commands to tell each other what they have to do to arrive at the party on time. Ex: **E1: ¡Sal del baño ya! E2: ¡No me grites! E1: Pero tengo que maquillarme. E2: Maquíllate más tarde. Yo necesito ducharme.**

Extra Practice Review the verbs in **Contextos** and informal commands by stating a verb, then calling on a volunteer to make an affirmative command using that verb. Call on a second volunteer to counter with a negative command.

11.2 Por and para

ANTE TODO Unlike English, Spanish has two words that mean *for*: **por** and **para**. These two prepositions are not interchangeable. Study the charts to see how they are used.

Es para usted. Es un cliente de don Paco.

Álex habla por teléfono.

Por is used to indicate...

1. Motion or a general location . . . .
(around, through, along, by)

La excursión nos llevó **por** el centro.
The tour took us through downtown.

Pasamos **por** el parque y **por** el río.
We passed by the park and along the river.

2. Duration of an action . . . .
(for, during, in)

Estuve en la Patagonia **por** un mes.
I was in Patagonia for a month.

Ana navegó la red **por** la tarde.
Ana surfed the net in the afternoon.

3. Reason or motive for an action . . . .
(because of, on account of, on behalf of)

Lo hizo **por** su familia.
She did it on behalf of her family.

Papá llegó a casa tarde **por** el tráfico.
Dad arrived home late because of the traffic.

4. Object of a search . . . .
(for, in search of)

Vengo **por** ti a las ocho.
I'm coming for you at eight.

Javier fue **por** su cámara digital.
Javier went in search of his digital camera.

5. Means by which something is done . . . .
(by, by way of, by means of)

Ellos viajan **por** la autopista.
They travel by (by way of) the highway.

¿Hablaste con la policía **por** teléfono?
Did you talk to the police by (on the) phone?

6. Exchange or substitution . . . .
(for, in exchange for)

Le di dinero **por** la videocasetera.
I gave him money for the VCR.

Muchas gracias **por** el cederrón.
Thank you very much for the CD-ROM.

7. Unit of measure . . . .
(per, by)

José manejaba a 120 kilómetros **por** hora.
José was driving 120 kilometers per hour.

¡ATENCIÓN!

Por is also used in several idiomatic expressions, including:
por aquí *around here*
por ejemplo *for example*
por eso *that's why; therefore*
por fin *finally*

¡ATENCIÓN!

Remember that when giving an exact time, **de** is used instead of **por** before **la mañana**, **la tarde**, etc.

La clase empieza a las nueve **de** la mañana.

• • •

In addition to **por**, **durante** is also commonly used to mean *for* when referring to time.

Esperé al mecánico **durante** cincuenta minutos.

TEACHING OPTIONS

TPR Call out a sentence, omitting either **por** or **para**. If students think **por** should be used in the sentence, they raise one hand. If they think **para** should be used, they raise two hands. Avoid cases where either **por** or **para** could be used. Ex: **Tengo que leer el capítulo 11 _____ mañana.** (two hands) **Jimena trabaja _____ la noche.** (one hand) **Estaba en Buenos Aires _____ el mes de marzo.** (one hand)

Game Divide the class into four or five teams, giving each team a large piece of paper. Call out a use of either **por** or **para**. Teams have one minute to write as many sentences as they can, employing that use. Check answers by having a volunteer read his or her team's sentences. Give a point for each correct sentence. Keep score on the board. The team with the most correct sentences wins.

Suggestions
- Create a matching activity for the uses of **para**. Write sentences exemplifying each use of **para** listed, but not in the order they are given in the text. Ex: **1. El señor López compró el Ferrari para Mariana. 2. Este autobús va para Corrientes. 3. Para don Francisco, conducir un autobús no es nada difícil. 4. Don Francisco trabaja para Ecuatur. 5. Estudia para llegar a ser ingeniero. 6. El baúl es para las maletas. 7. Tengo que pagar la multa para el lunes.** Call on individual students to match each sentence with its usage.
- Have students make two flashcards. On one they write **por** and on the other **para**. Call out one of the uses for either word. Students show the appropriate card. Then call on a volunteer to write a sentence illustrating that use on the board. The class determines whether the sentence is correct or not.
- Use magazine pictures to practice example sentences demonstrating the uses of **por** and **para**. Ex: **Este señor hace la cena para su esposa. Los novios montan a caballo por el campo.**

Para is used to indicate...

1. **Destination** . . . .
   (*toward, in the direction of*)

   Salimos **para** Córdoba el sábado.
   We are leaving for Córdoba on Saturday.

2. **Deadline or a specific time in the future** . .
   (*by, for*)

   Él va a arreglar el carro **para** el viernes.
   He will fix the car by Friday.

3. **Purpose or goal** + [*infinitive*] . . . .
   (*in order to*)

   Juan estudia **para** (ser) mecánico.
   Juan is studying to be a mechanic.

4. **Purpose** + [*noun*] . . . .
   (*for, used for*)

   Es una llanta **para** el carro.
   It's a tire for the car.

5. **The recipient of something** . . . .
   (*for*)

   Compré una impresora **para** mi hijo.
   I bought a printer for my son.

6. **Comparison with others or an opinion** . .
   (*for, considering*)

   Para un joven, es demasiado serio.
   For a young person, he is too serious.

   Para mí, esta lección no es difícil.
   For me, this lesson isn't difficult.

7. **In the employ of** . . . .
   (*for*)

   Sara trabaja **para** Telecom Argentina.
   Sara works for Telecom Argentina.

▶ In many cases it is grammatically correct to use either **por** or **para** in a sentence. The meaning of the sentence is different, however, depending on which preposition is used.

Caminé **por** el parque.
I walked through the park.

Caminé **para** el parque.
I walked to (toward) the park.

Trabajó **por** su padre.
He worked for (in place of) his father.

Trabajó **para** su padre.
He worked for his father('s company).

¡INTÉNTALO!   Completa estas frases con las preposiciones **por** o **para**.

1. Fuimos al cibercafé __por__ la tarde.
2. Necesitas un módem __para__ navegar en la red.
3. Entraron __por__ la puerta.
4. Quiero un pasaje __para__ Buenos Aires.
5. __Para__ arrancar el carro, necesito la llave.
6. Arreglé el televisor __para__ mi amigo.
7. Estuvieron nerviosos __por__ el examen.
8. ¿No hay una gasolinera __por__ aquí?
9. Esta computadora es __para__ usted.
10. Juan está enfermo. Tengo que trabajar __por__ él.
11. Estuvimos en Cancún __por__ dos meses.
12. __Para__ mí, el español es difícil.
13. Tengo que estudiar la lección __para__ el lunes.
14. Voy a ir __por__ la carretera.
15. Compré dulces __para__ mi novia.
16. Compramos el auto __por__ un buen precio.

TEACHING OPTIONS

Extra Practice Give each student in the class a strip of paper on which you have written one of the uses of **por** or **para**, or a sentence that is an example of one of the uses. Have students circulate around the room until they find the person who has the match for their use or sentence. After everyone has found a partner, the pairs read their sentences and uses to the class.

Pairs/Game Have students create cards for a memory game. There should be one card for each use of **por** and **para**, and one card with a sentence illustrating each use, for a total of 28 cards. When finished, students lay all the cards face down. Then, taking turns, students uncover two cards at a time, trying to match a use to a sentence. The student with the most matches wins.

1 Expansion Have students list the uses of **por** and **para** in the paragraph. Then ask them to work in pairs to add sentences to the paragraph, employing the remaining uses of **por** and **para**. (Remaining uses of **por**: reason or motive, object of search, means, unit of measure; remaining uses of **para**: destination, deadline, purpose + [*noun*], comparison, employment.)

2 Suggestions
• Model the activity by creating a sentence with an element from each column. Ask a volunteer to explain your choice of **por** or **para**. Possible sentences: **Fuimos al mercado para comprar frutas por la mañana. Fueron a Buenos Aires por tres días para divertirse.**
• Divide the class into groups of three. Groups should write as many sentences as they can by combining elements from each column in a given amount of time. The group with the most correct sentences wins.

3 Expansion Have students take turns with a partner to expand their descriptions to a short oral narrative. After each drawing has been described, ask students to pick two or three of their narratives and link them into a story.

Práctica

1 Completar Completa este párrafo con las preposiciones **por** o **para**.

El mes pasado mi esposo y yo hicimos un viaje a Buenos Aires y sólo pagamos dos mil dólares (1)_por_ los pasajes. Estuvimos en Buenos Aires (2)_por_ una semana y recorrimos toda la ciudad. Durante el día caminamos (3)_por_ la plaza San Martín, el microcentro y el barrio de La Boca, donde viven muchos artistas. (4)_Por_ la noche fuimos a una tanguería, que es una especie de teatro (5)_para_ mirar a la gente bailar tango. Dos días después decidimos hacer una excursión (6)_por_ las pampas (7)_para_ ver el paisaje y un rodeo con gauchos. Alquilamos (*we rented*) un carro y manejamos (8)_por_ todas partes y pasamos unos días muy agradables. El último (*last*) día que estuvimos en Buenos Aires fuimos a Galerías Pacífico (9)_para_ comprar recuerdos (*souvenirs*) (10)_para_ nuestros hijos y nietos. Compramos tantos regalos que tuvimos que pagar impuestos (*duties*) cuando pasamos (11)_por_ la aduana al regresar.

2 Oraciones Crea frases originales con los elementos de las columnas. Une los elementos usando **por** o **para**. Answers will vary.

> **modelo**
> Fuimos a Mar del Plata por razones de salud para visitar a un especialista.

(No) fuimos al mercado	por/para	comprar frutas	por/para	¿?
(No) fuimos a las montañas	por/para	tres días	por/para	¿?
(No) fuiste a Mar del Plata	por/para	razones de salud	por/para	¿?
(No) fueron a Buenos Aires	por/para	tomar el sol	por/para	¿?

NOTA CULTURAL

Mar del Plata es un centro turístico en la costa de Argentina. La ciudad es conocida como "la perla del Atlántico" y todos los años muchos turistas visitan sus playas y casinos.

3 Describir Usa **por** o **para** y el tiempo presente para describir estos dibujos.

Answers will vary.

1. _____   2. _____   3. _____

4. _____   5. _____   6. _____

TEACHING OPTIONS

Large Group Have students create ten questions for a survey about the use of modern technology. Questions should include as many uses of **por** and **para** as possible. When finished, have students administer their survey to five different people in the room, then compile their results. Ex: **¿Por cuántos minutos al día hablas por teléfono celular?**

Extra Practice Ask students to imagine they are explaining to a younger sibling how to maintain the family car and why certain types of maintenance are necessary. Students should employ as many different uses of **por** and **para** in their explanations as possible.

Comunicación

4 **Descripciones** Usa **por** o **para** y completa estas frases de una manera (*manner*) lógica. Luego, compara tus respuestas con las de un(a) compañero/a. Answers will vary.

1. En casa, hablo con mis amigos…
2. Mi padre/madre trabaja…
3. Ayer fui al taller…
4. Los miércoles tengo clases…
5. A veces voy a la biblioteca…
6. Esta noche tengo que estudiar…
7. Necesito… dólares…
8. Compré un regalo…
9. Mi mejor amigo/a estudia…
10. Necesito hacer la tarea…

5 **Situación** En parejas, dramaticen esta situación. Utilicen muchos ejemplos de **por** y **para**. Answers will vary.

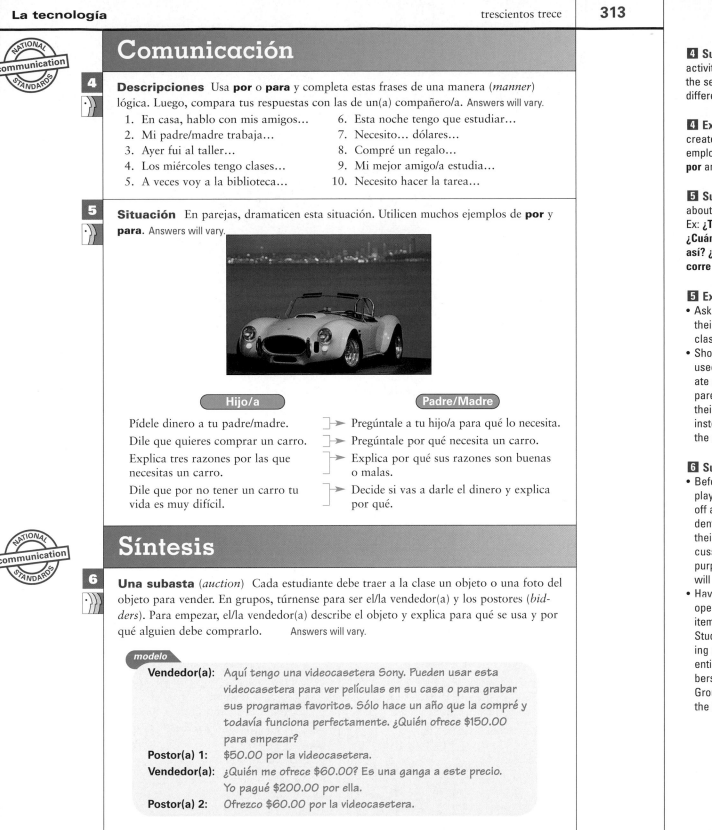

Hijo/a

Pídele dinero a tu padre/madre.

Dile que quieres comprar un carro.

Explica tres razones por las que necesitas un carro.

Dile que por no tener un carro tu vida es muy difícil.

Padre/Madre

→ Pregúntale a tu hijo/a para qué lo necesita.

→ Pregúntale por qué necesita un carro.

→ Explica por qué sus razones son buenas o malas.

→ Decide si vas a darle el dinero y explica por qué.

Síntesis

6 **Una subasta** (*auction*) Cada estudiante debe traer a la clase un objeto o una foto del objeto para vender. En grupos, túrnense para ser el/la vendedor(a) y los postores (*bidders*). Para empezar, el/la vendedor(a) describe el objeto y explica para qué se usa y por qué alguien debe comprarlo. Answers will vary.

> **modelo**
>
> **Vendedor(a):** Aquí tengo una videocasetera Sony. Pueden usar esta videocasetera para ver películas en su casa o para grabar sus programas favoritos. Sólo hace un año que la compré y todavía funciona perfectamente. ¿Quién ofrece $150.00 para empezar?
>
> **Postor(a) 1:** $50.00 por la videocasetera.
>
> **Vendedor(a):** ¿Quién me ofrece $60.00? Es una ganga a este precio. Yo pagué $200.00 por ella.
>
> **Postor(a) 2:** Ofrezco $60.00 por la videocasetera.

---

4 **Suggestion** Model the activity by completing one of the sentence starters in two different ways.

4 **Expansion** Have students create new sentences, employing additional uses of **por** and **para**.

5 **Suggestion** Ask students about the car in the picture. Ex: **¿Te gusta este carro? ¿Cuánto se paga por un carro así? ¿A cuántas millas por hora corre este carro?**

5 **Expansion**
- Ask volunteers to role-play their conversations for the class.
- Showing a picture of an old used car, ask students to create new conversations. The parents are offering to buy their son/daughter this car instead of the one shown in the activity.

6 **Suggestions**
- Before the bidding begins, display the items to be auctioned off and name them. Invite students to walk around with their group members and discuss what the items are, their purposes, and how much they will pay for them.
- Have groups prepare the opening statements for the items their members brought. Students then take turns opening up the bidding for the entire class. Non-group members may bid on each item. Group members bid to keep the bidding alive.

Small Groups Have students create a television advertisement for a car or piece of technological equipment. Students should: describe the item, why the customer should buy it, and how much it costs, explain that the item is on sale only until a certain date, and detail any possible trade-ins. Students should use **por** and **para** when possible in their ad.

Extra Practice For students still having trouble distinguishing between **por** and **para**, have them create a mnemonic device, like a story or chant, for remembering the different uses. Ex: **Vine por la tarde y busqué por el parque, por el río y por el centro. Busqué por horas. Viajé por carro, por tren y por avión.** Do the same for **para**.

11.3 Reciprocal reflexives

ANTE TODO In **Lección 7**, you learned that reflexive verbs indicate that the subject of a sentence does the action to itself. Reciprocal reflexives, on the other hand, express a shared or reciprocal action between two or more people or things. In this context, the pronoun means *(to) each other* or *(to) one another*.

Luis y Marta **se** miran en el espejo.
Luis and Marta look at themselves in the mirror.

Luis y Marta **se** miran.
Luis and Marta look at each other.

▶ Only the plural forms of the reflexive pronouns (**nos, os, se**) are used to express reciprocal actions because the action must involve more than one person or thing.

Cuando **nos vimos** en la calle, **nos abrazamos**.
When we saw each other on the street, we hugged one another.

Ustedes **se** van a **encontrar** en el cibercafé, ¿no?
You are meeting each other at the cybercafé, right?

Nos ayudamos cuando usamos la computadora.
We help each other when we use the computer.

Las amigas **se saludaron** y **se besaron**.
The friends greeted each other and kissed one another.

¡ATENCIÓN!

Here is a list of common verbs that can express reciprocal actions:
abrazar(se) *to hug; to embrace (each other)*
ayudar(se) *to help (each other)*
besar(se) *to kiss (each other)*
encontrar(se) *to meet (each other); run into (each other)*
saludar(se) *to greet (each other)*

¡INTÉNTALO! Indica el reflexivo recíproco adecuado y el presente o el pretérito de estos verbos.

El presente

1. (escribir) Los novios <u>se escriben</u> .
   Nosotros <u>nos escribimos</u> .
   Ana y Ernesto <u>se escriben</u> .
2. (escuchar) Mis tíos <u>se escuchan</u> .
   Nosotros <u>nos escuchamos</u> .
   Ellos <u>se escuchan</u> .
3. (ver) Nosotros <u>nos vemos</u> .
   Fernando y Tomás <u>se ven</u> .
   Ustedes <u>se ven</u> .
4. (llamar) Ellas <u>se llaman</u> .
   Mis hermanos <u>se llaman</u> .
   Pepa y yo <u>nos llamamos</u> .

El pretérito

1. (saludar) Nicolás y tú <u>se saludaron</u> .
   Nuestros vecinos <u>se saludaron</u> .
   Nosotros <u>nos saludamos</u> .
2. (hablar) Los amigos <u>se hablaron</u> .
   Elena y yo <u>nos hablamos</u> .
   Nosotras <u>nos hablamos</u> .
3. (conocer) Alberto y yo <u>nos conocimos</u> .
   Ustedes <u>se conocieron</u> .
   Ellos <u>se conocieron</u> .
4. (encontrar) Ana y Javier <u>se encontraron</u> .
   Los primos <u>se encontraron</u> .
   Mi hermana y yo <u>nos encontramos</u> .

Práctica

1 **Un amor recíproco** Describe a Laura y a Elián usando los verbos recíprocos.

> **modelo**
> Laura veía a Elián todos los días. Elián veía a Laura todos los días.
> *Laura y Elián se veían todos los días.*

1. Laura conocía bien a Elián. Elián conocía bien a Laura.
   Laura y Elián se conocían bien.
2. Laura miraba a Elián con amor. Elián la miraba con amor también.
   Laura y Elián se miraban con amor.
3. Laura entendía bien a Elián. Elián entendía bien a Laura.
   Laura y Elián se entendían bien.
4. Laura hablaba con Elián todas las noches por teléfono. Elián hablaba
   con Laura todas las noches por teléfono.
   Laura y Elián se hablaban todas las noches por teléfono.
5. Laura ayudaba a Elián con sus problemas. Elián la ayudaba también
   con sus problemas.
   Laura y Elián se ayudaban con sus problemas.

2 **Describir** Mira los dibujos y describe lo que estas personas hicieron.

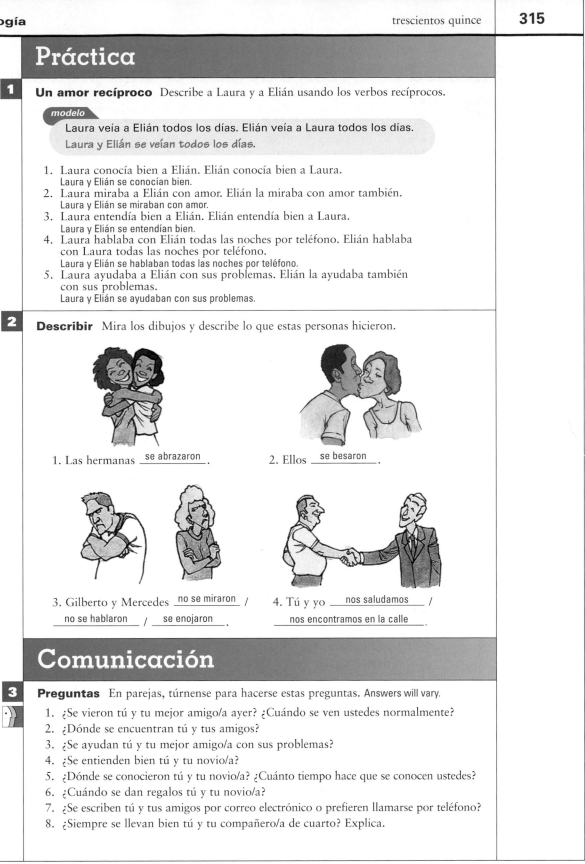

1. Las hermanas __se abrazaron__.

2. Ellos __se besaron__.

3. Gilberto y Mercedes __no se miraron__ / __no se hablaron__ / __se enojaron__.

4. Tú y yo __nos saludamos__ / __nos encontramos en la calle__.

Comunicación

3 **Preguntas** En parejas, túrnense para hacerse estas preguntas. Answers will vary.

1. ¿Se vieron tú y tu mejor amigo/a ayer? ¿Cuándo se ven ustedes normalmente?
2. ¿Dónde se encuentran tú y tus amigos?
3. ¿Se ayudan tú y tu mejor amigo/a con sus problemas?
4. ¿Se entienden bien tú y tu novio/a?
5. ¿Dónde se conocieron tú y tu novio/a? ¿Cuánto tiempo hace que se conocen ustedes?
6. ¿Cuándo se dan regalos tú y tu novio/a?
7. ¿Se escriben tú y tus amigos por correo electrónico o prefieren llamarse por teléfono?
8. ¿Siempre se llevan bien tú y tu compañero/a de cuarto? Explica.

NATIONAL communication STANDARDS

---

1 Suggestion Review conjugations of the imperfect tense before beginning the activity.

1 Expansion
• Have students expand upon the sentences to create a story about Laura and Elián falling in love.
• Have students rewrite the sentences, imagining that they are talking about themselves and their significant other, a close friend, or a relative.

2 Suggestion Have pairs choose a drawing and create the story of what the characters did leading up to the moment pictured and what they did after that. Ask pairs to share their stories and have the class vote for the most original or funniest one.

3 Suggestions
• Ask students to read through the questions and prepare short answers before talking to their partner.
• Encourage students to verify what they hear by paraphrasing or summarizing their partners' responses.

3 Expansion Have students ask follow-up questions after their partner has answered the original ones. Ex: **¿A qué hora se vieron ayer? ¿Dónde se vieron? ¿Por qué se vieron ayer? ¿Para qué se ven ustedes normalmente?**

TEACHING OPTIONS

Game Divide the class into teams of four to play a guessing game. Write a verb on the board. Teams have twenty seconds to come up with a famous couple or two famous people or entities that behave or feel that way toward each other. The verb may be in the present, imperfect, or preterite tense. Ex: **quererse— Romeo y Julieta se querían.** All teams with a correct answer earn a point.

TPR Call on a pair of volunteers to act out a reciprocal action. The class will guess the action, using the verb in a sentence.
Small groups Ask students to summarize the action of their favorite love story, soap opera, or television drama. They should try to use as many reciprocal reflexives as possible in their summary.

Section Goals

In **Estructura 11.4** students will learn:
- the stressed possessive adjectives and pronouns
- placement of stressed possessive adjectives

Instructional Resources

WB/VM: Workbook, pp. 133–134
Lab Manual, p. 66
*Lab CD/MP3 **Lección 11***
IRM: ¡Inténtalo! & Práctica
Answers, pp. 189–190;
Tapescript, pp. 49–53
Info Gap Activities Booklet,
pp. 43–44
Interactive CD-ROM
Companion website:
www.vistahigherlearning.com
Presentations CD-ROM

Suggestions

- Ask a few questions that involve possessive adjectives and respond to student answers with statements that involve the stressed possessive pronouns. Write each stressed pronoun you introduce on the board as you say it. Ex: _____ , **¿es éste tu lápiz? (Sí.) Pues, este lápiz es tuyo, _____ .** Show your own pencil. **Éste es mi lápiz. Este lápiz es mío.**

- Write the masculine forms of the stressed possessive adjectives/pronouns on the board, and ask volunteers to give the feminine and plural forms. Emphasize that when a stressed possessive adjective is used, the word it modifies is preceded by an article.

11.4 Stressed possessive adjectives and pronouns

ANTE TODO In contrast to English, Spanish has two types of possessive adjectives: the unstressed (or short) forms you learned in **Lección 3** and the stressed (or long) forms. The stressed possessive adjectives are used for emphasis or to express the English phrases *of mine, of yours, of his,* and so on.

Stressed possessive adjectives

Masculine singular	Feminine singular	Masculine plural	Feminine plural	
mío	mía	míos	mías	*my; (of) mine*
tuyo	tuya	tuyos	tuyas	*your; (of) yours (fam.)*
suyo	suya	suyos	suyas	*your; (of) yours (form.); his; (of) his; her; (of) hers; its*
nuestro	nuestra	nuestros	nuestras	*our; (of) ours*
vuestro	vuestra	vuestros	vuestras	*your; (of) yours (fam.)*
suyo	suya	suyos	suyas	*your; (of) yours (form.); their; (of) theirs*

¡ATENCIÓN!

Used with **un/una**, these possessives are similar in meaning to the English expression *of mine/yours/etc.*

Juancho es un amigo mío.
Juancho is a friend of mine.

▶ Stressed possessive adjectives must agree in gender and number with the nouns they modify.

su impresora   la impresora **suya**
her printer   *her printer*

nuestros televisores   los televisores **nuestros**
our television sets   *our television sets*

▶ Stressed possessive adjectives are placed after the noun they modify, while unstressed possessive adjectives are placed before the noun.

Son **mis** llaves.   Son las llaves **mías**.
They are my keys.   *They are my keys.*

▶ A definite article, an indefinite article, or a demonstrative adjective usually precedes a noun modified by a stressed possessive adjective.

Me encantan { **unos** discos compactos **tuyos**.   *I love some of your CDs.*
             los discos compactos **tuyos**.   *I love your CDs.*
             estos discos compactos **tuyos**. *I love these CDs of yours.*

▶ Since **suyo, suya, suyos,** and **suyas** have more than one meaning, you can avoid confusion by using the construction: [*article*] + [*noun*] + **de** + [*subject pronoun*].

el teclado **suyo** → el teclado **de él/ella**   *his/her keyboard*
                            el teclado **de usted**   *your keyboard*
                            el teclado **de ellos/ellas** *their keyboard*
                            el teclado **de ustedes**   *your keyboard*

CONSÚLTALO

This is the same construction you learned in **Lección 3** for clarifying **su** and **sus**. To review unstressed possessive adjectives, see **Estructura 3.2**, p. 75.

TEACHING OPTIONS

TPR Place different objects and/or photos of objects in a large bag. Ask students to retrieve one item from the bag. The students then mime how to use the item. Have volunteers use the name(s) of the student(s) miming (to state to whom the item belongs) and guess what the item is. Ex: **Es el carro de _____ y de _____. Es el carro suyo.**

Extra Practice Refer students to the chart of possessive adjectives on this page. Call out a noun and subject, then ask students to tell you which adjective they would use. Ex: **discos compactos, ustedes (suyos)**

Possessive pronouns

▶ Possessive pronouns are used to replace a noun + [*possessive adjective*]. In Spanish, the possessive pronouns have the same forms as the stressed possessive adjectives, and they are preceded by a definite article.

la calculadora **nuestra**	**la nuestra**
el *fax* **tuyo**	**el tuyo**
los archivos **suyos**	**los suyos**

▶ A possessive pronoun agrees in number and gender with the noun it replaces.

—Aquí está **mi coche**. ¿Dónde está **el tuyo**?
Here's my car. Where is yours?

—¿Tienes **las revistas** de Carlos?
Do you have Carlos' magazines?

—**El mío** está en el taller de mi hermano.
Mine is at my brother's garage.

—No, pero tengo **las nuestras**.
No, but I have ours.

¡ATENCIÓN!

The definite article (**el/la**) is usually omitted when a stressed possessive follows the verb **ser**.

Perdone, ¿pero **es suya** esta cámara?

No, no **es mía**.

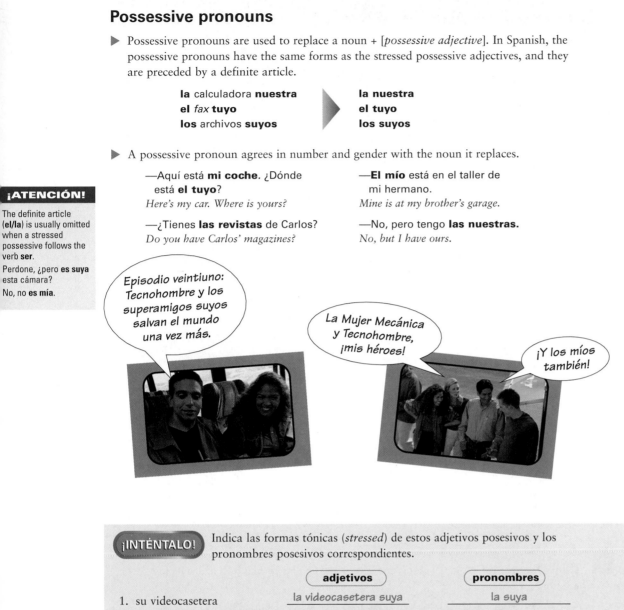

Episodio veintiuno: Tecnohombre y los superamigos suyos salvan el mundo una vez más.

La Mujer Mecánica y Tecnohombre, ¡mis héroes!

¡Y los míos también!

¡INTÉNTALO!   Indica las formas tónicas (*stressed*) de estos adjetivos posesivos y los pronombres posesivos correspondientes.

	adjetivos	pronombres
1. su videocasetera	la videocasetera suya	la suya
2. mi televisor	el televisor mío	el mío
3. nuestros discos compactos	los discos compactos nuestros	los nuestros
4. tus calculadoras	las calculadoras tuyas	las tuyas
5. su monitor	el monitor suyo	el suyo
6. mis videos	los videos míos	los míos
7. nuestra impresora	la impresora nuestra	la nuestra
8. tu estéreo	el estéreo tuyo	el tuyo
9. nuestro cederrón	el cederrón nuestro	el nuestro
10. mi computadora	la computadora mía	la mía

Suggestions

• Use a ball (or balled-up piece of paper) to practice possessives. Call out a sentence using an unstressed possessive adjective. Toss the ball to a student who restates the sentence, using a stressed possessive adjective. That student, in turn, tosses the ball to another student, who states the sentence using a possessive pronoun and tosses the ball back to you. Ex: **Nuestra impresora es nueva. La impresora nuestra es nueva. La nuestra es nueva.**

• Ask students questions using unstressed possessive adjectives or the [*article*] + [*noun*] + **de** construction before a name, having them answer with a possessive pronoun. Ex: **Es tu cuaderno, ¿verdad? (Sí, es el mío.) Clase, ¿son éstos sus exámenes? (Sí, son los nuestros.) Ésta es la mochila negra de ____ , ¿no? (No, no es la suya. La mochila roja es la suya.)**

• Point out that the function of the stressed possessives is to give emphasis. They are often used to point out contrasts. Ex: **¿Tu carro es azul? Pues, el carro mío es rojo. ¿Tu cámara digital no es buena? La mía es excelente.**

TEACHING OPTIONS

Video Replay the **Fotonovela**, having students listen for each use of an unstressed possessive adjective and write down the sentence in which it occurs. Next, have students rewrite those sentences using a stressed possessive adjective. Then, discuss how the use of stressed possessive adjectives affected the meaning or fluidity of the sentences.

Pairs Tell students that their laundry has gotten mixed up with their roommates' and since they are the same size and have the same tastes in clothing, they cannot tell what belongs to whom. Have them ask each other questions about different articles of clothing. Ex: —**¿Son tuyos estos pantalones de rayas? —Sí, son míos. —Y ¿estos calcetines rojos son tuyos? —Sí, son míos, pero esta camisa grandísima no es mía.**

Práctica

1 Frases Forma frases con las siguientes palabras. Usa el presente.

1. Un / amiga / suyo / vivir / Mendoza Una amiga suya vive en Mendoza.
2. ¿Me / prestar / calculadora / tuyo? ¿Me prestas la calculadora tuya?
3. El / coche / suyo / nunca / funcionar / bien El coche suyo nunca funciona bien.
4. No / nos / interesar / problemas / suyo No nos interesan los problemas suyos.
5. Yo / querer / cámara digital / mío / ahora mismo Yo quiero la cámara digital mía ahora mismo.
6. Un / amigos / nuestro / manejar / como / loco Unos amigos nuestros manejan como locos.

2 ¿Es suyo? Un policía ha capturado al hombre que robó (*robbed*) en tu casa. Ahora quiere saber qué cosas son tuyas. Túrnate con un(a) compañero/a para hacer el papel del policía y usa las pistas (*clues*) para contestar las preguntas.

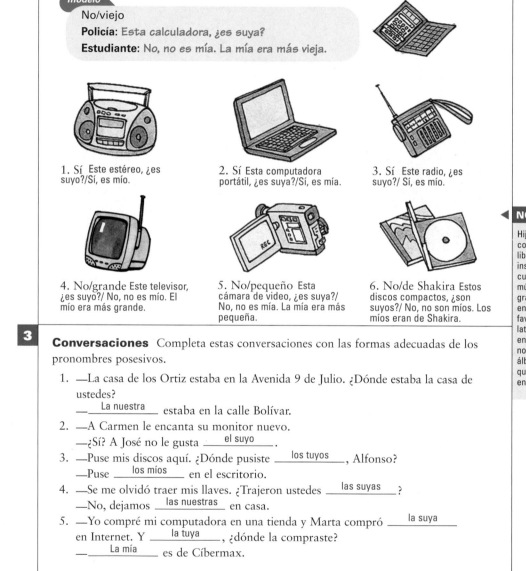

modelo
No/viejo
Policía: Esta calculadora, ¿es suya?
Estudiante: No, no es mía. La mía era más vieja.

1. Sí Este estéreo, ¿es suyo?/Sí, es mío.

2. Sí Esta computadora portátil, ¿es suya?/Sí, es mía.

3. Sí Este radio, ¿es suyo?/ Sí, es mío.

4. No/grande Este televisor, ¿es suyo?/ No, no es mío. El mío era más grande.

5. No/pequeño Esta cámara de video, ¿es suya?/ No, no es mía. La mía era más pequeña.

6. No/de Shakira Estos discos compactos, ¿son suyos?/ No, no son míos. Los míos eran de Shakira.

3 Conversaciones Completa estas conversaciones con las formas adecuadas de los pronombres posesivos.

1. —La casa de los Ortiz estaba en la Avenida 9 de Julio. ¿Dónde estaba la casa de ustedes?
   —__La nuestra__ estaba en la calle Bolívar.
2. —A Carmen le encanta su monitor nuevo.
   —¿Sí? A José no le gusta __el suyo__.
3. —Puse mis discos aquí. ¿Dónde pusiste __los tuyos__, Alfonso?
   —Puse __los míos__ en el escritorio.
4. —Se me olvidó traer mis llaves. ¿Trajeron ustedes __las suyas__?
   —No, dejamos __las nuestras__ en casa.
5. —Yo compré mi computadora en una tienda y Marta compró __la suya__ en Internet. Y __la tuya__, ¿dónde la compraste?
   —__La mía__ es de Cíbermax.

Comunicación

4 Identificar Trabajen en grupos. Cada estudiante da tres objetos. Pongan (*Put*) todos los objetos juntos. Luego, un(a) estudiante escoge uno o dos objetos y le pregunta a otro/a si esos objetos son suyos. Usen los adjetivos posesivos en sus preguntas.

Answers will vary.

> **modelo**
>
> **Estudiante 1:** Felipe, ¿son tuyos estos discos compactos?
> **Estudiante 2:** Sí, son míos.
> No, no son míos. Son los discos compactos de Bárbara.

5 Comparar Trabajen en parejas. Intenta (*Try to*) convencer a tu compañero/a de que algo que tú tienes es mejor que el que él/ella tiene. Pueden hablar de sus carros, estéreos, discos compactos, clases, horarios o trabajos. Answers will vary.

> **modelo**
>
> **Estudiante 1:** Mi computadora tiene una pantalla de quince pulgadas (*inches*). ¿Y la tuya?
> **Estudiante 2:** La mía es mejor porque tiene una pantalla de diecisiete pulgadas.
> **Estudiante 1:** Pues la mía...

Síntesis

6 Inventos locos En grupos pequeños, lean la descripción de este invento fantástico. Después diseñen su propio invento y expliquen por qué es mejor que el de los demás grupos. Utilicen los posesivos, **por** y **para** y el vocabulario de **Contextos**.

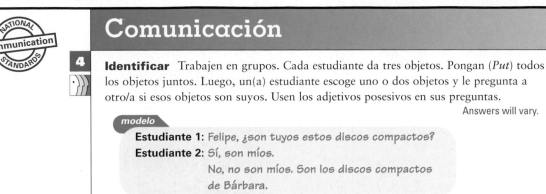

Nuestro celular tiene conexión a Internet, ¿y el tuyo?

Este teléfono celular es mucho mejor que el tuyo por estas razones:

- El nuestro tiene capacidad para guardar un millón de mensajes electrónicos.
- El celular nuestro toma video.
- Da la temperatura.
- Funciona como control remoto para la tele.
- También arranca el coche y toca música como un *walkman*.

Sirve para todo.

Oferta: $45 dólares por mes (con un contrato mínimo de dos años)

Para más información, llama al 607-362-1990 o visita nuestro sitio web www.telefonoloco.com

---

4 Suggestion If students cannot bring in three objects, have them either find photos of objects or draw them. Students should find one feminine, one masculine, and one plural object to do the activity.

5 Suggestion Before beginning the activity, have students make a list of objects to compare. Next, have them brainstorm as many different qualities or features of those objects as they can. Finally, have them list adjectives that they might use to compare the objects they have chosen.

5 Expansion Have pairs who had a heated discussion perform it for the class.

6 Expansion Have students change their ad to market their product for television or radio.

Suggestion See the Information Gap Activities Booklet for an additional activity to practice the material presented in this section.

TEACHING OPTIONS

Large Group Ask each student to bring in a photo of an object. Tell students not to tell anyone what their object is, and place it in a large sack. Call students up one at a time to choose a photo from the sack. Students then circulate around the classroom, trying to find the owner of their photo. Ex: **¿Es tuyo este disco compacto? (No, no es mío./Sí, es mío.)**

Extra Practice Have students imagine that they are salespersons at a car dealership and they are writing a letter to a customer explaining why their cars are better than those of the other two dealerships in town. Students should compare several attributes of the cars and use stressed possessive adjectives and pronouns when appropriate.

Lectura

Antes de leer

Estrategia
Recognizing borrowed words

One way languages grow is by borrowing words from each other. English words that relate to technology are often borrowed by Spanish and other languages throughout the world. Sometimes the words are modified slightly to fit the sounds of the languages that borrow them. When reading in Spanish, you can often increase your understanding by looking for words borrowed from English or other languages you know.

Examinar el texto

Mira brevemente° la selección. ¿De qué trata°? ¿Cómo lo sabes?

Buscar

Esta lectura contiene varias palabras tomadas° del inglés. Trabaja con un(a) compañero/a para encontrarlas. Internet, fax, Deep Blue

Predecir

Trabaja con un(a) compañero/a para contestar las siguientes preguntas. Answers will vary.

1. En la foto, ¿quiénes participan en el juego?
2. ¿Jugabas en una computadora cuando eras niño/a? ¿Juegas ahora?
3. ¿Cómo cambiaron las computadoras y la tecnología en los años 80? ¿En los años 90?
4. ¿Qué tipo de "inteligencia" tiene una computadora?
5. ¿Qué significa "inteligencia artificial" para ti?

recursos

vistahigher
learning.com

brevemente *briefly* ¿De qué trata? *What is it about?* tomadas *taken*

Inteligencia y memoria: la inteligencia artificial por Alfonso Santamaría

Una de las principales características de la película de ciencia ficción *2001: una odisea del espacio*, es la gran inteligencia de su protagonista no humano, la computadora HAL-9000. Para muchas personas, la genial película de Stanley Kubrick es una reflexión sobre la evolución de la inteligencia, desde que el hombre utilizó por primera vez un hueso como herramienta° hasta la llegada de la inteligencia artificial (I.A.).

Ahora que vivimos en el siglo XXI, un mundo en el que Internet y el *fax* son ya comunes, podemos preguntarnos: ¿consiguieron los científicos especialistas en I.A. crear una computadora como HAL? La respuesta es no. Hoy día no existe una computadora con las capacidades intelectuales de HAL porque todavía no existen *inteligencias*

herramienta *tool* sentido común *common sense* desarrollo *development* ajedrez *chess*

Después de leer

¿Cierto o falso?

Indica si cada frase es cierta o falsa. Corrige las frases falsas.

Cierta 1. La computadora HAL-9000 era muy inteligente.

Falsa 2. Deep Blue es un buen ejemplo de la inteligencia artificial general. Deep Blue es un buen ejemplo de la inteligencia artificial especializada.

Falsa 3. El maestro de ajedrez Garry Kasparov le ganó a Deep Blue en 1997. Deep Blue le ganó a Garry Kasparov en 1997.

Cierta 4. Las computadoras no tienen la creatividad de Mozart o Picasso.

Falsa 5. Hoy hay computadoras como HAL-9000. Las computadoras con la inteligencia de HAL-9000 son pura ciencia ficción.

...rtificiales *generales* que demuestren lo que lamamos "sentido común"°. Sin embargo, la I.A. está progresando mucho en el desarrollo° de las inteligencias especializadas. El ejemplo más famoso es Deep Blue, la computadora de IBM especializada en jugar al ajedrez°.

La idea de crear una máquina con capacidad para jugar al ajedrez se originó en 1950. En esa década, el científico Claude Shannon desarrolló una teoría que se convirtió en realidad en 1967, cuando apareció el primer programa que permitió a una computadora competir, aunque sin éxito°, en un campeonato° de ajedrez. Más de veinte años después, un grupo de expertos en I.A. fue al centro de investigación

Thomas J. Watson de Nueva York para desarrollar Deep Blue, la computadora que en 1997 derrotó° al campeón mundial de ajedrez, Garry Kasparov. Esta extraordinaria computadora pudo ganarle al maestro ruso de ajedrez porque estaba diseñada para procesar 200 millones de jugadas° por segundo. Además, Deep Blue guardaba en su memoria una recopilación de los movimientos de ajedrez más brillantes de toda la historia, entre ellos los que Kasparov efectuó en sus competiciones anteriores.

Para muchas personas la victoria de Deep Blue sobre Kasparov simbolizó la victoria de la inteligencia artificial sobre la del ser humano°. Debemos reconocer los grandes avances científicos en el área de las computadoras y las ventajas° que pueden traernos en un futuro, pero también tenemos que entender sus limitaciones. Las computadoras generan nuevos modelos con conocimientos° muy definidos, pero todavía no tienen sentido común: una computadora como Deep Blue puede ganar una partida° de ajedrez, pero no puede explicar la diferencia entre una reina° y un peón°. Tampoco puede crear algo nuevo y original a partir de lo establecido, como hicieron Mozart o Picasso.

Las inteligencias artificiales especializadas son una realidad. ¿Pero una inteligencia como la de HAL-9000? Pura ciencia ficción. ◼

...xito *success* campeonato *championship* derrotó *defeated* jugadas *moves* la del ser humano *that of the human being* ventajas *advantages* ...onocimientos *knowledge* partida *match* reina *queen* peón *pawn*

Preguntas

Contesta las preguntas.

1. ¿Qué tipo de inteligencia se relaciona con HAL-9000?
   La inteligencia artificial general se relaciona con HAL-9000.

2. ¿Qué tipo de inteligencia tienen las computadoras como Deep Blue? Las computadoras como Deep Blue tienen una inteligencia especializada.

3. ¿Cuándo se originó la idea de crear una máquina para jugar al ajedrez? La idea de crear una máquina para jugar al ajedrez se originó en 1950.

4. ¿Qué compañía inventó Deep Blue? IBM inventó Deep Blue.

5. ¿Por qué Deep Blue le pudo ganar a Garry Kasparov? Deep Blue le ganó a Garry Kasparov porque podía procesar 200 millones de jugadas por segundo.

Conversar

En grupos pequeños, hablen de los siguientes temas. Answers will vary.

1. ¿Son las computadoras más inteligentes que los seres humanos?

2. ¿Para qué cosas son mejores las computadoras, y para qué cosas son mejores los seres humanos? ¿Por qué?

3. En el futuro, ¿van a tener las computadoras la inteligencia de los seres humanos? ¿Cuándo?

Section Goal

In **Panorama**, students will read about the geography, history, and culture of Argentina.

Instructional Resources

Transparencies, #5, #6, #43
WB/VM: Workbook, pp. 135–136;
Video Activities, pp. 247–248
***Panorama cultural** DVD/Video*
Interactive CD-ROM
IRM: Videoscript, p. 113;
***Panorama cultural** Translations,*
p. 135
Companion website:
www.vistahigherlearning.com
Presentations CD-ROM

Suggestions

- Have students look at the map of Argentina or project **Transparency #43**. Guide students to recognize Argentina's great size and the variety of topographical features, such as mountains (**los Andes**), vast plains (**las pampas**), and large rivers.
- Point out that Argentina is one of the largest beef producers in the world and that **gauchos** have played an important role in the culture of the country.
- **Bariloche** is an important winter recreation area. Remind students that June–August is winter in the southern hemisphere.

El país en cifras Patagonia is very sparsely populated, but **Buenos Aires** is a metropolis about the size of New York City. Invite students to mention anything they know about Argentina.

¡Increíble pero cierto! Under the leadership of General José de San Martín, Argentina won its independence from Spain on July 9, 1816. Like Simón Bolívar, San Martín is a well-known figure in Latin America.

Argentina

NATIONAL connections cultures STANDARDS

El país en cifras

▶ **Área:** 2.780.400 km² (1.074.000 millas²)
Argentina es el país de habla española más grande del mundo. Su territorio es dos veces el tamaño° de Alaska.

▶ **Población:** 39.302.000

▶ **Capital:** Buenos Aires—12.439.000
En Buenos Aires vive cerca del cuarenta por ciento de la población total del país. La ciudad es conocida° como el "París de Suramérica" por el estilo parisino° de muchas de sus calles y edificios.

Buenos Aires

▶ **Ciudades principales:**
Córdoba—1.458.000, Rosario—1.370.000, Mendoza—1.025.000

SOURCE: Population Division, UN Secretariat

▶ **Moneda:** peso argentino

▶ **Idiomas:** español (oficial), guaraní

Bandera de Argentina

Argentinos célebres

▶ **Jorge Luis Borges,** escritor (1899–1986)
▶ **María Eva Duarte de Perón ("Evita"),** primera dama° (1919–1952)
▶ **Mercedes Sosa,** cantante (1935–)
▶ **Gato Barbieri,** saxofonista (1934–)

tamaño *size*   conocida *known*   parisino *Parisian*   primera dama *First Lady*
ancha *wide*   lado *side*   mide *it measures*   campo *field*

¡Increíble pero cierto!

La Avenida 9 de Julio en Buenos Aires es la calle más ancha° del mundo. De lado° a lado mide° cerca de 140 metros, lo que es equivalente a un campo° y medio de fútbol. Su nombre conmemora el Día de la Independencia de Argentina.

Gaucho de la Patagonia

BOLIVIA

PARAGUAY

ESTADOS UNIDOS

OCÉANO ATLÁNTICO

OCÉANO PACÍFICO

AMÉRICA DEL SUR

ARGENTINA

San Miguel De Tucumán

Las cat de Ig

Córdoba

La Cordillera de los Andes

Aconcagua

Rosario

Río Paraná

URUGU

Mendoza

CHILE

Buenos Aires

Mar del Pla

La Pampa

San Carlos de Bariloche

Océano Atlántico

Montañas de Patagonia

Patagonia

Vista de San Carlos de Bariloche

Tierra del Fuego

recursos

WB pp. 135–136	VM pp. 247–248	I CD-ROM Lección 11	vistahigh learning.c

---

TEACHING OPTIONS

Worth Noting The Argentinian cowboy, the **gaucho**, has played as significant a role in the folklore of Argentina as the cowboy of the Old West has played in that of the United States. Two classic works of Argentinian literature focus on the gaucho. *El gaucho Martín Fierro*, an epic poem by José Hernández (1834–1886), celebrates the gaucho's fiercely independent way of life, whereas Domingo Sarmiento's (1811–1888) biography,

Facundo: Civilización y barbarie, describes the nomadic, uneducated gauchos as hindrances in Argentina's pursuit of economic, social, and political progress.

Extra Practice Have students listen to a song on one of the many recordings by singer Mercedes Sosa. Then, have pairs work together to transcribe the lyrics. Invite volunteers to share their work with the class.

Historia • Inmigración europea

Se dice que Argentina es el país más "europeo" de toda Latinoamérica, porque después del año 1880, una gran cantidad de inmigrantes dejó Europa para establecerse en este país. Las diferentes culturas de estos inmigrantes, que venían de Italia, Alemania, España e Inglaterra, han dejado una profunda huella° en la música, el cine, el arte y la arquitectura de Argentina.

Artes • El tango

El tango, un baile con sonidos y ritmos de origen africano, italiano y español, es uno de los símbolos culturales más importantes de Argentina. Se originó entre los porteños°, muchos de ellos inmigrantes, en la década de 1880. Se hizo popular en París y más tarde entre la clase alta de Argentina. En un principio°, el tango era un baile provocativo y violento, pero se hizo más romántico durante los años 30. Hoy día es popular en muchas partes del mundo°.

Lugares • Las cataratas de Iguazú

Entre las fronteras de Argentina, Paraguay y Brasil, al norte de Buenos Aires y cerca de la confluencia° de los ríos Iguazú y Paraná, están las famosas cataratas° de Iguazú. Estas extensas cataratas tienen unos 70 m (230 pies) de altura° y, en época de lluvias, llegan a medir 4 km (2,5 mi) de ancho. Situadas en el Parque Nacional Iguazú, las cataratas son uno de los sitios turísticos más visitados de Suramérica.

¿Qué aprendiste? Responde a las preguntas con una frase completa.

1. ¿Qué porcentaje de la población de Argentina vive en la capital?
   Cerca del cuarenta por ciento de la población de Argentina vive en la capital.
2. ¿Quién es Mercedes Sosa?
   Mercedes Sosa es una cantante argentina.
3. Se dice que Argentina es el país más europeo de América Latina. ¿Por qué? Se dice que Argentina es el país más europeo de América Latina porque muchos inmigrantes europeos se establecieron allí.
4. ¿Qué tipo de baile es uno de los símbolos culturales más importantes de Argentina?
   El tango es uno de los símbolos culturales más importantes de la Argentina.
5. ¿Dónde y cuándo se originó el tango?
   El tango se originó entre los porteños en la década de 1880.
6. ¿Cómo era el tango originalmente?
   El tango era un baile provocativo y violento.
7. ¿En qué parque nacional están las cataratas de Iguazú?
   Las cataratas de Iguazú están en el Parque Nacional Iguazú.

Ceramista en
Buenos Aires

Conexión Internet Investiga estos temas en el sitio **www.vistahigherlearning.com.**

1. Busca información sobre el tango. ¿Te gustan los ritmos y sonidos del tango? ¿Por qué? ¿Se baila el tango en tu comunidad?
2. ¿Quiénes fueron Juan y Eva Perón y qué importancia tienen en la historia de Argentina?

han dejado una profunda huella *have left a deep mark*   porteños *people of Buenos Aires*   En un principio *At first*   mundo *world* confluencia *junction*   cataratas *waterfalls*   altura *height*

Inmigración europea Among the European immigrants who arrived in waves on Argentina's shores were thousands of Jews. An interesting chapter in the history of the **pampas** features Jewish **gauchos**. A generous pre-Zionist philanthropist purchased land for Jews who settled on the Argentine grasslands. At one time, the number of Yiddish-language newspapers in Argentina was second only to that of New York City.

El tango The great classic interpreter of tango was Carlos Gardel (1890–1935). If possible, bring in a recording of his version of a tango such as **"Cuesta abajo"** or **"Volver."** A modern exponent of tango was Astor Piazzola (1921–1992). His **tango nuevo** has found interpreters such as cellist Yo-Yo Ma and the Kronos Quartet. For more information about **el tango**, you may want to play the **Panorama cultural** video for this lesson.

Las cataratas de Iguazú In the **Guaraní** language, **Iguazú** means *big water*. The falls are three times wider than Niagara and have been declared a World Heritage Site by UNESCO. Iguazú National Park was established in 1934 to protect and preserve this natural treasure.

Conexión Internet Students will find supporting Internet activities and links at **www.vistahigherlearning.com.**

Variación léxica Argentinians frequently use the word ¡che! to get the attention of someone they are talking to. **Che** also serves as a kind of spoken exclamation point with which Argentinians pepper their speech. This is so noticeable to outsiders that Argentinians are often given the nickname **Che** in other parts of the Spanish-speaking world. Another notable feature of Argentinian Spanish is the existence, alongside **tú**, of **vos** as the second-person singular familiar pronoun. **Vos** is also heard in other parts of Latin America, and it is accompanied by corresponding verb forms in the present tense. Here are some equivalents: **vos contás / tú cuentas, vos pensás / tú piensas, vos sos / tú eres, vos ponés / tú pones, vos venís / tú vienes.**

Uruguay

National Standards: connections cultures

El país en cifras

▶ **Área:** 176.220 km² (68.039 millas²) *el tamaño° del estado de Washington*
▶ **Población:** 3.455.000
▶ **Capital:** Montevideo—1.352.000

Casi la mitad° de la población de Uruguay vive en Montevideo. Situada en la desembocadura° del famoso Río de la Plata, esta ciudad cosmopolita e intelectual es también un destino popular para las vacaciones, debido a sus numerosas playas de arena° blanca que se extienden hasta la ciudad de Punta del Este.

▶ **Ciudades principales:** Salto—77.000, Paysandú—75.000, Las Piedras—61.000, Rivera—55.000
SOURCE: Population Division, UN Secretariat

▶ **Moneda:** peso uruguayo
▶ **Idiomas:** español (oficial)

Bandera de Uruguay

Uruguayos célebres

▶ **Horacio Quiroga,** escritor (1878–1937)
▶ **Juana de Ibarbourou,** escritora (1895–1979)
▶ **Mario Benedetti,** escritor (1920–)
▶ **Cristina Peri Rossi,** escritora y profesora (1941–)

tamaño *size* mitad *half* desembocadura *mouth* arena *sand* avestruz *ostrich* no voladora *flightless* medir *measure* cotizado *valued*

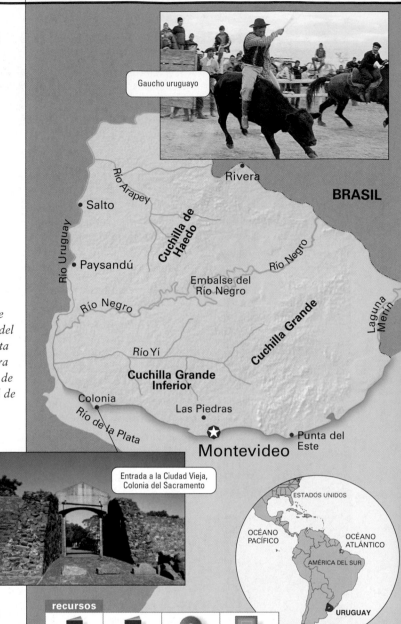
Gaucho uruguayo
BRASIL
Montevideo
Entrada a la Ciudad Vieja, Colonia del Sacramento

recursos
WB pp. 137–138 | VM pp. 249–250 | I CD-ROM Lección 11 | vistahigher learning.com

¡Increíble pero cierto!

En Uruguay hay muchos animales curiosos, entre ellos el ñandú. De la misma especie del avestruz°, el ñandú es el ave no voladora° más grande del hemisferio occidental. Puede llegar a medir° dos metros. Normalmente, va en grupos de veinte o treinta y vive en el campo. Es muy cotizado° por su carne, sus plumas y sus huevos.

Costumbres • La carne y el mate

La gran importancia de la producción ganadera° en las economías de Uruguay y Argentina se refleja en sus hábitos culinarios. Para los uruguayos, como para los argentinos, la carne de res es un elemento esencial de la dieta diaria. Algunos platos representativos son el asado°, la parrillada° y el chivito°. El mate, una infusión similar al té, es también muy típico de esta región. Es una bebida de origen indígena que está muy presente en la vida social y familiar de estos países aunque, curiosamente, no se sirve en bares o restaurantes.

Deportes • El fútbol

El fútbol es, sin lugar a dudas, el deporte nacional de Uruguay. La afición a este deporte se inició hace mucho en Uruguay. En 1891, se formó el primer equipo de fútbol uruguayo y, en 1930, el país fue la sede° de la primera copa mundial. A partir de los años treinta se inició el período profesional del fútbol uruguayo. El equipo nacional ha conseguido° grandes éxitos a lo largo de los años: dos campeonatos olímpicos en 1923 y 1928, y dos campeonatos mundiales en 1930 y 1950.

Costumbres • El Carnaval

El Carnaval de Montevideo es el más largo del mundo y uno de los mejores de Suramérica. Dura° unos cuarenta días y cuenta con la participación de casi todos los habitantes de la ciudad. Durante el Carnaval, hay desfiles°, bailes y música en las calles de su capital. La celebración más conocida es el *Desfile de las Llamadas*, en el que participan bailarines que desfilan al ritmo del candombe, un colorido baile de tradición africana.

¿Qué aprendiste? Responde a las preguntas con una frase completa.

1. ¿Qué tienen en común los uruguayos célebres mencionados en la página 324?
   Son escritores.
2. ¿Cuál es el elemento esencial de la dieta uruguaya?
   La carne de res es esencial en la dieta uruguaya.
3. ¿En qué países es importante la producción ganadera?
   La producción ganadera es importante en Uruguay y Argentina.
4. ¿Qué es el mate?
   El mate es una bebida indígena que es similar al té.
5. ¿Cuándo se formó el primer equipo uruguayo de fútbol?
   En 1891 se formó el primer equipo de fútbol uruguayo.
6. ¿Cuándo se celebró la primera Copa Mundial de fútbol?
   La primera Copa Mundial se celebró en 1930.
7. ¿Cómo se llama la celebración más conocida del Carnaval de Montevideo?
   La celebración más conocida del Carnaval de Montevideo se llama El Desfile de las Llamadas.
8. ¿Cuántos días dura el Carnaval de Montevideo?
   El Carnaval de Montevideo dura unos cuarenta días.

Edificio del Parlamento en Montevideo

Conexión Internet Investiga estos temas en el sitio **www.vistahigherlearning.com.**

1. Uruguay es conocido como un país de muchos escritores. Busca información sobre uno de ellos y escribe una biografía.
2. Investiga cuáles son las comidas y bebidas favoritas de los uruguayos. Descríbelas e indica cuáles quieres probar y por qué.

....

ganadera *cattle (adj.)* asado *barbecue* parrillada *beef platter* chivito *goat* sede *site* ha conseguido *has achieved*
Dura *It lasts* desfiles *parades*

La carne y el mate A legend from the **guaraní** people of Uruguay says that **yerba mate** was a gift from the god **Pa'i Shume**. Traditionally, the **yerba mate** leaves are packed into a **mate**—a cup made from a gourd—and hot water is poured over them. The infusion is sipped through a **bombilla**—a metal straw with a built-in tea strainer. The **mate** is refilled and drained several times, passing from hand to hand among a group of friends or family.

El fútbol Uruguayan women have made their mark in soccer. Although the International Federation of Football Association (FIFA) established a women's league in 1982, it was not until 1985 that the first women's league—from Brazil—was formally established. The women's league of Uruguay now participates in international soccer play, showing that Uruguayan women can be just as fanatical as the men when it comes to **fútbol**.

El Carnaval Like the rest of Latin America, Uruguay also imported slaves from Africa during the colonial period. The music of the African-influenced **candombe** culture is popular with Uruguayans from all sectors of society.

Conexión Internet Students will find supporting Internet activities and links at **www.vistahigherlearning.com**.

Suggestion You may want to wrap up this section by playing the **Panorama cultural** video footage for this lesson.

TEACHING OPTIONS

Worth Noting Uruguay is similar to its larger neighbor, Argentina, in many ways: the Uruguayans also love the **tango** and **yerba mate**, play the Argentine card game **truco**, and include meat as a major part of their diet. Historically, cattle ranching, the culture of the **gaucho**, and the great cattle ranches (called **estancias**) have been important elements in the Uruguayan national fabric. Another, less pleasant, similarity was in the Dirty War (**Guerra sucia**) waged by an Uruguayan military dictatorship against domestic dissidents during the 1970s and 80s. In 1984 the military allowed the election of a civilian government. In 1989 that government was peacefully succeeded by another. Today, presidential and parliamentary elections are held every five years.

La tecnología

la calculadora	calculator
la cámara digital, de video	digital, video camera
el canal	(TV) channel
el cibercafé	cybercafé
la contestadora	answering machine
el control remoto	remote control
el disco compacto	compact disc
el estéreo	stereo
el *fax*	fax (machine)
el radio	radio (set)
el teléfono (celular)	(cell) telephone
la televisión por cable	cable television
el televisor	televison set
el tocadiscos compacto	compact disc player
el video(casete)	video(cassette)
la videocasetera	VCR
el *walkman*	walkman
apagar	to turn off
funcionar	to work
llamar	to call
poner, prender	to turn on
sonar (o:ue)	to ring
descompuesto/a	not working; out of order
lento/a	slow
lleno/a	full

La computadora

el archivo	file
arroba	@ symbol
el cederrón	CD-ROM
la computadora (portátil)	(portable) computer; (laptop)
la dirección electrónica	e-mail address
el disco compacto	compact disc
la impresora	printer
Internet	Internet
el monitor	(computer) monitor
la página principal	home page
la pantalla	screen
el programa de computación	software
el ratón	mouse
la red	network; Web
el reproductor de DVD	DVD player
el sitio web	website
el teclado	keyboard
borrar	to erase
descargar	to download
grabar	to record
guardar	to save
imprimir	to print
navegar (en Internet)	to surf (the Internet)
quemar	to burn (a CD)

El carro

la autopista, la carretera	highway
el baúl	trunk
la calle	street
el capó, el cofre	hood
el carro, el coche	car
la circulación, el tráfico	traffic
el garaje, el taller (mecánico)	garage; (mechanic's) repair shop
la gasolina	gasoline
la gasolinera	gas station
la licencia de conducir	driver's license
la llanta	tire
el/la mecánico/a	mechanic
el parabrisas	windshield
la policía	police (force)
la velocidad máxima	speed limit
el volante	steering wheel
arrancar	to start
arreglar	to fix; to arrange
bajar(se) de	to get off of/out of (a vehicle)
conducir, manejar	to drive
estacionar	to park
llenar (el tanque)	to fill (the tank)
parar	to stop
revisar (el aceite)	to check (the oil)
subir(se) a	to get on/into (a vehicle)

Verbos

abrazar(se)	to hug; to embrace (each other)
ayudar(se)	to help (each other)
besar(se)	to kiss (each other)
encontrar(se) (o:ue)	to meet (each other); to run into (each other)
saludar(se)	to greet (each other)

Otras palabras y expresiones

por aquí	around here
por ejemplo	for example
por eso	that's why; therefore
por fin	finally

Por and *para*	See pages 310–311.
Stressed possessive adjectives and pronouns	See pages 316–317.
Expresiones útiles	See page 303.

recursos

LM p. 66 | Lab CD/MP3 Lección 11 | Vocab CD Lección 11

La vivienda

12

Communicative Goals

You will learn how to:

- Welcome people to your home
- Describe your house or apartment
- Talk about household chores
- Give instructions

A PRIMERA VISTA

- ¿Está el chico en casa?
- ¿Tiene una casa moderna o vieja?
- ¿Tiene un teléfono celular en la mano?
- ¿Se va a vestir para ir al trabajo o al gimnasio?

Lesson Goals

In **Lección 12** students will be introduced to the following:
- terms for parts of a house
- names of common household objects
- terms for household chores
- relative pronouns
- formal commands
- object pronouns with formal commands
- present subjunctive
- subjunctive with verbs and expressions of will and influence
- locating the main parts of a sentence
- using idea maps
- writing a lease agreement
- using visual cues while listening
- cultural and geographic information about Panama
- cultural and geographic information about El Salvador

A primera vista Here are some additional questions you can ask based on the photo: **¿Dónde vives? ¿Con quién vives? ¿Cómo es la casa tuya? ¿Qué haces en casa por la noche? ¿Qué haces los fines de semana? ¿Tienes una computadora en casa? ¿Qué otros productos tecnológicos tienes? ¿Cómo te vistes cuando estás en casa? ¿Comes en casa con mucha frecuencia? ¿Qué te gusta comer cuando estás en casa?**

INSTRUCTIONAL RESOURCES

Workbook/Video Manual: WB Activities, pp. 139–154
Laboratory Manual: Lab Activities, pp. 67–72
Workbook/Video Manual: Video Activities, pp. 217–218; pp. 251–254
Instructor's Resource Manual: **Vocabulario adicional**, p. 166; **¡Inténtalo!** & **Práctica** Answers, pp. 191–192; **Fotonovela** Translations, p. 125; Textbook CD

Tapescript, p. 82; Lab CDs Tapescript, pp. 54–58; **Fotonovela** Videoscript, p. 100; **Panorama cultural** Videoscript, p. 114; **Pan. cult.** Translations, p. 136
Info Gap Activities Booklet, pp. 45–48
Overhead Transparencies: #3, #4, #45, #46, #47, #48, #49
Lab Audio CD/MP3 **Lección 12**

Panorama cultural DVD/Video
Fotonovela DVD/Video
Testing Program, pp. 133–144
Testing Program Audio CD
Test Files CD-ROM
Test Generator
Companion website

Presentations CD-ROM
Textbook CD
Vocabulary CD
Interactive CD-ROM
Video CD-ROM
Web-SAM

Section Goals

In **Contextos**, students will learn and practice:
- names of rooms in a home
- names of common household objects
- terms for household chores

Instructional Resources
Transparencies, #45, #46
Textbook Activities CD
Vocabulary CD
WB/VM: Workbook, pp. 139–140
Lab Manual, p. 67
Lab CD/MP3 Lección 12
IRM: Vocab. adicional,
p. 166; Práctica Answers,
p.191; Tapescript, pp. 54–58; p. 82
Info Gap Activities Booklet,
pp. 45–46
Interactive CD-ROM
Companion website:
www.vistahigherlearning.com
Presentations CD-ROM

Suggestions

- Project **Transparency #45** and describe the house, naming the kinds of rooms and introducing those that are not shown. Ex: **Ésta es la casa de los Hernández. Hay una sala grande, un dormitorio, una oficina, una cocina y un altillo. También hay un cuarto de baño, un sótano, un patio y un garaje, pero no vemos estos cuartos en la ilustración.**

- Project **Transparency #45.** Ask open-ended questions about the house and housework. Ex: **¿Dónde se pone la comida después de regresar del supermercado? ¿Qué se hace en la oficina?** Personalize questions, getting students to talk to you and one another about themselves and their living arrangements. Ex: _____, **¿vives en una residencia o en un apartamento? ¿Cuántos cuartos hay? Y tú,** _____, **¿vives en un apartamento con cinco cuartos?**

Note: At this point you may want to present **Vocabulario adicional: Más vocabulario para el hogar**, from the IRM.

La vivienda

Más vocabulario

las afueras	suburbs; outskirts
el alquiler	rent (payment)
el ama (*m., f.*) de casa	housekeeper; caretaker
el barrio	neighborhood
el edificio de apartamentos	apartment building
el/la vecino/a	neighbor
la vivienda	housing
el balcón	balcony
el cuarto	room
la entrada	entrance
la escalera	stairs; stairway
el garaje	garage
el jardín	garden; yard
el pasillo	hallway
el patio	patio; yard
el sótano	basement; cellar
la cafetera	coffee maker
el electrodoméstico	electrical appliance
el horno (de microondas)	(microwave) oven
la lavadora	washing machine
la luz	light, electricity
la secadora	clothes dryer
la tostadora	toaster
el cartel	poster
la mesita de noche	night stand
los muebles	furniture
alquilar	to rent
mudarse	to move (from one house to another)

Variación léxica

alcoba, dormitorio ⟷ aposento (*Rep. Dom.*); recámara (*Méx.*)

apartamento ⟷ departamento (*Arg., Chile*); piso (*Esp.*)

lavar los platos ⟷ lavar/fregar los trastes (*Amér. C., Rep. Dom.*)

recursos

TEXT CD Lección 12	WB pp. 139–140	LM p. 67	Lab CD/MP3 Lección 12	I CD-ROM Lección 12	Vocab CD Lección 12

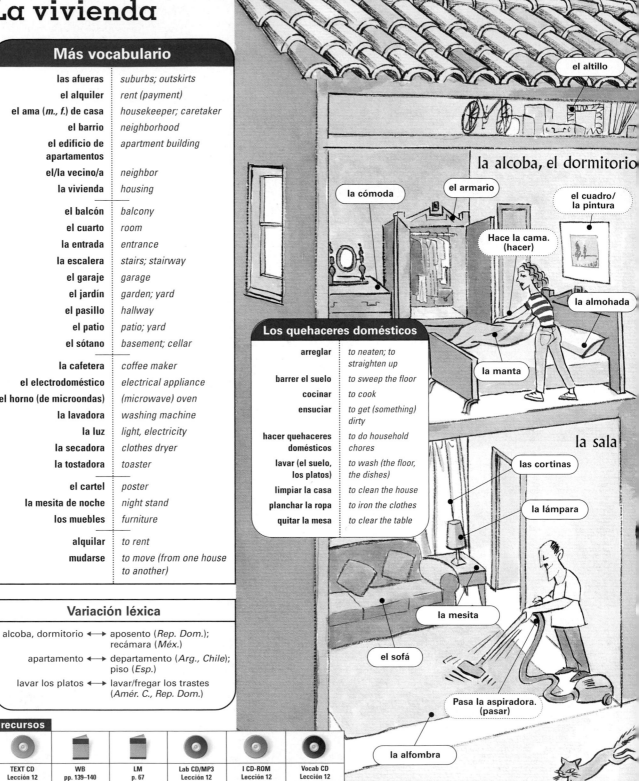

el altillo

la alcoba, el dormitorio

la cómoda — el armario — el cuadro/ la pintura

Hace la cama. (hacer)

la almohada

la manta

Los quehaceres domésticos

arreglar	to neaten; to straighten up
barrer el suelo	to sweep the floor
cocinar	to cook
ensuciar	to get (something) dirty
hacer quehaceres domésticos	to do household chores
lavar (el suelo, los platos)	to wash (the floor, the dishes)
limpiar la casa	to clean the house
planchar la ropa	to iron the clothes
quitar la mesa	to clear the table

la sala

las cortinas

la lámpara

la mesita

el sofá

Pasa la aspiradora. (pasar)

la alfombra

TEACHING OPTIONS

Extra Practice Ask students to complete these analogies.
1. aspiradora : _____ :: lavadora : ropa (alfombra) (*aspiradora* es a _____ como *lavadora* es a *ropa*)
2. frío : calor :: congelador : _____ (horno)
3. cama : alcoba :: _____ : oficina (escritorio)
4. platos : cocina :: carro : _____ (garaje)

Variación léxica Ask heritage speakers to tell the class any other terms they use to refer to rooms in a home. Ex: **alcoba, dormitorio = aposento** (D.R.), **recámara** (Mex.); **lavar los platos = fregar los trastes** (D.R.). Also ask heritage speakers to describe typical homes in Spanish-speaking countries.

Práctica

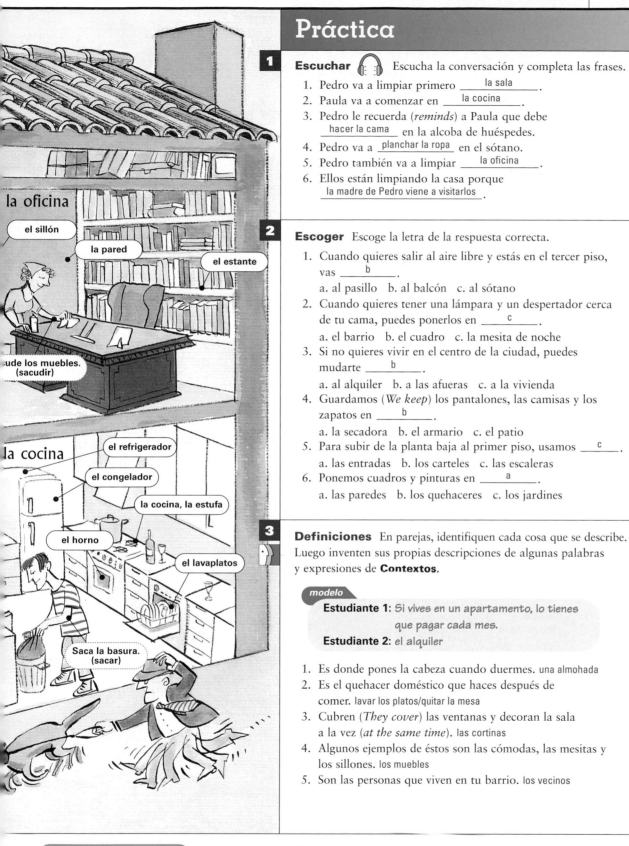

la oficina

el sillón

la pared

el estante

...ude los muebles. (sacudir)

la cocina

el refrigerador

el congelador

la cocina, la estufa

el horno

el lavaplatos

Saca la basura. (sacar)

1 Escuchar 🎧 Escucha la conversación y completa las frases.

1. Pedro va a limpiar primero ___la sala___ .
2. Paula va a comenzar en ___la cocina___ .
3. Pedro le recuerda (*reminds*) a Paula que debe ___hacer la cama___ en la alcoba de huéspedes.
4. Pedro va a ___planchar la ropa___ en el sótano.
5. Pedro también va a limpiar ___la oficina___ .
6. Ellos están limpiando la casa porque ___la madre de Pedro viene a visitarlos___ .

2 Escoger Escoge la letra de la respuesta correcta.

1. Cuando quieres salir al aire libre y estás en el tercer piso, vas ___b___ .
   a. al pasillo   b. al balcón   c. al sótano
2. Cuando quieres tener una lámpara y un despertador cerca de tu cama, puedes ponerlos en ___c___ .
   a. el barrio   b. el cuadro   c. la mesita de noche
3. Si no quieres vivir en el centro de la ciudad, puedes mudarte ___b___ .
   a. al alquiler   b. a las afueras   c. a la vivienda
4. Guardamos (*We keep*) los pantalones, las camisas y los zapatos en ___b___ .
   a. la secadora   b. el armario   c. el patio
5. Para subir de la planta baja al primer piso, usamos ___c___ .
   a. las entradas   b. los carteles   c. las escaleras
6. Ponemos cuadros y pinturas en ___a___ .
   a. las paredes   b. los quehaceres   c. los jardines

3 Definiciones En parejas, identifiquen cada cosa que se describe. Luego inventen sus propias descripciones de algunas palabras y expresiones de **Contextos**.

> **modelo**
> **Estudiante 1:** Si vives en un apartamento, lo tienes que pagar cada mes.
> **Estudiante 2:** el alquiler

1. Es donde pones la cabeza cuando duermes. una almohada
2. Es el quehacer doméstico que haces después de comer. lavar los platos/quitar la mesa
3. Cubren (*They cover*) las ventanas y decoran la sala a la vez (*at the same time*). las cortinas
4. Algunos ejemplos de éstos son las cómodas, las mesitas y los sillones. los muebles
5. Son las personas que viven en tu barrio. los vecinos

TEACHING OPTIONS

Small Groups Have groups of three interview each other about their dream house, one conducting the interview, one answering, and one taking notes. At three-minute intervals have students switch roles until each has been interviewer, interviewee, and note-taker. Then pair up the groups and have them report to one another using their notes.

Game Ask students to bring in pictures of mansions, castles, or palaces. Divide the class into teams of three, and have each team write a description of the rest of the residence that is not visible. Have each group read its description aloud. To determine the winner, ask the students to vote for the best description.

Suggestion Project **Transparency #46** and ask volunteers to name the items on the table. Then talk about the uses of the silverware (**cubiertos**), glassware (**cristalería**), and china (**vajilla**) pictured. Ex: **La copa sirve para tomar vino, pero la taza es para el café o el té. La cuchara sirve para tomar sopa. El tenedor sirve para llevar a la boca la carne y el pescado.**

4 Expansion
• Ask volunteers to answer questions modeled on the partial sentences in **Actividad 4.** Ex: **¿Qué se necesita para comer la carne? Para comer un helado, ¿qué se necesita?**
• Using magazine pictures, ask students what utensils are needed. Ex: **¿Qué se necesita para comer este plato de espaguetis? (Un tenedor y una cuchara)**

5 Suggestion Before breaking the class into groups, model the activity using your own situation. Ex: **En casa, mi marido siempre pasa la aspiradora, pero yo sacudo los muebles. Mi hijo saca la basura cada noche. Cada uno hace su cama antes de salir de la casa por la mañana.**

5 Expansion Ask students to name the worst possible place to have to do each of the chores listed. Ex: **¿Cuál es el lugar donde menos te gustaría sacar la basura? (Yankee Stadium después de la Serie Mundial) ¿Cuál es el lugar donde menos te gustaría pasar la aspiradora? (la Casa Blanca)**

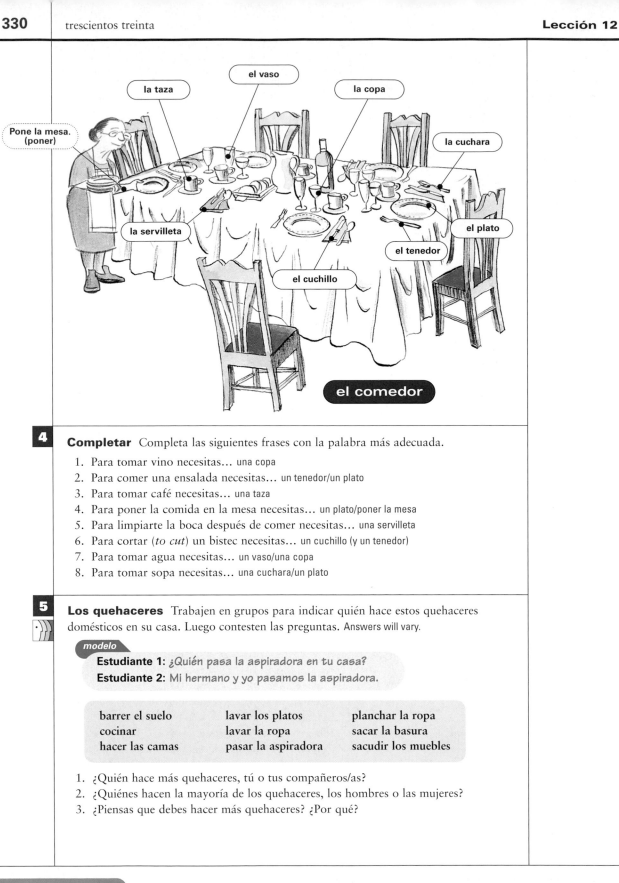

la taza · el vaso · la copa · Pone la mesa. (poner) · la cuchara · la servilleta · el tenedor · el plato · el cuchillo · **el comedor**

4 **Completar** Completa las siguientes frases con la palabra más adecuada.

1. Para tomar vino necesitas… una copa
2. Para comer una ensalada necesitas… un tenedor/un plato
3. Para tomar café necesitas… una taza
4. Para poner la comida en la mesa necesitas… un plato/poner la mesa
5. Para limpiarte la boca después de comer necesitas… una servilleta
6. Para cortar (*to cut*) un bistec necesitas… un cuchillo (y un tenedor)
7. Para tomar agua necesitas… un vaso/una copa
8. Para tomar sopa necesitas… una cuchara/un plato

5 **Los quehaceres** Trabajen en grupos para indicar quién hace estos quehaceres domésticos en su casa. Luego contesten las preguntas. Answers will vary.

> **modelo**
> **Estudiante 1:** ¿Quién pasa la aspiradora en tu casa?
> **Estudiante 2:** Mi hermano y yo pasamos la aspiradora.

barrer el suelo	lavar los platos	planchar la ropa
cocinar	lavar la ropa	sacar la basura
hacer las camas	pasar la aspiradora	sacudir los muebles

1. ¿Quién hace más quehaceres, tú o tus compañeros/as?
2. ¿Quiénes hacen la mayoría de los quehaceres, los hombres o las mujeres?
3. ¿Piensas que debes hacer más quehaceres? ¿Por qué?

TEACHING OPTIONS

Extra Practice Have students describe their homes. They should specify who does chores and in which rooms. Have them compare their descriptions with several different classmates.

Extra Practice Write these partial sentences on the board, and have the students complete them with appropriate chores. **1. Antes de pasar la aspiradora, tienes que… (sacudir los muebles.) 2. Después de lavar y secar la ropa, normalmente… (tienes que plancharla.) 3. Después de comer, tienes que… (lavar los platos.) 4. Tienes que levantarte antes de… (hacer la cama.) 5. Antes de sentarte a comer, tienes que… (poner la mesa.)**

Comunicación

communication NATIONAL STANDARDS

6 **La vida doméstica** En parejas, describan las habitaciones que ven en estas fotos. Identifiquen y describan cinco muebles o adornos (*accessories*) de cada foto y digan dos quehaceres que se pueden hacer en cada habitación. Answers will vary.

7 **Mi apartamento** Dibuja el plano de un apartamento amueblado (*furnished*) imaginario y escribe los nombres de las habitaciones y de los muebles. En parejas, pónganse espalda contra espalda (*sit back to back*). Uno/a de los/las dos describe su apartamento mientras su compañero/a lo dibuja según (*according to*) la descripción. Cuando terminen, miren el segundo dibujo. ¿Es similar al dibujo original? Hablen de los cambios que se necesitan hacer para mejorar el dibujo. Repitan la actividad intercambiando los papeles (*roles*). Answers will vary.

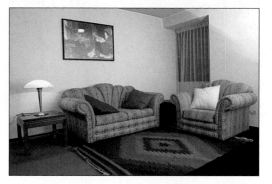

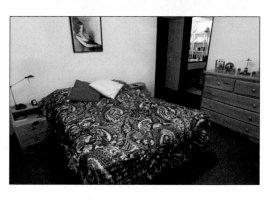

CONSÚLTALO

To review bathroom-related vocabulary, see **Lección 7, Contextos,** p. 182.

8 **¡Corre, corre!** Tu profesor(a) va a darte una serie incompleta de dibujos que forman una historia. Tú y tu compañero/a tienen dos series diferentes. Descríbanse los dibujos para completar la historia.

modelo

Estudiante 1: Marta quita la mesa.
Estudiante 2: Francisco...

6 Suggestions
- Model the activity using a magazine picture. Ex: **¡Qué comedor más desordenado! ¡Es un desastre! Alguien debe quitar los platos sucios de la mesa. También es necesario sacudir los muebles y pasar la aspiradora. La mesa y las sillas son muy bonitas, pero el comedor está muy sucio ahora.**
- Give students three minutes to look at the pictures and brainstorm possible answers before assigning pairs.

7 Suggestions
- Draw a map of a three-room apartment on the board. Ask volunteers to describe it.
- Have students draw their maps before you assign pairs. Make sure they understand the activity so that their maps do not become too complicated.

7 Expansion
- Have students make the suggested changes on their maps and repeat the activity again with a different partner.
- Have pairs repeat the activity, drawing maps of their real apartments.

8 Suggestion Divide the class into pairs and distribute the handouts from the Information Gap Activities Booklet that correspond to this activity. Give students ten minutes to complete this activity.

8 Expansion Have pairs tell each other about an occasion when they have had to clean up the house or apartment for a particular reason. Ask them to share their stories with the class.

TEACHING OPTIONS

Extra Practice Have students complete this cloze activity: **La vida doméstica de un estudiante universitario puede ser un desastre, ¿no? Nunca hay tiempo para hacer los ____ (quehaceres) domésticos. Sólo ____ (pasa) la aspiradora una vez al semestre y nunca ____ (sacude) los muebles. Los ____ (platos) sucios se acumulan en la ____ (cocina). Saca la ropa de la ____ (secadora) y se la pone sin ____ (planchar). Y, ¿por qué hacer la ____ (cama)? Se va a acostar en ella de nuevo este mismo día, ¿no?**

Game Have students bring in real estate ads. Ask teams of three to write a description of a property. Teams then take turns reading their descriptions aloud. Other teams guess the price. The team that guesses the amount closest to the real price, without going over, scores a point.

Section Goals

In **Fotonovela** students will:
- receive comprehensible input from free-flowing discourse
- learn functional phrases that preview lesson grammatical structures

Instructional Resources

WB/VM: Video Activities, pp. 217–218
***Fotonovela** DVD/Video (Start 01:04:59)*
***Fotonovela** Video CD-ROM*
*IRM: **Fotonovela** Translations, p. 125, Videoscript, p. 100 Interactive CD-ROM*

Video Recap: Lección 11

Before doing this **Fotonovela** section, review the previous one with this activity.

1. ¿Qué hace Álex con sus amigos todos los días? (hablan por teléfono Internet)

2. ¿Por qué sabe Inés mucho de mecánica? (trabajó en el taller de su tío)

3. ¿Qué problema tiene el autobús? (el alternador está quemado)

4. ¿Quién es el señor Fonseca? (un mecánico de Ibarra, amigo de don Francisco)

5. ¿Cómo va a ayudar el señor Fonseca? (va a arreglar el autobús allí mismo)

Video Synopsis

Don Francisco and the students go to the house where they will stay before their hike. The housekeeper shows the students around the house. Don Francisco tells the students to help with the chores, and he advises them that their guide for the hike will arrive at seven the next morning.

Suggestions

- Have your students guess what happens in this **Fotonovela** episode, based on its title and the video stills.
- Ask the class if this **Fotonovela** episode was what they expected, based on the predictions they made.

¡Les va a encantar la casa!

Don Francisco y los estudiantes llegan a Ibarra.

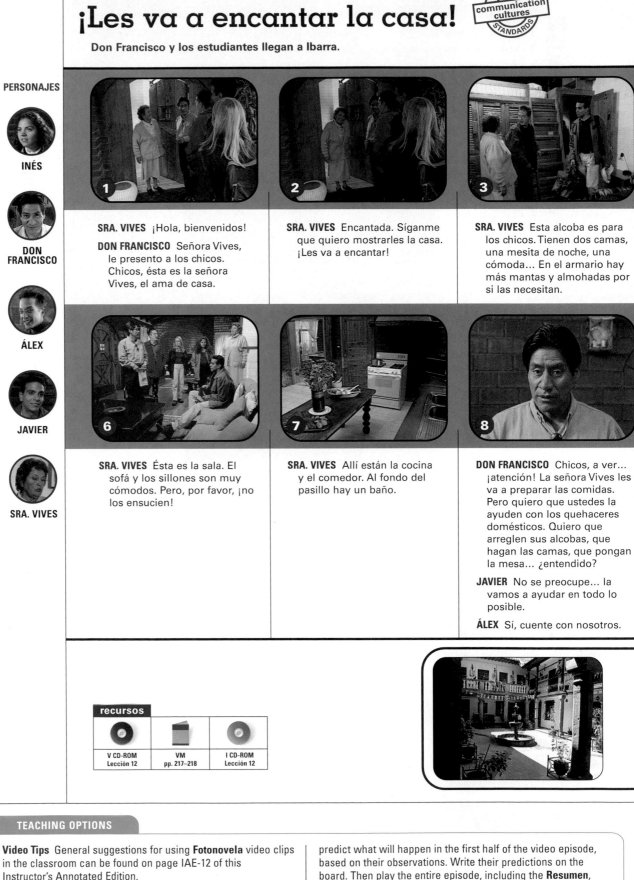

PERSONAJES

INÉS

DON FRANCISCO

ÁLEX

JAVIER

SRA. VIVES

1.
SRA. VIVES ¡Hola, bienvenidos!
DON FRANCISCO Señora Vives, le presento a los chicos. Chicos, ésta es la señora Vives, el ama de casa.

2.
SRA. VIVES Encantada. Síganme que quiero mostrarles la casa. ¡Les va a encantar!

3.
SRA. VIVES Esta alcoba es para los chicos. Tienen dos camas, una mesita de noche, una cómoda... En el armario hay más mantas y almohadas por si las necesitan.

6.
SRA. VIVES Ésta es la sala. El sofá y los sillones son muy cómodos. Pero, por favor, ¡no los ensucien!

7.
SRA. VIVES Allí están la cocina y el comedor. Al fondo del pasillo hay un baño.

8.
DON FRANCISCO Chicos, a ver... ¡atención! La señora Vives les va a preparar las comidas. Pero quiero que ustedes la ayuden con los quehaceres domésticos. Quiero que arreglen sus alcobas, que hagan las camas, que pongan la mesa... ¿entendido?
JAVIER No se preocupe... la vamos a ayudar en todo lo posible.
ÁLEX Sí, cuente con nosotros.

recursos

V CD-ROM	VM	I CD-ROM
Lección 12	pp. 217–218	Lección 12

TEACHING OPTIONS

Video Tips General suggestions for using **Fotonovela** video clips in the classroom can be found on page IAE-12 of this Instructor's Annotated Edition.
¡Les va a encantar la casa! Play the last half of the **Lección 12** video episode, except the **Resumen** segment. Have your students summarize what they see and hear. Then, have the class predict what will happen in the first half of the video episode, based on their observations. Write their predictions on the board. Then play the entire episode, including the **Resumen**, and, through discussion, guide the class to a correct summary of the plot.

SRA. VIVES Javier, no ponga las maletas en la cama. Póngalas en el piso, por favor.

SRA. VIVES Tomen ustedes esta alcoba, chicas.

INÉS Insistimos en que nos deje ayudarla a preparar la comida.

SRA. VIVES No, chicos, no es para tanto, pero gracias por la oferta. Descansen un rato que seguramente están cansados.

ÁLEX Gracias. A mí me gustaría pasear por la ciudad.

INÉS Perdone, don Francisco, ¿a qué hora viene el guía mañana?

DON FRANCISCO ¿Martín? Viene temprano, a las siete de la mañana. Les aconsejo que se acuesten temprano esta noche. ¡Nada de televisión ni de conversaciones largas!

ESTUDIANTES ¡Ay, don Francisco!

Enfoque cultural Las viviendas

Del mismo modo que en los países hispanos era típico construir las ciudades en torno a una plaza central, también era frecuente construir las casas alrededor de un patio abierto central. Aunque esta arquitectura tradicional ya no es muy común, la importancia del patio sigue intacta en la cultura hispana. No es extraño ver crecer árboles de mangos y de aguacates en los patios de las casas de los países tropicales de Latinoamérica. En el sur de España, los geranios y otras flores alegran los balcones y terrazas de las viviendas.

Expresiones útiles

Welcoming people
▶ ¡Bienvenido(s)/a(s)!
Welcome!

Showing people around the house
▶ Síganme... que quiero mostrarles la casa.
Follow me... I want to show you the house.
▶ Esta alcoba es para los chicos.
This bedroom is for the guys.
▶ Ésta es la sala.
This is the living room.
▶ Allí están la cocina y el comedor.
The kitchen and dining room are over there.
▶ Al fondo del pasillo hay un baño.
At the end of the hall there is a bathroom.

Telling people what to do
▶ Quiero que la ayude(n) con los quehaceres domésticos.
I want you to help her with the household chores.
▶ Quiero que arregle(n) su(s) alcoba(s).
I want you to straighten your room(s).
▶ Quiero que haga(n) las camas.
I want you to make the beds.
▶ Quiero que ponga(n) la mesa.
I want you to set the table.
▶ Cuente con nosotros.
You can count on us.
▶ Insistimos en que nos deje ayudarla a preparar la comida.
We insist that you let us help you make the food.
▶ Le (Les) aconsejo que se acueste(n) temprano.
I recommend that you go to bed early.

Other expressions
▶ No es para tanto.
It's not a big deal.
▶ Gracias por la oferta.
Thanks for the offer.

Suggestion Have the class read through the entire **Fotonovela**, with volunteers playing the various parts. You may want to point out the form **gustaría** in the caption under video still 9. Explain to students that it is the conditional of **gustar** and that they will learn more about it in **Estructura 15.1**. Tell them that **me gustaría** means *I'd like*.

Expresiones útiles Point out that the verbs **Síganme** and **Cuente** are command forms. Have the class guess which is an **usted** command and which is an **ustedes** command. Then point out the sentences that begin with **Quiero que...**, **Insistimos en que...**, and **Le(s) aconsejo que...**. Explain that these sentences are examples of the present subjunctive with verbs of will or influence. Write two or three of these sentences on the board. Point out that the main clause in each sentence contains a verb of will or influence, while the subordinate clause contains a verb in the present subjunctive. Tell your students that they will learn more about these concepts in **Estructura**.

The Affective Dimension Tell students that travelers in a foreign country may feel culture shock for a while. These feelings are normal and tend to diminish with time.

Enfoque cultural The "traditional" houses built around patios described here have ancient roots, going back to the style of houses built by the Romans. The traditional Spanish house made a very clear separation between the interior of the house, which was a private and protected space, and the street, which was public and exposed. Modern residents of large cities in Spanish-speaking countries often live in apartments, which may be rented but are sometimes owned by the occupants. Explain that the first floor (**planta baja**) of many multistory buildings is occupied by places of business, while the upper floors consist of apartments. Point out that it is not unusual for an apartment dweller in the United States or Canada to refer to his or her home as a house; explain that in Spanish-speaking countries, the word **casa** is often used in the same way.

Expansion Present these as items 6-7: 6. Álex quiere descansar. (Falso. Álex quiere pasear por la ciudad.) 7. Martín va a llegar mañana a las cuatro de la tarde. (Falso. Martín va a llegar a las siete de la mañana.)

Suggestion Have the class skim the **Fotonovela** on pages 332–333 before they begin this activity.

Expansion Write these additional items on the board: 6. Ésta es la alcoba de las chicas. (Sra. Vives) 7. El guía va a llegar a las siete de la mañana. (don Francisco) 8. ¿Quieren descansar un rato? (Sra. Vives) 9. Chicos, les presento a la señora Vives. (don Francisco)

Expansion Ask pairs to come up with lists of other household chores that can be done in each of the rooms. Have them share their answers with the class. Keep count of the items on their lists to find out which pair came up with the most correct possibilities.

Possible Response
E1: Quiero mostrarte mi casa. Ésta es la sala. Me gusta mirar la televisión allí. Aquí está la oficina. Allí hablo por teléfono y trabajo en la computadora. Éste es el garaje. Es donde tengo mis dos coches. Y aquí está la cocina, donde preparo las comidas. Quiero que me ayudes a sacudir los muebles y pasar la aspiradora.
E2: Está bien. Ahora quiero mostrarte mi apartamento....

Reacciona a la fotonovela

1 **¿Cierto o falso?** Indica si lo que dicen las siguientes frases es **cierto** o **falso**. Corrige las frases falsas.

	Cierto	Falso
1. Las alcobas de los estudiantes tienen dos camas, dos mesitas de noche y una cómoda. Tienen sólo una mesita de noche.	○	●
2. La señora Vives no quiere que Javier ponga las maletas en la cama.	●	○
3. El sofá y los sillones están en la sala.	●	○
4. Los estudiantes tienen que sacudir los muebles y sacar la basura. Tienen que arreglar las alcobas, hacer las camas y poner la mesa.	○	●
5. Los estudiantes van a preparar las comidas. La señora Vives va a preparar las comidas.	○	●

2 **Identificar** Identifica quién puede decir las siguientes frases.

1. Nos gustaría preparar la comida esta noche. ¿Le parece bien a usted? Inés
2. Miren, si quieren otra almohada o manta, hay más en el armario. Sra. Vives
3. Tranquilo, tranquilo, que nosotros vamos a ayudarla muchísimo. Javier
4. Tengo ganas de caminar un poco por la ciudad. Álex
5. No quiero que nadie mire la televisión esta noche. ¡Tenemos que levantarnos temprano mañana! don Francisco

ÁLEX   JAVIER   INÉS   DON FRANCISCO   SRA. VIVES

3 **Completar** Los estudiantes y la señora Vives están haciendo los quehaceres. Adivina en qué cuarto está cada uno de ellos.

1. Inés limpia el congelador. Inés está en __la cocina__.
2. Javier limpia el escritorio. Javier está en __la oficina__.
3. Álex pasa la aspiradora debajo de la mesa y las sillas. Álex está en __el comedor__.
4. La señora Vives sacude el sillón. La señora Vives está en __la sala__.
5. Don Francisco no está haciendo nada. Él está dormido en __el dormitorio/ la alcoba__.

4 **Mi casa** Dibuja el plano (*floor plan*) de una casa o de un apartamento. Puede ser el plano de la casa o del apartamento donde vives o de donde te gustaría vivir. Después, trabajen en parejas y describan lo que se hace en cuatro de las habitaciones. Para terminar, pídanse (*ask for*) ayuda para hacer dos quehaceres domésticos. Pueden usar estas frases en su conversación. Answers will vary.

> Al fondo hay...   Por favor, ayúdame con...
> Allí yo (preparo la comida).   Quiero mostrarte...
> Ésta es (la cocina).   Quiero que me ayudes a (sacar la basura).

TEACHING OPTIONS

TPR Have the class label various parts of the classroom with the names of rooms one would typically find in a house. Then have groups of three perform a skit in which the owner of the house is showing it to two inquisitive exchange students who are going to be spending the semester there. Give the groups time to prepare.

Game Have each of your students write a few sentences that one of the characters in this **Fotonovela** episode would say. They can look at the **Fotonovela** for ideas, but they should not copy sentences from it word for word. Then have each student read his or her sentences to the class. The class will guess which character would say those sentences.

Ortografía

Las mayúsculas y las minúsculas

Here are some of the rules that govern the use of capital letters (**mayúsculas**) and lowercase letters (**minúsculas**) in Spanish.

Los estudiantes llegaron al aeropuerto a las dos. Luego fueron al hotel.

In both Spanish and English, the first letter of every sentence is capitalized.

Rubén Blades   **Panamá**   **Colón**   **los Andes**

The first letter of all proper nouns (names of people, countries, cities, geographical features, etc.) is capitalized.

Cien años de soledad   *Don Quijote de la Mancha*
El País   *Muy Interesante*

The first letter of the first word in titles of books, films, and works of art is generally capitalized, as well as the first letter of any proper names. In newspaper and magazine titles, as well as other short titles, the initial letter of each word is often capitalized.

---

la señora Ramos   **don Francisco**
el presidente   **Sra. Vives**

Titles associated with people are *not* capitalized unless they appear as the first word in a sentence. Note, however, that the first letter of an abbreviated title is capitalized.

Último   **Álex**   **MENÚ**   **PERDÓN**

Accent marks should be retained on capital letters. In practice, however, this rule is often ignored.

---

lunes   **viernes**   **marzo**   **primavera**

The first letter of days, months, and seasons is not capitalized.

---

español   **estadounidense**   **japonés**   **panameños**

The first letter of nationalities and languages is not capitalized.

Práctica Corrige las mayúsculas y minúsculas incorrectas.

1. soy lourdes romero. Soy Colombiana.
   Soy Lourdes Romero. Soy colombiana.
2. éste Es mi Hermano álex.
   Éste es mi hermano Álex.
3. somos De panamá. Somos de Panamá.
4. ¿es ud. La sra. benavides?
   ¿Es Ud. la Sra. Benavides?
5. ud. Llegó el Lunes, ¿no?
   Ud. llegó el lunes, ¿no?

Palabras desordenadas Lee el diálogo de las serpientes. Ordena las letras para saber de qué palabras se trata. Después escribe las letras indicadas para descubrir por qué llora Pepito.

m n a a P á ⬭ ⬚ ⬚ ⬚ ⬚ ⬚

s t e m r a ⬭ ⬚ ⬚ ⬚ ⬚ ⬚

i g s l é n ⬚ ⬚ ⬭ ⬚ ⬚ ⬚

y a U r u g u ⬚ ⬚ ⬚ ⬭ ⬚ ⬚ ⬚

r o ñ e s a ⬚ ⬚ ⬚ ⬚ ⬚ ⬭

¡ ⬚orque ⬚⬚e acabo de morder° la ⬚ ⬚en ⬚u ⬚⬚!

venenosas *venomous*   morder *to bite*

¡Porque me acabo de morder la lengua!

Respuestas: Panamá, martes, inglés, Uruguay, señora.

Speech bubbles in illustrations:

Herrera, ¿que somos osas°?

Sí, Pepito. ¿Por qué lloras?

Section Goal

In **Ortografía** students will learn about the rules for capitalization in Spanish.

Instructional Resource
Interactive CD-ROM

Suggestions

- Explain that, in a few Spanish city and country names, the definite article is considered part of the name, and thus is capitalized. Ex: **La Habana, La Coruña, La Haya, El Salvador**
- Spanish treatment of titles of books, film, and works of art differs from English. In Spanish, only the first word and any proper noun gets an initial capital. Spanish treatment of the names of newspapers and magazines is the same as in English. Tell students that *El País* is a newspaper and *Muy Interesante* is a magazine. All the items mentioned are italicized in print.
- After going through the explanation, write example titles, names, sentences, etc., all in lower case, on the board. Then, ask pairs to decide which letters should be capitalized.
- Point out that **Ortografía** replaces **Pronunciación** in the Student Edition for **Lecciones 10–15**, but not in the Lab Manual. The **Recursos** box references the **Pronunciación** sections found in all lessons of the Lab Manual.

TEACHING OPTIONS

Pairs Have your students work in pairs to circle all the capital letters in the **Enfoque cultural** on page 333. Then have them explain why each of these letters is capitalized.

Extra Practice Give this sentence to the class as a dictation: **El doctor Guzmán, el amigo panameño de la señora Rivera, llegó a Quito el lunes doce de mayo.** Tell the class to abbreviate all titles. To allow your students time to write, read the sentence twice slowly and once at full speed.

12.1 Relative pronouns

NATIONAL comparisons STANDARDS

ANTE TODO In both English and Spanish, relative pronouns are used to combine two sentences or clauses that share a common element, such as a noun or pronoun. Study the following diagram.

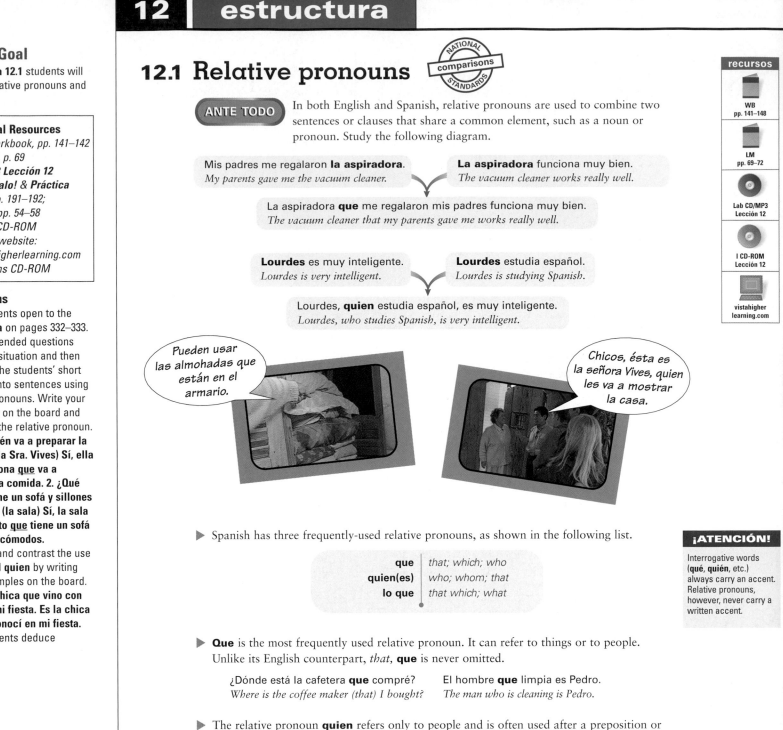

Mis padres me regalaron **la aspiradora**.
My parents gave me the vacuum cleaner.

La aspiradora funciona muy bien.
The vacuum cleaner works really well.

La aspiradora **que** me regalaron mis padres funciona muy bien.
The vacuum cleaner that my parents gave me works really well.

Lourdes es muy inteligente.
Lourdes is very intelligent.

Lourdes estudia español.
Lourdes is studying Spanish.

Lourdes, **quien** estudia español, es muy inteligente.
Lourdes, who studies Spanish, is very intelligent.

Pueden usar las almohadas que están en el armario.

Chicos, ésta es la señora Vives, quien les va a mostrar la casa.

▶ Spanish has three frequently-used relative pronouns, as shown in the following list.

que	*that; which; who*
quien(es)	*who; whom; that*
lo que	*that which; what*

¡ATENCIÓN!

Interrogative words (**qué**, **quién**, etc.) always carry an accent. Relative pronouns, however, never carry a written accent.

▶ **Que** is the most frequently used relative pronoun. It can refer to things or to people. Unlike its English counterpart, *that*, **que** is never omitted.

¿Dónde está la cafetera **que** compré?
Where is the coffee maker (that) I bought?

El hombre **que** limpia es Pedro.
The man who is cleaning is Pedro.

▶ The relative pronoun **quien** refers only to people and is often used after a preposition or the personal **a**. Note that **quien** has only two forms: **quien** (singular) and **quienes** (plural).

¿Son las chicas **de quienes** me hablaste la semana pasada?
Are they the girls (that) you told me about last week?

Eva, **a quien** conocí anoche, es mi nueva vecina.
Eva, whom I met last night, is my new neighbor.

Section Goal

In **Estructura 12.1** students will learn the relative pronouns and their use.

Instructional Resources
*WB/VM: Workbook, pp. 141–142
Lab Manual, p. 69
Lab CD/MP3 Lección 12
IRM: ¡Inténtalo! & Práctica
Answers, pp. 191–192;
Tapescript, pp. 54–58
Interactive CD-ROM
Companion website:
www.vistahigherlearning.com
Presentations CD-ROM*

Suggestions
• Have students open to the **Fotonovela** on pages 332–333. Ask open-ended questions about the situation and then rephrase the students' short answers into sentences using relative pronouns. Write your sentences on the board and underline the relative pronoun. Ex: **1. ¿Quién va a preparar la comida? (la Sra. Vives) Sí, ella es la persona que va a preparar la comida. 2. ¿Qué cuarto tiene un sofá y sillones cómodos? (la sala) Sí, la sala es el cuarto que tiene un sofá y sillones cómodos.**
• Compare and contrast the use of **que** and **quien** by writing some examples on the board. Ex: **Es la chica que vino con Carlos a mi fiesta. Es la chica a quien conocí en mi fiesta.** Have students deduce the rule.

TEACHING OPTIONS

Extra Practice Write these sentences on the board, and have students supply the correct relative pronoun:
1. Hay una escalera _____ sube al primer piso. (que)
2. Elena es la muchacha a _____ le presté la aspiradora. (quien)
3. ¿Dónde pusiste la ropa _____ acabas de quitarte? (que)
4. ¿Cuál es el señor a _____ le alquilas tu casa? (quien)

5. La cómoda _____ compramos la semana pasada está en el dormitorio de mi hermana. (que)
Heritage Speakers Have heritage speakers create descriptions of favorite gathering places in their home communities using complex sentences with relative pronouns. Possible sites might be the local parish, the town square, or a favorite park.

▶ **Quien(es)** is occasionally used instead of **que** in clauses set off by commas.

> Lola, **quien** es cubana, es médica.
> *Lola, who is Cuban, is a doctor.*

> Su tía, **que** es alemana, ya llegó.
> *His aunt, who is German, already arrived.*

▶ Unlike **que** and **quien(es)**, **lo que** doesn't refer to a specific noun. It refers to an idea, a situation, or a past event and means *what*, *that which*, or *the thing that*.

Este mercado tiene todo lo que Inés necesita.

A la señora Vives no le gustó lo que hizo Javier.

Lo que me molesta es el calor.
What bothers me is the heat.

Lo que quiero es una casa.
What I want is a house.

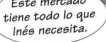**¡INTÉNTALO!** Completa las siguientes oraciones con pronombres relativos.

1. Voy a utilizar los platos _____que_____ me regaló mi abuela.
2. Ana comparte un apartamento con la chica a _____quien_____ conocimos en la fiesta de Jorge.
3. Esta oficina tiene todo _____lo que_____ necesitamos.
4. Puedes estudiar en el dormitorio _____que_____ está a la derecha de la cocina.
5. Los señores _____que_____ viven en esa casa acaban de llegar de Centroamérica.
6. Los niños a _____quienes_____ viste en nuestro jardín son mis sobrinos.
7. La piscina _____que_____ ves desde la ventana es la piscina de mis vecinos.
8. Fue Úrsula _____quien_____ ayudó a mamá a limpiar el refrigerador.
9. Ya te dije que fue mi padre _____quien_____ alquiló el apartamento.
10. _____Lo que_____ te dijo Pablo no es cierto.
11. Tengo que sacudir los muebles _____que_____ están en el altillo una vez al mes.
12. No entiendo por qué no lavaste los vasos _____que_____ están sucios.
13. La mujer a _____quien_____ saludaste vive en las afueras.
14. ¿Sabes _____lo que_____ necesita este dormitorio? ¡Unas cortinas!
15. No quiero volver a hacer _____lo que_____ hice ayer.
16. No me gusta vivir con personas a _____quienes_____ no conozco.

Práctica

1 **Combinar** Combina elementos de la columna A y la columna B para formar oraciones lógicas.

A	**B**
1. Ése es el hombre ___d___.	a. con quien bailaba es mi vecina
2. La mujer ___a___.	b. que te compró Cecilia
3. No traje ___e___.	c. quien canta mis canciones (*songs*) favoritas, es de Panamá
4. ¿Te gusta la tostadora ___b___?	d. que arregló mi lavadora
5. ¿Cómo se llama el programa ___g___?	e. lo que necesito para la clase de matemáticas
6. Rubén Blades, ___c___.	f. que comiste en el restaurante
	g. que viste en la televisión anoche

2 **Completar** Completa la historia sobre la casa que Jaime y Tina quieren comprar, usando los pronombres relativos **que, quien, quienes** o **lo que.**

1. Jaime y Tina son los chicos a ___quienes___ conocí la semana pasada.
2. Quieren comprar una casa ___que___ está en las afueras de la ciudad.
3. Es una casa ___que___ era de una artista famosa.
4. La artista, a ___quien___ yo conocía, murió el año pasado y no tenía hijos.
5. Ahora se vende la casa con todos los muebles ___que___ ella tenía.
6. La sala tiene una alfombra ___que___ ella trajo de Kuwait.
7. La casa tiene muchos estantes, ___lo que___ a Tina le encanta.

3 **Combinar** Javier y Ana acaban de casarse y han comprado una casa y muchas otras cosas. Combina sus declaraciones para formar una sola oración con los pronombres relativos **que, quien(es)** y **lo que.**

> **modelo**
> Vamos a usar los vasos nuevos mañana. Los pusimos en el comedor.
> *Mañana vamos a usar los vasos nuevos que pusimos en el comedor.*

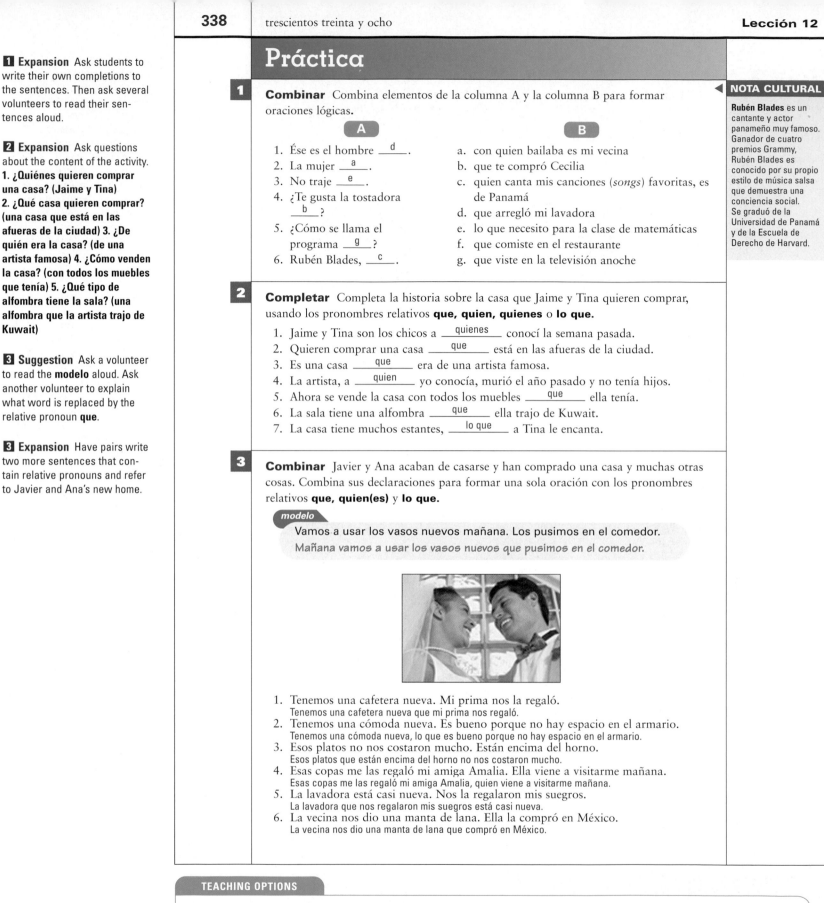

1. Tenemos una cafetera nueva. Mi prima nos la regaló.
   Tenemos una cafetera nueva que mi prima nos regaló.
2. Tenemos una cómoda nueva. Es bueno porque no hay espacio en el armario.
   Tenemos una cómoda nueva, lo que es bueno porque no hay espacio en el armario.
3. Esos platos no nos costaron mucho. Están encima del horno.
   Esos platos que están encima del horno no nos costaron mucho.
4. Esas copas me las regaló mi amiga Amalia. Ella viene a visitarme mañana.
   Esas copas me las regaló mi amiga Amalia, quien viene a visitarme mañana.
5. La lavadora está casi nueva. Nos la regalaron mis suegros.
   La lavadora que nos regalaron mis suegros está casi nueva.
6. La vecina nos dio una manta de lana. Ella la compró en México.
   La vecina nos dio una manta de lana que compró en México.

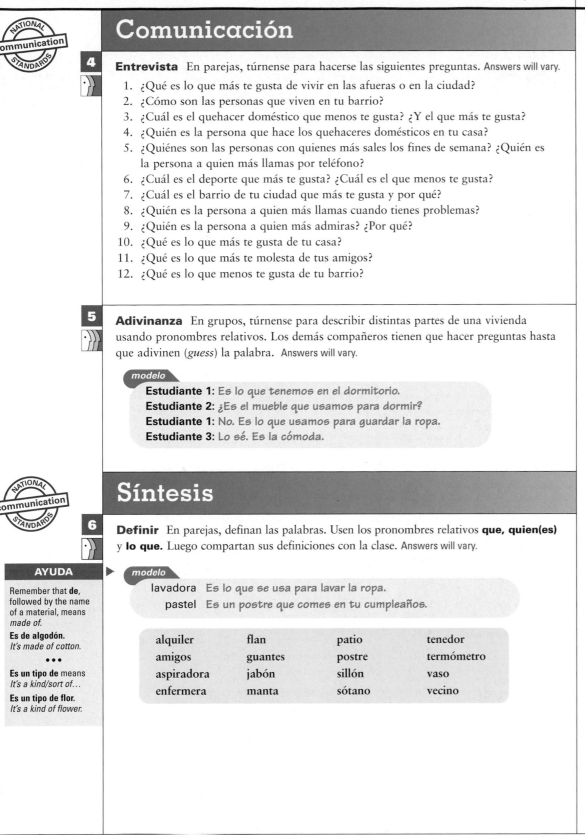

Comunicación

4 **Entrevista** En parejas, túrnense para hacerse las siguientes preguntas. Answers will vary.

1. ¿Qué es lo que más te gusta de vivir en las afueras o en la ciudad?
2. ¿Cómo son las personas que viven en tu barrio?
3. ¿Cuál es el quehacer doméstico que menos te gusta? ¿Y el que más te gusta?
4. ¿Quién es la persona que hace los quehaceres domésticos en tu casa?
5. ¿Quiénes son las personas con quienes más sales los fines de semana? ¿Quién es la persona a quien más llamas por teléfono?
6. ¿Cuál es el deporte que más te gusta? ¿Cuál es el que menos te gusta?
7. ¿Cuál es el barrio de tu ciudad que más te gusta y por qué?
8. ¿Quién es la persona a quien más llamas cuando tienes problemas?
9. ¿Quién es la persona a quien más admiras? ¿Por qué?
10. ¿Qué es lo que más te gusta de tu casa?
11. ¿Qué es lo que más te molesta de tus amigos?
12. ¿Qué es lo que menos te gusta de tu barrio?

5 **Adivinanza** En grupos, túrnense para describir distintas partes de una vivienda usando pronombres relativos. Los demás compañeros tienen que hacer preguntas hasta que adivinen (*guess*) la palabra. Answers will vary.

> **modelo**
> **Estudiante 1:** Es lo que tenemos en el dormitorio.
> **Estudiante 2:** ¿Es el mueble que usamos para dormir?
> **Estudiante 1:** No. Es lo que usamos para guardar la ropa.
> **Estudiante 3:** Lo sé. Es la cómoda.

Síntesis

6 **Definir** En parejas, definan las palabras. Usen los pronombres relativos **que, quien(es)** y **lo que.** Luego compartan sus definiciones con la clase. Answers will vary.

> **modelo**
> lavadora   Es lo que se usa para lavar la ropa.
> pastel   Es un postre que comes en tu cumpleaños.

alquiler	flan	patio	tenedor
amigos	guantes	postre	termómetro
aspiradora	jabón	sillón	vaso
enfermera	manta	sótano	vecino

4 Suggestion Have students take notes on the answers provided by their partners to use in expansion activities.

4 Expansion
• Have pairs team up to form groups of four. Each student will report on his or her partner, using the information obtained in the interview.
• Have pairs of students write four more questions modeled on the activity. Ask each pair to exchange its questions with another.

5 Expansion Have groups choose their three best **adivinanzas** and present them to the rest of the class.

6 Expansion Have pairs choose one of the items listed in the activity and develop a magazine ad. Their ad should include three sentences with relative pronouns.

TEACHING OPTIONS

Small Groups Have students bring in pictures of houses (exterior only). Have them work in groups of three to write a description of what they imagine the interiors to be like. Remind them to use relative pronouns in their descriptions.
Extra Practice For practice in listening comprehension, prepare short descriptions of five easily recognizable residences like the White House, Alcatraz prison, and Buckingham Palace. Write

their names on the board in random order. Then read your descriptions as a dictation, having students copy your description and match it to the appropriate name. Ex: **Es un castillo que está situado en una pequeña montaña cerca del Océano Pacífico de California. Lo construyó un norteamericano considerado bastante excéntrico. Es un sitio que visitan muchos turistas cada año.** (Hearst Castle)

Section Goals

In **Estructura 12.2** students will learn:
• formal commands
• use of object pronouns with formal commands

Instructional Resources
WB/VM: Workbook, pp. 143–144
Lab Manual, p. 70
*Lab CD/MP3 **Lección 12***
IRM: ¡Inténtalo! & Práctica
Answers, pp. 191–192;
Tapescript, pp. 54–58
Info Gap Activities Booklet,
pp. 47–48
Interactive CD-ROM
Companion website:
www.vistahigherlearning.com
Presentations CD-ROM

Suggestions

• Model the use of formal commands with simple examples using TPR and gestures. Ex: **Levántense. Siéntense.** Then point to individual students. Ex: _____ , **levántese.** Give other commands using **salga/salgan, vuelva/vuelvan,** and **venga/vengan.**

• Write these sentences on the board, contrasting their meaning with the examples in the text: **Habla con ellos. Come frutas y verduras. Lavan los platos ahora mismo. Beben menos té y café.**

• Consolidate by having volunteers give the command forms for other verbs, such as **alquilar, correr,** or **imprimir.**

12.2 Formal commands

ANTE TODO As you learned in **Lección 11**, the command forms are used to give orders or advice. Formal commands are used with people you address as **usted** or **ustedes.** Observe the following examples, then study the chart.

Hable con ellos, don Francisco.
Talk with them, don Francisco.

Laven los platos ahora mismo.
Wash the dishes right now.

Coma frutas y verduras.
Eat fruits and vegetables.

Beban menos té y café.
Drink less tea and coffee.

CONSEJOS

Learning these command forms will be very helpful since the same forms are used for the subjunctive, which you will begin learning in the next section.

Formal commands (*Ud.* and *Uds.*)

Infinitive	Present tense *yo* form	*Ud.* command	*Uds.* command
limpiar	limpi**o**	limpi**e**	limpi**en**
barrer	barr**o**	barr**a**	barr**an**
sacudir	sacud**o**	sacud**a**	sacud**an**
decir (e:i)	dig**o**	dig**a**	dig**an**
pensar (e:ie)	piens**o**	piens**e**	piens**en**
volver (o:ue)	vuelv**o**	vuelv**a**	vuelv**an**
servir (e:i)	sirv**o**	sirv**a**	sirv**an**

▶ The **Ud.** and **Uds.** commands, like the negative **tú** commands, are formed by dropping the final **–o** of the **yo** form of the present tense. For **–ar** verbs, add **–e** or **–en**. For **–er** and **–ir** verbs, add **–a** or **–an**.

No se preocupe… La vamos a ayudar en todo lo posible.

Sí, cuente con nosotros.

▶ Verbs with irregular **yo** forms maintain the same irregularity in their formal commands. These verbs include **conducir, conocer, decir, hacer, ofrecer, oír, poner, salir, tener, traducir, traer, venir,** and **ver.**

Oiga, don Francisco…
Listen, don Francisco…

Ponga la mesa, por favor.
Set the table, please.

¡Salgan inmediatamente!
Leave immediately!

Hagan la cama antes de salir.
Make the bed before leaving.

▶ Note also that stem-changing verbs maintain their stem-changes in **Ud.** and **Uds.** commands.

e:ie	o:ue	e:i

No **pierda** la llave.
Cierren la puerta.

Vuelva temprano, joven.
Duerman bien, chicos.

Sirva la sopa, por favor.
Repitan las frases.

TEACHING OPTIONS

Video Replay the **Fotonovela** video segment, having students focus on formal commands. Ask them to write down each formal command that they hear. Then form groups of three and have students compare their lists.

TPR Have students stand. Using the verbs presented in the discussion of formal commands, give commands at random (Ex: **Barra el suelo. Lave los platos. Sacuda los muebles.**) and point to a student who should perform the appropriate gesture. Keep the pace rapid. Vary by calling out names of more than one student. (Ex: **Pongan la mesa. Hagan la cama.**)

▶ Verbs ending in **-car, -gar,** and **-zar** have a spelling change in the command forms.

sa**car**	**c** → **qu**	sa**qu**e, sa**qu**en
ju**gar**	**g** → **gu**	jue**gu**e, jue**gu**en
almor**zar**	**z** → **c**	almuer**c**e, almuer**c**en

▶ The following verbs have irregular formal commands.

Infinitive	Ud. command	Uds. command
dar	**dé**	**den**
estar	**esté**	**estén**
ir	**vaya**	**vayan**
saber	**sepa**	**sepan**
ser	**sea**	**sean**

▶ To make a formal command negative, simply place **no** before the verb.

No ponga las maletas en la cama.   **No ensucien** los sillones.
Don't put the suitcases on the bed.   *Don't dirty the armchairs.*

▶ In affirmative commands, reflexive, indirect, and direct object pronouns are always attached to the end of the verb.

Siénten**se**, por favor.   Acuésten**se** ahora.
Síga**me,** Laura.   Pónga**las** en el suelo, por favor.

▶ In negative commands, these pronouns always precede the verb.

No **se** preocupe.   No **los** ensucien.
No **me lo** dé.   No **nos las** traigan.

▶ **Ud.** and **Uds.** can be used with the command forms to strike a more formal tone. In such instances they follow the command form.

Muéstrele usted la foto a su amigo.   **Tomen ustedes** esta alcoba.
Show the photo to your friend.   *Take this bedroom.*

¡INTÉNTALO!   Indica cuáles son los mandatos afirmativos y negativos correspondientes.

1. escucharlo (Ud.) ___Escúchelo___. ___No lo escuche___.
2. decírmelo (Uds.) ___Díganmelo___. ___No me lo digan___.
3. salir (Ud.) ___Salga___. ___No salga___.
4. servírnoslo (Uds.) ___Sírvannoslo___. ___No nos lo sirvan___.
5. barrerla (Ud.) ___Bárrala___. ___No la barra___.
6. hacerlo (Ud.) ___Hágalo___. ___No lo haga___.
7. ir (Uds.) ___Vayan___. ___No vayan___.
8. sentarse (Uds.) ___Siéntense___. ___No se sienten___.

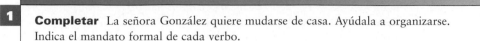

Práctica

1 **Completar** La señora González quiere mudarse de casa. Ayúdala a organizarse. Indica el mandato formal de cada verbo.

1. __Lea__ los anuncios (*ads*) del periódico y __guárdelos__. (leer, guardar)
2. __Vaya__ personalmente y __vea__ las casas usted misma. (ir, ver)
3. Decida qué casa quiere y __llame__ al agente. __Pídale__ un contrato de alquiler. (llamar, pedirle)
4. __Contrate__ un camión (*truck*) para ese día y __pregúnteles__ la hora exacta de llegada. (contratar, preguntarles)
5. El día de la mudanza (*On moving day*) __esté__ tranquila. __Vuelva__ a revisar su lista para completar todo lo que tiene que hacer. (estar, volver)
6. Primero, __dígales__ a todos en casa que usted va a estar ocupada. No __les diga__ que usted va a hacerlo todo. (decirles, decirles)
7. __Saque__ la ropa con tiempo para hacer las maletas tranquilamente. No __les haga__ las maletas a sus hijos. (sacar, hacerles)
8. No __se preocupe__. __Sepa__ que todo va a salir bien. (preocuparse, saber)

2 **¿Qué dicen?** Mira los dibujos y escribe un mandato lógico para cada uno. Usa palabras que aprendiste en **Contextos**. Answers will vary; suggested answers below.

1. __Abran sus libros, por favor.__

2. __Cierre la puerta. ¡Hace frío!__

3. __Traiga usted la cuenta, por favor.__

4. __La cocina está sucia. Bárranla, por favor.__

5. __Duerma bien, niña.__

6. __Arreglen el cuarto, por favor. Está desordenado.__

Comunicación

3 Solucionar Trabajen en parejas para presentar los siguientes problemas. Un(a) estudiante presenta los problemas de la columna A y el/la otro/a los de la columna B. Usen mandatos formales y túrnense para ofrecer soluciones. Answers will vary.

> **modelo**
>
> **Estudiante 1:** Vilma se torció un tobillo jugando al tenis. Es la tercera vez.
> **Estudiante 2:** No juegue más al tenis. / Vaya a ver a un especialista.

A

1. Se me perdió el libro de español con todas mis notas.
2. A Vicente se le cayó la botella de vino para la cena.
3. ¿Cómo? ¿Se le olvidó traer el traje de baño a la playa?
4. Se nos quedaron los pasajes en la casa. El avión sale en una hora.

B

1. Mis hijas no se levantan temprano. Siempre llegan tarde a la escuela.
2. A mi abuela le robaron (*stole*) las maletas. Era su primer día de vacaciones.
3. Nuestra casa es demasiado pequeña para nuestra familia.
4. Me preocupo constantemente por Roberto. Trabaja demasiado.

4 Conversaciones En parejas, escojan dos situaciones y preparen conversaciones para presentar a la clase. Usen mandatos formales. Answers will vary.

> **modelo**
>
> **Lupita:** Señor Ramírez, siento mucho llegar tan tarde. Mi niño se enfermó. ¿Qué debo hacer?
> **Sr. Ramírez:** No se preocupe. Siéntese y descanse un poco.

SITUACIÓN 1 Profesor Rosado, no vine la semana pasada porque el equipo jugaba en Boquete. ¿Qué debo hacer para ponerme al día (*catch up*)?

SITUACIÓN 2 Los invitados de la boda llegan a las cuatro de la tarde, la mesa está sin poner y el champán sin servir. Los camareros apenas están llegando. ¿Qué deben hacer los camareros?

SITUACIÓN 3 Mi novio es un poco aburrido. No le gustan ni el cine, ni los deportes, ni salir a comer. Tampoco habla mucho. ¿Qué puedo hacer o qué le puedo decir?

SITUACIÓN 4 Tengo que preparar una presentación para mañana sobre el Canal de Panamá. ¿Por dónde comienzo?

NOTA CULTURAL

El 31 de diciembre de 1999, los Estados Unidos cedió control del **Canal de Panamá** al gobierno de Panamá, terminando así casi 100 años de administración estadounidense.

Síntesis

5 Presentar En grupos, preparen un anuncio (*ad*) de televisión para presentar a la clase. El anuncio debe tratar de (*be about*) un detergente, un electrodoméstico, o una agencia inmobiliaria (*real estate agency*). Usen mandatos, los pronombres relativos **(que, quien(es)** o **lo que)** y el **se** impersonal. Answers will vary.

> **modelo**
>
> Compre el lavaplatos Siglo XXI. Tiene todo lo que usted desea. Es el lavaplatos que mejor funciona. Venga a verlo ahora mismo... No pierda ni un minuto más. Se aceptan tarjetas de crédito.

Sidebar (right column):

3 Suggestion Ask volunteers to offer other suggestions for the problem in the **modelo**. Ex: **Tenga usted más cuidado. Compre nuevos zapatos de tenis.**

3 Expansion Ask pairs to pick their most humorous or unusual response to present to the class.

4 Expansion Have pairs write another scenario on a sheet of paper. Then ask them to exchange papers with another pair and give them two minutes to prepare another dialogue. Have them act out their dialogues for the authors.

5 Suggestion Divide the class into small groups. Have them choose a product or business and brainstorm positive attributes that they want to advertise.

5 Expansion
- Ask groups to share their commercials with the class.
- Have groups videotape their ads outside of class. Encourage them to be creative.

The Affective Dimension
Students may feel more comfortable speaking if they assume the personae of celebrity endorsers when presenting the television commercial.

Suggestion See the Information Gap Activities Booklet for an additional activity to practice the material presented in this section.

TEACHING OPTIONS

Heritage Speakers Have heritage speakers write a description of a household item commonly found in their homes, but not typically in other communities. Ex: **comal, molcajete, cafetera exprés, paellera,** and so forth. Have them read their descriptions to the class. Then, have them use formal commands to share with the class a recipe that calls for using one of the items described.

Pairs Have pairs of students write a series of commands for a famous sports figure. Ex: (John McEnroe) **No se enoje. Tenga paciencia. Escuche a los árbitros. No tire la raqueta.**

Section Goals

In **Estructura 12.3** students will learn:
- present subjunctive of regular verbs
- present subjunctive of stem-changing verbs
- irregular verbs in the present subjunctive

Instructional Resources

WB/VM: Workbook, pp. 145–146
Lab Manual, p. 71
*Lab CD/MP3 **Lección 12***
*IRM: ¡**Inténtalo!** & **Práctica***
Answers, pp. 191–192;
Tapescript, pp. 54–58
Interactive CD-ROM
Companion website:
www.vistahigherlearning.com
Presentations CD-ROM

Suggestions

- Write sentences like these on the board in two columns labeled *Indicative* and *Subjunctive*. Column 1: **1. Mi esposo lava los platos. 2. Mi esposo barre el suelo. 3. Mi esposo cocina.** Column 2: **1. Mi esposo quiere que yo lave los platos. 2. Mi esposo quiere que yo barra el suelo. 3. Mi esposo quiere que yo cocine.** Underline **yo lave**, asking students what the indicative form would be. Do the same for the other sentences.
- Check for understanding by asking volunteers to give subjunctive forms of other regular verbs from this lesson such as **planchar, barrer,** and **sacudir**.

12.3 The present subjunctive

ANTE TODO With the exception of commands, all of the verb forms you have been using have been in the indicative mood. The indicative is used to state facts and to express actions or states that the speaker considers to be real and definite. In contrast, the subjunctive mood expresses the speaker's attitudes toward events, as well as actions or states the speaker views as uncertain or hypothetical.

Quiero que ustedes ayuden con los quehaceres domésticos.

Insistimos en que nos deje ayudarla a preparar la comida.

Present subjunctive of regular verbs

		hablar	comer	escribir
SINGULAR FORMS	yo	habl**e**	com**a**	escrib**a**
	tú	habl**es**	com**as**	escrib**as**
	Ud./él/ella	habl**e**	com**a**	escrib**a**
PLURAL FORMS	nosotros/as	habl**emos**	com**amos**	escrib**amos**
	vosotros/as	habl**éis**	com**áis**	escrib**áis**
	Uds./ellos/ellas	habl**en**	com**an**	escrib**an**

▶ The present subjunctive is formed very much like **usted** and **ustedes** and *negative* **tú** commands. From the **yo** form of the present indicative, drop the **-o** ending, and replace it with the subjunctive endings.

INFINITIVE	PRESENT INDICATIVE	VERB STEM	PRESENT SUBJUNCTIVE
hablar	**hablo**	**habl-**	**hable**
comer	**como**	**com-**	**coma**
escribir	**escribo**	**escrib-**	**escriba**

▶ The present subjunctive endings are:

–ar verbs

–e	–emos
–es	–éis
–e	–en

–er and –ir verbs

–a	–amos
–as	–áis
–a	–an

¡LENGUA VIVA!

You may think that English has no subjunctive, but it does! It used to be very common but now survives mostly in set expressions such as *if I were you* and *be that as it may.*

CONSEJOS

Note that, in the present subjunctive, **–ar** verbs use endings normally associated with present tense **–er** and **–ir** verbs and vice versa. Note also that the **yo** form is the same as the **Ud./él/ella** form.

TEACHING OPTIONS

Large Group You will need a ball (or balled-up piece of paper) for this activity. Have students arrange their chairs in a circle. Then say an infinitive of a regular verb and a subject pronoun. Ex: **alquilar / nosotros**. Throw the ball to a student. He or she must provide the correct subjunctive form (**alquilemos**).

Extra Practice Create sentences that use the subjunctive. Say the sentence, and have students repeat. Then call out a different subject for the subordinate clause. Have students then say the sentence with the new subject, making all other necessary changes. Ex: **Quiero que ustedes trabajen mucho. Javier. (Quiero que Javier trabaje mucho.) Quiero que lleguen temprano. Nosotras. (Quiero que lleguemos temprano.)**

Suggestions
- It may be helpful for students to be aware of how English uses the subjunctive mood. Ex: *I wish she were here. I insist that he take notes. I suggest you be there tomorrow. If it were me, I would be happy. Be that as it may . . . .*
- Emphasize the stem changes that occur in the **nosotros/as** and **vosotros/as** forms of –ir stem-changing verbs.

▶ Verbs with irregular **yo** forms show the same irregularity in all forms of the present subjunctive.

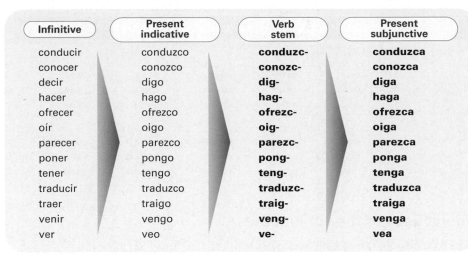

Infinitive	Present indicative	Verb stem	Present subjunctive
conducir	conduzco	conduzc-	conduzca
conocer	conozco	conozc-	conozca
decir	digo	dig-	diga
hacer	hago	hag-	haga
ofrecer	ofrezco	ofrezc-	ofrezca
oír	oigo	oig-	oiga
parecer	parezco	parezc-	parezca
poner	pongo	pong-	ponga
tener	tengo	teng-	tenga
traducir	traduzco	traduzc-	traduzca
traer	traigo	traig-	traiga
venir	vengo	veng-	venga
ver	veo	ve-	vea

▶ Verbs ending in **-car, -gar,** and **-zar** have a spelling change in all forms of the present subjunctive.

sacar:	sa**qu**e, sa**qu**es, sa**qu**e, sa**qu**emos, sa**qu**éis, sa**qu**en
jugar:	jue**gu**e, jue**gu**es, jue**gu**e, ju**gu**emos, ju**gu**éis, jue**gu**en
almorzar:	almuer**c**e, almuer**c**es, almuer**c**e, almor**c**emos, almor**c**éis, almuer**c**en

Present subjunctive of stem-changing verbs

¡ATENCIÓN!

Note that stem-changing verbs and verbs that have a spelling change have the same ending as regular verbs in the present subjunctive.

▶ **-Ar** and **-er** stem-changing verbs have the same stem changes in the subjunctive as they do in the present indicative.

pensar (e:ie):	p**ie**nse, p**ie**nses, p**ie**nse, pensemos, penséis, p**ie**nsen
mostrar (o:ue):	m**ue**stre, m**ue**stres, m**ue**stre, mostremos, mostréis, m**ue**stren
entender (e:ie):	ent**ie**nda, ent**ie**ndas, ent**ie**nda, entendamos, entendáis, ent**ie**ndan
volver (o:ue):	v**ue**lva, v**ue**lvas, v**ue**lva, volvamos, volváis, v**ue**lvan

▶ **–Ir** stem-changing verbs have the same stem changes in the subjunctive as they do in the present indicative, but in addition, the **nosotros/as** and **vosotros/as** forms undergo a stem change. The unstressed **e** changes to **i,** while the unstressed **o** changes to **u.**

pedir (e:i):	p**i**da, p**i**das, p**i**da, p**i**damos, p**i**dáis, p**i**dan
sentir (e:ie):	s**ie**nta, s**ie**ntas, s**ie**nta, s**i**ntamos, s**i**ntáis, s**ie**ntan
dormir (o:ue):	d**ue**rma, d**ue**rmas, d**ue**rma, d**u**rmamos, d**u**rmáis, d**ue**rman

TEACHING OPTIONS

Pairs Have pairs of students role-play landlord/landlady and new resident. Students should refer to the **Fotonovela** as a model. Give pairs sufficient time to plan and practice. When all pairs have completed the activity, ask a few of them to introduce their characters and perform the conversation for the whole class.

Extra practice Ask students to compare family members' attitudes toward domestic life using the subjunctive. Ex: **Los padres quieren que los hijos... Los hijos insisten en que...** Their comparative study should reflect values in their communities.

Irregular verbs in the present subjunctive

▶ The following five verbs are irregular in the present subjunctive.

Irregular verbs in the present subjunctive

		dar	estar	ir	saber	ser
SINGULAR FORMS	yo	dé	esté	vaya	sepa	sea
	tú	des	estés	vayas	sepas	seas
	Ud./él/ella	dé	esté	vaya	sepa	sea
PLURAL FORMS	nosotros/as	demos	estemos	vayamos	sepamos	seamos
	vosotros/as	deis	estéis	vayáis	sepáis	seáis
	Uds./ellos/ellas	den	estén	vayan	sepan	sean

General uses of the subjunctive

▶ The subjunctive is mainly used to express: 1) will and influence, 2) emotion, 3) doubt, disbelief, and denial, and 4) indefiniteness and nonexistence.

▶ The subjunctive is most often used in sentences that consist of a main clause and a subordinate clause. The main clause contains a verb or expression that triggers the use of the subjunctive. The conjunction **que** connects the subordinate clause to the main clause.

Main clause	Connector	Subordinate clause
Es muy importante	que	**vayas** al hotel ahora mismo.

▶ These impersonal expressions are always followed by clauses in the subjunctive:

Es bueno que...	**Es malo que...**	**Es necesario que...**
It's good that...	_It's bad that..._	_It's necessary that..._
Es importante que...	**Es mejor que...**	**Es urgente que...**
It's important that...	_It's better that..._	_It's urgent that..._

¡INTÉNTALO!   Indica el presente de subjuntivo de los siguientes verbos.

1. (alquilar, beber, vivir)   que yo _____ alquile, beba, viva
2. (estudiar, aprender, asistir)   que tú _____ estudies, aprendas, asistas
3. (encontrar, poder, dormir)   que él _____ encuentre, pueda, duerma
4. (hacer, tener, venir)   que nosotras _____ hagamos, tengamos, vengamos
5. (dar, hablar, escribir)   que ellos _____ den, hablen, escriban
6. (pagar, empezar, buscar)   que ustedes _____ paguen, empiecen, busquen
7. (ser, ir, saber)   que yo _____ sea, vaya, sepa
8. (estar, dar, oír)   que tú _____ estés, des, oigas
9. (arreglar, leer, abrir)   que nosotros _____ arreglemos, leamos, abramos
10. (cantar, leer, vivir)   que ellas _____ canten, lean, vivan

Práctica

1 **Completar** Completa las oraciones conjugando los verbos entre paréntesis. Luego empareja las oraciones del primer grupo con las del segundo grupo.

 **A**

1. Es mejor que ____cenemos____ en casa. (nosotros, cenar) b
2. Es importante que ____visites____ las casas colgantes de Cuenca. (tú, visitar) c
3. Señora, es urgente que le ____saque____ la muela. Parece que tiene una infección. (yo, sacar) e
4. Es malo que Ana les ____dé____ tantos dulces a los niños. (dar) a
5. Es necesario que ____lleguen____ a la una de la tarde. (ustedes, llegar) f
6. Es importante que ____nos acostemos____ temprano. (nosotros, acostarse) d

B

a. Es importante que ____coman____ más verduras. (ellos, comer)
b. No, es mejor que ____salgamos____ a comer a un restaurante. (nosotros, salir)
c. Y yo creo que es bueno que ____vaya____ a Madrid después. (yo, ir)
d. En mi opinión, no es necesario que ____durmamos____ tanto. (nosotros, dormir)
e. ¿Ah, sí? ¿Es necesario que me ____tome____ un antibiótico también? (yo, tomar)
f. Para llegar a tiempo, es necesario que ____almorcemos____ temprano. (nosotros, almorzar)

NOTA CULTURAL

Las casas colgantes (*hanging*) de Cuenca, España, son muy famosas. Estas casas están situadas en un acantilado (*cliff*) y forman parte del paisaje (*landscape*) de la ciudad.

Comunicación

2 **Minidiálogos** En parejas, completen los minidiálogos con expresiones impersonales de una manera lógica. Answers will vary.

> **modelo**
> **Miguelito:** Mamá, no quiero arreglar mi cuarto.
> **Señora Casas:** Es necesario que lo arregles. Y es importante que sacudas los muebles también.

1. **MIGUELITO** Mamá, no quiero estudiar. Quiero salir a jugar con mis amigos.
   SRA. CASAS _____

2. **MIGUELITO** Mamá, es que no me gustan las verduras. Prefiero comer pasteles.
   SRA. CASAS _____

3. **MIGUELITO** ¿Tengo que poner la mesa, mamá?
   SRA. CASAS _____

4. **MIGUELITO** No me siento bien, mamá. Me duele todo el cuerpo y tengo fiebre.
   SRA. CASAS _____

3 **Entrevista** Trabajen en parejas. Entrevístense usando estas preguntas. Expliquen sus respuestas. Answers will vary.

1. ¿Es importante que los niños ayuden con los quehaceres domésticos?
2. ¿Es urgente que los norteamericanos aprendan otras lenguas?
3. Si un(a) norteamericano/a quiere aprender francés, ¿es mejor que lo aprenda en Francia?
4. En su universidad, ¿es necesario que los estudiantes vivan en residencias estudiantiles?
5. ¿Es importante que todos los estudiantes asistan a la universidad?

---

1 **Expansion** After students have paired the sentences from each group, have them continue a couple of the short conversations with two more sentences using the subjunctive. Ex: **No es posible que encontremos un restaurante con mesas libres a las siete. Es mejor que salgamos ahora mismo para no tener ese problema.**

2 **Expansion**
- Ask volunteers to share their mini-dialogues with the rest of the class.
- Ask questions about Miguelito and Señora Casas using the subjunctive. Ex: **¿En qué insiste la señora Casas? (Insiste en que Miguelito arregle su cuarto; coma verduras; ponga la mesa.) ¿Qué quiere Miguelito? (Quiere salir a jugar; comer pasteles.)**

3 **Expansion** Ask students to report on their partners' answers using complete sentences and explanations. Ex: **¿Qué opina ____ sobre los quehaceres de los niños? ¿Cree que es importante que ayuden?**

Heritage Speakers Have heritage speakers write ten sentences comparing mainstream social practices with those of their cultural communities. Ex: **Aquí, es correcto que una señora le extienda la mano a un caballero. En nuestra cultura se considera mala educación que un caballero no le extienda la mano a una señora primero.**

Small Groups Divide the class into groups of four. Assign each group one of the following personal characteristics: **apariencia física; dinero; inteligencia; personalidad.** Have groups use the subjunctive to write sentences about the importance or unimportance of this trait for certain individuals. Ex: **Para ser presidente es importante que una persona sea inteligente.**

Section Goals

In **Estructura 12.4** students will learn:
• the subjunctive with verbs and expressions of will and influence
• common verbs of will and influence

Instructional Resources
Transparency #47
WB/VM: Workbook, pp. 147–148
Lab Manual, p. 72
Lab CD/MP3 Lección 12
IRM: ¡Inténtalo! & Práctica
Answers, pp. 191–192;
Tapescript, pp. 54–58
Interactive CD-ROM
Companion website:
www.vistahigherlearning.com
Presentations CD-ROM

Suggestions

• Write the word **Recomenda-ciones** on the board. Ask volunteers for household tips and write them on the board in the infinitive with the student's name in parentheses. Ex: **Hacer todos los quehaceres los sábados** (Paul) **Lavar los platos en el lavaplatos** (Sara). When you have approximately ten suggestions, begin rephrasing them using verbs of will and influence with subordinate clauses. Ex: **Paul nos aconseja que hagamos todos los quehaceres los sábados. Sara recomienda que lavemos los platos en el lavaplatos.** After you have modeled several responses, ask volunteers to continue. Give them cues such as:
¿Qué sugiere _____ ?
• Go through the lists of verbs of will and influence and impersonal expressions that generally take the subjunctive, giving examples of their use and asking volunteers for others.
• Have a volunteer read the advertisement for Dentabrit and explain what the subject of each clause is.

12.4 Subjunctive with verbs of will and influence

ANTE TODO You will now learn how to use the subjunctive with verbs and expressions of will and influence.

Quiero que tengas dientes más blancos.

▶ Verbs of will and influence are often used when someone wants to affect the actions or behavior of other people.

Enrique **quiere** que salgamos a cenar.
Enrique wants us to go out to dinner.

Paola **prefiere** que cenemos en casa.
Paola prefers that we have dinner at home.

▶ Here is a list of widely used verbs of will and influence.

	Verbs of will and influence		
aconsejar	*to advise*	**pedir** (e:i)	*to ask (for)*
desear	*to wish; to desire*	**preferir** (e:ie)	*to prefer*
importar	*to be important; to matter*	**prohibir**	*to prohibit*
		querer (e:ie)	*to want*
insistir (en)	*to insist (on)*	**recomendar** (e:ie)	*to recommend*
mandar	*to order*	**rogar** (o:ue)	*to beg; to plead*
necesitar	*to need*	**sugerir** (e:ie)	*to suggest*

▶ Some impersonal expressions, such as **es necesario que, es importante que, es mejor que,** and **es urgente que,** are considered expressions of will or influence.

▶ When the main clause contains an expression of will or influence, the subjunctive is required in the subordinate clause, provided that the two clauses have different subjects.

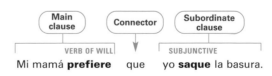

Mi mamá **prefiere**   que   yo **saque** la basura.

TEACHING OPTIONS

Small Groups Have groups of three write nine sentences, each of which uses a different verb of will and influence with the subjunctive. Ask volunteers to write some of their group's best sentences on the board. Work with the whole class to read the sentences and correct any errors.
Extra Practice Have students finish the following incomplete sentences. **1. Yo insisto en que mis amigos… 2. No quiero que**

mi familia… **3. Para mí es importante que el amor… 4. Prefiero que mi residencia… 5. Mi novio/a no quiere que yo… 6. Los profesores siempre recomiendan a los estudiantes que… 7. El doctor sugiere que nosotros… 8. Mi madre me ruega que… 9. El policía manda que los estudiantes… 10. El fotógrafo prefiere que nosotras…**

Quiero que arreglen sus alcobas, que hagan las camas, que pongan la mesa...

...y les aconsejo que se acuesten temprano esta noche.

▶ Indirect object pronouns are often used with the verbs **aconsejar, importar, mandar, pedir, prohibir, recomendar, rogar,** and **sugerir.**

Te aconsejo que estudies.
I advise you to study.

Le sugiero que vaya a casa.
I suggest that he go home.

Les recomiendo que barran el suelo.
I recommend that you sweep the floor.

Le ruego que no venga.
I beg him not to come.

▶ Note that all the forms of **prohibir** in the present tense carry a written accent, except for the **nosotros** form: **prohíbo, prohíbes, prohíbe, prohibimos, prohibís, prohíben.**

Ella les **prohíbe** que miren la televisión.
She prohibits them from watching television.

Nos **prohíben** que nademos en la piscina.
They prohibit that we swim in the pool.

▶ The infinitive is used with words or expressions of will and influence, if there is no change of subject in the sentence.

No quiero **sacudir** los muebles.
I don't want to dust the furniture.

Paco prefiere **descansar.**
Paco prefers to rest.

Es importante **sacar** la basura.
It's important to take out the trash.

No es necesario **quitar** la mesa.
It's not necessary to clear the table.

¡INTÉNTALO! Completa cada oración con la forma correcta del verbo entre paréntesis.

1. Te sugiero que ___vayas___ (ir) con ella al supermercado.
2. Él necesita que yo le ___preste___ (prestar) dinero.
3. No queremos que tú ___hagas___ (hacer) nada especial para nosotros.
4. Mis papás quieren que yo ___limpie___ (limpiar) mi cuarto.
5. Nos piden que la ___ayudemos___ (ayudar) a preparar la comida.
6. Quieren que tú ___saques___ (sacar) la basura todos los días.
7. Quiero ___descansar___ (descansar) esta noche.
8. Es importante que ustedes ___limpien___ (limpiar) los estantes.
9. Su tía les manda que ___pongan___ (poner) la mesa.
10. Te aconsejo que no ___salgas___ (salir) con él.
11. Mi tío insiste en que mi prima ___haga___ (hacer) la cama.
12. Prefiero ___ir___ (ir) al cine.
13. Es necesario ___estudiar___ (estudiar).
14. Recomiendo que ustedes ___pasen___ (pasar) la aspiradora.

Suggestions
• Have a volunteer read aloud the examples in the captions to the video stills. Point out that in each example the subject of the verb in the main clause is different from the subject of the verb in the subordinate clause.
• Elicit indirect object pronouns with verbs of influence by making statements that give advice and asking students for advice. Ex: **Yo siempre les aconsejo a mis estudiantes que estudien mucho. ¿Qué me recomiendan ustedes a mí?** Continue: **1. Mi coche no arranca cuando hace mucho frío. ¿Qué me recomiendas, ____? 2. Mi apartamento está siempre desordenado. ¿Qué me aconsejan? 3. Voy a tener huéspedes este fin de semana. ¿Qué nos sugieren que hagamos?**
• Write the following sentences on the board: **Quiero que almuerces en la cafetería. Quiero almorzar en la cafetería.** Ask a volunteer to explain why an infinitive is used in the second sentence instead of the subjunctive.

TEACHING OPTIONS

Extra Practice Create sentences that follow the pattern of the sentences in **¡Inténtalo!** Say the sentence, have students repeat it, then give a different subject pronoun for the subordinate clause, varying the person and number. Have students then say the sentence with the new subject, changing pronouns and verbs as necessary.

TPR Have students stand. At random call out implied commands using statements with verbs of will or influence and actions that can be mimed. Ex: **Quiero que laves los platos. Insisto en que hagas la cama.** When you make a statement, point to a student to mime the action. Also use plural statements and point to more than one student. When you use negative statements, indicated students should do nothing. Keep the pace rapid.

Práctica

1 **Completar** Completa el diálogo con palabras de la lista.

cocina	haga	quiere	sea
comas	ponga	saber	ser
diga	prohíbe	sé	vaya

IRENE Tengo problemas con Vilma. Sé que debo hablar con ella. ¿Qué me recomiendas que le (1)__diga__?

JULIA Pues, necesito (2)__saber__ más antes de darte consejos.

IRENE Bueno, para empezar me (3)__prohíbe__ que traiga dulces a la casa.

JULIA Pero chica, tiene razón. Es mejor que tú no (4)__comas__ cosas dulces.

IRENE Sí, ya lo sé. Pero quiero que (5)__sea__ más flexible. Además, insiste en que yo (6)__haga__ todo en la casa.

JULIA Yo (7)__sé__ que Vilma (8)__cocina__ y hace los quehaceres todos los días.

IRENE Sí, pero siempre que hay fiesta me pide que (9)__ponga__ los cubiertos y las copas en la mesa y que (10)__vaya__ al sótano por las servilletas y los platos. ¡Es lo que más odio: ir al sótano!

JULIA Mujer, ¡Vilma sólo (11)__quiere__ que ayudes en la casa!

2 **Aconsejar** En parejas, lean lo que dice cada persona. Luego den consejos lógicos usando verbos como **aconsejar, recomendar** y **prohibir**. Sus consejos deben ser diferentes de lo que la persona quiere hacer. Answers will vary.

> **modelo**
> **Isabel:** Quiero conseguir un comedor con los muebles más caros del mundo.
> **Consejo:** Te aconsejamos que consigas unos muebles menos caros.

1. **DAVID** Pienso poner el cuadro del lago de Maracaibo en la cocina.
2. **SARA** Voy a ir a la gasolinera para comprar unas copas de cristal elegantes.
3. **SR. ALARCÓN** Insisto en comenzar a arreglar el jardín en marzo.
4. **SRA. VILLA** Quiero ver las tazas y los platos de la tienda El Ama de Casa Feliz.
5. **DOLORES** Voy a poner servilletas de tela (*cloth*) para los cuarenta invitados.
6. **SR. PARDO** Pienso poner todos mis muebles nuevos en el altillo.
7. **SRA. GONZÁLEZ** Hay una fiesta en mi casa esta noche pero no quiero arreglar la casa.
8. **CARLITOS** Hoy no tengo ganas de hacer las camas ni de quitar la mesa.

NOTA CULTURAL

En el **lago de Maracaibo**, en Venezuela, hay casas suspendidas sobre el agua que se llaman palafitos. Los palafitos son reminiscentes de la ciudad italiana de Venecia, de donde viene el nombre "Venezuela", que significa "pequeña Venecia".

3 **Preguntas** En parejas, túrnense para contestar las preguntas. Usen el subjuntivo. Answers will vary.

1. ¿Te dan consejos tus amigos/as? ¿Qué te aconsejan? ¿Aceptas sus consejos? ¿Por qué?
2. ¿Qué te sugieren tus profesores que hagas antes de terminar los cursos que tomas?
3. ¿Insisten tus amigos/as en que salgas mucho con ellos?
4. ¿Qué quieres que te regalen tu familia y tus amigos/as en tu cumpleaños?
5. ¿Qué le recomiendas tú a un(a) amigo/a que no quiere salir los sábados con su novio/a?
6. ¿Qué les aconsejas a los nuevos estudiantes de tu universidad?

TEACHING OPTIONS

Small Groups Have small groups prepare skits in which a group of roommates is discussing how to divide the household chores equitably. Give groups time to prepare and practice their skits before presenting them to the class.

Game Give pairs of students five minutes to write a conversation in which they use logically as many of the verbs of will and influence with the subjunctive as they can. After the time is up, ask pairs the number of subjunctive constructions using verbs of will and influence they used in their conversations. Have the top three or four perform their conversations for the class.

Comunicación

4 **Inventar** En parejas, preparen una lista de seis personas famosas. Un(a) estudiante da el nombre de una persona famosa y el/la otro/a le da un consejo. Answers will vary.

> **modelo**
>
> **Estudiante 1:** Judge Judy.
> **Estudiante 2:** Le recomiendo que sea más simpática con la gente.
> **Estudiante 2:** Leonardo DiCaprio.
> **Estudiante 1:** Le aconsejo que haga más películas.

5 **Ayudar** En parejas, miren la ilustración. Imaginen que Gerardo es su hermano y necesita ayuda para arreglar su casa y resolver sus problemas románticos y económicos. Usen expresiones impersonales y verbos como **aconsejar**, **sugerir** y **recomendar**. Answers will vary.

> **modelo**
>
> Es mejor que arregles el apartamento más a menudo.
> Te aconsejo que no dejes para mañana lo que puedes hacer hoy.

Síntesis

6 **La doctora Salvamórez** Hernán tiene problemas con su novia y le escribe a la doctora Salvamórez, columnista del periódico *Panamá y su gente*. Ella responde a las cartas de personas con problemas románticos. En parejas, lean la carta de Hernán y después usen el subjuntivo para escribir los consejos de la doctora. Answers will vary.

> Estimada doctora Salvamórez:
>
> Mi novia nunca quiere que yo salga de casa. No le molesta que vengan mis amigos a visitarme. Pero insiste en que nosotros sólo miremos los programas de televisión que ella quiere. Necesita saber dónde estoy en cada momento, y yo necesito que ella me dé un poco de independencia. ¿Qué hago?
>
> Hernán

4 **Suggestion** Ask volunteers to read the **modelo** aloud and provide other suggestions for Judge Judy and Leonardo DiCaprio.

4 **Expansion** Ask each pair to pick out their favorite response and share it with the class. Have everyone vote for the most clever, most shocking, or funniest suggestion.

5 **Suggestion** Before beginning the activity, project **Transparency #47** and ask volunteers to describe the drawing, naming everything they see and all the chores that need to be done.

5 **Expansion** Have students change partners and take turns playing the roles of Gerardo and one sibling giving him advice. Ex: **Te sugiero que pongas la pizza en la basura.**

6 **Expansion**
- Have pairs compare their responses in groups of four. Ask groups to choose which among all of the suggestions are the most likely to work for Hernán and have them share these with the class.
- Have pairs choose a famous couple in history or fiction. Ex: Romeo and Juliet or Napoleon and Josephine. Then have them write a letter from one of the couples to **doctora Salvamórez**. Finally, have them exchange their letters with another pair and write the corresponding responses from the doctor.

TEACHING OPTIONS

Heritage Speakers Have heritage speakers write a list of ten suggestions for other class members participating in an exchange program in their cultural communities. Their suggestions should focus on participating in daily activities and chores in their host families' homes.

Large Group Write the names of famous historical figures on individual sticky notes and place them on the students' backs. The students should circulate around the room giving each other advice that will help them guess their "identity."

Section Goals

In **Lectura** students will:
- learn to locate the main parts of a sentence
- read a content-rich text with long sentences

Instructional Resource
Companion website:
www.vistahigherlearning.com

Estrategia Tell students that if they have trouble reading long sentences in Spanish, they should pause to identify the main verb of the sentence and its subject. They should then reread the entire sentence.

Examinar el texto Students should see from the layout (cover page with title, photo, and phone numbers; interior pages with an introduction and several headings followed by short paragraphs) that this is a brochure. Revealing cognates are: **información** (cover) and **residencia oficial del Presidente de Panamá** (introduction).

¿Probable o improbable? Ask volunteers to read aloud each item and give the answer. Have a volunteer rephrase the improbable statement so that it is probable.

Frases largas Ask pairs to suggest a couple of long sentences. Have them point out the main verb and subject.

Lectura

Antes de leer

Estrategia
Locating the main parts of a sentence

Did you know that a text written in Spanish is an average of 15% longer than the same text written in English? Because the Spanish language tends to use more words to express ideas, you will often encounter long sentences when reading in Spanish. Of course, the length of sentences varies with genre and with authors' individual styles. To help you understand long sentences, identify the main parts of the sentence before trying to read it in its entirety. First locate the main verb of the sentence, along with its subject, ignoring any words or phrases set off by commas. Then reread the sentence, adding details like direct and indirect objects, transitional words, and prepositional phrases.

Examinar el texto

Mira el formato de la lectura. ¿Qué tipo de documento es? ¿Qué cognados encuentras en la lectura? ¿Qué te dicen sobre el tema de la selección?

¿Probable o improbable?

Mira brevemente el texto e indica si las frases son probables o improbables.

1. Este folleto° es de interés turístico. probable
2. Describe un edificio moderno cubano. improbable
3. Incluye algunas explicaciones de arquitectura. probable
4. Espera atraer° a visitantes al lugar. probable

Frases largas

Mira el texto y busca algunas frases largas. Con un(a) compañero/a, identifiquen las partes principales de la frase y después examinen las descripciones adicionales. ¿Qué significan las frases?

recursos

vistahigher
learning.com

folleto *brochure*   atraer *to attract*   épocas *time periods*

Bienvenidos al
Palacio de Las Garzas

El palacio está abierto de martes a domingo.
Para más información,
llame al teléfono 507-226-7000.
También puede solicitar° un folleto
a la casilla° 3467,
Ciudad de Panamá, Panamá.

Después de leer

Ordenar

Pon los eventos en el orden cronológico adecuado.

_3_ El palacio se convirtió en residencia presidencial.

_2_ Durante diferentes épocas°, maestros, médicos y banqueros practicaron su profesión en el palacio.

_4_ El doctor Belisario Porras ocupó el palacio por primera vez.

_1_ Los colonizadores construyeron el palacio.

_5_ Se renovó el palacio.

_6_ Los turistas pueden visitar el palacio de martes a domingo.

TEACHING OPTIONS

Heritage Speakers Ask heritage speakers to give a brief presentation about the official residence of the president of their home country. Tell them to include if it is possible to visit the residence, and, if so, their recommendations to visitors about what rooms and objects are particularly noteworthy and should not be missed. If it is possible, they should illustrate their presentation with photographs or brochures.

Extra Practice Have students work in pairs to write ten suggestions, recommendations, or statements using the subjunctive for what their idea of a dream house (**la casa de mis sueños**) would be like. Ex: **Para mí es importante que haya una piscina de tamaño olímpico en la casa de mis sueños. Recomiendo que la cocina sea grande porque me gusta cocinar. Es necesario que tenga varias alcobas porque siempre tengo huéspedes.**

El Palacio de Las Garzas° es la residencia oficial del Presidente de Panamá desde 1903. Fue construido en 1673 para ser la casa de un gobernador español. Con el paso de los años fue almacén, escuela, hospital, aduana, banco y por último, palacio presidencial.

En la actualidad el edificio tiene tres pisos, pero los planos originales muestran una construcción de un piso con un gran patio en el centro. La restauración del palacio comenzó en el año 1922 y los trabajos fueron realizados por el arquitecto Villanueva-Myers y el pintor Roberto Lewis. El palacio, un monumento al estilo colonial, todavía conserva su elegancia y buen gusto, y es una de las principales atracciones turísticas del barrio Casco Viejo°.

Planta baja
El patio de las Garzas

Una antigua puerta de hierro° recibe a los visitantes. El patio interior todavía conserva los elementos originales de la construcción: piso de mármol°, columnas de perla gris y una magnífica fuente de agua en el centro. Aquí están las nueve garzas que le dan el nombre al palacio y que representan las nueve provincias de Panamá.

Primer piso
El salón Amarillo

Aquí el turista puede visitar una galería de cuarenta y un retratos° de gobernadores y personajes ilustres de Panamá. La principal atracción de este salón es el sillón presidencial, que se usa especialmente cuando hay cambio de presidente. Otros atractivos de esta área son el comedor de Los Tamarindos, que se destaca° por la elegancia de sus muebles y sus lámparas de cristal, y el patio andaluz, con sus coloridos mosaicos que representan la unión de la cultura indígena y la española.

El salón Dr. Belisario Porras

Este elegante y majestuoso salón es uno de los lugares más importantes del Palacio de Las Garzas. Lleva su nombre en honor al doctor Belisario Porras, quien fue tres veces presidente de Panamá (1912–1916, 1918–1920 y 1920–1924).

Segundo piso

Es el área residencial del palacio y el visitante no tiene acceso a ella. Los armarios, las cómodas y los espejos de la alcoba fueron comprados en Italia y Francia por el presidente Porras, mientras que las alfombras, cortinas y frazadas° son originarias de España.

solicitar *request* casilla *post office box* Garzas *Herons* Casco Viejo *Old Quarter* hierro *iron* mármol *marble* retratos *portraits* se destaca *stands out* frazadas *blankets*

Preguntas
Contesta las preguntas.

1. ¿Qué sala es notable por sus muebles elegantes y sus lámparas de cristal? el comedor de Los Tamarindos
2. ¿En qué parte del palacio se encuentra la residencia del presidente? en el segundo piso
3. ¿Dónde empiezan los turistas su visita al palacio? en el patio de las Garzas
4. ¿En qué lugar se representa artísticamente la rica herencia cultural de Panamá? en el patio andaluz
5. ¿Qué salón honra la memoria de un gran panameño? el salón Dr. Belisario Porras
6. ¿Qué partes del palacio te gustaría más visitar? ¿Por qué? Explica tu respuesta. Answers will vary.

Conversación
En grupos de tres o cuatro estudiantes, hablen sobre lo siguiente: Answers will vary.

1. ¿Qué tiene en común el Palacio de Las Garzas con otras residencias presidenciales u otras casas muy grandes?
2. ¿Te gustaría vivir en el Palacio de Las Garzas? ¿Por qué?
3. Imagina que puedes diseñar tu palacio ideal. Describe los planos para cada piso del palacio.

Escritura

Estrategia
Using idea maps

How do you organize ideas for a first draft? Often, the organization of ideas represents the most challenging part of the process. Idea maps are useful for organizing pertinent information. Imagine that you are writing a description of your family. Here is an example of an idea map you might use, changing facts to fit your own situation.

MAPA DE IDEAS

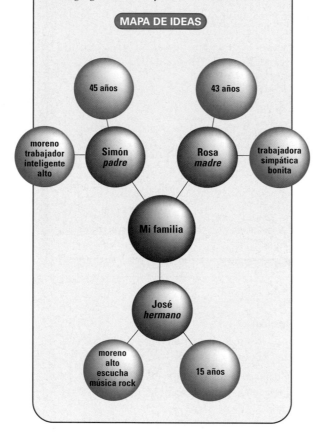

Section Goals

In **Escritura** students will:
• learn to use idea maps
• integrate **Lección 12** vocabulary and structures
• write a lease agreement

Estrategia Have your students create their idea maps in Spanish. English idea maps are likely to include items for which students do not have structures or vocabulary. Some students may find it helpful to create their idea maps with note cards, writing each idea on a separate card. This facilitates rearrangements and experiments with various types of organization.

Tema
• Review with students the details suggested for inclusion in the lease agreement. You may wish to present these terms students can use in their agreements: **arrendatario/a** (*tenant*); **arrendador(a)** (*landlord*); **propietario/a** (*owner*); **estipulaciones** (*stipulations*); **parte** (*party*); **de anticipación**, **de antelación** (*in advance*).
• Provide students with samples of legal documents in Spanish. (Many legal forms are downloadable from the Internet.) Go over the format of these documents with students, clarifying legal terminology as necessary.

Suggestion Tell students to consult the **Plan de Escritura** in **Apéndice A**, page 448, for step-by-step writing instructions. You might also tell them to refer to the **Organizing information logically** strategy in **Apéndice A**, page 449.

Tema

Escribir un contrato de arrendamiento

Eres el/la administrador(a)° de un edificio de apartamentos. Prepara un contrato de arrendamiento° para los nuevos inquilinos°. El contrato debe incluir los siguientes detalles:

► La dirección° del apartamento y del/de la administrador(a)
► Las fechas del contrato
► El precio del alquiler y el día que se debe pagar
► El precio del depósito
► Información y reglas° acerca de:
   la basura
   el correo
   los animales domésticos
   el ruido°
   los servicios° de electricidad y agua
   el uso de electrodomésticos
► Otros aspectos importantes de la vida comunitaria

administrador(a) *manager* contrato de arrendamiento *lease* inquilinos *tenants* dirección *address* reglas *rules* ruido *noise* servicios *utilities*

TEACHING OPTIONS

Proofreading Activity Copy these sentences containing mistakes onto the board or a transparency as a proofreading activity to do with the whole class.
1. El agente nos recomienda que buscamos una casa de las afueras, la que no me gusta nada.
2. Nuestros amigos Panameños acaban de encontrar en el centro lo qué buscaban.
3. ¿Es ésta la casa de quien me hablaste el Lunes?
4. Es necesario que Uds. pasan al balcón para ver el océano pacífico.
5. Por favor, entran Uds. en la sala y observan que es grande.
6. Los martínez, quiénes conocieron ayer, son sus vecinos.
7. ¿Sepan Uds. que el vecino del otro lado sea muy famoso?

Escuchar

NATIONAL • STANDARDS • communication

Estrategia
Using visual cues

Visual cues like illustrations and headings provide useful clues about what you will hear.

To practice this strategy, you will listen to a passage related to the following photo. Jot down the clues the photo gives you as you listen.

Preparación

Mira el dibujo. ¿Qué pistas te da para comprender la conversación que vas a escuchar? ¿Qué significa *bienes raíces*?

18G

Bienes raíces

Se vende.
4 alcobas, 3 baños, cocina moderna, jardín con árboles frutales.
B/. 225.000

Se alquila.
2 alcobas, 1 baño. Balcón. Urbanización Las Brisas. B/. 525

Ahora escucha 🎧

Mira los anuncios de esta página y escucha la conversación entre el señor Núñez, Adriana y Felipe. Luego indica si cada descripción se refiere a la casa ideal de Adriana y Felipe, a la casa del anuncio° o al apartamento del anuncio.

Frases	La casa ideal	La casa del anuncio	El apartamento del anuncio
Es barato.	___	___	✔
Tiene cuatro alcobas.	___	✔	___
Tiene una oficina.	✔	___	___
Tiene un balcón.	___	___	✔
Tiene una cocina moderna.	___	✔	___
Tiene un jardín muy grande.	___	✔	___
Tiene un patio.	✔	___	___

Comprensión

Preguntas

1. ¿Cuál es la relación entre el señor Núñez, Adriana y Felipe? ¿Cómo lo sabes? El Sr. Núñez es el padre de Adriana y Felipe es su esposo.
2. ¿Qué diferencia de opinión hay entre Adriana y Felipe sobre dónde quieren vivir? Felipe prefiere vivir en la ciudad, pero Adriana quiere vivir en las afueras.
3. Usa la información de los dibujos y la conversación para entender lo que dice Adriana al final. ¿Qué significa "todo a su debido tiempo"? Answers will vary.

Conversación En parejas, túrnense para hacer y responder a las preguntas. Answers will vary.

1. ¿Qué tienen en común el apartamento y la casa del anuncio con el lugar donde tú vives?
2. ¿Qué piensas de la recomendación del señor Núñez?
3. ¿Qué tipo de sugerencias te da tu familia sobre dónde vivir?
4. ¿Dónde prefieres vivir tú, en un apartamento o en una casa? Explica por qué.

recursos

TEXT CD
Lección 12

anuncio *advertisement*

A: Es importante que tengamos una oficina para mí y un patio para las plantas.
S: Como no tienen mucho dinero ahorrado, es mejor que alquilen un apartamento pequeño por un tiempo. Así pueden ahorrar su dinero para comprar la casa ideal. Miren este apartamento. Tiene un balcón precioso y está en un barrio muy

seguro y bonito. Y el alquiler es muy razonable.
F: Adriana, me parece que tu padre tiene razón. Con un alquiler tan barato, podemos comprar muebles y también ahorrar dinero cada mes.
A: ¡Ay!, quiero mi casa. Pero, bueno, ¡todo a su debido tiempo!

Section Goal

In **Panorama**, students will read about the geography and culture of Panama.

Instructional Resources

Transparencies, #3, #4, #48
WB/VM: Workbook, pp. 149–150;
Video Activities, pp. 251–252
Panorama cultural *DVD/Video*
Interactive CD-ROM
IRM: Videoscript, p. 114;
Panorama cultural *Translations,*
p. 136
Companion website:
www.vistahigherlearning.com
Presentations CD-ROM

Suggestion Have students look at the map of Panama or project **Transparency #48** and discuss the physical features of the country. Point out the bodies of water that run along the coasts of Panama, and the canal that cuts through the isthmus (**istmo**). Then, have students look at the call-out photos and read the captions. Point out that the Kuna people live on the San Blas islands in the Caribbean Sea.

El país en cifras Mention that the national currency, the balboa, is named for **Vasco Núñez de Balboa**, who explored the Isthmus of Panama in 1501. Tell students that **Chibcha** is a major indigenous language group, with dialects spoken by native people from central Colombia through eastern Nicaragua. After reading about the **Panameños célebres**, ask students to share what they know about the individuals listed and how they learned about them.

¡Increíble pero cierto! The opening of the Panama Canal not only dramatically reduced the distance ships had to travel to get from the Atlantic Ocean to the Pacific, it also provided a much safer route than the stormy, perilous route around Cape Horn and through the Straits of Magellan.

Panamá

NATIONAL connections cultures STANDARDS

El país en cifras

▸ **Área:** 78.200 km² (30.193 millas²), *aproximadamente el área de Carolina del Sur*

▸ **Población:** 3.067.000

▸ **Capital:** La ciudad de Panamá—1.299.000

▸ **Ciudades principales:** Colón—138.000, David—125.000

SOURCE: Population Division, UN Secretariat

▸ **Moneda:** balboa; Es equivalente al dólar estadounidense. *En Panamá circulan los billetes de dólar estadounidense. El país centroamericano, sin embargo, acuña° sus propias monedas. "El peso" es una moneda grande equivalente a cincuenta centavos°. La moneda de cinco centavos es llamada frecuentemente "real".*

▸ **Idiomas:** español (oficial), chibcha, inglés *La mayoría de los panameños es bilingüe. La lengua materna del 14% de los panameños es el inglés.*

Bandera de Panamá

Panameños célebres

▸ **Rod Carew,** beisbolista (1945–)

▸ **Mireya Moscoso,** política (1946–)

▸ **Rubén Blades,** músico y político (1948–)

acuña *mints* centavos *cents*
actualmente *currently*
peaje *toll* promedio *average*

recursos

| WB pp. 149–150 | VM p. 251–252 | I CD-ROM Lección 12 | vistahigher learning.com |

Un turista disfruta del bosque tropical colgado de un cable.

Mujer kuna lavando una mola

COSTA RICA

Lago Gatún

Canal de Panamá

Islas Sa Blas

Bocas del Toro

Mar Caribe

Colón

Cordillera de San Bla

Río Chep

Serranía de Tabasarái

David

Río Cobre

Ciudad de Panamá

Isla del Rey

Océano Pacífico

Golfo de Panamá

Isla de Coiba

ESTADOS UNIDOS

OCÉANO ATLÁNTICO

PANAMÁ

AMÉRICA DEL SUR

Ruinas de un fuerte panameño

¡Increíble pero cierto!

¿Conocías estos datos sobre el Canal de Panamá?

• Gracias al Canal de Panamá, el viaje en barco de Nueva York a Tokio es 3.000 millas más corto.
• Su construcción costó 639 millones de dólares.
• Actualmente° lo usan 38 barcos al día.
• El peaje° promedio° cuesta 40.000 dólares.

Tokio

Nueva York

PANAMÁ

TEACHING OPTIONS

Heritage Speakers Invite Panamanian students or heritage speakers who have visited Panama to share information about language patterns there. Have these students talk about what languages they speak at home, what language is usually learned first, how English speakers acquire English, and so forth.
Extra Practice Rubén Blades changed the world of salsa music by introducing lyrics with social import into what had previously

been simply dance music. If possible, bring in his recording *Buscando América*, and have students listen to "**El Padre Antonio y su monaguillo Andrés**," based on the story of Archbishop Romero of El Salvador. Or, listen to the story of "**Pedro Navaja**" on *Siembra*, Blades' classic collaboration with Willie Colón. Have students write a summary of the song in English, or describe how Blades' salsa differs from traditional "romantic" salsa.

Lugares • El Canal de Panamá

El Canal de Panamá conecta el océano Pacífico con el océano Atlántico. Se empezó a construir en 1903 y se terminó diez años después. Es la fuente° principal de ingresos° del país, gracias al dinero que se recibe de los más de 12.000 buques° que pasan anualmente por el canal.

Artes • La mola

La mola es una forma de arte textil de los kunas, una tribu indígena que vive en las islas San Blas, en Panamá. Las molas se hacen con capas° y fragmentos de tela° de colores vivos°. Sus diseños son muchas veces abstractos, inspirados en las formas del coral. Las molas tradicionales son las más apreciadas y sus diseños son completamente geométricos. Antes sólo se usaban como ropa, pero hoy día también se usan para decorar las casas.

Deportes • El buceo

Panamá, cuyo° nombre significa "lugar de muchos peces°", es un sitio excelente para los aficionados del buceo, el buceo con esnórkel y la pesca. Las playas en los dos lados del istmo°, el mar Caribe a un lado y el océano Pacífico al otro, son muy variadas. Unas están destinadas al turismo y otras tienen un gran valor° ecológico, por la diversidad de su vida marina, abundante en arrecifes° de coral. En la playa Bluff, por ejemplo, se pueden observar cuatro especies de tortugas° en peligro° de extinción.

COLOMBIA

Vista de la Ciudad de Panamá

¿Qué aprendiste? Responde a las preguntas con una frase completa.

1. ¿Cuál es la lengua materna del catorce por ciento de los panameños?
   El inglés es la lengua materna del catorce por ciento de los panameños.
2. ¿A qué unidad monetaria (*monetary unit*) es equivalente el balboa?
   El balboa es equivalente al dólar estadounidense.
3. ¿Qué océanos une el Canal de Panamá?
   El Canal de Panamá une los océanos Atlántico y Pacífico.
4. ¿Quién es Rubén Blades?
   Rubén Blades es un músico y político panameño.
5. ¿Qué son las molas?
   Las molas son una forma de arte textil común entre los kunas.
6. ¿Cómo son los diseños de las molas?
   Sus diseños son abstractos.
7. ¿Para qué se usaban las molas antes?
   Las molas se usaban como ropa.
8. ¿Cómo son las playas de Panamá?
   Son muy variadas; unas están destinadas al turismo, otras tienen valor ecológico.
9. ¿Qué significa "Panamá"?
   "Panamá" significa "lugar de muchos peces".

Conexión Internet Investiga estos temas en el sitio **www.vistahigherlearning.com**.

1. Investiga la historia de las relaciones entre Panamá y los Estados Unidos y la decisión de devolver (*give back*) el Canal de Panamá. ¿Estás de acuerdo con la decisión? Explica tu opinión.
2. Investiga los kunas u otro grupo indígena de Panamá. ¿En qué partes del país viven? ¿Qué lenguas hablan? ¿Cómo es su cultura?

fuente *source*   ingresos *income*   buques *ships*   capas *layers*   tela *fabric*   vivos *bright*   cuyo *whose*   peces *fish*
istmo *isthmus*   valor *value*   arrecifes *reefs*   tortugas *turtles*   peligro *danger*

El Canal de Panamá The Panama Canal is a lake-and-lock type of canal, connecting the Atlantic and Pacific oceans at one of the lowest points on the Continental Divide. It is about 40 miles long and is one of the two most strategic waterways on earth (the Suez Canal is the other).

La mola The Kuna people originally lived on mainland Panama, but preferred to move to the San Blas islands, where they could maintain their way of life. Elaborate traditions accompany every life-cycle event in Kuna culture, and many of these ceremonies are depicted on the elaborate appliqué **molas**.

El buceo An excellent place for diving in Panama is the **Parque Nacional Bastimentos**, in the **Archipiélago de Bocas del Toro**. In this nature reserve, turtles nest on some of the beaches. Its coral reefs are home to more than 200 species of tropical fish, in addition to lobsters and other sea life; manatees also inhabit these waters. The park is also known for its mangroves, which offer snorkelers another aquatic experience. For more information about **el buceo** and other ocean sports, you may want to play the **Panorama cultural** video for this lesson.

Conexión Internet Students will find supporting Internet activities and links at **www.vistahigherlearning.com**.

Worth Noting The Kuna people have a strong, rich oral tradition. During regular community meetings, ritual forms of speaking, including storytelling and speeches, are presented by community elders. It is only over the past decade that a written form of the Kuna language has been developed by outsiders. However, as Spanish—and even English—begin to encroach more and more into Kuna Yala (the Kuna name for their home-land), linguistic anthropologists have highlighted the urgency of recording and preserving the rich Kuna oral tradition, fearing that the traditional Kuna language and culture will begin to be diluted by outside influences.

Section Goal

In **Panorama**, students will read about the geography and culture of El Salvador.

Instructional Resources
Transparencies, #3, #4, #49
WB/VM: Workbook, pp. 151–152;
Video Activities, pp. 253–254
***Panorama cultural** DVD/Video*
Interactive CD-ROM
IRM: Videoscript, p. 114;
***Panorama cultural** Translations,*
p. 136
Companion website:
www.vistahigherlearning.com
Presentations CD-ROM

Suggestion Have students look at the map of El Salvador or project **Transparency #49**. Draw students' attention to the number of active volcanoes in El Salvador. Tell students that because of the fertility of El Salvador's volcanic soil, the country has a strong agricultural sector which, in turn, has promoted a large population. Have students look at the inset map as you point out that El Salvador is the only Central American country without a Caribbean coast. Look at the photos and ask volunteers to read the captions.

El país en cifras El Salvador's overpopulation, chronic economic problems, and lack of social justice resulted, in the early 1970s, in social disturbances that the government put down with brutal force.

¡Increíble pero cierto! In the town of Concepción de Ataco, another legend claims that on the **Cerro la Empalizada** there is a cave containing plants that disorient anyone who steps on them.

El Salvador

NATIONAL connections cultures STANDARDS

El país en cifras

▶ **Área:** 21.040 km² (8.124 millas²), *el tamaño° de Massachusetts*
▶ **Población:** 6.876.000

El Salvador es el país centroamericano más pequeño y el más densamente° poblado. Su población, al igual que la de Honduras, es muy homogénea: casi el 95 por ciento de la población es mestiza.

▶ **Capital:** San Salvador—1.533.000
▶ **Ciudades principales:** Soyapango—252.000, Santa Ana—202.000, San Miguel—183.000, Mejicanos—145.000

SOURCE: Population Division, UN Secretariat

▶ **Moneda:** colón, dólar estadounidense
▶ **Idiomas:** español (oficial), náhuatl, lenca

Bandera de El Salvador

Salvadoreños célebres

▶ **Óscar Romero,** arzobispo° y activista por los derechos humanos° (1917–1980)
▶ **Claribel Alegría,** poeta, novelista y cuentista (1924–)
▶ **Roque Dalton,** poeta, ensayista y novelista (1935–1975)
▶ **María Eugenia Brizuela,** política (1956–)

Óscar Romero

tamaño *size* densamente *densely* arzobispo *archbishop*
derechos humanos *human rights* Laguna *Lagoon* sirena *mermaid*

Ruinas de Tazumal

Salvadoreña secando hamacas (*hammocks*)

GUATEMALA

Lago de Guija
Río de la Paz
Río Lempa
Santa Ana
Volcán de San Salvador
Mejicanos Ilobasco
San Salvador
Soyapango
Volcán de San Vicente
La Libertad
Río Lempa
Volcán de San Miguel
San Miguel
Río Torola
Río Goascorán
HONDURAS
Golfo de Fonseca
Océano Pacífico

Aeropuerto Ilopango en San Salvador

ESTADOS UNIDOS
OCÉANO ATLÁNTICO
EL SALVADOR
OCÉANO PACÍFICO
AMÉRICA DEL SUR

recursos

| WB pp. 151–152 | VM pp. 253–254 | I CD-ROM Lección 12 | vistahigher learning.com |

¡Increíble pero cierto!

El rico folklore salvadoreño se basa sobre todo en sus extraordinarios recursos naturales. Por ejemplo, según una leyenda, las muertes que se producen en la Laguna° de Alegría tienen su explicación en la existencia de una sirena° solitaria que vive en el lago y captura a los jóvenes atractivos.

TEACHING OPTIONS

Worth Noting Government repression in El Salvador intensified resistance, and by the mid-1970s a civil war was being fought between government forces and the FMLN, an armed guerrilla movement. Among the many martyrs of the war was the Archbishop of San Salvador, Óscar Romero. A descendent of the privileged class in El Salvador, Romero came to champion the cause of peace and social justice for the poor. This position made him the target of reactionary elements. On March 24, 1980, Archbishop Romero was assassinated while saying mass in the Cathedral of San Salvador. His life and death became an inspiration for those seeking social justice. Still, it was only in 1991 that a cease-fire brought an end to the civil war.

Deportes • El *surfing*

El Salvador, con unos 300 kilómetros de costa en el Océano Pacífico, es un gran centro de *surfing* por la calidad° y consistencia de sus olas°. *La Libertad* es la playa que está más cerca de la capital, y allí las condiciones son perfectas para el *surfing*. Por eso vienen surfistas de todo el mundo a este pequeño pueblo salvadoreño. Los fines de semana hay muchísima gente en *La Libertad* y por eso muchos surfistas van al oeste, por la *Costa del Bálsamo*, donde las olas son buenas y hay menos gente.

Naturaleza • El Parque Nacional Montecristo

El Parque Nacional Montecristo se encuentra en el norte del país. Es conocido también como El Trifinio porque es el punto donde se unen° Guatemala, Honduras y El Salvador. Este bosque está a una altitud de 2.400 metros (7.900 pies). Recibe 200 centímetros (80 pulgadas°) de lluvia al año y con frecuencia tiene una humedad° relativa del 100 por ciento. Sus altísimos árboles forman una bóveda° que la luz del sol no puede traspasar°. Allí hay muchas especies interesantes de plantas y animales, como orquídeas, hongos°, monos araña°, pumas, quetzales y tucanes.

Artes • La artesanía° de Ilobasco

Ilobasco es un pueblo famoso por sus objetos de arcilla° y por los artículos de cerámica pintados a mano. Los productos más tradicionales de Ilobasco son los juguetes°, los adornos° y los utensilios de cocina. Se ofrecen excursiones en las que se puede observar paso a paso° la fabricación de estos productos. Las "sorpresas" de Ilobasco, pequeñas piezas° de cerámica en cuyo interior están representadas escenas de la vida diaria, son especialmente populares.

¿Qué aprendiste? Responde a las preguntas con una frase completa.

1. ¿Qué es el náhuatl?
   El náhuatl es un idioma que se habla en El Salvador.

2. ¿Quien es María Eugenia Brizuela?
   María Eugenia Brizuela es una política salvadoreña.

3. Hay muchos lugares ideales para el *surfing* en El Salvador. ¿Por qué? Hay muchos lugares ideales para el *surfing* porque El Salvador recibe algunas de las mejores olas del océano Pacífico.

4. ¿A qué altitud se encuentra el parque Montecristo? Se encuentra a una altitud de 2.400 metros.

5. ¿Cuáles son algunos de los animales y las plantas que se encuentran en el bosque?
   En el bosque hay orquídeas, hongos, monos araña, pumas, quetzales y tucanes.

6. ¿Por qué al Parque Nacional Montecristo se le llama también El Trifinio? Al Parque Nacional Montecristo también se le llama El Trifinio porque es el punto donde se unen Guatemala, Honduras y El Salvador.

7. ¿Por qué es famoso el pueblo de Ilobasco? El pueblo de Ilobasco es famoso por los objetos de arcilla y por los artículos de cerámica pintados a mano.

8. ¿Qué se puede ver en una excursión a Ilobasco? En una excursión a Ilobasco se puede ver la fabricación de los artículos de cerámica paso a paso.

9. ¿Qué son las "sorpresas" de Ilobasco? Las "sorpresas" son pequeñas piezas de cerámica en cuyo interior están representadas escenas de la vida diaria.

Conexión Internet Investiga estos temas en el sitio **www.vistahigherlearning.com.**

1. El Parque Nacional Montecristo es una reserva natural; busca información sobre otros parques o zonas protegidas en El Salvador. ¿Cómo son estos lugares? ¿Qué tipos de plantas y animales se encuentran allí?

2. Busca información sobre museos u otros lugares turísticos en San Salvador (u otra ciudad de El Salvador).

calidad *quality* olas *waves* se unen *come together* pulgadas *inches* humedad *humidity* bóveda *canopy* traspasar *pierce* hongos *fungi* monos araña *spider monkeys* artesanía *crafts* arcilla *clay* juguetes *toys* adornos *ornaments* paso a paso *step by step* piezas *pieces*

El *surfing* Tell students that La Libertad is a relatively small town that sees a large influx of beach-goers, not just surfers during the weekends and holidays. Black, volcanic sand covers the beach of La Libertad. About five miles east lies Zunzal beach, which, during Holy Week (**Semana Santa**) each year, is the site of international surfing competitions.

El Parque Nacional Montecristo The Montecristo cloud forest (**bosque nuboso**) is a protected area at the point where El Salvador, Honduras, and Guatemala meet. The point, at the summit of Montecristo, is called **El Trifinio**. The cloud forest receives close to 80 inches of rain per year and the average relative humidity is 100%. Visitors have access to Montecristo only between October and March. The rest of the year it is closed to visitors.

La artesanía de Ilobasco Ilobasco is a crafts village that specializes in ceramic ware. **Sorpresas** are one of the most famous items. They are miniscule, intricate scenes and figures inside egg-shaped shells about the size of a walnut. Every year on September 29th, a crafts fair is held, drawing thousands of visitors from around the world.

Conexión Internet Students will find supporting Internet activities and links at **www.vistahigherlearning.com.**

TEACHING OPTIONS

Variación léxica Pupusa is the name given to the Salvadoran version of the **tortilla**. In fact, **pupusas** are made by putting a filling such as red beans, onions, garlic, and cheese on one uncooked tortilla, laying another tortilla over it, and pressing the two together so they adhere, and then frying both in hot oil. Served sizzling from the fryer, **pupusas** are delicious. They are so popular that in El Salvador there are many stores, called **pupuserías**, that specialize in them. And if you visit a neighborhood in the United States where Salvadorans have settled, you will inevitably find a **pupusería**.

You may want to play the **Panorama cultural** video for this lesson that shows how **pupusas** are prepared.

Instructional Resources
Vocabulary CD
Lab Manual, p. 72
*Lab CD/MP3 **Lección 12***
IRM: Tapescript, pp. 54–58
*Testing Program: **Pruebas**,*
pp. 133–144
Testing Program Audio CD
Test Files CD-ROM
Test Generator

Las viviendas

las afueras	suburbs; outskirts
el alquiler	rent (payment)
el ama (*m., f.*) de casa	housekeeper; caretaker
el barrio	neighborhood
el edificio de apartamentos	apartment building
el/la vecino/a	neighbor
la vivienda	housing
alquilar	to rent
mudarse	to move (from one house to another)

Los cuartos y otros lugares

la alcoba, el dormitorio	bedroom
el altillo	attic
el balcón	balcony
la cocina	kitchen
el comedor	dining room
el cuarto	room
la entrada	entrance
la escalera	stairs; stairway
el garaje	garage
el jardín	garden; yard
la oficina	office
el pasillo	hallway
el patio	patio; yard
la sala	living room
el sótano	basement; cellar

Los muebles y otras cosas

la alfombra	carpet; rug
la almohada	pillow
el armario	closet
el cartel	poster
la cómoda	chest of drawers
las cortinas	curtains
el cuadro	picture
el estante	bookcase; bookshelves
la lámpara	lamp
la luz	light; electricity
la manta	blanket
la mesita	end table
la mesita de noche	night stand
los muebles	furniture
la pared	wall
la pintura	painting; picture
el sillón	armchair
el sofá	couch; sofa

Los electrodomésticos

la cafetera	coffee maker
la cocina, la estufa	stove
el congelador	freezer
el electrodoméstico	electric appliance
el horno (de microondas)	(microwave) oven
la lavadora	washing machine
el lavaplatos	dishwasher
el refrigerador	refrigerator
la secadora	clothes dryer
la tostadora	toaster

La mesa

la copa	wineglass; goblet
la cuchara	(table or large) spoon
el cuchillo	knife
el plato	plate
la servilleta	napkin
la taza	cup
el tenedor	fork
el vaso	glass

Los quehaceres domésticos

arreglar	to neaten; to straighten up
barrer el suelo	to sweep the floor
cocinar	to cook
ensuciar	to get (something) dirty
hacer la cama	to make the bed
hacer quehaceres domésticos	to do household chores
lavar (el suelo, los platos)	to wash (the floor, the dishes)
limpiar la casa	to clean the house
pasar la aspiradora	to vacuum
planchar la ropa	to iron the clothes
poner la mesa	to set the table
quitar la mesa	to clear the table
sacar la basura	to take out the trash
sacudir los muebles	to dust the furniture

Verbos y expresiones verbales

aconsejar	to advise
insistir (en)	to insist (on)
mandar	to order
recomendar (e:ie)	to recommend
rogar (o:ue)	to beg; to plead
sugerir (e:ie)	to suggest
Es bueno que…	It's good that…
Es importante que…	It's important that…
Es malo que…	It's bad that…
Es mejor que…	It's better that…
Es necesario que…	It's necessary that…
Es urgente que…	It's urgent that…

Relative pronouns	See page 336.
Expresiones útiles	See page 333.

recursos

| LM p. 72 | Lab CD/MP3 Lección 12 | Vocab CD Lección 12 |

La naturaleza

Communicative Goals

You will learn how to:

- Talk about and discuss the environment
- Express your beliefs and opinions about issues

Lesson Goals

In **Lección 13** students will be introduced to the following:

- terms to describe nature and the environment
- conservation and recycling terms
- subjunctive with verbs and expressions of emotion
- subjunctive with verbs and expressions of doubt, disbelief, and denial
- expressions of certainty
- subjunctive with conjunctions
- infinitives with conjunctions
- forming regular past participles
- irregular past articiples
- past participles used as adjectives
- recognizing the purpose of a text
- cultural, geographic, and historical information about Colombia
- cultural, geographic, and historical information about Honduras

A primera vista Here are some additional questions you can ask based on the photo: **¿Vives en la ciudad? ¿En las afueras? ¿En el campo? ¿Te gusta pasar tiempo fuera de la casa? ¿Por qué? ¿Tienes algún pasatiempo? ¿Cuál? ¿Dónde lo practicas? ¿Puedes escalar montañas? ¿Te gusta acampar? ¿Dónde puedes hacer estas actividades? ¿Adónde prefieres ir de vacaciones?**

A PRIMERA VISTA
- ¿Son excursionistas?
- ¿Es importante que usen zapatos deportivos?
- ¿Se llevan bien o mal?
- ¿Se divierten?

INSTRUCTIONAL RESOURCES

Workbook/Video Manual: WB Activities, pp. 155–168
Laboratory Manual: Lab Activities, pp. 73–78
Workbook/Video Manual: Video Activities, pp. 219–220; pp. 255–258
Instructor's Resource Manual: **Vocabulario adicional**, p. 167; **¡Inténtalo!** & **Práctica** Answers, p. 193; **Fotonovela** Translations, pp. 125–126; Textbook CD

Tapescript, p. 83; Lab CDs Tapescript, pp. 59–62; **Fotonovela** Videoscript, pp. 101–102; **Panorama cultural** Videoscript, p. 115; **Pan. cult.** Translations, p.137
Info Gap Activities Booklet, pp. 49–52
Overhead Transparencies: #3, #4, #5, #6, #50–#53
Lab Audio CD/MP3 **Lección 13**

Panorama cultural DVD/Video
Fotonovela DVD/Video
Testing Program, pp. 145–156
Testing Program Audio CD
Test Files CD-ROM
Test Generator
Companion website

Presentations
  CD-ROM
Textbook CD
Vocabulary CD
Interactive CD-ROM
Video CD-ROM
Web-SAM

La naturaleza

Más vocabulario

el animal	animal
el bosque (tropical)	(tropical; rain) forest
el desierto	desert
la naturaleza	nature
la planta	plant
la región	region; area
la selva, la jungla	jungle
la tierra	land; soil
el cielo	sky
la estrella	star
la luna	moon
el mundo	world
la conservación	conservation
la contaminación (del aire; del agua)	(air; water) pollution
la deforestación	deforestation
la ecología	ecology
el ecoturismo	ecotourism
la energía (nuclear; solar)	(nuclear; solar) energy
la extinción	extinction
la lluvia (ácida)	(acid) rain
el medio ambiente	environment
el peligro	danger
el recurso natural	natural resource
la solución	solution
el gobierno	government
la ley	law
la población	population
puro/a	pure

Variación léxica

césped ←→ pasto (*Perú*); grama (*Venez., Col.*); zacate (*Méx.*)

recursos

TEXT CD Lección 13	WB pp. 155–156	LM p. 73	Lab CD/MP3 Lección 13	I CD-ROM Lección 13	Vocab CD Lección 13

el ave, el pájaro
el cráter
el volcán
el pez
la vaca
el árbol
el césped, la hierba
el perro
el gato

Práctica

la nube
el sol
el valle
el sendero
el lago
la piedra
el río
la flor

1 **Escuchar**  Mientras escuchas las frases, anota los sustantivos (*nouns*) que se refieren a las plantas, los animales, la tierra y el cielo.

Plantas	Animales	Tierra	Cielo
flores	perro	valle	sol
hierba	gatos	volcán	nubes
árboles	vacas	bosques tropicales	estrellas

2 **Seleccionar** Selecciona la palabra que no está relacionada con cada grupo.

1. estrella • gobierno • luna • sol gobierno
2. gatos • peces • perros • hierba hierba
3. contaminación • extinción • ecoturismo • deforestación ecoturismo
4. lago • río • mar • peligro peligro
5. vaca • gato • pájaro • población población
6. conservación • lluvia ácida • ecología • recurso natural lluvia ácida
7. cielo • cráter • aire • nube cráter
8. desierto • solución • selva • bosque solución
9. nube • cielo • lluvia • piedra piedra
10. flor • césped • sendero • árbol sendero

3 **Definir** Trabaja con un(a) compañero/a para definir o describir cada palabra. Sigue el modelo. Answers will vary.

modelo
Estudiante 1: ¿Qué es el cielo?
Estudiante 2: El cielo está sobre la tierra y tiene nubes.

1. la población
2. un valle
3. la lluvia
4. la naturaleza
5. un desierto
6. la extinción
7. la ecología
8. un sendero

4 **Describir** Trabajen en parejas para describir las siguientes fotos. Answers will vary.

1 **Suggestion** Check the answers orally with the class.

1 **Tapescript** 1. Mi novio siempre me compra flores para nuestro aniversario. 2. Cuando era pequeño jugaba con mi perro todo el tiempo. 3. Javier prefiere jugar al fútbol norteamericano sobre hierba natural. 4. Antes de las vacaciones, los estudiantes tomaban el sol en el parque. 5. No puedo visitarte porque soy alérgico a los gatos. 6. Durante la tormenta, las nubes grises cubrían toda la ciudad. 7. Cerca de la casa de mi hermana hay un valle donde siempre hay muchas vacas. 8. Algunas noches vamos al campo para ver las estrellas. 9. El Puracé es un volcán activo en los Andes colombianos. 10. Los árboles de los bosques tropicales contienen las curas para muchas enfermedades. *Textbook Activities CD*

2 **Suggestion** Have students give answers and state a category for each group. Ex: **1. Cosas que están en el cielo.**

3 **Expansion** Have pairs read their definitions aloud in random order for the class to guess which term is being described.

4 **Suggestion** Have pairs include this in the descriptions: objects in the photos, the colors, what the weather is like, the time of day, the country where the photo was taken. Ask students to pick a description to present to the class.

4 **Expansion** Ask students to imagine the photos were taken on a recent vacation. Have them write a brief essay about their vacation, incorporating their descriptions.

Suggestion Involve students in a discussion about recycling and conservation. Project **Transparency #51** and ask volunteers to describe what is happening in the drawing. Ask: **¿Quién me quiere describir lo que se ve en la ilustración? ¿Qué hace la señora de la izquierda? (Recicla una lata de aluminio.)** Cover the active vocabulary, then guide the conversation toward students' own experiences and opinions. Ask questions like the following: **¿Tiene un buen programa de reciclaje nuestra ciudad? ¿Qué hacen ustedes para reducir la contaminación del medio ambiente? ¿Qué hace la universidad? ¿Cómo estamos afectados por la contaminación en nuestra ciudad/región? ¿Cuál es el mayor problema ecológico de nuestra región? ¿Qué evitan ustedes por razones ecológicas?**

5 Expansion
• Ask questions that require students to recycle the activity's vocabulary. Ex: **¿Qué debemos hacer para mantener las calles limpias de basura? ¿Para qué trabajan los científicos? ¿Por qué es necesario que trabajemos para proteger el medio ambiente?**
• Have students write five more original sentences, using different forms of the verbs. Ask volunteers to share their sentences with the class.

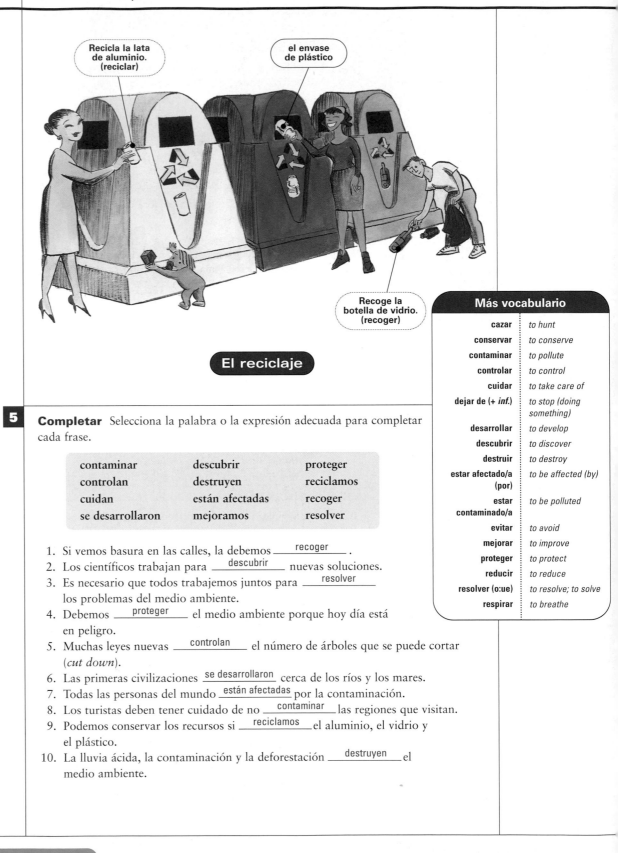

El reciclaje

Más vocabulario

cazar	to hunt
conservar	to conserve
contaminar	to pollute
controlar	to control
cuidar	to take care of
dejar de (+ inf.)	to stop (doing something)
desarrollar	to develop
descubrir	to discover
destruir	to destroy
estar afectado/a (por)	to be affected (by)
estar contaminado/a	to be polluted
evitar	to avoid
mejorar	to improve
proteger	to protect
reducir	to reduce
resolver (o:ue)	to resolve; to solve
respirar	to breathe

5 **Completar** Selecciona la palabra o la expresión adecuada para completar cada frase.

contaminar	descubrir	proteger
controlan	destruyen	reciclamos
cuidan	están afectadas	recoger
se desarrollaron	mejoramos	resolver

1. Si vemos basura en las calles, la debemos __recoger__ .
2. Los científicos trabajan para __descubrir__ nuevas soluciones.
3. Es necesario que todos trabajemos juntos para __resolver__ los problemas del medio ambiente.
4. Debemos __proteger__ el medio ambiente porque hoy día está en peligro.
5. Muchas leyes nuevas __controlan__ el número de árboles que se puede cortar (*cut down*).
6. Las primeras civilizaciones __se desarrollaron__ cerca de los ríos y los mares.
7. Todas las personas del mundo __están afectadas__ por la contaminación.
8. Los turistas deben tener cuidado de no __contaminar__ las regiones que visitan.
9. Podemos conservar los recursos si __reciclamos__ el aluminio, el vidrio y el plástico.
10. La lluvia ácida, la contaminación y la deforestación __destruyen__ el medio ambiente.

TEACHING OPTIONS

Pairs Have pairs of students write each vocabulary word from this page on index cards. Pairs then shuffle the cards and take turns drawing from the stack. The student who draws a card then must make a comment about conservation or the environment, using the word he or she has drawn. One partner writes down the other's comment. After students finish the stack, call on volunteers to share their comments.

Small Groups Divide the class into groups of three or four. Have each group make a list of eight environmental problems in the region. Ask groups to trade lists. Have them write solutions to the problems on the list they receive, and then give the lists back to the original group. After reading the solutions, the original groups should give reasons why the solutions are good or not.

Comunicación

NATIONAL communication STANDARDS

6

¿Es importante? Lee el siguiente párrafo y después contesta las preguntas con un(a) compañero/a. *Some answers will vary.*

Los problemas del medio ambiente

importantísimo	
muy importante	
importante	
poco importante	
no es importante	

la deforestación   los animales en peligro de extinción   la contaminación del aire   la contaminación del agua   la basura en las ciudades

Para celebrar El día de la tierra, una estación de radio colombiana hizo una pequeña encuesta (*survey*) entre estudiantes universitarios, donde les preguntaron sobre los problemas del medio ambiente. Se les preguntó cuáles creían que eran los cinco problemas más importantes del medio ambiente. Ellos también tenían que decidir el orden de importancia de estos problemas, del uno al cinco.

Los resultados probaron (*proved*) que la mayoría de los estudiantes están preocupados por la contaminación del aire. Muchos mencionaron que no hay aire puro en las ciudades. El problema número dos para los estudiantes es que los ríos y los lagos están afectados por la contaminación. La deforestación quedó como el problema número tres, la basura en las ciudades el número cuatro y los animales en peligro de extinción el número cinco.

1. ¿Según la encuesta, qué problema consideran más grave? ¿Qué problema consideran menos grave? la contaminación del aire; los animales en peligro de extinción
2. ¿Cómo creen que se puede evitar o resolver el problema más importante?
3. ¿Es necesario resolver el problema menos importante? ¿Por qué?
4. ¿Consideran ustedes que existen los mismos problemas en su comunidad? Den algunos ejemplos.

7

Situaciones Trabajen en grupos pequeños para representar las siguientes situaciones. *Answers will vary.*
1. Un(a) representante de una agencia ambiental (*environmental*) habla con el/la presidente/a de una compañía industrial que está contaminando un río o el aire.
2. Un(a) guía de ecoturismo habla con un grupo sobre cómo disfrutar (*enjoy*) de la naturaleza y conservar el medio ambiente.
3. Un(a) representante de la universidad habla con un grupo de nuevos estudiantes sobre la campaña (*campaign*) ambiental de la universidad y trata de reclutar (*tries to recruit*) miembros para un club que trabaja para la protección del medio ambiente.

8

Escribir una carta Trabajen en parejas para escribir una carta a una empresa real o imaginaria que esté contaminando el medio ambiente. Expliquen las consecuencias que sus acciones van a tener para el medio ambiente. Sugiéranle algunas ideas para que solucionen el problema. Utilicen por lo menos diez palabras de **Contextos**. *Answers will vary.*

TEACHING OPTIONS

Heritage Speakers Ask heritage speakers to interview family members or people in their community about the environmental challenges in the region they come from. Encourage them to find out how the problems impact the land and the people. Have students report their findings to the class.

Large Groups Write environmental problems and possible solutions on separate index cards. Ex: **la destrucción de los bosques** – **reducir las áreas de deforestación; la contaminación de los ríos** – **controlar el tipo de sustancias que hay en el agua.** Hand the cards out to students. Students with problem cards ask their classmates questions until they find a viable solution.

---

6 Expansion Divide the class into groups of five to discuss follow-up questions 2–4. Groups should reach a consensus for each question, then report to the class.

7 Suggestion Divide the class into groups of three. Have each group choose a situation, but make sure that all situations are covered. Have students take turns playing each role. After groups have had time to prepare their situations, have some of them present their skits to the class.

8 Suggestions
• Remind students that a business letter in Spanish begins with a salutation such as **Estimado(s) señor(es)** and ends with a closing such as **Atentamente**.
• With the whole class, brainstorm a list of agencies or companies that are known to be environmentally conscious. Ask the class to categorize the companies by the steps they take to protect the environment. Then divide the class into pairs and have them choose a company for the activity.

¡Qué paisaje más hermoso!

Martín y los estudiantes visitan el sendero en las montañas.

NATIONAL STANDARDS
communication
cultures

Section Goals

In **Fotonovela** students will:
• receive comprehensible input from free-flowing discourse
• learn functional phrases that preview lesson grammatical structures

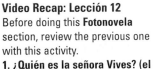

Instructional Resources
WB/VM: Video Activities,
pp. 219–220
***Fotonovela** DVD/Video*
(Start 01:10:38)
***Fotonovela** Video CD-ROM*
*IRM: **Fotonovela** Translations,*
pp. 125–126, Videoscript, pp.
101–102
Interactive CD-ROM

Video Recap: Lección 12
Before doing this **Fotonovela** section, review the previous one with this activity.
1. ¿Quién es la señora Vives? (el ama de casa)
2. ¿Qué muebles tiene la alcoba de los chicos? (dos camas, una mesita de noche, una cómoda, un armario)
3. ¿Qué quiere don Francisco que hagan los chicos? (quiere que ayuden a la señora Vives con los quehaceres domésticos)
4. ¿Por qué les aconseja don Francisco a los chicos que se acuesten temprano? (porque Martín, el guía, viene a las siete de la mañana)

Video Synopsis Don Francisco introduces the students to Martín, who will be their guide on the hike. Martín takes the students to the site of the hike, where they discuss the need for environmental protection.

Suggestions

• Have your students scan this **Fotonovela** episode and list words related to nature and the environment. Then have them predict what will happen in this episode. Write down their predictions.
• Quickly review the guesses your students made about the **Fotonovela**. Through discussion, guide the class to a correct summary of the plot.

PERSONAJES

MAITE

INÉS

DON FRANCISCO

ÁLEX

JAVIER

MARTÍN

1 **DON FRANCISCO** Chicos, les presento a Martín Dávalos, el guía de la excursión. Martín, nuestros pasajeros—Maite, Javier, Inés y Álex.

2 **MARTÍN** Mucho gusto. Voy a llevarlos al área donde vamos a ir de excursión mañana. ¿Qué les parece?
ESTUDIANTES ¡Sí! ¡Vamos!

3 **MAITE** ¡Qué paisaje más hermoso!
INÉS No creo que haya lugares más bonitos en el mundo.

6 **JAVIER** Entiendo que mañana vamos a cruzar un río. ¿Está contaminado?
MARTÍN En las montañas el río no parece estar afectado por la contaminación. Cerca de las ciudades, sin embargo, el río tiene bastante contaminación.

7 **ÁLEX** ¡Qué aire tan puro se respira aquí! No es como en la Ciudad de México... Tenemos un problema gravísimo de contaminación.
MARTÍN A menos que resuelvan ese problema, los habitantes van a sufrir muchas enfermedades en el futuro.

8 **INÉS** Creo que todos debemos hacer algo para proteger el medio ambiente.
MAITE Yo creo que todos los países deben establecer leyes que controlen el uso de automóviles.

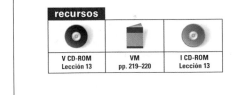

recursos

| V CD-ROM Lección 13 | VM pp. 219–220 | I CD-ROM Lección 13 |

TEACHING OPTIONS

Video Tips General suggestions for using video clips in the classroom can be found on page IAE-12 of this Instructor's Annotated Edition.

¡Qué paisaje más hermoso! Play the video episode and have your students give you a "play-by-play" description of the action. Write their descriptions on the board. Then replay it, asking the class to list any key words they hear. Write some of their key words on the board. Finally, discuss the material on the board with the class and guide the class toward a correct summary of the plot.

MARTÍN Esperamos que ustedes se diviertan mucho, pero es necesario que cuiden la naturaleza.

JAVIER Se pueden tomar fotos, ¿verdad?

MARTÍN Sí, con tal de que no toques las flores o las plantas.

ÁLEX ¿Hay problemas de contaminación en esta región?

MARTÍN La contaminación es un problema en todo el mundo. Pero aquí tenemos un programa de reciclaje. Si ves por el sendero botellas, papeles o latas, recógelos.

JAVIER Pero Maite, ¿tú vas a dejar de usar tu carro en Madrid?

MAITE Pues voy a tener que usar el metro... Pero tú sabes que mi coche es tan pequeñito... casi no contamina nada.

INÉS ¡Ven, Javier!

JAVIER ¡¡Ya voy!!

Enfoque cultural El ecoturismo

La contaminación es un problema en todo el mundo, incluyendo los países hispanohablantes. Sin embargo (*However*), el ecoturismo enseña a los turistas y a los habitantes de las regiones turísticas la importancia de cuidar el medio ambiente. El ecoturismo es muy popular en los bosques tropicales de países como Costa Rica y Perú, donde hay animales y plantas que están en peligro de extinción. Gracias al ecoturismo, los dueños de las tiendas de estas zonas turísticas son sus mismos habitantes, lo cual evita que el turismo altere estas regiones.

Expresiones útiles

Talking about the environment

▶ **¿Hay problemas de contaminación en esta región?**
Are there problems with pollution in this region/area?

▷ **La contaminación es un problema en todo el mundo.**
Pollution is a problem throughout the world.

▶ **¿Está contaminado el río?**
Is the river polluted?

▷ **En las montañas el río no parece estar afectado por la contaminación.**
In the mountains, the river does not seem to be affected by pollution.

▷ **Cerca de las ciudades el río tiene bastante contaminación.**
Near the cities, the river is pretty polluted.

▶ **¡Qué aire tan puro se respira aquí!**
The air you breathe here is so pure!

▶ **Puedes tomar fotos, con tal de que no toques las plantas.**
You can take pictures, provided that you don't touch the plants.

▶ **Es necesario que cuiden la naturaleza.**
It's necessary that you take care of nature/respect the environment.

▶ **Tenemos un problema gravísimo de contaminación.**
We have an extremely serious problem with pollution.

▶ **A menos que resuelvan el problema, los habitantes van a sufrir muchas enfermedades.**
Unless they solve the problem, the inhabitants are going to suffer many illnesses.

▶ **Tenemos un programa de reciclaje.**
We have a recycling program.

▶ **Si ves por el sendero botellas, papeles o latas, recógelos.**
If you see bottles, papers, or cans along the trail, pick them up.

Suggestions
• Continue the conversation that you began in **Contextos** about the state of the environment in your area. Integrate **Expresiones útiles** into the conversation. Ex: **¿Cuál es el mayor problema de contaminación en esta región? ¿Qué creen ustedes que debemos hacer para proteger el medio ambiente?**
• Have the class work in groups to read through the entire **Fotonovela** aloud, with volunteers playing the various parts.

Expresiones útiles Draw attention to the question **¿Está contaminado el río?** Tell the class that **contaminado** is a past participle of the verb **contaminar** and that it is used here as an adjective. Have the class look at video still 3 of the **Fotonovela**. Explain that **No creo que haya lugares más bonitos en el mundo** is an example of the present subjunctive used with an expression of doubt. In video still 4, point out that **Esperamos que ustedes se diviertan mucho** is an example of the present subjunctive with a verb of emotion. Draw attention to **con tal de que no toques las flores** in video still 4 and **a menos que resuelvan ese problema** in video still 7; explain that **con tal de que** and **a menos que** are conjunctions that are always followed by the subjunctive. Tell your students that they will learn more about these concepts in **Estructura**.

TEACHING OPTIONS

Enfoque cultural Many governments in the Spanish-speaking world have established national parks and biological reserves to preserve their natural treasures. Costa Rica and Ecuador, of course, are famous for their protection of ecological treasures, but there are also other famous examples. **El Yunque**, located near San Juan, Puerto Rico, also known as the **Bosque Nacional del Caribe**, preserves a tract of the Caribbean rain for-est. **Parque Nacional Manu**, in Peru's Amazon basin, is famous for its brilliantly-colored macaws, jaguars, ocelots, otters, and alligators. **Parque Nacional Canaima**, in the Guiana highlands of Venezuela, is home of the microecologies of the **tepuyes** and **Salto Ángel**, the highest waterfall in the world. **Parque Nacional Torres del Paine** in Chilean Patagonia contains some of the most spectacularly rugged crags in the southern Andes.

Reacciona a la fotonovela

1 **Seleccionar** Selecciona la respuesta más lógica para cada frase.

1. Martín va a llevar a los estudiantes al lugar donde van a ____c____.
   a. contaminar el río b. bailar c. ir de excursión

2. El río está más afectado por la contaminación ____b____.
   a. cerca de los bosques b. en las ciudades c. en las montañas

3. Martín quiere que los estudiantes ____a____.
   a. limpien los senderos b. descubran nuevos senderos c. no usen sus autos

4. La naturaleza está formada por ____c____.
   a. los ríos, las montañas y las leyes b. los animales, las latas y los ríos
   c. los lagos, los animales y las plantas

5. La contaminación del aire puede producir ____b____.
   a. problemas del estómago b. enfermedades respiratorias c. enfermedades mentales

2 **Identificar** Identifica quién puede decir las siguientes frases. Puedes usar cada nombre más de una vez.

1. Es necesario que hagamos algo por el medio ambiente, ¿pero qué? Inés
2. En mi ciudad es imposible respirar aire limpio. ¡Está muy contaminado! Álex
3. En el futuro, a causa del problema de la contaminación, las personas van a tener problemas de salud. Martín
4. El metro es una excelente alternativa al coche. Maite
5. ¿Está limpio o contaminado el río? Javier
6. Es importante reciclar latas y botellas. Martín
7. De todos los lugares del mundo, me parece que éste es el mejor. Inés
8. Como todo el mundo usa automóviles, debemos establecer leyes para controlar cómo y cuándo usarlos. Maite

ÁLEX   INÉS

MAITE

MARTÍN   JAVIER

◀ **NOTA CULTURAL**

En la capital de México existe la ley de "Hoy no circula" la cual controla el uso de **los automóviles**. Las personas no pueden manejar su carro un día a la semana. Por ejemplo, los automóviles con placas (*plates*) que terminan en 5 y 6 no pueden circular los lunes.

3 **Preguntas** Responde a las siguientes preguntas usando la información de **Fotonovela**.

1. Según Martín, ¿qué es necesario que hagan los estudiantes? ¿Qué no pueden hacer?
   Es necesario que cuiden la naturaleza. No pueden tocar las plantas ni las flores.
2. ¿Qué problemas del medio ambiente mencionan Martín y los estudiantes?
   Hay problemas de contaminación del aire y de los ríos.
3. ¿Qué cree Maite que deben hacer los países?
   Los países deben establecer leyes que controlen el uso de los automóviles.
4. ¿Qué cosas se pueden reciclar? Menciona tres.
   Se pueden reciclar las botellas, los papeles y las latas.
5. ¿Qué otro medio de transporte importante dice Maite que hay en Madrid?
   Dice que el metro es importante.

4 **El medio ambiente** En parejas, discutan algunos problemas ambientales y sus posibles soluciones. Usen las siguientes preguntas y frases en su conversación.
Answers will vary.
- ¿Hay problemas de contaminación donde vives?
- Tenemos un problema muy grave de contaminación de...
- ¿Cómo podemos resolver los problemas de la contaminación?

---

1 Expansion Have students use the subject of the sentence in each item to write new sentences that incorporate words from **Contextos**.

2 Expansion Have pairs come up with a response that Martín would give for each of the comments listed in the activity, with the exception of items 3 and 6.

3 Expansion Have pairs use the answers to the questions as if they were lines of dialogue, incorporating them into a conversation, different from the one in the episode, among the **Fotonovela** characters. Have pairs perform their conversation for the class.

4 Possible Response
E1: ¿Hay problemas de contaminación donde vives?
E2: Sí, tenemos un problema muy grave de contaminación de los ríos. Hay muchos papeles, botellas y latas en los ríos. En las montañas, los ríos no están afectados por la contaminación pero en las ciudades, sí. ¿En tu región hay problemas de contaminación?
E1: Sí, tenemos un problema gravísimo de contaminación del aire. ¡No se puede respirar aire puro! Esto causa enfermedades para los habitantes.
E2: Qué terrible. ¿Cómo podemos resolver los problemas de la contaminación?
E1: Bueno, nosotros tenemos un programa de reciclaje ahora. Reciclamos papeles, latas y botellas de vidrio y plástico. También algunas personas tratan de no usar el auto. Usan el metro o caminan al trabajo o a la universidad.

The Affective Dimension
Many students feel nervous when called on to give an answer or to read aloud. You can minimize this source of anxiety by asking for volunteers and by having students work in pairs or groups.

TEACHING OPTIONS

Extra Practice You may want to use the sentences in **Actividad 1** or **Actividad 2** on this page for a dictation activity. Have your students close their books, then read each sentence twice slowly and once at regular speed. Then have students open their books and correct any errors in their work.

Small Groups Have your students work in groups of three to write a short article about their environmental concerns for a local newsletter (**boletín informativo**). Their articles should include a description of a few environmental problems and some suggestions for solving them. When groups have finished, have them share their articles with the rest of the class.

Ortografía

Los signos de puntuación

In Spanish, as in English, punctuation marks are important because they help you express your ideas in a clear, organized way.

> **No podía ver las llaves. Las buscó por los estantes, las mesas, las sillas, el suelo; minutos después, decidió mirar por la ventana. Allí estaban…**

The **punto y coma (;)**, the **tres puntos (…)**, and the **punto (.)** are used in very similar ways in Spanish and English.

> **Argentina, Brasil, Paraguay y Uruguay son miembros de Mercosur.**

In Spanish, the **coma (,)** is not used before **y** or **o** in a series.

13,5%	**29,2°**	**3.000.000**	**$2.999,99**

In numbers, Spanish uses a **coma** where English uses a decimal point and a **punto** where English uses a comma.

¿**Cómo te llamas**?   **¿Dónde está?**   **¡Ven aquí!**   **Hola**

Questions in Spanish are preceded and followed by **signos de interrogación (¿ ?)**, and exclamations are preceded and followed by **signos de exclamación (¡ !)**.

Práctica Lee el párrafo e indica los signos de puntuación necesarios. Answers will vary.

Ayer recibí la invitación de boda de Marta mi amiga colombiana inmediatamente empecé a pensar en un posible regalo fui al almacén donde Marta y su novio tenían una lista de regalos había de todo copas cafeteras tostadoras finalmente decidí regalarles un perro ya sé que es un regalo extraño pero espero que les guste a los dos

¿Palabras de amor? El siguiente diálogo tiene diferentes significados (*meanings*) dependiendo de los signos de puntuación que utilices y el lugar donde los pongas. Intenta encontrar los diferentes significados. Answers will vary.

JULIÁN	me quieres
MARISOL	no puedo vivir sin ti
JULIÁN	me quieres dejar
MARISOL	no me parece mala idea
JULIÁN	no eres feliz conmigo
MARISOL	no soy feliz

Section Goal

In **Ortografía** students will learn the use of punctuation marks in Spanish.

Instructional Resource
Interactive CD-ROM

Suggestions

- Explain that ellipsis marks are used in Spanish to indicate omissions and hesitations, but that there is no space before or between the marks in Spanish. There is, however, a space after them.
- Model reading the numerical examples. Ex: **13,5% = trece coma cinco por ciento; 29,2° = veintinueve coma dos grados.** Write numbers on the board for translations into Spanish. Ex: 89.3%; 5,020,307; $13.50; 0.49%.
- Explain that the inverted question mark or exclamation point does not always come at the beginning of a sentence, but at the beginning of the part of the sentence where the question or exclamation begins. Ex:
  —**¿Cómo estás, Mirta?**
  —**¡Súper bien, Andrés! Y tú, ¿cómo estás?**
  —**No me siento bien y me duele la cabeza, ¡caramba!**
- Point out that **Ortografía** replaces **Pronunciación** in the Student Edition for **Lecciones 10–15**, but not in the Lab Manual. The **Recursos** box references the **Pronunciación** sections found in all lessons of the Lab Manual.

¿Palabras de amor? Two possibilities for punctuation:

J: ¿Me quieres?
M: ¡No puedo vivir sin ti!
J: ¿Me quieres dejar?
M: No. Me parece mala idea.
J: ¿No eres feliz conmigo?
M: No. Soy feliz.

J: ¿Me quieres?
M: No. Puedo vivir sin ti.
J: ¡Me quieres dejar!
M: No me parece mala idea.
J: ¿No eres feliz conmigo?
M: No soy feliz.

Pairs Have pairs write example sentences for each of the four punctuation rules explained in **Ortografía**. Then ask volunteers to write their sentences on the board.

Extra Practice Go over the **¿Palabras de amor?** dialogue and point out how it can be punctuated in different ways to express opposite meanings. Reinforce this point by having your students work in pairs to dramatize the dialogue in both ways. Ask a few pairs to present the contrasting dialogues to the class.

13.1 The subjunctive with verbs of emotion

NATIONAL STANDARDS comparisons

recursos

WB
pp. 157–164

LM
pp. 75–78

Lab CD/MP3
Lección 13

I CD-ROM
Lección 13

vistahigher
learning.com

ANTE TODO In the previous lesson, you learned how to use the subjunctive with expressions of will and influence. You will now learn how to use the subjunctive with verbs and expressions of emotion.

Main clause		Subordinate clause
Marta **espera**	que	yo **vaya** al lago este fin de semana.

▶ When the verb in the main clause of a sentence expresses an emotion or feeling such as hope, fear, joy, pity, surprise, etc., the subjunctive is required in the subordinate clause.

Nos alegramos de que te **gusten** las flores.
We are happy that you like the flowers.

Siento que tú no **puedas** venir mañana.
I'm sorry that you can't come tomorrow.

Temo que Ana no **pueda** ir mañana con nosotros.
I'm afraid that Ana won't be able to go with us tomorrow.

Le **sorprende** que Juan **sea** tan joven.
It surprises him that Juan is so young.

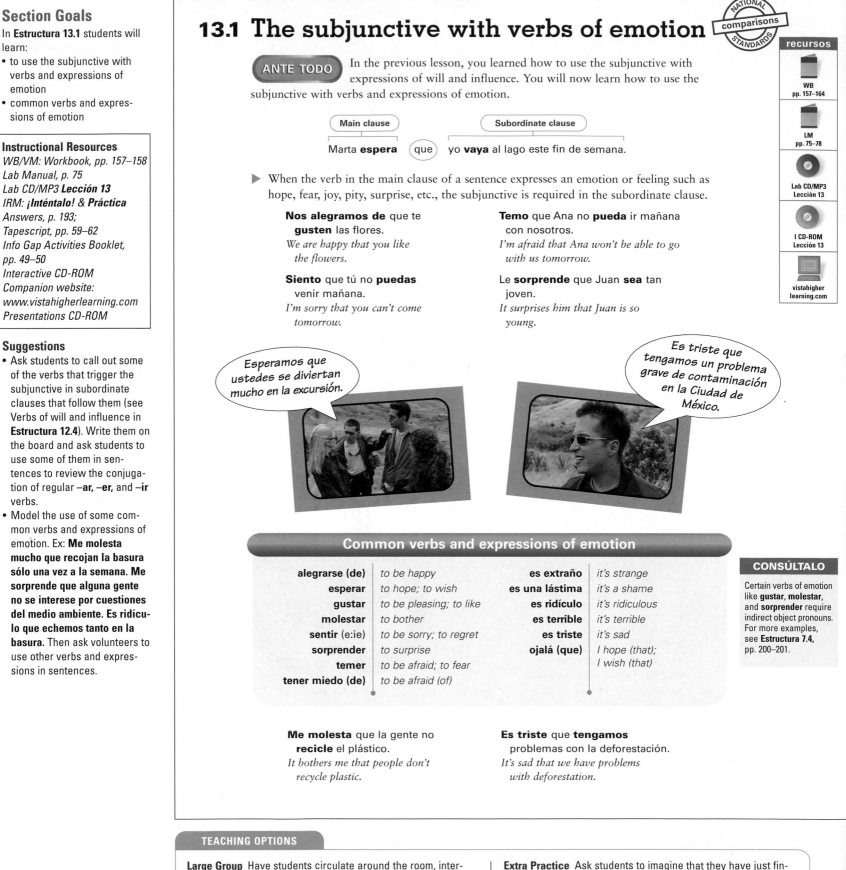

Esperamos que ustedes se diviertan mucho en la excursión.

Es triste que tengamos un problema grave de contaminación en la Ciudad de México.

Common verbs and expressions of emotion

alegrarse (de)	to be happy	**es extraño**	it's strange
esperar	to hope; to wish	**es una lástima**	it's a shame
gustar	to be pleasing; to like	**es ridículo**	it's ridiculous
molestar	to bother	**es terrible**	it's terrible
sentir (e:ie)	to be sorry; to regret	**es triste**	it's sad
sorprender	to surprise	**ojalá (que)**	I hope (that); I wish (that)
temer	to be afraid; to fear		
tener miedo (de)	to be afraid (of)		

CONSÚLTALO

Certain verbs of emotion like **gustar**, **molestar**, and **sorprender** require indirect object pronouns. For more examples, see **Estructura 7.4**, pp. 200–201.

Me molesta que la gente no **recicle** el plástico.
It bothers me that people don't recycle plastic.

Es triste que **tengamos** problemas con la deforestación.
It's sad that we have problems with deforestation.

▶ As with expressions of will and influence, the infinitive, not the subjunctive, is used after an expression of emotion when there is no change of subject from the main clause to the subordinate clause. Compare these sentences.

Temo **llegar** tarde.
I'm afraid I'll arrive late.

Temo que mi novio **llegue** tarde.
I'm afraid my boyfriend will arrive late.

▶ The expression **ojalá (que)** means *I hope* or *I wish*, and it is always followed by the subjunctive. Note that the use of **que** with this expression is optional.

Ojalá (que) se conserven
nuestros recursos naturales.
I hope (that) our natural resources will be conserved.

Ojalá (que) recojan la basura
hoy.
I hope (that) they collect the garbage today.

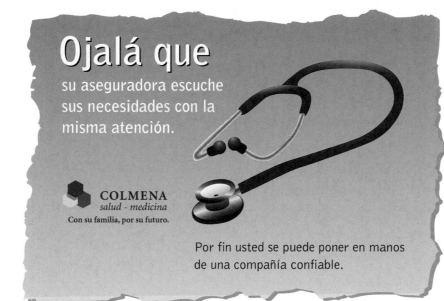

Ojalá que
su aseguradora escuche
sus necesidades con la
misma atención.

COLMENA
salud - medicina
Con su familia, por su futuro.

Por fin usted se puede poner en manos
de una compañía confiable.

¡INTÉNTALO! Completa las oraciones con las formas correctas de los verbos.

1. Ojalá que ellos __descubran__ (descubrir) nuevas formas de energía.
2. Espero que Ana nos __ayude__ (ayudar) a recoger la basura en la carretera.
3. Es una lástima que la gente no __recicle__ (reciclar) más.
4. Esperamos __proteger__ (proteger) el aire de nuestra comunidad.
5. Me alegro de que mis amigos __quieran__ (querer) conservar la naturaleza.
6. A mis padres les gusta que nosotros __participemos__ (participar) en programas de conservación.
7. Es malo __contaminar__ (contaminar) el medio ambiente.
8. Espero que tú __vengas__ (venir) a la reunión (*meeting*) del Club de Ecología.
9. Siento que nuestras ciudades __estén__ (estar) afectadas por la contaminación.
10. Ojalá que yo __pueda__ (poder) hacer algo para reducir la contaminación.

Suggestions
• Compare and contrast the use of the infinitive and the subjunctive with examples like the following: **Juan espera hacer algo para aliviar el problema de la contaminación ambiental. Juan espera que el gobierno haga algo para aliviar el problema de la contaminación ambiental.** Then proceed: **¿Es terrible no reciclar? ¿Es terrible que yo no recicle? ¿Les molesta sentarse aquí? ¿Les molesta que nos sentemos aquí?**
• Use a ball (or balled-up piece of paper) to expand on the **¡Inténtalo!** activity. Read the beginning of one of the sentences (the words before the blank) and toss the ball to one of your students, who should then complete the sentence in an original manner using the correct subjunctive form of a verb or an infinitive.

The Affective Dimension
Reassure students they will feel more comfortable with the subjunctive as they continue studying Spanish.

TEACHING OPTIONS

Extra Practice Have students look at the drawing for **Contextos** on pages 362–363. Ask them to imagine they are one of the people pictured. Then have them write five sentences about how they feel from the point of view of that person. Ex: **Espero que a Alicia le guste la comida. Ojalá que ella no pierda las llaves del carro esta vez. Es ridículo que llevemos el perro y el gato a un picnic.**

Pairs Have students write five sentences describing nature or the environment. Students then read their sentences to a partner who will respond to each one, expressing a feeling or hope. Ex: **Hay muchos animales que están en peligro de extinción. (Es terrible que haya muchos animales en peligro de extinción.)**

Práctica

1 Completar Completa el diálogo con palabras de la lista. Compara tus respuestas con las de un(a) compañero/a.

Bogotá, Colombia

alegro	molesta	salga
encuentren	ojalá	tengo miedo de
estén	puedan	vayan
lleguen	reduzcan	visitar

OLGA Me alegro de que Adriana y Raquel (1)___vayan___ a Colombia. ¿Van a estudiar?

SARA Sí. Es una lástima que (2)___lleguen___ una semana tarde. Ojalá que la universidad las ayude a buscar casa. (3)___Tengo miedo de___ que no consigan dónde vivir.

OLGA Me (4)___molesta___ que seas tan pesimista, pero sí, yo también espero que (5)___encuentren___ gente simpática y que hablen mucho español.

SARA Sí, ojalá. Van a hacer un estudio sobre la deforestación en las costas. Es triste que en tantos países los recursos naturales (6)___estén___ en peligro.

OLGA Pues, me (7)___alegro___ de que no se queden mucho en la capital por la contaminación. (8)___Ojalá___ tengan tiempo de viajar por el país.

SARA Sí, espero que (9)___puedan___ por lo menos ir a la costa. Sé que también esperan (10)___visitar___ la Catedral de Sal de Zipaquirá.

2 Transformar Transforma los siguientes elementos en frases completas para formar un diálogo entre Juan y la madre de Raquel. Añade palabras si es necesario. Luego, con un(a) compañero/a, presenta el diálogo a la clase. Some answers will vary.

1. Juan, / esperar / (tú) escribirle / Raquel. / Ser / tu / novia. / Ojalá / no / sentirse / sola. Juan, espero que (tú) le escribas a Raquel. Es tu novia. Ojalá (que) no se sienta sola.

2. molestarme / (usted) decirme / lo que / tener / hacer. / Ahora / mismo / le / estar / escribiendo. Me molesta que (Ud.) me diga lo que tengo que hacer. Ahora mismo le estoy escribiendo.

3. alegrarme / oírte / decir / eso. / Ser / terrible / estar / lejos / cuando / nadie / recordarte. Me alegra oírte decir eso. Es terrible estar lejos cuando nadie te recuerda.

4. señora, / ¡yo / tener / miedo / (ella) no recordarme / mí! / Ser / triste / estar / sin / novia. Señora, ¡yo tengo miedo de que (ella) no me recuerde a mí! Es triste estar sin novia.

5. ser / ridículo / (tú) sentirte / así. / Tú / saber / ella / querer / casarse / contigo. Es ridículo que te sientas así. Tú sabes que ella quiere casarse contigo.

6. ridículo / o / no, / sorprenderme / (todos) preocuparse / ella / y / (nadie) acordarse / mí. Ridículo o no, me sorprende que todos se preocupen por ella y nadie se acuerde de mí.

Comunicación

3 **Comentar** En parejas, túrnense para formar oraciones sobre su ciudad, sus clases, su gobierno o algún otro tema, usando expresiones como **me alegro de que, temo que** y **es extraño que.** Luego reaccionen a los comentarios de su compañero/a.   Answers will vary.

> **modelo**
>
> **Estudiante 1:** Me alegro de que vayan a limpiar el río.
> **Estudiante 2:** Yo también. Me preocupa que el agua del río esté tan sucia.

4 **Contestar** Lee el mensaje electrónico que Raquel le escribió a su novio Juan. Luego, en parejas, contesten el mensaje usando expresiones como **me sorprende que, me molesta que** y **es una lástima que.** Answers will vary.

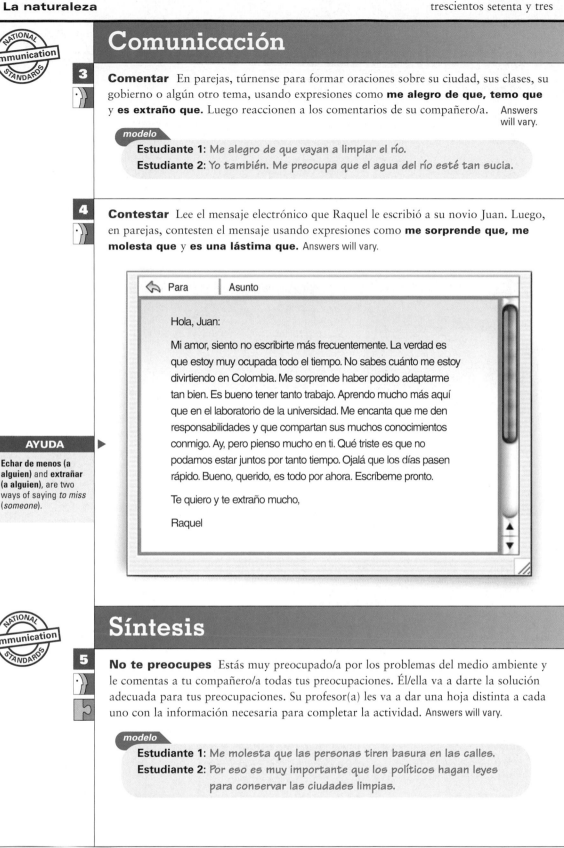

Para | **Asunto**

Hola, Juan:

Mi amor, siento no escribirte más frecuentemente. La verdad es que estoy muy ocupada todo el tiempo. No sabes cuánto me estoy divirtiendo en Colombia. Me sorprende haber podido adaptarme tan bien. Es bueno tener tanto trabajo. Aprendo mucho más aquí que en el laboratorio de la universidad. Me encanta que me den responsabilidades y que compartan sus muchos conocimientos conmigo. Ay, pero pienso mucho en ti. Qué triste es que no podamos estar juntos por tanto tiempo. Ojalá que los días pasen rápido. Bueno, querido, es todo por ahora. Escríbeme pronto.

Te quiero y te extraño mucho,

Raquel

> **AYUDA**
>
> **Echar de menos (a alguien)** and **extrañar (a alguien),** are two ways of saying *to miss* (*someone*).

Síntesis

5 **No te preocupes** Estás muy preocupado/a por los problemas del medio ambiente y le comentas a tu compañero/a todas tus preocupaciones. Él/ella va a darte la solución adecuada para tus preocupaciones. Su profesor(a) les va a dar una hoja distinta a cada uno con la información necesaria para completar la actividad. Answers will vary.

> **modelo**
>
> **Estudiante 1:** Me molesta que las personas tiren basura en las calles.
> **Estudiante 2:** Por eso es muy importante que los políticos hagan leyes para conservar las ciudades limpias.

Suggestions (sidebar)

3 Suggestions
- Before starting the activity, have students divide a sheet of paper into four columns, with these headings: **nuestra ciudad, las clases, el gobierno**, and another subject of their choosing. Ask them to brainstorm topics or issues for each column.
- Have groups write statements about these issues and then hand them off to another group for its reactions. The second group should write down their comments and exchange them with the first group.

4 Expansion In pairs, have students tell each other about a memorable e-mail that they have written. Using verbs and expressions of emotion, partners must respond to the e-mail as if they had received it. Wherever applicable, ask pairs to compare their partners' responses with the ones they actually received from the real recipients.

5 Suggestion Divide the class into pairs and distribute the handouts from the Information Gap Activities Booklet that correspond to this activity. Give the students ten minutes to complete this activity.

5 Expansion Have students work in groups of three to create a public service announcement. Groups should choose one of the ecological problems they mentioned in the activity, and include the proposed solutions for that problem in their announcement.

TEACHING OPTIONS

Small Groups Divide students into groups of three. Have students write three predictions about the future on separate pieces of paper and put them in a sack. Students take turns drawing predictions and reading them to the group. Group members respond with an appropriate expression of emotion. Ex: **Voy a ganar millones de dólares algún día. (Me alegro que vayas a ganar millones de dólares.)**

Extra Practice Ask students to imagine that they are world leaders speaking at an environmental summit. Have students deliver a short speech to the class about some of the world's environmental problems and how they hope to solve them. Students should use as many verbs and expressions of emotion as possible.

Section Goals

In **Estructura 13.2** students will learn:
• to use the subjunctive with verbs and expressions of doubt, disbelief, and denial
• common verbs and expressions of doubt, disbelief, and denial
• expressions of certainty

Instructional Resources
WB/VM: Workbook, pp. 159–160
Lab Manual, p. 76
Lab CD/MP3 **Lección 13**
IRM: **¡Inténtalo!** & **Práctica**
Answers, p. 193;
Tapescript, pp. 59–62
Interactive CD-ROM
Companion website:
www.vistahigherlearning.com
Presentations CD-ROM

Suggestions
• Introduce a few of the expressions of doubt, disbelief, or denial by talking about a topic familiar to the whole class.
Ex: **Dudo que el equipo de baloncesto vaya a ganar el partido este fin de semana. Es probable que el equipo contrario gane. No es cierto que el entrenador de nuestro equipo sea tan bueno como se dice.** As you introduce each expression of doubt, disbelief, or denial, write it on the board, making sure that everyone understands its meaning and recognizes the subjunctive verb in the subordinate clause.
• Ask volunteers to read the captions to the video stills, having them identify the phrase that triggers the subjunctive and the verb in the subjunctive.

13.2 The subjunctive with doubt, disbelief, and denial

ANTE TODO Just as the subjunctive is required with expressions of emotion, influence, and will, it is also used with expressions of doubt, disbelief, and denial.

Main clause		Subordinate clause
Dudan	que	su hijo les **diga** la verdad.

▶ The subjunctive is always used in a subordinate clause when there is a change of subject and the expression in the main clause implies negation or uncertainty.

No creo que haya lugares más bonitos en el mundo.

Dudo que el río esté contaminado aquí en las montañas.

▶ Here is a list of some common expressions of doubt, disbelief, or denial.

Expressions of doubt, disbelief, or denial

dudar	to doubt	**no es seguro**	it's not certain
negar (e:ie)	to deny	**no es verdad**	it's not true
no creer	not to believe	**es imposible**	it's impossible
no estar seguro/a (de)	not to be sure	**es improbable**	it's improbable
no es cierto	it's not true; it's not certain	**(no) es posible**	it's (not) possible
		(no) es probable	it's (not) probable

El gobierno **niega** que el agua **esté** contaminada.
The government denies that the water is contaminated.

Dudo que el gobierno **resuelva** el problema.
I doubt that the government will solve the problem.

Es probable que **haya** menos bosques y selvas en el futuro.
It's probable that there will be fewer forests and jungles in the future.

No es verdad que mi hermano **estudie** ecología.
It's not true that my brother studies ecology.

¡LENGUA VIVA!

In English, the expression *it is probable* indicates a fairly high degree of certainty. In Spanish, however, **es probable** implies uncertainty and therefore triggers the subjunctive in the subordinate clause: **Es muy probable que venga Elena.**

TEACHING OPTIONS

Extra Practice Write these statements on the board, then ask students to write their reactions using a different expression of doubt, disbelief, or denial for each. **1. Muchos tipos de peces viven en el desierto. 2. El cielo se está cayendo. 3. Plantas enormes crecen en la luna. 4. Los carros pequeños no contaminan. 5. No hay ningún animal en peligro de extinción.**

Pairs Ask students to write five absurd statements. Students react to their partners' statements with an expression of doubt, disbelief, or denial as their partner reads them aloud. Ex: **Unos hombres verdes vienen a visitarme todos los días. (No creo que unos hombres verdes vengan a visitarte todos los días.)**

▶ The indicative is used in a subordinate clause when there is no doubt or uncertainty in the main clause. Here is a list of some expressions of certainty.

Expressions of certainty

creer	*to believe*	**es cierto**	*it's true; it's certain*
no cabe duda de	*there is no doubt*	**es obvio**	*it's obvious*
no dudar	*not to doubt*	**es seguro**	*it's certain*
no hay duda de	*there is no doubt*	**es verdad**	*it's true*
no negar (e:ie)	*not to deny*	**estar seguro/a (de)**	*to be sure*

No negamos que **hay** demasiados carros en las carreteras.
We don't deny that there are too many cars on the highways.

Es verdad que Colombia **es** un país bonito.
It's true that Colombia is a beautiful country.

No hay duda de que el Amazonas **es** uno de los ríos más largos.
There is no doubt that the Amazon is one of the longest rivers.

Es obvio que los tigres **están** en peligro de extinción.
It's obvious that tigers are in danger of extinction.

▶ In affirmative sentences, the verb **creer** expresses belief or certainty, so it is followed by the indicative. In negative sentences, however, when doubt is implied, **creer** is followed by the subjunctive.

No creo que **haya** vida en el planeta Marte.
I don't believe that there is life on the planet Mars.

Creo que **debemos** usar exclusivamente la energía solar.
I believe we should use solar energy exclusively.

▶ The expressions **quizás** and **tal vez** are usually followed by the subjunctive because they imply doubt about something.

Quizás haga sol mañana.
Perhaps it will be sunny tomorrow.

Tal vez veamos la luna esta noche.
Perhaps we will see the moon tonight.

¡INTÉNTALO! Completa estas frases con la forma correcta del verbo.

1. Dudo que ellos __trabajen__ (trabajar).
2. Es cierto que él __come__ (comer) mucho.
3. Es imposible que ellos __salgan__ (salir).
4. Es probable que ustedes __ganen__ (ganar).
5. No creo que ella __vuelva__ (volver).
6. Es posible que nosotros __vayamos__ (ir).
7. Dudamos que tú __recicles__ (reciclar).
8. Creo que ellos __juegan__ (jugar) al fútbol.
9. No niego que ustedes __estudian__ (estudiar).
10. Es posible que ella no __venga__ (venir) a casa.
11. Es probable que ellos __duerman__ (dormir).
12. Es posible que Marta __llame__ (llamar).
13. Tal vez Juan no nos __oiga__ (oír).
14. No es cierto que ellos nos __ayuden__ (ayudar).
15. Es obvio que Luis __se aburre__ (aburrirse).
16. Creo que Juana __va__ (ir) a casarse.

Práctica

1 Expansion Have pairs prepare another conversation between Raúl and his father using expressions of doubt, disbelief, and denial as well as expressions of certainty. This time, Raúl is explaining the advantages of the Internet to his reluctant father and trying to persuade him to use it. Have pairs act out the conversation for the class.

2 Expansion
• Continue the activity by making other false statements. Ex: **Voy a hacer una excursión a la Patagonia mañana. Mi abuela sólo come pasteles y cebollas.**
• Ask students to write down two true sentences and two false ones. Encourage them to write statements that are all relatively likely. Have partners read their sentences to each other in random order. Pairs must express whether they think their partners' statements are true or false by using sentences with expressions of doubt, disbelief, and denial or expressions of certainty. Ex: **Mañana tengo que ir al médico. (Dudo que tengas que ir al médico.)** The student who stumps his or her partner with all four statements wins. Have pairs share the most challenging sentences with the class.

1 **Escoger** Escoge las respuestas correctas para completar el diálogo. Luego dramatiza el diálogo con un(a) compañero/a.

RAÚL Ustedes dudan que yo realmente (1) __estudie__ (estudio/estudie). No niego que a veces me (2) __divierto__ (divierto/divierta) demasiado, pero no cabe duda de que (3) __tomo__ (tomo/tome) mis estudios en serio. Estoy seguro de que cuando me vean graduarme van a pensar de manera diferente. Creo que no (4) __tienen__ (tienen/tengan) razón con sus críticas.

PAPÁ Es posible que tu mamá y yo no (5) __tengamos__ (tenemos/tengamos) razón. Es cierto que a veces (6) __dudamos__ (dudamos/dudemos) de ti. Pero no hay duda de que te (7) __pasas__ (pasas/pases) toda la noche en Internet y oyendo música. No es nada seguro que (8) __estés__ (estás/estés) estudiando.

RAÚL Es verdad que (9) __uso__ (uso/use) mucho la computadora pero, ¡piensen! ¿No es posible que (10) __sea__ (es/sea) para buscar información para mis clases? ¡No hay duda de que Internet (11) __es__ (es/sea) el mejor recurso del mundo! Es obvio que ustedes (12) __piensan__ (piensan/piensen) que no hago nada, pero no es cierto.

PAPÁ No dudo que esta conversación nos (13) __va__ (va/vaya) a ayudar. Pero tal vez esta noche (14) __puedas__ (puedes/puedas) trabajar sin música. ¿Está bien?

2 **Dudas** Carolina es una chica que siempre miente. Expresa tus dudas sobre lo que Carolina está diciendo ahora. Usa las expresiones entre paréntesis para tus respuestas.

> **modelo**
> El próximo año mi familia y yo vamos de vacaciones por diez meses. (dudar)
> ¡Ja! Dudo que vayan de vacaciones por ese tiempo. ¡Ustedes no son ricos!

1. Estoy escribiendo una novela en español. (no creer)
   No creo que estés escribiendo una novela en español.
2. Mi tía es la directora del *Sierra Club*. (no ser verdad)
   No es verdad que tu tía sea la directora del Sierra Club.
3. Dos profesores míos juegan para los Osos *(Bears)* de Chicago. (ser imposible)
   Es imposible que dos profesores tuyos jueguen para los Osos.
4. Mi mejor amiga conoce al chef Emeril. (no ser cierto)
   No es cierto que tu mejor amiga conozca al chef Emeril.
5. Mi padre es dueño del Centro Rockefeller. (no ser posible)
   No es posible que tu padre sea dueño del Centro Rockefeller.
6. Yo ya tengo un doctorado *(doctorate)* en lenguas. (ser improbable)
   Es improbable que tengas un doctorado en lenguas.

AYUDA

Some useful expressions to say that you don't believe someone:
¡Qué va!
¡Imposible!
¡No te creo!
¡Es mentira!

TEACHING OPTIONS

Large Groups Divide the class into groups of six to stage an environmental debate. Some groups should play the role of environmental advocates while others represent industrialists and big business. Have students take turns presenting a policy platform for the group they represent. When they are finished, opposing groups express their doubts, disbeliefs, and denials.

Heritage Speakers Ask heritage speakers to write an editorial about a current event or political issue in their community. In the body of their essay, students should include expressions of certainty as well as expressions of doubt, disbelief, or denial.

Comunicación

3 **Entrevista** En parejas, imaginen que trabajan para un periódico y que tienen que hacerle una entrevista a la conservacionista Mary Axtmann, la coordinadora del programa Ciudadanos Pro Bosque San Patricio, en Puerto Rico. Escriban seis preguntas para la entrevista después de leer las declaraciones de Mary Axtmann. Al final, inventen las respuestas de Axtmann. Answers will vary.

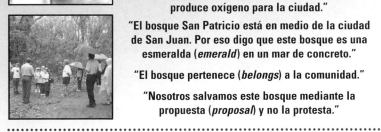

Declaraciones de Mary Axtmann:

"...que el bosque es un recurso ecológico educativo para la comunidad."

"El bosque San Patricio es un pulmón (*lung*) que produce oxígeno para la ciudad."

"El bosque San Patricio está en medio de la ciudad de San Juan. Por eso digo que este bosque es una esmeralda (*emerald*) en un mar de concreto."

"El bosque pertenece (*belongs*) a la comunidad."

"Nosotros salvamos este bosque mediante la propuesta (*proposal*) y no la protesta."

4 **Adivinar** Escribe cinco oraciones sobre tu vida presente y futura. Cuatro deben ser falsas y sólo una debe ser cierta. Presenta tus oraciones al grupo. El grupo adivina (*guesses*) cuál es la oración cierta y expresa sus dudas sobre las oraciones falsas. Answers will vary.

AYUDA

Here are some useful verbs for talking about plans:

esperar → *to hope*
querer → *to want*
pretender → *to intend*
pensar → *to plan*

Note that **pretender** and *pretend* are false cognates. To say *to pretend*, use the verb **fingir**.

> **modelo**
> **Estudiante 1:** Quiero irme un año a la selva a trabajar.
> **Estudiante 2:** Dudo que te guste vivir en la selva.
> **Estudiante 3:** En cinco años voy a ser presidente de los Estados Unidos.
> **Estudiante 2:** No creo que seas presidente de los Estados Unidos en cinco años. ¡Tal vez en treinta!

Síntesis

5 **Intercambiar** En grupos, escriban un párrafo sobre los problemas del medio ambiente en su estado o en su comunidad. Compartan su párrafo con otro grupo, que va a ofrecer opiniones y soluciones. Luego presenten su párrafo, con las opiniones y soluciones del otro grupo, a la clase. Answers will vary.

---

3 Suggestion Before starting, have the class brainstorm different topics that might be discussed with Mary Axtmann.

3 Expansion Ask pairs to act out their interviews for the class.

4 Suggestion Ask students to choose a secretary to write down the group members' true statements to present to the class.

5 Suggestion Assign students to groups of four. Ask group members to appoint a mediator to lead the discussion, a secretary to write the paragraph, a checker to proofread what was written, and a stenographer to take notes on the opinions and solutions of the other group.

5 Expansion Have students create a poster illustrating the environmental problems in their community and proposing possible solutions.

TEACHING OPTIONS

Small Groups Assign scenarios to groups of three. Have students take turns playing a reporter interviewing the other two about what is happening in each situation. The interviewees should use expressions of certainty or doubt, disbelief, and denial when responding to the reporter's questions. Possible scenarios: protest in favor of animal rights, a volcano about to erupt, a local ecological problem, a vacation in the mountains.

Game Divide the class into two teams. Team A writes sentences with expressions of certainty while Team B writes sentences with expressions of doubt, disbelief, or denial. Put all the sentences in a hat. Students take turns drawing sentences for their team and stating the opposite of what the sentence says. The team with the most sentences using the correct mood wins.

13.3 The subjunctive with conjunctions

ANTE TODO In both Spanish and English, conjunctions are words or phrases that connect other words and clauses in sentences. Certain conjunctions commonly introduce adverbial clauses, which describe *how*, *why*, *when*, and *where* an action takes place.

Main clause	Conjunction	Adverbial clause
Vamos a visitar a Carlos	**antes de que**	**regrese** a California.

> Se pueden tomar fotos, ¿verdad?

> Sí, con tal de que no toques ni las flores ni las plantas.

> A menos que resuelvan el problema de la contaminación, los habitantes van a sufrir muchas enfermedades en el futuro.

▶ The subjunctive is used to express a hypothetical situation, uncertainty as to whether an action or event will take place, or a condition that may or may not be fulfilled.

Voy a dejar un recado **en caso de que Gustavo me llame.**
I'm going to leave a message in case Gustavo calls me.

Voy al supermercado **para que tengas** algo de comer.
I'm going to the store so that you'll have something to eat.

▶ Here is a list of the conjunctions that always require the subjunctive.

Conjunctions that require the subjunctive

a menos que	*unless*	**en caso (de) que**	*in case (that)*
antes (de) que	*before*	**para que**	*so that*
con tal (de) que	*provided that*	**sin que**	*without*

Algunos animales van a morir **a menos que** haya leyes para protegerlos.
Some animals are going to die unless there are laws to protect them.

Ellos nos llevan a la selva **para que** veamos las plantas tropicales.
They are taking us to the jungle so that we may see the tropical plants.

▶ The infinitive is used after the prepositions **antes de, para**, and **sin** when there is no change of subject.

Te llamamos **antes de salir** de la casa.
We will call you before leaving the house.

Te llamamos mañana **antes de que salgas.**
We will call you tomorrow before you leave.

Conjunctions with subjunctive or indicative

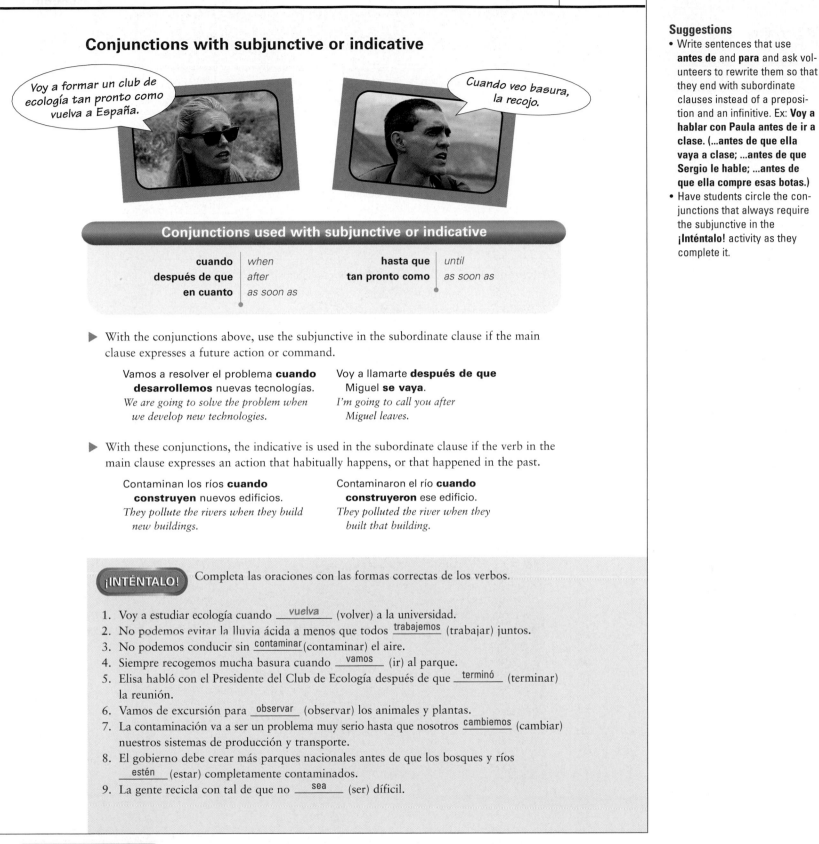

> *Voy a formar un club de ecología tan pronto como vuelva a España.*

> *Cuando veo basura, la recojo.*

Conjunctions used with subjunctive or indicative

cuando	*when*	**hasta que**	*until*
después de que	*after*	**tan pronto como**	*as soon as*
en cuanto	*as soon as*		

▶ With the conjunctions above, use the subjunctive in the subordinate clause if the main clause expresses a future action or command.

Vamos a resolver el problema **cuando desarrollemos** nuevas tecnologías.	Voy a llamarte **después de que** Miguel **se vaya**.
We are going to solve the problem when we develop new technologies.	*I'm going to call you after Miguel leaves.*

▶ With these conjunctions, the indicative is used in the subordinate clause if the verb in the main clause expresses an action that habitually happens, or that happened in the past.

Contaminan los ríos **cuando construyen** nuevos edificios.	Contaminaron el río **cuando construyeron** ese edificio.
They pollute the rivers when they build new buildings.	*They polluted the river when they built that building.*

¡INTÉNTALO!   Completa las oraciones con las formas correctas de los verbos.

1. Voy a estudiar ecología cuando __vuelva__ (volver) a la universidad.
2. No podemos evitar la lluvia ácida a menos que todos __trabajemos__ (trabajar) juntos.
3. No podemos conducir sin __contaminar__ (contaminar) el aire.
4. Siempre recogemos mucha basura cuando __vamos__ (ir) al parque.
5. Elisa habló con el Presidente del Club de Ecología después de que __terminó__ (terminar) la reunión.
6. Vamos de excursión para __observar__ (observar) los animales y plantas.
7. La contaminación va a ser un problema muy serio hasta que nosotros __cambiemos__ (cambiar) nuestros sistemas de producción y transporte.
8. El gobierno debe crear más parques nacionales antes de que los bosques y ríos __estén__ (estar) completamente contaminados.
9. La gente recicla con tal de que no __sea__ (ser) difícil.

Práctica

1 Completar La señora Montero habla de una excursión que quiere hacer con su familia. Completa las oraciones con la forma correcta de cada verbo.

1. Voy a llevar a mis hijos al parque para que ___aprendan___ (aprender) sobre la naturaleza.
2. Voy a pasar todo el día allí a menos que ___haga___ (hacer) mucho frío.
3. En bicicleta podemos explorar el parque sin ___caminar___ (caminar) demasiado.
4. Vamos a bajar al cráter con tal de que no se ___prohíba___ (prohibir).
5. Siempre llevamos al perro cuando ___vamos___ (ir) al parque.
6. No pensamos ir muy lejos en caso de que ___llueva___ (llover).
7. Vamos a almorzar a la orilla (*shore*) del río cuando nosotros ___terminemos___ (terminar) de preparar la comida.
8. Mis hijos van a dejar todo limpio antes de ___salir___ (salir) del parque.

2 Oraciones Completa las siguientes oraciones de una manera lógica. Answers will vary.

1. No podemos controlar la contaminación del aire a menos que...
2. Voy a reciclar los productos de papel y de vidrio en cuanto...
3. Debemos comprar coches eléctricos tan pronto como...
4. Protegemos los animales en peligro de extinción para que...
5. Mis amigos y yo vamos a recoger la basura de la universidad después de que...
6. No podemos desarrollar nuevas fuentes (*sources*) de energía sin...
7. Hay que eliminar la contaminación del agua para...
8. No podemos proteger la naturaleza sin que...

3 Recursos naturales En parejas, lean la información sobre algunos de los recursos naturales de Guinea Ecuatorial. Luego hablen de los temas y den soluciones a los problemas presentados. Usen el subjuntivo y las conjunciones. Answers will vary.

GUINEA ECUATORIAL

Bosque lluvioso tropical
En su denso bosque lluvioso (*rain*) tropical hay más de 140 especies de árboles, entre las más importantes están el okume, el nogal africano y varios tipos de caoba. Existe una intensa deforestación por parte de grandes compañías internacionales, y la reforestación de los bosques es mínima.

Parque Nacional Monte Alen
Este parque tiene un territorio montañoso con cascadas (*waterfalls*) y rápidos en sus ríos. Aquí viven muchos tipos de plantas y animales típicas del bosque lluvioso, pero también especies únicas de la zona de Guinea Ecuatorial. Este parque tiene más de cien especies de mamíferos (*mammals*).

El 10% del territorio del país es considerado área protegida.

El petróleo
El cacao (*cocoa bean*) y otros productos agrícolas eran la base de la economía del país hasta que en 1995 se encontró petróleo (*oil*) en el Golfo de Guinea. Desde entonces, este recurso natural es el principal producto de exportación del país. Muchas empresas (*businesses*) internacionales están invirtiendo (*investing*) en la industria petrolera y energética olvidando la industria agrícola.

NOTA CULTURAL

Guinea Ecuatorial es un país en la costa oeste (*west*) de África. Su capital es Malabo, en la isla de Bioko. Uno de sus idiomas oficiales es el español. Su área es un poco más pequeña que el área de Maryland. En su territorio hay montañas, volcanes y un bosque lluvioso tropical.

Comunicación

4 **Preguntas** En parejas, túrnense para hacerse las siguientes preguntas. Answers will vary.

1. ¿Qué haces cada noche antes de acostarte?
2. ¿Qué haces después de salir de la universidad?
3. ¿Qué hace tu familia para que puedas asistir a la universidad?
4. ¿Qué piensas hacer tan pronto como te gradúes?
5. ¿Qué quieres hacer mañana, a menos que haga mal tiempo?
6. ¿Qué haces en tus clases sin que los profesores lo sepan?

5 **Comparar** En parejas, comparen una actividad rutinaria que ustedes hacen con algo que van a hacer en el futuro. Usen palabras de la lista. Answers will vary.

> **modelo**
>
> **Estudiante 1:** El sábado vamos al lago. Tan pronto como volvamos, vamos a estudiar para el examen.
> **Estudiante 2:** Todos los sábados llevo a mi primo al parque para que juegue. Pero el sábado que viene, con tal de que no llueva, lo voy a llevar a las montañas.

antes de	después de que	hasta que	sin (que)
antes de que	en caso de que	para (que)	tan pronto como

Síntesis

¡LENGUA VIVA!

Tic-tac-toe has various names in the Spanish-speaking world, including **tres en raya, tres en línea, ta-te-ti, gato, la vieja,** and **triqui-triqui.**

6 **Tres en raya** (*Tic-Tac-Toe*) Formen dos equipos. Una persona comienza una frase y otra persona de su equipo la termina usando palabras de la gráfica. El primer equipo que forme tres oraciones seguidas (*in a row*) gana el tres en raya. Hay que usar la conjunción o la preposición y el verbo correctamente. Si no, ¡no cuenta! Answers will vary.

> **modelo**
>
> *Equipo 1*
> **Estudiante 1:** Dudo que podamos eliminar la deforestación...
> **Estudiante 2:** sin que nos ayude el gobierno.
> *Equipo 2*
> **Estudiante 1:** Creo que podemos conservar nuestros recursos naturales...
> **Estudiante 2:** con tal de que todos hagamos algo para ayudar.

cuando	con tal de que	para que
antes de que	para	sin que
hasta que	en caso de que	antes de

4 Expansion When pairs have finished asking and answering the questions, work with the whole class, asking several individuals each of the questions and asking other students to react to their responses. Ex: ____ **hace aeróbicos antes de acostarse. ¿Quién más hace ejercicio? ¡Uf! Hacer ejercicio me parece excesivo. ¿Quiénes ven la tele? ¿Nadie lee un libro antes de acostarse?**

5 Suggestion Have partners compare the routines of other people they know and what they are going to do in the future. Have them do the same with celebrities, taking guesses about their routines.

6 Suggestion Have groups prepare tic-tac-toe cards like the one shown in the activity.

6 Expansion Regroup the students to do a second round of tic-tac-toe.

Suggestion See the Information Gap Activities Booklet for an additional activity to practice the material presented in this section.

TEACHING OPTIONS

Heritage Speakers Ask heritage speakers if they ever played tic-tac-toe when growing up. What did they call it? Was it one of the names listed in **¡Lengua viva!**? Ask them the names of other childhood games they played and to describe them. Are the games similar to those played by the native English speakers in the class?

Pairs Ask partners to interview each other about what they must do today for their future goals to become a reality. Students should state what their goals are, the necessary conditions to achieve them, and talk about obstacles they may encounter. Students should use as many conjunctions as possible in their interviews. Have pairs present their interviews.

Section Goals

In **Estructura 13.4** students will learn:
- to form regular past participles
- irregular past participles
- to use past participles as adjectives

Instructional Resources
WB/VM: Workbook, pp. 163–164
Lab Manual, p. 78
Lab CD/MP3 Lección 13
IRM: ¡Inténtalo! & Práctica
Answers, p. 193;
Tapescript, pp. 59–62
Interactive CD-ROM
Companion website:
www.vistahigherlearning.com
Presentations CD-ROM

Suggestions

- Use magazine pictures to review some of the following regular past participles students have learned as adjectives: **aburrido, afectado, avergonzado, cansado, casado, cerrado, desordenado, enamorado, enojado, equivocado, mareado, ocupado, ordenado, preocupado.** As you review these forms, have students indicate the corresponding infinitives.
- Check for understanding by calling out known infinitives and asking volunteers to give their past participles. Ex: **mirar, comprender, escribir**
- Practice irregular forms by asking students to finish incomplete sentences. Ex: **Esas piñatas son ____ en México. (hechas) La biblioteca está ____ toda la noche. (abierta)**

13.4 Past participles used as adjectives

ANTE TODO In **Lección 5**, you learned about present participles (**estudiando**). Both Spanish and English have past participles. The past participles of English verbs often end in **–ed** (*to turn* ➤ *turned*), but many are also irregular (*to buy* ➤ *bought; to drive* ➤ *driven*).

▶ In Spanish, regular **–ar** verbs form the past participle with **–ado**. Regular **–er** and **–ir** verbs form the past participle with **–ido**.

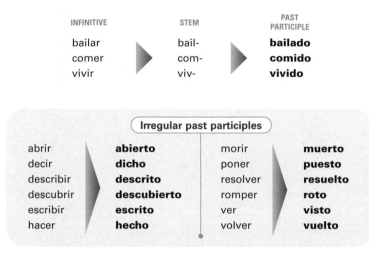

INFINITIVE	STEM	PAST PARTICIPLE
bailar	bail-	**bailado**
comer	com-	**comido**
vivir	viv-	**vivido**

Irregular past participles

abrir	**abierto**	morir	**muerto**
decir	**dicho**	poner	**puesto**
describir	**descrito**	resolver	**resuelto**
descubrir	**descubierto**	romper	**roto**
escribir	**escrito**	ver	**visto**
hacer	**hecho**	volver	**vuelto**

¡ATENCIÓN!

The past participles of –er and –ir verbs whose stems end in –a, –e, or –o carry a written accent mark on the i of the –ido ending.

caer	**caído**
creer	**creído**
leer	**leído**
oír	**oído**
reír	**reído**
sonreír	**sonreído**
traer	**traído**

▶ In Spanish, as in English, past participles can be used as adjectives. They are often used with the verb **estar** to describe a condition or state that results from an action. Like other Spanish adjectives, they must agree in gender and number with the nouns they modify.

Ella vio una botella **rota** en la playa.
She saw a broken bottle on the beach.

Me gusta usar papel **reciclado.**
I like to use recycled paper.

Tenemos la mesa **puesta** y la cena **hecha.**
We have the table set and dinner made.

Este río ya no está **contaminado.**
This river is no longer contaminated.

CONSEJOS

You already know several participles used as adjectives: **aburrido, interesado, nublado, perdido,** etc.
• • •
Note that all irregular past participles except **dicho** and **hecho** end in –**to**.

¡INTÉNTALO! Indica la forma correcta del participio pasado de estos verbos.

1. hablar ___hablado___
2. beber ___bebido___
3. decidir ___decidido___
4. romper ___roto___
5. escribir ___escrito___
6. cantar ___cantado___
7. oír ___oído___
8. traer ___traído___

9. correr ___corrido___
10. leer ___leído___
11. ver ___visto___
12. hacer ___hecho___
13. morir ___muerto___
14. reír ___reído___
15. mirar ___mirado___
16. abrir ___abierto___

TEACHING OPTIONS

Extra Practice To provide oral practice with past participle agreement, create substitution drills. Ex: *Felipe* **está enojado.** (*Lupe/Los estudiantes/Mis hermanas/El profesor*) Say a sentence and have students repeat. Say a cue. Have students replace the subject of the original sentence with the cued subject and make any other necessary changes.

Game Divide the class into teams of five and have each team sit in a row. The first person in the row has a blank piece of paper. Have five infinitives in mind. Call out one of them. Allow the student with the paper ten seconds to write down the past participle of the infinitive and pass the paper to the next in row. The team with the most correct responses wins.

Práctica

1

Completar Completa estas frases con la forma adecuada del participio pasado del
▶ verbo que está entre paréntesis.

1. Nuestra excursión a la selva ya está ___preparada___ (preparar).
2. Todos los detalles están ___escritos___ (escribir) en español.
3. Tenemos que comprar los pasajes, pero Sara no encuentra el mapa. ¡Oh no! Creo que estamos ___perdidos___ (perder).
4. Sabemos que la agencia de viajes está en una plaza muy ___conocida___ (conocer), la Plaza Bolívar. Está ___abierta___ (abrir) de nueve a tres.
5. El nombre de la agencia está ___escrito___ (escribir) en el letrero y en la acera (*sidewalk*).
6. Pero ya son las tres y diez.... que mala suerte. Seguramente la oficina ya está ___cerrada___ (cerrar).

2

Preparativos Tú y tu compañero/a van a hacer un viaje. Túrnense para hacerse las siguientes preguntas sobre los preparativos (*preparations*). Usen el participio pasado en sus respuestas.

> **modelo**
> **Estudiante 1:** ¿Compraste los pasajes del avión?
> **Estudiante 2:** Sí, los pasajes ya están comprados.

1. ¿Hiciste las maletas?
   Sí, las maletas ya están hechas.
2. ¿Confirmaste las reservaciones para el hotel?
   Sí, las reservaciones ya están confirmadas.
3. ¿Compraste tus medicinas?
   Sí, las medicinas ya están compradas.
4. ¿Lavaste la ropa?
   Sí, la ropa ya está lavada.
5. ¿Apagaste todas las luces?
   Sí, las luces ya están apagadas.
6. ¿Cerraste bien la puerta?
   Sí, la puerta ya está cerrada.

Comunicación

3

Describir Tú y un(a) compañero/a son agentes de policía y tienen que investigar un crimen. Miren el dibujo y describan lo que encontraron en la habitación del señor Villalonga. Usen el participio pasado en la descripción. Luego, comparen su descripción con la de otra pareja. Answers will vary.

> **modelo**
> La puerta del baño no estaba cerrada.

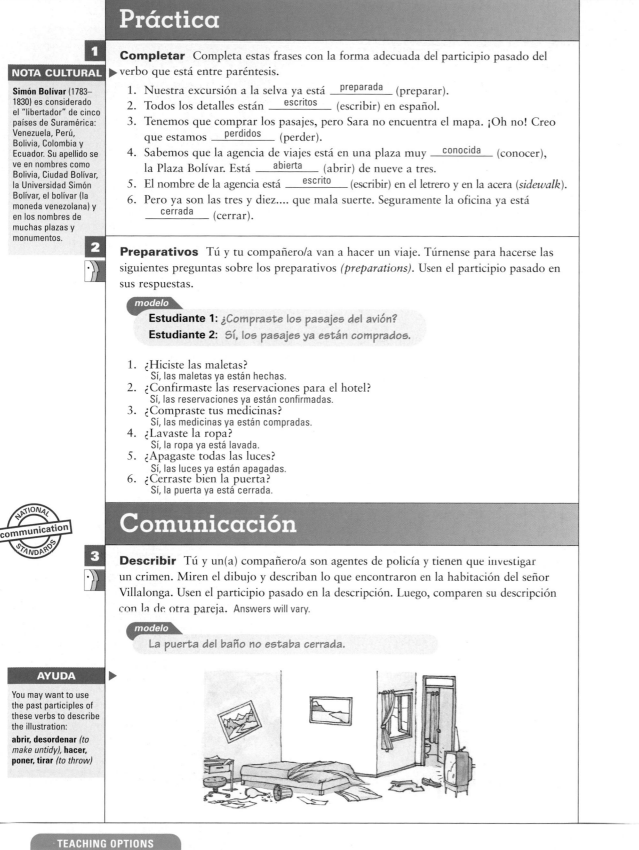

---

1 Expansion Have pairs make a list of new nouns of different gender and/or number, one for each item in the activity, to replace the original nouns being modified by past participles. They should double-check that the new sentences will make sense. Have them exchange their list with another pair, who should rewrite the sentences making all necessary changes, then return them to the first pair for correction.

2 Expansion Have students redo this activity using a negative response and a different past participle used as an adjective to provide a reason. Ex: **No, no están hechas porque la ropa no está limpia. No, no están confirmadas porque el teléfono del hotel está ocupado.**

3 Suggestion Before assigning the activity to pairs, allow students a couple of minutes to take notes about the crime scene.

3 Expansion Have students give their answers in round-robin format. Remind them that each contribution has to contain new information not already supplied by another pair.

TEACHING OPTIONS

Pairs Have pairs make a promotional flyer for a new environmentally-friendly business or association in town. Their flyers should include at least three past participles used as adjectives. When they have finished, circulate the flyers in the class.

Game Divide the class into teams of three. Each team should think of a famous place. Encourage them to use vocabulary from **Contextos**. The other teams will take turns asking questions about the place. Questions can only be answered with **sí/no** and each one should have a past participle used as an adjective. Ex: **¿Está abierto al público? ¿Es conocido solamente en este país?** The first team to guess the identity of the place wins a point.

Lectura

Antes de leer

Estrategia
Recognizing the purpose of a text

When you are faced with an unfamiliar text, it is important to determine the writer's purpose. If you are reading an editorial in a newspaper, for example, you know that the journalist's objective is to persuade you of his or her point of view. Identifying the purpose of a text will help you better comprehend its meaning.

Examinar el texto
Utiliza las estrategias de lectura para familiarizarte con el texto. Después contesta las siguientes preguntas y compara tus respuestas con las de un(a) compañero/a.
- ¿De qué trata la lectura?°
- ¿Es una fábula°, un poema, un artículo de periódico…?
- ¿Cómo lo sabes?

Predicciones
Lee estas predicciones sobre la lectura e indica si estás de acuerdo° con ellas. Después compara tus opiniones con las de un(a) compañero/a.
1. La lectura trata del medio ambiente.
2. La autora se preocupa por la contaminación.
3. Habla de la naturaleza y de los seres humanos.
4. Tiene opiniones muy fuertes.

Determinar el propósito
Con un(a) compañero/a, hablen de los posibles propósitos° del texto. Consideren estas preguntas:
- ¿Qué te dice el género° del texto sobre los posibles propósitos del texto?
- ¿Piensas que el texto puede tener más de un propósito? ¿Por qué?

recursos

vistahigher
learning.com

¿De qué trata la lectura? *What is the reading about?*
fábula *fable* estás de acuerdo *you agree*
propósitos *purposes* género *type*

Todos contra la contaminación

Gloria Fuertes

La escritora española Gloria Fuertes nació el 28 de julio de 1917 y murió en 1988. En 1950 publicó su primer libro de poesía y desde entonces escribió poemas para niños y para adultos. De 1960 a 1963 vivió en los Estados Unidos donde dio clases de literatura en varias universidades. A partir de los años setenta trabajó en programas para niños en Televisión Española.

Que los hombres no manchen° los ríos.
Que los hombres no manchen el mar.
Que los niños no maltraten° los árboles.
Que los hombres no ensucien la ciudad.

(No quererse es lo que más contamina,
sobre el barco o bajo la mina°).

Que los tigres no tengan garras°,
que los países no tengan guerras°.

Que los niños no maten pájaros,
que los gatos no maten ratones°
y sobre todo, que los hombres
no maten hombres.

manchen *pollute*   maltraten *mistreat*   mina *mine*
garras *claws*   guerras *wars*   ratones *mice*

Después de leer

¿Cierto o falso?

Indica si lo que se dice es **cierto** o **falso**. Corrige las afirmaciones falsas.

1. La autora cree que los hombres no manchan los ríos.
   Falso. La autora quiere que los hombres no manchen los ríos.
2. Ella piensa que las ciudades están limpias.
   Falso. La autora piensa que los hombres ensucian la ciudad.
3. Ella quiere que los países no tengan guerras.
   Cierto.
4. Según ella, es importante que los hombres no se maten.
   Cierto.
5. Dice que los gatos no matan los ratones.
   Falso. Quiere que los gatos no maten los ratones.

Contestar

Contesta estas preguntas. Answers will vary.

1. ¿Cuáles son tres de los problemas que menciona la poeta?
2. ¿Qué crees que quiere decir la poeta en los siguientes versos: "No quererse es lo que más contamina, sobre el barco o bajo la mina"?
3. ¿Tienen importancia las repeticiones en el poema? Explica por qué.
4. Explica qué significan para ti los últimos versos del poema.

Ser poeta

En grupos, un(a) estudiante asume el papel de la poeta de "Todos contra la contaminación". Los/Las otros/as estudiantes le hacen preguntas sobre las ideas y los sentimientos expresados en su poema. Answers will vary.

Un grupo de poetas

El poema de Gloria Fuertes habla de algunos problemas del medio ambiente. En grupos pequeños escojan uno de los problemas mencionados y escriban un poema sobre ese tema. Altérnense para escribir un verso cada vez que sea su turno. Compartan su poema con la clase cuando lo terminen. Answers will vary.

¿Cierto o falso? After the false statements have been identified and corrected, summarize the poem by having pairs rewrite them. Have them use the subjunctive after verbs and expressions of emotion, doubt, disbelief, and denial, as well as after conjunctions. Ex: **La autora duda que los hombres no manchen los ríos.**

Contestar Divide the class into groups of four to compare and debate individuals' answers to the questions. Assign a moderator to help the group reach as much consensus as possible on each question and then relate the group's opinions to the class.

Ser poeta Have groups act out their interviews in front of the class. After the role-play, encourage the rest of the class to ask additional questions or make additional comments.

Un grupo de poetas After groups have written and presented their poems to the class, re-assign groups so that each student in the new groups represents a different topic from the poem. Have these new groups write a second poem incorporating ideas about all the topics represented.

TEACHING OPTIONS

Extra Practice Ask students to look for other poems in Spanish. Have them check for poems written originally in Spanish as well as those that have been translated. Have them read the poems to the class.

Heritage Speakers Ask heritage speakers if they know of a traditional poem or song in Spanish significant to their community or have heard someone in their family reciting or singing one. If so, encourage them to bring copies of it to class and read it aloud. Ask them to explain its importance and whether it is passed on from one generation to the next.

Section Goal

In **Panorama** students will read about the geography, history, and culture of Colombia.

Instructional Resources
Transparencies, #5, #6, #52
WB/VM: Workbook, pp. 165–166;
Video Activities, pp. 255–256
Panorama cultural *DVD/Video*
Interactive CD-ROM
IRM: Videoscript, p. 115;
Panorama cultural *Translations,*
p. 137
Companion website:
www.vistahigherlearning.com
Presentations CD-ROM

Suggestion Have students look at the map of Colombia or project **Transparency #52** and talk about the physical features of the country. Point out the three parallel ranges of the Andes in the west, and the Amazon Basin in the east and south. After students look at the call-out photos and read the captions, point out that there are no major cities in the eastern half of the country. Ask students to suggest reasons for the lack of population there.

El país en cifras After reading the **Población** section, ask students what the impact might be of having 55% of the nation's territory unpopulated, and the sort of problems this might create for a national government. Remind students that **chibcha** is spoken as far north as Nicaragua. **Araucano** is a language spoken by indigenous people of the Andes.

¡Increíble pero cierto! In their desperation to uncover the gold from Lake Guatavita, Spaniards made several attempts to drain the lake. Around 1545, Hernán Pérez de Quesada set up a bucket brigade that lowered the water level by several meters, allowing gold to be gathered.

Colombia

El país en cifras

▸ **Área:** 1.138.910 km² (439.734 millas²), *tres veces el área de Montana*

▸ **Población:** 45.580.000
De todos los países de habla hispana, sólo México tiene más habitantes° que Colombia. Casi toda la población colombiana vive en las áreas montañosas y la costa occidental° del país. Aproximadamente el 55% de la superficie° del país está sin poblar°.

▸ **Capital:** Santa Fe de Bogotá—7.596.000

▸ **Ciudades principales:** Cali—2.583.000, Medellín—3.237.000, Barranquilla—1.918.000, Cartagena—1.002.000

SOURCE: Population Division, UN Secretariat

Medellín

▸ **Moneda:** peso colombiano
▸ **Idiomas:** español (oficial)

Bandera de Colombia

Colombianos célebres

▸ **Edgar Negret,** escultor°, pintor (1920–)
▸ **Gabriel García Márquez,** escritor (1928–)
▸ **Juan Pablo Montoya,** automovilista (1975–)
▸ **Shakira,** cantante (1977–)

habitantes *inhabitants* occidental *western* superficie *surface*
sin poblar *unpopulated* escultor *sculptor* dioses *gods*
arrojaban *threw* cacique *chief* llevó *led* de oro *golden*

¡Increíble pero cierto!

En el siglo XVI los exploradores españoles oyeron la leyenda de El Dorado. Esta leyenda cuenta que los indios, como parte de un ritual en honor a los dioses°, arrojaban° oro a la laguna de Guatavita y el cacique° se sumergía en sus aguas cubierto de oro. Aunque esto era cierto, muy pronto la exageración llevó° al mito de una ciudad de oro°.

Plaza Bolívar, Bogotá

Baile típico de Barranquilla

Barranquilla
Cartagena
Mar Caribe
PANAMÁ
VENEZUELA

Sierra Nevada de Santa Marta
Río Magdalena

ESTADOS UNIDOS
OCÉANO ATLÁNTICO
COLOMBIA
OCÉANO PACÍFICO
AMÉRICA DEL SUR

Cordillera Occidental de los Andes
Cordillera Central de los Andes

Medellín
Río Meta

Volcán Nevado del Huila
Cali
Bogotá

Cordillera Oriental de los Andes

Océano Pacífico

Cultivo de caña de azúcar cerca de Cali

ECUADOR

recursos

| WB pp. 165–166 | VM pp. 255–256 | I CD-ROM Lección 13 | vistahigher learning.com |

PERÚ

Laguna de Guatavita

Lugares • El Museo del Oro

El famoso Museo del Oro° del Banco de la República fue fundado° en Bogotá en 1939 para preservar las piezas de orfebrería° de la época precolombina. En el museo, que tiene más de 30.000 piezas de oro, se pueden ver joyas°, ornamentos religiosos y figuras que sirvieron de ídolos. El cuidado con el que se hicieron los objetos de oro refleja la creencia° de las tribus indígenas de que el oro era la expresión física de la energía creadora° de los dioses°.

Literatura • Gabriel García Márquez (1928–)

Gabriel García Márquez, ganador del Premio Nobel de Literatura en 1982, es uno de los escritores contemporáneos más importantes del mundo. García Márquez publicó su primer cuento° en 1947, cuando era estudiante universitario. Su libro más conocido, *Cien años de soledad*, está escrito en el estilo° literario llamado "realismo mágico", un estilo que mezcla° la realidad con lo irreal y lo mítico°.

Historia • Cartagena de Indias

Los españoles fundaron la ciudad de Cartagena de Indias en 1533 y construyeron a su lado la fortaleza° más grande de las Américas, el Castillo de San Felipe de Barajas. En la ciudad de Cartagena se conservan° muchos edificios de la época colonial, como iglesias, monasterios, palacios y mansiones. Cartagena es conocida también por el Festival de Música del Caribe y su prestigioso Festival Internacional de Cine.

¿Qué aprendiste? Responde a las preguntas con una frase completa.

1. ¿Cuáles son las principales ciudades de Colombia? Las principales ciudades de Colombia son Santa Fe de Bogotá, Cali, Medellín, Barranquilla y Cartagena.

2. ¿Qué país de habla hispana tiene más habitantes que Colombia? México tiene más habitantes que Colombia.

3. ¿Quién es Edgar Negret? Edgar Negret es un escultor y pintor colombiano.

4. ¿Para qué fue fundado el Museo del Oro? El Museo del Oro fue fundado para preservar las piezas de orfebrería de la época precolombina.

5. ¿Qué tipos de objetos hay en el Museo del Oro? En el Museo del Oro hay joyas, ornamentos religiosos y figuras que sirvieron de ídolos.

6. ¿Quién ganó el Premio Nobel de Literatura en 1982? Gabriel García Márquez ganó el Premio Nobel de Literatura en 1982.

7. ¿Cuál es el libro más famoso de García Márquez? *Cien años de soledad* es el libro más famoso de García Márquez.

8. ¿Qué es el "realismo mágico"? El "realismo mágico" es un estilo literario que mezcla la realidad con lo irreal y lo mítico.

9. ¿Qué construyeron los españoles al lado de la ciudad de Cartagena de Indias? Los españoles construyeron el Castillo de San Felipe de Barajas al lado de Cartagena de Indias.

10. ¿Qué festivales internacionales se celebran en Cartagena? Se celebran el Festival Internacional de Cine y el Festival de Música del Caribe.

Conexión Internet Investiga estos temas en el sitio **www.vistahigherlearning.com**.

1. Busca información sobre las ciudades más grandes de Colombia. ¿Qué lugares de interés hay en estas ciudades? ¿Qué puede hacer un(a) turista en estas ciudades?

2. Busca información sobre pintores y escultores colombianos como Edgar Negret, Débora Arango o Fernando Botero. ¿Cuáles son algunas de sus obras más conocidas? ¿Cuáles son sus temas?

Oro *Gold* fundado *founded* orfebrería *goldsmithing* joyas *jewels* creencia *belief* creadora *creative* dioses *gods* cuento *story* estilo *style* mezcla *mixes* mítico *mythical* fortaleza *fortress* se conservan *are preserved*

El Museo del Oro In pre-Columbian times, the native peoples from different regions of Colombia developed distinct styles of working with gold. Some preferred to melt copper into the metal before working it, some pounded the gold, while others poured it into molds. If possible, bring in photos of pre-Columbian gold work.

Gabriel García Márquez García Márquez was raised primarily by his maternal grandparents, who made a profound impression upon his life and his literature. His grandfather was a man of strong ideals and a military hero. His grandmother held fast to many superstitious folk beliefs, which she espoused as gospel. Both of these elements surface in García Márquez' magical realism.

Cartagena de Indias Because Cartagena de Indias was the point of departure for shipments of Andean gold to Spain, it was the frequent target of pirate attacks from the 16th through the 18th centuries. It was besieged on five occasions. The most famous siege was led by the English pirate Sir Francis Drake, in 1586. He held the city for 100 days, until the residents surrendered to him some 100,000 pieces of gold!

Conexión Internet Students will find supporting Internet activities and links at **www.vistahigherlearning.com**.

Suggestion You may want to wrap up this section by playing the **Panorama cultural** video footage for this lesson.

ASIL

TEACHING OPTIONS

Worth Noting Colombia, like other mountainous countries near the equator, does not experience the four seasons that are known in parts of the United States and Canada. The average temperature of a given location does not vary much during the course of a year. Climate, however, changes dramatically with elevation, the higher altitudes being cooler than the low-lying ones. While the average temperature at sea level is 86°, 57° is the average temperature in Bogotá, the third highest capital in the world, behind La Paz, Bolivia, and Quito, Ecuador. When Colombians speak of **verano** or **invierno**, they are referring to the dry season (**verano**) and the rainy season (**invierno**). When these seasons occur varies from one part of the country to another. In the Andean region, the **verano**, or dry season, generally falls between December and March.

Section Goal

In **Panorama** students will read about the economy and culture of Honduras.

Instructional Resources
Transparencies, #3, #4, #53
WB/VM: Workbook, pp. 167–168;
Video Activities, pp. 257–258
***Panorama cultural** DVD/Video*
Interactive CD-ROM
IRM: Videoscript, p. 115;
***Panorama cultural** Translations,*
p. 137
Companion website:
www.vistahigherlearning.com
Presentations CD-ROM

Suggestion Have students look at the map of Honduras or project **Transparency #53** and talk about the physical features of the country. Hills and mountains cover three quarters of Honduras, with lowlands found only along coastal areas and in major river valleys. Deforestation is a major environmental challenge in Honduras. If deforestation continues at the current rate of 300 square kilometers per year, Honduras will have no trees left by 2020.

El país en cifras After reading about the indigenous populations of Honduras, tell students that the **miskito** people are also found along the Caribbean coast of Nicaragua. After students read about **Idiomas**, point out that **garífuna** speakers are descendants of indigenous Caribs who intermarried with African slaves following the shipwreck of a slaving ship some 300 years ago.

¡Increíble pero cierto!
Although the Honduran justice system is not famous for its fairness, the case of the artisan prisoners at the **Penitenciaría Central de Tegucigalpa** is a surprising example of business ethics. All profits from the sale of the crafts go directly to the creators: the prisoners themselves.

Honduras

El país en cifras

▶ **Área:** 112.492 km² (43.870 millas²), *un poco más grande que Tennessee*

▶ **Población:** 7.199.000
Cerca del 90 por ciento de la población de Honduras es mestiza. Todavía hay pequeños grupos indígenas como los jicaque, los miskito y los paya, que han mantenido su cultura sin influencias exteriores y que no hablan español.

▶ **Capital:** Tegucigalpa—1.120.000

Tegucigalpa

▶ **Ciudades principales:** San Pedro Sula—470.000, El Progreso—81.000, La Ceiba—72.000

SOURCE: Population Division, UN Secretariat

▶ **Moneda:** lempira

▶ **Idiomas:** español (oficial), miskito, garífuna

Bandera de Honduras

Hondureños célebres

▶ **José Antonio Velásquez,** pintor (1906–1983)
▶ **Argentina Díaz Lozano,** escritora (1917–1999)
▶ **Carlos Roberto Reina,** juez° y presidente del país (1926–2003)
▶ **Roberto Sosa,** escritor (1930–)

juez judge *presos prisoners* *madera wood* *hamacas hammocks* *artesanía crafts*

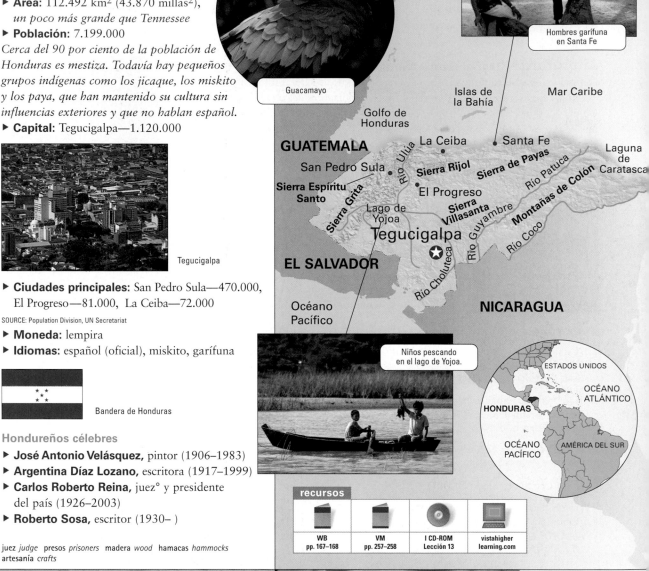
Guacamayo
Hombres garífuna en Santa Fe
Niños pescando en el lago de Yojoa.

GUATEMALA
Golfo de Honduras
Islas de la Bahía
Mar Caribe
La Ceiba
Santa Fe
San Pedro Sula
Río Ulúa
Sierra Rijol
Sierra de Payas
Laguna de Caratasca
Sierra Espíritu Santo
El Progreso
Río Patuca
Montañas de Colón
Sierra Grita
Lago de Yojoa
Sierra Villasanta
Río Guyambre
Tegucigalpa
Río Coco
EL SALVADOR
Río Choluteca
NICARAGUA
Océano Pacífico

ESTADOS UNIDOS
OCÉANO ATLÁNTICO
HONDURAS
OCÉANO PACÍFICO
AMÉRICA DEL SUR

recursos
| WB pp. 167–168 | VM pp. 257–258 | I CD-ROM Lección 13 | vistahigher learning.com |

¡Increíble pero cierto!

Los presos° de la Penitenciaría Central de Tegucigalpa hacen objetos de madera°, hamacas° y hasta instrumentos musicales. Sus artesanías° son tan populares que los funcionarios de la prisión han abierto una pequeña tienda donde los turistas pueden regatear con este especial grupo de artesanos.

TEACHING OPTIONS

Worth Noting It was in Honduras, on his fourth voyage of discovery, that Christopher Columbus first set foot on the mainland of the continent that would become known as the Americas. On August 14, 1502, the navigator landed at a site near the town of Trujillo and named the country **Honduras** (*depths*) because of the deep waters along the northern Caribbean coast.

Extra Practice Have students choose one of the people in **Hondureños** célebres to find out more about his or her work. They should report their findings to the class.

Lugares • Copán

Copán es el sitio arqueológico más importante de Honduras, y para los que estudian la cultura maya, es uno de los más fascinantes de la región. Aproximadamente en 400 d.C., la ciudad era muy grande, con más de 150 edificios y plazas, patios, templos y canchas° para el juego de pelota°. Copán es famoso por las esculturas pintadas que adornan sus edificios; por los cetros° ceremoniales de piedra finamente° esculpidos; y por el templo llamado Rosalila.

Economía • Las plantaciones de bananas

Hoy día las bananas son la exportación principal de Honduras. Hace más de cien años que tienen un papel fundamental en la historia económica y política del país. En 1889, la Standard Fruit Company empezó a exportar bananas a Nueva Orleans y la fruta resultó tan popular que rápidamente empezó a generar° grandes beneficios° para la Standard Fruit y para la United Fruit Company, otra compañía° norteamericana. Debido al° enorme poder° económico que tenían en el país, estas compañías intervinieron° muchas veces en la política hondureña.

Artes • José Antonio Velásquez (1906–1983)

José Antonio Velásquez fue uno de los pintores primitivistas° más famosos de su tiempo. Se le compara con pintores europeos del mismo género°, como Paul Gauguin o Emil Nolde, porque en su arte representaba lo más concreto de la vida diaria que lo rodeaba°. Se nota fácilmente el énfasis del pintor en los detalles° de la escena°. En su pintura desaparecen° casi totalmente los juegos de perspectiva, y los colores utilizados en los paisajes son puros.

San Antonio de Oriente,
José Antonio Velásquez, 1957.

¿Qué aprendiste? Responde a las preguntas con una frase completa.

1. ¿Qué es la lempira?
   La lempira es la moneda nacional de Honduras.
2. ¿Por qué es famoso Copán? Copán es famoso por las esculturas pintadas,
   por los centros ceremoniales y por el templo Rosalila.
3. ¿Dónde está el templo Rosalila?
   El templo Rosalila está en Copán.
4. ¿Cuál es la exportación principal de Honduras?
   Las bananas son la exportación principal de Honduras.
5. ¿Qué hizo la Standard Fruit Company? La Standard Fruit Company exportaba bananas de Honduras
   e intervino muchas veces en la política hondureña.
6. ¿Cómo es el estilo de José Antonio Velásquez?
   El estilo de Velásquez es primitivista.

Conexión Internet Investiga estos temas en el sitio **www.vistahigherlearning.com**.

1. ¿Cuáles son algunas de las exportaciones principales de Honduras, además de las bananas?
   ¿A qué países exporta Honduras sus productos?
2. Busca información sobre Copán u otro sitio arqueológico en Honduras. En tu opinión,
   ¿cuáles son los aspectos más interesantes del sitio?

....

canchas *courts*   juego de pelota *pre-Columbian ceremonial ball game*   cetros *scepters*   finamente *in a refined way*   generar *to generate*   beneficios *profits*   compañía *company*   Debido al *Due to*   poder *power*   intervinieron *intervened*   pintores primitivistas *primitivist painters*   género *genre*   rodeaba *surrounded*   detalles *details*   escena *scene*   desaparecen *disappear*

Copán Recent archaeological studies have focused on the abrupt disappearance of the Mayans from **Copán** around the ninth century C.E. Findings indicate that the Mayan dynasty suffered a sudden collapse that left the **Copán** valley virtually depopulated within a century. For more information about **Copán**, you may want to play the **Panorama cultural** video for this lesson.

Las plantaciones de bananas When Hurricane Mitch struck Central America in October 1998, it not only wiped out much of the infrastructure of Honduras, but also destroyed 60% of the projected agricultural exports. Instead of the 33 million boxes of bananas projected for export in 1999, only 4 million boxes were exported. The banana industry is still trying to recover from this major setback.

José Antonio Velásquez The primitive style established by José Antonio Velásquez is now being carried on by his son, Tulio Velásquez. Tulio was taught by his father, and had his first exhibition in 1959. Since then, his primitive art has been exhibited throughout the Americas, in Europe, and in Asia. Have students view works by each artist and then write a brief comparison of their styles.

Conexión Internet Students will find supporting Internet activities and links at **www.vistahigherlearning.com**.

Worth Noting Honduras was among the hardest hit of the Central American nations when Hurricane Mitch struck in late October 1998. Major roadways and bridges were destroyed, entire communities were covered in mud, and an air of hopelessness and desperation pervaded the country. With one of the lowest per capita income levels and one of the highest illiteracy rates in Central America, Hondurans were already struggling

before the devastation of Mitch. Despite international aid, reconstruction is slow and the level of desperation in Honduras has been reflected in the increase in violent crime.
Heritage Speakers Ask heritage speakers to research one of the Honduran topics mentioned in **Panorama** and write a three-paragraph essay about it. They may then present their findings orally to the class.

Instructional Resources
Vocabulary CD
Lab Manual, p. 78
*Lab CD/MP3 **Lección 13***
IRM: Tapescript, pp. 59–62
*Testing Program: **Pruebas**,*
pp. 145–156
Testing Program Audio CD
Test Files CD-ROM
Test Generator

La naturaleza

el árbol	tree
el bosque (tropical)	(tropical; rain) forest
el césped, la hierba	grass
el cielo	sky
el cráter	crater
el desierto	desert
la estrella	star
la flor	flower
el lago	lake
la luna	moon
el mundo	world
la naturaleza	nature
la nube	cloud
la piedra	stone
la planta	plant
la región	region; area
el río	river
la selva, la jungla	jungle
el sendero	trail; trailhead
el sol	sun
la tierra	land; soil
el valle	valley
el volcán	volcano

Los animales

el animal	animal
el ave, el pájaro	bird
el gato	cat
el perro	dog
el pez	fish
la vaca	cow

El medio ambiente

la conservación	conservation
la contaminación (del aire; del agua)	(air; water) pollution
la deforestación	deforestation
la ecología	ecology
el ecoturismo	ecotourism
la energía (nuclear, solar)	(nuclear, solar) energy
el envase	container
la extinción	extinction
el gobierno	government
la lata	(tin) can
la ley	law
la lluvia (ácida)	(acid) rain
el medio ambiente	environment
el peligro	danger
la población	population
el reciclaje	recycling
el recurso natural	natural resource
la solución	solution
cazar	to hunt
conservar	to conserve
contaminar	to pollute
controlar	to control
cuidar	to take care of
dejar de (+ *inf.*)	to stop (doing something)
desarrollar	to develop
descubrir	to discover
destruir	to destroy
estar afectado/a (por)	to be affected (by)
estar contaminado/a	to be polluted
evitar	to avoid
mejorar	to improve
proteger	to protect
reciclar	to recycle
recoger	to pick up
reducir	to reduce
resolver (o:ue)	to resolve; to solve
respirar	to breathe
de aluminio	(made) of aluminum
de plástico	(made) of plastic
de vidrio	(made) of glass
puro/a	pure

Las emociones

alegrarse (de)	to be happy
esperar	to hope; to wish
sentir (e:ie)	to be sorry; to regret
temer	to fear
es extraño	it's strange
es una lástima	it's a shame
es ridículo	it's ridiculous
es terrible	it's terrible
es triste	it's sad
ojalá (que)	I hope (that); I wish (that)

Las dudas y certezas

(no) creer	(not) to believe
(no) dudar	(not) to doubt
(no) negar (e:ie)	(not) to deny
es imposible	it's impossible
es improbable	it's improbable
es obvio	it's obvious
no cabe duda de	there is no doubt
no hay duda de	there is no doubt
(no) es cierto	it's (not) certain
(no) es posible	it's (not) possible
(no) es probable	it's (not) probable
(no) es seguro	it's (not) certain
(no) es verdad	it's (not) true

Conjunciones

a menos que	unless
antes (de) que	before
con tal (de) que	provided (that)
cuando	when
después de que	after
en caso (de) que	in case (that)
en cuanto	as soon as
hasta que	until
para que	so that
sin que	without
tan pronto como	as soon as

Past participles used as adjectives	See page 382.
Expresiones útiles	See page 367.

recursos

| LM p. 78 | Lab CD/MP3 Lección 13 | Vocab CD Lección 13 |

En la ciudad

14

Communicative Goals

You will learn how to:
- Give advice to others
- Give and receive directions
- Discuss daily chores

contextos

pages 392–395
- City life
- Daily chores
- Money and banking
- At a post office

fotonovela

pages 396–399

In preparation for the hike, Álex and Maite decide to go food shopping. On their way downtown, they ask a young man for directions.

estructura

pages 400–411
- The subjunctive in adjective clauses
- **Nosotros/as** commands
- The future

adelante

pages 412–413

Lectura: Read a short story by Marco Denevi.

panorama

pages 414–417

Featured country: Venezuela
- Oil • Caracas: A modern metropolis • Simón Bolívar

Featured country: República Dominicana
- Santo Domingo • Baseball
- Dancing merengue

Lesson Goals

In **Lección 14** students will be introduced to the following:
- names of commercial establishments
- banking terminology
- citing locations
- subjunctive in adjective clauses
- **nosotros/as** commands
- future tense
- identifying a narrator's point of view
- cultural, geographic, economic, and historical information about Venezuela
- cultural, geographic, and historical information about the Dominican Republic

A primera vista Here are some additional questions you can ask based on the photo: ¿Vives en una ciudad? ¿Cuál? ¿Cómo es la vida en la ciudad? ¿Cómo es la vida en el campo? ¿Prefieres vivir ahí? ¿Por qué? ¿Es posible que no haya contaminación en una ciudad? ¿Cómo? ¿Qué responsabilidades tienen las personas que viven en una ciudad para proteger el medio ambiente?

A PRIMERA VISTA
- ¿Viven estas personas en un bosque, un pueblo o una ciudad?
- ¿Dónde están, en una calle o en un sendero?
- ¿Es limpio o sucio el lugar donde están?
- ¿Es posible que haya contaminación en esta ciudad?

INSTRUCTIONAL RESOURCES

Workbook/Video Manual: WB Activities, pp. 169–180
Laboratory Manual: Lab Activities, pp. 79–83
Workbook/Video Manual: Video Activities, pp. 221–222, pp. 259–262
Instructor's Resource Manual: **Hojas de actividades**, p. 149; Vocabulario adicional, p. 168; ¡Inténtalo! & **Práctica Answers**, p. 194; **Fotonovela** Translations,

p. 126; Textbook CD Tapescript, p. 84; Lab CDs Tapescript, pp. 63–66; **Fotonovela** Videoscript, pp. 103–104; **Panorama cultural** Videoscript, p. 116; **Pan. cult.** translations, p. 138
Info Gap Activities Booklet, pp. 53–58
Overhead Transparencies: , #3–#6, #54–#57
Lab Audio CD/MP3 **Lección 14**

Panorama cultural DVD/Video
Fotonovela DVD/Video
Testing Program, pp. 157–168
Testing Program Audio CD
Test Files CD-ROM
Test Generator
Companion website

Presentations
CD-ROM
Textbook CD
Vocabulary CD
Interactive CD-ROM
Video CD-ROM
Web-SAM

Section Goals

In **Contextos** students will learn and practice:
• names of commercial establishments
• banking terminology
• citing locations

Instructional Resources
Transparencies, #54, #55
Textbook Activities CD
Vocabulary CD
WB/VM: Workbook, pp. 169–170
Lab Manual, p. 79
Lab CD/MP3 **Lección 14**
IRM: Vocab. adicional, p. 168;
Práctica *Answers, p. 194;*
Tapescript, pp. 63–66; p. 84
Interactive CD-ROM
Companion website:
www.vistahigherlearning.com
Presentations CD-ROM

Suggestions

• Using realia or magazine pictures, ask volunteers to identify the items. Ex: **carne, zapato, pan**. As students give their answers, write the names of corresponding establishments on the board (**carnicería, zapatería, panadería**). Then present banking vocabulary by miming common transactions. Ex: **Cuando necesito dinero, voy al banco. Escribo un cheque y lo cobro.**
• Project **Transparency #54**. Have students refer to the picture to answer your questions about it. Ex: **¿Dónde queda el cajero automático? ¿Qué tienda queda entre la lavandería y la carnicería? ¿Qué establecimiento se encuentra encima del supermercado? Las dos señoras frente a la estatua, ¿de qué hablan? ¿Qué tipo de transacciones pueden hacerse en un banco?**

Successful Language Learning Ask students to imagine how they would use this vocabulary when traveling.

Note: At this point you may want to present **Vocabulario adicional: Más vocabulario para la ciudad**, from the IRM.

En la ciudad

Más vocabulario

la frutería	fruit store
la heladería	ice cream shop
la pastelería	pastry shop
la pescadería	fish market
la cuadra	(city) block
la dirección	address
la esquina	corner
el estacionamiento	parking lot
derecho	straight (ahead)
enfrente de	opposite; facing
hacia	toward
cruzar	to cross
doblar	to turn
hacer diligencias	to run errands
quedar	to be located
el cheque (de viajero)	(traveler's) check
la cuenta corriente	checking account
la cuenta de ahorros	savings account
ahorrar	to save (money)
cobrar	to cash (a check)
depositar	to deposit
firmar	to sign
llenar (un formulario)	to fill out (a form)
pagar a plazos	to pay in installments
pagar al contado, en efectivo	to pay in cash
pedir prestado	to borrow
pedir un préstamo	to apply for a loan
ser gratis	to be free of charge

Variación léxica

cuadra ←→ manzana (*Esp.*)
direcciones ←→ indicaciones (*Esp.*)
doblar ←→ girar; virar; voltear
hacer diligencias ←→ hacer mandados

recursos

TEXT CD Lección 14	WB pp. 169–170	LM p. 79	Lab CD/MP3 Lección 14	I CD-ROM Lección 14	Vocab CD Lección 14

la peluquería, el salón de belleza

el banco

el supermercado

la panadería

la joyería

el cajero automático

Da direcciones. (dar)

Está perdida. (estar)

TEACHING OPTIONS

Heritage Speakers Have heritage speakers write about shopping and banking customs in their home communities. Have them mention such things as business hours and the prevalence of specialty shops compared to supermarkets or department stores. Encourage them to compare and contrast customs cross-generationally as well as cross-culturally.

Pairs Have students individually draw schematic maps of a couple of blocks around a city square, labeling every establishment and naming the streets. Then have them each write a description of the location of each establishment and exchange it with a partner. They then use the partner's descriptions to recreate the city map on which the description is based. Afterward, partners compare the two sets of maps.

Práctica

el letrero

la carnicería

la zapatería

la lavandería

1 Escuchar 🎧 Mira el dibujo de las páginas 392 y 393. Luego escucha las frases e indica si lo que dice cada una es **cierto** o **falso**.

	Cierto	Falso		Cierto	Falso
1.	○	☑	6.	☑	○
2.	☑	○	7.	☑	○
3.	○	☑	8.	○	☑
4.	☑	○	9.	○	☑
5.	○	☑	10.	☑	○

2 Seleccionar Selecciona los lugares de la lista en los que haces las siguientes diligencias.

banco	joyería	pescadería
carnicería	lavandería	salón de belleza
frutería	pastelería	zapatería

1. comprar galletas pastelería
2. comprar manzanas frutería
3. comprar un collar (*necklace*) joyería
4. cortarte (*to cut*) el pelo salón de belleza
5. lavar la ropa lavandería
6. comprar pescado pescadería
7. comprar pollo carnicería
8. comprar sandalias zapatería

3 Completar Llena los espacios en blanco con las palabras más adecuadas.

1. El banco me regaló un reloj. Fue ____gratis____.
2. Me gusta ____ahorrar____ dinero, pero no me molesta gastarlo.
3. La cajera me dijo que tenía que ____firmar____ el cheque en el dorso (*on the back*) para cobrarlo.
4. Para pagar con un cheque, necesito tener dinero en mi ____cuenta corriente____.
5. Mi madre va a un ____cajero automático____ para obtener dinero en efectivo cuando el banco está cerrado.
6. Cada viernes, Julio lleva su cheque al banco y lo ____cobra____ para tener dinero en efectivo.
7. Cada viernes Ana lleva su cheque al banco y lo ____deposita____ en su cuenta de ahorros.
8. Anoche en el restaurante, Marco ____pagó en efectivo/al contado____ en vez de usar una tarjeta de crédito.
9. Cuando viajas, es buena idea llevar cheques ____de viajero____.
10. Para pedir un préstamo, Miguel y Susana tuvieron que ____llenar____ cuatro formularios.

ESTE SUR NORTE OESTE

1 Suggestion Help students check their answers by reading each statement in the tapescript to the class and asking volunteers to say whether it is true or false. Have students correct the false statements.

1 Tapescript 1. El supermercado queda al este de la plaza, al lado de la joyería. 2. La zapatería está al lado de la carnicería. 3. El banco queda al sur de la plaza. 4. Cuando sales de la zapatería, la lavandería está a su lado. 5. La carnicería está al lado del banco. 6. Cuando sales de la joyería, el cajero automático está a su lado. 7. No hay ninguna heladería cerca de la plaza. 8. La joyería está al oeste de la peluquería. 9. Hay una frutería al norte de la plaza. 10. No hay ninguna pastelería cerca de la plaza.
Textbook Activities CD

2 Expansion After students finish, ask them what else could be bought in the establishments listed. Ex: **¿Qué más podemos comprar en la pastelería?**

3 Expansion Ask students to compare and contrast two different facets of banking. Ex: ATM vs. traditional tellers; credit card vs. check; savings account vs. checking account. Have them work in groups of three to make a list of **Ventajas** and **Desventajas**.

TEACHING OPTIONS

Game Play **Concentración**. On eight cards, write names of types of commercial establishments. On another eight cards, draw or paste a picture that matches each commercial establishment. Place the cards face-down in four rows of four. In pairs, students select two cards. If the two cards match, the pair keeps them. If the two cards do not match, students replace them in their original position. The pair with the most cards at the end wins.

Pairs Have each student write a shopping list (**lista de la compra/lista del mandado**) with ten items. Have students include items found in different stores. Then have them exchange their shopping list with a partner. Using the shopping list received, each student tells his or her partner where to go to get each item. Ex: **unas botas nuevas → Para comprar unas botas nuevas, tienes que ir a la zapatería que queda en la calle ____.**

Suggestion Project
Transparency #55 and ask students questions about the picture to elicit active vocabulary. **¿Qué hace la señora en la ventanilla? Y la gente que espera detrás de ella, ¿qué hace?** When you have covered the vocabulary, involve students in a conversation about mail and the post office. Ex: **Necesito estampillas. ¿Dónde está la oficina de correos que está más cerca de aquí? A mí me parece que la carta es una forma de escritura en vías de extinción. Desde que uso el correo electrónico, casi nunca escribo cartas. ¿Quiénes todavía escriben cartas?**

4 Expansion
• After you have gone over the activity, have students practice the conversation with a partner.
• Have pairs create short conversations similar to the one presented in the activity, but set in a different place of business. Ex: **el salón de belleza, la pescadería.**

5 Suggestions
• Create a word bank of useful phrases on the board. Ask volunteers to suggest expressions and grammatical constructions that will help students develop their role-plays.
• Go over the new vocabulary once again by asking questions. Ex: **¿Cuándo pedimos un préstamo? ¿Los cheques son para una cuenta corriente o una cuenta de ahorros?**

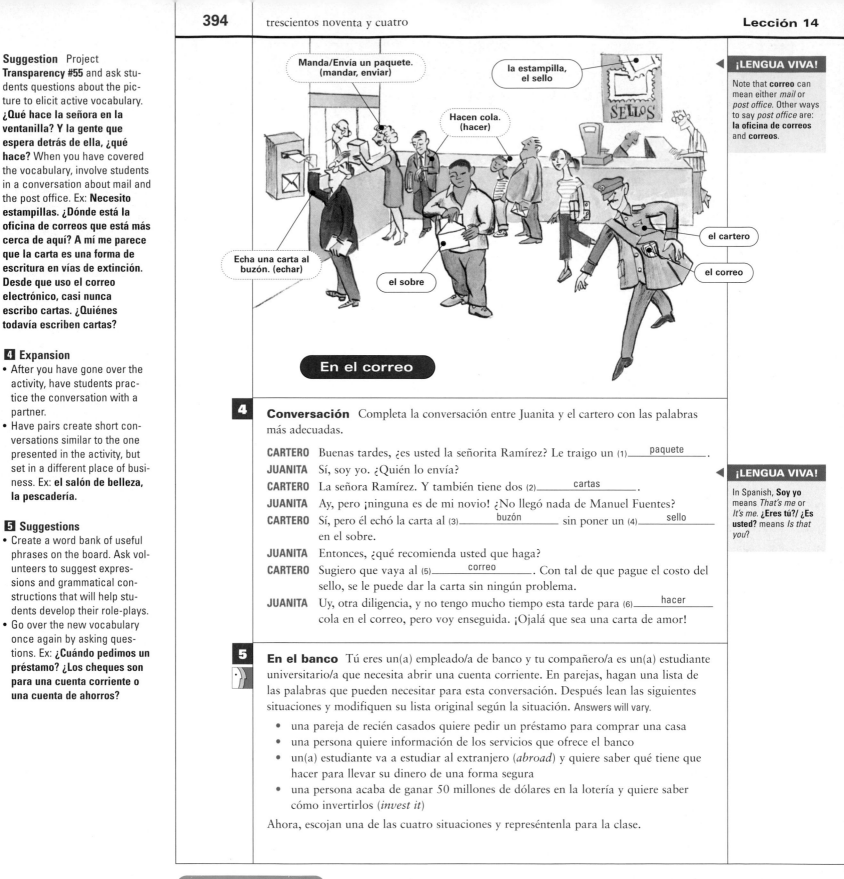

Manda/Envía un paquete. (mandar, enviar)

la estampilla, el sello

SELLOS

Hacen cola. (hacer)

el cartero

el correo

Echa una carta al buzón. (echar)

el sobre

En el correo

4 **Conversación** Completa la conversación entre Juanita y el cartero con las palabras más adecuadas.

CARTERO Buenas tardes, ¿es usted la señorita Ramírez? Le traigo un (1)_____paquete_____.

JUANITA Sí, soy yo. ¿Quién lo envía?

CARTERO La señora Ramírez. Y también tiene dos (2)_____cartas_____.

JUANITA Ay, pero ¡ninguna es de mi novio! ¿No llegó nada de Manuel Fuentes?

CARTERO Sí, pero él echó la carta al (3)_____buzón_____ sin poner un (4)_____sello_____ en el sobre.

JUANITA Entonces, ¿qué recomienda usted que haga?

CARTERO Sugiero que vaya al (5)_____correo_____. Con tal de que pague el costo del sello, se le puede dar la carta sin ningún problema.

JUANITA Uy, otra diligencia, y no tengo mucho tiempo esta tarde para (6)_____hacer_____ cola en el correo, pero voy enseguida. ¡Ojalá que sea una carta de amor!

5 **En el banco** Tú eres un(a) empleado/a de banco y tu compañero/a es un(a) estudiante universitario/a que necesita abrir una cuenta corriente. En parejas, hagan una lista de las palabras que pueden necesitar para esta conversación. Después lean las siguientes situaciones y modifiquen su lista original según la situación. Answers will vary.

• una pareja de recién casados quiere pedir un préstamo para comprar una casa
• una persona quiere información de los servicios que ofrece el banco
• un(a) estudiante va a estudiar al extranjero (*abroad*) y quiere saber qué tiene que hacer para llevar su dinero de una forma segura
• una persona acaba de ganar 50 millones de dólares en la lotería y quiere saber cómo invertirlos (*invest it*)

Ahora, escojan una de las cuatro situaciones y represéntenla para la clase.

TEACHING OPTIONS

Extra Practice Ask students to surf the Internet for banks in Spanish-speaking countries. Have them write a summary of services, rates, and hours, offered by the bank.

Game Divide the class into two teams. They should sit in a row facing one another so that a person from team A is directly across from a person from team B. Begin with the first two students and work your way down the row. Say a word, and the first one to make an association with a different word wins a point for his or her team. Ex: You say: **correos.** The first person from team B answers: **sello.** Team B wins one point.

NATIONAL
communication
STANDARDS

Comunicación

6 **Diligencias** En parejas, decidan quién va a hacer cada diligencia y cuál es la manera más rápida de llegar a los diferentes lugares desde el campus. Answers will vary.

¡ATENCIÓN!

Note these different meanings:

quedar *to be located; to be left over; to fit*

quedarse *to stay, to remain*

modelo

Cobrar unos cheques
Estudiante 1: *Yo voy a cobrar unos cheques. ¿Cómo llego al banco?*
Estudiante 2: *Conduce hacia el norte hasta cruzar la calle Oak.*
El banco queda en la esquina a la izquierda.

1. Enviar un paquete
2. Comprar botas nuevas
3. Comprar un pastel de cumpleaños
4. Lavar unas camisas
5. Comprar helado
6. Cortarte (*to cut*) el pelo

7 **El Hatillo** Trabajen en parejas para representar los papeles (*roles*) de un(a) turista que está perdido/a en El Hatillo y de un(a) residente de la ciudad que quiere ayudarlo/la.

Answers will vary.

NOTA CULTURAL ▶

El Hatillo es un pueblo cerca de Caracas popular por su arquitectura pintoresca, sus restaurantes y sus tiendas de artesanía.

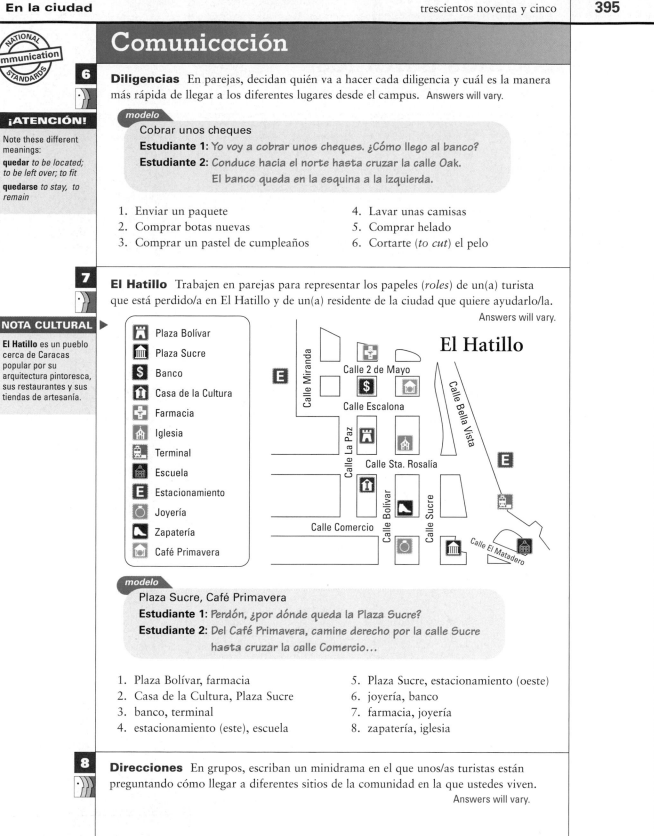

modelo

Plaza Sucre, Café Primavera
Estudiante 1: *Perdón, ¿por dónde queda la Plaza Sucre?*
Estudiante 2: *Del Café Primavera, camine derecho por la calle Sucre*
hasta cruzar la calle Comercio...

1. Plaza Bolívar, farmacia
2. Casa de la Cultura, Plaza Sucre
3. banco, terminal
4. estacionamiento (este), escuela
5. Plaza Sucre, estacionamiento (oeste)
6. joyería, banco
7. farmacia, joyería
8. zapatería, iglesia

8 **Direcciones** En grupos, escriban un minidrama en el que unos/as turistas están preguntando cómo llegar a diferentes sitios de la comunidad en la que ustedes viven.

Answers will vary.

6 Suggestion Draw a map of your campus and nearby streets with local commerce, asking students to direct you. Ex: **¿En qué calle queda el banco más cercano? ¿Qué tienda se encuentra en la esquina de _____ y _____?**

7 Suggestions
• Go over the icons in the legend to the map, finding the places each represents.
• Explain that the task is to give directions to the first place from the second place. Ask students to find **Café Primavera** and **Plaza Sucre** on the map.

7 Expansion Ask students to research **El Hatillo** on the Internet.

8 Suggestions
• As a class, brainstorm different tourist sites in and around your area. Write them on the board.
• Using one of the sites listed on the board, model the activity by asking volunteers to give driving directions from campus.

TEACHING OPTIONS

TPR Have students work in pairs. One partner is blindfolded and the other gives directions to get from one place in the classroom to another. For example: **Te voy a decir cómo llegar de tu escritorio a la puerta del salón. Camina derecho cinco pasos. Da tres pasos a la izquierda y luego dobla a la derecha y camina cuatro pasos para que no choques con el escritorio. Estás cerca de la puerta. Sigue derecho dos pasos más. Allí está la puerta.**

Game Divide the class into teams of three. Each must write directions to a particular commercial establishment close to campus. The teams read their directions, and the other teams try to guess what errand they are running. Each team that guesses correctly wins a point. The team with the most points wins.

14 | fotonovela

Section Goals

In **Fotonovela** students will:
• receive comprehensible input from free-flowing discourse
• learn functional phrases that preview lesson grammatical structures

Instructional Resources
WB/VM: Video Activities, pp. 221–222
***Fotonovela** DVD/Video (Start 01:16:02)*
***Fotonovela** Video CD-ROM*
*IRM: **Fotonovela** Translations, p. 126, Videoscript, pp. 103–104*
Interactive CD-ROM

Video Recap: Lección 13
Before doing this **Fotonovela** section, review the previous one with this activity.
1. ¿Adónde lleva Martín a los chicos? (al área donde van a ir de excursión)
2. ¿Qué dice él de la contaminación en la región? (es un problema en todo el mundo; tienen un programa de reciclaje)
3. ¿Qué dice Martín de la contaminación del río? (en las montañas no está contaminado; cerca de las ciudades tiene bastante contaminación)
4. ¿Qué va a hacer Maite para proteger el medio ambiente? (va a usar el metro)

Video Synopsis
Don Francisco and Martín advise the students about things they need for the hike. Álex and Maite decide to go to the supermarket, the bank, and the post office. They get lost downtown, but a young man gives them directions. After finishing their errands, Álex and Maite return to the house.

Suggestions
• Ask students to predict what they would see and hear in an episode in which the main characters get lost while running errands. Then, ask them a few questions to help them summarize this episode.
• Ask for volunteers to list a few expressions that would be used to get directions. Then ask for volunteers to give you directions to a nearby location.

Estamos perdidos.

Maite y Álex hacen diligencias en el centro.

(NATIONAL communication cultures STANDARDS)

PERSONAJES

MAITE

INÉS

DON FRANCISCO

ÁLEX

JAVIER

MARTÍN

JOVEN

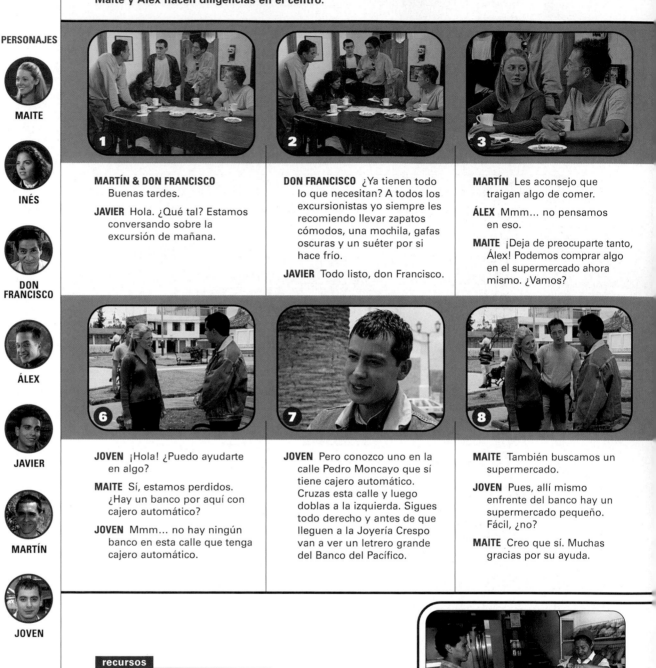

MARTÍN & DON FRANCISCO Buenas tardes.

JAVIER Hola. ¿Qué tal? Estamos conversando sobre la excursión de mañana.

DON FRANCISCO ¿Ya tienen todo lo que necesitan? A todos los excursionistas yo siempre les recomiendo llevar zapatos cómodos, una mochila, gafas oscuras y un suéter por si hace frío.

JAVIER Todo listo, don Francisco.

MARTÍN Les aconsejo que traigan algo de comer.

ÁLEX Mmm... no pensamos en eso.

MAITE ¡Deja de preocuparte tanto, Álex! Podemos comprar algo en el supermercado ahora mismo. ¿Vamos?

JOVEN ¡Hola! ¿Puedo ayudarte en algo?

MAITE Sí, estamos perdidos. ¿Hay un banco por aquí con cajero automático?

JOVEN Mmm... no hay ningún banco en esta calle que tenga cajero automático.

JOVEN Pero conozco uno en la calle Pedro Moncayo que sí tiene cajero automático. Cruzas esta calle y luego doblas a la izquierda. Sigues todo derecho y antes de que lleguen a la Joyería Crespo van a ver un letrero grande del Banco del Pacífico.

MAITE También buscamos un supermercado.

JOVEN Pues, allí mismo enfrente del banco hay un supermercado pequeño. Fácil, ¿no?

MAITE Creo que sí. Muchas gracias por su ayuda.

recursos

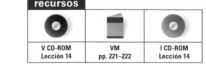

| V CD-ROM Lección 14 | VM pp. 221–222 | I CD-ROM Lección 14 |

Video Tips General suggestions for using video clips in the classroom can be found on page IAE-12 of this Instructor's Annotated Edition.

Estamos perdidos Play the **Resumen** segment of this video module without sound and ask the class to summarize what they see. Ask them to predict the content of the main video episode based on what they see in the **Resumen**. Write their predictions on the board. Then play the main video episode and the **Resumen** with sound. Finally, through questions and discussion, lead the class to a correct summary of the plot.

ÁLEX ¡Excelente idea! En cuanto termine mi café te acompaño.

MAITE Necesito pasar por el banco y por el correo para mandar unas cartas.

ÁLEX Está bien.

ÁLEX ¿Necesitan algo del centro?

INÉS ¡Sí! Cuando vayan al correo, ¿pueden echar estas postales al buzón? Además necesito unas estampillas.

ÁLEX Por supuesto.

MAITE Ten, guapa, tus sellos.

INÉS Gracias, Maite. ¿Qué tal les fue en el centro?

MAITE ¡Súper bien! Fuimos al banco y al correo. Luego en el supermercado compramos comida para la excursión. Y antes de regresar, paramos en una heladería.

MAITE ¡Ah! Y otra cosa. Cuando llegamos al centro conocimos a un joven muy simpático que nos dio direcciones. Era muy amable... ¡y muy guapo!

Enfoque cultural Las tiendas especializadas

La popularidad de los supermercados está aumentando (*growing*) en los países hispanos, pero todavía muchas personas van a tiendas especializadas para comprar comidas como la carne, el pescado, el pan y los dulces. La pulpería, por ejemplo, es una tienda típica de las zonas rurales de algunos países de Latinoamérica. La gente va a una pulpería para tomar una bebida o comprar productos esenciales. Otra tienda típica de algunos países hispanos es la rosticería, donde se asan (*roast*) y se venden carnes para llevar (*takeout*).

Expresiones útiles

Giving advice

▶ **Les recomiendo/Hay que llevar zapatos cómodos.**
I recommend that you/It's necessary to wear comfortable shoes.

▶ **Les aconsejo que traigan algo de comer.**
I advise you to bring something to eat.

Talking about errands

▶ **Necesito pasar por el banco.**
I need to go by the bank.

▷ **En cuanto termine mi café te acompaño.**
As soon as I finish my coffee, I'll go with you.

Getting directions

▶ **Estamos perdidos.**
We're lost.

▶ **¿Hay un banco por aquí con cajero automático?**
Is there a bank around here with an ATM?

▷ **Crucen esta calle y luego doblen a la izquierda/derecha.**
Cross this street and then turn to the left/right.

▷ **Sigan todo derecho.**
Go straight ahead.

▷ **Antes de que lleguen a la joyería van a ver un letrero grande.**
Before you get to the jewelry store, you're going to see a big sign.

▶ **¿Por dónde queda el supermercado?**
Where is the supermarket?

▷ **Está a dos cuadras de aquí.**
It's two blocks from here.

▷ **Queda en la calle Flores.**
It's on Flores street.

▷ **Pues, allí mismo enfrente del banco hay un supermercado.**
Well, right in front of the bank there is a supermarket.

Reacciona a la fotonovela

CONSÚLTALO

To review the use of verbs like **insistir**, see **Estructura 12.4**, p. 348.

1 ¿Cierto o falso? Decide si lo que dicen las siguientes frases es **cierto** o **falso**. Corrige las frases falsas.

	Cierto	Falso	
1. Don Francisco insiste en que los excursionistas lleven una cámara.	○	☑	Don Francisco recomienda que los excursionistas lleven zapatos cómodos, una mochila, gafas oscuras y un suéter.
2. Inés escribió unas postales y ahora necesita mandarlas por correo.	☑	○	
3. El joven dice que el Banco del Atlántico tiene un cajero automático.	○	☑	El Banco del Pacífico tiene un cajero automático.
4. Enfrente del banco hay una heladería.	○	☑	Enfrente del banco hay un supermercado pequeño.

2 Ordenar Pon los eventos de la **Fotonovela** en el orden correcto.

a. Un joven ayuda a Álex y a Maite a encontrar el banco porque están perdidos. _3_
b. Álex y Maite comen un helado. _6_
c. Inés les da unas postales a Maite y a Álex para echar al buzón. _2_
d. Maite y Álex van al banco y al correo. _4_
e. Álex termina su café. _1_
f. Maite y Álex van al supermercado y compran comida. _5_

3 Otras diligencias En parejas, hagan una lista de las diligencias que Maite, Álex, Inés y Javier necesitan hacer para completar las siguientes actividades. Answers will vary.

1. ir de excursión
2. pedir una beca (*scholarship*)
3. visitar una nueva ciudad
4. abrir una cuenta corriente
5. celebrar el cumpleaños de Maite
6. comprar una nueva computadora portátil

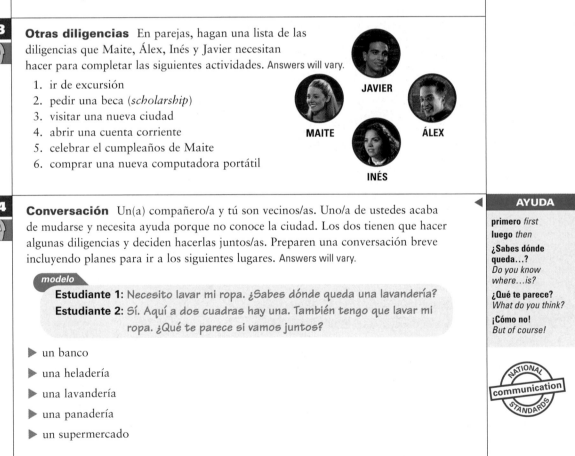

JAVIER
MAITE
ÁLEX
INÉS

4 Conversación Un(a) compañero/a y tú son vecinos/as. Uno/a de ustedes acaba de mudarse y necesita ayuda porque no conoce la ciudad. Los dos tienen que hacer algunas diligencias y deciden hacerlas juntos/as. Preparen una conversación breve incluyendo planes para ir a los siguientes lugares. Answers will vary.

modelo
> **Estudiante 1:** Necesito lavar mi ropa. ¿Sabes dónde queda una lavandería?
> **Estudiante 2:** Sí. Aquí a dos cuadras hay una. También tengo que lavar mi ropa. ¿Qué te parece si vamos juntos?

▶ un banco
▶ una heladería
▶ una lavandería
▶ una panadería
▶ un supermercado

AYUDA

primero *first*
luego *then*
¿Sabes dónde queda...? *Do you know where...is?*
¿Qué te parece? *What do you think?*
¡Cómo no! *But of course!*

NATIONAL communication STANDARDS

---

1 **Expansion** Give these to the class as items 5-6: **5. El joven llevó a Álex y a Maite al banco. (Falso. El joven les dio direcciones.) 6. Después de hacer sus diligencias, Maite y Álex fueron a una heladería. (Cierto.)**

2 **Suggestion** Have your students write these sentences on separate slips of paper so that they can rearrange them until they determine the correct order.

3 **Expansion** Have pairs come up with an additional situation and then make a list of the errands the **Fotonovela** characters need to run in order to complete it. Then have them read the list of errands aloud so the class can guess what the situation might be.

4 **Possible Response**
E1: Voy al supermercado y a la heladería. ¿Quieres ir conmigo?
E2: Sí, en cuanto termine mi almuerzo te acompaño.
E1: Necesito pasar por el banco porque necesito dinero.
E2: Yo también necesito ir al banco. ¿Hay un banco por aquí con cajero automático?
E1: Hay un cajero automático a tres cuadras de aquí. Queda en la calle Libertad.
E2: También necesito ir a la lavandería y al correo para mandar unas cartas.
E1: Ningún problema... el correo y la lavandería están cerca del banco.
E2: Oye, ¿qué vas a hacer esta noche?
E1: Voy a ir a la fiesta que celebran para un amigo. ¿Quieres ir?
E2: ¡Sí, gracias!

TEACHING OPTIONS

Game Prepare several sets of directions that explain how to get to well-known places on campus or in your community, without mentioning the destinations by name. Read each set of directions aloud and ask the class to tell you where they would end up if they followed your directions.

Pairs Ask pairs to create a skit in which a tourist asks for directions in a Spanish-speaking country. Give the class sufficient time to prepare and rehearse the skits, then ask for a few volunteers to present their skits to the class.

Ortografía

Las abreviaturas

In Spanish, as in English, abbreviations are often used in order to save space and time while writing. Here are some of the most commonly used abbreviations in Spanish.

usted ⟶ Ud.   ustedes ⟶ Uds.

As you have already learned, the subject pronouns **usted** and **ustedes** are often abbreviated.

don ⟶ D.	doña ⟶ Dña.	doctor(a) ⟶ Dr(a).
señor ⟶ Sr.	señora ⟶ Sra.	señorita ⟶ Srta.

These titles are frequently abbreviated.

centímetro ⟶ cm	metro ⟶ m	kilómetro ⟶ km
litro ⟶ l	gramo ⟶ g, gr	kilogramo ⟶ kg

The abbreviations for these units of measurement are often used, but without periods.

por ejemplo ⟶ p. ej.   página(s) ⟶ pág(s).

These abbreviations are often seen in books.

derecha ⟶ dcha.	izquierda ⟶ izq., izqda.
código postal ⟶ C.P.	número ⟶ n.°

These abbreviations are often used in mailing addresses.

> Sra. Emilia F. Bazán
> Cía. Romero, S.A.
> 3396
> Calle Lozano, n.° 37
> Caracas, Venezuela

Banco ⟶ Bco.	Compañía ⟶ Cía.
cuenta corriente ⟶ c/c.	Sociedad Anónima (*Inc.*) ⟶ S.A.

These abbreviations are frequently used in the business world.

Práctica   Escribe otra vez la siguiente información usando las abreviaturas adecuadas.

1. doña María   Dña.
2. señora Pérez   Sra.
3. Compañía Mexicana de Inversiones   Cía.
4. usted   Ud.
5. Banco de Santander   Bco.
6. doctor Medina   Dr.
7. Código Postal 03697   C.P.
8. cuenta corriente número 20-453   c/c., n.°

Emparejar   En la tabla hay 9 abreviaturas. Empareja los cuadros necesarios para formarlas.   S.A., Bco., cm, Dña., c/c., dcha., Srta., C.P., Ud.

S.	c.	C.	c	co.	U
B	c/	Sr	A.	D	dc
ta.	P.	ña.	ha.	m	d.

recursos

| LM p. 80 | Lab CD/MP3 Lección 14 | I CD-ROM Lección 14 |

14.1 The subjunctive in adjective clauses

NATIONAL STANDARDS comparisons

ANTE TODO In **Lección 13**, you learned that the subjunctive is used in adverbial clauses after certain conjunctions. You will now learn how the subjunctive can be used in adjective clauses to express that the existence of someone or something is uncertain or indefinite.

recursos

WB
pp. 171–176

LM
pp. 81–83

Lab CD/MP3
Lección 14

I CD-ROM
Lección 14

vistahigher
learning.com

¿Hay un banco por aquí que tenga cajero automático?

No hay ningún banco en esta calle que tenga cajero automático.

▶ The subjunctive is used in an adjective (or subordinate) clause that refers to a person, place, thing, or idea that either does not exist or whose existence is uncertain or indefinite. In the examples below, compare the differences in meaning between the statements using the indicative and those using the subjunctive.

¡ATENCIÓN!

Adjective clauses are subordinate clauses that modify a noun or pronoun in the main clause of a sentence. That noun or pronoun is called the *antecedent*.

Indicative	Subjunctive
Necesito **el libro** que **tiene** información sobre Venezuela. *I need **the book** that has information about Venezuela.*	Necesito **un libro** que **tenga** información sobre Venezuela. *I need **a book** that has information about Venezuela.*
Quiero vivir en **esta casa** que **tiene** jardín. *I want to live in this house that has a garden.*	Quiero vivir en **una casa** que **tenga** jardín. *I want to live in a house that has a garden.*
En mi barrio, hay **una heladería** que **vende** helado de mango. *In my neighborhood, there's an ice cream store that sells mango ice cream.*	En mi barrio no hay **ninguna heladería** que **venda** helado de mango. *In my neighborhood, there are no ice cream stores that sell mango ice cream.*

▶ When the adjective clause refers to a person, place, thing, or idea that is clearly known, certain, or definite, the indicative is used.

Quiero ir **al supermercado** que **vende** productos venezolanos. *I want to go to the supermarket that sells Venezuelan products.*	Conozco **a alguien** que **va** a esa peluquería. *I know someone who goes to that beauty salon.*
Busco **al profesor** que **enseña** japonés. *I'm looking for the professor who teaches Japanese.*	Tengo **un amigo** que **vive** cerca de mi casa. *I have a friend who lives near my house.*

▶ The personal **a** is not used with direct objects that are hypothetical people. However, as you learned in **Lección 7**, **alguien** and **nadie** are always preceded by the personal **a** when they function as direct objects.

Necesitamos **un empleado** que **sepa** usar computadoras.
We need an employee who knows how to use computers.

Necesitamos **al empleado** que **sabe** usar computadoras.
We need the employee who knows how to use computers.

Buscamos **a alguien** que **pueda** cocinar.
We're looking for someone who can cook.

No conocemos **a nadie** que **pueda** cocinar.
We don't know anyone who can cook.

▶ The subjunctive is commonly used in questions with adjective clauses when the speaker is trying to find out information about which he or she is uncertain. However, if the person who responds to the question knows the information, the indicative is used.

—¿Hay un parque que **esté** cerca de nuestro hotel?
Is there a park that's near our hotel?

—Sí, hay un parque que **está** muy cerca del hotel.
Yes, there's a park that's very near the hotel.

SECCIÓN AMARILLA

Busque cualquier información que necesite.

¡INTÉNTALO!   Escoge entre el subjuntivo o el indicativo para completar cada oración.

1. Necesito una persona que ___pueda___ (puede/pueda) cantar bien.
2. Buscamos a alguien que ___tenga___ (tiene/tenga) paciencia.
3. ¿Hay restaurantes aquí que ___sirvan___ (sirven/sirvan) comida japonesa?
4. Tengo una amiga que ___saca___ (saca/saque) fotografías muy bonitas.
5. Hay una carnicería que ___está___ (está/esté) cerca de aquí.
6. No vemos ningún apartamento que nos ___interese___ (interesa/interese).
7. Conozco a un estudiante que ___come___ (come/coma) hamburguesas todos los días.
8. ¿Hay alguien que ___diga___ (dice/diga) la verdad?

---

1 Suggestion Briefly review the use of the indicative and subjunctive in adjective clauses. Write two contrasting sentences on the board. Ex: **Conozco una pastelería donde sirven café. No hay ninguna pastelería en este barrio donde sirvan café.** Then ask volunteers to explain why the indicative or subjunctive was used in each sentence.

2 Suggestion Have volunteers write each "rehydrated" sentence on the board. Ask other volunteers to point out why the subjunctive or indicative was used in each sentence.

2 Expansion Ask pairs to invent an ending to Marta's day of running errands by writing a few sentences using the subjunctive in adjective clauses. Ex: **No encuentro una estación de metro que quede cerca. Hay un taxi en la esquina que está esperando.**

3 Suggestions
• Ask volunteers to discuss the types of information found in classified ads. Write them on the board.
• Have students do the activity by studying the ads for a few minutes and then discussing them with a partner without referring back to them.

3 Expansion Have pairs compose their own classified ad for one of the topics listed on the board but not covered in the activity.

Práctica

1 Completar Completa estas frases con la forma correcta del indicativo o del subjuntivo de los verbos entre paréntesis.

1. Buscamos un hotel que ____tenga____ (tener) piscina.
2. ¿Sabe usted dónde ____queda____ (quedar) el Correo Central?
3. ¿Hay algún buzón por aquí donde yo ____pueda____ (poder) echar una carta?
4. Ana quiere ir a la carnicería que ____está____ (estar) en la avenida Lecuna.
5. Encontramos un restaurante que ____sirve____ (servir) comida venezolana típica.
6. ¿Conoces a alguien que ____sepa____ (saber) mandar un *fax* por computadora?
7. Necesitas al empleado que ____entiende____ (entender) este nuevo programa de computación.
8. No hay nada en este mundo que ____sea____ (ser) gratis.

2 Oraciones Marta está haciendo diligencias en Caracas con una amiga. Forma frases con los siguientes elementos, usando el presente del indicativo o del subjuntivo. Haz los cambios que sean necesarios.

1. yo / conocer / un / panadería / que / vender / pan / cubano
   Yo conozco una panadería que vende pan cubano.
2. ¿hay / alguien / que / saber / dirección / de / un / buen / carnicería?
   ¿Hay alguien que sepa la dirección de una buena carnicería?
3. yo / querer / comprarle / mi / hija / un / zapatos / que / gustar
   Yo quiero comprarle a mi hija unos zapatos que le gusten.
4. Ella / no / encontrar / nada / que / gustar / en / ese / zapatería
   Ella no encuentra nada que le guste en esa zapatería.
5. ¿tener / dependientas / algo / que / ser / más / barato?
   ¿Tienen las dependientas algo que sea más barato?
6. ¿conocer / tú / alguno / banco / que / ofrecer / cuentas / corriente / gratis?
   ¿Conoces tú algún banco que ofrezca cuentas corrientes gratis?
7. nosotras / no / conocer / nadie / que / hacer / tanto / diligencias / como / nosotras
   Nosotras no conocemos a nadie que haga tantas diligencias como nosotras.
8. nosotras / necesitar / un / línea / de / metro / que / nos / llevar / a / casa
   Nosotras necesitamos una línea de metro que nos lleve a casa.

NOTA CULTURAL

El **metro** de Caracas empezó a funcionar en 1983, después de varios años de intensa publicidad para promoverlo (*promote it*). El arte fue un recurso importante en la promoción del metro, y en las estaciones se pueden admirar obras (*works*) de famosos escultores venezolanos como Carlos Cruz-Diez y Jesús Rafael Soto.

3 Anuncios clasificados En parejas, lean estos anuncios y luego describan el tipo de persona u objeto que se busca. Answers will vary.

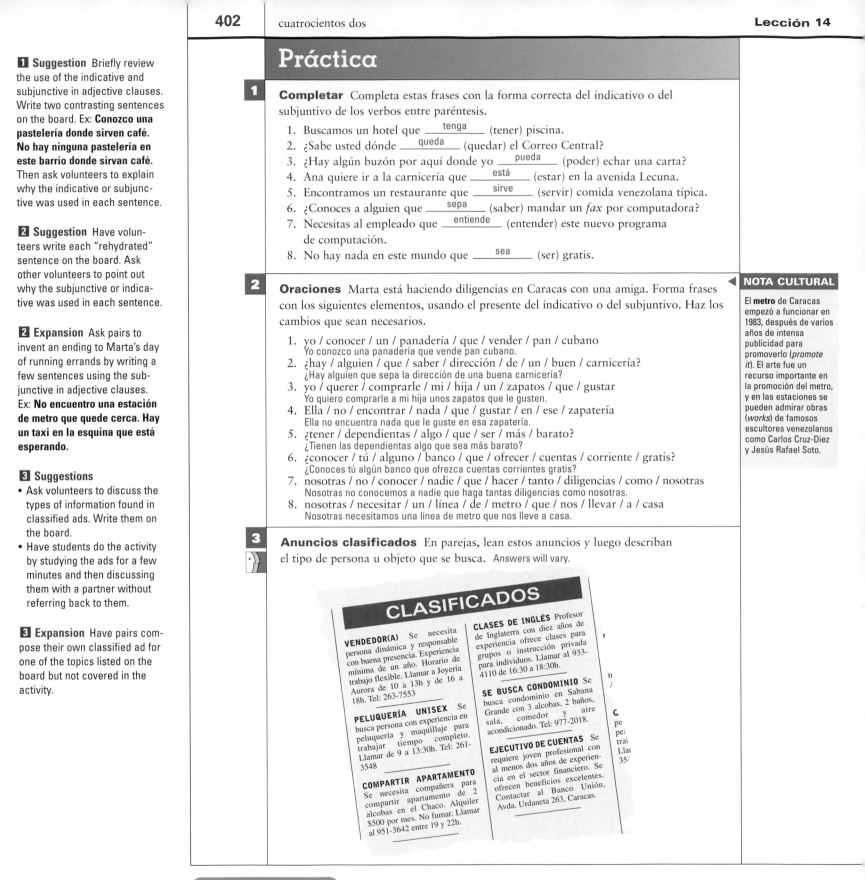

CLASIFICADOS

VENDEDOR(A) Se necesita persona dinámica y responsable con buena presencia. Experiencia mínima de un año. Horario de trabajo flexible. Llamar a Joyería Aurora de 10 a 13h y de 16 a 18h. Tel: 263-7553

PELUQUERÍA UNISEX Se busca persona con experiencia en peluquería y maquillaje para trabajar tiempo completo. Llamar de 9 a 13:30h. Tel: 261-3548

COMPARTIR APARTAMENTO Se necesita compañera para compartir apartamento de 2 alcobas en el Chaco. Alquiler $500 por mes. No fumar. Llamar al 951-3642 entre 19 y 22h.

CLASES DE INGLÉS Profesor de Inglaterra con diez años de experiencia ofrece clases para grupos o instrucción privada para individuos. Llamar al 933-4110 de 16:30 a 18:30h.

SE BUSCA CONDOMINIO Se busca condominio en Sabana Grande con 3 alcobas, 2 baños, sala, comedor y aire acondicionado. Tel: 977-2018.

EJECUTIVO DE CUENTAS Se requiere joven profesional con al menos dos años de experiencia en el sector financiero. Se ofrecen beneficios excelentes. Contactar al Banco Unión, Avda. Urdaneta 263, Caracas.

TEACHING OPTIONS

Pairs Have students write a description of the kind of place where they would like to vacation, using the subjunctive. Then have them exchange papers and make suggestions as to places that satisfy the desired characteristics. Ex: **Quiero ir de vacaciones a un lugar donde pueda esquiar en julio. → Bariloche, Argentina es un lugar donde puedes esquiar en julio.**

Extra Practice Here are five sentences to use as a dictation. Read each twice, pausing at natural breaks during the second reading to allow students time to write. 1. **¿Conoces una peluquería donde un corte de pelo no sea muy caro?** 2. **Sí, el salón de belleza que está al lado del banco tiene precios bajos.** 3. **No hay otra peluquería que tenga tan buen servicio.** 4. **Gracias, tú siempre me das consejos que me ayudan.** 5. **Espero que te guste la peluquería.**

Comunicación

4 Completar Completa estas frases de una manera lógica. Luego, compara tus respuestas con las de un(a) compañero/a. Answers will vary.

1. Deseo un trabajo *(job)* que…
2. Algún día espero tener un apartamento (una casa) que…
3. Mis padres buscan un carro que…, pero yo quiero un carro que…
4. Tengo un(a) novio/a que…
5. Un consejero/a *(advisor)* debe ser una persona que…
6. Me gustaría conocer a alguien que…
7. En esta clase no hay nadie que…
8. No tengo ningún profesor que…

5 Encuesta Tu profesor(a) va a darte una hoja de actividades. Circula por la clase y pregúntales a tus compañeros/as si conocen a alguien que haga cada actividad de la lista. Si responden que sí, pregúntales quién es y anota sus respuestas. Luego informa a la clase de los resultados de tu encuesta. Answers will vary.

> **modelo**
> Trabajar en un supermercado
> **Estudiante 1:** ¿Conoces a alguien que trabaje en un supermercado?
> **Estudiante 2:** Sí, conozco a alguien que trabaja en un supermercado. Es mi hermano menor.

Actividades	Nombres	Respuestas
1. Dar direcciones buenas		
2. Hablar japonés		
3. Graduarse este año		
4. Necesitar un préstamo		
5. Pedir prestado un carro		
6. Odiar ir de compras		
7. Ser venezolano/a		
8. Manejar una motocicleta		
9. Trabajar en una zapatería		
10. No tener tarjeta de crédito		

Síntesis

6 Busca los cuatro Tu profesor te va a dar una hoja con ocho anuncios clasificados y a tu compañero/a otra hoja con ocho anuncios distintos a los tuyos. Háganse preguntas para encontrar los cuatro anuncios de cada hoja que tienen su respuesta en la otra. Answers will vary.

> **modelo**
> **Estudiante 1:** ¿Hay alguien que necesite una alfombra?
> **Estudiante 2:** No, no hay nadie que necesite una alfombra.

TEACHING OPTIONS

Video Show the **Fotonovela** video module again to give students more input on the use of the subjunctive in adjective clauses. Stop the video where appropriate to discuss why the subjunctive or indicative was or was not used.

Small Groups Ask students to bring in travel brochures or tourist information from the Internet. Divide the class into groups of four and have them write a short radio spot for one of the tourist locations using only the subjunctive and formal commands.

4 Suggestion Model the activity by giving a personal example. Write, for example, **No conozco ningún restaurante cercano que…** on the board, then complete the sentence. Ex: **No conozco ningún restaurante cercano que sirva comida venezolana. No conozco ningún restaurante cercano que tenga un patio grande.**

4 Expansion Assign students to groups of six. Have each student compare his or her responses with those of the rest of the group. Then ask the group to pick two responses and make a visual representation of them. Designate a student from each group to show the visual for the class to guess what the response was. Guesses should include an adjective clause.

5 Suggestion Distribute the **Hojas de actividades** from the IRM that correspond to this activity.

5 Expansion Have pairs write six original sentences with adjective clauses based on the answers of the **encuesta**. Three sentences should have subordinate clauses in the subjunctive and three in the indicative.

6 Suggestion Divide the class into pairs and distribute the handouts from the Information Gap Activities Booklet that correspond to this activity. Give students ten minutes to complete this activity.

6 Expansion Have pairs write counterparts for two of the ads that do not have them. One ad should be for someone wanting to buy something and the other for someone wanting to sell something.

Section Goal

In **Estructura 14.2** students will learn **nosotros/as** commands.

Instructional Resources

WB/VM: Workbook, pp. 173–174
Lab Manual, p. 82
Lab CD/MP3 Lección 14
IRM: ¡Inténtalo! & Práctica
Answers, p. 194; Tapescript,
pp. 63–66
Info Gap Activities Booklet,
pp. 55–56
Interactive CD-ROM
Companion website:
www.vistahigherlearning.com
Presentations CD-ROM

Suggestions

• Model the **nosotros/as** commands by making suggestions to the whole class. Begin by having students respond to **tú** and **Uds.** commands, and then add commands for the class as a whole. Ex: ____ , **abre el libro.** ____ **y** ____ , **abran el libro. Ahora todos, abramos el libro. Abrámoslo.**

• Check comprehension by asking volunteers to convert **vamos a** + [*infinitive*] suggestions into **nosotros/as** commands.

Successful Language Learning Ask your students how they might use the **nosotros/as** commands when they are out with a group of Spanish speakers.

14.2 Nosotros/as commands

ANTE TODO You have already learned familiar (**tú**) commands and formal (**Ud./Uds.**) commands. You will now learn **nosotros/as** commands, which are used to give orders or suggestions that include yourself and other people.

▶ **Nosotros/as** commands correspond to the English *Let's.*

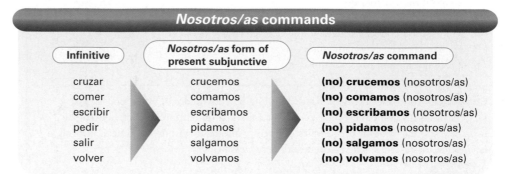

Infinitive	Nosotros/as form of present subjunctive	Nosotros/as command
cruzar	crucemos	**(no) crucemos** (nosotros/as)
comer	comamos	**(no) comamos** (nosotros/as)
escribir	escribamos	**(no) escribamos** (nosotros/as)
pedir	pidamos	**(no) pidamos** (nosotros/as)
salir	salgamos	**(no) salgamos** (nosotros/as)
volver	volvamos	**(no) volvamos** (nosotros/as)

▶ As the chart shows, both affirmative and negative **nosotros/as** commands are generally formed by using the first-person plural form of the present subjunctive.

Crucemos la calle.
Let's cross the street.

No crucemos la calle.
Let's not cross the street.

▶ The affirmative *Let's* + [*verb*] command may also be expressed with **vamos a** + [*infinitive*]. Remember, however, that **vamos a** + [*infinitive*] can also mean *we are going to (do something).* Context and tone of voice determine which meaning is being expressed.

Vamos a cruzar la calle.
Let's cross the street.

Vamos a trabajar mucho.
We're going to work a lot.

▶ To express *Let's go*, the present indicative form of **ir** (**vamos**) is used, not the subjunctive. For the negative command, however, the subjunctive is used.

Vamos a la pescadería.
Let's go to the fishmarket.

No vayamos a la pescadería.
Let's not go to the fish market.

CONSÚLTALO

Remember that stem-changing **–ir** verbs have an additional stem change in the **nosotros/as** and **vosotros/as** forms of the present subjunctive. To review these forms, see **Estructura 12.3**, p. 344.

¿Quieres ir al supermercado?

¡Excelente idea! ¡Vamos!

TEACHING OPTIONS

TPR Brainstorm gestures related to the active vocabulary in **Lección 14**. Have students stand. At random call out **nosotros/as** commands. All students should perform the appropriate gesture. Keep the pace rapid. Ex: **Echemos una carta al buzón. Hagamos cola. Firmemos un cheque. Paguemos en efectivo. Pidamos un préstamo. Llenemos un formulario.**

Extra Practice To provide oral practice with **nosotros/as** commands, create sentences with **vamos a** before the name of a business. Ex: **Vamos al banco. Vamos a la peluquería.** Say the sentence, have students repeat it, then call on individual students to add an appropriate **nosotros/as** command form. Ex: **Saquemos dinero. Cortémonos el pelo.**

▶ Object pronouns are attached to affirmative **nosotros/as** commands. A written accent is added to maintain original stress.

Firmemos el cheque. ———▶ **Firmémoslo.**
Let's sign the check. *Let's sign it.*

Escribamos a Ana y Raúl. ———▶ **Escribámosles.**
Let's write to Ana and Raúl. *Let's write to them.*

▶ Object pronouns are placed in front of negative **nosotros/as** commands.

No **les paguemos** el préstamo. No **se lo digamos** a ellos.
Let's not pay them the loan. *Let's not tell them.*

No **lo compremos.** No **se la presentemos.**
Let's not buy it. *Let's not introduce her.*

▶ When **nos** or **se** are attached to an affirmative **nosotros/as** command, the final **–s** is dropped from the verb ending.

Sentémonos allí. **Démoselo** a ella.
Let's sit there. *Let's give it to her.*

▶ The **nosotros/as** command form of **irse** (*to go away*) is **vámonos**. It's negative form is **no nos vayamos**.

¡**Vámonos** de vacaciones! **No nos vayamos** de aquí.
Let's go away on vacation! *Let's not go away from here.*

BANCOSUR. LLÁMANOS.

¡INTÉNTALO! Indica los mandatos afirmativos y negativos de la primera persona del plural (**nosotros/as**) de los siguientes verbos.

1. estudiar _estudiemos, no estudiemos_
2. cenar _cenemos, no cenemos_
3. leer _leamos, no leamos_
4. decidir _decidamos, no decidamos_
5. decir _digamos, no digamos_
6. cerrar _cerremos, no cerremos_
7. levantarse _levantémonos, no nos levantemos_
8. irse _vámonos, no nos vayamos_
9. depositar _depositemos, no depositemos_
10. quedarse _quedémonos, no nos quedemos_
11. pedir _pidamos, no pidamos_
12. vestirse _vistámonos, no nos vistamos_

TEACHING OPTIONS

Pairs Have pairs create an ad similar to the one on this page, using **nosotros/as** commands. Then have them exchange their ads with another pair who corrects them. Finally, have some pairs share their ads with the class.

Small Groups In groups of three, Student A writes a sentence that contains **nosotros/as** commands with direct and indirect objects (not pronouns). Ex: **Firmemos el cheque.** Student B must express the sentence using pronouns. Ex: **Firmémoslo.** Student C must express the sentence negatively. Ex: **No lo firmemos.** They should continue, switching roles and writing new sentences until the group has written six sentences.

Práctica

1

Completar Completa esta conversación con mandatos usando **nosotros/as.** Luego, representa la conversación con un(a) compañero/a.

MARÍA Sergio, ¿quieres hacer diligencias ahora o por la tarde?

SERGIO No (1)_las dejemos_ (dejarlas) para más tarde. (2)_Hagámoslas_ (Hacerlas) ahora. ¿Qué tenemos que hacer?

MARÍA Necesito comprar sellos.

SERGIO Yo también. (3)_Vamos_ (Ir) al correo.

MARÍA Pues, antes de ir al correo, necesito sacar dinero de mi cuenta corriente.

SERGIO Bueno, (4)_busquemos_ (buscar) un cajero automático.

MARÍA ¿Tienes hambre?

SERGIO Sí. (5)_Crucemos_ (Cruzar) la calle y (6)_entremos_ (entrar) en ese café.

MARÍA Buena idea.

SERGIO ¿Nos sentamos aquí?

MARÍA No, no (7)_nos sentemos_ (sentarse) aquí; (8)_sentémonos_ (sentarse) enfrente de la ventana.

SERGIO ¿Qué pedimos?

MARÍA (9)_Pidamos_ (Pedir) café y pan dulce.

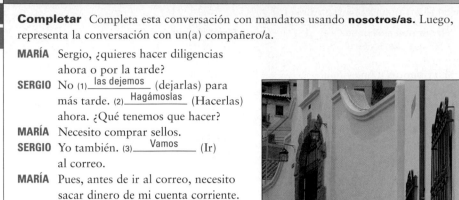

2

Responder Responde a cada mandato usando **nosotros/as** según las indicaciones. Sustituye los sustantivos por los objetos directos e indirectos.

> **modelo**
> Vamos a vender el carro. (Sí)
> *Sí, vendámoslo.*

1. Vamos a levantarnos a las seis. (Sí) Sí, levantémonos a las seis.
2. Vamos a enviar los paquetes. (No) No, no los enviemos.
3. Vamos a depositar el cheque. (Sí) Sí, depositémoslo.
4. Vamos al supermercado. (No) No, no vayamos al supermercado.
5. Vamos a mandar esta tarjeta postal a nuestros amigos. (No) No, no se la mandemos.
6. Vamos a limpiar la habitación. (Sí) Sí, limpiémosla.
7. Vamos a mirar la televisión. (No) No, no la miremos.
8. Vamos a bailar. (Sí) Sí, bailemos.
9. Vamos a pintar la sala. (No) No, no la pintemos.
10. Vamos a comprar estampillas. (Sí) Sí, comprémoslas.

---

1 Expansion
- Encourage pairs performing in front of the class to ad-lib additional material as they see fit.
- Give the class situations for students to solve by using **nosotros/as** commands. Ex: **Tenemos un examen mañana. (Estudiemos el subjuntivo.) La comida en la cafetería es muy mala. (No comamos allí todos los días.)**

2 Expansion For each item, have pairs come up with another logical **nosotros/as** command. Ex: **Vamos a levantarnos a las seis. (Sí, levantémonos a las seis. Y acostémonos temprano por la noche.)**

TEACHING OPTIONS

Heritage Speakers Ask heritage speakers to write a conversation using **nosotros/as** commands. The topic of the conversation should be typical errands run in their home communities. Have them read their conversations to the class, making sure to note any new vocabulary on the board.

Game Divide the class into teams of three. Teams will take turns responding to your cues with a **nosotros/as** command. Ex: **Necesitamos pan. (Vamos a la panadería.)** Give the cue. Allow the teams to confer and come up with a team answer, and then call on a team. Each correct answer earns a point.

Comunicación

communication — NATIONAL STANDARDS

3 **Sugerencias** Tú y tu compañero/a están de vacaciones en Caracas y se hacen sugerencias para resolver las situaciones que se presentan. Inventen mandatos afirmativos o negativos usando **nosotros/as**. Answers will vary.

> **modelo**
> Se nos olvidaron las tarjetas de crédito.
> *Paguemos en efectivo./No compremos más regalos.*

A

1. El museo está a sólo una cuadra de aquí.
2. Tenemos hambre.
3. Hay mucha cola en el cine.

B

1. Tenemos muchos cheques de viajero.
2. Tenemos prisa para llegar al cine.
3. Estamos cansados y queremos dormir.

4 **Decisiones** Trabajen en grupos pequeños. Ustedes están en Caracas por dos días. Lean esta página de una guía turística sobre la ciudad y decidan qué van a hacer hoy por la mañana, por la tarde y por la noche. Hagan oraciones con mandatos afirmativos o negativos usando **nosotros/as.** Answers will vary.

> **modelo**
> *Visitemos el Museo de Arte Contemporáneo Sofía Imber*
> *esta tarde. Quiero ver las esculturas de Jesús Rafael Soto.*

NOTA CULTURAL ▶

El venezolano **Jesús Rafael Soto** (1923–) es un escultor y pintor moderno. Sus obras cinéticas (*kinetic works*) frecuentemente incluyen formas que brillan (*shimmer*) y vibran.

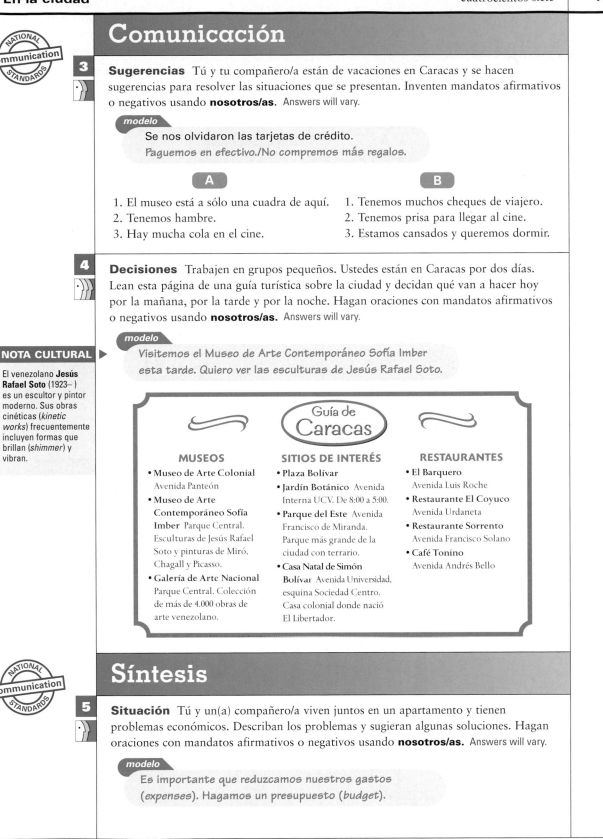

Guía de Caracas

MUSEOS
- **Museo de Arte Colonial** Avenida Panteón
- **Museo de Arte Contemporáneo Sofía Imber** Parque Central. Esculturas de Jesús Rafael Soto y pinturas de Miró, Chagall y Picasso.
- **Galería de Arte Nacional** Parque Central. Colección de más de 4.000 obras de arte venezolano.

SITIOS DE INTERÉS
- **Plaza Bolívar**
- **Jardín Botánico** Avenida Interna UCV. De 8:00 a 5:00.
- **Parque del Este** Avenida Francisco de Miranda. Parque más grande de la ciudad con terrario.
- **Casa Natal de Simón Bolívar** Avenida Universidad, esquina Sociedad Centro. Casa colonial donde nació El Libertador.

RESTAURANTES
- **El Barquero** Avenida Luis Roche
- **Restaurante El Coyuco** Avenida Urdaneta
- **Restaurante Sorrento** Avenida Francisco Solano
- **Café Tonino** Avenida Andrés Bello

Síntesis

communication — NATIONAL STANDARDS

5 **Situación** Tú y un(a) compañero/a viven juntos en un apartamento y tienen problemas económicos. Describan los problemas y sugieran algunas soluciones. Hagan oraciones con mandatos afirmativos o negativos usando **nosotros/as.** Answers will vary.

> **modelo**
> *Es importante que reduzcamos nuestros gastos*
> *(expenses). Hagamos un presupuesto (budget).*

14.3 The future

ANTE TODO   You have already learned ways of expressing the near future in Spanish. You will now learn how to form and use the future tense. Compare the different ways of expressing the future in Spanish and English.

Section Goals

In **Estructura 14.3** students will learn:
• the future
• irregular verbs in the future
• the future as a means of expressing conjecture or probability

Instructional Resources

*WB/VM: Workbook, pp. 175–176
Lab Manual, p. 83
Lab CD/MP3 **Lección 16**
IRM: ¡Inténtalo! & Práctica
Answers, p. 194; Tapescript,
pp. 63–66
Info Gap Activities Booklet,
pp. 57–58
Interactive CD-ROM
Companion website:
www.vistahigherlearning.com
Presentations CD-ROM*

Suggestions

• Ask students about their future activities using **ir a +** [*infinitive*]. After they answer, repeat the information using the future. Ex: **Mis amigos y yo almorzaremos a la una.**
• Review the **ir / ir a +** [*infinitive*] constructions to express the future in Spanish using the information in **Ante todo**. Then, work through the paradigm for the formation of the future. Go over regular and irregular verbs in the future point-by-point, calling students' attention to the information in **¡Atención!**
• Check for understanding by asking volunteers to give different forms of verbs not listed. Ex: **ahorrar, comer, vivir.**

Present indicative	**Present subjunctive**
Voy al cine mañana.	Ojalá **vaya al cine** mañana.
I'm going to the movies tomorrow.	*I hope I will go to the movies tomorrow.*

ir a + [infinitive]	**Future**
Voy a ir al cine.	**Iré** al cine.
I'm going to go to the movies.	*I will go to the movies.*

Future tense

		estudiar	**aprender**	**recibir**
SINGULAR FORMS	yo	estudiar**é**	aprender**é**	recibir**é**
	tú	estudiar**ás**	aprender**ás**	recibir**ás**
	Ud./él/ella	estudiar**á**	aprender**á**	recibir**á**
PLURAL FORMS	nosotros/as	estudiar**emos**	aprender**emos**	recibir**emos**
	vosotros/as	estudiar**éis**	aprender**éis**	recibir**éis**
	Uds./ellos/ellas	estudiar**án**	aprender**án**	recibir**án**

CONSÚLTALO

To review **ir a +** [*infinitive*], see **Estructura 4.1**, p. 102.

▶ In Spanish, the future is a simple tense that consists of one word, whereas in English it is made up of the auxiliary verb *will* or *shall*, and the main verb.

    ¿Cuándo **cobrarás** el cheque?   Mañana **abriré** una cuenta corriente.
    When will you cash the check?   *Tomorrow I will open a checking account.*

¡ATENCIÓN!

Note that all of the future endings have a written accent except the **nosotros/as** form.

▶ The future endings are the same for regular and irregular verbs. For regular verbs, simply add the endings to the infinitive. For irregular verbs, add the endings to the irregular stem.

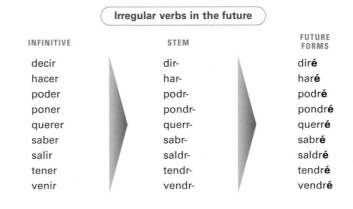

Irregular verbs in the future

INFINITIVE	STEM	FUTURE FORMS
decir	dir-	dir**é**
hacer	har-	har**é**
poder	podr-	podr**é**
poner	pondr-	pondr**é**
querer	querr-	querr**é**
saber	sabr-	sabr**é**
salir	saldr-	saldr**é**
tener	tendr-	tendr**é**
venir	vendr-	vendr**é**

TEACHING OPTIONS

Extra Practice To provide oral practice with the future, create sentences that follow the pattern of the sentences in the examples. Say the sentence, have students repeat it, then change the subject. Have students then say the sentence with the new subject, changing the verb as necessary.

Game Divide the class into teams of six. Each team should have a piece of paper. When you give an infinitive in Spanish, the first team member will write the **yo** form of the verb and pass the paper to the second member, who will write the **tú** form, and so forth. The first team to finish the entire paradigm correctly wins a point. The team with the most points wins.

▶ The future of **hay** (*inf.* **haber**) is **habrá** (*there will be*).

| La próxima semana **habrá** un nuevo director. *Next week there will be a new director.* | **Habrá** más formularios en el correo. *There will be more forms at the post office.* |

▶ Although the English word *will* can refer to future time, it also refers to someone's willingness to do something. In this case, Spanish uses **querer** + [*infinitive*], not the future tense.

| **¿Quieres llamarme**, por favor? *Will you please call me?* | **¿Quieren** ustedes **escucharnos**, por favor? *Will you please listen to us?* |

COMPARE & CONTRAST

In Spanish, the future tense has an additional use: expressing conjecture or probability. English sentences involving expressions such as *I wonder, I bet, must be, may, might,* and *probably* are often translated into Spanish using the *future of probability.*

| —¿Dónde **estarán** mis llaves? *I wonder where my keys are.* | —¿Qué hora **será**? *What time can it be? (I wonder what time it is.)* |
| —**Estarán** en la cocina. *They're probably in the kitchen.* | —**Serán** las once o las doce. *It must be (It's probably) eleven or twelve.* |

Note that although the future tense is used, these verbs express conjecture about *present* conditions, events, or actions.

CONSÚLTALO

To review these conjunctions of time, see **Estructura 13.3**, pp. 378–379.

▶ The future may also be used in the main clause of sentences in which the present subjunctive follows a conjunction of time such as **cuando, después (de) que, en cuanto, hasta que,** and **tan pronto como.**

| **Cuando llegues** a casa, **hablaremos**. *When you get home, we will talk.* | **Nos verás en cuanto entres** en la cafetería. *You'll see us as soon as you enter the cafeteria.* |

¡INTÉNTALO!   Conjuga los verbos entre paréntesis en futuro.

1. yo _____ dejaré, correré, pediré _____ (dejar, correr, pedir)
2. tú _____ cobrarás, beberás, vivirás _____ (cobrar, beber, vivir)
3. Lola _____ hará, pondrá, vendrá _____ (hacer, poner, venir)
4. nosotros _____ tendremos, diremos, querremos _____ (tener, decir, querer)
5. ustedes _____ irán, serán, estarán _____ (ir, ser, estar)
6. usted _____ firmará, comerá, repetirá _____ (firmar, comer, repetir)
7. yo _____ sabré, saldré, podré _____ (saber, salir, poder)
8. tú _____ encontrarás, jugarás, servirás _____ (encontrar, jugar, servir)

Suggestions

• Go over the future of **haber**. Remind students that **hay/habrá** has only one form and does not agree with any element in a sentence.
• Go over the explanation of **querer** + [*infinitive*].
• Explain the use of the future for expressing conjecture, which English generally expresses with the present tense. Use magazine pictures to get students to express speculation about what characters are thinking or going to do. Ex: **¿Qué estará pensando la mujer que hace cola en el banco? (Estará pensando que ya es tarde para su cita en el salón de belleza.) ¿Quiénes serán esos chicos que corren por la calle? (Serán estudiantes de otra escuela.)**
• Go over the use of the future in the main clause of sentences in which the present subjunctive follows a conjunction of time. Check for understanding by asking individuals to supply the main clause to prompts of present subjunctive clauses. Ex: **En cuanto pueda... ; Tan pronto como me lo digas...**
• Ask students to answer questions about the future of the **Fotonovela** characters. Ex: **¿Quién tendrá la profesión más interesante? ¿Por qué? ¿Quién será más feliz?**

TEACHING OPTIONS

Pairs Ask pairs to write ten academic resolutions for the upcoming semester using the future. Ex: **Haré dos o tres borradores de cada composición. Practicaremos el español con los estudiantes hispanos.**

Extra Practice Ask students to finish the following sentences logically: **1. En cuanto encuentre trabajo,... 2. Tan pronto como termine mis estudios,... 3. El día que me toque la lotería,... 4. Cuando lleguen las vacaciones,... 5. Hasta que tenga mi propio (*own*) apartamento,...**

- Before beginning the activity, briefly explain the subtle difference between the future with **ir a** + [*infinitive*] and the simple future.
- Have two volunteers read the **modelo**. Change the subject of the sentence and ask a volunteer for the new sentence. Ex: **Celia va a hacer unas compras. (Hará unas compras).**

1 Expansion For further oral practice, read these additional items to the class: **7. Después de cinco años Álvaro y yo vamos a tener nuestra propia casa. 8. La casa va a estar en un lugar bonito. 9. Ustedes van a querer visitarnos. 10. Vamos a jubilarnos cuando tengamos sesenta años.**

2 Expansion Have partners tell each other about a real person they have seen somewhere but to whom they have never spoken. Have them speculate about that person. Ex: **Será el dueño del restaurante. Trabajará hasta muy tarde cada noche. Vivirá en las afueras de la ciudad.** Then, have pairs share their speculations with the class.

3 Suggestion Before beginning the activity, give students a few minutes to brainstorm about the categories before assigning pairs.

3 Expansion
- After completing the activity, have students share their predictions with the class. Write some of the predictions on the board.
- Have pairs complete this activity predicting the future of a celebrity. Then have the class try to guess the identity of each celebrity.

Successful Language Learning Ask your students how they could use Spanish in their present or future careers.

Práctica

1 **Planes** Celia está hablando de sus planes. Repite lo que dice, usando el tiempo futuro.

> **modelo**
> Hoy voy a hacer unas compras.
> Hoy haré unas compras.

1. Voy a pasar por el banco a cobrar un cheque. Pasaré por el banco a cobrar un cheque.
2. Mi hermana va a venir conmigo al supermercado. Mi hermana vendrá conmigo al supermercado.
3. Vamos a buscar las mejores rebajas. Buscaremos las mejores rebajas.
4. Voy a comprarme unas botas. Me compraré unas botas.
5. Después voy a volver a casa y me voy a duchar. Después volveré a casa y me ducharé.
6. Seguramente mis amigos me van a llamar para salir esta noche. Seguramente mis amigos me llamarán para salir esta noche.

2 **¿Quién será?** En parejas, imaginen que están en un café y ven entrar a un hombre o una mujer. Imaginen cómo será su vida y utilicen el futuro de probabilidad en su conversación. Usen estas preguntas como guía y después lean su conversación delante de la clase. Answers will vary.

> **modelo**
> **Estudiante 1:** ¿Será simpático?
> **Estudiante 2:** Creo que no, está muy serio. Será antipático.

- ¿Estará soltero/a?
- ¿Cuántos años tendrá?
- ¿Vivirá por aquí cerca?
- ¿Será famoso/a?
- ¿Será de otro país?
- ¿Con quién vivirá?
- ¿Estará esperando a alguien?
  ¿A quién?

3 **¿Qué pasará?** Imagina que tienes que adivinar (*to predict*) el futuro de tu compañero/a. En parejas, túrnense para hablar sobre cada una de estas categorías usando el futuro. Answers will vary.

> **modelo**
> **Estudiante 1:** ¿Seré rico? ¿Tendré una casa grande?
> **Estudiante 2:** Mmm... tendrás muy poco dinero durante los próximos cinco años, pero después serás muy, muy rico con una casa enorme. Luego te mudarás a una isla desierta (*deserted*) donde conocerás a...

▶ Amor
▶ Dinero
▶ Salud
▶ Trabajo
▶ Vivienda

Small Groups Divide the class into small groups. Have students take turns telling the group three things they will do next summer or next year. Ex: **Viajaré a Europa. Trabajaré en un banco.** Have students report back to the class what their group members will do.

Extra Practice To provide more practice with the future, give students oral prompts with a future date. Ex: **En el año 2020...** Provide the prompt and then call on individual students to complete the sentence using the future. (**...nadie manejará un coche. ... usted vivirá en Costa Rica.**)

Comunicación

4

Conversar Tú y tu compañero/a viajarán a la República Dominicana por siete días. En parejas, indiquen lo que harán y no harán. Digan dónde, cómo, con quién o en qué fechas lo harán, usando el anuncio (*ad*) como guía. Pueden usar sus propias ideas también.

Answers will vary.

modelo

Estudiante 1: ¿Qué haremos el martes?
Estudiante 2: Visitaremos el Jardín Botánico.
Estudiante 1: Pues, tú visitarás el Jardín Botánico y yo caminaré por el Mercado Modelo.

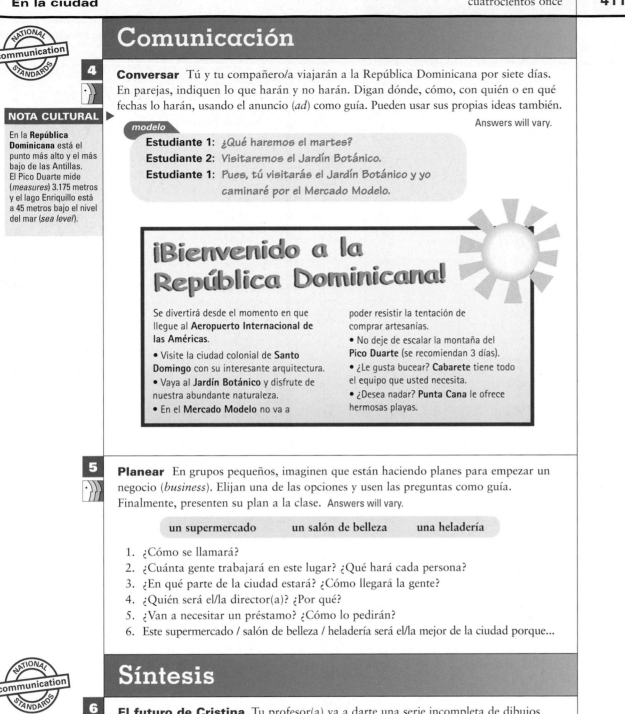

¡Bienvenido a la República Dominicana!

Se divertirá desde el momento en que llegue al **Aeropuerto Internacional de las Américas**.

• Visite la ciudad colonial de **Santo Domingo** con su interesante arquitectura.

• Vaya al **Jardín Botánico** y disfrute de nuestra abundante naturaleza.

• En el **Mercado Modelo** no va a poder resistir la tentación de comprar artesanías.

• No deje de escalar la montaña del **Pico Duarte** (se recomiendan 3 días).

• ¿Le gusta bucear? **Cabarete** tiene todo el equipo que usted necesita.

• ¿Desea nadar? **Punta Cana** le ofrece hermosas playas.

5

Planear En grupos pequeños, imaginen que están haciendo planes para empezar un negocio (*business*). Elijan una de las opciones y usen las preguntas como guía. Finalmente, presenten su plan a la clase. Answers will vary.

un supermercado   un salón de belleza   una heladería

1. ¿Cómo se llamará?
2. ¿Cuánta gente trabajará en este lugar? ¿Qué hará cada persona?
3. ¿En qué parte de la ciudad estará? ¿Cómo llegará la gente?
4. ¿Quién será el/la director(a)? ¿Por qué?
5. ¿Van a necesitar un préstamo? ¿Cómo lo pedirán?
6. Este supermercado / salón de belleza / heladería será el/la mejor de la ciudad porque...

Síntesis

6

El futuro de Cristina Tu profesor(a) va a darte una serie incompleta de dibujos sobre el futuro de Cristina. Tú y tu compañero/a tienen dos series diferentes. Háganse preguntas y respondan de acuerdo a los dibujos para completar la historia.

modelo

Estudiante 2: ¿Qué hará Cristina en el año 2015?
Estudiante 1: Ella se graduará en el año 2015.

Sidebar (right column):

4 Suggestions
• Encourage pairs to review the ad before they complete the activity.
• If you have any students from the Dominican Republic in your class, or if any of your students have visited the Dominican Republic, ask them to talk about the places named in the ad.

4 Expansion Have several pairs present their conversations to the class.

5 Expansion Have groups develop a visual aid to accompany their presentation to the class.

6 Suggestion Divide the class into pairs and distribute the handouts from the Information Gap Activities Booklet that correspond to this activity. Give the students ten minutes to complete it.

6 Expansion
• Have students change partners, and have the new pairs use the future to retell the story without looking at the drawings. Later, ask students if any aspects of their second partner's version of the story differed from the version they created with their first partner.
• Have pairs pick a person who is currently in the news. Have them write predictions about his or her future and then share their predictions with the class.

Game Use a ball (or balled-up piece of paper) to practice the simple future forms. Say an infinitive of a known verb followed by a subject pronoun. Ex: **tener (Uds.)** Toss the ball to a student who must give the simple future of the verb in the indicated form. (**tendrán**) When the student has given the appropriate form, he or she tosses the ball back to you. Include verbs from all conjugations and those that have irregular futures. Keep the pace rapid.

Large Groups Assign a century to each corner of the room. Ex: 23rd century. Tell students they are going to go into the future in a time machine (**máquina de transporte a través del tiempo**). They should pick which year they would like to visit and go to that corner. Once assembled, each group should develop a summary of life in their century. After groups have finished, call on a spokesperson in each group to report to the class.

Section Goals

In **Lectura** students will:
• learn the strategy of identifying a narrator's point of view
• read an authentic narrative in Spanish

Instructional Resource
Companion website:
www.vistahigherlearning.com

Estrategia Tell students that recognizing the point of view from which a narrative is told will help them comprehend it. Write the following first sentences of two narratives on the board and ask students to identify the point of view.

Cristóbal Colón vio por primera vez el territorio de Venezuela el 1° de agosto de 1498 en su tercer viaje al Nuevo Mundo.

Muy pronto tuvimos que reconocer que no íbamos a solucionar el caso sin mucho trabajo.

Examinar el texto Ask students to read the first paragraph of "**Grandezas de la burocracia**" and determine whether the narrative is written from the first- or third-person point of view.

Seleccionar Have pairs work through this activity together. If they have difficulty answering any question, suggest that one of the partners read aloud corresponding portions of the text.

Suggestion Point out the forms **permitiera, dignase,** and **estuviese** in the reading. Explain that they are forms of the past subjunctive. Tell your students they can probably figure out the meaning of these words using context clues and the glosses.

Lectura

Antes de leer

communication cultures NATIONAL STANDARDS

Estrategia
Identifying point of view

You can understand a narrative more completely if you identify the point of view of the narrator. You can do this by simply asking yourself from whose perspective the story is being told. Some stories are narrated in the first person. That is, the narrator is a character in the story, and everything you read is filtered through that person's thoughts, emotions, and opinions. Other stories have an omniscient narrator who is not one of the story's characters and who reports the thoughts and actions of all the characters.

Examinar el texto

Lee brevemente el cuento. ¿De qué trata? ¿Cómo lo sabes? ¿Se narra en primera persona o tiene un narrador omnisciente? ¿Cómo lo sabes?

Seleccionar

Completa cada frase con la información adecuada.

1. Los personajes° son ____a____.
   a. árabes b. franceses c. argentinos
2. Abderrahmán era ____b____.
   a. el ingeniero más sabio de los árabes
   b. un califa importante
   c. supervisor de la construcción de la ciudad
3. El cuento° tiene que ver° con ____a____.
   a. la construcción de una ciudad
   b. los problemas del califa con su esposa
   c. la burocracia en Bagdad
4. El supervisor de la construcción prometió terminar el proyecto dentro de ____c____.
   a. diez años b. cuatro años c. un año

recursos

vistahigher learning.com

personajes *characters* cuento *story*
tiene que ver con *has to do with*

GRANDEZAS° DE LA BUROCRACIA

Marco Denevi

Marco Denevi nació en Buenos Aires, Argentina, en 1922 y murió en la misma ciudad en 1998. Su novela Rosaura a las diez lo llevó a la fama en 1955. Escribió cuentos, novelas, obras teatrales y, a partir de 1980°, se dedicó a escribir periodismo político. La obra de Denevi, candidato al Premio Nobel de Literatura, se caracteriza por su ingenio° y sentido del humor.

Después de leer

Completar

Completa cada frase con la información adecuada. Answers will

1. Abderrahmán quería fundar _____.
2. Kamaru-l-Akmar prometió _____.
3. Después del primer año, Kamaru-l-Akmar pidió _____.
4. Abderrahmán se enojó porque _____.
5. Cuando Abderrahmán vio la ciudad, dijo que _____.
6. Mientras planeaban la futura ciudad, los ingenieros y arquitectos construyeron _____.

Cuentan que Abderrahmán decidió fundar° la ciudad más hermosa del mundo, para lo cual mandó llamar a una multitud de ingenieros, de arquitectos y de artistas a cuya cabeza estaba Kamaru-l-Akmar, el primero y el más sabio° de los ingenieros árabes.

Kamaru-l-Akmar prometió que en un año la ciudad estaría edificada°, con sus alcázares°, sus mezquitas° y jardines más bellos que los de Susa y Ecbatana y aun° que los de Bagdad. Pero solicitó al califa° que le permitiera construirla con entera libertad y fantasía y según sus propias ideas, y que no se dignase verla sino una vez que estuviese concluida°. Abderrahmán, sonriendo, accedió.

Al cabo del° primer año Kamaru-l-Akmar pidió otro año de prórroga°, que el califa gustosamente le concedió. Esto se repitió varias veces. Así transcurrieron° no menos de diez años. Hasta que Abderrahmán, encolerizado°, decidió ir a investigar.

Cuando llegó, una sonrisa le borró el ceño adusto°. ¡Es la más hermosa ciudad que han contemplado ojos mortales! —le dijo a Kamaru-l-Akmar—. ¿Por qué no me avisaste que estaba construida?

Kamaru-l-Akmar inclinó la frente° y no se atrevió° a confesar al califa que lo que estaba viendo eran los palacios y jardines que los ingenieros, arquitectos y demás artistas habían levantado para sí mismos mientras estudiaban los planes de la futura ciudad.

Así fue construida Zahara, a orillas del° Guadalquivir.

grandezas *grandeurs* a partir de 1980 *from 1980 on*
ingenio *creativity* fundar *to found* sabio *wise*
estaría edificada *would be built* alcázares *fortresses*
mezquitas *mosques* aun *even* califa *caliph (an Islamic leader)*
sino una vez que estuviese concluida *until it was finished*
Al cabo del *At the end of* prórroga *extension*
transcurrieron *passed* encolerizado *angry*
le borró el ceño adusto *wiped the stern frown off his face*
frente *forehead* no se atrevió *didn't dare* a orillas de *on the shores of*

Contestar

Contesta estas preguntas. Answers will vary.

1. Describe al califa y a Kamaru-l-Akmar. ¿Qué tipo de personas crees que son? Explica tu respuesta.
2. ¿Por qué el ingeniero no quiere que Abderrahmán vea la ciudad antes de que termine la construcción? Explica tu respuesta.
3. ¿Qué significa la palabra **burocracia**? Da algunos ejemplos.
4. ¿Por qué este cuento se llama *Grandezas de la burocracia*?
5. ¿Crees que el narrador de este cuento está a favor° o en contra de° la burocracia? Explica tu opinión.

Diálogo

Trabaja con un(a) compañero/a para preparar una conversación en tres partes, basándose en la lectura. Después presenten la conversación a la clase. Answers will vary.

▸ Primera parte: El califa habla con el más sabio de los ingenieros sobre la ciudad que quiere fundar.
▸ Segunda parte: Kamaru-l-Akmar pide la séptima prórroga y explica por qué es necesaria. El califa se la concede pero no está muy contento.
▸ Tercera parte: Abderrahmán y Kamaru-l-Akmar visitan el lugar de construcción en el décimo año.

a favor de *in favor of*   en contra de *against*

Venezuela

El país en cifras

▶ **Área:** 912.050 km² (352.144 millas²), *aproximadamente dos veces el área de California*
▶ **Población:** 26.468.000
▶ **Capital:** Caracas—3.261.000
▶ **Ciudades principales:** Maracaibo—2.172.000, Valencia—2.320.000, Maracay—1.249.000, Barquisimeto—1.005.000

SOURCE: Population Division, UN Secretariat

▶ **Moneda:** bolívar
▶ **Idiomas:** español (oficial), arahuaco, caribe
El yanomami es uno de los idiomas indígenas que se habla en Venezuela. La cultura de los yanomami tiene su centro en el sur de Venezuela, en el bosque tropical. Son cazadores° y agricultores y viven en comunidades de hasta 400 miembros.

Bandera de Venezuela

Venezolanos célebres

▶ **Teresa Carreño,** compositora y pianista (1853–1917)
▶ **Rómulo Gallegos,** escritor y político (1884–1969)
▶ **Andrés Eloy Blanco,** poeta (1897–1955)
▶ **Baruj Benacerraf,** científico (1920–)
Baruj Benacerraf, junto con dos de sus colegas, recibió el Premio Nobel por sus investigaciones en el campo° de la inmunología y las enfermedades autoinmunes. Nacido en Caracas, Benacerraf también vivió en París y reside ahora en los Estados Unidos.

cazadores *hunters* campo *field* caída *drop* catarata *waterfall*

¡Increíble pero cierto!

Con una caída° de 979 m (3.212 pies) desde la meseta de Auyan Tepuy, Salto Ángel (*Angel Falls*), en Venezuela, es la catarata° más alta del mundo, ¡diecisiete veces más alta que las cataratas del Niágara! James C. Angel la descubrió en 1937. Los indígenas de la zona la denominan Churún Merú.

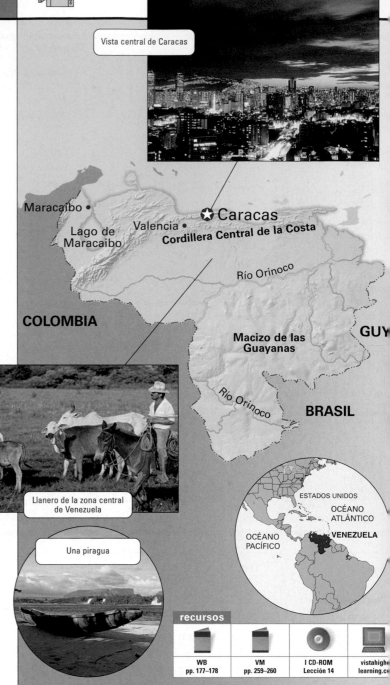

Vista central de Caracas

Maracaibo
Lago de Maracaibo
Valencia
☆ Caracas
Cordillera Central de la Costa
Río Orinoco
COLOMBIA
Macizo de las Guayanas
GUY
Río Orinoco
BRASIL

Llanero de la zona central de Venezuela

ESTADOS UNIDOS
OCÉANO ATLÁNTICO
OCÉANO PACÍFICO
VENEZUELA

Una piragua

Economía • El petróleo

La industria petrolera° es muy importante para la economía venezolana. La mayor concentración de petróleo se encuentra debajo del lago Maracaibo, el lago más grande de Suramérica. En 1976 se nacionalizaron las empresas° petroleras y pasaron a ser propiedad° del estado con el nombre de *Petróleos de Venezuela*. Este producto representa más del 70% de las exportaciones del país, siendo Estados Unidos su principal comprador°.

Actualidades • Caracas

El *boom* petrolero de los años cincuenta transformó a Caracas en una ciudad cosmopolita. Sus rascacielos° y excelentes sistemas de transporte la hacen una de las ciudades más modernas de Latinoamérica. El metro, construido en 1983, es uno de los más modernos del mundo y sus extensas carreteras y autopistas conectan la ciudad con el interior del país. El corazón de la ciudad es el Parque Central, una zona de centros comerciales, tiendas, restaurantes y clubes.

Historia • Simón Bolívar (1783–1830)

A finales del siglo° XVIII, Venezuela, al igual que otros países suramericanos, todavía estaba bajo el dominio de la corona° española. El general Simón Bolívar, nacido en Caracas, es llamado "El Libertador" porque fue el líder del movimiento independentista suramericano en el área que hoy es Venezuela, Colombia, Ecuador, Perú y Bolivia.

¿Qué aprendiste? Responde a las preguntas con una frase completa.

1. ¿Cuál es la moneda de Venezuela?
   La moneda de Venezuela es el bolívar.
2. ¿Quién fue Rómulo Gallegos?
   Rómulo Gallegos fue un escritor y político venezolano.
3. ¿Cuál es el lago más grande de Suramérica?
   El lago Maracaibo es el lago más grande de Suramérica.
4. ¿Cuál es el producto más exportado de Venezuela?
   El producto más exportado de Venezuela es el petróleo.
5. ¿Qué ocurrió en 1976 con las empresas petroleras?
   En 1976 las empresas petroleras se nacionalizaron.
6. ¿Cómo se llama la capital de Venezuela?
   La capital de Venezuela se llama Caracas.
7. ¿Qué hay en el Parque Central de Caracas?
   Hay centros comerciales, tiendas, restaurantes y clubes.
8. ¿Por qué es conocido Simón Bolívar como "El Libertador"?
   Simón Bolívar es conocido como "El Libertador" porque fue el líder del movimiento independentista suramericano.

Tejedor° en Los Aleros, aldea° en los Andes de Venezuela

Conexión Internet Investiga estos temas en el sitio **www.vistahigherlearning.com**.

1. Busca información sobre Simón Bolívar. ¿Cuáles son algunos de los episodios más importantes de su vida? ¿Crees que Bolívar fue un estadista (*statesman*) de primera categoría? ¿Por qué?
2. Prepara un plan para un viaje de ecoturismo por el Orinoco. ¿Qué quieres ver y hacer durante la excursión? ¿Por qué?

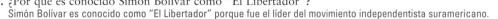

industria petrolera *oil industry* empresas *companies* propiedad *property* comprador *buyer* rascacielos *skyscrapers*
siglo *century* corona *crown* tejedor *weaver* aldea *village*

Section Goal

In **Panorama** students will read about the geography and culture of the Dominican Republic.

Instructional Resources
Transparencies, #3, #4, #57
WB/VM: Workbook, pp. 179–180;
Video Activities, pp. 261–262
***Panorama cultural** DVD/Video*
Interactive CD-ROM
IRM: Videoscript, p. 116;
***Panorama cultural** Translations,*
p. 138
Companion website:
www.vistahigherlearning.com
Presentations CD-ROM

Suggestion Have students look at the map of the Dominican Republic or project **Transparency #57** and talk about the physical features of the country. Ask students to note that many cities are located along the coast or close to it. Point out that there are rugged mountains through the center of the country, with fertile valleys interspersed.

El país en cifras After reading **Población,** point out to students that the neighboring country of Haiti is the poorest in the Western Hemisphere. Ask students to speculate about how that fact might impact the Dominican Republic. After reading **Idiomas,** the information that Haitian Creole (Kreyol) is widely spoken should confirm that there is a major Haitian presence in the Dominican Republic.

¡Increíble pero cierto! The actual whereabouts of the remains of Christopher Columbus are a matter of dispute. While Santo Domingo claims to house them, the navigator died in Spain and there is an elaborate tomb said to be his in the cathedral of Seville.

La República Dominicana

El país en cifras

▸ **Área:** 48.730 km² (18.815 millas²), *el área combinada de New Hampshire y Vermont*

▸ **Población:** 9.026.000

La isla La Española, llamada así tras° el primer viaje de Cristóbal Colón, estuvo bajo el completo dominio de la corona° española hasta 1697, cuando la parte oeste de la isla pasó a ser propiedad° francesa. Hoy día está dividida políticamente en dos países, La República Dominicana en la zona este y Haití en el oeste.

SOURCE: Population Division, UN Secretariat

▸ **Capital:** Santo Domingo—2.889.000
La mitad° de la población de la República Dominicana vive en la capital.

▸ **Ciudades principales:** Santiago de los Caballeros—897.000, La Vega—335.000, Puerto Plata—255.000, San Pedro de Macorís—213.000

▸ **Moneda:** peso dominicano

▸ **Idiomas:** español (oficial), criollo haitiano

Bandera de la
República Dominicana

Dominicanos célebres

▸ **Juan Pablo Duarte,** político y padre de la patria° (1808–1876)

▸ **Celeste Woss y Gil,** pintora (1891–1985)

▸ **Juan Luis Guerra,** compositor y cantante de merengue (1956–)

tras *after* corona *crown* propiedad *property* mitad *half*
padre de la patria *founding father* fortaleza *fortress*
se construyó *was built* naufragó *shipwrecked* enterrado *buried*

¡Increíble pero cierto!

La primera fortaleza° del Nuevo Mundo se construyó° en la República Dominicana en 1492 cuando la Santa María, uno de los tres barcos de Cristóbal Colón, naufragó° allí. Aunque la fortaleza, hecha con los restos del barco, fue destruida por tribus indígenas. Colón quería ser enterrado° allí.

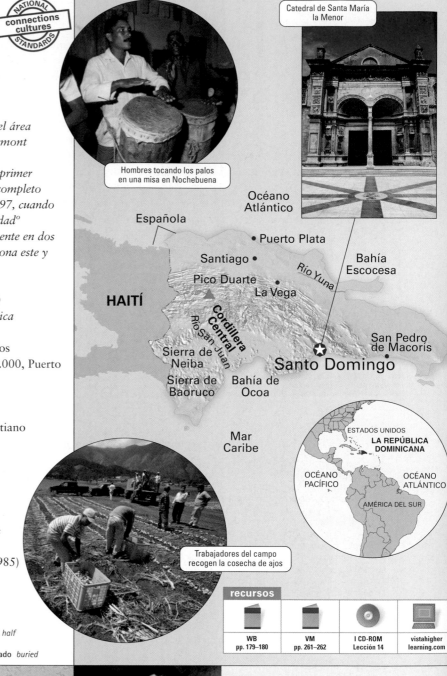

Catedral de Santa María la Menor

Hombres tocando los palos en una misa en Nochebuena

Océano Atlántico

Española

Puerto Plata

Santiago

Bahía Escocesa

Río Yuna

Pico Duarte

La Vega

HAITÍ

Cordillera Central

Río San Juan

Sierra de Neiba

San Pedro de Macorís

Santo Domingo

Sierra de Baoruco

Bahía de Ocoa

Mar Caribe

ESTADOS UNIDOS

LA REPÚBLICA DOMINICANA

OCÉANO PACÍFICO

OCÉANO ATLÁNTICO

AMÉRICA DEL SUR

Trabajadores del campo recogen la cosecha de ajos

recursos

WB pp. 179–180	VM pp. 261–262	I CD-ROM Lección 14	vistahigher learning.com

---

TEACHING OPTIONS

Variación léxica Although the Arawak and Taíno people who were indigenous to Hispaniola were virtually eliminated following the European conquest, Caribbean Spanish continues to be marked by lexical items from these cultures. Point out these words of Native American origin that have entered Spanish: **ají, cacique, canoa, hamaca, huracán** *(chili pepper, political leader, canoe, hammock, hurricane).*

Extra Practice Bring in recordings by Juan Luis Guerra, such as his 1998 release ***Ni es lo mismo ni es igual.*** Invite students to follow the printed lyrics as they listen to a track such as **"Mi PC."** Then, have students work together to create an English translation of the song.

Ciudades • Santo Domingo

La zona colonial de Santo Domingo, fundada en 1496, posee° algunas de las construcciones más antiguas del hemisferio. Gracias a las restauraciones°, la arquitectura de la ciudad es famosa no sólo por su belleza sino también por el buen estado de sus edificios. Entre sus sitios más visitados se cuentan° la Calle de las Damas, llamada así porque allí paseaban las señoras de la corte del Virrey; el Alcázar de Colón, un palacio construido en 1509 por Diego Colón, hijo de Cristóbal; y la Fortaleza Ozama, la más vieja de las Américas, construida en 1503.

Deportes • El béisbol

El béisbol es un deporte muy practicado en el Caribe. Los primeros países hispanos en tener una liga fueron Cuba y México, donde se empezó a jugar al béisbol en el siglo° XIX. Hoy día este deporte es una afición° nacional en la República Dominicana. Pedro Martínez y Manny Ramírez son sólo dos de los muchísimos beisbolistas dominicanos que han alcanzado° enorme éxito° e inmensa popularidad entre los aficionados.

Artes • El merengue

El merengue, una música para bailar originaria de la República Dominicana, tiene sus raíces° en el campo. Tradicionalmente las canciones hablaban de los problemas sociales de los campesinos°. Sus instrumentos eran el acordeón, el saxofón, el bajo°, el guayano° y la tambora, un tambor° característico del lugar. Entre 1930 y 1960, el merengue se popularizó en las ciudades y adoptó un tono más urbano. En este período empezaron a formarse grandes orquestas°. Uno de los cantantes° más famosos y que más ha ayudado a internacionalizar esta música es Juan Luis Guerra.

¿Qué aprendiste? Responde a las preguntas con una frase completa.

1. Aproximadamente ¿qué porcentaje de la población vive en la capital?
   Aproximadamente el 50 por ciento de la población vive en la capital.
2. ¿Cuándo se fundó la ciudad de Santo Domingo?
   Santo Domingo se fundó en 1496.
3. ¿Qué es el Alcázar de Colón?
   El Alcázar de Colón es un palacio construido en 1509 por Diego Colón, hijo de Cristóbal.
4. Nombra dos beisbolistas famosos de la República Dominicana.
   Dos beisbolistas famosos de la República Dominicana son Pedro Martínez y Manny Ramírez.
5. ¿De qué hablaban las canciones de merengue tradicionales?
   Las canciones de merengue tradicionales hablaban de los problemas sociales de los campesinos.
6. ¿Qué instrumentos se utilizaban para tocar (*play*) el merengue?
   Se utilizaban el acordeón, el saxofón, el bajo, el guayano y/o la tambora.
7. ¿Cuándo se transformó el merengue en un estilo más urbano?
   El merengue se transformó en un estilo más urbano entre los años 30 y 60.
8. ¿Qué cantante ha ayudado a internacionalizar el merengue?
   Juan Luis Guerra ha ayudado a internacionalizar el merengue.

Conexión Internet Investiga estos temas en el sitio **www.vistahigherlearning.com**.

1. Busca más información sobre la isla La Española. ¿Cómo son las relaciones entre la República Dominicana y Haití?
2. Busca más información sobre la zona colonial de Santo Domingo: la Catedral de Santa María, la Casa de Bastidas o el Panteón Nacional. ¿Cómo son estos edificios? ¿Te gustan? Explica tus respuestas.

....

posee *possesses*   restauraciones *restorations*   se cuentan *are included*   siglo *century*   afición *love*   han alcanzado *have reached*
éxito *success*   raíces *roots*   campesinos *rural people*   bajo *bass*   guayano *metal scraper*   tambor *drum*   orquestas *orchestras*
cantantes *singers*

Santo Domingo UNESCO has declared Santo Domingo a World Heritage site because of the abundance of historical architecture. Efforts are being made to restore buildings to their original grandeur, and to "correct" restorations made in the past that were not true to original architectural styles.

El béisbol Like many other Dominicans, baseball player Sammy Sosa's first baseball glove was a milk carton, his bat was a stick, and the ball was a rolled-up sock wound with tape. Sosa has not forgotten the difficult conditions experienced by most Dominicans. After a devastating hurricane swept the island, Sosa's charitable foundation raised $700,000 for reconstruction.

El merengue The **merengue** synthesizes elements of the cultures that make up the Dominican Republic's heritage. The gourd scraper—or **güiro**—comes from the Arawak people, the **tambora**—a drum unique to the Dominican Republic—is part of the nation's African legacy, the stringed instruments were adapted from the Spanish guitar, and the accordion was introduced by German merchants. Once students hear this quick-paced music, they will understand how it came to be named after meringue—a dessert made by furiously beating egg whites! For more information about **el merengue** and **la bachata**, you may want to play the **Panorama cultural** video for this lesson.

Conexión Internet Students will find supporting Internet activities and links at **www.vistahigherlearning.com**.

En la ciudad

el banco	bank
la carnicería	butcher shop
el correo	post office
el estacionamiento	parking lot
la frutería	fruit store
la heladería	ice cream shop
la joyería	jewelry store
la lavandería	laundromat
la panadería	bakery
la pastelería	pastry shop
la peluquería, el salón de belleza	beauty salon
la pescadería	fish market
el supermercado	supermarket
la zapatería	shoe store
hacer cola	to stand in line
hacer diligencias	to run errands

En el banco

el cajero automático	ATM
la cuenta corriente	checking account
la cuenta de ahorros	savings account
el cheque (de viajero)	(traveler's) check
ahorrar	to save (money)
cobrar	to cash (a check)
depositar	to deposit
firmar	to sign
llenar (un formulario)	to fill out (a form)
pagar a plazos	to pay in installments
pagar al contado, en efectivo	to pay in cash
pedir prestado	to borrow
pedir un préstamo	to apply for a loan
ser gratis	to be free of charge

Las direcciones

la cuadra	(city) block
la dirección	address
la esquina	corner
el letrero	sign
cruzar	to cross
dar direcciones	to give directions
doblar	to turn
estar perdido/a	to be lost
quedar	to be located
(al) este	(to the) east
(al) norte	(to the) north
(al) oeste	(to the) west
(al) sur	(to the) south
derecho	straight (ahead)
enfrente de	opposite; facing
hacia	toward

Expresiones útiles	See page 397.

En el correo

el cartero	mail carrier
el correo	mail/post office
el paquete	package
la estampilla, el sello	stamp
el sobre	envelope
echar (una carta) al buzón	to put (a letter) in the mailbox; to mail
enviar, mandar	to send; to mail

recursos
LM p. 83 | Lab CD/MP3 Lección 14 | Vocab CD Lección 14

El bienestar

15

Communicative Goals

You will learn how to:

- **Talk about health, well-being, and nutrition**
- **Talk about physical activities**

Lesson Goals

In **Lección 15** students will be introduced to the following:
- terms for health and exercise
- nutrition terms
- conditional tense
- present perfect
- past perfect
- making inferences
- listing key words when writing
- writing a personal fitness plan
- listening for the gist and for cognates
- cultural, geographic, and historical information about Bolivia
- cultural, geographic, and historical information about Paraguay

A primera vista Here are some additional questions you can ask based on the photo: **¿Crees que tienes buena salud? ¿Cómo lo sabes? ¿Vas al gimnasio regularmente? ¿Usas tu carro para hacer diligencias, o caminas? ¿Qué haces cuando te sientes nervioso/a o cansado/a? ¿Es importante que desayunes todas las mañanas? ¿Qué comes durante el día? ¿Cuántas horas duermes cada noche? ¿Conoces algún programa que ofrezca buenas ideas para mejorar la salud? ¿Cuál?**

A PRIMERA VISTA
- **¿Practicará ella deportes frecuentemente?**
- **¿Es activa o sedentaria?**
- **¿Es probable que le importe su salud?**

INSTRUCTIONAL RESOURCES

Workbook/Video Manual: WB Activities, pp. 181–194
Laboratory Manual: Lab Activities, pp. 85–89
Workbook/Video Manual: Video Activities, pp. 223–224; pp. 263–266
Instructor's Resource Manual: **Hojas de actividades**, pp. 150–152; **Vocabulario adicional**, p. 169; **¡Inténtalo!** & **Práctica** Answers, p. 195; **Fotonovela** Translations,

p. 127; Textbook CD Tapescript, p. 85; Lab CDs Tapescript, pp. 67–70; **Fotonovela** Videoscript, p. 105; **Panorama cultural** Videoscript, p. 117; **Pan. cult.** Translations, p. 139
Info Gap Activities Booklet, pp. 59–62
Overhead Transparencies: #5, #6, #58, #59, #60, #61
Lab Audio CD/MP3 **Lección 15**
Panorama cultural DVD/Video

Fotonovela DVD/Video
Testing Program, pp. 169–180; 193–204; 229–240
Testing Program Audio CD
Test Files CD-ROM
Test Generator
Companion website

Presentations CD-ROM
Textbook CD
Vocabulary CD
Interactive CD-ROM
Video CD-ROM
Web-SAM

Section Goals

In **Contextos** students will learn and practice:

• vocabulary used to talk about health and exercise

• vocabulary used to discuss nutrition and a healthy diet

Instructional Resources

Transparencies, #58, #59
Textbook Activities CD
Vocabulary CD
WB/VM: Workbook, pp. 181–182
Lab Manual, p. 85
Lab CD/MP3 **Lección 15**
IRM: **Vocab. adicional,** *p. 169;*
Práctica *Answers, p. 195;*
Tapescript, pp. 67–70; p. 85
Info Gap Activities Booklet,
pp. 59–60
Interactive CD-ROM
Companion website:
www.vistahigherlearning.com
Presentations CD-ROM

Suggestions

• Write **hacer ejercicios** on the board, then ask personalized questions such as the following, writing new vocabulary on the board: **¿Quiénes hacen ejercicios regularmente? ¿Hacen ejercicios aeróbicos? ¿Quiénes levantan pesas? ¿Quiénes no hacen ejercicios nunca?** Tell students that they are going to learn vocabulary related to exercise and nutrition.

• Project **Transparency #58.** Give the people in the transparency names and make statements and ask questions about their activities. Ex: **El señor Garza es teleadicto. Él no hace ejercicios. Ve televisión y come papitas fritas. ¿Es activo o sedentario? ¿Lleva una vida sana?** After you have gone over the active vocabulary, ask students personalized questions about their exercise habits. Ex: **¿Qué hacen para aliviar el estrés? ____, ¿qué haces para aliviar el estrés? ¿Creen que se puede hacer demasiada gimnasia? ¿Creen que es más importante ser flexible o ser fuerte?**

• Point out the *no smoking* sign at the top right of the drawing. Explain to students that the infinitive, instead of a command form, is often found on public signs to express prohibitions or instructions. Ex: **No fumar.**

El bienestar

Más vocabulario

adelgazar	*to lose weight; to slim down*
aliviar el estrés	*to reduce stress*
aliviar la tensión	*to reduce tension*
apurarse, darse prisa	*to hurry; to rush*
aumentar de peso, engordar	*to gain weight*
calentarse (e:ie)	*to warm up*
disfrutar (de)	*to enjoy; to reap the benefits (of)*
entrenarse	*to practice; to train*
estar a dieta	*to be on a diet*
estar en buena forma	*to be in good shape*
hacer gimnasia	*to work out*
llevar una vida sana	*to lead a healthy lifestyle*
mantenerse en forma	*to stay in shape*
sufrir muchas presiones	*to be under a lot of pressure*
tratar de (+ *inf.*)	*to try (to do something)*
la droga	*drug*
el/la drogadicto/a	*drug addict*
activo/a	*active*
débil	*weak*
en exceso	*in excess; too much*
flexible	*flexible*
fuerte	*strong*
sedentario/a	*sedentary; related to sitting*
tranquilo/a	*calm; quiet*
el bienestar	*well-being*

Variación léxica

hacer ejercicios ⟷ hacer aeróbic (*Esp.*)
aeróbicos

entrenador ⟷ monitor

el teleadicto

Hace ejercicios de estiramiento. (hacer)

la clase de ejercicios aeróbicos

Suda. (sudar)

Hace ejercicio. (hacer)

el entrenador

el músculo

la cinta caminadora

recursos

| TEXT CD Lección 15 | WB pp. 181–182 | LM p. 85 | Lab CD/MP3 Lección 15 | I CD-ROM Lección 15 | Vocab CD Lección 15 |

TEACHING OPTIONS

TPR Ask students to stand. Call out commands based on the lesson vocabulary. Ex: **¡Levanten pesas! ¡Hagan ejercicios aeróbicos! ¡Apúrense! ¡Descansen!** Working with students, invent a gesture to mime each activity. When you have invented gestures to cover all the vocabulary, carry out a TPR activity with the class. Keep the pace rapid. Vary singular and plural commands.

Variación léxica Direct students attention to this box. Ask heritage speakers if they can think of additional terms related to fitness, health, and well-being.

No fumar.

el masaje

Hace ejercicios aeróbicos.
(hacer)

Levanta pesas.
(levantar)

Práctica

1

Escuchar 🎧 Mira el dibujo en las páginas 420 y 421. Luego escucha las frases e indica si lo que se dice en cada frase es **cierto** o **falso**.

	Cierto	Falso		Cierto	Falso
1.	○	◉	6.	○	◉
2.	○	◉	7.	○	◉
3.	◉	○	8.	◉	○
4.	◉	○	9.	○	◉
5.	◉	○	10.	○	◉

2

Identificar Identifica el opuesto (*opposite*) de cada palabra.

> apurarse   fuerte
> disfrutar   mantenerse en forma
> engordar   sedentario
> estar enfermo   sufrir muchas presiones
> flexible   tranquilo

1. activo sedentario
2. adelgazar engordar
3. aliviar el estrés sufrir muchas presiones
4. débil fuerte
5. ir despacio apurarse
6. estar sano estar enfermo
7. nervioso tranquilo
8. ser teleadicto mantenerse en forma

3

Combinar Combina palabras de cada columna para formar diez frases lógicas sobre el bienestar.

1. David levanta pesas   j   a. aumentó de peso.
2. Estás en buena forma   f   b. estiramiento.
3. Felipe se lastimó   h   c. fuertes.
4. José y Rafael   g   d. presiones.
5. María y yo somos   c   e. porque quieren adelgazar.
6. Mi hermano   a   f. porque haces ejercicio.
7. Sara hace ejercicios de   b   g. sudan mucho en el gimnasio.
8. Mis primas están a dieta   e   h. un músculo de la pierna.
9. Para llevar una vida sana,   i   i. no se debe fumar.
10. Ellos sufren muchas   d   j. y corre mucho.

1 Suggestion Check answers by reading each item individually and asking volunteers to say whether the statement is true or false. Have students change the false statements to make them true.

1 Tapescript 1. Se puede fumar dentro del gimnasio. 2. El teleadicto está en buena forma. 3. Los músculos del entrenador son grandes. 4. La mujer que está corriendo también está sudando. 5. Se puede recibir un masaje en el Gimnasio Sucre. 6. Hay cuatro hombres en la clase de ejercicios aeróbicos. 7. El hombre que levanta pesas lleva una vida muy sedentaria. 8. La instructora de la clase de ejercicios aeróbicos lleva una vida muy activa. 9. El hombre que mira televisión está a dieta. 10. No hay nadie en el gimnasio que haga ejercicios de estiramiento.
Textbook Activities CD

2 Expansion Have students use each pair of opposite terms in sentences illustrating their contrasting meanings. Ex: **José está muy nervioso porque no estudió para el examen. Roberto estudió por dos horas; por eso está tranquilo.**

3 Expansion Have students create their own original endings for each of the sentence fragments in the left column.

Successful Language Learning Mention that working out to a Spanish-language exercise program would be excellent listening practice.

Note: At this point you may want to present **Vocabulario adicional: Más vocabulario para el bienestar**, from the IRM.

TEACHING OPTIONS

Pairs Have pairs of students interview each other about what they do to stay in shape. Interviewers should also find out how often their partner does these things and when he or she did them over the past week. Ask students to write a brief report summarizing the interview.

Game Divide the class into teams of three. Ask a team to leave the room while the class chooses a vocabulary word or expression. When the team returns, they must try to guess it by asking the class yes or no questions. If the team guesses the word within ten questions, the team gets a point. Ex: **¿Es un lugar? ¿Describe a una persona? ¿Es una acción? ¿Es algo bueno para el bienestar?**

- Project **Transparency #59.** First, ask open-ended or yes/no questions that elicit the names of the foods depicted. Ex: **¿Qué es esto? (un huevo) Y esto al lado del queso, ¿son papas fritas?** Then ask students either/or questions to elicit the vocabulary in **La nutrición.** Ex: **¿La carne tiene proteínas o vitaminas? ¿Las bebidas alcohólicas tienen colesterol o no?** Continue asking for information or opinions. Ex: **¿Cuáles son algunas comidas que tienen colesterol? La cafeína, ¿creen que es una droga? ¿Por qué?**
- Point out that although English *alcohol* contains three syllables, Spanish **alcohol** is pronounced as two syllables.

4 Expansion After checking each item, ask students a personal question based on the information in that item, or have them comment on that information. Ex: **¿Comen ustedes comidas con mucha proteína después de hacer ejercicio? ¿Piensan que es buena idea comer comidas de todos los grupos alimenticios? ¿Por qué?**

Ayuda Present the vocabulary using the words in sentences that describe your eating or physical activity patterns.

5 Suggestion Have students discuss each question thoroughly before they move on to the next one. Also have them note opinions, ideas, and habits they have in common.

5 Expansion As students share their answers with the class, have a volunteer write down any common themes that stand out. Have a class discussion about these themes and their origins.

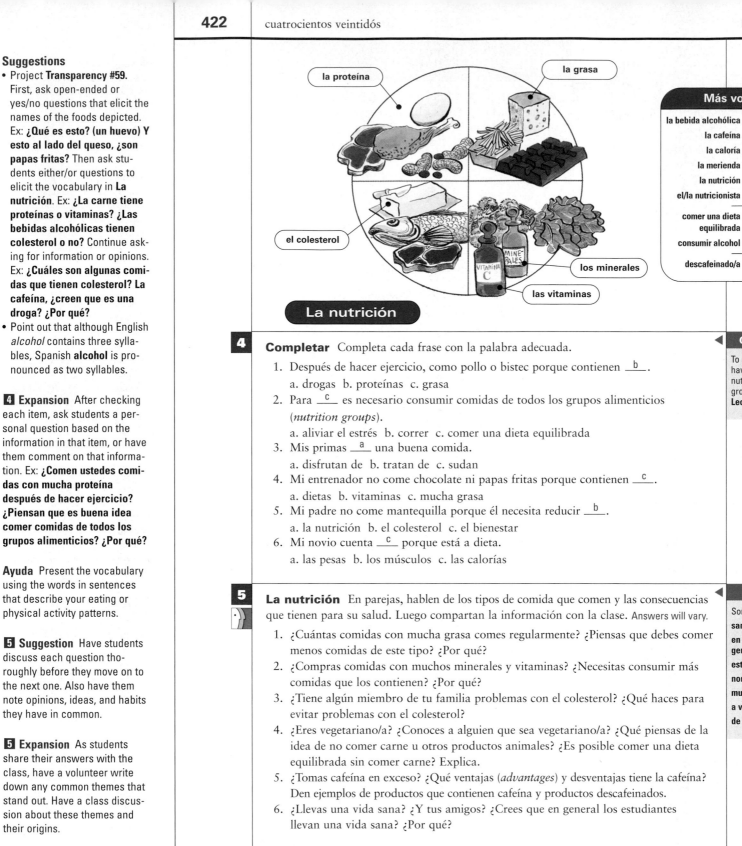

Más vocabulario	
la bebida alcohólica	*alcoholic beverage*
la cafeína	*caffeine*
la caloría	*calorie*
la merienda	*afternoon snack*
la nutrición	*nutrition*
el/la nutricionista	*nutritionist*
comer una dieta equilibrada	*to eat a balanced diet*
consumir alcohol	*to consume alcohol*
descafeinado/a	*decaffeinated*

La nutrición

4 **Completar** Completa cada frase con la palabra adecuada.
1. Después de hacer ejercicio, como pollo o bistec porque contienen __b__.
   a. drogas b. proteínas c. grasa
2. Para __c__ es necesario consumir comidas de todos los grupos alimenticios (*nutrition groups*).
   a. aliviar el estrés b. correr c. comer una dieta equilibrada
3. Mis primas __a__ una buena comida.
   a. disfrutan de b. tratan de c. sudan
4. Mi entrenador no come chocolate ni papas fritas porque contienen __c__.
   a. dietas b. vitaminas c. mucha grasa
5. Mi padre no come mantequilla porque él necesita reducir __b__.
   a. la nutrición b. el colesterol c. el bienestar
6. Mi novio cuenta __c__ porque está a dieta.
   a. las pesas b. los músculos c. las calorías

CONSÚLTALO

To review what you have learned about nutrition and food groups, see **Contextos Lección 8**, pp. 210–213.

5 **La nutrición** En parejas, hablen de los tipos de comida que comen y las consecuencias que tienen para su salud. Luego compartan la información con la clase. Answers will vary.
1. ¿Cuántas comidas con mucha grasa comes regularmente? ¿Piensas que debes comer menos comidas de este tipo? ¿Por qué?
2. ¿Compras comidas con muchos minerales y vitaminas? ¿Necesitas consumir más comidas que los contienen? ¿Por qué?
3. ¿Tiene algún miembro de tu familia problemas con el colesterol? ¿Qué haces para evitar problemas con el colesterol?
4. ¿Eres vegetariano/a? ¿Conoces a alguien que sea vegetariano/a? ¿Qué piensas de la idea de no comer carne u otros productos animales? ¿Es posible comer una dieta equilibrada sin comer carne? Explica.
5. ¿Tomas cafeína en exceso? ¿Qué ventajas (*advantages*) y desventajas tiene la cafeína? Den ejemplos de productos que contienen cafeína y productos descafeinados.
6. ¿Llevas una vida sana? ¿Y tus amigos? ¿Crees que en general los estudiantes llevan una vida sana? ¿Por qué?

AYUDA

Some useful words:
sano = saludable
en general = por lo general
estricto
normalmente
muchas veces
a veces
de vez en cuando

TEACHING OPTIONS

Extra Practice Make a series of statements about healthy and unhealthy habits. Have students call out **bueno** if the habit is healthy and **malo** if it is not. Ex: **Antes de hacer ejercicio, siempre como comidas con mucha grasa. (malo) Consumo muy poco alcohol. (bueno)**

Heritage Speakers Ask heritage speakers to interview friends and relatives about their exercise and dietary habits. Have them also find out whether attitudes regarding diet and exercise are the same among their Spanish-speaking acquaintances as those among their English-speaking ones. Have students report their findings to the class.

Comunicación

6 **Un anuncio** En grupos de cuatro, imaginen que son dueños/as de un gimnasio con un equipo (*equipment*) moderno, entrenadores calificados y un(a) nutricionista. Preparen y presenten un anuncio para la televisión que hable del gimnasio y atraiga (*attracts*) a una gran variedad de nuevos clientes. No se olviden de presentar la siguiente información:

Answers will vary.

► Las ventajas de estar en buena forma
► El equipo que tienen
► Los servicios y clases que ofrecen
► Las características únicas del gimnasio
► La dirección y el teléfono del gimnasio
► El precio para los socios (*members*) del gimnasio

7 **Recomendaciones para la salud** En parejas, imaginen que están preocupados con los malos hábitos de un(a) amigo/a suyo/a que no está bien últimamente (*lately*). Escriban y representen una conversación en la cual hablan de lo que está pasando en la vida de su amigo/a y los cambios que necesita hacer para llevar una vida sana. Answers will vary.

8 **El teleadicto** Con un(a) compañero/a, representen los papeles (*play the roles*) de un(a) nutricionista y un(a) teleadicto/a. La persona sedentaria habla de sus malos hábitos en las comidas y de que no hace ejercicio. También dice que toma demasiado café y que siente mucho estrés. El/La nutricionista le sugiere una dieta equilibrada con bebidas descafeinadas y una rutina para mantenerse en buena forma. El/La teleadicto/a le da las gracias por su ayuda. Answers will vary.

9 **El gimnasio perfecto** Tú y tu compañero/a quieren encontrar el gimnasio perfecto. Tú tienes el anuncio del gimnasio *Bienestar* y tu compañero tiene el del gimnasio *Músculos*. Hazle preguntas a tu compañero/a sobre las actividades que se ofrecen en el otro gimnasio. Tu profesor(a) le va a dar a cada uno de ustedes una hoja distinta con la información necesaria para completar la actividad. Answers will vary.

> **modelo**
> **Estudiante 1:** *¿Se ofrecen clases para levantar pesas?*
> **Estudiante 2:** *Sí, se ofrecen clases todos los lunes a las seis de la tarde para levantar pesas.*

---

6 Suggestions
• If possible, have students visit health clubs in your area to gather advertising brochures and/or fitness magazines to help them brainstorm ideas for their commercial.
• Have groups write their advertisement so that each student gets to speak for an equal amount of time.

7 Suggestions
• Suggest that students use expressions of doubt followed by the subjunctive or expressions of certainty. Review the verbs and expressions on pages 374–375 as necessary.
• Have students discuss at least five bad habits their friend has, explain why he or she has them, and what he or she did unsuccessfully to overcome them. Then, have students discuss possible ways of successfully overcoming each habit.

8 Suggestion Review the verbs and expressions of will and influence on pages 348–349 before doing the activity.

8 Expansion Have students conduct a follow-up interview which takes place one month after the initial meeting.

9 Suggestion Divide the class into pairs and distribute the handouts from the Information Gap Activities Booklet that correspond to this activity. Give students ten minutes to complete this activity.

9 Expansion
• Have pairs work in groups to discuss which gym they personally would join and why.
• Have groups compare the gyms described in the activity with the campus gym and share their comparisons with the class.

TEACHING OPTIONS

Pairs Have students imagine that they are personal lifestyle consultants. Have them give their partner a set of ten guidelines on how to begin a comprehensive health program. Suggestions should be made regarding diet, aerobic exercise, strength training, flexibility training, and stress management. Have students switch roles.

Extra Practice Ask students to write down five personal goals for achieving or maintaining a healthy lifestyle. Then have them write a brief paragraph explaining why they want to attain these goals and how they plan to achieve them. Call on volunteers to share their goals with the class.

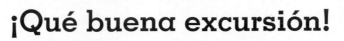

Section Goals

In **Fotonovela** students will:
- receive comprehensible input from free-flowing discourse
- learn functional phrases that preview lesson grammatical structures

Instructional Resources
WB/VM: Video Activities, pp. 223–224
***Fotonovela** DVD/Video (Start 01:22:22)*
***Fotonovela** Video CD-ROM*
*IRM: **Fotonovela** Translations, p. 127, Videoscript, p. 105*
Interactive CD-ROM

Video Recap: Lección 14
Before doing this **Fotonovela** section, review the previous one with this activity.
1. ¿Qué recomienda don Francisco que lleven todos los excursionistas? (zapatos cómodos, una mochila, gafas oscuras y un suéter)
2. ¿Qué quiere Inés que Álex y Maite le compren en el centro? (unas estampillas/unos sellos)
3. ¿Por qué hablaron Maite y Álex con un joven? (porque estaban perdidos)
4. ¿Dónde estaba el supermercado? (enfrente del banco)

Video Synopsis Martín leads the students in some warm-up stretches before the hike. During the hike, the students chat, take pictures, and admire their surroundings. Afterward, they talk about the wonderful time they had. Don Francisco tells the group it is time to go back for dinner.

Suggestions
- Have students read only the first statement in each numbered frame of this **Fotonovela** episode. Then have them predict the content of the episode, based only on those sentences. Write down their predictions.
- Quickly review the predictions your students made about the **Fotonovela**. Through discussion, help the class summarize the plot.

¡Qué buena excursión!

Martín y los estudiantes van de excursión a las montañas.

PERSONAJES

MAITE

INÉS

DON FRANCISCO

ÁLEX

JAVIER

MARTÍN

1
MARTÍN Buenos días, don Francisco.
DON FRANCISCO ¡Hola, Martín!
MARTÍN Ya veo que han traído lo que necesitan. ¡Todos han venido muy bien equipados!

2
MARTÍN Muy bien. ¡Atención, chicos! Primero hagamos algunos ejercicios de estiramiento...

3
MARTÍN Es bueno que se hayan mantenido en buena forma. Entonces, jóvenes, ¿ya están listos?
JAVIER ¡Sí, listísimos! No puedo creer que finalmente haya llegado el gran día.

6
DON FRANCISCO ¡Hola! ¡Qué alegría verlos! ¿Cómo les fue en la excursión?
JAVIER Increíble, don Efe. Nunca había visto un paisaje tan espectacular. Es un lugar estupendo. Saqué mil fotos y tengo montones de escenas para dibujar.

7
MAITE Nunca había hecho una excursión. ¡Me encantó! Cuando vuelva a España, voy a tener mucho que contarle a mi familia.

8
INÉS Ha sido la mejor excursión de mi vida. Amigos, Martín, don Efe, mil gracias.

recursos

| V CD-ROM Lección 15 | VM pp. 223–224 | I CD-ROM Lección 15 |

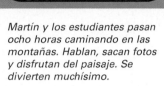

MARTÍN ¡Fabuloso! ¡En marcha, pues!

DON FRANCISCO ¡Adiós! ¡Cuídense!

Martín y los estudiantes pasan ocho horas caminando en las montañas. Hablan, sacan fotos y disfrutan del paisaje. Se divierten muchísimo.

ÁLEX Sí, gracias, Martín. Gracias por todo.

MARTÍN No hay de qué. Ha sido un placer.

DON FRANCISCO Chicos, pues, es hora de volver. Creo que la señora Vives nos ha preparado una cena muy especial.

Enfoque cultural Para estar en buena forma

Cada país del mundo hispano tiene deportes populares diferentes. En Argentina, por ejemplo, se juega mucho al fútbol, en Venezuela se juega al béisbol y en Colombia y España hay muchos aficionados al ciclismo. Otro deporte conocido en el mundo hispano es el jai alai, que es un juego de pelota originario del País Vasco (España). Su nombre significa "día de fiesta" en vascuence y es un deporte que se practica también en México, en la Florida, en Rhode Island y en Connecticut (EE.UU.).

Expresiones útiles

Getting ready to start a hike
▶ **Ya veo que han traído lo que necesitan.**
I see that you have brought what you need.
▶ **¡Todos han venido muy bien equipados!**
Everyone has come very well equipped!
▶ **Primero hagamos algunos ejercicios de estiramiento.**
First let's do some stretching exercises.
▶ **No puedo creer que finalmente haya llegado el gran día.**
I can't believe that the big day has finally arrived.
▶ **¿(Están) listos?**
(Are you) ready?
▷ **¡En marcha, pues!**
Let's get going, then!

Talking about a hike
▶ **¿Cómo les fue en la excursión?**
How did the hike go?
▷ **Nunca había visto un paisaje tan espectacular.**
I had never seen such spectacular scenery.
▷ **Nunca había hecho una excursión. ¡Me encantó!**
I had never gone on a hike before. I loved it!
▷ **Ha sido la mejor excursión de mi vida.**
It's been the best hike of my life.

Courtesy expressions
▶ **Gracias por todo.**
Thanks for everything.
▶ **Ha sido un placer.**
It's been a pleasure.
▶ **¡Cuídense!**
Take care!

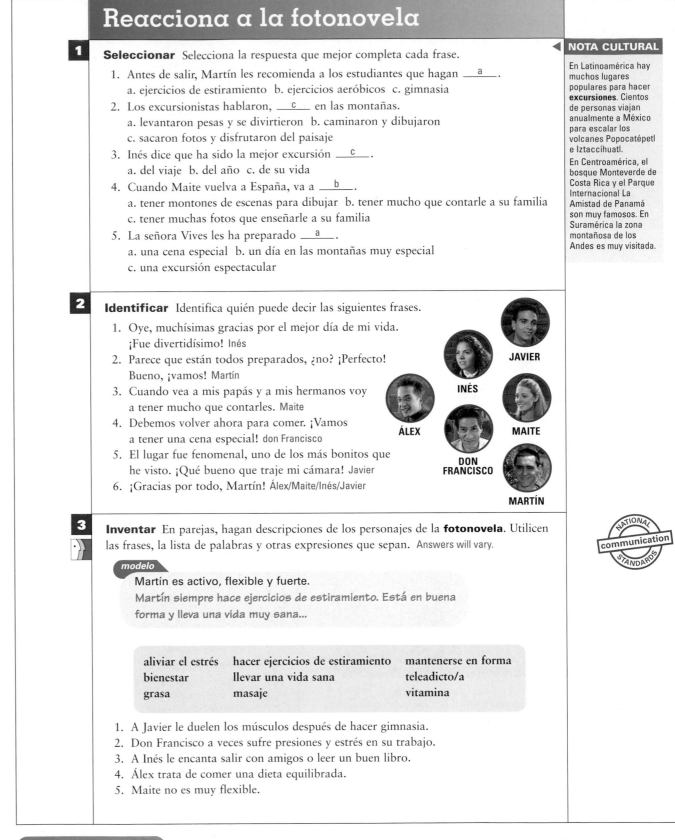

Reacciona a la fotonovela

1 **Seleccionar** Selecciona la respuesta que mejor completa cada frase.

1. Antes de salir, Martín les recomienda a los estudiantes que hagan ___a___.
   a. ejercicios de estiramiento b. ejercicios aeróbicos c. gimnasia
2. Los excursionistas hablaron, ___c___ en las montañas.
   a. levantaron pesas y se divirtieron b. caminaron y dibujaron
   c. sacaron fotos y disfrutaron del paisaje
3. Inés dice que ha sido la mejor excursión ___c___.
   a. del viaje b. del año c. de su vida
4. Cuando Maite vuelva a España, va a ___b___.
   a. tener montones de escenas para dibujar b. tener mucho que contarle a su familia
   c. tener muchas fotos que enseñarle a su familia
5. La señora Vives les ha preparado ___a___.
   a. una cena especial b. un día en las montañas muy especial
   c. una excursión espectacular

2 **Identificar** Identifica quién puede decir las siguientes frases.

1. Oye, muchísimas gracias por el mejor día de mi vida. ¡Fue divertidísimo! Inés
2. Parece que están todos preparados, ¿no? ¡Perfecto! Bueno, ¡vamos! Martín
3. Cuando vea a mis papás y a mis hermanos voy a tener mucho que contarles. Maite
4. Debemos volver ahora para comer. ¡Vamos a tener una cena especial! don Francisco
5. El lugar fue fenomenal, uno de los más bonitos que he visto. ¡Qué bueno que traje mi cámara! Javier
6. ¡Gracias por todo, Martín! Álex/Maite/Inés/Javier

JAVIER
INÉS
ÁLEX
MAITE
DON FRANCISCO
MARTÍN

3 **Inventar** En parejas, hagan descripciones de los personajes de la **fotonovela**. Utilicen las frases, la lista de palabras y otras expresiones que sepan. Answers will vary.

> **modelo**
> Martín es activo, flexible y fuerte.
> *Martín siempre hace ejercicios de estiramiento. Está en buena forma y lleva una vida muy sana...*

aliviar el estrés	hacer ejercicios de estiramiento	mantenerse en forma
bienestar	llevar una vida sana	teleadicto/a
grasa	masaje	vitamina

1. A Javier le duelen los músculos después de hacer gimnasia.
2. Don Francisco a veces sufre presiones y estrés en su trabajo.
3. A Inés le encanta salir con amigos o leer un buen libro.
4. Álex trata de comer una dieta equilibrada.
5. Maite no es muy flexible.

NOTA CULTURAL

En Latinoamérica hay muchos lugares populares para hacer **excursiones**. Cientos de personas viajan anualmente a México para escalar los volcanes Popocatépetl e Iztaccíhuatl.

En Centroamérica, el bosque Monteverde de Costa Rica y el Parque Internacional La Amistad de Panamá son muy famosos. En Suramérica la zona montañosa de los Andes es muy visitada.

---

1 **Expansion** Have the class work in pairs or small groups to write a question that would elicit each statement.

2 **Expansion**
• Give these to class as items 7-8: **7. Bueno, chicos… hay que hacer unos ejercicios antes de empezar. (Martín) 8. ¿Qué tal les fue en la excursión? (don Francisco)**
• Have your students close their books, then give them these sentences as a dictation. Read each sentence twice slowly and then once at regular speed so that the class will have time to write.

3 **Suggestion** Ask your students a few questions using words from the word bank. Ex: **¿Comes mucha grasa? ¿Qué es un teleadicto? ¿Cómo te mantienes en forma? ¿Qué haces para mantenerte en forma?**

3 **Expansion** Have pairs write sentences using any leftover words from the word bank. Ask volunteers to share their sentences with the class.

TEACHING OPTIONS

Extra Practice Ask the class a few additional questions about the **Fotonovela**. Ex: **¿Qué hicieron Martín y los chicos antes de empezar la excursión? (Hicieron unos ejercicios de estiramiento.) ¿Qué hicieron los estudiantes durante la excursión? (Caminaron, hablaron, sacaron fotos y miraron el paisaje.)**

Pairs Have pairs prepare a television program in which a traveler is interviewed about a recent hiking trip. Give them time to prepare and rehearse; then ask for volunteers to present their programs to the class. Alternately, you may want the students to videotape their programs and play them for the class.

Ortografía

Las letras b y v

Since there is no difference in pronunciation between the Spanish letters **b** and **v**, spelling words that contain these letters can be tricky. Here are some tips.

nombre	**blusa**	**absoluto**	**descubrir**

The letter **b** is always used before consonants.

bonita	**botella**	**buscar**	**bienestar**

At the beginning of words, the letter **b** is usually used when it is followed by the letter combinations -**on**, -**or**, -**ot**, -**u**, -**ur**, -**us**, -**ien**, and -**ene**.

bonita buscar voy vamos

adelgazaba	**disfrutaban**	**ibas**	**íbamos**

The letter **b** is used in the verb endings of the imperfect tense for –**ar** verbs and the verb **ir**.

voy	**vamos**	**estuvo**	**tuvieron**

The letter **v** is used in the present tense forms of **ir** and in the preterite forms of **estar** and **tener**.

octavo	**huevo**	**activa**	**grave**

The letter **v** is used in these noun and adjective endings: -**avo/a**, -**evo/a**, -**ivo/a**, -**ave**, -**eve**.

Práctica Completa las palabras con las letras **b** o **v**.

1. Una _v_ez me lastimé el _b_razo cuando esta_b_a _b_uceando.
2. Manuela se ol_v_idó sus li_b_ros en el auto_b_ús.
3. Ernesto tomó el _b_orrador y se puso todo _b_lanco de tiza.
4. Para tener una _v_ida sana y saluda_b_le necesitas tomar _v_itaminas.
5. En mi pue_b_lo hay un _b_ule_v_ar que tiene muchos ár_b_oles.

El ahorcado (*Hangman*) Juega al ahorcado para adivinar las palabras.

1. _n_ _u_ _b_ _e_ _s_   Están en el cielo. nubes
2. _b_ _u_ _z_ _ó_ _n_   Relacionado con el correo buzón
3. _b_ _o_ _t_ _e_ _l_ _l_ _a_   Está llena de líquido. botella
4. _n_ _i_ _e_ _v_ _e_   Fenómeno meteorológico nieve
5. _v_ _e_ _n_ _t_ _a_ _n_ _a_ _s_   Los "ojos" de la casa ventanas

recursos

LM p. 86	Lab CD/MP3 Lección 15	I CD-ROM Lección 15

Section Goal

In **Ortografía** students will learn about the spelling of words that contain **b** and **v**.

Instructional Resource
Interactive CD-ROM

Suggestions

• Ask the class if **b** or **v** is used before a consonant. Then say the words **nombre, blusa, absoluto,** and **descubrir** and have volunteers write them on the board.

• Write the words **bonita, botella, buscar,** and **bienestar** on the board. Ask the class to explain why these words are spelled with **b**.

• Ask the class if **b** or **v** is used in the endings of –**ar** verbs and the verb **ir** in the imperfect tense. Then say the words **adelgazaba, disfrutaban, ibas,** and **íbamos** and ask for volunteers to write them on the board.

• Ask why the words **voy, vamos, estuvo,** and **tuvieron** are spelled with **v** and have volunteers write them on the board.

• Write the words **octavo, huevo, activa,** and **grave** on the board and ask the class to explain why these words are spelled with **v**.

• Point out that **Ortografía** replaces **Pronunciación** in the Student Edition for **Lecciones 10–15,** but not in the Lab Manual. The **Recursos** box references the **Pronunciación** sections found in all lessons of the Lab Manual.

TEACHING OPTIONS

Small Groups On the board, write these sentences:
1. Doña __ioleta era muy acti__a y lle__aba una __ida muy sana. 2. Siempre comía __ien y nunca toma__a __ino ni refrescos. 3. Nunca fuma__a e i__a al gimnasio todos los días para hacer ejercicios aeró__icos. Have your students work in groups to fill in the missing letters.

Pairs Have partners use **Vocabulario** at the back of the book to help them write five sentences that contain words with **b** and **v**. Encourage students to use as many of these words as they can. They should leave blanks in place of these letters, as in **Práctica**. Then have pairs exchange papers and complete the words.

Section Goals

In **Estructura 15.1** students will learn:
• to use the conditional
• to make polite requests and hypothesize about past conditions

Instructional Resources

WB/VM: Workbook, pp. 183–184
Lab Manual, p. 87
*Lab CD/MP3 **Lección 15***
*IRM: **Hojas de actividades**, pp. 150–151; ¡Inténtalo! & Práctica Answers, p. 195; Tapescript, pp. 67–70*
Interactive CD-ROM
Companion website:
www.vistahigherlearning.com
Presentations CD-ROM

Suggestions

• Ask students to imagine they are on the trip with the **Fotonovela** characters. Ask them what they would like to do there. Ex: **¿Qué te gustaría hacer o ver en Ecuador? A mí me gustaría ir de excursión. ¿Y a ti?** Tell students that **gustaría** is a polite form of **gustar**. The conditional is used to make polite requests.
• Ask volunteers to read the captions to the video stills and indicate which verbs are in the conditional.
• Point out that, as in the future, there is only one set of endings in the conditional.
• Check for understanding by citing an infinitive and a subject pronoun while pointing to a specific student. The student should respond with the conditional form. Ex: **decir / nosotros (diríamos); venir / tú (vendrías)**
• Ask students what the future form of **hay** is. Then ask them what they would expect the conditional form to be.

15.1 The conditional

> **ANTE TODO** The conditional tense in Spanish expresses what you *would do* or what *would happen* under certain circumstances.

The conditional tense

		visitar	comer	escribir
SINGULAR FORMS	yo	visitar**ía**	comer**ía**	escribir**ía**
	tú	visitar**ías**	comer**ías**	escribir**ías**
	Ud./él/ella	visitar**ía**	comer**ía**	escribir**ía**
PLURAL FORMS	nosotros/as	visitar**íamos**	comer**íamos**	escribir**íamos**
	vosotros/as	visitar**íais**	comer**íais**	escribir**íais**
	Uds./ellos/ellas	visitar**ían**	comer**ían**	escribir**ían**

recursos

WB
pp. 183–188

LM
pp. 87–89

Lab CD/MP3
Lección 15

I CD-ROM
Lección 15

vistahigher
learning.com

¿Volverías a este lugar?

Sí, me gustaría volver pronto a este lugar.

▶ The conditional tense is formed much like the future tense. The endings are the same for all verbs, both regular and irregular. For regular verbs, you simply add the appropriate endings to the infinitive.

▶ For irregular verbs add the conditional endings to the irregular stems.

INFINITIVE	STEM	CONDITIONAL	INFINITIVE	STEM	CONDITIONAL
decir	dir–	dir**ía**	querer	querr–	querr**ía**
hacer	har–	har**ía**	saber	sabr–	sabr**ía**
poder	podr–	podr**ía**	salir	saldr–	saldr**ía**
poner	pondr–	pondr**ía**	tener	tendr–	tendr**ía**
haber	habr–	habr**ía**	venir	vendr–	vendr**ía**

> **¡ATENCIÓN!**
> The polite expressions **Me gustaría...** (*I would like...*) and **Te gustaría** (*You would like...*) are commonly used examples of the conditional.

> **¡ATENCIÓN!**
> All forms of the conditional have an accent mark.
> • • •
> The infinitive of **hay** is **haber**, so its conditional form is **habría**.

▶ While in English the conditional is a compound verb form made up of the auxiliary verb *would* and a main verb, in Spanish it is a simple verb form that consists of one word.

Yo no **iría** a ese gimnasio.
I would not go to that gym.

¿**Vendrías** conmigo a la clase de yoga?
Would you go with me to yoga class?

TEACHING OPTIONS

Game Line students up in teams of six several feet from the board. Write an infinitive on the board and call out **¡Empieza!** The first team members race to the board and write the **yo** form of the verb in the conditional, then pass the chalk to the next team members, who write the **tú** form, and so on. The team that finishes first and has all the forms correct wins the round.

Extra Practice Ask students what they would or would not do over the next six months if they could do anything their hearts desired and money and time were no object. Ex: **Yo viajaría por todo el mundo.** Call on volunteers to read their sentences, then ask the class comprehension questions about what was said. Ex: **¿Qué harían _____ y _____?**

▶ The conditional is commonly used to make polite requests.

¿**Podrías** abrir la ventana, por favor?
Would you open the window, please?

¿**Sería** tan amable de venir a mi oficina?
Would you be so kind as to come to my office?

CONSEJOS

Keep in mind the two parallel combinations shown in these sentences:

1) present tense in main clause → future tense in subordinate clause

2) past tense in main clause → conditional tense in subordinate clause

▶ In Spanish, as in English, the conditional expresses the future in relation to a past action or state of being. In other words, the future indicates what *will happen* whereas the conditional indicates what *would happen.*

Creo que mañana **hará** sol.
I think it will be sunny tomorrow.

Creía que hoy **haría** sol.
I thought it would be sunny today.

▶ The English *would* is often used with a verb to express the conditional, but it can also mean *used to*, in the sense of past habitual action. To express past habitual actions, Spanish uses the imperfect, not the conditional.

Íbamos a correr al parque los sábados.
We would go running to the park on Saturdays.

De adolescente **entrenaba** todos lo días.
As a teenager, I used to work out every day.

Sin ti, no sé qué haría.
Sólo tú sabes ordenar mi vida.
Computadoras de Bolsillo Vargas
MM-3000

COMPARE & CONTRAST

In **Lección 14**, you learned the *future of probability.* Spanish also has the *conditional of probability,* which expresses conjecture or probability about a past condition, event, or action. Compare these Spanish and English sentences.

Serían las once de la noche cuando Elvira me llamó.
It must have been (It was probably) 11 p.m. when Elvira called me.

Sonó el teléfono. ¿**Llamaría** Emilio para cancelar nuestra cita?
The phone rang. I wondered if it was Emilio calling to cancel our date.

Note that English conveys conjecture or probability with phrases such as *I wondered if, probably,* and *must have been.* In contrast, Spanish gets these same ideas across with conditional forms.

¡INTÉNTALO! Indica la forma apropiada del condicional de los verbos que están entre paréntesis.

1. Yo ___escucharía, leería, me apuraría___ (escuchar, leer, apurarse)
2. Tú ___te mantendrías, comprenderías, compartirías___ (mantenerse, comprender, compartir)
3. Marcos ___pondría, vendría, querría___ (poner, venir, querer)
4. Nosotras ___seríamos, sabríamos, iríamos___ (ser, saber, ir)
5. Ustedes ___adelgazarían, deberían, sufrirían___ (adelgazar, deber, sufrir)
6. Ella ___saldría, podría, haría___ (salir, poder, hacer)
7. Yo ___tendría, trataría, fumaría___ (tener, tratar, fumar)
8. Tú ___dirías, verías, engordarías___ (decir, ver, engordar)

Suggestions
• Discuss the use of the conditional in polite requests. Remind students of the forms **me gustaría** and **te gustaría**, which they have already seen in the **Fotonovela**. You might point out that usage tends to occur in set expressions, such as ¿**Podrías... ?** ¿**Sería usted tan amable de... ?** ¿**Tendrían ustedes la bondad de... ?** ¿**Me harías el favor de... ?**
• Explain the concept of the conditional as *the future of the past.* Explain that the conditional is used to express some action that was yet to occur at some past time, and give examples. Ex: **1. Creo que me mantendré en forma. Creía que me mantendría en forma. 2. Sé que te adelgazarás. Sabía que te adelgazarías.**
• Remind students of the future of probability. Point out that the conditional of probability functions just like it but in the context of the past. Compare the second example in the Compare & Contrast chart to this one: **Suena el teléfono. ¿Será Emilio para cancelar nuestra cita?**

TEACHING OPTIONS

Extra Practice Tell students to imagine that their families have come into a great deal of money. Ask them to write ten sentences describing what they and their family members would do with the money. Students should try to use as many different verbs and conjugations as possible. Ex: **Mi familia y yo ayudaríamos a los artistas de nuestra ciudad.**

Pairs Have students work together to role-play interviewing a personal trainer. Interviewers should ask the trainer what he or she would do to help get them in shape. Have pairs play both roles.

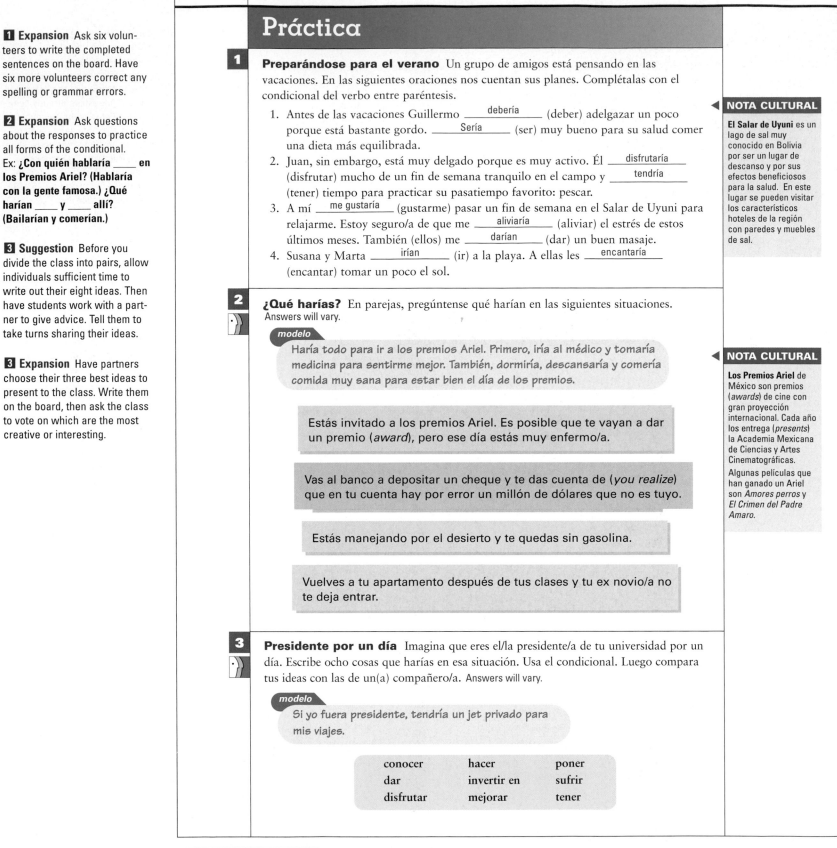

Práctica

1

Preparándose para el verano Un grupo de amigos está pensando en las vacaciones. En las siguientes oraciones nos cuentan sus planes. Complétalas con el condicional del verbo entre paréntesis.

1. Antes de las vacaciones Guillermo ___debería___ (deber) adelgazar un poco porque está bastante gordo. ___Sería___ (ser) muy bueno para su salud comer una dieta más equilibrada.

2. Juan, sin embargo, está muy delgado porque es muy activo. Él ___disfrutaría___ (disfrutar) mucho de un fin de semana tranquilo en el campo y ___tendría___ (tener) tiempo para practicar su pasatiempo favorito: pescar.

3. A mí ___me gustaría___ (gustarme) pasar un fin de semana en el Salar de Uyuni para relajarme. Estoy seguro/a de que me ___aliviaría___ (aliviar) el estrés de estos últimos meses. También (ellos) me ___darían___ (dar) un buen masaje.

4. Susana y Marta ___irían___ (ir) a la playa. A ellas les ___encantaría___ (encantar) tomar un poco el sol.

2

¿Qué harías? En parejas, pregúntense qué harían en las siguientes situaciones. *Answers will vary.*

modelo

Haría todo para ir a los premios Ariel. Primero, iría al médico y tomaría medicina para sentirme mejor. También, dormiría, descansaría y comería comida muy sana para estar bien el día de los premios.

Estás invitado a los premios Ariel. Es posible que te vayan a dar un premio (*award*), pero ese día estás muy enfermo/a.

Vas al banco a depositar un cheque y te das cuenta de (*you realize*) que en tu cuenta hay por error un millón de dólares que no es tuyo.

Estás manejando por el desierto y te quedas sin gasolina.

Vuelves a tu apartamento después de tus clases y tu ex novio/a no te deja entrar.

3

Presidente por un día Imagina que eres el/la presidente/a de tu universidad por un día. Escribe ocho cosas que harías en esa situación. Usa el condicional. Luego compara tus ideas con las de un(a) compañero/a. *Answers will vary.*

modelo

Si yo fuera presidente, tendría un jet privado para mis viajes.

conocer	hacer	poner
dar	invertir en	sufrir
disfrutar	mejorar	tener

Comunicación

4 Conversaciones Tu profesor(a) te dará una hoja de actividades. En ella se presentan dos listas con diferentes problemas que supuestamente tienen los estudiantes. En parejas, túrnense para explicar los problemas de su lista; uno/a cuenta lo que le pasa y el/la otro/a dice lo que haría en esa situación usando la frase "Yo en tu lugar..." (*If I were you...*)

Answers will vary.

> **modelo**
>
> **Estudiante 1:** ¡Qué problema! Mi novio/a no me habla desde el domingo.
> **Estudiante 2:** Yo en tu lugar no le diría nada por unos días para ver qué pasa.

5 Roberto en el gimnasio Roberto es una persona muy sedentaria. El médico le dice que tiene que adelgazar para mejorar su salud. Dile ocho cosas que tú harías si fueras él. Usa el condicional. Después, compara tus sugerencias con las del resto de la clase.
Answers will vary.

> **modelo**
>
> Si yo fuera tú, vería menos la televisión e iría a una clase de ejercicios aeróbicos.

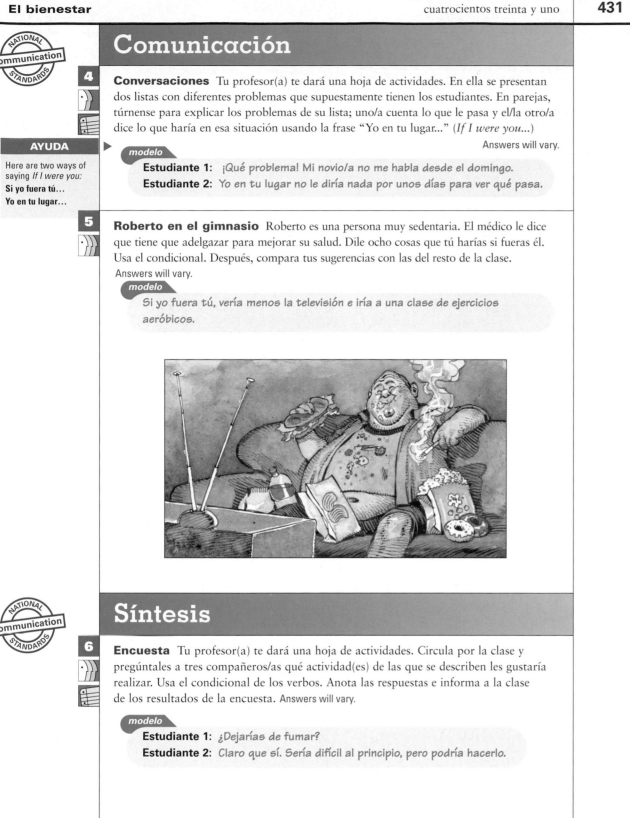

Síntesis

6 Encuesta Tu profesor(a) te dará una hoja de actividades. Circula por la clase y pregúntales a tres compañeros/as qué actividad(es) de las que se describen les gustaría realizar. Usa el condicional de los verbos. Anota las respuestas e informa a la clase de los resultados de la encuesta. Answers will vary.

> **modelo**
>
> **Estudiante 1:** ¿Dejarías de fumar?
> **Estudiante 2:** Claro que sí. Sería difícil al principio, pero podría hacerlo.

Sidebar

4 Suggestion Distribute the **Hojas de actividades** from the IRM that correspond to this activity.

4 Expansion Working with the whole class, name a problem from one of the lists and ask several volunteers to share the suggestions they received. Encourage other students to comment on the suggestions, going through several problems this way.

5 Suggestion Go over the directions with the class. Work with the class to brainstorm a list of Roberto's problems. Write them on the board. Give students time to write eight pieces of advice.

6 Suggestion Distribute the **Hojas de actividades** from the IRM that correspond to this activity.

6 Expansion Encourage students to add two more activities to their list.

Section Goal

In **Estructura 15.2** students will learn the use of the present perfect.

Instructional Resources

WB/VM: Workbook, pp. 185–186
Lab Manual, p. 88
Lab CD/MP3 Lección 15
IRM: ¡Inténtalo! & Práctica
Answers, p. 195; Tapescript, pp. 67–70
Interactive CD-ROM
Companion website: www.vistahigherlearning.com
Presentations CD-ROM

Suggestions

• Have students turn to pages 424–425. Ask them to read the **Fotonovela** again and write down the past participles they find. Ask students if they are used as adjectives or as parts of verbs.

• Model the present perfect by making statements about what you and others in the class have done, or by asking students questions. Ex: **Yo he preparado una lección. Ustedes han leído la sección de Estructura, ¿verdad? ¿Quién no la ha leído?**

Consúltalo Tell students that while the present perfect is generally used in Spanish just as it is in English, the expression *to have just* done something is expressed in Spanish by **acabar de** + [*infinitive*]. Write the following sentences on the board and contrast them: **Acabo de venir del gimnasio. / He venido del gimnasio.**

15.2 The present perfect

ANTE TODO In **Lección 13**, you learned how to form past participles. You will now learn how to form the present perfect indicative (**el pretérito perfecto de indicativo**), a compound tense that uses the past participle. The present perfect is used to talk about what someone *has done*. In Spanish, it is formed with the present tense of the auxiliary verb **haber** and a past participle.

> *Ya veo que han traído todo lo que necesitan.*

> *Todos han venido muy bien equipados.*

Present indicative of *haber*

Singular forms		Plural forms	
yo	**he**	nosotros/as	**hemos**
tú	**has**	vosotros/as	**habéis**
Ud./él/ella	**ha**	Uds./ellos/ellas	**han**

Tú no **has aumentado** de peso.
You haven't gained weight.

Yo ya **he leído** esos libros.
I've already read those books.

¿**Ha asistido** Juan a la clase de ejercicios aeróbicos?
Has Juan attended the aerobics class?

Hemos conocido al entrenador.
We have met the trainer.

CONSÚLTALO

To review what you have learned about participles, see **Estructura 13.4**, p. 382.

▶ The past participle does not change in form when it is part of the present perfect tense; it only changes in form when it is used as an adjective.

Clara **ha abierto** las ventanas.
Clara has opened the windows.

Yo **he cerrado** la puerta del gimnasio.
I've closed the door to the gym.

Las ventanas están **abiertas.**
The windows are open.

La puerta del gimnasio está **cerrada.**
The door to the gym is closed.

▶ In Spanish, the present perfect indicative is generally used just as it is used in English: to talk about what someone has done or what has occurred. It usually refers to the recent past.

He trabajado cuarenta horas esta semana.
I have worked forty hours this week.

¿Cuál es el último libro que **has leído**?
What is the last book that you have read?

CONSÚLTALO

Remember that the Spanish equivalent of the English *to have just (done something)* is **acabar de** + [*infinitive*]. Do not use the present perfect to express that English structure.

Juan acaba de llegar.
Juan has just arrived.
See **Estructura 6.3**, p. 167.

TEACHING OPTIONS

Extra Practice Ask students what they have done over the past week to lead a healthy lifestyle. Ask follow-up questions to elicit a variety of different conjugations of the present perfect.
Ex: **¿Qué han hecho esta semana pasada para llevar una vida sana? Y tú, ____, ¿qué has hecho?, ¿Qué ha hecho ____ esta semana?**

Pairs Ask students to tell their partner five things they have done in the past to stay in shape. Partners repeat back what the students have said, using the **tú** form of the present perfect.
Ex: **He levantado pesas. (Muy bien. Has levantado pesas.)**

▶ In English, the auxiliary verb and the past participle are often separated. In Spanish, however, these two elements—**haber** and the past participle—cannot be separated by any word.

Siempre **hemos vivido** en Bolivia.
We have always lived in Bolivia.

Usted nunca **ha venido** a mi oficina.
You have never come to my office.

Creo que la señora Vives nos ha preparado una cena muy especial.

Gracias, Martín.

No hay de qué. Ha sido un placer.

▶ The word **no** and any object or reflexive pronouns are placed immediately before **haber.**

Yo **no he comido** la merienda.
I haven't eaten the snack.

Susana ya **se ha entrenado**.
Susana has already trained.

¿Por qué **no la has comido**?
Why haven't you eaten it?

Ellos **no lo han terminado**.
They haven't finished it.

▶ Note that *to have* can be either a main verb or an auxiliary verb in English. As a main verb, it corresponds to **tener,** while as an auxiliary, it corresponds to **haber.**

Tengo muchos amigos.
I have a lot of friends.

He tenido mucho éxito.
I have had a lot of success.

▶ To form the present perfect of **hay,** use the third person singular of **haber (ha) + habido.**

Ha habido muchos problemas con el nuevo profesor.
There have been a lot of problems with the new professor.

Ha habido un accidente en la calle Central.
There has been an accident on Central Street.

¡INTÉNTALO!   Indica el pretérito perfecto de indicativo de los siguientes verbos.

1. yo   he disfrutado, he comido, he vivido   (disfrutar, comer, vivir)
2. tú   has traído, has adelgazado, has compartido   (traer, adelgazar, compartir)
3. usted   ha venido, ha estado, ha corrido   (venir, estar, correr)
4. ella   ha leído, ha resuelto, ha puesto   (leer, resolver, poner)
5. ellos   han dicho, han roto, han hecho   (decir, romper, hacer)
6. nosotros   nos hemos mantenido, nos hemos dormido   (mantenerse, dormirse)
7. yo   he estado, he escrito, he visto   (estar, escribir, ver)
8. él   ha vivido, ha corrido, ha muerto   (vivir, correr, morir)

Suggestions

- Ask students questions in the present perfect with indirect and direct objects. Ex: ____, **¿has estudiado bien la lección?** (Sí, **la he estudiado bien.**) ____, **¿has entendido todo lo que te he dicho?** (No, **no lo he entendido todo.**) **¿Todos me han entregado el trabajo de hoy?** (Sí, todos **se lo hemos entregado.**)
- Explain that although an adverb can never appear between **haber** and its past participle, it may appear in other positions in the sentence to change emphasis. Ex: **Hemos vivido siempre en Bolivia. Siempre hemos vivido en Bolivia.**
- Practice adverb placement by supplying an adverb for each item in **¡Inténtalo!** Ex: siempre **(siempre he disfrutado/he disfrutado siempre)**

TEACHING OPTIONS

Large Groups Divide the class into three groups. Have students write down five physical activities. Then have them ask each of their group members if they have ever done those activities and record their answers. Ex: **¿Has hecho ejercicios de estiramiento alguna vez? ¿Has levantado pesas? ¿Has hecho ejercicios en un gimnasio?**

Extra Practice Draw a time line on the board. On the far right of the line, write **el presente**. Just to the left of that point, write **el pasado muy reciente**. To the left of that, write **el pasado reciente**. Then to the far left, write **el pasado**. Make a statement using the preterite, the present perfect, or **acabar de** + [*infinitive*]. Have students indicate on the timeline when the action took place.

1 Expansion Have students write five original sentences using the present perfect to describe their past health and that of their friends and family members.

Ayuda Practice the expressions by using sentences that describe your and your students' lives. Ex: **He viajado a España un par de veces. ¿Quién ha viajado a España muchas veces?**

2 Expansion
• Ask students follow-up questions about their responses.
• Have partners elaborate on their responses by asking each other questions about what they have done. Ex: —¿**Has buceado?** —**Sí, he buceado varias veces.** —¡**Qué suerte! ¿Dónde has buceado, en el Caribe?**

3 Expansion
• Take a survey of the answers given and write the results on the board. Then ask volunteers to summarize the results. Ex: **Casi todos hemos dejado de tomar refrescos.**
• Ask students to give examples of the benefits of adopting some of the healthy habits listed. Ex: **Ahora puedo subir las escaleras hasta el quinto piso sin llegar cansado/a.**

Práctica

1 **Completar** Estas oraciones describen el bienestar o los problemas de unos estudiantes. Completa las oraciones con el pretérito perfecto de indicativo de los verbos de la lista.

adelgazar	comer	llevar
aumentar	hacer	sufrir

1. Luisa __ha sufrido__ muchas presiones este año.
2. Juan y Raúl __han aumentado__ de peso porque no hacen ejercicio.
3. Pero María y yo __hemos adelgazado__ porque trabajamos en exceso y nos olvidamos de comer.
4. Desde siempre, yo __he llevado__ una vida muy sana.
5. Pero tú y yo no __hemos hecho__ gimnasia este semestre.

2 **¿Qué has hecho?** Indica si has hecho lo siguiente. Answers will vary.

> **modelo**
> Escalar una montaña
> Sí, he escalado varias montañas./No, no he escalado nunca una montaña.

1. Jugar al baloncesto
2. Viajar a Bolivia
3. Conocer a una persona famosa
4. Levantar pesas
5. Comer un insecto
6. Recibir un masaje
7. Aprender un segundo idioma
8. Bailar salsa
9. Ver una película española
10. Escuchar música latina
11. Estar despierto 24 horas
12. Bucear

AYUDA

You may use some of these expressions in your answers:
una vez *once*
un par de veces *a couple of times*
algunas veces *a few times*
varias veces *several times*
muchas veces *many times; often*

3 **La vida sana** En parejas, túrnense para hacer preguntas sobre el tema de la vida sana. Sean creativos. Answers will vary.

> **modelo**
> Encontrar un gimnasio
> **Estudiante 1:** ¿Has encontrado un buen gimnasio cerca de tu casa?
> **Estudiante 2:** Yo no he encontrado un gimnasio pero sé que debo buscar uno.

1. Tratar de estar en forma
2. Estar a dieta los últimos dos meses
3. Dejar de tomar refrescos
4. Hacerse una prueba del colesterol
5. Entrenarse cinco días a la semana
6. Cambiar de una vida sedentaria a una vida activa
7. Tomar vitaminas por las noches y por las mañanas
8. Hacer ejercicio para aliviar la tensión
9. Consumir mucha proteína
10. Dejar de fumar

TEACHING OPTIONS

Small Groups Divide the class into groups of four to write and perform skits in which one student plays a personal trainer, another plays a nutritionist, and the other two play clients. The personal trainer and nutritionist ask the clients whether they have done the things they have recommended. The clients explain what they have done and make excuses for what they have not done.

Pairs Have students discuss with a classmate five things they have already done today. Ex: **He estudiado la lección para esta clase. He ido al gimnasio. He ido a una clase de ejercicios aeróbicos. He almorzado con unos amigos. He escrito una carta a mis abuelos. ¿Qué has hecho tú?**

Comunicación

4 **Descripción** En parejas, describan lo que ha(n) hecho y no ha(n) hecho la(s) persona(s) en cada dibujo. Usen la imaginación. Answers will vary.

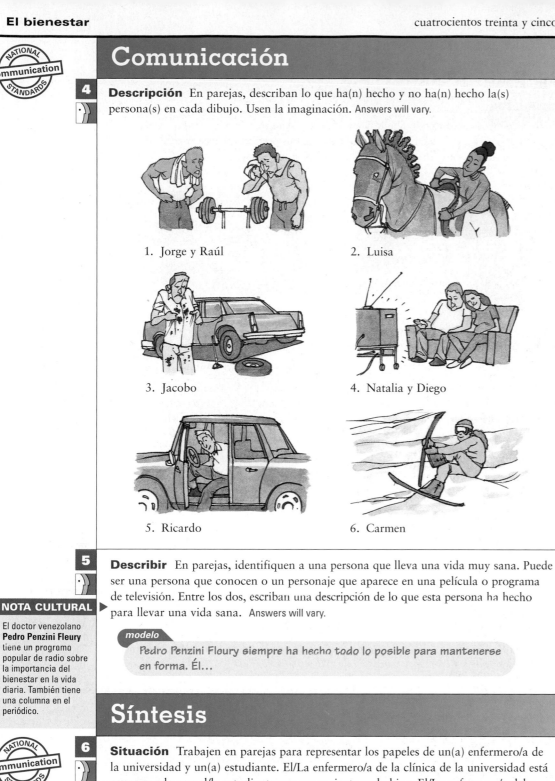

1. Jorge y Raúl

2. Luisa

3. Jacobo

4. Natalia y Diego

5. Ricardo

6. Carmen

5 **Describir** En parejas, identifiquen a una persona que lleva una vida muy sana. Puede ser una persona que conocen o un personaje que aparece en una película o programa de televisión. Entre los dos, escriban una descripción de lo que esta persona ha hecho para llevar una vida sana. Answers will vary.

> *modelo*
> Pedro Penzini Fleury siempre ha hecho todo lo posible para mantenerse en forma. Él...

NOTA CULTURAL

El doctor venezolano **Pedro Penzini Fleury** tiene un programa popular de radio sobre la importancia del bienestar en la vida diaria. También tiene una columna en el periódico.

Síntesis

6 **Situación** Trabajen en parejas para representar los papeles de un(a) enfermero/a de la universidad y un(a) estudiante. El/La enfermero/a de la clínica de la universidad está conversando con el/la estudiante que no se siente nada bien. El/La enfermero/a debe averiguar de dónde viene el problema e investigar los hábitos del/de la estudiante. El/La estudiante le explica lo que ha hecho en los últimos meses y cómo se ha sentido. Luego el/la enfermero/a le da recomendaciones al/a la estudiante de cómo llevar una vida más sana. Answers will vary.

---

4 Suggestion Before beginning the activity, ask volunteers to describe the people in each drawing and how they feel.

5 Suggestion Have pairs describe eight different things their chosen person has done that exemplifies a healthy lifestyle. Remind them to include introductory and concluding statements in their description.

5 Expansion Have students choose someone who is the exact opposite of the healthy person they chose earlier and write a description of what that person has done that exemplifies an unhealthy lifestyle.

6 Expansion While pairs are performing their role-plays for the class, stop the action after the patient has described his or her symptoms and what he or she has done in the last few months. Ask the audience to make a diagnosis. Then have the players finish their presentation.

Suggestion See the Information Gap activities booklet for an additional activity to practice the material presented in this section.

TEACHING OPTIONS

Game Have students write three important things they have done over the past year on a slip of paper and put it in a box. Ex: **Este año he creado un sitio web.** Have students draw a paper from the box, then circulate around the room, asking students if they have done the activities listed, until they find the person who wrote the slip of paper. The first person to find a match wins.

Heritage Speakers Have heritage speakers interview someone who has immigrated from a Spanish-speaking country to the United States or Canada to find out how that person's life has changed since moving. Students should find out how the interviewee's physical activity and diet have changed. Have students present their findings in a brief written report.

Section Goal

In **Estructura 15.3** students will learn the use of the past perfect tense.

Instructional Resources

WB/VM: Workbook, pp. 187–188
Lab Manual, p. 89
Lab CD/MP3 Lección 15
IRM: ¡Inténtalo! & Práctica
Answers, p. 195; Tapescript, pp. 67–70
Interactive CD-ROM
Companion website:
www.vistahigherlearning.com
Presentations CD-ROM

Suggestions

• Introduce the past perfect tense by making statements about the past that are true for you. Write examples of the past perfect on the board as you use them. Ex: **Esta mañana vine a la universidad en la bicicleta de mi hijo. Nunca antes había venido en bicicleta. Por lo general, vengo en carro. Muchas veces antes había caminado y también había venido en autobús cuando tenía prisa, pero nunca en bicicleta.**

• Check for comprehension of **ya** by contrasting it with **nunca**. Ex: **Antes del semestre pasado, nunca había enseñado este curso, pero ya había enseñado otros cursos de español.**

Successful Language Learning Tell your students to imagine how they might use the past perfect to tell someone about their lives.

15.3 The past perfect

ANTE TODO The past perfect indicative (**el pretérito pluscuamperfecto de indicativo**) is used to talk about what someone *had done* or what *had occurred* before another past action, event, or state. Like the present perfect, the past perfect uses a form of **haber**—in this case, the imperfect—plus the past participle.

> Nunca había visto un paisaje tan espectacular.

> Nunca había hecho una excursión.

Past perfect indicative

		cerrar	perder	asistir
SINGULAR FORMS	yo	**había** cerrado	**había** perdido	**había** asistido
	tú	**habías** cerrado	**habías** perdido	**habías** asistido
	Ud./él/ella	**había** cerrado	**había** perdido	**había** asistido
PLURAL FORMS	nosotros/as	**habíamos** cerrado	**habíamos** perdido	**habíamos** asistido
	vosotros/as	**habíais** cerrado	**habíais** perdido	**habíais** asistido
	Uds./ellos/ellas	**habían** cerrado	**habían** perdido	**habían** asistido

Antes de 2003, **había vivido** en La Paz.
Before 2003, I had lived in La Paz.

Cuando llegamos, Luis ya **había salido.**
When we arrived, Luis had already left.

▶ The past perfect is often used with the word **ya** (*already*) to indicate that an action, event, or state had already occurred before another. Remember that, unlike its English equivalent, **ya** cannot be placed between **haber** and the past participle.

Ella **ya había salido** cuando llamaron.
She had already left when they called.

Cuando llegué, Raúl **ya se había acostado.**
When I arrived, Raúl had already gone to bed.

¡ATENCIÓN!

The past perfect is often used in conjunction with **antes de** + [*noun*] or **antes de** + [*infinitive*] to describe when the action(s) occurred.

Antes de este año, nunca había estudiado español.
Before this year, I had never studied Spanish.

Luis me había llamado antes de venir.
Luis had called me before he came.

¡INTÉNTALO! Indica el pretérito pluscuamperfecto de indicativo de cada verbo.

1. Nosotros ya _habíamos cenado_ (cenar) cuando nos llamaron.
2. Antes de tomar esta clase, yo no _había estudiado_ (estudiar) nunca el español.
3. Antes de ir a México, ellos nunca _habían ido_ (ir) a otro país.
4. Eduardo nunca _se había entrenado_ (entrenarse) tanto en invierno.
5. Tú siempre _habías llevado_ (llevar) una vida sana antes del año pasado.
6. Antes de conocerte, yo ya te _había visto_ (ver) muchas veces.

TEACHING OPTIONS

Extra Practice Have students write sentences, using the past perfect and each of the following twice: **antes de** + [*infinitive*], **antes de que** + [*conjugated verb*], the preterite, and the imperfect. Have students peer edit their work before sharing their sentences with the class. Ex: **Nuestros bisabuelos ya habían muerto cuando éramos niños.**

TPR Make a series of statements about the past, using two different verbs. After making a statement, call out the infinitive of one of the verbs. If that action occurred before the other one, have students raise one finger. If it occurred after the other action, have them raise two fingers. Ex: **Tomás ya había bajado de la montaña cuando empezó a nevar. Empezar.** (two fingers)

Práctica

1

Completar Completa los minidiálogos con las formas correctas del pretérito pluscuamperfecto de indicativo.

NOTA CULTURAL

La yerba mate, una bebida similar al té, es muy popular en Argentina, Uruguay y Paraguay. Se dice que controla el estrés, la obesidad, y que estimula el sistema inmunológico.

Tradicionalmente, se toma en una calabaza (*gourd*) con una bombilla filtrante (*tea-filtering straw*).

1. **SARA**   Antes de cumplir los 15 años, ¿<u>habías estudiado</u> (estudiar) tú otra lengua?
   JOSÉ   Sí, <u>había tomado</u> (tomar) clases de inglés y de italiano.

2. **DOLORES**   Antes de ir a Argentina, ¿<u>habían probado</u> (probar) tú y tu familia el mate?
   TOMÁS   Sí, ya <u>habíamos tomado</u> (tomar) mate muchas veces.

3. **ANTONIO**   Antes de este año, ¿<u>había corrido</u> (correr) usted en un maratón?
   SRA. VERA   No, nunca lo <u>había hecho</u> (hacer).

4. **SOFÍA**   Antes de su enfermedad, ¿<u>había sufrido</u> (sufrir) muchas presiones tu tío?
   IRENE   Sí… y él nunca <u>se había mantenido</u> (mantenerse) en buena forma.

2

Tu vida Indica si ya habías hecho las siguientes cosas antes de cumplir los 16 años. Answers will vary.

1. Hacer un viaje en avión
2. Escribir un poema
3. Enamorarte
4. Tomar clases de aeróbicos
5. Montar a caballo
6. Escalar una montaña
7. Manejar un carro
8. Navegar en la red
9. Ir de pesca

Comunicación

3

Gimnasio Olímpico En parejas, lean el anuncio y contesten las preguntas.

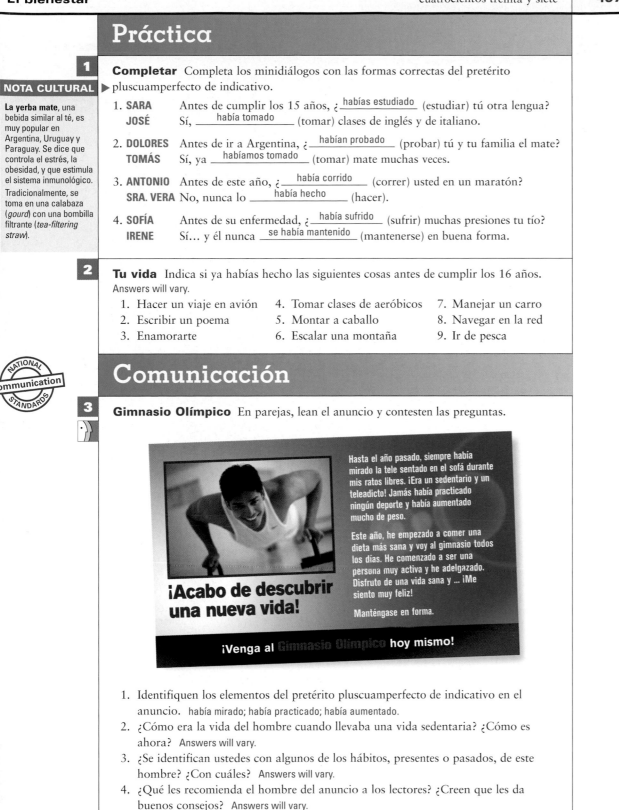

Hasta el año pasado, siempre había mirado la tele sentado en el sofá durante mis ratos libres. ¡Era un sedentario y un teleadicto! Jamás había practicado ningún deporte y había aumentado mucho de peso.

Este año, he empezado a comer una dieta más sana y voy al gimnasio todos los días. He comenzado a ser una persona muy activa y he adelgazado. Disfruto de una vida sana y … ¡Me siento muy feliz!

Manténgase en forma.

¡Acabo de descubrir una nueva vida!

¡Venga al Gimnasio Olímpico hoy mismo!

1. Identifiquen los elementos del pretérito pluscuamperfecto de indicativo en el anuncio. había mirado; había practicado; había aumentado.
2. ¿Cómo era la vida del hombre cuando llevaba una vida sedentaria? ¿Cómo es ahora? Answers will vary.
3. ¿Se identifican ustedes con algunos de los hábitos, presentes o pasados, de este hombre? ¿Con cuáles? Answers will vary.
4. ¿Qué les recomienda el hombre del anuncio a los lectores? ¿Creen que les da buenos consejos? Answers will vary.

---

1 Expansion
• Have students pick one of the interchanges and expand upon it to create a conversation with six lines.
• Have students create an original conversation like the ones in the activity. Call on volunteers to perform them for the class.

2 Suggestion Ask students questions to elicit the answers for the activity. Ex: **¿Quién había hecho un viaje en avión antes de cumplir los 16 años?** Ask follow-up questions to elicit other conjugations of the past perfect. Ex: **Entonces, ¿quiénes habían hecho un viaje en avión antes de cumplir los 16 años? (____ y ____ habían hecho…)**

3 Suggestion Before beginning the activity, survey the class to find out who exercises regularly and/or carefully watches what he or she eats. Ask these students to use the past perfect to say what they had done in their life prior to starting their fitness or diet program. Ex: **Había comido pastel de chocolate todos los días.**

3 Expansion Have groups create an ad for a different type of health-related business, for instance a vegetarian restaurant.

TEACHING OPTIONS

Pairs Have students imagine they have joined a gym for the first time and are telling a friend about their new experiences. Ask students to tell their partner five things they had never done before going to a gym. Ex: **Nunca había sudado tanto antes de empezar a ir al gimnasio.**

Large Groups Divide the class into groups of six for a game of "one-upmanship." The first student states something he or she had done before a certain event in his or her past. The second student tells what the first one had done, then counters with something even more outrageous that he or she had done, and so on, until everyone has participated. Ex: ____ **había…, pero yo había…**

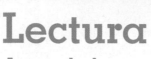

Lectura

Antes de leer

Estrategia
Making inferences

For dramatic effect and to achieve a smoother writing style, authors often do not explicitly supply the reader with all the details of a story or poem. Clues in the text can help you infer those things the writer chooses not to state in a direct manner. You simply "read between the lines" to fill in the missing information and draw conclusions. To practice making inferences, read the following statement:

A Liliana le encanta ir al gimnasio. Hace años que empezó a levantar pesas.

Based on this statement alone, what inferences can you draw about Liliana?

El título

Sin leer el texto del poema, lee el título. Piensa en las cosas de la vida que una persona no escoge. Haz una lista.

_____
_____
_____
_____
_____

Examinar el texto

Lee el poema brevemente y haz una lista de algunos de los cognados y de otras palabras que conoces. Según esta lista, ¿de qué trata el poema?

_____ _____
_____ _____
_____ _____

recursos

vistahigher
learning.com

Uno no escoge

Gioconda Belli

La escritora nicaragüense Gioconda Belli nació en Managua en 1948. Durante la lucha° de revolución de su país, Belli vivió en México en donde escribió su novela Línea de fuego. *Con esta novela ganó el premio Las Américas en 1978. La obra de Belli rompe con las estructuras tradicionales y expresa la urgencia de un cambio social en su país.*

Uno no escoge el país donde nace;
pero ama el país donde ha nacido.

Uno no escoge el tiempo para venir al mundo;
pero debe dejar huella° de su tiempo.

Nadie puede evadir su responsabilidad.

Nadie puede taparse° los ojos, los oídos,
enmudecer° y cortarse° las manos.

Todos tenemos un deber de amor que cumplir,
una historia que nacer
una meta° que alcanzar°.

No escogimos el momento para venir al mundo:
ahora podemos hacer el mundo
en que nacerá° y crecerá°
la semilla° que trajimos con nosotros.

°cha *fight* dejar huella *leave a mark* taparse *to cover up*
°mudecer *to fall silent* cortarse *to cut* meta *goal* alcanzar *to reach*
°cerá *will be born* crecerá *will grow* la semilla *seed*

Después de leer

¿Cierto o falso?

Indica si estos comentarios sobre el texto son **ciertos** o **falsos**.

	Cierto	Falso
1. Podemos escoger el país donde nacemos.	○	☑
2. No es necesario hacer algo importante en la vida.	○	☑
3. Debemos ser responsables.	☑	○
4. No debemos dejar de ver, escuchar y saber lo que pasa en el mundo.	☑	○
5. Debemos ignorar el amor.	○	☑
6. Cada persona tiene importancia en el mundo.	☑	○

Inferencias

Contesta estas preguntas. Answers will vary.

1. ¿Cuál es el tema principal del poema?
2. ¿Estás de acuerdo con las ideas de la poeta?
3. ¿Por qué crees que escribió el poema?
4. Después de leer, ¿has cambiado tu opinión sobre el significado del título? ¿Qué piensas ahora?

Analizar

El poema está compuesto de seis partes. Con un(a) compañero/a, traten de escribir el significado de cada una de las partes. Después, compartan sus ideas con la clase. Answers will vary.

Preguntas

Contesta estas preguntas. Answers will vary.

1. ¿Cuáles son tus metas personales?
2. ¿Tienes muchas responsabilidades? ¿Cuáles son?
3. ¿Crees que lo que haga una persona puede cambiar el mundo? ¿Por qué?
4. ¿Crees que Gioconda Belli es una líder en cuestiones de bienestar social en su país? Explica tu respuesta.

¿Cierto o falso? Have pairs correct the false statements. Then, have them locate the lines in the poem that corroborate each one. Have pairs read these lines aloud to ensure that everyone in the class chose the same ones. Have students solve any discrepancies.

Inferencias Much of the poem's message lies in ideas that are not explicitly stated. Have groups discuss these implied ideas and develop them as a collection of explicit statements. Ask students to imagine how they would be expressed if included in the poem as additional lines. Then, have each group rewrite a longer version of the poem incorporating the new statements.

Analizar Have each student come up with a title for his or her favorite section of the poem. Then, in groups of four, have them compare their titles and explain why they apply well to aspects of their own life. Once all students have had a chance to speak, have them work individually to write a short poem about themselves based on one of the titles.

Preguntas Have small groups choose a respected politician, media celebrity, or other philanthropist who has done admirable work for a humanitarian cause. Have them answer items 1–3 as if they were this person.

Section Goals

In **Escritura** students will:
- learn about listing key words as a writing strategy
- integrate **Lección 15** vocabulary and structures
- write a personal fitness plan in Spanish

Estrategia Go over this writing strategy with your students, stressing that they should write their key words in Spanish whenever possible. Encourage students to rely primarily on vocabulary they already know when preparing their list of key words. They should consult the dictionary only if they need a word that they consider central to their writing. Remind them about the correct use of Spanish-English dictionaries and explain that spending too much time looking through a dictionary could sidetrack them and make them lose the focus of the writing activity.

Tema Review the three suggested categories of details to include, clarifying any unfamiliar vocabulary. Then, have volunteers make up questions or use the ones on this page to interview you regarding your personal fitness plan.

Suggestion Tell your students that they can consult the **Plan de Escritura** in **Apéndice A**, page 448, for step-by-step writing instructions.

Escritura

communication STANDARDS NATIONAL

Estrategia
Listing key words

Before beginning your first draft, you may find it helpful to make a list of key words you can use while writing.

If you prepare a list of potentially useful words ahead of time, you may find it easier to avoid using the dictionary while writing your first draft. You will probably also learn a few new Spanish words while preparing your list of key words.

Listing useful vocabulary is also a valuable organizational strategy, since the act of brainstorming key words will help you to form ideas about your topic. In addition, a list of key words can help you avoid redundancy when you write.

If you were writing a description of what you do to stay fit, your list of key words would probably include terms related to nutrition, exercise, and stress management. What are a few of the words you might include?

1. _____
2. _____
3. _____
4. _____
5. _____
6. _____

Tema

Escribir un plan personal de bienestar

Desarrolla un plan personal para mejorar tu bienestar, tanto físico como emocional. Tu plan debe describir:

1. Lo que has hecho para mejorar tu bienestar y llevar una vida sana
2. Lo que no has podido hacer todavía
3. Las actividades que debes hacer en los próximos meses

Considera también la siguiente lista de preguntas.

La nutrición

▸ ¿Comes una dieta equilibrada?
▸ ¿Consumes suficientes vitaminas y minerales? ¿Consumes demasiada grasa?
▸ ¿Quieres aumentar de peso o adelgazar?
▸ ¿Qué puedes hacer para mejorar tu dieta?

El ejercicio

▸ ¿Haces ejercicio? ¿Con qué frecuencia?
▸ ¿Vas al gimnasio? ¿Qué tipo de ejercicios haces allí?
▸ ¿Practicas algún deporte?
▸ ¿Qué puedes hacer para mejorar tu bienestar físico?

El estrés

▸ ¿Sufres muchas presiones?
▸ ¿Qué actividades o problemas te causan estrés?
▸ ¿Qué haces (o debes hacer) para aliviar el estrés y sentirte más tranquilo/a?
▸ ¿Qué puedes hacer para mejorar tu bienestar emocional?

TEACHING OPTIONS

Proofreading Activity Copy the following sentences containing mistakes onto the board or a transparency as a proofreading activity to do with the whole class.

1. ¿Tu padre ha tenidos problemas con el colesterol? Espero que deja de comer comidas grasosas.
2. Ya tengo trabajado cuarenta horas esta semana y todavía no tengo terminado.

3. Guillermo ha un plan para aliviar el estrés. Había sufrido mucho del estrés recientemente.
4. Me alegro que has dejado de fumar y por fin has empezado a llevar una vida sana.
5. El gimnasio ya ha cerrado antes de que he llegado.

Escuchar

Estrategia

Listening for the gist/ Listening for cognates

Combining these two strategies is an easy way to get a good sense of what you hear. When you listen for the gist, you get the general idea of what you're hearing, which allows you to interpret cognates and other words in a meaningful context. Similarly, the cognates give you information about the details of the story that you might not have understood when listening for the gist.

🎧 To practice these strategies, you will listen to a short paragraph. Write down the gist of what you hear and jot down a few cognates. Based on the gist and the cognates, what conclusions can you draw about what you heard?

Preparación

Mira la foto. ¿Qué pistas° te da de lo que vas a oír?

Ahora escucha 🎧

Escucha lo que dice Ofelia Cortez de Bauer. Anota algunos de los cognados que escuchas y también la idea general del discurso°. Answers will vary.

_____

_____

_____

_____

Idea general: _____

Ahora contesta las siguientes preguntas.

1. ¿Cuál es el género° del discurso?
2. ¿Cuál es el tema?
3. ¿Cuál es el propósito°?

Comprensión

¿Cierto o falso?

Indica si lo que dicen las siguientes frases es **cierto** o **falso**. Corrige las oraciones que son falsas.

	Cierto	Falso
1. La señora Bauer habla de la importancia de estar en buena forma y de hacer ejercicio.	☑	○
2. Según ella, lo más importante es que lleves el programa sugerido por los expertos. Lo más importante es que lleves un programa variado que te guste.	○	☑
3. La señora Bauer participa en actividades individuales y de grupo.	☑	○
4. El único objetivo del tipo de programa que ella sugiere es adelgazar. Los objetivos de su programa son: condicionar el sistema cardiopulmonar, aumentar la fuerza muscular y mejorar la flexibilidad.	○	☑

Preguntas Answers will vary.

1. Imagina que el programa de radio sigue. Según las pistas que ella dio, ¿qué vas a oír en la segunda parte?
2. ¿A qué tipo de público° le interesa el tema del que habla la señora Bauer?
3. ¿Sigues los consejos de la señora Bauer? Explica tu respuesta.
4. ¿Qué piensas de los consejos que ella da? ¿Hay otra información que ella debía haber incluido°?

pistas *clues* discurso *speech* género *genre* propósito *purpose* público *audience* debía haber incluido *should have included*

recursos

TEXT CD Lección 15

Luego levanto pesas y termino haciendo estiramientos de los músculos. Los fines de semana me mantengo activa pero hago una variedad de cosas de acuerdo a lo que quiere hacer la familia. A veces practico la natación; otras, vamos de excursión al campo, por ejemplo.
Como les había dicho la semana pasada, como unas 1.600 calorías al día, mayormente alimentos con poca grasa y sin sal.

Disfruto mucho del bienestar que estos hábitos me producen. Ahora iremos a unos anuncios de nuestros patrocinadores. Cuando regresemos, voy a contestar sus preguntas acerca del ejercicio, la dieta o el bienestar en general. El teléfono es el 43.89.76. No se vayan. Ya regresamos con mucha más información.

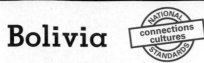

Bolivia

NATIONAL STANDARDS connections cultures

El país en cifras

▶ **Área:** 1.098.580 km² (424.162 millas²), *equivalente al área total de Francia y España*

▶ **Población:** 9.275.000

Los indígenas quechua y aimará constituyen más de la mitad° de la población de Bolivia. Estos grupos indígenas han mantenido sus culturas y lenguas tradicionales. Las personas de descendencia indígena y europea representan la tercera parte de la población. El 15% restante° es gente de descendencia europea nacida en Latinoamérica. Una gran mayoría de los bolivianos, más o menos el 70%, vive en el altiplano°.

▶ **Capital:** La Paz, sede° del gobierno, capital administrativa—1.662.000; Sucre, sede del Tribunal Supremo, capital constitucional y judicial—195.000

▶ **Ciudades principales:** Santa Cruz de la Sierra—1.286.000, Cochabamba—794.000, Oruro—202.000, Potosí—124.000

SOURCE: Population Division, UN Secretariat

▶ **Moneda:** peso boliviano

▶ **Idiomas:** español (oficial), aimará (oficial), quechua (oficial)

Bandera de Bolivia

Mujer indígena con bebé

Bolivianos célebres

▶ **Jesús Lara,** escritor (1898–1980)
▶ **Víctor Paz Estenssoro,** político y presidente (1907–2001)
▶ **María Luisa Pacheco,** pintora (1919–1982)
▶ **Matilde Casazola,** poeta (1942–)

la mitad *half* restante *remaining* altiplano *high plateau*
sede *seat* paraguas *umbrella* cascada *waterfall*

Plaza San Francisco

Vista de la ciudad de Sucre

PERÚ — BRASIL — Río Beni — Río Mamoré — Illampu — Lago Titicaca — La Paz — Cordillera Oriental de los Andes — Tiahuanaco — Río Desaguadero — Cordillera Central de los Andes — Oruro — Río Grande — Santa Cruz de la Sierra — Lago Poopó — Sucre — Cochabamba — Potosí — Río Pilcomayo — PARAGUAY — ARGENTINA — CHILE

ESTADOS UNIDOS — OCÉANO ATLÁNTICO — OCÉANO PACÍFICO — BOLIVIA

recursos

WB pp. 189–190	VM pp. 263–264	I CD-ROM Lección 15	vistahigher learning.com

¡Increíble pero cierto!

La Paz es la capital más alta del mundo. Su aeropuerto está situado a una altitud de 3.600 m. (12.000 pies). Ah, y si viajas en carro hasta La Paz, ¡no te olvides del paraguas°! En la carretera, que cruza 9.000 metros de densa selva, te encontrarás con una cascada°.

Section Goal
In **Panorama** students will read about the geography and culture of Bolivia.

Instructional Resources
*Transparencies, #5, #6, #60
WB/VM: Workbook, pp. 189–190;
Video Activities, pp. 263–264
Panorama cultural DVD/Video
Interactive CD-ROM
IRM: Videoscript, p. 117;
Panorama cultural Translations,
p. 139
Companion website:
www.vistahigherlearning.com
Presentations CD-ROM*

Suggestion Have students look at the map of Bolivia or project **Transparency #60**. Note that Bolivia is a completely land-locked country. Have students name the five countries that share its borders. Point out Bolivia's three main regions: the Andes region, the high plain (**altiplano**), and the Amazon basin. Ask students to read aloud the places labeled on the map, and to identify whether place names are in Spanish or in an indigenous language.

El país en cifras Have volunteers create a pie chart that represents Bolivia's ethnic makeup as described in the **Población** section. As students read about the **Ciudades principales**, have them locate each city on the map. As students read about **Idiomas**, point out that **quechua** was the language of the ancient Incan empire.

¡Increíble pero cierto!
Visitors to La Paz and other Andean cities often experience **el soroche**, or altitude sickness. Andean natives typically develop increased lung capacity and a greater capacity for diffusing oxygen to the body, helping to compensate for decreased oxygen levels at these heights.

TEACHING OPTIONS

Heritage Speakers Another way to become acquainted with the traditions of Bolivia's different regions is through regional dances. The **cueca collasuyo** is a traditional dance from the **altiplano** region, while the **cueca chapaca** is from the **Chaco** area. The **jiringueros del Bení** is traditionally performed by rubber tappers from the Amazon area. Invite students familiar with these traditional dances to share some of their basic steps with the class.

Worth Noting To give students the opportunity to listen to the sounds of **quechua** or **aimará**, as well as the music of the Andes, bring in recordings made by Andean musicians, such as **los Kjarkas** or **Inkuyo**. Some recordings may include lyrics in the original language and in translation.

Lugares • El lago Titicaca

Titicaca, situado en los Andes de Bolivia y Perú, es el lago navegable más alto del mundo y está a una altitud de 3.815 metros (12.500 pies). También es el segundo lago más grande, después del lago Maracaibo, de Suramérica, con un área de más de 8.000 km² (3.000 millas²). La mitología inca cuenta° que los hijos del dios° Sol emergieron de las profundas aguas del lago Titicaca para fundar° su imperio°. Los indígenas de la zona todavía hacen botes° de totora° a la manera° antigua y los usan para navegar las claras aguas del lago.

Artes • La música andina

La música andina, compartida por Bolivia, Perú, Ecuador, Chile y Argentina, es el aspecto más conocido de su folklore. Hay muchos conjuntos° profesionales que dan a conocer° esta música popular, de origen indígena, alrededor° del mundo. Uno de los grupos más importantes son los Kjarkas, que llevan más de veinticinco años actuando en los escenarios internacionales. Los instrumentos típicos que se usan son la zampoña y la quena (dos tipos de flauta°), el arpa°, el bombo°, la guitarra y el charango, que es una pequeña guitarra andina.

Historia • Tiahuanaco

Tiahuanaco, que significa "Ciudad de los dioses", es un sitio arqueológico de ruinas preincaicas situado cerca de La Paz y del lago Titicaca. Se piensa que los antepasados° de los indígenas aimará fundaron este centro ceremonial hace unos 15.000 años. En el año 1100 d.C., la ciudad tenía más o menos 60.000 habitantes. En este sitio se pueden ver el Templo de Kalasasaya, el Monolito Ponce, el Templete Subterráneo, la Puerta del Sol y la Puerta de la Luna. La Puerta del Sol es un impresionante monumento que tiene tres metros de alto y cuatro de ancho° y que pesa aproximadamente 10 toneladas.

¿Qué aprendiste? Responde a las preguntas con una frase completa.

1. ¿Qué idiomas se hablan en Bolivia?
   En Bolivia se hablan español, quechua y aimará.
2. ¿Dónde vive la mayoría de los bolivianos?
   La mayoría de los bolivianos vive en el altiplano.
3. ¿Cuál es la capital administrativa de Bolivia?
   La capital administrativa de Bolivia es La Paz.
4. ¿Cómo se llama la moneda de Bolivia?
   La moneda de Bolivia es el peso boliviano.
5. Según la mitología inca, ¿qué ocurrió en el lago Titicaca? Los hijos del dios Sol emergieron del lago para fundar su imperio.

6. ¿Qué hacen los indios con la totora?
   Los indios hacen botes de totora.
7. ¿Qué es la quena?
   La quena es un tipo de flauta.
8. ¿Qué es el charango?
   El charango es una pequeña guitarra andina.
9. ¿Qué es la Puerta del Sol? La Puerta del Sol es un monumento que está en Tiahuanaco.
10. ¿Cómo se llama el sitio arqueológico situado cerca de La Paz y del lago Titicaca?
    El sitio arqueológico situado cerca de La Paz y del lago Titicaca se llama Tiahuanaco.

Conexión Internet Investiga estos temas en el sitio **www.vistahigherlearning.com**.

1. Busca información sobre un(a) boliviano/a célebre. ¿Cuáles son algunos de los episodios más importantes de su vida? ¿Qué ha hecho esta persona? ¿Por qué es célebre?
2. Busca información sobre Tiahuanaco u otro sitio arqueológico en Bolivia. ¿Qué han descubierto los arqueólogos en ese sitio?

cuenta *tells the story* dios *god* fundar *to found* imperio *empire* botes *rowboats* totora *reed* manera *way* conjuntos *groups*
dan a conocer *make known* alrededor *around* flauta *flute* arpa *harp* bombo *drum* antepasados *ancestors* ancho *wide*

TEACHING OPTIONS

Worth Noting Teams of scientists are currently extracting sediment samples from Titicaca's lake bed to study the history of climatological change in the region. Such research may help scientists build models to analyze contemporary trends in global climate change.

Worth Noting Students might like to learn this indigenous riddle about the **armadillo**, the animal whose outer shell is used to make the body of the **charango**, a small ten-stringed guitar used in Andean music:
Vive en el cerro, lejos del mar.
De concha el saco sin abrochar.
Cuando se muere... ¡pues a cantar!

Section Goal

In **Panorama** students will read about the geography and culture of Paraguay.

Instructional Resources
Transparencies, #5, #6, #61
WB/VM: Workbook, pp. 191–192;
Video Activities, pp. 265–266
***Panorama cultural** DVD/Video*
Interactive CD-ROM
IRM: Videoscript, p. 117;
***Panorama cultural** Translations,*
p. 139
Companion website:
www.vistahigherlearning.com
Presentations CD-ROM

Suggestion Have students look at the map of Paraguay or project **Transparency #61**. Note that the major population centers lie east of the Paraguay River, which divides the country in two. West of the river is the **Gran Chaco**, a sparsely populated and largely infertile region.

El país en cifras As you read **Idiomas**, point out that **guaraní** is also spoken in neighboring Bolivia, Brazil, and Argentina. However, as an officially bilingual nation, Paraguay has the largest concentration of Guaraní speakers. As students read **Paraguayos célebres**, let them know that writer **Augusto Roa Bastos** is well known throughout Latin America as both a poet and novelist. His novels *Yo, el Supremo* and *Hijo de hombre* deal with the turbulent and difficult history of Paraguay.

¡Increíble pero cierto! Like Paraguay, several other Spanish-speaking countries impose fines on citizens for not voting. Ask students to research and name these countries. Ask the class if they think that such a measure should be implemented here to improve voter turnout at the polls.

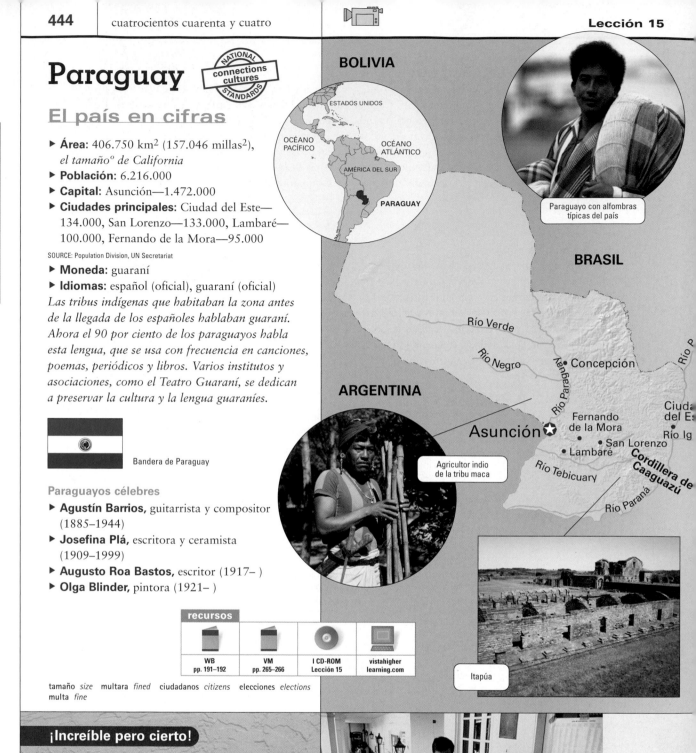

Paraguay

El país en cifras

▶ **Área:** 406.750 km² (157.046 millas²), *el tamaño° de California*
▶ **Población:** 6.216.000
▶ **Capital:** Asunción—1.472.000
▶ **Ciudades principales:** Ciudad del Este—134.000, San Lorenzo—133.000, Lambaré—100.000, Fernando de la Mora—95.000

SOURCE: Population Division, UN Secretariat

▶ **Moneda:** guaraní
▶ **Idiomas:** español (oficial), guaraní (oficial)

Las tribus indígenas que habitaban la zona antes de la llegada de los españoles hablaban guaraní. Ahora el 90 por ciento de los paraguayos habla esta lengua, que se usa con frecuencia en canciones, poemas, periódicos y libros. Varios institutos y asociaciones, como el Teatro Guaraní, se dedican a preservar la cultura y la lengua guaraníes.

Bandera de Paraguay

Paraguayos célebres

▶ **Agustín Barrios,** guitarrista y compositor (1885–1944)
▶ **Josefina Plá,** escritora y ceramista (1909–1999)
▶ **Augusto Roa Bastos,** escritor (1917–)
▶ **Olga Blinder,** pintora (1921–)

Paraguayo con alfombras típicas del país

Agricultor indio de la tribu maca

Itapúa

recursos			
WB pp. 191–192	VM pp. 265–266	I CD-ROM Lección 15	vistahigher learning.com

tamaño size   multara fined   ciudadanos citizens   elecciones elections   multa fine

¡Increíble pero cierto!

¿Te imaginas qué pasaría si el gobierno multara° a los ciudadanos° que no van a votar? En Paraguay, es una obligación. Ésta es una ley nacional, que otros países también tienen, para obligar a los ciudadanos a participar en las elecciones°. En Paraguay los ciudadanos que no van a votar tienen que pagar una multa° al gobierno.

Artesanía° • El ñandutí

El ñandutí es la forma artesanal más conocida de Paraguay. Es un fino encaje° hecho a mano, que generalmente tiene forma circular. En guaraní, su nombre significa telaraña° y se llama así porque imita su trazado°. Estos encajes suelen ser blancos, pero también los hay de colores, y sus diseños° pueden tener formas geométricas o florales. Aunque el ñandutí es originario de Itaguá, con el tiempo ha llegado a ser muy conocido en toda Suramérica.

Ciencias • La represa Itaipú

La represa° Itaipú, la obra° hidroeléctrica más ambiciosa hasta nuestros días, se encuentra en la frontera° entre Paraguay y Brasil. Su construcción se inició en 1974 y duró once años. Durante los primeros cinco años, se usó suficiente concreto como para construir un edificio de 350 pisos. El proyecto dio trabajo a 100.000 paraguayos. En 1984 se puso en funcionamiento la Central Hidroeléctrica de Itaipú, la mayor del mundo. Gracias a su cercanía a las famosas Cataratas de Iguazú, muchos turistas visitan la Central, atraídos° por lo imponente de su construcción.

Naturaleza • Los ríos Paraguay y Paraná

Los ríos Paraguay y Paraná sirven de frontera natural entre Paraguay y Argentina, y son las principales rutas de transporte dentro de Paraguay. El río Paraná tiene unos 3.200 km navegables, y por esta ruta pasan barcos de más de 5.000 toneladas que pueden ir desde el estuario° del Río de la Plata hasta la ciudad de Asunción. El río Paraguay divide el Gran Chaco, una zona poco poblada, de la meseta° Paraná, donde vive la mayoría de los paraguayos.

¿Qué aprendiste? Responde a las preguntas con una frase completa.

1. ¿Quién es Augusto Roa Bastos?
   Augusto Roa Bastos es un escritor paraguayo.
2. ¿Cómo se llama la moneda de Paraguay?
   La moneda de Paraguay se llama guaraní.
3. ¿Qué es el ñandutí?
   El ñandutí es un tipo de encaje.
4. ¿De dónde es originario el ñandutí?
   El ñandutí es originario de Itaguá.
5. ¿Qué forma imita el ñandutí?
   Imita la forma de una telaraña.
6. En total, ¿cuántos años tomó la construcción de la represa Itaipú?
   La construcción de la represa Itaipú tomó 11 años.
7. ¿A cuántos paraguayos dio trabajo la construcción de la represa?
   La construcción de la represa dio trabajo a 100.000 paraguayos.
8. ¿Qué países separan los ríos Paraguay y Paraná?
   Los ríos Paraguay y Paraná separan a Argentina y Paraguay.
9. ¿Qué distancia se puede navegar por el Paraná?
   Se pueden navegar 3.200 km.

Conexión Internet Investiga estos temas en el sitio **www.vistahigherlearning.com**.

1. Busca información sobre Alfredo Stroessner, el ex-presidente de Paraguay. ¿Por qué se le considera un dictador?
2. Busca información sobre la historia de Paraguay. En tu opinión, ¿cuáles fueron los episodios decisivos en su historia?

---

artesanía *crafts*   encaje *lace*   telaraña *spiderweb*   trazado *outline; design*   diseños *designs*   represa *dam*   obra *work (construction)*
frontera *border*   atraídos *attracted; drawn*   estuario *estuary*   meseta *plateau*

El ñandutí In recent years, the number of traditional **ñandutí** makers has been in serious decline. The artisans of **Itaguá** grew tired of the low levels of compensation they received, and many have turned to other more profitable sources of income. Formal instruction in the skill of making **ñandutí** has even been incorporated in the curriculum of local handicraft schools in an effort to keep this traditional art alive.

La represa Itaipú The **Itaipú** dam project is a joint venture between Brazil and Paraguay, and has been remarkably successful. By 1995, four years after it went into production, the dam generated 25% of Brazil's energy supply, and 78% of Paraguay's. Annual electrical output continues to increase yearly.

Los ríos Paraguay y Paraná The Paraná River in particular was a highway for the settlement of Paraguay. Along its banks, between the 16th and late 18th centuries, the Jesuits organized their Guaraní-speaking parishioners into small, self-supporting city-states built around mission settlements, similar to the Franciscan mission system in California during the same period.

Conexión Internet Students will find supporting Internet activities and links at **www.vistahigherlearning.com**.

Instructional Resources
Vocabulary CD
Lab Manual, p. 89
Lab CD/MP3 Lección 15
IRM: Tapescript, pp. 67–70
Testing Program: Pruebas,
pp. 169–180; Exámenes,
pp. 193–204; pp. 229–240
Testing Program Audio CD
Test Files CD-ROM
Test Generator

El bienestar

el bienestar	well-being
la droga	drug
el/la drogadicto/a	drug addict
el masaje	massage
el/la teleadicto/a	couch potato
adelgazar	to lose weight; to slim down
aliviar el estrés	to reduce stress
aliviar la tensión	to reduce tension
apurarse, darse prisa	to hurry; to rush
aumentar de peso, engordar	to gain weight
disfrutar (de)	to enjoy; to reap the benefits (of)
estar a dieta	to be on a diet
(no) fumar	(not) to smoke
llevar una vida sana	to lead a healthy lifestyle
sufrir muchas presiones	to be under a lot of pressure
tratar de (+ inf.)	to try (to do something)
activo/a	active
débil	weak
en exceso	in excess; too much
flexible	flexible
fuerte	strong
sedentario/a	sedentary; related to sitting
tranquilo/a	calm; quiet

En el gimnasio

la cinta caminadora	treadmill
la clase de ejercicios aeróbicos	aerobics class
el/la entrenador(a)	trainer
el músculo	muscle
calentarse (e:ie)	to warm up
entrenarse	to practice; to train
estar en buena forma	to be in good shape
hacer ejercicio	to exercise
hacer ejercicios aeróbicos	to do aerobics
hacer ejercicios de estiramiento	to do stretching exercises
hacer gimnasia	to work out
levantar pesas	to lift weights
mantenerse en forma	to stay in shape
sudar	to sweat

La nutrición

la bebida alcohólica	alcoholic beverage
la cafeína	caffeine
la caloría	calorie
el colesterol	cholesterol
la grasa	fat
la merienda	afternoon snack
el mineral	mineral
la nutrición	nutrition
el/la nutricionista	nutritionist
la proteína	protein
la vitamina	vitamin
comer una dieta equilibrada	to eat a balanced diet
consumir alcohol	to consume alcohol
descafeinado/a	decaffeinated

Expresiones útiles	See page 425.

recursos

| LM p. 89 | Lab CD/MP3 Lección 15 | Vocab CD Lección 15 |

Plan de escritura

 Ideas y organización

Begin by organizing your writing materials. If you prefer to write by hand, you may want to have a few spare pens and pencils on hand, as well as an eraser or correction fluid. If you prefer to use a word-processing program, make sure you know how to use Spanish accent marks, the **tilde,** and Spanish punctuation marks. Then make a list of the resources you can consult while writing. Finally, make a list of the basic ideas you want to cover. Beside each idea, jot down a few Spanish words and phrases you may want to use while writing.

 Primer borrador

Write your first draft, using the resources and ideas you gathered in **Ideas y organización.**

3 Comentario

Exchange papers with a classmate and comment on each other's work, using these questions as a guide. Begin by mentioning what you like about your classmate's writing.

a.   How can your classmate make his or her writing clearer, more logical, or more organized?

b.   What suggestions do you have for making the writing more interesting or complete?

c.   Do you see any spelling or grammatical errors?

4 Redacción

Revise your first draft, keeping in mind your classmate's comments. Also, incorporate any new information you may have. Before handing in the final version, review your work using these guidelines:

a.   Make sure each verb agrees with its subject. Then check the gender and number of each article, noun, and adjective.

b.   Check your spelling and punctuation.

c.   Consult your **Anotaciones para mejorar la escritura** (see description below) to avoid repetition of previous errors.

5 Evaluación y progreso

You may want to share what you've written with a classmate, a small group, or the entire class. After your instructor has returned your paper, review the comments and corrections. On a separate sheet of paper, write the heading **Anotaciones para mejorar** (*Notes for improving*) **la escritura** and list your most common errors. Place this list and your corrected document in your writing portfolio (**Carpeta de trabajos**) and consult it from time to time to gauge your progress.

Algunas estrategias

Considering audience and purpose

Before you write, think about what you are writing and the people for whom you are writing it. Try to write in a way that would appeal to and meet the needs of your audience.

Organizing information logically

There are many ways to organize your writing. You may, for example, want to organize your information chronologically (e.g., events in the history of a country), sequentially (e.g., steps in a recipe), or in order of importance. Some people prepare an outline before they write. Others jot information down on note cards and then arrange the note cards in a logical order. If you are organizing information chronologically or sequentially, you may want to use adverbs or adverbial phrases (e.g., **primero, luego, entonces, más tarde, al final**) to indicate the sequence in which events occurred.

Improving your style

You can improve your style by using complex sentences and avoiding redundancies. You can use linking words (e.g., **pero, y, o**) to connect simple sentences and create more complex ones. To avoid redundancy with verbs and nouns, consult a **diccionario de sinónimos.** You can also avoid redundancy by replacing nouns with direct object pronouns, possessive adjectives, demonstrative adjectives, and pronouns. For example: Have you seen my racket? I can't seem to find it anywhere. Do you mind if I borrow yours?

Doing a comparative analysis

You may want to create a Venn diagram in order to organize your information visually before comparing or contrasting people, places, objects, events, or issues. To create a Venn diagram, draw two circles that overlap and label the top of each circle with the names of the people or things you are comparing. In the outer rings of the two circles, list the differences between the people or things. Then list their similarities where the two circles overlap. When you write a comparative analysis or give your opinions, be sure to express yourself clearly and support your ideas with appropriate details, facts, examples, and other forms of evidence.

Writing strong introductions and conclusions

Introductions and conclusions focus the reader's attention on your topic. The introduction previews the topic and informs your reader of the important points that will be covered. The conclusion concisely sums up the information. A compelling fact or statistic, a humorous anecdote, or a question directed to the reader are all interesting ways to begin or end your writing.

Spanish Terms for Direction Lines and Classroom Use

Below is a list of useful terms that you might hear your instructor say in class. It also includes Spanish terms that appear in the direction lines of your textbook.

En las instrucciones *In direction lines*

Camina/Caminen por la clase.	*Walk around the classroom.*
Ciertas o falsas	*True or false*
Cierto o falso	*True or false*
Circula/Circulen por la clase.	*Walk around the classroom.*
Completa las oraciones de una manera lógica.	*Complete the sentences logically.*
Con un(a) compañero/a...	*With a classmate...*
Contesta las preguntas.	*Answer the questions.*
Corrige las frases falsas.	*Correct the false statements.*
Di/ Digan...	*Say...*
En grupos...	*In groups...*
En parejas...	*In pairs...*
Entrevista ...	*Interview...*
Forma oraciones completas.	*Create/Make complete sentences.*
Háganse preguntas.	*Ask each other questions.*
Haz el papel de...	*Play the role of...*
Haz los cambios necesarios.	*Make the necessary changes.*
Indica/Indiquen si las oraciones...	*Indicate if the sentences...*
Lee/Lean en voz alta.	*Read aloud.*
...que mejor completa...	*...that best completes...*
Reúnete...	*Get together...*
Toma nota...	*Take note...*
Tomen apuntes.	*Take notes.*
Túrnense...	*Take turns...*

Palabras útiles *Useful words*

el anuncio	*advertisement/ad*
los apuntes	*notes*
el borrador	*draft*
la concordancia	*agreement*
el contenido	*contents*
eficaz	*efficient*
la encuesta	*survey*
el equipo	*team*
el esquema	*outline*
el folleto	*brochure*
las frases	*statements*
la hoja de actividades	*activity sheet/ handout*
la hoja de papel	*piece of paper*
la información errónea	*incorrect information*
el/la lector(a)	*reader*
la lectura	*reading*
las oraciones	*sentences*
la ortografía	*spelling*
las palabras útiles	*useful words*
el papel	*role*
el párrafo	*paragraph*
el paso	*step*
la(s) persona(s) descrita(s)	*the person (people) described*
la pista	*clue*
por ejemplo	*for example*
el propósito	*purpose*
los recursos	*resources*
el reportaje	*report*
los resultados	*results*
según	*according to*
siguiente	*following*
la sugerencia	*suggestion*
el sustantivo	*noun*
el tema	*topic*
último	*last*
el último recurso	*last resort*

Verbos útiles *Useful verbs*

adivinar	*to guess*
anotar	*to jot down*
añadir	*to add*
apoyar	*to support*
averiguar	*to find out*
combinar	*to combine*
compartir	*to share*
comprobar (o:ue)	*to check*
corregir (e:i)	*to correct*
crear	*to create*
devolver	*to return*
doblar	*to fold*
dramatizar	*to act out*
elegir	*to choose/select*
emparejar	*to match*
entrevistar	*to interview*
escoger	*to choose*
identificar	*to identify*
incluir	*to include*
informar	*to report*
intentar	*to try*
intercambiar	*to exchange*
investigar	*to research*
marcar	*to mark*
preguntar	*to ask*
recordar (o:ue)	*to remember*
responder	*to answer*
revisar	*to revise*
seguir	*to follow*
seleccionar	*to select*
subrayar	*to underline*
traducir	*to translate*
tratar de	*to be about*

Expresiones útiles *Useful expressions*

Ahora mismo.	*Right away.*
¿Cómo no?	*But of course.*
¿Cómo se dice _____ en español?	*How do you say _____ in Spanish?*
¿Cómo se escribe _____?	*How do you spell _____?*
¿Comprende(n)?	*Do you understand?*
Con gusto.	*With pleasure.*
Con permiso.	*Excuse me.*
De acuerdo.	*Okay.*
De nada.	*You're welcome.*
¿De veras?	*Really?*
¿En qué página estamos?	*What page are we on?*
¿En serio?	*Seriously?*
Enseguida.	*Right away.*
Más despacio, por favor.	*Slower, please.*
Muchas gracias.	*Thanks a lot.*
No entiendo.	*I don't understand.*
No hay de qué.	*Don't mention it.*
No importa.	*No problem./It doesn't matter.*
¡No me digas!	*You don't say.*
No sé.	*I don't know.*
¡Ojalá!	*Hopefully!*
Perdone.	*Pardon me.*
Por favor.	*Please.*
Por supuesto.	*Of course.*
¡Qué bien!	*Great!*
¡Qué gracioso!	*How funny!*
¡Qué pena!	*What a pain!*
¿Qué significa _____?	*What does _____ mean?*
Repite, por favor.	*Please repeat.*
Tengo una pregunta.	*I have a question.*
¿Tiene(n) alguna pregunta?	*Do you have any questions?*
Vaya(n) a la página dos.	*Go to page 2.*

Glossary of Grammatical Terms

ADJECTIVE A word that modifies, or describes, a noun or pronoun.

muchos libros	un hombre rico
many books	*a rich man*

las mujeres **altas**
*the **tall** women*

Demonstrative adjective An adjective that specifies which noun a speaker is referring to.

esta fiesta	**ese** chico
this party	*that boy*

aquellas flores
those flowers

Possessive adjective An adjective that indicates ownership or possession.

mi mejor vestido	Éste es **mi** hermano.
my best dress	*This is **my** brother.*

Stressed possessive adjective A possessive adjective that emphasizes the owner or possessor.

Es un libro **mío**.
*It's **my** book./It's a book **of mine**.*

Es amiga **tuya**; yo no la conozco.
*She's a friend **of yours**; I don't know her.*

ADVERB A word that modifies, or describes, a verb, adjective, or other adverb.

Pancho escribe **rápidamente**.
*Pancho writes **quickly**.*

Este cuadro es **muy** bonito.
*This picture is **very** pretty.*

ARTICLE A word that points out a noun in either a specific or a non-specific way.

Definite article An article that points out a noun in a specific way.

el libro	la maleta
the book	*the suitcase*

los diccionarios	las palabras
the dictionaries	*the words*

Indefinite article An article that points out a noun in a general, non-specific way.

un lápiz	**una** computadora
a pencil	*a computer*

unos pájaros	**unas** escuelas
some birds	*some schools*

CLAUSE A group of words that contains both a conjugated verb and a subject, either expressed or implied.

Main (or Independent) clause A clause that can stand alone as a complete sentence.

Pienso ir a cenar pronto.
I plan to go to dinner soon.

Subordinate (or Dependent) clause A clause that does not express a complete thought and therefore cannot stand alone as a sentence.

Trabajo en la cafetería **porque necesito dinero para la escuela**.
*I work in the cafeteria **because I need money for school**.*

COMPARATIVE A construction used with an adjective or adverb to express a comparison between two people, places, or things.

Este programa es **más interesante** que el otro.
*This program is **more interesting** than the other one.*

Tomás no es **tan alto como** Alberto.
*Tomás is not **as tall as** Alberto.*

CONJUGATION A set of the forms of a verb for a specific tense or mood or the process by which these verb forms are presented.

Preterite conjugation of **cantar**:

canté	cantamos
cantaste	cantasteis
cantó	cantaron

CONJUNCTION A word used to connect words, clauses, or phrases.

Susana es de Cuba **y** Pedro es de España.
*Susana is from Cuba **and** Pedro is from Spain.*

No quiero estudiar **pero** tengo que hacerlo.
*I don't want to study, **but** I have to.*

CONTRACTION The joining of two words into one. The only contractions in Spanish are **al** and **del**.

Mi hermano fue **al** concierto ayer.
*My brother went **to the** concert yesterday.*

Saqué dinero **del** banco.
*I took money **from the** bank.*

DIRECT OBJECT A noun or pronoun that directly receives the action of the verb.

Tomás lee **el libro**.   **La** pagó ayer.
*Tomás reads **the book**.   She paid **it** yesterday.*

GENDER The grammatical categorizing of certain kinds of words, such as nouns and pronouns, as masculine, feminine, or neuter.

Masculine
articles **el, un**
pronouns **él, lo, mío, éste, ése, aquél**
adjective **simpático**

Feminine
articles **la, una**
pronouns **ella, la, mía, ésta, ésa, aquélla**
adjective **simpática**

IMPERSONAL EXPRESSION A third-person expression with no expressed or specific subject.

Es muy importante.   Llueve mucho.
It's very important.   It's raining hard.

Aquí **se habla** español.
*Spanish **is spoken** here.*

INDIRECT OBJECT A noun or pronoun that receives the action of the verb indirectly; the object, often a living being, to or for whom an action is performed.

Eduardo **le** dio un libro **a Linda**.
*Eduardo gave a book **to Linda**.*

La profesora **me** dio una C en el examen.
*The professor gave **me** a C on the test.*

INFINITIVE The basic form of a verb. Infinitives in Spanish end in **-ar**, **-er**, or **-ir**.

hablar   correr   abrir
to speak   to run   to open

INTERROGATIVE An adjective or pronoun used to ask a question.

¿**Quién** habla?   ¿**Cuántos** compraste?
***Who** is speaking?   **How many** did you buy?*

¿**Qué** piensas hacer hoy?
***What** do you plan to do today?*

INVERSION Changing the word order of a sentence, often to form a question.

Statement: Elena pagó la cuenta del restaurante.

Inversion: ¿Pagó Elena la cuenta del restaurante?

MOOD A grammatical distinction of verbs that indicates whether the verb is intended to make a statement or command or to express a doubt, emotion, or condition contrary to fact.

Imperative mood Verb forms used to make commands.

Di la verdad.   Caminen ustedes conmigo.
Tell the truth.   Walk with me.

¡Comamos ahora!
Let's eat now!

Indicative mood Verb forms used to state facts, actions, and states considered to be real.

Sé que **tienes** el dinero.
*I know that **you have** the money.*

Subjunctive mood Verb forms used principally in subordinate (dependent) clauses to express wishes, desires, emotions, doubts, and certain conditions, such as contrary-to-fact situations.

Prefieren que **hables** en español.
*They prefer that **you speak** in Spanish.*

Dudo que Luis **tenga** el dinero necesario.
*I doubt that Luis **has** the necessary money.*

NOUN A word that identifies people, animals, places, things, and ideas.

hombre   gato
man   cat

México   casa
Mexico   house

libertad   libro
freedom   book

NUMBER A grammatical term that refers to singular or plural. Nouns in Spanish and English have number. Other parts of a sentence, such as adjectives, articles, and verbs, can also have number.

Singular	Plural
una cosa	**unas** cosas
a thing	*some things*
el profesor	**los** profesores
the professor	*the professors*

NUMBERS Words that represent amounts.

Cardinal numbers Words that show specific amounts.

cinco minutos
five minutes

el año **dos mil cuatro**
the year **2004**

Ordinal numbers Words that indicate the order of a noun in a series.

el **cuarto** jugador   la **décima** hora
*the **fourth** player*   *the **tenth** hour*

PAST PARTICIPLE A past form of the verb used in compound tenses. The past participle may also be used as an adjective, but it must then agree in number and gender with the word it modifies.

Han **buscado** por todas partes.
*They have **searched** everywhere.*

Yo no había **estudiado** para el examen.
*I hadn't **studied** for the exam.*

Hay una **ventana abierta** en la sala.
*There is an **open window** in the living room.*

PERSON The form of the verb or pronoun that indicates the speaker, the one spoken to, or the one spoken about. In Spanish, as in English, there are three persons: first, second, and third.

Person	Singular	Plural
1st	**yo** *I*	**nosotros/as** *we*
2nd	**tú, Ud.** *you*	**vosotros/as, Uds.** *you*
3rd	**él, ella** *he/she*	**ellos, ellas** *they*

PREPOSITION A word or words that describe(s) the relationship, most often in time or space, between two other words.

Anita es **de** California.
*Anita is **from** California.*

La chaqueta está **en** el carro.
*The jacket is **in** the car.*

Marta se peinó **antes de** salir.
*Marta combed her hair **before** going out.*

PRESENT PARTICIPLE In English, a verb form that ends in *-ing*. In Spanish, the present participle ends in **-ndo**, and is often used with **estar** to form a progressive tense.

Mi hermana está **hablando** por teléfono ahora mismo.
*My sister is **talking** on the phone right now.*

PRONOUN A word that takes the place of a noun or nouns.

Demonstrative pronoun A pronoun that takes the place of a specific noun.

Quiero **ésta.**
*I want **this one.***

¿Vas a comprar **ése?**
*Are you going to buy **that one?***

Juan prefirió **aquéllos.**
*Juan preferred **those** (over there).*

Object pronoun A pronoun that functions as a direct or indirect object of the verb.

Te digo la verdad.
*I'm telling **you** the truth.*

Me lo trajo Juan.
*Juan brought **it** to **me.***

Reflexive pronoun A pronoun that indicates that the action of a verb is performed by the subject on itself. These pronouns are often expressed in English with *-self: myself, yourself,* etc.

Yo **me bañé** antes de salir.
*I bathed **(myself)** before going out.*

Elena **se acostó** a las once y media.
*Elena **went to bed** at eleven-thirty.*

Relative pronoun A pronoun that connects a subordinate clause to a main clause.

El chico **que** nos escribió viene a visitar mañana.
*The boy **who** wrote us is coming to visit tomorrow.*

Ya sé **lo que** tenemos que hacer.
*I already know **what** we have to do.*

Subject pronoun A pronoun that replaces the name or title of a person or thing, and acts as the subject of a verb.

Tú debes estudiar más.
***You** should study more.*

Él llegó primero.
***He** arrived first.*

SUBJECT A noun or pronoun that performs the action of a verb and is often implied by the verb.

María va al supermercado.
***María** goes to the supermarket.*

(Ellos) Trabajan mucho.
***They** work hard.*

Esos **libros** son muy caros.
*Those **books** are very expensive.*

SUPERLATIVE A word or construction used with an adjective or adverb to express the highest or lowest degree of a specific quality among three or more people, places, or things.

De todas mis clases, ésta es la **más interesante**.
*Of all my classes, this is the **most interesting**.*

Raúl es el **menos simpático** de los chicos.
*Raúl is the **least pleasant** of the boys.*

TENSE A set of verb forms that indicates the time of an action or state: past, present, or future.

Compound tense A two-word tense made up of an auxiliary verb and a present or past participle. In Spanish, there are two auxiliary verbs: **estar** and **haber**.

En este momento, **estoy estudiando**.
*At this time, **I am studying**.*

El paquete no **ha llegado** todavía.
*The package **has not arrived** yet.*

Simple tense A tense expressed by a single verb form.

María **estaba** mal anoche.
*María **was** ill last night.*

Juana **hablará** con su mamá mañana.
*Juana **will** speak with her mom tomorrow.*

VERB A word that expresses actions or states-of-being.

Auxiliary verb A verb used with a present or past participle to form a compound tense. **Haber** is the most commonly used auxiliary verb in Spanish.

Los chicos **han** visto los elefantes.
*The children **have** seen the elephants.*

Espero que **hayas** comido.
*I hope you **have** eaten.*

Reflexive verb A verb that describes an action performed by the subject on itself and is always used with a reflexive pronoun.

Me compré un carro nuevo.
*I **bought myself** a new car.*

Pedro y Adela **se levantan** muy temprano.
*Pedro and Adela **get (themselves) up** very early.*

Spelling change verb A verb that undergoes a predictable change in spelling, in order to reflect its actual pronunciation in the various conjugations.

practicar	c→qu	practico	practiqué
dirigir	g→j	dirigí	dirijo
almorzar	z→c	almorzó	almorcé

Stem-changing verb A verb whose stem vowel undergoes one or more predictable changes in the various conjugations.

entender (e:ie)	entiendo
pedir (e:i)	piden
dormir (o:ue, u)	duermo, durmieron

Verb Conjugation Tables

The verb lists

The list of verbs below, and the model-verb tables that start on page 458 show you how to conjugate every verb taught in **PANORAMA**. Each verb in the list is followed by a model verb conjugated according to the same pattern. The number in parentheses indicates where in the verb tables you can find the conjugated forms of the model verb. If you want to find out how to conjugate **divertirse**, for example, look up number 33, **sentir**, the model for verbs that follow the **e:ie** stem-change pattern.

How to use the verb tables

In the tables you will find the infinitive, present and past participles, and all the simple forms of each model verb. The formation of the compound tenses of any verb can be inferred from the table of compound tenses, pages 458–459, either by combining the past participle of the verb with a conjugated form of **haber** or by combining the present participle with a conjugated form of **estar**.

---

abrazar (z:c) like cruzar (37)

abrir like vivir (3) *except* past participle is abierto

aburrir(se) like vivir (3)

acabar de like hablar (1)

acampar like hablar (1)

acompañar like hablar (1)

aconsejar like hablar (1)

acordarse (o:ue) like contar (24)

acostarse (o:ue) like contar (24)

adelgazar (z:c) like cruzar (37)

afeitarse like hablar (1)

ahorrar like hablar (1)

alegrarse like hablar (1)

aliviar like hablar (1)

almorzar (o:ue) like contar (24) *except* (z:c)

alquilar like hablar (1)

andar like hablar (1) *except* preterite stem is anduv–

anunciar like hablar (1)

apagar (g:gu) like llegar (41)

aplaudir like vivir (3)

apreciar like hablar (1)

aprender like comer (2)

apurarse like hablar (1)

arrancar (c:qu) like tocar (43)

arreglar like hablar (1)

asistir like vivir (3)

aumentar like hablar (1)

ayudar(se) like hablar (1)

bailar like hablar (1)

bajar(se) like hablar (1)

bañarse like hablar (1)

barrer like comer (2)

beber like comer (2)

besar(se) like hablar (1)

borrar like hablar (1)

brindar like hablar (1)

bucear like hablar (1)

buscar (c:qu) like tocar (43)

caber (4)

caer(se) (5)

calentarse (e:ie) like pensar (30)

calzar (z:c) like cruzar (37)

cambiar like hablar (1)

caminar like hablar (1)

cantar like hablar (1)

casarse like hablar (1)

cazar (z:c) like cruzar(37)

celebrar like hablar (1)

cenar like hablar (1)

cepillarse like hablar (1)

cerrar (e:ie) like pensar (30)

cobrar like hablar (1)

cocinar like hablar (1)

comenzar (e:ie) (z:c) like empezar (26)

comer (2)

compartir like vivir (3)

comprar like hablar (1)

comprender like comer (2)

comprometerse like comer (2)

comunicarse (c:qu) like tocar (43)

conducir (c:zc) (6)

confirmar like hablar (1)

conocer (c:zc) (35)

conseguir (e:i) like seguir (32)

conservar like hablar (1)

consumir like vivir (3)

contaminar like hablar (1)

contar (o:ue) (24)

controlar like hablar (1)

correr like comer (2)

costar (o:ue) like contar (24)

creer (y) (36)

cruzar (z:c) (37)

cubrir like vivir (3) *except* past participle is cubierto

cuidar like hablar (1)

cumplir like vivir (3)

dañar like hablar (1)

dar (7)

deber like comer (2)

decidir like vivir (3)

decir (e:i) (8)

declarar like hablar (1)

dejar like hablar (1)

depositar like hablar (1)

desarrollar like hablar (1)

desayunar like hablar (1)

descansar like hablar (1)

descargar like hablar (1)

describir like vivir (3) *except* past participle is descrito

descubrir like vivir (3) *except* past participle is descubierto

desear like hablar (1)

despedirse (e:i) like pedir (29)

despertarse (e:ie) like pensar (30)

destruir (y) (38)

dibujar like hablar (1)

dirigir (g:j) like vivir (3) *except* (g:j)

disfrutar like hablar (1)

divertirse (e:ie) like sentir (33)

divorciarse like hablar (1)

doblar like hablar (1)

doler (o:ue) like volver (34) *except* past participle is regular

dormir(se) (o:ue) (25)

ducharse like hablar (1)

dudar like hablar (1)

durar like hablar (1)

echar like hablar (1)

elegir (e:i) like pedir (29) *except* (g:j)

emitir like vivir (3)

empezar (e:ie) (z:c) (26)

enamorarse like hablar (1)

encantar like hablar (1)

encontrar(se) (o:ue) like contar (24)

enfermarse like hablar (1)

engordar like hablar (1)

enojarse like hablar (1)

enseñar like hablar (1)

ensuciar like hablar (1)

entender (e:ie) (27)

entrenarse like hablar (1)

entrevistar like hablar (1)

enviar (envío) (39)

escalar like hablar (1)

escoger (g:j) like proteger (42)

escribir like vivir (3) except past participle is escrito

escuchar like hablar (1)

esculpir like vivir (3)

esperar like hablar (1)

esquiar (esquío) like enviar (39)

establecer (c:zc) like conocer (35)

estacionar like hablar (1)

estar (9)

estornudar like hablar (1)

estudiar like hablar (1)

evitar like hablar (1)

explicar (c:qu) like tocar (43)

explorar like hablar (1)

faltar like hablar (1)

fascinar like hablar (1)

firmar like hablar (1)

fumar like hablar (1)

funcionar like hablar (1)

ganar like hablar (1)

gastar like hablar (1)

grabar like hablar (1)

graduarse (gradúo) (40)

guardar like hablar (1)

gustar like hablar (1)

haber (hay) (10)

hablar (1)

hacer (11)

importar like hablar (1)

imprimir like vivir (3)

informar like hablar (1)

insistir like vivir (3)

interesar like hablar (1)

invertir (e:ie) like sentir (33)

invitar like hablar (1)

ir(se) (12)

jubilarse like hablar (1)

jugar (u:ue) (g:gu) (28)

lastimarse like hablar (1)

lavar(se) like hablar (1)

leer (y) like creer (36)

levantar(se) like hablar (1)

limpiar like hablar (1)

llamar(se) like hablar (1)

llegar (g:gu) (41)

llenar like hablar (1)

llevar(se) like hablar (1)

llover (o:ue) like volver (34) except past participle is regular

luchar like hablar (1)

mandar like hablar (1)

manejar like hablar (1)

mantener(se) (e:ie) like tener (20)

maquillarse like hablar (1)

mejorar like hablar (1)

merendar (e:ie) like pensar (30)

mirar like hablar (1)

molestar like hablar (1)

montar like hablar (1)

morir (o:ue) like dormir (25) except past participle is muerto

mostrar (o:ue) like contar (24)

mudarse like hablar (1)

nacer (c:zc) like conocer (35)

nadar like hablar (1)

navegar (g:gu) like llegar (41)

necesitar like hablar (1)

negar (e:ie) like pensar (30) except (g:gu)

nevar (e:ie) like pensar (30)

obedecer (c:zc) like conocer (35)

obtener (e:ie) like tener (20)

ocurrir like vivir (3)

odiar like hablar (1)

ofrecer (c:zc) like conocer (35)

oír (y) (13)

olvidar like hablar (1)

pagar (g:gu) like llegar (41)

parar like hablar (1)

parecer (c:zc) like conocer (35)

pasar like hablar (1)

pasear like hablar (1)

patinar like hablar (1)

pedir (e:i) (29)

peinarse like hablar (1)

pensar (e:ie) (30)

perder (e:ie) like entender (27)

pescar (c:qu) like tocar (43)

pintar like hablar (1)

planchar like hablar (1)

poder (o:ue) (14)

poner(se) (15)

practicar (c:qu) like tocar (43)

preferir (e:ie) like sentir (33)

preguntar like hablar (1)

preocuparse like hablar (1)

preparar like hablar (1)

presentar like hablar (1)

prestar like hablar (1)

probar(se) (o:ue) like contar (24)

prohibir like vivir (3)

proteger (g:j) (42)

publicar (c:qu) like tocar (43)

quedar(se) like hablar (1)

quemar like hablar (1)

querer (e:ie) (16)

quitar(se) like hablar (1)

recetar like hablar (1)

recibir like vivir (3)

reciclar like hablar (1)

recoger (g:j) like proteger (42)

recomendar (e:ie) like pensar (30)

recordar (o:ue) like contar (24)

reducir (c:zc) like conducir (6)

regalar like hablar (1)

regatear like hablar (1)

regresar like hablar (1)

reír(se) (e:i) (31)

relajarse like hablar (1)

renunciar like hablar (1)

repetir (e:i) like pedir (29)

resolver (o:ue) like volver (34)

respirar like hablar (1)

revisar like hablar (1)

rogar (o:ue) like contar (24) except (g:gu)

romper(se) like comer (2) except past participle is roto

saber (17)

sacar (c:qu) like tocar (43)

sacudir like vivir (3)

salir (18)

saludar(se) like hablar (1)

secar(se) (c:q) like tocar (43)

seguir (e:i) (32)

sentarse (e:ie) like pensar (30)

sentir(se) (e:ie) (33)

separarse like hablar (1)

ser (19)

servir (e:i) like pedir (29)

solicitar like hablar (1)

sonar (o:ue) like contar (24)

sonreír (e:i) like reír(se) (31)

sorprender like comer (2)

subir like vivir (3)

sudar like hablar (1)

sufrir like vivir (3)

sugerir (e:ie) like sentir (33)

suponer like poner (15)

temer like comer (2)

tener (e:ie) (20)

terminar like hablar (1)

tocar (c:qu) (43)

tomar like hablar (1)

torcerse (o:ue) like volver (34) except (c:z) and past participle is regular; e.g. yo tuerzo

toser like comer (2)

trabajar like hablar (1)

traducir (c:zc) like conducir (6)

traer (21)

transmitir like vivir (3)

tratar like hablar (1)

usar like hablar (1)

vender like comer (2)

venir (e:ie) (22)

ver (23)

vestirse (e:i) like pedir (29)

viajar like hablar (1)

visitar like hablar (1)

vivir (3)

volver (o:ue) (34)

votar like hablar (1)

Regular verbs: simple tenses

			INDICATIVE				SUBJUNCTIVE		IMPERATIVE
Infinitive	Present	Imperfect	Preterite	Future	Conditional	Present	Past	
1 hablar	hablo	hablaba	hablé	hablaré	hablaría	hable	hablara	
	hablas	hablabas	hablaste	hablarás	hablarías	hables	hablaras	habla tú (no hables)
	habla	hablaba	habló	hablará	hablaría	hable	hablara	hable Ud.
Participles:	hablamos	hablábamos	hablamos	hablaremos	hablaríamos	hablemos	habláramos	hablemos
hablando	habláis	hablabais	hablasteis	hablaréis	hablaríais	habléis	hablarais	hablad (no habléis)
hablado	hablan	hablaban	hablaron	hablarán	hablarían	hablen	hablaran	hablen Uds.
2 comer	como	comía	comí	comeré	comería	coma	comiera	
	comes	comías	comiste	comerás	comerías	comas	comieras	come tú (no comas)
	come	comía	comió	comerá	comería	coma	comiera	coma Ud.
Participles:	comemos	comíamos	comimos	comeremos	comeríamos	comamos	comiéramos	comamos
comiendo	coméis	comíais	comisteis	comeréis	comeríais	comáis	comierais	comed (no comáis)
comido	comen	comían	comieron	comerán	comerían	coman	comieran	coman Uds.
3 vivir	vivo	vivía	viví	viviré	viviría	viva	viviera	
	vives	vivías	viviste	vivirás	vivirías	vivas	vivieras	vive tú (no vivas)
	vive	vivía	vivió	vivirá	viviría	viva	viviera	viva Ud.
Participles:	vivimos	vivíamos	vivimos	viviremos	viviríamos	vivamos	viviéramos	vivamos
viviendo	vivís	vivíais	vivisteis	viviréis	viviríais	viváis	vivierais	vivid (no viváis)
vivido	viven	vivían	vivieron	vivirán	vivirían	vivan	vivieran	vivan Uds.

All verbs: compound tenses

PERFECT TENSES

	INDICATIVE						SUBJUNCTIVE	
Present Perfect		**Past Perfect**		**Future Perfect**		**Conditional Perfect**	**Present Perfect**	**Past Perfect**
he	hablado	había	hablado	habré	hablado	habría	hablado	haya	hablado	hubiera	hablado
has	comido	habías	comido	habrás	comido	habrías	comido	hayas	comido	hubieras	comido
ha	vivido	había	vivido	habrá	vivido	habría	vivido	haya	vivido	hubiera	vivido
hemos		habíamos		habremos		habríamos		hayamos		hubiéramos	
habéis		habíais		habréis		habríais		hayáis		hubierais	
han		habían		habrán		habrían		hayan		hubieran	

PROGRESSIVE TENSES

	INDICATIVE				SUBJUNCTIVE	
Present Progressive	Past Progressive		Future Progressive	Conditional Progressive	Present Progressive	Past Progressive
estoy	estaba		estaré	estaría	esté	estuviera
estás	estabas	hablando	estarás	estarías	estés	estuvieras
está	estaba	comiendo	estará	estaría	esté hablando	estuviera
estamos	estábamos	viviendo	estaremos	estaríamos	estemos comiendo	estuviéramos
estáis	estabais		estaréis	estaríais	estéis viviendo	estuvierais
estan	estaban		estarán	estarían	estén	estuvieran

Irregular verbs

		INDICATIVE					SUBJUNCTIVE		IMPERATIVE
Infinitive	Present	Imperfect	Preterite	Future	Conditional		Present	Past	
4 caber	**quepo**	cabía	**cupe**	**cabré**	**cabría**		**quepa**	**cupiera**	
	cabes	cabías	**cupiste**	**cabrás**	**cabrías**		**quepas**	**cupieras**	cabe tú (no **quepas**)
	cabe	cabía	**cupo**	**cabrá**	**cabría**		**quepa**	**cupiera**	**quepa** Ud.
Participles:	cabemos	cabíamos	**cupimos**	**cabremos**	**cabríamos**		**quepamos**	**cupiéramos**	**quepamos**
cabiendo	cabéis	cabíais	**cupisteis**	**cabréis**	**cabríais**		**quepáis**	**cupierais**	cabed (no **quepáis**)
cabido	caben	cabían	**cupieron**	**cabrán**	**cabrían**		**quepan**	**cupieran**	**quepan** Uds.
5 caer(se)	**caigo**	caía	**caí**	caeré	caería		**caiga**	**cayera**	
	caes	caías	**caíste**	caerás	caerías		**caigas**	**cayeras**	cae tú (no **caigas**)
	cae	caía	**cayó**	caerá	caería		**caiga**	**cayera**	**caiga** Ud.
Participles:	caemos	caíamos	**caímos**	caeremos	caeríamos		**caigamos**	**cayéramos**	**caigamos**
cayendo	caéis	caíais	**caísteis**	caeréis	caeríais		**caigáis**	**cayerais**	caed (no **caigáis**)
caído	caen	caían	**cayeron**	caerán	caerían		**caigan**	**cayeran**	**caigan** Uds.
6 conducir	**conduzco**	conducía	**conduje**	conduciré	conduciría		**conduzca**	**condujera**	
(c:zc)	conduces	conducías	**condujiste**	conducirás	conducirías		**conduzcas**	**condujeras**	conduce tú (no **conduzcas**)
	conduce	conducía	**condujo**	conducirá	conduciría		**conduzca**	**condujera**	**conduzca** Ud.
Participles:	conducimos	conducíamos	**condujimos**	conduciremos	conduciríamos		**conduzcamos**	**condujéramos**	**conduzcamos**
conduciendo	conducís	conducíais	**condujisteis**	conduciréis	conduciríais		**conduzcáis**	**condujerais**	conducid (no **conduzcáis**)
conducido	conducen	conducían	**condujeron**	conducirán	conducirían		**conduzcan**	**condujeran**	**conduzcan** Uds.

7 — dar (Participles: dando, dado)

	Present	Imperfect	Preterite	Future	Conditional	Subj. Present	Subj. Past	Imperative
	doy	daba	di	daré	daría	dé	diera	
	das	dabas	diste	darás	darías	des	dieras	da tú (no des)
	da	daba	dio	dará	daría	dé	diera	dé Ud.
	damos	dábamos	dimos	daremos	daríamos	demos	diéramos	demos
	dais	dabais	disteis	daréis	daríais	deis	dierais	dad (no deis)
	dan	daban	dieron	darán	darían	den	dieran	den Uds.

8 — decir (e:i) (Participles: diciendo, dicho)

	Present	Imperfect	Preterite	Future	Conditional	Subj. Present	Subj. Past	Imperative
	digo	decía	dije	diré	diría	diga	dijera	
	dices	decías	dijiste	dirás	dirías	digas	dijeras	di tú (no digas)
	dice	decía	dijo	dirá	diría	diga	dijera	diga Ud.
	decimos	decíamos	dijimos	diremos	diríamos	digamos	dijéramos	digamos
	decís	decíais	dijisteis	diréis	diríais	digáis	dijerais	decid (no digáis)
	dicen	decían	dijeron	dirán	dirían	digan	dijeran	digan Uds.

9 — estar (Participles: estando, estado)

	Present	Imperfect	Preterite	Future	Conditional	Subj. Present	Subj. Past	Imperative
	estoy	estaba	estuve	estaré	estaría	esté	estuviera	
	estás	estabas	estuviste	estarás	estarías	estés	estuvieras	está tú (no estés)
	está	estaba	estuvo	estará	estaría	esté	estuviera	esté Ud.
	estamos	estábamos	estuvimos	estaremos	estaríamos	estemos	estuviéramos	estemos
	estáis	estabais	estuvisteis	estaréis	estaríais	estéis	estuvierais	estad (no estéis)
	están	estaban	estuvieron	estarán	estarían	estén	estuvieran	estén Uds.

10 — haber (Participles: habiendo, habido)

	Present	Imperfect	Preterite	Future	Conditional	Subj. Present	Subj. Past	Imperative
	he	había	hube	habré	habría	haya	hubiera	
	has	habías	hubiste	habrás	habrías	hayas	hubieras	
	ha	había	hubo	habrá	habría	haya	hubiera	
	hemos	habíamos	hubimos	habremos	habríamos	hayamos	hubiéramos	
	habéis	habíais	hubisteis	habréis	habríais	hayáis	hubierais	
	han	habían	hubieron	habrán	habrían	hayan	hubieran	

11 — hacer (Participles: haciendo, hecho)

	Present	Imperfect	Preterite	Future	Conditional	Subj. Present	Subj. Past	Imperative
	hago	hacía	hice	haré	haría	haga	hiciera	
	haces	hacías	hiciste	harás	harías	hagas	hicieras	haz tú (no hagas)
	hace	hacía	hizo	hará	haría	haga	hiciera	haga Ud.
	hacemos	hacíamos	hicimos	haremos	haríamos	hagamos	hiciéramos	hagamos
	hacéis	hacíais	hicisteis	haréis	haríais	hagáis	hicierais	haced (no hagáis)
	hacen	hacían	hicieron	harán	harían	hagan	hicieran	hagan Uds.

12 — ir (Participles: yendo, ido)

	Present	Imperfect	Preterite	Future	Conditional	Subj. Present	Subj. Past	Imperative
	voy	iba	fui	iré	iría	vaya	fuera	
	vas	ibas	fuiste	irás	irías	vayas	fueras	ve tú (no vayas)
	va	iba	fue	irá	iría	vaya	fuera	vaya Ud.
	vamos	íbamos	fuimos	iremos	iríamos	vayamos	fuéramos	vamos
	vais	ibais	fuisteis	iréis	iríais	vayáis	fuerais	id (no vayáis)
	van	iban	fueron	irán	irían	vayan	fueran	vayan Uds.

13 — oír (y) (Participles: oyendo, oído)

	Present	Imperfect	Preterite	Future	Conditional	Subj. Present	Subj. Past	Imperative
	oigo	oía	oí	oiré	oiría	oiga	oyera	
	oyes	oías	oíste	oirás	oirías	oigas	oyeras	oye tú (no oigas)
	oye	oía	oyó	oirá	oiría	oiga	oyera	oiga Ud.
	oímos	oíamos	oímos	oiremos	oiríamos	oigamos	oyéramos	oigamos
	oís	oíais	oísteis	oiréis	oiríais	oigáis	oyerais	oíd (no oigáis)
	oyen	oían	oyeron	oirán	oirían	oigan	oyeran	oigan Uds.

14 poder (o:ue)
Participles: pudiendo, podido

	INDICATIVE					SUBJUNCTIVE		IMPERATIVE
	Present	Imperfect	Preterite	Future	Conditional	Present	Past	
	puedo	podía	pude	podré	podría	pueda	pudiera	
	puedes	podías	pudiste	podrás	podrías	puedas	pudieras	puede tú (no puedas)
	puede	podía	pudo	podrá	podría	pueda	pudiera	pueda Ud.
	podemos	podíamos	pudimos	podremos	podríamos	podamos	pudiéramos	podamos
	podéis	podíais	pudisteis	podréis	podríais	podáis	pudierais	poded (no podáis)
	pueden	podían	pudieron	podrán	podrían	puedan	pudieran	puedan Uds.

15 poner
Participles: poniendo, puesto

	INDICATIVE					SUBJUNCTIVE		IMPERATIVE
	Present	Imperfect	Preterite	Future	Conditional	Present	Past	
	pongo	ponía	puse	pondré	pondría	ponga	pusiera	
	pones	ponías	pusiste	pondrás	pondrías	pongas	pusieras	pon tú (no pongas)
	pone	ponía	puso	pondrá	pondría	ponga	pusiera	ponga Ud.
	ponemos	poníamos	pusimos	pondremos	pondríamos	pongamos	pusiéramos	pongamos
	ponéis	poníais	pusisteis	pondréis	pondríais	pongáis	pusierais	poned (no pongáis)
	ponen	ponían	pusieron	pondrán	pondrían	pongan	pusieran	pongan Uds.

16 querer (e:ie)
Participles: queriendo, querido

	INDICATIVE					SUBJUNCTIVE		IMPERATIVE
	Present	Imperfect	Preterite	Future	Conditional	Present	Past	
	quiero	quería	quise	querré	querría	quiera	quisiera	
	quieres	querías	quisiste	querrás	querrías	quieras	quisieras	quiere tú (no quieras)
	quiere	quería	quiso	querrá	querría	quiera	quisiera	quiera Ud.
	queremos	queríamos	quisimos	querremos	querríamos	queramos	quisiéramos	queramos
	queréis	queríais	quisisteis	querréis	querríais	queráis	quisierais	quered (no queráis)
	quieren	querían	quisieron	querrán	querrían	quieran	quisieran	quieran Uds.

17 saber
Participles: sabiendo, sabido

	INDICATIVE					SUBJUNCTIVE		IMPERATIVE
	Present	Imperfect	Preterite	Future	Conditional	Present	Past	
	sé	sabía	supe	sabré	sabría	sepa	supiera	
	sabes	sabías	supiste	sabrás	sabrías	sepas	supieras	sabe tú (no sepas)
	sabe	sabía	supo	sabrá	sabría	sepa	supiera	sepa Ud.
	sabemos	sabíamos	supimos	sabremos	sabríamos	sepamos	supiéramos	sepamos
	sabéis	sabíais	supisteis	sabréis	sabríais	sepáis	supierais	sabed (no sepáis)
	saben	sabían	supieron	sabrán	sabrían	sepan	supieran	sepan Uds.

18 salir
Participles: saliendo, salido

	INDICATIVE					SUBJUNCTIVE		IMPERATIVE
	Present	Imperfect	Preterite	Future	Conditional	Present	Past	
	salgo	salía	salí	saldré	saldría	salga	saliera	
	sales	salías	saliste	saldrás	saldrías	salgas	salieras	sal tú (no salgas)
	sale	salía	salió	saldrá	saldría	salga	saliera	salga Ud.
	salimos	salíamos	salimos	saldremos	saldríamos	salgamos	saliéramos	salgamos
	salís	salíais	salisteis	saldréis	saldríais	salgáis	salierais	salid (no salgáis)
	salen	salían	salieron	saldrán	saldrían	salgan	salieran	salgan Uds.

19 ser
Participles: siendo, sido

	INDICATIVE					SUBJUNCTIVE		IMPERATIVE
	Present	Imperfect	Preterite	Future	Conditional	Present	Past	
	soy	era	fui	seré	sería	sea	fuera	
	eres	eras	fuiste	serás	serías	seas	fueras	sé tú (no seas)
	es	era	fue	será	sería	sea	fuera	sea Ud.
	somos	éramos	fuimos	seremos	seríamos	seamos	fuéramos	seamos
	sois	erais	fuisteis	seréis	seríais	seáis	fuerais	sed (no seáis)
	son	eran	fueron	serán	serían	sean	fueran	sean Uds.

20 tener (e:ie)
Participles: teniendo, tenido

	INDICATIVE					SUBJUNCTIVE		IMPERATIVE
	Present	Imperfect	Preterite	Future	Conditional	Present	Past	
	tengo	tenía	tuve	tendré	tendría	tenga	tuviera	
	tienes	tenías	tuviste	tendrás	tendrías	tengas	tuvieras	ten tú (no tengas)
	tiene	tenía	tuvo	tendrá	tendría	tenga	tuviera	tenga Ud.
	tenemos	teníamos	tuvimos	tendremos	tendríamos	tengamos	tuviéramos	tengamos
	tenéis	teníais	tuvisteis	tendréis	tendríais	tengáis	tuvierais	tened (no tengáis)
	tienen	tenían	tuvieron	tendrán	tendrían	tengan	tuvieran	tengan Uds.

21   traer

Infinitive / Participles	INDICATIVE					SUBJUNCTIVE		IMPERATIVE
	Present	Imperfect	Preterite	Future	Conditional	Present	Past	
traer	traigo	traía	traje	traeré	traería	traiga	trajera	
	traes	traías	trajiste	traerás	traerías	traigas	trajeras	trae tú (no traigas)
	trae	traía	trajo	traerá	traería	traiga	trajera	traiga Ud.
Participles:	traemos	traíamos	trajimos	traeremos	traeríamos	traigamos	trajéramos	traigamos
trayendo	traéis	traíais	trajisteis	traeréis	traeríais	traigáis	trajerais	traed (no traigáis)
traído	traen	traían	trajeron	traerán	traerían	traigan	trajeran	traigan Uds.

22   venir (e:ie)

Infinitive / Participles	INDICATIVE					SUBJUNCTIVE		IMPERATIVE
	Present	Imperfect	Preterite	Future	Conditional	Present	Past	
venir (e:ie)	vengo	venía	vine	vendré	vendría	venga	viniera	
	vienes	venías	viniste	vendrás	vendrías	vengas	vinieras	ven tú (no vengas)
	viene	venía	vino	vendrá	vendría	venga	viniera	venga Ud.
Participles:	venimos	veníamos	vinimos	vendremos	vendríamos	vengamos	viniéramos	vengamos
viniendo	venís	veníais	vinisteis	vendréis	vendríais	vengáis	vinierais	venid (no vengáis)
venido	vienen	venían	vinieron	vendrán	vendrían	vengan	vinieran	vengan Uds.

23   ver

Infinitive / Participles	INDICATIVE					SUBJUNCTIVE		IMPERATIVE
	Present	Imperfect	Preterite	Future	Conditional	Present	Past	
ver	veo	veía	vi	veré	vería	vea	viera	
	ves	veías	viste	verás	verías	veas	vieras	ve tú (no veas)
	ve	veía	vio	verá	vería	vea	viera	vea Ud.
Participles:	vemos	veíamos	vimos	veremos	veríamos	veamos	viéramos	veamos
viendo	veis	veíais	visteis	veréis	veríais	veáis	vierais	ved (no veáis)
visto	ven	veían	vieron	verán	verían	vean	vieran	vean Uds.

Stem-changing verbs

24   contar (o:ue)

Infinitive / Participles	INDICATIVE					SUBJUNCTIVE		IMPERATIVE
	Present	Imperfect	Preterite	Future	Conditional	Present	Past	
contar (o:ue)	cuento	contaba	conté	contaré	contaría	cuente	contara	
	cuentas	contabas	contaste	contarás	contarías	cuentes	contaras	cuenta tú (no cuentes)
	cuenta	contaba	contó	contará	contaría	cuente	contara	cuente Ud.
Participles:	contamos	contábamos	contamos	contaremos	contaríamos	contemos	contáramos	contemos
contando	contáis	contabais	contasteis	contaréis	contaríais	contéis	contarais	contad (no contéis)
contado	cuentan	contaban	contaron	contarán	contarían	cuenten	contaran	cuenten Uds.

25   dormir (o:ue)

Infinitive / Participles	INDICATIVE					SUBJUNCTIVE		IMPERATIVE
	Present	Imperfect	Preterite	Future	Conditional	Present	Past	
dormir (o:ue)	duermo	dormía	dormí	dormiré	dormiría	duerma	durmiera	
	duermes	dormías	dormiste	dormirás	dormirías	duermas	durmieras	duerme tú (no duermas)
	duerme	dormía	durmió	dormirá	dormiría	duerma	durmiera	duerma Ud.
Participles:	dormimos	dormíamos	dormimos	dormiremos	dormiríamos	durmamos	durmiéramos	durmamos
durmiendo	dormís	dormíais	dormisteis	dormiréis	dormiríais	durmáis	durmierais	dormid (no durmáis)
dormido	duermen	dormían	durmieron	dormirán	dormirían	duerman	durmieran	duerman Uds.

26   empezar (e:ie) (c)

Infinitive / Participles	INDICATIVE					SUBJUNCTIVE		IMPERATIVE
	Present	Imperfect	Preterite	Future	Conditional	Present	Past	
empezar (e:ie) (c)	empiezo	empezaba	empecé	empezaré	empezaría	empiece	empezara	
	empiezas	empezabas	empezaste	empezarás	empezarías	empieces	empezaras	empieza tú (no empieces)
	empieza	empezaba	empezó	empezará	empezaría	empiece	empezara	empiece Ud.
Participles:	empezamos	empezábamos	empezamos	empezaremos	empezaríamos	empecemos	empezáramos	empecemos
empezando	empezáis	empezabais	empezasteis	empezaréis	empezaríais	empecéis	empezarais	empezad (no empecéis)
empezado	empiezan	empezaban	empezaron	empezarán	empezarían	empiecen	empezaran	empiecen Uds.

27 entender (e:ie)
Participles: entendiendo, entendido

	INDICATIVE					SUBJUNCTIVE		IMPERATIVE
	Present	Imperfect	Preterite	Future	Conditional	Present	Past	
	entiendo	entendía	entendí	entenderé	entendería	entienda	entendiera	
	entiendes	entendías	entendiste	entenderás	entenderías	entiendas	entendieras	entiende tú (no entiendas)
	entiende	entendía	entendió	entenderá	entendería	entienda	entendiera	entienda Ud.
	entendemos	entendíamos	entendimos	entenderemos	entenderíamos	entendamos	entendiéramos	entendamos
	entendéis	entendíais	entendisteis	entenderéis	entenderíais	entendáis	entendierais	entended (no entendáis)
	entienden	entendían	entendieron	entenderán	entenderían	entiendan	entendieran	entiendan Uds.

28 jugar (u:ue) (gu)
Participles: jugando, jugado

	INDICATIVE					SUBJUNCTIVE		IMPERATIVE
	Present	Imperfect	Preterite	Future	Conditional	Present	Past	
	juego	jugaba	jugué	jugaré	jugaría	juegue	jugara	
	juegas	jugabas	jugaste	jugarás	jugarías	juegues	jugaras	juega tú (no juegues)
	juega	jugaba	jugó	jugará	jugaría	juegue	jugara	juegue Ud.
	jugamos	jugábamos	jugamos	jugaremos	jugaríamos	juguemos	jugáramos	juguemos
	jugáis	jugabais	jugasteis	jugaréis	jugaríais	juguéis	jugarais	jugad (no juguéis)
	juegan	jugaban	jugaron	jugarán	jugarían	jueguen	jugaran	jueguen Uds.

29 pedir (e:i)
Participles: pidiendo, pedido

	INDICATIVE					SUBJUNCTIVE		IMPERATIVE
	Present	Imperfect	Preterite	Future	Conditional	Present	Past	
	pido	pedía	pedí	pediré	pediría	pida	pidiera	
	pides	pedías	pediste	pedirás	pedirías	pidas	pidieras	pide tú (no pidas)
	pide	pedía	pidió	pedirá	pediría	pida	pidiera	pida Ud.
	pedimos	pedíamos	pedimos	pediremos	pediríamos	pidamos	pidiéramos	pidamos
	pedís	pedíais	pedisteis	pediréis	pediríais	pidáis	pidierais	pedid (no pidáis)
	piden	pedían	pidieron	pedirán	pedirían	pidan	pidieran	pidan Uds.

30 pensar (e:ie)
Participles: pensando, pensado

	INDICATIVE					SUBJUNCTIVE		IMPERATIVE
	Present	Imperfect	Preterite	Future	Conditional	Present	Past	
	pienso	pensaba	pensé	pensaré	pensaría	piense	pensara	
	piensas	pensabas	pensaste	pensarás	pensarías	pienses	pensaras	piensa tú (no pienses)
	piensa	pensaba	pensó	pensará	pensaría	piense	pensara	piense Ud.
	pensamos	pensábamos	pensamos	pensaremos	pensaríamos	pensemos	pensáramos	pensemos
	pensáis	pensabais	pensasteis	pensaréis	pensaríais	penséis	pensarais	pensad (no penséis)
	piensan	pensaban	pensaron	pensarán	pensarían	piensen	pensaran	piensen Uds.

31 reír(se) (e:i)
Participles: riendo, reído

	INDICATIVE					SUBJUNCTIVE		IMPERATIVE
	Present	Imperfect	Preterite	Future	Conditional	Present	Past	
	río	reía	reí	reiré	reiría	ría	riera	
	ríes	reías	reíste	reirás	reirías	rías	rieras	ríe tú (no rías)
	ríe	reía	rió	reirá	reiría	ría	riera	ría Ud.
	reímos	reíamos	reímos	reiremos	reiríamos	riamos	riéramos	riamos
	reís	reíais	reísteis	reiréis	reiríais	riáis	rierais	reíd (no riáis)
	ríen	reían	rieron	reirán	reirían	rían	rieran	rían Uds.

32 seguir (e:i) (gu)
Participles: siguiendo, seguido

	INDICATIVE					SUBJUNCTIVE		IMPERATIVE
	Present	Imperfect	Preterite	Future	Conditional	Present	Past	
	sigo	seguía	seguí	seguiré	seguiría	siga	siguiera	
	sigues	seguías	seguiste	seguirás	seguirías	sigas	siguieras	sigue tú (no sigas)
	sigue	seguía	siguió	seguirá	seguiría	siga	siguiera	siga Ud.
	seguimos	seguíamos	seguimos	seguiremos	seguiríamos	sigamos	siguiéramos	sigamos
	seguís	seguíais	seguisteis	seguiréis	seguiríais	sigáis	siguierais	seguid (no sigáis)
	siguen	seguían	siguieron	seguirán	seguirían	sigan	siguieran	sigan Uds.

33 sentir (e:ie)
Participles: sintiendo, sentido

	INDICATIVE					SUBJUNCTIVE		IMPERATIVE
	Present	Imperfect	Preterite	Future	Conditional	Present	Past	
	siento	sentía	sentí	sentiré	sentiría	sienta	sintiera	
	sientes	sentías	sentiste	sentirás	sentirías	sientas	sintieras	siente tú (no sientas)
	siente	sentía	sintió	sentirá	sentiría	sienta	sintiera	sienta Ud.
	sentimos	sentíamos	sentimos	sentiremos	sentiríamos	sintamos	sintiéramos	sintamos
	sentís	sentíais	sentisteis	sentiréis	sentiríais	sintáis	sintierais	sentid (no sintáis)
	sienten	sentían	sintieron	sentirán	sentirían	sientan	sintieran	sientan Uds.

Infinitive	INDICATIVE					SUBJUNCTIVE		IMPERATIVE
	Present	Imperfect	Preterite	Future	Conditional	Present	Past	
34 volver (o:ue)	**vuelvo**	volvía	volví	volveré	volvería	**vuelva**	volviera	
	vuelves	volvías	volviste	volverás	volverías	**vuelvas**	volvieras	**vuelve** tú (no **vuelvas**)
	vuelve	volvía	volvió	volverá	volvería	**vuelva**	volviera	**vuelva** Ud.
	volvemos	volvíamos	volvimos	volveremos	volveríamos	volvamos	volviéramos	volvamos
	volvéis	volvíais	volvisteis	volveréis	volveríais	volváis	volvierais	volved (no volváis)
Participles:	**vuelven**	volvían	volvieron	volverán	volverían	**vuelvan**	volvieran	**vuelvan** Uds.
volviendo **vuelto**								

Verbs with spelling changes only

Infinitive	INDICATIVE					SUBJUNCTIVE		IMPERATIVE
	Present	Imperfect	Preterite	Future	Conditional	Present	Past	
35 conocer (c:zc)	**conozco**	conocía	conocí	conoceré	conocería	**conozca**	conociera	
	conoces	conocías	conociste	conocerás	conocerías	**conozcas**	conocieras	conoce tú (no **conozcas**)
	conoce	conocía	conoció	conocerá	conocería	**conozca**	conociera	**conozca** Ud.
	conocemos	conocíamos	conocimos	conoceremos	conoceríamos	**conozcamos**	conociéramos	**conozcamos**
Participles:	conocéis	conocíais	conocisteis	conoceréis	conoceríais	**conozcáis**	conocierais	conoced (no **conozcáis**)
conociendo conocido	conocen	conocían	conocieron	conocerán	conocerían	**conozcan**	conocieran	**conozcan** Uds.
36 creer (y)	creo	creía	**creí**	creeré	creería	crea	**creyera**	
	crees	creías	**creíste**	creerás	creerías	creas	**creyeras**	cree tú (no creas)
	cree	creía	**creyó**	creerá	creería	crea	**creyera**	crea Ud.
Participles:	creemos	creíamos	**creímos**	creeremos	creeríamos	creamos	**creyéramos**	creamos
creyendo	creéis	creíais	**creísteis**	creeréis	creeríais	creáis	**creyerais**	creed (no creáis)
creído	creen	creían	**creyeron**	creerán	creerían	crean	**creyeran**	crean Uds.
37 cruzar (c)	cruzo	cruzaba	**crucé**	cruzaré	cruzaría	**cruce**	cruzara	
	cruzas	cruzabas	cruzaste	cruzarás	cruzarías	**cruces**	cruzaras	cruza tú (no **cruces**)
	cruza	cruzaba	cruzó	cruzará	cruzaría	**cruce**	cruzara	**cruce** Ud.
Participles:	cruzamos	cruzábamos	cruzamos	cruzaremos	cruzaríamos	**crucemos**	cruzáramos	**crucemos**
cruzando	cruzáis	cruzabais	cruzasteis	cruzaréis	cruzaríais	**crucéis**	cruzarais	cruzad (no **crucéis**)
cruzado	cruzan	cruzaban	cruzaron	cruzarán	cruzarían	**crucen**	cruzaran	**crucen** Uds.
38 destruir (y)	**destruyo**	destruía	destruí	destruiré	destruiría	**destruya**	**destruyera**	
	destruyes	destruías	destruiste	destruirás	destruirías	**destruyas**	**destruyeras**	**destruye** tú (no **destruyas**)
	destruye	destruía	**destruyó**	destruirá	destruiría	**destruya**	**destruyera**	**destruya** Ud.
Participles:	destruimos	destruíamos	destruimos	destruiremos	destruiríamos	**destruyamos**	**destruyéramos**	**destruyamos**
destruyendo	destruis	destruíais	destruisteis	destruiréis	destruiríais	**destruyáis**	**destruyerais**	destruid (no **destruyáis**)
destruido	**destruyen**	destruían	**destruyeron**	destruirán	destruirían	**destruyan**	**destruyeran**	**destruyan** Uds.
39 enviar (envío)	**envío**	enviaba	envié	enviaré	enviaría	**envíe**	enviara	
	envías	enviabas	enviaste	enviarás	enviarías	**envíes**	enviaras	**envía** tú (no **envíes**)
	envía	enviaba	envió	enviará	enviaría	**envíe**	enviara	**envíe** Ud.
Participles:	enviamos	enviábamos	enviamos	enviaremos	enviaríamos	**enviemos**	enviáramos	enviemos
enviando	enviáis	enviabais	enviasteis	enviaréis	enviaríais	**enviéis**	enviarais	enviad (no **enviéis**)
enviado	**envían**	enviaban	enviaron	enviarán	enviarían	**envíen**	enviaran	**envíen** Uds.

Infinitive	INDICATIVE					SUBJUNCTIVE		IMPERATIVE
	Present	Imperfect	Preterite	Future	Conditional	Present	Past	
40 graduarse (gradúo) **Participles:** graduando graduado	**gradúo** **gradúas** **gradúa** graduamos graduáis **gradúan**	graduaba graduabas graduaba graduábamos graduabais graduaban	gradué graduaste graduó graduamos graduasteis graduaron	graduaré graduarás graduará graduaremos graduaréis graduarán	graduaría graduarías graduaría graduaríamos graduaríais graduarían	**gradúe** **gradúes** **gradúe** graduemos graduéis **gradúen**	graduara graduaras graduara graduáramos graduarais graduaran	**gradúa** tú (no **gradúes**) **gradúe** Ud. graduemos graduad (no graduéis) **gradúen** Uds.
41 llegar (gu) **Participles:** llegando llegado	llego llegas llega llegamos llegáis llegan	llegaba llegabas llegaba llegábamos llegabais llegaban	**llegué** llegaste llegó llegamos llegasteis llegaron	llegaré llegarás llegará llegaremos llegaréis llegarán	llegaría llegarías llegaría llegaríamos llegaríais llegarían	**llegue** **llegues** **llegue** **lleguemos** **lleguéis** **lleguen**	llegara llegaras llegara llegáramos llegarais llegaran	llega tú (no **llegues**) **llegue** Ud. **lleguemos** llegad (no **lleguéis**) **lleguen** Uds.
42 proteger (j) **Participles:** protegiendo protegido	**protejo** proteges protege protegemos protegéis protegen	protegía protegías protegía protegíamos protegíais protegían	protegí protegiste protegió protegimos protegisteis protegieron	protegeré protegerás protegerá protegeremos protegeréis protegerán	protegería protegerías protegería protegeríamos protegeríais protegerían	**proteja** **protejas** **proteja** **protejamos** **protejáis** **protejan**	protegiera protegieras protegiera protegiéramos protegierais protegieran	protege tú (no **protejas**) **proteja** Ud. **protejamos** proteged (no **protejáis**) **protejan** Uds.
43 tocar (qu) **Participles:** tocando tocado	toco tocas toca tocamos tocáis tocan	tocaba tocabas tocaba tocábamos tocabais tocaban	**toqué** tocaste tocó tocamos tocasteis tocaron	tocaré tocarás tocará tocaremos tocaréis tocarán	tocaría tocarías tocaría tocaríamos tocaríais tocarían	**toque** **toques** **toque** **toquemos** **toquéis** **toquen**	tocara tocaras tocara tocáramos tocarais tocaran	toca tú (no **toques**) **toque** Ud. **toquemos** tocad (no **toquéis**) **toquen** Uds.

Guide to Vocabulary

Note on alphabetization

Formerly, **ch**, **ll**, and **ñ** were considered separate letters in the Spanish alphabet, **ch** appearing after **c**, **ll** after **l**, and **ñ** after **n**. In current practice, for purposes of alphabetization, **ch** and **ll** are not treated as separate letters, but **ñ** still follows **n**. Therefore, in this glossary you will find that **año**, for example, appears after **anuncio**.

Abbreviations used in this glossary

adj.	adjective	*form.*	formal	*pl.*	plural
adv.	adverb	*indef.*	indefinite	*poss.*	possessive
art.	article	*interj.*	interjection	*prep.*	preposition
conj.	conjunction	*i.o.*	indirect object	*pron.*	pronoun
def.	definite	*m.*	masculine	*ref.*	reflexive
d.o.	direct object	*n.*	noun	*sing.*	singular
f.	feminine	*obj.*	object	*sub.*	subject
fam.	familiar	*p.p.*	past participle	*v.*	verb

Spanish-English

A

a *prep.* at; to 1
   ¿A qué hora...? At what time...? 1
   a bordo aboard 1
   a dieta on a diet 15
   a la derecha to the right 2
   a la izquierda to the left 2
   a la plancha grilled 8
   a la(s) + (time) at + (time) 1
   a menos que unless 13
   a menudo *adv.* often 10
   a nombre de in the name of 5
   a plazos in installments 14
   A sus órdenes. At your service. 11
   a tiempo *adv.* on time 10
   a veces *adv.* sometimes 10
   a ver let's see 2
¡Abajo! *adv.* Down!
abeja *f.* bee
abierto/a *adj.* open 5, 13
abogado/a *m., f.* lawyer
abrazar(se) *v.* to hug; to embrace (each other) 11
abrazo *m.* hug
abrigo *m.* coat 6
abril *m.* April 5
abrir *v.* to open 3
abuelo/a *m., f.* grandfather; grandmother 3
abuelos *pl.* grandparents 3
aburrido/a *adj.* bored; boring 5
aburrir *v.* to bore 7
aburrirse *v.* to get bored
acabar de (+ inf.) *v.* to have just done something 6
acampar *v.* to camp 5
accidente *m.* accident 10
acción *f.* action

   de acción action (genre)
aceite *m.* oil 8
ácido/a *adj.* acid 13
acompañar *v.* to go with; to accompany 14
aconsejar *v.* to advise 12
acontecimiento *m.* event
acordarse (de) (o:ue) *v.* to remember 7
acostarse (o:ue) *v.* to go to bed 7
activo/a *adj.* active 15
actor *m.* actor
actriz *f.* actor
actualidades *f., pl.* news; current events
acuático/a *adj.* aquatic 4
adelgazar *v.* to lose weight; to slim down 15
además (de) *adv.* furthermore; besides 10
adicional *adj.* additional
adiós *m.* goodbye 1
adjetivo *m.* adjective
administración de empresas *f.* business administration 2
adolescencia *f.* adolescence 9
¿adónde? *adv.* (to) where? (destination) 2
aduana *f.* customs 5
aeróbico/a *adj.* aerobic 15
aeropuerto *m.* airport 5
afectado/a *adj.* affected 13
afeitarse *v.* to shave 7
aficionado/a *adj.* fan 4
afirmativo/a *adj.* affirmative
afueras *f., pl.* suburbs; outskirts 12
agencia de viajes *f.* travel agency 5
agente de viajes *m., f.* travel agent 5
agosto *m.* August 5
agradable *adj.* pleasant
agua *f.* water 8

   agua mineral mineral water 8
ahora *adv.* now 2
   ahora mismo right now 5
ahorrar *v.* to save (money) 14
ahorros *m.* savings 14
aire *m.* air 5
ajo *m.* garlic 8
al *(contraction of* **a + el**) 2
   al aire libre open-air 6
   al contado in cash 14
   (al) este (to the) east 14
   al fondo (de) at the end (of) 12
   al lado de beside 2
   (al) norte (to the) north 14
   (al) oeste (to the) west 14
   (al) sur (to the) south 14
alcoba *f.* bedroom 12
alcohol *m.* alcohol 15
alcohólico/a *adj.* alcoholic 15
alegrarse (de) *v.* to be happy 13
alegre *adj.* happy; joyful 5
alegría *f.* happiness 9
alemán, alemana *adj.* German 3
alérgico/a *adj.* allergic 10
alfombra *f.* carpet; rug 12
algo *pron.* something; anything 7
algodón *m.* cotton 6
alguien *pron.* someone; somebody; anyone 7
algún, alguno/a(s) *adj.* any; some 7
alimento *m.* food
   alimentación *f.* diet
aliviar *v.* to reduce 15
   aliviar el estrés/la tensión to reduce stress/tension 15
allí *adv.* there 5
   allí mismo right there 14
almacén *m.* department store 6
almohada *f.* pillow 12
almorzar (o:ue) *v.* to have lunch 4
almuerzo *m.* lunch 8

aló *interj.* hello (*on the telephone*) 11
alquilar *v.* to rent 12
alquiler *m.* rent (payment) 12
alternador *m.* alternator 11
altillo *m.* attic 12
alto/a *adj.* tall 3
aluminio *m.* aluminum 13
ama de casa *m., f.* housekeeper; caretaker 12
amable *adj.* nice; friendly 5
amarillo/a *adj.* yellow 6
amigo/a *m., f.* friend 3
amistad *f.* friendship 9
amor *m.* love 9
anaranjado/a *adj.* orange 6
andar en patineta to skateboard 4
animal *m.* animal 13
aniversario (de bodas) *m.* (wedding) anniversary 9
anoche *adv.* last night 6
anteayer *adv.* the day before yesterday 6
antes *adv.* before 7
　antes (de) que *conj.* before 13
　antes de *prep.* before 7
antibiótico *m.* antibiotic 10
antipático/a *adj.* unpleasant 3
anunciar *v.* to announce; to advertise
anuncio *m.* advertisement
año *m.* year 5
el año pasado *last* year 6
apagar *v.* to turn off 11
aparato *m.* appliance
apartamento *m.* apartment 12
apellido *m.* last name 3
apenas *adv.* hardly; scarcely 10
aplaudir *v.* to applaud
apreciar *v.* to appreciate
aprender (a + *inf.*) *v.* to learn 3
apurarse *v.* to hurry; to rush 15
aquel, aquella *adj.* that; those (over there) 6
aquél, aquélla *pron.* that; those (over there) 6
aquello *neuter, pron.* that; that thing; that fact 6
aquellos/as *pl. adj.* that; those (over there) 6
aquéllos/as *pl. pron.* those (ones) (over there) 6
aquí *adv.* here 1
　Aquí está... Here it is... 5
　Aquí estamos en... Here we are at/in... 2
　aquí mismo right here 11
árbol *m.* tree 13
archivo *m.* file 11
armario *m.* closet 12
arqueólogo/a *m., f.* archaeologist
arquitecto/a *m., f.* architect
arrancar *v.* to start (*a car*) 11
arreglar *v.* to fix; to arrange 11; to neaten; to straighten up 12

arriba *adv.* up
arroba *f.* @ symbol 11
arroz *m.* rice 8
arte *m.* art 2
artes *f., pl.* arts
artesanía *f.* craftsmanship; crafts
artículo *m.* article
artista *m., f.* artist 3
artístico/a *adj.* artistic
arvejas *m.* peas 8
asado/a *adj.* roast 8
ascenso *m.* promotion
ascensor *m.* elevator 5
así *adv.* like this; so (*in such a way*) 10
　así así so so
asistir (a) *v.* to attend 3
aspiradora *f.* vacuum cleaner 12
aspirante *m. f.* candidate; applicant
aspirina *f.* aspirin 10
atún *m.* tuna 8
aumentar *v.* **de peso** to gain weight 15
aumento *m.* increase
　aumento de sueldo pay raise
aunque although
autobús *m.* bus 1
automático/a *adj.* automatic
auto(móvil) *m.* auto(mobile) 5
autopista *f.* highway 11
ave *f.* bird 13
avenida *f.* avenue
aventura *f.* adventure
　de aventura adventure (genre)
avergonzado/a *adj.* embarrassed 5
avión *m.* airplane 5
¡Ay! *interj.* Oh!
　¡Ay, qué dolor! Oh, what pain!
ayer *adv.* yesterday 6
ayudar(se) *v.* to help (each other) 11, 12
azúcar *m.* sugar 8
azul *adj. m., f.* blue 6

B

bailar *v.* to dance 2
bailarín/bailarina *m., f.* dancer
baile *m.* dance
bajar(se) de *v.* to get off of/out of (a vehicle) 11
bajo/a *adj.* short (*in height*) 3
bajo control under control 7
balcón *m.* balcony 12
baloncesto *m.* basketball 4
banana *f.* banana 8
banco *m.* bank 14
banda *f.* band

bandera *f.* flag
bañarse *v.* to bathe; to take a bath 7
baño *m.* bathroom 7
barato/a *adj.* cheap 6
barco *m.* boat 5
barrer *v.* to sweep 12
　barrer el suelo *v.* to sweep the floor 12
barrio *m.* neighborhood 12
bastante *adv.* enough; rather 10; pretty; quite 13
basura *f.* trash 12
baúl *m.* trunk 11
beber *v.* to drink 3
bebida *f.* drink 8
　bebida alcohólica *f.* alcoholic beverage 15
béisbol *m.* baseball 4
bellas artes *f., pl.* fine arts
belleza *f.* beauty 14
beneficio *m.* benefit
besar(se) *v.* to kiss (each other) 11
beso *m.* kiss 9
biblioteca *f.* library 2
bicicleta *f.* bicycle 4
bien *adj.* well 1
bienestar *m.* well-being 15
bienvenido(s)/a(s) *adj.* welcome 12
billete *m.* paper money; ticket
billón *m.* trillion
biología *f.* biology 2
bisabuelo/a *m.* great-grandfather/ great-grandmother 3
bistec *m.* steak 8
bizcocho *m.* biscuit
blanco/a *adj.* white 6
bluejeans *m., pl.* jeans 6
blusa *f.* blouse 6
boca *f.* mouth 10
boda *f.* wedding 9
boleto *m.* ticket
bolsa *f.* purse, bag 6
bombero/a *m., f.* firefighter
bonito/a *adj.* pretty 3
borrador *m.* eraser 2
borrar *v.* to erase 11
bosque *m.* forest 13
　bosque tropical tropical forest; rainforest 13
bota *f.* boot 6
botella *f.* bottle 9
　botella de vino bottle of wine 9
botones *m., f. sing.* bellhop 5
brazo *m.* arm 10
brindar *v.* to toast (*drink*) 9
bucear *v.* to scuba dive 4
bueno *adv.* well 2
buen, bueno/a *adj.* good 3, 6
　¡Buen viaje! Have a good trip! 1
　buena forma good shape (*physical*) 15
　Buena idea. Good idea. 4
　Buenas noches. Good evening;

Good night. 1
Buenas tardes. Good afternoon. 1
buenísimo extremely good
¿Bueno? Hello. (*on telephone*) 11
Buenos días. Good morning. 1
bulevar *m.* boulevard
buscar *v.* to look for 2
buzón *m.* mailbox 14

C

caballo *m.* horse 5
cabaña *f.* cabin 5
cabe: no cabe duda de there's no doubt 13
caber *v.* to fit
cabeza *f.* head 10
cada *adj. m., f.* each 6
caerse *v.* to fall (down) 10
café *m.* café 4; *adj. m., f.* brown 6; *m.* coffee 8
cafeína *f.* caffeine 14
cafetera *f.* coffee maker 12
cafetería *f.* cafeteria 2
caído/a *p.p.* fallen 13
caja *f.* cash register 6
cajero/a *m., f.* cashier 14
    cajero automático *m.* ATM 14
calcetín *m.* sock 6
calculadora *f.* calculator 11
caldo *m.* soup 8
    caldo de patas *m.* beef soup 8
calentarse *v.* to warm up 15
calidad *f.* quality 6
calle *f.* street 11
calor *m.* heat 4
caloría *f.* calorie 15
calzar *v.* to take size... shoes 6
cama *f.* bed 5
cámara digital *f.* digital camera 11
cámara de video *f.* videocamera 11
camarero/a *m., f.* waiter 8
camarón *m.* shrimp 8
cambiar (de/en) *v.* to change 9
cambio *m.* **de moneda** currency exchange
caminar *v.* to walk 2
camino *m.* road; path
camión *m* truck; bus
camisa *f.* shirt 6
camiseta *f.* t-shirt 6
campo *m.* countryside 5
canadiense *adj.* Canadian 3
canal *m.* channel (TV)
canción *f.* song
candidato/a *m., f.* candidate
cansado/a *adj.* tired 5
cantante *m., f.* singer
cantar *v.* to sing 2
capital *f.* capital (city) 1
capó *m.* hood 11
cara *f.* face 7

caramelo *m.* caramel 9
carne *f.* meat 8
    carne de res *f.* beef 8
carnicería *f.* butcher shop 14
caro/a *adj.* expensive 6
carpintero/a *m., f.* carpenter
carrera *f.* career
carretera *f.* highway 11
carro *m.* car; automobile 11
carta *f.* letter 4; (*playing*) card 5
cartel *m.* poster 12
cartera *f.* wallet 6
cartero *m.* mail carrier 14
casa *f.* house; home 2
casado/a *adj.* married 9
casarse (con) *v.* to get married (to) 9
casi *adv.* almost 10
catorce *adj.* fourteen 1
cazar *v.* to hunt 13
cebolla *f.* onion 8
cederrón *m.* CD-ROM 11
celebrar *v.* to celebrate 9
celular *adj.* cellular 11
cena *f.* dinner 8
cenar *v.* to have dinner 2
centro *m.* downtown 4
    centro comercial shopping mall 6
cepillarse los dientes/el pelo *v.* to brush one's teeth/one's hair 7
cerámica *f.* pottery
cerca de *prep.* near 2
cerdo *m.* pork 8
cereales *m., pl.* cereal; grains 8
cero *m.* zero 1
cerrado/a *adj.* closed 5, 14
cerrar (e:ie) *v.* to close 4
cerveza *f.* beer 8
césped *m.* grass 13
ceviche *m.* marinated fish dish 8
    ceviche de camarón *m.* lemon-marinated shrimp 8
chaleco *m.* vest
champán *m.* champagne 9
champiñón *m.* mushroom 8
champú *m.* shampoo 7
chaqueta *f.* jacket 6
chau *fam. interj.* bye 1
cheque *m.* (bank) check 14
    cheque (de viajero) *m.* (traveler's) check 14
chévere *adj., fam.* terrific
chico/a *adj.* boy/girl 1
chino/a *adj.* Chinese 3
chocar (con) *v.* to run into
chocolate *m.* chocolate 9
choque *m.* collision
chuleta *f.* chop (*food*) 8
    chuleta de cerdo *f.* pork chop 8
cibercafé *m.* cybercafé 11
ciclismo *m.* cycling 4
cielo *m.* sky 13
cien(to) one hundred 2, 6

ciencia *f.* science 2
    de ciencia ficción *f.* science fiction (genre)
científico/a *m., f.* scientist
cierto *m.* certain 13
    Es cierto. It's certain. 13
    No es cierto. It's not certain. 13
cinco five 1
cincuenta fifty 2
cine *m.* movie theater 4
cinta *f.* (audio)tape
cinta caminadora *f.* treadmill 15
cinturón *m.* belt 6
circulación *f.* traffic 11
cita *f.* date; appointment 9
ciudad *f.* city 4
ciudadano/a *m., f.* citizen
Claro (que sí). *fam.* Of course.
clase *f.* class 2
    clase de ejercicios aeróbicos *f.* aerobics class 15
clásico/a *adj.* classical
cliente/a *m., f.* customer 6
clínica *f.* clinic 10
cobrar *v.* to cash (a check) 14
coche *m.* car; automobile 11
cocina *f.* kitchen; stove 12
cocinar *v.* to cook 12
cocinero/a *m., f.* cook, chef
cofre *m.* hood 14
cola *f.* line 14
colesterol *m.* cholesterol 15
color *m.* color 6
comedia *f.* comedy; play
comedor *m.* dining room 12
comenzar (e:ie) *v.* to begin 4
comer *v.* to eat 3
comercial *adj.* commercial; business-related
comida *f.* food; meal 8
como like; as 8
¿cómo? what?; how? 1
    ¿Cómo es...? What's... like? 3
    ¿Cómo está usted? *form.* How are you? 1
    ¿Cómo estás? *fam.* How are you? 1
    ¿Cómo les fue...? *pl.* How did ... go for you? 15
    ¿Cómo se llama (usted)? (*form.*) What's your name? 1
    ¿Cómo te llamas (tú)? (*fam.*) What's your name? 1
cómoda *f.* chest of drawers 12
cómodo/a *adj.* comfortable 5
compañero/a de clase *m., f.* classmate 2
compañero/a de cuarto *m., f.* roommate 2
compañía *f.* company; firm
compartir *v.* to share 3
completamente *adv.* completely
compositor(a) *m., f.* composer
comprar *v.* to buy 2
compras *f., pl.* purchases 5

ir de compras go shopping 5
comprender *v.* to understand 3
comprobar *v.* to check
comprometerse (con) *v.* to get engaged (to) 9
computación *f.* computer science 2
computadora *f.* computer 1
computadora portátil *f.* portable computer; laptop 11
comunicación *f.* communication
comunicarse (con) *v.* to communicate (with)
comunidad *f.* community 1
con *prep.* with 2
  Con él/ella habla. This is he/she. (*on telephone*) 11
  con frecuencia *adv.* frequently 10
  Con permiso. Pardon me; Excuse me. 1
  con tal (de) que provided (that) 13
concierto *m.* concert
concordar *v.* to agree
concurso *m.* game show; contest
conducir *v.* to drive 8, 11
conductor(a) *m., f.* driver 1
confirmar *v.* to confirm 5
confirmar *v.* **una reservación** *f.* to confirm a reservation 5
confundido/a *adj.* confused 5
congelador *m.* freezer 12
congestionado/a *adj.* congested; stuffed-up 10
conmigo *pron.* with me 4, 9
conocer *v.* to know; to be acquainted with 8
conocido *adj.; p.p.* known
conseguir (e:i) *v.* to get; to obtain 4
consejero/a *m., f.* counselor; advisor
consejo *m.* advice 6
conservación *f.* conservation 13
conservar *v.* to conserve 13
construir *v.* to build
consultorio *m.* doctor's office 10
consumir *v.* to consume 15
contabilidad *f.* accounting 2
contador(a) *m., f.* accountant
contaminación *f.* pollution 13
  contaminación del aire/del agua air/water pollution 13
contaminado/a *adj.* polluted 13
contaminar *v.* to pollute 13
contar *v.* to count; to tell 4
contar (con) *v.* to count (on) 12
contento/a *adj.* happy; content 5
contestadora *f.* answering machine 11
contestar *v.* to answer 2
contigo *fam. pron.* with you 9
contratar *v.* to hire
control *m.* control 7
  control remoto remote control 11
controlar *v.* to control 13

conversación *f.* conversation 2
conversar *v.* to converse, to chat 2
copa *f.* wineglass; goblet 12
corazón *m.* heart 10
corbata *f.* tie 6
corredor(a) *m., f.* **de bolsa** stockbroker
correo *m.* mail; post office 14
  correo electrónico *m.* e-mail 4
correr *v.* to run 3
cortesía *f.* courtesy
cortinas *f., pl.* curtains 12
corto/a *adj.* short (*in length*) 6
cosa *f.* thing 1
costar (o:ue) *f.* to cost 6
cráter *m.* crater 13
creer *v.* to believe 13
  creer (en) *v.* to believe (in) 3
  no creer (en) *v.* not to believe (in) 13
creído/a *adj., p.p.* believed 13
crema de afeitar *f.* shaving cream 7
crimen *m.* crime; murder
cruzar *v.* to cross 14
cuaderno *m.* notebook 1
cuadra *f.* (city) block 14
¿cuál(es)? which?; which ones? 2
  ¿Cuál es la fecha (de hoy)? What is the date (today)? 5
cuadro *m.* picture 12
cuadros *m., pl.* plaid 6
cuando when 7; 13
¿cuándo? when? 2
¿cuánto(s)/a(s)? how much/how many? 1
  ¿Cuánto cuesta...? How much does... cost? 6
  ¿Cuántos años tienes? How old are you? 3
cuarenta forty 2
cuarto de baño *m.* bathroom 7
cuarto *m.* room 7; 12
cuarto/a *adj.* fourth 5
  menos cuarto quarter to (time)
  y cuarto quarter after (time) 1
cuatro four 1
cuatrocientos/as *m., f.* four hundred 6
cubiertos *m., pl.* silverware
cubierto/a *p.p.* covered
cubrir *v.* to cover
cuchara *f.* (table or large) spoon 12
cuchillo *m.* knife 12
cuello *m.* neck 10
cuenta *f.* bill 9; account 14
  cuenta corriente *f.* checking account 14
  cuenta de ahorros *f.* savings account 14
cuento *m.* story
cuerpo *m.* body 10
cuidado *m.* care 3
cuidar *v.* to take care of 13
  ¡Cuídense! Take care! 14

cultura *f.* culture
cumpleaños *m., sing.* birthday 9
cumplir años *v.* to have a birthday 9
cuñado/a *m., f.* brother-in-law; sister-in-law 3
currículum *m.* résumé
curso *m.* course 2

D

danza *f.* dance
dañar *v.* to damage; to breakdown 10
dar *v.* to give 6, 9
  dar direcciones *v.* to give directions 14
  dar consejos *v.* to give advice 6
  darse con *v.* to bump into; to run into (something) 10
  darse prisa *v.* to hurry; to rush 15
de *prep.* of; from 1
  ¿De dónde eres? *fam.* Where are you from? 1
  ¿De dónde es usted? *form.* Where are you from? 1
  ¿De parte de quién? Who is calling? (*on telephone*) 11
  ¿de quién...? whose...? (*sing.*) 1
  ¿de quiénes...? whose...? (*pl.*) 1
  de algodón (made of) cotton 6
  de aluminio (made of) aluminum 13
  de buen humor in a good mood 5
  de compras shopping 5
  de cuadros plaid 6
  de excursión hiking 4
  de hecho in fact
  de ida y vuelta roundtrip 5
  de la mañana in the morning; A.M. 1
  de la noche in the evening; at night; P.M. 1
  de la tarde in the afternoon; in the early evening; P.M. 1
  de lana (made of) wool 6
  de lunares polka-dotted 6
  de mal humor in a bad mood 5
  de mi vida of my life 15
  de moda in fashion 6
  De nada. You're welcome. 1
  De ninguna manera. No way.
  de niño/a as a child 10
  de parte de on behalf of 11
  de plástico (made of) plastic 13
  de rayas striped 6
  de repente suddenly 6
  de seda (made of) silk 6
  de vaqueros western (genre)
  de vez en cuando from time to time 10
  de vidrio (made of) glass 13

debajo de *prep.* below; under 2
deber (+ *infin.*) *v.* should; must 3;
  Debe ser... It must be... 6
deber *m.* responsibility; obligation
debido a due to (the fact that)
débil *adj.* weak 15
decidido/a *adj.* decided 14
decidir (+ *infin.*) *v.* (to decide) 3
décimo/a *adj.* tenth 5
decir *v.* **(que)** to say (that);
  to tell (that) 4, 9
  decir la verdad to tell the
    truth 4
  decir mentiras to tell lies 4
  decir que to say that 4
declarar *v.* to declare; to say
dedo *m.* finger 10
deforestación *f.* deforestation 13
dejar *v.* to let 12; to quit; to leave
  behind
  dejar de *(+ inf.)* *v.* to stop
    (*doing something*) 13
  dejar una propina *v.* to leave
    a tip 9
del (*contraction of* **de** + **el**) of
  the; from the 1
delante de *prep.* in front of 2
delgado/a *adj.* thin; slender 3
delicioso/a *adj.* delicious 8
demás *adj.* the rest
demasiado *adj., adv.* too much 6
dentista *m., f.* dentist 10
dentro de (diez años) within
  (ten years); inside
dependiente/a *m., f.* clerk 6
deporte *m.* sport 4
deportista *m.* sports person
deportivo/a *adj.* sports-related 4
depositar *v.* to deposit 14
derecha *f.* right 2
derecho *adj.* straight (ahead) 14
  a la derecha de to the right of 2
derechos *m.* rights
desarrollar *v.* to develop 13
desastre (natural) *m.* (natural)
  disaster
desayunar *v.* to have breakfast 2
desayuno *m.* breakfast 8
descafeinado/a *adj.* decaffeinated 15
descansar *v.* to rest 2
descargar *v.* to download 11
descompuesto/a *adj.* not working; out-of-order 11
describir *v.* to describe 3
descrito/a *p.p.* described 13
descubierto/a *p.p.* discovered 13
descubrir *v.* to discover 13
desde from 6
desear *v.* to wish; to desire 2
desempleo *m.* unemployment
desierto *m.* desert 13
(des)igualdad *f.* (in)equality
desordenado/a *adj.* disorderly 5
despacio *adv.* slowly 10

despedida *f.* farewell; goodbye
despedir (e:i) *v.* to fire
despedirse (de) (e:i) *v.* to say
  goodbye (to) 7
despejado/a *adj.* clear (*weather*)
despertador *m.* alarm clock 7
despertarse (e:ie) *v.* to wake up 7
después *adv.* afterwards; then 7
  después de after 7
  después de que *conj.* after 13
destruir *v.* to destroy 13
detrás de *prep.* behind 2
día *m.* day 1
día de fiesta holiday 9
diario *m.* diary 1; newspaper
diario/a *adj.* daily 7
dibujar *v.* to draw 2
dibujo *m.* drawing
  dibujos animados *m., pl.* car-
    toons
diccionario *m.* dictionary 1
dicho/a *p.p.* said 13
diciembre *m.* December 5
dictadura *f.* dictatorship
diecinueve nineteen 1
dieciocho eighteen 1
dieciséis sixteen 1
diecisiete seventeen 1
diente *m.* tooth 7
dieta *f.* diet 15
  comer una dieta equilibrada
    to eat a balanced diet 15
diez ten 1
difícil *adj.* difficult; hard 3
Diga. Hello. (*on telephone*) 11
diligencia *f.* errand 14
dinero *m.* money 6
dirección *f.* address 14
  dirección electrónica *f.* e-mail
    address 11
direcciones *f., pl.* directions 14
director(a) *m., f.* director; (*musical*) conductor
dirigir *v.* to direct
disco compacto compact disc
  (CD) 11
discriminación *f.* discrimination
discurso *m.* speech
diseñador(a) *m., f.* designer
diseño *m.* design
disfrutar (de) *v.* to enjoy; to reap
  the benefits (of) 15
diversión *f.* fun activity; entertainment; recreation 4
divertido/a *adj.* fun 7
divertirse (e:ie) *v.* to have fun 9
divorciado/a *adj.* divorced 9
divorciarse (de) *v.* to get
  divorced (from) 9
divorcio *m.* divorce 9
doblar *v.* to turn 14
doble *adj.* double
doce twelve 1
doctor(a) *m., f.* doctor 3
documental *m.* documentary

documentos de viaje *m., pl.*
  travel documents
doler (o:ue) *v.* to hurt 10
dolor *m.* ache; pain 10
  dolor de cabeza *m.* headache 10
doméstico/a *adj.* domestic 12
domingo *m.* Sunday 2
don/doña *title of respect used
  with a person's first name* 1
donde *prep.* where
  ¿Dónde está...? Where is...? 2
  ¿dónde? where? 1
dormir (o:ue) *v.* to sleep 4
dormirse (o:ue) *v.* to go to sleep;
  to fall asleep 7
dormitorio *m.* bedroom 12
dos two 1
  dos veces *f.* twice; two times 6
doscientos/as two hundred 6
drama *m.* drama; play
dramático/a *adj.* dramatic
dramaturgo/a *m., f.* playwright
droga *f.* drug 15
drogadicto/a *adj.* drug addict 15
ducha *f.* shower 7
ducharse *v.* to shower; to take a
  shower 7
duda *f.* doubt 13
dudar *v.* to doubt 13
  no dudar *v.* not to doubt 13
dueño/a *m., f.* owner; landlord 8
dulces *m., pl.* sweets; candy 9
durante *prep.* during 7
durar *v.* to last

E

e *conj.* (*used instead of* **y** *before
  words beginning with* **i** *and* **hi**)
  and 4
echar *v.* to throw 14
  echar (una carta) al buzón *v.*
    to throw (a letter) in the
    mailbox 14
ecología *f.* ecology 13
economía *f.* economics 2
ecoturismo *m.* ecotourism 13
Ecuador *m.* Ecuador 1
ecuatoriano/a *adj.* Ecuadorian 3
edad *f.* age 9
edificio *m.* building 12
(en) efectivo *m.* cash 6
ejercicio *m.* exercise 15
  ejercicios aeróbicos *m.*
    aerobic exercises 15
  ejercicios de estiramiento
    stretching exercises 15
ejército *m.* army
el *m., sing., def. art.* the 1
él *sub. pron.* he 1; *adj. pron.* him
elecciones *f. pl.* election
electricista *m., f.* electrician
electrodoméstico *m.* electric
  appliance 12

elegante *adj. m., f.* elegant 6
elegir *v.* to elect
ella *sub. pron.* she 1; *obj. pron.* her
ellos/as *sub. pron.* they 1; them 1
embarazada *adj.* pregnant 10
emergencia *f.* emergency 10
emitir *v.* to broadcast
emocionante *adj. m., f.* exciting
empezar (e:ie) *v.* to begin 4
empleado/a *m., f.* employee 5
empleo *m.* job; employment
empresa *f.* company; firm
en *prep.* in; on 2
　en casa at home 7
　en caso (de) que in case
　　(that) 13
　en cuanto as soon as 13
　en efectivo in cash 14
　en exceso in excess; too
　　much 15
　en línea in-line 4
　¡En marcha! Let's get going! 15
　en mi nombre in my name
　en punto on the dot; exactly;
　　sharp (*time*) 1
　en qué in what; how 2
　¿En qué puedo servirles?
　　How can I help you? 5
enamorado/a (de) *adj.* in love
　(with) 5
enamorarse (de) *v.* to fall in love
　(with) 9
encantado/a *adj.* delighted;
　pleased to meet you 1
encantar *v.* to like very much; to
　love (*inanimate things*) 7
　¡Me encantó! I loved it! 15
encima de *prep.* on top of 2
encontrar (o:ue) *v.* to find 4
encontrar(se) (o:ue) *v.* to meet
　(each other); to run into (each
　other) 11
encuesta *f.* poll; survey
energía *f.* energy 13
　energía nuclear nuclear
　　energy 13
　energía solar solar energy 13
enero *m.* January 5
enfermarse *v.* to get sick 10
enfermedad *f.* illness 10
enfermero/a *m., f.* nurse 10
enfermo/a *adj.* sick 10
enfrente de *adv.* opposite; facing 14
engordar *v.* to gain weight 15
enojado/a *adj.* mad; angry 5
enojarse (con) *v.* to get angry
　(with) 7
ensalada *f.* salad 8
enseguida *adv.* right away 9
enseñar *v.* to teach 2
ensuciar *v.* to get (something)
　dirty 12
entender (e:ie) *v.* to understand 4
entonces *adv.* then 7
entrada *f.* entrance 12; ticket
entre *prep.* between; among 2

entremeses *m., pl.* hors
　d'oeuvres 8
entrenador(a) *m., f.* trainer 15
entrenarse *v.* to practice; to train 15
entrevista *f.* interview
entrevistador(a) *m., f.* interviewer
entrevistar *v.* to interview
envase *m.* container 13
enviar *v.* to send; to mail 14
equilibrado/a *adj.* balanced 15
equipado/a *adj.* equipped 15
equipaje *m.* luggage 5
equipo *m.* team 4
equivocado/a *adj.* wrong 5
eres *fam.* you are 1
es he/she/it is 1
　Es bueno que... It's good
　　that... 12
　Es de... He/She is from... 1
　Es extraño It's strange 13
　Es importante que... It's
　　important that... 12
　Es imposible It's impossible 13
　Es improbable It's
　　improbable 13
　Es malo que... It's bad
　　that... 12
　Es mejor que... It's better
　　that... 12
　Es necesario que... It's
　　necessary that... 12
　Es obvio. It's obvious. 13
　Es ridículo. It's ridiculous. 13
　Es seguro. It's sure. 13
　Es terrible. It's terrible. 13
　Es triste. It's sad. 13
　Es urgente que... It's urgent
　　that... 12
　Es la una. It's one o'clock. 1
　Es una lástima. It's a
　　shame. 13
　Es verdad. It's true. 13
esa(s) *f., adj.* that; those 6
ésa(s) *f., pron.* those (ones) 6
escalar *v.* to climb 4
　escalar montañas *v.* to climb
　　mountains 4
escalera *f.* stairs; stairway 12
escoger *v.* to choose 8
escribir *v.* to write 3
　escribir un mensaje
　　electrónico to write an
　　e-mail message 4
　escribir una carta to write a
　　letter 4
　escribir una (tarjeta) postal
　　to write a postcard 4
escrito/a *p.p.* written 13
escritor(a) *m., f* writer
escritorio *m.* desk 2
escuchar *v.* to listen to
　escuchar la radio to listen (to)
　　the radio 2
　escuchar música to listen (to)
　　music 2
escuela *f.* school 1

esculpir *v.* to sculpt
escultor(a) *m., f.* sculptor
escultura *f.* sculpture
ese *m., sing., adj.* that 6
ése *m., sing., pron.* that (one) 6
eso *neuter, pron.* that;
　that thing 6
esos *m., pl., adj.* those 6
ésos *m., pl., pron.* those (ones) 6
España *f.* Spain 1
español *m.* Spanish (*language*) 2
español(a) *adj. m., f.* Spanish 3
espárragos *m., pl.* asparagus 8
especialización *f.* major 2
espectacular *adj.* spectacular 15
espectáculo *m.* show
espejo *m.* mirror 7
esperar *v.* to hope; to wish 13
　esperar (+ infin.) *v.* to wait
　　(for); to hope 2
esposo/a *m., f.* husband/wife;
　spouse 3
esquí (acuático) *m.* (water)
　skiing 4
esquiar *v.* to ski 4
esquina *m.* corner 14
está he/she/it is, you are
　Está (muy) despejado. It's
　　(very) clear. (*weather*)
　Está (muy) nublado. It's
　　(very) cloudy. (*weather*) 5
　Está bien. That's fine. 11
esta(s) *f., adj.* this; these 6
　esta noche tonight 4
ésta(s) *f., pron.* this (one); these
　(ones) 6
　Ésta es... *f.* This is...
　　(*introducing someone*) 1
establecer *v.* to start, to establish
estación *f.* station; season 5
　estación de autobuses
　　bus station 5
　estación del metro subway
　　station 5
　estación de tren train
　　station 5
estacionamiento *m.* parking
　lot 14
estacionar *v.* to park 11
estadio *m.* stadium 2
estado civil *m.* marital status 9
Estados Unidos *m.* (EE.UU.;
　E.U.) United States 1
estadounidense *adj. m., f.* from
　the United States 3
estampado/a *adj.* print
estampilla *f.* stamp 14
estante *m.* bookcase;
　bookshelves 12
estar *v.* to be 2
　estar a (veinte kilómetros)
　　de aquí. to be (20 kilometers)
　　from here 11
　estar a dieta to be on a diet 15
　estar aburrido/a to be
　　bored 5

estar afectado/a (por) to be affected (by) 13
estar bajo control to be under control 7
estar cansado/a to be tired 5
estar contaminado/a to be polluted 13
estar de acuerdo to agree
  Estoy (completamente) de acuerdo. I agree (completely)
  No estoy de acuerdo. I don't agree.
estar de moda to be in fashion 6
estar de vacaciones *f., pl.* to be on vacation 5
estar en buena forma to be in good shape 15
estar enfermo/a to be sick 10
estar listo/a to be ready 15
estar perdido/a to be lost 14
estar roto/a to be broken 10
estar seguro/a to be sure 5
estar torcido/a to be twisted; to be sprained 10
  No está nada mal. It's not at all bad. 5
estatua *f.* statue
este *m.* east 14; umm
este *m., sing., adj.* this 6
éste *m., sing., pron.* this (one) 6
  Éste es... *m.* This is... (introducing someone) 1
estéreo *m.* stereo 11
estilo *m.* style
estiramiento *m.* stretching 15
esto *neuter pron.* this; this thing 6
estómago *m.* stomach 10
estornudar *v.* to sneeze 10
estos *m., pl., adj.* these 6
éstos *m., pl., pron.* these (ones) 6
estrella *f.* star 13
  estrella de cine *m., f.* movie star
estrés *m.* stress 15
estudiante *m., f.* student 1, 2
estudiantil *adj. m., f.* student 2
estudiar *v.* to study 2
estufa *f.* stove 12
estupendo/a *adj.* stupendous 5
etapa *f.* stage 9
evitar *v.* to avoid 13
examen *m.* test; exam 2
  examen médico physical exam 10
excelente *adj. m., f.* excellent 5
exceso *m.* excess; too much 15
excursión *f.* hike; tour; excursion 4
excursionista *m., f.* hiker 4
éxito *m.* success
experiencia *f.* experience
explicar *v.* to explain 2
explorar *v.* to explore
expresión *f.* expression

extinción *f.* extinction 13
extranjero/a *adj.* foreign
extraño/a *adj.* strange 13

F

fabuloso/a *adj* fabulous 5
fácil *adj.* easy 3
falda *f.* skirt 6
faltar *v.* to lack; to need 7
familia *f.* family 3
famoso/a *adj.* famous
farmacia *f.* pharmacy 10
fascinar *v.* to fascinate 7
favorito/a *adj.* favorite 4
fax *m.* fax (machine) 11
febrero *m.* February 5
fecha *f.* date 5
feliz *adj.* happy 5
  ¡Felicidades! Congratulations! (*for an event such as a birthday or anniversary*) 9
  ¡Felicitaciones! Congratulations! (*for an event such as an engagement or a good grade on a test*) 9
  ¡Feliz cumpleaños! Happy birthday! 9
fenomenal *adj.* great, phenomenal 5
feo/a *adj.* ugly 3
festival *m.* festival
fiebre *f.* fever 10
fiesta *f.* party 9
fijo/a *adj.* fixed, set 6
fin *m.* end 4
  fin de semana weekend 4
finalmente *adv.* finally 15
firmar *v.* to sign (*a document*) 14
física *f.* physics 2
flan (de caramelo) *m.* baked (caramel) custard 9
flexible *adj.* flexible 15
flor *f.* flower 13
folklórico/a *adj.* folk; folkloric
folleto *m.* brochure
fondo *m.* end 12
forma *f.* shape 15
formulario *m.* form 14
foto(grafía) *f.* photograph 1
francés, francesa *adj. m., f.* French 3
frecuentemente *adv.* frequently 10
frenos *m., pl.* brakes
fresco/a *adj.* cool 5
frijoles *m., pl.* beans 8
frío/a *adj.* cold 5
frito/a *adj.* fried 8
fruta *f.* fruit 8
frutería *f.* fruit store 14
frutilla *f.* strawberry 8
fuente de fritada *f.* platter of fried food
fuera *adv.* outside
fuerte *adj. m., f.* strong 15

fumar *v.* to smoke 15
  (no) fumar *v.* (not) to smoke 15
funcionar *v.* to work; to function 11
fútbol *m.* soccer 4
  fútbol americano *m.* football 4
futuro/a *adj.* future
  en el futuro in the future

G

gafas (de sol) *f., pl.* (sun)glasses 6
gafas (oscuras) *f., pl.* (sun)glasses 6
galleta *f.* cookie 9
ganar *v.* to win 4; to earn (money)
ganga *f.* bargain 6
garaje *m.* garage; (mechanic's) repair shop; 11 garage (*in a house*) 12
garganta *f.* throat 10
gasolina *f.* gasoline 11
gasolinera *f.* gas station 11
gastar *v.* to spend (*money*) 6
gato *m.* cat 13
gemelo/a *m., f.* twin 3
gente *f.* people 3
geografía *f.* geography 2
gerente *m., f.* manager
gimnasio *m.* gymnasium 4
gobierno *m.* government 13
golf *m.* golf 4
gordo/a *adj.* fat 3
grabadora *f.* tape recorder 1
grabar *v.* to record 11
gracias *f., pl.* thank you; thanks 1
  Gracias por todo. Thanks for everything. 9, 15
  Gracias una vez más. Thanks again. 9
graduarse (de/en) *v.* to graduate (from/in) 9
gran, grande *adj.* big 3
grasa *f.* fat 15
gratis *adj. m., f.* free of charge 14
grave *adj.* grave; serious 10
gravísimo/a *adj.* extremely serious 13
grillo *m.* cricket
gripe *f.* flu 10
gris *adj. m., f.* gray 6
gritar *v.* to scream 7
guantes *m., pl.* gloves 6
guapo/a *adj.* handsome; good-looking 3
guardar *v.* to save (on a computer) 11
guerra *f.* war
guía *m., f.* guide
gustar *v.* to be pleasing to; to like 7
  Me gustaría... I would like...
gusto *m.* pleasure
  El gusto es mío. The pleasure is mine. 1

Gusto de verlo/la. *(form.)* It's nice to see you.
Gusto de verte. *(fam.)* It's nice to see you.
Mucho gusto. Pleased to meet you. 1
¡Qué gusto volver a verlo/la! *(form.)* I'm happy to see you again!
¡Qué gusto volver a verte! *(fam.)* I'm happy to see you again!

H

haber *(aux.)* *v.* to have *(done something)* 15
   Ha sido un placer. It's been a pleasure. 15
habitación *f.* room 5
   habitación doble double room 5
   habitación individual single room 5
hablar *v.* to talk; to speak 2
hacer *v.* to do; to make; 4
   Hace buen tiempo. The weather is good. 5
   Hace (mucho) calor. It's (very) hot. *(weather)* 5
   Hace fresco. It's cool. *(weather)* 5
   Hace (mucho) frío. It's very cold. *(weather)* 5
   Hace mal tiempo. The weather is bad. 5
   Hace (mucho) sol. It's (very) sunny. *(weather)* 5
   Hace (mucho) viento. It's (very) windy. *(weather)* 5
   hacer cola to stand in line 14
   hacer diligencias to run errands 14
   hacer ejercicio to exercise 15
   hacer ejercicios aeróbicos to do aerobics 15
   hacer ejercicios de estiramiento to do stretching exercises 15
   hacer el papel (de) to play the role (of)
   hacer gimnasia to work out 15
   hacer juego (con) to match (with) 6
   hacer la cama to make the bed 12
   hacer las maletas to pack (one's) suitcases 5
   hacer quehaceres domésticos to do household chores 12
   hacer turismo to go sightseeing 5
   hacer un viaje to take a trip 5
   hacer una excursión to go on a hike; to go on a tour 5

hacia *prep.* toward 14
hambre *f.* hunger 3
hamburguesa *f.* hamburger 8
hasta *prep.* until 6; toward
   Hasta la vista. See you later. 1
   Hasta luego. See you later. 1
   Hasta mañana. See you tomorrow. 1
   hasta que until 13
   Hasta pronto. See you soon. 1
hay there is; there are 1
   Hay (mucha) contaminación. It's (very) smoggy.
   Hay (mucha) niebla. It's (very) foggy. 5
   Hay que It is necessary that
   No hay duda de There's no doubt 13
   No hay de qué. You're welcome. 1
hecho/a *p.p.* done 13
heladería *f.* ice cream shop 14
helado/a *adj.* iced 8
helado *m.* ice cream 9
hermanastro/a *m., f.* stepbrother/stepsister 3
hermano/a *m., f.* brother/sister 3
hermano/a mayor/menor *m., f.* older/younger brother/sister 3
hermanos *m., pl.* siblings (brothers and sisters) 3
hermoso/a *adj.* beautiful 6
hierba *f.* grass 13
hijastro/a *m., f.* stepson/stepdaughter 3
hijo/a *m., f.* son/daughter 3
   hijo/a único/a *m., f.* only child 3
   hijos *m., pl.* children 3
historia *f.* history 2; story
hockey *m.* hockey 4
hola *interj.* hello; hi 1
hombre *m.* man 1
   hombre de negocios *m.* businessman
hora *f.* hour 1; the time
horario *m.* schedule 2
horno *m.* oven 12
   horno de microondas *m.* microwave oven 12
horror *m.* horror
   de horror horror (genre)
hospital *m.* hospital 10
hotel *m.* hotel 5
hoy *adv.* today 2
   hoy día *adv.* nowadays
   Hoy es... Today is... 2
huelga *f.* strike (labor)
hueso *m.* bone 10
huésped *m., f.* guest 5
huevo *m.* egg 8
humanidades *f., pl.* humanities 2
huracán *m.* hurricane

I

ida *f.* one way *(travel)*
idea *f.* idea 4
iglesia *f.* church 4
igualdad *f.* equality
igualmente *adv.* likewise 1
impermeable *m.* raincoat 6
importante *adj. m., f.* important 3
importar *v.* to be important to; to matter 7
imposible *adj. m., f.* impossible 13
impresora *f.* printer 11
imprimir *v.* to print 11
improbable *adj. m., f.* improbable 13
impuesto *m.* tax
incendio *m.* fire
increíble *adj. m., f.* incredible 5
individual *adj.* private *(room)* 5
infección *f.* infection 10
informar *v.* to inform
informe *m.* report; paper *(written work)*
ingeniero/a *m., f.* engineer 3
inglés *m.* English *(language)* 2
inglés, inglesa *adj.* English 3
inodoro *m.* toilet 6
insistir (en) *v.* to insist (on) 12
inspector(a) de aduanas *m., f.* customs inspector 5
inteligente *adj. m., f.* intelligent 3
intercambiar *v.* to exchange
interesante *adj. m., f.* interesting 3
interesar *v.* to be interesting to; to interest 7
(inter)nacional *adj. m., f.* (inter)national
Internet *m.* Internet 11
inundación *f.* flood
invertir (e:ie) *v.* to invest
invierno *m.* winter 5
invitado/a *m., f.* guest *(at a function)* 9
invitar *v.* to invite 9
inyección *f.* injection 10
ir *v.* to go 4
   ir a (+ *inf.*) to be going to do something 4
   ir de compras to go shopping 5
   ir de excursión (a las montañas) to go for a hike (in the mountains) 4
   ir de pesca to go fishing 5
   ir de vacaciones to go on vacation 5
   ir en autobús to go by bus 5
   ir en auto(móvil) to go by auto(mobile); to go by car 5
   ir en avión to go by plane 5
   ir en barco to go by boat 5
   ir en metro to go by subway 5
   ir en motocicleta to go by

motorcycle 5
ir en taxi to go by taxi 5
ir en tren to go by train 5
irse *v.* to go away; to leave 7
italiano/a *adj.* Italian 3
izquierdo/a *adj.* left 2
a la izquierda de to the left of 2

J

jabón *m.* soap 7
jamás *adv.* never; not ever 7
jamón *m.* ham 8
japonés, japonesa *adj.* Japanese 3
jardín *m.* garden; yard 12
jefe, jefa *m., f.* boss
joven *adj. m., f.* young 3
joven *m., f.* youth; young person 1
joyería *f.* jewelry store 14
jubilarse *v.* to retire (*from work*) 9
juego *m.* game
jueves *m., sing.* Thursday 2
jugador(a) *m., f.* player 4
jugar (u:ue) *v.* to play 4
jugar a las cartas *f. pl.* to play cards 5
jugo *m.* juice 8
jugo de fruta *m.* fruit juice 8
julio *m.* July 5
jungla *f.* jungle 13
junio *m.* June 5
juntos/as *adj.* together 9
juventud *f.* youth 9

K

kilómetro *m.* kilometer 11

L

la *f., sing., def. art.* the 1
la *f., sing., d.o. pron.* her, it, *form.* you 5
laboratorio *m.* laboratory 2
lago *m.* lake 13
lámpara *f.* lamp 12
lana *f.* wool 6
langosta *f.* lobster 8
lápiz *m.* pencil 1
largo/a *adj.* long (*in length*) 6
las *f., pl., def. art.* the 1
las *f., pl., d.o.pron.* them; *form.* you 5
lástima *f.* shame 13
lastimarse *v.* to injure oneself 10
lastimarse el pie to injure one's foot 10
lata *f.* (*tin*) can 13
lavabo *m.* sink 7

lavadora *f.* washing machine 12
lavandería *f.* laundromat 14
lavaplatos *m., sing.* dishwasher 12
lavar *v.* to wash 12
lavarse *v.* to wash oneself 7
lavarse la cara to wash one's face 7
lavarse las manos to wash one's hands 7
le *sing., i.o. pron.* to/for him, her, *form.* you 6
Le presento a... *form.* I would like to introduce... to you. 1
lección *f.* lesson 1
leche *f.* milk 8
lechuga *f.* lettuce 8
leer *v.* to read 3
leer correo electrónico to read e-mail 4
leer un periódico to read a newspaper 4
leer una revista to read a magazine 4
leído/a *p.p.* read 13
lejos de *prep.* far from 2
lengua *f.* language 2
lenguas extranjeras *f., pl.* foreign languages 2
lentes de contacto *m., pl.* contact lenses 6
lentes (de sol) (sun)glasses 6
lento/a *adj.* slow 11
les *pl., i.o. pron.* to/for them, *form.* you 6
letrero *m.* sign 14
levantar *v.* to lift 15
levantar pesas to lift weights 15
levantarse *v.* to get up 7
ley *f.* law 13
libertad *f.* liberty; freedom
libre *adj. m., f.* free 4
librería *f.* bookstore 2
libro *m.* book 2
licencia de conducir *f.* driver's license 11
limón *m.* lemon 8
limpiar *v.* to clean 12
limpiar la casa *v.* to clean the house 12
limpio/a *adj.* clean 5
línea *f.* line 4
listo/a *adj.* ready; smart 5
literatura *f.* literature 2
llamar *v.* to call 11
llamar por teléfono to call on the phone
llamarse *v.* to be called; to be named 7
llanta *f.* tire 11
llave *f.* key 5
llegada *f.* arrival 5
llegar *v.* to arrive 2
llenar *v.* to fill 11, 14
llenar el tanque to fill the

tank 11
llenar (un formulario) to fill out (a form) 14
lleno/a *adj.* full 11
llevar *v.* to carry 2; *v.* to wear; to take 6
llevar una vida sana to lead a healthy lifestyle 15
llevarse bien/mal (con) to get along well/badly (with) 9
llover (o:ue) *v.* to rain 5
Llueve. It's raining. 5
lluvia *f.* rain 13
lluvia ácida acid rain 13
lo *m., sing. d.o. pronoun.* him, it, *form.* you 5
¡Lo hemos pasado de película! We've had a great time!
¡Lo hemos pasado maravillosamente! We've had a great time!
lo mejor the best (thing)
Lo pasamos muy bien. We had a good time.
lo peor the worst (thing)
lo que that which; what 12
Lo siento. I'm sorry. 1
Lo siento muchísimo. I'm so sorry. 4
loco/a *adj.* crazy 6
locutor(a) *m., f.* (TV or radio) announcer
lomo a la plancha *m.* grilled flank steak 8
los *m., pl., def. art.* the 1
los *m.pl., d.o. pron.* them, *form.* you 5
luchar (contra/por) *v.* to fight; to struggle (against/for)
luego *adv.* then 7; *adv.* later 1
lugar *m.* place 4
luna *f.* moon 13
lunares *m.* polka dots 6
lunes *m., sing.* Monday 2
luz *f.* light; electricity 12

M

madrastra *f.* stepmother 3
madre *f.* mother 3
madurez *f.* maturity; middle age 9
maestro/a *m., f.* teacher
magnífico/a *adj.* magnificent 5
maíz *m.* corn 8
mal, malo/a *adj.* bad 3
maleta *f.* suitcase 1
mamá *f.* mom 1
mandar *v.* to order 12; to send; to mail 14
manejar *v.* to drive 11
manera *f.* way
mano *f.* hand 1
¡Manos arriba! Hands up!

manta *f.* blanket 12
mantener *v.* to maintain 15
  mantenerse en forma to stay in shape 15
mantequilla *f.* butter 8
manzana *f.* apple 8
mañana *f.* morning, a.m. 1; tomorrow 1
mapa *m.* map 2
maquillaje *m.* make-up 7
maquillarse *v.* to put on makeup 7
mar *m.* sea 5
maravilloso/a *adj.* marvelous 5
mareado/a *adj.* dizzy; nauseated 10
margarina *f.* margarine 8
mariscos *m., pl.* shellfish 8
marrón *adj. m., f.* brown 6
martes *m., sing.* Tuesday 2
marzo *m.* March 5
más *pron.* more 2
  más de (+ *number*) more than 8
  más tarde later 7
  más... que more... than 8
masaje *m.* massage 15
matemáticas *f., pl.* mathematics 2
materia *f.* course 2
matrimonio *m.* marriage 9
máximo/a *adj.* maximum 11
mayo *m.* May 5
mayonesa *f.* mayonnaise 8
mayor *adj.* older 3
  el/la mayor *adj.* eldest 8; oldest
me *pron.* me 6
  Me duele mucho. It hurts me a lot. 10
  Me gusta... I like... 2
  No me gustan nada. I don't like them at all. 2
  Me gustaría(n)... I would like... 15
  Me llamo... My name is... 1
  Me muero por... I'm dying to (for)...
mecánico/a *m., f.* mechanic 11
mediano/a *adj.* medium
medianoche *f.* midnight 1
medias *f., pl.* pantyhose, stockings 6
medicamento *m.* medication 10
medicina *f.* medicine 10
médico/a *m., f.* doctor 3; *adj.* medical 10
medio/a *adj.* half 3
  medio ambiente *m.* environment 13
  medio/a hermano/a *m., f.* half-brother/half-sister 3
  mediodía *m.* noon 1
  medios de comunicación *m., pl.* means of communication; media

y media thirty minutes past the hour (time) 1
mejor *adj.* better 8
  el/la mejor *m., f.* the best 8
mejorar *v.* to improve 13
melocotón *m.* peach 8
menor *adj.* younger 3
  el/la menor *m., f.* youngest 8
menos *adv.* less 10
  menos cuarto... menos quince... quarter to... (*time*) 1
  menos de (+ *number*) fewer than 8
  menos... que less... than 8
mensaje electrónico *m.* e-mail message 4
mentira *f.* to lie 4
menú *m.* menu 8
mercado *m.* market 6
  mercado al aire libre open-air market 6
merendar *v.* to snack 8; to have an afternoon snack
merienda *f.* afternoon snack 15
mes *m.* month 5
mesa *f.* table 2
mesita *f.* end table 12
  mesita de noche night stand 12
metro *m.* subway 5
mexicano/a *adj.* Mexican 3
México *m.* Mexico 1
mí *pron. obj. of prep.* me 8
mi(s) *poss. adj.* my 3
microonda *f.* microwave 12
  horno de microondas *m.* microwave oven 12
miedo *m.* fear 3
mientras *adv.* while 10
miércoles *m., sing.* Wednesday 2
mil *m.* one thousand 6
  mil millones billion
  Mil perdones. I'm so sorry. (*lit.* A thousand pardons.) 4
milla *f.* mile 11
millón *m.* million 6
millones (de) *m.* millions (of) 6
mineral *m.* mineral 15
minuto *m.* minute 1
mío(s)/a(s) *poss.* my; (of) mine 11
mirar *v.* to look (at); to watch 2
  mirar (la) televisión to watch television
mismo/a *adj.* same 3
mochila *f.* backpack 2
moda *f.* fashion 6
módem *m.* modem
moderno/a *adj.* modern
molestar *v.* to bother; to annoy 7
monitor *m.* (computer) monitor 11
  monitor(a) *m., f.* trainer
montaña *f.* mountain 4
montar a caballo *v.* to ride a horse 5
monumento *m.* monument 4

mora *f.* blackberry 8
morado/a *adj.* purple 6
moreno/a *adj.* brunet(te) 3
morir (o:ue) *v.* to die 8
mostrar (o:ue) *v.* to show 4
motocicleta *f.* motorcycle 5
motor *m.* motor
muchacho/a *m., f.* boy; girl 3
mucho/a *adj., adv.* a lot of; much 2; many 3
  muchas veces *adv.* a lot; many times 10
  Muchísimas gracias. Thank you very, very much. 9
  Mucho gusto. Pleased to meet you. 1
  (Muchas) gracias. Thank you (very much); Thanks (a lot). 1
muchísimo very much 2
mudarse *v.* to move (from one house to another) 12
muebles *m., pl.* furniture 12
muela *f.* tooth 10
muerte *f.* death 9
muerto/a *p.p.* died 13
mujer *f.* woman 1
  mujer de negocios *f.* business woman
  mujer policía *f.* female police officer
multa *f.* fine
mundial *adj. m., f.* worldwide
mundo *m.* world 13
municipal *adj. m., f.* municipal
músculo *m.* muscle 15
museo *m.* museum 4
música *f.* music 2
musical *adj. m., f.* musical
músico/a *m., f.* musician
muy *adv.* very 1
  Muy amable. That's very kind of you. 5
  (Muy) bien, gracias. (Very) well, thanks. 1

N

nacer *v.* to be born 9
nacimiento *m.* birth 9
nacional *adj. m., f.* national
nacionalidad *f.* nationality 1
nada nothing 1; not anything 7
  nada mal not bad at all 5
nadar *v.* to swim 4
nadie *pron.* no one, nobody, not anyone 7
naranja *f.* orange 8
nariz *f.* nose 10
natación *f.* swimming 4
natural *adj. m., f.* natural 13
naturaleza *f.* nature 13
navegar (en Internet) *v.* to surf (the Internet) 11
Navidad *f.* Christmas 9

necesario/a *adj.* necessary 12
necesitar (+ inf.) *v.* to need 2
negar (e:ie) *v.* to deny 13
  no negar (e:ie) *v.* not to deny 13
negativo/a *adj.* negative
negocios *m., pl.* business; commerce
negro/a *adj.* black 6
nervioso/a *adj.* nervous 5
nevar (e:ie) *v.* to snow 5
  Nieva. It's snowing. 5
ni...ni neither... nor 7
niebla *f.* fog
nieto/a *m., f.* grandson/granddaughter 3
nieve *f.* snow
ningún, ninguno/a(s) *adj.* no; none; not; any 7
ningún problema no problem 7
niñez *f.* childhood 9
niño/a *m., f.* child 3
no no; not 1
  No cabe duda de... There is no doubt... 13
  No es así. That's not the way it is.
  No es para tanto. It's not a big deal. 12
  No es seguro. It's not sure. 13
  No es verdad. It's not true. 13
  No está nada mal. It's not bad at all. 5
  no estar de acuerdo to disagree
  No estoy seguro. I'm not sure.
  (no) hay there is (not); there are (not) 1
  No hay de qué. You're welcome. 1
  No hay duda de... There is no doubt... 13
  ¡No me diga(s)! You don't say! 11
  No me gustan nada. I don't like them at all. 2
  no muy bien not very well 1
  ¿no? right? 1
  No quiero. I don't want to. 4
  No sé. I don't know.
  No se preocupe. (*form.*) Don't worry. 7
  No te preocupes. (*fam.*) Don't worry. 7
  no tener razón to be wrong 3
noche *f.* night 1
nombre *m.* name 1
norte *m.* north 14
norteamericano/a *adj.* (North) American 3
nos *pron.* us 6
  Nos divertimos mucho. We had a lot of fun.
  Nos vemos. See you. 1

nosotros/as *sub. pron.* we 1; *ob. pron.* us
noticias *f., pl.* news
noticiero *m.* newscast
novecientos/as *adj.* nine hundred 6
noveno/a *adj.* ninth 5
noventa ninety 2
noviembre *m.* November 5
novio/a *m., f.* boyfriend/girlfriend 3
nube *f.* cloud 13
nublado/a *adj.* cloudy 5
  Está (muy) nublado. It's very cloudy. 5
nuclear *adj. m. f.* nuclear 13
nuera *f.* daughter-in-law 3
nuestro(s)/a(s) *poss. adj.* our 3; (of ours) 11
nueve nine 1
nuevo/a *adj.* new 6
número *m.* number 1
  número (shoe) size 6
nunca *adj.* never; not ever 7
nutrición *f.* nutrition 15
nutricionista *m., f.* nutritionist 15

O

o or 7
o... o ; either... or 7
obedecer (c:zc) *v.* to obey
obra *f.* work (*of art, literature, music, etc.*)
  obra maestra *f.* masterpiece
obtener *v.* to obtain; to get
obvio/a *adj.* obvious 13
océano *m.* ocean 5
ochenta eighty 2
ocho *m.* eight 1
ochocientos/as *adj.* eight hundred 6
octavo/a *adj.* eighth 5
octubre *m.* October 5
ocupación *f.* occupation
ocupado/a *adj.* busy 5
ocurrir *v.* to occur; to happen
odiar *v.* to hate 9
oeste *m.* west 14
oferta *f.* offer 12
oficina *f.* office 12
oficio *m.* trade
ofrecer (c:zc) *v.* to offer 8
oído *m.* (sense of) hearing; inner ear 10
  oído *p.p.* heard 13
oír *v.* to hear 4
  Oigan. *form., pl.* Listen. (*in conversation*)
  Oye. *fam., sing.* Listen. (*in conversation*) 1
ojalá (que) *interj.* I hope (that); I wish (that) 13
ojo *m.* eye 10

olvidar *v.* to forget 10
once eleven 1
ópera *f.* opera
operación *f.* operation 10
ordenado/a *adj.* orderly 5
ordinal *adj.* ordinal (*number*)
oreja *f.* (outer) ear 10
orquesta *f.* orchestra
ortografía *f.* spelling
  ortográfico/a *adj.* spelling
os *fam., pl. pron.* you 6
otoño *m.* autumn 5
otro/a *adj.* other; another 6
  otra vez again

P

paciente *m., f.* patient 10
padrastro *m.* stepfather 3
padre *m.* father 3
  padres *m., pl.* parents 3
pagar *v.* to pay 6, 9
  pagar a plazos to pay in installments 14
  pagar al contado to pay in cash 14
  pagar en efectivo to pay in cash 14
  pagar la cuenta to pay the bill 9
página *f.* page 11
  página principal *f.* home page 11
país *m.* country 1
paisaje *m.* landscape 5
pájaro *m.* bird 13
palabra *f.* word 1
pan *m.* bread 8
  pan tostado *m.* toasted bread 8
panadería *f.* bakery 14
pantalla *f.* screen 11
pantalones *m., pl.* pants 6
  pantalones cortos *m., pl.* shorts 6
pantuflas *f.* slippers 7
papa *f.* potato 8
  papas fritas *f., pl.* fried potatoes; French fries 8
papá *m.* dad 3
  papás *m., pl.* parents 3
papel *m.* paper 2; *m.* role
papelera *f.* wastebasket
paquete *m.* package 14
par *m.* pair 6
para *prep.* for; in order to; by; used for; considering 11
  para que so that 13
parabrisas *m., sing.* windshield 11
parar *v.* to stop 11
parecer *v.* to seem 8
pared *f.* wall 12
pareja *f.* (married) couple; partner 9
parientes *m., pl.* relatives 3
parque *m.* park 4

párrafo *m.* paragraph
parte: de parte de on behalf of 11
partido *m.* game; match (*sports*) 4
pasado/a *adj.* last; past 6
   pasado *p.p.* passed
pasaje *m.* ticket 5
   pasaje de ida y vuelta *m.*
    roundtrip ticket 5
pasajero/a *m., f.* passenger 1
pasaporte *m.* passport 5
pasar *v.* to go through 5
   pasar la aspiradora to
    vacuum 12
   pasar por el banco to go by
    the bank 14
   pasar por la aduana to go
    through customs 5
   pasar tiempo to spend time 4
   pasarlo bien/mal to have a
    good/bad time 9
pasatiempo *m.* pastime; hobby 4
pasear *v.* to take a walk; to
   stroll 4
   pasear en bicicleta to ride a
    bicycle 4
   pasear por to walk around 4
pasillo *m.* hallway 12
pasta *f.* **de dientes** toothpaste 7
pastel *m.* cake; pie 9
   pastel de chocolate *m.*
    chocolate cake 9
   pastel de cumpleaños *m.*
    birthday cake 9
pastelería *f.* pastry shop 14
pastilla *f.* pill; tablet 10
patata *f.* potato; 8
   patatas fritas *f., pl.* fried
    potatoes; French fries 8
patinar (en línea) *v.* to skate
   (in-line) 4
patineta *f.* skateboard 4
patio *m.* patio; yard 12
pavo *m.* turkey 8
paz *f.* peace
pedir (e:i) *v.* to ask for; to request
   4; to order (*food*) 8
   pedir prestado *v.* to borrow 14
   pedir un préstamo *v.* to apply
    for a loan 14
peinarse *v.* to comb one's hair 7
película *f.* movie 4
peligro *m.* danger 13
peligroso/a *adj.* dangerous
pelirrojo/a *adj.* red-haired 3
pelo *m.* hair 7
pelota *f.* ball 4
peluquería *f.* beauty salon 14
peluquero/a *m., f.* hairdresser
penicilina *f.* penicillin 10
pensar (e:ie) *v.* to think 4
   pensar (+ inf.) *v.* to intend to 4;
    to plan to (*do something*)
   pensar en *v.* to think about
pensión *f.* boardinghouse
peor *adj.* worse 8

el/la peor *adj.* the worst 8
pequeño/a *adj.* small 3
pera *f.* pear 8
perder (e:ie) *v.* to lose; to miss 4
perdido/a *adj.* lost 14
Perdón. Pardon me.;
   Excuse me. 1
perezoso/a *adj.* lazy
perfecto/a *adj.* perfect 5
periódico *m.* newspaper 4
periodismo *m.* journalism 2
periodista *m., f.* journalist 3
permiso *m.* permission
pero *conj.* but 2
perro *m.* dog 13
persona *f.* person 3
personaje *m.* character
   personaje (principal) *m.*
    (main) character
pesas *f. pl.* weights 15
pesca *f.* fishing 5
pescadería *f.* fish market 14
pescado *m.* fish (*cooked*) 8
pescador(a) *m., f.* fisherman/
   fisherwoman
pescar *v.* to fish 5
peso *m.* weight 15
pez *m.* fish (*live*) 13
pie *m.* foot 10
piedra *f.* stone 13
pierna *f.* leg 10
pimienta *f.* black pepper 8
pintar *v.* to paint
pintor(a) *m., f.* painter
pintura *f.* painting; picture 12
piña *f.* pineapple 8
piscina *f.* swimming pool 4
piso *m.* floor (*of a building*) 5
pizarra *f.* blackboard 2
placer *m.* pleasure 15
   Ha sido un placer. It's been a
    pleasure. 15
planchar la ropa *v.* to iron the
   clothes 12
planes *m., pl.* plans 4
planta *f.* plant 13
   planta baja *f.* ground floor 5
plástico *m.* plastic 13
plato *m.* dish (*in a meal*) 8; *m.*
   plate 12
   plato principal *m.* main dish 8
playa *f.* beach 5
plaza *f.* city or town square 4
plazos *m., pl.* periods; time 14
pluma *f.* pen 2
población *f.* population 13
pobre *adj. m., f.* poor 6
pobreza *f.* poverty
poco/a *adj.* little; few 5
poder (o:ue) *v.* to be able to;
   can 4
poema *m.* poem
poesía *f.* poetry
poeta *m., f.* poet
policía *f.* police (force) 11

política *f.* politics
político/a *m., f.* politician; *adj.*
   political
pollo *m.* chicken 8
   pollo asado *m.* roast chicken 8
ponchar *v.* to go flat
poner *v.* to put; to place 4; *v.* to
   turn on (*electrical appliances*) 11
   poner la mesa *v.* to set the
    table 12
   poner una inyección *v.* to give
    an injection 10
ponerse (+ adj.) *v.* to become
   (+ *adj.*) 7; to put on 7
por *prep.* in exchange for; for;
   by; in; through; around; along;
   during; because of; on account
   of; on behalf of; in search of;
   by way of; by means of 11
   por aquí around here 11
   por avión by plane
   por ejemplo for example 11
   por eso that's why;
    therefore 11
   Por favor. Please. 1
   por fin finally 11
   por la mañana in the
    morning 7
   por la noche at night 7
   por la tarde in the afternoon 7
   por lo menos *adv.* at least 10
   ¿por qué? why? 2
   Por supuesto. Of course.
   por teléfono by phone; on the
    phone
   por último finally 7
porque *conj.* because 2
portátil *m.* portable 11
porvenir *m.* future
   ¡Por el porvenir! Here's to the
    future!
posesivo/a *adj.* possessive 3
posible *adj.* possible 13
   Es posible. It's possible. 13
   No es posible. It's not possible.
   13
postal *f.* postcard 4
postre *m.* dessert 9
practicar *v.* to practice 2
   practicar deportes *m., pl.* to
    play sports 4
precio (fijo) *m.* (fixed; set)
   price 6
preferir (e:ie) *v.* to prefer 4
pregunta *f.* question
preguntar *v.* to ask (*a question*) 2
premio *m.* prize; award
prender *v.* to turn on 11
prensa *f.* press
preocupado/a (por) *adj.* worried
   (about) 5
preocuparse (por) *v.* to worry
   (about) 7
preparar *v.* to prepare 2
preposición *f.* preposition

presentación *f.* introduction
presentar *v.* to introduce
to put on (*a performance*)
Le presento a... I would like to introduce (name) to you... (*form.*) 1
Te presento a... I would like to introduce (name) to you... (*fam.*) 1
presiones *f., pl.* pressures 15
prestado/a *adj.* borrowed
préstamo *m.* loan 14
prestar *v.* to lend; to loan 6
primavera *f.* spring 5
primer, primero/a *adj.* first 5
primo/a *m., f.* cousin 3
principal *adj. m., f.* main 8
prisa *f.* haste 3
darse prisa *v.* to hurry; to rush 15
probable *adj. m., f.* probable 13
Es probable. It's probable. 13
No es probable. It's not probable. 13
probar (o:ue) *v.* to taste; to try 8
probarse (o:ue) *v.* to try on 7
problema *m.* problem 1
profesión *f.* profession 3
profesor(a) *m., f.* teacher 1, 2
programa *m.* 1
programa de computación *m.* software 11
programa de entrevistas *m.* talk show
programador(a) *m., f.* programmer 3
prohibir *v.* to prohibit 10; 12 to forbid
pronombre *m.* pronoun
pronto *adv.* soon 10
propina *f.* tip 9
propio/a *adj.* own
proteger *v.* to protect 13
proteína *f.* protein 15
próximo/a *adj.* next
prueba *f.* test; quiz 2
psicología *f.* psychology 2
psicólogo/a *m., f.* psychologist
publicar *v.* to publish
público *m.* audience
pueblo *m.* town 4
puerta *f.* door 2
Puerto Rico *m.* Puerto Rico 1
puertorriqueño/a *adj.* Puerto Rican 3
pues *conj.* well 2
puesto *m.* position; job
puesto/a *p.p.* put 13
puro/a *adj.* pure 13

que *pron.* that; which; who 12
¡Qué...! How...! 3
¡Qué dolor! What pain!
¡Qué ropa más bonita! What pretty clothes! 6
¡Qué sorpresa! What a surprise!
¿qué? what? 1
¿Qué día es hoy? What day is it? 2
¿Qué hay de nuevo? What's new? 1
¿Qué hora es? What time is it? 1
¿Qué les parece? What do you (*pl.*) think?
¿Qué pasa? What's happening? What's going on? 1
¿Qué pasó? What happened? 11
¿Qué precio tiene? What is the price?
¿Qué tal...? How are you?; How is it going? 1; How is/are . . . ? 2
¿Qué talla lleva/usa? What size do you wear? 6
¿Qué tiempo hace? How's the weather? 5
¿En qué...? In which...? 2
quedar *v.* to be left over; to fit (*clothing*) 7; to be left behind; to be located 14
quedarse *v.* to stay; to remain 7
quehaceres domésticos *m., pl.* household chores 12
quemado/a *adj.* burned (out) 11
quemar *v.* to burn (a CD) 11
querer (e:ie) *v.* to want; to love 4
queso *m.* cheese 8
quien(es) *pron.* who; whom; that 12
¿Quién es...? Who is...? 1
¿Quién habla? Who is speaking? (*telephone*) 11
¿quién(es)? who?; whom? 1
química *f.* chemistry 2
quince fifteen 1
menos quince quarter to (time) 1
y quince quarter after (time) 1
quinceañera *f.* young woman's fifteenth birthday celebration/fifteen-year old girl 9
quinientos/as *adj.* five hundred 6
quinto/a *adj.* fifth 5
quisiera *v.* I would like
quitar la mesa *v.* to clear the table 12
quitarse *v.* to take off 7
quizás *adv.* maybe 5

racismo *m.* racism
radio *f.* radio (*medium*)
radio *m.* radio (set) 11
radiografía *f.* X-ray 10
rápido/a *adv.* quickly 10
ratón *m.* mouse 11
ratos libres *m., pl.* spare (free) time 4
raya *f.* stripe 6
razón *f.* reason 3
rebaja *f.* sale 6
recado *m.* (telephone) message 11
receta *f.* prescription 10
recetar *v.* to prescribe 10
recibir *v.* to receive 3
reciclaje *m.* recycling 13
reciclar *v.* to recycle 13
recién casado/a *m., f.* newlywed 9
recoger *v.* to pick up 13
recomendar (e:ie) *v.* to recommend 8, 12
recordar (o:ue) *v.* to remember 4
recorrer *v.* to tour an area
recurso *m.* resource 13
recurso natural *m.* natural resource 13
red *f.* network; Web 11
reducir *v.* to reduce 13
refresco *m.* soft drink 8
refrigerador *m.* refrigerator 12
regalar *v.* to give (a gift) 9
regalo *m.* gift 6
regatear *v.* to bargain 6
región *f.* region; area 13
regresar *v.* to return 2
regular *adj. m., f.* so so.; OK 1
reído *p.p.* laughed 13
reírse (e:i) *v.* to laugh 9
relaciones *f., pl.* relationships 9
relajarse *v.* to relax 9
reloj *m.* clock; watch 2
renunciar (a) *v.* to resign (from)
repetir (e:i) *v.* to repeat 4
reportaje *m.* report
reportero/a *m., f.* reporter; journalist
representante *m., f.* representative
reproductor de DVD *m.* DVD player 11
resfriado *m.* cold (*illness*) 10
residencia estudiantil *f.* dormitory 2
resolver (o:ue) *v.* to resolve; to solve 13
respirar *v.* to breathe 13
respuesta *f.* answer
restaurante *m.* restaurant 4
resuelto/a *p.p.* resolved 13
reunión *f.* meeting
revisar *v.* to check 11

revisar el aceite *v.* to check the oil 11
revista *f.* magazine 4
rico/a *adj.* rich 6; *adj.* tasty; delicious 8
ridículo *adj.* ridiculous 13
río *m.* river 13
riquísimo/a *adj.* extremely delicious 8
rodilla *f.* knee 10
rogar (o:ue) *v.* to beg; to plead 12
rojo/a *adj.* red 6
romántico/a *adj.* romantic
romper (con) *v.* to break up (with) 9
romper(se) *v.* to break 10
romperse la pierna *v.* to break one's leg 10
ropa *f.* clothing; clothes 6
ropa interior *f.* underwear 6
rosado/a *adj.* pink 6
roto/a *adj.* broken 10, 13
rubio/a *adj.* blond(e) 3
ruso/a *adj.* Russian 3
rutina *f.* routine 7
rutina diaria *f.* daily routine 7

S

sábado *m.* Saturday 2
saber *v.* to know; to know how 8
saber (+ adj.) to taste + (adj.) 8
saber + a to taste like 8
sabroso/a *adj.* tasty; delicious 8
sacar *v.* to take out
sacar fotos to take photos 5
sacar la basura to take out the trash 12
sacar(se) una muela to have a tooth removed 10
sacudir *v.* to dust 12
sacudir los muebles to dust the furniture 12
sal *f.* salt 8
sala *f.* living room 12; room
sala de emergencia(s) emergency room 10
salario *m.* salary
salchicha *f.* sausage 8
salida *f.* departure; exit 5
salir *v.* to leave 4; to go out
salir (con) to go out (with); to date 9
salir de to leave from
salir para to leave for (*a place*)
salmón *m.* salmon 8
salón de belleza *m.* beauty salon 14
salud *f.* health 10
saludable *adj.* healthy 10
saludar(se) *v.* to greet (each other) 11

saludo *m.* greeting 1
saludos a... greetings to... 1
sandalia *f.* sandal 6
sandía *f.* watermelon 8
sándwich *m.* sandwich 8
sano/a *adj.* healthy 10
se *ref.pron.* himself, herself, itself, *form.* yourself, themselves, yourselves 7
se *impersonal* one 10
Se nos dañó... The... broke down. 11
Se hizo... He/she/it became...
Se nos pinchó una llanta. We had a flat tire. 11
secadora *f.* clothes dryer 12
secarse *v.* to dry (oneself) 7
sección de (no) fumar *f.* (non) smoking section 8
secretario/a *m., f.* secretary
secuencia *f.* sequence
sed *f.* thirst 3
seda *f.* silk 6
sedentario/a *adj.* sedentary; related to sitting 15
seguir (e:i) *v.* to follow; to continue 4
según according to
segundo/a *adj.* second 5
seguro/a *adj.* sure 5
seis six 1
seiscientos/as *adj.* six hundred 6
sello *m.* stamp 14
selva *f.* jungle 13
semana *f.* week 2
fin *m.* **de semana** weekend 4
semana *f.* **pasada** last week 6
semestre *m.* semester 2
sendero *m.* trail; trailhead 13
sentarse (e:ie) *v.* to sit down 7
sentir(se) (e:ie) *v.* to feel 7; to be sorry; to regret 13
señor (Sr.); don *m.* Mr.; sir 1
señora (Sra.) *f.* Mrs.; ma'am 1
señorita (Srta.) *f.* Miss 1
separado/a *adj.* separated 9
separarse (de) *v.* to separate (from) 9
septiembre *m.* September 5
séptimo/a *adj.* seventh 5
ser *v.* to be 1
ser aficionado/a (a) to be a fan (of) 4
ser alérgico/a (a) to be allergic (to) 10
ser gratis to be free of charge 14
serio/a *adj.* serious
servilleta *f.* napkin 12
servir (e:i) *v.* to serve 8; to help 5
sesenta sixty 2
setecientos/as *adj.* seven hundred 6
setenta seventy 2
sexismo *m.* sexism

sexto/a *adj.* sixth 5
sí *adv.* yes 1
si *conj.* if 4
SIDA *m.* AIDS
sido *p.p.* been 15
siempre *adv.* always 7
siete seven 1
silla *f.* seat 2
sillón *m.* armchair 12
similar *adj. m., f.* similar
simpático/a *adj.* nice; likeable 3
sin *prep.* without 2, 13
sin duda without a doubt
sin embargo however
sin que *conj.* without 13
sino but (rather) 7
síntoma *m.* symptom 10
sitio *m.* **web**; website 11
situado/a *p.p.* located
sobre *m.* envelope 14; *prep.* on; over 2
sobrino/a *m., f.* nephew; niece 3
sociología *f.* sociology 2
sofá *m.* couch; sofa 12
sol *m.* sun 4; 5; 13
solar *adj. m., f.* solar 13
soldado *m., f.* soldier
soleado/a *adj.* sunny
solicitar *v.* to apply (*for a job*)
solicitud (de trabajo) *f.* (job) application
sólo *adv.* only 3;
solo *adj.* alone
soltero/a *adj.* single 9
solución *f.* solution 13
sombrero *m.* hat 6
Son las dos. It's two o'clock. 1
sonar (o:ue) *v.* to ring 11
sonreído *p.p.* smiled 13
sonreír (e:i) *v.* to smile 9
sopa *f.* soup 8
sorprender *v.* to surprise 9
sorpresa *f.* surprise 9
sótano *m.* basement; cellar 12
soy I am 1
Soy yo. That's me. 1
Soy de... I'm from... 1
su(s) *poss. adj.* his; her; its; *form.* your; their; 3
subir(se) a *v.* to get on/into (*a vehicle*) 11
sucio/a *adj.* dirty 5
sucre *m.* Former Ecuadorian currency 6
sudar *v.* to sweat 15
suegro/a *m., f.* father-in-law; mother-in-law 3
sueldo *m.* salary
suelo *m.* floor 12
sueño *n.* sleep 3
suerte *f.* luck 3
suéter *m.* sweater 6
sufrir *v.* to suffer 10
sufrir muchas presiones to be under a lot of pressure 15

sufrir una enfermedad to suffer an illness 10
sugerir (e:ie) *v.* to suggest 12
supermercado *m.* supermarket 14
suponer *v.* to suppose 4
sur *m.* south 14
sustantivo *m.* noun
suyo(s)/a(s) *poss.* (of) his/her; (of) hers; (of) its; (of) *form.* your, (of) yours, (of) their 11

tal vez *adv.* maybe 5
talentoso/a *adj.* talented
talla *f.* size 6
  talla grande *f.* large 6
taller *m.* **mecánico** garage; mechanic's repairshop 11
también *adv.* also; too 2; 7
tampoco *adv.* neither; not either 7
tan *adv.* so
  tan pronto como as soon as 13
  tan... como as... as 8
tanque *m.* tank 11
tanto *adv.* so much
  tanto... como as much... as 8
  tantos/as... como as many... as 8
tarde *adv.* late 7
  tarde *f.* afternoon; evening; P.M. 1
tarea *f.* homework 2
tarjeta *f.* (post) card 4
tarjeta de crédito *f.* credit card 6
tarjeta postal *f.* postcard 4
taxi *m.* taxi 5
taza *f.* cup 12
te *fam. pron.* you 6
  Te presento a... I would like to introduce you to... 1
  ¿Te gustaría? Would you like to? 15
  ¿Te gusta(n)...? Do you like... ? 2
té *m.* tea 8
  té helado *m.* iced tea 8
teatro *m.* theater
teclado *m.* keyboard 11
técnico/a *m., f.* technician
tejido *m.* weaving
teleadicto/a *m., f.* couch potato 15
teléfono (celular) *m.* (cell) telephone 11
telenovela *f.* soap opera
teletrabajo *m.* telecommuting
televisión *f.* television 11
televisión por cable *f.* cable television 11
televisor *m.* television set 11
temer *v.* to fear 13

temperatura *f.* temperature 10
temprano *adv.* early 7
tenedor *m.* fork 12
tener *v.* to have 3
  tener... años to be... years old 3
  Tengo... años. I'm... years old. 3
  tener (mucho) calor to be (very) hot 3
  tener (mucho) cuidado to be (very) careful 3
  tener dolor to have a pain 10
  tener éxito to be successful
  tener fiebre to have a fever 10
  tener (mucho) frío to be (very) cold 3
  tener ganas de (+ *inf.*) to feel like (*doing something*) 3
  tener (mucha) hambre *f.* to be (very) hungry 3
  tener (mucho) miedo (de) to be (very) afraid (of); to be (very) scared (of) 3
  tener miedo (de) que to be afraid that
  tener planes *m., pl.* to have plans 4
  tener (mucha) prisa to be in a (big) hurry 3
  tener que (+ *inf.*) *v.* to have to (*do something*) 3
  tener razón *f.* to be right 3
  tener (mucha) sed *f.* to be (very) thirsty 3
  tener (mucho) sueño to be (very) sleepy 3
  tener (mucha) suerte to be (very) lucky 3
  tener tiempo to have time 4
  tener una cita to have a date; to have an appointment 9
tenis *m.* tennis 4
tensión *f.* tension 15
tercer, tercero/a *adj.* third 5
terminar *v.* to end; to finish 2
  terminar de (+*inf.*) *v.* to finish (*doing something*) 4
terremoto *m.* earthquake
terrible *adj. m., f.* terrible 13
ti *prep., obj. of prep., fam.* you
tiempo *m.* time 4; weather 5
  tiempo libre free time 4
tienda *f.* shop; store 6
  tienda de campaña tent
tierra *f.* land; soil 13
tinto/a *adj.* red (wine) 8
tío/a *m., f.* uncle; aunt 3
tíos *m.* aunts and uncles 3
título *m.* title
tiza *f.* chalk 2
toalla *f.* towel 7
tobillo *m.* ankle 10
tocadiscos compacto *m.* compact-disc player 11

tocar *v.* to play (*a musical instrument*) ; to touch 13
todavía *adv.* yet; still 5
todo *m.* everything 5
  en todo el mundo throughout the world 13
  Todo está bajo control. Everything is under control. 7
  todo derecho straight (ahead) 14
  ¡Todos a bordo! All aboard! 1
todo/a *adj.* all 4; whole
todos *m., pl.* all of us; *m., pl.* everybody; everyone
todos los días *adv.* every day 10
tomar *v.* to take; to drink 2
  tomar clases *f., pl.* to take classes 2
  tomar el sol to sunbathe 4
  tomar en cuenta take into account
  tomar fotos *f., pl.* to take photos 5
  tomar la temperatura to take someone's temperature 10
tomate *m.* tomato 8
tonto/a *adj.* silly; foolish 3
torcerse (o:ue) (el tobillo) *v.* to sprain (one's ankle) 10
torcido/a *adj.* twisted; sprained 10
tormenta *f.* storm
tornado *m.* tornado
tortilla *f.* kind of flat bread 8
  tortillas de maíz flat bread made of corn flour 8
tos *f., sing.* cough 10
toser *v.* to cough 10
tostado/a *adj.* toasted 8
tostadora *f.* toaster 12
trabajador(a) *adj.* hard-working 3
trabajar *v.* to work 2
trabajo *m.* job; work
traducir *v.* to translate 8
traer *v.* to bring 4
tráfico *m.* traffic 11
tragedia *f.* tragedy
traído/a *p.p.* brought 13
traje *m.* suit 6
  traje (de baño) *m.* (bathing) suit 6
tranquilo/a *adj.* calm; quiet 15
  Tranquilo. Don't worry.; Be cool. 7
transmitir to broadcast
tratar de (+ *inf.*) *v.* to try (*to do something*) 15
Trato hecho. You've got a deal.
trece thirteen 1
treinta thirty 1, 2
  y treinta thirty minutes past the hour (time) 1
tren *m.* train 5
tres three 1
trescientos/as *adj.* three

hundred 6
trimestre *m.* trimester; quarter 2
triste *adj.* sad 5
tú *fam. sub. pron.* you 1
   Tú eres... You are... 1
tu(s) *fam. poss. adj.* your 3
turismo *m.* tourism 5
turista *m., f.* tourist 1
turístico/a *adj.* touristic
tuyo(s)/a(s) *fam. poss. pron.*
   your; (of) yours 11

U

Ud. *form. sing.* you 1
Uds. *form., pl.* you 1
último/a *adj.* last
un, uno/a *indef. art.* a; one 1
   uno/a *m., f., sing. pron.* one
      a la una at one o'clock 1
   una vez más one more time 9
   una vez once; one time 6
único/a *adj.* only 3
universidad *f.* university;
   college 2
unos/as *m., f., pl. indef. art.*
   some 1
   unos/as *pron.* some 1
urgente *adj.* urgent 12
usar *v.* to wear; to use 6
usted (Ud.) *form. sing.* you 1
   ustedes (Uds.) *form., pl.* you 1
útil *adj.* useful
uva *f.* grape 8

V

vaca *f.* cow 13
vacaciones *f. pl.* vacation 5
valle *m.* valley 13
vamos let's go 4
vaquero *m.* cowboy
   de vaqueros *m., pl.* western
      (genre)
varios/as *adj. m. f., pl.* various 8
vaso *m.* glass 12
veces *f., pl.* times 6
vecino/a *m., f.* neighbor 12
veinte twenty 1
veinticinco twenty-five 1
veinticuatro twenty-four 1
veintidós twenty-two 1
veintinueve twenty-nine 1
veintiocho twenty-eight 1
veintiséis twenty-six 1
veintisiete twenty-seven 1
veintitrés twenty-three 1
veintiún, veintiuno/a *adj.*
   twenty-one 1
vejez *f.* old age 9
velocidad *f.* speed 11
   velocidad máxima *f.* speed
      limit 11

vendedor(a) *m., f.* salesperson 6
vender *v.* to sell 6
venir *v.* to come 3
ventana *f.* window 2
ver *v.* to see 4
   ver películas *f., pl.* to see
      movies 4
   a ver *v.* let's see 2
verano *m.* summer 5
verbo *m.* verb
verdad *f.* truth 4
   ¿verdad? right? 1
verde *adj., m. f.* green 6
verduras *pl., f.* vegetables 8
vestido *m.* dress 6
vestirse (e:i) *v.* to get dressed 7
vez *f.* time 6
viajar *v.* to travel 2
viaje *m.* trip 5
viajero/a *m., f.* traveler 5
vida *f.* life 9
video(casete) *m.* video
   (cassette) 11
videocasetera *f.* VCR 11
videoconferencia *f.* videoconference
vidrio *m.* glass 13
viejo/a *adj.* old 3
viento *m.* wind 5
viernes *m., sing.* Friday 2
vinagre *m.* vinegar 8
vino *m.* wine 8
   vino blanco *m.* white wine 8
   vino tinto *m.* red wine 8
violencia *f.* violence
visitar *v.* to visit 4
   visitar monumentos *m., pl.*
      to visit monuments 4
visto/a *p.p.* seen 13
vitamina *f.* vitamin 15
viudo/a *adj.* widower/widow 9
vivienda *f.* housing 12
vivir *v.* to live 3
vivo/a *adj.* bright; lively; living
volante *m.* steering wheel 11
volcán *m.* volcano 13
vóleibol *m.* volleyball 4
volver (o:ue) *v.* to return 4
volver a ver(te, lo, la) *v.* to see
   (you, him, her) again
vos *pron.* you
vosotros/as *form., pl.* you 1
votar *v.* to vote
vuelta *f.* return trip
vuelto/a *p.p.* returned 13
vuestro(s)/a(s) *poss. adj.* your 3;
   (of) yours *fam.* 11

W

walkman *m.* walkman 11

Y

y *conj.* and 1
   y cuarto quarter after (time) 1
   y media half-past (time) 1
   y quince quarter after (time) 1
   y treinta thirty (minutes past
      the hour) 1
   ¿Y tú? *fam.* And you? 1
   ¿Y usted? *form.* And you? 1
ya *adv.* already 6
yerno *m.* son-in-law 3
yo *sub. pron.* I 1
   Yo soy... I'm... 1
yogur *m.* yogurt 8

Z

zanahoria *f.* carrot 8
zapatería *f.* shoe store 14
zapatos (de tenis) *m., pl.* (tennis)
   shoes, sneakers 6

English-Spanish

A

a **un/a** *m., f., sing.; indef. art.* 1
@ *(symbol)* **arroba** *f.* 11
A.M. **mañana** *f.* 1
able: be able to **poder (o:ue)** *v.* 4
aboard **a bordo** 1
accident **accidente** *m.* 10
accompany **acompañar** *v.* 14
account **cuenta** *f.* 14
   on account of **por** *prep.* 11
accountant **contador(a)** *m., f.*
accounting **contabilidad** *f.* 2
ache **dolor** *m.* 10
acid **ácido/a** *adj.* 13
   acid rain **lluvia ácida** 13
acquainted: be acquainted with
   conocer *v.* 8
action (genre) **de acción** *f.*
active **activo/a** *adj.* 15
actor **actor** *m.,* **actriz** *f.*
addict *(drug)* **drogadicto/a**
   adj. 15
additional **adicional** *adj.*
address **dirección** *f.* 14
adjective **adjetivo** *m.*
adolescence **adolescencia** *f.* 9
adventure (genre) **de aventura** *f.*
advertise **anunciar** *v.*
advertisement **anuncio** *m.*
advice **consejo** *m.* 6
   give advice **dar consejos** 6
advise **aconsejar** *v.* 12
advisor **consejero/a** *m., f.*
aerobic **aeróbico/a** *adj.* 15
   to do aerobics **hacer ejercicios**
     aeróbicos 15
   aerobics class **clase de**
     ejercicios aeróbicos 15
affected **afectado/a** *adj.* 13
   be affected (by) **estar** *v.*
     afectado/a (por) 13
affirmative **afirmativo/a** *adj.*
afraid: be (very) afraid (of) **tener**
   (mucho) miedo (de) 3
   be afraid that **tener miedo**
     (de) que
after **después de** *prep.* 7;
   después de que *conj.* 14
afternoon **tarde** *f.* 1
afterward **después** *adv.* 7
again **otra vez**
age **edad** *f.* 9
agree **concordar** *v.*
agree **estar** *v.* **de acuerdo**
   I agree (completely). **Estoy**
     (completamente) de
     acuerdo.
   I don't agree. **No estoy de**
     acuerdo.
agreement **acuerdo** *m.*
AIDS **SIDA** *m.*

air **aire** *m.* 13
   air pollution **contaminación**
     del aire 13
airplane **avión** *m.* 5
airport **aeropuerto** *m.* 5
alarm clock **despertador** *m.* 7
alcohol **alcohol** *m.* 15
   to consume alcohol **consumir**
     alcohol 15
alcoholic **alcohólico/a** *adj.* 15
all **todo/a** *adj.* 4
   All aboard! **¡Todos a bordo!** 1
   all of us **todos** 1
   all over the world **en todo el**
     mundo
allergic **alérgico/a** *adj.* 10
   be allergic (to) **ser alérgico/a**
     (a) 10
alleviate **aliviar** *v.*
almost **casi** *adv.* 10
alone **solo/a** *adj.*
along **por** *prep.* 11
already **ya** *adv.* 6
also **también** *adv.* 2; 7
alternator **alternador** *m.* 11
although *conj.* **aunque**
aluminum **aluminio** *m.* 13
   (made of) aluminum **de**
     aluminio 13
always **siempre** *adv.* 7
American (*North*) **norteameri-**
   cano/a *adj.* 3
among **entre** *prep.* 2
amusement **diversión** *f.*
and **y** 1, **e** (*before words beginning*
   with i or hi) 4
   And you? **¿Y tú?** *fam.* 1;
     ¿Y usted? *form.* 1
angry **enojado/a** *adj.* 5
   get angry (with) **enojarse** *v.*
     (con) 7
animal **animal** *m.* 13
ankle **tobillo** *m.* 10
anniversary **aniversario** *m.* 9
   (wedding) anniversary **aniver-**
     sario *m.* **(de bodas)** 9
announce **anunciar** *v.*
announcer (*TV/radio*) **locutor(a)**
   m., f.
annoy **molestar** *v.* 7
another **otro/a** *adj.* 6
answer **contestar** *v.* 2;
   respuesta *f.*
answering machine **contestadora**
   f. 11
antibiotic **antibiótico** *m.* 10
any **algún, alguno/a(s)** *adj.* 7
anyone **alguien** *pron.* 7
anything **algo** *pron.* 7
apartment **apartamento** *m.* 12
apartment building **edificio de**
   apartamentos 12
appear **parecer** *v.*
appetizers **entremeses** *m., pl.*
applaud **aplaudir** *v.*

apple **manzana** *f.* 8
appliance (electric) **elec-**
   trodoméstico *m.* 12
applicant **aspirante** *m., f.*
application **solicitud** *f.*
   job application **solicitud de**
     trabajo
apply (*for a job*) **solicitar** *v.*
   apply for a loan **pedir** *v.*
     préstamo 14
appointment **cita** *f.* 9
   have an appointment **tener** *v.*
     una cita 9
appreciate **apreciar** *v.*
April **abril** *m.* 5
aquatic **acuático/a** *adj.*
archaeologist **arqueólogo/a**
   m., f.
architect **arquitecto/a** *m., f.*
area **región** *f.* 13
arm **brazo** *m.* 10
armchair **sillón** *m.* 12
army **ejército** *m.*
around **por** *prep.* 11
   around here **por aquí** 11
arrange **arreglar** *v.* 11
arrival **llegada** *f.* 5
arrive **llegar** *v.* 2
art **arte** *m.* 2
   (fine) arts **bellas artes** *f., pl.*
article *m.* **artículo**
artist **artista** *m., f.* 3
artistic **artístico/a** *adj.*
arts **artes** *f., pl.*
as **como** 8
   as... as **tan... como** 8
   as a child **de niño/a** 10
   as many... as **tantos/as...**
     como 8
   as much... as **tanto...**
     como 8
   as soon as **en cuanto** *conj.* 13;
     tan pronto como *conj.* 13
ask (*a question*) *v.* **preguntar** *v.* 2
   ask for **pedir (e:i)** *v.* 4
asparagus **espárragos** *m., pl.* 8
aspirin **aspirina** *f.* 10
at **a** *prep.* 1
   at + *time* **a la(s)** + *time* 1
   at home **en casa** 7
   at least **por lo menos** 10
   at night **por la noche** 7
   at the end (of) **al fondo (de)** 12
   At what time...? **¿A qué**
     hora...? 1
   At your service. **A sus**
     órdenes. 11
ATM **cajero automático** *m.* 14
attend **asistir (a)** *v.* 3
attic **altillo** *m.* 12
attract **atraer** *v.* 4
audience **público** *m.*
August **agosto** *m.* 5
aunt **tía** *f.* 3

aunts and uncles **tíos** *m., pl.* 3
automatic **automático/a** *adj.*
automobile **automóvil** *m.* 5;
    carro *m.*; **coche** *m.* 11
autumn **otoño** *m.* 5
avenue **avenida** *f.*
avoid **evitar** *v.* 13
award **premio** *m.*

B

backpack **mochila** *f.* 2
bad **mal, malo/a** *adj.* 3
    It's bad that... **Es malo**
      que... 12
    It's not at all bad. **No está**
      nada mal. 5
bag **bolsa** *f.* 6
bakery **panadería** *f.* 14
balanced **equilibrado/a** *adj.* 15
    to eat a balanced diet **comer**
      una dieta equilibrada 15
balcony **balcón** *m.* 12
ball **pelota** *f.* 4
banana **banana** *f.* 8
band **banda** *f.*
bank **banco** *m.* 14
bargain **ganga** *f.* 6; **regatear** *v.* 6
baseball (*game*) **béisbol** *m.* 4
basement **sótano** *m.* 12
basketball (*game*) **baloncesto** *m.* 4
bathe **bañarse** *v.* 7
(bathing) suit **traje** *m.* **(de baño)** 6
bathroom **baño** *m.* 7; **cuarto de**
    baño *m.* 7
be **ser** *v.* 1; **estar** *v.* 2
be... years old **tener... años** 3
beach **playa** *f.* 5
beans **frijoles** *m., pl.* 8
beautiful **hermoso/a** *adj.* 6
beauty **belleza** *f.* 14
    beauty salon **peluquería** *f.* 14;
      salón *m.* **de belleza** 14
because **porque** *conj.* 2
    because of **por** *prep.* 11
become (+ *adj.*) **ponerse (+ *adj.*)**
    7; **convertirse** *v.*
bed **cama** *f.* 5
    go to bed **acostarse (o:ue)** *v.* 7
bedroom **alcoba** *f.*, **dormitorio**
    m. 12; **recámara** *f.*
beef **carne de res** *f.* 8
    beef soup **caldo de patas** 8
been **sido** *p.p.* 15
beer **cerveza** *f.* 8
before **antes** *adv.* 7; **antes de**
    prep. 7; **antes (de) que**
      conj. 13
behalf: on behalf of **de parte**
    de 11
behind **detrás de** *prep.* 2

believe (in) **creer** *v.* **(en)** 3; **creer**
    v. 13
    not to believe **no creer** 13
believed **creído/a** *p.p.* 13
bellhop **botones** *m., f. sing.* 5
below **debajo de** *prep.* 2
belt **cinturón** *m.* 6
benefit **beneficio** *m.*
beside **al lado de** *prep.* 2
besides **además (de)** *adv.* 10
best **mejor** *adj.*
    the best **el/la mejor** *m., f.* 8
      lo mejor *neuter*
better **mejor** *adj.* 8
    It's better that... **Es mejor**
      que... 12
between **entre** *prep.* 2
beverage **bebida** *f.*
    alcoholic beverage **bebida**
      alcohólica *f.* 15
bicycle **bicicleta** *f.* 4
big **gran, grande** *adj.* 3
bill **cuenta** *f.* 9
billion: billion **mil millones**
biology **biología** *f.* 2
bird **ave** *f.* 13; **pájaro** *m.* 13
birth **nacimiento** *m.* 9
birthday **cumpleaños** *m., sing.* 9
    birthday cake **pastel de**
      cumpleaños 9
    have a birthday **cumplir** *v.*
      años 9
biscuit **bizcocho** *m.*
black **negro/a** *adj.* 6
blackberry **mora** *f.* 8
blackboard **pizarra** *f.* 2
blanket **manta** *f.* 12
block (city) **cuadra** *f.* 14
blond(e) **rubio/a** *adj.* 3
blouse **blusa** *f.* 6
blue **azul** *adj. m., f.* 6
boarding house **pensión** *f.*
boat **barco** *m.* 5
body **cuerpo** *m.* 10
bone **hueso** *m.* 10
book **libro** *m.* 2
bookcase **estante** *m.* 12
bookshelves **estante** *m.* 12
bookstore **librería** *f.* 2
boot **bota** *f.* 6
bore **aburrir** *v.* 7
bored **aburrido/a** *adj.* 5
    be bored **estar** *v.* **aburrido/a** 5
    get bored **aburrirse** *v.*
boring **aburrido/a** *adj.* 5
born: be born **nacer** *v.* 9
borrow **pedir prestado** 14
borrowed **prestado/a** *adj.*
boss **jefe** *m.*, **jefa** *f.*
bother **molestar** *v.* 7
bottle **botella** *f.* 9
    bottle (of wine) **botella (de**
      vino) 9
bottom **fondo** *m.*
boulevard **bulevar** *m.*

boy **chico** *m.* 1; **muchacho** *m.* 3
boyfriend **novio** *m.* 3
brakes **frenos** *m., pl.*
bread **pan** *m.* 8
break **romper** *v.* 10
    break (one's leg) **romperse (la**
      pierna) 10
    break down **dañar** *v.* 10
    The... broke down. **Se nos**
      dañó el/la... 11
    break up (with) **romper** *v.*
      (con) 9
breakfast **desayuno** *m.* 2, 8
    have breakfast **desayunar** *v.* 2
breathe **respirar** *v.* 13
bring **traer** *v.* 4
broadcast **transmitir** *v.*;
    emitir *v.*
brochure **folleto** *m.*
broken **roto/a** *adj.* 10, 13
    be broken **estar roto/a** 10
brother **hermano** *m.* 3
    brother-in-law **cuñado** *m., f.* 3
    brothers and sisters **hermanos**
      m., pl. 3
brought **traído** *p.p.* 13
brown **café** *adj.* 6; **marrón** *adj.* 6
brunet(te) **moreno/a** *adj.* 3
brush **cepillar** *v.* 7
    brush one's hair **cepillarse el**
      pelo 7
    brush one's teeth **cepillarse los**
      dientes 7
build **construir** *v.* 4
building **edificio** *m.* 12
bump into (something accidentally)
    darse con 10; (someone)
    encontrarse *v.* 11
burn (a CD) **quemar** *v.* 11
burned (out) **quemado/a** *adj.* 11
bus **autobús** *m.* 1
    bus station **estación** *f.* **de**
      autobuses 5
business **negocios** *m. pl.*
    business administration **admi-**
      nistración *f.* **de empresas** 2
    business-related **comercial** *adj.*
businessperson **hombre** *m.*
    /mujer *f.* **de negocios**
busy **ocupado/a** *adj.* 5
but **pero** *conj.* 2; (rather) **sino**
    conj. (in negative sentences) 7
butcher shop **carnicería** *f.* 14
butter **mantequilla** *f.* 8
buy **comprar** *v.* 2
by **por** *conj.* 11; **para** *prep.* 11
    by means of **por** *prep.* 11
    by phone **por teléfono** 11
    by plane **en avión** 5
    by way of **por** *prep.* 11
bye **chau** *interj. fam.* 1

C

cabin **cabaña** *f.* 5
cable television **televisión** *f.*
  por cable *m.* 11
café **café** *m.* 4
cafeteria **cafetería** *f.* 2
caffeine **cafeína** *f.* 15
cake **pastel** *m.* 9
  (chocolate) cake **pastel (de
  chocolate)** *m.* 9
calculator **calculadora** *f.* 11
call **llamar** *v.* 11
  call on the phone **llamar por
  teléfono**
  be called **llamarse** *v.* 7
calm **tranquilo/a** *adj.* 15
calorie **caloría** *f.* 15
camera **cámara** *f.* 11
camp **acampar** *v.* 5
can **lata** *f.* 13
can **poder (o:ue)** *v.* 4
Canadian **canadiense** *adj.* 3
candidate **aspirante** *m. f.*; candidate **candidato/a** *m., f.*
candy **dulces** *m., pl.* 9
capital (*city*) **capital** *f.* 1
car **coche** *m.* 11; **carro** *m.* 11;
  auto(móvil) *m.* 5
caramel **caramelo** *m.* 9
card **tarjeta** *f.* 4; (*playing*)
  carta *f.* 5
care **cuidado** *m.* 3
  take care of **cuidar** *v.* 13
  Take care! **¡Cuídense!** *v.* 15
career **carrera** *f.*
careful: be (very) careful **tener** *v.*
  (mucho) cuidado 3
caretaker **ama** *m., f.* **de casa** 12
carpenter **carpintero/a** *m., f.*
carpet **alfombra** *f.* 12
carrot **zanahoria** *f.* 8
carry **llevar** *v.* 2
cartoons **dibujos** *m, pl.* **animados**
case: in case (that) **en caso (de)
  que** 13
cash (a check) **cobrar** *v.* 14;
  cash **(en) efectivo** 6
  cash register **caja** *f.* 6
  pay in cash **pagar** *v.* 6 **al
  contado** 14; **pagar en efectivo**
  14
cashier **cajero/a** *m., f.*
cat **gato** *m.* 13
CD-ROM **cederrón** *m.* 11
celebrate **celebrar** *v.* 9
celebration **celebración** *f.*
  young woman's fifteenth
    birthday celebration
    quinceañera *f.* 9
cellar **sótano** *m.* 12
cellular **celular** *adj.* 11
  cellular telephone **teléfono
  celular** *m.* 11

cereal **cereales** *m., pl.* 8
certain **cierto** *m.*; **seguro** *m.* 13
  It's (not) certain. **(No) Es
  cierto/seguro.** 13
chalk **tiza** *f.* 2
champagne **champán** *m.* 9
change **cambiar** *v.* **(de)** 9
channel (*TV*) **canal** *m.*
character (*fictional*) **personaje** *m.*
  (main) character *m.* **personaje
  (principal)**
chat **conversar** *v.* 2
chauffeur **conductor(a)** *m., f.* 1
cheap **barato/a** *adj.* 6
check **comprobar** *v.*; **revisar** *v.*
  11; (*bank*) **cheque** *m.* 14
  check the oil **revisar el aceite**
  11
checking account **cuenta** *f.*
  corriente 14
cheese **queso** *m.* 8
chef **cocinero/a** *m., f.*
chemistry **química** *f.* 2
chest of drawers **cómoda** *f.* 12
chicken **pollo** *m.* 8
child **niño/a** *m., f.* 3
childhood **niñez** *f.* 9
children **hijos** *m., pl.* 3
Chinese **chino/a** *adj.* 3
chocolate **chocolate** *m.* 9
  chocolate cake **pastel** *m.* **de
  chocolate** 9
cholesterol **colesterol** *m.* 15
choose **escoger** *v.* 8
chop (*food*) **chuleta** *f.* 8
Christmas **Navidad** *f.* 9
church **iglesia** *f.* 4
citizen **ciudadano/a** *m., f.*
city **ciudad** *f.* 4
class **clase** *f.* 2
  take classes **tomar clases** 2
classical **clásico/a** *adj.*
classmate **compañero/a** *m., f.* **de
  clase** 2
clean **limpio/a** *adj.* 5;
  limpiar *v.* 12
  clean the house *v.* **limpiar la
  casa** 12
clear (*weather*) **despejado/a** *adj.*
  clear the table **quitar la
  mesa** 12
  It's (very) clear. (*weather*)
  Está (muy) despejado.
clerk **dependiente/a** *m., f.* 6
climb **escalar** *v.* 4
  climb mountains **escalar
  montañas** 4
clinic **clínica** *f.* 10
clock **reloj** *m.* 2
close **cerrar (e:ie)** *v.* 4
closed **cerrado/a** *adj.* 5
closet **armario** *m.* 12
clothes **ropa** *f.* 6
  clothes dryer **secadora** *f.* 12
clothing **ropa** *f.* 6

cloud **nube** *f.* 13
cloudy **nublado/a** *adj.* 5
  It's (very) cloudy. **Está (muy)
  nublado.** 5
coat **abrigo** *m.* 6
coffee **café** *m.* 8
  coffee maker **cafetera** *f.* 12
cold **frío** *m.* 5;
  (*illness*) **resfriado** *m.* 10
  be (*feel*) (very) cold **tener
  (mucho) frío** 3
  It's (very) cold. (*weather*) **Hace
  (mucho) frío.** 5
college **universidad** *f.* 2
collision **choque** *m.*
color **color** *m.* 6
comb one's hair **peinarse** *v.* 7
come **venir** *v.* 3
comedy **comedia** *f.* .
comfortable **cómodo/a** *adj.* 5
commerce **negocios** *m., pl.*
commercial **comercial** *adj.*
communicate (with) **comunicarse**
  v. **(con)**
communication **comunicación** *f.*
  means of communication
    medios *m. pl.* **de comuni-
    cación**
community **comunidad** *f* .1
compact disc (CD) **disco** *m.* **compacto** 11
  compact disc player **tocadiscos**
  m. sing. **compacto** 11
company **compañía** *f.*; **empresa** *f.*
comparison **comparación** *f.*
completely **completamente**
  adv.
composer **compositor(a)** *m., f.*
computer **computadora** *f.* 1
  computer disc **disco** *m.*
  computer monitor **monitor**
  m. 11
  computer programmer **progra-
  mador(a)** *m., f.* 3
  computer science **computación**
  f. 2
concert **concierto** *m.*
conductor (*musical*) **director(a)**
  m., f.
confirm **confirmar** *v.* 5
  confirm a reservation **confirmar
  una reservación** 5
confused **confundido/a** *adj.* 5
congested **congestionado/a**
  adj. 10
Congratulations! (*for an event such
  as a birthday or anniversary*)
    ¡Felicidades! 9; (*for an
    event such as an engagement
    or a good grade on a test*)
    f., pl. **¡Felicitaciones!** 9
conservation **conservación** *f.* 13
conserve **conservar** *v.* 13
considering **para** *prep.* 11
consume **consumir** *v.* 15

contact lenses **lentes** *m. pl.* **de contacto** 6
container **envase** *m.* 13
contamination **contaminación** *f.*
content **contento/a** *adj.* 5
contest **concurso** *m.*
continue **seguir (e:i)** *v.* 4
control **control** *m.*; **controlar** *v.* 13
  be under control **estar bajo control** 7
conversation **conversación** *f.* 1
converse **conversar** *v.* 2
cook **cocinar** *v.* 12; **cocinero/a** *m., f.*
cookie **galleta** *f.* 9
cool **fresco/a** *adj.* 5
  It's cool. *(weather)* **Hace fresco.** 5
corn **maíz** *m.* 8
corner **esquina** *m.* 14
cost **costar (o:ue)** *v.* 6
cotton **algodón** *f.* 6
  (made of) cotton **de algodón** 6
couch **sofá** *m.* 12
couch potato **teleadicto/a** *m., f.* 15
cough **tos** *f.* 10; **toser** *v.* 10
counselor **consejero/a** *m., f.*
count (on) **contar** *v.* **(con)** 4, 12
country *(nation)* **país** *m.* 1
countryside **campo** *m.* 5; **paisaje** *m.* 5
(married) couple **pareja** *f.* 9
course **curso** *m.* 2; **materia** *f.* 2
courtesy **cortesía** *f.*
cousin **primo/a** *m., f.* 3
cover **cubrir** *v.*
covered **cubierto** *p.p.*
cow **vaca** *f.* 13
crafts **artesanía** *f.*
craftsmanship **artesanía** *f.*
crater **cráter** *m.* 13
crazy **loco/a** *adj.* 6
create **crear** *v.*
credit **crédito** *m.* 6
  credit card **tarjeta** *f.* **de crédito** 6
crime **crimen** *m.*
cross **cruzar** *v.* 14
culture **cultura** *f.*
cup **taza** *f.* 12
currency exchange **cambio** *m.* **de moneda**
current events **actualidades** *f., pl.*
curtains **cortinas** *f., pl.* 12
custard *(baked)* **flan** *m.* 9
custom **costumbre** *f.* 1
customer **cliente/a** *m., f.* 6
customs **aduana** *f.* 5
  customs inspector **inspector(a)** *m., f.* **de aduanas** 5
cybercafé **cibercafé** *m.* 11
cycling **ciclismo** *m.* 4

D

dad **papá** *m.* 3
daily **diario/a** *adj.* 7
  daily routine **rutina** *f.* **diaria** 7
damage **dañar** *v.* 10
dance **bailar** *v.* 2; **danza** *f.*; **baile** *m.*
dancer **bailarín/bailarina** *m. f.*
danger **peligro** *m.* 13
dangerous **peligroso/a** *adj.*
date *(appointment)* **cita** *f.* 9; *(calendar)* **fecha** *f.* 5; *(someone)* **salir** *v.* **con (alguien)** 9
  date: have a date **tener una cita** 9
daughter **hija** *f.* 3
  daughter-in-law **nuera** *f.* 3
day **día** *m.* 1
  day before yesterday **anteayer** *adv.* 6
deal **trato** *m.*
  You've got a deal! **¡Trato hecho!**
  It's not a big deal. **No es para tanto.** 12
death **muerte** *f.* 9
decaffeinated **descafeinado/a** *adj.* 15
December **diciembre** *m.* 5
decide **decidir** *v.* **(+ *inf.*)** 3
decided **decidido/a** *adj. p.p.* 14
declare **declarar** *v.*
deforestation **deforestación** *f.* 13
delicious **delicioso/a** *adj.* 8; **rico/a** *adj.* 8; **sabroso/a** *adj.* 8
delighted **encantado/a** *adj.* 1
dentist **dentista** *m., f.* 10
deny **negar (e: ie)** *v.* 13
  not to deny **no dudar** 13
department store **almacén** *m.* 6
departure **salida** *f.* 5
deposit **depositar** *v.* 14
describe **describir** *v.* 3
described **descrito/a** *p.p.* 13
desert **desierto** *m.* 13
design **diseño** *m.*
designer **diseñador(a)** *m., f.*
desire **desear** *v.* 2
desk **escritorio** *m.* 2
dessert **postre** *m.* 9
destroy **destruir** *v.* 13
develop **desarrollar** *v.* 13
diary **diario** *m.* 1
dictatorship **dictadura** *f.*
dictionary **diccionario** *m.* 1
die **morir (o:ue)** *v.* 8
died **muerto/a** *p.p.* 13
diet **dieta** *f.* 15; **alimentación**
  balanced diet **dieta equilibrada** 15
  be on a diet **estar a dieta** 15
difficult **difícil** *adj. m., f.* 3
digital camera **cámara** *f.* **digital** 11
dining room **comedor** *m.* 12

dinner **cena** *f.* 2, 8
  have dinner **cenar** *v.* 2
direct **dirigir** *v.*
directions **direcciones** *f., pl.* 14
  give directions **dar direcciones** 14
director **director(a)** *m., f.*
dirty **ensuciar** *v.*; **sucio/a** *adj.* 5
  get (something) dirty **ensuciar** *v.* 12
disagree **no estar de acuerdo**
disaster **desastre** *m.*
discover **descubrir** *v.* 13
discovered **descubierto** *p.p.* 13
discrimination **discriminación** *f.*
dish **plato** *m.* 8; 12
  main dish *m.* **plato principal** 8
dishwasher **lavaplatos** *m., sing.* 12
disk **disco** *m.*
disorderly **desordenado/a** *adj.* 5
dive **bucear** *v.* 4
divorce **divorcio** *m.* 9
divorced **divorciado/a** *adj.* 9
  get divorced (from) **divorciarse** *v.* **(de)** 9
dizzy **mareado/a** *adj.* 10
do **hacer** *v.* 4
  do aerobics **hacer ejercicios aeróbicos** 15
  do household chores **hacer quehaceres domésticos** 12
  do stretching exercises **hacer ejercicios de estiramiento** 15
  (I) don't want to. **No quiero.** 4
doctor **doctor(a)** *m., f.* 3; **médico/a** *m., f.* 3
documentary *(film)* **documental** *m.*
dog **perro** *m.* 13
domestic **doméstico/a** *adj.*
  domestic appliance **electrodoméstico** *m.* 12
done **hecho/a** *p.p.* 13
door **puerta** *f.* 2
dormitory **residencia** *f.* **estudiantil** 2
double **doble** *adj.* 5
  double room **habitación** *f.* **doble** 5
doubt **duda** *f.* 13; **dudar** *v.* 13
  not to doubt 13
  There is no doubt **No cabe duda de** 13; **No hay duda de** 13
Down with… ! **¡Abajo el/la…!**
download **descargar** *v.* 11
downtown **centro** *m.* 4
drama **drama** *m.*
dramatic **dramático/a** *adj.*
draw **dibujar** *v.* 2
drawing **dibujo** *m.*
dress **vestido** *m.* 6
  get dressed **vestirse (e:i)** *v.* 7
drink **beber** *v.* 3; **bebida** *f.* 8;

tomar *v.* 2
  Do you want something to drink? **¿Quieres algo de tomar?**
drive **conducir** *v.* 8; **manejar** *v.* 11
driver **conductor(a)** *m., f.* 1
drug *f.* **droga** 15
  drug addict **drogadicto/a** *adj.* 15
dry (oneself) **secarse** *v.* 7
due to **por** *prep.*
  due to the fact that **debido a**
during **durante** *prep.* 7; **por** *prep.* 11
dust **sacudir** *v.* 12
  dust the furniture **sacudir los muebles** 12
DVD player **reproductor** *m.* **de DVD** 11
dying: I'm dying to (for)... **me muero por...**

E

each **cada** *adj. m., f.* 6
eagle **águila** *f.*
ear (outer) **oreja** *f.* 10
early **temprano** *adv.* 7
earn **ganar** *v.*
earthquake **terremoto** *m.*
ease **aliviar** *v.*
east **este** *m.* 14
  to the east **al este** 14
easy **fácil** *adj. m., f.* 3
eat **comer** *v.* 3
ecology **ecología** *f.* 13
economics **economía** *f.* 2
ecotourism **ecoturismo** *m.* 13
Ecuador **Ecuador** *m.* 1
Ecuadorian **ecuatoriano/a** *adj.* 3
effective **eficaz** *adj. m., f.*
egg **huevo** *m.* 8
eight **ocho** 1
eight hundred **ochocientos/as** 6
eighteen **dieciocho** 1
eighth **octavo/a** 5
eighty **ochenta** 2
either... or **o... o** *conj.* 7
eldest **el/la mayor** 8
elect **elegir** *v.*
election **elecciones** *f. pl.*
electric appliance **electrodoméstico** *m.* 12
electrician **electricista** *m., f.*
electricity **luz** *f.* 12
elegant **elegante** *adj. m., f.* 6
elevator **ascensor** *m.* 5
eleven **once** 1
e-mail **correo** *m.* **electrónico** 4
e-mail address **dirrección** *f.* **electrónica** 11
  e-mail message **mensaje** *m.* **electrónico**
read e-mail **leer** *v.* **el correo electrónico** 4

embarrassed **avergonzado/a** *adj.* 5
embrace (each other) **abrazar(se)** *v.* 11
emergency **emergencia** *f.* 10
  emergency room **sala** *f.* **de emergencia** 10
employee **empleado/a** *m., f.* 5
employment **empleo** *m.*
end **fin** *m.* 4; **terminar** *v.* 2
  end table **mesita** *f.* 12
energy **energía** *f.* 13
engaged: get engaged (to) **comprometerse** *v.* **(con)** 9
engineer **ingeniero/a** *m., f.* 3
English (*language*) **inglés** *m.* 2; **inglés, inglesa** *adj.* 3
enjoy **disfrutar** *v.* **(de)** 15
enough **bastante** *adv.* 10
entertainment **diversión** *f.* 4
entrance **entrada** *f.* 12
envelope **sobre** *m.* 14
environment **medio ambiente** *m.* 13
equality **igualdad** *f.*
equipped **equipado/a** *adj.* 15
erase **borrar** *v.* 11
eraser **borrador** *m.* 2
errand *f.* **diligencia** 14
establish **establecer** *v.*
evening **tarde** *f.* 1
event **acontecimiento** *m.*
every day **todos los días** 10
everybody **todos** *m., pl.*
everything **todo** *m.* 5
  Everything is under control. **Todo está bajo control.** 7
exactly **en punto** 1
exam **examen** *m.* 2
excellent **excelente** *adj.* 5
excess **exceso** *m.* 15
  in excess **en exceso** 15
exchange **intercambiar** *v.*
  in exchange for **por** 11
exciting **emocionante** *adj. m., f.*
excursion **excursión** *f.*
excuse **disculpar** *v.*
Excuse me. (*May I?*) **Con permiso.** 1; (*I beg your pardon.*) **Perdón.** 1
exercise **ejercicio** *m.* 15
  hacer ejercicio 15
exit **salida** *f.* 5
expensive **caro/a** *adj.* 6
experience **experiencia** *f.*
explain **explicar** *v.* 2
explore **explorar** *v.*
expression **expresión** *f.*
extinction **extinción** *f.* 13
extremely delicious **riquísimo/a** *adj.* 8
extremely serious **gravísimo** *adj.* 13
eye **ojo** *m.* 10

F

fabulous **fabuloso/a** *adj* 5
face **cara** *f.* 7
facing **enfrente de** *prep.* 14
fact: in fact **de hecho**
fall (down) **caerse** *v.* 10
  fall asleep **dormirse (o:ue)** *v.* 7
  fall in love (with) **enamorarse** *v.* **(de)** 9
  fall (season) **otoño** *m.* 5
fallen **caído** *p.p.* 13
family **familia** *f.* 3
famous **famoso/a** *adj.*
fan **aficionado/a** *adj.* 4
  be a fan (of) **ser aficionado/a (a)** 4
far from **lejos de** *prep.* 2
farewell **despedida** *f.*
fascinate **fascinar** *v.* 7
fashion **moda** *f.* 6
  be in fashion **estar de moda** 6
fast **rápido/a** *adj.* 10
fat **gordo/a** *adj.* 3; **grasa** *f.* 15
father **padre** *m.* 3
father-in-law **suegro** *m.* 3
favorite **favorito/a** *adj.* 4
fax (machine) *fax* *m.* 11
fear **miedo** *m.* 3; fear **temer** *v.* 13
February **febrero** *m.* 5
feel **sentir(se) (e:ie)** *v.* 7
  feel like (*doing something*) **tener ganas de (+ *inf.*)** 3
festival **festival** *m.*
fever **fiebre** *f.* 10
  have a fever **tener** *v.* **fiebre** 10
few **pocos/as** *adj. pl.*
  fewer than **menos de (+ *number*)** 8
field: major field of study **especialización** *f.*
fifteen **quince** 1
  young woman's fifteenth birthday celebration **quinceañera** *f.* 9
  fifteen-year-old girl **quinceañera** *f.*
fifth **quinto/a** 5
fifty **cincuenta** 2
fight (for/against) **luchar** *v.* **(por/contra)**
figure (*number*) **cifra** *f.*
file **archivo** *m.* 11
fill **llenar** *v.* 11
  fill out (a form) **llenar (un formulario)** 14
  fill the tank **llenar** *v.* **el tanque** 11
finally **finalmente** *adv.* 15; **por último** 7; **por fin** 11
find **encontrar (o:ue)** *v.* 4
  find (each other) **encontrar(se)** *v.*
fine arts **bellas artes** *f., pl.*
fine **multa** *f.*
  That's fine. **Está bien.** 11
finger **dedo** *m.* 10
finish **terminar** *v.* 2

finish (*doing something*)
    terminar *v.* **de (+** *inf.*) 4
fire **incendio** *m.*; **despedir (e:i)**
firefighter **bombero/a** *m., f.*
firm **compañia** *f.*; **empresa** *f.*
first **primer, primero/a** *adj.* 5
fish (*food*) **pescado** *m.* 8; **pescar**
    v. 5; (*live*) **pez** *m.* 13
    fish market **pescadería** *f.* 14
fisherman **pescador** *m.*
fisherwoman **pescadora** *f.*
fishing **pesca** *f.* 5
fit (*clothing*) **quedar** *v.* 7
five **cinco** 1
five hundred **quinientos/as** 6
fix (*put in working order*) **arreglar**
    v. 11
fixed **fijo/a** *adj.* 6
flag **bandera** *f.*
flank steak **lomo** *m.* 8
flat tire: We had a flat tire. **Se nos**
    pinchó una llanta. 11
flexible **flexible** *adj.* 15
flood **inundación** *f.*
floor (*of a building*) **piso** *m.* 5;
    suelo *m.* 12
    ground floor **planta baja** *f.* 5
    top floor **planta** *f.* **alta**
flower **flor** *f.* 13
flu **gripe** *f.* 10
fog **niebla** *f.* 5
foggy: It's (very) foggy. **Hay**
    (mucha) niebla. 5
folk **folklórico/a** *adj.*
follow **seguir (e:i)** *v.* 4
food **comida** *f.* 8; **alimento**
foolish **tonto/a** *adj.* 3
foot **pie** *m.* 10
football **fútbol** *m.* **americano** 4
for **para** *prep.* 11; **por** *prep.* 11
    for example **por ejemplo** 11
    for me **para mí** 8
forbid **prohibir** *v.* 10, 12
foreign **extranjero/a** *adj.*
    foreign languages **lenguas**
    f. pl. **extranjeras** 2
forest **bosque** *m.* 13
forget **olvidar** *v.* 10
fork **tenedor** *m.* 12
form **formulario** *m.* 14
forty **cuarenta** *m.* 2
four **cuatro** 1
four hundred **cuatrocientos/as** 6
fourteen **catorce** 1
fourth **cuarto/a** *m., f.* 5
free **libre** *adj. m., f.* 4
    be free (of charge) **ser gratis** 14
    free time **tiempo libre** 4; spare
    (free) time **ratos libres** 4
freedom **libertad** *f.*
freezer **congelador** *m.* 12
French **francés, francesa** *adj.* 3
    French fries **papas** *f., pl* **fritas** 8
    patatas *f., pl* **fritas** 8
frequently **frecuentemente** *adv.*

10; **con frecuencia** *adv.* 10
Friday **viernes** *m., sing.* 2
fried **frito/a** *adj.* 8
    fried potatoes **papas** *f., pl.*
    fritas 8; **patatas** *f., pl.*
    fritas 8
friend **amigo/a** *m., f.* 3
friendly **amable** *adj. m., f.* 5
friendship **amistad** *f.* 9
from **de** *prep.* 1; **desde** *prep.* 6
    from the United States
    estadounidense *m., f. adj.* 3
    from time to time **de vez en**
    cuando 10
    He/She/It is from... **Es de...**;
    I'm from... **Soy de...** 1
fruit **fruta** *f.* 8
    fruit juice **jugo** *m.* **de fruta** 8
    fruit store **frutería** *f.* 14
full **lleno/a** *adj.* 11
fun **divertido/a** *adj.* 7
    fun activity **diversión** *f.* 4
    have fun **divertirse (e:ie)** *v.* 9
function **funcionar** *v.*
furniture **muebles** *m., pl.* 12
furthermore **además (de)** *adv.* 10
future **futuro** *adj.*; **porvenir** *m.*
    Here's to the future! **¡Por el**
    porvenir!
    in the future **en el futuro**

G

gain weight **aumentar** *v.* **de peso**
    15; **engordar** 15
game **juego** *m.*; (*match*)
    partido *m.* 4
    game show **concurso** *m.*
garage (*in a house*) **garaje** *m.* 12;
    garaje *m.* 11; **taller**
    (mecánico) 12
garden **jardín** *m.* 12
garlic **ajo** *m.* 8
gas station **gasolinera** *f.* 11
gasoline **gasolina** *f.* 11
geography **geografía** *f.* 2
German **alemán, alemana** *adj.* 3
get **conseguir (e:i)** *v.* 4; **obtener** *v.*
    get along well/badly with
    llevarse bien/mal con 9
    get bored **aburrirse** *v.*
    get off (a vehicle) **bajar(se)** *v.*
    (de) 11
    get on/into (a vehicle) **subir(se)**
    v. **a** 11
    get out of (a vehicle) **bajar(se)**
    v. **(de)** 11
    get up **levantarse** *v.* 7
gift **regalo** *m.* 6
girl **chica** *f.* 1; **muchacha** *f.* 3
girlfriend **novia** *f.* 3
give **dar** *v.* 6, 9;
    (*as a gift*) **regalar** 9
glass (*drinking*) **vaso** *m.* 12; **vidrio**

m. 13
    (made of) glass **de vidrio** 13
glasses **gafas** *f., pl.* 6
    (sun)glasses **gafas** *f., pl.*
    (oscuras/de sol) 6
gloves **guantes** *m., pl.* 6
go **ir** *v.* 4
    go away **irse** 7
    go by boat **ir en barco** 5
    go by bus **ir en autobús** 5
    go by car **ir en auto(móvil)** 5
    go by motorcycle **ir en**
    motocicleta 5
    go by plane **ir en avión** 5
    go by subway **ir en metro** 5
    go by taxi **ir en taxi** 5
    go by the bank **pasar por el**
    banco 14
    go by train **ir en tren** 5
    go down; **bajar(se)** *v.* 11
    go fishing **ir** *v.* **de pesca** 5
    go on a hike (in the mountains)
    ir de excursión (a las mon-
    tañas) 4; **hacer una excur-**
    sión 5
    go out **salir** *v.* 9
    go out (with) **salir** *v.* **(con)** 9
    go through customs **pasar** *v.*
    por la aduana 5
    go up **subir** *v.* 11
    go with **acompañar** *v.* 14
    Let's go. **Vamos.** 4
goblet **copa** *f.* 12
going to: be going to (*do*
    something) **ir a (+** *inf.*) 4
golf **golf** *m.* 4
good **buen, bueno/a** *adj.* 3, 6
    Good afternoon. **Buenas**
    tardes. 1
    Good evening. **Buenas**
    noches. 1
    Good idea. **Buena idea.** 4
    Good morning. **Buenos días.** 1
    Good night. **Buenas noches.** 1
    It's good that... **Es bueno**
    que... 12
goodbye **adiós** *m.* 1
    say goodbye (to) **despedirse** *v.*
    (de) (e:i) 7
good-looking **guapo/a** *adj.* 3
government **gobierno** *m.* 13
graduate (from/in) **graduarse** *v.*
    (de/en) 9
grains **cereales** *m., pl.* 8
granddaughter **nieta** *f.* 3
grandfather **abuelo** *m.* 3
grandmother **abuela** *f.* 3
grandparents **abuelos** *m. pl.* 3
grandson **nieto** *m.* 3
grape **uva** *f.* 8
grass **césped** *m.* 13; **hierba** *f.* 13
grave **grave** *adj.* 10
gray **gris** *adj. m., f.* 6
great **fenomenal** *adj. m., f.* 5
great-grandfather **bisabuelo** *m.* 3

great-grandmother **bisabuela** *f.* 3
green **verde** *adj. m., f.* 6
greet (each other) **saludar(se)**
   v. 11
greeting **saludo** *m.* 1
   Greetings to... **Saludos a...** 1
grilled (*food*) **a la plancha** 8
   grilled flank steak **lomo a la**
     plancha 8
ground floor **planta baja** *f.* 5
guest (*at a house/hotel*) **huésped**
   m., f. 5 (*invited to a function*)
   invitado/a *m., f.* 9
guide **guía** *m., f.* 13
gymnasium **gimnasio** *m.* 4

H

hair **pelo** *m.* 7
hairdresser **peluquero/a** *m., f.*
half **medio/a** *adj.* 3
   half-brother **medio hermano** 3;
   half-sister **media hermana** 3
   half-past... (*time*) **...y**
     media 1
hallway **pasillo** *m.* 12
ham **jamón** *m.* 8
hamburger **hamburguesa** *f.* 8
hand **mano** *f.* 1
Hands up! **¡Manos arriba!**
handsome **guapo/a** *adj.* 3
happen **ocurrir** *v.*
Happy birthday! **¡Feliz**
   cumpleaños! 9
happy **alegre** *adj.* 5; **contento/a**
   adj. 5; **feliz** *adj. m., f.* 5
   be happy **alegrarse** *v.* (**de**) 13
hard **difícil** *adj. m., f.* 3
hard-working **trabajador(a)**
   adj. 3
hardly **apenas** *adv.* 10
haste **prisa** *f.* 3
hat **sombrero** *m.* 6
hate **odiar** *v.* 9
have **tener** *v.* 3
   have time **tener tiempo** 4
   have to (*do something*) **tener**
     que (**+ *inf.***) 3; **deber** (**+ *inf.***)
   have a tooth removed **sacar(se)**
     una muela 10
he **él** 1
head **cabeza** *f.* 10
headache **dolor de cabeza** *m.* 10
health **salud** *f.* 10
healthy **saludable** *adj. m., f.* 10;
   sano/a *adj.* 10
   lead a healthy lifestyle **llevar** *v.*
     una vida sana 15
hear **oír** *v.* 4
heard **oído** *p.p.* 13
hearing: sense of hearing **oído**
   m. 10
heart **corazón** *m.* 10
heat **calor** *m.* 5

Hello. **Hola.** 1; (*on the telephone*)
   Aló. 11; **¿Bueno?** 11; **Diga.** 11
help **ayudar** *v.* 12; **servir (e:i)** *v.* 5
   help each other **ayudarse** *v.* 11
her **su(s)** *poss.* 3; (*of*) hers
   suyo(s)/a(s) *poss.* 11
here *adv.* **aquí** 1
   Here it is. **Aquí está.** 5
   Here we are at/in... **Aquí**
     estamos en... 2
Hi. **Hola.** 1
highway **autopista** *f.* 11;
   carretera *f.* 11
hike **excursión** *f.* 4
   go on a hike **hacer una excur-**
     sión 5; **ir de excursión** 4
hiker **excursionista** *m., f.* 4
hiking **de excursión** 4
hire **contratar** *v.*
his **su(s)** *poss. adj.* 3; (*of*) his
   suyo(s)/a(s) *poss. pron.* 11
history **historia** *f.* 2
hobby **pasatiempo** *m.* 4
hockey **hockey** *m.* 4
holiday **día** *m.* **de fiesta** 9
home **casa** *f.* 2
   home page **página** *f.*
     principal 11
homework **tarea** *f.* 2
hood **capó** *m.* 11; **cofre** *m.* 11
hope **esperar** *v.* (**+ *inf.***) 2;
   esperar *v.* 13
   I hope (that) **Ojalá (que)** 13
horror (*genre*) **de horror** *m.*
hors d'oeuvres **entremeses** *m.*,
   pl. 8
horse **caballo** *m.* 5
hospital **hospital** *m.* 10
hot: be (*feel*) (very) hot **tener**
   (mucho) calor 3
   It's (very) hot. **Hace (mucho)**
     calor. 5
hotel **hotel** *m.* 5
hour **hora** *f.* 1
house **casa** *f.* 2
household chores **quehaceres** *m.*
   pl. **domésticos** 12
housekeeper **ama** *m., f.* **de casa** 12
housing **vivienda** *f.* 12
How...! **¡Qué...!** 3
   how **¿cómo?** *adv.* 1
   How are you? **¿Qué tal?** 1
   How are you? **¿Cómo estás?**
     fam. 1
   How are you? **¿Cómo está**
     usted? *form.* 1
   How can I help you? **¿En qué**
     puedo servirles? 5
   How did it go for you...?
     ¿Cómo le/les fue...? 15
   How is it going? **¿Qué tal?** 1
   How is/are...? **¿Qué tal...?** 2
   How is the weather like? **¿Qué**
     tiempo hace? 15
   How many? **¿Cuánto(s)/a(s)?** 1

How much does... cost?
   ¿Cuánto cuesta...? 6
How old are you? **¿Cuántos**
   años tienes? *fam.* 3
however **sin embargo**
hug (each other) **abrazar(se)** *v.* 11
humanities **humanidades** *f., pl.* 2
hunger **hambre** *f.* 3
hundred **cien, ciento** *m.* 2, 6
hungry: be (very) hungry **tener** *v.*
   (mucha) hambre 3
hunt **cazar** *v.* 13
hurricane **huracán** *m.*
hurry **apurarse** *v.* 15; **darse prisa**
   v. 15
   be in a (big) hurry **tener** *v.*
     (mucha) prisa 3
hurt **doler (o:ue)** *v.* 10
   It hurts me a lot... **Me duele**
     mucho... 10
husband **esposo** *m.* 3

I

I **Yo** 1
I am... **Yo soy...** 1
I hope (that) **Ojalá (que)** *interj.* 13
I wish (that) **Ojalá (que)** *interj.* 13
ice cream **helado** *m.* 9
   ice cream shop **heladería** *f.* 14
iced **helado/a** *adj.* 9
   iced tea **té** *m.* **helado** 8
idea **idea** *f.* 4
if **si** *conj.* 4
illness **enfermedad** *f.* 10
important **importante** *adj.* 3
   be important to **importar** *v.* 7
   It's important that... **Es impor-**
     tante que... 12
impossible **imposible** *adj.* 13
   It's impossible. **Es imposible.** 13
improbable **improbable** *adj.* 13
   It's improbable. **Es improbable.**
   13
improve **mejorar** *v.* 13
in **en** *prep.* 2; **por** *prep.* 11
   in the afternoon **de la tarde** 1;
     por la tarde 7
   in a bad mood **de mal humor** 5
   in the direction of **para** *prep.* 1;
   in the early evening **de la tarde** 1
   in the evening **de la noche** 1;
     por la tarde 7
   in a good mood **de buen**
     humor 1
   in the morning **de la mañana** 1;
     por la mañana 7
   in love (with) **enamorado/a**
     (de) 5
   in search of **por** *prep.* 11
in front of **delante de** *prep.* 2
increase **aumento** *m.*
incredible **increíble** *adj.* 5
inequality **desigualdad** *f.*

infection **infección** *f.* 10
inform **informar** *v.*
injection **inyección** *f.* 10
   give an injection *v.* **poner una inyección** 10
injure (oneself) **lastimarse** 10
   injure (one's foot) **lastimarse** *v.* **(el pie)** 10
inner ear **oído** *m.* 10
inside **dentro** *adv.*
insist (on) **insistir** *v.* **(en)** 12
installments: pay in installments **pagar** *v.* **a plazos** 14
intelligent **inteligente** *adj.* 3
intend to **pensar** *v.* **(+ inf.)** 4
interest **interesar** *v.* 7
interesting **interesante** *adj.* 3
   be interesting to **interesar** *v.* 7
(inter)national **(inter)nacional** *adj. m., f.*
Internet **Internet** *m.* 11
interview **entrevista** *f.;* interview **entrevistar** *v.*
interviewer **entrevistador(a)** *m., f.*
introduction **presentación** *f.*
   I would like to introduce (name) to you... **Le presento a...** *form.* **Te presento a...** *fam.*
invest **invertir (e:ie)** *v.*
invite **invitar** *v.* 9
iron (clothes) **planchar** *v.* **la ropa** 12
Italian **italiano/a** *adj.* 3
its **su(s)** *poss. adj.* 3, **suyo(s)/a(s)** *poss. pron.* 11
It's me. **Soy yo.** 1

J

jacket **chaqueta** *f.* 6
January **enero** *m.* 5
Japanese **japonés, japonesa** *adj.* 3
jeans **bluejeans** *m., pl.* 6
jewelry store **joyería** *f.* 14
job **empleo** *m.;* **puesto** *m.;* **trabajo** *m.*
   job application **solicitud** *f.* **de trabajo**
jog **correr** *v.*
journalism **periodismo** *m.* 2
journalist **periodista** *m., f.* 3; **reportero/a** *m., f.*
joy **alegría** *f.* 9
   give joy **dar** *v.* **alegría** 9
joyful **alegre** *adj.* 5
juice **jugo** *m.* 8
July **julio** *m.* 5
June **junio** *m.* 5
jungle **selva, jungla** *f.* 13
just **apenas** *adv.*
   have just (done something) **acabar de (+ inf.)** 6

K

key **llave** *f.* 5
keyboard **teclado** *m.* 11
kilometer **kilómetro** *m.* 11
kind: That's very kind of you. **Muy amable.** 5
kiss **beso** *m.* 9; (each other) **besar(se)** *v.* 11
kitchen **cocina** *f.* 12
knee **rodilla** *f.* 10
knife **cuchillo** *m.* 12
know **saber** *v.* 8; **conocer** *v.* 8
know how **saber** *v.* 8

L

laboratory **laboratorio** *m.* 2
lack **faltar** *v.* 7
lake **lago** *m.* 13
lamp **lámpara** *f.* 12
land **tierra** *f.* 13
landlord **dueño/a** *m., f.* 8
landscape **paisaje** *m.* 5
language **lengua** *f.* 2
laptop (computer) **computadora** *f.* **portátil** 11
large (clothing size) **talla grande** 6
last **durar** *v.;* **pasado/a** *adj.* 6; **último/a** *adj.*
   last name **apellido** *m.* 3
   last night **anoche** *adv.* 6
   last week **semana** *f.* **pasada** 6
   last year **año** *m.* **pasado** 6
late **tarde** *adv.* 7
later **más tarde** 7
   See you later. **Hasta la vista.** 1; **Hasta luego.** 1
laugh **reírse (e:i)** *v.* 9
laughed **reído** *p.p.* 13
laundromat **lavandería** *f.* 14
law **ley** *f.* 13
lawyer **abogado/a** *m., f.*
lazy **perezoso/a** *adj.*
learn **aprender** *v.* **(a + inf.)** 3
least, at **por lo menos** *adv.* 10
leave **salir** *v.* 4; **irse** *v.* 7
   leave a tip **dejar una propina** 9
   leave behind **dejar** *v.*
   leave for (a place) **salir para**
   leave from **salir de**
left **izquierdo/a** *adj.* 2
   be left over **quedar** *v.* 7
   to the left of **a la izquierda de** 2
leg **pierna** *f.* 10
lemon **limón** *m.* 8
lend **prestar** *v.* 6
less **menos** *adv.* 10
   less... than **menos... que** 8
   less than **menos de (+ number)**
lesson **lección** *f.* 1
let **dejar** *v.* 12

---

let's see **a ver** 2
letter **carta** *f.* 4, 14
lettuce **lechuga** *f.* 8
liberty **libertad** *f.*
library **biblioteca** *f.* 2
license (driver's) **licencia** *f.* **de conducir** 11
lie **mentira** *f.* 4
life **vida** *f.* 9
   of my life **de mi vida** 15
lifestyle: lead a healthy lifestyle **llevar una vida sana** 15
lift **levantar** *v.* 15
   lift weights **levantar pesas** 15
light **luz** *f.* 12
like **como** *prep.* 8; **gustar** *v.* 7
   I like... **Me gusta(n)...** 2
   like this **así** *adv.* 10
   like very much *v.* **encantar** 7
   Do you like...? **¿Te gusta(n)...?** 2
likeable **simpático/a** *adj.* 3
likewise **igualmente** *adv.* 1
line **línea** *f.* 4; **cola** (queue) *f.* 14
listen (to) **escuchar** *v.* 2
   Listen! (command) **¡Oye!** *fam., sing.* 1; **¡Oigan!** *form., pl.*
   listen to music **escuchar música** 2
   listen (to) the radio **escuchar la radio** 2
literature **literatura** *f.* 2
little (quantity) **poco/a** *adj.* 5; **poco** *adv.* 10
live **vivir** *v.* 3
living room **sala** *f.* 12
loan **préstamo** *m.* 14; **prestar** *v.* 6, 14
lobster **langosta** *f.* 8
located **situado/a** *adj.*
   be located **quedar** *v.* 14
long (in length) **largo/a** *adj.* 6
look (at) **mirar** *v.* 2
look for **buscar** *v.* 2
lose **perder (e:ie)** *v.* 4
   lose weight **adelgazar** *v.* 15
lost **perdido/a** *adj.* 14
   be lost **estar perdido/a** 14
lot, a **muchas veces** *adv.* 10
lot of, a **mucho/a** *adj.* 2, 3
love (another person) **querer (e:ie)** *v.* 4; (inanimate objects) **encantar** *v.* 7 ; **amor** *m.* 9
   in love **enamorado/a** *adj.* 5
   I loved it! **¡Me encantó!** 15
luck **suerte** *f.* 3
lucky: be (very) lucky **tener (mucha) suerte** 3
luggage **equipaje** *m.* 5
lunch **almuerzo** *m.* 8
   have lunch **almorzar (o:ue)** *v.* 4

M

ma'am **señora (Sra.)** *f.* 1
mad **enojado/a** *adj.* 5
magazine **revista** *f.* 4
magnificent **magnífico/a** *adj.* 5
mail **correo** *m.* 14; **enviar** *v.*,
  mandar *v.* 14
  mail carrier **cartero** *m.* 14
mailbox **buzón** *m.* 14
main **principal** *adj. m., f.* 8
maintain **mantener** *v.* 15
major **especialización** *f.* 2
make **hacer** *v.* 4
  make the bed **hacer la cama** 12
make-up **maquillaje** *m.* 7
  to put on make-up **maquillarse**
    v. 7
man **hombre** *m.* 1
manager **gerente** *m., f.*
many **mucho/a** *adj.* 3
  many times **muchas veces** 10
map **mapa** *m.* 2
March **marzo** *m.* 5
margarine **margarina** *f.* 8
marinated fish **ceviche** *m.* 8
  lemon-marinated shrimp
    ceviche *m.* **de camarón** 8
marital status **estado** *m.* **civil** 9
market **mercado** *m.* 6
  (open air) market **mercado (al**
    aire libre) 6
marriage **matrimonio** *m.* 9
married **casado/a** *adj.* 9
  get married (to) **casarse** *v.*
    (con) 9
marvelous **maravilloso/a** *adj.* 5
marvelously **maravillosamente**
  adv.
massage **masaje** *m.* 15
masterpiece **obra maestra** *f.*
match (*sports*) **partido** *m.* 4
  match **hacer** *v.* **juego (con)** 6
mathematics **matemáticas**
  f., pl. 2
matter **importar** *v.* 7
maturity **madurez** *f.* 9
maximum **máximo/a** *m.* 11
May **mayo** *m.* 5
maybe **tal vez** 5; **quizás** 5
mayonnaise **mayonesa** *f.* 8
(to, for) me **me** *pron.* 6
meal **comida** *f.* 8
means of communication **medios**
  m. pl. **de comunicación**
meat **carne** *f.* 8
mechanic **mecánico/a** *m., f.* 11
  mechanic's repair shop **taller**
    mecánico 11
media **medios** *m., pl.* **de**
  comunicación
medical **médico/a** *adj.* 10
medication **medicamento** *m.* 10
medicine **medicina** *f.* 10
medium **mediano/a** *adj.*

meet (each other) **encontrar(se)**
  v. 11; **conocerse(se)** *v.* 8
meeting **reunión** *f.*
menu **menú** *m.* 8
message (*telephone*) **recado** *m.* 11,
  mensaje *m.*
Mexican **mexicano/a** *adj.* 3
Mexico **México** *m.* 1
microwave **microonda** *f.* 12
  microwave oven **horno** *m.* **de**
    microondas 12
middle age **madurez** *f.* 9
midnight **medianoche** *f.* 1
mile **milla** *f.* 11
milk **leche** *f.* 8
million **millón** *m.* 6
million of **millón de** *m.* 6
mine **mío(s)/a(s)** *poss.* 11
mineral **mineral** *m.* 15
  mineral water **agua** *f.*
    mineral 8
minute **minuto** *m.* 1
mirror **espejo** *m.* 7
Miss **señorita (Srta.)** *f.* 1
miss **perder** *v.* 4
mistaken **equivocado/a** *adj.*
modem **módem** *m.*
modern **moderno/a** *adj.*
molar **muela** *f.* 10
mom **mamá** *f.* 3
Monday **lunes** *m., sing.* 2
money **dinero** *m.* 6
monitor **monitor** *m.* 11
month **mes** *m.* 5
monument **monumento** *m.* 4
moon **luna** *f.* 13
more **más**
  more... than **más... que** 8
  more than **más de (+** *number***)** 8
morning **mañana** *f.* 1
mother **madre** *f.* 3
mother-in-law **suegra** *f.* 3
motor **motor** *m.*
motorcycle **motocicleta** *f.* 5
mountain **montaña** *f.* 4
mouse **ratón** *m.* 11
mouth **boca** *f.* 10
move (*from one house to another*)
  mudarse *v.* 12
movie **película** *f.* 4
  movie star **estrella** *f.* **de**
    cine
  movie theater **cine** *m.* 4
Mr. **señor (Sr.)** *m.* 1
Mrs. **señora (Sra.)** *f.* 1
much **mucho/a** *adj.* 2, 3
  very much **muchísimo/a** *adj.* 2
municipal **municipal** *adj. m., f.*
murder **crimen** *m.*
muscle **músculo** *m.* 15
museum **museo** *m.* 4
mushroom **champiñón** *m.* 8
music **música** *f.* 2
musical **musical** *adj.*
musician **músico/a** *m., f.*

must **deber** *v.* (**+** *inf.*) 3
  It must be... **Debe ser...** 6
my **mi(s)** *poss. adj.* 3; **mío(s)/a(s)**
  poss. pron. 11

N

name **nombre** *m.* 1
  in the name of **a nombre de** 5
  last name *m.* **apellido**
  My name is... **Me llamo...** 1
  be named **llamarse** *v.* 7
napkin **servilleta** *f.* 12
national **nacional** *adj. m., f.*
nationality **nacionalidad** *f.* 1
natural **natural** *adj. m., f.* 13
(natural) disaster **desastre** *m.*
  (natural)
  natural resource **recurso** *m.*
    natural 13
nature **naturaleza** *f.* 13
nauseated **mareado/a** *adj.* 10
near **cerca de** *prep.* 2
neaten **arreglar** *v.* 12
necessary **necesario/a** *adj.* 12
  It is necessary that...
    Es necesario que... 12;
    Hay que
neck **cuello** *m.* 10
need **faltar** *v.* 7; **necesitar** *v.* 2
negative **negativo/a** *adj.*
neighbor **vecino/a** *m., f.* 12
neighborhood **barrio** *m.* 12
neither... nor **ni... ni** *conj.* 7; neither **tampoco** *adv.* 7
nephew **sobrino** *m.* 3
nervous **nervioso/a** *adj.* 5
network **red** *f.* 11
never **nunca** *adj.* 7; **jamás** 7
new **nuevo/a** *adj.* 6
newlywed **recién casado/a**
  m., f. 9
news **noticias** *f., pl.*;
  actualidades *f., pl.*
newscast **noticiero** *m.*
newspaper **periódico** 4; **diario** *m.*
next **próximo/a** *adj.*
  next to **al lado de** *prep.* 2
nice **simpático/a** *adj.* 3; **amable**
  adj. m., f. 5
niece **sobrina** *f.* 3
night **noche** *f.* 1
  night stand **mesita** *f.* **de**
    noche 12
nine **nueve** 1
nine hundred **novecientos/as** 6
nineteen **diecinueve** 1
ninety **noventa** 2
ninth **noveno/a** 5
no **no** 1; **ningún, ninguno/a(s)**
  adj. 7
  no one **nadie** *pron.* 7
  No problem. **Ningún**
    problema. 7

no way **de ninguna manera**
nobody **nadie** 7
none **ningún, ninguno/a(s)** *adj.* 7
noon **mediodía** *m.* 1
nor **ni** *conj.* 7
north **norte** *m.* 14
  to the north **al norte** 14
nose **nariz** *f.* 10
not **no** 1
  not any **ningún, ninguno/a(s)** *adj.* 7
  not anyone **nadie** *pron.* 7
  not anything **nada** *pron.* 7
  not bad at all **nada mal** 5
  not either **tampoco** *adv.* 7
  not ever **nunca** *adv.* 7; **jamás** *adv.* 7
  not very well **no muy bien** 1
  not working **descompuesto/a** *adj.* 11
notebook **cuaderno** *m.* 1
nothing **nada** 1; 7
noun **sustantivo** *m.*
November **noviembre** *m.* 5
now **ahora** *adv.* 2
nowadays **hoy día** *adv.*
nuclear **nuclear** *adj. m., f.* 13
  nuclear energy **energía nuclear** 13
number **número** *m.* 1
nurse **enfermero/a** *m., f.* 10
nutrition **nutrición** *f.* 15
nutritionist **nutricionista** *m., f.* 15

O

o'clock: It's… o'clock **Son las…** 1
  It's one o'clock. **Es la una.** 1
obey **obedecer (c:zc)** *v.*
obligation **deber** *m.*
obtain **conseguir (e:i)** *v.* 4; **obtener** *v.*
obvious **obvio/a** *adj.* 13
  it's obvious **es obvio** 13
occupation **ocupación** *f.*
occur **ocurrir** *v.*
ocean **océano** *m.* 5
October **octubre** *m.* 5
of **de** *prep.* 1
  Of course. **Claro que sí.; Por supuesto.**
offer **oferta** *f.* 12; **ofrecer (c:zc)** *v.* 8
office **oficina** *f.* 12
  doctor's office **consultorio** *m.* 10
often **a menudo** *adv.* 10
Oh! **¡Ay!**
oil **aceite** *m.* 8
OK **regular** *adj.* 1
  It's okay. **Está bien.**
old **viejo/a** *adj.* 3; old age **vejez** *f.* 9

older **mayor** *adj. m., f.* 3
  older brother, sister **hermano/a mayor** *m., f.* 3
oldest **el/la mayor** 8
on **en** *prep.* 2: **sobre** *prep.* 2
  on behalf of **por** *prep.* 11
  on the dot **en punto** 1
  on time **a tiempo** 10
  on top of **encima de** 2
once **una vez** 6
one **un, uno/a** *m., f., sing. pron.* 1
  one hundred **cien(to)** 6
  one million **un millón** *m.* 6
  one more time **una vez más** 9
  one thousand **mil** 6
  one time **una vez** 6
  one way (*travel*) **ida** *f.*
onion **cebolla** *f.* 8
only **sólo** *adv.* 3; **único/a** *adj.* 3
  only child **hijo/a único/a** *m., f.* 3
open **abierto/a** *adj.* 5, 13; **abrir** *v.* 3
open-air **al aire libre** 6
opera **ópera** *f.*
operation **operación** *f.* 10
opposite **en frente de** *prep.* 14
or **o** *conj.* 7
orange **anaranjado/a** *adj.* 6; **naranja** *f.* 8
orchestra **orquesta** *f.*
order **mandar** 12; (*food*) **pedir (e:i)** *v.* 8
  in order to **para** *prep.* 11
orderly **ordenado/a** *adj.* 5
ordinal (*numbers*) **ordinal** *adj.*
other **otro/a** *adj.* 6
our **nuestro(s)/a(s)** *poss. adj.* 3; *poss. pron.* 11
out of order **descompuesto/a** *adj.* 11
outside **fuera** *adv.*
outskirts **afueras** *f., pl.* 12
oven **horno** *m.* 12
over **sobre** *prep.* 2
own **propio/a** *adj.*
owner **dueño/a** *m., f* 8

P

p.m. **tarde** *f.* 1
pack (*one's suitcases*) **hacer** *v.* **las maletas** 5
package **paquete** *m.* 14
page **página** *f.* 11
pain **dolor** *m.* 10
  have a pain **tener** *v.* **dolor** 10
paint **pintar** *v.*
painter **pintor(a)** *m., f.*
painting **pintura** *f.* 12
pair **par** *m.* 6
pants **pantalones** *m., pl.* 6
pantyhose **medias** *f., pl.* 6
paper **papel** *m.* 2; (*report*)

informe *m.*
  paper money **billete** *m.*
paragraph **párrafo** *m.*
Pardon me. (*May I?*) **con permiso** 1; (*Excuse me.*) Pardon me. **Perdón.** 1
parents **padres** *m., pl.* 3; **papás** *m., pl.* 3
park **estacionar** *v.* 11; **parque** *m.* 4
parking lot **estacionamiento** *m.* 14
partner (*one of a married couple*) **pareja** *f.* 9
party **fiesta** *f.* 9
passed **pasado/a** *p.p.*
passenger **pasajero/a** *m., f.* 1
passport **pasaporte** *m.* 5
past **pasado/a** *adj.* 6
pastime **pasatiempo** *m.* 4
pastry shop **pastelería** *f.* 14
patient **paciente** *m., f.* 10
patio **patio** *m.* 12
pay **pagar** *v.* 6
  pay in cash **pagar** *v.* **al contado; pagar en efectivo** 14
  pay in installments **pagar** *v.* **a plazos** 14
  pay the bill **pagar la cuenta** 9
peas **arvejas** *m.* 8
peace **paz** *f.*
peach **melocotón** *m.* 8
pear **pera** *f.* 8
pen **pluma** *f.* 2
pencil **lápiz** *m.* 1
penicillin **penicilina** *f.* 10
people **gente** *f.* 3
pepper (*black*) **pimienta** *f.* 8
pcr **por** *prep.* 11
perfect **perfecto/a** *adj.* 5
perhaps **quizás** 5; **tal vez** 5
permission **permiso** *m.*
person **persona** *f.* 3
pharmacy **farmacia** *f.* 10
phenomenal **fenomenal** *adj.* 5
photograph **foto(grafía)** *f.* 1
physical (*exam*) **examen** *m.* **médico** 10
physician **doctor(a), médico/a** *m., f.* 3
physics **física** *f. sing.* 2
pick up **recoger** *v.* 13
picture **cuadro** *m.* 12; **pintura** *f.* 12
pie **pastel** *m.* 9
pill (*tablet*) **pastilla** *f.* 10
pillow **almohada** *f.* 12
pineapple **piña** *f.* 8
pink **rosado/a** *adj.* 6
place **lugar** *m.* 4; **poner** *v.* 4
plaid **de cuadros** 6
plans **planes** *m., pl.* 4
  have plans **tener planes** 4
plant **planta** *f.* 13
plastic **plástico** *m.* 13
  (made of) plastic **de plástico** 13

plate **plato** *m.* 12
  platter of fried food **fuente** *f.*
  de fritada
play **drama** *m.*; **comedia** *f.*; **jugar**
  (u:ue) *v.* 4; (*a musical*
  instrument) **tocar** *v.*; (*a role*)
  hacer el papel de; (*cards*)
  jugar a (las cartas) 5; (*sports*)
  practicar deportes 4
player **jugador(a)** *m., f.* 4
playwright **dramaturgo/a**
  m., f.
plead **rogar (o:ue)** *v.* 12
pleasant **agradable** *adj. m., f.*
Please. **Por favor.** 1
Pleased to meet you. **Mucho**
  gusto. 1; **Encantado/a.** *adj.* 1
pleasing: be pleasing to **gustar** *v.* 7
pleasure **gusto** *m.* 1; **placer** *m.* 15
  It's a pleasure to... **Gusto de**
  (+ inf.)
  It's been a pleasure. **Ha sido un**
  placer. 15
  The pleasure is mine. **El gusto**
  es mío. 1
poem **poema** *m.*
poet **poeta** *m., f.*
poetry **poesía** *f.*
police (force) **policía** *f.* 11
  police officer **policía** *m.*, **mujer**
  policía *f.*
political **político/a** *adj.*
politician **político/a** *m., f.*
politics **política** *f.*
polka-dotted **de lunares** 6
poll **encuesta** *f.*
pollute **contaminar** *v.* 13
polluted **contaminado/a** *m., f.* 13
  be polluted **estar contami-**
  nado/a 13
pollution **contaminación** *f.* 13
pool **piscina** *f.* 4
poor **pobre** *adj.* 6
population **población** *f.* 13
pork **cerdo** *m.* 8
  pork chop **chuleta** *f.* **de**
  cerdo 8
portable **portátil** *adj.* 11
  portable computer **computa-**
  dora *f.* **portátil** 11
position **puesto** *m.*
possessive **posesivo/a** *adj.* 3
possible **posible** *adj.* 13
  It's (not) possible. **(No) Es**
  posible. 13
post office **correo** *m.* 14
postcard **postal** *f.* 4; **tarjeta**
  postal *f.* 4
poster **cartel** *m.* 12
potato **papa** *f.* 8; **patata** *f.* 8
pottery **cerámica** *f.* 15
practice **entrenarse** *v.* 15;
  practicar *v.* 2
prefer **preferir (e:ie)** *v.* 4
pregnant **embarazada** *adj. f.* 10

prepare **preparar** *v.* 2
preposition **preposición** *f.*
prescribe (*medicine*) **recetar** *v.* 10
prescription **receta** *f.* 10
present **regalo** *m.*; **presentar** *v.*
pressure **presión** *f.*
  be under a lot of pressure **sufrir**
  muchas presiones 15
pretty **bonito/a** *adj.* 3; **bastante**
  adv. 13
price **precio** *m.* 6
  (fixed, set) price **precio** *m.* **fijo** 6
print **estampado/a** *adj.*;
  imprimir *v.* 11
printer **impresora** *f.* 11
private (*room*) **individual** *adj.*
prize **premio** *m.*
probable **probable** *adj.* 13
  It's (not) probable. **(No) Es**
  probable. 13
problem **problema** *m.* 1
profession **profesión** *f.* 3
professor **profesor(a)** *m., f.*
program **programa** *m.* 1
programmer **programador(a)**
  m., f. 3
prohibit **prohibir** *v.* 10
promotion (*career*) **ascenso** *m.*
pronoun **pronombre** *m.*
protect **proteger** *v.* 13
protein **proteína** *f.* 15
provided (that) **con tal (de) que**
  conj. 13
psychologist **psicólogo/a**
  m., f.
psychology **psicología** *f.* 2
publish **publicar** *v.*
Puerto Rican **puertorriqueño/a**
  adj. 3
Puerto Rico **Puerto Rico** *m.* 1
pull a tooth **sacar una muela**
purchases **compras** *f., pl.* 5
pure **puro/a** *adj.* 13
purple **morado/a** *adj.* 6
purse **bolsa** *f.* 6
put **poner** *v.* 4; **puesto/a** *p.p.* 13
  put (a letter) in the mailbox
  echar (una carta) al buzón
  14
  put on (*a performance*)
  presentar *v.*
  put on (*clothing*) **ponerse** *v.* 7
  put on makeup **maquillarse**
  v. 7

Q

quality **calidad** *f.* 6
quarter **trimestre** *m.* 2
  quarter after (*time*) **y cuarto** 1;
  y quince 1
  quarter to (*time*) **menos cuarto**
  1; **menos quince** 1
question **pregunta** *f.* 2

quickly **rápido** *adv.* 10
quiet **tranquilo/a** *adj.* 15
quit **dejar** *v.*
quiz **prueba** *f.* 2

R

racism **racismo** *m.*
radio (*medium*) **radio** *f.* 2
  radio (set) **radio** *m.* 11
rain **llover (o:ue)** *v.* 5; **lluvia** *f.* 13
  It's raining. **Llueve.** 5
raincoat **impermeable** *m.* 6
rainforest **bosque** *m.* **tropical** 13
raise (*salary*) **aumento de**
  sueldo
rather **bastante** *adv.* 10
read **leer** *v.* 3; **leído/a** *p.p.* 13
  read e-mail **leer correo**
  electrónico 4
  read a magazine **leer una**
  revista 4
  read a newspaper **leer un**
  periódico 4
ready **listo/a** *adj.*
  (Are you) ready? **¿(Están)**
  listos? 15
reap the benefits (of) *v.* **disfrutar**
  v. **(de)** 15
reason **razón** *f.*
receive **recibir** *v.* 3
recommend **recomendar (e:ie)**
  v. 8; 12
record **grabar** *v.* 11
recreation **diversión** *f.* 4
recycle **reciclar** *v.* 13
recycling **reciclaje** *m.* 13
red **rojo/a** *adj.* 6
red-haired **pelirrojo/a** *adj.* 3
reduce **reducir** *v.* 13
  reduce stress/tension **aliviar el**
  estrés/la tensión 15
refrigerator **refrigerador** *m.* 12
region **región** *f.* 13
regret **sentir (e:ie)** *v.* 13
related to sitting **sedentario/a**
  adj. 15
relationships **relaciones** *f., pl.* 9
relatives **parientes** *m., pl.* 3
relax **relajarse** *v.* 9
remain **quedarse** *v.* 7
remember **acordarse (o:ue)** *v.*
  (de) 7; **recordar (o:ue)** *v.* 4
remote control **control remoto**
  m. 11
rent **alquilar** *v.* 12; (payment)
  alquiler *m.* 12
repeat **repetir (e:i)** *v.* 4
report **informe** *m.*; **reportaje** *m.*
reporter **reportero/a** *m., f.*
representative **representante** *m., f.*
request **pedir (e:i)** *v.* 4
reservation **reservación** *f.* 5
resign (from) **renunciar (a)** *v.*

resolve **resolver (o:ue)** *v.* 13
resolved **resuelto/a** *p.p.* 13
resource **recurso** *m.* 13
responsibility **deber** *m.* **respons-abilidad** *f.*
rest **descansar** *v.* 2
   the rest **lo/los/las demás** *pron.*
restaurant **restaurante** *m.* 4
résumé **currículum** *m.*
retire (from work) **jubilarse** *v.* 9
return **regresar** *v.* 2; **volver (o:ue)** *v.* 4
   return trip **vuelta** *f.*
returned **vuelto/a** *p.p.* 13
rice **arroz** *m.* 8
rich **rico/a** *adj.* 6
ride a bicycle **pasear** *v.* **en bicicleta** 4
ride a horse **montar** *v.* **a caballo** 5
ridiculous **ridículo/a** *adj.* 13
   It's ridiculous. **Es ridículo.** 13
right **derecha** *f.* 2;
   right away **enseguida** *adv.* 9
   right here **aquí mismo** 11
   right now **ahora mismo** 5
   right there **allí mismo** 14
   be right **tener razón** 3
   to the right of **a la derecha de** 2
   right? (*question tag*) **¿no?** 1; **¿verdad?** 1
rights **derechos** *m.*
ring (*a doorbell*) **sonar (o:ue)** *v.* 11
river **río** *m.* 13
road **camino** *m.*
roast **asado/a** *adj.* 8
roast chicken **pollo** *m.* **asado** 8
rollerblade **patinar en línea** *v.* 4
romantic **romántico/a** *adj.*
room **habitación** *f.* 5; **cuarto** *m.* 7; 13
   living room **sala** *f.* 12
roommate **compañero/a** *m., f.* **de cuarto** 2
roundtrip **de ida y vuelta** 5
   roundtrip ticket **pasaje** *m.* **de ida y vuelta** 5
routine **rutina** *f.* 7
rug **alfombra** *f.* 12
run **correr** *v.* 3
   run errands **hacer diligencias** 14
   run into (*have an accident*) **chocar (con)** *v.*; (*meet accidentally*) **encontrar(se) (o:ue)** *v.* 11; (*run into something*) **darse (con)** 10
   run into (each other) **encontrar(se) (o:ue)** *v.* 11
rush **apurarse, darse prisa** *v.* 15
Russian **ruso/a** *adj.* 3

S

sad **triste** *adj.* 5; 13
   It's sad. **Es triste.** 13
said **dicho/a** *p.p.* 13
sake: for the sake of **por**
salad **ensalada** *f.* 8
salary **salario** *m.*; **sueldo** *m.*
sale **rebaja** *f.* 6
salesperson **vendedor(a)** *m., f.* 6
salmon **salmón** *m.* 8
salt **sal** *f.* 8
same **mismo/a** *adj.* 3
sandal **sandalia** *f.* 6
sandwich **sándwich** *m.* 8
Saturday **sábado** *m.* 2
sausage **salchicha** *f.* 8
save (*on a computer*) **guardar** *v.* 11; save (money) **ahorrar** *v.* 14
savings **ahorros** *m.* 14
   savings account **cuenta** *f.* **de ahorros** 14
say **decir** *v.* 4
say (that) **decir (que)** *v.* 4, 9
scarcely **apenas** *adv.* 10
scared: be (very) scared (of) **tener (mucho) miedo (de)** 3
schedule **horario** *m.* 2
school **escuela** *f.* 1
science *f.* **ciencia** 2
   science fiction **ciencia ficción** *f.*
scientist **científico/a** *m., f.*
screen **pantalla** *f.* 11
scuba dive **bucear** *v.* 4
sculpt **esculpir** *v.*
sculptor **escultor(a)** *m., f.*
sculpture **escultura** *f.*
sea **mar** *m.* 5
season **estación** *f.* 5
seat **silla** *f.* 2
second **segundo/a** *adj.* 5
secretary **secretario/a** *m., f.*
sedentary **sedentario/a** *adj.* 15
see **ver** *v.* 4
   see (you, him, her) again **volver a ver(te, lo, la)**
   see movies **ver películas** 4
   See you. **Nos vemos.** 1
   See you later. **Hasta la vista.** 1; **Hasta luego.** 1
   See you soon. **Hasta pronto.** 1
   See you tomorrow. **Hasta mañana.** 1
seem **parecer** *v.* 8
seen **visto/a** *p.p.* 13
sell **vender** *v.* 6
semester **semestre** *m.* 2
send **enviar; mandar** *v.* 14
separate (from) **separarse** *v.* (de) 9
separated **separado/a** *adj.* 9
September **septiembre** *m.* 5
sequence **secuencia** *f.*
serious **grave** *adj.* 10
serve **servir (e:i)** *v.* 8

set (*fixed*) **fijo** *adj.* 6
   set the table **poner la mesa** 12
seven **siete** 1
seven hundred **setecientos/as** 6
seventeen **diecisiete** 1
seventh **séptimo/a** 5
seventy **setenta** 2
sexism **sexismo** *m.*
shame **lástima** *f.* 13
   It's a shame. **Es una lástima.** 13
shampoo **champú** *m.* 7
shape **forma** *f.* 15
   be in good shape **estar en buena forma** 15
   stay in shape **mantenerse en forma** 15
share **compartir** *v.* 3
sharp (*time*) **en punto** 1
shave **afeitarse** *v.* 7
shaving cream **crema** *f.* **de afeitar** 7
she **ella** 1
shellfish **mariscos** *m., pl.* 8
ship **barco** *m.*
shirt **camisa** *f.* 6
shoe **zapato** *m.* 6
   shoe size **número** *m.* 6
   shoe store **zapatería** *f.* 14
   tennis shoes **zapatos** *m., pl.* **de tenis** 6
shop **tienda** *f.* 6
shopping, to go **ir de compras** 5
   shopping mall **centro comercial** *m.* 6
short (*in height*) **bajo/a** *adj.* 3; (*in length*) **corto/a** *adj.* 6
short story **cuento** *m.*
shorts **pantalones cortos** *m., pl.* 6
should (*do something*) **deber** *v.* (+ *infin.*) 3
show **espectáculo** *m.*; **mostrar (o:ue)** *v.* 4
   game show **concurso** *m.*
shower **ducha** *f.* 7; **ducharse** *v.* 7; **bañarse** *v.* 7
shrimp **camarón** *m.* 8
siblings **hermanos/as** *pl.* 3
sick **enfermo/a** *adj.* 10
   be sick **estar enfermo/a** 10
   get sick **enfermarse** *v.* 10
sightseeing: go sightseeing **hacer turismo** 5
sign **firmar** *v.* 14; **letrero** *m.* 14
silk **seda** *f.* 6; (made of) **de seda** 6
silly **tonto/a** *adj.* 3
silverware **cubierto** *m.*
since **desde** *prep.*
sing **cantar** *v.* 2
singer **cantante** *m., f.*
single **soltero/a** *adj.* 9
   single room **habitación** *f.* **individual** 5
sink **lavabo** *m.* 7

sir **señor (Sr.)** *m.* 1
sister **hermana** *f.* 3
sister-in-law **cuñada** *f.* 3
sit down **sentarse (e:ie)** *v.* 7
six **seis** 1
six hundred **seiscientos/as** 6
sixteen **dieciséis** 1
sixth **sexto/a** 5
sixty **sesenta** 2
size **talla** *f.* 6
   shoe size *m.* **número** 6
skate (in-line) **patinar (en línea)** 4
skateboard **andar en patineta**
   v. 4
ski **esquiar** *v.* 4
skiing **esquí** *m.* 4
   water-skiing **esquí** *m.*
     acuático 4
skirt **falda** *f.* 6
sky **cielo** *m.* 13
sleep **dormir (o:ue)** *v.* 4; **sueño**
   m. 3
   go to sleep **dormirse**
     (o:ue) *v.* 7
sleepy: be (very) sleepy **tener**
   (mucho) sueño 3
slender **delgado** *adj.* 3
slim down **adelgazar** *v.* 15
slippers **pantuflas** *f.* 7
slow **lento/a** *adj.* 11
slowly **despacio** *adv.* 10
small **pequeño/a** *adj.* 3
smart **listo/a** *adj.* 5
smile **sonreír (e:i)** *v.* 9
smiled **sonreído** *p.p.* 13
smoggy: It's (very) smoggy. **Hay**
   (mucha) contaminación.
smoke **fumar** *v.* 8, 15
   (not) to smoke **(no) fumar** 15
smoking section **sección** *f.* **de**
   fumar 8
   (non) smoking section *f.* **sección**
     de (no) fumar 8
snack **merendar** *v.* 8; afternoon
   snack **merienda** *f.* 15
   have a snack **merendar** *v.*
sneakers **los zapatos de tenis** 6
sneeze **estornudar** *v.* 10
snow **nevar (e:ie)** *v.* 5; **nieve** *f.*
snowing: It's snowing. **Nieva.** 5
so (*in such a way*) **así** *adv.* 10;
   tan *adv.*
   so much **tanto** *adv.*
   so so **regular** 1, **así así**
   so that **para que** *conj.* 13
soap **jabón** *m.* 7
   soap opera **telenovela** *f.*
soccer **fútbol** *m.* 4
sociology *f.* **sociología** 2
sock **calcetín** *m.* 6
sofa **sofá** *m.* 12
soft drink **refresco** *m.* 8
software **programa** *m.* **de**
   computación 11
soil **tierra** *f.* 13
solar **solar** *adj., m., f.* 13

solar energy **energía solar** 13
solution **solución** *f.* 13
solve **resolver (o:ue)** *v.* 13
some **algún, alguno/a(s)** *adj.* 7;
   unos/as *pron./ m., f., pl; indef.*
   art. 1
somebody **alguien** *pron.* 7
someone **alguien** *pron.* 7
something **algo** *pron.* 7
sometimes **a veces** *adv.* 10
son **hijo** *m.* 3
song **canción** *f.*
son-in-law **yerno** *m.* 3
soon **pronto** *adv.* 10
   See you soon. **Hasta pronto.** 1
sorry: be sorry **sentir (e:ie)** *v.* 13
   I'm sorry. **Lo siento.** 1
   I'm so sorry. **Mil perdones.;**
     Lo siento muchísimo. 4
soup **caldo** *m.* 8; **sopa** *f.* 8
south **sur** *m.* 14
   to the south **al sur** 14
Spain **España** *f.* 1
Spanish (*language*) **español** *m.* 2;
   español(a) *adj.* 3
spare (free) time **ratos libres** 4
speak **hablar** *v.* 2
specialization **especialización** *f.*
spectacular **espectacular** *adj. m.,*
   f. 15
speech **discurso** *m.*
speed **velocidad** *f.* 11
   speed limit **velocidad** *f.*
     máxima 11
spelling **ortografía** *f.,* **ortográfi-**
   co/a *adj.*
spend (*money*) **gastar** *v.* 6
   spend time **pasar tiempo** 4
spoon (*table or large*) **cuchara** *f.* 12
sport **deporte** *m.* 4
   sports-related **deportivo/a**
     adj. 4
spouse **esposo/a** *m., f.* 3
sprain (one's ankle) **torcerse**
   (o:ue) *v.* **(el tobillo)** 10
sprained **torcido/a** *adj.* 10
   be sprained **estar torcido/a** 10
spring **primavera** *f.* 5
(city or town) square **plaza** *f.* 4
stadium **estadio** *m.* 2
stage **etapa** *f.* 9
stairs **escalera** *f.* 12
stairway **escalera** *f.* 12
stamp **estampilla** *f.* 14; **sello**
   m. 14
stand in line **hacer** *v.* **cola** 14
star **estrella** *f.* 13
start (*a vehicle*) **arrancar** *v.* 11;
   establecer *v.*
state **estado** *m.*
station **estación** *f.* 5
statue **estatua** *f.*
status: marital status **estado** *m.*
   civil 9
stay **quedarse** *v.* 7
   stay in shape **mantenerse en**

   forma 15
steak **bistec** *m.* 8
steering wheel **volante** *m.* 11
step **etapa** *f.*
stepbrother **hermanastro** *m.* 3
stepdaughter **hijastra** *f.* 3
stepfather **padrastro** *m.* 3
stepmother **madrastra** *f.* 3
stepsister **hermanastra** *f.* 3
stepson **hijastro** *m.* 3
stereo **estéreo** *m.* 11
still **todavía** *adv.* 5
stockbroker **corredor(a)** *m., f.* **de**
   bolsa
stockings **medias** *f., pl.* 6
stomach **estómago** *m.* 10
stone **piedra** *f.* 13
stop **parar** *v.* 11
   stop (*doing something*) **dejar de**
     (+ inf.) 13
store **tienda** *f.* 6
storm **tormenta** *f.*
story **cuento** *m.;* **historia** *f.*
stove **cocina, estufa** *f.* 12
straight **derecho** *adj.* 14
   straight (ahead) **derecho** 14
straighten up **arreglar** *v.* 12
strange **extraño/a** *adj.* 13
   It's strange. **Es extraño.** 13
strawberry **frutilla** *f.* 8, **fresa**
street **calle** *f.* 11
stress **estrés** *m.* 15
stretching **estiramiento** *m.* 15
   to do stretching exercises **hacer**
     ejercicios
   m. pl. **de estiramiento** 15
strike (*labor*) **huelga** *f.*
stripe **raya** *f.* 6
   striped **de rayas** 6
stroll **pasear** *v.* 4
strong **fuerte** *adj.* 15
struggle (for) **luchar** *v.* **(por)**
student **estudiante** *m., f.* 1, 2;
   estudiantil *adj.* 2
study **estudiar** *v.* 2
stuffed-up (*sinuses*) **congestio-**
   nado/a *adj.* 10
stupendous **estupendo/a** *adj.* 5
style **estilo** *m.*
suburbs **afueras** *f., pl.* 12
subway **metro** *m.* 5
   subway station **estación** *f.*
     del metro 5
success **éxito** *m.*
successful: be successful **tener**
   éxito
such as **tales como**
suddenly **de repente** *adv.* 6
suffer **sufrir** *v.* 10
   suffer an illness **sufrir una**
     enfermedad 10
sufficient **bastante** *adj.*
sugar **azúcar** *m.* 8
suggest **sugerir (e:ie)** *v.* 12
suit **traje** *m.* 6
suitcase **maleta** *f.* 1

summer **verano** *m.* 5
sun **sol** *m.* 5; 13
sunbathe **tomar** *v.* **el sol** 4
Sunday **domingo** *m.* 2
(sun)glasses **gafas** *f., pl.*
 (oscuras/de sol) 6; **lentes** *m.*
 pl. **(de sol)** 6
sunny: It's (very) sunny. **Hace**
 (mucho) sol. 5
supermarket **supermercado**
 m. 14
suppose **suponer** *v.* 4
sure **seguro/a** *adj.* 5
 be sure **estar seguro/a** 5
surf (*the Internet*) **navegar** *v.* **(en**
 Internet) 11
surprise **sorprender** *v.* 9;
 sorpresa *f.* 9
survey **encuesta** *f.*
sweat **sudar** *v.* 15
sweater **suéter** *m.* 6
sweep the floor **barrer el suelo** 12
sweets **dulces** *m., pl.* 9
swim **nadar** *v.* 4
swimming **natación** *f.* 4
 swimming pool **piscina** *f.* 4
symptom **síntoma** *m.* 10

T

table **mesa** *f.* 2
tablespoon **cuchara** *f.* 12
tablet (*pill*) **pastilla** *f.* 10
take **tomar** *v.* 2; **llevar** *v.* 6;
 take care of **cuidar** 13
 take someone's temperature
  tomar la temperatura 10
 take (*wear*) a shoe size *v.*
  calzar 6
 take a bath **bañarse** *v.* 7
 take a shower **ducharse** *v.* 7
 take into account **tomar** *v.* **en**
  cuenta
 take off **quitarse** *v.* 7
 take out (*the trash*) *v.* **sacar (la**
  basura) 12
 take photos **tomar fotos** 5;
  sacar fotos 5
talented **talentoso/a** *adj.*
talk *v.* **hablar** 2
 talk show **programa** *m.* **de**
  entrevistas
tall **alto/a** *adj.* 3
tank **tanque** *m.* 11
tape (*audio*) **cinta** *f.*
 tape recorder **grabadora** *f.* 1
taste **probar (o:ue)** *v.* 8
 taste + (*adj.*) **saber + (adj.)** 8
 taste like **saber a** 8
tasty **rico/a** *adj.* 8; **sabroso/a** *adj.*
 8
tax **impuesto** *m.*
taxi **taxi** *m.* 5
tea **té** *m.* 8
teach **enseñar** *v.* 2

teacher **profesor(a)** *m., f.* 1;
 maestro/a *m., f.*
team **equipo** *m.* 4
technician **técnico/a** *m., f.*
telecommuting **teletrabajo** *m.*
telephone **teléfono** *m.* 11
 cellular telephone **teléfono** *m.*
  celular 11
television **televisión** *f.* 11
 television set **televisor** *m.* 11
tell **contar** *v.*; **decir** *v.* 4
tell (that) **decir** *v.* **(que)** 4, 9
 tell the truth **decir la verdad** 4
 tell lies **decir mentiras** 4
temperature **temperatura** *f.* 10
ten **diez** 1
tennis **tenis** *m.* 4
 tennis shoes **zapatos** *m., pl.* **de**
  tenis 6
tension **tensión** *f.* 15
tent **tienda** *f.* **de campaña**
tenth **décimo/a** 5
terrible **terrible** *adj. m., f.* 13
 It's terrible. **Es terrible.** 13
terrific **chévere** *adj.*
test **prueba** *f.* 2; **examen** *m.* 2
Thank you. *f., pl.* **Gracias.** 1
 Thank you (very much).
  (Muchas) gracias. 1
 Thank you very, very much.
  Muchísimas gracias. 9
 Thanks (a lot). **(Muchas)**
  gracias. 1
 Thanks again. (lit. Thanks one
  more time.) **Gracias una vez**
  más. 9
 Thanks for everything. **Gracias**
  por todo. 9, 15
that **que, quien, lo que** *pron.* 12
 that (one) **ése, ésa, eso**
  pron. 6; **ese, esa,** *adj.* 6
 that (*over there*) **aquél,**
  aquélla, aquello *pron.* 6;
  aquel, aquella *adj.* 6
 that which **lo que** *conj.* 12
 That's not the way it is. **No es**
  así.
 that's why **por eso** 11
the **el** *m.,* **la** *f. sing.,* **los** *m.,* **las** *f.*
 pl.
theater **teatro** *m.*
their **su(s)** *poss. adj.* 3;
 suyo(s)/a(s) *poss. pron.* 11
then **después** (*afterward*) *adv.* 7;
 entonces (*as a result*) *adv.* 7;
 luego (*next*) *adv.* 7; **pues**
 adv. 15
there **allí** *adv.* 5
 There is/are... **Hay...** 1;
 There is/are not... **No hay...** 1
therefore **por eso** 11
these **éstos, éstas** *pron.* 6;
 estos, estas *adj.* 6
they **ellos** *m.,* **ellas** *f. pron.*
thin **delgado/a** *adj.* 3

thing **cosa** *f.* 1
think **pensar (e:ie)** *v.* 4; (believe)
 creer *v.*
 think about **pensar en** *v.* 4
third **tercero/a** 5
thirst **sed** *f.* 3
thirsty: be (very) thirsty **tener**
 (mucha) sed 3
thirteen **trece** 1
thirty **treinta** 1, 2; thirty (*minutes*
 past the hour) **y treinta; y**
 media 1
this **este, esta** *adj.;* **éste, ésta,**
 esto *pron.* 6
 This is... (*introduction*)
  Éste/a es... 1
 This is he/she. (*on telephone*)
  Con él/ella habla. 11
those **ésos, ésas** *pron.* 6; **esos,**
 esas *adj.* 6
those (*over there*) **aquéllos,**
 aquéllas *pron.* 6; **aquellos,**
 aquellas *adj.* 6
thousand **mil** *m.* 6
three **tres** 1
three hundred **trescientos/as** 6
throat **garganta** *f.* 10
through **por** *prep.* 11
throughout: throughout the world
 en todo el mundo 13
throw **echar** *v.*
Thursday **jueves** *m., sing.* 2
thus (*in such a way*) **así** *adj.*
ticket **boleto** *m.;* **pasaje** *m.* 5
tie **corbata** *f.* 6
time **vez** *f.* 6; time **tiempo** *m.* 4
 buy on time **comprar a plazos**
  m., pl.
 have a good/bad time **pasarlo**
  bien/mal 9
 We had a great time. **Lo**
  pasamos de película.
 What time is it? **¿Qué hora**
  es? 1
 (At) What time...? **¿A qué**
  hora...? 1
times **veces** *f., pl.* 6
 many times **muchas veces** 10
 two times **dos veces** 6
tip **propina** *f.* 9
tire **llanta** *f.* 11
tired **cansado/a** *adj.* 5
 be tired **estar cansado/a** 5
title **título** *m.*
to **a** *prep.* 1
toast (*drink*) **brindar** *v.* 9
 toast **pan** *m.* **tostado**
toasted **tostado/a** *adj.* 8
 toasted bread **pan tostado** *m.* 8
toaster **tostadora** *f.* 12
today **hoy** *adv.* 2
 Today is... **Hoy es...** 2
together **juntos/as** *adj.* 9
toilet **inodoro** *m.* 7
tomato **tomate** *m.* 8
tomorrow **mañana** *f.* 1

See you tomorrow. **Hasta mañana.** 1
tonight **esta noche** *adv.* 4
too **también** *adv.* 2; 7
  too much **demasiado** *adv.* 6; **en exceso** 15
tooth **diente** *m.* 7; tooth **muela** *f.*
toothpaste **pasta** *f.* **de dientes** 7
tornado **tornado** *m.*
tortilla **tortilla** *f.* 8
touch **tocar** *v.* 13
tour an area **recorrer** *v*; **excursión** *f.* 4
  go on a tour **hacer una excursión** 5
tourism **turismo** *m.* 5
tourist **turista** *m., f.* 1; **turístico/a** *adj.*
toward **hacia** *prep.* 14; **para** *prep.* 11
towel **toalla** *f.* 7
town **pueblo** *m.* 4
trade **oficio** *m.*
traffic **circulación** *f.* 11; **tráfico** *m.* 11
  traffic signal **semáforo** *m.*
tragedy **tragedia** *f.*
trail **sendero** *m.* 13
  trailhead **sendero** *m.* 13
train **entrenarse** *v.* 15; **tren** *m.* 5
  train estation **estación** *f.* **(de) tren** *m.* 5
trainer **entrenador/a** *m., f.* 15
translate **traducir** *v.* 8
trash **basura** *f.* 12
travel **viajar** *v.* 2
  travel agency **agencia** *f.* **de viajes** 5
  travel agent **agente** *m., f.* **de viajes** 5
  travel documents **documentos** *pl. m.* **de viaje**
traveler **viajero/a** *m., f.* 5
  (traveler's) check **cheque (de viajero)** 14
treadmill **cinta caminadora** *f.* 15
tree **árbol** *m.* 13
trillion **billón** *m.*
trimester **trimestre** *m.* 2
trip **viaje** *m.* 5
  take a trip **hacer un viaje** 5
tropical forest **bosque** *m.* **tropical** 13
truck **camión** *m.*
true **verdad** *adj.* 13
  It's (not) true **(No) Es verdad** 13
trunk **baúl** *m.* 11
truth **verdad** *f.*
try **intentar** *v.*; **probar (o:ue)** *v.* 8
  try (*to do something*) **tratar de (+ *inf.*)** 15
  try on **probarse (o:ue)** *v.* 7
t-shirt **camiseta** *f.* 6
Tuesday **martes** *m., sing.* 2

tuna **atún** *m.* 8
turkey *m.* **pavo** 8
turn **doblar** *v.* 14
  turn off (*electricity/appliance*) **apagar** *v.* 11
  turn on (*electricity/appliance*) **poner** *v.* 11; **prender** *v.* 11
twelve **doce** 1
twenty **veinte** 1
twenty-eight **veintiocho** 1
twenty-five **veinticinco** 1
twenty-four **veinticuatro** 1
twenty-nine **veintinueve** 1
twenty-one **veintiún, veintiuno/a** 1
twenty-seven **veintisiete** 1
twenty-six **veintiséis** 1
twenty-three **veintitrés** 1
twenty-two **veintidós** 1
twice **dos veces** 6
twin **gemelo/a** *m., f.* 3
twisted **torcido/a** *adj.* 10; be twisted **estar torcido/a** 10
two **dos** 1
  two hundred **doscientos/as** 6
  two times **dos veces**

U

ugly **feo/a** *adj.* 3
uncle **tío** *m.* 3
under **bajo** *adv.* 7; **debajo de** *prep.* 2
understand **comprender** *v.* 3; **entender (e:ie)** *v.* 4
underwear **ropa interior** 6
unemployment **desempleo** *m.*
United States **Estados Unidos** *m. pl.* 1
university **universidad** *f.* 2
unless **a menos que** *adv.* 13
unmarried **soltero/a** *adj.* 9
unpleasant **antipático/a** *adj.* 3
until **hasta** *prep.* 6; **hasta que** *conj.* 13
up **arriba** *adv.* 15
urgent **urgente** *adj.* 12
  It's urgent that... **Es urgente que...** 12
us **nosotros,** (to, for) us *pl. pron.* 6
use **usar** *v.* 6
used for **para** *prep.* 11
useful **útil** *adj. m., f.*

V

vacation **vacaciones** *f. pl.* 5
  be on vacation **estar de vacaciones** 5
  go on vacation **ir de vacaciones** 5
vacuum **pasar** *v.* **la aspiradora** 12
  vacuum cleaner **aspiradora** *f.* 12

valley **valle** *m.* 13
various **varios/as** *adj. m., f. pl.* 8
VCR **videocasetera** *f.* 11
vegetables **verduras** *pl., f.* 8
verb **verbo** *m.*
very **muy** *adv.* 1
  very much **muchísimo** *adv.* 2
  (Very) well, thank you. **(Muy) bien gracias.** 1
vest **chaleco** *m.*
video **video** *m.* 1
  video camera **cámara** *f.* **de video** 11
  video(cassette) **video(casete)** *m.* 11
  videoconference **videoconferencia** *f.*
vinegar **vinagre** *m.* 8
violence **violencia** *f.*
visit **visitar** *v.* 4
  visit monuments **visitar monumentos** 4
vitamin **vitamina** *f.* 15
volcano **volcán** *m.* 13
volleyball **vóleibol** *m.* 4
vote **votar** *v.*

W

wait for **esperar** *v.* 2
waiter **camarero/a** *m., f.* 8
wake up **despertarse (e:ie)** *v.* 7
walk **caminar** *v.* 2
  take a walk **pasear** *v.* 4; walk around **pasear por** 4
walkman *walkman* *m.* 11
wall **pared** *f.* 12
wallet **cartera** *f.* 6
want **querer (e:ie)** *v.* 4
war **guerra** *f.*
warm (oneself) up **calentarse** *v.* 15
wash **lavar** *v.* 12
  wash one's face/hands **lavarse la cara/las manos** 7
  wash oneself *v.* **lavarse** 7
washing machine **lavadora** *f.* 12
wastebasket **papelera** *f.* 2
watch **mirar** *v.* 2; **reloj** *m.* 2
  watch television **mirar (la) televisión**
water **agua** *f.* 8
  water pollution **contaminación del agua** 13
  water-skiing *m.* **esquí acuático** 4
way **manera** *f.*
we **nosotros(as)** *m., f.* 1
weak **débil** *adj. m., f.* 15
wear **llevar** *v.* 6; **usar** 6
weather **tiempo** *m.*
  The weather is bad. **Hace mal tiempo.** 5
  The weather is good. **Hace buen tiempo.** 5

weaving **tejido** *m.*
Web **red** *f.* 11
website **sitio** *m.* **web** 11
wedding **boda** *f.* 9
Wednesday **miércoles** *m., sing.* 2
week **semana** *f.* 2
weekend **fin** *m.* **de semana** 4
weight **peso** *m.* 15
  lift weights **levantar** *v.* **pesas**
  f., pl. 15
welcome **bienvenido(s)/a(s)** *adj.*
  12
well **pues** *adv.* 2; **bueno** *adv.* 2;
  (Very) well, thanks. **(Muy) bien,**
  gracias.
well-being **bienestar** *m.* 15
well-organized **ordenado/a** *adj.* 5
west **oeste** *m.* 14
  to the west **al oeste** 14
western (*genre*) **de vaqueros**
what **lo que** 12
  what? **¿qué?** 1;
  At what time...? **¿A qué**
    hora...? 1
  What... ! **¡Qué...!**
  What a pleasure to... ! **¡Qué**
    gusto (+ *inf.***)...**
  What a surprise! **¡Qué**
    sorpresa!
  What day is it? **¿Qué día es**
    hoy? 2
  What did you say? **¿Cómo?**
  What do you think? **¿Qué**
    le/les *form.* **parece?**
  What happened? **¿Qué pasó?** 11
  What is the date (today)? **¿Cuál**
    es la fecha (de hoy)? 5
  What is the price? **¿Qué precio**
  tiene?
  What pain! **¡Qué dolor!**
  What pretty clothes! **¡Qué ropa**
  más bonita! 6
  What size do you take? **¿Qué**
    talla lleva/usa? 6
  What time is it? **¿Qué hora**
    es? 1
  What's going on? **¿Qué pasa?** 1
  What's happening? **¿Qué**
    pasa? 1
  What's. . . like? **¿Cómo es...?** 3
  What's new? **¿Qué hay de**
    nuevo? 1
  What's the weather like? **¿Qué**
    tiempo hace? 5
  What's wrong? **¿Qué pasó?** 11
  What's your name? **¿Cómo se**
    llama usted? *form.* 1
  What's your name? **¿Cómo te**
    llamas (tú)? *fam.* 1
when **cuando** *conj.* 7; 13
  When? **¿Cuándo?** 2
where **donde**
  where? (*destination*) **¿adónde?**
    2; (*location*)**¿dónde?** 1
  Where are you from? **¿De**

    dónde eres (tú)? *(fam.)* 1;
    ¿De dónde es (usted)?
    (form.) 1
  Where is...? **¿Dónde**
    está...? 2
  (to) where? **¿adónde?** 2
which **que** *pron.*
which? **¿cuál?** 2; **¿qué?** 2
  which one(s)? **¿cuáles?** 2
while **mientras** *adv.* 10
white **blanco/a** *adj.* 6
  white wine **vino blanco** 8
who **que** *pron.* 12; **quien(es)**
  pron. 12
  who? **¿quién(es)?** 1
Who is...? **¿Quién es...?** 1
  Who is calling? (*on telephone*)
    ¿De parte de quién? 11
  Who is speaking? (*on telephone*)
    ¿Quién habla? 11
whom **quien(es)** *pron.*
whole **todo/a** *adj.*
whose **¿de quién(es)?** 1
why? **¿por qué?** 2
widower/widow **viudo/a** *adj.* 9
wife **esposa** *f.* 3
win **ganar** *v.* 4
wind **viento** *m.* 5
window **ventana** *f.* 2
windshield **parabrisas** *m.,*
  sing. 11
windy: It's (very) windy. **Hace**
  (mucho) viento. 5
wine **vino** *m.* 8
  red wine **vino tinto** 8
  white wine **vino blanco** 8
wineglass **copa** *f.* 12
winter **invierno** *m.* 5
wish **desear** *v.* 2; **esperar** *v.* 13
  I wish (that) **Ojalá (que)** 13
with **con** *prep.* 2
  with me **conmigo** 4, 9
  with you **contigo** *fam.* 9
within (ten years) **dentro de (diez**
  años) *prep.*
without **sin** *prep.* 2
  sin que *conj.* 13
  without a doubt **sin duda**
woman **mujer** *f.* 1
wool **lana** *f.* 6
  (made of) wool **de lana** 6
word **palabra** *f.* 1
work **trabajar** *v.* 2; **funcionar** *v.*
  11; **trabajo** *m.*
  work (*of art, literature, music,*
    etc.) **obra** *f.*
  work out **hacer gimnasia** 15
world **mundo** *m.* 13
worldwide **mundial** *adj. m., f.*
worried (about) **preocupado/a**
  (por) *adj.* 5
worry (about) **preocuparse** *v.*
  (por) 7
  Don't worry. **No se preocupe.**
    form. 7; **Tranquilo.** *adj.*; **No**

    te preocupes. *fam.* 7
worse **peor** *adj. m., f.* 8
worst **el/la peor, lo peor** 8
Would you like to...? **¿Te gus-**
  taría...? *fam.* 4
write **escribir** *v.* 3
  write a letter/post card/e-mail
    message **escribir una**
    carta/(tarjeta) postal/
    mensaje electrónico 4
writer **escritor(a)** *m., f.*
written **escrito/a** *p.p.* 13
wrong **equivocado/a** *adj.* 5
  be wrong **no tener razón** 3

            X

X-ray **radiografía** *f.* 10

            Y

yard **jardín** *m.* 12; **patio** *m.* 12
year **año** *m.* 5
  be... years old **tener...**
    años 3
yellow **amarillo/a** *adj.* 6
yes **sí** *interj.* 1
yesterday **ayer** *adv.* 6
yet **todavía** *adv.* 5
yogurt **yogur** *m.* 8
You **tú** *fam.* **usted (Ud.)** *form.*
  sing. **vosotros/as** *m., f. fam.*
  ustedes (Uds.) *form.* 1; (to,
  for) you *fam. sing.* **te** *pl.* **os** 6;
  form. sing. **le** *pl.* **les** 6
You don't say! **¡No me digas!**
  fam.; **¡No me diga!** *form.* 11
You are. . . **Tú eres...** 1
You're welcome. **De nada.** 1; **No**
  hay de qué. 1
young **joven** *adj.* 3
  young person **joven** *m., f.* 1
  young woman **señorita**
    (Srta.) *f.*
younger **menor** *adj. m., f.* 3
younger: younger brother, sister *m.,*
  f. **hermano/a menor** 3
youngest **el/la menor** *m., f.* 8
your **su(s)** *poss. adj. form.* 3
  your **tu(s)** *poss. adj. fam. sing.* 3
  your **vuestro/a(s)** *poss. adj.*
    form. pl. 3
  your(s) *form.* **suyo(s)/a(s)**
    poss. pron. form. 11
  your(s) **tuyo(s)/a(s)** *poss.*
    fam. sing. 11
  your(s) **vuestro(s)/a(s)** *poss.*
    fam. 11
youth *f.* **juventud** 9

            Z

zero **cero** *m.* 1

Text Credits

384–385 © Gloria Fuertes. Reprinted by permission of Fundación Gloria Fuertes.

412–413 © Marco Denevi. Falsificaciones, Buenos Aires, Corregidor, 1999. Reprinted by permission of Editorial Corregidora.

438–439 © Gioconda Belli. Reprinted by permission of the author.

Fine Art Credits

59 Diego Velázquez. *Las meninas*. 1656. Derechos reservados © Museo Nacional del Prado, Madrid.

91 Oswaldo Guayasamín. *Madre y niño en azul*. 1986. Cortesía Fundación Guayasamín.
Quito, Ecuador.

118 Frida Kahlo. *Autorretrato con mono*. 1938. Oil on masonite, overall 16 X12" (40.64 x 30.48 cms). Albright-Knox Art Gallery, Buffalo, New York. Bequest of A. Conger Goodyear, 1966

389 José Antonio Velásquez. *San Antonio de Oriente*. 1957. Colección: Art Museum of the Americas, Organization of American States. Washington D.C.

Illustration Credits

Debra Spina Dixon: 410.

Hermann Mejía: 5, 12, 13, 15, 16, 20, 21, 44, 51, 65, 73 (b), 76, 84, 85, 103, 107, 114, 133, 136, 141, 145, 155, 173, 184, 185, 192, 202, 221, 235, 244, 252, 271, 281, 286, 287, 312, 315, 318, 319, 342, 351, 355, 376, 383, 431, 435.

Pere Virgili: 2–3, 32–33, 52, 55, 62–63, 73 (t), 94–95, 96, 122–123, 124, 125, 137, 140, 152–153, 154, 182–183, 210–211, 212, 242–243, 268–269, 298–299, 300, 328–329, 330, 362–363, 364, 392–393, 394, 420–421, 422.

Yayo: 9, 39, 69, 101, 131, 159, 189, 219, 249, 275, 305, 335, 369, 399,412–413, 427.

Photography Credits

Alamy Images: Cover © David Noton Photography.

Martín Bernetti: 1, 3, 4, 6 (b), 10 (l), 14, 17 (l, m), 28 (b), 34, 42, 47, 63, 64 (tl,tml, tmr, bml, bmr, br), 66 (b), 72, 79 (r), 80, 86, 87 (b), 89, 95 (b), 98, (b), 115, 116, 156 (b), 165, 169 (tl, tr, ml, mr), 170, 171, 176, 177, 186 (b), 191, 193 (l), 196, 197, 215, 245, 262, 272 (b), 279, 283, 302 (b), 314, 331, 332 (b), 354, 396, (b), 406, 423, 441.

Corbis: iii © Chuck Savage. 2 © John Henley. 10 (r) © José Luis Pelaez, Inc. 17 (r) © Charles Gupton. 28 (tr) © Robert Holmes. 29 (tr) © Tony Arruza. 36 (b) © Owen Franken. 48 © Charles Gupton. 58 (tl, tr) © Patrick Ward, (m) © Elke Stolzenberg, (b) © Reuters/Heino Kalis. 59 (tl) © Paul Almasy, (tr) © Jean-Pierre Lescourret, (mr) © Tony Arruza, (br) © Dave G. Houser. 61 © Ronnie Kaufman. 64 (tr) © LWA-Dann Tardif, (bl) © Ariel Skelley. 77 © Walter Hodges. 79 (l) Warren Morgan. 87 (t) © José Luis Pelaez, Inc.,

About the Authors

José A. Blanco founded Vista Higher Learning in 1998. A native of Barranquilla, Colombia, Mr. Blanco holds degrees in Literature and Hispanic Studies from Brown University and the University of California, Santa Cruz. He has worked as a writer, editor, and translator for Houghton Mifflin and D.C. Heath and Company and has taught Spanish at the secondary and university levels. Mr. Blanco is also the co-author of several other Vista Higher Learning programs: **Vistas** at the introductory level, **Ventanas, Facetas**, and **Enfoques** at the intermediate level, and **Revista** at the advanced conversation level.

Philip Redwine Donley received his M.A. in Hispanic Literature from the University of Texas at Austin in 1986 and his Ph.D. in Foreign Language Education from the University of Texas at Austin in 1997. Dr. Donley taught Spanish at Austin Community College, Southwestern University, and the University of Texas at Austin. He published articles and conducted workshops about language anxiety management, and the development of critical thinking skills, and was involved in research about teaching languages to the visually impaired. Dr. Donley was also the co-author of **Aventuras** and **Vistas**, two other introductory college Spanish textbook programs published by Vista Higher Learning.

About the Illustrators

Yayo, an internationally acclaimed illustrator, was born in Colombia. He has illustrated children's books, newspapers, and magazines, and has been exhibited around the world. He currently lives in Montreal, Canada.

Pere Virgili lives and works in Barcelona, Spain. His illustrations have appeared in textbooks, newspapers, and magazines throughout Spain and Europe.

Born in Caracas, Venezuela, **Hermann Mejía** studied illustration at the *Instituto de Diseño de Caracas*. Hermann currently lives and works in the United States.